T0189401

Lecture Notes in Computer Science   14601

Founding Editors

Gerhard Goos
Juris Hartmanis

The series Lecture Notes in Computer Science (LNCS), including its subseries Lecture Notes in Artificial Intelligence (LNAI) and Lecture Notes in Bioinformatics (LNBI), has established itself as a medium for the publication of new developments in computer science and information technology research, teaching, and education.

LNCS enjoys close cooperation with the computer science R & D community, the series counts many renowned academics among its volume editors and paper authors, and collaborates with prestigious societies. Its mission is to serve this international community by providing an invaluable service, mainly focused on the publication of conference and workshop proceedings and postproceedings. LNCS commenced publication in 1973.

Qiang Tang · Vanessa Teague
Editors

Public-Key Cryptography – PKC 2024

27th IACR International Conference
on Practice and Theory of Public-Key Cryptography
Sydney, NSW, Australia, April 15–17, 2024
Proceedings, Part I

 Springer

Editors
Qiang Tang
The University of Sydney
Sydney, NSW, Australia

Vanessa Teague
The Australian National University
Acton, ACT, Australia

ISSN 0302-9743   ISSN 1611-3349 (electronic)
Lecture Notes in Computer Science
ISBN 978-3-031-57720-8   ISBN 978-3-031-57718-5 (eBook)
https://doi.org/10.1007/978-3-031-57718-5

This Springer imprint is published by the registered company Springer Nature Switzerland AG
The registered company address is: Gewerbestrasse 11, 6330 Cham, Switzerland

Paper in this product is recyclable.

Preface

The 27th International Conference on Practice and Theory of Public-Key Cryptography (PKC 2024) was held in Sydney, Australia, on April 15–17, 2024. It was sponsored by the International Association for Cryptologic Research (IACR) and is the main IACR-sponsored conference with an explicit focus on public-key cryptography. PKC 2024 authors represented 24 different countries, bringing a vibrant international community of cryptography researchers to Australia.

The conference received 176 submissions, reviewed by the Program Committee of 68 cryptography experts (including four area chairs) working with 183 external reviewers. The reviewing process took two months and selected 54 papers to appear in PKC 2024. Papers were reviewed in the usual double-blind fashion with an average of just over three reviews per paper. Program committee members and general chairs were limited to 3 submissions (4 if all with students), and their submissions were scrutinized more closely. The two program chairs were not allowed to submit papers. PKC 2024 was the first major cryptography conferences to accept SoK papers.

PKC 2024 welcomed Nadia Heninger (University of California, San Diego) and Aggelos Kiayias (University of Edinburgh) as the invited speakers. The Program Committee also selected two best papers: *An algorithm for efficient detection of (N, N)-splittings and its application to the isogeny problem in dimension 2* by Maria Corte-Real Santos, Craig Costello and Sam Frengley, and *Quantum CCA-Secure PKE, Revisited* by Navid Alamati and Varun Maram.

The award committee (Masayuki Abe, Alexandra Boldyreva, Qiang Tang, Vanessa Teague, Moti Yung) also chose the PKC Test of Time Award for 2024.

PKC is a remarkable undertaking, possible only through the hard work and significant contributions of many people. We would like to express our sincere gratitude to all the authors, as well as to the Program Committee and external reviewers, session chairs and presenters. Special thanks to the area chairs: Steven Galbraith, Giuseppe Persiano, Kazue Sako and Vassilis Zikas. Their specialist knowledge and good judgement were critical for making good decisions.

Additionally, we would like to thank Willy Susilo, Fuchun Guo and the team at the University of Wollongong for making the general arrangements such a success. Also, as always, Kay McKelly and Kevin McCurley provided invaluable support for all things technical behind the scenes.

All of this happens against a backdrop in which even some democratic governments are working to undermine encrypted communications in the name of "safety." In Australia, exporting a new encryption algorithm without a permit can be punished with years in jail. Open, scientific, internationally collaborative research in cryptography is more important than ever.

We hope you enjoyed the conference and the warm welcome of Sydney.

April 2024

Qiang Tang
Vanessa Teague

Organization

General Chairs

Fuchun Guo   University of Wollongong, Australia
Willy Susilo   University of Wollongong, Australia

Program Committee Chairs

Qiang Tang   The University of Sydney, Australia
Vanessa Teague   Democracy Developers Ltd., The Australian National University and Thinking Cybersecurity Pty. Ltd., Australia

Steering Committee

Masayuki Abe   NTT, Japan
Alexandra Boldyreva   Georgia Tech, USA
Jung Hee Cheon   Seoul National University, South Korea
Yvo Desmedt   University of Texas at Dallas, USA
Goichiro Hanaoka   National Institute of Advanced Industrial Science and Technology, Japan
Tibor Jager   University of Wuppertal, Germany
Aggelos Kiayias   University of Edinburgh, UK
Vladimir Kolesnikov   Georgia Tech, USA
Tanja Lange   Eindhoven University of Technology, The Netherlands
Jiaxin Pan   NTNU, Norway & University of Kassel, Germany
David Pointcheval   École Normale Supérieure Paris, France
Qiang Tang   The University of Sydney, Australia
Vanessa Teague   Democracy Developers Ltd., The Australian National University and Thinking Cybersecurity Pty. Ltd., Australia
Moti Yung (Secretary)   Google Inc. & Columbia University, USA
Yuliang Zheng (Chair)   University of Alabama at Birmingham, USA

Area Chairs

Steven Galbraith

The University of Auckland,
Aotearoa-New Zealand
*Post-quantum cryptography, quantum
cryptography, Math & Attacks*

Giuseppe Persiano

University of Salerno, Italy and Google, USA
*Theoretical Foundations & Advanced
Primitives*

Kazue Sako

Waseda University, Japan
*Applied Cryptography, SNARKs & Verifiable
Computation*

Vassilis Zikas

Purdue University, USA
Multiparty computation & consensus

Program Committee

Divesh Aggarwal	National University of Singapore, Singapore
Christian Badertscher	Input Output Global, Switzerland
Foteini Baldimtsi	George Mason University, USA
Sofia Celi	Brave, Portugal
Suvradip Chakraborty	Visa Research, USA
Long Chen	Chinese Academy of Sciences, China
Yilei Chen	Tsinghua University, China
Rongmao Chen	National University of Defense Technology, China
Jung Hee Cheon	Seoul National University, Republic of Korea
Amy Corman	RMIT University, Australia
Luca De Feo	IBM Research Europe, Switzerland
Yi Deng	Chinese Academy of Sciences, China
Xiong Fan	Rutgers University, USA
Hanwen Feng	The University of Sydney, Australia
Rishab Goyal	University of Wisconsin-Madison, USA
Debayan Gupta	Ashoka University, India
Thomas Haines	The Australian National University, Australia
Goichiro Hanaoka	AIST, Japan
Cheng Hong	Ant Research, China
Tibor Jager	University of Wuppertal, Germany
Zhengzhong Jin	MIT, USA
Dmitry Khovratovich	Ethereum Foundation, Luxembourg
Fuyuki Kitagawa	NTT Social Informatics Laboratories, Japan

Jiaheng Zhang   National University of Singapore, Singapore
Dominique Schroeder   Friedrich-Alexander University of
                                  Erlangen-Nürnberg, Germany
Wessel van Woerden   University of Bordeaux, France

Additional Reviewers

Aydin Abadi
Behzad Abdolmaleki
Masayuki Abe
Miguel Ambrona
Arathi Arakala
Sven Argo
Benedikt Auerbach
Renas Bacho
Weihao Bai
Shi Bai
Fabio Banfi
Andrea Basso
Fabrice Benhamouda
Olivier Bernard
Daniel J. Bernstein
Siddhartha Bhoi
Alex Bienstock
Katharina Boudgoust
Charles Bouillaguet
Pedro Branco
Fabian Buschkowski
Rohit Chatterjee
Binyi Chen
Hyeongmin Choe
Arka Rai Choudhuri
Hao Chung
Michele Ciampi
Valerio Cini
Alexandru Cojocaru
Pierrick Dartois
Poulami Das
Koen de Boer
Paola de Perthuis
Benne de Weger
Giovanni Deligios
Lalita Devadas
Jesus Diaz

Jelle Don
Léo Ducas
Pranjal Dutta
Keita Emura
Daniel Escudero
Muhammed F. Esgin
Thomas Espitau
Prastudy Fauzi
Danilo Francati
Daniele Friolo
Yao Jiang Galteland
Gayathri Garimella
Riddhi Ghosal
Aarushi Goel
Lenaick Gouriou
Anna Guinet
Hui Guo
Kyoohyung Han
Lucjan Hanzlik
Charlotte Hoffmann
Alex Hoover
Yao-Ching Hsieh
David Hu
Zhicong Huang
Andreas Hülsing
Nikai Jagganath
Aayush Jain
Xiaoyu Ji
Haodong Jiang
Haohao Jiang
Ioanna Karantaidou
Sabyasachi Karati
Handan Kilinc Alper
Suhri Kim
Dongwoo Kim
Seongkwang Kim
Sungwook Kim

Miran Kim
Kamil Kluczniak
Anders Konrig
Swastik Kopparty
Alexis Korb
Abhiram Kothapalli
Elisabeth Krahmer
Sabrina Kunzweiler
Kaoru Kurosawa
Qiqi Lai
Georg Land
Changmin Lee
Yun Li
Yanan Li
Xiao Liang
Yao-Ting Lin
Qipeng Liu
Zeyu Liu
Weiran Liu
Fengrun Liu
Wen-jie Lu
Varun Madathil
Lorenzo Magliocco
Monosij Maitra
Easwar Mangipudi
Elisaweta Masserova
Takahiro Matsuda
Daniel McVicker
Simon-Philipp Merz
Ruiqi Mi
Peihan Miao
Arash Mirzaei
Anuja Modi
Johannes Mono
Ethan Mook
Kirill Morozov
Marta Mularczyk
Ky Nguyen
Ryo Nishimaki
Alice Pellet-Mary
Nikhil Pappu
Jeongeun Park
Guillermo Pascual Perez
Alain Passelegue
Rutvik Patel

Sihang Pu
Ludo Pulles
Octavio Pérez Kempner
Wei Qi
Tian Qiu
Wenjie Qu
Willy Quach
Ahmadreza Rahimi
Omar Renawi
Mahshid Riahinia
Jan Richter-Brockmann
Guilherme Rito
Damien Robert
Maxime Roméas
Lawrence Roy
Luigi Russo
Sagnik Saha
Yusuke Sakai
Robert Schaedlich
Sven Schäge
Jacob Schuldt
Mahdi Sedaghat
Sruthi Sekar
Joon Young Seo
Jun Jie Sim
Yongha Son
Bruno Sterner
Atsushi Takayasu
Gang Tang
Guofeng Tang
Yuhao Tang
Khai Hanh Tang
Stefano Tessaro
Junichi Tomida
Monika Trimoska
Yiannis Tselekounis
Akhil Vanukuri
Benedikt Wagner
Hendrik Waldner
Han Wang
Yuchen Wang
Li-Ping Wang
Zhedong Wang
Yi Wang
Jiabo Wang

Charlotte Weitkämper
Chenkai Weng
Jie Xu
Anshu Yadav
Aayush Yadav
Shota Yamada
Takashi Yamakawa
Dan Yamamoto
Zhaomin Yang

Yusuke Yoshida
Zuoxia Yu
Shang Zehua
Xinyu Zhang
Liangfeng Zhang
Raymond K. Zhao
Hong-Sheng Zhou
Tanping Zhou
Zidi Zhuang

Contents – Part I

Attacks

Signatures

On Proving Equivalence Class Signatures Secure from Non-interactive Assumptions

Balthazar Bauer[1]([✉]), Georg Fuchsbauer[2], and Fabian Regen[2]

[1] UVSQ, Versailles, France
balthazar.bauer@ens.fr
[2] TU Wien, Vienna, Austria
{georg.fuchsbauer,fabian.regen}@tuwien.ac.at

Abstract. Equivalence class signatures (EQS), introduced by Hanser and Slamanig (AC'14, J. Crypto'19), sign vectors of elements from a bilinear group. Their main feature is "adaptivity": given a signature on a vector, anyone can transform it to a (uniformly random) signature on any multiple of the vector. A signature thus authenticates equivalence classes and unforgeability is defined accordingly. EQS have been used to improve the efficiency of many cryptographic applications, notably (delegatable) anonymous credentials, (round-optimal) blind signatures, group signatures and anonymous tokens. EQS security implies strong anonymity (or blindness) guarantees for these schemes which holds against malicious signers without trust assumptions.

Unforgeability of the original EQS construction is proven directly in the generic group model. While there are constructions from standard assumptions, these either achieve prohibitively weak security notions (PKC'18) or they require a common reference string (AC'19, PKC'22), which reintroduces trust assumptions avoided by EQS.

In this work we ask whether EQS schemes that satisfy the original security model can be proved secure under standard (or even non-interactive) assumptions with standard techniques. Our answer is negative: assuming a reduction that, after running once an adversary breaking unforgeability, breaks a non-interactive computational assumption, we construct efficient meta-reductions that either break the assumption or break class-hiding, another security requirement for EQS.

1 Introduction

Structure-preserving signatures (SPS) [AFG+10] are defined over groups of prime order p equipped with a bilinear map (pairing), and their messages are group elements. *SPS on equivalence classes*, or equivalence class signatures (EQS) for short, introduced by Hanser and Slamanig [HS14] and later refined [FHS19], sign vectors of (non-zero) group elements, that is, messages are from $M = (\mathbb{G}^*)^\ell$ for a group $\mathbb{G}$ (where $\ell = 2$ suffices for most applications). Compared to standard signature schemes, EQS provide an additional functionality Adapt: given the public key, a signature σ on $m \in M$ and $\mu \in \mathbb{Z}_p^*$, Adapt returns, without requiring the signing key, a signature on the message $\mu \cdot m$. Signing $m \in M$ thus

© International Association for Cryptologic Research 2024
Q. Tang and V. Teague (Eds.): PKC 2024, LNCS 14601, pp. 3–36, 2024.
https://doi.org/10.1007/978-3-031-57718-5_1

authenticates the equivalence class $[m]_\sim$, where $m \sim m' :\Leftrightarrow \exists\, \mu \in \mathbb{Z}_p^* : m' = \mu \cdot m$. Unforgeability means that after querying signatures on (polynomially many) messages $m_1, m_2, \ldots$, no adversary can compute a signature for any m^* with $m^* \notin [m_1] \cup [m_2] \cup \ldots$

A second security notion is *class-hiding*, meaning that it is hard to distinguish a random message pair (m, m') from the same class (i.e., $m \sim m'$) from a random pair $(m, m') \leftarrow\!\!\$\, M \times M$. Note that this is equivalent to the hardness of the decisional Diffie-Hellman (DDH) problem in $\mathbb{G}$. The third property is *signature adaptation* (under malicious keys): it states that, even if a public key pk was set up maliciously, when running $\sigma' \leftarrow \mathsf{Adapt}(pk, m, \sigma, \mu)$ for a σ valid on m, then σ' is uniformly random in the set of all valid signatures on $\mu \cdot m$.

Together with class-hiding, this yields the following guarantee against malicious signers, which lies at the core of applications of EQS: after issuing a signature σ on a message m, when later given $\mu \cdot m$ and $\sigma' \leftarrow \mathsf{Adapt}(pk, m, \sigma, \mu)$ for $\mu \leftarrow\!\!\$\, \mathbb{Z}_p^*$, the signer cannot distinguish $(\sigma', \mu \cdot m)$ from a *random* signature on a *random* message $m' \leftarrow\!\!\$\, M$ valid under pk.

The original work [FHS19] gives a very efficient construction of EQS with signatures consisting of 2 elements from $\mathbb{G}$ and 1 from $\hat{\mathbb{G}}$ (the other source group of the asymmetric pairing). Unforgeability is proved directly in the generic group model [Nec94, Sho97, Mau05].

Applications of EQS. Since their introduction, equivalence class signatures have been used to instantiate numerous cryptographic concepts.

Anonymous Credentials. The first application of EQS were attribute-based credentials (ABC) [CL03]. In an ABC scheme, users are issued credentials for a set of attributes they possess. Users can then selectively disclose attributes, that is, *show* that they possess any subset of their attributes. Anonymity requires that no one can tell whether two showings were done by the same user and that they reveal nothing about the non-disclosed attributes.

To showcase the power of EQS, the authors [FHS19] use it to construct the first ABC scheme for which the communication complexity of showing a credential is independent of the number of (possessed or showed) attributes. In their scheme, a credential is an EQS signature σ on a (randomizable) commitment $c \in M$ to the user's attributes; when a user wants to prove she owns certain attributes, she adapts σ for $\mu \cdot c$ for $\mu \leftarrow\!\!\$\, \mathbb{Z}_p^*$ and opens the commitment $\mu \cdot c$ to the disclosed attributes. Anonymity (even against malicious credential issuers) follows from the adaptivity properties of EQS. Note that this construction avoids using zero-knowledge proofs to hide signatures, which are a source of inefficiency in many prior constructions. (Interactive proofs could still be required to prevent replay attacks.[1]) Slamanig and others added the possibility of revoking users to

---

[1] Note that the following simple pseudonym system from EQS would not use any ZK proofs during showing. A user creates $pk = sk \cdot g$, with party i she establishes pseudonym $(r_i \cdot g, r_i \cdot pk)$ for random r_i, and she transforms (via Adapt) signatures (credentials) on one pseudonym to another. ZK proofs (of DL-knowledge) would only be needed when establishing a new pseudonym.

the credential scheme [DHS15] and construct credentials that allow outsourcing of sensitive computation to a restricted device [HS21].

EQS were generalized by considering adaptivity within equivalence classes not only for messages but also for keys, termed "signatures with flexible public key" [BHKS18] or "mercurial signatures" [CL19, CL21, CLPK22]. Mercurial signatures were used to construct *delegatable* anonymous credentials [BCC+09] with non-interactive delegation [Fuc11]. New credentials constructions from EQS are still being proposed [MSBM23, MBG+23].

Group Signatures. EQS were used to construct efficient group signatures [DS16, CS20], in particular supporting dynamic adding of members [DS18]. Group signatures, as well as ring signatures, have also been constructed from the generalization of EQS to adaptable public keys [BHKS18].

Blind Signatures. Another line of research uses EQS to construct blind signatures, which let a user obtain a signature on a message that remains hidden from the signer. This builds on earlier work [BFPV13], which use randomizable zero-knowledge proofs [FP09] and thus require a trusted common reference string (CRS). In contrast, the EQS-based schemes [FHS15, FHKS16] do not assume common reference strings or random oracles and achieve blindness against malicious signers, leveraging the adaptivity property of EQS. Moreover, the schemes are round-optimal [Fis06], meaning the signing protocol consists of one message from the user to the signer and one message back; such schemes are thus *concurrently secure* [HKKL07] by default. Hanzlik [Han23] went further and uses the FHS EQS scheme to construct *non-interactive* blind signatures on random messages.

Other Cryptographic Primitives. EQS also yield [HRS15] verifiably encrypted signatures. *Access-control encryption* [DHO16] was efficiently instantiated using EQS [FGKO17], as well as [BLL+19] *sanitizable signatures* [ACdMT05] and privacy-preserving incentive systems from EQS [BEK+20]. The FHS scheme [FHS19] was used [HPP20] to instantiate highly scalable mix nets and [ST21] the anonymous authentication protocol *EPID*. It was also used for the most efficient instantiation of *anonymous counting tokens* [BRS23].

Constructions from Standard Assumptions. Despite applications of EQS requiring neither CRS nor random oracles, the first instantiation of EQS [FHS19] only has a proof in the generic group model (GGM). Therefore, calling constructions using that scheme "standard-model" has attracted some criticism [KM19]. This motivated the search for constructions from *falsifiable* [Nao03] assumptions, that is, assumptions where the challenger that sets up the problem instance can efficiently decide whether an adversary has broken the assumption. The assumption that a given EQS satisfies unforgeability is for example *not* falsifiable, since, by the class-hiding property, deciding whether the adversary's message lies in one of the queried classes is hard.

The first EQS from falsifiable assumptions was proposed by Fuchsbauer and Gay [FG18], based on Matrix-Diffie-Hellman assumptions [EHK+13]. However, its signatures can only be adapted once (after which they change format) and the scheme only satisfies a weakened security notion: when querying a signature, the unforgeability adversary must provide the discrete logarithms of the queried messages. Note that this unforgeability notion *is* efficiently decidable.[2]

Unfortunately, the notion of *signature adaption* that the scheme achieves assumes honest keys and honest signatures, which excludes all applications except to access control encryption, as later argued [KSD19].

Motivated by this, Khalili, Slamanig and Dakhilalian [KSD19] propose an EQS construction from the SXDH assumption (i.e., DDH is hard in $\mathbb{G}$ and $\hat{\mathbb{G}}$) with signatures in $\mathbb{G}^8 \times \hat{\mathbb{G}}^9$. Building on this work, Connolly, Lafourcade and Perez-Kempner [CLPK22] propose a more efficient scheme (with signatures in $\mathbb{G}^9 \times \hat{\mathbb{G}}^4$), which requires an additional assumption (extKerMDH). A drawback of both schemes is that they assume a trusted CRS to achieve signature adaption under malicious keys. Sadly, this foils the main security benefit of EQS-based constructions: anonymity guarantees (against blind signers or credential issuers, etc.) without any trust assumptions in the standard model. We note that for schemes with a uniform CRS (of group elements) the CRS could be generated "transparently" by hashing (into the group). Formally, one would then need to prove adaptation security in the ROM.

A recent work [BFR24] points out a flaw in the security proofs of the CRS-based schemes [KSD19, CLPK22] and thus their security is currently unclear. (A game hop in the unforgeability proofs modifies the adversary's view and the change in its advantage is then bounded by the advantage of a reduction in solving a computational problem. But since EQS-unforgeability is not efficiently decidable, the reduction would not be efficient.[3])

The current state of affairs remains thus that the only scheme enabling trust-less applications is FHS [FHS19], and it is only proven secure in the GGM. This poses two independent questions: can we prove stronger security guarantees for FHS; and do there exist more efficient schemes? Since any EQS scheme can be transformed into a structure-preserving signature (SPS) scheme without changing the signature format [FHS15], known impossibility results for SPS imply the following: First, the signature size of FHS is optimal, since 3 group elements per signature are necessary [AGHO11]. Second, FHS cannot be proven secure from a non-interactive assumption via an *algebraic* reduction, since this is the case for all 3-element schemes [AGO11].

---

[2] Consider $\ell = 2$. For all i, let $(x_{i,1}, x_{i,2}) \in (\mathbb{Z}_p^*)^2$ be the logarithms of the components of the queried message m_i (i.e., $m_{i,j} = x_{i,j} \cdot g$, where $\mathbb{G} = \langle g \rangle$). When the adversary returns a signature on $m^* = (m_1^*, m_2^*)$, it wins if $x_{i,2} \cdot m_1^* \neq x_{i,1} \cdot m_2^*$ for all i.

[3] In the hop from Game 2 to Game 3 [KSD19, Theorem 2], the distribution of the signatures output by the signing oracle is modified and thus $\mathcal{A}$'s advantage of breaking unforgeability could also change, without being efficiently detectable. However, the constructed reduction $\mathcal{B}_1$ (to the "core lemma", which relies on the computational hardness of Matrix-DDH [EHK+17]) only checks an (efficiently testable) property of $\mathcal{A}$'s forgery but not whether $\mathcal{A}$ was successful. The implication $\mathbf{Adv}_2 - \mathbf{Adv}_3 \leq \mathbf{Adv}_{\mathcal{B}_1}^{\text{core}}$ derived by the authors is thus not justified. As the proof of the second work [CLPK22, eprint, Appendix D] is virtually identical, the above applies as well.

Since the second result only applies to 3-element schemes, the question that has been open for a decade remains: do there exist (less efficient) instantiations of EQS with a security proof from a non-interactive assumption at all? We answer this in the negative for black-box reductions that run the unforgeability adversary once.

Impossibility Results. To prove our result, we use the meta-reduction technique: one assumes that a reduction $\mathcal{R}$ (with certain properties, such as being algebraic or being tight) exists; that is, when given access to an adversary that breaks the scheme, $\mathcal{R}$ can efficiently solve a (conjectured-to-be-hard) computational problem. One then derives a contradiction by showing how to use $\mathcal{R}$ to break a computational assumption. Building on earlier work [BV98], Coron [Cor02] first used this technique to show that there is no tight security proof for the RSA full-domain hash signature scheme. (A reduction has tightness ϕ if it can use an adversary breaking the scheme with probability ϵ to break the underlying assumption with probability at least $\phi \cdot \epsilon$). His result was later revisited by Kakvi and Kiltz [KK12].

Hofheinz, Jager and Knapp [HJK12] extended Coron's ideas to Waters signatures [Wat05] and, more generally, any *re-randomizable* signature scheme. These schemes let anyone transform a signature on a message into a random signature on that message. They show that a reduction can have tightness at most $\phi = 1/\Omega(q)$, where q is the number of signing queries, as follows. Assume there exists a reduction $\mathcal{R}$, which must thus break the computational assumption using the following (inefficient) adversary: $\mathcal{A}$ makes queries on random messages and then returns a random signature on a random message m^*. The authors construct a(n efficient) meta-reduction $\mathcal{M}$ that simulates $\mathcal{A}$: to obtain the signature on m^*, $\mathcal{M}$ *rewinds* $\mathcal{R}$, that is, it runs $\mathcal{R}$ again on the same randomness; $\mathcal{M}$ then queries a signature on m^*, randomizes it and returns it as the forgery in the first run (re-randomizability is thus crucial for the simulation of the adversary).

If the hardness assumption holds, then it must be the case that either $\mathcal{R}$ cannot provide a signature on m^*, or $\mathcal{R}$ cannot use the randomized signature to break the assumption. Intuitively, every message m is thus "signable" (i.e., the reduction can provide a signature), or "exploitable" (i.e., the reduction can use a forgery on m to break the assumption). The probability that all messages queried by $\mathcal{A}$ are signable and $\mathcal{A}$'s forgery is exploitable is thus bounded by the inverse of the number of signing queries, which yields the upper-bound on tightness. Since EQS are randomizable (by running Adapt with $\mu = 1$), this readily implies that EQS cannot be proven tightly secure.[4]

Meta-reductions have also been used to prove impossibility or optimality results about Schnorr signatures [PV05, Seu12, GBL08, FJS14], and more general statements [FF13]. Bader et al. [BJLS16] consider the multi-user setting and extend Coron's technique to other cryptographic primitives.

---

[4] Note that this does not extend to CRS-based EQS, since these are only guaranteed to be randomizable under a trusted CRS [KSD19]. As in the proof of impossibility of tightness [HJK12] the CRS is set up by the reduction, it might detect the meta-reduction's simulation.

Fischlin and Schröder [FS10] show that no three-move blind signature scheme can be proved secure from non-interactive assumptions if it satisfies certain conditions. One might wonder whether, together with the fact that EQS were used by FHS [FHS15] to construct round-optimal (i.e., two-move) blind signatures, this already implies the impossibility of EQS from non-interactive assumptions.

This is not the case. The blind-signature construction [FHS15] only satisfies computational blindness, a case Fischlin and Schröder deal with in their full version.[5] For their impossibility to hold, they must assume that blindness of the scheme holds relative to two oracles (Definition A.3 in the full version), of which "Σ^c_{sk}", given a public key, returns a matching secret key. For FHS this means solving discrete logarithms, which can be used to break blindness.[6]

Our Result

Statement. Our result can be (simplified and) summarized as follows (as done in Corollary 1):

Let Σ be an EQS scheme with signature-adaptivity under malicious keys. Let Π be a (non-interactive) computational problem and $\mathcal{R}$ be a reduction from Π that runs an adversary $\mathcal{A}$ against unforgeability of Σ once, so that if $\mathcal{A}$ wins with probability ϵ, then $\mathcal{R}$ breaks Π with probability at least $\phi \cdot \epsilon$. Then there exist an adversary $\mathcal{B}$ against unforgeability of Σ running in constant time, as well as the following, which run in time linear in that of $\mathcal{R}$: meta-reductions $\mathcal{M}$, attacking Π, and $\mathcal{D}$, attacking class-hiding (CH) of Σ, such that

$$\mathsf{Adv}^{\Pi}_{\mathcal{R}^{\mathcal{B}}} + \mathsf{Adv}^{\Pi}_{\mathcal{M}^{\mathcal{R}}} + \mathsf{Adv}^{\mathrm{CH}}_{\Sigma, \mathcal{D}^{\mathcal{R}}} \geq \phi^5/384 \ . \tag{1}$$

(By $\mathsf{Adv}^{\mathrm{X}}_{[\Sigma,]\mathcal{Y}}$ we denote $\mathcal{Y}$'s advantage in breaking the notion X [for scheme Σ] and $\mathcal{Y}^{\mathcal{Z}}$ denotes that $\mathcal{Y}$ has oracle access to $\mathcal{Z}$.)

This implies that if the reduction for unforgeability is successful (i.e., ϕ is not "small") then either Σ does not satisfy CH, or the problem Π is not hard. Considering asymptotic security would yield that if the three advantages in Eq. (1) are negligible then so will be the success probability of the reduction.

Implications for Extensions of EQS. Since mercurial signatures and "signatures with flexible public key" are EQS with additional functionality, one would expect our result to carry over. However, all existing constructions [CL19, BHKS18, CL21, CLPK22] only consider adaptation under honest keys (arguably, because

---

[5] https://www.cryptoplexity.informatik.tu-darmstadt.de/media/crypt/publications_1/fischlinthree-moves2010.pdf.

[6] Using their notation [FHS15], after receiving the user's protocol message $M = (sC, sP)$ the signer can use Σ^c_{sk} to compute s and thus C, and when later given a challenge message/blind-signature pair $(m, (\sigma, R, T))$, it checks if $C = mP + T$.

anonymity of the resulting delegatable credential schemes is only weak anyway), whereas our result requires adaptation under malicious keys.

Proof Ideas. The central idea for our impossibility result is to leverage the following discrepancy: for falsifiable assumptions the challenger can efficiently determine whether the adversary has won, whereas this cannot be efficiently done for unforgeability of an EQS scheme Σ. In particular, consider an unforgeability adversary $\mathcal{A}$ that queries a signature on a single message m and then returns a signature on some m^*. According to the definition of EQS-unforgeability, if $m \sim m^*$, that is, they are from the same class, then the adversary has not won; if $m \nsim m^*$ then it has won. Now consider a reduction $\mathcal{R}$ to a falsifiable assumption Π, which runs such an adversary. In case ($\nsim$) the reduction must break Π with good probability. However, whereas in case ($\sim$) it cannot: this is because a case-($\sim$) adversary $\mathcal{A}_\sim$ can be efficiently implemented using signature adaptation: it queries a signature on m and adapts it to one on m^*. The reduction combined with the adversary ($\mathcal{R}^{\mathcal{A}_\sim}$) would thus be an efficient algorithm for solving Π.

Distinguishing case ($\sim$) from ($\nsim$) corresponds to breaking class-hiding (CH), where CH is equivalent to DDH being hard in the underlying group. It seems thus that we can use reduction $\mathcal{R}$ to break CH, i.e., DDH: Construct the following meta-reduction $\mathcal{M}_1$ that is given (m, m^*) and has to decide if $m \sim m^*$: $\mathcal{M}_1$ queries a signature σ^* on m^*, rewinds the reduction, queries m and returns (m^*, σ^*). The meta-reduction concludes that $m \sim m^*$ iff $\mathcal{R}$ fails to solve Π.

A problem ignored so far is that a reduction will typically not be able to exploit a signature σ^* it created itself; otherwise, it could just solve Π on its own.[7] We thus define the adversaries $\mathcal{A}_\sim$ and $\mathcal{A}_\nsim$ simulated to $\mathcal{R}$ as follows: given the public key, they sample $m \leftarrow\!\!{\scriptstyle\$}\, M$ (where M is the message space) and query a signature on m; next they sample m^*: $\mathcal{A}_\sim$ samples $m^* \leftarrow\!\!{\scriptstyle\$}\, [m]$ and $\mathcal{A}_\nsim$ samples $m^* \leftarrow\!\!{\scriptstyle\$}\, M$; they then *sample a random signature σ^* from the set of all valid signatures on m^** and return σ^*. (This is analogous to the proof of the impossibility of tight reductions for re-randomizable signatures [HJK12].)

Define meta-reduction $\mathcal{M}_2$ as follows: given a class-hiding instance (m, m^*), it simulates $\mathcal{A}_\sim$ or $\mathcal{A}_\nsim$ (not knowing which) by obtaining a signature σ' on m^* via rewinding and using Adapt (with $\mu = 1$) to transform σ' to a uniform σ^*; decide according to whether $\mathcal{R}$ breaks Π.

This proof strategy only works for *perfect* reductions, which break Π whenever an adversary returns a forgery. Using the ideas for re-randomizable signatures [HJK12], this could be used to show that there are no tight reductions. However, we have not yet excluded the existence of non-tight reductions, such as *partitioning* reductions [Cor00,BLS01,Wat05]: given the problem instance, such

---

[7] The problem is that the definition of the adversary $\mathcal{A}$ simulated by $\mathcal{M}_1$ *depends* on $\mathcal{R}$ (as it uses a signature produced by $\mathcal{R}$). But a reduction only guarantees that when given any efficient adversary (defined independently of the reduction), it can use it to solve the problem. We must therefore start with defining $\mathcal{A}$ (who is not necessarily efficient, but whose behavior is precisely defined). Really we specify two adversaries, one simulated in the DDH case (not breaking the scheme) and one breaking the scheme.

reductions set up the public key (or program the random oracle in a way) so that they can answer signing queries for a subset S of messages, whereas for messages from another subset E, they can "exploit" forgeries to solve the problem.

Reductions that Partition Along Classes. To see how $\mathcal{M}_2$, defined above, fails for a non-tight reduction, assume $\mathcal{R}^p$ partitions the message space M "along classes", that is, if some m is in S (the set of "signable" messages) then all the messages of its class $[m]$ are, and if $m \in E$ (the set of "exploitable" messages) then $[m] \subseteq E$. We first observe that S and E must be (almost) disjoint, as otherwise $\mathcal{R}^p$ can solve the problem Π on its own (by producing a signature and then exploiting it). This case is reflected in the first term in Eq. (1) via an adversary $\mathcal{B}$ that simply aborts if it receives an invalid signature.

Applying $\mathcal{M}_2$ to $\mathcal{R}^p$ yields the following: if the signatures on m and m^* returned by $\mathcal{R}^p$ are valid, they both come from S, either in the same class or not; in both cases, since S and E are (almost) disjoint, σ^* will (almost certainly) not be exploitable by $\mathcal{R}^p$. Thus, $\mathcal{M}_2$ cannot exploit $\mathcal{R}^p$: either one of the signatures is invalid, or $\mathcal{R}^p$ will not solve the problem (no matter whether $m \sim m^*$ or not).

While this shows that the strategy $\mathcal{M}_2$ does not work for a reduction $\mathcal{R}^p$ that partitions along classes, a different meta-reduction $\mathcal{D}$ (which is the one used in our proof and appearing in Eq. (1)) can actually exploit $\mathcal{R}^p$ to distinguish classes: given an instance (m, m^*), $\mathcal{D}$ queries a signature on m, and (after rewinding) it queries a signature on m^*; if (a) one of them is valid and the other one isn't, it deduces that $m \not\sim m^*$, whereas if (b) they are both valid or both invalid, it guesses $m \sim m^*$. Since $\mathcal{R}^p$ partitions along classes, if ($\sim$) then (b) must occur, whereas if ($\not\sim$) then (a) occurs with good probability. For the last argument, we show, again via $\mathcal{B}$, that the sets S and E must both be "big" for a "good" reduction.

Other Reductions. So far, we have discussed that no reduction that partitions entire *classes* (into "simulatable" and "exploitable") can exist. The first question this raises is what to do about *non*-partitioning reductions. It turns out that we can view any reduction $\mathcal{R}$ as partitioning: let r be $\mathcal{R}$'s randomness given to it as explicit input and let st be $\mathcal{R}$'s internal state (which incorporates r) after returning the public key pk. For a fixed st, $\mathcal{R}$'s next step, $\mathcal{R}.\mathsf{sign}$ which takes input st and a query m and returns σ, is then a deterministic function.

For any (st, pk) we now define $S_{st,pk}$ as the set of messages m for which $\mathcal{R}.\mathsf{sign}(st, m)$ returns a signature valid under pk. Similarly, $\mathcal{R}.\mathsf{fin}$ taking a state and a forgery (m, σ) and returning a solution for Π is deterministic. We define $E_{st,pk}$ as the set of messages m^* for which, if $\mathcal{R}$ is given st and a *uniform* valid signature on m^*, it solves the Π-instance with a probability greater than a threshold we set.

It remains to show that a reduction $\mathcal{R}'$ that does *not* partition along classes cannot exist either. For such $\mathcal{R}'$, there are (many) classes which contain (many) messages in S as well as (many) messages in E. Now we can use *signature-adaptation* to directly attack the underlying problem Π (and thus, if the problem is hard to begin with, then no such reduction can exist). We construct a meta-reduction $\mathcal{M}$ (appearing in Eq. (1)) against Π, analogous to $\mathcal{R}^{\mathcal{A}_\sim}$ from the beginning of the proof intuition. Given an instance of Π, $\mathcal{M}$ runs $\mathcal{R}'$ to receive pk and queries a signature σ on a message $m \leftarrow_\$ M$; it then runs $\sigma^* \leftarrow$ Adapt(pk, m, σ, μ) for $\mu \leftarrow_\$ \mathbb{Z}_p^*$ and returns $(\mu \cdot m, \sigma^*)$.[8] The forgery returned by $\mathcal{M}$ is thus a uniform signature on a random message m^* in $[m]$. Thus, since there are many classes with many elements in S and many elements in E, there is a "good" probability that $m \in S$ and $m^* \in E$, meaning $\mathcal{R}'$ solves the problem instance.

Challenges. Turning the above intuition (with all its "many", "big", "almost certainly", etc.) into a rigorous proof turns out quite tricky. We need to argue that our meta-reductions really cover all possible reduction strategies. That is, show that if both $\mathcal{B}$ (the trivial adversary) and $\mathcal{M}$ (the meta-reduction that returns a forgery on a multiple of the queried message) fail then the correlation between classes and the partitioning by S and E must be high enough so $\mathcal{D}$ can decide whether two messages m and m^* are from the same class. What complicates the computation of probabilities are dependencies of random variables. Moreover, the above sets S and E depend on the intermediate values generated by the reduction (and these sets are of the form $S_{st,pk}$ and $E_{st,pk}$), whereas the success of the reduction is guaranteed for random st and pk.

Proof Overview. The first meta-reduction $\mathcal{M}_1$ (simulating $\mathcal{A}_\sim$ or $\mathcal{A}_{\not\sim}$) with which we started discussing proof ideas is not used in our proof. $\mathcal{M}_1$ only works for reductions that have both signable and exploitable signature in many classes, but for these, $\mathcal{M}$ (from two paragraphs above) can directly break Π: it runs the reduction on a problem instance, queries a signature on a random message m, adapts it to a random multiple $\mu \cdot m$, and returns it to the reduction. The latter solves the instance if m is signable ($m \in S$) and $\mu \cdot m$ is exploitable ($\mu \cdot m \in E$).

Using $\mathcal{M}$, our proof first establishes that for an exploitable message there cannot be many signable messages in the same class (Lemmas 1 and 2). This shows that (roughly) classes contain either signable or exploitable messages but not both. We also show that there must be many signable messages, as otherwise the reduction does not correctly simulate the game to the adversary (Lemma 3, which constructs a "trivial" adversary $\mathcal{B}$); moreover, there cannot be too few exploitable messages either, as otherwise the reduction is not successful (Lemmas 5 and 6).

Together, this yields that while overall there are many signable messages, there are also many classes that contain (almost) none (since the exploitable messages must also be somewhere). This can be leveraged by the meta-reduction $\mathcal{D}$ (also previously discussed) against class-hiding: given an instance (m, m^*), $\mathcal{D}$ asks the reduction for signatures on both. If exactly one of the messages is signable, then they are likely to be in different classes. This suffices to obtain an advantage solving class-hiding. (Note that $\mathcal{D}$ need not "fully" simulate an adversary outputting a forgery.)

---

[8] Really, $\mathcal{M}$ first rewinds $\mathcal{R}'$ and returns $(\mu \cdot m, \sigma^*)$ in an execution in which it did not query a signature ($\mathcal{M}$ thus differs from $\mathcal{A}_\sim$ defined earlier). The reason is that the signing query could modify the set E, which could foil our analysis. (This is also why $\mathcal{D}$, defined above, rewinds the reduction).

To make this argument formal, we port the above properties to the level of state/public-key pairs (st, pk), which corresponds to the point when the reduction starts running the adversary on pk. This is done to then leverage the conditional independence of uniformly sampled messages falling into S or E respectively in the proof. Let $I^{(S)}$ be the set of pairs (st, pk) for which there are "sufficiently many" signable messages and let $I^{(\cap)}$ be the set of pairs (st, pk) which have very few classes that have many signable and exploitable messages. We show that $I^{(S)}$ is large (Lemma 4), that $I^{(\cap)}$ is large (Lemmas 7 and 8) and their intersection is large (Lemma 9).

These lemmas yield that (for many state/public-key pairs) there is a correlation between whether two messages are in the same class and whether these two messages are signable, which is what the success of the meta-reduction $\mathcal{D}$ against class-hiding relies on. This is made formal in Theorem 1.

2 Preliminaries

2.1 Notation

For a prime p, by $\mathbb{Z}_p^*$ we denote the non-zero elements of the finite field $\mathbb{Z}_p :=$ $\mathbb{Z}/p\mathbb{Z}$. In this paper we will consider a fixed group $(\mathbb{G}, +)$ of prime order p. Define its non-zero elements $\mathbb{G}^* := \mathbb{G} \setminus \{0_\mathbb{G}\}$. We will denote by $k \cdot g := \sum_1^k g$. Note that $\mathbb{G}$ having prime order implies that for $g \neq 0_\mathbb{G}$ and $k \neq 0$ we have $k \cdot g \neq 0_\mathbb{G}$. We will naturally extend this operation to vectors by applying the operation "$\cdot$" defined above component-wise: for $m = (g_1, g_2) \in (\mathbb{G}^*)^2$ and $k \in \mathbb{Z}_p^*$ define $k \cdot m := (k \cdot g_1, k \cdot g_2)$. Let g denote a fixed generator of $\mathbb{G}$, which exists due to p being prime. For a set A denote by $\bar{A}$ the complement of A.

Assigning a value b to a variable a is denoted by $a := b$. When a denotes the output of a probabilistic algorithm B write $a \leftarrow B$, while drawing a value a uniformly from a finite set A is denoted by $a \leftarrow\!\!\$\ A$.

2.2 DDH

In this work we consider concrete security treatment, that is, we do not consider "negligible" advantages, but concretely relate the security of a scheme to the hardness of an underlying computational problem. The decisional Diffie-Hellamn (DDH) problem will be of central importance.

Definition 1. *Define for a group $\mathbb{G}$ of prime order p with g generating $\mathbb{G}$ the DDH-Game, played by an adversary $\mathcal{A}$ for $b \in \{0, 1\}$ as:*

$$\underline{\mathrm{DDH}_{\mathbb{G},\mathcal{A}}^b}$$

$1:\quad x, y, t \leftarrow\!\!\$\ \mathbb{Z}_p^*$

$2:\quad b' \leftarrow \mathcal{A}(\mathbb{G}, x \cdot g, y \cdot g, (bxy + (1-b)t) \cdot g)$

$3:\quad \textbf{return } b'$

Define the advantage of an adversary $\mathcal{A}$ as

$$\mathsf{Adv}_{\mathbb{G},\mathcal{A}}^{\mathrm{DDH}} := \left| \Pr\left[\mathrm{DDH}_{\mathbb{G},\mathcal{A}}^1 = 1\right] - \Pr\left[\mathrm{DDH}_{\mathbb{G},\mathcal{A}}^0 = 1\right] \right|.$$

2.3 EQS Signature Schemes

For concreteness, we consider Equivalence Class Signature schemes for the message space $M := (\mathbb{G}^*)^2$. (All our results easily generalize to $(\mathbb{G}^*)^\ell$ for $\ell > 2$). This message space is partitioned into equivalence classes by the following relation for $m, m' \in M$:

$$m \sim m' :\Leftrightarrow \exists \mu \in \mathbb{Z}_p^* : m' = \mu \cdot m.$$

Define the set of classes of M as $\mathcal{C} := M/_\sim$. An EQS Scheme for message space M consists of the following algorithms:

– Keygen(): a probabilistic algorithm that outputs a key pair (sk, pk) with $pk \in PK$, the public key space.
– Sign(sk, m): a probabilistic algorithm that takes a secret key sk and a message $m \in M$ and outputs a signature $\sigma \in \mathbb{S}$, where $\mathbb{S}$ is the (finite) signature space.
– Verify(pk, m, σ): a deterministic algorithm taking a public key pk, a message $m \in M$ and a signature σ and outputting 1 if the triple is valid and 0 otherwise.
– Adapt(pk, m, σ, μ): a probabilistic algorithm taking a public key pk, a message $m \in M$, a signature σ on m and a scalar $\mu \in \mathbb{Z}_p^*$ as inputs and outputting a signature $\sigma' \in \mathbb{S}$ on the message $\mu \cdot m$.

By [Keygen] we will denote the set of pairs (sk, pk) that have non-zero probability of being output by Keygen. The next definition ensures that Sign and Adapt generate valid signatures.

Definition 2. *An EQS scheme is* correct *if for all $m \in M$ and for all $(sk, pk) \in$ [Keygen] and for all $\mu \in \mathbb{Z}_p^*$ it holds that*

$$\Pr[\mathsf{Verify}(pk, m, \mathsf{Sign}(sk, m)) = 1] = 1 \qquad and$$
$$\Pr[\mathsf{Verify}(pk, \mu \cdot m, \mathsf{Adapt}(pk, m, \mathsf{Sign}(sk, m), \mu)) = 1] = 1.$$

The following definition [FHS19, Definition 20] guarantees that signatures returned by Adapt are distributed uniformly.

Definition 3. *An EQS scheme* perfectly adapts signatures under malicious keys *if for all tuples $(pk, m, \sigma, \mu) \in PK \times M \times \mathbb{S} \times \mathbb{Z}_p^*$ for which*

$$\mathsf{Verify}(pk, m, \sigma) = 1$$

the output of $\sigma' \leftarrow \mathsf{Adapt}(pk, m, \sigma, \mu)$ is a uniformly random element of $\mathbb{S}$ conditioned on $\mathsf{Verify}(pk, \mu \cdot m, \sigma') = 1$.

Unforgeability is defined via a game. It starts by generating a key pair and initializing the set Q of messages for whose class a query has been issued. It then hands over the public key to $\mathcal{A}$, giving it access to an oracle $\mathcal{O}$. The oracle, when queried with a message m, adds the class of m to Q. In the end $\mathcal{A}$ outputs a message/signature pair (m^*, σ^*), which is considered a forgery if it is valid and no oracle query has been asked on the equivalence class of m^*.

Definition 4. *For an EQS scheme Σ and for a forger $\mathcal{A}$ that has access to a signing oracle $\mathcal{O}$, which can modify the set Q and has access to sk, we define the UNF game as follows:*

$\underline{\text{UNF}_{\Sigma,\mathcal{A}}}$

1 : $(sk, pk) \leftarrow \mathsf{Keygen}()$

2 : $Q := \emptyset$

3 : $(m^*, \sigma^*) \leftarrow \mathcal{A}^{\mathcal{O}(\cdot)}(pk)$

4 : **return** $(\mathsf{Verify}(pk, m^*, \sigma^*) \wedge m^* \notin Q)$

$\underline{\mathcal{O}(m)}$

1 : $Q := Q \cup [m]$

2 : **return** $\mathsf{Sign}(sk, m)$

where $[m] := \{m' \in M \mid m \sim m'\}$ is the equivalence class of m. Define the advantage of an adversary $\mathcal{A}$ as

$$\mathsf{Adv}_{\Sigma,\mathcal{A}}^{\text{UNF}} := \Pr[\text{UNF}_{\Sigma,\mathcal{A}} = 1].$$

The next definition requires it to be hard to distinguish message pairs from the same class from random pairs.

Definition 5. *Let Σ be an EQS scheme with message space M. Define the Class-hiding game played by an adversary $\mathcal{D}$ for $b \in \{0,1\}$:*

$\underline{\text{CH}_{\Sigma,\mathcal{D}}^b}$

1 : $m \leftarrow\!\!\$\, M$

2 : $m_0 \leftarrow\!\!\$\, M$

3 : $m_1 \leftarrow\!\!\$\, [m]$

4 : $b' \leftarrow \mathcal{D}(m, m_b)$

5 : **return** b'

The advantage of $\mathcal{D}$ is defined as

$$\mathsf{Adv}_{\Sigma,\mathcal{D}}^{\text{CH}} := \left| \Pr\left[\text{CH}_{\Sigma,\mathcal{D}}^1 = 1 \right] - \Pr\left[\text{CH}_{\Sigma,\mathcal{D}}^0 = 1 \right] \right|.$$

The proof of the following is straightforward and given in [FHS19].

Proposition 1 ([FHS19, **Proposition 1**]). *Let $\mathbb{G}$ be a group of prime order p and Σ an EQS scheme with $M = (\mathbb{G}^*)^2$. Then Σ is class-hiding if and only if DDH is hard in $\mathbb{G}$, in particular, we have $\mathsf{Adv}_{\Sigma,\mathcal{A}}^{\text{CH}} = \mathsf{Adv}_{\mathbb{G},\mathcal{A}}^{\text{DDH}}$ for all $\mathcal{A}$.*

2.4   Computational Problems

The following definition is due to [HJK12].

Definition 6. *A computational problem $\Pi := (C_\Pi, S_\Pi)$ consists of a set of challenges C_Π and a family of sets of solutions S_Π for each challenge c, i.e. $S_\Pi := (S_c)_{c \in C_\Pi}$. Additionally, we require the existence of two deterministic (polynomial-time) algorithms.*

- Sample(ρ) *takes randomness ρ and outputs $c \in C_\Pi$.*
- Check(ρ, s) *takes randomness ρ and an element s and checks whether $s \in S_c$ for $c :=$ Sample(ρ).*

We will denote the randomness space of Sample *by* P. *For an algorithm $\mathcal{A}$ define the game Π played by $\mathcal{A}$ below.*

$$\underline{\Pi_{\mathcal{A}}}$$

$$
\begin{array}{ll}
1: & \rho \leftarrow_{\$} P \\
2: & c := \mathsf{Sample}(\rho) \\
3: & s \leftarrow \mathcal{A}(c) \\
4: & \mathbf{return}\ \mathsf{Check}(\rho, s)
\end{array}
$$

3   Our Impossibility Result

We strengthen our impossibility result in that we only consider adversaries that make one single signing query. That is, we show that even reductions that *only* work for single-query adversaries do not exist.

We will first establish some definitions and notations used throughout this section. Let R denote the randomness space of $\mathcal{R}$, then fixing its randomness $r \leftarrow_{\$} R$ lets us think of $\mathcal{R}$ as deterministic. When talking about a reduction $\mathcal{R}$ from Π to UNF that is being run by a meta-reduction $\mathcal{D}$, which simulates an adversary $\mathcal{A}$ for UNF that uses at most one signing query, we can think of $\mathcal{R}$ as split into three deterministic algorithms:

- $\mathcal{R}.\mathsf{init}(c, r)$: is the initialization routine of $\mathcal{R}$, which takes a challenge c of Π and some randomness $r \leftarrow_{\$} R$ and returns the state st of $\mathcal{R}$ and the public key pk of the UNF game;
- $\mathcal{R}.\mathsf{sign}(st, m)$: implements the signing oracle of $\mathcal{R}$. Given a state st which is output by $\mathcal{R}.\mathsf{init}$ and a message m it outputs a new state st' and a signature σ;
- $\mathcal{R}.\mathsf{fin}(st, m^*, \sigma^*)$: takes a state st returned by either $\mathcal{R}.\mathsf{init}$ or $\mathcal{R}.\mathsf{sign}$ (in the former case the adversary made no signing queries); it also takes a message m^* and a purported forgery σ^* for m^*. The algorithm then outputs its solution s to the problem c received in $\mathcal{R}.\mathsf{init}$.

Definition 7. *We say $\mathcal{R}$ reducing Π to UNF communicating with an adversary $\mathcal{A}$ for UNF has a (multiplicative) reduction tightness $\phi \in (0, 1]$ if the following holds:*

$$\phi \cdot \mathsf{Adv}_{\mathcal{A}}^{\mathrm{UNF}} \leq \mathsf{Adv}_{\mathcal{R}^{\mathcal{A}}}^{\Pi}.$$

To condense notation and make calculations more readable, we introduce the following shorthand.

Definition 8. *Define* Init *as the code fragment given below.*

$$\begin{array}{l} \hline \textsf{Init} \\ \hline r \leftarrow_\$ \textrm{R} \\ \rho \leftarrow_\$ \textrm{P} \\ c := \textsf{Sample}(\rho) \\ (st, pk) := \mathcal{R}.\textsf{init}(c, r) \\ \textbf{return } (st, pk) \\ \hline \end{array}$$

Definition 9. *Let Π be a computational problem. Let $\mathcal{R}$ be a reduction from Π to UNF with tightness ϕ. Given $(st, pk) \in [\textsf{Init}]$ we define for a message m the set of valid signatures $V_{m,pk} := \{\sigma \in \mathbb{S} \mid \textsf{Verify}(pk, m, \sigma) = 1\}$. We then define subsets of M:*

$$S_{st,pk} := \{m \in M \mid \mathcal{R}.\textsf{sign}(st, m) \in V_{m,pk}\},$$

$$E_{st,pk} := \left\{ m \in M \mid \Pr_{\sigma \leftarrow_\$ V_{m,pk}} [\textsf{Check}(\rho, \mathcal{R}.\textsf{fin}(st, (m, \sigma))) = 1] > \frac{\phi}{2} \right\},$$

where $S_{st,pk}$ (signable messages) corresponds to the set of messages for which $\mathcal{R}$ is able to provide a valid signature, and $E_{st,pk}$ (exploitable messages) corresponds to the set of messages for which $\mathcal{R}$ is "likely" to win game Π when given a uniform forgery on that message. Note that ρ is implicitly defined in the execution of $\textsf{Init}$.

The following result will show that whenever there is a message m that is "exploitable", then the probability of finding a multiple of m to be "signable" is bounded by the advantage of an efficient adversary winning Π. Intuitively this means that whenever we can find a message that $\mathcal{R}$ can sign, which can then be adapted into a message which $\mathcal{R}$ can exploit, then Π can be solved efficiently.

Lemma 1. *Let Σ be an EQS scheme that adapts perfectly under malicious keys (Definition 3). Let $\mathcal{R}$ be a reduction from Π to UNF running in time τ with reduction tightness ϕ. Then there exists a meta-reduction $\mathcal{M}$ running in time $\approx \tau$ such that*

$$\Pr\left[\begin{array}{l} (st, pk) \leftarrow \textsf{Init}, \\ m \leftarrow_\$ M, \mu \leftarrow_\$ \mathbb{Z}_p^* \end{array} : \mu \cdot m \in S_{st,pk} \wedge m \in E_{st,pk} \right] \leq \frac{2}{\phi} \textsf{Adv}_{\mathcal{M}^{\mathcal{R}}}^{\Pi}.$$

Proof. Consider the meta-reduction $\mathcal{M}^{\mathcal{R}}$ playing Π that rewinds $\mathcal{R}$ given in Fig. 1. Then it holds that

$$\begin{aligned} \textsf{Adv}_{\mathcal{M}^{\mathcal{R}}}^{\Pi} &= \Pr[\Pi_{\mathcal{M}^{\mathcal{R}}} = 1] \\ &\geq \Pr[\Pi_{\mathcal{M}^{\mathcal{R}}} = 1 \mid m \in S_{st,pk} \wedge \zeta \cdot m \in E_{st,pk}] \\ &\quad \cdot \Pr\left[\begin{array}{l} (st, pk) \leftarrow \textsf{Init}, \\ m \leftarrow_\$ M, \zeta \leftarrow_\$ \mathbb{Z}_p^* \end{array} : m \in S_{st,pk} \wedge \zeta \cdot m \in E_{st,pk} \right] \end{aligned}$$

by the definition of $E_{st,pk}$ we have that $\mathcal{R}$ wins with probability $\geq \frac{\phi}{2}$ when $\zeta \cdot m \in E_{st,pk}$. Therefore

$\mathcal{M}^{\mathcal{R}}(c)$

---

1   $r \leftarrow\!\!\$\ \mathrm{R}$

2   $(st, pk) := \mathcal{R}.\mathsf{init}(c, r)$

3   $m \leftarrow\!\!\$\ M$

4   $(st', \sigma) \leftarrow \mathcal{R}.\mathsf{sign}(st, m)$

5   **if** $\mathsf{Verify}(pk, m, \sigma) = 0$

6   **abort**

7   $\mu \leftarrow \mathbb{Z}_p^*$

8   $\sigma' := \mathsf{Adapt}(pk, m, \sigma, \mu)$

9   **return** $\mathcal{R}.\mathsf{fin}(st, \mu \cdot m, \sigma')$

Recall:

$\Pi_{\mathcal{M}^{\mathcal{R}}}$

---

1   $\rho \leftarrow\!\!\$\ \mathrm{P}$

2   $c := \mathsf{Sample}(\rho)$

3   $s \leftarrow \mathcal{M}^{\mathcal{R}}(c)$

4   **return** $\mathsf{Check}(\rho, s)$

Fig. 1. The meta-reduction $\mathcal{M}$

$$\mathsf{Adv}_{\mathcal{M}^{\mathcal{R}}}^{\Pi} \geq \frac{\phi}{2} \Pr\left[\begin{matrix}(st, pk) \leftarrow \mathsf{Init}, \\ m \leftarrow\!\!\$\ M, \zeta \leftarrow\!\!\$\ \mathbb{Z}_p^*\end{matrix} : m \in S_{st,pk} \wedge \zeta \cdot m \in E_{st,pk}\right]$$

$$= \frac{\phi}{2} \Pr\left[\begin{matrix}(st, pk) \leftarrow \mathsf{Init}, \\ m \leftarrow\!\!\$\ M, \mu \leftarrow\!\!\$\ \mathbb{Z}_p^*\end{matrix} : \mu \cdot m \in S_{st,pk} \wedge m \in E_{st,pk}\right].$$

□

The following result will be analogous to Lemma 1. It intuitively shows that if the problem Π is computationally hard then when sampling two random messages from an equivalence class, it is unlikely that the reduction can sign one of them while exploiting the other one to solve Π. In particular, we bound the probability that a random message is "signable" and there are many "exploitable" messages in its class, where "signable" and "exploitable" are as described in Definition 9. This is the case because when $\mathcal{R}$ is able to provide signatures on messages which can be adapted to exploitable ones, it could solve Π on its own.

Lemma 2. *Let Σ be an EQS scheme that adapts perfectly under malicious keys (Definition 3). Let $\mathcal{R}$ be a reduction from Π to UNF running in time τ with reduction tightness ϕ. Let $\delta \in [0, 1]$. Then there exists a meta-reduction $\mathcal{M}$ aiming to solve Π and running in time $\approx \tau$ such that*

$$\Pr\left[\begin{matrix}(st, pk) \leftarrow \mathsf{Init}, \\ m \leftarrow\!\!\$\ M\end{matrix} : m \in S_{st,pk} \wedge \frac{|E_{st,pk} \cap [m]|}{|[m]|} \geq \delta\right] \leq \frac{2}{\delta\phi}\mathsf{Adv}_{\mathcal{M}^{\mathcal{R}}}^{\Pi}.$$

Proof. Consider the meta-reduction $\mathcal{M}^{\mathcal{R}}$ playing Π that *rewinds* $\mathcal{R}$ which is given in Fig. 1 (note that $\mathcal{M}$ runs $\mathcal{R}.\mathsf{fin}$ on st and not st'). The reason for $\mathcal{M}$'s need to rewind $\mathcal{R}$ is that this allows us to view the sets $S_{st,pk}$ and $E_{st,pk}$ as fixed for each execution, as opposed to them changing after each call of the signing oracle. Then we can show the following.

$$\mathsf{Adv}^{\Pi}_{\mathcal{M}^{\mathcal{R}}} = \Pr[\Pi_{\mathcal{M}^{\mathcal{R}}} = 1]$$

$$\geq \Pr\left[\Pi_{\mathcal{M}^{\mathcal{R}}} = 1 \ \middle| \ m \in S_{st,pk} \wedge \frac{|E_{st,pk} \cap [m]|}{|[m]|} \geq \delta\right]$$

$$\cdot \Pr\left[\Pi_{\mathcal{M}^{\mathcal{R}}} : m \in S_{st,pk} \wedge \frac{|E_{st,pk} \cap [m]|}{|[m]|} \geq \delta\right]$$

$$\geq \Pr\left[\Pi_{\mathcal{M}^{\mathcal{R}}} = 1 \ \middle| \ m \in S_{st,pk} \wedge \frac{|E_{st,pk} \cap [m]|}{|[m]|} \geq \delta \wedge \mu \cdot m \in E_{st,pk}\right] \quad (a)$$

$$\cdot \Pr\left[\Pi_{\mathcal{M}^{\mathcal{R}}} : \mu \cdot m \in E_{st,pk} \ \middle| \ m \in S_{st,pk} \wedge \frac{|E_{st,pk} \cap [m]|}{|[m]|} \geq \delta\right] \quad (b)$$

$$\cdot \Pr\left[\Pi_{\mathcal{M}^{\mathcal{R}}} : m \in S_{st,pk} \wedge \frac{|E_{st,pk} \cap [m]|}{|[m]|} \geq \delta\right]$$

where $(b) \geq \delta$, while $(a) \geq \frac{\phi}{2}$ since $\mathcal{R}$ wins with probability $\frac{\phi}{2}$ if $\mu \cdot m \in E_{st,pk}$ and a uniformly random valid signature is given to $\mathcal{R}$, which is the case due to Σ fulfilling Definition 3. Therefore

$$\mathsf{Adv}^{\Pi}_{\mathcal{M}^{\mathcal{R}}} \geq \frac{\phi}{2}\delta\Pr\left[\begin{matrix}(st, pk) \leftarrow \mathsf{Init}, \\ m \leftarrow_\$ M\end{matrix} : m \in S_{st,pk} \wedge \frac{|E_{st,pk} \cap [m]|}{|[m]|} \geq \delta\right],$$

which concludes the lemma.   □

Having established how $E_{st,pk}$ is distributed with respect to $S_{st,pk}$, we will now shift our attention to $S_{st,pk}$, the set of all messages which $\mathcal{R}$ can sign. The first result will establish a lower bound on the expected size of $S_{st,pk}$. Intuitively, this bound exists since in order to simulate UNF $\mathcal{R}$ has to provide signatures on "many" messages.

Lemma 3. *Let Σ be an EQS scheme. Let $\mathcal{R}$ have a reduction tightness ϕ. Then there exists an adversary $\mathcal{B}$ running in constant time such that the probability of a uniformly sampled m falling into $S_{st,pk}$, as defined in Definition 9, is lower-bounded as follows:*

$$\Pr\left[\begin{matrix}(st, pk) \leftarrow \mathsf{Init}, \\ m \leftarrow_\$ M\end{matrix} : m \in S_{st,pk}\right] \geq \phi - \mathsf{Adv}^{\Pi}_{\mathcal{R}^{\mathcal{B}}}$$

Proof. Consider the unbounded adversary $\mathcal{U}_S$ (showing a bound on "S") playing UNF which is defined in Fig. 2. $\mathcal{U}_S$ wins with probability 1, since in the game UNF the signature returned by the oracle is always valid, and therefore $\mathcal{U}_S$ never aborts. Now define the efficient adversary $\mathcal{B}$ (Fig. 3), which queries a signature σ and then aborts. Conditioned on σ being invalid, $\mathcal{B}$ perfectly simulates $\mathcal{U}_S$. We obtain

$$\phi \leq \phi \cdot \mathsf{Adv}^{\mathsf{UNF}}_{\Sigma, \mathcal{U}_S}$$

$$\leq \mathsf{Adv}^{\Pi}_{\mathcal{R}^{\mathcal{U}_S}}$$

$$= \Pr\left[\begin{matrix}(st, pk) \leftarrow \mathsf{Init}, \\ (m', \sigma') \leftarrow \mathcal{U}_S^{\mathcal{R}.\mathsf{sign}(st,.)}(pk)\end{matrix} : \mathsf{Check}(\rho, \mathcal{R}.\mathsf{fin}(m', \sigma')) = 1\right],$$

$$\mathcal{U}_S^{\text{sign}(\cdot)}(pk)$$

1 $m \leftarrow\!\!\$\ M$

2 $\sigma \leftarrow \text{sign}(m)$

3 if $\text{Verify}(pk, m, \sigma) = 0$

4   abort

5 $m' \leftarrow\!\!\$\ M \setminus [m]$

6 $\sigma' \leftarrow\!\!\$\ V_{m',pk}$

7 return (m', σ')

$$\mathcal{B}^{\text{sign}(\cdot)}(pk)$$

1 $m \leftarrow\!\!\$\ M$

2 $\sigma \leftarrow \text{sign}(m)$

3 abort

Fig. 2. The unbounded adversary $\mathcal{U}_S$ **Fig. 3.** The a$\mathcal{B}$orting adversary $\mathcal{B}$

where ρ is implicitly defined in Init,

$$= \Pr[\Pi_{\mathcal{R}^{u_S}} = 1 \mid m \in \bar{S}_{st,pk}] \Pr\begin{bmatrix} (st, pk) \leftarrow \text{Init}, \\ m \leftarrow\!\!\$\ M \end{bmatrix} : m \in \bar{S}_{st,pk}\end{bmatrix}$$

$$+ \Pr[\Pi_{\mathcal{R}^{u_S}} = 1 \mid m \in S_{st,pk}] \Pr\begin{bmatrix} (st, pk) \leftarrow \text{Init}, \\ m \leftarrow\!\!\$\ M \end{bmatrix} : m \in S_{st,pk}\end{bmatrix}$$

where the m in the two left-handed factors refers to the one chosen in line 1 of $\mathcal{U}_S$, and due to $\mathcal{B}$ simulating $\mathcal{U}_S$ in the case where σ is invalid we get

$$= \Pr[\Pi_{\mathcal{R}^{\mathcal{B}}} = 1 \mid m \in \bar{S}_{st,pk}] \Pr\begin{bmatrix} (st, pk) \leftarrow \text{Init}, \\ m \leftarrow\!\!\$\ M \end{bmatrix} : m \in \bar{S}_{st,pk}\end{bmatrix}$$

$$+ \Pr[\Pi_{\mathcal{R}^{u_S}} = 1 \mid m \in S_{st,pk}] \Pr\begin{bmatrix} (st, pk) \leftarrow \text{Init}, \\ m \leftarrow\!\!\$\ M \end{bmatrix} : m \in S_{st,pk}\end{bmatrix}$$

$$\leq \text{Adv}_{\mathcal{R}^{\mathcal{B}}}^{\Pi} + \Pr\begin{bmatrix} (st, pk) \leftarrow \text{Init}, \\ m \leftarrow\!\!\$\ M \end{bmatrix} : m \in S_{st,pk}\end{bmatrix},$$

where the last inequality is due to

$$\Pr[\Pi_{\mathcal{R}^{\mathcal{B}}} = 1 \mid m \in \bar{S}_{st,pk}] \leq \frac{\text{Adv}_{\mathcal{R}^{\mathcal{B}}}^{\Pi}}{\Pr[m \in \bar{S}_{st,pk}]}.$$

□

The next statement will translate the previous lemma to a setting where we will fix (st, pk). Fixing (st, pk) will enable us to remove dependencies of events at the expense of an additional condition, namely that of the fixed state/public-key pair. This tradeoff is well worth it due to the following lemma allowing us to reason with a similar bound about a reduced but still "large" set of state/public-key pairs. The intuition is that if for a random state/public-key pair generated by the experiment there is a bound, then the set of state/public-key pairs for which a similar bound holds must be large. Since $S_{st,pk}$ is "big", there must also be "many" state/public-key pairs for which a slightly worse bound holds. We will denote subsets of [Init] with $I^{(x)}$, where x will identify the subset in question. For example the next lemma will define the subset for which the set $S_{st,pk}$ is "big".

Lemma 4. *Let Σ be an EQS scheme that adapts perfectly under malicious keys. Let $\mathcal{R}$ have a reduction tightness ϕ. Let $\mathcal{B}$ be as defined in Fig. 3. Define a subset of [Init] for which it is "likely" to sample a message in $S_{st,pk}$ conditioned on the given state and public key:*

$$I^{(S)} := \left\{ (st, pk) \middle| \Pr\left[m \leftarrow M : m \in S_{st,pk}\right] \geq \frac{\phi - \mathsf{Adv}_{\mathcal{R}^{\mathcal{B}}}^{\Pi}}{2} \right\}.$$

Then $\Pr[(st, pk) \leftarrow \mathsf{Init} : (st, pk) \in I^{(S)}] \geq \frac{\phi - \mathsf{Adv}_{\mathcal{R}^{\mathcal{B}}}^{\Pi}}{2}$.

Proof. From Lemma 3 we have

$$\phi - \mathsf{Adv}_{\mathcal{R}^{\mathcal{B}}}^{\Pi} \leq \Pr\left[\begin{matrix}(st, pk) \leftarrow \mathsf{Init}, \\ m \leftarrow_\$ M\end{matrix} : m \in S_{st,pk}\right]$$

$$= \sum_{(st,pk)} \Pr[(st, pk)] \Pr[m \leftarrow_\$ M : m \in S_{st,pk}]$$

$$= \sum_{(st,pk) \in I^{(S)}} \Pr[(st, pk)] \Pr[m \leftarrow_\$ M : m \in S_{st,pk}]$$

$$+ \sum_{(st,pk) \notin I^{(S)}} \Pr[(st, pk)] \Pr[m \leftarrow_\$ M : m \in S_{st,pk}]$$

$$\leq \Pr[(st, pk) \leftarrow \mathsf{Init} : (st, pk) \in I^{(S)}]$$

$$+ \frac{\phi - \mathsf{Adv}_{\mathcal{R}^{\mathcal{B}}}^{\Pi}}{2}(1 - \Pr[(st, pk) \leftarrow \mathsf{Init} : (st, pk) \in I^{(S)}]).$$

And therefore

$$\Pr[(st, pk) \leftarrow \mathsf{Init} : (st, pk) \in I^{(S)}] \geq \frac{\phi - \mathsf{Adv}_{\mathcal{R}^{\mathcal{B}}}^{\Pi}}{2}.$$

$\square$

Similar to Lemma 3 we can obtain a bound on the size of $E_{st,pk}$. An obvious observation is that in order for $\mathcal{R}$ to be successful, there must be many messages such that when given a forgery on said message it wins Π. This follows because $\mathcal{R}$ must keep its tightness guarantees even for very successful UNF-adversaries. This idea, captured rigorously, yields the next lemma.

Lemma 5. *Let Σ be an EQS scheme that adapts perfectly under malicious keys. Let $\mathcal{R}$ have a reduction tightness ϕ. Then the probability of sampling $m \in M$ and it falling into $E_{st,pk}$, as defined in Definition 9, is lower-bounded as follows:*

$$\Pr\left[\begin{matrix}(st, pk) \leftarrow \mathsf{Init}, \\ m \leftarrow_\$ M\end{matrix} : m \in E_{st,pk}\right] \geq \frac{\phi}{2}$$

Proof. Consider the unbounded adversary $\mathcal{U}_E$ (showing a bound on "E") playing the UNF game and not making any signing queries defined as follows:

$$\mathcal{U}_E(pk)$$

---

1 : $m \leftarrow\!\!\$ \, M$

2 : $\sigma \leftarrow\!\!\$ \, V_{m,pk}$

3 : **return** (m, σ)

Then $\mathcal{U}_E$ wins with probability 1. Note that $\mathcal{U}_E$ is inefficient because (for a secure scheme) one cannot efficiently sample from $V_{m,pk}$. We get

$$\phi = \phi \cdot \mathsf{Adv}^{\mathrm{UNF}}_{\Sigma, \mathcal{U}_E} \leq \mathsf{Adv}^{\Pi}_{\mathcal{R}^{\mathcal{U}_E}}$$

$$= \Pr\left[\begin{matrix}(st, pk) \leftarrow \mathsf{Init}, \\ (m, \sigma) \leftarrow \mathcal{U}_E(pk)\end{matrix} : \mathsf{Check}(\rho, \mathcal{R}.\mathsf{fin}(m, \sigma)) = 1\right]$$

$$\leq \Pr\left[\Pi_{\mathcal{R}^{\mathcal{U}_E}} = 1 \mid m \in E_{st,pk}\right] \cdot \Pr\left[\Pi_{\mathcal{R}^{\mathcal{U}_E}} : m \in E_{st,pk}\right]$$

$$+ \Pr\left[\Pi_{\mathcal{R}^{\mathcal{U}_E}} = 1 \mid m \in \bar{E}_{st,pk}\right] \cdot \Pr\left[\Pi_{\mathcal{R}^{\mathcal{U}_E}} : m \in \bar{E}_{st,pk}\right]. \quad (2)$$

Now by the definition of $E_{st,pk}$, if $\mathcal{R}$ is given a uniform forgery on a message m which is not in $E_{st,pk}$, then its winning probability is less than $\frac{\phi}{2}$, therefore

$$(2) \leq \Pr\left[\Pi_{\mathcal{R}^{\mathcal{U}_E}} : m \in E_{st,pk}\right] + \frac{\phi}{2}.$$

Rearranging yields the result.   □

We just showed that if $\mathcal{R}$ is "tight" then $E_{st,pk}$ is "big". We will lift this result onto a level of classes by showing that there also must be "many" classes C, which we will call "heavy", for which the proportion of $E_{st,pk}$-elements is "big". This partitioning of the message space will be denoted by the superscript (C), indicating that we are operating on the level of classes. This will essentially be done by a variation of a technical lemma known as either the *Splitting Lemma* or *Heavy Row Lemma*, for which a version can be found in [PS00, Lemma 7]. Note that our "rows" much rather resemble the classes into which M is partitioned as opposed to "rows" in a two dimensional representation of $(\mathbb{G}^*)^2$ with a basis (g, g), which would correspond to the setting common in the literature.

Additionally we will show, in the spirit of Lemma 2, that finding messages in a "heavy" class for which $\mathcal{R}$ can provide a signature can be used to solve Π.

Lemma 6. *Let Σ be an EQS scheme that adapts perfectly under malicious keys. Let $\mathcal{R}$ have a reduction tightness ϕ. Define for $(st, pk) \in [\mathsf{Init}]$ the set of $E_{st,pk}$-"heavy" classes*

$$E^{(C)}_{st,pk} := \left\{ m \in M \,\middle|\, \frac{|E_{st,pk} \cap [m]|}{|[m]|} \geq \frac{\phi}{4} \right\}.$$

Then

1. $\Pr[(st, pk) \leftarrow \mathsf{Init}, m \leftarrow_\$ M : m \in E_{st,pk}^{(C)}] \geq \frac{\phi}{4}$, and
2. $\Pr\left[(st, pk) \leftarrow \mathsf{Init}, m \leftarrow_\$ E_{st,pk}^{(C)} : m \in S_{st,pk}\right] \leq \frac{32}{\phi^3} \mathsf{Adv}_{\mathcal{MR}}^{\Pi}$.

Proof. To show that $E_{st,pk}^{(C)}$ is "big" assume towards a contradiction that $\Pr[(st, pk) \leftarrow \mathsf{Init}, m \leftarrow_\$ M : m \in E_{st,pk}^{(C)}] < \frac{\phi}{4}$. From Lemma 5 we get $\Pr[(st, pk) \leftarrow \mathsf{Init}, m \leftarrow_\$ M : m \in E_{st,pk}] \geq \phi/2$. Then since for m and μ uniformly chosen, $\mu \cdot m \in E_{st,pk}$ has the same probability as $m \in E_{st,pk}$ we get

$$
\begin{aligned}
\frac{\phi}{2} \leq {} & \Pr\begin{bmatrix} (st, pk) \leftarrow \mathsf{Init}, \\ m \leftarrow_\$ M, \mu \leftarrow_\$ \mathbb{Z}_p^* \end{bmatrix} : \mu \cdot m \in E_{st,pk} \end{bmatrix} \\
= {} & \Pr\begin{bmatrix} (st, pk) \leftarrow \mathsf{Init}, \\ m \leftarrow_\$ M, \mu \leftarrow_\$ \mathbb{Z}_p^* \end{bmatrix} : \mu \cdot m \in E_{st,pk} \,\Big|\, m \in E_{st,pk}^{(C)} \end{bmatrix} \\
& \cdot \Pr\begin{bmatrix} (st, pk) \leftarrow \mathsf{Init}, \\ m \leftarrow_\$ M, \mu \leftarrow_\$ \mathbb{Z}_p^* \end{bmatrix} : m \in E_{st,pk}^{(C)} \end{bmatrix} \\
& + \Pr\begin{bmatrix} (st, pk) \leftarrow \mathsf{Init}, \\ m \leftarrow_\$ M, \mu \leftarrow_\$ \mathbb{Z}_p^* \end{bmatrix} : \mu \cdot m \in E_{st,pk} \,\Big|\, m \notin E_{st,pk}^{(C)} \end{bmatrix} \\
& \cdot \Pr\begin{bmatrix} (st, pk) \leftarrow \mathsf{Init}, \\ m \leftarrow_\$ M, \mu \leftarrow_\$ \mathbb{Z}_p^* \end{bmatrix} : m \notin E_{st,pk}^{(C)} \end{bmatrix}. \quad (3)
\end{aligned}
$$

By the premise and since $m \notin E_{st,pk}^{(C)}$ implies that $\Pr_{\mu \in \mathbb{Z}_p^*}[\mu \cdot m \in E_{st,pk}] < \phi/4$ we get

$$(3) < \frac{\phi}{4} + \frac{\phi}{4} = \frac{\phi}{2},$$

a contradiction. This proves the first part.

To prove the second part, we apply Lemma 2 for $\delta := \frac{\phi}{4}$ to get

$$
\begin{aligned}
\frac{8}{\phi^2} \mathsf{Adv}_{\mathcal{MR}}^{\Pi} \geq {} & \Pr\begin{bmatrix} (st, pk) \leftarrow \mathsf{Init}, \\ m \leftarrow_\$ M \end{bmatrix} : m \in S_{st,pk} \wedge \frac{|E_{st,pk} \cap [m]|}{|[m]|} \geq \frac{\phi}{4} \end{bmatrix} \\
= {} & \Pr\begin{bmatrix} (st, pk) \leftarrow \mathsf{Init}, \\ m \leftarrow_\$ M \end{bmatrix} : m \in S_{st,pk} \wedge m \in E_{st,pk}^{(C)} \end{bmatrix} \\
= {} & \Pr\begin{bmatrix} (st, pk) \leftarrow \mathsf{Init}, \\ m \leftarrow_\$ M \end{bmatrix} : m \in S_{st,pk} \,\Big|\, m \in E_{st,pk}^{(C)} \end{bmatrix} \\
& \cdot \Pr\begin{bmatrix} (st, pk) \leftarrow \mathsf{Init}, \\ m \leftarrow_\$ M \end{bmatrix} : m \in E_{st,pk}^{(C)} \end{bmatrix} \\
= {} & \Pr\left[(st, pk) \leftarrow \mathsf{Init}, m \leftarrow_\$ E_{st,pk}^{(C)} : m \in S_{st,pk}\right] \\
& \cdot \Pr\begin{bmatrix} (st, pk) \leftarrow \mathsf{Init}, \\ m \leftarrow_\$ M \end{bmatrix} : m \in E_{st,pk}^{(C)} \end{bmatrix}. \quad (4)
\end{aligned}
$$

Using the first part of this lemma,

$$(4) \geq \Pr\left[(st, pk) \leftarrow \mathsf{Init}, m \leftarrow_\$ E_{st,pk}^{(C)} : m \in S_{st,pk}\right] \cdot \frac{\phi}{4}.$$

Rearranging yields

$$\Pr\left[(st, pk) \leftarrow \mathsf{Init}, m \leftarrow\!\!\$\, E_{st,pk}^{(C)} : m \in S_{st,pk}\right] \leq \frac{32}{\phi^3}\mathsf{Adv}_{\mathcal{MR}}^{\Pi},$$

which concludes the proof of the lemma.   □

Similar to Lemma 4 we will transform the statement we just obtained into a setting where we fix the state and public-key, and then show that many such pairs exist for which a weaker bound holds. Since we are concerned with the state/public-key pairs for which the intersection of $E_{st,pk}$-heavy classes and $S_{st,pk}$ is "small", we will denote this subset of $[\mathsf{Init}]$ with "∩".

Lemma 7. *Let Σ be an EQS scheme that adapts perfectly under malicious keys. Let $\mathcal{R}$ have a reduction tightness ϕ. Let $\mathcal{M}$ be the meta-reduction defined in Fig. 1. For $\delta \in [0, 1]$ define a subset of $[\mathsf{Init}]$ for which the size of the intersection of $E_{st,pk}^{(C)}$ and $S_{st,pk}$ obeys a weaker bound than the one in Lemma 6 once we condition the probability on that fixed state/public-key pair:*

$$I_\delta^{(\cap)} := \left\{(st, pk) \,\middle|\, \Pr\left[m \leftarrow\!\!\$\, E_{st,pk}^{(C)} : m \in S_{st,pk}\right] \leq \frac{32}{\delta\phi^3}\mathsf{Adv}_{\mathcal{MR}}^{\Pi}\right\}.$$

Then the probability of $(st, pk) \leftarrow \mathsf{Init}$ falling into $I_\delta^{(\cap)}$ has the following lower bound

$$\Pr[(st, pk) \leftarrow \mathsf{Init} : (st, pk) \in I_\delta^{(\cap)}] \geq 1 - \delta.$$

Proof. From Lemma 6 we get

$$\frac{32}{\phi^3}\mathsf{Adv}_{\mathcal{MR}}^{\Pi} \geq \Pr\left[(st, pk) \leftarrow \mathsf{Init}, m \leftarrow\!\!\$\, E_{st,pk}^{(C)} : m \in S_{st,pk}\right]$$

$$= \sum_{(st,pk)} \Pr[(st, pk)] \Pr\left[m \leftarrow\!\!\$\, E_{st,pk}^{(C)} : m \in S_{st,pk}\right]$$

$$\geq \sum_{(st,pk)\notin I_\delta^{(\cap)}} \Pr[(st, pk)] \Pr\left[m \leftarrow\!\!\$\, E_{st,pk}^{(C)} : m \in S_{st,pk}\right]$$

$$\geq \sum_{(st,pk)\notin I_\delta^{(\cap)}} \Pr[(st, pk)] \cdot \frac{32}{\delta\phi^3}\mathsf{Adv}_{\mathcal{MR}}^{\Pi}$$

$$= (1 - \Pr[(st, pk) \leftarrow \mathsf{Init} : (st, pk) \in I_\delta^{(\cap)}]) \cdot \frac{32}{\delta\phi^3}\mathsf{Adv}_{\mathcal{MR}}^{\Pi}.$$

Rearranging yields $\Pr[(st, pk) \leftarrow \mathsf{Init} : (st, pk) \in I_\delta^{(\cap)}] \geq 1 - \delta$.   □

In the same manner we can reason that if the bound from Lemma 7 holds for a random class, then a similar bound will hold for a "large" subset of classes when we fix the class.

Lemma 8. *Let Σ be an EQS scheme that adapts perfectly under malicious keys. Let $\mathcal{R}$ have a reduction tightness ϕ. Let $\mathcal{M}$ be the meta-reduction defined in Fig. 1. For $\delta \in [0,1]$, $(st, pk) \in I_\delta^{(\cap)}$ define the following subset of $\mathcal{C}$: all classes for which the intersection of $E_{st,pk}^{(C)}$ and $S_{st,pk}$ is bounded by a multiple of $\mathcal{M}$'s advantage*

$$\mathcal{C}_{st,pk,\delta}^{(\cap)} := \left\{ C \in \mathcal{C} \;\middle|\; \Pr\left[m \leftarrow\!\!{\$}\, E_{st,pk}^{(C)} : m \in S_{st,pk} \middle| m \in C \right] \leq \frac{64}{\delta\phi^3} \mathrm{Adv}_{\mathcal{M}\mathcal{R}}^{\Pi} \right\}.$$

Then $\Pr\left[(st, pk) \leftarrow \mathsf{Init}, m \leftarrow\!\!{\$}\, M : [m] \in \mathcal{C}_{st,pk,\delta}^{(\cap)} \right] \geq \frac{\phi}{8}.$

Proof. Let $(st, pk) \in I_\delta^{(\cap)}$ then by definition of $I_\delta^{(\cap)}$ in Lemma 7 we have

$$\frac{32}{\delta\phi^3} \mathrm{Adv}_{\mathcal{M}\mathcal{R}}^{\Pi} \geq \Pr\left[m \leftarrow\!\!{\$}\, E_{st,pk}^{(C)} : m \in S_{st,pk} \right]$$

$$\geq \sum_{C \notin \mathcal{C}_{st,pk,\delta}^{(\cap)}} \Pr[m \leftarrow\!\!{\$}\, E_{st,pk}^{(C)} : m \in C]$$

$$\cdot \Pr\left[m \leftarrow\!\!{\$}\, E_{st,pk}^{(C)} : m \in S_{st,pk} \middle| m \in C \right]$$

$$\geq \sum_{C \notin \mathcal{C}_{st,pk,\delta}^{(\cap)}} \Pr[m \leftarrow\!\!{\$}\, E_{st,pk}^{(C)} : m \in C] \frac{64}{\delta\phi^3} \mathrm{Adv}_{\mathcal{M}\mathcal{R}}^{\Pi}$$

$$= (1 - \Pr[m \leftarrow\!\!{\$}\, E_{st,pk}^{(C)} : [m] \in \mathcal{C}_{st,pk,\delta}^{(\cap)}]) \frac{64}{\delta\phi^3} \mathrm{Adv}_{\mathcal{M}\mathcal{R}}^{\Pi}$$

And therefore

$$\Pr[(st, pk) \leftarrow \mathsf{Init}, m \leftarrow\!\!{\$}\, E_{st,pk}^{(C)} : [m] \in \mathcal{C}_{st,pk,\delta}^{(\cap)}] \geq \frac{1}{2}$$

Now using this and Lemma 6 we get

$$\Pr\left[(st, pk) \leftarrow \mathsf{Init}, m \leftarrow\!\!{\$}\, M : [m] \in \mathcal{C}_{st,pk,\delta}^{(\cap)} \right]$$

$$\geq \Pr\left[\begin{matrix} (st, pk) \leftarrow \mathsf{Init}, \\ m \leftarrow\!\!{\$}\, E_{st,pk}^{(C)} \end{matrix} : [m] \in \mathcal{C}_{st,pk,\delta}^{(\cap)} \right] \Pr\left[\begin{matrix} (st, pk) \leftarrow \mathsf{Init}, \\ m \leftarrow\!\!{\$}\, M \end{matrix} : m \in E_{st,pk}^{(C)} \right]$$

$$\geq \frac{1}{2} \cdot \frac{\phi}{4} = \frac{\phi}{8}$$

concluding the proof. $\qquad\square$

Having established lower bounds on the sizes of both $I^{(S)}$ and $I_\delta^{(\cap)}$, we will reason that for an appropriate value for δ their intersection must be "large" as well. This intersection contains state/public-key pairs for which both $S_{st,pk}$ is big and $S_{st,pk}$ and $E_{st,pk}$ have a small intersection. This is of interest because the separation along classes will enable us to construct a reduction which leverages $\mathcal{R}$'s implicit separation of classes to break DDH.

Lemma 9. *Let Σ be an EQS scheme that adapts perfectly under malicious keys. Let $\mathcal{R}$ have a reduction tightness ϕ. Let $I^{(S)}$ be as defined in Lemma 4, $I_\delta^{(\cap)}$ be as defined in Lemma 7 and $\mathcal{B}$ be the aborting adversary defined in Fig. 3. Then for $\delta := \phi - \mathsf{Adv}_{\mathcal{R}^\mathcal{B}}^\Pi$ we get that $I^{(S)} \cap I_{\phi-\mathsf{Adv}_{\mathcal{R}^\mathcal{B}}^\Pi}^{(\cap)}$ is "big", namely*

$$|I^{(S)} \cap I_{\phi-\mathsf{Adv}_{\mathcal{R}^\mathcal{B}}^\Pi}^{(\cap)}| \geq \frac{\phi - \mathsf{Adv}_{\mathcal{R}^\mathcal{B}}^\Pi}{2}.$$

Proof. Fix $\delta := \phi - \mathsf{Adv}_{\mathcal{R}^\mathcal{B}}^\Pi$; then Lemma 7 and Lemma 4 yield

$$\overline{|I^{(S)} \cap I_\delta^{(\cap)}|} = |\overline{I^{(S)}} \cup \overline{I_\delta^{(\cap)}}| \leq |\overline{I^{(S)}}| + |\overline{I_\delta^{(\cap)}}|$$

$$\leq \frac{\phi - \mathsf{Adv}_{\mathcal{R}^\mathcal{B}}^\Pi}{2} + 1 - \phi + \mathsf{Adv}_{\mathcal{R}^\mathcal{B}}^\Pi = 1 - \frac{\phi - \mathsf{Adv}_{\mathcal{R}^\mathcal{B}}^\Pi}{2}.$$

And therefore $|I^{(S)} \cap I_{\phi-\mathsf{Adv}_{\mathcal{R}^\mathcal{B}}^\Pi}^{(\cap)}| \geq (\phi - \mathsf{Adv}_{\mathcal{R}^\mathcal{B}}^\Pi)/2$. $\square$

With many lemmas in the bag we can now tackle the main result of this work. The intuitive statement is that if $\mathcal{R}$ is "tight" then we can construct meta-reductions such that either one such meta-reduction will use $\mathcal{R}$ to win DDH, or a different meta-reduction will use $\mathcal{R}$ to win Π, or $\mathcal{R}$ is able to win Π itself (formally, with the help of an efficient but trivial adversary).

Theorem 1. *For all groups $\mathbb{G}$ and all EQS schemes Σ over $\mathbb{G}$ that adapt perfectly under malicious keys (as defined in Sect. 2.3), for all computational problems Π and all reductions $\mathcal{R}$ that reduce Π to UNF, running the adversary once, with a reduction tightness of ϕ and running in time τ, there exist meta-reductions $\mathcal{D}$ attacking DDH running in time $\approx 2\tau$ and $\mathcal{M}$ attacking Π running in time $\approx \tau$ as well as an adversary $\mathcal{B}$ attacking UNF of Σ running in constant time such that*

$$\mathsf{Adv}_{\mathbb{G},\mathcal{D}^\mathcal{R}}^{\mathsf{DDH}} + \frac{3\phi^3}{32}\mathsf{Adv}_{\mathcal{R}^\mathcal{B}}^\Pi + \frac{12}{\phi}\mathsf{Adv}_{\mathcal{M}^\mathcal{R}}^\Pi \geq \frac{\phi^4}{32}.$$

Proof Idea. Let's start by first giving an idea of the proof. For a reduction $\mathcal{R}$ having defined the sets $S_{st,pk}$ and $E_{st,pk}$ we have established that both these sets must be reasonably "large" if $\mathcal{R}$ is to be "successful". Now if it is the case that both of these sets are spread evenly across the message space, then there exist (many) classes with both elements of $S_{st,pk}$ and $E_{st,pk}$. This can be used to solve Π, as can be seen in the analysis of $\mathcal{M}$ defined in Fig. 1. On the other hand, if the sets are separated into different classes, then we can construct a meta-reduction $\mathcal{D}$ which extracts this information from $\mathcal{R}$ in order to reason about DDH. The main effort will be in establishing an appropriate lower bound on this latter process being successful.

The proof will use the following technical lemma.

Lemma 10. *Let I be a finite set of indices. Let $\lambda_i \geq 0$ for $i \in I$ with $\sum_i \lambda_i = 1$, $x_i \in [0,1]$ for $i \in I$, and $y := \sum_i \lambda_i x_i$. Then*

$$\sum_{i \in I} \lambda_i x_i^2 - y^2 = \sum_{i \in I} \lambda_i (x_i - y)^2.$$

Proof.

$$\sum_i \lambda_i(x_i - y)^2 = \sum_i \lambda_i(x_i^2 - 2x_iy + y^2) = \sum_i \lambda_i x_i^2 - 2y\sum_i \lambda_i x_i + y^2$$
$$= \sum_i \lambda_i x_i^2 - 2y^2 + y^2 = \sum_i \lambda_i x_i^2 - y^2.$$

□

$\mathcal{D}^{\mathcal{R}}(g, x \cdot g, y \cdot g, z \cdot g)$

1   $r \leftarrow\!\!\$\, R$ // where z = bxy + (1-b)t

2   $\rho \leftarrow\!\!\$\, P$

3   $c := \mathsf{Sample}(\rho)$

4   $(st, pk) := \mathcal{R}.\mathsf{init}(c, r)$

5   $\zeta \leftarrow\!\!\$\, \mathbb{Z}_p^*$

6   $m := \zeta \cdot (g, x \cdot g)$

7   $m' := (y \cdot g, z \cdot g)$

8   $\sigma \leftarrow \mathcal{R}.\mathsf{sign}(st, m)$

9   $\sigma' \leftarrow \mathcal{R}.\mathsf{sign}(st, m')$

10 **if** $\mathsf{Verify}(pk, m, \sigma) = \mathsf{Verify}(pk, m', \sigma')$:

11   **return** 1

12 **return** 0

Fig. 4. The DDH distinguisher $\mathcal{D}$

Proof of Theorem 1. Consider the efficient meta-reduction $\mathcal{D}$ which rewinds the reduction $\mathcal{R}$ and uses it in order to win the DDH-Game defined in Fig. 4. (Note that $\mathcal{D}$ runs $\mathcal{R}.\mathsf{sign}$ twice on the *same* value st.) The first four lines correspond to the Init experiment, in which $\mathcal{D}$ obtains the problem instance c for $\mathcal{R}$. It then groups its inputs into two messages m and m' and obtains a signature from $\mathcal{R}$ on both messages. If the validity of both signatures matches, then $\mathcal{D}$ outputs "DDH-pair". For a fixed $(st, pk) \in [\mathsf{Init}]$ we will write $\Pr[(st, pk)]$instead of $\Pr[(st', pk') \leftarrow \mathsf{Init} : (st', pk') = (st, pk)]$ to enhance readability. Then when $\mathcal{D}$ plays the DDH game on a "random" instance, it will be right with the following probability:

$$\Pr[\mathrm{DDH}_{\mathcal{D}}^0 = 0] = \Pr\left[\begin{matrix}(st, pk) \leftarrow \mathsf{Init}, \\ m, m' \leftarrow\$ M\end{matrix} : \left(m \in S_{st,pk} \wedge m' \in \bar{S}_{st,pk}\right)\right.$$
$$\left. \vee \left(m \in \bar{S}_{st,pk} \wedge m' \in S_{st,pk}\right)\right]$$
$$= 2\Pr\left[\begin{matrix}(st, pk) \leftarrow \mathsf{Init}, \\ m, m' \leftarrow\$ M\end{matrix} : m \in S_{st,pk} \wedge m' \in \bar{S}_{st,pk}\right] \tag{5}$$

Fixing (st, pk) will remove the dependency between the events $m \in S_{st,pk}$ and $m' \in \bar{S}_{st,pk}$, since m and m' are independent

$$(5) = 2\sum_{(st,pk)} \Pr[(st, pk)] \cdot \Pr\left[m, m' \leftarrow\$ M : m \in S_{st,pk} \wedge m' \in \bar{S}_{st,pk}\right]$$
$$= 2\sum_{(st,pk)} \Pr[(st, pk)] \cdot \Pr\left[m \leftarrow\$ M : m \in S_{st,pk}\right]$$
$$\cdot \Pr\left[m' \leftarrow\$ M : m' \in \bar{S}_{st,pk}\right]$$
$$= 2\sum_{(st,pk)} \Pr[(st, pk)] \cdot \Pr\left[m \leftarrow\$ M : m \in S_{st,pk}\right]$$
$$\cdot (1 - \Pr\left[m \leftarrow\$ M : m \in S_{st,pk}\right])$$
$$= 2\Pr\left[\begin{matrix}(st, pk) \leftarrow \mathsf{Init}, \\ m \leftarrow\$ M\end{matrix} : m \in S_{st,pk}\right]$$
$$- 2\sum_{(st,pk)} \Pr[(st, pk)] \cdot \Pr\left[m \leftarrow\$ M : m \in S_{st,pk}\right]^2 \tag{6}$$

On the other hand, when $\mathcal{D}$ plays the DDH game on a "DDH" instance, its guess will be wrong with the following probability:

$$\Pr[\mathrm{DDH}_{\mathcal{D}}^1 = 0] =$$
$$= \Pr\left[\begin{matrix}(st, pk) \leftarrow \mathsf{Init}, \\ m \leftarrow\$ M, \mu \leftarrow\$ \mathbb{Z}_p^*\end{matrix} : \left(m \in S_{st,pk} \wedge \mu \cdot m \in \bar{S}_{st,pk}\right)\right.$$
$$\left. \vee \left(m \in \bar{S}_{st,pk} \wedge \mu \cdot m \in S_{st,pk}\right)\right]$$
$$= 2\Pr\left[\begin{matrix}(st, pk) \leftarrow \mathsf{Init}, \\ m \leftarrow\$ M, \mu \leftarrow\$ \mathbb{Z}_p^*\end{matrix} : m \in \bar{S}_{st,pk} \wedge \mu \cdot m \in S_{st,pk}\right]$$
$$= 2\left(\Pr\left[\begin{matrix}(st, pk) \leftarrow \mathsf{Init}, \\ m \leftarrow\$ M, \mu \leftarrow\$ \mathbb{Z}_p^*\end{matrix} : m \in \bar{S}_{st,pk} \wedge \mu \cdot m \in S_{st,pk} \wedge m \in E_{st,pk}\right]\right.$$
$$\left. + \Pr\left[\begin{matrix}(st, pk) \leftarrow \mathsf{Init}, \\ m \leftarrow\$ M, \mu \leftarrow\$ \mathbb{Z}_p^*\end{matrix} : m \in \bar{S}_{st,pk} \wedge \mu \cdot m \in S_{st,pk} \wedge m \in \bar{E}_{st,pk}\right]\right) \tag{7}$$

For the second term in parenthesis we obtain the following upper bound.

$$\Pr\left[\begin{matrix}(st,pk)\leftarrow\mathsf{Init},\\ m\leftarrow_\$ M, \mu\leftarrow_\$\mathbb{Z}_p^*\end{matrix} : m\in\bar{S}_{st,pk}\wedge\mu\cdot m\in S_{st,pk}\wedge m\in\bar{E}_{st,pk}\right]$$

$$=\sum_{C\in\mathcal{C}}\frac{1}{|C|}\Pr\left[\begin{matrix}(st,pk)\leftarrow\mathsf{Init},\\ m\leftarrow_\$ M,\\ \mu\leftarrow_\$\mathbb{Z}_p^*\end{matrix} : m\in\bar{S}_{st,pk}\wedge m\in\bar{E}_{st,pk}\wedge\mu\cdot m\in S_{st,pk}\Bigg| m\in C\right]$$

$$=\sum_{C\in\mathcal{C}}\frac{1}{|C|}\sum_{(st,pk)}\Pr[(st,pk)]\Pr[m\leftarrow_\$ M,\mu\leftarrow_\$\mathbb{Z}_p^* : m\in\bar{S}_{st,pk}$$

$$\wedge m\in\bar{E}_{st,pk}\wedge\mu\cdot m\in S_{st,pk}\mid m\in C]$$

$$=\sum_{C\in\mathcal{C}}\frac{1}{|C|}\sum_{(st,pk)}\Pr[(st,pk)]\Pr[m\leftarrow_\$ M : m\in\bar{S}_{st,pk}$$

$$\wedge m\in\bar{E}_{st,pk}\mid m\in C]$$
$$\cdot\Pr\left[m\leftarrow_\$ M,\mu\leftarrow_\$\mathbb{Z}_p^* : \mu\cdot m\in S_{st,pk}\mid m\in C\right]$$

From $\bar{S}_{st,pk}\cap\bar{E}_{st,pk}\subseteq\bar{S}_{st,pk}$ and both m and $\mu\cdot m$ being a uniform element of a class C, we get

$$\leq\sum_{C\in\mathcal{C}}\frac{1}{|C|}\sum_{(st,pk)}\Pr[(st,pk)]\cdot\Pr\left[m\leftarrow_\$ M : m\in\bar{S}_{st,pk}\mid m\in C\right]$$

$$\cdot\Pr\left[m\leftarrow_\$ M : m\in S_{st,pk}\mid m\in C\right]$$

$$=\sum_{C\in\mathcal{C}}\frac{1}{|C|}\sum_{(st,pk)}\Pr[(st,pk)]\cdot(1-\Pr\left[m\leftarrow_\$ M : m\in S_{st,pk}\mid m\in C\right])$$

$$\cdot\Pr\left[m\leftarrow_\$ M : m\in S_{st,pk}\mid m\in C\right]$$

$$=\sum_{(st,pk)}\Pr[(st,pk)]\sum_{C\in\mathcal{C}}\frac{1}{|C|}(1-\Pr\left[m\leftarrow_\$ M : m\in S_{st,pk}\mid m\in C\right])$$

$$\cdot\Pr\left[m\leftarrow_\$ M : m\in S_{st,pk}\mid m\in C\right]$$

$$=\sum_{(st,pk)}\Pr[(st,pk)]\sum_{C\in\mathcal{C}}\frac{1}{|C|}\left(\Pr\left[m\leftarrow_\$ M : m\in S_{st,pk}\mid m\in C\right]\right.$$

$$\left.-\Pr\left[m\leftarrow_\$ M : m\in S_{st,pk}\mid m\in C\right]^2\right)$$

$$=\Pr\left[(st,pk)\leftarrow\mathsf{Init}, m\leftarrow_\$ M : m\in S_{st,pk}\right]$$

$$-\sum_{(st,pk)}\Pr[(st,pk)]\sum_{C\in\mathcal{C}}\frac{1}{|C|}\Pr\left[m\leftarrow_\$ M : m\in S_{st,pk}\mid m\in C\right]^2.$$

Plugging this result together with

$$\Pr\begin{bmatrix}(st,pk) \leftarrow \mathsf{Init}, \\ m \leftarrow_\$ M, \mu \leftarrow_\$ \mathbb{Z}_p^* \end{bmatrix} : m \in \bar{S}_{st,pk} \wedge \mu \cdot m \in S_{st,pk} \wedge m \in E_{st,pk}\end{bmatrix}$$

$$\leq \Pr\begin{bmatrix}(st,pk) \leftarrow \mathsf{Init}, \\ m \leftarrow_\$ M, \mu \leftarrow_\$ \mathbb{Z}_p^* \end{bmatrix} : \mu \cdot m \in S_{st,pk} \wedge m \in E_{st,pk}\end{bmatrix}$$

into Eq. (7), we obtain

$$\Pr[\mathrm{DDH}_{\mathcal{D}}^1 = 0]$$

$$\leq 2\Pr\begin{bmatrix}(st,pk) \leftarrow \mathsf{Init}, \\ m \leftarrow_\$ M, \mu \leftarrow_\$ \mathbb{Z}_p^* \end{bmatrix} : \mu \cdot m \in S_{st,pk} \wedge m \in E_{st,pk}\end{bmatrix}$$

$$+ 2\Pr\left[(st,pk) \leftarrow \mathsf{Init}, m \leftarrow_\$ M : m \in S_{st,pk}\right]$$

$$- 2 \sum_{(st,pk)} \Pr[(st,pk)] \sum_{C \in \mathcal{C}} \frac{1}{|\mathcal{C}|} \Pr\left[m \leftarrow_\$ M : m \in S_{st,pk} | m \in C\right]^2. \quad (8)$$

Putting Eqs. (6) and (8) together yields

$$\mathsf{Adv}_{\mathsf{G},\mathcal{D}^\mathcal{R}}^{\mathrm{DDH}} = \Pr[\mathrm{DDH}_{\mathcal{D}}^1 = 1] - \Pr[\mathrm{DDH}_{\mathcal{D}}^0 = 1]$$

$$= \Pr[\mathrm{DDH}_{\mathcal{D}}^0 = 0] - \Pr[\mathrm{DDH}_{\mathcal{D}}^1 = 0]$$

$$\geq 2\Pr\begin{bmatrix}(st,pk) \leftarrow \mathsf{Init}, \\ m \leftarrow_\$ M \end{bmatrix} : m \in S_{st,pk}\end{bmatrix}$$

$$- 2 \sum_{(st,pk)} \Pr[(st,pk)] \cdot \Pr\left[m \leftarrow_\$ M : m \in S_{st,pk}\right]^2$$

$$- 2\Pr\begin{bmatrix}(st,pk) \leftarrow \mathsf{Init}, \\ m \leftarrow_\$ M, \mu \leftarrow_\$ \mathbb{Z}_p^* \end{bmatrix} : \mu \cdot m \in S_{st,pk} \wedge m \in E_{st,pk}\end{bmatrix}$$

$$- 2\Pr\begin{bmatrix}(st,pk) \leftarrow \mathsf{Init}, \\ m \leftarrow_\$ M \end{bmatrix} : m \in S_{st,pk}\end{bmatrix}$$

$$+ 2 \sum_{(st,pk)} \Pr[(st,pk)] \sum_{C \in \mathcal{C}} \frac{1}{|\mathcal{C}|} \Pr\left[m \leftarrow_\$ M : m \in S_{st,pk} | m \in C\right]^2 \quad (9)$$

Lemma 1 yields $\Pr\begin{bmatrix}(st,pk) \leftarrow \mathsf{Init}, \\ m \leftarrow_\$ M, \mu \leftarrow_\$ \mathbb{Z}_p^* \end{bmatrix} : \mu \cdot m \in S_{st,pk} \wedge m \in E_{st,pk}\end{bmatrix} \leq \frac{2}{\phi}\mathsf{Adv}_{\mathcal{M}^\mathcal{R}}^{\Pi}$ with $\mathcal{M}$ as defined in Fig. 1, and therefore

$$(9) \geq 2 \sum_{(st,pk)} \Pr[(st,pk)] \left(\sum_{C \in \mathcal{C}} \frac{1}{|\mathcal{C}|} \Pr\left[m \leftarrow_\$ M : m \in S_{st,pk} | m \in C\right]^2 \right.$$

$$\left. - \Pr\left[m \leftarrow_\$ M : m \in S_{st,pk}\right]^2 \right) - \frac{4}{\phi}\mathsf{Adv}_{\mathcal{M}^\mathcal{R}}^{\Pi}. \quad (10)$$

Applying Lemma 10 for $I := \mathcal{C}$, $x_{\mathcal{C}} := \Pr\left[m \leftarrow_\$ M : m \in S_{st,pk} \,|\, m \in C\right]$, and $\lambda_{\mathcal{C}} := \frac{1}{|\mathcal{C}|}$ yields

$$(10) = 2 \sum_{(st,pk)} \Pr[(st,pk)] \sum_{C \in \mathcal{C}} \frac{1}{|\mathcal{C}|} \left(\Pr\left[m \leftarrow_\$ M : m \in S_{st,pk} \,|\, m \in C\right] \right.$$
$$\left. - \Pr\left[m \leftarrow_\$ M : m \in S_{st,pk}\right] \right)^2 - \frac{4}{\phi}\mathsf{Adv}_{\mathcal{MR}}^{\Pi}$$

$$= 2 \sum_{(st,pk)} \Pr[(st,pk)] \sum_{C \in \mathcal{C}} \frac{1}{|\mathcal{C}|} \left(\Pr\left[m \leftarrow_\$ M : m \in S_{st,pk}\right] \right.$$
$$\left. - \Pr\left[m \leftarrow_\$ M : m \in S_{st,pk} \,|\, m \in C\right] \right)^2 - \frac{4}{\phi}\mathsf{Adv}_{\mathcal{MR}}^{\Pi}.$$

Let $\mathcal{B}$ be the aborting adversary defined in Fig. 3. Let $\delta := \phi - \mathsf{Adv}_{\mathcal{RB}}^{\Pi}$. Then since $I := I^{(S)} \cap I^{(\cap)}_{\phi - \mathsf{Adv}_{\mathcal{RB}}^{\Pi}} \subseteq [\mathsf{Init}]$ and $\mathcal{C}^{(\cap)}_{st,pk} := \mathcal{C}^{(\cap)}_{st,pk,\phi - \mathsf{Adv}_{\mathcal{RA}}^{\Pi}} \subseteq \mathcal{C}$ we get

$$\geq 2 \sum_{(st,pk) \in I} \Pr[(st,pk)] \sum_{C \in \mathcal{C}^{(\cap)}_{st,pk}} \frac{1}{|\mathcal{C}|} \left(\Pr\left[m \leftarrow_\$ M : m \in S_{st,pk}\right] \right.$$
$$\left. - \Pr\left[m \leftarrow_\$ M : m \in S_{st,pk} \,|\, m \in C\right] \right)^2 - \frac{4}{\phi}\mathsf{Adv}_{\mathcal{MR}}^{\Pi}$$

by the definition of $I^{(S)}$ in Lemma 4 and by the definition of $\mathcal{C}^{(\cap)}_{st,pk}$ in Lemma 8 we get

$$\geq 2 \sum_{(st,pk) \in I} \Pr[(st,pk)] \sum_{C \in \mathcal{C}^{(\cap)}_{st,pk}} \frac{1}{|\mathcal{C}|}$$
$$\underbrace{\left(\frac{\phi - \mathsf{Adv}_{\mathcal{RB}}^{\Pi}}{2} - \frac{64}{(\phi - \mathsf{Adv}_{\mathcal{RB}}^{\Pi})\phi^3}\mathsf{Adv}_{\mathcal{MR}}^{\Pi} \right)^2}_{(*)} - \frac{4}{\phi}\mathsf{Adv}_{\mathcal{MR}}^{\Pi}. \qquad (11)$$

For the term $(*)$ we obtain the following bound by expanding the square and ignoring the squared terms:

$$(*) = \frac{\phi^2}{4} - \frac{\phi\mathsf{Adv}_{\mathcal{RB}}^{\Pi}}{2} + \left(\frac{\mathsf{Adv}_{\mathcal{RB}}^{\Pi}}{2}\right)^2 - \frac{64\mathsf{Adv}_{\mathcal{MR}}^{\Pi}}{\phi^3} + \left(\frac{64\mathsf{Adv}_{\mathcal{MR}}^{\Pi}}{(\phi - \mathsf{Adv}_{\mathcal{RB}}^{\Pi})\phi^3}\right)^2$$
$$\geq \frac{\phi^2}{4} - \frac{\phi\mathsf{Adv}_{\mathcal{RB}}^{\Pi}}{2} - \frac{64\mathsf{Adv}_{\mathcal{MR}}^{\Pi}}{\phi^3}$$

and therefore

$$(11) \geq 2 \sum_{(st,pk) \in I} \Pr[(st,pk)] \sum_{C \in \mathcal{C}^{(\cap)}_{st,pk}} \frac{1}{|\mathcal{C}|} \left(\frac{\phi^2}{4} - \frac{\phi}{2}\mathsf{Adv}_{\mathcal{RB}}^{\Pi} - \frac{64}{\phi^3}\mathsf{Adv}_{\mathcal{MR}}^{\Pi} \right)$$
$$- \frac{4}{\phi}\mathsf{Adv}_{\mathcal{MR}}^{\Pi}$$

Lemma 9 yields a bound on the size of $I = I^{(S)} \cap I^{(\cap)}_{\phi - \mathsf{Adv}^{\Pi}_{\mathcal{R}^{\mathcal{B}}}}$ while Lemma 8 gives a bound on the size of $\mathcal{C}^{(\cap)}_{st, pk}$. These facts combine to

$$\geq 2 \cdot \frac{\phi - \mathsf{Adv}^{\Pi}_{\mathcal{R}^{\mathcal{B}}}}{2} \cdot \frac{\phi}{8} \cdot \left(\frac{\phi^2}{4} - \frac{\phi}{2} \mathsf{Adv}^{\Pi}_{\mathcal{R}^{\mathcal{B}}} - \frac{64}{\phi^3} \mathsf{Adv}^{\Pi}_{\mathcal{M}^{\mathcal{R}}} \right) - \frac{4}{\phi} \mathsf{Adv}^{\Pi}_{\mathcal{M}^{\mathcal{R}}}$$

$$\geq \frac{\phi^4}{32} - \left(\frac{3\phi^3}{32} \mathsf{Adv}^{\Pi}_{\mathcal{R}^{\mathcal{B}}} + \frac{12}{\phi} \mathsf{Adv}^{\Pi}_{\mathcal{M}^{\mathcal{R}}} \right),$$

where the last inequality comes from discarding terms that contain products of advantages. Rearranging yields the result. □

Expanding denominators, upper-bounding $\phi \leq 1$, and using Proposition 1 stating equivalence of class-hiding and DDH, Theorem 1 implies the following:

Corollary 1. *For all EQS schemes Σ as defined in Sect. 2.3, for all computational problems Π and all reductions $\mathcal{R}$ that reduce Π to UNF, running the adversary once, with a reduction tightness of ϕ and running in time τ, there exist meta-reductions $\mathcal{D}$ attacking class-hiding of Σ running in time $\approx 2\tau$ and $\mathcal{M}$ attacking Π running in time $\approx \tau$ as well as an adversary $\mathcal{B}$ attacking UNF of Σ running in constant time such that*

$$\mathsf{Adv}^{CH}_{\Sigma, \mathcal{D}^{\mathcal{R}}} + \mathsf{Adv}^{\Pi}_{\mathcal{R}^{\mathcal{B}}} + \mathsf{Adv}^{\Pi}_{\mathcal{M}^{\mathcal{R}}} \geq \frac{\phi^5}{384}.$$

Therefore in an asymptotic setting where Σ is class-hiding (CH) and adapts perfectly under malicious keys, and $\mathcal{R}$ is an efficient reduction reducing a "hard" problem Π to UNF, Corollary 1 states that $\mathcal{R}$'s tightness ϕ is bound by the sum of the advantages of efficient reductions. Because of the hardness of CH and Π, we get that these advantages are negligible. Therefore also ϕ must be negligible, which yields that $\mathcal{R}$ is not a "useful" reduction.

Acknowledgments. This work was funded by the Vienna Science and Technology Fund (WWTF) [10.47379/VRG18002] and by the Austrian Science Fund (FWF) [10.55776/F8515-N]. The authors would like to thank the anonymous reviewers for their valuable comments and suggestions.

References

[ACdMT05] Ateniese, G., Chou, D.H., de Medeiros, B., Tsudik, G.: Sanitizable signatures. In: di Vimercati, S.C., Syverson, P., Gollmann, D. (eds.) ESORICS 2005. LNCS, vol. 3679, pp. 159–177. Springer, Heidelberg (2005). https://doi.org/10.1007/11555827_10

[AFG+10] Abe, M., Fuchsbauer, G., Groth, J., Haralambiev, K., Ohkubo, M.: Structure-preserving signatures and commitments to group elements. In: Rabin, T. (ed.) CRYPTO 2010. LNCS, vol. 6223, pp. 209–236. Springer, Heidelberg (2010). https://doi.org/10.1007/978-3-642-14623-7_12

[AGHO11] Abe, M., Groth, J., Haralambiev, K., Ohkubo, M.: Optimal structure-preserving signatures in asymmetric bilinear groups. In: Rogaway, P. (ed.) CRYPTO 2011. LNCS, vol. 6841, pp. 649–666. Springer, Heidelberg (2011). https://doi.org/10.1007/978-3-642-22792-9_37

[AGO11] Abe, M., Groth, J., Ohkubo, M.: Separating short structure-preserving signatures from non-interactive assumptions. In: Lee, D.H., Wang, X. (eds.) ASIACRYPT 2011. LNCS, vol. 7073, pp. 628–646. Springer, Heidelberg (2011). https://doi.org/10.1007/978-3-642-25385-0_34

[BCC+09] Belenkiy, M., Camenisch, J., Chase, M., Kohlweiss, M., Lysyanskaya, A., Shacham, H.: Randomizable proofs and delegatable anonymous credentials. In: Halevi, S. (ed.) CRYPTO 2009. LNCS, vol. 5677, pp. 108–125. Springer, Heidelberg (2009). https://doi.org/10.1007/978-3-642-03356-8_7

[BEK+20] Bobolz, J., Eidens, F., Krenn, S., Slamanig, D., Striecks, C.: Privacy-preserving incentive systems with highly efficient point-collection. In: Sun, H.-M., Shieh, S.-P., Gu, G., Ateniese, G. (eds.) ASIACCS 2020, October 2020, pp. 319–333. ACM Press (2020)

[BFPV13] Blazy, O., Fuchsbauer, G., Pointcheval, D., Vergnaud, D.: Short blind signatures. J. Comput. Secur. **21**(5), 627–661 (2013)

[BFR24] Bauer, B., Fuchsbauer, G., Regen, F.: On security proofs of existing equivalence class signature schemes. Cryptology ePrint Archive, Paper 2024/183 (2024). https://eprint.iacr.org/2024/183

[BHKS18] Backes, M., Hanzlik, L., Kluczniak, K., Schneider, J.: Signatures with flexible public key: introducing equivalence classes for public keys. In: Peyrin, T., Galbraith, S. (eds.) ASIACRYPT 2018, Part II. LNCS, vol. 11273, pp. 405–434. Springer, Cham (2018). https://doi.org/10.1007/978-3-030-03329-3_14

[BJLS16] Bader, C., Jager, T., Li, Y., Schäge, S.: On the impossibility of tight cryptographic reductions. In: Fischlin, M., Coron, J.-S. (eds.) EUROCRYPT 2016, Part II. LNCS, vol. 9666, pp. 273–304. Springer, Heidelberg (2016). https://doi.org/10.1007/978-3-662-49896-5_10

[BLL+19] Bultel, X., Lafourcade, P., Lai, R.W.F., Malavolta, G., Schröder, D., Thyagarajan, S.A.K.: Efficient invisible and unlinkable sanitizable signatures. In: Lin, D., Sako, K. (eds.) PKC 2019, Part I. LNCS, vol. 11442, pp. 159–189. Springer, Cham (2019). https://doi.org/10.1007/978-3-030-17253-4_6

[BLS01] Boneh, D., Lynn, B., Shacham, H.: Short signatures from the weil pairing. In: Boyd, C. (ed.) ASIACRYPT 2001. LNCS, vol. 2248, pp. 514–532. Springer, Heidelberg (2001). https://doi.org/10.1007/3-540-45682-1_30

[BRS23] Benhamouda, F., Raykova, M., Seth, K.: Anonymous counting tokens. IACR Cryptology ePrint Archive, p. 320 (2023, to appear at Asiacrypt 2023)

[BV98] Boneh, D., Venkatesan, R.: Breaking RSA may not be equivalent to factoring. In: Nyberg, K. (ed.) EUROCRYPT 1998. LNCS, vol. 1403, pp. 59–71. Springer, Heidelberg (1998). https://doi.org/10.1007/BFb0054117

[CL03] Camenisch, J., Lysyanskaya, A.: A signature scheme with efficient protocols. In: Cimato, S., Persiano, G., Galdi, C. (eds.) SCN 2002. LNCS, vol. 2576, pp. 268–289. Springer, Heidelberg (2003). https://doi.org/10.1007/3-540-36413-7_20

[CL19]   Crites, E.C., Lysyanskaya, A.: Delegatable anonymous credentials from mercurial signatures. In: Matsui, M. (ed.) CT-RSA 2019. LNCS, vol. 11405, pp. 535–555. Springer, Cham (2019). https://doi.org/10.1007/978-3-030-12612-4_27

[CL21]   Crites, E.C., Lysyanskaya, A.: Mercurial signatures for variable-length messages. In: PoPETs, vol. 2021, no. 4, pp. 441–463 (2021)

[CLPK22] Connolly, A., Lafourcade, P., Perez-Kempner, O.: Improved constructions of anonymous credentials from structure-preserving signatures on equivalence classes. In: Hanaoka, G., Shikata, J., Watanabe, Y. (eds.) Public-Key Cryptography, PKC 2022, Part I. LNCS vol. 13177, pp. 409–438. Springer, Heidelberg (2022). https://doi.org/10.1007/978-3-030-97121-2_15

[Cor00] Coron, J.-S.: On the exact security of full domain hash. In: Bellare, M. (ed.) CRYPTO 2000. LNCS, vol. 1880, pp. 229–235. Springer, Heidelberg (2000). https://doi.org/10.1007/3-540-44598-6_14

[Cor02] Coron, J.-S.: Optimal security proofs for PSS and other signature schemes. In: Knudsen, L.R. (ed.) EUROCRYPT 2002. LNCS, vol. 2332, pp. 272–287. Springer, Heidelberg (2002). https://doi.org/10.1007/3-540-46035-7_18

[CS20]   Clarisse, R., Sanders, O.: Group signature without random oracles from randomizable signatures. In: Nguyen, K., Wu, W., Lam, K.Y., Wang, H. (eds.) ProvSec 2020. LNCS, vol. 12505, pp. 3–23. Springer, Cham (2020). https://doi.org/10.1007/978-3-030-62576-4_1

[DHO16] Damgård, I., Haagh, H., Orlandi, C.: Access control encryption: enforcing information flow with cryptography. In: Hirt, M., Smith, A. (eds.) TCC 2016. LNCS, vol. 9986, pp. 547–576. Springer, Heidelberg (2016). https://doi.org/10.1007/978-3-662-53644-5_21

[DHS15] Derler, D., Hanser, C., Slamanig, D.: A new approach to efficient revocable attribute-based anonymous credentials. In: Groth, J. (ed.) IMACC 2015. LNCS, vol. 9496, pp. 57–74. Springer, Cham (2015). https://doi.org/10.1007/978-3-319-27239-9_4

[DS16]   Derler, D., Slamanig, D.: Fully-anonymous short dynamic group signatures without encryption. Cryptology ePrint Archive, Report 2016/154 (2016). https://eprint.iacr.org/2016/154

[DS18]   Derler, D., Slamanig, D.: Highly-efficient fully-anonymous dynamic group signatures. In: Kim, J., Ahn, G.-J., Kim, S., Kim, Y., López, J., Kim, T. (eds.) ASIACCS 18, April 2018, pp. 551–565. ACM Press (2018)

[EHK+13] Escala, A., Herold, G., Kiltz, E., Ràfols, C., Villar, J.: An algebraic framework for Diffie-Hellman assumptions. In: Canetti, R., Garay, J.A. (eds.) CRYPTO 2013, Part II. LNCS, vol. 8043, pp. 129–147. Springer, Heidelberg (2013). https://doi.org/10.1007/978-3-642-40084-1_8

[EHK+17] Escala, A., Herold, G., Kiltz, E., Ràfols, C., Villar, J.L.: An algebraic framework for Diffie-Hellman assumptions. J. Cryptol. 30(1), 242–288 (2017)

[FF13]   Fischlin, M., Fleischhacker, N.: Limitations of the meta-reduction technique: the case of Schnorr signatures. In: Johansson, T., Nguyen, P.Q. (eds.) EUROCRYPT 2013. LNCS, vol. 7881, pp. 444–460. Springer, Heidelberg (2013). https://doi.org/10.1007/978-3-642-38348-9_27

[FG18]   Fuchsbauer, G., Gay, R.: Weakly secure equivalence-class signatures from standard assumptions. In: Abdalla, M., Dahab, R. (eds.) PKC 2018, Part II. LNCS, vol. 10770, pp. 153–183. Springer, Cham (2018). https://doi.org/10.1007/978-3-319-76581-5_6

[FGKO17] Fuchsbauer, G., Gay, R., Kowalczyk, L., Orlandi, C.: Access control encryption for equality, comparison, and more. In: Fehr, S. (ed.) PKC 2017, Part II. LNCS, vol. 10175, pp. 88–118. Springer, Heidelberg (2017). https://doi.org/10.1007/978-3-662-54388-7_4

[FHKS16] Fuchsbauer, G., Hanser, C., Kamath, C., Slamanig, D.: Practical round-optimal blind signatures in the standard model from weaker assumptions. In: Zikas, V., De Prisco, R. (eds.) SCN 2016. LNCS, vol. 9841, pp. 391–408. Springer, Cham (2016). https://doi.org/10.1007/978-3-319-44618-9_21

[FHS15] Fuchsbauer, G., Hanser, C., Kamath, C., Slamanig, D.: Practical round-optimal blind signatures in the standard model from weaker assumptions. In: Zikas, V., De Prisco, R. (eds.) SCN 2016, Part II. LNCS, vol. 9841, pp. 391–408. Springer, Cham (2016). https://doi.org/10.1007/978-3-319-44618-9_21

[FHS19] Fuchsbauer, G., Hanser, C., Slamanig, D.: Structure-preserving signatures on equivalence classes and constant-size anonymous credentials. J. Cryptol. $32(2)$, 498–546 (2019)

[Fis06] Fischlin, M.: Round-optimal composable blind signatures in the common reference string model. In: Dwork, C. (ed.) CRYPTO 2006. LNCS, vol. 4117, pp. 60–77. Springer, Heidelberg (2006). https://doi.org/10.1007/11818175_4

[FJS14] Fleischhacker, N., Jager, T., Schröder, D.: On tight security proofs for Schnorr signatures. In: Sarkar, P., Iwata, T. (eds.) ASIACRYPT 2014, Part I. LNCS, vol. 8873, pp. 512–531. Springer, Heidelberg (2014). https://doi.org/10.1007/978-3-662-45611-8_27

[FP09] Fuchsbauer, G., Pointcheval, D.: Proofs on encrypted values in bilinear groups and an application to anonymity of signatures. In: Shacham, H., Waters, B. (eds.) Pairing 2009. LNCS, vol. 5671, pp. 132–149. Springer, Heidelberg (2009). https://doi.org/10.1007/978-3-642-03298-1_10

[FS10] Fischlin, M., Schröder, D.: On the impossibility of three-move blind signature schemes. In: Gilbert, H. (ed.) EUROCRYPT 2010. LNCS, vol. 6110, pp. 197–215. Springer, Heidelberg (2010). https://doi.org/10.1007/978-3-642-13190-5_10

[Fuc11] Fuchsbauer, G.: Commuting signatures and verifiable encryption. In: Paterson, K.G. (ed.) EUROCRYPT 2011. LNCS, vol. 6632, pp. 224–245. Springer, Heidelberg (2011). https://doi.org/10.1007/978-3-642-20465-4_14

[GBL08] Garg, S., Bhaskar, R., Lokam, S.V.: Improved bounds on security reductions for discrete log based signatures. In: Wagner, D. (ed.) CRYPTO 2008. LNCS, vol. 5157, pp. 93–107. Springer, Heidelberg (2008). https://doi.org/10.1007/978-3-540-85174-5_6

[Han23] Hanzlik, L.: Non-interactive blind signatures for random messages. In: Hazay, C., Stam, M. (eds.) EUROCRYPT 2023, Part V. LNCS, vol. 14008, pp. 722–752. Springer, Heidelberg (2023). https://doi.org/10.1007/978-3-031-30589-4_25

[HJK12] Hofheinz, D., Jager, T., Knapp, E.: Waters signatures with optimal security reduction. In: Fischlin, M., Buchmann, J., Manulis, M. (eds.) PKC 2012. LNCS, vol. 7293, pp. 66–83. Springer, Heidelberg (2012). https://doi.org/10.1007/978-3-642-30057-8_5

[HKKL07] Hazay, C., Katz, J., Koo, C.-Y., Lindell, Y.: Concurrently-secure blind signatures without random oracles or setup assumptions. In: Vadhan, S.P. (ed.) TCC 2007. LNCS, vol. 4392, pp. 323–341. Springer, Heidelberg (2007). https://doi.org/10.1007/978-3-540-70936-7_18

[HPP20] Hébant, C., Phan, D.H., Pointcheval, D.: Linearly-homomorphic signatures and scalable mix-nets. In: Kiayias, A., Kohlweiss, M., Wallden, P., Zikas, V. (eds.) PKC 2020, Part II. LNCS, vol. 12111, pp. 597–627. Springer, Cham (2020). https://doi.org/10.1007/978-3-030-45388-6_21

[HRS15] Hanser, C., Rabkin, M., Schröder, D.: Verifiably encrypted signatures: security revisited and a new construction. In: Pernul, G., Ryan, P.Y.A., Weippl, E. (eds.) ESORICS 2015, Part I. LNCS, vol. 9326, pp. 146–164. Springer, Cham (2015). https://doi.org/10.1007/978-3-319-24174-6_8

[HS14] Hanser, C., Slamanig, D.: Structure-preserving signatures on equivalence classes and their application to anonymous credentials. In: Sarkar, P., Iwata, T. (eds.) ASIACRYPT 2014, Part I. LNCS, vol. 8873, pp. 491–511. Springer, Heidelberg (2014). https://doi.org/10.1007/978-3-662-45611-8_26

[HS21] Hanzlik, L., Slamanig, D.: With a little help from my friends: constructing practical anonymous credentials. In: Vigna, G., Shi, E. (eds.) ACM CCS 2021, November 2021, pp. 2004–2023. ACM Press (2021)

[KK12] Kakvi, S.A., Kiltz, E.: Optimal security proofs for full domain hash, revisited. In: Pointcheval, D., Johansson, T. (eds.) EUROCRYPT 2012. LNCS, vol. 7237, pp. 537–553. Springer, Heidelberg (2012). https://doi.org/10.1007/978-3-642-29011-4_32

[KM19] Koblitz, N., Menezes, A.: Critical perspectives on provable security: fifteen years of "another look" papers. Cryptology ePrint Archive, Report 2019/1336 (2019). https://eprint.iacr.org/2019/1336

[KSD19] Khalili, M., Slamanig, D., Dakhilalian, M.: Structure-preserving signatures on equivalence classes from standard assumptions. In: Galbraith, S.D., Moriai, S. (eds.) ASIACRYPT 2019, Part III. LNCS, vol. 11923, pp. 63–93. Springer, Cham (2019). https://doi.org/10.1007/978-3-030-34618-8_3

[Mau05] Maurer, U.: Abstract models of computation in cryptography. In: Smart, N.P. (ed.) Cryptography and Coding 2005. LNCS, vol. 3796, pp. 1–12. Springer, Heidelberg (2005). https://doi.org/10.1007/11586821_1

[MBG+23] Mir, O., Bauer, B., Griffy, S., Lysyanskaya, A., Slamanig, D.: Aggregate signatures with versatile randomization and issuer-hiding multi-authority anonymous credentials. In: Meng, W., Jensen, C.D., Cremers, C., Kirda, E. (eds.) ACM CCS 2023, pp. 30–44. ACM (2023)

[MSBM23] Mir, O., Slamanig, D., Bauer, B., Mayrhofer, R.: Practical delegatable anonymous credentials from equivalence class signatures. Proc. Priv. Enhancing Technol. 2023(3), 488–513 (2023)

[Nao03] Naor, M.: On cryptographic assumptions and challenges. In: Boneh, D. (ed.) CRYPTO 2003. LNCS, vol. 2729, pp. 96–109. Springer, Heidelberg (2003). https://doi.org/10.1007/978-3-540-45146-4_6

[Nec94] Nechaev, V.I.: Complexity of a determinate algorithm for the discrete logarithm. Math. Notes 55(2), 165–172 (1994)

[PS00] Pointcheval, D., Stern, J.: Security arguments for digital signatures and blind signatures. J. Cryptol. 13(3), 361–396 (2000)

[PV05] Paillier, P., Vergnaud, D.: Discrete-log-based signatures may not be equivalent to discrete log. In: Roy, B. (ed.) ASIACRYPT 2005. LNCS, vol. 3788, pp. 1–20. Springer, Heidelberg (2005). https://doi.org/10.1007/11593447_1

[Seu12] Seurin, Y.: On the exact security of Schnorr-type signatures in the Random Oracle Model. In: Pointcheval, D., Johansson, T. (eds.) EUROCRYPT 2012. LNCS, vol. 7237, pp. 554–571. Springer, Heidelberg (2012). https://doi.org/10.1007/978-3-642-29011-4_33

[Sho97] Shoup, V.: Lower bounds for discrete logarithms and related problems. In: Fumy, W. (ed.) EUROCRYPT 1997. LNCS, vol. 1233, pp. 256–266. Springer, Heidelberg (1997). https://doi.org/10.1007/3-540-69053-0_18

[ST21] Sanders, O., Traoré, J.: EPID with malicious revocation. In: Paterson, K.G. (ed.) CT-RSA 2021. LNCS, vol. 12704, pp. 177–200. Springer, Cham (2021). https://doi.org/10.1007/978-3-030-75539-3_8

[Wat05] Waters, B.: Efficient identity-based encryption without Random Oracles. In: Cramer, R. (ed.) EUROCRYPT 2005. LNCS, vol. 3494, pp. 114–127. Springer, Heidelberg (2005). https://doi.org/10.1007/11426639_7

Fully Dynamic Attribute-Based Signatures for Circuits from Codes

San Ling[1]📧, Khoa Nguyen[2]📧, Duong Hieu Phan[3]📧, Khai Hanh Tang[1]📧,
Huaxiong Wang[1]📧, and Yanhong Xu[4](✉)📧

[1] Nanyang Technological University, 50 Nanyang Ave., Singapore 639798, Singapore
[2] University of Wollongong, Northfields Avenue, Wollongong, NSW 2522, Australia
[3] Telecom Paris, Institut Polytechnique de Paris, 19 place Marguerite Perey CS
20031, F-91123 Palaiseau Cedex, France
[4] Shanghai Jiao Tong University, 800 Dongchuan Road, Shanghai 200240, China
yanhong.xu@sjtu.edu.cn

Abstract. Attribute-Based Signature (ABS), introduced by Maji et al.
(CT-RSA'11), is an advanced privacy-preserving signature primitive that
has gained a lot of attention. Research on ABS can be categorized into
three main themes: expanding the expressiveness of signing policies,
enabling new functionalities, and providing more diversity in terms of
computational assumptions. We contribute to the development of ABS in
all three dimensions, by providing a fully dynamic ABS scheme for arbitrary circuits from codes. The scheme is the first ABS from code-based
assumptions and also the first ABS system offering the `full dynamicity`
functionality (i.e., attributes can be enrolled and revoked simultaneously).
Moreover, the scheme features much shorter signature size than a lattice-
based counterpart proposed by El Kaafarani and Katsumata (PKC'18).

In the construction process, we put forward a new theoretical abstraction of Stern-like zero-knowledge (ZK) protocols, which are the major
tools for privacy-preserving cryptography from codes. Our main insight
here actually lies in the questions we ask about the fundamental principles of Stern-like protocols that have remained unchallenged since their
conception by Stern at CRYPTO'93. We demonstrate that these long-
established principles are not essential, and then provide a refined framework generalizing existing Stern-like techniques and enabling enhanced
constructions.

1 Introduction

Attribute-Based Signatures. Introduced by Maji et al. [69], attribute-based
signature (ABS) is an advanced signature primitive that simultaneously provides fine-grained authentications and protects the privacy of signers. In an ABS
scheme, a user possessing an attribute x certified by an authority can anony-
mously sign message M along with a policy P, as long as x satisfies the given
policy, i.e., $P(x) = 1$. Thanks to its versatility and privacy-preserving features,
ABS may find applications in various contexts, such as attribute-based mes-
saging, attribute-based authentication and trust negotiation, leaking secrets and

Q. Tang and V. Teague (Eds.): PKC 2024, LNCS 14601, pp. 37–73, 2024.
https://doi.org/10.1007/978-3-031-57718-5_2

non-transferable access control (see [54, 69] for comprehensive discussions). Since the pioneering work of Maji et al. [69], significant attention has been paid to the developments of ABS systems, which can be categorized into the following three major research themes.

Similar to other access-control primitives, a prominent line of work in ABS is devoted to expanding the expressiveness of the class of signing policies a given ABS can allow. Okamoto and Takashima [76] proposed efficient ABS schemes for non-monotone access structures, improving Maji et al.'s schemes that can only handle monotone ones. Systems allowing more expressive policy families, such as bounded-depth circuits [86], unbounded arithmetic branching programs [31] and non-deterministic finite automata [81], were subsequently developed. This line of research reached high success with constructions supporting very general policies, in the form of arbitrary circuits [37, 80] and Turing machines [81].

The second important direction focuses on defining and designing ABS systems with new functionalities. Examples of these features include decentralization [77] (that removes the need for a central authority), traceability [36, 38] (that incorporates a group-signature-like [27] opening mechanism), linkability [35, 88] (that allows to link two ABS signatures under certain conditions), forward security [90], hierarchy [33] and revocability [13, 46, 55, 84, 85]. Among them, revocability is arguably one of the most non-trivial functionalities to achieve. In the original model of ABS [69], the authority can enroll new signing keys for attributes, but the model does not support revocations of certified attributes. In fact, for advanced multi-user systems, efficient key revocation is a desirable feature (e.g., to address situations such as membership terminations or key misuses), yet typically challenging to realize, since one has to ensure that revoked keys are no longer usable without having to reinitialize the system or affecting other key owners. While in the related context of group signatures [27], nice solutions have been proposed, e.g., [16, 60, 61], existing proposals for ABS are still somewhat unsatisfactory. In a nutshell, they either suggest to revoke users' identities (which is an artificial and unnecessary concept in the ABS setting) instead of attributes; or they do not propose a clear model for handling revocations.

The third major research direction aims to provide more diversity regarding the pool of computational assumptions used to instantiate ABS. A long line of pairing-based constructions started with Maji et al.'s work [69]. The first scheme that does not rely on pairings was suggested by Herranz [49]. The recent emergence of post-quantum cryptography raised interest in designing ABS from post-quantum assumptions, and lattice-based constructions [7, 37, 46] have been introduced. To our knowledge, no other ABS from alternative post-quantum foundations, e.g., codes, multivariates, isogenies, has been proposed.

In this work, we aim to contribute to the development of ABS systems in all three dimensions discussed above. In terms of supporting techniques, we will also enhance the area of code-based zero-knowledge protocols, specifically, those that operate in Stern's framework [82, 83].

Code-Based and Stern-Like ZK Protocols. A beautiful and influential cryptographic notion introduced by Goldwasser, Micali and Rackoff [48], zero-knowledge (ZK) protocols allow to prove the truth of a statement without leaking any additional information. In the last three decades or so, ZK protocols have become a foundational subject of study and essential building blocks in the development of countless cryptographic constructions. Specifically, via the Fiat-Shamir transform [45], ZK protocols have been the basis for developing ordinary signature schemes, including those in NIST's Post-Quantum Cryptography project[1], such as Dilithium [34,67] and Picnic [25,52,91]. An equally important application domain of ZK protocols comprises privacy-preserving authentication systems, such as group signatures [27], ring signatures [79], anonymous credentials [26], functional signatures [20], policy-based signatures [8], mesh signatures [19], and – of our particular interest – attribute-based signatures [69].

In the context of code-based ZK, a recent line of work [14,24,42,43] has obtained efficient Fiat-Shamir-based ordinary signatures by cleverly employing the MPC-in-the-head paradigm [50] for variants of the Syndrome Decoding problem. However, for developing advanced code-based privacy-preserving cryptosystems, where sophisticated algebraic structures are required, the major technical stepping stone is still Stern's protocol [82,83].

The original protocol of Stern addresses the following relation

$$R_{\text{Stern}} = \left\{ \left((\mathbf{M}, \mathbf{v}), \mathbf{w} \right) \in (\mathbb{Z}_2^{D_0 \times D} \times \mathbb{Z}_2^{D_0}) \times \mathsf{B}(D, \omega) : \quad \mathbf{M} \cdot \mathbf{w} = \mathbf{v} \right\},$$

where $D, \omega \in \mathbb{Z}^+$ such that $D > \max\{D_0, \omega\}$, and $\mathsf{B}(D, \omega)$ denotes the set of all vectors in $\{0, 1\}^D$ having Hamming weight ω. The protocol is a Σ-protocol [29] in the generalized sense defined in [11,51] (where three valid transcripts are needed for extraction, instead of just two), and is based on the following two main ideas.

(i) To prove the linear equation $\mathbf{M} \cdot \mathbf{w} = \mathbf{v}$, use a uniformly random $\mathbf{r} \in \{0, 1\}^D$, and prove instead that $\mathbf{M} \cdot \mathbf{z} = \mathbf{M} \cdot \mathbf{r} \oplus \mathbf{v}$. Here, $\mathbf{z} = \mathbf{w} \oplus \mathbf{r}$, where $\oplus$ denotes the addition modulo 2, is uniformly random over $\{0, 1\}^D$, as $\mathbf{r}$ acts as a one-time pad.

(ii) To prove that $\mathbf{w} \in \mathsf{B}(D, \omega)$, use a uniformly random permutation ϕ in the symmetric group $\mathcal{S}_D$ to permute the coordinates of $\mathbf{w}$. The permuted vector $\mathbf{t} = \phi(\mathbf{w})$ is then uniformly distributed over $\mathsf{B}(D, \omega)$.

Moreover, the two ideas are compatible with each other thanks to the homomorphism $\phi(\mathbf{z}) = \phi(\mathbf{w}) \oplus \phi(\mathbf{r})$, since there are two different ways to compute $\phi(\mathbf{z})$, based on either $(\phi, \mathbf{z})$ or $(\phi(\mathbf{w}), \phi(\mathbf{r}))$. That is, the prover can show the honest computation of $\phi(\mathbf{z})$ via either of the pairs, depending on the verifier's challenge. Since 1993, there have been a large number of works built upon Stern's ideas. Most notably, they enabled privacy-preserving code-based constructions such as proofs of plaintext knowledge [71], proofs of valid openings for commitments and proofs for general relations [51] and committed Boolean functions [62], ring signatures [21,30,70,75], group signatures [2,40,41,75], group encryption [74], accumulators and range proofs [75].

---

[1] https://csrc.nist.gov/Projects/post-quantum-cryptography.

Stern's ideas have also been shown useful in the lattice setting, including the first proposals [53,64] of "exact" ZK protocols[2] for the Short Integer Solution [1] and Learning With Errors [78] problems, as well as the first lattice-based group signatures [58,59] without trapdoors [47], the first policy-based signatures [28], accountable tracing signatures [65], multimodal private signatures [72], bicameral and auditably private signatures [73].

In terms of developing Stern's framework, Libert et al. [56] proposed an abstraction of Stern-like protocols that captures the contexts where one's witness vectors may simultaneously be involved in many linear equations. In Libert et al.'s formulation, the set of valid witnesses is generalized from $B(D, \omega)$ to some set $\mathsf{VALID} \subset \{0,1\}^D$. Furthermore, to handle vectors $\mathbf{w}$ whose coordinates are arranged according to certain patterns, the random permutations applied to $\mathbf{w}$ are not necessarily uniform over $\mathcal{S}_D$, e.g., they could be uniformly random over some fine-grained subset $\mathcal{S}'$ of $\mathcal{S}_D$.

However, Libert et al.'s work as well as all other existing Stern-like protocols all methodically adhere to the two original ideas, namely, use uniformly random permutations of coordinates and uniformly random masking vectors over the entire space $\{0,1\}^D$. In this paper, we *challenge these fundamental ideas*. The new perspectives acquired during our revisiting process could then help us to move forward with new formulations, which in turn, could potentially inspire new and enhanced cryptographic applications, in particular, code-based ABS.

OUR CONTRIBUTIONS. We make several contributions to the area of attribute-based signatures. In the process, we also introduce new insights and techniques for Stern-like protocols, which help enhance our code-based ABS scheme and could be of independent interest. Our contributions are summarized as follows.

Contributions to Attribute-Based Signatures. Our results for ABS subsume all the three discussed aspects: additional functionality, expressiveness of signing policies and diversity of (post-quantum) computational assumptions.

We first propose a model for fully dynamic attribute-based signatures (FDABS). By "full dynamicity", we mean that the system simultaneously supports: (i) Dynamic enrollments of new attributes; (ii) Key updates for users who changed their attributes; and (iii) Revocations of expired/misused keys. Our model is equipped with rigorous definitions and stringent security requirements that extend the privacy and unforgeability notions put forward by Maji et al. [69] to the fully dynamic setting.

Next, we provide an instantiation of FDABS based on codes. Being the first code-based ABS, our scheme helps to enrich the pool of ABS from post-quantum assumptions. In terms of policy expressiveness, the scheme supports arbitrary Boolean circuits. In the quantum random oracle model (QROM), we prove that the scheme satisfies the proposed security requirements for FDABS, based on a well-studied variant of the Syndrome Decoding problem [5,6,12]. In terms of

---

[2] "Exactness" here roughly means that there is no difference between the language used for defining ZK and the one ensured by soundness. This is a desirable feature for lattice-based ZK proofs and arguments. See, e.g., [18,39,89].

efficiency, our scheme has signature size $\widetilde{\mathcal{O}}(C \cdot \lambda + \lambda^2)$, where C denotes the size of a circuit representing the signed policy, and λ is the security parameter.

Prior to our work, the only ABS construction for arbitrary circuits based on well-studied post-quantum assumptions is the one introduced in [37], which has signature size $\widetilde{\mathcal{O}}(C \cdot \lambda^2 + \lambda^3)$. Our signature size is smaller by a factor $\widetilde{\mathcal{O}}(\lambda)$, which is quite a surprising and counterintuitive feat, as code-based signatures are generally considered to be much inferior to their lattice-based counterparts in terms of efficiency. Here, the improvement is achieved thanks to an enhanced approach that allows us to prove circuit satisfiability in a direct manner and that is compatible with our refined abstraction of Stern (discussed below). In a nutshell, in [37] one has to commit to all the input and output wires of the circuit and prove relations among them in zero-knowledge with communication cost $\widetilde{\mathcal{O}}(\lambda^2)$ bits for each gate. Here, in contrast, we prove the circuit satisfiability directly (without relying on commitments) by reducing it to C simple binary equations that involve witness vectors constructed in a specific way. Then, our new Stern-like techniques help us to prove with communication cost 4 bits per gate for soundness error $2/3$ and $\mathcal{O}(\lambda)$ bits per gate for soundness error $2^{-\lambda}$. Moreover, while the ABS scheme in [37] was only analyzed in the ROM [9], our scheme here is proven secure in the QROM [15] and it is technically the first post-quantum ABS for arbitrary circuits.[3].

In Table 1, we provide a comparison among known ABS schemes for expressive policy classes and from well-established assumptions. Note that, while we obtain noticeable improvements over previous work, our scheme is still far from being practical (with an estimated signature size of tens MBs). We therefore mainly view our work as a theoretical one and consider the problem of designing practically usable post-quantum ABS for circuits as a fascinating open question.

Contributions to Stern-Like and Code-Based ZK Protocols. We revisit the fundamental ideas Stern introduced in his seminal work [82,83], namely, the uses of uniformly random permutations of coordinates and uniformly random masking vectors. Viewing them from new angles, we observe a highly intriguing fact: these ideas are not essential for Stern-like protocols! Indeed, we show that there are examples where it is unnecessary (and sub-optimal) to use a uniformly random masking $\mathbf{r}$ or a uniformly random permutation ϕ to hide witness vector $\mathbf{w}$. These new understandings inspire us to formulate an abstract ZK protocol for proving linear relations of binary witness vectors, with the following nice features.

- It captures previous approaches and techniques for Stern-like protocols, including Stern's original work [82,83], Libert et al.'s formulation [56], as well as those used in code-based constructions such as [2,40,51,70,71,74,75].

---

[3] To be fair, it could also be possible make the scheme in [37] secure in the QROM. Intuitively, the scheme also employs Stern-like protocols, and can as well benefit from the variant of Unruh's transform [87] presented in [44].

Table 1. A summary of known ABS for expressive policy classes and from well-established computational assumptions. For all schemes, λ denotes the security parameter. For [76], S denotes the access structure size; For [81], T and W denote the running time of a Turing machine and the input length of a finite automaton, respectively; For [31], L denotes the branching program length; For [86], D denotes the circuit depth; For [37,80] and ours, C denotes the circuit size.

Scheme	Policy expressiveness	Assumptions	SM/ (Q)ROM	Signature size	Fully dynamic
OT11 [76]	Non-monotone access structures	pairings	SM	$\mathcal{O}(S \cdot \lambda)$	✗
SAH16 [80]	Arbitrary circuits	pairings	SM	$\mathcal{O}(C \cdot \lambda)$	✗
SKAH18-1 [81]	Turing machines	pairings	SM	$\mathcal{O}(T^2 \cdot \lambda)$	✗
SKAH18-2 [81]	Non-deterministic finite automata	pairings	SM	$\mathcal{O}(W \cdot \lambda)$	✗
DOT19 [31]	Branching programs	pairings	SM	$\mathcal{O}(L \cdot \lambda)$	✗
Tsa17 [86]	Bounded-depth circuits	lattices	SM	$\widetilde{\mathcal{O}}(D \cdot \lambda)$	✗
EKK18 [37]	Arbitrary circuits	lattices	ROM	$\widetilde{\mathcal{O}}(C \cdot \lambda^2 + \lambda^3)$	✗
Ours	Arbitrary circuits	codes	QROM	$\widetilde{\mathcal{O}}(C \cdot \lambda + \lambda^2)$	✓

- It paves the way for the designs of more efficient protocols in which one may securely hide a witness vector **w** via non-traditional methods: a masking vector **r** that is not necessarily uniform, or a function $F(\cdot)$ that is not necessarily a permutation.

In particular, these new views allow us to obtain sub-protocols with enhanced efficiency for commonly seen statements in code-based privacy-preserving cryptography, such as proving knowledge of a binary vector of fixed Hamming weight [82,83] or with special arrangements of non-zero bits [40,58,75], or for handling products of secret bits [57]. These improved sub-routines are helpful for our instantiation of ABS from codes.

We would like to stress that our major innovation here actually lies in *the questions we ask* about the fundamental principles of Stern-like protocols that have been remaining unchallenged since their conception in 1993. Once the questions are spot on, the counterexamples as well as the refinements would come rather naturally and might look somewhat "simple" *in hindsight*. We also would like to admit that our refinements have not yielded a noteworthy efficiency improvement for the cryptographic applications we are currently aware of. In particular, our techniques of replacing uniform masks by odd-weight masks and replacing coordinate permutations by affine functions only give improvement factor $\mathcal{O}(1)$, which could be considered small – in theory and in practice. Nevertheless, we believe that our refined framework has the *potential* to enable more significant improvements for cryptographic applications, which we have been unable to fully exploit.

TECHNICAL OVERVIEW.   Let us give a high-level discussion for each of our technical contributions.

Defining FDABS. In order to bring full dynamicity into the context of ABS, we adapt the definitional framework of Bootle et al. [16,17] in their work on fully dynamic group signatures, which captures the two most commonly adopted approaches for revocations, namely, accumulator-based [23] and revocation-list-based [22]. Similar to [16,17], the lifetime of an FDABS system is divided into time epochs. We assume that the specification of the epochs (e.g., from 8:00:00 am UTC on Monday to 7:59:59 am UTC on next Monday) is publicly known. We also assume that the updated system information is announced at the beginning of each epoch and is publicly accessible. For example, such information may be appended to a public database at 8:00:00 am UTC on each Monday. Hence, the signers and verifiers are required to download the updated information at most once per epoch. Such a requirement is natural and necessary to formulate the correctness and security properties in the fully dynamic setting. In fact, unlike the partially dynamic setting (in which users can join the system at any time but cannot be revoked) – where the public parameters do not need to change over time, all known fully dynamic signatures inherently demand some updates of system information per time period: either in the form of an updated keys or updated lists of active/revoked users.

In our model, a signature Σ is always attached to a message-epoch pair (M, τ). To verify Σ, one should use the corresponding system information at epoch τ – which can be publicly downloaded if it has not been in one's local storage. We formalize the stringent security requirements of privacy and unforgeability for FDABS, which are extended from those in Maji et al.'s model [69].

Regarding privacy, the adversary is provided with the strongest capability: it is allowed to maliciously generate the keys of the authority and even the challenge attributes. Furthermore, different flavors of privacy are presented to capture different computational powers of the adversary.

In terms of unforgeability, we formulate a strict notion, in which an attribute is not authorized to sign unless it is not revoked and also active at the epoch associated with the signature. Furthermore, a signature generated at epoch τ should only be verified w.r.t. τ, i.e., verification w.r.t. any different epoch τ' should fail. This, in particular, eliminates the possibility that an attribute is used to sign before it is introduced into the system.

Designing Code-Based FDABS for Circuits. A typical approach for designing ABS is "sign-then-prove", which relies on an ordinary signature scheme and a zero-knowledge protocol. The signing key for an attribute $\mathbf{x}$ is then set as a signature $\mathbf{s}$ of the authority on "message" $\mathbf{x}$. When signing with policy P, one proves knowledge of a message-signature pair $(\mathbf{x}, \mathbf{s})$ that is valid under the authority's public key, and additionally proves that $P(\mathbf{x}) = 1$. This approach, in particular, was used in existing lattice-based ABS in the ROM [7,37,46].

In the code-based setting, however, ordinary signature schemes compatible with ZK proofs of a message-signature pair are currently unavailable. Note that the state-of-the-art code-based signature schemes, such as [4,14,24,32,42], resort to the (Q)ROM, and are unsuitable for our purpose – since it is not known how to efficiently prove in ZK the knowledge of a message hashed by a RO. Thus, at a high level, the current lack of code-based signature schemes in the standard model is arguably the major reason why constructing ABS from codes remains an open question to date.

To overcome the above issue, we start with a somewhat disparate approach, which we name "commit-then-accumulate-then-prove". Specifically, we employ different technical building blocks: an updatable Merkle-tree accumulator [74, 75], a commitment scheme [75] and a companion ZK protocol. The general idea is inspired by the constructions from [66,74], but here, we put commitments $\mathbf{d} = \mathsf{com}(\mathbf{x}, \mathbf{r})$ to attributes $\mathbf{x}$ at leaves of the tree. Then, when signing with policy P, one proves that: (i) $\mathbf{d}$ is contained in the tree; (ii) $\mathbf{d}$ is a valid commitment to some attribute $\mathbf{x}$; (iii) $\mathbf{x}$ satisfies the Boolean circuit relation $P(\mathbf{x}) = 1$. Here, (ii) can be viewed as a bridge connecting two layers (i) and (iii).

In fact, a ZK protocol for the combined relation above can be developed based on existing Stern-like techniques from [75] – for the Merkle trees and commitments, and [51] – for circuits. However, [51] requires to commit to all input and output wires in the circuit, which yields communication cost $\mathcal{O}(C \cdot \lambda^2)$ for the circuit layer (similar to the situation in [37]).

Fortunately, as we will discuss below, our refined framework for Stern-like protocols together with our techniques for proving $(x_1 \mathsf{\ NAND\ } x_2) \oplus x_3 = 0$ enable us to handle the NAND gates in the circuit and realize the sub-protocols in a much more efficient manner. In particular, we manage to reduce the communication cost for the circuit layer to $\mathcal{O}(C \cdot \lambda)$.

Let us now discuss how we enroll and revoke an attribute $\mathbf{x}$. Initially, all the leaves of the tree are associated with $\mathbf{0}$. To enroll $\mathbf{x}$, we commit it to $\mathbf{d}$, and add $\mathbf{d}$ to the tree if $\mathbf{d}$ has *odd Hamming weight* (which happens with probability negligibly close to $1/2$). To revoke $\mathbf{x}$, we set $\mathbf{d}$ back to $\mathbf{0}$ and update the tree accordingly. When signing, one additionally proves that attribute $\mathbf{x}$ is active (i.e., it has been enrolled and has not been revoked) by showing that $\mathbf{d}$ has odd weight – which then can be done very efficiently by proving that the inner product of $\mathbf{d}$ and the all-1 vector is 1. We remark that, in previous works [66,74], an active $\mathbf{d}$ was set to be non-zero, causing a relatively inefficient sub-protocol for proving $\mathbf{d} \neq \mathbf{0}$. That sub-protocol relies on an extension trick from [64]. The latter requires the use of a random permutation of bit-size $\mathcal{O}(n \log n)$, where n is the dimension of $\mathbf{d}$. Here, in contrast, by working with odd-weight $\mathbf{d}$, our cost is only n bits.

Revisiting Stern. Recall that Stern's two fundamental ideas [82,83] are to employ a one-time pad $\mathbf{r} \in \{0,1\}^D$ to additively mask witness $\mathbf{w}$, and to use a uniformly random permutation $\phi \in \mathcal{S}_D$ to permute the coordinates of $\mathbf{w}$.

Our first observation is that $\mathbf{r}$ does not necessarily have to be uniform over the entire space $\{0,1\}^D$. This sounds particularly counterintuitive (and contrary to the usual notion of one-time pads), but we can demonstrate that it is true when $\mathbf{w}$ has a specific constraint. For instance, let us consider the case $\mathbf{w} \in \mathsf{B}(D, \omega)$ as in [82,83], and denote by $\mathcal{B}_{\mathsf{even}}^D$ (resp., $\mathcal{B}_{\mathsf{odd}}^D$) the set of all length-$D$ vectors with even (resp., odd) Hamming weight. Then, if we use $\mathbf{r} \xleftarrow{\$} \mathcal{B}_{\mathsf{odd}}^D$ to mask $\mathbf{w}$, the sum $\mathbf{z} = \mathbf{w} \oplus \mathbf{r}$ will be uniformly random in the set $\mathcal{B}_q^D$, where $q = \mathsf{odd}$ if ω is an even integer and $q = \mathsf{even}$ otherwise. Here, we note that elements of $\mathcal{B}_{\mathsf{even}}^D$ and $\mathcal{B}_{\mathsf{odd}}^D$ can be described by $(D-1)$ bits instead of D bits, yielding smaller complexity.

Another example is for vectors of the form $\mathbf{w} = (\mathbf{w}_1 \| \cdots \| \mathbf{w}_D) \in \{0,1\}^{2D}$, where each $\mathbf{w}_i \in \{01, 10\}$, as considered in code-based privacy-preserving constructions like [40,75]. If for each $\mathbf{w}_i$, we apply a mask $\mathbf{r}_i \xleftarrow{\$} \{01, 10\}$, then the sum $\mathbf{z}_i = \mathbf{w}_i \oplus \mathbf{r}_i$ will be uniformly random over $\{00, 11\}$. Because elements of $\{01, 10\}$ and $\{00, 11\}$ can be represented by just 1 bit, we can reduce the communication cost for proving knowledge of $\mathbf{w}$ from $2D$ bits to D bits.

Inspired by the above observation, we suggest a new abstraction for Stern-like ZK protocols, in which we assume the existence of (possibly proper) subsets VALID, $\mathcal{R}$, $\mathcal{Z}$ of $\{0,1\}^D$, such that for all witness vectors $\mathbf{w} \in$ VALID, the distributions of $\{\mathbf{z} = \mathbf{w} \oplus \mathbf{r} \mid \mathbf{r} \xleftarrow{\$} \mathcal{R}\}$ and $\{\mathbf{z} \xleftarrow{\$} \mathcal{Z}\}$ are identical. We remark that, while this refined masking framework only helps to save a small portion of overall communication cost for our zero-knowledge protocols (Sect. 4), the underlying motive could potentially be more useful in related contexts. For example, if one only requires statistical closeness between the two distributions, then one might possibly work with sets $\mathcal{R}$, $\mathcal{Z}$ of smaller cardinalities, via techniques such as rejection samplings [32,67].

Next, we ask the question of whether it is really essential to employ permutations of coordinates to prove the membership of witness $\mathbf{w}$ in some predetermined set VALID, as done in all previous Stern-like protocols. To answer this question, we abstract out the properties we would need for a function F that can be used to prove $\mathbf{w} \in$ VALID and that is compatible with our linear masking framework discussed above. Let us define F as $F : \mathcal{S} \times \{0,1\}^D \to \{0,1\}^D$, where $\mathcal{S}$ is a finite set. Then, we would need F to satisfy the following requirements.

First, F must "behave nicely" w.r.t. the set VALID, namely, for all $\phi \in \mathcal{S}$, we require that $\mathbf{t} = F(\phi, \mathbf{w}) \in$ VALID if and only if $\mathbf{w} \in$ VALID and furthermore, $\mathbf{t}$ is uniform whenever ϕ is uniform (in their respective sets). Second, we define functions $F' : \mathcal{S} \times \mathcal{R} \to \mathcal{R}$ (for the mask $\mathbf{r}$) and $F'' : \mathcal{S} \times \mathcal{Z} \to \mathcal{Z}$ (for the sum $\mathbf{z}$), and demand that they together with F satisfy a "homomorphism" property:

$$F'(\phi, \mathbf{r}) \oplus F''(\phi, \mathbf{z}) = F(\phi, \mathbf{r} \oplus \mathbf{z}), \ \forall \ (\phi, \mathbf{r}, \mathbf{z}) \in \mathcal{S} \times \mathcal{R} \times \mathcal{Z}.$$

Our new formulations capture the case of Stern's original protocol, with $\mathcal{S} := \mathcal{S}_D$, $\mathcal{R} = \mathcal{Z} = \{0,1\}^D$ and $F(\phi, \cdot) = F'(\phi, \cdot) = F''(\phi, \cdot) = \phi(\cdot)$. These formulations are particularly helpful for a technical step in our protocol of Sect. 4.3, where we would like to prove knowledge of bits x_1, x_2, x_3 such that $(x_1 \text{ NAND } x_2) \oplus x_3 = 0$ and x_1, x_2, x_3 may satisfy other relations (e.g., they are committed and may appear in other wires in the considered circuit).

To the above end, we would need highly non-trivial definitions of the corresponding sets and functions. Specifically, letting $\bar{b} = b \oplus 1$ for any bit b, we encode (x_1, x_2, x_3) as $\mathbf{w} \in \{0,1\}^4$ of the form

$$\mathsf{ENC}(x_1, x_2, x_3) := [\ \bar{x}_1 \cdot \bar{x}_2 \oplus x_3 \mid \bar{x}_1 \cdot x_2 \oplus x_3 \mid x_1 \cdot \bar{x}_2 \oplus x_3 \mid x_1 \cdot x_2 \oplus x_3\ ]^\top.$$

Next, we define valid $:= \{\mathsf{ENC}(x_1, x_2, x_3) \mid (x_1, x_2, x_3) \in \{0,1\}^3\}$, and prove instead that $\mathbf{w} \in$ valid and its last coordinate is equal to 1.

In the process, we note that valid $= \mathcal{B}_{\text{odd}}^4$, allowing us to use our refined masking framework (with $\mathcal{R} = \mathcal{B}_{\text{odd}}^4$, $\mathcal{Z} = \mathcal{B}_{\text{even}}^4$) for proving linear equation $[0 \mid 0 \mid 0 \mid 1] \cdot \mathbf{w} = 1$ – which implies that the last coordinate of $\mathbf{w}$ is 1.

Meanwhile, we would need specifically designed functions F, F', F'' to prove that $\mathbf{w}$ is a well-formed element of valid. To this end, we employ a permuting function $T : \{0,1\}^2 \times \{0,1\}^4 \rightarrow \{0,1\}^4$, first suggested in [57], that, on input (e_1, e_2) and $\mathbf{y} = [y_{0,0} \mid y_{0,1} \mid y_{1,0} \mid y_{1,1}]^\top$, outputs $[y_{e_1,e_2} \mid y_{e_1,\bar{e}_2} \mid y_{\bar{e}_1,e_2} \mid y_{\bar{e}_1,\bar{e}_2}]^\top$. Then, we let $\mathcal{S} = \{0,1\}^3$ and define

$$F : \mathcal{S} \times \{0,1\}^4 \rightarrow \{0,1\}^4, \quad F((e_1,e_2,e_3),\mathbf{y}) = T((e_1,e_2),\mathbf{y}) + [e_3 \mid e_3 \mid e_3 \mid e_3]^\top;$$
$$F' : \mathcal{S} \times \mathcal{R} \rightarrow \mathcal{R}, \quad F'((e_1,e_2,e_3),\mathbf{r}) = T((e_1,e_2),\mathbf{r});$$
$$F'' : \mathcal{S} \times \mathcal{Z} \rightarrow \mathcal{Z}, \quad F''((e_1,e_2,e_3),\mathbf{z}) = T((e_1,e_2),\mathbf{z}) + [e_3 \mid e_3 \mid e_3 \mid e_3]^\top.$$

Now, it is crucial to remark that F does **not** act as a permutation of coordinates (due to the shift of $[e_3 \mid e_3 \mid e_3 \mid e_3]^\top$), but it interacts well with the set valid, since we have

$$F((e_1,e_2,e_3),\mathsf{ENC}(x_1,x_2,x_3)) = \mathsf{ENC}(x_1 \oplus e_1, x_2 \oplus e_2, x_3 \oplus e_3).$$

Moreover, F, F', F'' satisfy the described homomorphism property. As a result, we obtain a sub-protocol for proving $(x_1 \text{ NAND } x_2) \oplus x_3 = 0$, which can further be extended to additionally prove that x_1, x_2, x_3 satisfy other relations (by using the same bits e_1, e_2, e_3 at those places). We stress that techniques from [57] could also lead to a sub-protocol achieving the same goals, but our refinements here allow to save $1/2$ of the communication cost.

Encouraged by the above new insights, new formulations and their usefulness, we put forward a new abstract Stern-like ZK protocol. It serves as a blueprint for the development of the ZK protocol supporting our code-based FDABS construction. It also enables more efficient methods for proving knowledge of binary vectors satisfying various different constraints, and can be used to improve the efficiency of existing and future code-based privacy-preserving constructions.

2   Fully Dynamic Attribute-Based Signatures

In this section, we formalize the primitive of fully dynamic attribute-based signature (FDABS). An FDABS scheme involves the following entities: a trusted authority who initializes the system; an attribute-issuing authority who generates attribute keys and periodically announces updated system information; users/signers and signature verifiers.

We let $\mathcal{X}$ be the universe of possible attributes and $\mathcal{P} = \{P : \mathcal{X} \rightarrow \{0,1\}\}$ be a policy family. We say an attribute $x \in \mathcal{X}$ satisfies a policy $P \in \mathcal{P}$ if $P(x) = 1$.

2.1   Syntax

An FDABS scheme consists of the following polynomial-time algorithms.

$\mathsf{Setup}_{\mathsf{init}}(1^\lambda)$: This algorithm, run by a trusted authority, takes as input the security parameter 1^λ and generates public parameter pp. We assume that pp contains the description of an attribute space $\mathcal{X}$, a policy family $\mathcal{P}$, a time space $\mathcal{T}$, and a message space $\mathcal{M}$.

$\mathsf{Setup}_{\mathsf{auth}}(\mathsf{pp})$: This algorithm is run by an attribute-issuing authority. It takes as input pp and outputs a key pair $(\mathsf{mpk}, \mathsf{msk})$. The authority also initializes the system information info_0 and a public registration table **reg**. Note that the record stored in **reg** depends on the scheme specification and may be used by the authority for updating the system information. For simplicity, pp and mpk are inputs of the following algorithms even not explicitly written.

$\mathsf{AttrGen}(\mathsf{msk}, x, \mathsf{info}_{\tau_{\mathrm{current}}}, \mathbf{reg})$: This algorithm is run by the authority when receiving attribute key generation request from a user. It takes as input the authority's secret key msk, an attribute x and current system information $\mathsf{info}_{\tau_{\mathrm{current}}}$ and outputs an attribute key (or a signing key) sk_x to the user. The authority will then add a new record to the table **reg**.

$\mathsf{Update}(\mathsf{msk}, \mathcal{S}, \mathsf{info}_{\tau_{\mathrm{current}}}, \mathbf{reg})$: This algorithm is run by the authority who will advance the epoch and update system information. Given msk, a set $\mathcal{S} \subset \mathcal{X}$ of to-be-revoked attributes, $\mathsf{info}_{\tau_{\mathrm{current}}}$, and **reg**, the authority computes new system information $\mathsf{info}_{\tau_{\mathrm{new}}}$ and may also update **reg**. If there is no change to the system or $\mathcal{S}$ contains inactive attributes (which either have not been issued signing keys or have been revoked previously), this algorithm aborts.

$\mathsf{Sign}(\mathsf{sk}_x, M, P, \mathsf{info}_\tau)$: This algorithm is run by the user who possesses the signing key sk_x. Given sk_x, a message $M \in \mathcal{M}$, a policy $P \in \mathcal{P}$, and info_τ, it returns a signature Σ.

$\mathsf{Verify}(M, P, \mathsf{info}_\tau, \Sigma)$: This algorithm is run by any verifier. Given the inputs, it outputs a bit indicating the validity of signature Σ on message M with respect to policy P and system information info_τ.

Additional Algorithm. To ease the notion, we introduce another algorithm that will only be used in the definitions of security requirements.

$\mathsf{IsActive}(x, \mathsf{info}_\tau)$: This algorithm returns 1 if x has been issued a signing key and has not been revoked at time τ. We call x an active attribute. Otherwise, it returns 0 and we call x an inactive attribute.

Remark 1. Algorithm Update intends to capture all the changes to the activeness of attributes, which occur between epochs τ_{current} and τ_{new}. Since Update takes the registration table **reg** as an input, the changes it makes may include not only the revocations but also the enrollments and re-enrollments of attributes.

An attribute x could be active at epoch τ_1, revoked at epoch τ_2, and active again at epoch τ_3. To handle such dynamicity, we demand that each signature is bound to a specific epoch: a signature generated by x in epoch τ_1 should be rejected when verified w.r.t. to either τ_2 or τ_3 (even if x is active at τ_3).

Correctness. Basically, correctness of FDABS demands that: if x is active at time epoch τ and if $P(x) = 1$, then a signature $\Sigma \leftarrow \mathsf{Sign}(\mathsf{sk}_x, M, P, \mathsf{info}_\tau)$ should be accepted by $\mathsf{Verify}(M, P, \mathsf{info}_\tau, \Sigma)$. We model this requirement in an adversarial experiment $\mathbf{Exp}_{\mathcal{A}}^{\mathsf{correct}}(1^\lambda)$ in Fig. 1. Below, we define some oracles available to the adversary.

$\mathsf{AddHX}(x)$: This oracle issues a signing key for an attribute x at current time epoch τ_{current} when invoked by the adversary $\mathcal{A}$. If x has never been issued any signing key, it runs $\mathsf{sk}_x \leftarrow \mathsf{AttrGen}(\mathsf{msk}, x, \mathsf{info}_{\tau_{\mathsf{current}}}, \mathbf{reg})$ and adds x to an honestly maintained list HL. Otherwise, it returns $\perp$. Note that as in the algorithm $\mathsf{AttrGen}$, a new record is also added to $\mathbf{reg}$.

$\mathsf{Update}(\mathcal{S})$: This oracle allows $\mathcal{A}$ to remove a set $\mathcal{S}$ of active attributes from the system at current epoch. It executes $\mathsf{Update}(\mathsf{msk}, \mathcal{S}, \mathsf{info}_{\tau_{\mathsf{current}}}, \mathbf{reg})$ to get $\mathsf{info}_{\tau_{\mathsf{new}}}$, and may also update $\mathbf{reg}$ as specified in Update.

Definition 1. *Let* $\mathbf{Adv}_{\mathcal{A}}^{\mathsf{correct}}(1^\lambda) = \Pr[\mathbf{Expt}_{\mathcal{A}}^{\mathsf{correct}}(1^\lambda) = 1]$ *be the advantage of an adversary* $\mathcal{A}$ *against correctness of an FDABS scheme in experiment* $\mathbf{Expt}_{\mathcal{A}}^{\mathsf{correct}}(1^\lambda)$. *An FDABS scheme is correct if, for any PPT adversary* $\mathcal{A}$, *its advantage is negligible in* λ.

2.2   Formulation of the Security Requirements

Security requirements for static attribute-based signatures (see e.g., [69,80]) are perfect privacy and unforgeability. The former requires signatures not to reveal any information on the attribute beyond the fact that the attribute satisfies the policy. The latter requires that no colluding set of signers (even being able to see signatures on messages of their choices) can create valid signatures under a policy that is not satisfied by any individual attribute in the collusion. Below we carefully extend these two security requirements to the fully dynamic case.

Privacy. This notion is adapted from the static case and requires that signatures do not leak the underlying attributes. It protects the signer from a malicious adversary who tries to extract the attribute information from signatures. We model this requirement in adversarial experiments $\mathbf{Expt}_{\mathcal{A}}^{\mathsf{privacy}\text{-}b}(1^\lambda)$ for $b \in \{0, 1\}$. In the following, we define some oracles that will be used in the experiments.

$\mathsf{SndToHX}(x)$: This oracle simulates an honest user who requests an attribute key for x at τ_{current} from an adversarially controlled authority. It maintains a list CL. Let the output of this oracle be sk_x. It adds x to CL if sk_x is valid.

$\mathsf{Chal}_b(x_0, x_1, M, P, \tau)$: This is a challenge oracle that is called only once. It computes $\Sigma \leftarrow \mathsf{Sign}(\mathsf{sk}_{x_b}, M, P, \mathsf{info}_\tau)$ and outputs Σ if and only if $x_0, x_1 \in \mathcal{X}$, $M \in \mathcal{M}$ or $P \in \mathcal{P}$, $\tau \in \mathcal{T}$, $\mathsf{info}_\tau \neq \perp$, and $x_b \in \mathsf{CL}$, $P(x_b) = 1$, $\mathsf{IsActive}(x_b, \mathsf{info}_\tau) = 1$ for $b \in \{0, 1\}$.

In experiment $\mathbf{Expt}_{\mathcal{A}}^{\mathsf{privacy}\text{-}b}(1^\lambda)$, the adversary $\mathcal{A}$ fully controls the authority and enrolls honest users to the system by interacting with the oracle $\mathsf{SndToHX}$. We require $\mathcal{A}$ to output the randomness $\mathbf{r}$ used for generating the authority's key pair to verify its well-formedness. The adversary is also allowed to introduce fully corrupted users to and remove existing users from the system by updating info and **reg** at its will, so long as info and **reg** are well-formed.

Note that the two challenge attributes x_0, x_1 are required to be active at the challenge time τ. However, $\mathcal{A}$ could update the system (since it fully controls the authority) by revoking either attribute at an arbitrary time period $\tau' \neq \tau$. This does not help $\mathcal{A}$ to win the experiment, since revocation of sk_{x_0} or sk_{x_1} at time τ' does not affect the validity of signatures generated at challenge time τ.

Experiment $\mathbf{Expt}_{\mathcal{A}}^{\text{correct}}(1^\lambda)$

$\mathsf{pp} \leftarrow \mathsf{Setup}_{\text{init}}(1^\lambda)$;
$(\mathsf{mpk}, \mathsf{msk}) \leftarrow \mathsf{Setup}_{\text{auth}}(\mathsf{pp})$.
$\mathsf{HL} \leftarrow \emptyset$.
$(x, M, P, \tau) \leftarrow \mathcal{A}^{\mathsf{AddHX}, \mathsf{Update}}(\mathsf{pp}, \mathsf{mpk})$.
If $x \notin \mathcal{X}$ or $M \notin \mathcal{M}$ or $P \notin \mathcal{P}$
  or $\tau \notin \mathcal{T}$, return 0.
If $x \notin \mathsf{HL}$ or $\mathsf{info}_\tau = \perp$ or $P(x) = 0$ or
  $\mathsf{IsActive}(x, \mathsf{info}_\tau) = 0$, return 0.
$\Sigma \leftarrow \mathsf{Sign}(\mathsf{sk}_x, M, P, \mathsf{info}_\tau)$.
If $\mathsf{Verify}(M, P, \mathsf{info}_\tau, \Sigma) = 1$, return 0.
Else return 1.

Experiment $\mathbf{Expt}_{\mathcal{A}}^{\text{privacy-}b}(1^\lambda)$

$\mathsf{pp} \leftarrow \mathsf{Setup}_{\text{init}}(1^\lambda)$;
$((\mathsf{mpk}, \mathbf{r}), \mathsf{aux}) \leftarrow \mathcal{A}(\mathsf{pp}); \mathsf{CL} \leftarrow \emptyset$.
If mpk is not well-formed, return 0.

If info or **reg** is not well-formed
  at any epoch, return 0.
$b' \leftarrow \mathcal{A}^{\mathsf{SndToHX}, \mathsf{Chal}_b}(\mathsf{aux})$.
Return b'.

Experiment $\mathbf{Expt}_{\mathcal{A}}^{\text{unforge}}(1^\lambda)$

$\mathsf{pp} \leftarrow \mathsf{Setup}_{\text{init}}(1^\lambda)$;
$(\mathsf{mpk}, \mathsf{msk}) \leftarrow \mathsf{Setup}_{\text{auth}}(\mathsf{pp})$.
$\mathsf{HL} \leftarrow \emptyset, \mathsf{BL} \leftarrow \emptyset, \mathsf{SL} \leftarrow \emptyset$.
$(M, P, \tau, \Sigma) \leftarrow \mathcal{A}^{\mathsf{AddHX}, \mathsf{RevealX}, \mathsf{Sign}, \mathsf{Update}}(\mathsf{pp}, \mathsf{mpk})$.
If $M \notin \mathcal{M}$ or $P \notin \mathcal{P}$ or $\tau \notin \mathcal{T}$ return 0.
If $\mathsf{Verify}(M, P, \mathsf{info}_\tau, \Sigma) = 0$, return 0.
If $(M, P, \tau, \Sigma) \in \mathsf{SL}$, return 0.
If $\exists\, x \in \mathsf{BL}$ so that $P(x) = 1$ and
  $\mathsf{IsActive}(x, \mathsf{info}_\tau) = 1$, return 0.
Else return 1.

Fig. 1. Definitions of correctness, privacy and unforgeability of FDABS.

Definition 2. *Let the advantage of an adversary $\mathcal{A}$ against privacy be defined as $\mathbf{Adv}_{\mathcal{A}}^{\text{privacy}} = |\Pr[\mathbf{Expt}_{\mathcal{A}}^{\text{privacy-1}}(1^\lambda) = 1] - \Pr[\mathbf{Expt}_{\mathcal{A}}^{\text{privacy-0}}(1^\lambda) = 1]|$. An FDABS scheme is perfectly private (statistically private) if for any computationally unbounded adversary $\mathcal{A}$, the advantage of $\mathcal{A}$ is 0 (negligible in λ).*

Remark 2. Note that the above definitions on privacy are in the strongest sense. Slightly weaker requirement such as computational privacy, where the adversary is any PPT algorithm, might also be useful for most applications.

Unforgeability. This notion extends from the static case carefully to capture the full dynamicity. It protects the verifier from accepting a signature with respect to a policy not satisfied by any attribute in the colluding set. We model this requirement in experiment $\mathbf{Expt}_{\mathcal{A}}^{\text{unforge}}(1^\lambda)$ which utilizes oracles AddHX and Update, and the following oracles RevealX and Sign.

RevealX(x): This oracle allows the adversary to learn an honest attribute key. It maintains a list BL. When an attribute x is queried, it returns the corresponding attribute key sk_x and adds x to BL if $x \in \mathsf{HL}$, and aborts otherwise.

Sign(M, P, τ): This oracle allows the adversary to see a signature on any message
with respect to any policy and any time epoch of the adversary's choices. It
maintains a signature list SL. When a tuple (M, P, τ) is queried, it returns
$\Sigma \leftarrow$ Sign($\mathrm{sk}_x, M, P, \mathrm{info}_\tau$) with arbitrary sk_x such that $P(x) = 1$ and
IsActive(x, info_τ) $= 1$ and then adds (M, P, τ, Σ) to the list SL. If no such
x is found, it aborts.

Definition 3. *Let* $\mathbf{Adv}_{\mathcal{A}}^{\mathrm{unforge}} = \Pr[\mathbf{Expt}_{\mathcal{A}}^{\mathrm{unforge}}(1^\lambda) = 1]$ *be the advantage of
an adversary $\mathcal{A}$ against unforgeability in an FDABS scheme. The scheme is
unforgeable, if for any PPT adversary $\mathcal{A}$, the advantage of $\mathcal{A}$ is negligible in λ.*

3 Code-Based FDABS for Boolean Circuits

3.1 Preliminaries on Code-Based Cryptographic Tools

NOTATIONS. Let $a, b \in \mathbb{Z}$. Denote $[a, b]$ as the set $\{a, \ldots, b\}$. We simply write $[b]$
when $a = 1$. Let $\oplus$ denote the bit-wise addition operation modulo 2. If S is a finite
set, then $x \xleftarrow{\$} S$ means that x is chosen uniformly at random from S. Throughout
this paper, all vectors are column vectors. When concatenating vectors $\mathbf{x} \in
\{0,1\}^m$ and $\mathbf{y} \in \{0,1\}^k$, for simplicity, we use $(\mathbf{x}\|\mathbf{y}) \in \{0,1\}^{m+k}$ instead of
$(\mathbf{x}^\top\|\mathbf{y}^\top)^\top$. The Hamming weight of vector $\mathbf{x} \in \{0,1\}^m$ is denoted by $wt(\mathbf{x})$.
The Hamming distance between vectors $\mathbf{x}, \mathbf{y} \in \{0,1\}^m$ is denoted by $d_H(\mathbf{x}, \mathbf{y})$,
and is equal to $wt(\mathbf{x} \oplus \mathbf{y})$. Denote by $\mathsf{B}(n, \omega)$ the set of all binary vectors of
length n with Hamming weight ω.

Let $\mathbb{Z}^+$ be the set consisting of all positive integers. For $c \in \mathbb{Z}^+$ and k divisible
by c, define the following.

Regular(k, c) is the set containing all vectors of the form $\mathbf{w} = (\mathbf{w}_1\|\ldots\|\mathbf{w}_{\frac{k}{c}}) \in$
$\{0, 1\}^{2^c \cdot \frac{k}{c}}$ that consists of $\frac{k}{c}$ blocks, each of which is an element of $\mathsf{B}(2^c, 1)$.
We call $\mathbf{w}$ *regular word* if $\mathbf{w} \in$ Regular(k, c) for some k, c.

2-Regular(k, c) is the set of all $\mathbf{x} \in \{0, 1\}^{2^c \cdot \frac{k}{c}}$ such that there exist regular words
$\mathbf{v}, \mathbf{w} \in$ Regular(k, c) satisfying $\mathbf{x} = \mathbf{v} \oplus \mathbf{w}$. We call $\mathbf{x}$ a *2-regular word* if
$\mathbf{x} \in$ 2-Regular(k, c) for some k, c.

RE : $\{0, 1\}^k \to \{0, 1\}^{2^c \cdot \frac{k}{c}}$ is a regular encoding function mapping $\mathbf{x} \in \{0, 1\}^k$
to RE($\mathbf{x}$) $\in \{0, 1\}^{2^c \cdot \frac{k}{c}}$. Let $\mathbf{x} = (\mathbf{x}_1\|\ldots\|\mathbf{x}_{\frac{k}{c}})$, where $\mathbf{x}_j = [x_{j,1}\ldots|x_{j,c}]^\top$ for
all $j \in [1, \frac{k}{c}]$. Then, compute $t_j = \sum_{i=1}^{c} 2^{c-i} \cdot x_{j,i}$. Let re($\mathbf{x}_j$) $\in \mathsf{B}(2^c, 1)$ whose
sole 1 entry is at the t_j-th position for some $t_j \in [0, 2^c - 1]$. RE($\mathbf{x}$) is then
defined as $(\mathrm{re}(\mathbf{x}_1)\|\mathrm{re}(\mathbf{x}_2)\|\cdots\|\mathrm{re}(\mathbf{x}_{\frac{k}{c}})) \in$ Regular(k, c).

We now recall the 2-RNSD$_{n,k,c}$ problem, introduced by Augot, Finiasz and
Sendrier (AFS) [6]. The problem asks to find low-weight 2-regular codewords
in random binary linear codes, and is closely related to the Small Codeword
Problem [68] and binary Shortest Vector Problem [3], with an additional constraint that the solution codeword must be 2-regular.

Definition 4 ($2\text{-RNSD}_{n,k,c}$ **Problem**). *Given a uniformly random matrix* $\mathbf{B} \in \mathbb{Z}_2^{n \times m}$, *where* $m = 2^c \cdot k/c$, *find a non-zero vector* $\mathbf{z} \in 2\text{-Regular}(k, c) \subseteq \{0, 1\}^m$ *such that* $\mathbf{B} \cdot \mathbf{z} = \mathbf{0}$.

The problem is known to be NP-complete in the worst case [6]. In practice, for appropriate choices of n, k, c, the best known algorithms require exponential time in the security parameter. See [12] for a comprehensive discussion of known attacks and parameter settings.

Our construction below also employs an efficiently updatable code-based Merkle-tree accumulator and a commitment scheme from [74,75]. The accumulator consists of five algorithms TSetup, TAcc, TWitGen, TVerify, and TUpdate that can efficiently accumulate values, generate witnesses and update a value. The commitment scheme achieves statistical hiding by choosing appropriate parameters. Security of these two schemes relies on the security of 2-RNSD problems. Readers are referred to [74,75] or the full version [63] for more details.

3.2 Description of the Scheme

We now present our construction of a code-based ABS for arbitrary Boolean circuits. In the QROM, the scheme satisfies the security requirements defined in Sect. 2. The scheme makes use of the code-based updatable Merkle-tree accumulator and commitment scheme from [74,75], together with ZK protocols operating within our new framework of Stern from Sect. 4.1. Initially, the attribute-issuing authority maintains an all-zero Merkle tree. When a user possessing attribute $\mathbf{x}$ requests an attribute key, the authority computes a commitment $\mathbf{d} \in \{0, 1\}^n$ to $\mathbf{x}$ and adds $\mathbf{d}$ to the tree by associating it with a leaf. When signing a message with respect to policy P and time τ, the signer generates a NIZK argument to prove that (i) $\mathbf{d}$ is correctly accumulated to the current tree root; (ii) $\mathbf{d}$ is a valid commitment to $\mathbf{x}$; (iii) $\mathbf{x}$ satisfies P. Here the commitment acts as a connecting layer between (i) and (iii). Note that, our NIZK argument is obtained by applying the Unruh transform [44,87] to the refined Stern protocol, resulting in QROM security.

As in [66,74], we set the leaf nodes to all zero values $\mathbf{0}^n$ initially and change it back to $\mathbf{0}^n$ when an attribute is revoked. However, we enroll an attribute $\mathbf{x}$ to the system iff the commitment $\mathbf{d}$ has odd Hamming weight[4]. Next, when signing a message, the signer additionally proves that $\mathbf{d}$ has an odd Hamming weight. This is different from [66,74], where an active $\mathbf{d}$ is set to be non-zero. Our advantage here is that we can prove knowledge of an odd-weight $\mathbf{d}$ with cost only $\mathcal{O}(n)$ bits, while proving knowledge of a non-zero $\mathbf{d}$ would incur cost $\mathcal{O}(n \log n)$ bits.

$\mathsf{Setup}_{\mathsf{init}}(1^\lambda)$: Given the security parameter 1^λ, this algorithm performs the following steps.

---

[4] For the commitment scheme from [75], a commitment $\mathbf{d}$ to an arbitrary $\mathbf{x}$ is statistically close to uniform over $\mathbb{Z}_2^n$, thanks to a left-over hash lemma. Hence, it is expected to repeat the process around 2 times to obtain an odd-weight $\mathbf{d}$.

- Let $L = \mathsf{poly}(\lambda)$ be a positive integer. It then specifies the time space $\mathcal{T} = \{0, 1, 2, 3, \ldots\}$, the message space $\mathcal{M} = \{0, 1\}^*$, the attribute space $\mathcal{X} = \{0, 1\}^L$, and the policy family $\mathcal{P} = \{P : \mathcal{X} \to \{0, 1\}\}$ that consists of all possible polynomial-size Boolean circuits with L-bit input.
- Specify an integer $\ell = \ell(\lambda)$ that determines the maximum number $N = 2^\ell = \mathsf{poly}(\lambda)$ of potential attributes.
- Choose $n = \mathcal{O}(\lambda)$, $c = \mathcal{O}(1)$ such that c divides both L and n and set $m = 2 \cdot 2^c \cdot \frac{n}{c}$.
- Sample a random matrix $\mathbf{B} \xleftarrow{\$} \mathbb{Z}_2^{n \times m}$ that specifies a hash function $h_{\mathbf{B}}(\mathbf{x}) = \mathbf{B} \cdot \mathsf{RE}(\mathbf{x})$.
- Choose $k \geq n + 2\lambda + \mathcal{O}(1)$ such that c divides k. Let $m_0 = 2^c \cdot L/c$ and $m_1 = 2^c \cdot k/c$. Sample $\mathbf{C}_0 \xleftarrow{\$} \mathbb{Z}_2^{n \times m_0}$ and $\mathbf{C}_1 \xleftarrow{\$} \mathbb{Z}_2^{n \times m_1}$ that specifies a statistically hiding and computationally binding commitment scheme.
- Let $\mathsf{COM} : \{0, 1\}^* \times \{0, 1\}^k \to \{0, 1\}^n$ be the extended commitment scheme obtained by applying Merkle-Damgård technique to [74,75], which will be used in our zero-knowledge argument system (though not explicitly in the description below).
- Pick two secure hash functions $\mathcal{H}_G : \{0, 1\}^T \to \{0, 1\}^T$, for some positive integer T such that the bit size of each input queried to $\mathcal{H}_G$ is upper-bounded by T and T is super-logarithmic in λ, and $\mathcal{H}_{\mathsf{FS}} : \{0, 1\}^* \to \{1, 2, 3\}^\kappa$, where $\kappa = \mathcal{O}(\lambda)$, to be modeled as random oracles in the Unruh transform [44,87].

It then outputs public parameter

$$\mathsf{pp} = \{L, \mathcal{T}, \mathcal{M}, \mathcal{X}, \mathcal{P}, \ell, N, n, c, m, k, m_0, m_1, \mathbf{B}, \mathbf{C}_0, \mathbf{C}_1, \mathsf{COM}, \mathcal{H}_G, \mathcal{H}_{\mathsf{FS}}\}.$$

$\mathsf{Setup}_{\mathsf{auth}}(\mathsf{pp})$: This algorithm is run by the attribute-issuing authority. On input parameter pp, it runs $(\mathsf{mpk}, \mathsf{msk}) \leftarrow \mathsf{AuthGen}(\mathsf{pp})$[5]. In addition, it initializes the following.

- A registration table $\mathbf{reg} := (\mathbf{reg}[0], \ldots, \mathbf{reg}[N-1])$ so that $\mathbf{reg}[i][1] = \mathbf{0}^n$, $\mathbf{reg}[i][2] = -1$, and $\mathbf{reg}[i][3] = -1$ for all $i \in [0, N-1]$. Looking ahead, $\mathbf{reg}[i][1]$ will store a (non-zero) commitment of an attribute while $\mathbf{reg}[i][2]$ and $\mathbf{reg}[i][3]$ represent the epochs an attribute is enrolled in and removed from the system, respectively.
- A Merkle tree $\mathcal{MT}$ built on top of $\mathbf{reg}[0][1], \mathbf{reg}[1][1], \ldots, \mathbf{reg}[N-1][1]$. We remark that this $\mathcal{MT}$ is all-zero at this stage. However, it will be eventually updated either when an attribute is enrolled in or revoked from the system.
- A counter of enrolled attributes $j := 0$, initial time epoch $\tau = 0$, and initial system information $\mathsf{info}_0 = \emptyset$.

---

[5] Here, we assume the existence of a functionality $\mathsf{AuthGen}$, which enables an attribute-issuing authority's key pair to be derived as $(\mathsf{mpk}, \mathsf{msk}) \leftarrow \mathsf{AuthGen}(1^\lambda)$. In practice, the authority may use an ordinary signature with verifying-signing key pair $(\mathsf{mpk}, \mathsf{msk})$ to authenticate the updated system information.

The authority will then publish public key mpk and broadcast $\mathbf{reg}$ and info_0 while keeping $\mathcal{MT}$ and j for itself. We assume that both $\mathbf{reg}$ and info are visible to everyone but only editable by a party who owns msk. It is further required that one can efficiently verify the well-formedness of $\mathbf{reg}$ and info.

AttrGen(msk, $\mathbf{x}$, $\mathsf{info}_{\tau_{\text{current}}}$, $\mathbf{reg}$): When a user requests an attribute key for his provided attribute $\mathbf{x} \in \{0,1\}^L$ at current epoch τ_{current}, the authority executes this algorithm and proceeds as follows.

1. Issue an identifier for this attribute $\mathbf{x}$ as the binary representation of j, denoted as $\mathsf{bin}(j) \in \{0,1\}^\ell$.

2. Sample randomness $\mathbf{r} \overset{\$}{\leftarrow} \{0,1\}^k$ and compute a commitment of $\mathbf{x}$ as $\mathbf{d} = \mathbf{C}_0 \cdot \mathsf{RE}(\mathbf{x}) \oplus \mathbf{C}_1 \cdot \mathsf{RE}(\mathbf{r})$. Repeat the process until the weight of $\mathbf{d}$ is odd. Return $\mathsf{sk}_\mathbf{x} = (\mathbf{x}, \mathbf{r}, \mathsf{bin}(j))$ to the user. From now on, we write $\mathsf{sk}_{\mathbf{x}_j} = (\mathbf{x}_j, \mathbf{r}_j, \mathsf{bin}(j))$ to distinguish signing keys of different attributes.

3. Update $\mathcal{MT}$ by running the algorithm $\mathsf{TUpdate}_\mathbf{B}(\mathsf{bin}(j), \mathbf{d})$, register the attribute to $\mathbf{reg}$ as $\mathbf{reg}[j][1] = \mathbf{d}$, $\mathbf{reg}[j][2] = \tau_{\text{current}}$, and increase the counter j to $j+1$.

Update(msk, $\mathcal{S}$, $\mathsf{info}_{\tau_{\text{current}}}$, $\mathbf{reg}$): This algorithm is run by the authority to update the system and advance the epoch. Let $\mathcal{S} = \{\mathbf{x}_{i_1}, \ldots, \mathbf{x}_{i_r}\}$ contain attributes to be revoked. If there exists $t \in [1, r]$ so that $\mathsf{IsActive}(\mathbf{x}_{i_t}, \mathsf{info}_{\tau_{\text{current}}}) = 0$, this algorithm aborts. Otherwise it performs the following steps.

1. For each $t \in [1, r]$, run $\mathsf{TUpdate}_\mathbf{B}(\mathsf{bin}(i_t), \mathbf{0}^n)$ to update $\mathcal{MT}$ and set $\mathbf{reg}[i_t][3] = \tau_{\text{new}}$.

2. Note that all the zero leaves in updated $\mathcal{MT}$ are associated with either revoked attributes or non-registered attributes. In other words, only active attributes have their odd-weight commitments, denoted as $\{\mathbf{d}_j\}$, accumulated in the root $\mathbf{u}_{\tau_{\text{new}}}$ of the updated tree.

   For each j, let $w^{(j)} \in \mathbb{Z}_2^\ell \times (\mathbb{Z}_2^n)^\ell$ be the witness for the fact that $\mathbf{d}_j$ is accumulated in $\mathbf{u}_{\tau_{\text{new}}}$. (This can be obtained via algorithm $\mathsf{TWitGen}_\mathbf{B}$). The authority then announces the updated system information as

$$\mathsf{info}_{\tau_{\text{new}}} = (\mathbf{u}_{\tau_{\text{new}}}, \{w^{(j)}\}_j).$$

We remark that unnecessary for a signer or a verifier to download $\mathsf{info}_{\tau_{\text{new}}}$ as a whole. In fact, as we describe below, a signer with an active attribute only needs to download its corresponding witness $w^{(j)}$ of $\mathcal{O}(\lambda \cdot \ell)$ bits once so as to sign messages at time τ_{new}. Meanwhile, it suffices for a verifier to download $\mathbf{u}_{\tau_{\text{new}}}$ of $\mathcal{O}(\lambda)$ bits to verify all signatures associated with τ_{new}.

Sign($\mathsf{sk}_{\mathbf{x}_j}$, M, P, info_τ): This algorithm is run by a user possessing an attribute key $\mathsf{sk}_{\mathbf{x}_j} = (\mathbf{x}_j, \mathbf{r}_j, \mathsf{bin}(j))$ who wishes to sign a message with respect to a policy P. It aborts if $P(\mathbf{x}_j) = 0$ or info_τ does not include a witness containing $\mathsf{bin}(j)$. Otherwise, it proceeds as below.

1. Download $\mathbf{u}_\tau$ and the witness $w^{(j)} = (\mathsf{bin}(j), (\mathbf{w}_\ell, \ldots, \mathbf{w}_1))$ from info_τ.

2. Generate a proof to show the possession of tuple

$$\xi = (\mathbf{d}_j, \mathbf{x}_j, \mathbf{r}_j, \mathsf{bin}(j), \mathbf{w}_\ell, \ldots, \mathbf{w}_1) \tag{1}$$

   such that

(a) $\mathbf{d}_j$ is correctly accumulated in the root $\mathbf{u}_\tau$, i.e.,

$$\mathsf{TVerify}_\mathbf{B}(\mathbf{u}_\tau, \mathbf{d}_j, \mathsf{bin}(j), (\mathbf{w}_\ell, \ldots, \mathbf{w}_1)) = 1.$$

(b) $\mathbf{d}_j$ is an odd-weight commitment of $\mathbf{x}_j$, i.e.,

$$\mathbf{d}_j = \mathbf{C}_0 \cdot \mathsf{RE}(\mathbf{x}_j) \oplus \mathbf{C}_1 \cdot \mathsf{RE}(\mathbf{r}_j) \text{ and } wt(\mathbf{d}_j) = 1 \bmod 2.$$

(c) The attribute $\mathbf{x}_j$ satisfies the claimed policy P. In other words, $P(\mathbf{x}_j) = 1$.

To this end, we run the Stern-like protocol in Sect. 4.3. It is repeated κ times to achieve negligible soundness error and made non-interactive via Unruh transform. The resultant NIZK proof is

$$\Pi = (\{\mathsf{CMT}_i\}_{i=1}^\kappa, \{\overline{\mathsf{RSP}}_{i,j}\}_{i\in[1,\kappa], j\in\{1,2,3\}\setminus\{\mathsf{ch}_i\}}, \mathsf{CH}, \{\mathsf{RSP}_{i,\mathsf{ch}_i}\}_{i=1}^\kappa)$$

where, for all $i \in [1, \kappa]$ and all $j \in \{1, 2, 3\}$, $\mathsf{RSP}_{i,j}$ is a response with respect to CMT_i and challenge j, $\overline{\mathsf{RSP}}_{i,j} = \mathcal{H}_G(\mathsf{RSP}_{i,j})$, and

$$\mathsf{CH} = [\mathsf{ch}_1 | \ldots | \mathsf{ch}_\kappa]^\top$$
$$:= \mathcal{H}_{\mathsf{FS}}(\{\mathsf{CMT}_i\}_{i=1}^\kappa, \{\overline{\mathsf{RSP}}_{i,j}\}_{i\in[1,\kappa], j\in\{1,2,3\}}, M, P, \tau, \mathbf{u}_\tau, \mathbf{B}, \mathbf{C}_0, \mathbf{C}_1)$$
$$\in \{1, 2, 3\}^\kappa.$$

Notice that $\overline{\mathsf{RSP}}_{i,\mathsf{ch}_i}$, for all $i \in [1, \kappa]$, are excluded from Π since it can be recovered by invoking $\mathcal{H}_G(\mathsf{RSP}_{i,\mathsf{ch}_i})$.

3. Return signature as $\Sigma = \Pi$.

Verify$(M, P, \mathsf{info}_\tau, \Sigma)$: This algorithm checks the validity of the message signature pair (M, Σ) with respect to the policy P and time epoch τ. It parses $\Sigma = (\{\mathsf{CMT}_i\}_{i=1}^\kappa, \{\overline{\mathsf{RSP}}_{i,j}\}_{i\in[1,\kappa], j\in\{1,2,3\}\setminus\{\mathsf{ch}_i\}}, \mathsf{CH}, \{\mathsf{RSP}_{i,\mathsf{ch}_i}\}_{i=1}^\kappa)$ and performs the following steps.

1. Download $\mathbf{u}_\tau$ from info_τ.
2. Compute $\overline{\mathsf{RSP}}_{i,\mathsf{ch}_i} := \mathcal{H}_G(\mathsf{RSP}_{i,\mathsf{ch}_i})$ for all $i \in [1, \kappa]$.
3. If $\mathsf{CH} \neq \mathcal{H}_{\mathsf{FS}}(\{\mathsf{CMT}_i\}_{i=1}^\kappa, \{\overline{\mathsf{RSP}}_{i,j}\}_{i\in[1,\kappa], j\in\{1,2,3\}}, M, P, \tau, \mathbf{u}_\tau, \mathbf{B}, \mathbf{C}_0, \mathbf{C}_1)$, return 0.
4. Parse $\mathsf{CH} = [\mathsf{ch}_1 | \ldots | \mathsf{ch}_\kappa]^\top$.
5. For $i \in [1, \kappa]$, verify the validity of $\mathsf{RSP}_{i,\mathsf{ch}_i}$ with respect to commitment CMT_i and challenge value ch_i. If any of the verifications does not hold, return 0. Else return 1.

3.3 Analysis of the Scheme

Efficiency. The efficiency of our construction is summarized as follows.

- The public parameter includes several matrices and has bit size $\mathcal{O}(\lambda^2 + \lambda \cdot L)$.
- The attribute key $\mathsf{sk}_\mathbf{x}$ has bit size $\mathcal{O}(\lambda + L)$.
- At each epoch, the signer downloads data of bit size $\mathcal{O}(\lambda \cdot \ell) = \mathcal{O}(\lambda \cdot \log \lambda)$ while the verifier downloads data of bit size $\mathcal{O}(\lambda)$.

– The bit-size of signature Σ is $\mathcal{O}(\zeta + T) \cdot \kappa = \mathcal{O}(L + |P| + \lambda \cdot \log \lambda + T) \cdot \mathcal{O}(\lambda)$, where T is the output size of $\mathcal{H}_G$, ζ is the average communication cost of the protocol in Sect. 4.3 and $|P|$ is the size of a circuit representing P.

Correctness. We show that the construction is correct with probability 1. In fact, experiment $\mathbf{Expt}_{\mathcal{A}}^{\text{correct}}(1^{\lambda})$ outputs 1, i.e., the adversary breaks correctness, iff $\mathcal{A}$ outputs a tuple $(\mathbf{x}, M, P, \tau)$ with $P(\mathbf{x}) = 1$ and $\mathsf{IsActive}(\mathbf{x}, \mathsf{info}_{\tau}) = 1$ such that an honestly generated signature Σ is invalid. However, due to perfect correctness of the underlying NIZK protocol, the signature Σ is always valid.

Security. In Theorem 1, we prove that our construction satisfies the security requirements proposed in Sect. 2.2, based on the hardness of the 2-RNSD problems associated with parameters $(n, 2n, c)$ and $(n, L + k, c)$.

Theorem 1. *In the QROM, the described FDABS scheme satisfies statistical privacy and unforgeability assuming the hardness of* 2-RNSD *problems.*

The proof of Theorem 1 (see the full version [63]) relies on the following facts.

1. The employed Stern-like protocol described in Sect. 4.3 is statistical ZK and sound, based on the security of the underlying commitment COM.
2. The Merkle tree accumulator is secure, which relies on the hardness of the 2-RNSD$_{n,2n,c}$ problem.
3. The commitment scheme used to commit the attributes is statistically hiding and computationally binding, which relies on the hardness of the 2-RNSD$_{n,L+k,c}$ problem.

We now present how to simulate an FDABS signature, without using a witness, that is statistically indistinguishable from a real one by programming the hash function $\mathcal{H}_{\mathsf{FS}}$. Then we show how to extract a valid witness of form (1) from a valid signature by programming $\mathcal{H}_G$. These are essential in proving Theorem 1.

Simulating an FDABS Signature. Let $M, P, \tau, \mathbf{u}_{\tau}, \mathbf{B}, \mathbf{C}_0, \mathbf{C}_1$ be the public input involving a signing process and SIM is the simulator of the Stern protocol from Theorem 2. The simulator $\mathsf{SIM}_{\mathsf{fdabs}}$ is described in Fig. 2.

It is straightforward to verify that the above simulated signature is statistically indistinguishable from a real one, assuming the special honest-verifier ZK property of our Stern protocol in Fig. 4.

Extracting a Witness from an FDABS Signature. To be able to extract a witness from an FDABS message-signature pair (M, Σ) with respect to a policy P, we follow [44,87] to simulate random oracle $\mathcal{H}_G$ as a polynomial p_G over $\mathrm{GF}(2^T)$ of a sufficiently large degree, in particular, degree at least $2q_G - 1$, such that it is perfectly indistinguishable from a random function. Here q_G is an upper bound on the number of queries from all possible parties to $\mathcal{H}_G$, and T should be super-logarithmic in λ. From previous results [10], the inverse function p_G^{-1} can be efficiently computed.

Let $M, P, \tau, \mathbf{u}_{\tau}, \mathbf{B}, \mathbf{C}_0, \mathbf{C}_1, \Sigma$ be public input and $\mathcal{E}$ be the extractor of the protocol from Theorem 2. Our extractor $\mathcal{E}_{\mathsf{fdabs}}$ is formally described in Fig. 3.

Inputs: $M, P, \tau, \mathbf{u}_\tau, \mathbf{B}, \mathbf{C}_0, \mathbf{C}_1$.
Our simulator $\mathsf{SIM}_{\mathsf{fdabs}}$ works as follows.

1. Sample $\mathsf{CH} := [\mathsf{ch}_1 | \ldots | \mathsf{ch}_\kappa]^\top \xleftarrow{\$} \{1, 2, 3\}^\kappa$.
2. For each $i \in [1, \kappa]$:
   (a) Run SIM of the Stern protocol from Theorem 2, to obtain simulated transcript $(\mathsf{CMT}_i, \mathsf{ch}_i, \mathsf{RSP}_{i,\mathsf{ch}_i})$.
   (b) Compute $\overline{\mathsf{RSP}}_{i,\mathsf{ch}_i} := \mathcal{H}_G(\mathsf{RSP}_{i,\mathsf{ch}_i})$.
   (c) $\overline{\mathsf{RSP}}_{i,j} \xleftarrow{\$} \{0,1\}^T$ for all $j \in \{1, 2, 3\} \setminus \{\mathsf{ch}_i\}$.
3. Program $\mathcal{H}_{\mathsf{FS}}(\{\mathsf{CMT}_i\}_{i=1}^\kappa, \{\overline{\mathsf{RSP}}_{i,j}\}_{i\in[1,\kappa], j\in\{1,2,3\}}, M, P, \tau, \mathbf{u}_\tau, \mathbf{B}, \mathbf{C}_0, \mathbf{C}_1) := \mathsf{CH}$.
4. Return a simulated FDABS signature

$$\Pi = (\{\mathsf{CMT}_i\}_{i=1}^\kappa, \{\overline{\mathsf{RSP}}_{i,j}\}_{i\in[1,\kappa], j\in\{1,2,3\}\setminus\{\mathsf{ch}_i\}}, \mathsf{CH}, \{\mathsf{RSP}_{i,\mathsf{ch}_i}\}_{i=1}^\kappa)$$

where $\mathsf{CH} = [\mathsf{ch}_1 | \ldots | \mathsf{ch}_\kappa]^\top$.

Fig. 2. Simulator $\mathsf{SIM}_{\mathsf{fdabs}}$ of FDABS.

Inputs: $M, P, \tau, \mathbf{u}_\tau, \mathbf{B}, \mathbf{C}_0, \mathbf{C}_1, \Sigma, \mathcal{H}_G = p_G$.
Our extractor $\mathcal{E}_{\mathsf{fdabs}}$ works as follows.

1. Parse $\Sigma = (\{\mathsf{CMT}_i\}_{i=1}^\kappa, \{\overline{\mathsf{RSP}}_{i,j}\}_{i\in[1,\kappa], j\in\{1,2,3\}\setminus\{\mathsf{ch}_i\}}, \mathsf{CH}, \{\mathsf{RSP}_{i,\mathsf{ch}_i}\}_{i=1}^\kappa)$. Return 0 if $\mathsf{Verify}(M, P, \mathsf{info}_\tau, \Sigma) = 0$. Otherwise $\mathsf{RSP}_{i,\mathsf{ch}_i}$ is a valid response with respect to commitment CMT_i and challenge ch_i for all $i \in [1, \kappa]$.
2. For all $i \in [1, \kappa]$ and $j \in \{1, 2, 3\} \setminus \{\mathsf{ch}_i\}$, compute $\mathsf{RSP}_{i,j} := p_G^{-1}(\overline{\mathsf{RSP}}_{i,j})$. Then $\mathsf{CH} = [\mathsf{ch}_1 | \ldots | \mathsf{ch}_\kappa]^\top$ coincides with $\mathcal{H}_{\mathsf{FS}}(\{\mathsf{CMT}_i\}_{i=1}^\kappa, \{\overline{\mathsf{RSP}}_{i,j}\}_{i\in[1,\kappa], j\in\{1,2,3\}}, M, P, \tau, \mathbf{u}_\tau, \mathbf{B}, \mathbf{C}_0, \mathbf{C}_1)$.
3. Let $t^* \in [1, \kappa]$ such that $\mathsf{RSP}_{t^*,1}, \mathsf{RSP}_{t^*,2}, \mathsf{RSP}_{t^*,3}$ are three valid responses for challenges $\{1, 2, 3\}$ with respect to CMT_{t^*}. If no such t^* exists, abort.
4. Let $\mathbf{w}' \leftarrow \mathcal{E}(\mathsf{CMT}_{t^*}, \mathsf{RSP}_{t^*,1}, \mathsf{RSP}_{t^*,2}, \mathsf{RSP}_{t^*,3})$.
5. By "backtracking" the transformation steps we have performed, we are able to extract $\xi' = (\mathbf{d}', \mathbf{x}', \mathbf{r}', \mathsf{bin}(j'), \mathbf{w}'_\ell, \ldots, \mathbf{w}'_1)$ from $\mathbf{w}'$ for $\mathsf{R}_{\mathsf{fdabs}}$.
6. Return ξ'.

Fig. 3. Extractor $\mathcal{E}_{\mathsf{fdabs}}$ of FDABS.

Assuming the online extractability of the Unruh transform [44,87], and the special soundness of our Stern protocol in Fig. 4, the above extractor $\mathcal{E}_{\mathsf{fdabs}}$ outputs ξ' such that all the conditions specified in Sign algorithm from Sect. 3.2. In particular, the existence of t^* at Step 3 is guaranteed by the online extractability of the Unruh transform.

4   Supporting Zero-Knowledge Protocols

This section provides the supporting ZK layer for the FDABS scheme described in Sect. 3. We first present our refined abstraction of Stern's protocol in Sect. 4.1.

Then, in Sect. 4.2, we discuss our enhancement of previous Stern-like techniques in light of the refined abstraction. Then, the ZK protocol used in the signing algorithm of the proposed FDABS is presented in Sect. 4.3, as a special instance of the abstraction.

4.1 A Refined Abstraction of Stern's Protocol

Here, we present our refined framework for Stern-like protocols. As discussed in Sect. 1, our approach significantly departs from Stern's original work [82,83] and Libert et al.'s abstraction [56], in two fundamental aspects: we do not require that additive masking vectors to be uniformly random in the whole space, and we do not even assume that the functions applied to witness vectors are random permutations of coordinates.

Let $D \in \mathbb{Z}^+$ and VALID, $\mathcal{R}$, $\mathcal{Z}$ be subsets of $\{0,1\}^D$. Let $\mathcal{S}$ be a finite set, and F, F', F'' be functions with domains/ranges defined as follows:

$$F : \mathcal{S} \times \{0,1\}^D \ \rightarrow \ \{0,1\}^D; \quad F' : \mathcal{S} \times \mathcal{R} \ \rightarrow \ \mathcal{R}; \quad F'' : \mathcal{S} \times \mathcal{Z} \ \rightarrow \ \mathcal{Z}.$$

We assume VALID, $\mathcal{R}$, $\mathcal{Z}$, $\mathcal{S}$, and F, F', F'' satisfy the following 4 conditions.

(1) "Homomorphism": For all $(\phi, \mathbf{r}, \mathbf{z}) \in \mathcal{S} \times \mathcal{R} \times \mathcal{Z}$, $F'(\phi, \mathbf{r}) \oplus F''(\phi, \mathbf{z}) = F(\phi, \mathbf{r} \oplus \mathbf{z})$.

(2) "Closure of F w.r.t. VALID": For all $(\phi, \mathbf{w}) \in \mathcal{S} \times \{0,1\}^D$, $\mathbf{w} \in$ VALID $\Longleftrightarrow$ $F(\phi, \mathbf{w}) \in$ VALID.

(3) For all $\mathbf{w} \in$ VALID, the distributions of $\{\mathbf{t} = F(\phi, \mathbf{w}) \mid \phi \xleftarrow{\$} \mathcal{S}\}$ and $\{\mathbf{t} \xleftarrow{\$}$ VALID$\}$ are identical.

(4) For all $\mathbf{w} \in$ VALID, the distributions of $\{\mathbf{z} = \mathbf{w} \oplus \mathbf{r} \mid \mathbf{r} \xleftarrow{\$} \mathcal{R}\}$ and $\{\mathbf{z} \xleftarrow{\$} \mathcal{Z}\}$ are identical.

Let $D_0 \in \mathbb{Z}^+$ such that $D_0 \le D$. We aim to construct a Σ-protocol for the following abstract relation:

$$R_{\text{abstract}} = \{((\mathbf{M}, \mathbf{v}), \mathbf{w}) \in (\mathbb{Z}_2^{D_0 \times D} \times \mathbb{Z}_2^{D_0}) \times \text{VALID} : \mathbf{M} \cdot \mathbf{w} = \mathbf{v}\}.$$

The interaction between prover $\mathcal{P}$ and verifier $\mathcal{V}$ is described in Fig. 4. The protocol employs an auxiliary string commitment scheme COM that is statistically hiding and computationally binding, and that has commitment size n bits and randomness size r bits. (Such a commitment scheme can be obtained based on codes, see [75, Section 3.1].)

Theorem 2. *Assume that the auxiliary string commitment scheme* COM *is statistically hiding and computationally binding. Then the protocol in Fig. 4 is a Σ-protocol for the relation* R_{abstract} *with perfect completeness and average communication cost ζ bits, where*

$$\zeta = 3n + 2r + \frac{\log(|\text{VALID}|) + 2\log(|\mathcal{R}|) + \log(|\mathcal{Z}|) + 2\log(|\mathcal{S}|)}{3}. \tag{2}$$

In particular, the protocol satisfies

Inputs: The common input is $(\mathbf{M}, \mathbf{v}) \in \mathbb{Z}_2^{D_0 \times D} \times \mathbb{Z}_2^{D_0}$. Prover's witness is $\mathbf{w} \in \mathsf{VALID}$.

1. **Commitment:** Prover samples $\mathbf{r} \xleftarrow{\$} \mathcal{R}$, $\phi \xleftarrow{\$} \mathcal{S}$ and randomness ρ_1, ρ_2, ρ_3 for COM. Then it sends commitment $\mathsf{CMT} = (C_1, C_2, C_3)$ to the verifier, where

$$C_1 = \mathsf{COM}(\phi, \ \mathbf{M} \cdot \mathbf{r}; \ \rho_1), \quad C_2 = \mathsf{COM}(F'(\phi, \mathbf{r}); \ \rho_2),$$
$$C_3 = \mathsf{COM}(F''(\phi, \mathbf{w} \oplus \mathbf{r}); \ \rho_3).$$

2. **Challenge:** The verifier sends a challenge $Ch \xleftarrow{\$} \{1, 2, 3\}$ to the prover.
3. **Response:** Depending on Ch, the prover sends RSP computed as follows:
   - $Ch = 1$: Let $\mathbf{t} = F(\phi, \mathbf{w})$, $\mathbf{y} = F'(\phi, \mathbf{r})$, and RSP $= (\mathbf{t}, \mathbf{y}, \rho_2, \rho_3)$.
   - $Ch = 2$: Let $\psi = \phi$, $\mathbf{z} = \mathbf{w} \oplus \mathbf{r}$, and RSP $= (\psi, \mathbf{z}, \rho_1, \rho_3)$.
   - $Ch = 3$: Let $\chi = \phi$, $\mathbf{s} = \mathbf{r}$, and RSP $= (\chi, \mathbf{s}, \rho_1, \rho_2)$.

Verification: Receiving RSP, the verifier proceeds as follows:

   - $Ch = 1$: Check that $\mathbf{t} \in \mathsf{VALID}$, $\mathbf{y} \in \mathcal{R}$, and that $C_2 = \mathsf{COM}(\mathbf{y}; \ \rho_2)$, $C_3 = \mathsf{COM}(\mathbf{t} \oplus \mathbf{y}; \ \rho_3)$.
   - $Ch = 2$: Check that $\psi \in \mathcal{S}$, $\mathbf{z} \in \mathcal{Z}$, and that $C_1 = \mathsf{COM}(\psi, \ \mathbf{M} \cdot \mathbf{z} \oplus \mathbf{v}; \ \rho_1)$, $C_3 = \mathsf{COM}(F''(\psi, \mathbf{z}); \ \rho_3)$.
   - $Ch = 3$: Check that $\chi \in \mathcal{S}$, $\mathbf{s} \in \mathcal{R}$, and that $C_1 = \mathsf{COM}(\chi, \ \mathbf{M} \cdot \mathbf{s}; \ \rho_1)$, $C_2 = \mathsf{COM}(F'(\chi, \mathbf{s}); \ \rho_2)$.

In each case, the verifier outputs 1 if and only if all the conditions hold.

Fig. 4. A Σ-protocol for the relation $\mathrm{R_{abstract}}$.

- **Special honest-verifier ZK.** *There exists a PPT simulator that, on input $(\mathbf{M}, \mathbf{v})$ and $Ch \in \{1, 2, 3\}$, outputs an accepted transcript statistically close to that produced by the real prover.*
- **Special soundness.** *There exists a PPT extractor $\mathcal{E}$ that, on input a commitment CMT and 3 valid responses $(\mathrm{RSP}_1, \mathrm{RSP}_2, \mathrm{RSP}_3)$ to all 3 possible values of Ch, outputs $\mathbf{w}' \in \mathsf{VALID}$ such that $\mathbf{M} \cdot \mathbf{w}' = \mathbf{v}$.*

Proof. The proof uses the conditions **(1)-(4)** specified above, as well as the statistical hiding and computational binding properties of COM.

Completeness. An honest prover with witness $\mathbf{w} \in \mathsf{VALID}$ such that $\mathbf{M} \cdot \mathbf{w} = \mathbf{v}$ will always get accepted by the verifier. Apart from the checks for well-formedness of C_1, C_2, C_3, it suffices to note the following points.

- **Case $Ch = 1$.** We have $\mathbf{t} = F(\phi, \mathbf{w}) \in \mathsf{VALID}$ by condition **(2)**, and $\mathbf{y} = F'(\phi, \mathbf{r}) \in \mathcal{R}$, by the definition of F'. Furthermore, by condition **(4)**, we know that $\mathbf{z} = \mathbf{w} \oplus \mathbf{r} \in \mathcal{Z}$, and then, by condition **(1)**, we have

$$\mathbf{y} \oplus F''(\phi, \mathbf{w} \oplus \mathbf{r}) = F'(\phi, \mathbf{r}) \oplus F''(\phi, \mathbf{z}) = F(\phi, \mathbf{r} \oplus \mathbf{z}) = F(\phi, \mathbf{w}) = \mathbf{t},$$

which implies that $F''(\phi, \mathbf{w} \oplus \mathbf{r}) = \mathbf{t} \oplus \mathbf{y}$.

– **Case** $Ch = 2$. We have $\mathbf{z} = \mathbf{w} \oplus \mathbf{r} \in \mathcal{Z}$. Since $\mathbf{v} = \mathbf{M} \cdot \mathbf{w}$, it holds that

$$\mathbf{M} \cdot \mathbf{z} \oplus \mathbf{v} = \mathbf{M} \cdot (\mathbf{w} \oplus \mathbf{r}) \oplus \mathbf{v} = \mathbf{M} \cdot \mathbf{w} \oplus \mathbf{M} \cdot \mathbf{r} \oplus \mathbf{v} = \mathbf{M} \cdot \mathbf{r}.$$

Honest-Verifier ZK. We construct a simulator SIM that, on input $(\mathbf{M}, \mathbf{v})$ and $Ch \in \{1, 2, 3\}$, returns a transcript statistically close to the real one produced by an honest prover. Depending on the value of Ch, SIM proceeds as follows.

– **Case** $Ch = 1$. SIM samples $\mathbf{t} \xleftarrow{\$} \mathsf{VALID}$, $\phi \xleftarrow{\$} \mathcal{S}$, $\mathbf{r} \xleftarrow{\$} \mathcal{R}$ and randomness ρ_1, ρ_2, ρ_3 for COM. Then it computes $\mathbf{y} = F'(\phi, \mathbf{r})$ and commitment $\mathsf{CMT} = (C'_1, C'_2, C'_3)$ where $C'_1 = \mathsf{COM}(0; \rho_1)$, $C'_2 = \mathsf{COM}(\mathbf{y}; \rho_2)$ and $C'_3 = \mathsf{COM}(\mathbf{t} \oplus \mathbf{y}; \rho_3)$. It defines $\mathsf{RSP} = (\mathbf{t}, \mathbf{y}, \rho_2, \rho_3)$. By condition **(3)**, the distribution of $\mathbf{t}$ is identical to that of the real transcript. Also, $\mathbf{y}$ is computed in the same way as in the real transcript.

– **Case** $Ch = 2$. SIM samples $\psi \xleftarrow{\$} \mathcal{S}$, $\mathbf{z} \xleftarrow{\$} \mathcal{Z}$ and randomness ρ_1, ρ_2, ρ_3 for COM. Then it computes commitment $\mathsf{CMT} = (C'_1, C'_2, C'_3)$ where $C'_1 = \mathsf{COM}(\psi, \mathbf{M} \cdot \mathbf{z} \oplus \mathbf{v}; \rho_2)$, $C'_2 = \mathsf{COM}(0; \rho_2)$, $C'_3 = \mathsf{COM}(F''(\psi, \mathbf{z}); \rho_3)$, and response $\mathsf{RSP} = (\psi, \mathbf{z}, \rho_1, \rho_3)$. Here, note that the simulated $\mathbf{z}$ and the one in real transcript are both uniformly random over $\mathcal{Z}$, by condition **(4)**.

– **Case** $Ch = 3$. SIM samples $\psi \xleftarrow{\$} \mathcal{S}$, $\mathbf{s} \xleftarrow{\$} \mathcal{R}$ and randomness ρ_1, ρ_2, ρ_3 for COM. Then it computes commitment $\mathsf{CMT} = (C'_1, C'_2, C'_3)$ where $C'_1 = \mathsf{COM}(\chi, \mathbf{M} \cdot \mathbf{s}; \rho_1)$, $C'_2 = \mathsf{COM}(F'(\chi, \mathbf{s}); \rho_2)$ and $C'_3 = \mathsf{COM}(0; \rho_3)$, and response $\mathsf{RSP} = (\chi, \mathbf{s}, \rho_1, \rho_2)$.

In every case, SIM outputs the simulated transcript $(\mathsf{CMT}, Ch, \mathsf{RSP})$. It then follows from the statistical hiding property of COM that the distributions of simulated and real transcripts are statistically close.

Special Soundness. Let $\mathsf{RSP}_1 = (\mathbf{t}, \mathbf{y}, \rho_2, \rho_3)$, $\mathsf{RSP}_2 = (\psi, \mathbf{z}, \rho_1, \rho_3)$ and $\mathsf{RSP}_3 = (\chi, \mathbf{s}, \rho_1, \rho_2)$ be the 3 valid responses to the same commitment $\mathsf{CMT} = (C_1, C_2, C_3)$ with respect to all 3 values of Ch. Then, the following conditions hold.

$$\begin{cases} \mathbf{t} \in \mathsf{VALID}, \;\; \mathbf{y} \in \mathcal{R}, \;\; \mathbf{z} \in \mathcal{Z}, \;\; \mathbf{s} \in \mathcal{R}, \;\; \psi \in \mathcal{S}, \;\; \chi \in \mathcal{S}, \\ C_1 = \mathsf{COM}(\psi, \mathbf{M} \cdot \mathbf{z} \oplus \mathbf{v}; \; \rho_1) = \mathsf{COM}(\chi, \mathbf{M} \cdot \mathbf{s}; \; \rho_1), \\ C_2 = \mathsf{COM}(\mathbf{y}; \; \rho_2) = \mathsf{COM}(F'(\chi, \mathbf{s}); \; \rho_2), \\ C_3 = \mathsf{COM}(\mathbf{t} \oplus \mathbf{y}; \; \rho_3) = \mathsf{COM}(F''(\psi, \mathbf{z}); \; \rho_3). \end{cases}$$

Since COM is computationally binding, we deduce that

$$\mathbf{t} \in \mathsf{VALID}, \;\; \psi = \chi, \;\; \mathbf{M} \cdot \mathbf{z} \oplus \mathbf{v} = \mathbf{M} \cdot \mathbf{s}, \;\; \mathbf{y} = F'(\chi, \mathbf{s}), \;\; \mathbf{t} \oplus \mathbf{y} = F''(\psi, \mathbf{z}).$$

By condition **(1)**, we have

$$\mathbf{t} = \mathbf{y} \oplus (\mathbf{t} \oplus \mathbf{y}) = \mathbf{y} \oplus F''(\psi, \mathbf{z}) = F'(\psi, \mathbf{s}) \oplus F''(\psi, \mathbf{z}) = F(\psi, \mathbf{s} \oplus \mathbf{z}).$$

Since $\mathbf{t} \in \mathsf{VALID}$, condition **(2)** implies that $\mathbf{w}' := \mathbf{s} \oplus \mathbf{z} \in \mathsf{VALID}$. Moreover, as $\mathbf{M} \cdot \mathbf{z} \oplus \mathbf{v} = \mathbf{M} \cdot \mathbf{s}$, we deduce that $\mathbf{M} \cdot \mathbf{w}' = \mathbf{M} \cdot (\mathbf{s} \oplus \mathbf{z}) = \mathbf{v}$. In other words, we have $((\mathbf{M}, \mathbf{v}), \mathbf{w}') \in \mathsf{R}_{\text{abstract}}$.

4.2 Stern-Like Techniques: Previous Ideas and Our Enhancements

Techniques for Handling Arbitrary Binary Vectors. To prove knowledge of a vector $\mathbf{x} \in \{0,1\}^n$, define the following extension Encode and a function F_{bin}.

- For $\mathbf{x} = [x_1|\dots|x_n]^\top$, let $\text{Encode}(\mathbf{x}) = [\bar{x}_1|x_1|\dots|\bar{x}_n|x_n]^\top \in \{0,1\}^{2n}$.
- Let $\mathbf{I}_n^* \in \mathbb{Z}_2^{n \times 2n}$ be an extension of the identity matrix $\mathbf{I}_n$, obtained by inserting a zero-column $\mathbf{0}^n$ right before each column of $\mathbf{I}_n$. Form a new matrix $\mathbf{M} = \mathbf{M}_0 \cdot \mathbf{I}_n^* \in \mathbb{Z}_2^{D_0 \times 2n}$. Therefore, $\mathbf{x} = \mathbf{I}_n^* \cdot \text{Encode}(\mathbf{x})$ and $\mathbf{M}_0 \cdot \mathbf{x} = \mathbf{v}$ is equivalent to $\mathbf{M} \cdot \text{Encode}(\mathbf{x}) = \mathbf{v}$.
- For $\mathbf{b} = [b_1|\dots|b_n]^\top \in \{0,1\}^n$ and $\mathbf{w} = [w_{1,0}|w_{1,1}|\dots|w_{n,0}|w_{n,1}]^\top \in \{0,1\}^{2n}$, define a function $F_{\text{bin}} : \{0,1\}^n \times \{0,1\}^{2n} \to \{0,1\}^{2n}$ as $F_{\text{bin}}(\mathbf{b}, \mathbf{w}) = [w_{1,b_1}|w_{1,\bar{b}_1}|\dots|w_{n,b_n}|w_{n,\bar{b}_n}]^\top$. It can be verified that for all $\mathbf{b} \in \{0,1\}^n$ and all $\mathbf{w}, \mathbf{w}' \in \{0,1\}^{2n}$, the following holds:

$$F_{\text{bin}}(\mathbf{b}, \mathbf{w}) \oplus F_{\text{bin}}(\mathbf{b}, \mathbf{w}') = F_{\text{bin}}(\mathbf{b}, \mathbf{w} \oplus \mathbf{w}'). \tag{3}$$

Define $\text{valid}_{\text{bin}} = \{\mathbf{w} : \exists\, \mathbf{x} \in \{0,1\}^n \text{ s.t. } \mathbf{w} = \text{Encode}(\mathbf{x})\}$. Then. $\forall \mathbf{x}, \mathbf{b} \in \{0,1\}^n$,

$$\mathbf{w} = \text{Encode}(\mathbf{x}) \in \text{valid}_{\text{bin}} \iff F_{\text{bin}}(\mathbf{b}, \mathbf{w}) = \text{Encode}(\mathbf{x} \oplus \mathbf{b}) \in \text{valid}_{\text{bin}}. \tag{4}$$

In Stern's framework (see e.g. [58]), to prove knowledge of $\mathbf{x}$, the prover extends $\mathbf{x}$ to $\mathbf{w} \in \text{valid}_{\text{bin}}$ and shows that $\mathbf{w}$ is indeed from the set $\text{valid}_{\text{bin}}$ by using equivalence (4). In addition, if $\mathbf{b}$ is chosen randomly, it perfectly hides $\mathbf{w}$ and hence $\mathbf{x}$. Furthermore, to prove in ZK that the linear equation holds, the prover samples a masking vector $\mathbf{r}_w \xleftarrow{\$} \mathcal{R} = \{0,1\}^{2n}$ and convinces the verifier that $\mathbf{M} \cdot (\mathbf{w} \oplus \mathbf{r}_w) = \mathbf{M} \cdot \mathbf{r}_w \oplus \mathbf{v}$. We can see that the number of masking bits is $2n$. We now present our refined techniques so that n bits suffice.

Our Techniques. Before presenting our techniques, let us define some notions.

- Let $\mathcal{B}_{\text{odd}}^k = \{\mathbf{y} \in \{0,1\}^k : wt(\mathbf{y}) = 1 \bmod 2\}$ and $\mathcal{B}_{\text{even}}^k = \{\mathbf{y} \in \{0,1\}^k : wt(\mathbf{y}) = 0 \bmod 2\}$.
- For simplicity, denote by $\mathcal{B} = (\mathcal{B}_{\text{odd}}^k\|\dots\|\mathcal{B}_{\text{odd}}^k) \subset \{0,1\}^{k \cdot k_0}$ the set that contains all vectors of the form $\mathbf{y} = (\mathbf{y}_1\|\dots\|\mathbf{y}_{k_0})$, where each $\mathbf{y}_i \in \mathcal{B}_{\text{odd}}^k$.

We aim to reduce the above statement, i.e., proving knowledge of $\mathbf{w} = \text{Encode}(\mathbf{x})$ so that it satisfies the equation $\mathbf{M} \cdot \mathbf{w} = \mathbf{v}$, to an instance of the abstract relation $\mathrm{R}_{\text{abstract}}$ from Sect. 4.1. To this end, let $\mathcal{S}_{\text{bin}} = \{0,1\}^n$ and

$$\mathcal{R}_{\text{bin}} = (\mathcal{B}_{\text{odd}}^2\|\dots\|\mathcal{B}_{\text{odd}}^2) \subset \{0,1\}^{2 \cdot n}, \quad \mathcal{Z}_{\text{bin}} = (\mathcal{B}_{\text{even}}^2\|\dots\|\mathcal{B}_{\text{even}}^2) \subset \{0,1\}^{2 \cdot n}.$$

$F'_{\text{bin}} : \mathcal{S}_{\text{bin}} \times \mathcal{R}_{\text{bin}} \to \mathcal{R}_{\text{bin}}$ and $F''_{\text{bin}} : \mathcal{S}_{\text{bin}} \times \mathcal{Z}_{\text{bin}} \to \mathcal{Z}_{\text{bin}}$ are defined as $F'_{\text{bin}}(\mathbf{b}, \mathbf{w}) = F_{\text{bin}}(\mathbf{b}, \mathbf{w})$ and $F''_{\text{bin}}(\mathbf{b}, \mathbf{w}) = F_{\text{bin}}(\mathbf{b}, \mathbf{w})$, respectively. Since $F_{\text{bin}}(\mathbf{b}, \cdot)$ is indeed a permutation, then $F'_{\text{bin}}(\mathbf{b}, \mathbf{w}) \in \mathcal{R}_{\text{bin}}$ if $\mathbf{w} \in \mathcal{R}_{\text{bin}}$ and $F''_{\text{bin}}(\mathbf{b}, \mathbf{w}) \in \mathcal{Z}_{\text{bin}}$ if $\mathbf{w} \in \mathcal{Z}_{\text{bin}}$. Thus, these two functions are well defined.

We now demonstrate that the four conditions specified in Sect. 4.1 are all satisfied. First, "homomorphism" and "closure of F with respect to $\mathsf{valid}_{\mathsf{bin}}$" are satisfied due to (3) and (4), respectively. Next, observe that $\mathcal{R}_{\mathsf{bin}} = \mathsf{valid}_{\mathsf{bin}}$ and for any $\mathbf{w} = \mathsf{Encode}(\mathbf{x}) \in \mathsf{valid}_{\mathsf{bin}}$, we have[6]

$$\{\mathbf{t} = F_{\mathsf{bin}}(\mathbf{b}, \mathbf{w}) \mid \mathbf{b} \xleftarrow{\$} \mathcal{S}_{\mathsf{bin}}\} \equiv \{\mathbf{t} = \mathsf{Encode}(\mathbf{b} \oplus \mathbf{x}) \mid \mathbf{b} \xleftarrow{\$} \{0,1\}^n\}$$

$$\equiv \{\mathbf{t} = \mathsf{Encode}(\ \mathbf{b}\ ) \mid \mathbf{b} \xleftarrow{\$} \{0,1\}^n\}$$

$$\equiv \{\mathbf{t} \mid \mathbf{t} \xleftarrow{\$} \mathsf{valid}_{\mathsf{bin}}\};$$

$$\{\mathbf{z} = \mathbf{w} \oplus \mathbf{r} \mid \mathbf{r} \xleftarrow{\$} \mathcal{R}_{\mathsf{bin}}\} \equiv \{\mathbf{z} = \mathbf{w} \oplus (\mathbf{r}_1 \| \ldots \| \mathbf{r}_n) \mid \forall\ i \in [1,n]:\ \mathbf{r}_i \xleftarrow{\$} \mathcal{B}^2_{\mathsf{odd}}\}$$

$$\equiv \{\mathbf{z} = (\mathbf{z}_1 \| \ldots \| \mathbf{z}_n) \mid \forall\ i \in [1,n]:\ \mathbf{z}_i \xleftarrow{\$} \mathcal{B}^2_{\mathsf{even}}\}$$

$$\equiv \{\mathbf{z} \mid \mathbf{z} \xleftarrow{\$} \mathcal{Z}_{\mathsf{bin}}\}.$$

Thus, the remaining two conditions hold. Therefore, we have successfully reduced the above statement to an instance of $\mathrm{R}_{\mathrm{abstract}}$. Now the prover can simply run the protocol as described in Fig. 4, in which the cost of communicating masking vectors is $\log(|\mathcal{R}_{\mathsf{bin}}|) = n$ bits, reduced from $2n$ bits.

Techniques for Handling Regular Words. Let $\mathbf{M} \cdot \mathsf{RE}(\mathbf{x}) = \mathbf{v}$ for $\mathbf{M} \in \mathbb{Z}_2^{D_0 \times 2^c \cdot n/c}$, $\mathbf{x} \in \mathbb{Z}_2^n$ and $\mathbf{v} \in \mathbb{Z}_2^{D_0}$. To prove knowledge of a regular word $\mathbf{w} = \mathsf{RE}(\mathbf{x})$ we recall the following notions from [75].

- For $\mathbf{b} = [b_1 | \ldots | b_c]^\top \in \{0,1\}^c$, $\mathbf{w} = [w_{0,0,\ldots,0} | \ldots | w_{i_1,i_2,\ldots,i_c} | \ldots | w_{1,1,\ldots,1}]^\top \in \{0,1\}^{2^c}$, define a function $f_{\mathsf{re}} : \{0,1\}^c \times \{0,1\}^{2^c} \to \{0,1\}^{2^c}$ as $f_{\mathsf{re}}(\mathbf{b}, \mathbf{w}) = [w'_{0,0,\ldots,0} | \ldots | w'_{i_1,i_2,\ldots,i_c} | \ldots | w'_{1,1,\ldots,1}]^\top$ satisfying

$$w'_{i_1,i_2,\ldots,i_c} = w_{i_1 \oplus b_1, i_2 \oplus b_2, \ldots, i_c \oplus b_c}$$

for each $[i_1 | \ldots | i_c]^\top \in \{0,1\}^c$. It is verifiable that for any $\mathbf{x}, \mathbf{b} \in \{0,1\}^c$,

$$\mathbf{w} = \mathsf{re}(\mathbf{x}) \iff f_{\mathsf{re}}(\mathbf{b}, \mathbf{w}) = \mathsf{re}(\mathbf{x} \oplus \mathbf{b}). \tag{5}$$

- For $\mathbf{b} = (\mathbf{b}_1 \| \ldots \| \mathbf{b}_{n/c}) \in \{0,1\}^n$ containing n/c blocks of size c and for $\mathbf{w} = (\mathbf{w}_1 \| \ldots \| \mathbf{w}_{n/c}) \in \{0,1\}^{2^c \cdot n/c}$ containing n/c blocks of size 2^c, define $F_{\mathsf{re}} : \{0,1\}^n \times \{0,1\}^{2^c \cdot n/c} \to \{0,1\}^{2^c \cdot n/c}$ as

$$F_{\mathsf{re}}(\mathbf{b}, \mathbf{w}) = (\ f_{\mathsf{re}}(\mathbf{b}_1, \mathbf{w}_1) \| \ldots \| f_{\mathsf{re}}(\mathbf{b}_{n/c}, \mathbf{w}_{n/c})\ ).$$

One can check that for all $\mathbf{b} \in \{0,1\}^n$, all $\mathbf{w}, \mathbf{w}' \in \{0,1\}^{2^c \cdot n/c}$,

$$F_{\mathsf{re}}(\ \mathbf{b},\ \mathbf{w}\ ) \oplus F_{\mathsf{re}}(\ \mathbf{b},\ \mathbf{w}'\ ) = F_{\mathsf{re}}(\ \mathbf{b},\ \mathbf{w} \oplus \mathbf{w}'\ ). \tag{6}$$

Define $\mathsf{valid}_{\mathsf{re}} = \{\mathbf{w} : \exists\ \mathbf{x} \in \{0,1\}^n\ \text{s.t.}\ \mathbf{w} = \mathsf{RE}(\mathbf{x})\}$. For any $\mathbf{x}, \mathbf{b} \in \{0,1\}^n$, it follows immediately from (5) that the following equivalence holds,

$$\mathbf{w} = \mathsf{RE}(\mathbf{x}) \in \mathsf{valid}_{\mathsf{re}} \iff F_{\mathsf{re}}(\mathbf{b}, \mathbf{w}) = \mathsf{RE}(\mathbf{x} \oplus \mathbf{b}) \in \mathsf{valid}_{\mathsf{re}}. \tag{7}$$

---

[6] We use the "$\equiv$" sign to represent that two distributions are identical.

Equivalence (7) is fundamental in Stern's framework for proving knowledge of a regular word $\mathbf{w} = \mathsf{RE}(\mathbf{x})$. The prover first samples a random $\mathbf{b}$ and shows to the verifier that $F_{\mathsf{re}}(\mathbf{b}, \mathbf{w}) \in \mathsf{valid}_{\mathsf{re}}$. The verifier should be convinced that $\mathbf{w} \in \mathsf{valid}_{\mathsf{re}}$ as well. In addition, the uniformity of $\mathbf{b}$ perfectly hides $\mathbf{w}$. Furthermore, to prove in ZK that the equation holds, the prover randomly chooses a masking vector $\mathbf{r}_w \xleftarrow{\$} \mathcal{R} = \{0,1\}^{2^c \cdot n/c}$ and persuades the verifier that $\mathbf{M} \cdot (\mathbf{w} \oplus \mathbf{r}_w) = \mathbf{M} \cdot \mathbf{r}_w \oplus \mathbf{v}$.

Note that the number of bits to represent $\mathbf{r}_w$ is $2^c \cdot n/c$. We now present our refined techniques to reduce the cost of communicating masking vectors.

Our Techniques. As in the case of handling arbitrary binary vectors, the goal is to reduce the considered statement to an instance of $\mathrm{R}_{\mathsf{abstract}}$. Let

$$\mathcal{R}_{\mathsf{re},n} = (\mathcal{B}_{\mathsf{odd}}^{2^c} \| \cdots \| \mathcal{B}_{\mathsf{odd}}^{2^c}) \subset \{0,1\}^{2^c \cdot n/c},$$
$$\mathcal{Z}_{\mathsf{re},n} = (\mathcal{B}_{\mathsf{even}}^{2^c} \| \cdots \| \mathcal{B}_{\mathsf{even}}^{2^c}) \subset \{0,1\}^{2^c \cdot n/c}, \quad \mathcal{S}_{\mathsf{re}} = \{0,1\}^n.$$

Define $F'_{\mathsf{re}} : \mathcal{S}_{\mathsf{re}} \times \mathcal{R}_{\mathsf{re}} \to \mathcal{R}_{\mathsf{re}}$, $F''_{\mathsf{re}} : \mathcal{S}_{\mathsf{re}} \times \mathcal{Z}_{\mathsf{re}} \to \mathcal{Z}_{\mathsf{re}}$ as $F'_{\mathsf{re}}(\mathbf{b}, \mathbf{w}) = F_{\mathsf{re}}(\mathbf{b}, \mathbf{w})$ and $F''_{\mathsf{re}}(\mathbf{b}, \mathbf{w}) = F_{\mathsf{re}}(\mathbf{b}, \mathbf{w})$, respectively. These functions are well defined because F_{re} is a permutation.

We now verify that the requirements in Sect. 4.1 all hold. Due to (6) and (7), "homomorphism" and "closure of F with respect to $\mathsf{valid}_{\mathsf{re}}$" are met. Next, let $\mathbf{x} = (\mathbf{x}_1 \| \cdots \| \mathbf{x}_{n/c}) \in \{0,1\}^n$ where all $\mathbf{x}_i$ have the same length. For $\mathbf{w} = \mathsf{RE}(\mathbf{x}) = (\mathsf{re}(\mathbf{x}_1) \| \cdots \| \mathsf{re}(\mathbf{x}_{n/c})) \in \mathsf{valid}_{\mathsf{re}}$, we have $\mathsf{re}(\mathbf{x}_i) \in \mathcal{B}_{\mathsf{odd}}^{2^c}$ and:

$$\{\mathbf{t} = F_{\mathsf{re}}(\mathbf{b}, \mathbf{w}) \mid \mathbf{b} \xleftarrow{\$} \mathcal{S}_{\mathsf{re}}\} \equiv \{\mathbf{t} = \mathsf{RE}(\mathbf{b} \oplus \mathbf{x}) \mid \mathbf{b} \xleftarrow{\$} \{0,1\}^n\}$$
$$\equiv \{\mathbf{t} = \mathsf{RE}(\mathbf{b}) \mid \mathbf{b} \xleftarrow{\$} \{0,1\}^n\}$$
$$\equiv \{\mathbf{t} \mid \mathbf{t} \xleftarrow{\$} \mathsf{valid}_{\mathsf{re}}\};$$
$$\{\mathbf{z} = \mathbf{w} \oplus \mathbf{r} \mid \mathbf{r} \xleftarrow{\$} \mathcal{R}_{\mathsf{re},n}\} \equiv \{\mathbf{z} = (\mathsf{re}(\mathbf{x}_i) \oplus \mathbf{r}_i)_{i=1}^{n/c} \mid \forall\, i \in [1, n/c] : \mathbf{r}_i \xleftarrow{\$} \mathcal{B}_{\mathsf{odd}}^{2^c}\}$$
$$\equiv \{\mathbf{z} = (\mathbf{z}_1 \| \cdots \| \mathbf{z}_{n/c}) \mid \forall\, i \in [1, n/c] : \mathbf{z}_i \xleftarrow{\$} \mathcal{B}_{\mathsf{even}}^{2^c}\}$$
$$\equiv \{\mathbf{z} \mid \mathbf{z} \xleftarrow{\$} \mathcal{Z}_{\mathsf{re},n}\}.$$

Therefore, the last two conditions are satisfied as well. The prover and verifier now interact as in Fig. 4, which incurs masking vectors of length $(2^c - 1) \cdot n/c$ rather than $2^c \cdot n/c$ since $\log(|\mathcal{R}_{\mathsf{re},n}|) = (2^c - 1) \cdot n/c$.

At the first glance, the size of $\mathcal{R}_{\mathsf{re},n}$ is not lowered significantly. We, however, remark that this is indeed optimal. Let $\mathcal{B}^{2^c} \subset \{0,1\}^{2^c}$ and $\mathcal{R}' = (\mathcal{B}^{2^c} \| \cdots \| \mathcal{B}^{2^c}) \subset \{0,1\}^{2^c \cdot n/c}$. Consider two arbitrary $\mathbf{w}, \mathbf{w}' \in \mathsf{valid}_{\mathsf{re}}$, the fourth condition required by $\mathrm{R}_{\mathsf{abstract}}$ implies that for all $i \in [1, n/c]$:

$$\{\, \mathbf{z}_i = \mathsf{re}(\mathbf{x}_i) \oplus \mathbf{r}_i \mid \mathbf{r}_i \xleftarrow{\$} \mathcal{B}^{2^c} \,\} \equiv \{\, \mathbf{z}'_i = \mathsf{re}(\mathbf{x}'_i) \oplus \mathbf{r}'_i \mid \mathbf{r}'_i \xleftarrow{\$} \mathcal{B}^{2^c} \,\}. \quad (8)$$

Also note that $\{\mathsf{re}(\mathbf{x}_0) : \mathbf{x}_0 \in \{0,1\}^c\}$ forms a basis of the vector space $\{0,1\}^{2^c}$. Note that if $\mathcal{B}^{2^c}$ ever contains a single vector with odd weight, then $\mathcal{B}^{2^c}$ contains all vectors with odd weight, i.e., $\mathcal{B}^{2^c} \supseteq \mathcal{B}_{\mathsf{odd}}^{2^c}$. Thus, the size of $\mathcal{R}_{\mathsf{re},n}$ is optimal.

We also remark that the size of $\mathcal{R}_{re,n}$ is optimal only because we transform the considered statement to an instance of $R_{abstract}$. It remains open if we can further reduce the size of $\mathcal{R}_{re,n}$ by considering a different abstract relation.

Techniques for Handling Bit Multiplication. Let $M_0 \cdot (x_1 \cdot x_2) = v$ for $M_0 \in \mathbb{Z}_2^{D_0 \times 1}$, $x_1, x_2 \in \{0,1\}$ and $v \in \mathbb{Z}_2^{D_0}$. To prove knowledge of $x_3 = x_1 \cdot x_2$, Libert et al. [57] proposed the following notations and techniques.

- For bits $x_1, x_2, x_3 = x_1 \cdot x_2$, denote $\mathsf{ext}(x_1, x_2) = [\,\overline{x}_1 \cdot \overline{x}_2 \mid \overline{x}_1 \cdot x_2 \mid x_1 \cdot \overline{x}_2 \mid x_1 \cdot x_2\,]^\top \in \{0,1\}^4$ as the extension of x_3. Then $x_3 = [\,0 \mid 0 \mid 0 \mid 1\,] \cdot \mathsf{ext}(x_1, x_2)$.
- For $b = [\,b_1 \mid b_2\,]^\top \in \{0,1\}^2$ and $w = [\,w_{0,0} \mid w_{0,1} \mid w_{1,0} \mid w_{1,1}\,]^\top \in \{0,1\}^4$, define a function $F_{\mathsf{mult}} : \{0,1\}^2 \times \{0,1\}^4 \to \{0,1\}^4$ as

$$F_{\mathsf{mult}}(b, w) = [\,w_{b_1,b_2} \mid w_{b_1,\overline{b}_2} \mid w_{\overline{b}_1,b_2} \mid w_{\overline{b}_1,\overline{b}_2}\,]^\top.$$

Define $\mathsf{valid}_{\mathsf{mult}} = \{w : \exists\ x_1, x_2 \in \{0,1\}\ \text{s.t.}\ w = \mathsf{ext}(x_1, x_2)\}$. Then for any $x = [\,x_1 \mid x_2\,]^\top \in \{0,1\}^2$, and $b = [\,b_1 \mid b_2\,]^\top \in \{0,1\}^2$,

$$w = \mathsf{ext}(x_1, x_2) \in \mathsf{valid}_{\mathsf{mult}} \Leftrightarrow F_{\mathsf{mult}}(b, w) = \mathsf{ext}(b_1 \oplus x_1, b_2 \oplus x_2) \in \mathsf{valid}_{\mathsf{mult}}. \quad (9)$$

Equivalence (9) is essential in Stern's framework to prove knowledge of x_3 such that $x_3 = x_1 \cdot x_2$. In addition, the prover samples a random masking vector $r \in \mathcal{R} = \{0,1\}^4$ and shows to the verifier that $M \cdot (\mathsf{ext}(x_1, x_2) \oplus r) = M \cdot r \oplus v$, where $M = M_0 \cdot [0|0|0|1] \in \mathbb{Z}_2^{D_0 \times 4}$.

Here, 4 bits are needed to represent r. We will show how to reduce to 3 bits.

Our Techniques. Let $\mathcal{R}_{\mathsf{mult}} = \mathcal{B}_{\mathsf{odd}}^4$, $\mathcal{Z}_{\mathsf{mult}} = \mathcal{B}_{\mathsf{even}}^4$, $\mathcal{S}_{\mathsf{mult}} = \mathbb{Z}_2^2$. Define

$$F_{\mathsf{mult}}' : \mathcal{S}_{\mathsf{mult}} \times \mathcal{R}_{\mathsf{mult}} \to \mathcal{R}_{\mathsf{mult}} : F_{\mathsf{mult}}'(b, w) = F_{\mathsf{mult}}(b, w);$$
$$F_{\mathsf{mult}}'' : \mathcal{S}_{\mathsf{mult}} \times \mathcal{Z}_{\mathsf{mult}} \to \mathcal{Z}_{\mathsf{mult}} : F_{\mathsf{mult}}''(b, w) = F_{\mathsf{mult}}(b, w).$$

These two functions are well defined since F_{mult} is actually a permutation. Now we show that the four requirements in Sect. 4.1 are satisfied. For all $b \in \mathcal{S}_{\mathsf{mult}}$, $w \in \mathcal{R}_{\mathsf{mult}}$ and $w' \in \mathcal{Z}_{\mathsf{mult}}$, it is not hard to see that $F_{\mathsf{mult}}'(b, w) \oplus F_{\mathsf{mult}}''(b, w') = F_{\mathsf{mult}}(b, w \oplus w')$. Next, equivalence (9) shows that F_{mult} is closed with respect to $\mathsf{valid}_{\mathsf{mult}}$. For all $w \in \mathsf{valid}_{\mathsf{mult}}$, note that $\{t = F_{\mathsf{mult}}(b, w) : b \in \mathcal{S}_{\mathsf{mult}}\} = \mathsf{valid}_{\mathsf{mult}}$. It then follows that the third condition holds. Finally, $wt(w) = 1 \bmod 2$ for all $w \in \mathsf{valid}_{\mathsf{mult}}$. Thus, the distributions $\{z = w \oplus r | r \xleftarrow{\$} \mathcal{R}_{\mathsf{mult}}\}$ and $\{z | z \xleftarrow{\$} \mathcal{Z}_{\mathsf{mult}}\}$ are identical for all $w \in \mathsf{valid}_{\mathsf{mult}}$. Therefore, we have successfully reduced the above statement to an instance of $R_{abstract}$. Therefore, to prove knowledge of x_3 such that $x_3 = x_1 \cdot x_2$ for $x_1, x_2 \in \{0,1\}$ it suffices to sample a masking value r_w from $\mathcal{R}_{\mathsf{mult}}$. As a result, 3 bits are sufficient to represent r_w since $\log |\mathcal{R}_{\mathsf{mult}}| = 3$.

4.3 Supporting Zero-Knowledge Protocol for Algorithm Sign

This section presents the zero-knowledge protocol invoked by the signer who executes the algorithm Sign in Sect. 3.2. Let $L, \ell, N, n, c, m, k, m_0, m_1$ as specified in Sect. 3.2. For completeness, the protocol is summarized below.

- The public input consists of P, $\mathbf{u}_\tau$, $\mathbf{B}$, $\mathbf{C}_0$, $\mathbf{C}_1$.
- The secret input consists of $\xi = (\mathbf{d}_j, \mathbf{x}_j, \mathbf{r}_j, \mathsf{bin}(j), \mathbf{w}_\ell, \ldots, \mathbf{w}_1)$.
- The goal of the prover is to prove in ZK that
  - $\mathbf{d}_j$ is correctly accumulated in the root $\mathbf{u}_\tau$, i.e.,

$$\mathsf{TVerify}_{\mathbf{B}}(\mathbf{u}_\tau, \mathbf{d}_j, \mathsf{bin}(j), (\mathbf{w}_\ell, \ldots, \mathbf{w}_1)) = 1. \tag{10}$$

  - $\mathbf{d}_j$ is an odd-weight commitment of $\mathbf{x}_j$, i.e.,

$$\mathbf{d}_j = \mathbf{C}_0 \cdot \mathsf{RE}(\mathbf{x}_j) \oplus \mathbf{C}_1 \cdot \mathsf{RE}(\mathbf{r}_j) \text{ and } wt(\mathbf{d}_j) = 1 \bmod 2.$$

  - The attribute $\mathbf{x}_j$ satisfies the claimed policy P, i.e., $P(\mathbf{x}_j) = 1$.

Let $\mathsf{R}_{\mathsf{fdabs}}$ be the corresponding relation. Our strategy is to reduce $\mathsf{R}_{\mathsf{fdabs}}$ to an instance of $\mathsf{R}_{\mathsf{abstract}}$ from Sect. 4.1. We remark that we will transform the secret input to a secret vector $\mathbf{w}_{\mathsf{fdabs}} \in \{0,1\}^{D_{\mathsf{fdabs}}}$ and design a masking vector space $\mathcal{R}_{\mathsf{fdabs}}$ such that the $\log(|\mathcal{R}_{\mathsf{fdabs}}|)$ is strictly smaller than D_{fdabs}.

Handling the Accumulator Layer. In [75], Nguyen et al. devised a statistical zero-knowledge argument of knowledge that allows a prover $\mathcal{P}$ to convince a verifier $\mathcal{V}$ in ZK that $\mathcal{P}$ knows a value that was honestly accumulated in the root of the Merkle tree. Using the techniques presented in Sect. 4.2, we are able to obtain a protocol with fewer communication cost. Specifically, proving knowledge of $\mathbf{d}_j, \mathsf{bin}(j), \mathbf{w}_\ell, \ldots, \mathbf{w}_1$ such that (10) holds is the same as proving knowledge of $\mathbf{w}_{\mathsf{acc}} \in \{0,1\}^{D_{\mathsf{acc}}}$ such that $\mathbf{M}_{\mathsf{acc}} \cdot \mathbf{w}_{\mathsf{acc}} = \mathbf{v}_{\mathsf{acc}}$ for $\mathbf{M}_{\mathsf{acc}} \in \mathbb{Z}_2^{\ell n \times D_{\mathsf{acc}}}$, $\mathbf{v}_{\mathsf{acc}} \in \mathbb{Z}_2^{\ell n}$, $\mathbf{w}_{\mathsf{acc}} \in \{0,1\}^{D_{\mathsf{acc}}}$, and $D_{\mathsf{acc}} = 2\ell m + 2(\ell-1)n$. In addition, the sets $\mathsf{valid}_{\mathsf{acc}}$, $\mathcal{R}_{\mathsf{acc}}$, $\mathcal{Z}_{\mathsf{acc}}$, $\mathcal{S}_{\mathsf{acc}}$, and the functions F_{acc}, F'_{acc}, F''_{acc} are given so that the accumulator layer is reduced to an instance of $\mathsf{R}_{\mathsf{abstract}}$. Particularly, $\log|\mathcal{R}_{\mathsf{acc}}| = 2\ell m + (\ell-1)n < D_{\mathsf{acc}}$. Details can be found in the full version [63].

Handling the Commitment Layer. We will employ the techniques presented in Sect. 4.2 to prove knowledge of regular words $\mathsf{RE}(\mathbf{x}_j)$ and $\mathsf{RE}(\mathbf{r}_j)$. We now show how to prove that $\mathbf{d}_j$ has odd weight. To this end, observe that

$$wt(\mathbf{d}_j) = 1 \bmod 2 \iff \mathbf{1}^{1 \times n} \cdot \mathbf{d}_j = 1 \bmod 2. \tag{11}$$

Let $\mathbf{y}_\ell = \mathsf{Encode}(\mathbf{d}_j) \in \mathbb{Z}_2^{2n}$. We have $\mathbf{d}_j = \mathbf{I}_n^* \cdot \mathbf{y}_\ell$ and $\mathbf{M}_1 \cdot \mathbf{y}_\ell = 1$, where $\mathbf{M}_1 = \mathbf{1}^{1 \times n} \cdot \mathbf{I}_n^* \in \mathbb{Z}_2^{1 \times 2n}$. Therefore, the commitment layer is now equivalent to proving knowledge of $\mathbf{y}_\ell, \mathsf{RE}(\mathbf{x}_j), \mathsf{RE}(\mathbf{r}_j)$ such that

$$\mathbf{M}_1 \cdot \mathbf{y}_\ell = 1 \text{ and } \mathbf{C}_0 \cdot \mathsf{RE}(\mathbf{x}_j) \oplus \mathbf{C}_1 \cdot \mathsf{RE}(\mathbf{r}_j) \oplus \mathbf{I}_n^* \cdot \mathbf{y}_\ell = \mathbf{0}^n. \tag{12}$$

Through some basic algebra, one can form public matrix $\mathbf{M}_{\mathsf{com}} \in \mathbb{Z}_2^{(n+1) \times D_{\mathsf{com}}}$ and vector $\mathbf{v}_{\mathsf{com}} \in \mathbb{Z}_2^{n+1}$, secret $\mathbf{w}_{\mathsf{com}} = (\mathbf{y}_\ell \| \mathsf{RE}(\mathbf{x}_j) \| \mathsf{RE}(\mathbf{r}_j)) \in \mathbb{Z}_2^{D_{\mathsf{com}}}$ with $D_{\mathsf{com}} = 2n + m_0 + m_1$ such that (12) is equivalent to $\mathbf{M}_{\mathsf{com}} \cdot \mathbf{w}_{\mathsf{com}} = \mathbf{v}_{\mathsf{com}}$.

Handling the Policy Layer. To prove knowledge of $\mathbf{x}_j$ so that it satisfies the policy P, we first convert P to a Boolean circuit C entirely represented by NAND gates. Next we show knowledge of each wire value so that the output of C is 1 and that for each triple (x_1, x_2, x_3) connected by a NAND gate, $x_1 \cdot x_2 \oplus x_3 = 1$.

Note that the above transformation of the policy circuit P to C is for presentation purpose. In fact, for a triple (x_1, x_2, x_3) connected by an AND gate and an OR gate, we have $x_1 \cdot x_2 \oplus x_3 = 0$ and $x_1 \cdot x_2 \oplus x_3 \oplus x_1 \oplus x_2 = 0$, respectively; for (x_1, x_2) connected by a NOT gate, we have $x_1 \oplus x_2 = 1$. Therefore, we can use the same techniques that handle the NAND gates and arbitrary binary vectors to handle $x_1 \cdot x_2 \oplus x_3$ and the linear terms x_1, x_2, respectively. Therefore, it will not be an issue even if there is a blowup in C's size due to the transformation.

Now, let us present the notations and techniques for handling NAND triples.

– For $x_1, x_2, x_3 \in \{0, 1\}$, let

$$X = \mathsf{ENC}(x_1, x_2, x_3) = [\, \overline{x}_1 \cdot \overline{x}_2 \oplus x_3 \mid \overline{x}_1 \cdot x_2 \oplus x_3 \mid x_1 \cdot \overline{x}_2 \oplus x_3 \mid x_1 \cdot x_2 \oplus x_3 \,]^\top \in \mathbb{Z}_2^4.$$

It is easy to see that $[\, 0 \mid 0 \mid 0 \mid 1 \,] \cdot X = x_1 \cdot x_2 \oplus x_3$.

– Define $\mathsf{valid}_{\mathsf{nand}} = \{X : \exists\, x_1, x_2, x_3 \in \mathbb{Z}_2 \text{ s.t. } X = \mathsf{ENC}(x_1, x_2, x_3)\}$. It is worth noting that $\mathsf{valid}_{\mathsf{nand}} = \mathcal{B}_{\mathsf{odd}}^4$, i.e., the set that contains all length-4 binary vectors with odd weight. Set $\mathcal{R}_{\mathsf{nand}} = \mathcal{B}_{\mathsf{odd}}^4$, $\mathcal{Z}_{\mathsf{nand}} = \mathcal{B}_{\mathsf{even}}^4$, $\mathcal{S}_{\mathsf{nand}} = \mathbb{Z}_2^3$.

– Let $\mathbf{b} = [\, b_1 \mid b_2 \mid b_3 \,]^\top \in \mathbb{Z}_2^3$ and $X = [\, x_{0,0} \mid x_{0,1} \mid x_{1,0} \mid x_{1,1} \,]^\top \in \mathbb{Z}_2^4$, define $F_{\mathsf{nand}} : \mathcal{S}_{\mathsf{nand}} \times \mathbb{Z}_2^4 \to \mathbb{Z}_2^4$ as

$$F_{\mathsf{nand}}(\mathbf{b}, X) = [\, x_{b_1, b_2} \oplus b_3 \mid x_{b_1, \overline{b}_2} \oplus b_3 \mid x_{\overline{b}_1, b_2} \oplus b_3 \mid x_{\overline{b}_1, \overline{b}_2} \oplus b_3 \,]^\top,$$

$F'_{\mathsf{nand}} : \mathcal{S}_{\mathsf{nand}} \times \mathcal{R}_{\mathsf{nand}} \to \mathcal{R}_{\mathsf{nand}}$ as $F'_{\mathsf{nand}}(\mathbf{b}, X) = [\, x_{b_1, b_2} \mid x_{b_1, \overline{b}_2} \mid x_{\overline{b}_1, b_2} \mid x_{\overline{b}_1, \overline{b}_2} \,]^\top$, and $F''_{\mathsf{nand}} : \mathcal{S}_{\mathsf{nand}} \times \mathcal{Z}_{\mathsf{nand}} \to \mathcal{Z}_{\mathsf{nand}}$ as

$$F''_{\mathsf{nand}}(\mathbf{b}, X) = F_{\mathsf{nand}}(\mathbf{b}, X) = [\, x_{b_1, b_2} \mid x_{b_1, \overline{b}_2} \mid x_{\overline{b}_1, b_2} \mid x_{\overline{b}_1, \overline{b}_2} \,]^\top \oplus [\, b_3 \mid b_3 \mid b_3 \mid b_3 \,]^\top.$$

First, we show that F'_{nand} and F''_{nand} are well defined. Note that $F'_{\mathsf{nand}}(\mathbf{b}, \cdot)$ is indeed a permutation, thus $X \in \mathcal{R}_{\mathsf{nand}}$ implies $F'_{\mathsf{nand}}(\mathbf{b}, X) \in \mathcal{R}_{\mathsf{nand}}$. Regarding F''_{nand}, it suffices to see that $[\, b_3 \mid b_3 \mid b_3 \mid b_3 \,]^\top \in \mathcal{Z}_{\mathsf{nand}}$.

Next, we will demonstrate that the four conditions specified in Sect. 4.1 with respect to $\mathsf{valid}_{\mathsf{nand}}, \mathcal{R}_{\mathsf{nand}}, \mathcal{Z}_{\mathsf{nand}}, \mathcal{S}_{\mathsf{nand}}$ and $F_{\mathsf{nand}}, F'_{\mathsf{nand}}, F''_{\mathsf{nand}}$ are satisfied. Looking ahead, this is crucial in reducing $\mathsf{R}_{\mathsf{fdabs}}$ to an instance of $\mathsf{R}_{\mathsf{abstract}}$.

For all $\mathbf{b} = [\, b_1 \mid b_2 \mid b_3 \,]^\top \in \mathcal{S}_{\mathsf{nand}}$, and $X \in \mathcal{R}_{\mathsf{nand}}$, $X' \in \mathcal{Z}_{\mathsf{nand}}$,

$$\begin{aligned}
F_{\mathsf{nand}}(\mathbf{b}, X \oplus X') &= [\, x_{b_1, b_2} \mid x_{b_1, \overline{b}_2} \mid x_{\overline{b}_1, b_2} \mid x_{\overline{b}_1, \overline{b}_2} \,]^\top \\
&\oplus [\, x'_{b_1, b_2} \mid x'_{b_1, \overline{b}_2} \mid x'_{\overline{b}_1, b_2} \mid x'_{\overline{b}_1, \overline{b}_2} \,]^\top \oplus [\, b_3 \mid b_3 \mid b_3 \mid b_3 \,]^\top \\
&= F'_{\mathsf{nand}}(\mathbf{b}, X) \oplus F''_{\mathsf{nand}}(\mathbf{b}, X').
\end{aligned}$$

Thus, "homomorphism" is satisfied. Also, due to the design of F_{nand}, it is not hard to verify that for all $\mathbf{b} \in \mathcal{S}_{\mathsf{nand}}$, all $X \in \mathbb{Z}_2^4$, the equivalence $X \in \mathsf{valid}_{\mathsf{nand}} \iff F_{\mathsf{nand}}(\mathbf{b}, X) \in \mathsf{valid}_{\mathsf{nand}}$ holds. Therefore, "closure of F_{nand} with respect to $\mathsf{valid}_{\mathsf{nand}}$" is also fulfilled. Finally, observe that for all $X \in \mathsf{valid}_{\mathsf{nand}}$,

$\{F_{\mathsf{nand}}(\mathbf{b}, X) : \mathbf{b} \in \mathcal{S}_{\mathsf{nand}}\} = \mathsf{valid}_{\mathsf{nand}}$, $\{\mathbf{z} = X + \mathbf{r} : \mathbf{r} \in \mathcal{B}_{\mathsf{odd}}^4 = \mathcal{R}_{\mathsf{nand}}\} = \mathcal{B}_{\mathsf{even}}^4 = \mathcal{Z}_{\mathsf{nand}}$. Therefore, the last two conditions are satisfied as well. Being prepared with the above technique, we are ready to describe the transformations for the policy layer.

Let K be the number of NAND gates in C. We distinguish the input wires, the internal wires, and the output wire by $1, \ldots, L, L+1, \ldots, L+K$, where $1, \ldots, L$ are the input wires, $L+1, \ldots, L+K-1$ are the internal wires while $L+K$ is the output wire. The topology of C is specified by two publicly known functions g, h mapping $\{1, \ldots, K\} \to \{1, \ldots, L+K-1\}$. Given an L-bit input $(x_1, \ldots, x_L)$, the assignments to non-input wires in C are denoted as $x_{L+1}, \ldots, x_{L+K}$ and are as computed $x_{L+i} = x_{g(i)} \ \mathsf{NAND} \ x_{h(i)}$ for $i \in [1, K]$. Equivalently,

$$\begin{cases} x_{g(1)} \cdot x_{h(1)} \oplus x_{L+1} = 1, \\ \cdots \\ x_{g(K-1)} \cdot x_{h(K-1)} \oplus x_{L+K-1} = 1, \\ x_{g(K)} \cdot x_{h(K)} \oplus x_{L+K} = 1. \end{cases} \qquad (13)$$

Thus, the policy layer is equivalent to proving knowledge of $x_1, x_2, \ldots, x_{L+K-1}$, and $x_{L+K} = 1$ such that equations in (13) hold. For every $i \in [1, K-1]$, let $X_i = \mathsf{ENC}(x_{g(i)}, x_{h(i)}, x_{L+i})$ and $X_K = \mathsf{ext}(x_{g(K)}, x_{h(K)})$. Denote $\mathbf{h}_4 = [0 \,|\, 0 \,|\, 0 \,|\, 1] \in \mathbb{Z}_2^{1 \times 4}$. Then (13) is equivalent to

$$\mathbf{h}_4 \cdot X_1 = 1, \ \ldots, \ \mathbf{h}_4 \cdot X_{K-1} = 1, \ \mathbf{h}_4 \cdot X_K = 0. \qquad (14)$$

Through some basic algebra, one can form public matrix $\mathbf{M}_{\mathsf{cir}} \in \mathbb{Z}_2^{K \times 4K}$ and vector $\mathbf{v}_{\mathsf{cir}} \in \mathbb{Z}_2^K$, secret vector $\mathbf{w}_{\mathsf{cir}} = (X_1 \| \ldots \| X_{K-1} \| X_K) \in \mathbb{Z}_2^{4K}$ such that (14) is equivalent to $\mathbf{M}_{\mathsf{cir}} \cdot \mathbf{w}_{\mathsf{cir}} = \mathbf{v}_{\mathsf{cir}}$.

Putting it Together. We are ready to transform the considered relation $\mathsf{R}_{\mathsf{fdabs}}$ into one equation of the desired form $\mathbf{M}_{\mathsf{fdabs}} \cdot \mathbf{w}_{\mathsf{fdabs}} = \mathbf{v}_{\mathsf{fdabs}}$. The first step is to form appropriate public $\mathbf{M}_{\mathsf{fdabs}} \in \mathbb{Z}_2^{D_0 \times D_{\mathsf{fdabs}}}$ and $\mathbf{v}_{\mathsf{fdabs}} \in \mathbb{Z}_2^{D_0}$, and secret $\mathbf{w}_{\mathsf{fdabs}} \in \{0,1\}^{D_{\mathsf{fdabs}}}$, with $D_0 = \ell n + n + 1 + K$ and $D_{\mathsf{fdabs}} = D_{\mathsf{acc}} + D_{\mathsf{com}} + 4K$, and $\mathbf{w}_{\mathsf{fdabs}}$ being the following form:

$$\mathbf{w}_{\mathsf{fdabs}} = (\, \mathbf{w}_{\mathsf{acc}} \,\|\, \mathbf{y}_\ell \,\|\, \mathsf{RE}(\mathbf{x}_j) \,\|\, \mathsf{RE}(\mathbf{r}_j) \,\|\, X_1 \,\|\, \ldots \,\|\, X_{K-1} \,\|\, X_K \,), \qquad (15)$$

so that $\mathbf{M}_{\mathsf{fdabs}} \cdot \mathbf{w}_{\mathsf{fdabs}} = \mathbf{v}_{\mathsf{fdabs}}$. The next step is to specify the sets $\mathsf{valid}_{\mathsf{fdabs}}$, $\mathcal{R}_{\mathsf{fdabs}}$, $\mathcal{Z}_{\mathsf{fdabs}}$, $\mathcal{S}_{\mathsf{fdabs}}$, and $F_{\mathsf{fdabs}}, F'_{\mathsf{fdabs}}, F''_{\mathsf{fdabs}}$ such that the four constraints in Sect. 4.1 are satisfied. Once we have reduced the considered statement to an instance of $\mathsf{R}_{\mathsf{abstract}}$, the prover and verifier can run the protocol in Fig. 4. Due to space limit, details are deferred to the full version [63].

Acknowledgements. We thank the anonymous reviewers for their helpful comments and suggestions. The work of Yanhong Xu was supported in part by the National Key Research and Development Program under Grant 2022YFA1004900. San Ling, Khai Hanh Tang and Huaxiong Wang were supported by Singapore Ministry of Education

Academic Research Fund Tier 2 Grant MOE2019-T2-2-083. Duong Hieu Phan was supported in part by the "Banque Publique d'Investissement" under the VisioConfiance project. This research is supported by the National Research Foundation, Singapore under its Strategic Capability Research Centres Funding Initiative. Any opinions, findings and conclusions or recommendations expressed in this material are those of the authors and do not reflect the views of National Research Foundation, Singapore.

References

1. Ajtai, M.: Generating hard instances of lattice problems (extended abstract). In: Symposium on the Theory of Computing - STOC 1996, pp. 99–108. ACM (1996)
2. Alamélou, Q., Blazy, O., Cauchie, S., Gaborit, P.: A code-based group signature scheme. Des. Codes Cryptogr. **82**(1–2), 469–493 (2017)
3. Applebaum, B., Haramaty, N., Ishai, Y., Kushilevitz, E., Vaikuntanathan, V.: Low-complexity cryptographic hash functions. In: Innovations in Theoretical Computer Science Conference - ITCS 2017, vol. 67 of LIPIcs, pp. 7:1–7:31. Schloss Dagstuhl - Leibniz-Zentrum für Informatik (2017)
4. Aragon, N., Blazy, O., Gaborit, P., Hauteville, A., Zémor, G.: Durandal: a rank metric based signature scheme. In: Ishai, Y., Rijmen, V. (eds.) EUROCRYPT 2019. LNCS, vol. 11478, pp. 728–758. Springer, Cham (2019). https://doi.org/10.1007/978-3-030-17659-4_25
5. Augot, D., Finiasz, M., Sendrier, N.: A fast provably secure cryptographic hash function. IACR Cryptol. ePrint Arch. 2003/230 (2003)
6. Augot, D., Finiasz, M., Sendrier, N.: A family of fast syndrome based cryptographic hash functions. In: Dawson, E., Vaudenay, S. (eds.) Mycrypt 2005. LNCS, vol. 3715, pp. 64–83. Springer, Heidelberg (2005). https://doi.org/10.1007/11554868_6
7. Bansarkhani, R.E., El Kaafarani, A.: Post-quantum attribute-based signatures from lattice assumptions. IACR Cryptol. ePrint Arch. 2016/823 (2016)
8. Bellare, M., Fuchsbauer, G.: Policy-based signatures. In: Krawczyk, H. (ed.) PKC 2014. LNCS, vol. 8383, pp. 520–537. Springer, Heidelberg (2014). https://doi.org/10.1007/978-3-642-54631-0_30
9. Bellare, M., Rogaway, P.: Random oracles are practical: a paradigm for designing efficient protocols. In: Denning, D.E., Pyle, R., Ganesan, R., Sandhu, R.S., Ashby, V. (eds.) Conference on Computer and Communications Security - CCS 1993, pp. 62–73. ACM (1993)
10. Ben-Or, M.: Probabilistic algorithms in finite fields. In: Annual Symposium on Foundations of Computer Science - FOCS 1981, pp. 394–398. IEEE Computer Society (1981)
11. Benhamouda, F., Camenisch, J., Krenn, S., Lyubashevsky, V., Neven, G.: Better zero-knowledge proofs for lattice encryption and their application to group signatures. In: Sarkar, P., Iwata, T. (eds.) ASIACRYPT 2014. LNCS, vol. 8873, pp. 551–572. Springer, Heidelberg (2014). https://doi.org/10.1007/978-3-662-45611-8_29
12. Bernstein, D.J., Lange, T., Peters, C., Schwabe, P.: Faster 2-regular information-set decoding. In: Chee, Y.M., et al. (eds.) IWCC 2011. LNCS, vol. 6639, pp. 81–98. Springer, Heidelberg (2011). https://doi.org/10.1007/978-3-642-20901-7_5
13. Biçer, O., Küpçü, A.: Versatile ABS: usage limited, revocable, threshold traceable, authority hiding, decentralized attribute based signatures. IACR Cryptol. ePrint Arch. 2019/203 (2019)

14. Bidoux, L., Gaborit, P., Kulkarni, M., Mateu, V.: Code-based signatures from new proofs of knowledge for the syndrome decoding problem. Des. Codes Cryptogr. **91**(2), 497–544 (2023)
15. Boneh, D., Dagdelen, Ö., Fischlin, M., Lehmann, A., Schaffner, C., Zhandry, M.: Random oracles in a quantum world. In: Lee, D.H., Wang, X. (eds.) ASIACRYPT 2011. LNCS, vol. 7073, pp. 41–69. Springer, Heidelberg (2011). https://doi.org/10.1007/978-3-642-25385-0_3
16. Bootle, J., Cerulli, A., Chaidos, P., Ghadafi, E., Groth, J.: Foundations of fully dynamic group signatures. In: Manulis, M., Sadeghi, A.-R., Schneider, S. (eds.) ACNS 2016. LNCS, vol. 9696, pp. 117–136. Springer, Cham (2016). https://doi.org/10.1007/978-3-319-39555-5_7
17. Bootle, J., Cerulli, A., Chaidos, P., Ghadafi, E., Groth, J.: Foundations of fully dynamic group signatures. J. Cryptol. **33**(4), 1822–1870 (2020)
18. Bootle, J., Lyubashevsky, V., Seiler, G.: Algebraic techniques for short(er) exact lattice-based zero-knowledge proofs. In: Boldyreva, A., Micciancio, D. (eds.) CRYPTO 2019. LNCS, vol. 11692, pp. 176–202. Springer, Cham (2019). https://doi.org/10.1007/978-3-030-26948-7_7
19. Boyen, X.: Mesh signatures. In: Naor, M. (ed.) EUROCRYPT 2007. LNCS, vol. 4515, pp. 210–227. Springer, Heidelberg (2007). https://doi.org/10.1007/978-3-540-72540-4_12
20. Boyle, E., Goldwasser, S., Ivan, I.: Functional signatures and pseudorandom functions. In: Krawczyk, H. (ed.) PKC 2014. LNCS, vol. 8383, pp. 501–519. Springer, Heidelberg (2014). https://doi.org/10.1007/978-3-642-54631-0_29
21. Branco, P., Mateus, P.: A code-based linkable ring signature scheme. In: Baek, J., Susilo, W., Kim, J. (eds.) ProvSec 2018. LNCS, vol. 11192, pp. 203–219. Springer, Cham (2018). https://doi.org/10.1007/978-3-030-01446-9_12
22. Bresson, E., Stern, J.: Efficient revocation in group signatures. In: Kim, K. (ed.) PKC 2001. LNCS, vol. 1992, pp. 190–206. Springer, Heidelberg (2001). https://doi.org/10.1007/3-540-44586-2_15
23. Camenisch, J., Lysyanskaya, A.: Dynamic accumulators and application to efficient revocation of anonymous credentials. In: Yung, M. (ed.) CRYPTO 2002. LNCS, vol. 2442, pp. 61–76. Springer, Heidelberg (2002). https://doi.org/10.1007/3-540-45708-9_5
24. Carozza, E., Couteau, G., Joux, A.: Short signatures from regular syndrome decoding in the head. In: Hazay, C., Stam, M. (eds.) EUROCRYPT 2023. LNCS, vol. 14008, pp. 532–563. Springer, Cham (2023). https://doi.org/10.1007/978-3-031-30589-4_19
25. Chase, M., et al.: Post-quantum zero-knowledge and signatures from symmetric-key primitives. In: Conference on Computer and Communications Security - CCS 2017, pp. 1825–1842. ACM (2017)
26. Chaum, D.: Security without identification: transaction systems to make big brother obsolete. Commun. ACM **28**(10), 1030–1044 (1985)
27. Chaum, D., van Heyst, E.: Group signatures. In: Davies, D.W. (ed.) EUROCRYPT 1991. LNCS, vol. 547, pp. 257–265. Springer, Heidelberg (1991). https://doi.org/10.1007/3-540-46416-6_22
28. Cheng, S., Nguyen, K., Wang, H.: Policy-based signature scheme from lattices. Des. Codes Cryptogr. **81**(1), 43–74 (2016)
29. Cramer, R.: Modular Design of Secure yet Practical Cryptographic Protocols. Ph.D. thesis, Jan. 1997 (1997)

30. Dallot, L., Vergnaud, D.: Provably secure code-based threshold ring signatures. In: Parker, M.G. (ed.) IMACC 2009. LNCS, vol. 5921, pp. 222–235. Springer, Heidelberg (2009). https://doi.org/10.1007/978-3-642-10868-6_13

31. Datta, P., Okamoto, T., Takashima, K.: Efficient attribute-based signatures for unbounded arithmetic branching programs. In: Lin, D., Sako, K. (eds.) PKC 2019. LNCS, vol. 11442, pp. 127–158. Springer, Cham (2019). https://doi.org/10.1007/978-3-030-17253-4_5

32. Debris-Alazard, T., Sendrier, N., Tillich, J.-P.: Wave: a new family of trapdoor one-way preimage sampleable functions based on codes. In: Galbraith, S.D., Moriai, S. (eds.) ASIACRYPT 2019. LNCS, vol. 11921, pp. 21–51. Springer, Cham (2019). https://doi.org/10.1007/978-3-030-34578-5_2

33. Drăgan, C.-C., Gardham, D., Manulis, M.: Hierarchical attribute-based signatures. In: Camenisch, J., Papadimitratos, P. (eds.) CANS 2018. LNCS, vol. 11124, pp. 213–234. Springer, Cham (2018). https://doi.org/10.1007/978-3-030-00434-7_11

34. Ducas, L., et al.: Crystals-dilithium: a lattice-based digital signature scheme. IACR Trans. Cryptogr. Hardw. Embed. Syst. 2018(1), 238–268 (2018)

35. El Kaafarani, A., Chen, L., Ghadafi, E., Davenport, J.: Attribute-based signatures with user-controlled linkability. In: Gritzalis, D., Kiayias, A., Askoxylakis, I. (eds.) CANS 2014. LNCS, vol. 8813, pp. 256–269. Springer, Cham (2014). https://doi.org/10.1007/978-3-319-12280-9_17

36. El Kaafarani, A., Ghadafi, E., Khader, D.: Decentralized traceable attribute-based signatures. In: Benaloh, J. (ed.) CT-RSA 2014. LNCS, vol. 8366, pp. 327–348. Springer, Cham (2014). https://doi.org/10.1007/978-3-319-04852-9_17

37. El Kaafarani, A., Katsumata, S.: Attribute-based signatures for unbounded circuits in the ROM and efficient instantiations from lattices. In: Abdalla, M., Dahab, R. (eds.) PKC 2018. LNCS, vol. 10770, pp. 89–119. Springer, Cham (2018). https://doi.org/10.1007/978-3-319-76581-5_4

38. Escala, A., Herranz, J., Morillo, P.: Revocable attribute-based signatures with adaptive security in the standard model. In: Nitaj, A., Pointcheval, D. (eds.) AFRICACRYPT 2011. LNCS, vol. 6737, pp. 224–241. Springer, Heidelberg (2011). https://doi.org/10.1007/978-3-642-21969-6_14

39. Esgin, M.F., Nguyen, N.K., Seiler, G.: Practical exact proofs from lattices: new techniques to exploit fully-splitting rings. In: Moriai, S., Wang, H. (eds.) ASIACRYPT 2020. LNCS, vol. 12492, pp. 259–288. Springer, Cham (2020). https://doi.org/10.1007/978-3-030-64834-3_9

40. Ezerman, M.F., Lee, H.T., Ling, S., Nguyen, K., Wang, H.: A provably secure group signature scheme from code-based assumptions. In: Iwata, T., Cheon, J.H. (eds.) ASIACRYPT 2015. LNCS, vol. 9452, pp. 260–285. Springer, Heidelberg (2015). https://doi.org/10.1007/978-3-662-48797-6_12

41. Ezerman, M.F., Lee, H.T., Ling, S., Nguyen, K., Wang, H.: Provably secure group signature schemes from code-based assumptions. IEEE Trans. Inf. Theory 66(9), 5754–5773 (2020)

42. Feneuil, T., Joux, A., Rivain, M.: Syndrome decoding in the head: shorter signatures from zero-knowledge proofs. In: Dodis, Y., Shrimpton, T. (eds.) CRYPTO 2022. LNCS, vol. 13508, pp. 541–572. Springer, Cham (2022). https://doi.org/10.1007/978-3-031-15979-4_19

43. Feneuil, T., Joux, A., Rivain, M.: Shared permutation for syndrome decoding: new zero-knowledge protocol and code-based signature. Des. Codes Cryptogr. 91(2), 563–608 (2023)

44. Feng, H., Liu, J., Wu, Q.: Secure stern signatures in quantum random oracle model. In: Lin, Z., Papamanthou, C., Polychronakis, M. (eds.) ISC 2019. LNCS, vol. 11723, pp. 425–444. Springer, Cham (2019). https://doi.org/10.1007/978-3-030-30215-3_21

45. Fiat, A., Shamir, A.: How to prove yourself: practical solutions to identification and signature problems. In: Odlyzko, A.M. (ed.) CRYPTO 1986. LNCS, vol. 263, pp. 186–194. Springer, Heidelberg (1987). https://doi.org/10.1007/3-540-47721-7_12

46. Gardham, D., Manulis, M.: Revocable hierarchical attribute-based signatures from lattices. In: Ateniese, G., Venturi, D. (eds.) ACNS 2022. LNCS, vol. 13269, pp. 459–479. Springer, Cham (2022). https://doi.org/10.1007/978-3-031-09234-3_23

47. Gentry, C., Peikert, C., Vaikuntanathan, V.: Trapdoors for hard lattices and new cryptographic constructions. In: Symposium on Theory of Computing - STOC 2008, pp. 197–206. ACM (2008)

48. Goldwasser, S., Micali, S., Rackoff, C.: The knowledge complexity of interactive proof systems. SIAM J. Comput. **18**(1), 186–208 (1989)

49. Herranz, J.: Attribute-based signatures from RSA. Theor. Comput. Sci. **527**, 73–82 (2014)

50. Ishai, Y., Kushilevitz, E., Ostrovsky, R., Sahai, A.: Zero-knowledge from secure multiparty computation. In: Symposium on Theory of Computing - STOC 2007, pp. 21–30. ACM (2007)

51. Jain, A., Krenn, S., Pietrzak, K., Tentes, A.: Commitments and efficient zero-knowledge proofs from learning parity with noise. In: Wang, X., Sako, K. (eds.) ASIACRYPT 2012. LNCS, vol. 7658, pp. 663–680. Springer, Heidelberg (2012). https://doi.org/10.1007/978-3-642-34961-4_40

52. Katz, J., Kolesnikov, V., Wang, X.: Improved non-interactive zero knowledge with applications to post-quantum signatures. In: Conference on Computer and Communications Security - CCS 2018, pp. 525–537. ACM (2018)

53. Kawachi, A., Tanaka, K., Xagawa, K.: Concurrently secure identification schemes based on the worst-case hardness of lattice problems. In: Pieprzyk, J. (ed.) ASIACRYPT 2008. LNCS, vol. 5350, pp. 372–389. Springer, Heidelberg (2008). https://doi.org/10.1007/978-3-540-89255-7_23

54. Li, J., Au, M.H., Susilo, W., Xie, D., Ren, K.: Attribute-based signature and its applications. In: Symposium on Information, Computer and Communications Security - ASIACCS 2010, pp. 60–69. ACM (2010)

55. Lian, Y., Xu, L., Huang, X.: Attribute-based signatures with efficient revocation. In: International Conference on Intelligent Networking and Collaborative Systems - INCoS 2013, pp. 573–577. IEEE (2013)

56. Libert, B., Ling, S., Mouhartem, F., Nguyen, K., Wang, H.: Signature schemes with efficient protocols and dynamic group signatures from lattice assumptions. In: Cheon, J.H., Takagi, T. (eds.) ASIACRYPT 2016. LNCS, vol. 10032, pp. 373–403. Springer, Heidelberg (2016). https://doi.org/10.1007/978-3-662-53890-6_13

57. Libert, B., Ling, S., Mouhartem, F., Nguyen, K., Wang, H.: Zero-knowledge arguments for matrix-vector relations and lattice-based group encryption. Theor. Comput. Sci. **759**, 72–97 (2019)

58. Libert, B., Ling, S., Nguyen, K., Wang, H.: Zero-knowledge arguments for lattice-based accumulators: logarithmic-size ring signatures and group signatures without trapdoors. In: Fischlin, M., Coron, J.-S. (eds.) EUROCRYPT 2016. LNCS, vol. 9666, pp. 1–31. Springer, Heidelberg (2016). https://doi.org/10.1007/978-3-662-49896-5_1

59. Libert, B., Ling, S., Nguyen, K., Wang, H.: Zero-knowledge arguments for lattice-based accumulators: Logarithmic-size ring signatures and group signatures without trapdoors. J. Cryptol. **36**(3), 23 (2023)
60. Libert, B., Peters, T., Yung, M.: Group signatures with almost-for-free revocation. In: Safavi-Naini, R., Canetti, R. (eds.) CRYPTO 2012. LNCS, vol. 7417, pp. 571–589. Springer, Heidelberg (2012). https://doi.org/10.1007/978-3-642-32009-5_34
61. Libert, B., Peters, T., Yung, M.: Scalable group signatures with revocation. In: Pointcheval, D., Johansson, T. (eds.) EUROCRYPT 2012. LNCS, vol. 7237, pp. 609–627. Springer, Heidelberg (2012). https://doi.org/10.1007/978-3-642-29011-4_36
62. Ling, S., Nguyen, K., Phan, D.H., Tang, H., Wang, H.: Zero-knowledge proofs for committed symmetric Boolean functions. In: Cheon, J.H., Tillich, J.-P. (eds.) PQCrypto 2021 2021. LNCS, vol. 12841, pp. 339–359. Springer, Cham (2021). https://doi.org/10.1007/978-3-030-81293-5_18
63. Ling, S., Nguyen, K., Phan, D.H., Tang, K.H., Wang, H., Xu, Y.: Fully dynamic attribute-based signatures for circuits from codes. *IACR Cryptol. ePrint Arch.*, page 022 (2024)
64. Ling, S., Nguyen, K., Stehlé, D., Wang, H.: Improved zero-knowledge proofs of knowledge for the ISIS problem, and applications. In: Kurosawa, K., Hanaoka, G. (eds.) PKC 2013. LNCS, vol. 7778, pp. 107–124. Springer, Heidelberg (2013). https://doi.org/10.1007/978-3-642-36362-7_8
65. Ling, S., Nguyen, K., Wang, H., Xu, Y.: Accountable tracing signatures from lattices. In: Matsui, M. (ed.) CT-RSA 2019. LNCS, vol. 11405, pp. 556–576. Springer, Cham (2019). https://doi.org/10.1007/978-3-030-12612-4_28
66. Ling, S., Nguyen, K., Wang, H., Xu, Y.: Lattice-based group signatures: achieving full dynamicity (and deniability) with ease. Theor. Comput. Sci. **783**, 71–94 (2019)
67. Lyubashevsky, V.: Lattice signatures without trapdoors. In: Pointcheval, D., Johansson, T. (eds.) EUROCRYPT 2012. LNCS, vol. 7237, pp. 738–755. Springer, Heidelberg (2012). https://doi.org/10.1007/978-3-642-29011-4_43
68. Lyubashevsky, V., Micciancio, D.: Asymptotically efficient lattice-based digital signatures. J. Cryptol. **31**(3), 774–797 (2018)
69. Maji, H.K., Prabhakaran, M., Rosulek, M.: Attribute-based signatures. In: Kiayias, A. (ed.) CT-RSA 2011. LNCS, vol. 6558, pp. 376–392. Springer, Heidelberg (2011). https://doi.org/10.1007/978-3-642-19074-2_24
70. Melchor, C.A., Cayrel, P., Gaborit, P., Laguillaumie, F.: A new efficient threshold ring signature scheme based on coding theory. IEEE Trans. Inf. Theory **57**(7), 4833–4842 (2011)
71. Morozov, K., Takagi, T.: Zero-knowledge protocols for the McEliece encryption. In: Susilo, W., Mu, Y., Seberry, J. (eds.) ACISP 2012. LNCS, vol. 7372, pp. 180–193. Springer, Heidelberg (2012). https://doi.org/10.1007/978-3-642-31448-3_14
72. Nguyen, K., Guo, F., Susilo, W., Yang, G.: Multimodal private signatures. In: Dodis, Y., Shrimpton, T. (eds.) CRYPTO 2022. LNCS, vol. 13508, pp. 792–822. Springer, Cham (2022). https://doi.org/10.1007/978-3-031-15979-4_27
73. Nguyen, K., Roy, P.S., Susilo, W., Xu, Y.: Bicameral and auditably private signatures. In: Guo, J., Steinfeld, R. (eds.) ASIACRYPT 2023. LNCS, vol. 14439, pp. 313–347. Springer, Singapore (2023). https://doi.org/10.1007/978-981-99-8724-5_10
74. Nguyen, K., Safavi-Naini, R., Susilo, W., Wang, H., Xu, Y., Zeng, N.: Group encryption: full dynamicity, message filtering and code-based instantiation. In: Garay, J.A. (ed.) PKC 2021. LNCS, vol. 12711, pp. 678–708. Springer, Cham (2021). https://doi.org/10.1007/978-3-030-75248-4_24

75. Nguyen, K., Tang, H., Wang, H., Zeng, N.: New code-based privacy-preserving cryptographic constructions. In: Galbraith, S.D., Moriai, S. (eds.) ASIACRYPT 2019. LNCS, vol. 11922, pp. 25–55. Springer, Cham (2019). https://doi.org/10.1007/978-3-030-34621-8_2

76. Okamoto, T., Takashima, K.: Efficient attribute-based signatures for non-monotone predicates in the standard model. In: Catalano, D., Fazio, N., Gennaro, R., Nicolosi, A. (eds.) PKC 2011. LNCS, vol. 6571, pp. 35–52. Springer, Heidelberg (2011). https://doi.org/10.1007/978-3-642-19379-8_3

77. Okamoto, T., Takashima, K.: Decentralized attribute-based signatures. In: Kurosawa, K., Hanaoka, G. (eds.) PKC 2013. LNCS, vol. 7778, pp. 125–142. Springer, Heidelberg (2013). https://doi.org/10.1007/978-3-642-36362-7_9

78. Regev, O.: On lattices, learning with errors, random linear codes, and cryptography. J. ACM **56**(6), 341–3440 (2009)

79. Rivest, R.L., Shamir, A., Tauman, Y.: How to leak a secret. In: Boyd, C. (ed.) ASIACRYPT 2001. LNCS, vol. 2248, pp. 552–565. Springer, Heidelberg (2001). https://doi.org/10.1007/3-540-45682-1_32

80. Sakai, Y., Attrapadung, N., Hanaoka, G.: Attribute-based signatures for circuits from bilinear map. In: Cheng, C.-M., Chung, K.-M., Persiano, G., Yang, B.-Y. (eds.) PKC 2016. LNCS, vol. 9614, pp. 283–300. Springer, Heidelberg (2016). https://doi.org/10.1007/978-3-662-49384-7_11

81. Sakai, Y., Katsumata, S., Attrapadung, N., Hanaoka, G.: Attribute-based signatures for unbounded languages from standard assumptions. In: Peyrin, T., Galbraith, S. (eds.) ASIACRYPT 2018. LNCS, vol. 11273, pp. 493–522. Springer, Cham (2018). https://doi.org/10.1007/978-3-030-03329-3_17

82. Stern, J.: A new identification scheme based on syndrome decoding. In: Stinson, D.R. (ed.) CRYPTO 1993. LNCS, vol. 773, pp. 13–21. Springer, Heidelberg (1994). https://doi.org/10.1007/3-540-48329-2_2

83. Stern, J.: A new paradigm for public key identification. IEEE Trans. Inf. Theory **42**(6), 1757–1768 (1996)

84. Su, Q., Zhang, R., Xue, R., Li, P.: Revocable attribute-based signature for blockchain-based healthcare system. IEEE Access **8**, 127884–127896 (2020)

85. Tate, S.R., Vishwanathan, R.: Expiration and revocation of keys for attribute-based signatures. In: Samarati, P. (ed.) DBSec 2015. LNCS, vol. 9149, pp. 153–169. Springer, Cham (2015). https://doi.org/10.1007/978-3-319-20810-7_10

86. Tsabary, R.: An equivalence between attribute-based signatures and homomorphic signatures, and new constructions for both. In: Kalai, Y., Reyzin, L. (eds.) TCC 2017. LNCS, vol. 10678, pp. 489–518. Springer, Cham (2017). https://doi.org/10.1007/978-3-319-70503-3_16

87. Unruh, D.: Non-interactive zero-knowledge proofs in the quantum random oracle model. In: Oswald, E., Fischlin, M. (eds.) EUROCRYPT 2015. LNCS, vol. 9057, pp. 755–784. Springer, Heidelberg (2015). https://doi.org/10.1007/978-3-662-46803-6_25

88. Urquidi, M., Khader, D., Lancrenon, J., Chen, L.: Attribute-based signatures with controllable linkability. In: Yung, M., Zhang, J., Yang, Z. (eds.) INTRUST 2015. LNCS, vol. 9565, pp. 114–129. Springer, Cham (2016). https://doi.org/10.1007/978-3-319-31550-8_8

89. Yang, R., Au, M.H., Zhang, Z., Xu, Q., Yu, Z., Whyte, W.: Efficient lattice-based zero-knowledge arguments with standard soundness: construction and applications. In: Boldyreva, A., Micciancio, D. (eds.) CRYPTO 2019. LNCS, vol. 11692, pp. 147–175. Springer, Cham (2019). https://doi.org/10.1007/978-3-030-26948-7_6

90. Yuen, T.H., Liu, J.K., Huang, X., Au, M.H., Susilo, W., Zhou, J.: Forward secure attribute-based signatures. In: Chim, T.W., Yuen, T.H. (eds.) ICICS 2012. LNCS, vol. 7618, pp. 167–177. Springer, Heidelberg (2012). https://doi.org/10.1007/978-3-642-34129-8_15

91. G. Zaverucha, M. Chase, D. Derler, S. Goldfeder, C. Orlandi, S. Ramacher, C. Rechberger, D. Slamanig, J. Katz, X. Wang, et al. Picnic. *NIST Post-Quantum Standardization Project Round 3*, 2017

On Instantiating Unleveled Fully-Homomorphic Signatures from Falsifiable Assumptions

Romain Gay[1] and Bogdan Ursu[2]([✉]) [ID]

[1] IBM Research, Zurich, Switzerland
rga@zurich.ibm.com
[2] Consensys, Fort Worth, USA
bogdan.ursu@consensys.net

Abstract. We build the first *unleveled* fully homomorphic signature scheme in the standard model. Our scheme is not constrained by any a-priori bound on the depth of the functions that can be homomorphically evaluated, and relies on subexponentially-secure indistinguishability obfuscation, fully-homomorphic encryption and a non-interactive zero-knowledge (NIZK) proof system with composable zero-knowledge. Our scheme is also the first to satisfy the strong security notion of context-hiding for an unbounded number of levels, ensuring that signatures computed homomorphically do not leak the original messages from which they were computed. All building blocks are instantiable from falsifiable assumptions in the standard model, avoiding the need for knowledge assumptions.

The main difficulty we overcome stems from the fact that bootstrapping, which is a crucial tool for obtaining unleveled fully homomorphic encryption (FHE), has no equivalent for homomorphic signatures, requiring us to use novel techniques.

1 Introduction

Fully Homomorphic Signatures. A signature scheme is said to be homomorphic when given signatures $\sigma_1, \ldots, \sigma_n$ of messages $m_1, \ldots, m_n$, it is possible to publicly compute a signature σ_f of the message $f(m_1, \ldots, m_n)$ for any function f. This evaluated signature σ_f is verified with respect to the verification key of the scheme, the message $m = f(m_1, \ldots, m_n)$ and the function f.

Given a set of signatures $\sigma_1, \ldots, \sigma_n$, unforgeability prevents an adversary from deriving a signature σ_f that verifies with respect to a function f and a message $y \neq f(m_1, \ldots, m_n)$. In other words, the signature certifies that the message corresponds to the proper evaluation of the function f on the original messages.

Akin to homomorphic encryption, the signing algorithm is a homomorphism from the message space to the signature space. Computing the addition of signatures $\sigma_1 \boxplus \sigma_2$ results in the signature of the message $m_1 + m_2$, where $\boxplus$ and $+$

The corresponding author is based in Zurich, Switzerland, and this work was carried out during his time at ETH Zurich.

© International Association for Cryptologic Research 2024
Q. Tang and V. Teague (Eds.): PKC 2024, LNCS 14601, pp. 74–104, 2024.
https://doi.org/10.1007/978-3-031-57718-5_3

denote the addition in the signature and message space, respectively. The same goes for multiplication. Schemes equipped with a ring homomorphism (with both addition and multiplication) are referred to as *fully* homomorphic, since these operations are sufficient to capture all possible Boolean functions.

Applications of FHS. Homomorphic signatures are applicable in a wide range of scenarios, such as:

- Integrity for Network Coding. Network performances can be improved by encoding ongoing messages into vectors and letting each node perform linear operations on these encodings, instead of simply forwarding them. Unfortunately, because these encodings are modified by every node, the integrity property is lost when using traditional signatures. Homomorphic signatures (or their secret-key counterpart, as in [AB09]) that support linear operations can be used to preserve integrity throughout the network. In particular, each node updates not only the encoded messages, but also the homomorphic signatures associated with them.
- Verifying Delegated Computations. A client that wishes to delegate some computation on his data to a cloud provider could authenticate it via homomorphic signatures, then send it away to the cloud. The cloud performs the computation and updates the signatures accordingly, then sends the result back to the client, who can then verify the evaluated signature. If verification is successful, then the client is guaranteed that the cloud computed the intended function on the data. It is the perfect complement to fully homomorphic encryption (FHE), which preserves the confidentiality of the data in use, but not its integrity.
- Anonymous Credentials. Consider the scenario where a user obtains signatures $\sigma_1, \ldots, \sigma_n$ of her credentials $m_1, \ldots, m_n$, produced by some authority (the authority is associated to the vk of the signature scheme). Later on, the user is asked by a service provider (say, an insurance company) to prove that her credentials satisfy a policy expressed by a predicate P. The user can compute the signature σ_P and send it to the provider. If this signature verifies successfully with respect to vk and the message 1 (the output of the predicate should be 1), then it proves the user's credentials fulfill the policy. Assuming the homomorphic signatures satisfy some mild re-randomizability property (so that evaluated signatures look fresh), this does not reveal the underlying credentials to the provider (only that they satisfy the policy). Giving the policy explicitly to the user provides some transparency (for instance, the predicate P can be signed by a trusted regulator, ensuring the insurance company is not performing some discriminatory screening). We can even evaluate a function f on the signatures that not only indicates whether the user is eligible to an insurance scheme, but also outputs the price to be paid based on the credentials.

State of the Art. The first construction of homomorphic signatures [AB09] was limited to additive homomorphism in the secret-key setting i.e. it is a message authentication (MAC) scheme. Later on, [BF11a] built the first homomorphic signature for constant-degree polynomials, subsequently improved by [CFW14].

In [GW13], the authors built the first fully homomorphic MAC from FHE, while [CF13] built an homomorphic MAC with better efficiency for a restricted class of functions. Then, [GVW15] built the first leveled fully homomorphic signature (FHS) scheme.

All existing works suffer from the fact that the depth of the functions that can be homomorphically evaluated is bounded at setup. In other words, these are *leveled* FHS. This stands in contrast with FHE, where *unleveled* schemes can be obtained via bootstrapping [Gen09] and circular security. Bootstrapping requires an FHE encryption of the secret decryption key, and relies on evaluating homomorphically the (shallow) decryption algorithm to "refresh" ciphertexts. This idea is not straightforwardly transferable to the signature case, and unleveled FHS have so far been elusive.

Another approach to building FHS is to use Succinct Arguments of Knowledge (SNARKs) for NP, but this requires the use of strong knowledge assumptions, which we discuss in more detail in the full version of this paper [GU23].

Given this state of affair, a natural question comes up:

Can we build unleveled FHS from falsifiable assumptions?

This was left as an open problem in [GVW15], and has remained unsolved until our construction.

Our Result. We answer the question positively. Namely, we build the first *unleveled* FHS from falsifiable assumptions, in the standard model. Our feasibility result relies on indistinguishability obfuscation (iO), of which promising constructions appeared recently in [BDGM20a, JLS21, GP21, WW21, AP20, BDGM20b, DQV+21, JLS22], unleveled fully homomorphic encryption and a non-interactive zero-knowledge proof system (NIZK). While iO is not a falsifiable assumption itself[1], most of the iO candidates rely on falsifiable assumptions. The second building block, fully-homomorphic encryption, can be instantiated using circularly-secure LWE [GSW13], and alternatively using indistinguishability obfuscation [CLTV15]. Instantiating the FHE scheme using [CLTV15] yields a fully homomorphic signature construction that does not require any circular security assumption.

Building Blocks. We give more details on the building blocks, and the assumptions over which they can be instantiated. To build our FHS, we use an unleveled Fully-Homomorphic Encryption (FHE) scheme, which can be chosen to be either:

- a variant of the FHE scheme from [GSW13], slightly modified to ensure that it has unique random coins (which is needed for technical reasons in the proof). This scheme can be built from circularly-secure LWE.
- the FHE scheme of [CLTV15], which is instantiable using subexponentially-secure iO and a re-randomizable public-key encryption scheme. This second type of FHE scheme does not require a circular assumption. Moreover, the

---

[1] Formally, the iO security game does not fulfill falsifiability because the challenger cannot efficiently check that the circuits submitted by the adversary are functionally equivalent.

re-randomizable encryption scheme can be any one of the following: Goldwasser-Micali [GM82], ElGamal [ElG85], Paillier [Pai99] or Damgard-Jurik [DJ01] (which are secure assuming QR, DDH, or DCR).

Moreover, we rely on Non-Interactive Zero Knowledge (NIZK) proof systems satisfying a proof of knowledge property and composable zero-knowledge, which can also be built from subexponentially secure iO and lossy trapdoor functions [HU19]. Lossy trapdoor functions can be based on a multitude of standard assumptions such as DDH, k-LIN, QR or DCR. Other NIZK systems also offer the properties required, but from bilinear maps [GS08].

The NIZKs above [HU19, GS08] allow that the common reference string (CRS) can be either generated honestly to be binding, which ensures soundness (i.e. the fact that only true statements can be proved), or alternatively, the CRS is generated in a hiding way, providing a simulation mode that ensures zero-knowledge. In fact, the binding CRS is generated together with an extraction trapdoor that can be used to extract efficiently a witness from any valid proof (thereby ensuring that the statement proved is indeed true). The simulated CRS is generated together with a simulation trapdoor. In this case, the simulation trapdoor can be used to generate proofs on any statement (without requiring a witness). The two modes (real or simulated) are computationally indistinguishable.

Technical Overview

Overview of Our Construction. The verification key vk of our scheme contains several FHE encryptions of an arbitrary message (for example the message equals to 0). The number of such encryptions, N, determines the arity of the functions that can be homomorphically evaluated. We require that the FHE is unleveled. This differs from the FHS scheme from [GVW15] which uses homomorphic commitments instead of FHE encryptions. They crucially rely on the fact that these commitments are non-binding, which prevents from bootstrapping and only yields leveled FHS. To produce signatures, we rely on the NIZK proof system. To sign a message m_i for $i = 1, \ldots, N$, the signer produces a simulated proof stating (falsely) that the i'th encryption from vk, which we denote by ct_i, is an FHE encryption of m_i. This can be done since the NIZK common reference string CRS is simulated with an associated simulation trapdoor td_{sim}. Creating these simulated proofs requires the trapdoor, which is set to be the signing key. A signature is simply the ZK proof π_i stating that the ciphertext ct_i is an encryption of m_i. To homomorphically evaluate a function f on signatures $\sigma_1, \ldots, \sigma_N$ of the messages $m_1, \ldots, m_N$, we use an obfuscated circuit containing the simulation trapdoor td_{sim} that, given as input the tuple $(\sigma_1, m_1, \ldots, \sigma_n, m_n, f)$, first checks that the signatures σ_i are valid ZK proofs (of false statements), by running the verification algorithm of the NIZK proof system. If the check is successful, then it homomorphically evaluates the function f on the FHE encryptions $ct_1, \ldots, ct_N$ that are part of vk, which yields an

FHE ciphertext ct_f. It also generates a proof π that ct_f is an FHE encryption of $f(m_1, \ldots, m_n)$, using $\mathsf{td}_{\mathsf{sim}}$. The signature σ_f is set to be the proof π, which the evaluation circuit outputs. To verify a signature σ_f with respect to a function f and a value y, the verifier algorithm computes ct_f by evaluating f on the FHE encryptions $\mathsf{ct}_1, \ldots, \mathsf{ct}_N$ from vk and verifies that σ is a valid proof stating that ct_f is an FHE encryption of y.

Let us now have a look at the proof of unforgeability. For simplicity, we consider the selective setting, where the adversary first sends messages $m_1^\star, \ldots, m_n^\star$, then receives vk and the signatures $\sigma_1^\star, \ldots, \sigma_n^\star$. Finally, the adversary sends a forgery (σ_f, f, y). It wins if the signature σ_f verifies successfully with respect to vk, f, y and $y \neq f(m_1^\star, \ldots, m_n^\star)$. The first step of the proof is to switch the FHE encryptions $\mathsf{ct}_1 \ldots \mathsf{ct}_N$ of 0 in the vk to FHE encryptions of $m_1^\star, \ldots, m_n^\star$, respectively. This way, we can change the signatures $\sigma_i^\star$ to proofs that are computed using a witness (where the witness is the randomness used to compute the FHE encryptions in vk). The main implication is that we do not need to simulate proofs using $\mathsf{td}_{\mathsf{sim}}$ anymore. The intent is to get rid of $\mathsf{td}_{\mathsf{sim}}$ altogether and switch to an honestly computed CRS so that we can use the soundness of the NIZK to prevent forgeries. Unfortunately it is not clear at this point how to remove $\mathsf{td}_{\mathsf{sim}}$ from Eval, the obfuscated circuit that performs the homomorphic evaluations. What if we use proofs of knowledge? This way, if the signatures input to the Eval algorithm are valid ZK proofs, then Eval can efficiently extract witnesses (i.e. randomness of the corresponding FHE ciphertexts), which can be used to compute the randomness of the evaluated FHE ciphertext. This requires a so-called randomness homomorphism of the FHE scheme. Namely, given the secret key of the FHE sk, randomness r_1, r_2 and messages m_1, m_2 such that $\mathsf{ct}_1 = \mathsf{FHE.Enc}(\mathsf{pk}, m_1; r_1)$ and $\mathsf{ct}_2 = \mathsf{FHE.Enc}(\mathsf{pk}, m_2; r_2)$, one can compute a randomness r such that $\mathsf{FHE.EvalNAND}(\mathsf{ct}_1, \mathsf{ct}_2) = \mathsf{FHE.Enc}(\mathsf{pk}, \mathsf{NAND}; r)$. A stronger property where a randomness r can be computed only using the pk is satisfied by most lattice-based FHE schemes (e.g. [GSW13]) and the secret-key variant is satisfied by the FHE scheme from [CLTV15]. Then, Eval can use this randomness r as a witness to produce the ZK proof that constitutes the evaluated signature σ_f.

This approach runs into a circular issue: while it is true that the $\sigma_i^\star$ are proofs that are computed without $\mathsf{td}_{\mathsf{sim}}$, to use the proof of knowledge property and extract witnesses, we need to first remove $\mathsf{td}_{\mathsf{sim}}$ and switch to an honestly generated CRS. To do so, we need Eval to produce the signatures σ_f without $\mathsf{td}_{\mathsf{sim}}$, but using witnesses instead, which already requires the proof of knowledge property and an honest CRS.

To solve this circular issue, our scheme uses a different NIZK proof system for each depth level of the circuit that is homomorphically evaluated. That is, to evaluate a function f, represented as a depth d circuit, we evaluate the circuit gate by gate. Starting at the level 0, signatures $\sigma_1, \ldots, \sigma_n$ of messages $m_1, \ldots, m_n$ are ZK proofs stating (falsely) that the FHE ciphertexts $\mathsf{ct}_1, \ldots, \mathsf{ct}_N$ from vk are encryptions of $m_1, \ldots, m_n$, respectively, computed using crs_0, a simulated crs, together with a simulation trapdoor $\mathsf{td}_{\mathsf{sim}}^0$. Then Eval takes as input these level

0 signatures $\sigma_1, \ldots, \sigma_n$, the messages $m_1, \ldots, m_n$ and a n-ary gate g, verifies that the σ_i are valid proofs, computes the gate g on the messages which yields the value $y = g(m_1, \ldots, m_n)$, homomorphically evaluates g on the ciphertexts $\mathsf{ct}_1, \ldots, \mathsf{ct}_n$ which yields ct_g, and computes a ZK proof π stating that ct_g is an FHE encryption of y using crs_1, a simulated crs, together with a simulation trapdoor $\mathsf{td}_{\mathsf{sim}}^1$. The Eval algorithm performs just one more level of the homomorphic computation. It is repeated many times to obtain the final signature σ_f for the function f. To keep track of the gate-by-gate evaluation of the circuit, each signature will be of the form $\sigma = (\pi, i, \mathsf{ct})$, where $i \in \mathbb{N}$ indicates the level of the signature, π is a proof computed using $(\mathsf{crs}_i, \mathsf{td}_{\mathsf{sim}}^i)$, and ct is an homomorphically evaluated ciphertext (if $i = 0$ it is one ciphertext from vk). This way, Eval takes as input signatures of level i, and outputs signatures of level $i + 1$.

To prove the unforgeability of this scheme, as before, we start by replacing the FHE ciphertexts $\mathsf{ct}_1, \ldots, \mathsf{ct}_N$ from the vk to encryptions of the messages $m_1^\star, \ldots, m_N^\star$ chosen by the adversary, using the semantic security of FHE. Then, we generate level 0 signatures using witnesses (the randomness used to compute the ct_i) instead of $\mathsf{td}_{\mathsf{sim}}^0$. At this point, we can switch crs_0 to a real CRS, generated along with an extraction trapdoor, since $\mathsf{td}_{\mathsf{sim}}^0$ is not used anymore. The rest of the proof proceeds using a hybrid argument over all the levels $i = 1, \ldots, d$ where d is the (unbounded) depth of the circuit chosen by the adversary. By induction, we assume crs_i is generated honestly along with an extraction trapdoor $\mathsf{td}_{\mathsf{ext}}^i$. Therefore, we can switch the way Eval computes the ZK proof for the level $i + 1$. Instead of using a simulation trapdoor $\mathsf{td}_{\mathsf{sim}}^{i+1}$ with respect to crs_{i+1} and computing simulated proofs, it instead extracts witnesses from the level i signatures using $\mathsf{td}_{\mathsf{ext}}^i$, and uses them to compute the proofs without the trapdoor $\mathsf{td}_{\mathsf{sim}}^{i+1}$. At this point $\mathsf{td}_{\mathsf{sim}}^{i+1}$ is not used anymore so we can also switch crs_{i+1} to a real CRS, and go to the next step until we reach the depth of the function f chosen by the adversary.

While using a different CRS for each level seems to solve the circularity issue, this approach creates another problem: if we simply generate all crs_i for all levels in advance and put them in vk, we necessarily have to bound the maximum depth of the functions that can be homomorphically evaluated. In other words, we have a leveled FHS. To avoid that, Eval samples the crs_i on the fly using a pseudorandom function (the key of the PRF is hard-coded in the obfuscated circuit Eval). This complicates the security proof, but it can be made to work using puncturing techniques. Namely, to switch crs_i from a simulated to real CRS and use the proof of knowledge property of the proof system associated to crs_i, we need crs_i to be generated with truly random coins, as opposed to a PRF. We simply hard-code the PRF value on i, puncture the PRF key, and switch the value to random (this is a standard technique for security proofs using iO, see for instance [SW14]). The crucial fact that makes these techniques applicable is that at any point in our security proof, we only require the CRS of one specific level to be generated with truly random coins. That is, we only need to hard-code the value of one CRS to perform the hybrid argument that goes over each level one by one. Ultimately, we show that the CRS for the last level, which corresponds to the depth of f chosen by the adversary, is generated honestly, and the soundness of the proof system directly prevents any successful FHS forgery.

High-Level Description of our FHS Scheme. In this description, SimSetup generates a simulated CRS with an associated simulation trapdoor $\mathsf{td}_{\mathsf{sim}}$. In the unforgeability proof, we will use the honest variant Setup that generates a real CRS along with an extraction trapdoor $\mathsf{td}_{\mathsf{ext}}$. For simplicity, we consider an algorithm Eval that only evaluates binary NAND gates (this is without loss of generality). Our scheme is as follows:

- $\mathsf{vk} = (\mathsf{FHE.Enc}(0), \dots, \mathsf{FHE.Enc}(0), \mathsf{crs}_0)$, where $(\mathsf{crs}_0, \mathsf{td}_{\mathsf{sim}}^0) \leftarrow \mathsf{SimSetup}(1^\lambda)$, where $\lambda \in \mathbb{N}$ denotes the security parameter. The verification key vk contains N FHE encryptions of 0, namely $\mathsf{ct}_1 \dots \mathsf{ct}_N$.
- $\mathsf{sk} = K$, where K is a PRF key.
- $\mathsf{EvalNAND}\Big((\sigma_0, m_0), (\sigma_1, m_1)\Big) = \widetilde{\mathcal{C}_{[\mathsf{td}_{\mathsf{sim}}^0, K]}}\Big((\sigma_0, m_0), (\sigma_1, m_1)\Big)$, where $\widetilde{\mathcal{C}_{[\mathsf{td}_{\mathsf{sim}}^0, K]}}$ denotes an obfuscation of the circuit $\mathcal{C}_{[\mathsf{td}_{\mathsf{sim}}^0, K]}$ that has the values $\mathsf{td}_{\mathsf{sim}}^0$ and K hard-coded, described in Fig. 1 below, σ_0 and σ_1 are signatures of level $i \in \mathbb{N}$ of the messages m_0 and m_1 respectively, and a binary NAND gate is homomorphically evaluated.
- $\mathsf{Verify}(\sigma_f, f, y)$: parses σ_f as (ct, π, d). Proof π is a ZK proof with respect to crs_d where d is the depth of f and $(\mathsf{crs}_d, \mathsf{td}_d) = \mathsf{SimSetup}(1^\lambda; \mathsf{PRF}_K(i))$, i.e. SimSetup is run on the pseudorandom coins $\mathsf{PRF}_K(d)$. Then, it homomorphically evaluates f on the ciphertexts $\mathsf{ct}_i = \mathsf{FHE.Enc}(0)$ from vk to obtain ct_f. It checks that π is a valid proof stating that ct_f is an encryption of y, with respect to crs_d (it outputs 1 if the check passes, 0 otherwise). Note that the ciphertext ct that is part of the signature is not used by Verify. It is only useful if extra homomorphically evaluation are to be performed on the evaluated signature.

$\mathcal{C}_{[\mathsf{td}_0, K]}((\sigma_0, m_0), (\sigma_1, m_1))$:

It parses $\sigma_0 = (\pi_0, i, \mathsf{ct}_0)$ and $\sigma_1 = (\mathsf{ct}_1, \pi_1, i)$ where $i \in \mathbb{N}$ denotes the level of these signatures, $\mathsf{ct}_0, \mathsf{ct}_1$ denotes FHE ciphertexts, and π_0, π_1 denotes ZK proofs.

- If $i > 0$, then it computes $(\mathsf{crs}_i, \mathsf{td}_{\mathsf{sim}}^i) = \mathsf{SimSetup}(1^\lambda; \mathsf{PRF}_K(i))$ and $(\mathsf{crs}_{i+1}, \mathsf{td}_{\mathsf{sim}}^{i+1}) = \mathsf{SimSetup}(1^\lambda; \mathsf{PRF}_K(i+1))$.
- If $i = 0$, then it only computes $(\mathsf{crs}_{i+1}, \mathsf{td}_{\mathsf{sim}}^{i+1}) = \mathsf{SimSetup}(1^\lambda; \mathsf{PRF}_K(i+1))$, since crs_0 has already been generated (it is part of vk).

Then it checks that π_b is a valid proof stating that ct_b is a ciphertext of m_b, with respect to crs_i, for all $b \in \{0, 1\}$. If any of these checks fail, it outputs $\bot$. Otherwise, it evaluates homomorphically the NAND gate on the ciphertexts ct_0 and ct_1 to obtain ct, computes $m = \mathsf{NAND}(m_0, m_1)$, and produces a proof π stating that ct is a encryption of m, using the trapdoor $\mathsf{td}_{\mathsf{sim}}^{i+1}$. It then outputs $\sigma = (\mathsf{ct}, \pi, i+1)$.

Fig. 1. Circuit $\mathcal{C}_{[\mathsf{td}_0, K]}(\cdot, \cdot)$ used by Eval.

We summarize the unforgeability proof using the list of hybrid games presented in Fig. 2. Note that $G_{3.0} = G_2$, and in the last game $G_{3.d}$, where d denotes the depth of the function f chosen by the adversary, security simply follows from the soundness of the level d NIZK.

Complexity Leveraging and Adaptive Security. In the overview above, we skipped over some technical details. In the unforgeability proof of our FHS scheme, the challenger that interacts with the adversary does not know in advance the depth d of the function f chosen. To solve this problem, the challenger chooses a super-polynomial e.g. $2^{\omega(\log \lambda)}$ number of levels to perform the hybrid argument sketched above. This gives a super-polynomial security loss, which is why we require subexponential security of the underlying assumptions. A similar complexity leveraging argument can be used to obtain adaptive security, where the adversary is not restricted to choose the messages $m_1^\star, \ldots, m_N^\star$ before seeing the verification key of the scheme. The challenger guesses in advance the messages and acts as though the adversary were selective. The security loss due to the guessing argument is 2^N, which we can accommodate by choosing appropriately large parameters, relying again on the subexponential security of the underlying building blocks.

Unique Randomness. For technical reasons, we require additionally that the FHE has unique randomness: given a message m and a ciphertext

---

- G_0: vk = $\{\mathsf{FHE.Enc}(0)\}_i$, $(\mathsf{crs}_0, \mathsf{td}_{\mathsf{sim}}^0) \leftarrow \mathsf{SimSetup}(1^\lambda)$, $\sigma_i^\star$ simulated with $\mathsf{td}_{\mathsf{sim}}^0$. // original security game.

- G_1: vk = $\{\mathsf{FHE.Enc}(m_i^\star)\}_i$, $(\mathsf{crs}_0, \mathsf{td}_{\mathsf{sim}}^0) \leftarrow \mathsf{SimSetup}(1^\lambda)$, $\sigma_i^\star$ simulated with $\mathsf{td}_{\mathsf{sim}}^0$.   // security of FHE

- G_2: vk = $\{\mathsf{FHE.Enc}(m_i^\star; r_i)\}_i$, $(\mathsf{crs}_0, \mathsf{td}_{\mathsf{ext}}^0) \leftarrow \mathsf{Setup}(1^\lambda)$, $\sigma_i^\star$ proved with r_i.   // real CRS

- $G_{3.\ell}$:   // games defined for all $\ell = 0, \ldots, d$, where d is the depth of f
Eval uses the obfuscation of the following circuit which has
the pair $(\mathsf{crs}_\ell, \mathsf{td}_{\mathsf{ext}}^\ell) \leftarrow \mathsf{Setup}(1^\lambda)$ and the PRF key K hard-coded:
$C_{[\mathsf{crs}_\ell, \mathsf{td}_{\mathsf{ext}}^\ell, K]}((\sigma_0, m_0), (\sigma_1, m_1))$:
- Parse $\sigma_b = (\mathsf{ct}_b, \pi_b, j)$, for $b \in \{0, 1\}$
- Compute $\mathsf{ct} = \mathsf{FHE.Eval}(\mathsf{NAND}, \mathsf{ct}_0, \mathsf{ct}_1)$
- If $j < \ell$, then compute $(\mathsf{crs}_j, \mathsf{td}_{\mathsf{ext}}^j) = \mathsf{Setup}(1^\lambda; \mathsf{PRF}_K(j))$,
    extract witnesses (r_0, r_1) from (π_0, π_1) using $\mathsf{td}_{\mathsf{ext}}^j$,
    compute r such that $\mathsf{ct} = \mathsf{FHE.Enc}(\mathsf{NAND}(m_0, m_1); r)$ using r_0, r_1, m_0, m_1,
    compute a proof π that ct encrypts $\mathsf{NAND}(m_0, m_1)$ using r.
- If $j \geq \ell$, then compute $(\mathsf{crs}_{j+1}, \mathsf{td}_{\mathsf{sim}}^{j+1}) = \mathsf{SimSetup}(1^\lambda; \mathsf{PRF}_K(j+1))$
    and compute the proof π with $\mathsf{td}_{\mathsf{sim}}^{j+1}$ instead.
- Output $\sigma = (\pi, \mathsf{ct}, j+1)$.

Fig. 2. Hybrid games for the selective unforgeability proof of our FHS. We denote by $m_i^\star$ the message sent by the adversary, by $\sigma_i^\star$ the signatures it receives, by $\mathsf{SimSetup}$ the algorithm that generates a simulated CRS with a trapdoor $\mathsf{td}_{\mathsf{sim}}$, by $\mathsf{Setup}(1^\lambda)$ the honest variant that generates a real CRS together with an extraction trapdoor and by K a puncturable PRF key. We denote by $\mathsf{Setup}(1^\lambda; r)$ the algorithm Setup run with coins r (which can be truly random or pseudo random). When omitted, truly random coins are implicitly used. We use the same notations when writing $\mathsf{SimSetup}(1^\lambda; r)$ or $\mathsf{FHE.Enc}(m; r)$.

ct = Enc(pk, m; r) there cannot be another randomness $r' \neq r$ such that Enc(pk, m; r') = ct. In the full version of this paper [GU23], we show that a slight modification of the GSW FHE scheme [GSW13] directly achieves such a property. We also show that the FHE from [CLTV15] can be adapted straightforwardly to obtain unique randomness. Simply put, their scheme relies on iO and a re-randomizable encryption scheme (such as Goldwasser Micali, ElGamal, Paillier or Damgard-Jurik). If the latter has unique randomness, then the resulting FHE also has this property.

Related Works. The work of [JMSW02] introduced a similar notion of homomorphic signature but where the verification algorithm does not take the function f as an input. That is, signatures can be manipulated homomorphically, thereby changing the underlying message being signed, but the verification does not track which function was applied. In that case, the notion of unforgeability only makes sense when the homomorphism property is limited, so that from a set of signatures, one can only get a signature on some but not all messages. Typically, the messages are vectors, and given signatures on vectors $\mathbf{v}_1, \ldots, \mathbf{v}_n$, only signatures on the linear combinations of the vectors $\mathbf{v}_1, \ldots, \mathbf{v}_n$ can be obtained. In particular if n is less than the dimension of the vectors, then there are some vectors for which signatures cannot be generated (those outside the span of $\mathbf{v}_1, \ldots, \mathbf{v}_n$) and the unforgeability property is meaningful. These are referred to as linearly homomorphic signatures, such as in [BF11b, Fre12, ALP13, LPJY15, CFN15, CLQ16, HPP20]. This is similar to the notion of equivalence-class signatures [HS14, FHS19, FG18, KSD19], where signatures can be combined homomorphically within a given equivalence class, but forgeries outside the class are prohibited. The notion also requires a re-randomizability property, and is used in particular for anonymous credentials.

Other works [LTWC18, FP18, AP19, SBB19] consider the multi-key extension of homomorphic signatures, where the signatures to be homomorphically evaluated come from different users with different signing keys.

In [BFS14], the authors provide a fully-homomorphic signature from lattices that has the advantage of being adaptively secure (where the adversary can send the messages of her choice after receiving the verification key in the security game). In [CFN18], the authors study the security notions of homomorphic signatures in the adaptive setting, provide a simpler and stronger definition, and a compiler that generically strengthens the security of a scheme. The work of [Tsa17] establishes an equivalence between homomorphic signatures and the related notion of attribute-based signatures, and provides new constructions for both.

Another recent line of work [CFT22, BCFL23] on functional commitments also addresses the problem of homomorphic signatures. [BCFL23] instantiates the framework of [CFT22] with a functional commitment for circuits of unbounded depth, resulting in a homomorphic signature that supports circuits of unbounded depth (though the circuit width is bounded). In this way, [BCFL23] proposes schemes based on new falsifiable assumptions which rely on pairings and lattices (the pairing assumption holds in the bilinear generic group model, while the lattice one is an extension of the k-R-ISIS assumption of [ACL+22]). Comparing our work to [BCFL23], our basic scheme only relies on a bound on the input size[2]. Moreover, our scheme allows for arbitrary compositions of signatures, as was the case in [GVW15]. The signatures in [BCFL23] can be composed only sequentially, by feeding an entire signature as the input to another circuit (given a signature σ for $y = f(m)$, their scheme can compute a signature σ' for $z = g(y)$. Namely, the resulting signature σ' is with respect to z, circuit $g \circ f$ and input m).

As we mentioned already earlier, [CLTV15] builds an unleveled FHE scheme from subexponentially secure iO and re-randomizable encryption. Remarkably, their FHE does not require any circular security assumption, since it does not rely on the bootstrapping technique. Although we use a similar technical complexity leveraging argument to handle unbounded depth, the technical similarities end here.

Fully-Homomorphic Signatures from SNARKs. It was claimed in previous works [GW13,GVW15] that FHS can be built using succinct arguments of knowledge (SNARKs) for NP. This comes at a cost: in the FHS regime, that would mean using unfalsifiable assumptions (even in the random oracle model), as we explain in further details in the full version of this paper [GU23]. This stands in contrast with our scheme that can be instantiated from falsifiable assumptions, since general indistinguishability obfuscation itself can be built from falsifiable assumptions [JLS21,GP21,JLS22].

Full Context-Hiding. Our FHS scheme is also the first to achieve a strong notion of context hiding, more powerful than the one achieved by [GVW15]. Consider a signature σ for $m = f(m_1 \ldots m_N)$, which was obtained by homomorphically evaluating a function f for signature-message pairs $(\sigma_1, m_1) \ldots (\sigma_N, m_N)$. Full context-hiding[3] guarantees that the signature σ only certifies m and does not leak any information on messages $m_1 \ldots m_N$. A signature σ in [GVW15] is not context-hiding, but can be post-processed into another signature σ' that achieves context-hiding, at the cost that the homomorphism property is broken: no homomorphic operations can be applied on σ'.

In contrast, our FHS construction achieves full context hiding for signatures at all levels out-of-the-box, and context-hiding signatures can be homomorphically combined for an unbounded number of times. Our construction is the first to achieve this stronger notion of context-hiding in the standard model. More details can be found in the full version of this paper [GU23].

Roadmap. In Sect. 2 we define the building blocks used in our construction, then we describe our scheme in Sect. 3 and prove its security in Sect. 4.

Due to space limitations, some of our results are deferred to the full version of this paper [GU23] which contains:

---

[2] Our bound on the input size can be removed using random oracles, as in [GVW15].

[3] Previous work [GVW15] refers to this notion as context hiding. We use the modifier "full" to differentiate from its weak context hiding counterpart.

- a description of several schemes that satisfy unique randomness, a property needed from the FHE building block in the proof.
- a variation of the scheme that supports datasets of unbounded length, albeit by relying on the use of the random oracle model.
- an analysis of the context-hiding security of our scheme.
- a detailed description of how SNARKs can be used to build FHS. While such an approach would be much more practical in terms of the efficiency of the scheme, there would also be drawbacks with respect to the falsifiability of the assumptions used.
- a brief description of multi-data FHS, which allows for the signing of multiple datasets by associating each one with a label (the label is an arbitrary binary string, for example an encoding of a filename or a timestamp). Signing and verification is done with respect to the label, but the scheme uses the same signing and verification key for multiple labels. A generic transformation from single-data to multi-data FHS is known due to [GVW15] and is recalled in the full version of this paper [GU23].

2   Preliminaries

Notation. Throughout this paper, λ denotes the security parameter. For all $n \in \mathbb{N}$, $[n]$ denotes the set $\{1, \ldots, n\}$. An algorithm is said to be *efficient* if it is a probabilistic polynomial time (PPT) algorithm. A function $f : \mathbb{N} \to \mathbb{N}$ is *negligible* if for any polynomial p there exists a bound $B > 0$ such that, for any integer $k \geq B$, $f(k) \leq 1/|p(k)|$. An event depending on λ occurs with *overwhelming probability* when its probability is at least $1 - \mathsf{negl}(\lambda)$ for a negligible function negl. Given a finite set S, the notation $x \leftarrow_{\mathrm{R}} S$ means a uniformly random assignment of an element of S to the variable x. For all probabilistic algorithms $\mathcal{A}$, all inputs x, we denote by $y \leftarrow \mathcal{A}(x)$ the process of running $\mathcal{A}$ on x and assigning the output to y. The notation $\mathcal{A}^{\mathcal{O}}$ indicates that the algorithm $\mathcal{A}$ is given an oracle access to $\mathcal{O}$. For all algorithm $\mathcal{A}, \mathcal{B}, \ldots$, all inputs $x, y, \ldots$ and all predicates P, we denote by $\Pr[a \leftarrow \mathcal{A}(x); b \leftarrow \mathcal{B}(a); \ldots : \mathsf{P}(a, b, \ldots)]$ the probability that the predicate P holds on the values $a, b, \ldots$ computed by first running $\mathcal{A}$ on x, then $\mathcal{B}$ on y and a, and so forth. For two distributions D_1, D_2, we denote by $\Delta(D_1, D_2)$ their statistical distance. We denote by $\mathcal{D}_1 \approx_c \mathcal{D}_2$ two computationally indistinguishable distribution ensembles $\mathcal{D}_1$ and $\mathcal{D}_2$. We denote by $\mathcal{D}_1 \approx_s \mathcal{D}_2$ two statistically close ensembles.

Subexponential Security. The security definitions we consider will require that for every efficient algorithm $\mathcal{A}$, there exists some negligible function negl such that for all $\lambda \in \mathbb{N}$, $\mathcal{A}$ succeeds in "breaking security" w.r.t. the security parameter λ with probability at most $\mathsf{negl}(\lambda)$. All the definitions that we consider can be extended to consider subexponential security; this is done by requiring the existence of a constant $\varepsilon > 0$, such that for every PPT algorithm $\mathcal{A}$, $\mathcal{A}$ succeeds in "breaking security" w.r.t. the security parameter λ with probability at most $2^{-\lambda^{\varepsilon}}$. The security notion of obfuscation (Sect. 2.3) and NIZK

(Sect. 2.4) are traditionally defined for *non-uniform* adversaries. We write our security definitions for uniform adversaries for simplicity, but they can be easily adapted to non-uniform adversaries.

2.1 Puncturable Pseudorandom Functions

A pseudorandom function (PRF) is a tuple of PPT algorithms (PRF.KeyGen, PRF.Eval) where PRF.KeyGen generates a key which is used by PRF.Eval to evaluate outputs. The core property of PRFs states that for a random choice of key, the outputs of PRF.Eval are pseudo-random. Puncturable PRFs (pPRFs) have the additional property that keys can be generated *punctured* at any input x in the domain. As a result, the punctured key can be used to evaluate the PRF at all inputs but x. Moreover, revealing the punctured key does not violate the pseudorandomness of the image of x. This notion can be generalized to allow they key to be punctured at multiple points.

As observed in [BW13, BGI14, KPTZ13], it is possible to construct such punctured PRFs for the original PRF construction of [GGM84], which can be based on any one-way functions [HILL99]. While this PRFs support puncturing for a polynomial number of times, in this paper we only to puncture at sets that contain at most two points.

Definition 1 (Puncturable Pseudorandom Function). *A puncturable pseudorandom function (pPRF) is a triple of PPT algorithms* (PRF.KeyGen, PRF.Puncture, PRF.Eval) *such that:*

- PRF.KeyGen(1^λ): *on input the security parameter, it outputs a key K in the key space $\mathcal{K}_\lambda$. It also defines a domain $\mathcal{X}_\lambda$, a range $\mathcal{Y}_\lambda$ and a punctured key space $\mathcal{K}_\lambda^*$.*
- PRF.Puncture(K, S): *on input a key $K \in \mathcal{K}_\lambda$, a set $S \subseteq \mathcal{X}_\lambda$, it outputs a punctured key $K\{S\} \in \mathcal{K}_\lambda^*$,*
- PRF.Eval(K, x): *on input a key K (punctured or not, i.e. $K \in \mathcal{K}_\lambda \cup \mathcal{K}_\lambda^*$), and a point $x \in \mathcal{X}_\lambda$, it outputs a value in $\mathcal{Y}_\lambda$.*

We require the PPR algorithms to meet the following conditions:

Functionality Preserved under Puncturing. *For all $\lambda \in \mathbb{N}$, for all subsets $S \subseteq \mathcal{X}_\lambda$,*

$$\Pr[K \leftarrow \mathsf{PRF.KeyGen}(1^\lambda), K\{S\} \leftarrow \mathsf{PRF.Puncture}(K, S):$$
$$\forall x' \in \mathcal{X}_\lambda \setminus S \colon \mathsf{PRF.Eval}(K, x') = \mathsf{PRF.Eval}(K\{S\}, x')] = 1.$$

Pseudorandom at Punctured Points. *For every stateful PPT adversary $\mathcal{A}$ and every security parameter $\lambda \in \mathbb{N}$, the advantage of $\mathcal{A}$ in Exp-pPRF (described in Fig. 3) is negligible, namely:*

$$\mathsf{Adv_{cPRF}}(\lambda, \mathcal{A}) := \left| \Pr[\mathsf{Exp\text{-}pPRF}(1^\lambda, \mathcal{A}) = 1] - \tfrac{1}{2} \right| \le \mathsf{negl}(\lambda).$$

For ease of notation we often write $\mathsf{PRF}(\cdot, \cdot)$ instead of $\mathsf{PRF}.\mathsf{Eval}(\cdot, \cdot)$. When S is a singleton set $S = \{x\}$, we denote the punctured key at S as $K\{S\} = K\{x\}$, and when $S = \{x_1, x_2\}$, we denote $K\{S\} = K\{x_1, x_2\}$.

Theorem 2. [GGM84, BW13, BGI14, KPTZ13] *Consider a fixed polynomial $p(\lambda)$, and two arbitrary polynomials $n(\lambda), m(\lambda)$ in the security parameter λ. If one-way functions exist, then there exists a puncturable PRF family that maps $n(\lambda)$ bits to $m(\lambda)$ bits and which supports punctured sets S of $p(\lambda)$ size.*

As explained at the beginning of this section, in this paper we use puncturing for sets that contain at most two elements.

$$
\begin{array}{|l|}
\hline
\text{Experiment Exp-pPRF}(1^\lambda, \mathcal{A}) \\
\hline
S \leftarrow \mathcal{A}(1^\lambda) \\
b \leftarrow_{\mathrm{R}} \{0, 1\} \\
K \leftarrow \mathsf{PRF}.\mathsf{KeyGen}(1^\lambda) \\
K\{S\} \leftarrow \mathsf{PRF}.\mathsf{Puncture}(K, S) \\
Y = \emptyset \\
\text{for all } x \in S \\
\quad y_0 \leftarrow \mathsf{PRF}.\mathsf{Eval}(K, x) \\
\quad y_1 \leftarrow_{\mathrm{R}} \mathcal{Y}_\lambda \\
\quad Y = Y \bigcup \{y_b\} \\
b' \leftarrow \mathcal{A}(K\{S\}, Y) \\
\text{Return } b = b' \\
\hline
\end{array}
$$

Fig. 3. Experiment $\mathsf{Exp\text{-}pPRF}(1^\lambda, \mathcal{A})$ for the pseudo-randomness at punctured points.

2.2 Fully Homomorphic Encryption

We recall the definition of unleveled FHE here, where there is no a-priori bound on the depth of circuits that can be homomorphically evaluated. For simplicity we consider messages to be bits.

Definition 3 (Fully Homomorphic Encryption). *A fully homomorphic encryption scheme* FHE *is a tuple of* PPT *algorithms* (FHE.KeyGen, FHE.Enc, FHE.Dec, FHE.Eval), *where:*

- FHE.KeyGen(1^λ): *outputs a public encryption/evaluation key* pk *and a secret key* sk.
- FHE.Enc(pk, m): *outputs an encryption* ct *of message* $m \in \{0, 1\}$. *We denote by* $\mathcal{R}$ *the randomness space of* FHE.Enc.
- FHE.Dec$(\mathsf{sk}, \mathsf{ct})$: *uses* sk *to decrypt* ct. *It outputs a message.*
- FHE.Eval$(\mathsf{pk}, f, \mathsf{ct}_1 \ldots \mathsf{ct}_N)$: *it is a deterministic algorithm that takes as input a circuit* f *of arity* N, *and employs* pk *to compute an evaluated ciphertext* ct_f.

An FHE scheme must satisfy the following requirements:

Encryption Correctness. For all $\lambda \in \mathbb{N}$, all messages $m \in \{0,1\}$, all $(\mathsf{pk}, \mathsf{sk})$ in the support of $\mathsf{FHE.KeyGen}(1^\lambda)$, all ciphertexts ct in the support of $\mathsf{FHE.Enc}(\mathsf{pk}, m)$, we have $\mathsf{FHE.Dec}(\mathsf{sk}, \mathsf{ct}) = m$.

Evaluation Correctness. For all $\lambda \in \mathbb{N}$, all $(\mathsf{pk}, \mathsf{sk})$ in the support of $\mathsf{FHE.KeyGen}(1^\lambda)$, all messages $m_1, \ldots, m_N \in \{0,1\}$, all ciphertexts $(\mathsf{ct}_1 \ldots \mathsf{ct}_N)$ such that $\mathsf{FHE.Dec}(\mathsf{sk}, \mathsf{ct}_i) = m_i$ for all $i \in [N]$, all circuits f of arity N, it holds that:
$$\mathsf{FHE.Dec}(\mathsf{sk}, \mathsf{FHE.Eval}(\mathsf{pk}, f, \mathsf{ct}_1 \ldots \mathsf{ct}_N)) = f(m_1, \ldots, m_N).$$

Randomness Homomorphism. There exists an efficient deterministic algorithm $\mathsf{FHE.EvalRand}$ such that for all $\lambda \in \mathbb{N}$, all $(\mathsf{pk}, \mathsf{sk})$ in the support of $\mathsf{Setup}(1^\lambda)$, all messages $m_1, \ldots, m_N \in \{0,1\}$ and randomness $r_1, \ldots, r_N \in \mathcal{R}$, all circuits f of arity N, writing $r_f = \mathsf{FHE.EvalRand}(\mathsf{sk}, \mathsf{pk}, r_1, \ldots, r_N, m_1, \ldots, m_N, f)$ and $\mathsf{ct}_i = \mathsf{FHE.Enc}(\mathsf{pk}, m_i; r_i)$ for all $i \in [N]$, we have:

$$\mathsf{FHE.Enc}(\mathsf{pk}, f(m_1, \ldots, m_N); r_f) = \mathsf{FHE.Eval}(\mathsf{pk}, f, \mathsf{ct}_1, \ldots, \mathsf{ct}_N).$$

For most lattice-based FHE schemes, such as [GSW13], a stronger property holds: $\mathsf{EvalRand}$ can be publicly evaluated from the initial randomness and messages, and does not require sk (only pk). Nevertheless, the FHE scheme based on iO from [CLTV15] does require the use of the secret key to compute the evaluated randomness (which will consist of the key of a puncturable PRF). Both variants can be used as a building block in our construction.

Unique Randomness. For all $\lambda \in \mathbb{N}$, all $(\mathsf{pk}, \mathsf{sk})$ in the support of $\mathsf{FHE.KeyGen}(1^\lambda)$, all messages $m \in \{0,1\}$, all $r \in \mathcal{R}$ where $\mathcal{R}$ denotes the randomness space, there is no $r' \in \mathcal{R}$ such that $r' \neq r$ and $\mathsf{Enc}(\mathsf{pk}, m; r) = \mathsf{Enc}(\mathsf{pk}, m; r')$.

Selective IND-CPA Security. For any PPT adversary $\mathcal{A}$, we require that $\mathsf{Adv}^{\mathsf{FHE}}_{\mathsf{IND\text{-}CPA}}(\lambda, \mathcal{A})$ in the experiment $\mathsf{Exp\text{-}IND\text{-}CPA}$ from Fig. 4 is negligible, namely:

$$\mathsf{Adv}^{\mathsf{FHE}}_{\mathsf{IND\text{-}CPA}}(\lambda, \mathcal{A}) := \left| \Pr[\mathsf{Exp\text{-}IND\text{-}CPA}^{\mathsf{FHE}}(1^\lambda, \mathcal{A}) = 1] - \frac{1}{2} \right| \leq \mathsf{negl}(\lambda)$$

Experiment $\mathsf{Exp\text{-}IND\text{-}CPA}^{\mathsf{FHE}}(1^\lambda, \mathcal{A})$
$(m_0, m_1) \leftarrow \mathcal{A}(1^\lambda);$
$(\mathsf{pk}, \mathsf{sk}) \leftarrow \mathsf{FHE.Setup}(1^\lambda)$
$b \leftarrow_{\mathrm{R}} \{0,1\}$
$\mathsf{ct} \leftarrow \mathsf{FHE.Enc}(\mathsf{pk}, m_b)$
$b' \leftarrow \mathcal{A}(\mathsf{pk}, \mathsf{ct})$
Return $b = b'$

Fig. 4. Experiment Exp-IND-CPA for the selective indistinguishable security of FHE.

2.3 Indistinguishability Obfuscation

We recall the definition of indinstuighuishability obfuscation, originally from [BGI+01].

Definition 4 (Indistinguishability Obfuscator). *An indistinguishability obfuscator for a circuit class $\{\mathcal{C}_\lambda\}_{\lambda \in \mathbb{N}}$ is an efficient algorithm iO such that:*

- **Perfect correctness:** *for all $\lambda \in \mathbb{N}$, all $C \in \mathcal{C}_\lambda$, all inputs x, we have:*

$$\Pr[C' \leftarrow \mathsf{iO}(1^\lambda, C) : C'(x) = C(x)] = 1$$

- **Security:** *for all efficient algorithms $\mathcal{A}$, there exists a negligible function negl such that for all $\lambda \in \mathbb{N}$, all pairs of circuits $C_0, C_1 \in \mathcal{C}_\lambda$ such that $C_0(x) = C_1(x)$ for all inputs x, we have:*

$$\mathsf{Adv}^{\mathsf{iO}}(\lambda, \mathcal{A}) := |\Pr[\mathcal{A}(\mathsf{iO}(1^\lambda, C_0)) = 1] - \Pr[\mathcal{A}(\mathsf{iO}(1^\lambda, C_1)) = 1]| \leq \mathsf{negl}(\lambda)$$

2.4 Non-interactive Zero Knowledge Proofs

Given a binary relation $R : \mathcal{X} \times \mathcal{W} \to \{0, 1\}$ defined over a set of statements $\mathcal{X}$ and a set of witnesses $\mathcal{W}$, let $\mathcal{L}_R$ be the language defined as $\mathcal{L}_R = \{x \in \mathcal{X} \mid \exists w \in \mathcal{W} : R(x, w) = 1\}$. A Non-Interactive Zero Knowledge proof system for the binary relation R (originally introduced in [BFM88]) allows a prover in possession of a statement x and a witness w such that $R(x, w) = 1$ to produce a proof that convinces a verifier of the fact that $x \in L_R$ without revealing any information about w. The soundness property ensures that no proof can convince the verifier of the validity of a false statement, i.e. a statement $x \notin L_R$. We require the existence of an extractor that efficiently gets a witness from a valid proof π of a statement x, using an extraction trapdoor. Such proof systems are called *proofs of knowledge*. We focus on NIZK for relations R where the size of all statements and witnesses are bounded, which we call *size-bounded* relation. We now give the formal definition of NIZK proof of knowledge.

Definition 5 (NIZK-PoK). *Let R be a size-bounded relation. A Non-Interactive Zero-Knowledge Proof of Knowledge (NIZK-PoK) for R consists of the following PPT algorithms:*

- Setup(1^λ): *on input the security parameter, it outputs a common reference string crs and an extraction trapdoor $\mathsf{td}_{\mathsf{ext}}$.*
- Prove(crs, x, w): *on input crs, a statement x and a witness w, it outputs an argument π.*
- Verify(crs, x, π): *on input crs, a statement x and an argument π, it deterministically outputs a bit representing acceptance (1) or rejection (0).*

The PPT algorithms satisfy the following properties.

Composable Zero-Knowledge. There exist two PPT algorithms SimSetup and Sim such that for all PPT adversaries $\mathcal{A}$, the following advantages $\mathsf{Adv}_{\Pi}^{\mathsf{crs}}(\lambda, \mathcal{A})$ and $\mathsf{Adv}_{\Pi}^{\mathsf{ZK}}(\lambda, \mathcal{A})$ are negligible in λ:

$$\mathsf{Adv}_{\Pi}^{\mathsf{crs}}(\lambda, \mathcal{A}) = \left| 1/2 - \Pr \left[(\mathsf{crs}, \mathsf{td}_{\mathsf{ext}}) \leftarrow \mathsf{Setup}(1^\lambda), (\mathsf{crs}_{\mathsf{sim}}, \mathsf{td}_{\mathsf{sim}}) \leftarrow \mathsf{SimSetup}(1^\lambda), \right. \right.$$
$$\left. \left. b \leftarrow \{0,1\}, \mathsf{crs}_0 = \mathsf{crs}, \mathsf{crs}_1 = \mathsf{crs}_{\mathsf{sim}}, b' \leftarrow \mathcal{A}(\mathsf{crs}_b) : b' = b \right] \right|.$$

$$\mathsf{Adv}_{\Pi}^{\mathsf{ZK}}(\lambda, \mathcal{A}) = \left| 1/2 - \Pr \left[(x, w) \leftarrow \mathcal{A}(1^\lambda), (\mathsf{crs}_{\mathsf{sim}}, \mathsf{td}_{\mathsf{sim}}) \leftarrow \mathsf{SimSetup}(1^\lambda), \right. \right.$$
$$\pi_0 \leftarrow \mathsf{Prove}(\mathsf{crs}_{\mathsf{sim}}, x, w), \pi_1 \leftarrow \mathsf{Sim}(\mathsf{crs}_{\mathsf{sim}}, \mathsf{td}_{\mathsf{sim}}, x),$$
$$\left. \left. b \leftarrow \{0,1\}, b' \leftarrow \mathcal{A}(\mathsf{crs}_{\mathsf{sim}}, \mathsf{td}_{\mathsf{sim}}, \pi_b) : R(x, w) = 1 \wedge b' = b \right] \right|.$$

Completeness on Simulated CRS. For all efficient adversaries $\mathcal{A}$, the following advantage is negligible in the security parameter $\lambda \in \mathbb{N}$: $\Pr \left[(x, w) \leftarrow \mathcal{A}(1^\lambda), (\mathsf{crs}_{\mathsf{sim}}, \mathsf{td}_{\mathsf{sim}}) \leftarrow \mathsf{NIZK.SimSetup}(1^\lambda), \pi \leftarrow \mathsf{NIZK.Prove}(\mathsf{crs}_{\mathsf{sim}}, x, w) : R(x, w) = 1 \wedge \mathsf{NIZK.Verify}(\mathsf{crs}_{\mathsf{sim}}, x, \pi) = 0 \right]$.

Knowledge-Soundness. There exists an efficient algorithm Extract such that the following probability $\nu_{\mathsf{sound}}(\lambda)$ is a negligible function of $\lambda \in \mathbb{N}$, defined as:

$$\nu_{\mathsf{sound}}(\lambda) = \Pr \left[(\mathsf{crs}, \mathsf{td}_{\mathsf{ext}}) \leftarrow \mathsf{Setup}(1^\lambda) : \exists \, \pi, x, w \in \mathsf{Supp}(\mathsf{Extract}(\mathsf{crs}, \mathsf{td}_{\mathsf{ext}}, x, \pi)) \right.$$
$$\left. s.t. \, \mathsf{Verify}(\mathsf{crs}, x, \pi) = 1 \wedge R(x, w) = 0 \right].$$

We say *subexponential* knowledge-soundness holds if ν_{sound} is subexponential in the security parameter λ.

2.5 Fully Homomorphic Signatures

We recall the definition of Fully-Homomorphic Signature (FHS), which was originally given in [BF11a]. When many datasets are present, the signing algorithm takes as an additional input a tag τ that identifies the dataset that is being signed. Only signatures issued for the same tag can be combined together. For simplicity, we focus on the single dataset setting here (where there are no tags), since [GVW15] showed how to generically transform any FHS for single dataset to many datasets. This transformation relies on regular (non-homomorphic) signature schemes. Again for simplicity, we focus on bit messages and Boolean functions.

Definition 6 (FHS, Single Dataset). *An FHS scheme is a tuple of* PPT *algorithms* $\Sigma = (\mathsf{KeyGen}, \mathsf{Sign}, \mathsf{Verify}, \mathsf{Eval})$, *such that:*

- $\mathsf{KeyGen}(1^\lambda, 1^N)$: *on input the security parameter* λ *and a data-size bound* N, *it generates a public verification key* vk, *along with a secret signing key* sk.

- Sign(sk, m, i): *on input the secret key* sk, *a message* $m \in \{0, 1\}$ *and an index* $i \in [N]$, *it outputs a signature* σ.
- Eval(vk, f, $(m_1, \sigma_1), \ldots, (m_N, \sigma_N)$): *on input the public key* vk, *a function* f *of arity* N *and pairs* (m_i, σ_i), *it deterministically outputs an evaluated signature* σ *of the message* $f(m_1, \ldots, m_N)$.
- Verify(vk, f, y, σ) : *on input the public key* vk, *a function* f, *a value* y *and a signature* σ, *it outputs a bit.* 0 *means the signature* σ *is deemed invalid,* 1 *means it is considered valid.*

The algorithms satisfy the following properties.

Perfect Signing Correctness. For all $\lambda, N \in \mathbb{N}$, all pairs (vk, sk) in the support of KeyGen($1^\lambda, 1^N$), all $i \in [N]$, all messages $m \in \{0, 1\}$, all signatures σ in the support of Sign(sk, m, i), we have Verify(vk, id_i, m, σ) $= 1$, where id_i is the projection function that takes N messages $m_1, \ldots, m_N \in \{0, 1\}$, and outputs the i'th message m_i.

In our scheme, we achieve a weaker, computational variant of the correctness property, which roughly states that an efficient algorithm cannot find messages (with more than negligible probability) on which properly generated signatures do not verify successfully.

Computational Signing Correctness. For all efficient algorithms $\mathcal{A}$, the following probability, defined for all $\lambda, N \in \mathbb{N}$ is negligible in λ: $\Pr[(\mathsf{vk}, \mathsf{sk}) \leftarrow \mathsf{Setup}(1^\lambda, 1^N), (m_1, \ldots, m_N) \leftarrow \mathcal{A}(\mathsf{vk}), \forall i \in [N], \sigma_i \leftarrow \mathsf{Sign}(\mathsf{sk}, m_i, i) : \exists i \in [N] \text{ s.t. } \mathsf{Verify}(\mathsf{vk}, \mathrm{id}_i, m_i, \sigma_i) = 0]$.

Perfect Evaluation Correctness. For all $\lambda, N \in \mathbb{N}$, all pairs (vk, sk) in the support of KeyGen($1^\lambda, 1^N$), all messages $m_1, \ldots, m_N \in \{0, 1\}$, all signatures $\sigma_1, \ldots, \sigma_N$ in the support of Sign(sk, m_1), $\ldots$, Sign(sk, m_N) respectively, for all functions f of arity N, writing $\sigma_f = \mathsf{Eval}(\mathsf{vk}, f, (\sigma_1, m_1), \ldots, (\sigma_N, m_N))$ and $y = f(m_1, \ldots, m_N)$, we have Verify(vk, f, y, σ_f) $= 1$. Moreover, it is possible to perform additional homomorphic operations on signatures that have already been evaluated on. That is, correctness holds when functions are composed. Namely, for all $\ell \in \mathbb{N}$, all functions g of arity ℓ, all tuples $(\sigma_1, f_1, m_1), \ldots, (\sigma_\ell, f_\ell, m_\ell)$ such that for all $i \in [\ell]$, Verify(vk, f_i, m_i, σ_i) $= 1$, writing $\mathsf{Eval}(\mathsf{vk}, g, (m_1, \sigma_1), \ldots, (m_\ell, \sigma_\ell)) = \sigma$ and $y = g(m_1, \ldots, m_\ell)$, we have Verify(vk, g, y, σ) $= 1$.

Similarly to signing correctness, we define a computational variant of the evaluation correctness. For simplicity, we split the property into two properties: the first is a computational evaluation correctness that only consider one-shot homomorphic evaluation, but does not take into account the possibility of performing homomorphic evaluations in several steps, i.e. composing functions. The second property, called weak context hiding, states that composing functions using Eval many times yields the same signature as using Eval once on the composed function. The (non-weak) context hiding property additionally requires that evaluated signatures be independent of the underlying dataset, apart from the output of the evaluated function.

Computational Evaluation Correctness. For all efficient algorithms $\mathcal{A}$, the following probability, defined for all $\lambda, N \in \mathbb{N}$, is negligible in λ: $\Pr[(\mathsf{vk}, \mathsf{sk}) \leftarrow \mathsf{Setup}(1^\lambda, 1^N), (m_1, \ldots, m_N, f) \leftarrow \mathcal{A}(\mathsf{vk}), \forall i \in [N], \sigma_i \leftarrow \mathsf{Sign}(\mathsf{sk}, m_i, i), \sigma_f \leftarrow \mathsf{Eval}(\mathsf{vk}, f, (m_1, \sigma_1), \ldots, (m_N, \sigma_N)), y = f(m_1, \ldots, m_N) : \mathsf{Verify}(\mathsf{vk}, f, y, \sigma_f) = 0]$.

Weak Context Hiding. For all $\lambda, N, t, \ell \in \mathbb{N}$, all $(\mathsf{vk}, \mathsf{sk})$ in the support of $\mathsf{Setup}(1^\lambda, 1^N)$, all messages $m_1, \ldots, m_t \in \{0,1\}$, functions $\theta_1, \ldots, \theta_t$ and signatures $\sigma_1, \ldots, \sigma_t$ such that for all $i \in [t]$, $\mathsf{Verify}(\mathsf{vk}, \theta_i, m_i, \sigma_i) = 1$, all t-ary functions $f_1, \ldots, f_\ell$, all ℓ-ary functions g, we have:

$$\sigma_{g \circ \vec{f}} = \sigma_h,$$

where $\sigma_{g \circ \vec{f}} = \mathsf{Eval}(\mathsf{vk}, g, (\sigma_{f_1}, f_1(\vec{m})), \ldots, (\sigma_{f_\ell}, f_\ell(\vec{m})))$, $\sigma_{f_j} = \mathsf{Eval}(\mathsf{vk}, f_j, (\sigma_1, m_1), \ldots, (\sigma_t, m_t))$ for all $j \in [\ell]$, $\sigma_h = \mathsf{Eval}(\mathsf{vk}, h, (\sigma_1, m_1), \ldots, (\sigma_t, m_t))$, h is the t-ary function defined on any input $m_1, \ldots, m_t$ as $h(\vec{m}) = g(f_1(\vec{m}), \ldots, f_\ell(\vec{m})))$, which we denote by $h = g \circ \vec{f}$. We are also using the notation $\vec{m} = (m_1, \ldots, m_t)$.

Pre-processing. The scheme can be endowed with a pre-processing algorithm Process. Just like the FHS scheme from [GVW15], our Verify algorithm works in two steps. The first step only depends on the inputs vk and f. Thus, it can be run offline, before knowing the signature σ and message y to verify. It produces a short processed vk, denoted by α_f (whose size is independent of the size of f). This first phase constitutes the Process algorithm. The second, online step takes as input α_f, y and σ and outputs a bit. The online step runs in time independent of the complexity of f.

Adaptive Unforgeability. For all stateful PPT adversaries $\mathcal{A}$ and all data bound $N \in \mathbb{N}$, the advantage $\mathsf{Adv}_\Sigma^{\mathsf{forg}}(\lambda, \mathcal{A})$ defined below is a negligible function of the security parameter $\lambda \in \mathbb{N}$:

$$\mathsf{Adv}_\Sigma^{\mathsf{forg}}(\lambda, \mathcal{A}) = \Pr\Big[(\mathsf{sk}, \mathsf{vk}) \leftarrow \mathsf{Setup}(1^\lambda, 1^N), (m_1, \ldots, m_N) \leftarrow \mathcal{A}(\mathsf{vk}),$$
$$\forall i \in [N], \sigma_i \leftarrow \mathsf{Sign}(\mathsf{sk}, m_i, i), (f, y, \sigma^\star) \leftarrow \mathcal{A}(\sigma_1, \ldots, \sigma_N) :$$
$$\mathsf{Verify}(\mathsf{vk}, f, y, \sigma^\star) = 1 \wedge y \neq f(m_1, \ldots, m_n)\Big].$$

Selective unforgeability is defined identically except the adversary $\mathcal{A}$ must send the messages $m_1, \ldots, m_n$ of its choice *before* seeing the public key vk.

3   Construction

We describe our unleveled FHS scheme in Fig. 5. We choose to focus on single dataset FHS (as per Definition 6) rather that multi datasets for simplicity, since the work of [GVW15] presents a generic transformation from single to multi datasets, relying only on (non-homomorphic) signatures. Our FHS is for bit messages, and can evaluate arbitrary Boolean circuits. Without loss of generality, we focus on evaluating binary NAND gates.

We use a puncturable PRF, an indistinguishability obfuscator iO, an FHE scheme and a NIZK-PoK as building blocks, whose definition are given in the previous section. Our construction can be implemented using the dual-mode NIZK from [GS08] (from pairings) or [HU19] (from iO and lossy trapdoor functions), for instance. The FHE can be implemented using most lattice-based FHE (with bootstrapping since the FHE must be unleveled, which requires circular security), or with the construction from [CLTV15], which does not require any circularity assumption (it relies on iO and lossy trapdoor functions). Altogether, if we use the NIZK from [HU19] and the FHE from [CLTV15] we obtain our main result, which follows from Theorem 12 (unforgeability of our FHS).

Theorem 7 (Main Result). *Assume the existence of subexponentially secure iO and lossy trapdoor functions. Then subexponentially adaptively unforgeable unleveled FHS exist.*

3.1   Choice of Parameters

In our FHS, we rely on building blocks PRF, iO, NIZK, FHE that are subexponentially secure, that is, for which efficient adversaries can succeed with at most advantage $2^{-\kappa^\varepsilon}$ in breaking the security, for a constant $\varepsilon > 0$, where κ is the parameter chosen to run the setup of these primitives. We denote by κ_1 the parameter used for FHE and by κ_2 the parameter used for PRF, iO, and NIZK. Correctness is satisfied as long as the Eqs. (1) and (2) hold. Adaptive unforgeability is satisfied as long as the Eq. (3) holds. These equations are simultaneously satisfied when:

$$\kappa_1 = (N + \log N + 2\log^2 \lambda)^{1/\varepsilon}$$
$$\kappa_2 = \left(|ct| + N + \log N + 2\log^2 \lambda + O(1)\right)^{1/\varepsilon}$$

where $|ct|$ denotes the size of the FHE ciphertexts.

3.2   Correctness of the FHS

In this section we prove the computational signing correctness, the computational evaluation correctness, the weak context hiding and the pre-processing property of our scheme, all given in Definition 6.

FHS.KeyGen$(1^\lambda, 1^N)$	GenCRS(level)
$(\mathsf{fpk}, \mathsf{fsk}) \leftarrow \mathsf{FHE.Setup}(1^{\kappa_1})$	Hardcoded: key K_1
$\{\mathsf{ct}'_i \leftarrow \mathsf{FHE.Enc}(0)\}_{i \in \{1...N\}}$	$r = \mathsf{PRF}(K_1, \mathsf{level})$
$K_1, K_2 \leftarrow \mathsf{PRF.KeyGen}(1^{\kappa_2})$	$(\mathsf{crs}_{\mathsf{sim}}, \mathsf{td}_{\mathsf{sim}}) = \mathsf{NIZK.SimSetup}(1^{\kappa_2}; r)$
$\mathsf{Obf}_{\mathsf{GenCRS}} \leftarrow \mathsf{iO}(1^{\kappa_2}, \mathsf{PubGenCRS})$	Return $(\mathsf{crs}_{\mathsf{sim}}, \mathsf{td}_{\mathsf{sim}})$
$\mathsf{Obf}_{\mathsf{Eval}} \leftarrow \mathsf{iO}(1^{\kappa_2}, \mathsf{EvalNAND})$	
$\mathsf{vk} = (\mathsf{fpk}, \{\mathsf{ct}'_i\}, \mathsf{Obf}_{\mathsf{GenCRS}}, \mathsf{Obf}_{\mathsf{Eval}})$	PubGenCRS(level)
$\mathsf{sk} = (K_1, K_2, \mathsf{fsk})$	$(\mathsf{crs}_{\mathsf{sim}}, \mathsf{td}_{\mathsf{sim}}) = \mathsf{GenCRS}(\mathsf{level})$
Return $(\mathsf{vk}, \mathsf{sk})$	Return $\mathsf{crs}_{\mathsf{sim}}$
FHS.Sign(sk, m, i)	EvalNAND$((\sigma_0, m_0), (\sigma_1, m_1))$
$(\mathsf{crs}_{\mathsf{sim}}, \mathsf{td}_{\mathsf{sim}}) = \mathsf{GenCRS}(0)$	Hardcoded: key K_2
$\pi \leftarrow \mathsf{NIZK.Sim}(\mathsf{crs}_{\mathsf{sim}}, \mathsf{td}_{\mathsf{sim}}, \mathsf{stat}_{m, \mathsf{ct}'_i})$	Parse σ_b as $(\mathsf{ct}_b, \pi_b, \mathsf{level}_b)$, for $b \in \{0, 1\}$
$\sigma = (\mathsf{ct}'_i, \pi, 0)$	Return $\perp$ if $\mathsf{level}_0 \neq \mathsf{level}_1$
Return σ	$\mathsf{level} = \mathsf{level}_0$
	$(\mathsf{crs}_{\mathsf{sim}}, \mathsf{td}_{\mathsf{sim}}) = \mathsf{GenCRS}(\mathsf{level})$
FHS.Verify$(\mathsf{vk}, f, y, \sigma)$	If $\mathsf{NIZK.Verify}(\mathsf{crs}_{\mathsf{sim}}, \mathsf{stat}_{m_b, \mathsf{ct}_b}, \pi_b) = 0$
Parse σ as $(\mathsf{ct}, \pi, \mathsf{level})$	$\quad$ for some $b \in \{0, 1\}$ then return $\perp$
$\mathsf{ct}_f = \mathsf{FHE.Eval}(\mathsf{fpk}, f, \mathsf{ct}'_1, \ldots, \mathsf{ct}'_N)$	$\mathsf{ct} = \mathsf{FHE.Eval}(\mathsf{fpk}, \mathsf{NAND}, \mathsf{ct}_0, \mathsf{ct}_1)$
$\mathsf{crs} = \mathsf{Obf}_{\mathsf{GenCRS}}(\mathsf{level})$	$m = \mathsf{NAND}(m_0, m_1)$
Return $\mathsf{NIZK.Verify}(\mathsf{crs}, \mathsf{stat}_{y, \mathsf{ct}_f}, \pi)$	$(\mathsf{crs}'_{\mathsf{sim}}, \mathsf{td}'_{\mathsf{sim}}) = \mathsf{GenCRS}(\mathsf{level} + 1)$
	$\rho = \mathsf{PRF}(K_2, (m, \mathsf{ct}, \mathsf{level} + 1))$
FHS.Eval$(\mathsf{vk}, f, (m_1, \sigma_1) \ldots (m_N, \sigma_N))$	$\pi = \mathsf{NIZK.Sim}(\mathsf{crs}'_{\mathsf{sim}}, \mathsf{td}'_{\mathsf{sim}}, \mathsf{stat}_{m, \mathsf{ct}}; \rho)$
Evaluate each NAND gate of f	$\sigma = (\mathsf{ct}, \pi, \mathsf{level} + 1)$
$\quad$ using $\mathsf{Obf}_{\mathsf{Eval}}$ and return the result.	Return σ

Fig. 5. Fully-homomorphic signature scheme $\mathsf{FHS} = (\mathsf{FHS.KeyGen}, \mathsf{FHS.Sign}, \mathsf{FHS.}$ $\mathsf{Verify}, \mathsf{FHS.Eval})$. PRF is a puncturable pseudo-random function, NIZK is a proof of knowledge (NIZK PoK), FHE is a fully-homomorphic encryption scheme, and iO is an indistinguishability obfuscator. By $\mathsf{stat}_{m, \mathsf{ct}}$ we denote the statement which claims that $\exists\, r \in \mathcal{R}$ such that $\mathsf{ct} = \mathsf{FHE.Enc}(\mathsf{fpk}, m; r)$, where $\mathcal{R}$ denotes the randomness space of the FHE encryption algorithm. Parameters $\kappa(\lambda) = (N + 2\log^2 \lambda + 5)^{1/\varepsilon}$, where $\varepsilon > 0$ is a constant whose existence is ensure by the subexponential security of the underlying building blocks.

Lemma 8 (Computational Signing Correctness). *The FHS scheme from Fig. 5 satisfies the computational signing correctness as per Definition 6, assuming NIZK satisfies the subexponential composable zero-knowledge and completeness on simulated crs properties (as per Definition 5), FHE satisfies the subexponential (selective) IND-CPA security (as per Definition 3), PRF satisfies the subexponential pseudorandomness at punctured points and the functionality preservation under puncturing (as per Definition 1) and iO satisfies the correctness and subexponential security properties (as per Definition 4).*

Proof. We first explain how to prove the computational signing property in the selective case, where $\mathcal{A}$ sends the messages $m_1, \ldots, m_N \in \{0, 1\}$ before receiving vk. In this case, we can prove correctness using a hybrid argument, where we first switch the ciphertexts ct'_i from vk to FHE.Enc($fpk, m_i; r_i$), using the selective IND-CPA security of FHE. Then, we want to change the way FHS.Sign(sk, m_i, i) computes the ZK proofs, using $\pi \leftarrow$ NIZK.Prove($crs_{sim}, stat_{m_i, ct'_i}, r_i$), where r_i is a witness for $stat_{m_i, ct'_i}$, instead of producing $\pi \leftarrow$ NIZK.Sim($crs_{sim}, td_{sim}, stat_{m_i, ct'_i}$). This change would be justified by the composable zero knowledge property of NIZK. Finally, we would conclude the correctness proof using the completeness of NIZK on the simulated crs_{sim}. To perform these changes, we first need to puncture the PRF key K_1 on the point 0, and hardcode the pair $(crs_{sim}, td_{sim}) =$ NIZK.SimSetup($1^{\kappa_2};$ PRF($K_1, 0$)) in the obfuscated circuits (which relies on the functionality preservation under puncturing of PRF and the security of iO), then switch the value PRF($K_1, 0$) to truly random (which relies on the pseudorandomness at punctured points of PRF). Then, we can switch the way the proof π is computed by FHS.Sign(sk, m_i, i) as we explained, using the composable zero-knowledge property of NIZK. Finally use the completeness on simulated crs property of NIZK. To obtain correctness in the adaptive case, where $\mathcal{A}$ can choose the messages $m_1, \ldots, m_N$ after seeing vk, we simply guess all the messages m_i in advance, which incurs a security loss of 2^N. Since we assume subexponential security of the underlying building blocks, we know that an adversary against the selective correctness can only succeed with a probability $N \cdot 2^{-\kappa_1^\varepsilon} + 4 \cdot 2^{-\kappa_2^\varepsilon}$ for $\varepsilon > 0$ where κ_1 is the parameter used for FHE, and κ_2 is the parameter used for NIZK, PRF and iO. Note that ε does not depend on N, so we can choose κ_1, κ_2 as polynomials in the security parameter λ and the arity N such that $2^N(N \cdot 2^{-\kappa_1^\varepsilon} + 4 \cdot 2^{-\kappa_2^\varepsilon})$ is a negligible function of λ, e.g.

$$\kappa_1, \kappa_2 \geq (N + \log N + \log^2 \lambda)^{1/\varepsilon}. \tag{1}$$

Lemma 9 (Computational Evaluation Correctness). *The FHS scheme from Fig. 5 satisfies the computational evaluation correctness as per Definition 6, assuming NIZK satisfies the subexponential zero-knowledge and and completeness on simulated crs properties (as per Definition 5), FHE satisfies the subexponential (selective) IND-CPA security and the randomness homomorphism properties (as per Definition 3), PRF satisfies the subexponential pseudorandomness at punctured points and the functionality preservation under puncturing (as per Definition 1) and iO satisfies the subexponential security and the perfect correctness properties (as per Definition 4).*

Proof. First, we prove the evaluation correctness in the selective case where the adversary $\mathcal{A}$ sends the messages $m_1, \ldots, m_N$ and the depth d of the circuit f before seeing the public key vk. Then, $\mathcal{A}$ receives vk and chooses the circuit f of depth d. To obtain computational evaluation correctness in the adaptive setting where $\mathcal{A}$ can choose f and the messages $m_1, \ldots, m_N$ after seeing vk (as per Definition 3), we will use a guessing argument together with the subexponential security of the underlying building blocks similarly than for proving the signing correctness. Namely, we choose a superpolynomial function $L(\lambda)$, e.g. $L(\lambda) = 2^{\log^2 \lambda}$ and we guess the messages $m_1, \ldots, m_N$ at random over $\{0, 1\}^N$ and the depth d at random between 1 and $L(\lambda)$. Because we choose $L(\lambda)$ superpolynomial, we know that the depth d chosen by $\mathcal{A}$ is less than $L(\lambda)$, so the guess of the depth is correct with probability $1/L(\lambda)$. Overall the guessing incurs a security loss of $2^N L(\lambda)$.

Now we prove the selective variant of computational evaluation soundness. To begin with, we switch the ciphertexts ct'_i in vk to FHE encryptions of m_i of the form $\mathsf{FHE.Enc}(\mathsf{fpk}, m_i; r_i)$, using the selective IND-CPA security of FHE, just as in the computational signing correctness proof. Moreover, by perfect correctness of iO, we know that an evaluated signature $\sigma_f = \mathsf{Eval}(\mathsf{vk}, f, (\sigma_1, m_1), \ldots, (\sigma_N, m_N))$ is of the form $\sigma_f = (\mathsf{ct}, \pi, d)$ where $\mathsf{ct} = \mathsf{FHE.Eval}(\mathsf{fpk}, f, \mathsf{ct}'_1, \ldots \mathsf{ct}'_N)$, and d is the depth of f. By evaluation correctness of FHE, we know that ct is an encryption of the message $f(m_1, \ldots, m_N)$. In fact, by the randomness homomorphism property of FHE, we know that $\mathsf{ct} = \mathsf{FHE.Enc}(\mathsf{fpk}, f(m_1, \ldots, m_N); r_f)$ where $r_f = \mathsf{FHE.EvalRand}(\mathsf{fsk}, r_1, \ldots, r_N, m_1, \ldots, m_N, f)$. Then, we want to switch the way the proof π in σ_f is computed: using NIZK.Prove and the witness r_f instead of using NIZK.Sim and the simulation trapdoor $\mathsf{td}_{\mathsf{sim}}$. This switch would be justified by the composable zero-knowledge property of NIZK. We would then conclude the proof using the completeness of NIZK on simulated crs. Only to use these properties of NIZK, we first need to generate $(\mathsf{crs}_{\mathsf{sim}}, \mathsf{td}_{\mathsf{sim}})$ of level d using truly random coins, as opposed to pseudo-random. As typical, this requires puncturing the PRF key K_1 and hardcoding the pair $(\mathsf{crs}_{\mathsf{sim}}, \mathsf{td}_{\mathsf{sim}}) = \mathsf{NIZK.Setup}(1^{\kappa_2}; \mathsf{PRF}(K_1, d))$ in the obfuscated circuits (thanks to the security of iO and the functionality preservation under puncturing of PRF), then switching the value $\mathsf{PRF}(K_1, d)$ to truly random (thanks to the pseudo-randomness at punctured points property of PRF). Afterwards, we can use the properties of NIZK to conclude the proof, as we explained.

Since we assume subexponential security of the underlying building blocks, we know that an adversary against the selective computational evaluation correctness can only succeed with a probability $N \cdot 2^{-\kappa_1^\varepsilon} + 4 \cdot 2^{-\kappa_2^\varepsilon}$ for $\varepsilon > 0$ where κ_1 is the parameter used for FHE, and κ_2 is the parameter used for NIZK, PRF and iO. Note that ε does not depend on N, so we can choose κ_1, κ_2 as polynomials in the security parameter λ and the arity N such that $2^N L(\lambda)(N \cdot 2^{-\kappa_1^\varepsilon} + 4 \cdot 2^{-\kappa_2^\varepsilon})$ is a negligible function of λ, e.g.

$$\kappa_1, \kappa_2 \geq (N + \log N + 2 \log^2 \lambda)^{1/\varepsilon}. \tag{2}$$

Lemma 10 (Weak Context Hiding). *The FHS scheme from Fig. 5 satisfies the weak context hiding property as per Definition 6, assuming the perfect correctness of iO.*

Proof. This property follows straightforwardly from the description of the Eval algorithm and the correctness of iO. Indeed, Eval evaluates circuits gate by gate, using the EvalNAND algorithm (see Fig. 5), which performs deterministic evaluation on the FHE ciphertext, and then derive a ZK proof deterministically from the statement and the depth level (using PRF on the key K_2). Thus, we have $\sigma_{g \circ f} = \sigma_h$.

Lemma 11 (Pre-processing). *The FHS scheme from Fig. 5 satisfies the pre-processing property as per Definition 6.*

Proof. This simply follows from the description of FHS.Verify. First, during a pre-processing phase, it computes the values ct_f and crs from vk and f. This can be performed offline, since it does not require to know the message y and the signature σ. The result is a short pre-processed key $\alpha_f = (ct_f, crs)$. Then, during the online phase, FHS.Verify uses α_f, σ and y to run the NIZK.Verify algorithm. The running time of this online phase is independent from the size or depth of f.

4   Proof of Unforgeability

Theorem 12 (Adaptive Unforgeability). *Assuming subexponential security of* PRF, FHE, iO, *and* NIZK, *the FHS from Fig. 5 satisfies subexponential unforgeability as per Definition 6.*

Proof of Theorem 12. We first prove the selective unforgeability (as per Definition 6), where the adversary $\mathcal{A}$ must send the messages $m_1, \ldots, m_N$ before receiving vk. Then we show how to obtain adaptive unforgeability using a guessing argument and the subexponential security of the underlying building blocks (just as in the proof of computational signing and evaluation correctness in the previous section).

To prove unforgeability in the selective setting, we use a sequence of hybrid games, starting with G_0, defined exactly as the selective unforgeability game from Definition 6. For any game G_i, we denote by $Adv_i(\mathcal{A})$ the advantage of $\mathcal{A}$ in G_i, that is, $\Pr[G_i(1^\lambda, \mathcal{A}) = 1]$, where the probability is taken over the random coins of G_i and $\mathcal{A}$. Before we proceed to describe the other hybrids, we make several technical remarks.

Remark 13. When we hardcode a value in a subprogram, it is understood that this value is also hardcoded in all the programs that run it, and if a PRF key K is punctured in a subprogram, it is also punctured in all the programs that run it.

Remark 14 (Padding the programs). The security of iO can only be invoked for programs of the same size. For brevity, we assume without loss of generality that all programs in the security proof are padded to the size of the longest program. Since our hybrids extend up to a superpolynomial level $L(\lambda) = 2^{\omega(\log \lambda)}$, this implies a small increase in the programs contained in the real verification key (since the last hybrid must keep track of the level, and its bit representation requires $\omega(\log \lambda)$ bits). For example, choosing $L(\lambda) = 2^{\log^2 \lambda}$ would only incur a multiplicative increase by a factor of $\log^2 \lambda$ bits.

Remark 15 (Bounding the Sizes of Punctured PRF Keys). The security proof will require that PRF keys K_1 and K_2 are punctured at levels $i = 0 \ldots L(\lambda)$, where $L(\lambda) = 2^{\log^2 \lambda}$. Puncturing increases the size of the keys. In existing constructions of PRFs (e.g. [GGM84]), the size of the punctured keys only grows logarithmically with the number of levels This results in a size-increase of the keys (and therefore of the programs) of up to $O(\log^2 \lambda)$. In particular, it is important to note that this size increase is independent of the value of the specific level at which the adversary will output a forgery.

- **Game G_1**: same as G_0, except that we change the FHS.KeyGen algorithm. Instead of computing the ct'_i in the verification key as encryptions of 0, we compute $ct'_i \leftarrow$ FHE.Enc$(m_i; r_i)$, where m_i are the messages sent by $\mathcal{A}$. The randomness r_i used to compute the ciphertext ct'_i is stored in the secret key sk.

Lemma 16 (From G_0 to G_1). *For every* PPT *adversary* $\mathcal{A}$, *there exists a* PPT *adversary* $\mathcal{B}$, *such that:* $|\mathsf{Adv}_0(\mathcal{A}) - \mathsf{Adv}_1(\mathcal{A})| \leq \mathsf{Adv}^{\mathsf{FHE}}_{\mathsf{IND\text{-}CPA}}(\kappa_1, \mathcal{B})$.

Proof. The reduction $\mathcal{B}$ starts by sending $(0 \ldots 0)$ and $(m_1 \ldots m_N)$ to the IND-CPA challenger. It receives $(ct'_1 \ldots ct'_N)$, which it embeds in the vk. During the execution of FHS.KeyGen, all the other obfuscated programs in vk are generated as before, but using the ciphertexts received from the challenger.

- **Game G_2**: same as G_1, except that we change the FHS.Sign algorithm and replace it with HybridSign, defined in Fig. 6. The latter computes the signatures $\sigma_1, \ldots, \sigma_N$ sent to $\mathcal{A}$ (after $\mathcal{A}$ sends the messages $m_1, \ldots, m_N$) as $\sigma_i = (ct'_i, \pi_i, 0)$ where $ct'_i =$ FHE.Enc$(\mathsf{fpk}, m_i; r_i)$ is the i'th FHE encryption contained in vk, 0 indicates the level, and π_i is computed using the witness r_i (which is stored in sk), instead of using a simulation trapdoor.

Lemma 17 (From G_1 to G_2). *For every PPT adversary* $\mathcal{A}$, *there exist PPT adversaries* $\mathcal{B}_1$, $\mathcal{B}_2$, $\mathcal{B}_3$ *such that:*

$$|\mathsf{Adv}_1(\mathcal{A}) - \mathsf{Adv}_2(\mathcal{A})| \leq 2\big(\mathsf{Adv}_{\mathsf{cPRF}}(\kappa_2, \mathcal{B}_1) + \mathsf{Adv}_{\mathsf{iO}}(\kappa_2, \mathcal{B}_2)\big) + N \cdot \mathsf{Adv}_{\mathsf{ZK}}(\kappa_2, \mathcal{B}_3).$$

Proof. To switch from proofs π_i generated using NIZK.Sim and the simulation trapdoor $\mathsf{td}_{\mathsf{sim}}$ to proofs generated using NIZK.Prove and the witnesses r_i, as described in Fig. 6, we want to use the composable zero-knowledge property of NIZK. To do so, we first have to hard-code the pair $(\mathsf{crs}_{\mathsf{sim}}, \mathsf{td}_{\mathsf{sim}}) =$ NIZK.SimSetup$(1^{\kappa_2}; \mathsf{PRF}(K_1, 0))$ in the obfuscated circuit instead of using the key K_1 on the point 0. To generate the pairs $(\mathsf{crs}_{\mathsf{sim}}, \mathsf{td}_{\mathsf{sim}})$ for all other levels $i \neq 0$, we compute $(\mathsf{crs}_{\mathsf{sim}}, \mathsf{td}_{\mathsf{sim}}) =$ NIZK.SimSetup$(1^{\kappa_2}; \mathsf{PRF}(K_1\{0\}, i))$, where $K_1\{0\}$ is a key punctured at the point 0. Because puncturing preserves the functionality of PRF (as per Definition 1), this does not change the input/output behavior of the obfuscated circuit. Thus we can use the iO security to argue that this change is computational undetectable by the adversary. Then, we switch the hardcoded pair $(\mathsf{crs}_{\mathsf{sim}}, \mathsf{td}_{\mathsf{sim}}) =$ NIZK.SimSetup$(1^{\kappa_2}; \mathsf{PRF}(K_1, 0))$ to $(\mathsf{crs}_{\mathsf{sim}}, \mathsf{td}_{\mathsf{sim}}) =$ NIZK.SimSetup$(1^{\kappa_2}; r_0)$, where r_0 is truly random. This is possible by the pseudorandomness property at punctured points of PRF. Then, we use the composable zero-knowledge property of NIZK to switch π_i to $\pi_i \leftarrow$

NIZK.Prove(crs_{sim}, $stat_{ct'_i, m_i}$, r_i) for all $i \in [N]$. Finally we switch back the generation of the pairs (crs_{sim}, td_{sim}) using pseudo-random coins for all levels (instead of using truly random coins for the level 0) and we unpuncture the key K_1.

HybridSign(sk, m_i, i)

$crs_{sim} = PubGenCRS(0)$

$\pi_i \leftarrow$ NIZK.Prove(crs, $stat_{m_i, ct'_i}$, r_i)

$\sigma_i = (ct'_i, \pi_i, 0)$

Return σ_i

Fig. 6. In G_2, we replace the FHS.Sign algorithm with HybridSign. Changes are highlighted in gray.

- **Game $G_{3,\ell}$:** At this point, the proof proceeds in a series of $L(\lambda) = 2^{\log^2 \lambda}$ hybrids where $G_{3,\ell}$ is defined for all $\ell = \{0, \ldots, L(\lambda)\}$ identically to G_2, except that:
  1. the program GenCRS is replaced by HybridGenCRS$^\ell$, described in Fig. 7. The latter generates a crs with an extraction trapdoor using NIZK.Setup on any level $< \ell$, and generates a simulated crs with a simulation trapdoor using NIZK.SimSetup on any level $\geq \ell$.
  2. the program EvalNAND is replaced by HybridEvalNAND$^\ell$, described in Fig. 7. For any level $< \ell$, the latter generates proofs for the next level using witnesses obtained using an extraction trapdoor and the randomness homomorphic property of FHE. For any level $\geq \ell$, it generates proofs for the next level using a simulation trapdoor.
  Note that $G_{3,0} = G_2$. In Theorem 18, we prove that for all $\ell \in \{0, \ldots, L(\lambda) - 1\}$, $G_{3,\ell} \approx_c G_{3,\ell+1}$.
- **Game G_4:** same as $G_{3,L(\lambda)}$, except the game guesses the depth of the function f chosen by the adversary $\mathcal{A}$ for his forgery, by sampling $d^\star \leftarrow_R \{1, \ldots, L(\lambda)\}$. At the end of the game, $\mathcal{A}$ sends the forgery $(f, y, \sigma^\star)$. If $d^\star \neq d$, then the game G_4 outputs 0. Otherwise it proceeds as in $G_{3,L(\lambda)}$. Since $L(\lambda)$ has been chosen super polynomial in λ, we know that the function f has depth $d \leq L(\lambda)$. Thus, with probability $1/L(\lambda)$, the guess is correct, i.e. we have $d^\star = d$. Therefore,

$$\mathsf{Adv}_4(\mathcal{A}) = \frac{\mathsf{Adv}_{3,L(\lambda)}(\mathcal{A})}{L(\lambda)}.$$

- **Game G_5:** same as G_4, except we puncture the key K_1 at $d^\star$ and hardcode the value $PRF(K_1, d^\star)$ in the obfuscated circuit. Since puncturing preserve the functionality, we can use the security of iO to argue that there exists a PPT adversary $\mathcal{B}_5$ such that:

$$|\mathsf{Adv}_5(\mathcal{A}) - \mathsf{Adv}_4(\mathcal{A})| = \mathsf{Adv}_{iO}(\kappa_2, \mathcal{B}_5).$$

– **Game G_6**: same as G_5, except we change the value $\mathsf{PRF}(K_1, d^\star)$ hardcoded in the obfuscated circuit is turned to a truly random value. By the pseudorandomness of PRF on punctured points, we know there exists a PPT $\mathcal{B}_6$ such that:

$$|\mathsf{Adv}_6(\mathcal{A}) - \mathsf{Adv}_5(\mathcal{A})| = \mathsf{Adv}_{\mathsf{cPRF}}(\kappa_2, \mathcal{B}_6).$$

We now proceed to bound $\mathsf{Adv}_6(\mathcal{A})$. By the knowledge soundness property of NIZK, we know that $\mathsf{Adv}_6(\mathcal{A}) \leq \nu_{\mathsf{sound}}(\kappa_2)$. Putting things together, we have $\mathsf{Adv}_4(\mathcal{A}) \leq \nu_{\mathsf{sound}}(\kappa) + \mathsf{Adv}_{\mathsf{cPRF}}(\kappa_2, \mathcal{B}_6) + \mathsf{Adv}_{\mathsf{iO}}(\kappa_2, \mathcal{B}_5)$ and $\mathsf{Adv}_3(\mathcal{A}) = L(\lambda)\mathsf{Adv}_4(\mathcal{A})$. Together with the result of Theorem 18, we have:

$$\begin{aligned}
\mathsf{Adv}_0(\mathcal{A}) \leq &(2^{|\mathsf{ct}|+2} + L(\lambda) + 8)\mathsf{Adv}_{\mathsf{iO}}(\kappa_2, \mathcal{B}_1) + (2^{|\mathsf{ct}|+2} + L(\lambda) + 6)\mathsf{Adv}_{\mathsf{cPRF}}(\kappa_2, \mathcal{B}_2) \\
&+ \mathsf{Adv}_{\mathsf{crs}}(\kappa_2, \mathcal{B}_3) + (2^{|\mathsf{ct}|+1} + N)\mathsf{Adv}_{\mathsf{ZK}}(\kappa_2, \mathcal{B}_4) \\
&+ (L(\lambda) + 2)\nu_{\mathsf{sound}}(\kappa_2) + \mathsf{Adv}_{\mathsf{IND\text{-}CPA}}^{\mathsf{FHE}}(\kappa_1, \mathcal{B}_5).
\end{aligned}$$

The subexponential security of the building blocks implies that there exists a constant $\varepsilon > 0$ such that $\mathsf{Adv}_{\mathsf{iO}}(\kappa_2, \mathcal{B}_1), \mathsf{Adv}_{\mathsf{cPRF}}(\kappa_2, \mathcal{B}_2), \mathsf{Adv}_{\mathsf{crs}}(\kappa_2, \mathcal{B}_3),$ $\mathsf{Adv}_{\mathsf{ZK}}(\kappa_2, \mathcal{B}_4), \nu_{\mathsf{sound}}(\kappa_2) \leq 2^{-\kappa_2^\varepsilon}$ and $\mathsf{Adv}_{\mathsf{IND\text{-}CPA}}^{\mathsf{FHE}}(\kappa_1, \mathcal{B}_5) \leq 2^{-\kappa_1^\varepsilon}$. Thus, we have

$$\mathsf{Adv}_0(\mathcal{A}) \leq 2^{-\kappa_2^\varepsilon}(5 \cdot 2^{|\mathsf{ct}|+1} + 3L(\lambda) + N + 17) + 2^{-\kappa_1^\varepsilon}.$$

Since we chose $L(\lambda) = \log^2 \lambda$, selective security can be achieved by choosing for instance

$$\kappa_2 \geq (|\mathsf{ct}| + \log N + 2\log^2 \lambda + O(1))^{1/\varepsilon},$$
$$\kappa_1 \geq (\log^2 \lambda)^{1/\varepsilon}.$$

To achieve adaptive unforgeability, we use the same guessing technique as for the proof of computation correctness (both signing and evaluation) in the previous section. Namely, we simply guess the messages $m_1^\star, \ldots, m_N^\star \leftarrow_{\mathsf{R}} \{0, 1\}$ in advance, then proceed as in the selective game (but with the guesses $m_i^\star$ instead of the real messages chosen by the adversary). If the guess is correct, we have the same advantage as in the selective security game. If the guess is incorrect, the game outputs 0. This guessing argument incurs a security loss of 2^N. That is, the advantage of an adaptive adversary $\mathcal{A}$ against the unforgeability of our FHS is less than 2^N times the security loss in the selective setting written above. Therefore, adaptive unforgeability can be achieved by choosing for instance

$$\kappa_2 \geq (|\mathsf{ct}| + N + \log N + 2\log^2 \lambda + O(1))^{1/\varepsilon}, \quad \kappa_1 \geq (N + \log^2 \lambda)^{1/\varepsilon} \quad (3)$$

This concludes the unforgeability proof. $\square$

Theorem 18 (From $G_{3,\ell}$ to $G_{3,\ell+1}$). *For every PPT adversary $\mathcal{A}$, there exist PPT adversaries $\mathcal{B}_1, \mathcal{B}_2, \mathcal{B}_3, \mathcal{B}_4$, such that:*

$$\begin{aligned}
|\mathsf{Adv}_{3,\ell}(\mathcal{A}) - \mathsf{Adv}_{3,\ell+1}(\mathcal{A})| \leq &(2^{|\mathsf{ct}|+2} + 6)\mathsf{Adv}_{\mathsf{iO}}(\kappa_2, \mathcal{B}_1) + (2^{|\mathsf{ct}|+2} + \\
&4)\mathsf{Adv}_{\mathsf{cPRF}}(\kappa_2, \mathcal{B}_2) + 2^{|\mathsf{ct}|+1}\mathsf{Adv}_{\mathsf{ZK}}(\kappa_2, \mathcal{B}_3) + \mathsf{Adv}_{\mathsf{crs}}(\kappa_2, \mathcal{B}_4) + 2\nu_{\mathsf{sound}}(\kappa_2).
\end{aligned}$$

HybridGenCRS$^\ell$(level)

Hardcoded: key K_1
$s = \mathsf{PRF}(K_1, \mathsf{level})$
Return $(\mathsf{crs}, \mathsf{td}_{\mathsf{ext}}) = \mathsf{NIZK.Setup}(1^{\kappa_2}; s)$ for level $< \ell$
Return $(\mathsf{crs}_{\mathsf{sim}}, \mathsf{td}_{\mathsf{sim}}) = \mathsf{NIZK.SimSetup}(1^{\kappa_2}; s)$ for level $\geq \ell$

HybridEvalNAND$^\ell$$((\sigma_0, m_0), (\sigma_1, m_1))$

Hardcoded: key K_2
Parse σ_b as $(\mathsf{ct}_b, \pi_b, \mathsf{level}_b)$, for $b \in \{0, 1\}$
Return $\bot$ if $\mathsf{level}_0 \neq \mathsf{level}_1$
$j = \mathsf{level}_0$
$(\mathsf{crs}_j, \mathsf{td}_j) = \mathsf{HybridGenCRS}^\ell(j)$
If $\mathsf{NIZK.Verify}(\mathsf{crs}_j, \mathsf{stat}_{m_b, \mathsf{ct}_b}, \pi_b) = 0$ for some $b \in \{0, 1\}$ then output $\bot$
$\mathsf{ct} = \mathsf{FHE.Eval}(\mathsf{fpk}, \mathsf{NAND}, \mathsf{ct}_0, \mathsf{ct}_1)$
$m = \mathsf{NAND}(m_0, m_1)$
$(\mathsf{crs}_{j+1}, \mathsf{td}_{j+1}) = \mathsf{HybridGenCRS}^\ell(j + 1)$
$\rho = \mathsf{PRF}(K_2, (m, \mathsf{ct}, j + 1))$
If $j < \ell$
    $r_b = \mathsf{NIZK.Extract}(\mathsf{crs}_j, \mathsf{td}_j, \mathsf{stat}_{m_b, \mathsf{ct}_b}, \pi_b)$ for $b \in \{0, 1\}$
    $r = \mathsf{FHE.EvalRand}(\mathsf{fsk}, \mathsf{NAND}, r_1, r_2)$
    $\pi = \mathsf{NIZK.Prove}(\mathsf{crs}_{j+1}, \mathsf{stat}_{m, \mathsf{ct}}, r; \rho)$

If $j \geq \ell$
    $\pi = \mathsf{NIZK.Sim}(\mathsf{crs}_{j+1}, \mathsf{td}_{j+1}, \mathsf{stat}_{m, \mathsf{ct}}; \rho)$

$\sigma = (\mathsf{ct}, \pi, j + 1)$
Return σ

Fig. 7. Algorithms HybridGenCRS$^\ell$ and HybridEvalNAND$^\ell$, used in the games $\mathsf{G}_{3, \ell}$, for all $\ell \in \{0, \ldots, L(\lambda)\}$.

Due to space constraints, we provide the technical proof of this theorem in the full version of the paper [GU23].

Acknowledgements. We would like to thank Geoffroy Couteau and Dennis Hofheinz for their input during discussions that led to this work.

References

AB09. Agrawal, S., Boneh, D.: Homomorphic MACs: MAC-based integrity for network coding. In: Abdalla, M., Pointcheval, D., Fouque, P.-A., Vergnaud, D. (eds.) ACNS 2009. LNCS, vol. 5536, pp. 292–305. Springer, Heidelberg (2009). https://doi.org/10.1007/978-3-642-01957-9_18

ACL+22. Albrecht, M.R., Cini, V., Lai, R.W.F., Malavolta, G., Thyagarajan, S.A.: Lattice-based SNARKs: publicly verifiable, preprocessing, and recursively composable. In: Dodis, Y., Shrimpton, T. (eds.) Advances in Cryptology, CRYPTO 2022, Part II. LNCS, vol. 13508, pp. 102–132. Springer, Cham (2022). https://doi.org/10.1007/978-3-031-15979-4_4

ALP13. Attrapadung, N., Libert, B., Peters, T.: Efficient completely context-hiding quotable and linearly homomorphic signatures. In: Kurosawa, K., Hanaoka, G. (eds.) PKC 2013. LNCS, vol. 7778, pp. 386–404. Springer, Heidelberg (2013). https://doi.org/10.1007/978-3-642-36362-7_24

AP19. Aranha, D.F., Pagnin, E.: The simplest multi-key linearly homomorphic signature scheme. In: Schwabe, P., Thériault, N. (eds.) LATINCRYPT 2019. LNCS, vol. 11774, pp. 280–300. Springer, Cham (2019). https://doi.org/10.1007/978-3-030-30530-7_14

AP20. Agrawal, S., Pellet-Mary, A.: Indistinguishability obfuscation without maps: attacks and fixes for noisy linear FE. In: Canteaut, A., Ishai, Y. (eds.) EUROCRYPT 2020, Part I. LNCS, vol. 12105, pp. 110–140. Springer, Cham (2020). https://doi.org/10.1007/978-3-030-45721-1_5

BCFL23. Balbás, D., Catalano, D., Fiore, D., Lai, R.W.F.: Chainable functional commitments for unbounded-depth circuits. In: Rothblum, G., Wee, H. (eds.) Theory of Cryptography, TCC 2023. LNCS, vol. 14371, pp. 363–393. Springer, Cham (2023). https://doi.org/10.1007/978-3-031-48621-0_13

BDGM20a. Brakerski, Z., Döttling, N., Garg, S., Malavolta, G.: Candidate iO from homomorphic encryption schemes. In: Canteaut, A., Ishai, Y. (eds.) EUROCRYPT 2020, Part I. LNCS, vol. 12105, pp. 79–109. Springer, Cham (2020). https://doi.org/10.1007/978-3-030-45721-1_4

BDGM20b. Brakerski, Z., Döttling, N., Garg, S., Malavolta, G.: Factoring and pairings are not necessary for iO: circular-secure LWE suffices. Cryptology ePrint Archive (2020)

BF11a. Boneh, D., Freeman, D.M.: Homomorphic signatures for polynomial functions. In: Paterson, K.G. (ed.) EUROCRYPT 2011. LNCS, vol. 6632, pp. 149–168. Springer, Heidelberg (2011). https://doi.org/10.1007/978-3-642-20465-4_10

BF11b. Boneh, D., Freeman, D.M.: Linearly homomorphic signatures over binary fields and new tools for lattice-based signatures. In: Catalano, D., Fazio, N., Gennaro, R., Nicolosi, A. (eds.) PKC 2011. LNCS, vol. 6571, pp. 1–16. Springer, Heidelberg (2011). https://doi.org/10.1007/978-3-642-19379-8_1

BFM88. Blum, M., Feldman, P., Micali, S.: Non-interactive zero-knowledge and its applications (extended abstract). In: 20th ACM STOC, May 1988, pp. 103–112. ACM Press (1988)

BFS14. Boyen, X., Fan, X., Shi, E.: Adaptively secure fully homomorphic signatures based on lattices. Cryptology ePrint Archive, Paper 2014/916 (2014). https://eprint.iacr.org/2014/916

BGI+01. Barak, B., et al.: On the (im)possibility of obfuscating programs. In: Kilian, J. (ed.) CRYPTO 2001. LNCS, vol. 2139, pp. 1–18. Springer, Heidelberg (2001). https://doi.org/10.1007/3-540-44647-8_1

BGI14. Boyle, E., Goldwasser, S., Ivan, I.: Functional signatures and pseudorandom functions. In: Krawczyk, H. (ed.) PKC 2014. LNCS, vol. 8383, pp. 501–519. Springer, Heidelberg (2014). https://doi.org/10.1007/978-3-642-54631-0_29

BW13. Boneh, D., Waters, B.: Constrained pseudorandom functions and their applications. In: Sako, K., Sarkar, P. (eds.) ASIACRYPT 2013, Part II. LNCS, vol. 8270, pp. 280–300. Springer, Heidelberg (2013). https://doi.org/10.1007/978-3-642-42045-0_15

CF13.   Catalano, D., Fiore, D.: Practical homomorphic MACs for arithmetic circuits. In: Johansson, T., Nguyen, P.Q. (eds.) EUROCRYPT 2013. LNCS, vol. 7881, pp. 336–352. Springer, Heidelberg (2013). https://doi.org/10.1007/978-3-642-38348-9_21

CFN15. Catalano, D., Fiore, D., Nizzardo, L.: Programmable hash functions go private: constructions and applications to (homomorphic) signatures with shorter public keys. In: Gennaro, R., Robshaw, M. (eds.) CRYPTO 2015, Part II. LNCS, vol. 9216, pp. 254–274. Springer, Heidelberg (2015). https://doi.org/10.1007/978-3-662-48000-7_13

CFN18. Catalano, D., Fiore, D., Nizzardo, L.: On the security notions for homomorphic signatures. In: Preneel, B., Vercauteren, F. (eds.) ACNS 2018. LNCS, vol. 10892, pp. 183–201. Springer, Cham (2018). https://doi.org/10.1007/978-3-319-93387-0_10

CFT22. Catalano, D., Fiore, D., Tucker, I.: Additive-homomorphic functional commitments and applications to homomorphic signatures. In: Agrawal, S., Lin, D. (eds.) Advances in Cryptology, ASIACRYPT 2022, Part IV. LNCS, vol. 13794, pp. 159–188. Springer, Cham (2022). https://doi.org/10.1007/978-3-031-22972-5_6

CFW14. Catalano, D., Fiore, D., Warinschi, B.: Homomorphic signatures with efficient verification for polynomial functions. In: Garay, J.A., Gennaro, R. (eds.) CRYPTO 2014, Part I. LNCS, vol. 8616, pp. 371–389. Springer, Heidelberg (2014). https://doi.org/10.1007/978-3-662-44371-2_21

CLQ16. Chen, W., Lei, H., Qi, K.: Lattice-based linearly homomorphic signatures in the standard model. Theoret. Comput. Sci. **634**, 47–54 (2016)

CLTV15. Canetti, R., Lin, H., Tessaro, S., Vaikuntanathan, V.: Obfuscation of probabilistic circuits and applications. In: Dodis, Y., Nielsen, J.B. (eds.) TCC 2015, Part II. LNCS, vol. 9015, pp. 468–497. Springer, Heidelberg (2015). https://doi.org/10.1007/978-3-662-46497-7_19

DJ01.   Damgård, I., Jurik, M.: A generalisation, a simplification and some applications of Paillier's probabilistic public-key system. In: Kim, K. (ed.) PKC 2001. LNCS, vol. 1992, pp. 119–136. Springer, Heidelberg (2001). https://doi.org/10.1007/3-540-44586-2_9

DQV+21. Devadas, L., Quach, W., Vaikuntanathan, V., Wee, H., Wichs, D.: Succinct LWE sampling, random polynomials, and obfuscation. In: Nissim, K., Waters, B. (eds.) TCC 2021, Part II. LNCS, vol. 13043, pp. 256–287. Springer, Cham (2021). https://doi.org/10.1007/978-3-030-90453-1_9

ElG85. ElGamal, T.: A public key cryptosystem and a signature scheme based on discrete logarithms. IEEE Trans. Inf. Theor. **31**(4), 469–472 (1985)

FG18.   Fuchsbauer, G., Gay, R.: Weakly secure equivalence-class signatures from standard assumptions. In: Abdalla, M., Dahab, R. (eds.) PKC 2018, Part II. LNCS, vol. 10770, pp. 153–183. Springer, Cham (2018). https://doi.org/10.1007/978-3-319-76581-5_6

FHS19. Fuchsbauer, G., Hanser, C., Slamanig, D.: Structure-preserving signatures on equivalence classes and constant-size anonymous credentials. J. Cryptol. **32**(2), 498–546 (2019)

FP18.   Fiore, D., Pagnin, E.: Matrioska: a compiler for multi-key homomorphic signatures. In: Catalano, D., De Prisco, R. (eds.) SCN 2018. LNCS, vol. 11035, pp. 43–62. Springer, Cham (2018). https://doi.org/10.1007/978-3-319-98113-0_3

Fre12. Freeman, D.M.: Improved security for linearly homomorphic signatures: a generic framework. In: Fischlin, M., Buchmann, J., Manulis, M. (eds.) PKC 2012. LNCS, vol. 7293, pp. 697–714. Springer, Heidelberg (2012). https://doi.org/10.1007/978-3-642-30057-8_41

Gen09. Gentry, C.: Fully homomorphic encryption using ideal lattices. In: 41st ACM STOC, May/June 2009, pp. 169–178. ACM Press (2009)

GGM84. Goldreich, O., Goldwasser, S., Micali, S.: How to construct random functions (extended abstract). In: 25th FOCS, October 1984, pp. 464–479. IEEE Computer Society Press (1984)

GM82. Goldwasser, S., Micali, S.: Probabilistic encryption and how to play mental poker keeping secret all partial information. In: 14th ACM STOC, May 1982, pp. 365–377. ACM Press (1982)

GP21. Gay, R., Pass, R.: Indistinguishability obfuscation from circular security. In: 53rd ACM STOC, June 2021, pp. 736–749. ACM Press (2021)

GS08. Groth, J., Sahai, A.: Efficient non-interactive proof systems for bilinear groups. In: Smart, N. (ed.) EUROCRYPT 2008. LNCS, vol. 4965, pp. 415–432. Springer, Heidelberg (2008). https://doi.org/10.1007/978-3-540-78967-3_24

GSW13. Gentry, C., Sahai, A., Waters, B.: Homomorphic encryption from learning with errors: conceptually-simpler, asymptotically-faster, attribute-based. In: Canetti, R., Garay, J.A. (eds.) CRYPTO 2013, Part I. LNCS, vol. 8042, pp. 75–92. Springer, Heidelberg (2013). https://doi.org/10.1007/978-3-642-40041-4_5

GU23. Gay, R., Ursu, B.: On instantiating unleveled fully-homomorphic signatures from falsifiable assumptions. Cryptology ePrint Archive, Paper 2023/1818 (2023). https://eprint.iacr.org/2023/1818

GVW15. Gorbunov, S., Vaikuntanathan, V., Wichs, D.: Leveled fully homomorphic signatures from standard lattices. In: 47th ACM STOC, June 2015, pp. 469–477. ACM Press (2015)

GW13. Gennaro, R., Wichs, D.: Fully homomorphic message authenticators. In: Sako, K., Sarkar, P. (eds.) ASIACRYPT 2013, Part II. LNCS, vol. 8270, pp. 301–320. Springer, Heidelberg (2013). https://doi.org/10.1007/978-3-642-42045-0_16

HILL99. Håstad, J., Impagliazzo, R., Levin, L.A., Luby, M.: A pseudorandom generator from any one-way function. SIAM J. Comput. **28**(4), 1364–1396 (1999)

HPP20. Hébant, C., Phan, D.H., Pointcheval, D.: Linearly-homomorphic signatures and scalable mix-nets. In: Kiayias, A., Kohlweiss, M., Wallden, P., Zikas, V. (eds.) PKC 2020, Part II. LNCS, vol. 12111, pp. 597–627. Springer, Cham (2020). https://doi.org/10.1007/978-3-030-45388-6_21

HS14. Hanser, C., Slamanig, D.: Structure-preserving signatures on equivalence classes and their application to anonymous credentials. In: Sarkar, P., Iwata, T. (eds.) ASIACRYPT 2014, Part I. LNCS, vol. 8873, pp. 491–511. Springer, Heidelberg (2014). https://doi.org/10.1007/978-3-662-45611-8_26

HU19. Hofheinz, D., Ursu, B.: Dual-mode NIZKs from obfuscation. In: Galbraith, S.D., Moriai, S. (eds.) ASIACRYPT 2019, Part I. LNCS, vol. 11921, pp. 311–341. Springer, Cham (2019). https://doi.org/10.1007/978-3-030-34578-5_12

JLS21. Jain, A., Lin, H., Sahai, A.: Indistinguishability obfuscation from well-founded assumptions. In: 53rd ACM STOC, June 2021, pp. 60–73. ACM Press (2021)

JLS22. Jain, A., Lin, H., Sahai, A.: Indistinguishability obfuscation from LPN over $\mathbb{F}_p$, DLIN, and PRGs in NC^0. In: Dunkelman, O., Dziembowski, S. (eds.) Advances in Cryptology, EUROCRYPT 2022. LNCS, vol. 13275, pp. 670–699. Springer, Cham (2022). https://doi.org/10.1007/978-3-031-06944-4_23

JMSW02. Johnson, R., Molnar, D., Song, D., Wagner, D.: Homomorphic signature schemes. In: Preneel, B. (ed.) CT-RSA 2002. LNCS, vol. 2271, pp. 244–262. Springer, Heidelberg (2002). https://doi.org/10.1007/3-540-45760-7_17

KPTZ13. Kiayias, A., Papadopoulos, S., Triandopoulos, N., Zacharias, T.: Delegatable pseudorandom functions and applications. In: ACM CCS 2013, November 2013, pp. 669–684. ACM Press (2013)

KSD19. Khalili, M., Slamanig, D., Dakhilalian, M.: Structure-preserving signatures on equivalence classes from standard assumptions. In: Galbraith, S.D., Moriai, S. (eds.) ASIACRYPT 2019, Part III. LNCS, vol. 11923, pp. 63–93. Springer, Cham (2019). https://doi.org/10.1007/978-3-030-34618-8_3

LPJY15. Libert, B., Peters, T., Joye, M., Yung, M.: Linearly homomorphic structure-preserving signatures and their applications. Des. Codes Crypt. **77**(2), 441–477 (2015)

LTWC18. Lai, R.W.F., Tai, R.K.H., Wong, H.W.H., Chow, S.S.M.: Multi-key homomorphic signatures unforgeable under insider corruption. In: Peyrin, T., Galbraith, S. (eds.) ASIACRYPT 2018, Part II. LNCS, vol. 11273, pp. 465–492. Springer, Cham (2018). https://doi.org/10.1007/978-3-030-03329-3_16

Pai99. Paillier, P.: Public-key cryptosystems based on composite degree residuosity classes. In: Stern, J. (ed.) EUROCRYPT 1999. LNCS, vol. 1592, pp. 223–238. Springer, Heidelberg (1999). https://doi.org/10.1007/3-540-48910-X_16

SBB19. Schabhüser, L., Butin, D., Buchmann, J.: Context hiding multi-key linearly homomorphic authenticators. In: Matsui, M. (ed.) CT-RSA 2019. LNCS, vol. 11405, pp. 493–513. Springer, Cham (2019). https://doi.org/10.1007/978-3-030-12612-4_25

SW14. Sahai, A., Waters, B.: How to use indistinguishability obfuscation: deniable encryption, and more. In: 46th ACM STOC, May/June 2014, pp. 475–484. ACM Press (2014)

Tsa17. Tsabary, R.: An equivalence between attribute-based signatures and homomorphic signatures, and new constructions for both. In: Kalai, Y., Reyzin, L. (eds.) TCC 2017, Part II. LNCS, vol. 10678, pp. 489–518. Springer, Cham (2017). https://doi.org/10.1007/978-3-319-70503-3_16

WW21. Wee, H., Wichs, D.: Candidate obfuscation via oblivious LWE sampling. In: Canteaut, A., Standaert, F.-X. (eds.) EUROCRYPT 2021, Part III. LNCS, vol. 12698, pp. 127–156. Springer, Cham (2021). https://doi.org/10.1007/978-3-030-77883-5_5

Updatable Policy-Compliant Signatures

Christian Badertscher[1], Monosij Maitra[2,3], Christian Matt[4],
and Hendrik Waldner[5(✉)]

[1] Input Output, Zurich, Switzerland
`christian.badertscher@iohk.io`
[2] Ruhr-Universität Bochum, Bochum, Germany
`monosij.maitra@rub.de`
[3] Max Planck Institute for Security and Privacy, Bochum, Germany
[4] Primev, Steinhausen, Switzerland
`christian@primev.xyz`
[5] University of Maryland, College Park, MD, USA
`hwaldner@umd.edu`

Abstract. Policy-compliant signatures (PCS) are a recently introduced primitive by Badertscher et al. [TCC 2021] in which a central authority distributes secret and public keys associated with sets of attributes (e.g., nationality, affiliation with a specific department, or age) to its users. The authority also enforces a policy determining which senders can sign messages for which receivers based on a *joint* check of their attributes. For example, senders and receivers must have the same nationality, or only senders that are at least 18 years old can send to members of the computer science department. PCS further requires attribute-privacy – nothing about the users' attributes is revealed from their public keys and signatures apart from whether the attributes satisfy the policy or not. The policy in a PCS scheme is fixed once and for all during the setup. Therefore, a policy update requires a redistribution of all keys. This severely limits the practicality of PCS. In this work, we introduce the notion of *updatable policy-compliant signatures (UPCS)* extending PCS with a mechanism to efficiently update the policy without redistributing keys to all participants.

We define the notion of UPCS and provide the corresponding security definitions. We then provide a generic construction of UPCS based on digital signatures, a NIZK proof system, and a so-called secret-key two-input partially-hiding predicate encryption (2-PHPE) scheme. Unfortunately, the only known way to build the latter for general two-input predicates is using indistinguishability obfuscation. We show that the reliance on the heavy tool of 2-PHPE is inherent to build UPCS by proving that non-interactive UPCS implies 2-PHPE.

To circumvent the reliance on 2-PHPE, we consider *interactive* UPCS, which allows sender and receiver to interact during the message signing.

M. Maitra—Work done partially at Technische Universität Darmstadt, Germany.
C. Matt—Work done partially at Concordium, Zurich, Switzerland.
H. Waldner—Work done partially at the Max Planck Institute for Security and Privacy, Bochum, Germany.

Q. Tang and V. Teague (Eds.): PKC 2024, LNCS 14601, pp. 105–132, 2024.
https://doi.org/10.1007/978-3-031-57718-5_4

In this setting, we present two UPCS schemes: the first one requires only a digital signature scheme, a NIZK proof system, and secure two-party computation. This scheme works for arbitrary policies, but requires senders and receivers to engage in the two-party computation for each policy update. Our second scheme additionally requires a (single-input) predicate-encryption scheme and only requires the sender and receiver to interact ones independent of the updates. In contrast to 2-PHPE, single-input predicate encryption supporting certain predicate classes are known to exist (e.g., from pairings) under more concrete and well-understood assumptions.

1 Introduction

Policy-compliant signatures (PCS) [5] are credential-based, enhanced signature schemes in which a policy F governs signature generation: a party with attributes x (encoded in a privacy-preserving way in their public-key) that wishes to sign a message m destined for a receiving party with attributes y, is only ever able to produce a valid signature certifying this action if and only if $F(x, y) = 1$. This notion extends attribute-based signatures [26] and policy-based signatures [8] (which allow for policies based solely on the sender's attributes) and has interesting applications in corporate environments and financial applications including payment systems [5,6]. The reason is that this type of signature scheme is able to merge the act of signing (to unlock funds) with cryptographic compliance checks while still being publicly verifiable. Basic examples include enforcing that both parties are of a minimal legal age and operate in jurisdictions between which no sanctions exist, or to ensure that certain tokens are only spent in a prescribed context, such that between employees (e.g. of a state) and subsidized facilities/services where they obtain discounts. The scheme ensures that nothing more leaks than the mere validity of the statement, keeping the receiver's attributes hidden from the sender/signer at all times, meeting the promise to enforce compliance to a certain rule set in a privacy-preserving way. The policy in such systems can either be defined by a certain legal system (and implemented by an accredited credential issuer), or purely application-driven by a provider to govern the spending rights of domain-specific tokens. On a technical level, in a PCS scheme, a (credential) authority generates a master public and secret-key pair for a given policy, and then derives public and secret keys for each user and their attributes from the master secret key. A major practical limitation is that the policy is fixed at setup time (when generating the master keys), and consequently, all users need to get new key pairs if the policy gets changed, incurring a high communication cost. In the above mentioned applications, regularly new rules are put in place, which demands PCS to be more dynamic. Therefore, we introduce *updatable policy-compliant signatures (UPCS)* which allows authorities to update policies more efficiently, i.e., without updating the users' keys.

1.1 Updatable PCS Description

As a regular PCS scheme, a UPCS scheme has an algorithm Setup that an authority can use to generate a master public and secret key for an initial policy F_0. For a set of attributes x, the authority can then use the master secret key to generate a key pair corresponding to these attributes using KeyGen. An updatable PCS scheme has an additional procedure PolUpd that takes the master secret key and a new policy F' as an input and outputs a so-called update token $\text{tok}_{F'}$. Using the current update token, the secret key of the sender, and the public key of the receiver, the sender can sign a message by executing Sign and everyone can then verify the signature using the master public key, the current update token, and the public keys of the sender and receiver. The signature is valid if the signature and message have not been modified, and if the attributes of the sender and receiver satisfy the current policy associated with the update token $\text{tok}_{F'}$.

Security Requirements. As for regular policy-compliant signatures, UPCS security consists of two parts: unforgeability and privacy. Unforgeability captures what one can expect from any signature scheme, i.e., that no valid signature for a new message can be produced without knowledge of the secret key, even given access to a signing oracle for arbitrary messages. Additionally, unforgeability for (updatable) policy-compliant signatures prevents an adversary from creating a signature that verifies for a pair of public keys for a sender and a receiver with attributes not satisfying the policy. For *updatable* PCS, we require these properties to hold even if the adversary can adaptively update the policies. Furthermore, we require that an adversary is not able to generate a valid update token on its own. In particular, an adversary is prevented from producing a valid signature for an update token of an old policy, or an update token generated on its own, and attributes that do not satisfy it, even if these attributes satisfy a newer policy.

Privacy in this context refers to hiding the attributes of sender and receiver. This means an adversary, seeing signatures for a sender and receiver for different policies, should not learn anything about their attributes except for which of the considered policies they satisfy and what can be deduced from that. This must still hold if one of the two parties is corrupted, i.e., the attributes of the receiver are protected from a malicious sender and vice versa. We refer to this privacy property of attributes as attribute-hiding in the rest of the paper.

Below, we first motivate and provide some contextualization on policy updatability and then dive into the challenges and overview of our contributions.

1.2 On Policy Updatability

We start by discussing in more detail the importance of updates in the context of PCS [5] for its practical usage. UPCS improves the applicability of PCS and covers a blind spot in some novel applications of digital signatures. [5] laid the foundations for PCS and discussed such applications in detail, and [6] already provides first estimates on practicality. Our motivation for UPCS is to present it in an enriched model (e.g., with interactivity) which is necessary to unleash its potential in many more applications. We believe policy-updatability to be a critical stepping stone to push PCS further towards practice.

From the UPCS description above, we note that it is indeed necessary that the signer and the verifier need to be aware of the current update token. It is not the case though that all the parties in the system have to do some work with respect to the update token and there is no key update that needs to be executed. The only work that is needed in this step is done by the authority which is the generation of the update token. The complexity of the signing and the verification procedure remains the same for any update token. To minimize communication cost and make every user in the system aware of the current update token, the authority can post this token, for example, on a public bulletin-board. Or when using a blockchain, which is one area where (U)PCS could be applied to secure transactions [5], the most recent update token can be simply published inside the current block. This ensures that all parties in the system are aware of the same token. Further, our UPCS model does not enforce any specific requirements on the policy-update procedure, it is a standard probabilistic algorithm that can, in principle, produce the same update token multiple times. Hence, our definitions (and constructions) also allow for the reusability of update tokens.

We also note that UPCS can capture certain basic forms of revocation mechanisms by design – an updated policy may embed checks for revoked sender/receiver's attributes that never satisfy the new policy jointly with that of other parties in the system. In contrast, verifier-local revocation [10,20,24] requires verifiers to possess updated revocation lists. As UPCS signatures are valid subject to policies being satisfied *jointly* by sender and receiver's attributes, such revocation lists can vary across different verifiers and thus could get cumbersome to maintain. Similarly, server-aided revocation [13,14,25,27] is also inefficient as it additionally requires an (untrusted) server whereas the authority is supposed to update revocation lists periodically.

Finally, we do not consider delegation for UPCS in this paper. That is, we require all the updates to be driven by the authority. Nevertheless, one could imagine that the authority desires to delegate certain updates, i.e., allowing another party to generate update tokens for a *subclass* of the functionality. Such delegation capabilities maybe an interesting direction to explore in the future.

1.3   Challenges and Interactivity

Non-interactive Constructions. Policy-compliant signatures, as introduced in [5], are non-interactive in the sense that after receiving all relevant keys from the authority, parties can locally sign messages for arbitrary receivers and the resulting signatures can be verified by all other parties given only the pre-distributed public keys. In this work, we provide an updatable PCS scheme fitting this narrative. Our non-interactive construction relies on a regular signature scheme, a non-interactive zero-knowledge proof system, and a *secret-key* *two-input partially hiding predicate encryption (2-PHPE)* scheme. The latter is introduced in this work and corresponds to a weakened variant of two-input PE. The class of policies supported by our UPCS scheme directly corresponds to the set of predicates that the 2-PHPE scheme supports (see technical overview below for more details).

Our 2-PHPE needs to satisfy *strong* attribute-hiding (also known as *two-sided* security) [15,22], where no information about the hidden attribute is revealed beyond the output of the predicate.[1] Unfortunately, such 2-PHPE schemes can currently only be obtained using the strong assumption of indistinguishability obfuscation (*iO*) [16,21] which results in the immediate impracticality of the resulting schemes. This raises the question whether one can construct UPCS schemes without heavy tools such as 2-PHPE. We answer this question in the negative by proving that any non-interactive UPCS scheme can be used to construct a 2-PHPE scheme. Practically efficient non-interactive UPCS therefore appears to be out of reach with currently available techniques.

Interactive UPCS. Due to the negative result above, we relax the notion of UPCS to allow for interaction among the parties. Considering blockchain transactions as the main motivation for PCS [5], some sort of interaction between sender and receiver is already happening: before the sender can sign a transaction for a receiver, they have to obtain the correct address of the receiver and agree on the amount to be transferred. The relevant information for an interactive UPCS scheme can thus be integrated into an extension of an existing payment process.

Based on this insight, we present two interactive UPCS schemes with a different tradeoff between interactivity and efficiency: the first scheme is very simple and is based only on regular signature schemes, a non-interactive zero-knowledge proof system and a two-party computation protocol. Furthermore, it supports arbitrary (efficiently computable) policies. The downside of this scheme is that it requires one interaction between each sender and receiver every time the policy is updated. The second interactive scheme we present only requires a single interaction between sender and receiver and allows them to subsequently sign an unbounded number of messages even after policy updates. This scheme, however, requires a predicate-encryption (PE) scheme, and the supported class of policies depends on the predicates supported by the PE scheme. Both schemes are presented in more detail in the technical overview below.

1.4   Technical Overview

Defining UPCS and Its Security. Since we are interested in both, non-interactive as well as interactive UPCS schemes, we define UPCS in a generic way

---

[1] Strong attribute-hiding (predicate-only) PE allows an adversary to obtain secret keys for predicates that *can* decrypt a challenge ciphertext, but it is still required to hide any other information about the attributes.

such that both settings are covered. Our definition models UPCS as a message-driven protocol among a set of parties and a trusted authority $\mathfrak{A}$, all connected in a complete network consisting of pairwise point-to-point channels. Parties can receive instructions from the environment and subsequently can use the network to communicate with each other, and produce an output for the environment. We do not consider a dedicated adversary but consider the adversary to be part of the environment, as the dummy adversary in UC [12]. The environment can therefore corrupt any party except for the trusted authority $\mathfrak{A}$ to obtain full control over that party and learn all secrets of that party. For a fixed security parameter, we consider a family of attributes X, where $\mathcal{X}$ denotes the power-set of X, and a set of supported policies $\mathcal{F} = \{F\colon \mathcal{X} \times \mathcal{X} \to \{0,1\}\}$. In the beginning, the authority expects an input (SETUP, F_0) (from the environment) for some initial policy $F_0 \in \mathcal{F}$. It then produces a master key pair and an initial token tok_0. On input (UPDATE, F), the authority produces an update token tok_F. Furthermore, on input $(\text{KEYGEN}, P_i, x_i)$, the authority produces a key pair for the attributes x_i for party P_i (using the master secret key). This formally spawns this new party P_i initialized with this new key pair. Any party P_S can then receive inputs $(\text{SIGN}, \mathsf{tok}_F, \mathsf{pk}_R, m)$ instructing P_S to sign message m for a receiver P_R with public key pk_R relative to the policy update token tok_F, producing a signature σ. Any party (not just P_R) can then verify the signature via $(\text{VERIFY}, \mathsf{tok}_F, \mathsf{pk}_S, \mathsf{pk}_R, m, \sigma)$. Correctness of the UPCS scheme requires the result of the VERIFY instruction to be equal to $F(x_S, x_R)$, where x_S and x_R are the attributes of the sender and receiver, respectively. That is, the signature is valid if and only if the attributes of the sender and receiver satisfy the policy F. A non-interactive UPCS scheme simply corresponds to a scheme in which signing and verifying signatures are local operations, whereas interactive UPCS schemes allow interaction between sender and receiver.

Security of a UPCS scheme covers *unforgeability* and *attribute-hiding*. Unforgeability means that any environment can trigger any of the following events only with negligible probability: $(\text{VERIFY}, \mathsf{tok}_F, \mathsf{pk}_S, \mathsf{pk}_R, m, \sigma)$ returns 1 given pk_S or pk_R or tok_F that have not been output by KEYGEN or UPDATE, pk_S and pk_R correspond to attributes not satisfying the policy F corresponding to tok_F, or the sender S is uncorrupted and has not been instructed to sign the message m.

To define the attribute-hiding property, we introduce an additional instruction $(\text{TEST-KEYGEN}, P_i, (x_{i,0}, x_{i,1}))$ that internally does the same as $(\text{KEYGEN}, P_i, x_{i,b})$ for a uniformly random bit b. The goal of the environment is then to guess the bit b and we call the scheme attribute-hiding if this is only possible with negligible advantage over random guessing. For this definition, we exclude queries that would trivially allow an adversary to distinguish. That is, a party P_i can only be corrupted if the tested attributes $x_{i,0}$ and $x_{i,1}$ are equal, and we require all policies to be equal for all attributes involved in a SIGN query, or belonging to corrupted senders (who could sign themselves).

Two-Input Partially Hiding Predicate Encryption (2-PHPE). We use secret-key 2-PHPE to construct a non-interactive UPCS scheme. For a set of attributes X with powerset $\mathcal{X}$, consider a class of predicates $\mathcal{P} = \{P \colon \mathcal{X} \times \mathcal{X} \to \{0,1\}\}$. A 2-PHPE scheme for $\mathcal{P}$ allows an authority to generate a master secret key msk using the algorithm Setup. The obtained msk can then be used to generate keys sk_P for predicates $P \in \mathcal{P}$ via KeyGen(msk, P). The master secret key is also used to encrypt attributes $X \in \mathcal{X}$ and obtain a ciphertext $\mathsf{ct}_X = \mathsf{Encrypt}(\mathsf{msk}, X)$. In addition to encrypting, we also consider a method Encode to "encode" attributes $\widehat{X}$ using msk. In contrast to a ciphertext, an encoding $\mathsf{e}_{\widehat{X}}$ does not hide the attributes $\widehat{X}$ (hence the scheme is only partially hiding). Finally, there is an algorithm Decrypt that takes a secret key sk_P for a predicate P, an encoding e_{X_1} of X_1, and a ciphertext ct_{X_2} encrypting X_2. This algorithm outputs $P(X_1, X_2)$ with overwhelming probability.

Security of 2-PHPE is defined via a distinguishing game in which an adversary has access to KeyGen, Encode and Encrypt oracles, subject to some admissibility conditions. In particular, the adversary can obtain encryptions of $X_{2,b}$, when submitting $X_{2,0}$ and $X_{2,1}$ for uniformly chosen $b \in \{0,1\}$, along with encodings e_{X_1} and secret keys sk_P satisfying $P(X_1, X_{2,0}) = P(X_1, X_{2,1})$. The scheme is called *partially strong attribute-hiding*[2] if no PPT adversary has non-negligible advantage of determining b over random guessing.

To the best of our knowledge, the only known way to instantiate such a 2-PHPE for all predicates is via iO [16,21]. Furthermore, a *sub-exponentially* secure 2-PHPE supporting all boolean circuits actually implies iO. Even for a limited class of predicates (e.g., inner-products), a secret-key 2-PHPE with strong attribute-hiding yields a non-interactive UPCS for a class of policies captured by inner-products. One way to build such a 2-PHPE is using trilinear maps, where the linearity can be used to evaluate the inner-product of the vectors provided by the authority, the sender, and the receiver. Weakening the assumption to build it using bilinear maps, while satisfying attribute-hiding, seems challenging – the evaluation between the attributes of these three parties seems to require trilinearity. We leave overcoming this issue as an interesting open problem and refer to Sect. 4.1 (particularly to Remarks 2 and 3) for more details on this.

Non-interactive UPCS from 2-PHPE. Given a 2-PHPE scheme for a class of predicates $\mathcal{P}$, we can construct a non-interactive UPCS scheme for the same class of policies $\mathcal{F} = \mathcal{P}$. Our construction additionally assumes a NIZK proof system and a digital signature scheme. A token for a policy $F \in \mathcal{F}$ consists of a 2-PHPE secret key for the predicate F, signed by the authority using the digital signature scheme. A public key for attributes X consists of a digital signature public key and a ciphertext of X, both signed by the authority. The corresponding secret key instead contains an encoding of X (since it does not

---

[2] Note that the adversary may even learn sk_P for which $P(X_1, X_{2,b}) = 1, \forall b \in \{0,1\}$. This is referred to as strong attribute-hiding for the 2-PHPE scheme. For brevity, we call this attribute-hiding in the rest of the paper (except Sect. 4.1, where we again clarify this formally).

have to hide X) and additionally the secret key of the digital signature scheme. When S wants to sign a message for a receiver R, S proves, using the NIZK, knowledge of a secret key with a valid signature from the authority containing an encoding e_{X_1} such that 2-PHPE decryption of e_{X_1} and the ciphertext ct_{X_2} in the public key of R returns 1.

Unforgeability of the scheme follows from the correctness of the 2-PHPE scheme, the soundness of the NIZK proof, and unforgeability of the digital signature scheme. The attribute-hiding property of the UPCS scheme follows from the security of the 2-PHPE scheme and the zero-knowledge property of the NIZK. Note that all 2-PHPE keys, ciphertexts, and encodings are generated by the authority. Thus, a secret-key 2-PHPE scheme is sufficient. Furthermore, it is only necessary to hide the attributes in the receiver's public key since the sender's attributes are encoded in the UPCS secret key only known to the sender.

Non-interactive UPCS Implies 2-PHPE. Since 2-PHPE is a heavy tool, it would be desirable to construct a UPCS scheme without assuming 2-PHPE. Unfortunately, this is impossible for non-interactive UPCS schemes. We prove this by constructing a 2-PHPE scheme based on a non-interactive UPCS scheme, where the set of supported predicates exactly matches the set of supported policies of the assumed UPCS scheme. The basic idea of the construction is as follows: a 2-PHPE secret key for a policy P corresponds to a UPCS update token for the policy corresponding to P. To encode a set of attributes X_1, we generate a UPCS key pair for that attribute set, and the encoding consists of both the secret and public keys. To encrypt X_2, we also generate a UPCS key pair, but only include the public key in the ciphertext, to ensure that X_2 remains hidden. To decrypt a pair (e_{X_1}, ct_{X_2}), we use the secret key in e_{X_1} and the public key in ct_{X_2} to generate a UPCS signature (on a fixed message). We then verify this signature and output the bit that UPCS.Verify returns. Correctness of the UPCS scheme implies that the generated signature is valid if and only if $P(X_1, X_2) = 1$, which implies correctness of the 2-PHPE scheme. Security of the 2-PHPE scheme also directly follows from the attribute-hiding property of the UPCS scheme.

UPCS with Interaction After Each Policy Update. If we allow the sender and receiver to interact when signing for the first time after a policy update, it is rather easy to obtain a UPCS scheme. The basic idea is to let the parties jointly generate a non-interactive zero-knowledge (NIZK) proof that their attributes satisfy the current policy. More concretely, the scheme assumes a basic digital signature scheme, a NIZK proof system, and a secure two-party computation (2PC) protocol, and works as follows: on SETUP, the authority generates a CRS for the NIZK and key pairs of the digital signature scheme. The master public key consists of the CRS value and all signature public keys, the master secret key contains the corresponding secret keys, and the initial update token is a signature on the initial policy F_0 under the authority's signing key. UPDATE simply consists of signing the new policy. KEYGEN for attributes x first generates a regular signature key pair. The public key consists of the signature verification key signed by the authority, and the secret key consists of the signing key and the signed pair of verification key and attributes x. When a sender P_S wants to sign a message for a receiver P_R for the first time under the current policy, the two run the 2PC to produce a NIZK proof π for the statement that P_S and P_R know valid signatures from the authority on their verification keys together with attributes that satisfy the current policy. The UPCS signature of a message m then consists of π and a regular signature under the signing key of P_S of m, π, and the verification key of P_R. For future signatures, under the same policy, the proof π can be reused. Verification of a UPCS signature entails verifying the standard signature and the NIZK proof.

Unforgeability of the UPCS scheme is implied by unforgeability of the basic signature scheme and soundness of the NIZK proof. The zero-knowledge property of the proof further implies that a UPCS signature does not reveal anything about the attributes of the sender and receiver beyond the fact that they satisfy the current policy. Security of the 2PC finally implies that the attributes of the sender are hidden from the receiver and vice versa.

UPCS with One-Time Interaction. In the last step, we construct a UPCS scheme that requires only a single interaction between a pair of sender and receiver such that the sender can afterwards sign arbitrarily many messages for that receiver, even for future policy updates. This scheme combines ideas from our non-interactive scheme and the simple interactive one, but uses only a standard single-input predicate-encryption (PE) scheme. As in our non-interactive scheme, a policy update token consists of a signed PE secret key. Since UPCS policies take the attributes of the sender and receiver as separate inputs and the PE scheme only takes a single input, we concatenate the attributes of the sender and receiver into a single element and generate a PE secret key for the corresponding predicate that splits the input in half and then evaluates the corresponding two-input policy. In more detail, for a two-input policy F' that takes as an input two attribute sets X_S and X_R, we create a single-input function $\widehat{F}'$ that takes as an input a single set $X_{S,R}$ which is the disjoint union of the sender and receiver attributes, i.e. $X_{S,R} := \{(x,0)|x \in X_S\} \cup \{(x,1)|x \in X_R\}$. The function $\widehat{F}'$ then splits the input set $X_{S,R}$ into the two sets X_S and X_R, where attributes in X_S are of the form $(x,0)$ and attributes in X_R are of the form $(x,1)$, and then executes $F'(X_S, X_R)$. The set of supported policies in this scheme corresponds to all policies F' for which the PE scheme supports the corresponding $\widehat{F}'$. A UPCS secret key for a set of attributes X contains a signature from the authority on X together with a secret key for a digital signature scheme, and the corresponding public key contains the signed corresponding digital signature public key.

When a sender S wants to sign a message for a receiver R for the first time, they interact in a 2PC to first compute a PE ciphertext for the pair of attribute sets (X_S, X_R). Then, they produce a NIZK proof that the ciphertext was generated correctly using attributes with valid signatures from the authority for the corresponding public keys of S and R. To sign a message, the sender then produces a NIZK proof of knowledge of such a ciphertext and that the ciphertext decrypts to 1 using the PE secret key in the current policy update token.

If the scheme is implemented directly as described above, then, for the final signing of the message, the sender is required to generate a NIZK proof over another NIZK proof, namely that the known ciphertext comes with a valid NIZK proof from the 2PC that it is an encryption of the correct attributes. Since this can be rather inefficient (depending on the used NIZK scheme), we slightly modify the scheme to avoid this recursive proof. A seemingly simple solution would be to add the ciphertext generated in the 2PC in plain to a signature and then only prove that this ciphertext decrypts to 1. The problem with this approach is that now everyone can evaluate this ciphertext for all policies for which an update token exists, and not just those for which the sender generates a signature. This scheme therefore does not satisfy our privacy notion that only allows information leakage about the attributes that trivially follow from the usage of the scheme, and, in particular, hide policy evaluations for policies under which no signature has been generated. We avoid this issue by generating a commitment to the ciphertext in the 2PC, together with a proof that the commitment was generated correctly, and then add this commitment to each signature. A signature then contains two NIZK proofs, where the first one is taken directly from the 2PC, and the second one proves that the commitment is to a (secret) ciphertext that decrypts to 1 using the PE secret key for the current policy.

Instantiating PE. We also require a (strong) attribute-hiding, adaptively secure PE to instantiate the UPCS scheme with one-time interaction presented above. Such PE schemes exist based on pairings for inner-product (in the standard model) [28] and quadratic predicates (in the generic group model) [7,29]. We refer the reader to Sect. 5.1 for more details about the instantiation. The fact that the underlying PE schemes can be based on pairings highlights the practical potential of our UPCS with one-time interaction, i.e., one can, in principle, implement and benchmark the presented UPCS scheme, given efficient digital signatures and NIZK proofs that are compatible with the underlying pairing-based PE schemes. We leave a practical instantiation of this scheme as future work.

2   Preliminaries

In this section, we introduce the notation used in this work. For a full recap of all the used primitives, we refer to the full version.

Notation. We denote the security parameter with $\lambda \in \mathbb{N}$ and use 1^λ as its unary representation. We call a randomized algorithm $\mathcal{A}$ *probabilistic polynomial time* (PPT) if there exists a polynomial $p(\cdot)$ such that for every input x the running time of $\mathcal{A}(x)$ is bounded by $p(|x|)$. A function negl : $\mathbb{N} \to \mathbb{R}^+$ is called *negligible* if for every positive polynomial $p(\lambda)$, there exists $\lambda_0 \in \mathbb{N}$ such that for all $\lambda > \lambda_0$: $\mathrm{negl}(\lambda) < 1/p(\lambda)$. If clear from the context, we sometimes omit λ for improved readability. The set $\{1, \ldots, n\}$ is denoted as $[n]$ for $n \in \mathbb{N}$. For the equality check of two elements, we use "=". The assign operator is denoted with ":=", whereas randomized assignment is denoted with $a \leftarrow A$, with a randomized algorithm A and where the randomness is not explicit. If the randomness is explicit, we write $a := A(x; r)$ where x is the input and r is the randomness. For algorithms $\mathcal{A}$ and $\mathcal{B}$, we write $\mathcal{A}^{\mathcal{B}(\cdot)}(x)$ to denote that $\mathcal{A}$ gets x as an input and has black-box oracle access to $\mathcal{B}$, that is, the response for an oracle query q is $\mathcal{B}(q)$. For any probabilistic event E, we denote its complement by $\overline{\mathsf{E}}$. Furthermore, for the last construction that we present in the main body, we introduce the following notation:

$$X_s \dot{\cup} X_r := \{(x, 0) | x \in X_s\} \cup \{(x, 1) | x \in X_r\}.$$

3   A Model for Interactive and Non-interactive PCS with Updates

Here, we sketch a simple extension to the PCS setting that allows for interactive processes between protocol participants.

3.1   Model Basics

General Protocol Execution. We consider a standard real-world protocol execution as in [12] with a dynamic set of parties that are able to pass messages to each other. A protocol is an interactive program that specifies how incoming messages and inputs are processed, what outputs are generated and which messages are sent to which party. Protocols can be triggered (and protocol machines spawned) at a party by an external input, and/or due to incoming messages from the network. Upon each of these events, the protocol specification prescribes how information is processed, how the local state of the party is changed, whether output is given to the caller, or whether new messages are sent onto the network. Protocols can further trigger the start of sub-protocols, and several of these sub-protocols can be run simultaneously by any single party.

We follow the dynamic execution model defined in [12] where we simply merge the environment and the adversary into one entity (which is without loss of generality due to the completeness of the dummy adversary in UC). We thus assume a PPT adversary $\mathcal{A}$ that has full control over the basic communication network in that it can read, delay, delete, modify, and infect messages on the basic network. For some actions, parties are assumed to be connected by *secure channels*, in which case the adversary only learns that a message is being sent over that link without leaking the contents, and without the ability of the attacker to modify the content. The adversary also controls the scheduling of protocol events, including the initiation of protocols and providing their external inputs. The adversary can at any time decide to corrupt a party by a special request CORRUPT (except the trusted third party), in which case the entire private state is revealed (unless explicitly erased) together with all incoming and outgoing messages by this party. From this point on, the adversary is in full control of the protocol machine.

A General Model for PCS with Updates. We first define some notation. Let $\{X_\lambda\}_{\lambda\in\mathbb{N}}$ be a family of attributes and denote by $\mathcal{X}_\lambda$ the powerset of X_λ. Further let $\mathcal{F} = \{\mathcal{F}_\lambda\}_{\lambda\in\mathbb{N}}$ be a family of sets $\mathcal{F}_\lambda = \{F\colon \mathcal{X}_\lambda \times \mathcal{X}_\lambda \to \{0,1\}\}$ of policies/predicates. We omit λ in the subscripts from now on for the sake of simplicity and writing.

Policy-compliant signatures can be modeled as message-driven protocols, denoted PCS, where the set of parties consists of an authority $\mathfrak{A}$ and a set of users $P_1, \ldots, P_n$. The authority is a trusted entity that generates the setup of the system and generates the key-pair for the parties based on the attributes they are assigned to. More precisely, the authority is initially triggered by an input (SETUP, F) upon which it generates and outputs a master public key mpk and an additional token tok_0, an auxiliary value in anticipation of future policy updates. If the setup completes without failure, we say that the authority is initialized with policy F. After setup, the authority accepts inputs of the form (KEYGEN, P_i, x_i) upon which it has to generate the public-private key pair together with party P_i, potentially running an interactive sub-protocol over private channels with P_i. Such a user that completed this process, and thereby obtains a key pair ($\mathsf{pk}_i, \mathsf{sk}_i$) together with its attributes and the master public key is called initialized (with attributes x_i). Formally the user P_i signals the successful initialization by outputting (INITIALIZED, pk_i).

For policy updates, the authority accepts inputs of the form (UPDATE, F') and must output a so-called update token tok_e, where e is an increasing index corresponding to the number of times a policy has been updated.

Once a user is initialized it accepts two types of inputs in order to sign and verify signatures. On input (SIGN, tok, R, m) to party S, the party generates a signature σ, potentially after exchanging messages (i.e., running a sub-protocol) with the receiver R. Finally, on input (VERIFY, $\mathsf{tok}, \mathsf{pk}_S, \mathsf{pk}_R, m, \sigma$) for any combination of token, keys, message, and signature, the party locally produces a decision bit, where 0 indicates that the signature is invalid, and 1 indicates that the signature is valid with respect to the master public key mpk.

Concrete Protocol Descriptions in this Work. Not all steps above involve an interactive process between parties and hence many of the inputs to the protocol machines are answered directly by running algorithms which we can define following and extending the definition of [5]. In fact, our interactive schemes leverage a 2PC during signing between sender S and receiver R, while setup, key-generation, and verification are local operations (where in case of key-generation the keys are transmitted to the enrolled user). Thus, in order to define a full UPCS protocol, it is sufficient to specify the following tuple of algorithms:

Setup($1^\lambda, F$): On input a unary representation of the security parameter λ and an initial policy $F \in \mathcal{F}_\lambda$, output a master public and secret key pair (mpk, msk), and an initial token tok. This algorithm is run by $\mathfrak{A}$ upon input (SETUP, F).

PolUpd(msk, mpk, F'): On input the master secret and public key, msk and mpk, and a new policy F', output an update token tok. This algorithm is run by $\mathfrak{A}$ upon input (UPDATE, F').

KeyGen(msk, P_i, x_i): On input the master secret key msk and a set of attributes $x_i \in \mathcal{X}_\lambda$ for party P_i, output a public and secret key pair (pk, sk). This algorithm is run by $\mathfrak{A}$ upon input (KEYGEN, P_i, x_i). The authority then sends (mpk, pk, sk) to party P_i over a secure channel.

Verify(mpk, tok, pk_S, pk_R, m, σ): This is a deterministic algorithm, that on input a master public key mpk, a token tok, two public keys pk_S, pk_R, a signature σ on a message m, output either 0 or 1. This algorithms is executed upon input (VERIFY, tok, pk_S, pk_R, m, σ) by party P_i.

Finally, in the general case of an interactive signing process, we will define the following subprotocol:

Π_{sign}(mpk, tok, sk_S, pk_R, R, m): On input a master public key mpk, a token tok, a sender secret key sk_S and public key pk_R, a receiver identity, and a message m, this subprotocol, after termination, produces an output for the sender that is either a signature σ or $\perp$ (and no output for R). This subprotocol is invoked by S upon input (SIGN, tok, R, m).

In case signing is a non-interactive process as in [5], then the subprotocol Π_{sign} boils down to specifying an algorithm Sign just as in [5], where we assume that any public key pk_R issued by the authority $\mathfrak{A}$ toward a party P_i is associated to its identity in a certifiable way.[3] Obtaining a public key for a given identity can be accomplished by any out-of-band communication mechanism.

Sign(mpk, tok, sk_S, pk_R, m): On input a master public key mpk, a token tok, a sender secret key sk_S, a receiver public key pk_R, and a message m, output either a signature σ or $\perp$. This is run by S upon input (SIGN, tok, R, m), and where pk_R is the key issued to R by the authority (e.g. obtained from R).

3.2 Correctness and Security for PCS with Updates

PCS Correctness with Policy Updates. We first define the correctness of a (potentially interactive) updatable PCS scheme.

Definition 1. *An updatable PCS protocol π is called correct if the following property holds with overwhelming probability in the above experiment with respect to any PPT adversary: if d is the output by some initialized and honest party P_i upon input (VERIFY, tok, pk_S, pk_R, m, σ) and if it holds that*

1. *tok is the value output by $\mathfrak{A}$ on input (UPDATE, F) or (SETUP, F) for some policy F.*
2. *the public keys pk_S and pk_R belong to the initialized honest parties P_S and P_R computed as a result of invocations (KEYGEN, P_S, x_S), (KEYGEN, P_R, x_R), respectively; and*

---

[3] For example via a signature on the pair (pk_{P_i}, P_i).

3. the signature σ is the returned value by party P_S on input $(\text{SIGN}, \text{tok}, R, m)$,

then it must hold that $d = F(x_S, x_R)$.

Unforgeability. We capture unforgeability in this setting following [5], but cast in our model of execution.

Definition 2. *An updatable* PCS *protocol* π *is called unforgeable if no* PPT *adversary* $\mathcal{A}$ *is able to provoke the following event* E_{forge} *with better than negligible probability in the above experiment. Event* E_{forge} *occurs if an honest party* P_i *outputs a decision bit* $d = 1$ *on input* $(\text{VERIFY}, \text{tok}, \text{pk}_S, \text{pk}_R, m, \sigma)$ *where the following property holds:*

1. *The public key* pk_S *is associated with some initialized party* P_S *that is not corrupted and was never invoked on input* $(\text{SIGN}, \text{tok}, R, m)$; *or*
2. *the update token* tok *has never been computed by the authority* A *on any input* (UPDATE, F) *or* (SETUP, F); *or*
3. *the public key* pk_S *(resp.* pk_R*) does not belong to any initialized party* S *(resp.* R*) (by means of an invocation* (KEYGEN, S, x_S), *(resp.* (KEYGEN, R, x_R)*) to* $\mathfrak{A}$*); or*
4. *there is a policy* F *such that* tok *is the output by* $\mathfrak{A}$ *on input* (SETUP, F) *or* (UPDATE, F), *and there are attributes* x_S *and* x_R *associated to some initialized parties* S *and* R *with public keys* pk_S *and* pk_R, *respectively (as the result of inputs* (KEYGEN, S, x_S) *and* (KEYGEN, R, x_R) *to* $\mathfrak{A}$*), such that* $F(x_S, x_R) = 0$.

Attribute-Hiding. To define the attribute-hiding experiment, we extend the usual capabilities of the adversary by allowing it to perform a *test-key-gen* query. That is, in addition to its regular actions, the adversary $\mathcal{A}$ can initialize a party alternatively by $(\text{TEST-KEYGEN}, P_i, (x_{i,0}, x_{i,1}))$. At the onset of the experiment, a bit b is chosen uniformly at random. Upon a test-query $(\text{TEST-KEYGEN}, P_i, (x_{i,0}, x_{i,1}))$, party P_i executes the protocol action as if it received input $(\text{KEYGEN}, P_i, x_{i,b})$. In the following, we treat inputs of the form $(\text{KEYGEN}, P_i, x_i)$ made by $\mathcal{A}$ as if the adversary asked $(\text{TEST-KEYGEN}, P_i, (x_i, x_i))$. The adversary is allowed to execute all regular actions as defined above, but is not allowed to perform certain actions, involving any party P_i to which a test query $(\text{TEST-KEYGEN}, P_i, (x_{i,0}, x_{i,1}))$ has been issued, that would violate any of the conditions below:

1. $(\text{TEST-KEYGEN}, P_i, (x_{i,0}, x_{i,1}))$ is only issued for a corrupted P_i if $x_{i,0} = x_{i,1}$.
2. Vice-versa, the party P_i can only be corrupted in the execution if
   (a) it holds that $x_{i,0} = x_{i,1}$; and
   (b) For all other initialized parties P_j, initialized via $(\text{TEST-KEYGEN}, P_j, (x_{j,0}, x_{j,1}))$, it must hold that $F(x_{i,0}, x_{j,0}) = F(x_{i,1}, x_{j,1})$ for all policies F for which there is either the input (SETUP, F) or an input (UPDATE, F) to $\mathfrak{A}$.

3. For any signature produced by P_i via input $(\mathrm{SIGN}, \mathsf{tok}, P_j, m)$, where tok is a token for policy output by $\mathfrak{A}$ on input (UPDATE, F) or (SETUP, F), it must hold that $F(x_{i,0}, x_{j,0}) = F(x_{i,1}, x_{j,1})$.
4. For any signature produced by some honest party P_j toward P_i via an input $(\mathrm{SIGN}, \mathsf{tok}, P_i, m)$, where tok is as above, it must hold that $F(x_{j,0}, x_{i,0}) = F(x_{j,1}, x_{i,1})$.

An adversary is called valid, if it obeys the conditions with probability 1 over the randomness of the adversary and the protocol machines. At the end of its run, $\mathcal{A}$ outputs a bit b' (as a guess for b).

Definition 3. *An updatable PCS protocol π is called attribute-hiding if, for any valid PPT adversary $\mathcal{A}$ in the above extended experiment, the probability of event $b = b'$ is at most $1/2 + \mathrm{negl}(\lambda)$.*

4   Non-interactive Updatable Policy-Compliant Signatures

4.1   Two-Input Partially Hiding (Predicate-Only) Predicate Encryption

In this section, we formally define the notion of two-input partially hiding (predicate-only) predicate encryption (2-PHPE), which we use to build our non-interactive UPCS scheme in Sect. 4.2. As the name suggests, our 2-PHPE definition considers attribute-hiding only with respect to one slot of the predicate. We discuss this in more detail in Remark 2 after formally defining the primitive below.

Definition 4 (Two-input Partially-Hiding Predicate-Only Predicate Encryption). *Let $\{X_\lambda\}_{\lambda \in \mathbb{N}}$ be a family of attributes and denote by $\mathcal{X}_\lambda$ the powerset of X_λ. Further, let $\mathcal{P} = \{\mathcal{P}_\lambda\}_{\lambda \in \mathbb{N}}$ be a family of two-input predicate sets $\mathcal{P}_\lambda = \{P: \mathcal{X}_\lambda \times \mathcal{X}_\lambda \to \{0,1\}\}$. A two-input partially-hiding predicate-only predicate encryption (2-PHPE) scheme for the predicate class $\mathcal{P}_\lambda$ is given by a tuple of five PPT algorithms* 2-PHPE = (2-PHPE.Setup, 2-PHPE.KeyGen, 2-PHPE.Encode, 2-PHPE.Encrypt, 2-PHPE.Decrypt)[4]:

Setup(1^λ): *On input a unary representation of the security parameter λ, output public parameters* pp[5] *and a master secret key* msk.
KeyGen(msk, P): *On input* msk *and a predicate $P \in \mathcal{P}_\lambda$, output a secret key* sk_P.
Encode(msk, x_1): *On input* msk *and an attribute set $x_1 \in \mathcal{X}_\lambda$ (for slot 1), output an encoding e_{x_1} of x_1. (Note that e_{x_1} may not hide x_1.)*
Encrypt(msk, x_2): *On input* msk *and an attribute set $x_2 \in \mathcal{X}_\lambda$ (for slot 2), output a ciphertext* ct.
Decrypt(sk_P, (e_{x_1}, ct)): *On input a secret key sk_P, an encoded value e_{x_1} for slot 1 and a ciphertext* ct *for slot 2, output 0, 1 or $\perp$.*

---

[4] For readability, we will often drop the "2-PHPE." prefix when referring to its algorithms in this section.
[5] We assume pp to be an implicit input in all the other algorithms.

Correctness. A 2-PHPE *scheme for* $\mathcal{P}_\lambda$ *is correct, if for all* $(x_1, x_2) \in (\mathcal{X}_\lambda)^2, P \in \mathcal{P}_\lambda$, *for all* pp *and* msk *in the support of* Setup(1^λ), *all secret keys* sk$_P$ *in the support of* KeyGen(msk, P), *it holds that*

$$\Pr[\mathsf{Decrypt}(\mathsf{sk}_P, (\mathsf{Encode}(\mathsf{msk}, x_1), \mathsf{Encrypt}(\mathsf{msk}, x_2)))$$
$$= P(x_1, x_2)] \geq 1 - \mathrm{negl}(\lambda),$$

where the probability is over the random coins of Encode *and* Encrypt.

AH$_\beta^{\text{2-PHPE}}(1^\lambda, \mathcal{A})$

(pp, msk) $\leftarrow$ Setup(1^λ)

$\alpha \leftarrow \mathcal{A}^{\mathsf{KeyGen}(\mathsf{msk},\cdot),\mathsf{Encode}(\mathsf{msk},\cdot),\mathsf{QEncLR}_\beta(\cdot,\cdot)}(1^\lambda, \mathsf{pp})$

Output: α

Fig. 1. Partially-Hiding game of 2-PHPE.

Definition 5 (Indistinguishability-Based Partial Attribute-Hiding).
Let 2-PHPE = (Setup, KeyGen, Encode, Encrypt, Decrypt) *be a 2-PHPE scheme for a predicate class* $\mathcal{P}_\lambda$ *as defined in Definition 4. For* $\beta \in \{0,1\}$ *and for an adversary* $\mathcal{A}$, *we define an experiment* AH$_\beta^{\text{2-PHPE}}(1^\lambda, \mathcal{A})$ *(Fig. 1): The oracles* KeyGen(msk, $\cdot$) *and* Encode(msk, $\cdot$) *work exactly as the corresponding algorithms described in Definition 4 above. For any attribute-set pair* $(x_2^0, x_2^1) \in \mathcal{X}^2$ *for slot* 2, *define the oracle* QEncLR$_\beta(x_2^0, x_2^1) :=$ Encrypt$\left(\mathsf{msk}, x_2^\beta\right)$. *The adversary* $\mathcal{A}$ *in the above experiment may make an arbitrary polynomial number of queries adaptively to all its oracles before it outputs* α. *We call the adversary* $\mathcal{A}$ *valid, if for all predicates* $P \in \mathcal{P}_\lambda$ *queried to* KeyGen(msk, $\cdot$), *for all attribute sets* $x_1 \in \mathcal{X}$ *queried to* Encode(msk, $\cdot$) *and for all attribute-pairs* $(x_2^0, x_2^1) \in \mathcal{X}^2$ *queried to* QEncLR$_\beta(\cdot, \cdot)$, *it holds that* $P(x_1, x_2^0) = P(x_1, x_2^1)$. *We define the advantage of* $\mathcal{A}$ *as*

$$\mathsf{Adv}_{\text{2-PHPE},\mathcal{A}}^{\text{AH}}(1^\lambda) = |\Pr[\mathsf{AH}_0^{\text{2-PHPE}}(1^\lambda, \mathcal{A}) = 1] - \Pr[\mathsf{AH}_1^{\text{2-PHPE}}(1^\lambda, \mathcal{A}) = 1]|.$$

A 2-PHPE *scheme satisfies* partial attribute-hiding *security, if for any valid* PPT *adversary* $\mathcal{A}$, *there exists a negligible function* negl($\cdot$) *such that* $\mathsf{Adv}_{\text{2-PHPE},\mathcal{A}}^{\text{AH}}(1^\lambda) \leq \mathrm{negl}(\lambda)$.

Remark 1 (Asymmetric Evaluation). From Definition 4, we note that it is important for us to have the evaluation of any predicate P to be *asymmetric*. That is, given sk$_P$, an encoding e_{x_1} of attributes x_1 and a ciphertext ct encrypting attributes x_2, it is possible to learn $P(x_1, x_2)$ only and *not* $P(x_2, x_1)$. This is generally ensured by the syntax of any multi-input FE or PE by explicitly fixing the index associated to a ciphertext w.r.t. a slot [3,4,11,15]. For example, one way to do this for an n-input FE is to have the encryption algorithm take the index $i \in [n]$ as input along with a message and generate the slot i ciphertext as ct_i [11]. We keep this implicit in Definition 4 by denoting the attribute set for slot i as x_i for $i \in [2]$.

Remark 2 (Partial Attribute-Hiding). Note that for the first slot, the "encoding" e_{x_1} for attributes x_1 may not hide x_1, but still allows the evaluation of any predicate P, given a secret key sk_P and a ciphertext ct encrypting attributes x_2 with respect to the second slot. However, this encoding procedure needs the 2-PHPE master secret key and is thus a secret operation. The 2-PHPE security definition above further allows the adversary $\mathcal{A}$ to learn secret keys that decrypt successfully to 1. That is, for any of $\mathcal{A}$'s encoding query x_1 (to the $\mathsf{Encode}(\mathsf{msk}, \cdot)$ oracle) and any challenge query (x_2^0, x_2^1) (to the $\mathsf{QEncLR}_\beta(\cdot, \cdot)$ oracle), $\mathcal{A}$ may possess secret keys sk_P such that $P(x_1, x_2^b) = 1$ for all $b \in \{0,1\}$. Definition 5 thus requires (strong) attribute-hiding, but only with respect to the second slot.

Remark 3 (2-PHPE Instantiations and Implications). As stated in Remark 1, our 2-PHPE requires (strong) attribute-hiding for slot 2 whereas there are no privacy requirements on slot 1. 2-PHPE is thus a weaker variant of (and is implied by) the general two-input predicate encryption (2-PE) – a primitive that has recently been defined and studied under the more general framework of multi-input attribute-based and predicate encryption [1–3,15]. However, we believe there is no two-input (strong) attribute-hiding PE even for any specific class of predicates in any model under any assumptions.[6] (Realizing even 2-PHPE with strong attribute-hiding for inner-product predicates seems to require trilinear maps, which is a strong assumption. At a high level, a trilinear map allows to compute the inner-product functionality between vectors from three parties – the first and second party along with the secret key holder.) Currently, the only known way to build a (strong) attribute-hiding 2-PE (and 2-PHPE) scheme for all circuits is via iO for circuits [16,21] through two-input FE [4,9,17].

In terms of implications, we note that sub-exponentially secure, (strong) attribute-hiding 2-PHPE (even in the secret-key setting) for all circuits implies iO. To see this, we observe that (strong) attribute-hiding 2-PHPE implies PE with the same security (by simply ignoring the first input). Furthermore, (strong) attribute-hiding PE implies FE (where a secret key for some function with, say, n output bits corresponds to n PE secret keys for the individual bits). Finally, from [23], it follows that sub-exponentially secure, collusion-resistant, secret-key FE for all circuits implies iO.

---

[6] A recent work from [2] can be used to instantiate 2-PE from bilinear maps for inner-product predicates, but it does not support (strong) attribute-hiding. To the best of our knowledge, there are no (even one-input) PE schemes for general predicates based on standard assumptions satisfying this strong notion of privacy [18,19,30].

4.2 Non-interactive UPCS Scheme

In this section, we present our non-interactive updatable policy-compliant signature scheme. This scheme relies on the two-input partially-hiding predicate encryption scheme introduced in the previous section. A public key of a party in this scheme consists of the ciphertext ct encrypting its attributes as well as a verification key vk of a signature scheme. The corresponding secret key of this party contains the encoding of its attributes e_x and the signing key sk that corresponds to the verification key vk in the public key. Furthermore, the public key and the secret key of a party contain a signature of the authority that binds them together using the verification key vk, i.e. a signature in the public key that is generated for (vk, ct) and a signature in the secret key that is generated for (vk, e_x). These signatures are also used later to prove that the keys have been output by the authority.

To generate an update token in this scheme, the authority simply executes the key generation procedure of the two-input partially-hiding predicate encryption scheme for the update policy F' to generate the corresponding functional key $sk_{F'}$. Afterwards, this key is signed by the authority and together with this signature output as the update token.

If a sender now wants to generate a signature for a receiver, it uses its secret key (sk_S, e_S) together with the public key of the receiver $pk_R := (vk_R, ct_R)$ and the functional key $sk_{F'}$ that is part of the current token. In the first step, the sender verifies the signature of the receiver that is contained in its public key as well as the signature that has been generated for the update token $sk_{F'}$ to check their authenticity. Afterwards, the sender executes the decryption procedure of the two-input partially-hiding predicate encryption scheme using the functional key $sk_{F'}$, the ciphertext of the receiver ct_R, and its own encoding e_S to check if the sender and the receiver fulfill the current policy. If this is the case, then the sender generates a non-interactive zero-knowledge proof π over the output of the decryption procedure using the information of the receiver's public key, the update token and its own public and secret key. Here, the information contained in the public keys of the parties is used as part of the statement. The final signature σ, for a message m, is then generated by signing (m, pk_R, π) using the signing key sk of the sender.

To verify a signature, we start by verifying the signatures associated with the public keys of the sender and the receiver as well as the signature of the token for which it has been generated. If these verifications succeed, then the information inside the public keys and the token can be used to verify the proof π of the signature. In the last step, the signature σ generated over the proof and the message (m, pk_R, σ) is verified using the verification key of the sender vk_S. If all of these verification checks succeed, then the signature is deemed valid. We describe the formal scheme in Figs. 2 and 3.

Correctness and Security. The correctness of the scheme follows directly from the correctness of the underlying schemes, i.e., DS, NIZK and 2-PHPE. In terms of security, unforgeability follows from the unforgeability of the signature

$\underline{\text{Setup}(1^\lambda, F_{\text{init}} \in \mathcal{F}_\lambda):}$

$\text{CRS} \leftarrow \text{NIZK.Setup}(1^\lambda)$

$\text{msk}_{\text{PE}} \leftarrow \text{2-PHPE.Setup}(1^\lambda, \mathcal{F}_\lambda)$

$\text{sk}_{F_{\text{init}}} \leftarrow \text{2-PHPE.KeyGen}(\text{msk}_{\text{PE}},$
$\qquad\qquad\qquad\qquad F_{\text{init}})$

$(\text{vk}_{\text{pub}}, \text{sk}_{\text{pub}}) \leftarrow \text{DS}_{\text{pub}}.\text{Setup}(1^\lambda)$

$(\text{vk}_{\text{priv}}, \text{sk}_{\text{priv}}) \leftarrow \text{DS}_{\text{priv}}.\text{Setup}(1^\lambda)$

$(\text{vk}_{\text{tok}}, \text{sk}_{\text{tok}}) \leftarrow \text{DS}_{\text{tok}}.\text{Setup}(1^\lambda)$

$\sigma_{\text{tok}} \leftarrow \text{Sign}(\text{sk}_{\text{tok}}, (F_{\text{init}}, \text{sk}_{F_{\text{init}}}))$

$\text{mpk} := (\text{CRS}, \text{vk}_{\text{pub}}, \text{vk}_{\text{priv}}, \text{vk}_{\text{tok}})$

$\text{msk} := (\text{msk}_{\text{PE}}, \text{sk}_{\text{pub}}, \text{sk}_{\text{priv}}, \text{sk}_{\text{tok}})$

$\text{tok}_{\text{init}} := (F_{\text{init}}, \text{sk}_{F_{\text{init}}}, \sigma_{\text{tok}})$

Return $(\text{mpk}, \text{msk}), \text{tok}_{\text{init}}$

$\underline{\text{PolUpd}(\text{mpk}, \text{msk}, F'):}$

Parse $\text{mpk} := (\text{CRS}, \text{vk}_{\text{pub}}, \text{vk}_{\text{priv}})$

$\qquad \text{msk} = (\text{msk}_{\text{PE}}, \text{sk}_{\text{pub}}, \text{sk}_{\text{priv}})$

$\text{sk}_{F'} \leftarrow \text{2-PHPE.KeyGen}(\text{msk}_{\text{PE}}, F')$

$\sigma'_{\text{tok}} \leftarrow \text{DS}_{\text{tok}}.\text{Sign}(\text{sk}_{\text{tok}}, (F', \text{sk}_{F'}))$

Return $\text{tok}' := (F', \text{sk}_{F'}, \sigma'_{\text{tok}})$

$\underline{\text{KeyGen}(\text{msk}, P_i, x):}$

Parse $\text{msk} = (\text{msk}_{\text{PE}}, \text{sk}_{\text{pub}},$
$\qquad\qquad\qquad \text{sk}_{\text{priv}}, \text{sk}_{\text{tok}})$

$(\text{vk}_P, \text{sk}_P) \leftarrow \text{DS}_P.\text{Setup}(1^\lambda)$

$e_x \leftarrow \text{2-PHPE.Encode}(\text{msk}_{\text{PE}}, x)$

$\text{ct} \leftarrow \text{2-PHPE.Encrypt}(\text{msk}_{\text{PE}}, x)$

$\sigma_{\text{pub}} \leftarrow \text{Sign}(\text{sk}_{\text{pub}}, (\text{vk}_P, \text{ct}, P_i))$

$\sigma_{\text{priv}} \leftarrow \text{DS}_{\text{priv}}.\text{Sign}(\text{sk}_{\text{priv}}, (\text{vk}_P, e_x))$

$\text{pk} := (\text{vk}_P, \text{ct}, P_i, \sigma_{\text{pub}})$

$\text{sk} := (\text{vk}_P, \text{sk}_P, e_x, \sigma_{\text{priv}})$

Return (pk, sk)

$\underline{\text{Sign}(\text{mpk}, \text{tok}, \text{sk}, \text{pk}_R, m):}$

Parse $\text{mpk} = (\text{CRS}, \text{vk}_{\text{pub}},$
$\qquad\qquad\qquad \text{vk}_{\text{priv}}, \text{vk}_{\text{tok}})$

$\qquad \text{tok} = (F', \text{sk}_{F'}, \sigma_{\text{tok}})$

$\qquad \text{sk} = (\text{vk}_S, \text{sk}_S, e_x, \sigma_{\text{priv}})$

$\qquad \text{pk}_R = (\text{vk}_R, \text{ct}_R, P_R, \sigma_{\text{pub}})$

If $\text{Verify}(\text{vk}_{\text{pub}}, (\text{vk}_R, \text{ct}_R, P_R), \sigma^R_{\text{pub}})$

or $\text{Verify}(\text{vk}_{\text{tok}}, (F', \text{sk}_{F'}), \sigma_{\text{tok}}) = 0$

$\qquad$ Return $\bot$

$\pi \leftarrow \text{Prove}(\text{CRS}, (\text{vk}_{\text{priv}}, \text{sk}_{F'},$
$\qquad\qquad\qquad \text{vk}_S, \text{ct}_R), (e_x, \sigma_{\text{priv}})),$

$\qquad\qquad$ for R_{ZK} (defined in Figure 3)

Erase randomness used in Prove

$\sigma' \leftarrow \text{DS}_P.\text{Sign}(\text{sk}_S, (m, \text{pk}_R, \pi))$

Return $(m, \text{pk}_R, \sigma := (\pi, \sigma'))$

$\underline{\text{Verify}(\text{mpk}, \text{tok}, \text{pk}_S, \text{pk}_R, m, \sigma):}$

Parse $\text{mpk} = (\text{CRS}, \text{vk}_{\text{pub}},$
$\qquad\qquad\qquad \text{vk}_{\text{priv}}, \text{vk}_{\text{tok}})$

$\qquad \text{tok} = (F', \text{sk}_{F'}, \sigma_{\text{tok}})$

$\qquad \text{pk}_S = (\text{vk}_S, \text{ct}_S, P_S, \sigma^S_{\text{pub}})$

$\qquad \text{pk}_R = (\text{vk}_R, \text{ct}_R, P_R, \sigma^R_{\text{pub}})$

$\qquad \sigma = (\pi, \sigma')$

(Return 0 if parsing fails or $\sigma = \bot$)

Return $\text{Verify}(\text{vk}_{\text{tok}}, (F', \text{sk}_{F'}), \sigma_{\text{tok}})$

$\qquad \wedge \text{Verify}(\text{vk}_{\text{pub}}, (\text{vk}_R, \text{ct}_R), \sigma^R_{\text{pub}})$

$\qquad \wedge \text{Verify}(\text{vk}_{\text{pub}}, (\text{vk}_S, \text{ct}_S), \sigma^S_{\text{pub}})$

$\qquad \wedge \text{Verify}(\text{CRS}, (\text{vk}_{\text{priv}}, \text{vk}_S, \text{ct}_R), \pi)$

$\qquad \wedge \text{Verify}(\text{vk}_S, (m, \text{pk}_R, \pi), \sigma')$

Fig. 2. The setup, policy update, key generation and verification procedure of our non-interactive updatable policy-compliant signature scheme.

Relation R_{ZK}:

Instance: $x = (\mathsf{vk}_{\mathsf{priv}}, \mathsf{sk}_{F'}, \mathsf{vk}_S, \mathsf{ct}_R)$

Witness: $w = (\mathsf{e}_x, \sigma_{\mathsf{priv}})$

$R_{\mathrm{ZK}}(x, w) = 1$ if and only if:

   $\mathsf{DS}_{\mathsf{priv}}.\mathsf{Verify}(\mathsf{vk}_{\mathsf{priv}}, (\mathsf{vk}_S, \mathsf{e}_x), \sigma_{\mathsf{priv}}) = 1$ and $\mathsf{Dec}(\mathsf{sk}_F, (\mathsf{e}_x, \mathsf{ct}_R)) = 1$.

Fig. 3. Relation used for the NIZK in the signing procedure of the non-interactive UPCS scheme in Fig. 2.

schemes and the (knowledge) soundness of the NIZK proof. Attribute-hiding follows from the zero-knowledge property of NIZK and the partially attribute-hiding of 2-PHPE.

The formal security analysis of the scheme can be found in the full version.

4.3 Relationship Between UPCS and 2-PHPE

A compiler that realizes 2-PHPE from any *non-interactive* UPCS scheme, which we present in the full version, implies the equivalence of UPCS and 2-PHPE.

5 Interactive Updatable Policy-Compliant Signatures

In this section, we consider our interactive updatable policy-compliant signature schemes. Our first construction relies on signatures, non-interactive zero-knowledge proofs and two-party computation. This scheme requires interaction between the sender and the receiver in *each* update for a signature generation. We present this scheme as well as its security analysis in the full version of this work.

The second scheme only requires a *single* interaction between the sender and the receiver that allows a signature generation for all updates. To facilitate this, we require the same primitives as for the first scheme as well as a predicate encryption scheme. We present this scheme formally in the next section.

5.1 Interactive UPCS Using Predicate Encryption

Before presenting our scheme formally, we give an informal overview about how the scheme works. The public key of a party in the scheme consists of a verification key of a signature scheme vk and its secret key contains the corresponding signing key sk as well as its attribute set x. Additionally, the authority binds these keys together by generating signatures for both of them involving the verification key vk, i.e., it generates a signature over vk for the public key and a signature over (vk, x) for the secret key. Looking ahead, they are used inside the two-party computation protocol in the signature generation step to generate the predicate encryption ciphertext.

For the generation of an update token for a policy F', the authority first turns the two-input policy, that takes as an input two attribute sets X_S and X_R, into a single-input function $\widehat{F}'$ that takes as an input a single set $X_{S,R}$ which is a disjoint union of the sender and receiver attributes, i.e. $X_{S,R} := \{(x,0)|x \in X_S\} \cup \{(x,1)|x \in X_R\}$. The function $\widehat{F}'$ splits the input set $X_{S,R}$ into two sets X_S and X_R, where attributes in X_S are of the form $(x,0)$ and attributes in X_R are of the form $(x,1)$, and then executes $F'(X_S, X_R)$. This transformation is needed since, in this scheme, we rely only on a single-input PE scheme. Later, a functional key $\mathsf{sk}_{F'}$ for the policy $\widehat{F}'$ is generated and signed.

In the first step of the signature generation, the sender and the receiver interact in a 2PC protocol where the sender inputs its secret key $\mathsf{sk}_S := (\mathsf{vk}_S, x_S)$ and the public key of the receiver pk_R and the receiver inputs its secret key $\mathsf{sk}_R := (\mathsf{vk}_R, x_R)$ as well as the public key of the sender pk_S. Furthermore, both parties input the master public key of PE $\mathsf{mpk}_{\mathsf{PE}}$. The circuit that the 2PC protocol computes verifies, first, that the secret keys input by the parties correspond to the public keys, i.e., that sk_S corresponds to pk_S and sk_R corresponds to pk_R, by checking the contained information as well as verifying the signatures. Further, it also verifies that both parties have input the same master public key $\mathsf{mpk}_{\mathsf{PE}}$. Afterwards, it generates a PE ciphertext $\mathsf{ct}_{S,R}$ encrypting a concatenation (x_S, x_R) of the attributes of the sender x_S and the receiver x_R as well as a commitment $\mathsf{com}_{S,R}$ to the ciphertext $\mathsf{ct}_{S,R}$. In the last step of the 2PC protocol, a proof π' is generated that the commitment $\mathsf{com}_{S,R}$ commits to the ciphertext $\mathsf{ct}_{S,R}$ and that the ciphertext $\mathsf{ct}_{S,R}$ is honestly generated using the attributes x_S of the sender S and the attributes x_R of the receiver R.

The statement used in this proof involves the commitment $\mathsf{com}_{S,R}$ as well as the verification keys of the sender vk_S and the receiver vk_R. Finally, the commitment $\mathsf{com}_{S,R}$ as well as its randomness r_{com}, the ciphertext $\mathsf{ct}_{S,R}$ and the proof π are output to the sender.

The sender then generates the signature for a message m by first decrypting the obtained ciphertext $\mathsf{ct}_{S,R}$ using the functional key $\mathsf{sk}_{F'}$ of the current token and then proving, using a second zero-knowledge proof, that the commitment $\mathsf{com}_{S,R}$ commits to a ciphertext $\mathsf{ct}_{S,R}$ that decrypts to 1.

The commitment $\mathsf{com}_{S,R}$ as well as the token $\mathsf{sk}_{F'}$ are used as the statement and the randomness for the commitment r_{com} and the ciphertext $\mathsf{ct}_{S,R}$ are used as the witness. The final step of the signature generation consists of signing $(m, \mathsf{pk}_R, \pi := (\pi', \pi''))$, where π'' is the second proof generated as described above, using the signing key sk of the sender.

For every further signature generation between the same pair of parties the ciphertext $\mathsf{ct}_{S,R}$ and the commitment $\mathsf{com}_{S,R}$, and therefore the resulting proofs π' and π'', in case that the proof is generated under the same policy, can be reused. If a signature for the same pair of parties needs to be generated for a different policy, a new proof π'' needs to be generated and the remaining information can be reused.

The commitment is needed to ensure that the ciphertext is not revealed when a signature is generated. A revelation of the ciphertext would allow every other

Setup$(1^\lambda, F_{\text{init}})$:
$\text{CRS}_{\text{NIZK},1} \leftarrow \text{NIZK}_1.\text{Setup}(1^\lambda)$
for R^1_{ZK} (Fig. 6).
$\text{CRS}_{\text{NIZK},2} \leftarrow \text{NIZK}_2.\text{Setup}(1^\lambda)$
for R^2_{ZK} (Fig. 6).
$\text{CRS}_{\text{Com}} \leftarrow \text{Com}.\text{Setup}(1^\lambda)$
$(\text{mpk}_{\text{PE}}, \text{msk}_{\text{PE}}) \leftarrow \text{PE}.\text{Setup}(1^\lambda)$
$(\text{vk}_{\text{pub}}, \text{sk}_{\text{pub}}) \leftarrow \text{DS}_{\text{pub}}.\text{Setup}(1^\lambda)$
$(\text{vk}_{\text{priv}}, \text{sk}_{\text{priv}}) \leftarrow \text{DS}_{\text{priv}}.\text{Setup}(1^\lambda)$
$(\text{vk}_{\text{tok}}, \text{sk}_{\text{tok}}) \leftarrow \text{DS}_{\text{tok}}.\text{Setup}(1^\lambda)$
$\text{sk}_{F_{\text{init}}} \leftarrow \text{PE}.\text{KeyGen}(\text{msk}_{\text{PE}}, F_{\text{init}})$
$\sigma_{\text{tok}} \leftarrow \text{Sign}(\text{sk}_{\text{tok}}, (F_{\text{init}}, \text{sk}_{F_{\text{init}}}))$
$\text{CRS}_{\text{NIZK}} := \{\text{CRS}_{\text{NIZK},i}\}_{i \in [2]}$
$\text{mpk} = (\text{CRS}_{\text{NIZK}}, \text{CRS}_{\text{Com}},$
            $\text{mpk}_{\text{PE}}, \text{vk}_{\text{pub}}, \text{vk}_{\text{priv}}, \text{vk}_{\text{tok}})$
$\text{msk} := (\text{msk}_{\text{PE}}, \text{sk}_{\text{pub}}, \text{sk}_{\text{priv}}, \text{sk}_{\text{tok}})$
$\text{tok}_{\text{init}} := (F_{\text{init}}, \text{sk}_{F_{\text{init}}}, \sigma_{\text{tok}})$
Return $(\text{mpk}, \text{msk}), \text{tok}_{\text{init}}$

PolUpd$(\text{mpk}, \text{msk}, F_{\text{upd}})$
Parse $\text{mpk} := (\text{CRS}_{\text{NIZK}}, \text{CRS}_{\text{Com}},$
            $\text{mpk}_{\text{PE}}, \text{vk}_{\text{pub}}, \text{vk}_{\text{priv}}, \text{vk}_{\text{tok}})$
$\text{msk} := (\text{msk}_{\text{PE}}, \text{sk}_{\text{pub}},$
            $\text{sk}_{\text{priv}}, \text{sk}_{\text{tok}})$
Set $\widehat{F}_{\text{upd}}$ as the single input
function that splits its input into
two sets and then evaluates F_{upd}.
$\text{sk}_{F_{\text{upd}}} \leftarrow \text{PE}.\text{KeyGen}(\text{msk}_{\text{PE}}, \widehat{F}_{\text{upd}})$
$\sigma'_{\text{tok}} \leftarrow \text{Sign}(\text{sk}_{\text{tok}}, (F_{\text{upd}}, \text{sk}_{F_{\text{upd}}}))$
$\text{tok}_{\text{upd}} := (F_{\text{upd}}, \text{sk}_{F_{\text{upd}}}, \sigma'_{\text{tok}})$
Return tok_{upd}

KeyGen(msk, P_i, x):
Parse $\text{msk} := (\text{msk}_{\text{PE}}, \text{sk}_{\text{pub}}, \text{sk}_{\text{priv}})$
$(\text{vk}_{\text{P}}, \text{sk}_{\text{P}}) \leftarrow \text{DS}_{\text{P}}.\text{Setup}(1^\lambda)$
$\sigma_{\text{pub}} \leftarrow \text{DS}_{\text{pub}}.\text{Sign}(\text{sk}_{\text{pub}}, (\text{vk}_{\text{P}}, P_i))$
$\sigma_{\text{priv}} \leftarrow \text{DS}_{\text{priv}}.\text{Sign}(\text{sk}_{\text{priv}}, (\text{vk}_{\text{P}}, x))$
$\text{pk} := (\text{vk}_{\text{P}}, P_i, \sigma_{\text{pub}})$
$\text{sk} := (\text{vk}_{\text{P}}, \text{sk}_{\text{P}}, x, \sigma_{\text{priv}})$
Return (pk, sk)

Verify$(\text{mpk}, \text{tok}, \text{pk}_S, \text{pk}_R, m, \sigma)$:
Parse $\text{mpk} = (\text{CRS}_{\text{NIZK}}, \text{mpk}_{\text{PE}}$
                $\text{vk}_{\text{pub}}, \text{vk}_{\text{priv}}, \text{vk}_{\text{tok}})$
        $\text{tok} = (F, \text{sk}_F, \sigma_{\text{tok}}),$
        $\text{pk}_S = (\text{vk}_S, P_S, \sigma^S_{\text{pub}}),$
        $\text{pk}_R = (\text{vk}_R, P_R, \sigma^R_{\text{pub}}),$
        $\sigma = (\pi := (\text{com}_{S,R}, \pi', \pi''), \sigma')$
(Return 0 if parsing fails or $\sigma = \bot$)
Return $\text{Verify}(\text{vk}_{\text{tok}}, (F, \text{sk}_F, \sigma_{\text{tok}}))$
    $\wedge \text{Verify}(\text{vk}_{\text{pub}}, (\text{vk}_R, P_R), \sigma^R_{\text{pub}})$
    $\wedge \text{Verify}(\text{vk}_{\text{pub}}, (\text{vk}_S, P_S), \sigma^S_{\text{pub}})$
    $\wedge \text{Verify}(\text{CRS}_{\text{NIZK}}, (\text{vk}_{\text{priv}}, \text{vk}_S,$
                $\text{vk}_R, \text{com}_{S,R}), \pi')$
    $\wedge \text{NIZK}_{\text{NIZK}}.\text{Verify}(\text{CRS}_{\text{NIZK}},$
                $(\text{sk}_F, \text{com}_{S,R}), \pi'')$
    $\wedge \text{DS}_{\text{P}}.\text{Verify}(\text{vk}_S, (m, \text{pk}_R, \pi), \sigma')$

Fig. 4. The setup, policy update, key generation and verification procedures of our interactive PE-based UPCS scheme.

$\Pi_{\text{sign}}(\text{mpk}, \text{tok}, \text{sk}_S, \text{pk}_S, R, m)$ for signer S:

Parse $\text{mpk} = (\text{CRS}_{\text{NIZK}}, \text{CRS}_{\text{Com}}, \text{mpk}_{\text{PE}}, \text{vk}_{\text{pub}}, \text{vk}_{\text{priv}}, \text{vk}_{\text{tok}})$,
$\qquad \text{tok} = (F, \text{sk}_F, \sigma_{\text{tok}}), \text{sk}_S = (\text{vk}_\text{P}^S, \text{sk}_\text{P}^S, x_S, \sigma_{\text{priv}}^S), \text{pk}_S = (\text{vk}_\text{P}^S, P_S, \sigma_{\text{pub}}^S)$

Obtain $\text{pk}_R = (\text{vk}_\text{P}^R, P_R, \sigma_{\text{pub}}^R)$ from R (cf. Sec. 3)

Run decryption, if the algorithms were already executed by S and R.

S: Return $\perp$, if $\text{DS}_{\text{pub}}.\text{Verify}(\text{vk}_{\text{pub}}, (\text{vk}_\text{P}^R, P_R), \sigma_{\text{pub}}^R) = 0$.

R: Return $\perp$, if $\text{DS}_{\text{pub}}.\text{Verify}(\text{vk}_{\text{pub}}, (\text{vk}_\text{P}^S, P_S), \sigma_{\text{pub}}^S) = 0$.

S and R execute Π that computes the circuit described in Figure 5. After the execution of Π, S obtains $(\text{com}_{S,R}, \text{ct}_{S,R}, r_{\text{com}}, \pi')$.

If $\text{PE}.\text{Dec}(\text{sk}_F, \text{ct}_{S,R}) = 0$, return $\perp$.

S computes $\pi'' \leftarrow \text{NIZK}_2.\text{Prove}(\text{CRS}_{\text{NIZK},2}, (\text{CRS}_{\text{Com}}, \text{sk}_F, \text{com}_{S,R}), (\text{ct}_{S,R}, r_{\text{com}}))$ for the relation R_{ZK}^2 described in Figure 6 and erases the randomness used for the proof generation.

Compute $\sigma' \leftarrow \text{DS}_\text{P}.\text{Sign}(\text{sk}_\text{P}^S, (m, \text{pk}_R, \text{com}_{S,R}, \pi := (\pi', \pi'')))$,
set $\sigma := (\text{com}_{S,R}, \pi, \sigma')$, return (m, pk_R, σ)

Fig. 5. The signing procedure of our interactive PE-based UPCS scheme.

party in the system to evaluate every policy over the attributes of the parties that are involved in this single signature generation. Another alternative to prevent this leakage, if someone does not want to rely on a commitment scheme, is to generate the second proof for the relation that proves that the owned ciphertext decrypts to 1 and that the proof output by the two-party computation protocol verifies. This requires the generation of a proof of a proof which might be less efficient than a second proof that only proves some properties of the commitment. Therefore, we present the construction using the commitment scheme.

To verify a signature, the signatures associated with the public keys of the sender and receiver are verified, as well as the signature of the corresponding token. If these checks succeed, then the information in the public keys and the token can be used to verify the proofs π' and π'' of the signature. Lastly, the signature σ generated over the proof and the message $(m, \text{pk}_R, \pi := (\pi', \pi''))$ is verified using the sender's verification key vk_S. If all of these verifications succeed, the signature is deemed valid. We describe our formal scheme in Figs. 4, 5 and Fig. 7.

Correctness and Security. The correctness of the scheme from Figs. 4, 5 and Fig. 7 follows directly from the correctness of the underlying schemes, i.e., DS, NIZK, 2PC and PE. In terms of security, unforgeability follows from that of the signature schemes and the (knowledge) soundness of the NIZK proof and the

---

Circuit $C_{\mathsf{CRS_{NIZK,1}},\mathsf{mpk_{PE}},\mathsf{vk_{priv}}}$:

Inputs: S uses $(\mathsf{pk}_R := (\mathsf{vk}^R_{\mathsf{P},S}, P_R, \sigma^R_{\mathsf{pub},S}), \mathsf{sk}_S := (\mathsf{vk}^S_{\mathsf{P},S}, \cdot, x_S, \sigma^S_{\mathsf{priv}}),$
$\mathsf{mpk}_S := (\mathsf{CRS}^S_{\mathsf{NIZK}}, \mathsf{CRS}^S_{\mathsf{Com}}, \mathsf{mpk}^S_{\mathsf{PE}}, \cdot, \mathsf{vk}^S_{\mathsf{priv}}, \cdot)),$
R uses $(\mathsf{pk}_S := (\mathsf{vk}^S_{\mathsf{P},R}, P_S, \sigma^S_{\mathsf{pub},R}), \mathsf{sk}_R := (\mathsf{vk}^R_{\mathsf{P},R}, \cdot, x_R, \sigma^R_{\mathsf{priv}}),$
$\mathsf{mpk}_R := (\mathsf{CRS}^R_{\mathsf{NIZK}}, \mathsf{CRS}^R_{\mathsf{Com}}, \mathsf{mpk}^R_{\mathsf{PE}}, \cdot, \mathsf{vk}^R_{\mathsf{priv}}, \cdot))$

as its input.

For $P_i \in \{S, R\}$, check that:

- $\mathsf{mpk}_S = \mathsf{mpk}_R$,
- $\mathsf{vk}^{P_i}_{\mathsf{P},S} = \mathsf{vk}^{P_i}_{\mathsf{P},R}$,
- $\mathsf{Verify}(\mathsf{vk_{priv}}, (\mathsf{vk}^{P_i}_{\mathsf{P},P_i}, x_{P_i}), \sigma^{P_i}_{\mathsf{priv}}) = 1$,

with $\mathsf{CRS_{NIZK}} := \mathsf{CRS}^S_{\mathsf{NIZK}}, \mathsf{CRS_{Com}} := \mathsf{CRS}^S_{\mathsf{Com}}, \mathsf{mpk_{PE}} := \mathsf{mpk}^S_{\mathsf{PE}},$
$\mathsf{vk_{priv}} := \mathsf{vk}^R_{\mathsf{priv}}, \mathsf{vk}^{P_i}_{\mathsf{P}} := \mathsf{vk}^{P_i}_{\mathsf{P},P_i}.$

If any of these checks fails output $\bot$.

Else, compute:

- $\mathsf{ct}_{S,R} \leftarrow \mathsf{PE.Enc}(\mathsf{mpk_{PE}}, (x_S \dot{\cup} x_R); r_{\mathsf{Enc}})$, with $r_{\mathsf{Enc}} \leftarrow \{0,1\}^\lambda$
  and "$\dot{\cup}$" as in Section 2.
- $\mathsf{com}_{S,R} \leftarrow \mathsf{Com}(\mathsf{CRS_{Com}}, \mathsf{ct}_{S,R}; r_{\mathsf{com}})$, with $r_{\mathsf{com}} \leftarrow \{0,1\}^\lambda$.
- $\pi' \leftarrow \mathsf{NIZK_1.Prove}(\mathsf{CRS_{NIZK,1}}, (\mathsf{CRS_{Com}}, \mathsf{vk_{priv}}, \mathsf{vk}^S_{\mathsf{P}}, \mathsf{vk}^R_{\mathsf{P}}, \mathsf{com}_{S,R}),$
  $(x_S, x_R, \sigma^S_{\mathsf{priv}}, \sigma^R_{\mathsf{priv}}, \mathsf{ct}_{S,R}, r_{\mathsf{Enc}}, r_{\mathsf{com}}))$

for the relation R^1_{ZK} described in Figure 6.

Output: $(\mathsf{com}_{S,R}, \mathsf{ct}_{S,R}, r_{\mathsf{com}}, \pi)$ to S.

Fig. 6. The circuit that is being computed by the 2PC of the interactive UPCS scheme in Fig. 5.

binding property com. Further, the attribute-hiding of this UPCS follows from the simulatability of 2PC, zero-knowledge property of NIZK, the equivocality of the commitment Com, and the attribute-hiding of PE.

We refer to the full version for the formal security analysis.

PE Instantiations. For the interactive UPCS scheme described above, we require an attribute-hiding PE scheme with adaptive security. This primitive can be realized for *inner-product* predicates in the standard model using bilinear maps [28]. Such an instantiation allows for the evaluation of expressions such as $\langle (x, y), (u, v) \rangle = (\langle x, u \rangle + \langle y, v \rangle) \bmod \mathbb{Z}_q$, where $x \in \mathbb{Z}_q^n$ and $y \in \mathbb{Z}_q^n$ are the attributes associated with sender and receiver respectively, while $(u, v) \in \mathbb{Z}_q^{2n}$ defines the policy (for any $n \in \mathbb{N}$ and some prime q). The values x, y, u and v here are obtained by passing the attributes of the sender and the receiver, as well

$$\text{Relation } R^1_{\text{ZK}}:$$

Instance: $x = (\text{CRS}_{\text{Com}}, \text{vk}_{\text{priv}}, \text{vk}_P^S, \text{vk}_P^R, \text{com}_{S,R})$

Witness: $w = (x_S, x_R, \sigma_{\text{priv}}^S, \sigma_{\text{priv}}^R, \text{ct}_{S,R}, r_{\text{Enc}}, r_{\text{com}})$

$R_{\text{ZK}}(x, w) = 1$ if and only if:

$\quad \text{DS}_{\text{priv}}.\text{Verify}(\text{vk}_{\text{priv}}, (\text{vk}_P^P, x_P), \sigma_{\text{priv}}^P) = 1$, for $P \in \{S, R\}$,

$\quad \text{ct}_{S,R} := \text{PE.Enc}(\text{mpk}_{\text{PE}}, (x_S \dot\cup x_R); r_{\text{Enc}})$ and

$\quad \text{com}_{S,R} := \text{Com}(\text{CRS}_{\text{Com}}, \text{ct}_{S,R}; r_{\text{com}}).$

$$\text{Relation } R^2_{\text{ZK}}:$$

Instance: $x = (\text{CRS}_{\text{Com}}, \text{sk}_F, \text{com}_{S,R})$

Witness: $w = (\text{ct}_{S,R}, r_{\text{com}})$

$R_{\text{ZK}}(x, w) = 1$ if and only if:

$\quad \text{com} := \text{Com}(\text{CRS}_{\text{Com}}, \text{ct}_{S,R}, r_{\text{com}})$ and $\text{PE.Dec}(\text{sk}_F, \text{ct}_{S,R}) = 1.$

Fig. 7. Description of relation R^1_{ZK} for the NIZK used inside the 2PC (Fig. 6) and description of relation R^2_{ZK} for the NIZK used in the final signature generation (Fig. 5).

as the policy, through a *preprocessing* phase. Such a preprocessing procedure can be defined similarly as in [22, Sect. 5] and [5, Sect. 4.5] to realize more concrete policies.

We can also instantiate the underlying PE with an adaptively secure, attribute-hiding PE for *quadratic* predicates in the generic group model, again, based on pairings, from [7, Sect. 6] or [29, Sect. 3]. Concretely, having $\boldsymbol{x} \in \mathbb{Z}_q^{n_1}$ and $\boldsymbol{y} \in \mathbb{Z}_q^{n_2}$ (for some $n_1, n_2 \in \mathbb{N}$) as the sender's and receiver's attributes respectively, the policies P are described by matrices $\mathbf{F} \in \mathbb{Z}_q^{n_1 \times n_2}$ as $P((\boldsymbol{x}, \boldsymbol{y}), \mathbf{F}) = (\boldsymbol{x}^\top \mathbf{F} \boldsymbol{y}) \bmod \mathbb{Z}_q$. Such policies also capture richer functions like constant-depth boolean formulas or comparison predicates [7, Sect. 6.1].

These pairing-based PE schemes show that the presented UPCS scheme with one-time interaction can, in principle, be implemented and benchmarked for different classes of predicates, given efficient instantiations of digital signatures and NIZK proofs that are compatible with the underlying PE schemes.

Acknowledgments. The second author was partly supported by the European Union (ERC AdG REWORC - 101054911), and also by True Data 8 (Distributed Ledger & Multiparty Computation) under the Hessen State Ministry for Higher Education, Research and the Arts within their joint support of the National Research Center for Applied Cybersecurity ATHENE. The fourth author was supported by an MC2 postdoctoral fellowship.

References

1. Agrawal, S., Rossi, M., Yadav, A., Yamada, S.: Constant input attribute based (and predicate) encryption from evasive and tensor LWE. In: Handschuh, H., Lysyanskaya, A. (eds.) CRYPTO 2023 CRYPTO 2023. LNCS, 14084th edn., pp. 532–564. Springer, Cham (2023). https://doi.org/10.1007/978-3-031-38551-3_17
2. Agrawal, S., Tomida, J., Yadav, A.: Attribute-based multi-input FE (and more) for attribute-weighted sums. In: Handschuh, H., Lysyanskaya, A. (eds.) Advances in Cryptology, CRYPTO 2023. LNCS, vol. 14084, pp. 464–497. Springer, Cham (2023). https://doi.org/10.1007/978-3-031-38551-3_15
3. Agrawal, S., Yadav, A., Yamada, S.: Multi-input attribute based encryption and predicate encryption. In: Dodis, Y., Shrimpton, T. (eds.) Advances in Cryptology, CRYPTO 2022, Part I. LNCS, vol. 13507, pp. 590–621. Springer, Heidelberg (2022). https://doi.org/10.1007/978-3-031-15802-5_21
4. Ananth, P., Jain, A.: Indistinguishability obfuscation from compact functional encryption. In: Gennaro, R., Robshaw, M. (eds.) CRYPTO 2015, Part I. LNCS, vol. 9215, pp. 308–326. Springer, Heidelberg (2015). https://doi.org/10.1007/978-3-662-47989-6_15
5. Badertscher, C., Matt, C., Waldner, H.: Policy-compliant signatures. In: Nissim, K., Waters, B. (eds.) TCC 2021, Part III. LNCS, vol. 13044, pp. 350–381. Springer, Cham (2021). https://doi.org/10.1007/978-3-030-90456-2_12
6. Badertscher, C., Sedaghat, M., Waldner, H.: Fine-grained accountable privacy via unlinkable policy-compliant signatures. Cryptology ePrint Archive, Paper 2023/1070 (2023). https://eprint.iacr.org/2023/1070
7. Baltico, C.E.Z., Catalano, D., Fiore, D., Gay, R.: Practical functional encryption for quadratic functions with applications to predicate encryption. In: Katz, J., Shacham, H. (eds.) CRYPTO 2017, Part I. LNCS, vol. 10401, pp. 67–98. Springer, Cham (2017). https://doi.org/10.1007/978-3-319-63688-7_3
8. Bellare, M., Fuchsbauer, G.: Policy-based signatures. In: Krawczyk, H. (ed.) PKC 2014. LNCS, vol. 8383, pp. 520–537. Springer, Heidelberg (2014). https://doi.org/10.1007/978-3-642-54631-0_30
9. Bitansky, N., Vaikuntanathan, V.: Indistinguishability obfuscation from functional encryption. In: Guruswami, V. (ed.) 56th FOCS, October 2015, pp. 171–190. IEEE Computer Society Press (2015). https://doi.org/10.1109/FOCS.2015.20
10. Boneh, D., Shacham, H.: Group signatures with verifier-local revocation. In: Atluri, V., Pfitzmann, B., McDaniel, P. (eds.) ACM CCS 2004, October 2004, pp. 168–177. ACM Press (2004). https://doi.org/10.1145/1030083.1030106
11. Brakerski, Z., Komargodski, I., Segev, G.: Multi-input functional encryption in the private-key setting: stronger security from weaker assumptions. In: Fischlin, M., Coron, J.-S. (eds.) EUROCRYPT 2016, Part II. LNCS, vol. 9666, pp. 852–880. Springer, Heidelberg (2016). https://doi.org/10.1007/978-3-662-49896-5_30
12. Canetti, R.: Universally composable security: a new paradigm for cryptographic protocols. In: 42nd FOCS, October 2001, pp. 136–145. IEEE Computer Society Press (2001). https://doi.org/10.1109/SFCS.2001.959888
13. Cheng, L., Meng, F.: Server-aided revocable attribute-based encryption revised: multi-user setting and fully secure. In: Bertino, E., Shulman, H., Waidner, M. (eds.) ESORICS 2021, Part II. LNCS, vol. 12973, pp. 192–212. Springer, Cham (2021). https://doi.org/10.1007/978-3-030-88428-4_10

14. Cui, H., Deng, R.H., Li, Y., Qin, B.: Server-aided revocable attribute-based encryption. In: Askoxylakis, I., Ioannidis, S., Katsikas, S., Meadows, C. (eds.) ESORICS 2016, Part II. LNCS, vol. 9879, pp. 570–587. Springer, Cham (2016). https://doi.org/10.1007/978-3-319-45741-3_29

15. Francati, D., Friolo, D., Malavolta, G., Venturi, D.: Multi-key and multi-input predicate encryption from learning with errors. In: Proceedings of the 42nd Annual International Conference on the Theory and Applications of Cryptographic Techniques. Advances in Cryptology, EUROCRYPT 2023, Lyon, France, 23–27 April 2023, Part III. pp. 573–604. Springer, Cham (2023). https://doi.org/10.1007/978-3-031-30620-4_19

16. Garg, S., Gentry, C., Halevi, S., Raykova, M., Sahai, A., Waters, B.: Candidate indistinguishability obfuscation and functional encryption for all circuits. In: 54th FOCS, October 2013, pp. 40–49. IEEE Computer Society Press (2013). https://doi.org/10.1109/FOCS.2013.13

17. Goldwasser, S., Gordon, S.D., Goyal, V., Jain, A., Katz, J., Liu, F.-H., Sahai, A., Shi, E., Zhou, H.-S.: Multi-input functional encryption. In: Nguyen, P.Q., Oswald, E. (eds.) EUROCRYPT 2014. LNCS, vol. 8441, pp. 578–602. Springer, Heidelberg (2014). https://doi.org/10.1007/978-3-642-55220-5_32

18. Gorbunov, S., Vaikuntanathan, V., Wee, H.: Predicate encryption for circuits from LWE. In: Gennaro, R., Robshaw, M. (eds.) CRYPTO 2015, Part II. LNCS, vol. 9216, pp. 503–523. Springer, Heidelberg (2015). https://doi.org/10.1007/978-3-662-48000-7_25

19. Goyal, R., Koppula, V., Waters, B.: Lockable obfuscation. In: Umans, C. (ed.) 58th FOCS, October 2017, pp. 612–621. IEEE Computer Society Press (2017). https://doi.org/10.1109/FOCS.2017.62

20. Ishida, A., Sakai, Y., Emura, K., Hanaoka, G., Tanaka, K.: Fully anonymous group signature with verifier-local revocation. In: Catalano, D., De Prisco, R. (eds.) SCN 2018. LNCS, vol. 11035, pp. 23–42. Springer, Cham (2018). https://doi.org/10.1007/978-3-319-98113-0_2

21. Jain, A., Lin, H., Sahai, A.: Indistinguishability obfuscation from well-founded assumptions. In: Proceedings of the 53rd Annual ACM SIGACT Symposium on Theory of Computing, pp. 60–73 (2021)

22. Katz, J., Sahai, A., Waters, B.: Predicate encryption supporting disjunctions, polynomial equations, and inner products. In: Smart, N. (ed.) EUROCRYPT 2008. LNCS, vol. 4965, pp. 146–162. Springer, Heidelberg (2008). https://doi.org/10.1007/978-3-540-78967-3_9

23. Kitagawa, F., Nishimaki, R., Tanaka, K.: Obfustopia built on secret-key functional encryption. In: Nielsen, J.B., Rijmen, V. (eds.) EUROCRYPT 2018, Part II. LNCS, vol. 10821, pp. 603–648. Springer, Cham (2018). https://doi.org/10.1007/978-3-319-78375-8_20

24. Langlois, A., Ling, S., Nguyen, K., Wang, H.: Lattice-based group signature scheme with verifier-local revocation. In: Krawczyk, H. (ed.) PKC 2014. LNCS, vol. 8383, pp. 345–361. Springer, Heidelberg (2014). https://doi.org/10.1007/978-3-642-54631-0_20

25. Ling, S., Nguyen, K., Wang, H., Zhang, J.: Server-aided revocable predicate encryption: formalization and lattice-based instantiation. Comput. J. **62**(12), 1849–1862 (2019)

26. Maji, H.K., Prabhakaran, M., Rosulek, M.: Attribute-based signatures. In: Kiayias, A. (ed.) CT-RSA 2011. LNCS, vol. 6558, pp. 376–392. Springer, Heidelberg (2011). https://doi.org/10.1007/978-3-642-19074-2_24

27. Nguyen, K., Wang, H., Zhang, J.: Server-aided revocable identity-based encryption from lattices. In: Foresti, S., Persiano, G. (eds.) CANS 2016. LNCS, vol. 10052, pp. 107–123. Springer, Cham (2016). https://doi.org/10.1007/978-3-319-48965-0_7

28. Okamoto, T., Takashima, K.: Adaptively attribute-hiding (hierarchical) inner product encryption. In: Pointcheval, D., Johansson, T. (eds.) EUROCRYPT 2012. LNCS, vol. 7237, pp. 591–608. Springer, Heidelberg (2012). https://doi.org/10.1007/978-3-642-29011-4_35

29. Ryffel, T., Pointcheval, D., Bach, F., Dufour-Sans, E., Gay, R.: Partially encrypted deep learning using functional encryption. In: Wallach, H., Larochelle, H., Beygelzimer, A., d'Alché-Buc, F., Fox, E., Garnett, R. (eds.) Advances in Neural Information Processing Systems, vol. 32. Curran Associates, Inc. (2019). https://proceedings.neurips.cc/paper_files/paper/2019/file/9d28de8ff9bb6a3fa41fddfdc28f3bc1-Paper.pdf

30. Wichs, D., Zirdelis, G.: Obfuscating compute-and-compare programs under LWE. In: Umans, C. (ed.) 58th FOCS, October 2017, pp. 600–611. IEEE Computer Society Press (2017). https://doi.org/10.1109/FOCS.2017.61

Registered Attribute-Based Signature

Yijian Zhang[1], Jun Zhao[1], Ziqi Zhu[1], Junqing Gong[1,2(✉)], and Jie Chen[1(✉)]

[1] Shanghai Key Laboratory of Trustworthy Computing,
Software Engineering Institute, East China Normal University, Shanghai, China
`jqgong@sei.ecnu.edu.cn`, `s080001@e.ntu.edu.sg`
[2] Shanghai Qi Zhi Institute, Shanghai, China

Abstract. This paper introduces the notion of *registered attribute-based signature* (registered ABS). Distinctly different from classical *attribute-based signature* (ABS), registered ABS allows any user to generate their own public/secret key pair and register it with the system. The *key curator* is critical to keep the system flowing, which is a fully transparent entity that does not retain secrets. Our results can be summarized as follows.

- This paper provides the first *definition* of registered ABS, which has never been defined.
- This paper presents the first generic *fully secure* registered ABS over the prime-order group from k-Lin assumption under the standard model, which supports various classes of predicate.
- This paper gives the first concrete registered ABS scheme for *arithmetic branching program* (ABP), which achieves *full security* in the standard model.

Technically, our registered ABS is inspired by the blueprint of Okamoto and Takashima [PKC'11]. We convert the prime-order *registered attribute-based encryption* (registered ABE) scheme of Zhu et al. [ASIACRYPT'23] via predicate encoding to registered ABS by employing the technique of *re-randomization with specialized delegation*, while we employ the different dual-system method considering the property of registration. Prior to our work, the work of solving the key-escrow issue was presented by Okamoto and Takashima [PKC'13] while their work considered the weak adversary in the random oracle model.

Keywords: Registered Attribute-Based Signature · Predicate Encoding · Dual System Encryption

1 Introduction

Attribute-Based Signature. *Attribute-based signature* (ABS) [17, 18] provides the fine-grained control to authentication privileges while guaranteeing anonymous authentication of message, which extends the traditional digital signature [10]. In ABS for predicate $P : X \times Y \to \{0, 1\}$, the signer employs signing key sk_y, where $y \in Y$ is his/her attribute set, to sign message under policy $x \in X$

Q. Tang and V. Teague (Eds.): PKC 2024, LNCS 14601, pp. 133–162, 2024.
https://doi.org/10.1007/978-3-031-57718-5_5

only when $P(x, y) = 1$. Anyone can verify the signature by using solely public parameters. The basic security condition of ABS is *unforgeability*, i.e., an adversary holding a signing key with $P(x, y) = 0$ cannot generate a valid signature; furthermore, this should be ensured when the adversary has more than one key.

Decentralized Attribute-Based Signature. To circumvent the key escrow problem in ABS [8,9,20], Okamoto and Takashima introduced the notion of *decentralized ABS* [19] which means that different authorities with attributes can join the system instead of having only one central authority. However, decentralized ABS just solves the problem that attributes from the single part, but the keys come from different central authorities, and if a sufficient number of authorities are compromised or corrupted, then the scheme will no longer ensure unforgeability.

This Work. Recently, the notion of *registration-based encryption* (RBE) [13] and *registered attribute-based encryption* (registered ABE) [12,15,23] has been studied, which allows users in the system to generate their own public/secret keys and then register their public keys together with the key curator. The key curator keeps nothing about secrets in contrast to the conventional attribute authority. However, the feasibility of this strategy in ABS is still unknown and a natural question that arises is

Can we construct a registered attribute-based signature scheme that even supports monotone span program?

More details, in the *registered attribute-based signature* (registered ABS) scheme, each user can generate his/her own key pair (pk, sk) locally and register (pk, y) for some $y \in Y$ into the system. Registration is performed by the key curator in a public and deterministic manner, and will generate a master public key mpk for anyone who wants to verify the signature as a traditional ABS. Besides, during the registration phase, each user can obtain his/her own helper key hk from the curator, which can be used to generate signature for policy $x \in X$ with sk when $P(x, y) = 1$. Finally, as the number of user in the system increases, the curator may trigger an update to all users' helper keys.

1.1   Results

In this work, we have addressed the above question. We propose the first generic registered attribute-based signature via predicate encoding [6,22]. Our scheme relies on the well-known k-Lin assumption for $k \geq 1$ over the prime-order bilinear group in the standard model. Our contribution is as follows.

- This paper introduces the first definition of registered ABS, formalizing the fact that any user can generate their own public/secret key pair and register it with the system. Furthermore, we formalize a security notion of registered ABS, i.e., the signature is unforgeable against the adversary with corrupted user information.

– This paper proposes the first generic approach for registered ABS supporting various classes of predicate over the prime-order group under the standard model, while the previous scheme of decentralized ABS [19] relies on the random oracle model.
– This paper gives the first concrete registered ABS scheme for the expressive predicate *arithmetic branching program*(ABP). It is fully secure under the k-Lin assumption in the standard model.

We present a concrete comparison in Table 1. Although this table only involves [18,19], we note that other ABS constructions [3,9,20] published recently share similar properties and all of them suffer from key escrow issue.

Table 1. Comparison among prior works. Here, the column "Standard" denotes the standard model. "†" means that decentralized ABS is unable to completely eliminate key escrow issue since it still needs nontransparent authorities to store secret values.

Reference	Key-escrow	Standard	Assumption
ABS [18]	✗	✓	DLIN
Decentralized ABS [19]	†	✗	DLIN
Ours	✓	✓	k-Lin

1.2 Related Work

Since Maji et al. [17] put forward the notion of ABS, there exists two research lines on ABS. The first line is to enhance the expression ability of ABS schemes. Herranz et al. [14] proposed an ABS scheme with constant-size signatures supporting threshold predicate. Okamoto et al. [18] proposed a fully secure ABS scheme for non-monotone span program in the standard model. Attrapadung et al. [3] designed an ABS scheme with constant-size signatures that supports non-monotone span programs. Furthermore, Sakai et al. [20] built an ABS scheme supporting circuits via Groth-Sahai proofs over bilinear groups. Datta et al. [9] designed a fully secure ABS for ABP with unbounded multi-use of attributes. In these works, a central authority must be set to store master secret key. To tackle the key escrow problem, another line is to build decentralized ABS. Okamoto et al. [18] proposed the first decentralized multi-authority ABS scheme for non-monotone span programs while it is only provably secure under the random model. Our registered ABS can seen as an independent work of the second line.

Organization. We provide the technique overview in Sect. 2. We give the definition of (slotted) registered ABS in Sect. 3. The details of our slotted registered ABS are presented in Sect. 4. Besides, we derive a concrete slotted registered ABS scheme supporting expressive ABP in Sect. 5.

2   Technique Overview

In this work, we construct a *registered attribute-based signature* (registered ABS) via predicate encoding [6,22], and the scheme is based on well-known k-Lin assumption in the standard model. The design core of registered ABS is similar to [15,23], we start from slotted registered ABS and then convert it to the full-fledged registered ABS. Before going into the technical descriptions of the designing of primitives in registered setting, we first provide an overview of the notion of registered ABS.

2.1   Registered Attribute-Based Signature

Definition. We introduce the definition of registered ABS in the simplest setting, which is inspired by the idea of [15,23]. A registered ABS scheme for predicate $P : X \times Y \to \{0,1\}$ consists of the following six algorithms (Setup, Gen, Reg, Upd, Sig, Ver):

- Setup provides a common reference string crs for each user to register;
- Gen allows each user to generate their own public/secret key pair (pk, sk);
- Reg is a transparent and deterministic algorithm, which checks the validity of the registered user, and register user's pk and attribute $y \in Y$ into the master public key mpk; Upd returns helper key hk for the registered user;
- Sig with hk and user's secret key sk returns a signature on (x, m) when $P(x,y) = 1$, where $x \in X$ is the signature policy; Ver can check the validity of signature with just mpk.

Properties. Assuming $L \in \mathbb{N}$ denotes the user number in the registered ABS system, it has some essential efficiency requirements: the size of crs to be $\mathsf{poly}(\lambda, L)$ where λ is the security parameter of the system, and the size of mpk, hk to be $\mathsf{poly}(\lambda, P, \log L)$ where P is the size of predicate.

Furthermore, the security of registered ABS means *unforgeability* compared with the IND-security of registered ABE. It ensures that no one is able to forge a signature passing the verification without the knowledge of the sign secret key. Similar to registered ABE, the security model needs to consider both honest and corrupted users.

Generic Approach. We state that the "power-of-two" approach in [15] can be improved to derive a generic approach to obtaining registered ABS. The approach needs a new primitive, namely *slotted registered attribute-based signature* (slotted registered ABS), as the underlying block. Slotted registered ABS has the similar syntax as registered ABS except that it does not consider the update of public parameters.

Based on the "power-of-two" approach, we replace encryption and decryption algorithms with (Sig, Ver), so it is necessary to demonstrate the reduction from the unforgeability of registered ABS to the unforgeability of underlying slotted registered ABS. The proof relies on the fact that the signature and verification text in registered ABS consist of multiple copies of underlying slotted registered ABS. More details are available in the full version. Next, we will construct a slotted registered ABS based the techniques of predicate encoding.

2.2   Slotted Registered ABS

Firstly, let us define some notations, which will be used. Our slotted registered ABS relies on an asymmetric bilinear group $(p, \mathbb{G}_1, \mathbb{G}_2, \mathbb{G}_T, g_1, g_2, e)$ of prime-order p with pairing $e : \mathbb{G}_1 \times \mathbb{G}_2 \to \mathbb{G}_T$. For $s \in \{1, 2, T\}$ and $a \in \mathbb{Z}_p$, we define $[a]_s = g_s^a$ as the implicit representation of a in $\mathbb{G}_s$. Then, we give preliminary which is an important part of our slotted registered ABS.

Preliminary. For a predicate $P : X \times Y \to \{0, 1\}$, define a (n, n_c, n_k)-predicate encoding: For all $x \in X$, $y \in Y$, one can efficiently and deterministically find $\mathbf{C}_x \in \mathbb{Z}_p^{n \times n_c}$, $\mathbf{K}_y \in \mathbb{Z}_p^{n \times n_k}$, $\mathbf{a}_y \in \mathbb{Z}_p^{1 \times n_k}$ and $\mathbf{d}_{x,y} \in \mathbb{Z}_p^{n_c + n_k}$ that forms $\mathbf{M}_{x,y} = \begin{pmatrix} \mathbf{a}_y & \mathbf{0}_{n_c} \\ \mathbf{K}_y & \mathbf{C}_x \end{pmatrix}$ such that

- when $P(x, y) = 1$, we have $\mathbf{M}_{x,y} \mathbf{d}_{x,y}^\top = (1, 0, \ldots, 0)^\top$;
- when $P(x, y) = 0$, we have $\{x, y, \alpha, (\alpha \| \mathbf{w}) \mathbf{M}_{x,y}\} \approx_s \{x, y, \alpha, (0 \| \mathbf{w}) \mathbf{M}_{x,y}\}$ where $\mathbf{w} \leftarrow \mathbb{Z}_p^n$.

Initial Idea. Our initial idea is to apply Naor's paradigm [4,5], which has successfully transform some encryption schemes into signature's version [7,18, 19], on existing slotted registered ABE. For such purpose, we choose Zhu et al.'s slotted registered ABE [23] as our start point, because their construction is based on *predicate encoding* supporting a large number of expressive predicates, even including arithmetic branching programs (ABP).

Start From Slotted Registered ABE. In slotted registered ABE, after initializing the common reference string crs, all users can generate their own key pairs $(\mathsf{pk}_i, \mathsf{sk}_i)_{i \in [L]}$ and submit respective pk_i to the aggregator who subsequently outputs mpk and hk_i for user/slot i. The ciphertext ct_x is an encryption on (x, m) and can be decrypted correctly with $(\mathsf{sk}_i, \mathsf{hk}_i)$ if and only if $P(x, y_i) = 1$. We recap Zhu et al.'s slotted registered ABE construction based on predicate encoding as follows:

$$
\begin{aligned}
\mathsf{crs} : & \; [\alpha]_T, \{[v_j, \mathbf{w}_j]_1\}_{j \in [L]}, \{[r_i, r_i v_j, r_i \mathbf{w}_j, r_i v_i + \alpha]_2\}_{i \neq j}; \\
\mathsf{pk}_i : & \; [u_i]_1, \{[u_i r_j]_2\}_{j \neq i}; \\
\mathsf{sk}_i : & \; u_i; \\
\mathsf{mpk} : & \; [\textstyle\sum_j ((v_j + u_j) \mathbf{a}_{y_j} + \mathbf{w}_j \mathbf{K}_{y_j}), \textstyle\sum_j \mathbf{w}_j]_1, [\alpha]_T \\
\mathsf{hk}_i : & \; [r_i, r_i v_i + \alpha, r_i \textstyle\sum_{j \neq i} ((v_j + u_j) \mathbf{a}_{y_j} + \mathbf{w}_j \mathbf{K}_{y_j}), \; r_i \textstyle\sum_{j \neq i} \mathbf{w}_j]_2 \\
\mathsf{ct}_x : & \; [s, s \textstyle\sum_j ((v_j + u_j) \mathbf{a}_{y_j} + \mathbf{w}_j \mathbf{K}_{y_j}), \; s \textstyle\sum_j \mathbf{w}_j \mathbf{C}_x]_1, [s\alpha]_T \cdot \mathsf{m}
\end{aligned}
\tag{1}
$$

where for all $j \in [L]$, y_j is the attribute embedded in slot j; $\alpha, v_j, r_j, u_j \leftarrow \mathbb{Z}_p$ and $\mathbf{w}_j \in \mathbb{Z}_p^n$; $s \leftarrow \mathbb{Z}_p$ is the randomness in ct_x. As for decryption, it firstly computes the pairing result between hk_i and ct_x to cancel cross items from other slots

$j \in [L] \setminus \{i\}$, then proceed the decryption of predicate encoding on slot i. If $P(x, y_i) = 1$, just use $\mathsf{sk}_i = u_i$ to recover $[\alpha s]_T$ and thus obtain the message m.

First Try. Now, we make an attempt to transform the slotted registered ABE in (1) into a slotted registered ABS. Our strategy is to treat $(\mathsf{hk}_i, \mathsf{sk}_i)$ as the sign secret key of user i, and ct_x as the verification text ν, respectively. Here, sk_i should be privacy, while hk_i is publicly computed with crs and $(\mathsf{pk}_j)_{j \in [L] \setminus \{i\}}$. A signature $\sigma_{i,x,\mathsf{m}}$ is derived from $(\mathsf{sk}_i, \mathsf{hk}_i)$. Then it uses $(\mathsf{mpk}, x, \mathsf{m})$ to generate a verification text $\nu_{i^*,x^*,\mathsf{m}^*}$ to verify the validity of $\sigma_{i,x,\mathsf{m}}$. Intuitively, we have

$$\sigma_{i,x,\mathsf{m}} : [r_i, \boxed{u_i r_i} + r_i v_i + \alpha, r_i \sum_{j \neq i}((v_j + u_j)a_{y_j} + \mathbf{w}_j \mathbf{K}_{y_j}), \ r_i \sum_{j \neq i} \mathbf{w}_j \boxed{\mathbf{C}_x}]_2$$

$$\nu_{i^*,x^*,\mathsf{m}^*} : [s, s \sum_j((v_j + u_j)a_{y_j} + \mathbf{w}_j \mathbf{K}_{y_j}), \ s \sum_j \mathbf{w}_j \mathbf{C}_{x^*}]_1, [s\alpha]_T \cdot \mathsf{m}^*$$

where $\mathsf{crs}, \mathsf{mpk}, \mathsf{pk}_i, \mathsf{sk}_i$ and hk_i are identical to the equality (1). Observe that the verification process is identical to the decryption process in (1) except that it can directly recover m from ν without u_i, then checkout if $\mathsf{m} = \mathsf{m}^*$.

Actually, the above scheme is insecure, since the information of u_i is leaked from $\sigma_{i,x,\mathsf{m}}$. Note that any signature could be forged readily if $\mathsf{sk}_i = u_i$ is leaked. Besides, $\sigma_{i,x,\mathsf{m}}$ does not involve m and the generation is completely deterministic.

Second Try. Inspired by the "re-randomization" technique of [18], we state that $\sigma_{i,x,\mathsf{m}}$ actually plays a role as a special decryption key. Concretely, it should remain the decryption ability of $(\mathsf{sk}_i, \mathsf{hk}_i)$, but still preserve the privacy of sk_i to avoid the forgery. However, such technique cannot be trivially applied to our scheme, since our secret key is the secret value chosen by user, rather than the well-constructed secret key generated by authority. Therefore, the problem is how to generate desired signature and ensure security proof in our slotted registered ABS.

Our technique path is as follows: Firstly, to protect the confidentiality of u_i, we generate extra entropy by appending a new equality into the signature, which ensures adversary cannot obtain secret information from honest users. Secondly, the privacy of predicate encoding can ensure that adversary cannot obtain secret information from corrupted users. Finally, we use $(\mathsf{sk}_i, \mathsf{hk}_i)$ to delegate a new signature $\sigma_{i,x,\mathsf{m}}$ as follows:

$$\mathsf{pk}_i : [u_i, \boxed{c_i, d_i}]_1, \{[u_i r_j]_2\}_{j \neq i}; \qquad \mathsf{sk}_i : \ u_i, \boxed{c_i, d_i}$$

$$\sigma_{i,x,\mathsf{m}} : [\boxed{t}, r_i, \boxed{t(c_i + \mathsf{m} \cdot d_i)} + u_i r_i + r_i v_i + \alpha]_2,$$

$$[r_i \sum_{j \neq i}((v_j + u_j)a_{y_j} + \mathbf{w}_j \mathbf{K}_{y_j}), \ r_i \sum_{j \neq i} \mathbf{w}_j \mathbf{C}_x]_2$$

$$\nu_{i^*,x^*,\mathsf{m}^*} : [s, \boxed{s(c_{i^*} + \mathsf{m}^* \cdot d_{i^*})}, s \sum_j((v_j + u_j)a_{y_j} + \mathbf{w}_j \mathbf{K}_{y_j}), s \sum_j \mathbf{w}_j \mathbf{C}_{x^*}]_1, [s\alpha]_T$$

Here, we define a collusion-resistant hash function $\mathsf{H} : \{0,1\}^* \to \mathbb{Z}_p$, $\mathsf{m} \leftarrow \mathsf{H}(i, x, \mathsf{m})$ and $\mathsf{m}^* \leftarrow \mathsf{H}(i^*, x^*, \mathsf{m}^*)$, where i is more like a pseudo-identity. t is the randomness newly sampled in each signature. Observe that u_i has been totally hidden in the signature as long as $m \neq m^*$ (in the similar sense of [7]). Thus, we can ensure that the adversary has no ability to forge a valid signature unless slot i is corrupted. Observe that this construction is still unreasonable since the generation of ν_{i^*, x^*, m^*} needs both mpk and pk_{i^*}, which contradicts the definition of verification algorithm, but we can fix it by aggregating pk_i from all users.

Our Slotted Registered ABS. Finally, putting the above together, we obtain a new slotted registered ABS as follows:

$$\mathsf{crs} : [\alpha]_T, \{[v_j, \mathbf{w}_j]_1\}_{j \in [L]}, \{[r_i, r_i v_j, r_i \mathbf{w}_j, r_i v_i + \alpha]_2\}_{i \neq j}, \mathsf{H}$$

$$\mathsf{pk}_i : [u_i, c_i, d_i]_1, [c_i, d_i]_2, \{[u_i r_j]_2\}_{j \neq i}$$

$$\mathsf{sk}_i : u_i, c_i, d_i$$

$$\mathsf{mpk} : [\sum_j ((v_j + u_j) a_{y_j} + \mathbf{w}_j \mathbf{K}_{y_j}), \sum_j \mathbf{w}_j, \sum_j c_j, \sum_j d_j]_1, [\alpha]_T, \mathsf{H}$$

$$\mathsf{hk}_i : [r_i, r_i v_i + \alpha, r_i \sum_{j \neq i} ((v_j + u_j) a_{y_j} + \mathbf{w}_j \mathbf{K}_{y_j})]_2,$$

$$[r_i \sum_{j \neq i} \mathbf{w}_j, \sum_{j \neq i} c_j, \sum_{j \neq i} d_j]_2, \mathsf{H}$$

$$\sigma_{i,x,m} : [t, r_i, t(c_i + m \cdot d_i) + u_i r_i + r_i v_i + \alpha, t \sum_{j \neq i} (c_j + m \cdot d_j)]_2,$$

$$[r_i \sum_{j \neq i} ((v_j + u_j) a_{y_j} + \mathbf{w}_j \mathbf{K}_{y_j}), r_i \sum_{j \neq i} \mathbf{w}_j \mathbf{C}_x]_2$$

$$\nu_{i^*, x^*, m^*} : [s, s \sum_j (c_j + m^* \cdot d_j), s \sum_j ((v_j + u_j) a_{y_j} + \mathbf{w}_j \mathbf{K}_{y_j})]_1,$$

$$[s \sum_j \mathbf{w}_j \mathbf{C}_{x^*}]_1, [s\alpha]_T.$$

Then we apply the generic approach [6] from composite-order group to prime-order group to above construction, and obtain a secure slotted registered ABS based on k-Lin assumption under the standard model. We still adopt the dual system encryption as proof strategy, while it is quite distinct from previous works [18,19] since there is no longer authority holding secret keys in the system.

2.3 Discussion and Open Problem

Here, we discuss the future work about registered ABS.

– Our registered ABS achieves various classes of predicate even including span programs, but the concrete scheme for more expressive predicate (e.g., finite state automata and circuits) is still unknown.
– The signer anonymity of ABS says that the generated signature reveals no information on the signer's attribute other than the fact that the signature is valid. However, just as mentioned in [21], ABS schemes derived from ABE

generally do not provide anonymity property. This argument also works in our registered ABS, so we list the realization of signer anonymity in the standard model as one of future works.

- Our work opens a new and promising path for pairing-based research on registered ABS. An open question, however, is whether we can propose registered ABS under the LWE assumption. Furthermore, the size of crs is poly(λ, L) where λ is the security parameter of the system and L is the number of users, it is still an open problem to reduce the size of crs to poly(λ) under standard assumption.

3   Preliminaries

For a finite set S, we write $s \leftarrow S$ to denote that s is picked uniformly from finite set S. Then, we use $|S|$ to denote the size of S. Let $\approx_s$ stand for two distributions being statistically indistinguishable, and $\approx_c$ denote two distributions being computationally indistinguishable. We use lower-case boldface to denote vectors (e.g., $\mathbf{a}$) and upper-case boldface to denote matrices (e.g. $\mathbf{M}$), and use "$\|$" to denote vector/matrix concatenation (e.g. $\mathbf{A}\|\mathbf{B}$).

3.1   Prime-Order Bilinear Groups

A generator $\mathcal{G}$ takes as input a security parameter 1^λ and outputs a description $\mathbb{G} := (p, \mathbb{G}_1, \mathbb{G}_2, \mathbb{G}_T, e)$, where p is a prime, $\mathbb{G}_1$, $\mathbb{G}_2$ and $\mathbb{G}_T$ are cyclic groups of order p, and $e : \mathbb{G}_1 \times \mathbb{G}_2 \to \mathbb{G}_T$ is a non-degenerate bilinear map. Group operations in $\mathbb{G}_1$, $\mathbb{G}_2$, $\mathbb{G}_T$ and bilinear map e are computable in deterministic polynomial time in λ. Let $g_1 \in \mathbb{G}_1$, $g_2 \in \mathbb{G}_2$ and $g_T = e(g_1, g_2) \in \mathbb{G}_T$ be the respective generators, we employ *implicit representation* of group elements: for a matrix $\mathbf{M}$ over $\mathbb{Z}_p$, we define $[\mathbf{M}]_s = g_s^{\mathbf{M}}, \forall s \in \{1, 2, T\}$, where exponentiation is carried out component-wise. Given $[\mathbf{A}]_1, [\mathbf{B}]_2$ where $\mathbf{A}$ and $\mathbf{B}$ have proper sizes, we let $e([\mathbf{A}]_1, [\mathbf{B}]_2) = [\mathbf{AB}]_T$. We review *matrix Diffie-Hellman (MDDH) assumption* [11], which is implied by k-Lin [11].

Assumption 1 ((k, ℓ, d)-MDDH over $\mathbb{G}_s$, $s \in \{1, 2\}$). *Let $k, \ell, d \in \mathbb{N}$ with $k < \ell$. We say that the (k, ℓ, d)-MDDH assumption holds in $\mathbb{G}_s$ if for all PPT adversaries $\mathcal{A}$, the following advantage function is negligible in λ.*

$$\mathsf{Adv}^{\mathrm{MDDH}}_{\mathcal{A}, s, k, \ell, d}(\lambda) = \big| \Pr[\mathcal{A}(\mathbb{G}, [\mathbf{M}]_s, [\mathbf{SM}]_s) = 1] - \Pr[\mathcal{A}(\mathbb{G}, [\mathbf{M}]_s, [\mathbf{U}]_s) = 1] \big|$$

where $\mathbb{G} := (p, \mathbb{G}_1, \mathbb{G}_2, \mathbb{G}_T, e) \leftarrow \mathcal{G}(1^\lambda)$, $\mathbf{M} \leftarrow \mathbb{Z}_p^{k \times \ell}$, $\mathbf{S} \leftarrow \mathbb{Z}_p^{d \times k}$ and $\mathbf{U} \leftarrow \mathbb{Z}_p^{d \times \ell}$.

3.2   Slotted Registered Attribute-Based Signature

Algorithms. A slotted registered attribute-based signature (slotted registered ABS) for predicate $P : X \times Y \to \{0, 1\}$ consists of the following six efficient algorithms:

– Setup$(1^\lambda, P, 1^L) \to$ crs: It takes as input the security parameter 1^λ, description of predicate P and the upper bound 1^L of the number of slots, outputs a common reference string crs.
– Gen(crs, i) $\to$ (pk$_i$, sk$_i$): It takes as input crs and slot number $i \in [L]$, outputs key pair (pk$_i$, sk$_i$).
– IsValid(crs, i, pk$_i$) $\to 0/1$: It takes as input crs, i, pk$_i$ and outputs a bit indicating whether pk$_i$ is valid.
– Agg(crs, $\{$pk$_i, y_i\}_{i \in L}) \to$ (mpk, (hk$_j)_{j \in [L]}$): It takes as input crs and a series of pk$_i$ with $y_i \in Y$ for all $i \in [L]$, outputs master public key mpk and a series of helper keys hk$_j$ for all $j \in [L]$. This algorithm is deterministic.
– Sig(hk, sk, x, m) $\to \sigma$: It takes as input hk, sk, $x \in X$ and message m, outputs a signature σ.
– Ver(mpk, σ, x, m) $\to 0/1$: It takes as input hk, σ, $x \in X$, m and outputs a bit indicating whether σ is valid.

Completeness. For all $\lambda, L \in \mathbb{N}$, all P, and all $i \in [L]$, we have

$$\Pr[\text{IsValid}(\text{crs}, i, \text{pk}_i) = 1 | \text{crs} \leftarrow \text{Setup}(1^\lambda, P, 1^L); (\text{pk}_i, \text{sk}_i) \leftarrow \text{Gen}(\text{crs}, i)] = 1.$$

Correctness. For all $\lambda, L \in \mathbb{N}$, all P, and all $i \in [L]$, all crs $\leftarrow$ Setup$(1^\lambda, P, 1^L)$, all (pk$_{i^*}$, sk$_{i^*}$) $\leftarrow$ Gen(crs, i^*), all $\{$pk$_i\}_{i \in [L] \setminus \{i^*\}}$ such that IsValid(crs, i, pk$_i$) = 1, all $x \in X$ and $y_1, \ldots, y_L \in Y$ such that $P(x, y_{i^*}) = 1$, and all m, we have

$$\Pr\left[\text{Ver}(\text{mpk}, \sigma, x, \text{m}) = 1 \,\middle|\, \begin{array}{l} (\text{mpk}, (\text{hk}_j)_{j \in [L]}) \leftarrow \text{Agg}(\text{crs}, (\text{pk}_i, y_i)_{i \in [L]}); \\ \sigma \leftarrow \text{Sig}(\text{hk}, \text{sk}, x, \text{m}) \end{array}\right] = 1.$$

Compactness. For all $\lambda, L \in \mathbb{N}$, all P, and all $i \in [L]$, it holds that $|\text{mpk}| = \text{poly}(\lambda, P, \log L)$ and $|\text{hk}_i| = \text{poly}(\lambda, P, \log L)$.

Unforgeability. For any group of colluding signers, it is impossible to generate a valid signature on any message under any signing policy. Concretely, for all $\lambda \in \mathbb{N}$ and all efficient adversaries $\mathcal{A}$, the advantage

$$\left| \Pr\left[\text{Ver}(\text{mpk}, \sigma^*, x^*, \text{m}^*) = 1 \,\middle|\, \begin{array}{l} L \leftarrow \mathcal{A}(1^\lambda); \text{crs} \leftarrow \text{Setup}(1^\lambda, P, 1^L) \\ \{\text{pk}_i^*, y_i^*\}_{i \in [L]} \leftarrow \mathcal{A}^{\text{OGen}(\cdot), \text{OCor}(\cdot)}(\text{crs}) \\ (\text{mpk}, \{\text{hk}_j\}_{j \in [L]}) \leftarrow \text{Agg}(\text{crs}, \{\text{pk}_i^*, y_i^*\}_{i \in L}) \\ (i^*, x^*, \text{m}^*, \sigma^*) \leftarrow \mathcal{A}^{\text{OSig}(\cdot)}(\text{mpk}, \{\text{hk}_j\}_{j \in [L]}) \end{array}\right] - \frac{1}{2} \right|$$

is negligible in λ, where oracles OGen, OCor and OSig work with initial setting $\{\mathcal{D}_i = \emptyset\}_{i \in [L]}, \mathcal{C} = \emptyset$ and $\mathcal{S} = \emptyset$ as follows:

– OGen(i): run (pk$_i$, sk$_i$) $\leftarrow$ Gen(crs, i), set $\mathcal{D}_i[\text{pk}_i] = \text{sk}_i$ and return pk$_i$.
– OCor(i, pk): return $\mathcal{D}_i(\text{pk})$ and update $\mathcal{C} = \mathcal{C} \cup \{(i, \text{pk})\}$.
– OSig(i, x, m): Return Sig(mpk, $\mathcal{D}_i[\text{pk}_i^*], x, \text{m}$) and update $\mathcal{S} = \mathcal{S} \cup \{(i, x, \text{m})\}$.

and for all $i \in [L]$, we require that $\mathcal{D}_i[\text{pk}_i^*] \neq \bot$. For each query (i, x, m) to OSig, we have $P(x, y_i^*) = 1$. Besides, For the challenge $(i^*, x^*, \text{m}^*, \sigma^*)$,

– it holds that $(i^*, x^*, \text{m}^*) \notin \mathcal{S}$;
– if $(i^*, \text{pk}_{i^*}^*) \in \mathcal{C}$, it holds that $P(x^*, y_i^*) = 0$ for all $(i, \text{pk}_i^*) \in \mathcal{C}$.

3.3 Registered Attribute-Based Signature

Algorithms. A *registered attribute-based signature* for predicate $P : X \times Y \to \{0,1\}$ consists of six algorithms:

- Setup($1^\lambda, P$) $\to$ crs: It takes as input the security parameter 1^λ, description of predicate P, outputs a common reference string crs.
- Gen(crs, aux) $\to$ (pk, sk): It takes as input crs and the public state aux, outputs key pair (pk, sk).
- Reg(crs, aux, pk, y) $\to$ (mpk, aux$'$): It takes as input crs, aux, and pk along with $y \in Y$, outputs master public key mpk and updated state aux$'$.
- Upd(crs, aux, pk) $\to$ hk: It takes as input crs, aux, pk, outputs a helper key hk.
- Sig(mpk, hk, sk, x, m) $\to \sigma$/getupd: It takes as input mpk, hk, sk, $x \in X$ and message m, outputs a signature σ or a special symbol getupd to indicate that an updated helper key is need to generate the signature.
- Ver(mpk, σ, x, m) $\to$ 0/1: It takes as input mpk, σ, x, m and outputs 1 if σ is valid; otherwise, output 0.

Correctness. For all stateful adversary $\mathcal{A}$, the following advantage function is negligible in λ:

$$\Pr[b = 1 | \text{crs} \leftarrow \text{Setup}(1^\lambda, P); b = 0; \mathcal{A}^{\text{ORegNT}(\cdot,\cdot),\text{ORegT}(\cdot),\text{OSig}(\cdot,\cdot),\text{OVer}(\cdot,\cdot)}(\text{crs})]$$

where the oracles work as follows with initial setting aux $= \perp$, $\mathcal{S} = \emptyset$, $\mathcal{R} = \emptyset$ and $t = \perp$:

- ORegNT(pk, y): run (mpk, aux$'$) $\leftarrow$ Reg(crs, aux, pk, y), update aux $=$ aux$'$, append (mpk, aux) to $\mathcal{R}$ and return ($|\mathcal{R}|$, mpk, aux);
- ORegT(y^*):
  run (pk*, sk*) $\leftarrow$ Gen(crs, aux) , (mpk, aux$'$) $\leftarrow$ Reg(crs, aux, pk*, y^*), update aux $=$ aux$'$, compute hk* $\leftarrow$ Upd(crs, aux, pk*), append (mpk, aux) to $\mathcal{R}$, return ($t = |\mathcal{R}|$, mpk, aux, pk*, sk*, hk*).
- OSig(i, x, m): let $\mathcal{R}[i] = (\text{mpk}_i, \cdot)$ and run $\sigma \leftarrow$ Sig(mpk$_i$, hk*,sk*, x, m); If $\sigma =$ getupd, run hk* $\leftarrow$ Upd(crs, aux, pk*) and recompute $\sigma \leftarrow$ Sig(mpk$_i$, hk*, sk*, x, m). Then append (x, m, σ) to $\mathcal{S}$ and return ($|\mathcal{S}|, \sigma$);
- OVer(i, j): let $\mathcal{R}[i] = (\text{mpk}_i, \cdot)$ and $\mathcal{S}[j] = (x_j, m_j, \sigma_j)$, compute $b_j \leftarrow$ Ver(mpk$_i$, σ_j, x_j, m$_j$). If $b_j = 0$, set $b = 0$.

with the following restrictions:

- there exists one query to ORegT;
- for query $(i, x, \cdot)$ to OSig, it holds that $\mathcal{R}[i] \neq \perp$ and $P(x, y^*) = 1$;
- for query (i, j) to OVer, it holds that $t \leq i, \mathcal{R}[i] \neq \perp$ and $\mathcal{S}[j] \neq \perp$.

Compactness. Let $\mathcal{R}$ be defined as before. *Compactness* means that

$$|\text{mpk}_i| = \text{poly}(\lambda, P, \log i), \quad |\text{hk}^*| = \text{poly}(\lambda, P, \log |\mathcal{R}|);$$

where we let $\mathcal{R}[i] = (\text{mpk}_i, \cdot)$ for all $i \in [|\mathcal{R}|]$.

Update Efficiency. It means that the number of invocations of Upd in OSig is at most $O(\log |\mathcal{R}|)$ and each invocation runs in $\mathsf{poly}(\log |\mathcal{R}|)$ time (in RAM model).

Unforgeability. For all stateful adversary $\mathcal{A}$, the advantage

$$\left| \Pr \left[\mathsf{Ver}(\mathsf{mpk}, \sigma^*, x^*, m^*) = 1 \; \middle| \; \begin{array}{l} \mathsf{crs} \leftarrow \mathsf{Setup}(1^\lambda, P); \\ (i^*, x^*, m^*, \sigma^*) \leftarrow \mathcal{A}(\mathsf{crs}); \end{array} \right] - \frac{1}{2} \right|$$

is negligible in λ, where $\mathcal{A}$ has access to oracles $\mathsf{ORegHK}(\cdot), \mathsf{OCorHK}(\cdot)$ and $\mathsf{OSig}(\cdot, \cdot, \cdot)$. These oracles work with initially setting $\mathsf{aux}, \mathsf{mpk} = \perp$, $\mathcal{R} = \emptyset$, $\mathcal{C} = \emptyset$, $\mathcal{S} = \emptyset$ and a dictionary $\mathcal{K}$ with $\mathcal{K}[\mathsf{pk}] = $ for all possible pk:

- $\mathsf{ORegHK}(y)$:
  run $(\mathsf{pk}, \mathsf{sk}) \leftarrow \mathsf{Gen}(\mathsf{crs}, \mathsf{aux})$ and $(\mathsf{mpk}', \mathsf{aux}') \leftarrow \mathsf{Reg}(\mathsf{crs}, \mathsf{aux}, \mathsf{pk}, y)$, update $\mathsf{mpk} = \mathsf{mpk}', \mathsf{aux} = \mathsf{aux}', \mathcal{K}[\mathsf{pk}] = \mathcal{K}[\mathsf{pk}] \cup \{y\}$, append $(\mathsf{pk}, \mathsf{sk})$ to $\mathcal{R}$ and return $(|\mathcal{R}|, \mathsf{mpk}, \mathsf{aux}, \mathsf{pk})$;
- $\mathsf{OCor}(i)$: let $\mathcal{R}[i] = (\mathsf{pk}, \mathsf{sk})$, append pk to $\mathcal{C}$ and return sk;
- $\mathsf{OSig}(i, x, m)$: let $\mathcal{R}[i] = (\mathsf{pk}, \mathsf{sk})$, compute $\mathsf{hk} \leftarrow \mathsf{Upd}(\mathsf{crs}, \mathsf{aux}, \mathsf{pk})$ and run $\sigma \leftarrow \mathsf{Sig}(\mathsf{mpk}, \mathsf{hk}, \mathsf{sk}, x, m)$. Append (i, x, m) to $\mathcal{S}$ and return σ.

with the following restrictions:

- for query (i) to OCor or (i, x, m) to OSig, it holds that $\mathcal{R}[i] \neq \perp$. Besides, $\mathcal{R}[i^*] \neq \perp$;
- Let $\mathcal{R}[i] = (\mathsf{pk}, \mathsf{sk})$ and $\mathcal{K}[\mathsf{pk}] = y$, then it holds that $P(y, x) = 1$;
- Let $\mathcal{R}[i^*] = (\mathsf{pk}^*, \mathsf{sk}^*)$,
  - it holds that $(i^*, x^*, m^*) \notin \mathcal{S}$;
  - if $\mathsf{pk}^* \in \mathcal{C}$, it holds that $P(x^*, \mathcal{K}[\mathsf{pk}_i]) = 0$ for all $(\mathsf{pk}_i, \mathsf{sk}_i) \in \mathcal{R}$ such that $\mathsf{pk}_i \in \mathcal{C}$;

3.4 Predicate Encodings

We review the notion of predicate encoding [6,22,23]; for simplicity, we use the formulation in [1,2]. A predicate $P : X \times Y \to \{0, 1\}$ has a (n, n_c, n_k)-predicate encoding if: For all $x \in X$, $y \in Y$, there exist $\mathbf{C}_x \in \mathbb{Z}_p^{n \times n_c}$, $\mathbf{K}_y \in \mathbb{Z}_p^{n \times n_k}$, $\mathbf{a}_y \in \mathbb{Z}_p^{1 \times n_k}$, $\mathbf{d}_{x,y} \in \mathbb{Z}_p^{1 \times (n_k + n_c)}$ such that, letting

$$\mathbf{M}_{x,y} = \begin{pmatrix} \mathbf{a}_y & \mathbf{0}_{n_c} \\ \mathbf{K}_y & \mathbf{C}_x \end{pmatrix} \in \mathbb{Z}_p^{(1+n) \times (n_k + n_c)}$$

we have

- **correctness:** for $x \in X$ and $y \in Y$ such that $P(x, y) = 1$:

$$\mathbf{M}_{x,y} \mathbf{d}_{x,y}^\top = \mathbf{e}_1^\top;$$

- **security:** for $x \in X$ and $y \in Y$ such that $P(x, y) = 0$ and for all $\alpha \in \mathbb{Z}_p$:

$$\{x, y, \alpha, (\alpha \| \mathbf{w}) \mathbf{M}_{x,y}\} \approx_s \{x, y, \alpha, (0 \| \mathbf{w}) \mathbf{M}_{x,y}\}, \quad \mathbf{w} \leftarrow \mathbb{Z}_p^n.$$

Also, we require that (1) given P, one can efficiently determine n, n_c, n_k; (2) given x, one can efficiently compute $\mathbf{C}_x$; (3) given y, one can efficiently compute $\mathbf{K}_y$ and $\mathbf{a}_y$; (4) given both x and y, one can efficiently compute $\mathbf{d}_{x,y}$.

4 Slotted Registered ABS

In this section, we will propose a slotted registered ABS via predicate encoding under MDDH assumption.

4.1 Scheme

Our slotted registered ABS scheme from predicate encoding over prime-order bilinear group works as follows:

- Setup($1^\lambda, P, 1^L$): Run $\mathbb{G} := (p, \mathbb{G}_1, \mathbb{G}_2, \mathbb{G}_T, e) \leftarrow \mathcal{G}(1^\lambda)$ and select a collusion-resistant hash function $\mathsf{H} : \{0,1\}^* \to \mathbb{Z}_p$. Sample

$$\mathbf{A} \leftarrow \mathbb{Z}_p^{k \times (k+1)}, \mathbf{B} \leftarrow \mathbb{Z}_p^{(k+1) \times k}, \mathbf{k} \leftarrow \mathbb{Z}_p^{1 \times (k+1)}$$

  and compute parameter (n, n_c, n_k) from P. For all $i \in [L]$, sample

$$\mathbf{D}_i \leftarrow \mathbb{Z}_p^{k \times k}, \mathbf{V}_i \leftarrow \mathbb{Z}_p^{(k+1) \times (k+1)}, \mathbf{W}_i \leftarrow \mathbb{Z}_p^{(k+1) \times (k+1)n}, \mathbf{r}_i \leftarrow \mathbb{Z}_p^{1 \times k}.$$

  Set $\mathbf{B}_i = \mathbf{BD}_i$ for each $i \in [L]$ and output

$$\mathsf{crs} = \begin{pmatrix} [\mathbf{A}]_1, \{[\mathbf{AV}_i, \mathbf{AW}_i]_1, [\mathbf{Br}_i^\top, \mathbf{V}_i\mathbf{Br}_i^\top + \mathbf{k}^\top, \mathbf{B}_i]_2\}_{i \in [L]}, \\ \{[\mathbf{V}_i\mathbf{Br}_j^\top, \mathbf{W}_i(\mathbf{I}_n \otimes \mathbf{Br}_j^\top)]_2\}_{j \in [L], i \in [L] \backslash \{j\}}, [\mathbf{Ak}^\top]_T, \mathsf{H} \end{pmatrix}.$$

- Gen(crs, i): Sample $\mathbf{U}_i, \mathbf{Q}_i, \mathbf{T}_i \leftarrow \mathbb{Z}_p^{(k+1) \times (k+1)}$. Output

$$\mathsf{pk}_i = ([\mathbf{AU}_i, \mathbf{AQ}_i, \mathbf{AT}_i]_1, \{[\mathbf{U}_i\mathbf{Br}_j^\top, \mathbf{Q}_i\mathbf{B}_j, \mathbf{T}_i\mathbf{B}_j]_2\}_{j \in [L] \backslash \{i\}})$$

  and $\mathsf{sk}_i = (\mathbf{U}_i, \mathbf{Q}_i, \mathbf{T}_i)$.
- IsValid($\mathsf{crs}, i, \mathsf{pk}_i$): Parse the public key pk_i as follows $([\mathbf{AU}_i, \mathbf{AQ}_i, \mathbf{AT}_i]_1, \{[\mathbf{U}_i\mathbf{Br}_j^\top, \mathbf{Q}_i\mathbf{B}_j, \mathbf{T}_i\mathbf{B}_j]_2\}_{j \in [L] \backslash \{i\}})$. For each $j \in [L] \backslash \{i\}$, check

$$e([\mathbf{A}]_1, [\mathbf{U}_i\mathbf{Br}_j^\top]_2) \overset{?}{=} e([\mathbf{AU}_i]_1, [\mathbf{Br}_j^\top]_2),$$

$$e([\mathbf{A}]_1, [\mathbf{Q}_i\mathbf{B}_j]_2) \overset{?}{=} e([\mathbf{AQ}_i]_1, [\mathbf{B}_j]_2),$$

$$e([\mathbf{A}]_1, [\mathbf{T}_i\mathbf{B}_j]_2) \overset{?}{=} e([\mathbf{AT}_i]_1, [\mathbf{B}_j]_2).$$

  If the above checks pass, output 1; otherwise, output 0.
- Agg($\mathsf{crs}, \{\mathsf{pk}_i, y_i\}_{i \in L}$): For all $i \in [L]$, parse $\mathsf{pk}_i = ([\mathbf{AU}_i, \mathbf{AQ}_i, \mathbf{AT}_i]_1, \{[\mathbf{U}_i\mathbf{Br}_j^\top, \mathbf{Q}_i\mathbf{B}_j, \mathbf{T}_i\mathbf{B}_j]_2\}_{j \in [L] \backslash \{i\}})$ and compute $\mathbf{K}_{y_i}$ from y_i. Output

$$\mathsf{mpk} = \begin{pmatrix} [\mathbf{A}]_1, [\mathbf{Ak}^\top]_T, \mathsf{H}, \left[\sum_{j \in [L]} \mathbf{AQ}_j\right]_1, \left[\sum_{j \in [L]} \mathbf{AT}_j\right]_1, \left[\sum_{j \in [L]} \mathbf{AW}_j\right]_1, \\ \left[\sum_{j \in [L]} ((\mathbf{AV}_j + \mathbf{AU}_j)(\mathbf{a}_{y_j} \otimes \mathbf{I}_{k+1}) + \mathbf{AW}_j(\mathbf{K}_{y_j} \otimes \mathbf{I}_{k+1}))\right]_1 \end{pmatrix}$$

and for all $i \in [L]$, the hk_i is that

$$
\begin{pmatrix}
\mathsf{H}, [\mathbf{B}_i]_2, [\mathbf{Br}_i^\top]_2, [\mathbf{V}_i\mathbf{Br}_i^\top + \mathbf{k}^\top]_2, \left[\displaystyle\sum_{j\in[L]\setminus\{i\}} \mathbf{Q}_j\mathbf{B}_i\right]_2, \\[2em]
\left[\displaystyle\sum_{j\in[L]\setminus\{i\}} \mathbf{T}_j\mathbf{B}_i\right]_2, \left[\displaystyle\sum_{j\in[L]\setminus\{i\}} \mathbf{W}_j(\mathbf{I}_n \otimes \mathbf{Br}_i^\top)\right]_2, \\[2em]
\left[\displaystyle\sum_{j\in[L]\setminus\{i\}} (\mathbf{V}_j\mathbf{Br}_i^\top + \mathbf{U}_j\mathbf{Br}_i^\top)(\mathbf{I}_k \otimes \mathbf{a}_{y_j}) + \mathbf{W}_j(\mathbf{I}_n \otimes \mathbf{Br}_i^\top)(\mathbf{I}_k \otimes \mathbf{K}_{y_j})\right]_2
\end{pmatrix}.
$$

- $\mathsf{Sig}(\mathsf{hk}_i, \mathsf{sk}_i, x, \mathsf{m})$: Sample $\mathbf{t} \leftarrow \mathbb{Z}_p^{1\times k}$, and compute $\mathbf{C}_x$. Compute $[\mathbf{k}_0^\top]_2 = [\mathbf{B}_i\mathbf{t}^\top]_2, [\mathbf{k}_1^\top]_2 = [\mathbf{Br}_i^\top]_2$. Run $\mathsf{m} \leftarrow \mathsf{H}(i, \mathsf{m}, x)$ and generate

$$
\begin{pmatrix}
\underbrace{[\mathbf{V}_i\mathbf{Br}_i^\top + \mathbf{k}^\top + \mathbf{U}_i\mathbf{Br}_i^\top + (\mathbf{Q}_i\mathbf{B}_i\mathbf{t}^\top + \mathsf{m} \cdot \mathbf{T}_i\mathbf{B}_i\mathbf{t}^\top)]_2}_{\mathbf{k}_2^\top}, \\[2em]
\underbrace{\left[\displaystyle\sum_{j\in[L]\setminus\{i\}} (\mathbf{V}_j\mathbf{Br}_i^\top + \mathbf{U}_j\mathbf{Br}_i^\top)\mathbf{a}_{y_j} + \mathbf{W}_j(\mathbf{I}_n \otimes \mathbf{Br}_i^\top)\mathbf{K}_{y_j}\right]_2}_{\mathbf{K}_3}, \\[2em]
\underbrace{\left[\displaystyle\sum_{j\in[L]\setminus\{i\}} \mathbf{W}_j(\mathbf{I}_n \otimes \mathbf{Br}_i^\top)\mathbf{C}_x\right]_2}_{\mathbf{K}_4}, \underbrace{\left[\displaystyle\sum_{j\in[L]\setminus\{i\}} (\mathbf{Q}_j\mathbf{B}_i\mathbf{t}^\top + \mathsf{m} \cdot \mathbf{T}_j\mathbf{B}_i\mathbf{t}^\top)\right]}_{\mathbf{k}_5^\top}
\end{pmatrix}
$$

Output signature $\sigma_{i,x,\mathsf{m}} = ([\mathbf{k}_0^\top]_2, [\mathbf{k}_1^\top]_2, [\mathbf{k}_2^\top]_2, [\mathbf{K}_3]_2, [\mathbf{K}_4]_2, [\mathbf{k}_5^\top]_2)$.

- $\mathsf{Ver}(\mathsf{mpk}, \sigma_{i^*,x,\mathsf{m}}, x, \mathsf{m})$: Parse mpk as

$$
\begin{pmatrix}
[\mathbf{A}]_1, [\mathbf{Ak}^\top]_T, \mathsf{H}, \left[\displaystyle\sum_{j\in[L]} \mathbf{AQ}_j\right]_1, \left[\displaystyle\sum_{j\in[L]} \mathbf{AT}_j\right]_1, \left[\displaystyle\sum_{j\in[L]} \mathbf{AW}_j\right]_1, \\[2em]
\left[\displaystyle\sum_{j\in[L]} (\mathbf{AV}_j + \mathbf{AU}_j)(\mathbf{a}_{y_j} \otimes \mathbf{I}_{k+1}) + \mathbf{AW}_j(\mathbf{K}_{y_j} \otimes \mathbf{I}_{k+1})\right]_1
\end{pmatrix}
$$

and signature $\sigma_{i^*,x,\mathsf{m}} = ([\mathbf{k}_0^\top]_2, [\mathbf{k}_1^\top]_2, [\mathbf{k}_2^\top]_2, [\mathbf{K}_3]_2, [\mathbf{K}_4]_2, [\mathbf{k}_5^\top]_2)$. Then compute $\mathbf{C}_x$ and $\mathbf{d}_{x,y_{i^*}}$ from x and y_{i^*}. Run $\mathsf{m} \leftarrow \mathsf{H}(i^*, \mathsf{m}, x)$ and compute

$$
\begin{pmatrix}
\underbrace{[\mathbf{sA}]_1}_{\mathsf{v}_0}, \underbrace{\left[\displaystyle\sum_{j\in[L]} (\mathbf{sAQ}_j + \mathsf{m} \cdot \mathbf{sAT}_j)\right]_1}_{\mathsf{v}_1}, \underbrace{\left[\displaystyle\sum_{j\in[L]} \mathbf{sAW}_j(\mathbf{C}_x \otimes \mathbf{I}_{k+1})\right]_1}_{\mathsf{v}_2}, \\[2em]
\underbrace{\left[\displaystyle\sum_{j\in[L]} (\mathbf{sAV}_j + \mathbf{sAU}_j)(\mathbf{a}_{y_j} \otimes \mathbf{I}_{k+1}) + \mathbf{sAW}_j(\mathbf{K}_{y_j} \otimes \mathbf{I}_{k+1})\right]_1}_{\mathsf{v}_3}, \underbrace{[\mathbf{sAk}^\top]_T}_{\mathsf{v}_4}
\end{pmatrix}
$$

where $\mathbf{s} \leftarrow \mathbb{Z}_p^{1 \times k}$. Set the verification text $\nu_{i^*,x,\mathsf{m}} = ([\mathbf{v}_0]_1, [\mathbf{v}_1]_1, [\mathbf{v}_2]_1, [\mathbf{v}_3]_1, [v_4]_T)$. Recover

$$[\mathbf{z}]_T = e([\mathbf{v}_3 \| \mathbf{v}_2]_1, [\mathbf{I}_{n_k+n_c} \otimes \mathbf{k}_1^\top]_2), [z_2]_T = e([\mathbf{v}_0]_1, [\mathbf{K}_3 \| \mathbf{K}_4]_2)$$
$$[z_3]_T = e([\mathbf{v}_0]_1, [\mathbf{k}_2^\top]_2), [z_4]_T = e([\mathbf{v}_1]_1, [\mathbf{k}_0^\top]_2), [z_5]_T = e([\mathbf{v}_0]_1, [\mathbf{k}_5^\top]_2),$$
$$[z_6]_T = [z_3 - z_4 + z_5]_T, [z_7]_T = [(\mathbf{z}_1 - \mathbf{z}_2)\mathbf{d}_{x,y_{i^*}}^\top - z_6]_T$$

and check $[z_7]_T^{-1} \stackrel{?}{=} [v_4]_T$. If the above check passes, output 1; otherwise, output 0.

Correctness. For all $\lambda, L \in \mathbb{N}$, all P, all $i^* \in [L]$, all $\mathsf{crs} \leftarrow \mathsf{Setup}(1^\lambda, P, 1^L)$, all $(\mathsf{pk}_{i^*}, \mathsf{sk}_{i^*}) \leftarrow \mathsf{Gen}(\mathsf{crs}, i^*)$, all $\{\mathsf{pk}_i\}_{i \in [L] \setminus \{i^*\}}$ such that $\mathsf{IsValid}(\mathsf{crs}, i, \mathsf{pk}_i) = 1$, for all $y_1, \ldots, y_L \in Y$ and $x \in X$ with $P(x, y_{i^*}) = 1$ and all m, we have: $\sigma_{i^*,x,\mathsf{m}} = ([\mathbf{k}_0^\top]_2, [\mathbf{k}_1^\top]_2, [\mathbf{k}_2^\top]_2, [\mathbf{K}_3]_2, [\mathbf{K}_4]_2, [\mathbf{k}_5^\top]_2)$ and $\nu_{i^*,x,\mathsf{m}} = ([\mathbf{v}_0]_1, [\mathbf{v}_1]_1, [\mathbf{v}_2]_1, [\mathbf{v}_3]_1, [v_4]_1)$. We employ the predicate encoding as defined in Sect. 3.4, namely

$$\mathbf{M}_{x,y_i} = \begin{pmatrix} \mathbf{a}_{y_i} & \mathbf{0}_{n_c} \\ \mathbf{K}_{y_i} & \mathbf{C}_x \end{pmatrix}, \quad \forall i \in [L].$$

We obtain

$$\mathbf{z}_1 = \sum_{i \in [L]} (\mathbf{sAV}_i + \mathbf{sAU}_i \| \mathbf{sAW}_i)(\mathbf{M}_{x,y_i} \otimes \mathbf{I}_{k+1})(\mathbf{I}_{n_k+n_c} \otimes \mathbf{Br}_{i^*}^\top)$$

$$= \sum_{i \in [L]} (\mathbf{sAV}_i + \mathbf{sAU}_i \| \mathbf{sAW}_i)(\mathbf{I}_{1+n} \otimes \mathbf{Br}_{i^*}^\top)\mathbf{M}_{x,y_i}$$

$$= \sum_{i \in [L]} (\mathbf{sAV}_i\mathbf{Br}_{i^*}^\top + \mathbf{sAU}_i\mathbf{Br}_{i^*}^\top \| \mathbf{sAW}_i(\mathbf{I}_n \otimes \mathbf{Br}_{i^*}^\top))\mathbf{M}_{x,y_i}$$

$$\mathbf{z}_2 = \sum_{i \in [L] \setminus \{i^*\}} (\mathbf{sAV}_i\mathbf{Br}_{i^*}^\top + \mathbf{sAU}_i\mathbf{Br}_{i^*}^\top \| \mathbf{sAW}_i(\mathbf{I}_n \otimes \mathbf{Br}_{i^*}^\top))\mathbf{M}_{x,y_i}$$

$$z_3 = \mathbf{sAV}_{i^*}\mathbf{Br}_{i^*}^\top + \mathbf{sAk}^\top + \mathbf{sAU}_{i^*}\mathbf{Br}_{i^*}^\top + (\mathbf{sAQ}_{i^*}\mathbf{B}_{i^*}\mathbf{t}^\top + m \cdot \mathbf{sAT}_{i^*}\mathbf{B}_{i^*}\mathbf{t}^\top)$$

$$z_4 = \sum_{j \in [L]} (\mathbf{sAQ}_j\mathbf{B}_{i^*}\mathbf{t}^\top + m \cdot \mathbf{sAT}_j\mathbf{B}_{i^*}\mathbf{t}^\top)$$

$$z_5 = \sum_{j \in [L] \setminus \{i^*\}} (\mathbf{sAQ}_j\mathbf{B}_{i^*}\mathbf{t}^\top + m \cdot \mathbf{sAT}_j\mathbf{B}_{i^*}\mathbf{t}^\top)$$

$$(2)$$

and then

$$z_6 = z_3 - (z_4 - z_5) = \mathbf{sAV}_{i^*}\mathbf{Br}_{i^*}^\top + \mathbf{sAk}^\top + \mathbf{sAU}_{i^*}\mathbf{Br}_{i^*}^\top$$
$$z_7 = (\mathbf{z}_1 - \mathbf{z}_2)\mathbf{d}_{x,y_{i^*}}^\top - z_6 = -\mathbf{sAk}^\top$$

where

$$z_4 - z_5 = \mathbf{sAQ}_{i^*}\mathbf{B}_{i^*}\mathbf{t}^\top + m \cdot \mathbf{sAT}_{i^*}\mathbf{B}_{i^*}\mathbf{t}^\top.$$

Finally, we have $[z_7]_T^{-1} = [v_4]_T$. Notice that equality (2) follows from the property of tensor product: $(\mathbf{M} \otimes \mathbf{I})(\mathbf{I} \otimes \mathbf{a}^\top) = \mathbf{M} \otimes \mathbf{a}^\top = (\mathbf{I} \otimes \mathbf{a}^\top)\mathbf{M}$ for matrices of proper size; the computation of z_7 follows from the correctness of predicate encoding. This proves the correctness.

4.2   Security

Theorem 1. *The proposed slotted registered ABS scheme is unforgeable under MDDH assumption and collision-resistant hash functions.*

Game Sequence. We prove Theorem 1 via the following game sequences. Let L be the number of slots and i^* be the challenge slot, (x^*, m^*) be the challenge attribute and message pair; $(\mathsf{pk}_i^*, y_i^*)_{i \in [L]}$ be the challenge public keys and challenge "policy" to be registered. For all $i \in [L]$, $\mathcal{D}_i = \{\mathsf{pk}_i : \mathcal{D}_i[\mathsf{pk}_i] = \mathsf{sk}_i \neq \bot\}$ stores the response to $\mathsf{OGen}(i)$; $\mathcal{C}_i = \{\mathsf{pk}_i : (i, \mathsf{pk}_i) \in \mathcal{C}\}$ stores the response to $\mathsf{OCor}(i, \cdot)$. Define $Q = \sum_{i \in [L]} Q_i$ and $\sigma_{i,\kappa}$ as the κth ($\kappa \in [Q_i]$) signature query's result in slot i, where Q_i denotes the number of signature queries in slot i.

- G_0: Real Game. Recall that:
    - the common reference string is that

$$\mathsf{crs} = \begin{pmatrix} [\mathbf{A}]_1, \{[\mathbf{AV}_i, \mathbf{AW}_i]_1, [\mathbf{Br}_i^\top, \mathbf{V}_i\mathbf{Br}_i^\top + \mathbf{k}^\top, \mathbf{B}_i]_2\}_{i \in [L]}, \\ \{[\mathbf{V}_i\mathbf{Br}_j^\top, \mathbf{W}_i(\mathbf{I}_n \otimes \mathbf{Br}_j^\top)]_2\}_{j \in [L], i \in [L] \backslash \{j\}}, [\mathbf{Ak}^\top]_T, \mathsf{H} \end{pmatrix}.$$

    - For each $i \in [L]$, each public key $\mathsf{pk}_i \in \mathcal{D}_i$ is that

$$\mathsf{pk}_i = ([\mathbf{AU}_i, \mathbf{AQ}_i, \mathbf{AT}_i]_1, \{[\mathbf{U}_i\mathbf{Br}_j^\top, \mathbf{Q}_i\mathbf{B}_j, \mathbf{T}_i\mathbf{B}_j]_2\}_{j \in [L] \backslash \{i\}}).$$

    where the corresponding secret key is that $\mathsf{sk}_i = (\mathbf{U}_i, \mathbf{Q}_i, \mathbf{T}_i)$.
    - For each $i \in [L]$ and each $\kappa \in [Q_i]$, the κ-th query to $\mathsf{OSig}(i, x, \mathsf{m})$ will output the result $\sigma_{i,\kappa}$ as

$$\begin{pmatrix} \underbrace{[\mathbf{B}_i\mathbf{t}^\top]_2}_{\mathbf{k}_0^\top}, \underbrace{[\mathbf{Br}_i^\top]_2}_{\mathbf{k}_1^\top}, \underbrace{[\mathbf{V}_i\mathbf{Br}_i^\top + \mathbf{k}^\top + \mathbf{U}_i\mathbf{Br}_i^\top + (\mathbf{Q}_i\mathbf{B}_i\mathbf{t}^\top + m \cdot \mathbf{T}_i\mathbf{B}_i\mathbf{t}^\top)]_2}_{\mathbf{k}_2^\top} \\ \underbrace{\left[\sum_{j \in [L] \backslash \{i^*\}} (\mathbf{V}_j\mathbf{Br}_i^\top + \mathbf{U}_j\mathbf{Br}_i^\top)\mathbf{a}_{y_j} + \mathbf{W}_j(\mathbf{I}_n \otimes \mathbf{Br}_i^\top)\mathbf{K}_{y_j} \right]_2}_{\mathbf{K}_3}, \\ \underbrace{\left[\sum_{j \in [L] \backslash \{i\}} \mathbf{W}_j(\mathbf{I}_n \otimes \mathbf{Br}_i^\top)\mathbf{C}_x \right]_2}_{\mathbf{K}_4}, \underbrace{\left[\sum_{j \in [L] \backslash \{i\}} (\mathbf{Q}_j\mathbf{B}_i\mathbf{t}^\top + m \cdot \mathbf{T}_j\mathbf{B}_i\mathbf{t}^\top) \right]_2}_{\mathbf{k}_5^\top} \end{pmatrix}$$

    where $\mathbf{t} \leftarrow \mathbb{Z}_p^{1 \times k}$ and $m_{i,\kappa} \leftarrow \mathsf{H}(i, \mathsf{m}, x)$.
    - The challenge verification text is $\nu_{i^*, x^*, \mathsf{m}^*}^* = ([\mathbf{v}_0]_1, [\mathbf{v}_1]_1, [\mathbf{v}_2]_1, [\mathbf{v}_3]_1, [v_4]_T)$ where

$$\begin{pmatrix} \underbrace{[\mathsf{sA}]_1}_{\mathbf{v}_0}, \underbrace{\left[\sum_{j \in [L]} (\mathsf{sAQ}_j + m \cdot \mathsf{sAT}_j) \right]_1}_{\mathbf{v}_1}, \underbrace{\left[\sum_{j \in [L]} \mathsf{sAW}_j(\mathbf{C}_x \otimes \mathbf{I}_{k+1}) \right]_1}_{\mathbf{v}_2} \\ \underbrace{\left[\sum_{j \in [L]} (\mathsf{sAV}_j + \mathsf{sAU}_j)(\mathbf{a}_{y_j} \otimes \mathbf{I}_{k+1}) + \mathsf{sAW}_j(\mathbf{K}_{y_j} \otimes \mathbf{I}_{k+1}) \right]_1}_{\mathbf{v}_3}, \underbrace{[\mathsf{sAk}^\top]_T}_{v_4} \end{pmatrix}$$

notice that $\mathbf{s} \leftarrow \mathbb{Z}_p^{1 \times k}$ and $m^* \leftarrow \mathsf{H}(i^*, \mathsf{m}^*, x^*)$.

- G_1: Identical to G_0 except that we replace $\mathbf{sA}$ in challenge verification text with $\mathbf{c} \leftarrow \mathbb{Z}_p^{1 \times (k+1)}$. Then the challenge verification text is that

$$
\left(
\underbrace{[\boxed{\mathbf{c}}]_1}_{v_0},
\underbrace{\left[\sum_{j \in [L]} (\boxed{\mathbf{c}}\, \mathbf{Q}_j + m \cdot \boxed{\mathbf{c}}\, \mathbf{T}_j)\right]_1}_{v_1},
\underbrace{\left[\sum_{j \in [L]} \boxed{\mathbf{c}}\, \mathbf{W}_j(\mathbf{C}_x \otimes \mathbf{I}_{k+1})\right]_1}_{v_2}
\right.
$$
$$
\left.
\underbrace{\left[\sum_{j \in [L]} (\boxed{\mathbf{c}}\, \mathbf{V}_j + \boxed{\mathbf{c}}\, \mathbf{U}_j)(\mathbf{a}_{y_j} \otimes \mathbf{I}_{k+1}) + \boxed{\mathbf{c}}\, \mathbf{W}_j(\mathbf{K}_{y_j} \otimes \mathbf{I}_{k+1})\right]_1}_{v_3},
\underbrace{[\boxed{\mathbf{c}}\, \mathbf{k}^\top]_T}_{v_4}
\right).
$$

Observe that we have $\mathsf{G}_0 \approx_c \mathsf{G}_1$, which follows the MDDH assumption, ensuring that $([\mathbf{A}]_1, [\mathbf{sA}]_1 \approx_c [\mathbf{A}]_1, [\mathbf{c}]_1)$ where $\mathbf{A} \leftarrow \mathbb{Z}_p^{k \times (k+1)}, \mathbf{s} \leftarrow \mathbb{Z}_p^{1 \times k}$ and $\mathbf{c} \leftarrow \mathbb{Z}_p^{1 \times (k+1)}$. See Lemma 1 for more details.

- $\mathsf{G}_{2,\ell}(\ell \in [L])$: Identical to $\mathsf{G}_{2,\ell-1}$ except that we change crs into the following form:

$$
\mathsf{crs} = \left(
\begin{array}{l}
[\mathbf{A}]_1, \{[\mathbf{AV}_i, \mathbf{AW}_i]_1, [\mathbf{Br}_i^\top, \mathbf{V}_i\mathbf{Br}_i^\top + \boxed{\alpha \mathbf{c}^\perp} + \mathbf{k}^\top, \mathbf{B}_i]_2\}_{i \in [L]}, \\
\{[\mathbf{V}_i\mathbf{Br}_j^\top, \mathbf{W}_i(\mathbf{I}_n \otimes \mathbf{B}_j)]_2\}_{j \in [L], i \in [L] \setminus \{j\}}, [\mathbf{Ak}^\top]_T, \mathsf{H}
\end{array}
\right).
$$

where $\alpha_\ell \leftarrow \mathbb{Z}_p$ and $\mathbf{c}^\perp \leftarrow \mathbb{Z}_p^{2k+1}$ such that $\mathbf{Ac}^\perp = 0, \mathbf{cc}^\perp = 1$. Note that $\mathsf{G}_{2,0}$ is identical to G_1; we have $\mathsf{G}_{2,\ell-1} \approx_c \mathsf{G}_{2,\ell}$, see Sect. 4.3 for more details.

- G_3: Identical to G_{2,Q_L} except that we replace the verification text into the following form:

$$
\left(
\underbrace{[\boxed{\mathbf{c}}]_1}_{v_0},
\underbrace{\left[\sum_{j \in [L]} (\mathbf{cQ}_j + m \cdot \mathbf{cT}_j)\right]_1}_{v_1},
\underbrace{\left[\sum_{j \in [L]} \mathbf{cW}_j(\mathbf{C}_x \otimes \mathbf{I}_{k+1})\right]_1}_{v_2}
\right.
$$
$$
\left.
\underbrace{\left[\sum_{j \in [L]} (\mathbf{cV}_j + \mathbf{cU}_j)(\mathbf{a}_{y_j} \otimes \mathbf{I}_{k+1}) + \mathbf{cW}_j(\mathbf{K}_{y_j} \otimes \mathbf{I}_{k+1})\right]_1}_{v_3},
\underbrace{[\boxed{g^*}]_T}_{v_4}
\right).
$$

where g_T^* is sampled uniformly over G_T. We claim that $\mathsf{G}_{2,L} \approx_s \mathsf{G}_3$ which follows the following the statistical argument:

$$
(\mathbf{Ak}^\top, \mathbf{k}^\top + \alpha \mathbf{c}^\perp, \mathbf{ck}^\top) \approx_s (\mathbf{Ak}^\top, \mathbf{k}^\top, \mathbf{ck}^\top - \alpha)
$$

where $[\mathbf{ck}^\top - \alpha]_T$ is uniform, namely, g_T^*. See Lemma 4 for more details.

Observe that the advantage of $\mathcal{A}$ to forge a valid signature is negligible in G_3.

4.3   From $G_{2,\ell-1}$ to $G_{2,\ell}$

In this section, we prove $G_{2,\ell-1} \approx_c G_{2,\ell}$. Similar to [23], we consider the honest case and the corrupted case, respectively. For these two cases, we apply the following different strategies.

Honest Case. Here, only the challenger knows the secret key $\mathsf{sk}_\ell = (\mathbf{U}_\ell, \mathbf{Q}_\ell, \mathbf{T}_\ell)$ which is hidden from $\mathcal{A}$. We use the following sub-sequence of games for each $\ell \in \mathcal{D}_\ell \setminus \mathcal{C}_\ell$.

- $G_{2,\ell-1,0}$: Identical to $G_{2,\ell-1}$. Recall the crs is in the form

$$\mathsf{crs} = \left(\begin{array}{l} [\mathbf{Ak}^\top]_T, \mathsf{H}, [\mathbf{A}]_1, \{[\mathbf{AV}_i, \mathbf{AW}_i]_1, [\mathbf{B}_i]_2\}_{i\in[L]}, \\ \{[\mathbf{V}_i\mathbf{Br}_j^\top, \mathbf{W}_i(\mathbf{I}_n\otimes\mathbf{Br}_j^\top)]_2\}_{j\in[L],i\in[L]\setminus\{j\}}, \\ \{[\mathbf{Br}_i^\top, \mathbf{V}_i\mathbf{Br}_i^\top + \mathbf{k}^\top + \alpha\mathbf{c}^\perp]_2\}_{i<\ell}, [\,\mathbf{Br}_\ell^\top, \mathbf{V}_\ell\mathbf{Br}_\ell^\top + \mathbf{k}^\top\,]_2, \\ \{[\mathbf{Br}_i^\top, \mathbf{V}_i\mathbf{Br}_i^\top + \mathbf{k}^\top]_2\}_{i>\ell} \end{array} \right),$$

and the challenge verification text ν^* is that

$$\left([\mathbf{c}]_1, \left[\sum_{j\in[L]}(\mathbf{cQ}_j + m^*\cdot\mathbf{cT}_j) \right]_1, \left[\sum_{j\in[L]}\mathbf{cW}_j(\mathbf{C}_x\otimes\mathbf{I}_{k+1}) \right]_1, \right.$$
$$\left. \left[\sum_{j\in[L]}(\mathbf{cV}_j+\mathbf{cU}_j)(\mathbf{a}_{y_j}\otimes\mathbf{I}_{k+1}) + \mathbf{cW}_j(\mathbf{K}_{y_j}\otimes\mathbf{I}_{k+1}) \right]_1, [\mathbf{ck}^\top]_T \right).$$

Finally, for each $\kappa\in[Q_\ell]$, the corresponding signature $\sigma_{\ell,\kappa}$ is in the form:

$$\left(\begin{array}{l} [\mathbf{B}_\ell\mathbf{t}^\top]_2, [\mathbf{Br}_\ell^\top]_2, [\,\mathbf{V}_\ell\mathbf{Br}_\ell^\top + \mathbf{k}^\top + \mathbf{U}_\ell\mathbf{Br}_\ell^\top\,] + (\mathbf{Q}_\ell\mathbf{B}_\ell\mathbf{t}^\top + m_{\ell,\kappa}\cdot\mathbf{T}_\ell\mathbf{B}_\ell\mathbf{t}^\top)]_2, \\ \left[\sum_{j\in[L]\setminus\{\ell\}}(\mathbf{V}_j\mathbf{Br}_\ell^\top + \mathbf{U}_j\mathbf{Br}_\ell^\top)\mathbf{a}_{y_j} + \mathbf{W}_j(\mathbf{I}_n\otimes\mathbf{Br}_\ell^\top)\mathbf{K}_{y_j} \right]_2, \\ \left[\sum_{j\in[L]\setminus\{\ell\}}\mathbf{W}_j(\mathbf{I}_n\otimes\mathbf{Br}_\ell^\top)\mathbf{C}_x \right]_2, \left[\sum_{j\in[L]\setminus\{\ell\}}(\mathbf{Q}_j\mathbf{B}_\ell\mathbf{t}^\top + m_{\ell,\kappa}\cdot\mathbf{T}_j\mathbf{B}_\ell\mathbf{t}^\top) \right] \end{array} \right)$$

where $\mathbf{t}\leftarrow\mathbb{Z}_p^{1\times k}$ and $m_{\ell,\kappa}\leftarrow\mathsf{H}(\ell,\mathsf{m},x)$.
- $G_{2,\ell-1,\kappa}(\kappa\in[Q_\ell])$: Identical to $G_{2,\ell-1,\kappa-1}$ except that the signature $\sigma_{\ell,\kappa}$ is that

$$\left(\begin{array}{l} [\mathbf{B}_\ell\mathbf{t}^\top]_2, [\mathbf{Br}_\ell^\top]_2, \\ [\mathbf{V}_\ell\mathbf{Br}_\ell^\top + \mathbf{k}^\top + \mathbf{U}_\ell\mathbf{Br}_\ell^\top + \boxed{\beta_{\ell,\kappa}\mathbf{c}^\perp} + (\mathbf{Q}_\ell\mathbf{B}_\ell\mathbf{t}^\top + m_{\ell,\kappa}\cdot\mathbf{T}_\ell\mathbf{B}_\ell\mathbf{t}^\top)]_2, \\ \left[\sum_{j\in[L]\setminus\{\ell\}}(\mathbf{V}_j\mathbf{Br}_\ell^\top + \mathbf{U}_j\mathbf{Br}_\ell^\top)\mathbf{a}_{y_j} + \mathbf{W}_j(\mathbf{I}_n\otimes\mathbf{Br}_\ell^\top)\mathbf{K}_{y_j} \right]_2, \\ \left[\sum_{j\in[L]\setminus\{\ell\}}\mathbf{W}_j(\mathbf{I}_n\otimes\mathbf{Br}_\ell^\top)\mathbf{C}_x \right]_2, \left[\sum_{j\in[L]\setminus\{\ell\}}(\mathbf{Q}_j\mathbf{B}_\ell\mathbf{t}^\top + m_{\ell,\kappa}\cdot\mathbf{T}_j\mathbf{B}_\ell\mathbf{t}^\top) \right] \end{array} \right)$$

where $G_{2,\ell-1,\kappa-1} \approx_c G_{2,\ell-1,\kappa}$ for all $\kappa\in[Q_\ell]$; see Lemma 2 for more details.

- $\mathsf{G}_{2,\ell-1,Q_\ell+1}$: Identical to $\mathsf{G}_{2,\ell-1,Q_\ell}$ except that the item marked with dashed box in crs is that

$$[\,\boxed{\mathbf{d}_\ell^\top}\,,\mathbf{V}_\ell\,\boxed{\mathbf{d}_\ell^\top}\,+\mathbf{k}^\top]_2$$

where $\mathbf{d}_\ell \leftarrow \mathbb{Z}_p^{1\times(k+1)}$; correspondingly, for all $\kappa \in [Q_\ell]$, the item marked with dashed box in $\sigma_{\ell,\kappa}$ is that

$$[\mathbf{V}_\ell\,\boxed{\mathbf{d}_\ell^\top}\,+\mathbf{k}^\top+\mathbf{U}_\ell\,\boxed{\mathbf{d}_\ell^\top}\,+\beta_{\ell,\kappa}\mathbf{c}^\perp]_2.$$

We have $\mathsf{G}_{2,\ell-1,Q_\ell+1} \approx_c \mathsf{G}_{2,\ell-1,Q_\ell}$, which follows the MDDH assumption:

$$([\mathbf{B}]_2,[\mathbf{Br}_\ell^\top]_2) \approx_c ([\mathbf{B}]_2,[\mathbf{d}_\ell^\top]_2)$$

notice that $\mathbf{B} \leftarrow \mathbb{Z}_p^{(k+1)\times k}, \mathbf{r}_\ell \leftarrow \mathbb{Z}_p^{1\times(k+1)}$ and $\mathbf{d}_\ell \leftarrow \mathbb{Z}_p^{1\times k}$. See Lemma 3 for more details.
- $\mathsf{G}_{2,\ell-1,Q_\ell+2}$: Identical to $\mathsf{G}_{2,\ell-1,Q_\ell+1}$ except that the item marked with dashed box in crs is that

$$[\mathbf{d}_\ell^\top,\mathbf{V}_\ell\mathbf{d}_\ell^\top+\mathbf{k}^\top+\boxed{\alpha\mathbf{c}^\top}\,]_2.$$

We have $\mathsf{G}_{2,\ell-1,Q_\ell+1} \approx_s \mathsf{G}_{2,\ell-1,Q_\ell+2}$ which follows the following argument:

$$\begin{cases} \mathbf{A},\mathbf{B}_\ell,\mathbf{c}^\perp,\mathbf{d}_\ell^\top,\mathbf{AV}_\ell,\mathbf{V}_\ell\mathbf{B},\mathbf{V}_\ell\mathbf{d}_\ell^\top+bc^\perp\alpha;\quad \mathbf{AU}_\ell \quad //\mathsf{crs};\ \mathsf{pk}_i; \\ \mathbf{c},\mathbf{cV}_\ell+\mathbf{cU}_\ell;\quad \mathbf{d}_\ell^\top,\mathbf{U}_\ell\mathbf{d}_\ell^\top+\beta_{\ell,\kappa}\mathbf{c}^\perp \qquad\qquad //\nu^*;\ \sigma_{i,\kappa} \end{cases}$$

$$\approx_s \begin{cases} \mathbf{A},\mathbf{B}_\ell,\mathbf{c}^\perp,\mathbf{d}_\ell^\top,\mathbf{AV}_\ell,\mathbf{V}_\ell\mathbf{B},\mathbf{V}_\ell\mathbf{d}_\ell^\top+\boxed{v_\ell\mathbf{c}^\perp}+bc^\perp\alpha;\quad \mathbf{AU}_\ell \\ \mathbf{c},\mathbf{cV}_\ell+\mathbf{cU}_\ell+\boxed{v_\ell\mathbf{c}^\perp+u_\ell\mathbf{c}^\perp};\quad \mathbf{d}_\ell^\top,\mathbf{U}_\ell\mathbf{d}_\ell^\top+\boxed{u_\ell\mathbf{c}^\perp}+\beta_{\ell,\kappa}\mathbf{c}^\perp \end{cases}$$

$$\approx_s \begin{cases} \mathbf{A},\mathbf{B}_\ell,\mathbf{c}^\perp,\mathbf{d}_\ell^\top,\mathbf{AV}_\ell,\mathbf{V}_\ell\mathbf{B},\mathbf{V}_\ell\mathbf{d}_\ell^\top+v_\ell\mathbf{c}^\perp+\cancel{bc^\perp\alpha};\quad \mathbf{AU}_\ell \\ \mathbf{c},\mathbf{cV}_\ell+\mathbf{cU}_\ell+v_\ell\mathbf{c}^\perp+u_\ell\mathbf{c}^\perp;\quad \mathbf{d}_\ell^\top,\mathbf{U}_\ell\mathbf{d}_\ell^\top+u_\ell\mathbf{c}^\perp+\beta_{\ell,\kappa}\mathbf{c}^\perp \end{cases}$$

where $b \in \{0,1\}$.
- The first $\approx_s$ follows that:

$$\mathbf{V}_\ell \mapsto \mathbf{V}_\ell+\mathbf{c}^\perp v_\ell\mathbf{d}^\perp \quad \text{and} \quad \mathbf{U}_\ell \mapsto \mathbf{U}_\ell+\mathbf{c}^\perp u_\ell\mathbf{d}^\perp$$

where $\mathbf{c}^\perp \in \mathbb{Z}_p^{k+1}$ and $\mathbf{d}^\perp \in \mathbb{Z}_p^{1\times(k+1)}$ such that $\mathbf{Ac}^\perp = 0, \mathbf{cc}^\perp = 1, \mathbf{d}^\perp\mathbf{B} = 0, \mathbf{d}^\perp\mathbf{d}_\ell = 1$.
- The second $\approx_s$ holds since $\beta_{\ell,\kappa}$ is sampled randomly and hence preserve the privacy of u_ℓ. Then v_ℓ in crs also seems to be sampled randomly because u_ℓ hides v_ℓ in challenge verification text.
- $\mathsf{G}_{2,\ell-1,Q_\ell+3}$: Identical to $\mathsf{G}_{2,\ell-1,Q_\ell+2}$ except that the item marked with dashed box in crs is that

$$[\,\boxed{\mathbf{Br}_\ell^\top}\,,\mathbf{V}_\ell\,\boxed{\mathbf{Br}_\ell^\top}\,+\mathbf{k}^\top+\alpha\mathbf{c}^\perp]_2$$

where $\mathbf{B} \leftarrow \mathbb{Z}_p^{(k+1)\times k}, \mathbf{r}_\ell \leftarrow \mathbb{Z}_p^{1\times(k+1)}$ and $\mathbf{d}_\ell \leftarrow \mathbb{Z}_p^{1\times k}$; correspondingly, for all $\kappa \in [Q_\ell]$, the item marked with $\boxed{\text{dashed box}}$ in the $[\mathbf{k}_2^\top]_2$ of $\sigma_{\ell,\kappa}$ is that

$$[\mathbf{V}_\ell\,\boxed{\mathbf{Br}_\ell^\top} + \mathbf{k}^\top + \mathbf{U}_\ell\,\boxed{\mathbf{Br}_\ell^\top} + \beta_{\ell,\kappa}\mathbf{c}^\perp]_2.$$

We have $\mathsf{G}_{2,\ell-1,Q_\ell+2} \approx_c \mathsf{G}_{2,\ell-1,Q_\ell+3}$ which is symmetrical to $\mathsf{G}_{2,\ell-1,Q_\ell} \approx_c \mathsf{G}_{2,\ell-1,Q_\ell+1}$.

- $\mathsf{G}_{2,\ell-1,Q_\ell+4}$: Identical to $\mathsf{G}_{2,\ell-1,Q_\ell+3}$ except that the signature $\sigma_{\ell,\kappa}$ is that

$$\begin{pmatrix} [\mathbf{B}_\ell\mathbf{t}^\top]_2, [\mathbf{Br}_\ell^\top]_2, \\[2mm] [\mathbf{V}_\ell\mathbf{Br}_\ell^\top + \mathbf{k}^\top + \alpha\mathbf{c}^\perp + \mathbf{U}_\ell\mathbf{Br}_\ell^\top + \beta_{\ell,\kappa}\mathbf{c}^\perp + (\mathbf{Q}_\ell\mathbf{B}_\ell\mathbf{t}^\top + m_{\ell,\kappa}\cdot\mathbf{T}_\ell\mathbf{B}_\ell\mathbf{t}^\top)]_2, \\[2mm] \left[\displaystyle\sum_{j\in[L]\backslash\{\ell\}} (\mathbf{V}_j\mathbf{Br}_\ell^\top + \mathbf{U}_j\mathbf{Br}_\ell^\top)\mathbf{a}_{y_j} + \mathbf{W}_j(\mathbf{I}_n \otimes \mathbf{Br}_\ell^\top)\mathbf{K}_{y_j}\right]_2, \\[3mm] \left[\displaystyle\sum_{j\in[L]\backslash\{\ell\}} \mathbf{W}_j(\mathbf{I}_n \otimes \mathbf{Br}_\ell^\top)\mathbf{C}_x\right]_2, \left[\displaystyle\sum_{j\in[L]\backslash\{\ell\}} (\mathbf{Q}_j\mathbf{B}_\ell\mathbf{t}^\top + m_{\ell,\kappa}\cdot\mathbf{T}_j\mathbf{B}_\ell\mathbf{t}^\top)\right] \end{pmatrix}.$$

We say $\mathsf{G}_{2,\ell-1,Q_\ell+3} \approx_c \mathsf{G}_{2,\ell-1,Q_\ell+4}$ for all $\kappa \in [Q_\ell]$. The proof is symmetrical to $\mathsf{G}_{2,\ell-1,0} \approx_c \mathsf{G}_{2,\ell-1,Q_\ell}$. Notice that $\mathsf{G}_{2,\ell-1,Q_\ell+4} \equiv \mathsf{G}_{2,\ell}$.

So far, we have finished dealing with the honest case.

Corrupted Case. In the corrupted case, for each $\ell \in \mathcal{C}_\ell$, the secret key $\mathsf{sk}_\ell = (\mathbf{U}_\ell, \mathbf{Q}_\ell, \mathbf{T}_\ell)$ been known to the adversary, but it is required that $P(x^*, y_\ell) = 0$ for the challenge (x^*, m^*). We start with the following sub-games:

- $\mathsf{G}'_{2,\ell-1,0}$: Identical to $\mathsf{G}_{2,\ell-1}$. Recall the crs is in the form

$$\mathsf{crs} = \begin{pmatrix} [\mathbf{Ak}^\top]_T, \mathsf{H}, [\mathbf{A}]_1, \{[\mathbf{AV}_i, \mathbf{AW}_i]_1, [\mathbf{B}_i]_2\}_{i\in[L]}, \\ \{[\mathbf{V}_i\mathbf{Br}_j^\top, \mathbf{W}_i(\mathbf{I}_n \otimes \mathbf{Br}_j^\top)]_2\}_{j\in[L],i\in[L]\backslash\{j\}}, \\ \{[\mathbf{Br}_i^\top, \mathbf{V}_i\mathbf{Br}_i^\top + \mathbf{k}^\top + \alpha\mathbf{c}^\perp]_2\}_{i<\ell}, \boxed{[\mathbf{Br}_\ell^\top, \mathbf{V}_\ell\mathbf{Br}_\ell^\top + \mathbf{k}^\top]_2}, \\ \{[\mathbf{Br}_i^\top, \mathbf{V}_i\mathbf{Br}_i^\top + \mathbf{k}^\top]_2\}_{i>\ell} \end{pmatrix},$$

and the challenge verification text is that

$$\nu^* = \begin{pmatrix} [\mathbf{c}]_1, \left[\displaystyle\sum_{j\in[L]} (\mathbf{cQ}_j + \mathsf{m}^* \cdot \mathbf{cT}_j)\right]_1, \left[\displaystyle\sum_{j\in[L]} \mathbf{cW}_j(\mathbf{C}_x \otimes \mathbf{I}_{k+1})\right]_1, \\ \left[\displaystyle\sum_{j\in[L]} (\mathbf{cV}_j + \mathbf{cU}_j)(\mathbf{a}_{y_j} \otimes \mathbf{I}_{k+1}) + \mathbf{cW}_j(\mathbf{K}_{y_j} \otimes \mathbf{I}_{k+1})\right]_1, [\mathbf{ck}^\top]_T \end{pmatrix}.$$

- $\mathsf{G}'_{2,\ell-1,1}$: Identical to $\mathsf{G}'_{2,\ell-1,0}$ except that the item marked with $\boxed{\text{dashed box}}$ in crs is that

$$[\boxed{\mathbf{d}_\ell^\top}, \mathbf{V}_\ell\,\mathbf{d}_\ell^\top + \mathbf{k}^\top]_2.$$

We have $G'_{2,\ell-1,0} \approx_c G'_{2,\ell-1,1}$, which follows the MDDH assumption:

$$([\mathbf{B}]_2, [\mathbf{Br}_\ell^\top]_2) \approx_c ([\mathbf{B}]_2, [\mathbf{d}_\ell^\top]_2)$$

notice that $\mathbf{B} \leftarrow \mathbb{Z}_p^{(k+1)\times k}, \mathbf{r}_\ell \leftarrow \mathbb{Z}_p^{1\times(k+1)}$ and $\mathbf{d}_\ell \leftarrow \mathbb{Z}_p^{1\times k}$. The proof is analogous to $G_{2,\ell-1,\kappa} \approx_c G_{2,\ell-1,Q_\ell+1}$ in the honest case and can be followed via the Lemma 2.

- $G'_{2,\ell-1,2}$: Identical to $G'_{2,\ell-1,1}$ except that the item marked with $\dashbox{dashed box}$ in crs is that

$$[\mathbf{d}_\ell^\top, \mathbf{V}_\ell\mathbf{d}_\ell^\top + \mathbf{k}^\top + \boxed{\alpha\mathbf{c}^\perp}]_2.$$

We claim $G'_{2,\ell-1,2} \approx_s G'_{2,\ell-1,1}$ via the following argument ($b \in \{0,1\}$):

$$\left\{ \begin{array}{l} \mathbf{A}, \mathbf{B}_\ell, \mathbf{c}^\perp, \mathbf{d}_\ell^\top, \mathbf{AV}_\ell, \mathbf{AW}_\ell, \mathbf{V}_\ell\mathbf{B}, \mathbf{W}_\ell(\mathbf{I}_n \otimes \mathbf{B}), \mathbf{V}_\ell\mathbf{d}_\ell^\top + b\mathbf{c}^\perp\alpha \quad //\text{crs} \\ \mathbf{c}, \mathbf{cV}_\ell(\mathbf{a}_{y_\ell} \otimes \mathbf{I}_{k+1}) + \mathbf{cW}_\ell(\mathbf{K}_{y_\ell} \otimes \mathbf{I}_{k+1}) \qquad\qquad //\nu^* \\ \mathbf{cW}_\ell(\mathbf{C}_{x^*} \otimes \mathbf{I}_{k+1}) \end{array} \right.$$

$$\approx_s \left\{ \begin{array}{l} \mathbf{A}, \mathbf{B}_\ell, \mathbf{c}^\perp, \mathbf{d}_\ell^\top, \mathbf{AV}_\ell, \mathbf{AW}_\ell, \mathbf{V}_\ell\mathbf{B}, \mathbf{W}_\ell(\mathbf{I}_n \otimes \mathbf{B}), \mathbf{V}_\ell\mathbf{d}_\ell^\top + \boxed{v_\ell\mathbf{c}^\perp} + b\mathbf{c}^\perp\alpha \\ \mathbf{c}, \mathbf{cV}_\ell(\mathbf{a}_{y_\ell} \otimes \mathbf{I}_{k+1}) + \mathbf{cW}_\ell(\mathbf{K}_{y_\ell} \otimes \mathbf{I}_{k+1}) + \boxed{v_\ell\mathbf{a}_{y_\ell} \otimes \mathbf{d}^\perp + \mathbf{w}_\ell^\top\mathbf{K}_{y_\ell} \otimes \mathbf{d}^\perp}, \\ \mathbf{cW}_\ell(\mathbf{C}_{x^*} \otimes \mathbf{I}_{k+1}) + \boxed{\mathbf{w}_\ell^\top\mathbf{C}_{x^*} \otimes \mathbf{d}^\perp} \end{array} \right.$$

$$\approx_s \left\{ \begin{array}{l} \mathbf{A}, \mathbf{B}_\ell, \mathbf{c}^\perp, \mathbf{d}_\ell^\top, \mathbf{AV}_\ell, \mathbf{AW}_\ell, \mathbf{V}_\ell\mathbf{B}, \mathbf{W}_\ell(\mathbf{I}_n \otimes \mathbf{B}), \mathbf{V}_\ell\mathbf{d}_\ell^\top + v_\ell\mathbf{c}^\perp + b\mathbf{c}^\perp\alpha \\ \mathbf{c}, \mathbf{cV}_\ell(\mathbf{a}_{y_\ell} \otimes \mathbf{I}_{k+1}) + \mathbf{cW}_\ell(\mathbf{K}_{y_\ell} \otimes \mathbf{I}_{k+1}) + \cancel{v_\ell\mathbf{a}_{y_\ell} \otimes \mathbf{d}^\perp} + \mathbf{w}_\ell^\top\mathbf{K}_{y_\ell} \otimes \mathbf{d}^\perp, \\ \mathbf{cW}_\ell(\mathbf{C}_{x^*} \otimes \mathbf{I}_{k+1}) + \mathbf{w}_\ell^\top\mathbf{C}_{x^*} \otimes \mathbf{d}^\perp \end{array} \right.$$

$$\approx_s \left\{ \begin{array}{l} \mathbf{A}, \mathbf{B}_\ell, \mathbf{c}^\perp, \mathbf{d}_\ell^\top, \mathbf{AV}_\ell, \mathbf{AW}_\ell, \mathbf{V}_\ell\mathbf{B}, \mathbf{W}_\ell(\mathbf{I}_n \otimes \mathbf{B}), \mathbf{V}_\ell\mathbf{d}_\ell^\top + v_\ell\mathbf{c}^\perp + \cancel{b\mathbf{c}^\perp\alpha} \\ \mathbf{c}, \mathbf{cV}_\ell(\mathbf{a}_{y_\ell} \otimes \mathbf{I}_{k+1}) + \mathbf{cW}_\ell(\mathbf{K}_{y_\ell} \otimes \mathbf{I}_{k+1}) + \mathbf{w}_\ell^\top\mathbf{K}_{y_\ell} \otimes \mathbf{d}^\perp, \\ \mathbf{cW}_\ell(\mathbf{C}_{x^*} \otimes \mathbf{I}_{k+1}) + \mathbf{w}_\ell^\top\mathbf{C}_{x^*} \otimes \mathbf{d}^\perp \end{array} \right.$$

Observe that:
- The first $\approx_s$ follows that:

$$\mathbf{V}_\ell \mapsto \mathbf{V}_\ell + \mathbf{c}^\perp v_\ell\mathbf{d}^\perp \quad \text{and} \quad \mathbf{W}_\ell \mapsto \mathbf{W}_\ell + \mathbf{c}^\perp(\mathbf{w}_\ell^\top \otimes \mathbf{d}^\perp)$$

  where $v_\ell \leftarrow \mathbb{Z}_p$ and $\mathbf{w}_\ell \leftarrow \mathbb{Z}_p^n$.
- The second $\approx_s$ follows the α-*privacy* of predicate encoding since $P(x^*, y_\ell) = 0$.
- The last $\approx_s$ holds since v_ℓ is sampled randomly and only appears in crs.

- $G'_{2,\ell-1,3}$: Identical to $G'_{2,\ell-1,2}$ except that that the item marked with $\dashbox{dashed box}$ in crs is that

$$[\boxed{\mathbf{Br}_\ell^\top}, \mathbf{V}_\ell\boxed{\mathbf{Br}_\ell^\top} + \mathbf{k}^\top + \alpha\mathbf{c}^\perp]_2$$

where $\mathbf{B} \leftarrow \mathbb{Z}_p^{(k+1)\times k}, \mathbf{r}_\ell \leftarrow \mathbb{Z}_p^{1\times(k+1)}$ and $\mathbf{d}_\ell \leftarrow \mathbb{Z}_p^{1\times k}$. We have $G'_{2,\ell-1,2} \approx_c G'_{2,\ell-1,3}$, which follows the MDDH assumption:

$$([\mathbf{B}]_2, [\mathbf{Br}_\ell^\top]_2) \approx_c ([\mathbf{B}]_2, [\mathbf{d}_\ell^\top]_2).$$

The proof is analogous to $G_{2,\ell-1,Q_\ell+2} \approx_c G_{2,\ell-1,Q_\ell+3}$ in the honest case and can be followed via the Lemma 2.

Notice that $G'_{2,\ell-1,3} \equiv G'_{2,\ell}$. So far, we have finished dealing with the corrupted case. Finally, we prove $G_{2,\ell-1} \approx_c G_{2,\ell}$ for each $\ell \in \mathcal{D}_\ell$ or $\ell \in \mathcal{C}_\ell$ by the above strategies.

4.4   Lemmata

In the following, we use $\mathsf{Adv}_\mathcal{A}^i(\lambda)$ to denote the advantage of $\mathcal{A}$ in G_i.

Lemma 1 ($G_0 \approx_c G_1$).   *For any adversary $\mathcal{A}$, there exists algorithm $\mathcal{B}_1$ with close running time to $\mathcal{A}$ such that*

$$|\mathsf{Adv}_\mathcal{A}^0(\lambda) - \mathsf{Adv}_\mathcal{A}^1(\lambda)| \leq \mathsf{Adv}_{\mathcal{B}_1}^{\mathrm{MDDH}}(\lambda) + \mathsf{negl}(\lambda).$$

Proof. Recall that the difference between the two games is that we replace $[\mathbf{sA}]_1$ in G_0 with $[\mathbf{c}]_1$, where $\mathbf{A} \leftarrow \mathbb{Z}_p^{k \times (k+1)}, \mathbf{s} \leftarrow \mathbb{Z}_p^{1 \times k}$ and $\mathbf{c} \leftarrow \mathbb{Z}_p^{1 \times (k+1)}$. This follows from $(k, k+1, 1)$-MDDH assumption, which ensures that:

$$([\mathbf{A}]_1, [\mathbf{sA}]_1) \approx_c ([\mathbf{A}]_1, [\mathbf{c}]_1).$$

On input $([\mathbf{A}]_1, [\hat{\mathbf{t}}]_1)$ where $\hat{\mathbf{t}} = \mathbf{sA}$ or $\hat{\mathbf{t}} = \mathbf{c}$, algorithm $\mathcal{B}_1$ works as follows:

Setup. Sample

$$\mathbf{B} \leftarrow \mathbb{Z}_p^{(k+1) \times k}, \mathbf{k} \leftarrow \mathbb{Z}_p^{1 \times (k+1)}, \{\mathbf{D}_i \leftarrow \mathbb{Z}_p^{k \times k}, \mathbf{V}_i \leftarrow \mathbb{Z}_p^{(k+1) \times (k+1)},$$

$$\mathbf{W}_i \leftarrow \mathbb{Z}_p^{(k+1) \times (k+1)n}, \mathbf{r}_i \leftarrow \mathbb{Z}_p^{1 \times k}\}_{i \in [L]}.$$

Set $\mathbf{B}_i = \mathbf{B}\mathbf{D}_i$ for each $i \in [L]$ and output

$$\mathsf{crs} = \begin{pmatrix} [\mathbf{A}]_1, \{[\mathbf{AV}_i, \mathbf{AW}_i]_1, [\mathbf{Br}_i^\top, \mathbf{V}_i\mathbf{Br}_i^\top + \mathbf{k}^\top, \mathbf{B}_i]_2\}_{i \in [L]}, \\ \{[\mathbf{V}_i\mathbf{Br}_j^\top, \mathbf{W}_i(\mathbf{I}_n \otimes \mathbf{Br}_j^\top)]_2\}_{j \in [L], i \in [L]\backslash\{j\}}, [\mathbf{Ak}^\top]_T, \mathsf{H} \end{pmatrix}.$$

Query. Here, we deal with the query from $\mathcal{A}$.
  – For all $i \in [L]$ and each $(\mathsf{pk}_i, \mathsf{sk}_i) \in \mathcal{D}_i$ is generated honestly as :

$$\mathsf{pk}_i = ([\mathbf{AU}_i, \mathbf{AQ}_i, \mathbf{AT}_i]_1, \{[\mathbf{U}_i\mathbf{Br}_j^\top, \mathbf{Q}_i\mathbf{B}_j, \mathbf{T}_i\mathbf{B}_j]_2\}_{j \in [L]\backslash\{i\}})$$

and $\mathsf{sk}_i = (\mathbf{U}_i, \mathbf{Q}_i, \mathbf{T}_i)$ where $\mathbf{U}_i, \mathbf{Q}_i, \mathbf{T}_i \leftarrow \mathbb{Z}_p^{(k+1) \times (k+1)}$.

- For $\mathsf{OSig}(i,x,\mathsf{m})$, sample $\mathbf{t} \leftarrow \mathbb{Z}_p^{1\times k}$ and compute $\mathbf{C}_x$, output signature $\sigma_{i,x,\mathsf{m}}$ as

$$\begin{pmatrix} \underbrace{[\mathbf{B}_i\mathbf{t}^\top]_2}_{\mathbf{k}_0^\top}, \underbrace{[\mathbf{Br}_i^\top]_2}_{\mathbf{k}_1^\top}, \underbrace{[\mathbf{V}_i\mathbf{Br}_i^\top + \mathbf{k}^\top + \mathbf{U}_i\mathbf{Br}_i^\top + (\mathbf{Q}_i\mathbf{B}_i\mathbf{t}^\top + \mathsf{m}\cdot\mathbf{T}_i\mathbf{B}_i\mathbf{t}^\top)]_2}_{\mathbf{k}_2^\top} \\[2ex] \underbrace{\left[\sum_{j\in[L]\setminus\{i^*\}}(\mathbf{V}_j\mathbf{Br}_i^\top + \mathbf{U}_j\mathbf{Br}_i^\top)\mathbf{a}_{y_j} + \mathbf{W}_j(\mathbf{I}_n\otimes\mathbf{Br}_i^\top)\mathbf{K}_{y_j}\right]_2}_{\mathbf{K}_3}, \\[2ex] \underbrace{\left[\sum_{j\in[L]\setminus\{i\}}\mathbf{W}_j(\mathbf{I}_n\otimes\mathbf{Br}_i^\top)\mathbf{C}_x\right]_2}_{\mathbf{K}_4}, \underbrace{\left[\sum_{j\in[L]\setminus\{i\}}(\mathbf{Q}_j\mathbf{B}_i\mathbf{t}^\top + \mathsf{m}\cdot\mathbf{T}_j\mathbf{B}_i\mathbf{t}^\top)\right]_2}_{\mathbf{k}_5^\top} \end{pmatrix}$$

Challenge. On input challenge (i^*, x^*, m^*), output $\nu_{i^*,x,\mathsf{m}}$ as

$$\begin{pmatrix} \underbrace{[\hat{\mathbf{t}}]_1}_{\mathbf{v}_0}, \underbrace{\left[\sum_{j\in[L]}(\hat{\mathbf{t}}\mathbf{Q}_j + \mathsf{m}\cdot\hat{\mathbf{t}}\mathbf{T}_j)\right]_1}_{\mathbf{v}_1}, \underbrace{\left[\sum_{j\in[L]}\hat{\mathbf{t}}\mathbf{W}_j(\mathbf{C}_x\otimes\mathbf{I}_{k+1})\right]_1}_{\mathbf{v}_2} \\[2ex] \underbrace{\left[\sum_{j\in[L]}(\hat{\mathbf{t}}\mathbf{V}_j + \hat{\mathbf{t}}\mathbf{U}_j)(\mathbf{a}_{y_j}\otimes\mathbf{I}_{k+1}) + \hat{\mathbf{t}}\mathbf{W}_j(\mathbf{K}_{y_j}\otimes\mathbf{I}_{k+1})\right]_1}_{\mathbf{v}_3}, \underbrace{[\hat{\mathbf{t}}\mathbf{k}^\top]_T}_{v_4} \end{pmatrix}.$$

Observe that when $\hat{\mathbf{t}} = \mathbf{sA}$, the simulation is identical to G_0; when $\hat{\mathbf{t}} = \mathbf{c}$, the simulation is identical to G_1. This readily proves the lemma. $\qquad\square$

Lemma 2 ($\mathsf{G}_{2,\ell-1,\kappa-1} \approx_c \mathsf{G}_{2,\ell-1,\kappa}$). *For any adversary $\mathcal{A}$, there exists algorithm $\mathcal{B}_2$ with close running time to $\mathcal{A}$ such that*

$$|\mathsf{Adv}_{\mathcal{A}}^{2,\ell-1,\kappa-1}(\lambda) - \mathsf{Adv}_{\mathcal{A}}^{2,\ell-1,\kappa}(\lambda)| \leq 2\cdot\mathsf{Adv}_{\mathcal{B}_2}^{\mathsf{MDDH}}(\lambda) + \mathsf{negl}(\lambda).$$

Proof. The transition between $\mathsf{G}_{2,\ell-1,\kappa-1}$ and $\mathsf{G}_{2,\ell-1,\kappa}$ is similar to the secret key transition of IBE in [6]. Recall that in $\mathsf{G}_{2,\ell-1,\kappa-1}$, we have

- For all $i < \kappa$, the signature $\sigma_{\ell,i}$ is that

$$\begin{pmatrix} [\mathbf{B}_\ell\mathbf{t}^\top]_2, [\mathbf{Br}_\ell^\top]_2, \\[1ex] [\mathbf{V}_\ell\mathbf{Br}_\ell^\top + \mathbf{k}^\top + \mathbf{U}_\ell\mathbf{Br}_\ell^\top + \boxed{\beta_{\ell,i}\mathbf{c}^\perp} + (\mathbf{Q}_\ell\mathbf{B}_\ell\mathbf{t}^\top + m_{\ell,i}\cdot\mathbf{T}_\ell\mathbf{B}_\ell\mathbf{t}^\top)]_2, \\[1ex] \left[\sum_{j\in[L]\setminus\{\ell\}}(\mathbf{V}_j\mathbf{Br}_\ell^\top + \mathbf{U}_j\mathbf{Br}_\ell^\top)\mathbf{a}_{y_j} + \mathbf{W}_j(\mathbf{I}_n\otimes\mathbf{Br}_\ell^\top)\mathbf{K}_{y_j}\right]_2, \\[1ex] \left[\sum_{j\in[L]\setminus\{\ell\}}\mathbf{W}_j(\mathbf{I}_n\otimes\mathbf{Br}_\ell^\top)\mathbf{C}_x\right]_2, \left[\sum_{j\in[L]\setminus\{\ell\}}(\mathbf{Q}_j\mathbf{B}_\ell\mathbf{t}^\top + m_{\ell,\kappa}\cdot\mathbf{T}_j\mathbf{B}_\ell\mathbf{t}^\top)\right] \end{pmatrix}$$

where $\beta_{\ell,i} \leftarrow \mathbb{Z}_p$ and $\mathbf{B}_\ell = \mathbf{BD}_\ell$.

- For all $i \geq \kappa$, the signature $\sigma_{\ell,i}$ is that

$$
\begin{pmatrix}
[\mathbf{B}_\ell \mathbf{t}^\top]_2,\ [\mathbf{Br}_\ell^\top]_2,\ [\mathbf{V}_\ell \mathbf{Br}_\ell^\top + \mathbf{k}^\top + \mathbf{U}_\ell \mathbf{Br}_\ell^\top + (\mathbf{Q}_\ell \mathbf{B}_\ell \mathbf{t}^\top + m_{\ell,i} \cdot \mathbf{T}_\ell \mathbf{B}_\ell \mathbf{t}^\top)]_2, \\[2mm]
\left[\displaystyle\sum_{j \in [L] \setminus \{\ell\}} (\mathbf{V}_j \mathbf{Br}_\ell^\top + \mathbf{U}_j \mathbf{Br}_\ell^\top)\mathbf{a}_{y_j} + \mathbf{W}_j (\mathbf{I}_n \otimes \mathbf{Br}_\ell^\top)\mathbf{K}_{y_j} \right]_2, \\[3mm]
\left[\displaystyle\sum_{j \in [L] \setminus \{\ell\}} \mathbf{W}_j (\mathbf{I}_n \otimes \mathbf{Br}_\ell^\top)\mathbf{C}_x \right]_2,\ \left[\displaystyle\sum_{j \in [L] \setminus \{\ell\}} (\mathbf{Q}_j \mathbf{B}_\ell \mathbf{t}^\top + m_{\ell,i} \cdot \mathbf{T}_j \mathbf{B}_\ell \mathbf{t}^\top) \right]
\end{pmatrix}.
$$

The verification text ν^* is that

$$
\begin{pmatrix}
[\mathbf{c}]_1,\ \left[\displaystyle\sum_{j \in [L]} (\mathbf{cQ}_j + m^* \cdot \mathbf{cT}_j) \right]_1,\ \left[\displaystyle\sum_{j \in [L]} \mathbf{cW}_j (\mathbf{C}_x \otimes \mathbf{I}_{k+1}) \right]_1, \\[3mm]
\left[\displaystyle\sum_{j \in [L]} (\mathbf{cV}_j + \mathbf{cU}_j)(\mathbf{a}_{y_j} \otimes \mathbf{I}_{k+1}) + \mathbf{cW}_j (\mathbf{K}_{y_j} \otimes \mathbf{I}_{k+1}) \right]_1,\ [\mathbf{ck}^\top]_T
\end{pmatrix}.
$$

The only difference between $\mathsf{G}_{2,\ell-1,\kappa-1}$ and $\mathsf{G}_{2,\ell-1,\kappa}$ is the item $\boxed{[\beta_{\ell,\kappa}]_2}$ in $\sigma_{\ell,\kappa}$.
Since $\mathbf{B}_\ell = \mathbf{BD}_\ell$, we argue that for all $i \in [L]$, there exist $\overline{\mathbf{d}}_\ell^\perp$ such that $\overline{\mathbf{d}}_\ell^\perp \mathbf{B}_i = \mathbf{0}$ and $\overline{\mathbf{d}}_\ell^\perp \overline{\mathbf{d}}_{\ell,\kappa} = 1$, where $\overline{\mathbf{d}}_{\ell,\kappa} \leftarrow \mathbb{Z}_p^{1 \times (k+1)}$. We prove $\mathsf{G}_{2,\ell-1,\kappa-1} \approx_c \mathsf{G}_{2,\ell-1,\kappa}$ by the following argument ($\beta \in \{0,1\}$):

$$
\begin{cases}
\mathbf{A}, \mathbf{B}_\ell, \mathbf{c}^\perp;\quad \mathbf{AQ}_\ell, \mathbf{AT}_\ell, \mathbf{Q}_\ell \mathbf{B}, \mathbf{T}_\ell \mathbf{B}; & //\text{crs; pk}_\ell; \\
\mathbf{c}, \mathbf{cQ}_\ell + m^* \cdot \mathbf{cT}_\ell; & //\nu^* \\
\mathbf{B}_\ell \mathbf{t}^\top, \mathbf{Q}_\ell \mathbf{B}_\ell \mathbf{t}^\top + m_{\ell,\kappa} \cdot \mathbf{T}_\ell \mathbf{B}_\ell \mathbf{t}^\top + b\mathbf{c}^\perp \beta; & //\sigma_{\ell,\kappa}
\end{cases}
$$

$$
\approx_c
\begin{cases}
\mathbf{A}, \mathbf{B}_\ell, \mathbf{c}^\perp;\quad \mathbf{AQ}_\ell, \mathbf{AT}_\ell, \mathbf{Q}_\ell \mathbf{B}, \mathbf{T}_\ell \mathbf{B} \\
\mathbf{c}, \mathbf{cQ}_\ell + m^* \cdot \mathbf{cT}_\ell; \\
\boxed{\overline{\mathbf{d}}_{\ell,\kappa}^\top}, \mathbf{Q}_\ell \boxed{\overline{\mathbf{d}}_{\ell,\kappa}^\top} + m_{\ell,\kappa} \cdot \mathbf{T}_\ell \boxed{\overline{\mathbf{d}}_{\ell,\kappa}^\top} + b\mathbf{c}^\perp \beta;
\end{cases}
$$

$$
\approx_s
\begin{cases}
\mathbf{A}, \mathbf{B}_\ell, \mathbf{c}^\perp;\quad \mathbf{AQ}_\ell, \mathbf{AT}_\ell, \mathbf{Q}_\ell \mathbf{B}, \mathbf{T}_\ell \mathbf{B} \\
\mathbf{c}, \mathbf{cQ}_\ell + m^* \cdot \mathbf{cT}_\ell + \boxed{(q_{\ell,\kappa} + m^* \cdot t_{\ell,\kappa})\overline{\mathbf{d}}_\ell^\perp}; \\
\mathbf{d}_{\ell,\kappa}^\top, \mathbf{Q}_\ell \overline{\mathbf{d}}_{\ell,\kappa}^\top + m_{\ell,\kappa} \cdot \mathbf{T}_\ell \overline{\mathbf{d}}_{\ell,\kappa}^\top + b\mathbf{c}^\perp \beta + \boxed{(q_{\ell,\kappa} + m_{\ell,\kappa} \cdot t_{\ell,\kappa})\mathbf{c}^\perp};
\end{cases}
$$

$$
\approx_s
\begin{cases}
\mathbf{A}, \mathbf{B}_\ell, \mathbf{c}^\perp;\quad \mathbf{AQ}_\ell, \mathbf{AT}_\ell, \mathbf{Q}_\ell \mathbf{B}, \mathbf{T}_\ell \mathbf{B} \\
\mathbf{c}, \mathbf{cQ}_\ell + m^* \cdot \mathbf{cT}_\ell + (q_{\ell,\kappa} + m^* \cdot t_{\ell,\kappa})\mathbf{d}_\ell^\perp; \\
\overline{\mathbf{d}}_{\ell,\kappa}^\top, \mathbf{Q}_\ell \overline{\mathbf{d}}_{\ell,\kappa}^\top + m_{\ell,\kappa} \cdot \mathbf{T}_\ell \overline{\mathbf{d}}_{\ell,\kappa}^\top + \cancel{b\mathbf{c}^\perp \beta} + (q_{\ell,\kappa} + m_{\ell,\kappa} \cdot t_{\ell,\kappa})\mathbf{c}^\perp;
\end{cases}
$$

We justify each step as follows:

- The first $\approx_c$ follows from the MDDH assumption:

$$
([\mathbf{B}_\ell]_2, [\mathbf{B}_\ell \mathbf{t}^\top]_2) \approx_c ([\mathbf{B}_\ell]_2, [\overline{\mathbf{d}}_{\ell,\kappa}^\top]_2)
$$

where $\mathbf{B}_\ell \leftarrow \mathbb{Z}_p^{(k+1)\times k}$, $\mathbf{t} \leftarrow \mathbb{Z}_p^{1\times k}$ and $\overline{\mathbf{d}}_{\ell,\kappa} \leftarrow \mathbb{Z}_p^{1\times(k+1)}$.
- The second $\approx_s$ follows tha fact that:

$$\mathbf{Q}_\ell \mapsto \mathbf{Q}_\ell + \mathbf{c}^\perp q_{\ell,\kappa} \overline{\mathbf{d}}_{\ell,\kappa}^\perp \quad \text{and} \quad \mathbf{T}_\ell \mapsto \mathbf{T}_\ell + \mathbf{c}^\perp t_{\ell,\kappa} \overline{\mathbf{d}}_{\ell,\kappa}^\perp$$

where $\mathbf{c}^\perp \in \mathbb{Z}_p^{k+1}$ and $\overline{\mathbf{d}}_{\ell,\kappa}^\perp \in \mathbb{Z}_p^{1\times(k+1)}$ such that $\mathbf{A}\mathbf{c}^\perp = 0$, $\mathbf{c}\mathbf{c}^\perp = 1$, $\overline{\mathbf{d}}_{\ell,\kappa}^\perp \mathbf{B} = 0$, $\overline{\mathbf{d}}_{\ell,\kappa}^\perp \mathbf{d}_\ell = 1$.
- The last $\approx_s$ is straight-forward with the observation that item $(q_{\ell,\kappa} + m_{\ell,\kappa} \cdot t_{\ell,\kappa})\mathbf{c}^\perp$ hides the item $b\mathbf{c}^\perp \beta$.

This readily proves the lemma. $\qquad\qquad\qquad\qquad\qquad\qquad\qquad\qquad\qquad\square$

Lemma 3 ($\mathsf{G}_{2,\ell-1,Q_\ell} \approx_c \mathsf{G}_{2,\ell-1,Q_\ell+1}$). *For any adversary $\mathcal{A}$, there exists algorithm $\mathcal{B}_3$ with close running time to $\mathcal{A}$ such that*

$$|\mathsf{Adv}_{\mathcal{A}}^{2,\ell-1,Q_\ell}(\lambda) - \mathsf{Adv}_{\mathcal{A}}^{2,\ell-1,Q_\ell+1}(\lambda)| \leq \mathsf{Adv}_{\mathcal{B}_3}^{\mathrm{MDDH}}(\lambda) + \mathsf{negl}(\lambda).$$

Proof. This follows from the $(k, k+1, 1)$-MDDH assumption:

$$[\mathbf{B}]_2, [\mathbf{B}\mathbf{r}_\ell^\top]_2 \approx_c [\mathbf{B}]_2, [\mathbf{d}_\ell^\top]_2$$

where $\mathbf{B} \leftarrow \mathbb{Z}_p^{(k+1)\times k}$, $\mathbf{r}_\ell \leftarrow \mathbb{Z}_p^{1\times k}$ and $\mathbf{d}_\ell \leftarrow \mathbb{Z}_p^{1\times(k+1)}$. On input $[\mathbf{B}]_2, [\hat{\mathbf{t}}]_2$ where $\hat{\mathbf{t}}^\top = \mathbf{B}\mathbf{r}_\ell^\top$ or $\hat{\mathbf{t}}^\top = \mathbf{d}_\ell^\top$, the algorithm $\mathcal{B}_3$ works as follow:

Setup. Sample

$$\mathbf{A} \leftarrow \mathbb{Z}_p^{k\times(k+1)}, \quad \mathbf{k} \leftarrow \mathbb{Z}_p^{1\times(k+1)}, \quad \mathbf{c} \leftarrow \mathbb{Z}_p^{1\times(k+1)}, \quad \alpha \leftarrow \mathbb{Z}_p$$
$$\{\mathbf{D}_i \leftarrow \mathbb{Z}_p^{k\times k}, \quad \mathbf{V}_i \leftarrow \mathbb{Z}_p^{(k+1)\times(k+1)}, \quad \mathbf{W}_i \leftarrow \mathbb{Z}_p^{(k+1)\times(k+1)n}, \quad \mathbf{r}_i \leftarrow \mathbb{Z}_p^{1\times k}\}_{i\in[L]}$$

Set $[\mathbf{B}_i]_2 = [\mathbf{B}\mathbf{D}_i]_2$ for each $i \in [L]$ and output

$$\mathsf{crs} = \begin{pmatrix} [\mathbf{A}\mathbf{k}^\top]_T, \mathsf{H}, [\mathbf{A}]_1, \{[\mathbf{A}\mathbf{V}_i, \mathbf{A}\mathbf{W}_i]_1, [\mathbf{B}_i]_2\}_{i\in[L]}, \\ \{[\mathbf{V}_i\mathbf{B}\mathbf{r}_j^\top, \mathbf{W}_i(\mathbf{I}_n \otimes \mathbf{B}\mathbf{r}_j^\top)]_2\}_{j\in[L],i\in[L]\setminus\{j\}}, \\ \{[\mathbf{B}\mathbf{r}_i^\top, \mathbf{V}_i\mathbf{B}\mathbf{r}_i^\top + \mathbf{k}^\top + \alpha\mathbf{c}^\perp]_2\}_{i<\ell}, [\hat{\mathbf{t}}_\ell, \mathbf{V}_\ell\hat{\mathbf{t}}_\ell + \mathbf{k}^\top]_2, \\ \{[\mathbf{B}\mathbf{r}_i^\top, \mathbf{V}_i\mathbf{B}\mathbf{r}_i^\top + \mathbf{k}^\top]_2\}_{i>\ell} \end{pmatrix},$$

Query. Here, we deal with the query from $\mathcal{A}$.
- For all $i \in [L]$ and each $(\mathsf{pk}_i, \mathsf{sk}_i) \in \mathcal{D}_i$ is generated honestly as:
  - if $i \neq \ell$, the pk_i is that

$$([\mathbf{A}\mathbf{U}_i, \mathbf{A}\mathbf{Q}_i, \mathbf{A}\mathbf{T}_i]_1, \{[\mathbf{U}_i\mathbf{B}\mathbf{r}_j^\top, \mathbf{Q}_i\mathbf{B}_j, \mathbf{T}_i\mathbf{B}_j]_2\}_{j\in[L]\setminus\{i,\ell\}}, [\mathbf{U}_i\hat{\mathbf{t}}^\top]_2);$$

  - if $i = \ell$, the pk_ℓ is that

$$([\mathbf{A}\mathbf{U}_\ell, \mathbf{A}\mathbf{Q}_\ell, \mathbf{A}\mathbf{T}_\ell]_1, \{[\mathbf{U}_\ell\mathbf{B}\mathbf{r}_j^\top, \mathbf{Q}_\ell\mathbf{B}_j, \mathbf{T}_\ell\mathbf{B}_j]_2\}_{j\in[L]\setminus\{\ell\}});$$

where $\mathbf{U}_i, \mathbf{Q}_i, \mathbf{T}_i \leftarrow \mathbb{Z}_p^{(k+1)\times(k+1)}$.

- For $\mathsf{OSig}(\ell, x, \mathsf{m})$, sample $\mathbf{t} \leftarrow \mathbb{Z}_p^{1 \times k}$ and compute $\mathbf{C}_x$, output $\sigma_{\ell, x, \mathsf{m}}$ as

$$
\left(
\begin{array}{c}
[\mathbf{B}_\ell \mathbf{t}^\top]_2, [\hat{\mathbf{t}}^\top]_2, [\mathbf{V}_\ell \hat{\mathbf{t}}^\top + \mathbf{k}^\top + \mathbf{U}_\ell \hat{\mathbf{t}}^\top + (\mathbf{Q}_\ell \mathbf{B}_\ell \mathbf{t}^\top + \mathsf{m} \cdot \mathbf{T}_\ell \mathbf{B}_\ell \mathbf{t}^\top)]_2, \\[2mm]
\left[\displaystyle\sum_{j \in [L] \setminus \{\ell\}} (\mathbf{V}_j \hat{\mathbf{t}}^\top + \mathbf{U}_j \hat{\mathbf{t}}^\top) \mathbf{a}_{y_j} + \mathbf{W}_j (\mathbf{I}_n \otimes \hat{\mathbf{t}}^\top) \mathbf{K}_{y_j} \right]_2, \\[2mm]
\left[\displaystyle\sum_{j \in [L] \setminus \{\ell\}} \mathbf{W}_j (\mathbf{I}_n \otimes \hat{\mathbf{t}}^\top) \mathbf{C}_x \right]_2, \left[\displaystyle\sum_{j \in [L] \setminus \{\ell\}} (\mathbf{Q}_j \mathbf{B}_\ell \mathbf{t}^\top + \mathsf{m} \cdot \mathbf{T}_j \mathbf{B}_\ell \mathbf{t}^\top) \right]
\end{array}
\right).
$$

where $\mathsf{m} \leftarrow \mathsf{H}(i, \mathsf{m}, x)$.

Challenge. On input challenge (i^*, x^*, m^*), output $\nu_{i^*, x^*, \mathsf{m}^*}$ as

$$
\left(
\begin{array}{c}
[\mathbf{c}]_1, \left[\displaystyle\sum_{j \in [L]} (\mathbf{c}\mathbf{Q}_j + \mathsf{m} \cdot \mathbf{c}\mathbf{T}_j) \right]_1, \left[\displaystyle\sum_{j \in [L]} \mathbf{c}\mathbf{W}_j (\mathbf{C}_x \otimes \mathbf{I}_{k+1}) \right]_1 \\[2mm]
\left[\displaystyle\sum_{j \in [L]} (\mathbf{c}\mathbf{V}_j + \mathbf{c}\mathbf{U}_j)(\mathbf{a}_{y_j} \otimes \mathbf{I}_{k+1}) + \mathbf{c}\mathbf{W}_j (\mathbf{K}_{y_j} \otimes \mathbf{I}_{k+1}) \right]_1, [\mathbf{c}\mathbf{k}^\top]_T
\end{array}
\right).
$$

Observe that when $\hat{\mathbf{t}}^\top = \mathbf{B}\mathbf{r}_\ell^\top$, the simulation is identical to $\mathsf{G}_{2,\ell-1,Q_\ell}$; when $\hat{\mathbf{t}}^\top = \mathbf{d}_\ell^\top$, the simulation is identical to $\mathsf{G}_{2,\ell-1,Q_\ell+1}$. $\square$

Lemma 4 ($\mathsf{G}_{2,L} \approx_s \mathsf{G}_3$). *For any adversary $\mathcal{A}$, we have*

$$
|\mathsf{Adv}_{\mathcal{A}}^{2,L}(\lambda) - \mathsf{Adv}_{\mathcal{A}}^3(\lambda)| = 0
$$

Proof. First, in the process of simulating crs, we program $\mathbf{k}^\top$ in both $\mathsf{G}_{2,L}$ and G_3 as follow:

$$
\mathbf{k}^\top \mapsto \mathbf{k}^\top - \mathbf{c}^\perp \alpha
$$

where $\mathbf{k} \leftarrow \mathbb{Z}_p^{1 \times (k+1)}$, $\alpha \leftarrow \mathbb{Z}_p$. Under the fact that $\mathbf{A}\mathbf{c}^\perp = \mathbf{0}$, crs works as follow:

$$
\mathsf{crs} = \left(
\begin{array}{c}
[\mathbf{A}]_1, \{[\mathbf{A}\mathbf{V}_i, \mathbf{A}\mathbf{W}_i]_1, [\mathbf{B}\mathbf{r}_i^\top, \mathbf{V}_i \mathbf{B}\mathbf{r}_i^\top + \mathbf{k}^\top, \mathbf{B}_i]_2\}_{i \in [L]}, \\[2mm]
\{[\mathbf{V}_i \mathbf{B}\mathbf{r}_j^\top, \mathbf{W}_i (\mathbf{I}_n \otimes \mathbf{B}\mathbf{r}_j^\top)]_2\}_{j \in [L], i \in [L] \setminus \{j\}}, [\mathbf{A}\mathbf{k}^\top]_T, \mathsf{H}
\end{array}
\right).
$$

Then, α in the challenge verification text is that $[\mathbf{c}\mathbf{k}^\top - \alpha]_T$, where this follows from the fact that $\mathbf{c}\mathbf{c}^\perp = 1$. Furthermore, α only correlate to $[\mathbf{c}\mathbf{k}^\top - \alpha]_T$ in the challenge verification text. $[\alpha]_T$ is uniformly distributed over $\mathbb{G}_T$ which implies that the distribution of $[\mathbf{c}\mathbf{k}^\top - \alpha]_T$ is identical to a random coin in $\mathbb{G}_T$, just like in G_3. This readily proves the lemma. $\square$

5   Concrete Slotted Registered ABS

In this section, we will present a concrete slotted registered ABS for ABP, which derives from the generic scheme in Sect. 4. Note that other classes of predicate (e.g., inner-product, monotone span programs, and so on) can also be achieved in our slotted registered ABS, which will not be presented here due to the page limitation.

Preliminaries. An arithmetic span program [16], denoted by V, is defined by $(\mathbf{Y}, \mathbf{Z}) \in \mathbb{Z}_p^{m \times \ell} \times \mathbb{Z}_p^{m \times \ell}$ where

$$V(\mathbf{x}) = 1 \iff \mathbf{x} \in \mathbb{Z}_p^{1 \times m} \text{ satisfies } V \iff \mathbf{e}_1 \in \text{span}\langle \text{diag}(\mathbf{x}) \cdot \mathbf{Y} + \mathbf{Z} \rangle.$$

Here we use notation: $\text{diag}(\mathbf{x}) := \begin{pmatrix} x_1 & & \\ & \ddots & \\ & & x_m \end{pmatrix} \in \mathbb{Z}_p^{m \times m}$ for $\mathbf{x} = (x_1, \ldots, x_m)$

and note that $\text{diag}(\mathbf{x}) = \text{diag}(\mathbf{x})^\top$. And $\mathbf{e}_1 \in \text{span}\langle \text{diag}(\mathbf{x}) \cdot \mathbf{Y} + \mathbf{Z} \rangle$ means that there exists some $\boldsymbol{\omega} \in \mathbb{Z}_p^{1 \times m}$ such that $\mathbf{e}_1 = \boldsymbol{\omega}(\text{diag}(\mathbf{x}) \cdot \mathbf{Y} + \mathbf{Z})$

Recall the predicate encoding for ASP predicate (ciphertext-policy variant) in [6]: let $n = 2m + \ell$, $n_c = 2m$ and $n_k = m + 1$, define

$$\mathbf{C}_{\mathbf{Y},\mathbf{Z}} = \begin{pmatrix} \mathbf{I}_m & \mathbf{0}_{m \times m} \\ \mathbf{0}_{m \times m} & \mathbf{I}_m \\ \mathbf{Y}^\top & \mathbf{Z}^\top \end{pmatrix}, \quad \mathbf{K}_{\mathbf{x}} = \begin{pmatrix} \mathbf{0}_m^\top & \text{diag}(\mathbf{x}) \\ \mathbf{0}_m^\top & \mathbf{I}_m \\ \mathbf{e}_1^\top & \mathbf{0}_{\ell \times m} \end{pmatrix}, \quad \mathbf{a}_{\mathbf{x}} = (1 \| \mathbf{0}_m),$$

$$\mathbf{d}_{\mathbf{x},\mathbf{Y},\mathbf{Z}} = (1 \| \boldsymbol{\omega} \| - \boldsymbol{\omega} \cdot \text{diag}(\mathbf{x}) \| - \boldsymbol{\omega})$$

(3)

where $\mathbf{0}_m$ is a *row* zero vector of size m. Note that we work with *read-once* ASP as in [6].

Scheme. Our concrete slotted registered ABS for read-once ASP from SXDH assumption works as follows:

- Setup($1^\lambda, P, 1^L$): Run $\mathbb{G} := (p, \mathbb{G}_1, \mathbb{G}_2, \mathbb{G}_T, e) \leftarrow \mathcal{G}(1^\lambda)$ and select a collision-resistant hash function $\mathsf{H} : \{0,1\}^* \to \mathbb{Z}_p$. Sample

$$\mathbf{a} \leftarrow \mathbb{Z}_p^{1 \times 2}, \ \mathbf{b}^\top \leftarrow \mathbb{Z}_p^2, \ \mathbf{k} \leftarrow \mathbb{Z}_p^{1 \times 2}.$$

For all $i \in [L]$, sample

$$d_i, r_i \leftarrow \mathbb{Z}_p, \ \mathbf{V}_i \leftarrow \mathbb{Z}_p^{2 \times 2}, \ \mathbf{W}_i \leftarrow \mathbb{Z}_p^{2 \times 2(2m+\ell)}.$$

For all $i \in [L]$, write $\mathbf{b}_i^\top = d_i \mathbf{b}^\top$ and output

$$\mathsf{crs} = \begin{pmatrix} [\mathbf{a}]_1, \left\{ [\mathbf{a}\mathbf{V}_i, \mathbf{a}\mathbf{W}_i]_1, [\mathbf{b}^\top r_i, \mathbf{V}_i \mathbf{b}^\top r_i + \mathbf{k}^\top, \mathbf{b}_i^\top]_2 \right\}_{i \in [L]}, \\ \left\{ [\mathbf{V}_i \mathbf{b}^\top r_j, \mathbf{W}_i(\mathbf{I}_{2m+\ell} \otimes \mathbf{b}^\top r_j)]_2 \right\}_{j \in [L], i \in [L] \setminus \{j\}}, [\mathbf{a}\mathbf{k}^\top]_T, \mathsf{H} \end{pmatrix}$$

- Gen(crs, i): Sample $\mathbf{U}_i, \mathbf{Q}_i, \mathbf{T}_i \leftarrow \mathbb{Z}_p^{2 \times 2}$. Fetch $\{\mathbf{b}_i^\top\}_{i \in [L]}$ and $\{[\mathbf{b}^\top r_j]_2\}_{j \in [L] \setminus \{i\}}$ from crs and output

$$\mathsf{pk}_i = ([\mathbf{a}\mathbf{U}_i, \mathbf{a}\mathbf{Q}_i, \mathbf{a}\mathbf{T}_i]_1, \{[\mathbf{U}_i \mathbf{b}^\top r_j, \mathbf{Q}_i \mathbf{b}_j^\top, \mathbf{T}_i \mathbf{b}_j^\top]_2\}_{j \in [L] \setminus \{i\}})$$

and $\mathsf{sk}_i = (\mathbf{U}_i, \mathbf{Q}_i, \mathbf{T}_i)$.

- IsValid(crs, i, pk$_i$): Fetch $\{[\mathbf{b}^\top r_j, \mathbf{b}_j^\top]_2\}_{j\in[L]\setminus\{i\}}$ from crs and parse pk$_i$ = $([\mathbf{aU}_i, \mathbf{aQ}_i, \mathbf{aT}_i]_1, \{[\mathbf{U}_i\mathbf{b}^\top r_j, \mathbf{Q}_i\mathbf{b}_j^\top, \mathbf{T}_i\mathbf{b}_j^\top]_2\}_{j\in[L]\setminus\{i\}})$. For each $j \in [L] \setminus \{i\}$, check

$$e([\mathbf{a}]_1, [\mathbf{U}_i\mathbf{b}^\top r_j]_2) \overset{?}{=} e([\mathbf{aU}_i]_1, [\mathbf{b}^\top r_j]_2),$$

$$e([\mathbf{a}]_1, [\mathbf{Q}_i\mathbf{b}_j^\top]_2) \overset{?}{=} e([\mathbf{aQ}_i]_1, [\mathbf{b}_j^\top]_2),$$

$$e([\mathbf{a}]_1, [\mathbf{T}_i\mathbf{b}_j^\top]_2) \overset{?}{=} e([\mathbf{aT}_i]_1, [\mathbf{b}_j^\top]_2).$$

If all these checks pass, output 1; otherwise, output 0.
- Agg(crs, $(\mathsf{pk}_i, \mathbf{x}_i)_{i\in[L]}$): For all $i \in [L]$, compute $\mathbf{K}_{x_i}$ as in equality (3) and output:

$$\mathsf{mpk} = \left(\begin{array}{c} [\mathbf{a}]_1, [\mathbf{ak}^\top]_T, \mathsf{H}, \left[\sum_{j\in[L]} \mathbf{aQ}_j\right]_1, \left[\sum_{j\in[L]} \mathbf{aT}_j\right]_1, \left[\sum_{j\in[L]} \mathbf{aW}_j\right]_1, \\ \left[\sum_{j\in[L]}(\mathbf{aV}_j + \mathbf{aU}_j)((1\|\mathbf{0}_m) \otimes \mathbf{I}_2) + \mathbf{aW}_j\left(\mathbf{K}_{\mathbf{x}_j} \otimes \mathbf{I}_2\right)\right]_1 \end{array} \right)$$

and for all $i \in [L]$, compute hk$_i$ as

$$\left(\begin{array}{c} \mathsf{H}, [\mathbf{b}_i^\top]_2, [\mathbf{b}^\top r_i]_2, [\mathbf{V}_i\mathbf{b}^\top r_i + \mathbf{k}^\top]_2, \left[\sum_{j\in[L]\setminus\{i\}} \mathbf{Q}_j\mathbf{b}_i^\top\right]_2, \\ \left[\sum_{j\in[L]\setminus\{i\}} \mathbf{T}_j\mathbf{b}_i^\top\right]_2, \left[\sum_{j\in[L]\setminus\{i\}} \mathbf{W}_j(\mathbf{I}_{2m+\ell} \otimes \mathbf{b}^\top r_i)\right]_2, \\ \left[\sum_{j\in[L]\setminus\{i\}}(\mathbf{V}_j\mathbf{b}^\top r_i + \mathbf{U}_j\mathbf{b}^\top r_i)(1\|\mathbf{0}_m) + \mathbf{W}_j(\mathbf{I}_{2m+\ell} \otimes \mathbf{b}^\top r_i)\mathbf{K}_{\mathbf{x}_j}\right]_2 \end{array} \right).$$

- Sig(hk$_i$, sk$_i$, $(\mathbf{Y}, \mathbf{Z})$, m): Sample $t \leftarrow \mathbb{Z}_p$, run $h \leftarrow \mathsf{H}(i, \mathsf{m}, (\mathbf{Y}, \mathbf{Z}))$ and compute $\mathbf{C}_{\mathbf{Y},\mathbf{Z}}$ as in equality (3). Parse sk$_i$ = $(\mathbf{U}_i, \mathbf{Q}_i, \mathbf{T}_i)$, then compute $[\mathbf{k}_0^\top]_2 = [\mathbf{b}_i^\top t]_2$, $[\mathbf{k}_1^\top]_2 = [\mathbf{b}^\top r_i]_2$ and

$$[\mathbf{k}_2^\top]_2 = [\mathbf{V}_i\mathbf{b}^\top r_i + \mathbf{k}^\top + \mathbf{U}_i\mathbf{b}^\top r_i + (\mathbf{Q}_i\mathbf{b}_i^\top t + h \cdot \mathbf{T}_i\mathbf{b}_i^\top t)]_2,$$

$$[\mathbf{K}_3]_2 = \left[\sum_{j\in[L]\setminus\{i\}} (\mathbf{V}_j\mathbf{b}^\top r_i + \mathbf{U}_j\mathbf{b}^\top r_i)(1\|\mathbf{0}_m) + \mathbf{W}_j(\mathbf{I}_{2m+\ell} \otimes \mathbf{b}^\top r_i)\mathbf{K}_{\mathbf{x}_j}\right]_2,$$

$$[\mathbf{K}_4]_2 = \left[\sum_{j\in[L]\setminus\{i\}} \mathbf{W}_j(\mathbf{I}_{2m+\ell} \otimes \mathbf{b}^\top r_i)\mathbf{C}_{\mathbf{Y},\mathbf{Z}}\right]_2,$$

$$[\mathbf{k}_5^\top]_2 = \left[\sum_{j\in[L]\setminus\{i\}} (\mathbf{Q}_j\mathbf{b}_i^\top t + h \cdot \mathbf{T}_j\mathbf{b}_i^\top t)\right].$$

Output $\sigma_{i,(\mathbf{Y},\mathbf{Z}),\mathsf{m}} = ([\mathbf{k}_0^\top]_2, [\mathbf{k}_1^\top]_2, [\mathbf{k}_2^\top]_2, [\mathbf{K}_3]_2, [\mathbf{K}_4]_2, [\mathbf{k}_5^\top]_2)$.

- Ver($\mathsf{mpk}, \sigma_{i^*,(\mathbf{Y},\mathbf{Z}),\mathsf{m}}, (\mathbf{Y},\mathbf{Z}), \mathsf{m}$): Sample $s \leftarrow \mathbb{Z}_p$ and run $h^* \leftarrow \mathsf{H}(i^*, \mathsf{m}^*, (\mathbf{Y},\mathbf{Z}))$. Compute

$$[\mathbf{v}_0]_1 = [sa]_1, [\mathbf{v}_1]_1 = \left[\sum_{j\in[L]} (sa\mathbf{Q}_j + h^* \cdot sa\mathbf{T}_j) \right]_1,$$

$$[\mathbf{v}_2]_1 = \left[\sum_{j\in[L]} sa\mathbf{W}_j \left(\mathbf{C}_{\mathbf{Y},\mathbf{z}} \otimes \mathbf{I}_2 \right) \right]_1$$

$$[\mathbf{v}_3]_1 = \left[\sum_{j\in[L]} (sa\mathbf{V}_j + sa\mathbf{U}_j)((1\|\mathbf{0}_m) \otimes \mathbf{I}_2) + sa\mathbf{W}_j(\mathbf{K}_{\mathbf{x}_j} \otimes \mathbf{I}_2) \right]_1,$$

and $[v_4]_T = [\mathbf{sAk}^\top]_T$. Parse $\sigma_{i^*,(\mathbf{Y},\mathbf{Z}),\mathsf{m}} = ([\mathbf{k}_0^\top]_2, [\mathbf{k}_1^\top]_2, [\mathbf{k}_2^\top]_2, [\mathbf{K}_3]_2, [\mathbf{K}_4]_2, [\mathbf{k}_5^\top]_2)$ and compute $\boldsymbol{\omega}$ such that $\mathbf{e}_1 = \boldsymbol{\omega}(\mathsf{diag}(\mathbf{x}_{i^*}) \cdot \mathbf{Y} + \mathbf{Z})$. Then recover

$$[\mathbf{z}]_T = e([\mathbf{v}_3\|\mathbf{v}_2]_1, [\mathbf{I}_{3m+1} \otimes \mathbf{k}_1^\top]_2), \quad [z_2]_T = e([\mathbf{v}_0]_1, [\mathbf{K}_3\|\mathbf{K}_4]_2)$$
$$[z_3]_T = e([\mathbf{v}_0]_1, [\mathbf{k}_2^\top]_2), \quad [z_4]_T = e([\mathbf{v}_1]_1, [\mathbf{k}_0^\top]_2), \quad [z_5]_T = e([\mathbf{v}_0]_1, [\mathbf{k}_5^\top]_2),$$
$$[z_6]_T = [z_3 - z_4 + z_5]_T, \quad [z_7]_T = [(\mathbf{z}_1 - \mathbf{z}_2)(1\|\boldsymbol{\omega}\| - \boldsymbol{\omega} \cdot \mathsf{diag}(\mathbf{x})\| - \boldsymbol{\omega})^\top - z_6]_T$$

and check $[z_7]_T^{-1} \overset{?}{=} [v_4]_T$. If the above check passes, output 1; otherwise, output 0.

Acknowledgements. This work was supported in part by National Natural Science Foundation of China (61972156,62372180,62002120,62372175), NSFC-ISF Joint Scientific Research Program (61961146004), Innovation Program of Shanghai Municipal Education Commission (2021-01-07-00-08-E00101) and the "Digital Silk Road" Shanghai International Joint Lab of Trustworthy Intelligent Software (22510750100).

References

1. Abdalla, M., Catalano, D., Gay, R., Ursu, B.: Inner-product functional encryption with fine-grained access control. In: Moriai, S., Wang, H. (eds.) ASIACRYPT 2020, Part III. LNCS, vol. 12493, pp. 467–497. Springer, Cham (2020). https://doi.org/10.1007/978-3-030-64840-4_16

2. Ambrona, M., Barthe, G., Schmidt, B.: Generic transformations of predicate encodings: constructions and applications. In: Katz, J., Shacham, H. (eds.) CRYPTO 2017, Part I. LNCS, vol. 10401, pp. 36–66. Springer, Cham (2017). https://doi.org/10.1007/978-3-319-63688-7_2

3. Attrapadung, N., Hanaoka, G., Yamada, S.: Conversions among several classes of predicate encryption and applications to ABE with various compactness tradeoffs. In: Iwata, T., Cheon, J.H. (eds.) ASIACRYPT 2015, Part I. LNCS, vol. 9452, pp. 575–601. Springer, Heidelberg (2015). https://doi.org/10.1007/978-3-662-48797-6_24

4. Boneh, D., Franklin, M.: Identity-based encryption from the Weil pairing. In: Kilian, J. (ed.) CRYPTO 2001. LNCS, vol. 2139, pp. 213–229. Springer, Heidelberg (2001). https://doi.org/10.1007/3-540-44647-8_13

5. Boneh, D., Lynn, B., Shacham, H.: Short signatures from the Weil pairing. In: Boyd, C. (ed.) ASIACRYPT 2001. LNCS, vol. 2248, pp. 514–532. Springer, Heidelberg (2001). https://doi.org/10.1007/3-540-45682-1_30

6. Chen, J., Gay, R., Wee, H.: Improved dual system ABE in prime-order groups via predicate encodings. In: Oswald, E., Fischlin, M. (eds.) EUROCRYPT 2015, Part II. LNCS, vol. 9057, pp. 595–624. Springer, Heidelberg (2015). https://doi.org/10.1007/978-3-662-46803-6_20

7. Chen, J., Lim, H.W., Ling, S., Wang, H., Wee, H.: Shorter identity-based encryption via asymmetric pairings. Des. Codes Cryptogr. **73**, 911–947 (2014)

8. Datta, P., Dutta, R., Mukhopadhyay, S.: Short attribute-based signatures for arbitrary turing machines from standard assumptions. Des. Codes Cryptogr. **91**(5), 1845–1872 (2023)

9. Datta, P., Okamoto, T., Takashima, K.: Efficient attribute-based signatures for unbounded arithmetic branching programs. In: Lin, D., Sako, K. (eds.) PKC 2019, Part I. LNCS, vol. 11442, pp. 127–158. Springer, Cham (2019). https://doi.org/10.1007/978-3-030-17253-4_5

10. Diffie, W., Hellman, M.E.: New directions in cryptography. IEEE Trans. Inf. Theory **22**(6), 644–654 (1976)

11. Escala, A., Herold, G., Kiltz, E., Ràfols, C., Villar, J.: An algebraic framework for Diffie-Hellman assumptions. In: Canetti, R., Garay, J.A. (eds.) CRYPTO 2013, Part II. LNCS, vol. 8043, pp. 129–147. Springer, Heidelberg (2013). https://doi.org/10.1007/978-3-642-40084-1_8

12. Francati, D., Friolo, D., Maitra, M., Malavolta, G., Rahimi, A., Venturi, D.: Registered (inner-product) functional encryption. Cryptology ePrint Archive (2023)

13. Garg, S., Hajiabadi, M., Mahmoody, M., Rahimi, A.: Registration-based encryption: removing private-key generator from IBE. In: Beimel, A., Dziembowski, S. (eds.) TCC 2018, Part I. LNCS, vol. 11239, pp. 689–718. Springer, Cham (2018). https://doi.org/10.1007/978-3-030-03807-6_25

14. Herranz, J., Laguillaumie, F., Libert, B., Ràfols, C.: Short attribute-based signatures for threshold predicates. In: Dunkelman, O. (ed.) CT-RSA 2012. LNCS, vol. 7178, pp. 51–67. Springer, Heidelberg (2012). https://doi.org/10.1007/978-3-642-27954-6_4

15. Hohenberger, S., George, L., Waters, B., David, J.W.: Registered attribute-based encryption. In: Hazay, C., Stam, M. (eds.) EUROCRYPT 2023, Part III. LNCS, vol. 14006, pp. 511–542. Springer, Heidelberg (2023). https://doi.org/10.1007/978-3-031-30620-4_17

16. Ishai, Y., Wee, H.: Partial garbling schemes and their applications. In: Esparza, J., Fraigniaud, P., Husfeldt, T., Koutsoupias, E. (eds.) ICALP 2014. LNCS, vol. 8572, pp. 650–662. Springer, Heidelberg (2014). https://doi.org/10.1007/978-3-662-43948-7_54

17. Maji, H.K., Prabhakaran, M., Rosulek, M.: Attribute-based signatures: achieving attribute-privacy and collusion-resistance. IACR Cryptology ePrint Archive, p. 328 (2008)

18. Okamoto, T., Takashima, K.: Efficient attribute-based signatures for non-monotone predicates in the standard model. In: Catalano, D., Fazio, N., Gennaro, R., Nicolosi, A. (eds.) PKC 2011. LNCS, vol. 6571, pp. 35–52. Springer, Heidelberg (2011). https://doi.org/10.1007/978-3-642-19379-8_3

19. Okamoto, T., Takashima, K.: Decentralized attribute-based signatures. In: Kurosawa, K., Hanaoka, G. (eds.) PKC 2013. LNCS, vol. 7778, pp. 125–142. Springer, Heidelberg (2013). https://doi.org/10.1007/978-3-642-36362-7_9

20. Sakai, Y., Attrapadung, N., Hanaoka, G.: Attribute-based signatures for circuits from bilinear map. In: Cheng, C.-M., Chung, K.-M., Persiano, G., Yang, B.-Y. (eds.) PKC 2016, Part I. LNCS, vol. 9614, pp. 283–300. Springer, Heidelberg (2016). https://doi.org/10.1007/978-3-662-49384-7_11

21. Sakai, Y., Katsumata, S., Attrapadung, N., Hanaoka, G.: Attribute-based signatures for unbounded languages from standard assumptions. In: Peyrin, T., Galbraith, S. (eds.) ASIACRYPT 2018, Part II. LNCS, vol. 11273, pp. 493–522. Springer, Cham (2018). https://doi.org/10.1007/978-3-030-03329-3_17

22. Wee, H.: Dual system encryption via predicate encodings. In: Lindell, Y. (ed.) TCC 2014. LNCS, vol. 8349, pp. 616–637. Springer, Heidelberg (2014). https://doi.org/10.1007/978-3-642-54242-8_26

23. Zhu, Z., Zhang, K., Gong, J., Qian, H.: Registered ABE via predicate encodings. In: Guo, J., Steinfeld, R. (eds.) ASIACRYPT 2023. LNCS, vol. 14442, pp. 66–97. Springer, Singapore (2023). https://doi.org/10.1007/978-981-99-8733-7_3

Threshold Structure-Preserving Signatures: Strong and Adaptive Security Under Standard Assumptions

Aikaterini Mitrokotsa[1], Sayantan Mukherjee[2]($\boxtimes$), Mahdi Sedaghat[3], Daniel Slamanig[4], and Jenit Tomy[1]

[1] University of St. Gallen, St. Gallen, Switzerland
{aikaterini.mitrokotsa,jenit.tomy}@unisg.ch
[2] Indian Institute of Technology, Jammu, India
csayantan.mukherjee@gmail.com
[3] COSIC, KU Leuven, Leuven, Belgium
ssedagha@esat.kuleuven.be
[4] Research Institute CODE, Universität der Bundeswehr München, München, Germany
daniel.slamanig@unibw.de

Abstract. Structure-preserving signatures (SPS) have emerged as an important cryptographic building block, as their compatibility with the Groth-Sahai (GS) NIZK framework allows to construct protocols under standard assumptions with reasonable efficiency.

Over the last years there has been a significant interest in the design of threshold signature schemes. However, only very recently Crites et al. (ASIACRYPT 2023) have introduced threshold SPS (TSPS) along with a fully non-interactive construction. While this is an important step, their work comes with several limitations. With respect to the construction, they require the use of random oracles, interactive complexity assumptions and are restricted to so called indexed Diffie-Hellman message spaces. Latter limits the use of their construction as a drop-in replacement for SPS. When it comes to security, they only support static corruptions and do not allow partial signature queries for the forgery.

In this paper, we ask whether it is possible to construct TSPS without such restrictions. We start from an SPS from Kiltz, Pan and Wee (CRYPTO 2015) which has an interesting structure, but thresholdizing it requires some modifications. Interestingly, we can prove it secure in the strongest model (TS-UF-1) for fully non-interactive threshold signatures (Bellare et al., CRYPTO 2022) and even under fully adaptive corruptions. Surprisingly, we can show the latter under a standard assumption without requiring any idealized model. All known constructions of efficient threshold signatures in the discrete logarithm setting require interactive assumptions and idealized models.

Concretely, our scheme in type III bilinear groups under the SXDH assumption has signatures consisting of 7 group elements. Compared to the TSPS from Crites et al. (2 group elements), this comes at the cost of efficiency. However, our scheme is secure under standard assumptions, achieves strong and adaptive security guarantees and supports

© International Association for Cryptologic Research 2024
Q. Tang and V. Teague (Eds.): PKC 2024, LNCS 14601, pp. 163–195, 2024.
https://doi.org/10.1007/978-3-031-57718-5_6

general message spaces, i.e., represents a drop-in replacement for many SPS applications. Given these features, the increase in the size of the signature seems acceptable even for practical applications.

1 Introduction

STRUCTURE-PRESERVING SIGNATURES. Structure-preserving signature schemes (SPS for short) introduced by Abe et al. [4] are signatures defined over bilinear groups where the messages, public keys and signatures are required to be source group elements. Moreover, signature verification just consists of group membership testing and evaluating pairing product equations (PPE). SPS are very attractive as they can be combined with efficient pairing-based non-interactive zero-knowledge (NIZK) proofs due to Groth and Sahai (GS) [46]. This allows to construct many privacy-preserving cryptographic primitives and protocols under standard assumptions with reasonable practical efficiency.

SPS have been used in the literature to construct numerous cryptographic primitives and building blocks. Among them are many variants of signatures such as blind signatures [4,40], group signatures [4,56], traceable signatures [3], policy-compliant signatures [16,17], homomorphic and network coding signatures [13,55] and protocols such as anonymous credentials [26], delegatable anonymous credentials [39], compact verifiable shuffles [30] or anonymous e-cash [21]. Due to their wide range of applications, SPS have attracted significant research interest. Looking ahead to the threshold setting (i.e., TSPS), we note that typical applications of SPS in privacy-preserving applications are as follows: a user obtains a signature from some entity and then prove possession of a valid signature without revealing it using GS NIZK. Consequently, thresholdizing the SPS signing process does not have any impact on the remaining protocol and thus, TSPS can be considered a drop-in replacement for SPS.

The first SPS scheme presented by Abe et al. in [4] was followed by a line of research to obtain SPS with short signatures in the generic group model (GGM) [5,7,44,45], lower bounds [1,5,6], security under standard assumptions [2,25,47,50,51,56] as well as tight security reductions [8–10,31,42,49].

THRESHOLD SIGNATURES. Motivated by real-world deployments in decentralized systems such as distributed ledger technologies, cryptocurrencies, and decentralized identity management, the use of threshold cryptography [37] and in particular threshold signatures has become a very active field of research in the last years with a main focus on ECDSA [11,24,28,34,36,43,62], Schnorr [33,53] and BLS [14] signatures. We recall that an (n,t) threshold signature allows a set of n potential signers to jointly compute a signature for a message m, which verifies under a single verification key, as long as at least a threshold t many signers participate.

There are different types of constructions in the literature; ones that require multiple rounds of interaction (e.g., ECDSA [28,43]), ones that require a pre-processing round that does not depend on the message (often called non-interactive schemes), e.g,. FROST [53] and finally, ones that are fully non-interactive. The latter are schemes where all the participating signers can simply send a partial signature and the final signatures can then be combined from threshold many valid partial signatures, e.g., BLS [22].

SECURITY OF THRESHOLD SIGNATURES. Although many works on threshold signatures were known in the literature, the rigorous study of security notions was done only very recently. In particular, Bellare et al. in [18] studied a hierarchy of different notions of security for non-interactive schemes. As our work focuses on fully non-interactive schemes, we do not recall the entire hierarchy but only the ones relevant for this setting. In particular, the TS-UF-0 notion is the weaker one and prohibits adversaries from querying the signing oracle for partial signatures on the challenge message, i.e., the message corresponding to the forged signature. The stronger TS-UF-1 notion, which will be our main focus, allows adversaries to query the signing oracle up to $t - |\mathsf{CS}|$ times for partial signatures, even on the challenge message. Here CS with $|\mathsf{CS}| < t$ denotes the set of (statically corrupted) signers. Surprisingly, the majority of works on threshold signatures in the literature relied on weaker TS-UF-0-style notions instead of the much more realistic TS-UF-1 notion.

Another dimension in the security of threshold signatures is whether they support static or adaptive corruptions. In the case of static corruptions, the adversary has to declare the set of corrupted signers, CS, before seeing any parameters of the system apart from (n, t). In contrast, an adaptive adversary can choose the set of corrupted signers within a security game based on its view of the execution, which is a realistic assumption in the decentralized setting. All the notions in [18] consider only a static setting and refer to a complexity leveraging argument for adaptive security. Precisely, it suggests that for small number of parties, a guessing argument can yield adaptive security for any statically secure scheme with a loss of $\binom{n}{t-1}$, i.e., guessing the set of corrupted parties and aborting if the guess is wrong. However, this exponential loss of security can become significant as the number of parties increases, e.g., supporting $n \geq 1024$ (cf. [33]). While there are known generic techniques to lift statically secure schemes to adaptively secure ones [29,48,57], they all have undesirable side-effects such as relying on additional heavy tools, e.g., non-committing encryption [27], or relying on strong assumptions such as reliable erasure of secret states (cf. [33]).

Apart from the adaptively secure threshold RSA signatures [12], until recently there were no results on adaptively secure threshold signatures based on popular signature schemes in the discrete logarithm or pairing setting. Only very recently Bacho and Loss [14] as well as Crites et al. [33] have shown tight adaptive security for threshold versions of the popular BLS [23] and Schnorr schemes [60], respectively. Interestingly, all these adaptive security proofs need to rely on interactive assumptions and in particular variants of the One-More Discrete Logarithm Assumption [19], which is known as a strong assumption.

Only very recently and concurrent to this work, Bacho et al. [15] as well as Das and Ren [35] present schemes from standard and non-interactive assumptions in the pairing-free discrete logarithm setting and pairing setting, respectively. It is interesting that only few of the existing works achieve adaptive security under the TS-UF-1 notion, e.g., [14,35,54], with [54] being the only one from standard assumptions and without requiring idealized models.

THRESHOLD SPS. Recently, Crites et al. [32] have extended the concept of threshold signatures to threshold SPS (TSPS). They introduce a definitional framework for fully non-interactive TSPS and provide a construction that is proven secure in the Random Oracle Model (ROM) [20] under the hardness of a new interactive assumption, called the GPS_3 assumption, which is analyzed in the Algebraic Group Model (AGM) [41]. The authors start from an SPS proposed by Ghadafi [44], that is secure in the Generic Group Model (GGM), and introduce a message indexing technique to avoid non-linear operations in the signature components and thus to obtain a fully non-interactive threshold version. While the TSPS proposed in [32] is highly efficient and compact (only 2 group elements), the defined message space is restricted to a so called indexed Diffie-Hellman message space. This prevents its use as a drop-in-replacement for SPS in arbitrary applications of SPS that are desired to be thresholdized. Additionally, the security of their proposed TSPS is only shown in the TS-UF-0 model, i.e., under static corruptions.

1.1 Our Contributions

In this paper, we ask if it is possible to construct TSPS without the aforementioned restrictions and we answer this question affirmatively. We start with an observation that the SPS from Kiltz, Pan and Wee [51] has an interesting structure that makes it amenable for thresholdizing although this process requires some modifications of the original scheme. While Crites et al. [32] prove security in the TS-UF-0 model, i.e., under static corruptions, we are able to prove our construction is secure in the strongest model (TS-UF-1) for non-interactive threshold signatures [18] and even under fully adaptive corruptions (which we denote as adp-TS-UF-1 security). We provide a brief overview in Table 1 about our results.

Interestingly, we can do so by relying on standard assumptions, i.e., the Matrix Diffie-Hellman (MDDH) assumption family [38,58]. While this comes at some cost in concrete efficiency, as shown in Table 2, the overhead is still not significant. For instance, when instantiated in type III bilinear groups under the SXDH assumption ($k = 1$), then signatures consist of 7 group elements. When taking the popular BLS12-381 curve giving around 110 bit of security, this amounts to signatures of size around 380 bytes. Compared to 256 bytes for an RSA signature with comparable security (2048 bit modulus), this gives an increase of around 50%. This seems perfectly tolerable for most practical applications.

As can be seen from Table 2, an important benefit of our TSPS over the one by Crites et al. [32] is that it is not limited to an indexed Diffie-Hellman

Table 1. Overview of security notions and our results. t denotes the threshold, M^* the message corresponding to the forgery, S_1 the set recording signer indices of issued partial signatures and CS the set of corrupted signers.

Security Notion	Corruption Model	Winning Condition	Our Scheme (proof)
TS-UF-0	Static corruptions	$S_1(M^*) = \emptyset$	Theorem 1
TS-UF-1	Static corruptions	$|S_1(M^*)| < t - |\mathsf{CS}|$	Theorem 2
adp-TS-UF-1	Adaptive corruptions	$|S_1(M^*)| < t - |\mathsf{CS}|$	Theorem 3

message space, but works for arbitrary group message vectors. Thus, it represents a drop-in replacement for SPS when aiming to thresholdize its applications (such as anonymous credentials, e-cash, etc.). Moreover, we prove the unforgeability of the proposed TSPS scheme against an adaptive adversary under a stronger TS-UF-1 notion of security. We recall that in contrast, the TSPS proposed by Crites et al. in [32] only achieves TS-UF-0 security against a static adversary based on an interactive assumption, called GPS_3, in the AGM and ROM.

Table 2. Comparison with the existing threshold structure-preserving signature by Crites et al. [32]. iDH refers to the indexed Diffie-Hellman message spaces. ℓ is the length of the message vector to be signed. $|\mathbb{G}_i|$ denote the bit-length of elements in groups $\mathbb{G}_i$ for $i \in \{1, 2\}$. NI stands for Non-Interactive.

Scheme	Message Space	Signature Size	Number of Pairings	Security Notion	Security Model	Underlying Assumption
[32]	iDH	$2|\mathbb{G}_1|$	$\ell + 2$	TS-UF-0 (Static)	AGM+ ROM	GPS_3 (Interactive)
Ours	$\mathbb{G}_1$	$(3k+3)|\mathbb{G}_1|$ $+|\mathbb{G}_2|$	$5k+$ $\ell + 6$	TS-UF-1 (Adaptive)	Standard Model	$\mathcal{D}_k$-MDDH (NI)

1.2 Technical Overview

Considering the insights discussed in [32, Section 1], it can be deduced that a fully non-interactive TSPS scheme does not involve any non-linear operations during the partial signing phase. The use of non-linear operations prevents the reconstruction of the final signature from the partial signatures via Lagrange interpolation. These non-linear operations include the inversion of secret share keys (i.e., $[1/\mathsf{sk}_i]$), performing multiplication of distinct randomness and secret shares (i.e., $[r_i\mathsf{sk}_i]$), as well as raising either secret shares or distinct randomness to a power (e.g., $[\mathsf{sk}_i^\zeta]$ or $[r_i^\zeta]$ for any $\zeta > 1$). By employing an indexing approach, the authors in [32] were able to circumvent the need for multiplying randomness and secret keys, as required by Ghadafi's SPS [44]. In contrast, in our proposed TSPS scheme, we adopt a distinct perspective for avoiding the non-linear operations.

We start from an observation regarding the SPS construction of Kiltz *et al.* [51] which computes the first and second components of signature on a message $[\mathbf{m}]_1 \in \mathbb{G}_1^\ell$ as:

$$\text{KPW15}: (\sigma_1, \sigma_2) := \left(\underbrace{\left[(1\ \mathbf{m}^\top) \right]_1 \mathbf{K}}_{\text{SP-OTS}} + \overbrace{\mathbf{r}^\top \left[\mathbf{B}^\top (\mathbf{U} + \tau \cdot \mathbf{V}) \right]_1, \left[\mathbf{r}^\top \mathbf{B}^\top \right]_1}^{\text{randomized PRF}} \right),$$

where τ is a fresh random integer and $\mathbf{r}$ is a fresh random vector of proper size.[1] Additionally, the secret signing and verification keys are defined as follows:

$$\text{KPW15}: \mathsf{sk} := \left(\mathbf{K}, \left[\mathbf{B}^\top \mathbf{U} \right]_1, \left[\mathbf{B}^\top \mathbf{V} \right]_1, [\mathbf{B}]_1 \right),$$
$$\mathsf{vk} := \left([\mathbf{K}\mathbf{A}]_2, [\mathbf{U}\mathbf{A}]_2, [\mathbf{V}\mathbf{A}]_2, [\mathbf{A}]_2 \right),$$

where $\mathbf{K}, \mathbf{A}, \mathbf{B}, \mathbf{U}$ and $\mathbf{V}$ are random matrices of appropriate dimensions.

As noted by Kiltz *et al.* in their work [51], their SPS is build based on two fundamental primitives: (*i*) a structure-preserving one-time signature (SP-OTS), $\left(\left[(1\ \mathbf{m}^\top) \right]_1 \mathbf{K} \right)$, and (*ii*) a randomized pseudorandom function (PRF), $\left(\mathbf{r}^\top \left[\mathbf{B}^\top (\mathbf{U} + \tau \cdot \mathbf{V}) \right]_1, \left[\mathbf{r}^\top \mathbf{B}^\top \right]_1 \right)$. In their proof of security, we observe that both the building blocks are involved in a loose manner. In particular, in most of their proofs, the reduction samples the SP-OTS signing key $\mathbf{K}$. It is easy to verify that this observation still holds even when they are arguing about the security of the randomized PRF. Our approach in this work is motivated by this fact which further inspires us to modify Kiltz et al.'s SPS. This adjustment involves defining the secret key as $\mathsf{sk} := \mathbf{K}$ and transferring the remaining parameters to the set of public parameters, i.e., $\mathsf{pp} := ([\mathbf{A}]_2, [\mathbf{U}\mathbf{A}]_2, [\mathbf{V}\mathbf{A}]_2, [\mathbf{B}]_1, [\mathbf{B}^\top \mathbf{U}]_1, [\mathbf{B}^\top \mathbf{V}]_1)$ and the verification is defined as $\mathsf{vk} := [\mathbf{K}\mathbf{A}]_2$. This rather simple structure allows to obtain the first TSPS for general message spaces in the standard model that can withhold adaptive corruptions without the exponential degradation [18] and can be proven secure in the TS-UF-1 model.

Consider the following setting. Imagine there are n signers, each equipped with their own signing key, either obtained through the involvement of a trusted dealer or by conducting a Distributed Key Generation (DKG). Their collective objective is to generate a signature for a given message $[\mathbf{m}]_1 \in \mathbb{G}_1^\ell$. It is clear that the linear structure of the SP-OTS $\{ \left[(1\ \mathbf{m}^\top) \right]_1 \mathbf{K}_i \}_{i \in S}$ allows for effortless aggregation when dealing with a collection of them over any subset $S \subseteq [1, n]$. Since the random quantities τ_i and $\mathbf{r}_i$ are independently sampled from a uniform distribution by each signer $i \in [1, n]$, aggregating the PRF elements is still challenging. Consequently, we must explore potential modifications needed to

---

[1] Here we follow the group notation by Escala *et al.* [38]. See Definition 2 for more details.

enable the aggregation of these components in comparison to Kiltz et al.'s SPS. We choose to make the tag τ dependent on the message. Thus, the randomized PRF computed by every signer, while still being a random element in the respective space, now allows aggregation. Moreover, by establishing an injective mapping between $[\mathbf{m}]_1$ and τ, we can observe that the randomized PRF structure still guarantees the unforgeability in [51] when attempting to forge a signature on a distinct message. We employ a collision-resistant hash function (CRHF), $\mathcal{H}(.)$, to derive τ from $[\mathbf{m}]_1$. This gives the basis of our construction, where each signer $i \in [1, n]$ computes a partial signature on $[\mathbf{m}]_1$ as

$$(\sigma_1, \sigma_2) = \left(\left[[(1 \ \mathbf{m}^\top)] \right]_1 \mathbf{K}_i + \mathbf{r}_i^\top \left[\mathbf{B}^\top (\mathbf{U} + \tau \cdot \mathbf{V}) \right]_1 , \left[\mathbf{r}_i^\top \mathbf{B}^\top \right]_1 \right) .$$

Here the signer i is holding the secret share $\mathbf{K}_i$ and chooses a random quantity $\mathbf{r}_i$ of appropriate size and uses $\tau = \mathcal{H}([\mathbf{m}]_1)$. It is easy to verify that this signature can be aggregated in a non-interactive manner. Looking ahead, as a first step we prove that this construction achieves TS-UF-0 security, relying on the well-established and non-interactive standard assumption, i.e., the MDDH assumption.

In case of a TS-UF-1 adversary, we need to deal with the fact that the adversary is allowed to obtain partial signatures on the forged message $[\mathbf{m}^*]_1$. Let us first consider the case of static corruptions. We cannot apply the unforgeability of [51] here as it did not consider strong Uf-CMA security.[2] To overcome this problem, we introduce an information theoretic step to argue that given a number of partial signatures on the forged message $[\mathbf{m}^*]_1$ below the threshold, the adversary does not gather extra information. In particular, we use Shamir's secret reconstruction security to ensure that partial signatures do not really leak much information. In this argument, we implicitly use the "selective security" of Shamir's secret sharing where all the parties in the corrupted set are fixed at the start of the game.

In the case of adaptive corruptions, an adp-TS-UF-1 adversary not only is allowed to obtain partial signatures on the forged message $[\mathbf{m}^*]_1$, but also it can corrupt different users to get the corresponding secret keys within the security game, adaptively. We obviously could follow a standard guessing argument to achieve adp-TS-UF-1 security based on TS-UF-1 security. However, that direction unfortunately induces a significant security loss. We critically look at our proof of TS-UF-1 security we have briefly discussed above. To make our construction adp-TS-UF-1 secure, we show that it is sufficient to argue that the underlying secret sharing achieves "adaptive security". In this work, we indeed form an argument that Shamir's secret sharing achieves "adaptive security" which in turn makes our construction adp-TS-UF-1 secure.

Next, we provide a brief intuition of the formal argument for the "adaptive security" of Shamir's secret sharing. Informally speaking, we produce a reduction

---

[2] A signature is called strongly unforgeable when the adversary is not only incapable of producing a valid signature for a fresh message but also, it cannot generate a new signature for a challenge message M^*, by observing a valid signature for the same message M^*.

$\mathcal{B}$ to break the "selective security" of Shamir's secret sharing given an adaptive adversary $\mathcal{A}$ of the secret sharing. Being an information theoretic reduction, $\mathcal{B}$ basically runs the adaptive adversary $\mathcal{A}$ an exponential number of times. Since $\mathcal{B}$ chooses the target set S independently of $\mathcal{A}$'s run, the expected number of parallel runs of $\mathcal{A}$ required to ensure all the parties whose secrets $\mathcal{A}$ queried are indeed from S is upper bounded by exponential. Being an information theoretically secure secret sharing scheme, Shamir's secret sharing basically achieves "adaptive security" due to complexity leveraging but without any degradation in the advantage of the adversary. While we use Shamir secret sharing as our canonical choice, we believe that all information-theoretically secure Linear Secret Sharing schemes can be used instead.

2   Preliminaries

Notation. Throughout the paper, we let $\kappa \in \mathbb{N}$ denote the security parameter and 1^κ as its unary representation. Given a polynomial $p(\cdot)$, an efficient randomized algorithm, $\mathcal{A}$, is called *probabilistic polynomial time*, PPT in short, if its running time is bounded by a polynomial $p(|x|)$ for every input x. A function $\mathsf{negl} : \mathbb{N} \to \mathbb{R}^+$ is called *negligible* if for every positive polynomial $f(x)$, there exists x_0 such that for all $x > x_0$: $\mathsf{negl}(\kappa) < 1/f(x)$. If clear from the context, we sometimes omit κ for improved readability. The set $\{1, \ldots, n\}$ is denoted as $[1, n]$ for a positive integer n. For the equality check of two elements, we use "$=$". The assign operator is denoted with "$:=$", whereas the randomized assignment is denoted by $a \leftarrow A$, with a randomized algorithm A and where the randomness is not explicit. We use $\mathcal{D}_1 \approx_c \mathcal{D}_2$ to show two distributions like $\mathcal{D}_1$ and $\mathcal{D}_2$ are computationally indistinguishable.

Definition 1 (Secret Sharing). *For any two positive integers $n, t < n$, an $(n, t)_{\mathbb{Z}_p^{a \times b}}$-secret-sharing scheme over $\mathbb{Z}_p^{a \times b}$ for $a, b \in \mathbb{N}$ consists of two functions* Share *and* Rec. Share *is a randomized function that takes a secret $\mathbf{M} \in \mathbb{Z}_p^{a \times b}$ and outputs $(\mathbf{M}_1, \ldots, \mathbf{M}_n) \leftarrow \mathsf{Share}(\mathbf{M}, \mathbb{Z}_p^{a \times b}, n, t)$ where $\mathbf{M}_i \in \mathbb{Z}_p^{a \times b} \; \forall i \in [1, n]$. The pair of functions $(\mathsf{Share}, \mathsf{Rec})$ satisfy the following requirements.*

- **Correctness:** *For any secret $\mathbf{M} \in \mathbb{Z}_p^{a \times b}$ and a set of parties $\{i_1, i_2, \ldots, i_k\} \subseteq [1, n]$ such that $k \geq t$, we have*

$$\Pr[\mathsf{Rec}(\mathbf{M}_{i_1}, \ldots, \mathbf{M}_{i_k}) : (\mathbf{M}_1, \ldots, \mathbf{M}_n) \leftarrow \mathsf{Share}(\mathbf{M}, \mathbb{Z}_p^{a \times b}, n, t)) = \mathbf{M}] = 1 \ .$$

- **Security:** *For any secret $\mathbf{M} \in \mathbb{Z}_p^{a \times b}$ and a set of parties $S \subseteq [1, n]$ such that $|S| = k < t$, for all information-theoretic adversary $\mathcal{A}$ we have*

$$\Pr\left[S = \{i_i\}_{i \in [1,k]} \wedge \mathbf{M}^* = \mathbf{M} \; \middle| \; \begin{matrix} (\mathbf{M}_1, \ldots, \mathbf{M}_n) \leftarrow \mathsf{Share}(\mathbf{M}, \mathbb{Z}_p^{a \times b}, n, t) \\ S \leftarrow \mathcal{A}() \\ \mathbf{M}^* \leftarrow \mathcal{A}(\mathbf{M}_{i_1}, \ldots, \mathbf{M}_{i_k}) \end{matrix} \right] = 1/p \ .$$

We follow standard nomenclature to call this "selective security". In case of "adaptive security", $\mathcal{A}$ adaptively chooses $i_j \in [1, n]$ to get $\mathbf{M}_{i_j}$ one at a time.

We briefly recall the well-known secret sharing scheme due to Shamir [61]. In (n, t)-Shamir Secret Sharing, a secret s is shared to n parties via n evaluations of a polynomial of degree $(t - 1)$. Reconstruction of the secret is essentially Lagrange interpolation where one computes Lagrange polynomials $\{\lambda_{i_j}(x)\}_{j \in S}$ and linearly combine them with the given polynomial evaluations. The degree of the original polynomial confirms that one needs at least $|S| = t$ many polynomial evaluations. In this work, we use Shamir Secret Sharing to secret share a matrix of size $a \times b$, i.e., we use ab-many parallel instances of Shamir Secret Sharing. To keep our exposition simpler, we however assume that we have an (n, t)-Shamir Secret Sharing scheme (Share, Rec) which operates on matrices. Since, our work here uses Shamir Secret Sharing quite generically, it is convenient to make such abstraction without going into the details.

Definition 2 (Bilinear Groups). *Let an asymmetric bilinear group generator, $\mathsf{ABSGen}(1^\kappa)$, that returns a tuple $\mathcal{G} := (p, \mathbb{G}_1, \mathbb{G}_2, \mathbb{G}_T, \mathsf{P}_1, \mathsf{P}_2, e)$, such that $\mathbb{G}_1$, $\mathbb{G}_2$ and $\mathbb{G}_T$ are cyclic groups of the same prime order p such that there is no known homomorphism between $\mathbb{G}_1$ and $\mathbb{G}_2$. P_1 and P_2 are the generators of $\mathbb{G}_1$ and $\mathbb{G}_2$, respectively, where $e : \mathbb{G}_1 \times \mathbb{G}_2 \to \mathbb{G}_T$ is an efficiently computable (non-degenerate) bilinear map with the following properties:*

- $\forall\, a, b \in \mathbb{Z}_p,\ e([a]_1, [b]_2) = [ab]_T = e([b]_1, [a]_2)$,
- $\forall\, a, b \in \mathbb{Z}_p,\ e([a+b]_1, [1]_2) = e([a]_1, [1]_2)e([b]_1, [1]_2)$,

where we use an implicit representation of group elements, in which for $\zeta \in \{1, 2, T\}$ and an integer $\alpha \in \mathbb{Z}_p$, the implicit representation of integer α in group $\mathbb{G}_\zeta$ is defined by $[\alpha]_\zeta = \alpha \mathsf{P}_\zeta \in \mathbb{G}_\zeta$, where $\mathsf{P}_T = e(\mathsf{P}_1, \mathsf{P}_2)$. To be more general, the implicit representation of a matrix $\mathbf{A} = (\alpha_{ij}) \in \mathbb{Z}_p^{m \times n}$ in $\mathbb{G}_\zeta$ is defined by $[\mathbf{A}]_\zeta$ and we have:

$$[\mathbf{A}]_\zeta = \begin{pmatrix} \alpha_{1,1}\mathsf{P}_\zeta & \cdots & \alpha_{1,n}\mathsf{P}_\zeta \\ \alpha_{2,1}\mathsf{P}_\zeta & \cdots & \alpha_{2,n}\mathsf{P}_\zeta \\ \vdots & \ddots & \vdots \\ \alpha_{m,1}\mathsf{P}_\zeta & \cdots & \alpha_{m,n}\mathsf{P}_\zeta \end{pmatrix} .$$

For two matrices $\mathbf{A}$ and $\mathbf{B}$ with matching dimensions we define $e([\mathbf{A}]_1, [\mathbf{B}]_2) = [\mathbf{AB}]_T$.

Definition 3 (Matrix Distribution). *Let $k, \ell \in \mathbb{N}^*$ s.t. $k < \ell$. We call $\mathcal{D}_{\ell,k}$ a matrix distribution if it outputs matrices over $\mathbb{Z}_p^{\ell \times k}$ of full rank k in polynomial time. W.l.o.g, we assume the first k rows of matrix $\mathbf{A} \leftarrow \mathcal{D}_{\ell,k}$ form an invertible matrix. For $\ell = k + 1$, we write $\mathcal{D}_k$ in short.*

Next, we recall the Matrix Decisional Diffie-Hellman assumption, which defines over $\mathbb{G}_\zeta$ for any $\zeta = \{1, 2\}$ and states two distributions $([\mathbf{A}]_\zeta, [\mathbf{Ar}]_\zeta)$ and $([\mathbf{A}]_\zeta, [\mathbf{u}]_\zeta)$, where $\mathbf{A} \leftarrow \mathcal{D}_{\ell,k}, \mathbf{r} \leftarrow \mathbb{Z}_p^k, \mathbf{u} \leftarrow \mathbb{Z}_p^\ell$ are computationally indistinguishable.

Definition 4 ($\mathcal{D}_{\ell,k}$-Matrix Decisional Diffie-Hellman ($\mathcal{D}_{\ell,k}$-MDDH) Assumption [38]). *For a given security parameter κ, let $k, \ell \in \mathbb{N}^*$ s.t. $k < \ell$ and $\mathcal{D}_{\ell,k}$ be a matrix distribution, defined in Definition 3. We say $\mathcal{D}_{\ell,k}$-MDDH assumption over $\mathbb{G}_\zeta$ for $\zeta = \{1, 2\}$ holds, if for all PPT adversaries $\mathcal{A}$ we have:*

$$Adv_{\mathcal{D}_{\ell,k},\mathbb{G}_\zeta,\mathcal{A}}^{\mathsf{MDDH}}(\kappa) = \Big| \Pr\left[\mathcal{A}(\mathcal{G}, [\mathbf{A}]_\zeta, [\mathbf{Ar}]_\zeta) = 1\right]$$
$$- \Pr\left[\mathcal{A}(\mathcal{G}, [\mathbf{A}]_\zeta, [\mathbf{u}]_\zeta) = 1\right] \Big| \leq \mathsf{negl}(\kappa),$$

where $\mathcal{G} \leftarrow \mathsf{ABSGen}(1^\kappa)$, $\mathbf{A} \leftarrow \mathcal{D}_{\ell,k}, \mathbf{r} \leftarrow \mathbb{Z}_p^k$ and $\mathbf{u} \leftarrow \mathbb{Z}_p^\ell$.

Definition 5 ($\mathcal{D}_k$-Kernel Matrix Diffie-Hellman ($\mathcal{D}_k$-KerMDH) Assumption [58]). *For a given security parameter κ, let $k \in \mathbb{N}^*$ and $\mathcal{D}_k$ is a matrix distribution, defined in Definition 3. We say $\mathcal{D}_k$-KerMDH assumption over $\mathbb{G}_\zeta$ for $\zeta = \{1, 2\}$ holds, if for all PPT adversaries $\mathcal{A}$ we have:*

$$Adv_{\mathcal{D}_k,\mathbb{G}_\zeta,\mathcal{A}}^{\mathsf{KerMDH}}(\kappa) = \Pr\left[\mathbf{c} \in \mathsf{orth}(\mathbf{A}) \mid [\mathbf{c}]_{3-\zeta} \leftarrow \mathcal{A}(\mathcal{G}, [\mathbf{A}]_\zeta)\right] \leq \mathsf{negl}(\kappa) \cdot$$

The Kernel Matrix Diffie-Hellman assumption is a natural computational analog of the MDDH assumption. It is well-known that for all $k \geq 1$, $\mathcal{D}_k$-MDDH $\Rightarrow$ $\mathcal{D}_k$-KerMDH [51,58].

3   Threshold Structure-Preserving Signatures

In this section, we first present our security model for Threshold Structure-Preserving Signatures (TSPS) and then present our construction and prove its security.

3.1   TSPS: Syntax and Security Definitions

First, we recall the definition of the Threshold Structure-Preserving Signatures (TSPS) from [32] and their main security properties: correctness and threshold unforgeability. Informally, a threshold signature scheme enables a group of servers S of size n to collaboratively sign a message. In this paper, we assume the existence of a trusted dealer who shares the secret key among the signers. However, there are straightforward and well-known techniques in particular distributed key generation (DKG) protocols (e.g., [59]) that eliminate this needed trust.

Definition 6 (Threshold Structure-Preserving Signatures [32]). *Over a security parameter κ and a bilinear group, an (n, t)-TSPS contains the following PPT algorithms:*

- pp $\leftarrow$ Setup(1^κ): *The setup algorithm takes the security parameter κ as input and returns the set of public parameters pp as output.*

- $(\{\mathsf{sk}_i, \mathsf{vk}_i\}_{i \in [1,n]}, \mathsf{vk}) \leftarrow \mathsf{KeyGen}(\mathsf{pp}, n, t)$: *The key generation algorithm takes the public parameters* pp *along with two integers* n, t *s.t.* $1 \leq t \leq n$ *as inputs. It then returns secret/verification keys* $(\mathsf{sk}_i, \mathsf{vk}_i)$ *for* $i \in [1, n]$ *along with a global verification key* vk *as output.*
- $\Sigma_i \leftarrow \mathsf{ParSign}(\mathsf{pp}, \mathsf{sk}_i, [\mathbf{m}])$: *The partial signing algorithm takes* pp, *the* i^{th} *party's secret key,* sk_i, *and a message* $[\mathbf{m}] \in \mathcal{M}$ *as inputs. It then returns a partial signature* Σ_i *as output.*
- $0/1 \leftarrow \mathsf{ParVerify}(\mathsf{pp}, \mathsf{vk}_i, [\mathbf{m}], \Sigma_i)$: *The partial verification algorithm as a deterministic algorithm, takes* pp, *the* i^{th} *verification key,* vk_i, *and a message* $[\mathbf{m}] \in \mathcal{M}$ *along with partial signature* Σ_i *as inputs. It then returns 1 (accept), if the partial signature is valid and 0 (reject), otherwise.*
- $\Sigma \leftarrow \mathsf{CombineSign}(\mathsf{pp}, T, \{\Sigma_i\}_{i \in T})$: *The combine algorithm takes a set of partial signatures* Σ_i *for* $i \in T$ *along with* $T \subseteq [1, n]$ *and then returns an aggregated signature* Σ *as output.*
- $0/1 \leftarrow \mathsf{Verify}(\mathsf{pp}, \mathsf{vk}, [\mathbf{m}], \Sigma)$: *The verification algorithm as a deterministic algorithm, takes* pp, *the global verification key,* vk, *and message* $[\mathbf{m}] \in \mathcal{M}$ *along with an aggregated signature* Σ *as inputs. It then returns 1 (accept), if the aggregated signature is valid and 0 (reject), otherwise.*

Correctness. Correctness guarantees that a signature obtained from a set $T \subseteq [1, n]$ of honest signers always verifies for $|T| \geq t$.

Definition 7 (Correctness). *An* (n, t)-*TSPS scheme is called correct if we have:*

$$\Pr\left[\begin{array}{l} \forall\ \mathsf{pp} \leftarrow \mathsf{Setup}(1^\kappa), (\{\mathsf{sk}_i, \mathsf{vk}_i\}_{i \in [1,n]}, \mathsf{vk}) \leftarrow \mathsf{KeyGen}(\mathsf{pp}, n, t), [\mathbf{m}] \in \mathcal{M}, \\ \Sigma_i \leftarrow \mathsf{ParSign}(\mathsf{pp}, \mathsf{sk}_i, [\mathbf{m}])\ for\ i \in [1, n], \forall\ T \subseteq [1, n], |T| \geq t, \\ \Sigma \leftarrow \mathsf{CombineSign}\left(\mathsf{pp}, T, \{\Sigma_i\}_{i \in T}\right) : \mathsf{Verify}\left(\mathsf{pp}, \mathsf{vk}, [\mathbf{m}], \Sigma\right) = 1 \end{array}\right] = 1\ .$$

Unforgeability. Our security model for threshold unforgeability extends the one from Crites et al. [32]. Therefore, we need to recall a recent work by Bellare et al. [18], which investigates existing security notions and proposes stronger and more realistic security notions for threshold signatures under static corruptions. In particular, the authors in [18] present a hierarchy of different notions of security for non-interactive schemes. We focus on fully non-interactive schemes, i.e., ones that do not require one round of pre-processing, and thus in this paper only the TS-UF-0 and TS-UF-1 notions are relevant. The TS-UF-0 notion is a less stringent notion of unforgeability. In this context, if the adversary has previously seen a partial signature on a challenge message $[\mathbf{m}^*]$, the act of forging a signature for that specific message is considered as a trivial forgery. The security of the original TSPS is proved under this notion of unforgeability.

The stronger TS-UF-1 notion, which is our main focus, allows adversaries to query the signing oracle up to $t - |\mathsf{CS}|$ times for partial signatures, even on the challenge message. Here CS with $|\mathsf{CS}| < t$ denotes the set of (statically corrupted) signers. Moreover, the model in [18] as well as the TSPS construction in [32] only considers static corruptions. But we also integrate the core elements of the model introduced in the recent work by Crites et al. [33], adapted to fully non-interactive schemes, to support fully adaptive corruptions. Our model is depicted in Fig. 1. The dashed box as well as the solid white box in the winning condition apply to the TS-UF-0 and TS-UF-1 notions, respectively. Grey boxes are only present in the adaptive version of the game, i.e., adp-TS-UF-0 and adp-TS-UF-1.

Definition 8 (Threshold Unforgeability). *Let* TSPS = (Setup, KeyGen, ParSign, ParVerify, CombineSign, Verify) *be an* (n, t)-*TSPS scheme over message space* $\mathcal{M}$ *and let* prop $\in$ {TS-UF-b, adp-TS-UF-b}$_{b\in\{0,1\}}$. *The advantage of a PPT adversary* $\mathcal{A}$ *playing described security games in Fig. 1, is defined as,*

$$\mathbf{Adv}^{\mathsf{prop}}_{\mathsf{TSPS},\mathcal{A}}(\kappa) = \Pr\left[\mathbf{G}^{\mathsf{prop}}_{\mathsf{TS},\mathcal{A}}(\kappa) = 1\right] \ .$$

A TSPS achieves prop-security if we have, $\mathbf{Adv}^{\mathsf{prop}}_{\mathsf{TSPS},\mathcal{A}}(\kappa) \leq \mathsf{negl}(\kappa)$.

$\boxed{G^{\mathsf{TS\text{-}UF\text{-}0}}_{\mathsf{TS},\mathcal{A}}(\kappa)}$, $\boxed{G^{\mathsf{TS\text{-}UF\text{-}1}}_{\mathsf{TS},\mathcal{A}}(\kappa)}$, $\boxed{G^{\mathsf{adp\text{-}TS\text{-}UF\text{-}0}}_{\mathsf{TS},\mathcal{A}}(\kappa)}$, $\boxed{G^{\mathsf{adp\text{-}TS\text{-}UF\text{-}1}}_{\mathsf{TS},\mathcal{A}}(\kappa)}$:

pp $\leftarrow$ Setup(1^κ)

$(n, t, \mathsf{CS}, \mathsf{st}_0) \leftarrow \mathcal{A}(\mathsf{pp})$

$\mathsf{HS} := [1, n] \setminus \mathsf{CS}$

$(\mathsf{vk}, \{\mathsf{sk}_i\}_{i\in[1,n]}, \{\mathsf{vk}_i\}_{i\in[1,n]}) \leftarrow \mathsf{KeyGen}(\mathsf{pp}, n, t)$

$([\mathbf{m}^*], \Sigma^*, \mathsf{st}_1) \leftarrow \mathcal{A}^{\mathcal{O}^{\mathsf{PSign}}(.),\ \mathcal{O}^{\mathsf{Corrupt}}(.)}(\mathsf{st}_0, \mathsf{vk}, \{\mathsf{sk}_i\}_{i\in\mathsf{CS}}, \{\mathsf{vk}_i\}_{i\in[1,n]})$

return $\Big(\mathsf{Verify}(\mathsf{pp}, \mathsf{vk}, [\mathbf{m}^*], \Sigma^*) \wedge |\mathsf{CS}| < t \ \wedge$

$\qquad \Big(\boxed{S_1([\mathbf{m}^*]) = \emptyset} \vee \boxed{|S_1([\mathbf{m}^*])| < t - |\mathsf{CS}|}\Big)\Big)$

$\mathcal{O}^{\mathsf{PSign}}(i, [\mathbf{m}])$:	$\mathcal{O}^{\mathsf{Corrupt}}(k)$:
Assert $([\mathbf{m}] \in \mathcal{M} \wedge i \in \mathsf{HS})$	**if** $k \in \mathsf{CS}$:
$\Sigma_i \leftarrow \mathsf{ParSign}(\mathsf{pp}, \mathsf{sk}_i, [\mathbf{m}])$	$\qquad$ **return** $\perp$
if $\Sigma_i \neq \perp$:	**else** : $\mathsf{CS} \leftarrow \mathsf{CS} \cup \{k\}$
$\qquad S_1([\mathbf{m}]) \leftarrow S_1([\mathbf{m}]) \cup \{i\}$	$\qquad\qquad \mathsf{HS} \leftarrow \mathsf{HS} \setminus \{k\}$
return (Σ_i)	$\qquad\qquad$ **return** (sk_k)

Fig. 1. Games defining the $\boxed{\mathsf{TS\text{-}UF\text{-}0}}$, $\boxed{\mathsf{TS\text{-}UF\text{-}1}}$, $\boxed{\mathsf{adp\text{-}TS\text{-}UF\text{-}0}}$, and $\boxed{\mathsf{adp\text{-}TS\text{-}UF\text{-}1}}$ unforgeability notions of threshold signatures.

3.2   Core Lemma

Prior to introducing our construction, we first present the core lemma that forms a basis in the proofs of our proposed TSPS. It extends the core lemmas from [51, 52], however it is important to note that both of these schemes are standard SPS, where there was no need to simulate signatures on forged messages. In contrast, both the TS-UF-1 and adp-TS-UF-1 security models necessitate the simulation of partial signature queries on forged messages. Thus we define our core lemma with a key difference being the introduction of a new oracle, denoted as $\mathcal{O}^{**}(\cdot)$.

Lemma 1 (Core Lemma). *Let the game* $\mathbf{G}^{\mathsf{Core}}_{\mathcal{D}_k,\mathsf{ABSGen}}(\kappa)$ *be defined as Fig. 2. For any adversary* $\mathcal{A}$ *with the advantage of* $Adv^{\mathsf{Core}}_{\mathcal{D}_k,\mathsf{ABSGen},\mathcal{A}}(\kappa) := |\Pr[\mathbf{G}^{\mathsf{Core}}_{\mathcal{D}_k,\mathsf{ABSGen}}(\kappa)] - 1/2|$, *there exists an adversary* $\mathcal{B}$ *against the* $\mathcal{D}_k$-MDDH *assumption such that with the running time* $\mathbf{T}(\mathcal{A}) \approx \mathbf{T}(\mathcal{B})$ *it holds that*

$$Adv^{\mathsf{Core}}_{\mathcal{D}_k,\mathsf{ABSGen},\mathcal{A}}(\kappa) \leq 2q Adv^{\mathsf{MDDH}}_{\mathcal{D}_k,\mathbb{G}_1,\mathcal{B}}(\kappa) + q/p \,,$$

where q *is a bound on the number of queries requested by adversary* $\mathcal{A}$ *for oracle* $\mathcal{O}_b(\cdot)$. *Note that* $\mathcal{A}$ *can only query the other oracles only once.*

$\mathsf{Init}()$:

$\mathbf{A}, \mathbf{B} \leftarrow \mathcal{D}_k, \mathbf{U}, \mathbf{V} \leftarrow \mathbb{Z}_p^{(k+1)\times(k+1)}$

$\mathsf{vk} := (\mathbf{A}, \mathbf{UA}, \mathbf{VA}, [\mathbf{B}]_1, [\mathbf{B}^\top\mathbf{U}]_1, [\mathbf{B}^\top\mathbf{V}]_1)$

$b \leftarrow \{0,1\}$

Let $\mathbf{a}^\perp \leftarrow \mathbb{Z}_p^{1\times(k+1)}$ such that $\mathbf{a}^\perp\mathbf{A} = \mathbf{0}$

$q := 0, \mathcal{Q}_{\mathsf{tag}} := \emptyset$

return vk

$\mathcal{O}^*([\tau^*]_2)$:

return $[\mathbf{U} + \tau^*\mathbf{V}]_2$

$\mathcal{O}^{**}([\tau^*]_1)$:

return $\left[\mathbf{B}^\top(\mathbf{U} + \tau^*\mathbf{V})\right]_1$

$\mathcal{O}_b([\tau]_1)$:

$\mu \leftarrow \mathbb{Z}_p, \mathbf{r} \leftarrow \mathbb{Z}_p^k, q := q+1$

$\mathcal{Q}_{\mathsf{tag}} := \mathcal{Q}_{\mathsf{tag}} \cup \{\tau\}$

return $\left(\left[b\mu\mathbf{a}^\perp + \mathbf{r}^\top\mathbf{B}^\top(\mathbf{U} + \tau\mathbf{V})\right]_1, [\mathbf{r}^\top\mathbf{B}^\top]_1\right)$

Fig. 2. Game defining the core lemma, $\mathbf{G}^{\mathsf{Core}}_{\mathcal{D}_k,\mathsf{ABSGen}}(\kappa)$.

Proof Sketch. The proof of this lemma uses the proof of core lemma in [51,52]. The fundamental concept of these proofs is primarily an information-theoretic argument that $(\mathbf{t}^\top(\mathbf{U} + \tau\mathbf{V}), \mathbf{U} + \tau^*\mathbf{V})$ is identically distributed to $(\mu\mathbf{a}^{\perp\top} + \mathbf{t}^\top(\mathbf{U} + \tau\mathbf{V}), \mathbf{U} + \tau^*\mathbf{V})$ for $\mu \leftarrow \mathbb{Z}_p$, $\mathbf{a}^\perp, \mathbf{t} \leftarrow \mathbb{Z}_p^{k+1}$ and $\tau \neq \tau^*$. We use $\left[b\mu\mathbf{a}^{\perp\top} + \mathbf{t}^\top(\mathbf{U} + \tau\mathbf{V})\right]_1$ to simulate $\mathcal{O}_b([\tau]_1)$, $[\mathbf{U} + \tau^*\mathbf{V}]_2$ to simulate $\mathcal{O}^*([\tau^*]_2)$ and $\left[\mathbf{B}^\top(\mathbf{U} + \tau^*\mathbf{V})\right]_1$ to simulate $\mathcal{O}^{**}([\tau^*]_1)$. The detailed proof can be found in Sect. 3.5. $\square$

Setup(1^κ):

1: $\mathcal{G} := (p, \mathbb{G}_1, \mathbb{G}_2, \mathbb{G}_T, \mathsf{P}_1, \mathsf{P}_2, e) \leftarrow \mathsf{ABSGen}(1^\kappa)$.

2: $\mathbf{A}, \mathbf{B} \leftarrow \mathcal{D}_k$, $\mathbf{U}, \mathbf{V} \leftarrow \mathbb{Z}_p^{(k+1)\times(k+1)}$.

3: $\mathsf{pp} := \left([\mathbf{A}]_2, [\mathbf{UA}]_2, [\mathbf{VA}]_2, [\mathbf{B}]_1, [\mathbf{B}^\top\mathbf{U}]_1, [\mathbf{B}^\top\mathbf{V}]_1\right)$.

KeyGen(pp, n, t):

1: $\mathbf{K} \leftarrow \mathbb{Z}_p^{(\ell+1)\times(k+1)}$.

2: $\mathbf{K}_1, \ldots, \mathbf{K}_n \leftarrow \mathsf{Share}(\mathbf{K}, \mathbb{Z}_p^{(\ell+1)\times(k+1)}, n, t)$.

3: Set $\mathsf{vk} := [\mathbf{KA}]_2$ and $(\mathsf{sk}_i, \mathsf{vk}_i) := (\mathbf{K}_i, [\mathbf{K}_i\mathbf{A}]_2)$.

ParSign($\mathsf{pp}, \mathsf{sk}_i, [\mathbf{m}]_1$):

1: $\mathbf{r}_i \leftarrow \mathbb{Z}_p^k$.

2: $\tau := \mathcal{H}([\mathbf{m}]_1)$.

3: Output $\Sigma_i := (\sigma_1, \sigma_2, \sigma_3, \sigma_4)$ s.t.

4: $\sigma_1 := \left[\left(1\ \mathbf{m}^\top\right)\right]_1 \mathbf{K}_i + \mathbf{r}_i^\top \left[\mathbf{B}^\top(\mathbf{U} + \tau\mathbf{V})\right]_1$,

   $\sigma_2 := \left[\mathbf{r}_i^\top\mathbf{B}^\top\right]_1$,

   $\sigma_3 := \left[\tau\mathbf{r}_i^\top\mathbf{B}^\top\right]_1$,

   $\sigma_4 := [\tau]_2$.

ParVerify($\mathsf{pp}, \mathsf{vk}_i, [\mathbf{m}]_1, \Sigma_i$): Output 1 if the following checks hold; else output 0.

1: $e(\sigma_1, [\mathbf{A}]_2) = e\left(\left[\left(1\ \mathbf{m}^\top\right)\right]_1, \mathsf{vk}_i\right) \cdot e\left(\sigma_2, [\mathbf{UA}]_2\right) \cdot e\left(\sigma_3, [\mathbf{VA}]_2\right)$.

2: $e(\sigma_2, \sigma_4) = e(\sigma_3, [1]_2)$.

CombineSign($\mathsf{pp}, S, \{\Sigma_i\}_{i\in S}$):

1: Parse $\Sigma_i = (\sigma_{i,1}, \sigma_{i,2}, \sigma_{i,3}, \sigma_4)$ for all $i \in S$.

2: Compute Lagrange polynomials λ_i for $i \in S$.

3: Output $\Sigma := (\widehat{\sigma}_1, \widehat{\sigma}_2, \widehat{\sigma}_3, \widehat{\sigma}_4)$ s.t.

4: $\widehat{\sigma}_1 := \prod_{i\in S}\sigma_{i,1}^{\lambda_i} = \left[\left(1\ \mathbf{m}^\top\right)\sum_{i\in S}\lambda_i\mathbf{K}_i\right]_1 + \sum_{i\in S}\lambda_i\mathbf{r}_i^\top\left[\mathbf{B}^\top(\mathbf{U}+\tau\mathbf{V})\right]_1 =$

   $\left[\left(1\ \mathbf{m}^\top\right)\mathbf{K}\right]_1 + \mathbf{r}^\top\left[\mathbf{B}^\top(\mathbf{U}+\tau\mathbf{V})\right]_1$,

   $\widehat{\sigma}_2 := \prod_{i\in S}\sigma_{i,2}^{\lambda_i} = \left[\sum_{i\in S}\lambda_i\mathbf{r}_i^\top\mathbf{B}^\top\right]_1 = \left[\mathbf{r}^\top\mathbf{B}^\top\right]_1$,

   $\widehat{\sigma}_3 := \prod_{i\in S}\sigma_{i,3}^{\lambda_i} = \left[\sum_{i\in S}\tau\lambda_i\mathbf{r}_i^\top\mathbf{B}^\top\right]_1 = \left[\tau\mathbf{r}^\top\mathbf{B}^\top\right]_1$,

   $\widehat{\sigma}_4 := \sigma_4$.

Verify($\mathsf{pp}, \mathsf{vk}, [\mathbf{m}]_1, \Sigma$): Output 1 if the following checks satisfy; else output 0.

1: $e(\widehat{\sigma}_1, [\mathbf{A}]_2) = e\left(\left[\left(1\ \mathbf{m}^\top\right)\right]_1, \mathsf{vk}\right) \cdot e(\widehat{\sigma}_2, [\mathbf{UA}]_2) \cdot e(\widehat{\sigma}_3, [\mathbf{VA}]_2)$.

2: $e(\widehat{\sigma}_2, \widehat{\sigma}_4) = e(\widehat{\sigma}_3, [1]_2)$.

Fig. 3. Our proposed TSPS construction.

3.3   Our Threshold SPS Construction

Given a collision resistant hash function, $\mathcal{H} : \{0,1\}^* \rightarrow \mathbb{Z}_p$, and message space $\mathcal{M} := \mathbb{G}_1^\ell$, we present our (n,t)-TSPS construction in Fig. 3. This consists of six main PPT algorithms – Setup, KeyGen, ParSign, ParVerify, CombineSign and Verify, as defined in Definition 6. Similar to the settings of Bellare *et al.* [18], we also assume there is a dealer who is responsible for generating key pairs for all signers and a general verification key.

3.4   Security

Theorem 1. *Under the $\mathcal{D}_k$-MDDH Assumption in $\mathbb{G}_1$ and $\mathcal{D}_k$-KerMDH Assumption in $\mathbb{G}_2$, the proposed Threshold Structure-Preserving Signature construction in Fig. 3 achieves* TS-UF-0 *security against an efficient adversary making at most q partial signature queries.*

Proof. We prove the above theorem through a series of games and we use $\mathbf{Adv}_i$ to denote the advantage of the adversary $\mathcal{A}$ in winning the Game i. The games are described below.

Game 0. This is the TS-UF-0 security game described in Definition 8. As shown in Fig. 4, an adversary $\mathcal{A}$ after receiving the set of public parameters, pp, returns (n, t, CS), where n, t and CS represents the total number of signers, the threshold, and the set of corrupted signers, respectively. The adversary can query the partial signing oracle $\mathcal{O}^{\mathsf{PSign}}(\cdot)$ to receive partial signatures and q represents the total number of these queries. In the end, the adversary outputs a message $[\mathbf{m}^*]_1$ and a forged signature Σ^*.

Game 1. We modify the verification procedure to the one described in Fig. 5. Consider any forged message/signature pair $([\mathbf{m}^*]_1, \Sigma^* = (\widehat{\sigma}_1, \widehat{\sigma}_2, \widehat{\sigma}_3, \widehat{\sigma}_4))$, where $e(\widehat{\sigma}_2, \widehat{\sigma}_4) = e(\widehat{\sigma}_3, [1]_2)$, $|\mathsf{CS}| < t$ and $S_1([\mathbf{m}^*]_1) = \emptyset$. It is easy to observe that if the pair $([\mathbf{m}^*]_1, \Sigma^*)$ meets the Verify$^*(\cdot)$ criteria, outlined in Fig. 5, it also satisfies Verify$(\cdot)$ procedure, described in Fig. 4. This is primarily due to the fact that:

$$e(\widehat{\sigma}_1, [\mathbf{A}]_2) = e\left([(1\ \mathbf{m}^{*\top})]_1, [\mathbf{KA}]_2\right) \cdot e(\widehat{\sigma}_2, [\mathbf{UA}]_2) \cdot e(\widehat{\sigma}_3, [\mathbf{VA}]_2)$$
$$\Longleftarrow e(\widehat{\sigma}_1, [1]_2) = e([(1\ \mathbf{m}^{*\top})]_1, [\mathbf{K}]_2) \cdot e(\widehat{\sigma}_2, [\mathbf{U}]_2) \cdot e(\widehat{\sigma}_3, [\mathbf{V}]_2)$$
$$\Longleftrightarrow e(\widehat{\sigma}_1, [1]_2) = e([(1\ \mathbf{m}^{*\top})\ \mathbf{K}]_1, [1]_2) \cdot e(\widehat{\sigma}_2, [\mathbf{U} + \tau^*\mathbf{V}]_2) \cdot$$

Assume there exists a message/signature pair like $([\mathbf{m}^*]_1, \Sigma^* = (\widehat{\sigma}_1, \widehat{\sigma}_2, \widehat{\sigma}_3, \widehat{\sigma}_4))$ that satisifies Verify$(\cdot)$ and not Verify$^*(\cdot)$, then we can compute a non-zero vector $\mathbf{c}$ in the kernal of $\mathbf{A}$ as follows:

$$\mathbf{c} := \widehat{\sigma}_1 - ([(1\ \mathbf{m}^{*\top})\ \mathbf{K}]_1 + \widehat{\sigma}_2\mathbf{U} + \widehat{\sigma}_3\mathbf{V}) \in \mathbb{G}_1^{1 \times (k+1)}.$$

According to $\mathcal{D}_k$-KerMDH assumption over $\mathbb{G}_2$ described in Definition 5, computing such a vector $\mathbf{c}$ is considered computationally hard. Thus,

$$|\mathbf{Adv}_0 - \mathbf{Adv}_1| \leq Adv_{\mathcal{D}_k,\mathbb{G}_2,\mathcal{B}_0}^{\mathsf{KerMDH}}(\kappa) .$$

$G_0(\kappa)$:

1: $\mathcal{G} \leftarrow \mathsf{ABSGen}(1^\kappa)$,

2: $\mathbf{A}, \mathbf{B} \leftarrow \mathcal{D}_k$,

3: $\mathbf{U}, \mathbf{V} \leftarrow \mathbb{Z}_p^{(k+1)\times(k+1)}$.

4: $\mathsf{pp} := ([\mathbf{A}]_2, [\mathbf{UA}]_2, [\mathbf{VA}]_2, [\mathbf{B}]_1, [\mathbf{B}^\top \mathbf{U}]_1, [\mathbf{B}^\top \mathbf{V}]_1)$.

5: $(n, t, \mathsf{CS}, \mathsf{st}_0) \leftarrow \mathcal{A}(\mathsf{pp})$.

6: Assert $\mathsf{CS} \subset [1, n]$.

7: Sample $\mathbf{K} \leftarrow \mathbb{Z}_p^{(\ell+1)\times(k+1)}$.

8: $(\mathbf{K}_1, \ldots, \mathbf{K}_n) \leftarrow \mathsf{Share}(\mathbf{K}, \mathbb{Z}_p^{(\ell+1)\times(k+1)}, n, t)$.

9: $\mathsf{vk} := [\mathbf{KA}]_2$.

10: **for** $i \in [1, n]$:

11:    $\mathsf{sk}_i := \mathbf{K}_i,\ \mathsf{vk}_i := [\mathbf{K}_i \mathbf{A}]_2$.

12: $([\mathbf{m}^*]_1, \Sigma^*, \mathsf{st}_1) \leftarrow \mathcal{A}^{\mathcal{O}^{\mathsf{PSign}(\cdot)}}\left(\mathsf{st}_0, \mathsf{vk}, \{\mathsf{sk}_i\}_{i \in \mathsf{CS}}, \{\mathsf{vk}_i\}_{i \in [1,n]}\right)$.

13: **return** $(\mathsf{Verify}(\mathsf{pp}, \mathsf{vk}, [\mathbf{m}^*]_1, \Sigma^*) \wedge |\mathsf{CS}| < t \wedge S_1([\mathbf{m}^*]_1) = \emptyset)$

$\mathcal{O}^{\mathsf{PSign}}(i, [\mathbf{m}]_1)$:

1: Assert $\left([\mathbf{m}]_1 \in \mathcal{M} \wedge i \in \mathsf{HS}\right)$.

2: $\mathbf{r}_i \leftarrow \mathbb{Z}_p^k$.

3: $\tau := \mathcal{H}([\mathbf{m}]_1)$.

4: $\sigma_1 := \left[\left(1\ \mathbf{m}^\top\right)\mathbf{K}_i + \mathbf{r}_i^\top \mathbf{B}^\top (\mathbf{U} + \tau \mathbf{V})]\right]_1$,

   $\sigma_2 := [\mathbf{r}_i^\top \mathbf{B}^\top]_1$,

   $\sigma_3 := [\tau \mathbf{r}_i^\top \mathbf{B}^\top]_1$,

   $\sigma_4 := [\tau]_2$.

5: $\Sigma_i := (\sigma_1, \sigma_2, \sigma_3, \sigma_4)$.

6: **if** $\Sigma_i \neq \bot$:

7:    $S_1([\mathbf{m}]_1) := S_1([\mathbf{m}]_1) \cup \{i\}$.

8: **return** Σ_i

$\mathsf{Verify}(\mathsf{pp}, \mathsf{vk}, [\mathbf{m}^*]_1, \Sigma^*)$:

1: Parse Σ^* as $(\widehat{\sigma}_1, \widehat{\sigma}_2, \widehat{\sigma}_3, \widehat{\sigma}_4)$.

2: **return** $\Big(e(\widehat{\sigma}_1, [\mathbf{A}]_2) = e\left(\left[\left(1\ \mathbf{m}^{*\top}\right)\right]_1, [\mathbf{KA}]_2\right) \cdot e(\widehat{\sigma}_2, [\mathbf{UA}]_2) \cdot e(\widehat{\sigma}_3, [\mathbf{VA}]_2)$

   $\wedge\ e(\widehat{\sigma}_2, \widehat{\sigma}_4) = e(\widehat{\sigma}_3, [1]_2)\Big)$

Fig. 4. Game$_0$.

$\mathsf{Verify}^*(\mathsf{pp}, \mathsf{vk}, [\mathbf{m}^*]_1, \Sigma^*)$:

1: Parse Σ^* as $(\widehat{\sigma}_1, \widehat{\sigma}_2, \widehat{\sigma}_3, \widehat{\sigma}_4 = [\tau^*]_2)$.

2: **return** $\Big(e(\widehat{\sigma}_1, [1]_2) = e\left([(1\ \mathbf{m}^{*\top})\mathbf{K}]_1, [1]_2\right) \cdot e(\widehat{\sigma}_2, [\mathbf{U} + \tau^*\mathbf{V}]_2) \wedge$

$e(\widehat{\sigma}_2, \widehat{\sigma}_4) = e(\widehat{\sigma}_3, [1]_2)\Big)$

Fig. 5. Modifications in Game_1.

Game 2. On receiving a partial signature query on a message $[\mathbf{m}_i]_1$, the query list is updated to include the message $[\mathbf{m}_i]_1$ along with its corresponding tag, $\tau_i := \mathcal{H}([\mathbf{m}_i]_1)$. The challenger aborts if an adversary can generate two tuples $([\mathbf{m}_i]_1, \tau_i)$, $([\mathbf{m}_j]_1, \tau_j)$ with $[\mathbf{m}_i]_1 \neq [\mathbf{m}_j]_1$ and $\tau_i = \tau_j$. By the collision resistance property of the underlying hash function we have,

$$|\mathbf{Adv}_1 - \mathbf{Adv}_2| \leq Adv_{\mathcal{H}}^{\mathsf{CRHF}}(\kappa) \ .$$

Game 3. In this game, we introduce randomness to the partial signatures by adding $\mu\mathbf{a}^\perp$ to each partial signature, where μ is chosen uniformly at random and the vector $\mathbf{a}^\perp$ is a non-zero vector in the kernel of $\mathbf{A}$. The new partial signatures satisfy the verification procedure as $\mathbf{a}^\perp\mathbf{A} = \mathbf{0}$. Figure 6 describes the new partial signing oracle, $\mathcal{O}^{\mathsf{PSign}^*}(.)$.

$\mathcal{O}^{\mathsf{PSign}^*}(i, [\mathbf{m}]_1)$:

1: Assert $\big([\mathbf{m}]_1 \in \mathcal{M} \wedge i \in \mathsf{HS}\big)$.

2: $\mathbf{r}_i \leftarrow \mathbb{Z}_p^k, \tau := \mathcal{H}([\mathbf{m}]_1), \mu \leftarrow \mathbb{Z}_p$.

3: $\sigma_1 := [(1\ \mathbf{m}^\top)\mathbf{K}_i + \mu\mathbf{a}^\perp + \mathbf{r}_i^\top\mathbf{B}^\top(\mathbf{U} + \tau\mathbf{V})]_1$,

$\sigma_2 := [\mathbf{r}_i^\top\mathbf{B}^\top]_1$,

$\sigma_3 := [\tau\mathbf{r}_i^\top\mathbf{B}^\top]_1$,

$\sigma_4 := [\tau]_2$.

4: $\Sigma_i := (\sigma_1, \sigma_2, \sigma_3, \sigma_4)$.

5: **if** $\Sigma_i \neq \bot$:

6: $\quad S_1([\mathbf{m}]_1) := S_1([\mathbf{m}]_1) \cup \{i\}$.

7: **return** Σ_i

Fig. 6. Modifications in Game_3.

Lemma 2. $|\mathbf{Adv}_2 - \mathbf{Adv}_3| \leq 2q Adv_{\mathcal{D}_k, \mathbb{G}_1, \mathcal{B}_1}^{\mathsf{MDDH}}(\kappa) + q/p$.

Proof. We prove this lemma through a reduction to the core lemma, Lemma 1. Let us assume there exists an adversary $\mathcal{A}$ that can distinguish the games

$\mathcal{B}_1^{\mathsf{Init}(\cdot),\mathcal{O}_b(\cdot),\mathcal{O}^*(\cdot),\mathcal{O}^{**}(\cdot)}$:

1: Assert $\big([\mathbf{m}]_1 \in \mathcal{M} \ \wedge \ i \in \mathsf{HS}\big)$.

2: $(\mathbf{A}, \mathbf{UA}, \mathbf{VA}, [\mathbf{B}]_1, [\mathbf{B}^\top \mathbf{U}]_1, [\mathbf{B}^\top \mathbf{V}]_1) \leftarrow \mathsf{Init}()$.

3: $\mathsf{pp} := ([\mathbf{A}]_2, [\mathbf{UA}]_2, [\mathbf{VA}]_2, [\mathbf{B}]_1, [\mathbf{B}^\top \mathbf{U}]_1, [\mathbf{B}^\top \mathbf{V}]_1)$.

4: $(n, t, \mathsf{CS}, \mathsf{sto}) \leftarrow \mathcal{A}(\mathsf{pp})$.

5: Assert $\mathsf{CS} \subset [1, n]$.

6: Sample $\mathbf{K} \leftarrow \mathbb{Z}_p^{(\ell+1) \times (k+1)}$.

7: $(\mathbf{K}_1, \ldots, \mathbf{K}_n) \leftarrow \mathsf{Share}(\mathbf{K}, \mathbb{Z}_p^{(\ell+1) \times (k+1)}, n, t)$.

8: $\mathsf{vk} := [\mathbf{KA}]_2$.

9: **for** $i \in [1, n]$:

10:    $\mathsf{sk}_i := \mathbf{K}_i$, $\mathsf{vk}_i := [\mathbf{K}_i \mathbf{A}]_2$.

11: $(\mathbf{m}^*, \Sigma^*, \mathsf{st}_1) \leftarrow \mathcal{A}^{\mathcal{O}^{\mathsf{PSign}^*}(\cdot)}(\mathsf{sto}, \mathsf{vk}, \{\mathsf{sk}_i\}_{i \in \mathsf{CS}}, \{\mathsf{vk}_i\}_{i \in [1,n]})$.

12: Parse Σ^* as $(\hat{\sigma}_1, \hat{\sigma}_2, \hat{\sigma}_3, \hat{\sigma}_4)$

13: **if** $(\mathsf{Verify}^*(\mathsf{pp}, \mathsf{vk}, [\mathbf{m}^*]_1, \Sigma^*) \ \wedge \ |\mathsf{CS}| < t \ \wedge \ S_1([\mathbf{m}^*]_1) = \emptyset)$:

14:    result := true

15: **else** : result := false

16: **return** $\tilde{b} \leftarrow \mathcal{A}(\mathsf{result})$

$\mathcal{O}^{\mathsf{PSign}^*}(i, [\mathbf{m}]_1)$:

1: $\tau := \mathcal{H}([\mathbf{m}]_1)$.

2: $(val_1, val_2) \leftarrow \mathcal{O}_b(\tau)$.

3: $\sigma_1 := \left[\big(1 \ \mathbf{m}^\top\big) \mathbf{K}_i\right]_1 \cdot val_1$.
   $\sigma_2 := val_2$,
   $\sigma_3 := [\tau]_1 \cdot val_2$,
   $\sigma_4 := [\tau]_2$.

4: $\Sigma_i := (\sigma_1, \sigma_2, \sigma_3, \sigma_4)$.

5: **if** $\Sigma_i \neq \perp$:

6:    $S_1([\mathbf{m}]_1) := S_1([\mathbf{m}]_1) \cup \{i\}$.

7: **return** Σ_i

$\mathsf{Verify}^*(\mathsf{pp}, \mathsf{vk}, [\mathbf{m}^*]_1, \Sigma^*)$:

1: Parse Σ^* as $(\hat{\sigma}_1, \hat{\sigma}_2, \hat{\sigma}_3, \hat{\sigma}_4)$.

2: **return** $\Big(e(\hat{\sigma}_1, [1]_2) = e\left(\left[\big(1 \ \mathbf{m}^{*\top}\big) \mathbf{K}\right]_1, [1]_2\right) \cdot e(\hat{\sigma}_2, \mathcal{O}^*(\hat{\sigma}_4))$

$\wedge \ e(\hat{\sigma}_2, \hat{\sigma}_4) = e(\hat{\sigma}_3, [1]_2)\Big)$

Fig. 7. Reduction to the core lemma in Lemma 1.

Game_2 and Game_3, we can use it to build an adversary $\mathcal{B}_1$, defined in Fig. 7, which breaks the core lemma, Lemma 1. The adversary $\mathcal{B}_1$ has access to four oracles, $\mathsf{Init}(\cdot), \mathcal{O}_b(\cdot), \mathcal{O}^*(\cdot), \mathcal{O}^{**}(\cdot)$, however in this reduction, we only use the first three oracles, defined as follows:

Oracle $\mathsf{Init}(\cdot)$: The oracle Init provides the set of public parameters pp.
Oracle $\mathcal{O}_b(\cdot)$: On the i-th query to this oracle on $[\tau]_1$, it outputs $\left([b\mu\mathbf{a}^\perp + \mathbf{r}_i^\top \mathbf{B}^\top (\mathbf{U} + \tau \cdot \mathbf{V})]_1, [\mathbf{r}_i^\top \mathbf{B}^\top]_1\right)$ depending on a random bit b.
Oracle $\mathcal{O}^*(\cdot)$: On input $[\tau^*]_2$, it returns $[\mathbf{U} + \tau^* \mathbf{V}]_2$.

When the lemma challenger selects the challenge bit as $b = 0$, it leads to the game Game_2, and when $b = 1$, it results in the game Game_3. All the other values are simulated perfectly. Thus, $|\mathbf{Adv}_2 - \mathbf{Adv}_3| \leq Adv_{\mathcal{D}_k, \mathsf{ABSGen}, \mathcal{B}_1}^{\mathsf{Core}}(\kappa)$ holds and therefore we have,

$$|\mathbf{Adv}_2 - \mathbf{Adv}_3| \leq 2q Adv_{\mathcal{D}_k, \mathbb{G}_1, \mathcal{B}}^{\mathsf{MDDH}}(\kappa) + q/p \cdot \qquad \qquad \square$$

Game 4. In this game, we apply the modifications described in Fig. 8. Shamir secret sharing (see Definition 1) ensures that $(\mathbf{K}_1, \ldots, \mathbf{K}_n)$ in Game_3 and $(\widetilde{\mathbf{K}}_1, \ldots, \widetilde{\mathbf{K}}_n)$ in Game_4 have identical distributions. W.l.o.g, $\mathbf{K}_i$ in Game_3 and $\widetilde{\mathbf{K}}_i$ in Game_4 are identically distributed. In Game_4, on the other hand, $\widetilde{\mathbf{K}}_i$ and $\mathbf{K}_i = \widetilde{\mathbf{K}}_i - \mathbf{u}_i \mathbf{a}^\perp$ are identically distributed. Combining these observations, it follows that $\mathbf{K}_i$ in Game_3 and $\mathbf{K}_i$ in Game_4 are identically distributed for all $i \in [1, n]$. Consequently, it can be deduced that $\mathbf{K}$ in Game_3 and $\mathbf{K} + \mathbf{u}_0 \mathbf{a}^\perp$ in Game_4 are identically distributed. Therefore, this change is just a conceptual change and we have,

$$|\mathbf{Adv}_3 - \mathbf{Adv}_4| = 0 \cdot$$

Now, we give a bound on $\mathbf{Adv}_4$ via an information-theoretic argument. We first consider the information about $\mathbf{u}_0$ (and subsequently $\{\mathbf{u}_i\}_{i \in [1,n] \backslash \mathsf{CS}}$) leaked from vk (and subsequently $\{\mathsf{vk}_i\}_{i \in [1,n]}$) and partial signing queries:

- $\mathsf{vk} := [\mathbf{KA}]_2 = \left[\widetilde{\mathbf{K}}\mathbf{A}\right]_2$ and $\mathsf{vk}_i := [\mathbf{K}_i \mathbf{A}]_2 = \left[\widetilde{\mathbf{K}}_i \mathbf{A}\right]_2$ for all $i \in [1, n]$.
- The output of the jth partial signature query on $(i, [\mathbf{m}]_1)$ for $[\mathbf{m}]_1 \neq [\mathbf{m}^*]_1$ completely hides $\{\mathbf{u}_i\}_{i \in [1,n] \backslash \mathsf{CS}}$ (and subsequently $\mathbf{u}_0$ as the adversary has only $|\mathsf{CS}|$ many $\mathbf{u}_i$ with $|\mathsf{CS}| < t$), since

$$\left(1 \ \mathbf{m}^\top\right) \mathbf{K}_i + \mu_j \mathbf{a}^\perp = \left(1 \ \mathbf{m}^\top\right) \widetilde{\mathbf{K}}_i + \left(1 \ \mathbf{m}^\top\right) \mathbf{u}_i \mathbf{a}^\perp + \mu_j \mathbf{a}^\perp \ .$$

distributed identically to $\left(1 \ \mathbf{m}^\top\right) \widetilde{\mathbf{K}}_i + \mu_j \mathbf{a}^\perp$. This is because $\mu_j \mathbf{a}^\perp$ already hides $\left(1 \ \mathbf{m}^\top\right) \mathbf{u}_i \mathbf{a}^\perp$ for uniformly random $\mu_j \leftarrow \mathbb{Z}_p$.

The only way to successfully convince the verification to accept a signature Σ^* on $\mathbf{m}^*$, the adversary must correctly compute $\left(1 \ \mathbf{m}^{*\top}\right) (\mathbf{K} + \mathbf{u}_0 \mathbf{a}^\perp)$ and thus $\left(1 \ \mathbf{m}^{*\top}\right) \mathbf{u}_0$. Observe that, $\{\mathbf{u}_i\}_{i \in [1,n] \backslash \mathsf{CS}}$ (and thereby $\mathbf{u}_0$) are completely hidden to the adversary, $\left(1 \ \mathbf{m}^{*\top}\right) \mathbf{u}_0$ is uniformly random from $\mathbb{Z}_p$ from the adversary's viewpoint. Therefore, $\mathbf{Adv}_4 = 1/p$. $\qquad \square$

$\boxed{G_3(\kappa):}$ $\boxed{G_4(\kappa):}$

1: $\mathcal{G} \leftarrow \mathsf{ABSGen}(1^\kappa)$,

2: $\mathbf{A}, \mathbf{B} \leftarrow \mathcal{D}_k$,

3: $\mathbf{U}, \mathbf{V} \leftarrow \mathbb{Z}_p^{(k+1)\times(k+1)}$.

4: $\mathsf{pp} := ([\mathbf{A}]_2, [\mathbf{U}\mathbf{A}]_2, [\mathbf{V}\mathbf{A}]_2, [\mathbf{B}]_1, [\mathbf{B}^\top\mathbf{U}]_1, [\mathbf{B}^\top\mathbf{V}]_1)$.

5: $(n, t, \mathsf{CS}, \mathsf{st}_0) \leftarrow \mathcal{A}(\mathsf{pp})$.

6: Assert $\mathsf{CS} \subset [1, n]$.

7: Sample $\mathbf{K} \leftarrow \mathbb{Z}_p^{(\ell+1)\times(k+1)}$.

8: $(\mathbf{K}_1, \ldots, \mathbf{K}_n) \leftarrow \mathsf{Share}(\mathbf{K}, \mathbb{Z}_p^{(\ell+1)\times(k+1)}, n, t)$

   $\boxed{\text{Sample } \mathbf{u}_0 \leftarrow \mathbf{Z}_p^{\ell+1}}$

   $\boxed{(\mathbf{u}_1, \ldots, \mathbf{u}_n) \leftarrow \mathsf{Share}(\mathbf{u}_0, \mathbb{Z}_p^{(\ell+1)}, n, t)}$

   $\boxed{(\widetilde{\mathbf{K}}_1, \ldots, \widetilde{\mathbf{K}}_n) \leftarrow \mathsf{Share}(\mathbf{K}, \mathbb{Z}_p^{(\ell+1)\times(k+1)}, n, t)}$

   $\boxed{\mathbf{K}_i := \widetilde{\mathbf{K}}_i + \mathbf{u}_i \mathbf{a}^\perp, \forall i \in [1, n]}$

9: $\mathsf{vk} := [\mathbf{K}\mathbf{A}]_2$.

10: **for** $i \in [1, n]$:

11:     $\mathsf{sk}_i := \mathbf{K}_i, \mathsf{vk}_i := [\mathbf{K}_i\mathbf{A}]_2$.

12: $([\mathbf{m}^*]_1, \Sigma^*, \mathsf{st}_1) \leftarrow \mathcal{A}^{\mathcal{O}^{\mathsf{PSign}}(\cdot)}(\mathsf{st}_0, \mathsf{vk}, \{\mathsf{sk}_i\}_{i\in\mathsf{CS}}, \{\mathsf{vk}_i\}_{i\in[1,n]})$.

13: **return** $\left(\mathsf{Verify}^*(\mathsf{pp}, \mathsf{vk}, [\mathbf{m}^*]_1, \Sigma^*) \wedge |\mathsf{CS}| < t \wedge S_1([\mathbf{m}^*]_1) = \emptyset\right)$

$\mathsf{Verify}^*(\mathsf{pp}, \mathsf{vk}, [\mathbf{m}^*]_1, \Sigma^*):$

1: Parse Σ^* as $(\widehat{\sigma}_1, \widehat{\sigma}_2, \widehat{\sigma}_3, \widehat{\sigma}_4 = [\tau^*]_2)$.

2: **return** $\left(e(\widehat{\sigma}_1, [1]_2) = e\left(\left[\left(1\ \mathbf{m}^{*\top}\right)(\mathbf{K} + \boxed{\mathbf{u}_0\mathbf{a}^\perp})\right]_1, [1]_2\right) e(\widehat{\sigma}_2, [\mathbf{U} + \tau^*\mathbf{V}]_2)\right.$

$\left. \wedge\ e(\widehat{\sigma}_2, \widehat{\sigma}_4) = e(\widehat{\sigma}_3, [1]_2)\right)$

Fig. 8. Modification from Game$_3$ to Game$_4$.

Theorem 2. *Under the $\mathcal{D}_k$-MDDH Assumption in $\mathbb{G}_1$ and $\mathcal{D}_k$-KerMDH Assumption in $\mathbb{G}_2$, our Threshold Structure-Preserving Signature construction achieves* TS-UF-1 *security against an efficient adversary making at most q partial signature queries.*

Proof Sketch. The difference between TS-UF-0 and TS-UF-1 lies in the fact that, in the latter model, an adversary can request $\mathcal{O}^{\mathsf{PSign}}(\cdot)$ queries on $[\mathbf{m}^*]_1$ for which it aims to forge a signature. The natural restriction in Fig. 1 is expressed as $|S_1([\mathbf{m}^*]_1)| < t - |\mathsf{CS}|$, where t is the threshold value and the corrupted parties CS are fixed at the beginning of the game. As this security model allows partial signature oracle queries on $[\mathbf{m}^*]_1$, we next explore the changes we need to make on the proof of Theorem 1.

Game$_0$, Game$_1$ and Game$_2$ stay the same. To handle TS-UF-1 adversaries, we introduce an additional game Game$_2'$ to handle partial signature queries on the forged message. In Game$_2'$, the challenger makes a list of all the partial signature queries and guesses the message on which forgery will be done. However, the guess will be made on the list of partial signature queries. More precisely, let $\mathcal{A}$ make partial signature queries on $[\mathbf{m}_1]_1, \ldots, [\mathbf{m}_\mathcal{Q}]_1$ s.t. $\mathcal{Q} \leq q$, the challenger of Game$_2'$ rightly guesses the forged message with $1/\mathcal{Q}$ probability which introduces a degradation in the advantage. This small yet powerful modification allows the challenger in Game$_3$ to add a uniformly random quantity μ to partial signature oracle queries on $[\mathbf{m}]_1 \neq [\mathbf{m}^*]_1$. This concept is formulated by adding an additional line between lines number 2 and 3 in Fig. 6. In particular, the new Game$_3'$ (See Fig. 9) would set $\mu = 0$ if $[\mathbf{m}]_1 = [\mathbf{m}^*]_1$. Next, we give an intuitive explanation of the indistinguishability of Game$_2'$ and Game$_3'$ which basically is a modification of the proof of Lemma 2.

$\mathcal{O}^{\mathsf{PSign}^*}(i, [\mathbf{m}]_1)$:

1: assert $\big([\mathbf{m}]_1 \in \mathcal{M} \;\wedge\; i \in \mathsf{HS}\big)$
2: $\mathbf{r}_i \leftarrow \mathbb{Z}_p^k, \tau := \mathcal{H}([\mathbf{m}]_1), \mu \leftarrow \mathbb{Z}_p$ $\boxed{\text{If } [\mathbf{m}]_1 = [\mathbf{m}^*]_1, \text{ set } \mu := 0}$
3: $\sigma_1 := \big[(1\ \mathbf{m}^\top)\,\mathbf{K}_i + \mu \mathbf{a}^\perp + \mathbf{r}_i^\top \mathbf{B}^\top(\mathbf{U} + \tau \cdot \mathbf{V})\big]_1$,
    $\sigma_2 := [\mathbf{r}_i^\top \mathbf{B}^\top]_1$,
    $\sigma_3 := [\tau \mathbf{r}_i^\top \mathbf{B}^\top]_1$,
    $\sigma_4 := [\tau]_2$
4: $\Sigma_i := (\sigma_1, \sigma_2, \sigma_3, \sigma_4)$
5: if $\Sigma_i \neq \bot$:
6:     $S_1([\mathbf{m}]_1) := S_1([\mathbf{m}]_1) \cup \{i\}$
7: return Σ_i

Fig. 9. Game$_3'$ in the proof of Theorem 2.

The novelty of this research lies in the need to simulate partial signature queries on the forged message $[\mathbf{m}^*]_1$, a challenge not addressed in previous works like [51,52] upon which this study is based. It's important to mention that an extra oracle, termed $\mathcal{O}^{**}(\cdot)$, is sufficient for our objectives. On any partial signature query on the forged message $[\mathbf{m}^*]_1$, the reduction calls $\mathcal{O}^{**}([\tau^*]_1)$ for $\tau^* \leftarrow \mathcal{H}([\mathbf{m}^*]_1)$. Next we see that a single query to $\mathcal{O}^{**}([\tau^*]_1)$ is sufficient to handle multiple partial signature queries on $[\mathbf{m}^*]_1$. In particular, given a partial signature oracle query on $(i, [\mathbf{m}^*]_1)$, the reduction uses $\mathcal{O}^{**}(\cdot)$ of the so-called core-lemma (in Lemma 1) to get $\mathbf{X} = [\mathbf{B}^\top (\mathbf{U} + \tau^* \mathbf{V})]_1$, where $\tau^* = \mathcal{H}([\mathbf{m}^*]_1)$. The reduction then replies with $\left(\left[(1\ \mathbf{m}^{*\top}) \right]_1 \mathbf{K}_i + \mathbf{r}^\top \cdot \mathbf{X}, [\mathbf{r}^\top \mathbf{B}^\top]_1, [\tau^* \mathbf{r}^\top \mathbf{B}^\top]_1, [\tau^*]_2 \right)$ as a partial signature response to $\mathcal{A}$. Thus, a single call to $\mathcal{O}^{**}(\cdot)$ suffices to handle all partial signature queries on $[\mathbf{m}^*]_1$.

We define Game_4 as being identical to the proof of Theorem 1. In fact, the argument for the indistinguishability of Game_3 and Game_4 from the proof of Theorem 1 applies here as well. The argument that $\mathbf{Adv}_4$ is negligible however requires a small modification. Similar to the proof of Theorem 1, we can show that all verification keys vk and $\{\mathsf{vk}_i\}_{i \in [1,n]}$ stay the same. Furthermore, all partial signature queries on $[\mathbf{m}]_1 \neq [\mathbf{m}^*]_1$ do not leak any information about $\{\mathbf{u}_i\}_{i \in [1,n] \backslash \mathsf{CS}}$. Since, partial signature oracle queries are allowed on $[\mathbf{m}^*]_1$, observe that at most $\{\mathbf{u}_i\}_{i \in S_1([\mathbf{m}^*]_1)}$ are leaked to the adversary. To summarise, an adversary in $\mathsf{TS\text{-}UF\text{-}1}$ gets at most $\{\mathbf{u}_i\}_{i \in S_1([\mathbf{m}^*]_1) \sqcup \mathsf{CS}}$ even when it is unbounded. Due to the natural restriction, $|S_1([\mathbf{m}^*]_1)| + |\mathsf{CS}| < t$ ensures that $\mathbf{u}_0$ stays completely hidden to the adversary. Thus, $(1\ \mathbf{m}^{*\top})\,\mathbf{u}_0$ is uniformly random from $\mathbb{Z}_p$ from the adversary's viewpoint. Therefore, $\mathbf{Adv}_4 \leq 1/p$. $\qquad\square$

Theorem 3. *Under the $\mathcal{D}_k$-MDDH Assumption in $\mathbb{G}_1$ and $\mathcal{D}_k$-KerMDH Assumption in $\mathbb{G}_2$, the proposed Threshold Structure-Preserving Signature construction in Fig. 3 achieves $\mathsf{adp\text{-}TS\text{-}UF\text{-}1}$ security against an efficient adversary making at most q partial signature queries.*

Proof. The difference between $\mathsf{TS\text{-}UF\text{-}1}$ and $\mathsf{adp\text{-}TS\text{-}UF\text{-}1}$ is that an adversary of the later model has access to $\mathcal{O}^{\mathsf{Corrupt}}(.)$ oracle and can corrupt the honest signers, adaptively. As per Fig. 1, an $\mathsf{adp\text{-}TS\text{-}UF\text{-}1}$ adversary proposes a corrupted set CS at the start of the game which it updates incrementally as the game progresses. At the time of forgery, the natural restriction in Fig. 1 formulates as $|S_1([\mathbf{m}^*]_1)| < t - |\mathsf{CS}|$, where t is the threshold value and CS contains the list of corrupted signers at the forgery phase. Given that this security model permits an adversary to obtain the secret keys of users it may have queried using the $\mathcal{O}^{\mathsf{PSign}}(.)$ oracle in the past, our next step involves investigating the main modifications required for the proof in Theorem 2.

Game_0, Game_1, Game_2, and Game_2' stay the same. In the proof of Theorem 2, we also have showed that Game_2' and Game_3' to be indistinguishable due to the so-called core lemma, Lemma 1. We reuse the reduction in Fig. 7 towards this purpose. The reduction in Fig. 7 samples $\mathbf{K} \leftarrow \mathbb{Z}_p^{(\ell+1) \times (k+1)}$ and generates $(\mathbf{K}_1, \ldots, \mathbf{K}_n) \leftarrow \mathsf{Share}(\mathbf{K}, \mathbb{Z}_p^{(\ell+1) \times (k+1)}, n, t)$. Recall that, the $\mathsf{adp\text{-}TS\text{-}UF\text{-}1}$ adversary $\mathcal{A}$ of Lemma 2 corrupts a party $i \in [1, n]$ adaptively. Since the reduction of Lemma 2 already knows $\mathbf{K}_i$ in plain, it can handle the $\mathcal{O}^{\mathsf{Corrupt}}(.)$ oracle queries quite naturally.

The indistinguishability of Game_3 and Game_4 are argued exactly the same as in Theorem 2. We now focus on $\mathbf{Adv}_4$. In Game_4, the adversary gets to update CS adaptively. Intuitively, all $\mathbf{K}_i$ are independently sampled. Giving out a few of them to the adversary does not change the adversary's view. In the proof of Theorem 2, we already have managed to address partial signature queries on forged message. Except a few details, this ensures our proof will work out. We next give a formal argument.

We prove this theorem through a series of games and we use $\mathbf{Adv}_i$ to denote the advantage of the adversary $\mathcal{A}$ in winning the Game i. The games are described below.

Game 0. This is the adp-TS-UF-1 security game described in Definition 8. As shown in Fig. 10, an adversary $\mathcal{A}$ after receiving the set of public parameters, pp, returns (n, t, CS), where n, t and CS represents the total number of signers, the threshold, and the set of corrupted signers, respectively. The adversary can query the partial signing oracle $\mathcal{O}^{\mathsf{PSign}}(\cdot)$ to receive partial signatures. Let $\mathcal{Q}$ represent the number of distinct messages where partial signing queries are made. In the end, the adversary outputs a message $[\mathbf{m}^*]_1$ and a forged signature Σ^*.

Game 1. We modify the verification procedure to the one described in Fig. 11. Consider any forged message/signature pair $([\mathbf{m}^*]_1, \Sigma^* = (\hat{\sigma}_1, \hat{\sigma}_2, \hat{\sigma}_3, \hat{\sigma}_4))$ where $e(\hat{\sigma}_2, \hat{\sigma}_4) = e(\hat{\sigma}_3, [1]_2)$, $|\mathsf{CS}| < t$ and $S_1([\mathbf{m}^*]_1) = \emptyset$. Note that if the pair $([\mathbf{m}^*]_1, \Sigma^*)$ meets the $\mathsf{Verify}^*(\cdot)$ conditions, outlined in Fig. 11, it also satisfies $\mathsf{Verify}(\cdot)$ procedure, described in Fig. 10. This is primarily due to the fact that:

$$e(\hat{\sigma}_1, [\mathbf{A}]_2) = e\left([(1\ \mathbf{m}^{*\top})]_1, [\mathbf{KA}]_2\right) \cdot e(\hat{\sigma}_2, [\mathbf{UA}]_2) \cdot e(\hat{\sigma}_3, [\mathbf{VA}]_2)$$
$$\Longleftarrow e(\hat{\sigma}_1, [1]_2) = e([(1\ \mathbf{m}^{*\top})]_1, [\mathbf{K}]_2) \cdot e(\hat{\sigma}_2, [\mathbf{U}]_2) \cdot e(\hat{\sigma}_3, [\mathbf{V}]_2)$$
$$\Longleftrightarrow e(\hat{\sigma}_1, [1]_2) = e([(1\ \mathbf{m}^{*\top})\ \mathbf{K}]_1, [1]_2) \cdot e(\hat{\sigma}_2, [\mathbf{U} + \tau^*\mathbf{V}]_2) \cdot$$

Assume there exists a message/signature pair $([\mathbf{m}^*]_1, \Sigma^* = (\hat{\sigma}_1, \hat{\sigma}_2, \hat{\sigma}_3, \hat{\sigma}_4))$ that satisfies $\mathsf{Verify}(.)$ and not $\mathsf{Verify}^*(.)$, then we can compute a non-zero vector $\mathbf{c}$ in the kernel of $\mathbf{A}$ as follows:

$$\mathbf{c} := \hat{\sigma}_1 - \left([(1\ \mathbf{m}^{*\top})\ \mathbf{K}]_1 + \hat{\sigma}_2\mathbf{U} + \hat{\sigma}_3\mathbf{V}\right) \in \mathbb{G}_1^{1 \times (k+1)}.$$

According to $\mathcal{D}_k$-KerMDH assumption over $\mathbb{G}_2$ described in Definition 5, such a vector $\mathbf{c}$ is hard to compute. Thus,

$$|\mathbf{Adv}_0 - \mathbf{Adv}_1| \leq Adv_{\mathcal{D}_k, \mathbb{G}_2, \mathcal{B}_0}^{\mathsf{KerMDH}}(\kappa) \cdot$$

Game 2. On receiving a partial signature query on a message $[\mathbf{m}_i]_1$, a list is updated with the message $[\mathbf{m}_i]_1$ and the corresponding tag $\tau_i := \mathcal{H}([\mathbf{m}_i]_1)$. The challenger aborts if an adversary can generate two tuples $([\mathbf{m}_i]_1, \tau_i)$, $([\mathbf{m}_j]_1, \tau_j)$ with $[\mathbf{m}_i]_1 \neq [\mathbf{m}_j]_1$ and $\tau_i = \tau_j$. By the collision resistance property of the underlying hash function we have:

$$|\mathbf{Adv}_1 - \mathbf{Adv}_2| \leq Adv_{\mathcal{H}}^{\mathsf{CRHF}}(\kappa) \cdot$$

$G_0(\kappa)$:

1: $\mathcal{G} \leftarrow \mathsf{ABSGen}(1^\kappa)$,

2: $\mathbf{A}, \mathbf{B} \leftarrow \mathcal{D}_k$,

3: $\mathbf{U}, \mathbf{V} \leftarrow \mathbb{Z}_p^{(k+1)\times(k+1)}$.

4: $\mathsf{pp} := ([\mathbf{A}]_2, [\mathbf{UA}]_2, [\mathbf{VA}]_2, [\mathbf{B}]_1, [\mathbf{B}^\top\mathbf{U}]_1, [\mathbf{B}^\top\mathbf{V}]_1)$.

5: $(n, t, \mathsf{CS}, \mathsf{st}_0) \leftarrow \mathcal{A}(\mathsf{pp})$.

6: Assert $\mathsf{CS} \subset [1, n]$.

7: Sample $\mathbf{K} \leftarrow \mathbb{Z}_p^{(\ell+1)\times(k+1)}$.

8: $(\mathbf{K}_1, \ldots, \mathbf{K}_n) \leftarrow \mathsf{Share}(\mathbf{K}, \mathbb{Z}_p^{(\ell+1)\times(k+1)}, n, t)$.

9: $\mathsf{vk} := [\mathbf{KA}]_2$.

10: $\mathsf{sk}_i := \mathbf{K}_i$, $\mathsf{vk}_i := [\mathbf{K}_i\mathbf{A}]_2$ for $i \in [1, n]$.

11: $([\mathbf{m}^*]_1, \Sigma^*, \mathsf{st}_1) \leftarrow \mathcal{A}^{\mathcal{O}^{\mathsf{PSign}}(\cdot), \mathcal{O}^{\mathsf{Corrupt}}(\cdot)}(\mathsf{st}_0, \mathsf{vk}, \{\mathsf{sk}_i\}_{i\in\mathsf{CS}}, \{\mathsf{vk}_i\}_{i\in[1,n]})$.

12: **return** $\left(\mathsf{Verify}(\mathsf{pp}, \mathsf{vk}, [\mathbf{m}^*]_1, \Sigma^*) \wedge |\mathsf{CS}| < t \wedge S_1([\mathbf{m}^*]_1) = \emptyset \right)$

$\mathcal{O}^{\mathsf{PSign}}(i, [\mathbf{m}]_1)$:

1: Assert $\left([\mathbf{m}]_1 \in \mathcal{M} \wedge i \in \mathsf{HS}\right)$.

2: $\mathbf{r}_i \leftarrow \mathbb{Z}_p^k$.

3: $\tau := \mathcal{H}([\mathbf{m}]_1)$.

4: $\sigma_1 := \left[\left(1\ \mathbf{m}^\top\right)\mathbf{K}_i + \mathbf{r}_i^\top\mathbf{B}^\top(\mathbf{U} + \tau\mathbf{V}) \right]_1$.

   $\sigma_2 := [\mathbf{r}_i^\top\mathbf{B}^\top]_1$,

   $\sigma_3 := [\tau\mathbf{r}_i^\top\mathbf{B}^\top]_1$,

   $\sigma_4 := [\tau]_2$.

5: $\Sigma_i := (\sigma_1, \sigma_2, \sigma_3, \sigma_4)$.

6: **if** $\Sigma_i \neq \bot$:

7:    $S_1([\mathbf{m}]_1) := S_1([\mathbf{m}]_1) \cup \{i\}$.

8: **return** Σ_i

$\mathcal{O}^{\mathsf{Corrupt}}(j)$:

1: $\mathsf{CS} \leftarrow \mathsf{CS} \cup \{j\}$

2: $\mathsf{HS} \leftarrow \mathsf{CS} \setminus \{j\}$

3: **return** sk_j

$\mathsf{Verify}(\mathsf{pp}, \mathsf{vk}, [\mathbf{m}^*]_1, \Sigma^*)$:

1: Parse Σ^* as $(\hat\sigma_1, \hat\sigma_2, \hat\sigma_3, \hat\sigma_4)$.

2: **return** $\left(e(\hat\sigma_1, [\mathbf{A}]_2) = e\left(\left[\left(1\ \mathbf{m}^{*\top}\right)\right]_1, [\mathbf{KA}]_2 \right) \cdot e(\hat\sigma_2, [\mathbf{UA}]_2) \cdot e(\hat\sigma_3, [\mathbf{VA}]_2) \right.$

   $\left. \wedge\ e(\hat\sigma_2, \hat\sigma_4) = e(\hat\sigma_3, [1]_2) \right)$

Fig. 10. Game$_0$.

Verify*(pp, vk, $[\mathbf{m}^*]_1, \Sigma^*$):

1: Parse Σ^* as $(\widehat{\sigma}_1, \widehat{\sigma}_2, \widehat{\sigma}_3, \widehat{\sigma}_4 = [\tau^*]_2)$.

2: **return** $\Big(e(\widehat{\sigma}_1, [1]_2) = e\left([(1\ \mathbf{m}^{*\top})\, \mathbf{K}]_1, [1]_2\right) \cdot e(\widehat{\sigma}_2, [\mathbf{U} + \tau^*\mathbf{V}]_2) \ \wedge$

$$e(\widehat{\sigma}_2, \widehat{\sigma}_4) = e(\widehat{\sigma}_3, [1]_2) \Big)$$

Fig. 11. Modifications in Game$_1$.

Game 2'. In Game$_2'$, the challenger randomly chooses an index $j^* \leftarrow [1, Q]$ as its guess of the message on which the forgery will be done. This game is the same as Game 2 except that the challenger aborts the game immediately if forged message $[\mathbf{m}^*]_1 \neq [\mathbf{m}_{j^*}]_1$.

The challenger of Game$_2'$ rightly guesses the forged message $[\mathbf{m}^*]_1$ with $1/\mathcal{Q}$ probability which introduces a degradation in the advantage of Game$_2'$: $\mathbf{Adv}_{2'} = \frac{1}{\mathcal{Q}}\mathbf{Adv}_2$.

Game 3'. This game is same as Game$_2'$ except we introduce randomness to the partial signatures by adding $\mu a^\perp$ to each partial signature query on all messages $[\mathbf{m}]_1$ except $[\mathbf{m}]_1^*$ on which the forgery is done.

$\mathcal{O}^{\mathsf{PSign}^*}(i, [\mathbf{m}]_1)$:

1: assert $\left([\mathbf{m}]_1 \in \mathcal{M} \ \wedge \ i \in \mathsf{HS}\right)$

2: $\mathbf{r}_i \leftarrow \mathbb{Z}_p^k, \tau := \mathcal{H}([\mathbf{m}]_1), \mu \leftarrow \mathbb{Z}_p$ $\boxed{\text{If } [\mathbf{m}]_1 = [\mathbf{m}^*]_1, \text{ set } \mu := 0}$

3: $\sigma_1 := \left[(1\ \mathbf{m}^\top)\, \mathbf{K}_i + \mu a^\perp + \mathbf{r}_i^\top \mathbf{B}^\top (\mathbf{U} + \tau \cdot \mathbf{V})\right]_1$,

$\quad \sigma_2 := [\mathbf{r}_i^\top \mathbf{B}^\top]_1$,

$\quad \sigma_3 := [\tau \mathbf{r}_i^\top \mathbf{B}^\top]_1$,

$\quad \sigma_4 := [\tau]_2$

4: $\Sigma_i := (\sigma_1, \sigma_2, \sigma_3, \sigma_4)$

5: **if** $\Sigma_i \neq \perp$:

6: $\quad S_1([\mathbf{m}]_1) := S_1([\mathbf{m}]_1) \cup \{i\}$

7: **return** Σ_i

Fig. 12. Game$_3'$ in the proof of Theorem 3.

We show that, we can make a reduction algorithm $\mathcal{B}$ for the so-called core-lemma (in Lemma 1) using $\mathcal{A}$. At the start of the game, $\mathcal{B}$ randomly chooses an index $j^* \leftarrow [1, Q]$ as its guess of the message on which forgery will be done. If $[\mathbf{m}^*]_1 \neq [\mathbf{m}_{j^*}]_1 = [\mathbf{m}^*]_1$, $\mathcal{B}$ aborts. Otherwise, $\mathcal{B}$ outputs $\mathcal{A}$'s output as it is. In particular, $\mathcal{B}$ does the following:

1. $\mathcal{B}$ receives pp from the challenger.
2. $\mathcal{B}$ samples $\mathbf{K} \leftarrow \mathbb{Z}_p^{(\ell+1)\times(k+1)}$.
3. $\mathcal{B}$ then secret shares $\mathbf{K}$ into $(\mathbf{K}_1,\ldots,\mathbf{K}_n) \leftarrow \mathsf{Share}(\mathbf{K}, \mathbb{Z}_p^{(\ell+1)\times(k+1)}, n, t)$.
4. On a $\mathcal{O}^{\mathsf{Corrupt}}(.)$ oracle query on $j \in [1,n]$, $\mathcal{B}$ returns $\mathbf{K}_j$.
5. $\mathcal{B}$ simulates the partial signature query on $(i, [\mathbf{m}]_1)$ as following:
   - If $[\mathbf{m}]_1 = [\mathbf{m}^*]_1$, it makes a query (i, τ^*) on $\mathcal{O}^{**}(.)$ where $\tau^* \leftarrow \mathcal{H}([\mathbf{m}^*]_1)$.
     - Let $\mathcal{B}$ receives val as the response of the above queries.
     - $\mathcal{B}$ samples $\mathbf{r}_i \leftarrow \mathbb{Z}_p^k$ and returns $\Sigma_i := ([(1\ \mathbf{m}^\top)\,\mathbf{K}_i]_1 \cdot \mathbf{r}_i^\top \cdot val, \mathbf{r}_i^\top \cdot val, \tau \cdot \mathbf{r}_i^\top \cdot val, [\tau]_2)$ to $\mathcal{A}$ as the partial signature.
   - If $[\mathbf{m}]_1 \neq [\mathbf{m}^*]_1$, it makes a query (i, τ) on $\mathcal{O}^b(\cdot)$, where $\tau \leftarrow \mathcal{H}([\mathbf{m}]_1)$.
     - Let $\mathcal{B}$ receives (val_1, val_2) as the response of the above queries.
     - It returns $\Sigma_i := ([(1\ \mathbf{m}^\top)\,\mathbf{K}_i]_1 \cdot val_1, val_2, \tau \cdot val_2, [\tau]_2)$ to $\mathcal{A}$ as the partial signature.
6. On $\mathsf{Verify}^*(.)$ on $(\mathsf{vk}, [\mathbf{m}^*]_1, \Sigma^*)$, $\mathcal{B}$ queries on $\mathcal{O}^*(\cdot)$ on $[\tau^*]_2$ where $\tau^* \leftarrow \mathcal{H}([\mathbf{m}^*]_1)$.
   - Let Σ^* is $(\sigma_1, \sigma_2, \sigma_3, \sigma_4 = [\tau^*]_2)$.
   - Let $\mathcal{B}$ receives val as the response of the above query.
   - $\mathcal{B}$ verifies the signature: $e(\sigma_1, [1]_2) = e([(1\ \mathbf{m}^{*\top})\,\mathbf{K}]_1, [1]_2) \cdot e(\sigma_2, val) \wedge e(\sigma_2, \sigma_4) = e(\sigma_3, [1]_2)$.

Game_2' and Game_3' are indistinguishable due to the so-called core-lemma (in Lemma 1), then we have:

$$|\mathbf{Adv}_{2'} - \mathbf{Adv}_{3'}| \leq 2\mathcal{Q}Adv_{\mathcal{D}_k, \mathbb{G}_1, \mathcal{B}_1}^{\mathsf{MDDH}}(\kappa) + \mathcal{Q}/p \cdot$$

Game 4. This game is same as Game_3' except that $\{\mathbf{K}_i\}_{i\in[n]}$ are sampled. In particular, we sample $\mathbf{K}_i = \tilde{\mathbf{K}}_i + \mathbf{u}_i\mathbf{a}^\perp$ for $i \in [1,n]$.

Shamir secret sharing (see Definition 1) ensures that $(\mathbf{K}_1,\ldots,\mathbf{K}_n)$ in Game_3 and $(\tilde{\mathbf{K}}_1,\ldots,\tilde{\mathbf{K}}_n)$ in Game_4 are identically distributed. W.l.o.g, $\mathbf{K}_i$ in Game_3' and $\tilde{\mathbf{K}}_i$ in Game_4 are identically distributed. In Game_4, on the other hand, $\tilde{\mathbf{K}}_i$ and $\mathbf{K}_i = \tilde{\mathbf{K}}_i - \mathbf{u}_i\mathbf{a}^\perp$ are identically distributed. Considering both together, $\mathbf{K}_i$ is Game_3' and $\mathbf{K}_i$ in Game_4 are identically distributed for all $i \in [1,n]$. Thus further ensures that $\mathbf{K}$ in Game_3' and $\mathbf{K} + \mathbf{u}_0\mathbf{a}^\perp$ in Game_4 are identically distributed. Therefore, this change is just a conceptual change and $\mathbf{Adv}_{3'} - \mathbf{Adv}_4 = 0$.

Finally, we argue that $\mathbf{Adv}_4 = 1/p$. Notice that, the adversary gets to update CS adaptively. To complete the argument, we have to ensure that even after getting $\mathbf{K}_i = \tilde{\mathbf{K}}_i + \mathbf{u}_i\mathbf{a}^\perp$ for $i \in [\mathsf{CS}]$ chosen adaptively and even after having several partial signatures (possibly on the corrupted keys too), $\mathbf{u}_0$ is still hidden to the adversary.

- Firstly, vk and $\{\mathsf{vk}_i\}_{i\in[1,n]}$ do not leak anything about $\mathbf{u}_0$ and $\{\mathbf{u}_i\}_{i\in[1,n]}$ respectively. Note that, $\mathcal{A}$ gets $\mathsf{sk}_i = \mathbf{K}_i = \tilde{\mathbf{K}}_i + \mathbf{u}_i\mathbf{a}^\perp$ for $i \in [\mathsf{CS}]$ as a part of Input.

– The output of jth partial signature query on $(i, [\mathbf{m}]_1)$ for $[\mathbf{m}]_1 \neq [\mathbf{m}^*]_1$ completely hides $\{\mathbf{u}_i\}_{i \in [1,n] \setminus \mathsf{CS}}$ (and subsequently $\mathbf{u}_0$ as the adversary has only $|\mathsf{CS}|$ many $\mathbf{u}_i$ where $|\mathsf{CS}| < t$), since

$$\left(1\ \mathbf{m}^\top\right) \mathbf{K}_i + \mu_j \mathbf{a}^\perp = \left(1\ \mathbf{m}^\top\right) \widetilde{\mathbf{K}}_i + \left(1\ \mathbf{m}^\top\right) \mathbf{u}_i \mathbf{a}^\perp + \mu_j \mathbf{a}^\perp .$$

distributed identically to $\left(1\ \mathbf{m}^\top\right) \widetilde{\mathbf{K}}_i + \mu_j \mathbf{a}^\perp$. This is because $\mu_j \mathbf{a}^\perp$ already hides $\left(1\ \mathbf{m}^\top\right) \mathbf{u}_i \mathbf{a}^\perp$ for uniformly random $\mu_j \leftarrow \mathbb{Z}_p$.
– In case of the jth partial signature query on $(i, [\mathbf{m}^*]_1)$, observe that at most $\{\mathbf{u}_i\}_{i \in S_1([\mathbf{m}^*]_1)}$ are leaked to the adversary. To summarise, an adp-TS-UF-1 adversary gets at most $\{\mathbf{u}_i\}_{i \in S_1([\mathbf{m}^*]_1)}$ even when it is unbounded.
– Finally, we take a look at the corrupted set CS. We emphasize that this set was updated through out the game adaptively.

From the above discussion, it is clear that the information theoretically adversary can at most gets hold of $\{\mathbf{u}_i\}_{i \in S_1([\mathbf{m}^*]_1) \cup \mathsf{CS}}$ adaptively. Note that, the only way to sucessfuly convince the verification to accept a signature Σ^* on $\mathbf{m}^*$, the adversary must correctly compute $\left(1\ \mathbf{m}^{*\top}\right)\left(\mathbf{K} + \mathbf{u}_0 \mathbf{a}^\perp\right)$ and thus $\left(1\ \mathbf{m}^{*\top}\right) \mathbf{u}_0$. So the question now reduces to if the adversary can compute $\mathbf{u}_0$ from $\{\mathbf{u}_i\}_{i \in S_1([\mathbf{m}^*]_1) \cup \mathsf{CS}}$ which it got adaptively. Since Shamir secret sharing is information theoretically secure, the advantage of an adversary in case of selective corruption of users is same as the advantage of an adversary in case of adaptive corruption of users. Thus, $\mathbf{u}_0$ is completely hidden to the adaptive adversary, $\left(1\ \mathbf{m}^{*\top}\right) \mathbf{u}_0$ is uniformly random from $\mathbb{Z}_p$ from its viewpoint. Therefore, $\mathbf{Adv}_4 = 1/p$ (Fig. 12).

□

3.5   Proof of Core Lemma

Proof of Lemma 1. We proceed through a series of games from Game_0 to Game_q. Note that, Init outputs the same in all the games. In Game_i, the first i queries to the oracle $\mathcal{O}_b(.)$ are responded with $([\mu \mathbf{a}^\perp + \mathbf{r}^\top \mathbf{B}^\top (\mathbf{U} + \tau \mathbf{V})]_1, [\mathbf{r}^\top \mathbf{B}^\top]_1)$ and the next $q - i$ queries are responded with $([\mathbf{r}^\top \mathbf{B}^\top (\mathbf{U} + \tau \mathbf{V})]_1, [\mathbf{r}^\top \mathbf{B}^\top]_1)$. The intermediate games Game_i and Game_{i+1} respond differently to the $i + 1$-th query to $\mathcal{O}_b(.)$. The Game_i responds with $([\mathbf{r}^\top \mathbf{B}^\top (\mathbf{U} + \tau \mathbf{V})]_1, [\mathbf{r}^\top \mathbf{B}^\top]_1)$ whereas Game_{i+1} responds with $([\mu \mathbf{a}^\perp + \mathbf{r}^\top \mathbf{B}^\top (\mathbf{U} + \tau \mathbf{V})]_1, [\mathbf{r}^\top \mathbf{B}^\top]_1)$. We compute the advantage of the adversary in differentiating the two games below. The advantage of the adversary in Game_i is denoted by $\mathbf{Adv}_i$ for $i = 0, \ldots, q$. On querying $\mathcal{O}_b(\cdot)$, Game_i responds to $i + 1$-th query with

$$([\mathbf{r}^\top \mathbf{B}^\top (\mathbf{U} + \tau \mathbf{V})]_1, [\mathbf{r}^\top \mathbf{B}^\top]_1) ,$$

where $\mathbf{r} \leftarrow \mathbb{Z}_p^k$.

We define a sub-game $\mathsf{Game}_{i.1}$ where $[\mathbf{B}\mathbf{r}]_1$ is replaced with $[\mathbf{w}]_1$, $[\mathbf{w}]_1 \leftarrow \mathbb{G}_1^{k+1}$. From the MDDH assumption, a MDDH adversary cannot distinguish between the distributions $([\mathbf{B}]_1, [\mathbf{B}\mathbf{r}]_1)$ and $([\mathbf{B}]_1, [\mathbf{w}]_1)$. Thus,

$$([\mathbf{r}^\top \mathbf{B}^\top (\mathbf{U} + \tau \mathbf{V})]_1, [\mathbf{r}^\top \mathbf{B}^\top]_1) \approx_c ([\mathbf{w}^\top (\mathbf{U} + \tau \mathbf{V})]_1, [\mathbf{w}]_1) \cdot$$

All the other values can be perfectly simulated in the reduction by choosing $\mathbf{U}$ and $\mathbf{V}$ from the appropriate distributions. In the next sub-game $\mathsf{Game}_{i.2}$, we introduce the randomness $\mu \mathbf{a}^\perp$ to $[\mathbf{w}^\top (\mathbf{U} + \tau \mathbf{V})]_1$ and proceed to use an information-theoretic argument to bound the advantage in this experiment. As shown in [52], for every $\mathbf{A}, \mathbf{B} \leftarrow \mathcal{D}_k$, $\tau \neq \tau^*$, the following distributions are identically distributed

$$(\mathsf{vk}, [\mathbf{w}^\top (\mathbf{U} + \tau \mathbf{V})]_1, \mathbf{U} + \tau^* \mathbf{V}) \text{ and } (\mathsf{vk}, [\mu \mathbf{a}^\perp + \mathbf{w}^\top (\mathbf{U} + \tau \mathbf{V})]_1, \mathbf{U} + \tau^* \mathbf{V}) \cdot$$

with probability $1 - 1/p$ over $\mathbf{w}$. The values $[\mathbf{B}^\top \mathbf{U}]_1$ and $[\mathbf{B}^\top \mathbf{V}]_1$ are part of the public values $\mathsf{vk} := (\mathbf{A}, \mathbf{U}\mathbf{A}, \mathbf{V}\mathbf{A}, [\mathbf{B}]_1, [\mathbf{B}^\top \mathbf{U}]_1, [\mathbf{B}^\top \mathbf{V}]_1)$ and anyone can compute $[\mathbf{B}^\top (\mathbf{U} + \tau^* \mathbf{V})]_1$ corresponding to a τ^*. Thus, for $\tau \neq \tau^*$, we have the two following identical distributions:

$$
\begin{aligned}
&(\mathsf{vk}, [\mathbf{w}^\top (\mathbf{U} + \tau \mathbf{V})]_1, [\mathbf{U} + \tau^* \mathbf{V}]_2, [\mathbf{B}^\top (\mathbf{U} + \tau^* \mathbf{V})]_1) \text{ and} \\
&(\mathsf{vk}, [\mu \mathbf{a}^\perp + \mathbf{w}^\top (\mathbf{U} + \tau \mathbf{V})]_1, [\mathbf{U} + \tau^* \mathbf{V}]_2, [\mathbf{B}^\top (\mathbf{U} + \tau^* \mathbf{V})]_1) \cdot
\end{aligned}
\tag{1}
$$

From Equation (1), the subgames $\mathsf{Game}_{i.1}$ and $\mathsf{Game}_{i.2}$ are statistically close. We use the MDDH assumption again in the next sub-game $\mathsf{Game}_{i.3}$ and replace $[\mathbf{w}]_1$ with $[\mathbf{B}\mathbf{r}]_1$. The resulting distribution is

$$(\mathsf{vk}, [\mu \mathbf{a}^\perp + \mathbf{r}^\top \mathbf{B}^\top (\mathbf{U} + \tau \mathbf{V})]_1, [\mathbf{U} + \tau^* \mathbf{V}]_2, [\mathbf{B}^\top (\mathbf{U} + \tau^* \mathbf{V})]_1) \,,$$

which is same as Game_{i+1}. Thus, from the two MDDH instances as well as the information-theoretic argument,

$$|\mathbf{Adv}_i - \mathbf{Adv}_{i+1}| \leq 2 Adv_{\mathcal{D}_k, \mathbb{G}_1, \mathcal{B}}^{\mathsf{MDDH}}(\kappa) + 1/p \cdot$$

$\square$

4   Conclusion

In this paper, we give the first construction of a non-interactive threshold structure-preserving signature (TSPS) scheme from standard assumptions. We prove our construction secure in the adp-TS-UF-1 security model where the adversary is allowed to obtain partial signatures on the forged message and additionally allow the adversary to adaptively corrupt parties. Although the signatures are constant-size (and in fact quite small), we consider improving the efficiency of TSPS under standard assumptions as an interesting future work.

Acknowledgements. Mahdi Sedaghat was supported in part by the Research Council KU Leuven C1 on Security and Privacy for Cyber-Physical Systems and the Internet of Things with contract number C16/15/058 and by CyberSecurity Research Flanders with reference number VR20192203. Daniel Slamanig was supported by the Austrian Science Fund (FWF) and netidee SCIENCE PROFET (GA No. P31621-N38). His work was done while being affiliated with AIT Austrian Institute of Technology.

References

1. Abe, M., Ambrona, M., Ohkubo, M., Tibouchi, M.: Lower bounds on structure-preserving signatures for bilateral messages. In: Catalano, D., De Prisco, R. (eds.) SCN 2018. LNCS, vol. 11035, pp. 3–22. Springer, Cham (2018). https://doi.org/10.1007/978-3-319-98113-0_1

2. Abe, M., Chase, M., David, B., Kohlweiss, M., Nishimaki, R., Ohkubo, M.: Constant-size structure-preserving signatures: generic constructions and simple assumptions. In: Wang, X., Sako, K. (eds.) ASIACRYPT 2012. LNCS, vol. 7658, pp. 4–24. Springer, Heidelberg (2012). https://doi.org/10.1007/978-3-642-34961-4_3

3. Abe, M., Chow, S.S.M., Haralambiev, K., Ohkubo, M.: Double-trapdoor anonymous tags for traceable signatures. In: Lopez, J., Tsudik, G. (eds.) ACNS 2011. LNCS, vol. 6715, pp. 183–200. Springer, Heidelberg (2011). https://doi.org/10.1007/978-3-642-21554-4_11

4. Abe, M., Fuchsbauer, G., Groth, J., Haralambiev, K., Ohkubo, M.: Structure-preserving signatures and commitments to group elements. In: Rabin, T. (ed.) CRYPTO 2010. LNCS, vol. 6223, pp. 209–236. Springer, Heidelberg (2010). https://doi.org/10.1007/978-3-642-14623-7_12

5. Abe, M., Groth, J., Haralambiev, K., Ohkubo, M.: Optimal structure-preserving signatures in asymmetric bilinear groups. In: Rogaway, P. (ed.) CRYPTO 2011. LNCS, vol. 6841, pp. 649–666. Springer, Heidelberg (2011). https://doi.org/10.1007/978-3-642-22792-9_37

6. Abe, M., Groth, J., Ohkubo, M.: Separating short structure-preserving signatures from non-interactive assumptions. In: Lee, D.H., Wang, X. (eds.) ASIACRYPT 2011. LNCS, vol. 7073, pp. 628–646. Springer, Heidelberg (2011). https://doi.org/10.1007/978-3-642-25385-0_34

7. Abe, M., Groth, J., Ohkubo, M., Tibouchi, M.: Unified, minimal and selectively randomizable structure-preserving signatures. In: Lindell, Y. (ed.) TCC 2014. LNCS, vol. 8349, pp. 688–712. Springer, Heidelberg (2014). https://doi.org/10.1007/978-3-642-54242-8_29

8. Abe, M., Hofheinz, D., Nishimaki, R., Ohkubo, M., Pan, J.: Compact structure-preserving signatures with almost tight security. In: Katz, J., Shacham, H. (eds.) CRYPTO 2017, Part II. LNCS, vol. 10402, pp. 548–580. Springer, Cham (2017). https://doi.org/10.1007/978-3-319-63715-0_19

9. Abe, M., Jutla, C.S., Ohkubo, M., Pan, J., Roy, A., Wang, Y.: Shorter QA-NIZK and SPS with tighter security. In: Galbraith, S.D., Moriai, S. (eds.) ASIACRYPT 2019, Part III. LNCS, vol. 11923, pp. 669–699. Springer, Cham (2019). https://doi.org/10.1007/978-3-030-34618-8_23

10. Abe, M., Jutla, C.S., Ohkubo, M., Roy, A.: Improved (Almost) Tightly-Secure Simulation-Sound QA-NIZK with Applications. In: Peyrin, T., Galbraith, S. (eds.) ASIACRYPT 2018, Part I. LNCS, vol. 11272, pp. 627–656. Springer, Cham (2018). https://doi.org/10.1007/978-3-030-03326-2_21

11. Abram, D., Nof, A., Orlandi, C., Scholl, P., Shlomovits, O.: Low-bandwidth threshold ECDSA via pseudorandom correlation generators. In: 2022 IEEE Symposium on Security and Privacy. pp. 2554–2572. IEEE Computer Society Press (2022). https://doi.org/10.1109/SP46214.2022.9833559

12. Almansa, J.F., Damgard, I., Nielsen, J.B.: Simplified threshold RSA with adaptive and proactive security. In: Vaudenay, S. (ed.) EUROCRYPT 2006. LNCS, vol. 4004, pp. 593–611. Springer, Heidelberg (2006). https://doi.org/10.1007/11761679_35

13. Attrapadung, N., Libert, B., Peters, T.: Computing on authenticated data: new privacy definitions and constructions. In: Wang, X., Sako, K. (eds.) ASIACRYPT 2012. LNCS, vol. 7658, pp. 367–385. Springer, Heidelberg (2012). https://doi.org/10.1007/978-3-642-34961-4_23

14. Bacho, R., Loss, J.: On the adaptive security of the threshold BLS signature scheme. In: Yin, H., Stavrou, A., Cremers, C., Shi, E. (eds.) ACM CCS 2022. pp. 193–207. ACM Press (2022). https://doi.org/10.1145/3548606.3560656

15. Bacho, R., Loss, J., Tessaro, S., Wagner, B., Zhu, C.: Twinkle: threshold signatures from DDH with full adaptive security. Cryptology ePrint Archive, Paper 2023/1482 (2023). https://eprint.iacr.org/2023/1482

16. Badertscher, C., Matt, C., Waldner, H.: Policy-compliant signatures. In: Nissim, K., Waters, B. (eds.) TCC 2021, Part III. LNCS, vol. 13044, pp. 350–381. Springer, Cham (2021). https://doi.org/10.1007/978-3-030-90456-2_12

17. Badertscher, C., Sedaghat, M., Waldner, H.: Fine-grained accountable privacy via unlinkable policy-compliant signatures. Cryptology ePrint Archive, Paper 2023/1070 (2023). https://eprint.iacr.org/2023/1070

18. Bellare, M., Crites, E.C., Komlo, C., Maller, M., Tessaro, S., Zhu, C.: Better than advertised security for non-interactive threshold signatures. In: Dodis, Y., Shrimpton, T. (eds.) CRYPTO 2022, Part IV. LNCS, vol. 13510, pp. 517–550. Springer, Heidelberg (2022). https://doi.org/10.1007/978-3-031-15985-5_18

19. Bellare, M., Namprempre, C., Pointcheval, D., Semanko, M.: The one-more-RSA-inversion problems and the security of Chaum's blind signature scheme. J. Cryptol. **16**(3), 185–215 (2003). https://doi.org/10.1007/s00145-002-0120-1

20. Bellare, M., Rogaway, P.: Random oracles are practical: a paradigm for designing efficient protocols. In: Denning, D.E., Pyle, R., Ganesan, R., Sandhu, R.S., Ashby, V. (eds.) ACM CCS 93, pp. 62–73. ACM Press (Nov 1993). https://doi.org/10.1145/168588.168596

21. Blazy, O., Canard, S., Fuchsbauer, G., Gouget, A., Sibert, H., Traoré, J.: Achieving optimal anonymity in transferable e-cash with a judge. In: Nitaj, A., Pointcheval, D. (eds.) AFRICACRYPT 2011. LNCS, vol. 6737, pp. 206–223. Springer, Heidelberg (Jul (2011)

22. Boldyreva, A.: Threshold signatures, multisignatures and blind signatures based on the Gap-Diffie-Hellman-group signature scheme. In: Desmedt, Y.G. (ed.) PKC 2003. LNCS, vol. 2567, pp. 31–46. Springer, Heidelberg (2003). https://doi.org/10.1007/3-540-36288-6_3

23. Boneh, D., Lynn, B., Shacham, H.: Short signatures from the Weil pairing. In: Boyd, C. (ed.) ASIACRYPT 2001. LNCS, vol. 2248, pp. 514–532. Springer, Heidelberg (2001). https://doi.org/10.1007/3-540-45682-1_30

24. Bouez, A., Singh, K.: One round threshold ECDSA without roll call. In: Rosulek, M. (ed.) Topics in Cryptology - CT-RSA 2023. LNCS, vol. 13871, pp. 389–414. Springer, Cham (2023). https://doi.org/10.1007/978-3-031-30872-7_15

25. Camenisch, J., Dubovitskaya, M., Haralambiev, K.: Efficient structure-preserving signature scheme from standard assumptions. In: Visconti, I., De Prisco, R. (eds.) SCN 2012. LNCS, vol. 7485, pp. 76–94. Springer, Heidelberg (2012). https://doi.org/10.1007/978-3-642-32928-9_5

26. Camenisch, J., Dubovitskaya, M., Haralambiev, K., Kohlweiss, M.: Composable and modular anonymous credentials: definitions and practical constructions. In: Iwata, T., Cheon, J.H. (eds.) ASIACRYPT 2015, Part II. LNCS, vol. 9453, pp. 262–288. Springer, Heidelberg (2015). https://doi.org/10.1007/978-3-662-48800-3_11

27. Canetti, R., Feige, U., Goldreich, O., Naor, M.: Adaptively secure multi-party computation. In: 28th ACM STOC, pp. 639–648. ACM Press (1996). https://doi.org/10.1145/237814.238015

28. Canetti, R., Gennaro, R., Goldfeder, S., Makriyannis, N., Peled, U.: UC non-interactive, proactive, threshold ECDSA with identifiable aborts. In: Ligatti, J., Ou, X., Katz, J., Vigna, G. (eds.) ACM CCS 2020, pp. 1769–1787. ACM Press (2020). https://doi.org/10.1145/3372297.3423367

29. Canetti, R., Gennaro, R., Jarecki, S., Krawczyk, H., Rabin, T.: Adaptive security for threshold cryptosystems. In: Wiener, M. (ed.) CRYPTO 1999. LNCS, vol. 1666, pp. 98–116. Springer, Heidelberg (1999). https://doi.org/10.1007/3-540-48405-1_7

30. Chase, M., Kohlweiss, M., Lysyanskaya, A., Meiklejohn, S.: Malleable proof systems and applications. In: Pointcheval, D., Johansson, T. (eds.) EUROCRYPT 2012. LNCS, vol. 7237, pp. 281–300. Springer, Heidelberg (2012). https://doi.org/10.1007/978-3-642-29011-4_18

31. Couteau, G., Hartmann, D.: Shorter non-interactive zero-knowledge arguments and ZAPs for algebraic languages. In: Micciancio, D., Ristenpart, T. (eds.) CRYPTO 2020, Part III. LNCS, vol. 12172, pp. 768–798. Springer, Cham (2020). https://doi.org/10.1007/978-3-030-56877-1_27

32. Crites, E., Kohlweiss, M., Preneel, B., Sedaghat, M., Slamanig, D.: Threshold structure-preserving signatures. In: Guo, J., Steinfeld, R. (eds.) ASIACRYPT 2023. LNCS, pp. 348–382. Springer, Singapore (2023). https://doi.org/10.1007/978-981-99-8724-5_11

33. Crites, E., Komlo, C., Maller, M.: Fully adaptive Schnorr threshold signatures. In: Handschuh, H., Lysyanskaya, A. (eds.) CRYPTO 2023. LNCS, pp. 678–709. Springer, Cham (2023). https://doi.org/10.1007/978-3-031-38557-5_22

34. Dalskov, A., Orlandi, C., Keller, M., Shrishak, K., Shulman, H.: Securing DNSSEC keys via threshold ECDSA from generic MPC. In: Chen, L., Li, N., Liang, K., Schneider, S. (eds.) ESORICS 2020, Part II. LNCS, vol. 12309, pp. 654–673. Springer, Cham (2020). https://doi.org/10.1007/978-3-030-59013-0_32

35. Das, S., Ren, L.: Adaptively secure BLS threshold signatures from DDH and co-CDH. Cryptology ePrint Archive, Paper 2023/1553 (2023). https://eprint.iacr.org/2023/1553

36. Deng, Y., Ma, S., Zhang, X., Wang, H., Song, X., Xie, X.: Promise Σ-protocol: how to construct efficient threshold ECDSA from encryptions based on class Groups. In: Tibouchi, M., Wang, H. (eds.) ASIACRYPT 2021, Part IV. LNCS, vol. 13093, pp. 557–586. Springer, Cham (2021). https://doi.org/10.1007/978-3-030-92068-5_19

37. Desmedt, Y., Frankel, Y.: Threshold cryptosystems. In: Brassard, G. (ed.) CRYPTO 1989. LNCS, vol. 435, pp. 307–315. Springer, New York (1990). https://doi.org/10.1007/0-387-34805-0_28

38. Escala, A., Herold, G., Kiltz, E., Ràfols, C., Villar, J.L.: An algebraic framework for Diffie-Hellman assumptions. J. Cryptol. **30**(1), 242–288 (2017). https://doi.org/10.1007/s00145-015-9220-6

39. Fuchsbauer, G.: Commuting signatures and verifiable encryption. In: Paterson, K.G. (ed.) EUROCRYPT 2011. LNCS, vol. 6632, pp. 224–245. Springer, Heidelberg (2011). https://doi.org/10.1007/978-3-642-20465-4_14

40. Fuchsbauer, G., Hanser, C., Slamanig, D.: Practical round-optimal blind signatures in the standard model. In: Gennaro, R., Robshaw, M. (eds.) CRYPTO 2015, Part II. LNCS, vol. 9216, pp. 233–253. Springer, Heidelberg (2015). https://doi.org/10.1007/978-3-662-48000-7_12

41. Fuchsbauer, G., Kiltz, E., Loss, J.: The algebraic group model and its applications. In: Shacham, H., Boldyreva, A. (eds.) CRYPTO 2018, Part II. LNCS, vol. 10992, pp. 33–62. Springer, Cham (2018). https://doi.org/10.1007/978-3-319-96881-0_2

42. Gay, R., Hofheinz, D., Kohl, L., Pan, J.: More efficient (almost) tightly secure structure-preserving signatures. In: Nielsen, J.B., Rijmen, V. (eds.) EUROCRYPT 2018, Part II. LNCS, vol. 10821, pp. 230–258. Springer, Cham (2018). https://doi.org/10.1007/978-3-319-78375-8_8

43. Gennaro, R., Goldfeder, S.: Fast multiparty threshold ECDSA with fast trustless setup. In: Lie, D., Mannan, M., Backes, M., Wang, X. (eds.) ACM CCS 2018, pp. 1179–1194. ACM Press (2018). https://doi.org/10.1145/3243734.3243859

44. Ghadafi, E.: Short structure-preserving signatures. In: Sako, K. (ed.) CT-RSA 2016. LNCS, vol. 9610, pp. 305–321. Springer, Cham (2016). https://doi.org/10.1007/978-3-319-29485-8_18

45. Ghadafi, E.: More efficient structure-preserving signatures - or: bypassing the type-III lower bounds. In: Foley, S.N., Gollmann, D., Snekkenes, E. (eds.) ESORICS 2017, Part II. LNCS, vol. 10493, pp. 43–61. Springer, Cham (2017). https://doi.org/10.1007/978-3-319-66399-9_3

46. Groth, J., Sahai, A.: Efficient non-interactive proof systems for bilinear groups. In: Smart, N. (ed.) EUROCRYPT 2008. LNCS, vol. 4965, pp. 415–432. Springer, Heidelberg (2008). https://doi.org/10.1007/978-3-540-78967-3_24

47. Hofheinz, D., Jager, T.: Tightly secure signatures and public-key encryption. In: Safavi-Naini, R., Canetti, R. (eds.) CRYPTO 2012. LNCS, vol. 7417, pp. 590–607. Springer, Heidelberg (2012). https://doi.org/10.1007/978-3-642-32009-5_35

48. Jarecki, S., Lysyanskaya, A.: Adaptively secure threshold cryptography: introducing concurrency, removing erasures. In: Preneel, B. (ed.) EUROCRYPT 2000. LNCS, vol. 1807, pp. 221–242. Springer, Heidelberg (2000). https://doi.org/10.1007/3-540-45539-6_16

49. Jutla, C.S., Ohkubo, M., Roy, A.: Improved (almost) tightly-secure structure-preserving signatures. In: Abdalla, M., Dahab, R. (eds.) PKC 2018, Part II. LNCS, vol. 10770, pp. 123–152. Springer, Cham (2018). https://doi.org/10.1007/978-3-319-76581-5_5

50. Jutla, C.S., Roy, A.: Improved structure preserving signatures under standard bilinear assumptions. In: Fehr, S. (ed.) PKC 2017, Part II. LNCS, vol. 10175, pp. 183–209. Springer, Heidelberg (2017). https://doi.org/10.1007/978-3-662-54388-7_7

51. Kiltz, E., Pan, J., Wee, H.: Structure-preserving signatures from standard assumptions, revisited. In: Gennaro, R., Robshaw, M. (eds.) CRYPTO 2015, Part II. LNCS, vol. 9216, pp. 275–295. Springer, Heidelberg (2015). https://doi.org/10.1007/978-3-662-48000-7_14

52. Kiltz, E., Wee, H.: Quasi-adaptive NIZK for linear subspaces revisited. In: Oswald, E., Fischlin, M. (eds.) EUROCRYPT 2015, Part II. LNCS, vol. 9057, pp. 101–128. Springer, Heidelberg (2015). https://doi.org/10.1007/978-3-662-46803-6_4

53. Komlo, C., Goldberg, I.: FROST: flexible round-optimized Schnorr threshold signatures. In: Dunkelman, O., Jacobson, Jr., M.J., O'Flynn, C. (eds.) SAC 2020. LNCS, vol. 12804, pp. 34–65. Springer, Cham (2021). https://doi.org/10.1007/978-3-030-81652-0_2

54. Libert, B., Joye, M., Yung, M.: Born and raised distributively: fully distributed non-interactive adaptively-secure threshold signatures with short shares. Theor. Comput. Sci. **645**, 1–24 (2016)

55. Libert, B., Peters, T., Joye, M., Yung, M.: Linearly homomorphic structure-preserving signatures and their applications. In: Canetti, R., Garay, J.A. (eds.) CRYPTO 2013, Part II. LNCS, vol. 8043, pp. 289–307. Springer, Heidelberg (2013). https://doi.org/10.1007/978-3-642-40084-1_17

56. Libert, B., Peters, T., Yung, M.: Short group signatures via structure-preserving signatures: standard model security from simple assumptions. In: Gennaro, R., Robshaw, M. (eds.) CRYPTO 2015, Part II. LNCS, vol. 9216, pp. 296–316. Springer, Heidelberg (2015). https://doi.org/10.1007/978-3-662-48000-7_15

57. Lysyanskaya, A., Peikert, C.: Adaptive security in the threshold setting: from cryptosystems to signature schemes. In: Boyd, C. (ed.) ASIACRYPT 2001. LNCS, vol. 2248, pp. 331–350. Springer, Heidelberg (2001). https://doi.org/10.1007/3-540-45682-1_20

58. Morillo, P., Ràfols, C., Villar, J.L.: The kernel matrix Diffie-Hellman assumption. In: Cheon, J.H., Takagi, T. (eds.) ASIACRYPT 2016, Part I. LNCS, vol. 10031, pp. 729–758. Springer, Heidelberg (2016). https://doi.org/10.1007/978-3-662-53887-6_27

59. Pedersen, T.P.: Non-interactive and information-theoretic secure verifiable secret sharing. In: Feigenbaum, J. (ed.) CRYPTO 1991. LNCS, vol. 576, pp. 129–140. Springer, Heidelberg (1992). https://doi.org/10.1007/3-540-46766-1_9

60. Schnorr, C.P.: Efficient signature generation by smart cards. J. Cryptol. **4**(3), 161–174 (1991). https://doi.org/10.1007/BF00196725

61. Shamir, A.: How to share a secret. Commun. Assoc. Comput. Mach. **22**(11), 612–613 (1979)

62. Wong, H.W.H., Ma, J.P.K., Yin, H.H.F., Chow, S.S.M.: Real threshold ECDSA. In: 30th Annual Network and Distributed System Security Symposium, NDSS 2023, San Diego, California, USA, February 27 - March 3, 2023. The Internet Society (2023). https://www.ndss-symposium.org/ndss-paper/real-threshold-ecdsa/

Multi-Signatures for Ad-Hoc and Privacy-Preserving Group Signing

Anja Lehmann and Cavit Özbay[✉]

Hasso-Plattner-Institute, University of Potsdam, Potsdam, Germany
{anja.lehmann,cavit.oezbay}@hpi.de

Abstract. Multi-signatures allow to combine individual signatures from different signers on the same message into a short aggregated signature. Newer schemes further allow to aggregate the individual public keys, such that the combined signature gets verified against a short aggregated key. This makes them a versatile alternative to threshold or distributed signatures: the aggregated key can serve as group key, and signatures under that key can only be computed with the help of all signers. What makes multi-signatures even more attractive is their simple key management, as users can re-use the same secret key in several and ad-hoc formed groups. In that context, it will be desirable to not sacrifice privacy as soon as keys get re-used and ensure that users are not linkable across groups. In fact, when multi-signatures with key aggregation were proposed, it was claimed that aggregated keys hide the signers' identities or even the fact that it is a combined key at all. In our work, we show that none of the existing multi-signature schemes provide these privacy guarantees when keys get re-used in multiple groups. This is due to the fact that all known schemes deploy deterministic key aggregation. To overcome this limitation, we propose a new variant of *multi-signatures with probabilistic yet verifiable key aggregation*. We formally define the desirable privacy and unforgeability properties in the presence of key re-use. This also requires to adapt the unforgeability model to the group setting, and ensure that key-reuse does not weaken the expected guarantees. We present a simple BLS-based scheme that securely realizes our strong privacy and security guarantees. We also formalize and investigate the privacy that is possible by deterministic schemes, and prove that existing schemes provide the advertised privacy features as long as one public key remains secret.

1 Introduction

When cryptographic signatures and keys are used to protect high-value assets, it is often desirable to protect the access not only with a single, but with multiple keys. One of the most prominent applications of multi-key signing is public ledgers such as Bitcoin. Initially, a naive version of "multi-signatures" was proposed, where a single public key that protects an account gets replaced with a set of public keys, and transactions from that account require a set of respective signatures [1]. The key drawback of this approach is that signature and public

© International Association for Cryptologic Research 2024
Q. Tang and V. Teague (Eds.): PKC 2024, LNCS 14601, pp. 196–228, 2024.
https://doi.org/10.1007/978-3-031-57718-5_7

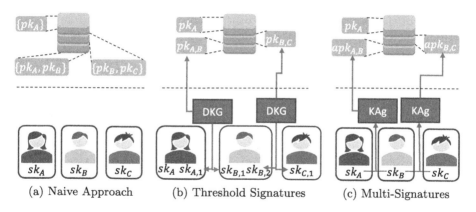

Fig. 1. Group signing approaches for the public ledger use case. Each figure presents a scenario which shows a public ledger with three users, Alice, Bob, and Charlie (from left to right) who hold accounts for user sets $\{Alice\}$, $\{Alice, Bob\}$, and $\{Bob, Charlie\}$. "DKG" and "KAg" stand for a distributed key generation protocol and the key aggregation process of multi-signatures with key aggregation, respectively.

key size, as well as signature verification costs, are linear in the group size. To improve the efficiency of the naive approach, the use of threshold signatures, such as Boldyreva's BLS-based scheme [11] or Schnorr-based FROST [24], was suggested in the Bitcoin standard [39].

Challenges in Key Management. While threshold signatures are more efficient than the naive approach, they come with challenges in key management – in particular in settings where a user is not part of a single signing group only, but wants to sign in *multiple* groups. Such a scenario is depicted in Fig. 1, where Fig. 1a employs the naive approach and Fig. 1b shows the implementation using threshold signatures.

In the naive solution, a group public key is simply the set of individual public keys. Thus, users could use the same secret key for multiple purposes and e.g., rely on a trusted hardware token to protect their individual long-term key. With threshold signatures, users need to manage *individual* key material for each group they are part of. For threshold signatures, this even requires a trusted dealer or an interactive key generation protocol.

In particular when dealing with end-users and not machines, convenient yet secure key management is crucial, and users should ideally be able to use a single long-term key for multiple accounts. In fact, this has very recently triggered a series of works, *multi-verse threshold signatures* (MTS), which allow signers to use a single long-term key to derive multiple "group" keys (or combined signatures) for arbitrary threshold structures [6,18,23]. However, all schemes require some level of interaction in the key aggregation algorithm and have a different focus from our work. We give a more detailed comparison in Sect. 1.3 and also include MTS in Fig. 2 for completeness.

Our work focuses on another – and conceptually much simpler – group signing solution: multi-signatures. They provide the long-term key support of the naive approach while enjoying the same compactness benefits as threshold signatures (but give up on the threshold setting).

Multi-signatures with Key Aggregation. Multi-signatures enable the efficient aggregation of individual signatures of n signers, each having an individual long-term key pair, on the *same* message m. The aggregated signature σ can be efficiently verified to be valid for all n signers. Secure multi-signatures have been constructed mostly from BLS, e.g., [36] and Schnorr signatures [10].

Originally, multi-signatures only considered the aggregation of signatures, but in 2019, Maxwell et al. [31] proposed a protocol that additionally combines the individual public keys into a short aggregated key apk. Verification of a multi-signature σ from n signers then requires only the aggregated public key apk. Computing apk needs to be done only once per group and several signatures of the same "group" can be verified using apk without needing the individual keys. After the initial work, several other schemes with key aggregation have been proposed [9,12,19,20,25,26,28,33,35]. These works were inspired by the public ledger application and have already seen real-world adoption. For instance, there is a proposal to include the multi-signature scheme MuSig2 of Nick et al. [33] into the Bitcoin standard. Another ledger technology, Cardano is also about to support MuSig2 [2]. Figure 1c shows how multi-signatures with key aggregation can be used in a public ledger to form group keys. Instead of creating dedicated secret keys for each group, signers can re-use a single key in multiple groups.

1.1 Ad-Hoc Group Signing with Long-Term Keys

The flexibility and convenience of multi-signatures bear the question of whether they already provide the optimal solution for applications that require compact group signing with long-term keys. We argue that this is not the case for existing multi-signatures, as unforgeability is not guaranteed to hold if keys are re-used, and any reasonable privacy is even impossible.

We start with a discussion of the desirable unforgeability and privacy guarantees in the context of flexible group signing with long-term keys, and explain what is satisfied by existing multi-signatures. For completeness, we also show in Fig. 2 how this compares to threshold signatures (that lack key re-use or simple verification) and the naive solution (allowing key re-use, but lacking compactness/efficiency).

From a practical perspective, we are interested in group signing solutions with the following properties:

Single long-term key: All users have an individual long-term key pair sk_i, pk_i that they generate (and use) autonomously. There is no trusted entity or joint protocol needed for key generation.
Ad-hoc groups: Users can use their single key to dynamically join *groups*, and do so repeatedly. A group is represented through an aggregated public

key apk that is derived from a set of public keys $PK = \{pk_i\}$. Signatures that verify under that group key can only be derived from the individual signatures of all members.

Standard verification: Verification of the groups' signature must be (somewhat) compatible with standard verification (e.g. Schnorr, ECDSA, or BLS).

Efficiency: A group's signature and public key size, and verification time must be independent of the group size.

In terms of security, we require the unforgeability of the groups' signatures. The challenge hereby is to understand and formalize the impact of re-using the same individual secret key in different signing groups. For applications such as public ledgers, it will be important that individual signature contributions are strictly bound to the group they were intended for. Otherwise, a signature on $m :=$ "Send \$10 to Eve" created by Alice to confirm the money transfer from her joint account with Bob, could be re-used to retrieve money from her individual account. Thus, for our group context, we required unforgeability:

Group unforgeability: It is infeasible to create a signature for message m and a group apk, when not all signers provided a signature for m *and apk*.

In existing works, this aspect is often not very explicit. While some target and realize group unforgeability [9,26,33–35,38], other works consider a weaker notion where signature contributions are not bound to a particular group [12, 19,20,25,28]. Thus, only some of the existing schemes provide the security that is necessary for public ledger applications, and developers must carefully read and understand the analyzed unforgeability guarantees. As a side contribution, our work conceptualizes the different unforgeability notions and also shows how weaker schemes can be lifted to achieve group unforgeability.

Note that group unforgeability also implicitly covers non-frameability, i.e., an honest user cannot be framed to be part of a group (i.e., apk) and participated in group signing, when she never did so. This is again crucial when dealing with long-term keys that will be clearly associated to individuals or legal entities, and gets re-used across groups. For the new type of multi-signatures we introduce here, this aspect requires more care and will therefore be discussed more explicitly throughout our work (yet formally is implied by group unforgeability).

The Need for Privacy. While the usage of multiple keys increases security, revealing information about this distribution might not be desired. For instance, revealing how many (and which) keys protect certain assets tells the adversary how many keys he has to compromise and possibly which are used more often and might be an easier or more lucrative target.

Most threshold signatures naturally hide who contributed to a particular signature, and multi-signatures with key aggregation gives rise to similar privacy features as they represent a signer group with a constant size public key. In the case of group signing with an *n-out-of-n* structure, the desire for privacy might be surprising at first. In the end, all signers must contribute to the signature, and one might think there is no need or chance for privacy at all.

However, one must distinguish between in- and outsiders here. Of course, the members of the group want to be aware who their co-signers are and there will be no privacy towards these insiders. To outsiders, i.e., non-group members, who only consume group keys and group signatures, this information is often not necessary. We believe that hiding information about the key structure should be the default, unless required otherwise.

In fact, Maxwell et al. [31] already advertised three privacy properties that multi-signatures with key aggregation allegedly provide: they do not leak any information about 1) the number of individual signers, 2) the identity of individual signers or 3) even whether a key and a corresponding signature are an aggregated key and signature, or standard ones. Previous works on aggregated signatures that implicitly used key aggregation also informally claimed similar features, e.g., that key aggregation hides the structure of the signers [3,37].

Having a single long-term key that is used in different groups now even amplifies the privacy need. Re-using the same key – which is desirable from a usability perspective – must not make the user's signature contributions traceable and linkable across groups. Thus, we set the privacy requirements as follows:

Outsider privacy: An aggregated public key apk (and corresponding signatures) leak no information about the underlying signers.

Unlinkability: The usage of the same long-term key in different groups cannot be linked. In fact, even when repeatedly signing with the same set of signers PK, users can decide to do so under the same apk or generate fresh apk's. Signatures under different apk's are fully unlinkable, i.e., they hide that they were generated by the same set of signers. This unlinkability holds for anyone that is not an insider in both groups.

No Privacy Yet. So far, no formal treatment of the already advertised privacy features for multi-signatures with key aggregation exist. However, even without a formal model, we can see that none of the existing schemes achieves any of the aforementioned privacy properties: all existing schemes have deterministic key aggregation. This makes any privacy properties of the aggregated keys (and associated signatures) impossible in a setting where the adversary knows the signers' individual public keys. Thus, privacy for such schemes can only hold in a model where at least some of the public keys (and their signatures) are considered to be secret. Given that a core benefit of multi-signatures is their flexible use, i.e., using the same long-term key for different group signing activities, assuming that public keys remain secret is clearly neither desirable nor realistic.

In summary, existing multi-signatures – despite being an attractive candidate for group signing – do not provide the privacy (and sometimes even security) guarantees that are needed in applications such as a public ledger. Therefore, our work addresses the following question:

How can we realize compact aggregated signatures that allow for key re-use across groups, yet guarantee strong privacy and security?

	Simple Vrfy	Compact	Key Re-Use	Group Unf	Privacy
Naive Appr. w. Key Prefix	✓	✗	✓	✓	✗
Threshold Signatures	✓	✓	✗	✓	✓
Multi-Signatures with KAg.	✓	✓	✓	(✗)	✗
Multiverse Threshold Sigs	✗	✓	✓	✗	(✗)
randBLS-1 (Section 5.1)	✓	✓	✓	✗	✓
randBLS-2 (Section 5.1)	✓	✓	✓	✓	✓

Fig. 2. Overview of approaches for group signing on public ledgers (see Sect. 1.3 for a more detailed discussion of multiverse threshold signatures). "✓", "✗", and "✗" mean the requirement is satisfied, only satisfied by some existing works, and not satisfied, respectively. randBLS-1 satisfies our strongest privacy notion, i.e., aggregated signatures are fully indistinguishable from standard BLS signatures. randBLS-2 uses key-prefixing to achieve the desired group unforgeability, which comes for the prize of not being identical to standard signatures. Apart from leaking the fact that signatures are aggregated, it still provides the desired privacy guarantees.

1.2   Our Contributions

Our work answers that question by introducing a new variant of multi-signatures that is flexible enough to realize ad-hoc group signing with long-term keys and ensure strong privacy and unforgeability. We formally define the desired security guarantees in a setting where long-term keys get re-used in multiple groups and propose two simple BLS-based constructions that satisfy them. In more detail, our work makes the following contributions:

Multi-signatures with Verifiable Key Aggregation. We introduce a new variant of multi-signatures that comes with verifiable key aggregation (MSvKA). The core idea is to remove the requirement that key aggregation KAg is deterministic, yet keep a way to verify whether an aggregated public key apk belongs to a certain set PK of public keys. We realize that by defining key aggregation to also output a proof π along with the aggregated key. An additional algorithm VfKAg verifies whether apk and PK belong together – but requires π as input. This allows us to later have different security and privacy guarantees for insiders (knowing π and wanting to verify their co-signers) and outsiders (not knowing π).

Unforgeability Framework & Transformations. As our core motivation is the use of multi-signatures for ad-hoc group signing, we define unforgeability for this targeted group context and in the presence of key re-use. Our framework provides a set of definitions, depending on how explicit the user's group intent is supposed to be. The strongest notion in our framework (UNF-3) captures the desired group unforgeability for insiders. It guarantees that if a signer wanted to contribute to a multi-signature for a particular group (expressed via apk), then her signature share cannot be reused in any other context. Our weaker versions (UNF-1/2) allow for more flexibility in the aggregation of individual signature contributions, and will be the right choice when the group context is not known when the individual signatures are computed.

We also show simple transformations to lift schemes with weak unforgeability guarantees to their stronger versions and to translate existing unforgeability results for deterministic schemes into our setting. Further, all our unforgeability definitions also implicitly cover *non-frameability*, i.e., it is guaranteed that an adversary cannot frame an honest user (by producing a malicious proof π) for a group signature she never contributed to.

Privacy Framework. Our core contribution is a definitional framework that defines the privacy guarantees users can expect, despite repeatedly using the same secret key in different groups. We follow the initially advertised properties and formalize three privacy goals: Set Privacy (SetPriv), Membership Privacy (MemPriv), and Full Privacy (FullPriv). All properties guarantee that signers can repeatedly use their long-term secret key in multiple groups without becoming traceable (except to someone who is an insider in all groups). The difference between the definitions is in what the aggregated keys and signatures are supposed to hide beyond that. Our strongest goal FullPriv requires the aggregated values to be fully indistinguishable from standard ones, whereas our weakest guarantee (MemPriv) only focuses on hiding whether a particular user is a member of a group or not, but signatures and keys can leak the group size or the fact that they are aggregates. The stronger properties are harder to achieve and we believe all definitions to have their individual benefits and applications.

All goals are stated in a strong adversarial model, where the adversary can freely interact with all individual signers, knows all their public keys and can request multi-signatures and even be an insider in their groups. This is called the Known-Public-Key (KPK) model. We also show that no multi-signature with deterministic key aggregation can achieve any privacy properties in KPK model.

New BLS Multi-signature with Strong Privacy. As our impossibility result rules out privacy for all existing schemes, we propose a new and simple variant of the BLS multi-signatures from Boneh et al. [12] that turns key aggregation into a probabilistic algorithm. We prove this scheme – called randBLS-1 – to satisfy the strongest FullPriv-KPK privacy and UNF-1 security (in the plain public key model). Using our generic unforgeability transform via key-prefixing, we show how this scheme can be turned into a variant randBLS-2 that achieves UNF-3 security while satisfying MemPriv-KPK and SetPriv-KPK (but no FullPriv privacy anymore, as it leaks the fact that it is an aggregated key/signature).

Weaker Model & Analysis of Existing Schemes. While privacy in the KPK model is the goal we aim for and achieve with our new constructions, it is not achievable by any existing construction due to their deterministic key aggregation: If the adversary knows all public keys, it is trivial to check whether an aggregated public key corresponds to a given set of individual public keys or not. To analyze the privacy properties of existing schemes, we also define the weaker "All-but-one" AbOPK versions of our three privacy properties, where at least one public key must remain secret. This secrecy requirement also comprises all (multi-)

signatures ever generated under that key, and thus any privacy in that model should be interpreted with great care.

We then show that the most common multi-signatures based on BLS and Schnorr signatures achieve the strongest possible privacy guarantees for a deterministic scheme, which is FullPriv-AbOPK. We also translate their known unforgeability results into our framework and discuss how key-prefixing might boost their unforgeability, which results in a slight privacy loss for BLS-based schemes.

1.3 Related Work

We now discuss the related work, with the most related result being for threshold signatures. While multi-signatures might appear to be the special case of n-out-of-n threshold signatures, they are actually considerably different. In a standard threshold signature scheme, there exists a dedicated key generation phase for all n signers that then can generate signatures for that particular (sub)group. In a multi-signature, there does not exist a phase that fixes n signers, and using the exact same setup, signers can create multi-signatures for arbitrary signer sets.

Unforgeability Hierarchy for Threshold Signatures. A recent work on threshold schemes by Bellare et al. [8] investigates the different levels of unforgeability they can achieve. They propose stronger notions that a signer, knowing the co-signers when creating a signature, produces signature shares that cannot be used to create a signature for any other signer set. This is similar to the stronger unforgeability notion that already existed for multi-signature and which we capture as MSdKA-UNF-2 and MSvKA-UNF-2/3. Their work focuses solely on unforgeability, but does not consider privacy – which is the focus of our work.

Accountable Subgroup Multi-signatures (ASM). First defined by Micali et al. [32], ASM signatures are a special type of multi-signature that strictly binds a signature to a certain subset of signers. This notion is similar to MSvKA-UNF-2 in Sect. 3, group unforgeability, or the strongest definition of Bellare et al. [8]. Still, ASM schemes focus only on accountability, whereas our focus is on privacy guarantees (in combination with unforgeability). Furthermore, ASM takes the signer subset as an input to the verification algorithm. Although this choice allows flexible threshold structures, it leaves no hope for any privacy property.

Recently, Baldimtsi et al. proposed *subset multi-signatures* [7] which adds a *subset key aggregation* algorithm to the subgroup multi-signatures. Thus, the signature verification only takes an aggregated public key instead of a subset of signers. Aggregated keys can provide threshold-like access structures in a fixed group to require that a message has been signed by a particular subset of the group. Although subset multi-signatures improve ASM's by providing compact public keys and a simple verification algorithm, they sacrifice group unforgeability. Finally, neither of the two schemes achieves the ad-hoc groups that multi-signatures provide: they can only serve subgroups/subsets of a constant signing group which is defined prior to any signing process.

Threshold Signatures with Private Accountability. While traditional threshold signatures offer private signatures where the signatures created by different subgroups are indistinguishable, ASM offer accountability. Boneh and Komlo [13], TAPS, proposes a more flexible option between threshold signatures and ASM. TAPS considers a single signer group and applies a dedicated key generation for this group like threshold signatures. Their main goal is to have privacy for outsiders of the signer group (and to some extent for insiders too), and accountability (with the help of an insider). To do so, they introduce dedicated parties of a Combiner and Tracer with designated secret keys. Li et al. [30] distributes the trust to the combiner and the tracer entities by applying threshold structures and relying on a private blockchain and dedicated hardware extensions.

Our work and TAPS have different privacy concerns: TAPS focuses on hiding which *subset* of a fixed group with an *t-out-of-n* structure created a certain signature. Multi-signatures only operate in *n-out-of-n* setting, so this privacy notion loses its meaning in the context of multi-signatures. We study a privacy notion in a setting with long-term keys to be used in multiple groups. This is an aspect that multi-signatures naturally provide unlike traditional threshold signatures or TAPS. Our privacy notion aims at hiding the structure of these multiple signing groups and re-using keys without being linkable. Finally, neither [13] nor [30] has a simple verification algorithm suitable for replacing a system solely relying on Schnorr or BLS signatures.

Multiverse Threshold Signature (MTS). Baird et al. [6] defined MTS enabling threshold signing with a single long-term secret key and allowing users to create aggregated keys for arbitrary threshold structure *t-out-of-n* and an arbitrary group of signers. Lee [27] proposed another MTS construction that improves key aggregation and signature combining performance. MTS aims at threshold schemes and is more flexible in that respect than our multi-signatures. They do not formalize or aim at privacy properties though, which is the focus of our work. Further, they only aim at a rather weak form of unforgeability that is similar to our UNF-1 notion, as it allows signature shares to be re-used in different contexts.

Concurrently, Garg et al. [23] and Das et al. [18] designed threshold signature schemes that work more classically for a fixed group of n parties, but support dynamic t values within that group by making the combine and verification algorithms depend on the threshold t. Thus, there is only a single group in which users have individual long-term keys (generated in a joined manner though), but the threshold in the combination and verification can vary. Although [23] informally discusses possible privacy extensions, this is not formalized and the given constructions do not prioritize privacy protection. Further, their unforgeability is again similar to our weakest notion only. While this is a desired feature for their setting, we aim at more restrictive signing, as our focus is on re-using the same key in *different* groups. Finally, we point out that none of these works meet our simplicity requirement as they use different verification algorithms than BLS signatures, making them unsuitable as a direct replacement in existing systems.

Signatures with Re-randomizable Keys. Fleischhacker et al. [22] proposed the concept of signatures with re-randomizable keys, where both the public and secret key allow for consistent re-randomization. These signatures naturally lend themselves for privacy-preserving applications and have sparked a line of research [4,15,17,21]. Building multi-signatures on top of signature schemes with re-randomizable keys could be an alternative way to achieve the functionality and privacy we aimed for, and might be an interesting direction for future work.

As demonstrated by our construction, it is not *necessary* though that the underlying key pairs allow for such re-randomization. From a practical perspective, our approach has two main advantages: 1) it requires a single re-randomization of the aggregated key instead of re-randomizing all public and secret keys for each group; 2) the long-term secret keys can be exposed through a plain sign-API, without the need of re-randomizing the secret key before each use.

2 Preliminaries

In this chapter, we state the notations and core building blocks we use throughout the paper. We also give a definition of multi-signatures with deterministic key aggregation and their known unforgeability models here.

Cyclic Groups and Pairing Groups. Throughout the paper we notate a prime order cyclic group generator GGen that outputs $\mathcal{G} = (\mathbb{G}, g, p)$ and bilinear pairing generator BGGen that outputs $\mathcal{BG} = (e, \mathbb{G}, \hat{\mathbb{G}}, g, \hat{g}, p)$ for the input security parameter. Formal definitions of these algorithms are in the full the paper [29].

We directly define the co-CDH assumption [12] on pairing groups.

Definition 1 (Co-CDH Assumption). *For all PPT adversaries $\mathcal{A}$ it holds that* $\Pr[\mathcal{BG} \leftarrow \mathsf{BGGen}(1^\lambda); a, b \leftarrow \mathbb{Z}_p; \hat{A} \leftarrow \mathcal{A}(\mathcal{BG}, g^a, g^b, \hat{g}^b) : \hat{A} = \hat{g}^{ab}] \leq \mathsf{negl}(\lambda)$

Traditional Signature Algorithms. Throughout the paper, we refer to traditional BLS and Schnorr signing algorithms using the following syntax. The public parameters of the BLS scheme and the Schnorr scheme contain the descriptions of a prime order bilinear group $\mathcal{BG}$ and a prime order group $\mathcal{G}$, respectively.

$\mathsf{BLSSign}(sk, m)$: Outputs $\mathsf{H}_0(m)^{sk}$.
$\mathsf{SchnorrSign}(sk, m)$: For $r \leftarrow \mathbb{Z}_p$, $R \leftarrow g^r$, and $c \leftarrow \mathsf{H}_0(R, g^{sk}, m)$, outputs $\sigma \leftarrow (z, R)$ where $z = r + c \cdot sk$.

Generalized Forking Lemma. The unforgeability proof of our new multi-signature requires the generalized forking lemma [5], and we refer the reader to the full paper [29] for its definition.

2.1 Multi-Signatures with Deterministic Key Aggregation

In this section, we define the existing variant for multi-signature with deterministic key aggregation (MSdKA) and two different versions of the unforgeability property that have been proposed in the literature.

There is actually no common and unified definition in the literature yet, e.g., works such as [12,16] do not make key aggregation or signature combination explicit at all. As both play a key role, we model them explicitly: key aggregation through function KAg and signature combination via the algorithm Combine. Also, we use the name MulSign instead of Sign, since we later want to express compatibility between a standard signing and the multi-sign operation.

Definition 2 (MSdKA with deterministic key aggregation). *Multi-signature MSdKA is a tuple of algorithms* (Pg, Kg, KAg, MulSign, Combine, Vf) *such that:*

$Pg(1^\lambda) \rightarrow pp$: *Outputs public parameters pp for security parameter 1^λ. We only make pp explicit in key generation and assume it to be an implicit input to all other algorithms.*

$Kg(pp) \rightarrow (sk, pk)$: *Probabilistic key generation, outputs key pair (sk, pk).*

$KAg(PK) \rightarrow apk$: *Deterministic key aggregation, that on input a set of public keys $PK = \{pk_i\}$, outputs an aggregated public key apk.*

$MulSign(sk_i, PK, m) \rightarrow s_i$: *(Possibly interactive) algorithm, that on input the secret key sk_i, message m and a set of public keys $PK = \{pk_i\}$ outputs a signature share s_i.*

$Combine(PK, \{s_i\}_{pk_i \in PK}) \rightarrow \sigma$: *On input a set of public keys $PK = \{pk_i\}$ and set of shares $\{s_i\}_{pk_i \in PK}$ outputs a combined signature σ for PK.*

$Vf(apk, \sigma, m) \rightarrow b$: *Verifies if σ is a valid signature on m for apk.*

A MSdKA must be correct, meaning that every combined multi-signature verifies correctly under the *apk* that belongs to the set of public keys the signature was created for. The correctness definition is available in the full version of the paper [29], and it also relies on the deterministic behaviour of the key aggregation.

Unforgeability Notions. For multi-signatures with deterministic key aggregation, there are two different variants for unforgeability. Both variants consider a single honest user with key pk^* that signs together with other users that are fully controlled by the adversary. The task of the adversary is to come up with a valid and non-trivial forgery (m, σ, PK), i.e., σ must verify correctly under $apk = KAg(PK)$ with $pk^* \in PK$ that includes the honest signer. The difference in both variants is how they define a *trivial* forgery.

The first definition, denoted as MSdKA-UNF-1 and first proposed by [36], only considers the message as authenticated information. That is re-using a signature obtained via $\mathcal{O}^{MulSign}$ for some (m, PK) and turning it into a valid signature for (m, PK') with $PK \neq PK'$ is *not* considered a valid forgery. A stronger version is MSdKA-UNF-2 (first used in [32]) which requires the tuple (m, PK) to be fresh. This ensures that each signature contribution of the honest signer is bound to the dedicated set PK it was intended for. Both games rely on the determinism of KAg and are shown in Fig. 3 and formally defined as follows:

Definition 3 (MSdKA Unforgeability-x). *A multi-signature scheme Π is x-unforgeable if for all PPT adversaries $\mathcal{A}$ $\Pr[Exp_{\Pi,\mathcal{A}}^{MSdKA\text{-}UNF\text{-}x}(\lambda) = 1] \leq negl(\lambda)$ for the experiment from Fig. 3.*

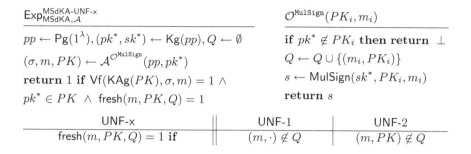

$\mathsf{Exp}_{\mathsf{MSdKA},\mathcal{A}}^{\mathsf{MSdKA\text{-}UNF\text{-}x}}$	$\mathcal{O}^{\mathtt{MulSign}}(PK_i, m_i)$
$pp \leftarrow \mathsf{Pg}(1^\lambda), (pk^*, sk^*) \leftarrow \mathsf{Kg}(pp), Q \leftarrow \emptyset$	**if** $pk^* \notin PK_i$ **then return** $\perp$
$(\sigma, m, PK) \leftarrow \mathcal{A}^{\mathcal{O}^{\mathtt{MulSign}}}(pp, pk^*)$	$Q \leftarrow Q \cup \{(m_i, PK_i)\}$
return 1 **if** $\mathsf{Vf}(\mathsf{KAg}(PK), \sigma, m) = 1 \wedge$	$s \leftarrow \mathsf{MulSign}(sk^*, PK_i, m_i)$
$pk^* \in PK \ \wedge \ \mathsf{fresh}(m, PK, Q) = 1$	**return** s

UNF-x		UNF-1	UNF-2
$\mathsf{fresh}(m, PK, Q) = 1$ **if**		$(m, \cdot) \notin Q$	$(m, PK) \notin Q$

Fig. 3. Unforgeability for MSdKA schemes with deterministic key aggregation.

For MSdKA, MSdKA-UNF-2 corresponds to the group unforgeability notion we discussed in Sect. 1.1. It is easy to see that MSdKA-UNF-2 implies MSdKA-UNF-1. Furthermore, MSdKA-UNF-2 is strictly stronger than MSdKA-UNF-1, which immediately follows from the fact that there are schemes that satisfy the weaker but not the stronger notion, such as BLS multi-signatures [12]. One can use a signature share of some pk for message m to create a BLS multi-signature for any set PK where $pk \in PK$. In the full paper [29], we discuss the relation between these notions, and provide a generic transformation which lifts a MSdKA-UNF-1 scheme with certain properties to a MSdKA-UNF-2 scheme, using key-prefixing.

Unforgeability (so far) Requires Deterministic KAg. Requiring deterministic key-aggregation seems to be mainly an artifact of the absence of a formal treatment of unforgeability of signatures with aggregated public keys. Even though the verification algorithm takes an aggregated public key apk as input, the unforgeability of these schemes has still been analyzed in the traditional multi-signature model (with no key aggregation!), where the adversary is asked to output n individual public keys, out of which at least one must be honest. Verification of the adversary's forgery is then done for the aggregated public key that is re-computed from these keys, which requires that key aggregation is deterministic.

This reveals an interesting conflict of unforgeability and privacy: For unforgeability it will be desirable – and in fact necessary – to check whether an aggregated key apk belongs to a certain set PK. This motivates the new type of multi-signature that makes this verification explicit, and allows for probabilistic schemes that will be necessary for any reasonable level of privacy.

3   Multi-Signatures with Verifiable Key Aggregation

As motivated in our introduction (and formally shown in the next section), the current definition of multi-signatures with explicit *deterministic* key aggregation makes it impossible to achieve any form of privacy when the adversary knows all the individual public keys. We therefore introduce a more generic variant of multi-signatures where key aggregation can be probabilistic and that allows for explicit verification of whether an apk is valid for a particular PK.

We start by defining the new syntax and also show how every multi-signature scheme with deterministic key aggregation can be recast in this syntax. We then define different types of unforgeability, which now comes with one more flavour as there is no unique binding between apk and PK anymore. Our unforgeability model also ensures that the more flexible verification cannot be misused to frame honest users, i.e., to incorrectly claim that an honest user is part of a group and corresponding signatures she never contributed to. The introduction of our privacy framework for such multi-signatures is given in the following section.

3.1 Syntax and Correctness

The first change to remove the requirement of *deterministic* key aggregation is to make KAg (possibly) probabilistic. This would not be sufficient, though, as we want to keep accountability for insiders, i.e., we need to check whether an aggregated key apk belongs to a certain set of public keys PK.

To allow this, we change the definition of key aggregation KAg to not only output the aggregated key apk but also a proof π. We further add an algorithm VfKAg that allows to verify whether apk belongs to PK using π. Thus, any insider knowing all keys and π can still verify the correctness of the key (towards them there is no key privacy), whereas outsiders only knowing apk and PK can (depending on the scheme) not tell whether they belong together or not.

Having no unique mapping between apk and PK anymore, as well as having a proof π, also requires changes to MulSign and Combine. Whereas the MSdKA version gives only PK as input to MulSign (as it uniquely defines apk), we will need to give the sign algorithm both PK and apk. We decided not to give π as input or enforce MulSign to check whether the key apk is correct. Instead, we assume signers to verify the correctness of the aggregated key explicitly (via VfKAg), and only run MulSign on verified keys. At some point in signing, this value π will be required though (in our concrete construction it will be the randomness used in key aggregation). This is happening in Combine which we give π as additional input. As Combine is run only once for a multi-signature, this choice has benefits for efficiency and practical security considerations, as it reduces the number of parties that need to keep and use π.

Definition 4 (MSvKA with verifiable key aggregation). *A multi-signature* MSvKA *is a tuple of algorithms* (Pg, Kg, KAg, VfKAg, MulSign, Combine, Vf) *s.t.:*

Pg(1^λ) → pp: *On input security parameter* 1^λ, *it outputs public parameters* pp.

Kg(pp) → (sk, pk): *Probabilistic key generation, outputs a key pair* (sk, pk).

KAg(PK) → (apk, π): *(Possibly probabilistic) key aggregation, that on input a set of public keys* $PK = \{pk_i\}$, *outputs an aggregated public key* apk *and a proof of aggregation* π.

VfKAg(PK, apk, π) → b: *Checks if* π *is a valid proof of aggregation for* PK *and* apk *and outputs the boolean result for it.*

MulSign(sk_i, PK, apk, m) → s_i: *(Possibly interactive) algorithm, that on input the secret key* sk_i, *message* m, *a set of public keys* $PK = \{pk_i\}$ *and aggregated key* apk *outputs a signature share* s_i.

Combine$(PK, \pi, \{s_i\}_{pk_i \in PK}) \to \sigma$: *On input a set of public keys* $PK = \{pk_i\}$
    and set of shares $\{s_i\}_{pk_i \in PK}$ *outputs a combined signature* σ *for* PK.
Vf$(apk, \sigma, m) \to b$: *Verifies if* σ *is a valid signature on* m *for* apk.

The correctness definition of MSvKA is in the full paper [29] and now covers
both VfKAg and Vf. Our new definition is a more general variant of multi-
signatures, and any previous scheme with deterministic key aggregation can be
turned into our more general variant as stated below. We will later show that
this transformation also preserves the unforgeability.

Construction 1 (MSdKA to MSvKA Transformation). *For a* MSdKA *sch-
eme* Π, *the* MSvKA *version with explicit key verification,* Π' *is defined as follows.
The algorithms* (Pg, Kg, Vf) *of* Π' *are identical to* Π. *The remaining algorithms
are:*

   Π'.KAg(PK): Set $apk \leftarrow \Pi$.KAg(PK). Set $\pi = \perp$ and output (apk, π).
   Π'.VfKAg(PK, apk, π): If $apk = \Pi$.KAg$(PK) \neq \perp$ output 1, else 0.
   Π'.MulSign(sk_i, PK, apk, m): Output $s_i \leftarrow \Pi$.MulSign(sk_i, PK, m).
   Π'.Combine$(PK, \pi, \{s_i\}_{pk_i \in PK})$: Outputs $\sigma \leftarrow \Pi$.Combine$(PK, \{s_i\}_{pk_i \in PK})$.

3.2 Unforgeability Notions

We again define all unforgeability definitions through a single game, where only
the freshness predicate differs depending on the unforgeability level. The main
game structure is similar to the definitions for deterministic schemes (Sect. 2.1):
the adversary gets a public key pk^* for an honest signer and oracle access to sk^*
via the signing oracle $\mathcal{O}^{\texttt{MulSign}}$. This oracle expects a message m, set of public
keys PK – now along with the aggregated public key apk and a proof π which
shows that apk and PK belong together and contain pk^*. After checking the
validity of the provided proof, the oracle computes and returns the honest user's
signature share. Further, when the adversary outputs his forgery, he must now
provide the aggregated key apk along with a proof π for the claimed group PK.
This is necessary as the winning condition will directly use apk when verifying
the signature, and we need to check that apk belongs to the group PK that
includes the honest signer, as otherwise "forging" would be trivial.

The strongest notion of our framework (MSvKA-UNF-3) guarantees that if a
signer wanted to contribute to a multi-signature for a particular group (expressed
via apk), then her signature share cannot be reused in any other context. This
is what we referred to as group unforgeability.

When aiming at a threshold/quorum setting of signatures, MSvKA-UNF-3
might not be desired though: therein a number of signers will sign the same
message, and as soon as the necessary amount exists, the aggregation into a
group signature should be possible. (So the different thresholds/quorums will be
represented by a set of possible apk's instead of a single on.) In such a scenario,
the users are not aware of their "co-signers" upon creation of their individual
signatures. To not exclude such applications, we also translate the classic notion

$\mathsf{Exp}_{\Pi,\mathcal{A}}^{\mathsf{MSvKA\text{-}UNF\text{-}x}}$	$\mathcal{O}^{\mathtt{MulSign}}(PK_i, apk_i, \pi_i, m_i)$
$pp \leftarrow \mathsf{Pg}(1^\lambda), (pk^*, sk^*) \leftarrow \mathsf{Kg}(pp), Q \leftarrow \emptyset$	**if** $pk^* \notin PK_i \vee \mathsf{VfKAg}(PK_i, apk_i, \pi_i) \neq 1$
$(\sigma, m, apk, \pi, PK) \leftarrow \mathcal{A}^{\mathcal{O}^{\mathtt{MulSign}}}(pp, pk^*)$	**then return** $\bot$
return 1 **if** $\mathsf{Vf}(apk, \sigma, m) = 1$	$Q \leftarrow Q \cup \{(m_i, PK_i, apk_i)\}$
$\wedge\ \mathsf{VfKAg}(PK, apk, \pi) = 1\ \wedge\ pk^* \in PK$	$s \leftarrow \mathsf{MulSign}(sk^*, PK_i, apk_i, m_i)$
$\wedge\ \mathsf{fresh}(m, PK, apk, Q) = 1$	**return** s

UNF-x	UNF-1	UNF-2	UNF-3
$\mathsf{fresh}(m, PK, apk, Q) = 1$ **if**	$(m, \cdot, \cdot) \notin Q$	$(m, PK, \cdot) \notin Q$	$(m, PK, apk) \notin Q$

Fig. 4. Unforgeability for MSvKA schemes with verifiable key aggregation.

of unforgeability (which was MSdKA-UNF-1 for deterministic schemes) to our setting, which yields the weakest definition denoted as MSvKA-UNF-1. Therein, there is no binding of a signature share or multi-signature to a particular *apk* but the property ensures that an adversary cannot create a message-signature pair that frames an honest user that has not signed the message.

For completeness, we also translate the existing unforgeability notion MSdKA -UNF-2 that binds signatures to the set of signers, i.e., PK (but not necessarily to *apk*) to our setting as MSvKA-UNF-2.

Non-frameability. Our unforgeability notion also guarantees non-frameability, i.e., an honest user cannot be framed (via VfKAg) for a signature she never contributed to. This aspect is modelled by the winning condition that comprises both verify algorithms, Vf (for signatures) and VfKAg (for the aggregated key). The adversary could always win if he is able to output a "forgery" σ for a key *apk* that he knows all secret keys for (then computing σ is trivial), yet he manages to produce a correct proof π s.t. $\mathsf{VfKAg}(PK, apk, \pi) = 1$ with $pk^* \in PK$. That is, $\mathcal{A}$ also wins if he produces a fraudulent proof π that frames the honest user.

Definition 5 (MSvKA Unforgeability-x). *A multi-signature scheme Π is x-unforgeable if for all PPT adversaries $\mathcal{A}$ in the experiment from Fig. 4 it holds that:* $\Pr[\mathsf{Exp}_{\Pi,\mathcal{A}}^{\mathsf{MSvKA\text{-}UNF\text{-}x}}(\lambda) = 1] \leq \mathsf{negl}(\lambda)$.

Relations and Transformations. It is easy to see that MSvKA-UNF-2 is strictly stronger than MSvKA-UNF-1. For MSvKA schemes that have deterministic key aggregation (which is still allowed, but not enforced) MSvKA-UNF-2 and MSvKA-UNF-3 are equivalent, whereas MSvKA-UNF-3 is strictly stronger than MSvKA-UNF-2 for schemes with probabilistic KAg. We further show how known unforgeability results for deterministic schemes can be translated into our setting, and how MSvKA unforgeability can be lifted from UNF-1 to UNF-3. An overview of these results is given in Fig. 5.

Translating MSdKA *into* MSvKA *Unforgeability.* We start by showing that the transformation given in Construction 1 not only transforms the syntax but also preserves the unforgeability. The simple proof is available in [29].

Theorem 1. *If Π' is the transformation from Construction 1 applied on a MSdKA scheme Π, then the following holds:*

- *If Π is MSdKA-UNF-2 secure, then Π' is MSvKA-UNF-3 secure,*
- *If Π is MSdKA-UNF-1 secure, then Π' is MSvKA-UNF-1 secure.*

Lifting MSvKA-UNF-1 *to* MSvKA-UNF-3 *Security.* A natural question is how weaker versions can be lifted to the strongest one. An immediate idea is to sign (m, PK, apk) instead of m only. Intuitively, this scheme would be UNF-3 secure as any forgery for a message $m' \neq m$ for the same PK and apk would also become a forgery for the UNF-1 secure scheme for the message (m', PK, apk). However, this scheme is not useful, as it requires the knowledge of the signer set PK during signature verification. This would immediately destroy the efficiency and privacy features that comes with the key aggregation.

We resolve this by merely signing (m, apk), and requiring an additional property on the underlying key aggregation mechanism. Similar to the binding property of commitments, we call this property *key binding*. Key binding requires that it is hard to find two distinct signer sets PK and PK' for an aggregated key apk. This property is formally defined in the full paper [29]. We show that this additional assumption is sufficient for the simple key-prefixing transformation to lift an UNF-1 secure scheme to UNF-3 security:

Construction 2 (UNF-1 to UNF-3 Transformation). *Let Π be a MSvKA-UNF-1 scheme. Then, we define Π' as stated follows: the algorithms $(\mathsf{Pg}, \mathsf{Kg}, \mathsf{KAg}, \mathsf{Combine})$ of Π' are exactly as in Π, and the remaining algorithms are:*

$\Pi'.\mathsf{MulSign}(sk_i, PK, apk, m)$: Returns $s_i \leftarrow \Pi.\mathsf{MulSign}(sk_i, PK, apk, (apk, m))$.
$\Pi'.\mathsf{Vf}(apk, \sigma, m)$: Outputs $b \leftarrow \Pi.\mathsf{Vf}(apk, \sigma, (apk, m))$.

Theorem 2. *If Π is a multi-signature that is MSvKA-UNF-1 secure and key binding, then Π' from Construction 2 is MSvKA-UNF-3 secure.*

The simple proof is delegated to the full paper [29]. In a nutshell, if the MSvKA-UNF-3 adversary can provide a valid forgery on fresh (m, PK, apk), then we are able to find either a valid MSvKA-UNF-1 forgery on message (m, apk) or a valid collision (PK, PK', π, π') against the key binding property of the scheme.

4 Privacy Framework for MSvKA

Being equipped with a definition of multi-signatures that allows probabilistic key aggregation, we can now turn to the privacy properties that have already been advertised for such schemes and are necessary for our envisioned application of privacy-preserving group signing. In this section, we provide a formal privacy framework, roughly following what was claimed in [31].

Fig. 5. Relation among unforgeability definitions. $A\overset{x}{\dashrightarrow}B$ means there is a generic construction of B from A relying on properties and/or theorems x. $A\to B$ means A implies B (any scheme has A, also has B). Finally, KEY-CF is nothing but the deterministic version of the key binding property (KEY-BND) which is available in the full paper [29].

Privacy Goals. We propose a hierarchy of definitions that aim at different strengths of privacy protection, which can be hiding the individual signers or, in the strongest variant, even hiding the fact that the signature and key are aggregated ones.

Full Privacy (FullPriv): One cannot tell whether a key and corresponding signature are a multi-signature with an aggregated key or stem from a standard signature algorithm.
Set Privacy (SetPriv): An aggregated key and corresponding signatures do not leak information about the underlying signer set (but can leak whether it is an aggregated one).
Membership Privacy (MemPriv): An aggregated key and corresponding signatures do not leak information about individual signers (but can leak the size of the group).

We show that FullPriv is the strongest notion and implies SetPriv, which in turn is strictly stronger than MemPriv. An advantage of FullPriv is that it allows for seamless integration into existing applications, as signatures and public keys have exactly the same form as standard ones. We decided to also formalize the weaker notions, as such strong FullPriv privacy might not be achievable (in particular for UNF-3-secure BLS signatures) or even desirable in some applications, e.g., when it should be clearly visible that the signature is a combined one. Both, SetPriv and MemPriv already capture the essential privacy guarantees we aimed for in the context of privacy-friendly group signing, and it will depend on the particular application which of the three properties is the "right" one.

Adversary Model. Given the ad-hoc nature of multi-signatures, the adversary should be able to interact with the individual signers freely, learn all their public keys, see their (multi)-signatures and even become insiders in some of her groups. All that must not allow the adversary to identify the user in groups he is not an insider in. This is what we capture as Known Public-keys (KPK) model for all three privacy properties. We will make this KPK-model explicit, as we will later also introduce a weaker "All-but-One" (AbOPK) model where at least one public key and associated signatures must remain secret. This weaker model is introduced to argue about the privacy of existing multi-signatures, as none of them satisfies the strong KPK version due to the deterministic key aggregation.

Unlinkability. Privacy in the KPK models presented in this section also captures unlinkability of individuals and groups. That is, if a signer re-uses the same key in several groups, the adversary cannot link her across the groups, unless he is an insider to all of them. Further, even the exact same group of signers can create different *apk*'s and signatures when desired. Only users that know the corresponding proof(s) π can tell that they originate from the same group, whereas anyone not being privy of the proofs cannot tell whether two multi-signatures stem from the same group of signers or not. Such unlinkability is guaranteed by any of the three properties mentioned above, the difference is merely whether signatures/keys also hide the group size or the fact that they are an aggregated one.

4.1 Security Games

The goal of our security games is to capture the privacy guarantees towards an *outsider* of a particular (challenge) group, while giving the adversary as much knowledge and power of the individual signers and their participation in other signing groups. An outsider of a group defined through the aggregated key *apk* knows all individual public keys, and can see combined signatures for arbitrary messages of his choice under that *apk* – but he does not learn the aggregation proof π for *apk* nor actively participates in the group signing for this key.

While the adversary must be an outsider to the challenge group (there is no privacy to insiders), he can be an insider in other groups that have a partial or even full overlap with some of the signers of the challenge group. Such an insider might learn the aggregation proofs, see the signing protocol transcripts or even be an active signer in groups that have an overlap with the challenge group.

A typical way to model these insider capabilities of the adversary, is to provide oracle access to all honest entities and their secret keys. Here, this would require to define oracles for key aggregation, multi- (and individual) signing for all possible group and corruption settings.

Another approach is to be as generous as possible, and give the adversary all (secret) keys not strictly necessary to achieve the desired security property. The knowledge of these keys then enable the adversary to internally run all interactions with the honest parties himself. The advantage is that it avoids the need to define a multitude of oracles and keep track of the made queries, which keeps the games much simpler. It also directly highlights the keys or values that are crucial for the targeted property.

In our work we follow the later approach, and give the adversary not only the public keys but even the secret keys of all honest entities. Thus, the only oracle we need to provide in our games is for the challenge group.

We start with the presentation of our definitions for set privacy (SetPriv) and membership privacy (MemPriv). Both require the indistinguishability of two

$\mathsf{Exp}^{\mathsf{X}}_{\Pi,\mathcal{A}}(\lambda)$

$b \leftarrow \{0,1\}, pp \leftarrow \mathsf{Pg}(1^{\lambda}), Q \leftarrow \emptyset, n \leftarrow \mathcal{A}(pp), \textbf{abort if } n \not> 0$

$(SK, PK) := (\{sk_i\}_{i\in[n]}, \{pk_i\}_{i\in[n]}) \leftarrow (\mathsf{Kg}(pp))_{i\in[n]}$

$(S_0, S_1) \leftarrow \mathcal{A}(SK\backslash\{sk_1\}, PK\backslash\{pk_1\}),\quad \textbf{, abort if } 1 \notin S_j \textbf{ for } j \in \{0,1\}$

$\boxed{\textbf{abort if } |S_j \setminus S_{1-j}| \neq 1 \textbf{ for } j \in \{0,1\}}$	$\mathcal{O}^{\mathsf{Chl}}(m)$
$(apk_b, \pi_b) \leftarrow \mathsf{KAg}(PK_{S_b})$	$\Sigma \leftarrow \{\mathsf{MulSign}(sk_i, PK_{S_b}, apk_b, m)\}_{sk_i \in SK_{S_b}}$
$b^* \leftarrow \mathcal{A}^{\mathcal{O}^{\mathsf{Chl}}(\cdot)}(apk_b), \textbf{ return } 1 \textbf{ if } b = b^*$	$\textbf{return } \sigma \leftarrow \mathsf{Combine}(PK_{S_b}, \pi_b, \Sigma)$

Fig. 6. This is the game for our Set and Membership Privacy definitions ($\mathsf{X} \in \{\mathsf{MemPriv}, \mathsf{SetPriv}\}$). The additional part for $\mathsf{X} = \mathsf{MemPriv}$ is shown in dashed box. Grayed parts correspond to additions for the All-but-One-Public-Key model (AbOPK) model which will be introduced in Sect. 6.

aggregated public keys and associated signatures, and only differ in the restriction on the challenge groups. Thus, we capture both through the same game and only need to include an extra restriction when expressing the $\mathsf{MemPriv}$ version.

Set Privacy. Our $\mathsf{SetPriv}$ definition captures that an aggregate key and signature do not leak *any* information about the underlying signer group. This includes membership of individual signers but also the group size, both are required to remain hidden. The corresponding game runs in three stages:

In the first stage, the adversary just outputs a value n, which sets the number of individual keys in the system. The challenger internally generates all key pairs and returns all key pairs (SK, PK) to the adversary. The knowledge of all secret and public keys allows $\mathcal{A}$ to generate aggregated keys (and corresponding proofs) for arbitrary groups, as well as generate individual and combined signatures for these aggregated keys.

In the second stage, the adversary is asked to output two challenge sets S_0 and S_1, which are the indices of the honest signers generated earlier. The challenger chooses a random bit b and uses S_b to generate the challenge public key apk_b and proof π_b. The adversary receives apk_b (but not π_b) and gets access to a challenge oracle $\mathcal{O}^{\mathsf{Chl}}$ which returns multi-signatures for apk_b (and π_b) for arbitrary messages chosen by $\mathcal{A}$.

As the adversary knows the secret keys of all signers, it can create aggregated keys, signatures, and signing protocol transcripts for both S_0 and S_1 himself. This models that the challenge public key and signatures must be unlinkable to the keys and signatures that originate from the same set of signers.

Finally, the task of the adversary is to output a bit b^* and he wins if $b^* = b$, i.e., if he can guess to which group of signers the challenge public key and signatures belong. A scheme is said to satisfy our $\mathsf{SetPriv}$ definition if $\mathcal{A}$'s winning probability is negligibly better than guessing.

Membership Privacy. This property is defined identically to SetPriv, but we no longer require the aggregated key and signature to hide the underlying group size. Thus, what membership privacy focuses on is hiding the identity of an individual signer within a group. To capture this (and not more), the definition must not allow an adversary to use any other difference between the two signer groups to infer information about a single user. We model this by asking the adversary to output two groups S_0 and S_1 that are identical, except for one user. That is, both groups must have the same size $|S_0| = |S_1| = k$ and $k - 1$ members of the two sets must be the same. This condition is checked via the line in the dashed box when the adversary outputs its challenge sets. Apart from that extra check, the game and the winning condition are the same as in SetPriv.

Definition 6 ({SetPriv, MemPriv}-KPK). *A* MSvKA *scheme Π has property* X $\in$ {SetPriv, MemPriv} *in the* KPK *model, if for all PPT adversaries $\mathcal{A}$ in* $\mathsf{Exp}_{\Pi,\mathcal{A}}^{\mathsf{X}}$ *from Fig. 6 :* $|\Pr[\mathsf{Exp}_{\Pi,\mathcal{A}}^{\mathsf{X}}(\lambda) = 1] - 1/2| \leq \mathsf{negl}(\lambda)$.

Full Privacy. We now turn to our strongest privacy property. Intuitively, this property guarantees that if the multi-signature uses the same verification algorithm as their "regular signature" analogue, they do not even leak information about whether the signature and key are aggregated ones or not.

This is a bit tricky to define though, as the definition of multi-signature schemes does not contain an algorithm for creating "standard" signatures. Hence, we first need to consider an additional algorithm that captures such a signing procedure with individual keys, which we call Sign. For the majority of existing schemes, this sign algorithm will be the standard BLS or Schnorr algorithm. The keys for the standard sign algorithm are the ones generated via MSvKA.Kg and it also uses the same verification algorithm MSvKA.Vf.

The detailed model is given in Definition 7 and starts by letting the adversary determine the number of signers for which the challenger then generates the individual keys. As in our previous models, $\mathcal{A}$ immediately gets the key pairs of the signers and these can be used to run KAg, MulSign, or Sign before deciding upon his challenge group. The main difference is in the challenge. Here the adversary is only asked to output a single challenge group S^* and either receives the aggregated public key $pk^* = apk^*$ of that group (if $b = 0$) or a freshly chosen individual public key $pk^* = pk$ (if $b = 1$). Consequently, the challenge oracle now either returns an aggregated signature for apk^* or a standard signature under sk, depending on the challenge bit.

Definition 7 (FullPriv-KPK). *A* MSvKA *scheme Π is fully private for algorithm* Sign *in the* KPK *model if for all PPT adversaries $\mathcal{A}$ in* $\mathsf{Exp}_{\Pi,\mathcal{A}}^{\mathsf{FullPriv\text{-}KPK}}$ *defined in Fig. 7 it holds that* $|\Pr[\mathsf{Exp}_{\Pi,\mathcal{A}}^{\mathsf{FullPriv\text{-}KPK}}(\lambda) = 1] - 1/2| \leq \mathsf{negl}(\lambda)$.

4.2 Impossibility Results and Relations

Before we investigate the relations among our different definitions, we want to stress the following obvious – yet impactful – impossibility result:

$\mathsf{Exp}_{\varPi,\mathcal{A}}^{\mathsf{FullPriv}}(\lambda)$

$b \leftarrow \{0,1\}, pp \leftarrow \mathsf{Pg}(1^\lambda), Q \leftarrow \emptyset, n \leftarrow \mathcal{A}(pp),$ **abort if** $n \not> 0$

$(SK, PK) := (\{sk_i\}_{i\in[n]}, \{pk_i\}_{i\in[n]}) \leftarrow (\mathsf{Kg}(pp))_{i\in[n]}$

$S^* \leftarrow \mathcal{A}(SK\backslash\{sk_1\}, PK\backslash\{pk_1\})$ **abort if** $1 \notin S^*$

if $b = 0$ then	$\mathcal{O}^{\mathrm{Chl}}(m)$
$(apk^*, \pi^*) \leftarrow \mathsf{KAg}(PK_{S^*}), pk^* \leftarrow apk^*$	**if** $b = 1$: **return** $\sigma \leftarrow \mathsf{Sign}(sk, m)$
if $b = 1$: $(sk, pk) \leftarrow \mathsf{Kg}(pp), pk^* \leftarrow pk$	$\Sigma \leftarrow \{\mathsf{MulSign}(sk_i, PK_{S^*}, apk^*, m)\}_{sk_i \in SK_{S^*}}$
$b^* \leftarrow \mathcal{A}^{\mathcal{O}^{\mathrm{Chl}}(\cdot)}(pk^*),$ **return** 1 if $b = b^*$	**return** $\sigma \leftarrow \mathsf{Combine}(PK_{S^*}, \pi^*, \Sigma)$

Fig. 7. Our FullPriv game capturing that aggregate signatures and keys are indistinguishable from standard ones. Grayed parts correspond to additions for the All-but-One-Public-Key model (AbOPK) model which will be introduced in Sect. 6.

Theorem 3. *No* MSvKA *schemes with deterministic key aggregation can satisfy the privacy properties* (FullPriv, SetPriv, MemPriv) *in the* KPK *model.*

Proof. As we will show that FullPriv and SetPriv are strictly stronger than MemPriv later in this section, we just prove that an MSvKA with deterministic key aggregation cannot satisfy MemPriv-KPK. We build a MemPriv-KPK adversary $\mathcal{A}$ as follows. $\mathcal{A}$ chooses $n = 3$, learns $\{(sk_i, pk_i)_{i=1,2,3}\}$, and submits the challenge sets $S_0 = \{1, 2\}$ and $S_1 = \{1, 3\}$. When $\mathcal{A}$ gets the challenge aggregated key apk_b, it checks whether $apk' = apk_b$ for $(apk', \_) := \mathsf{KAg}(\{pk_1, pk_2\})$. If the equality holds, the adversary outputs 0, and 1 otherwise. Due to the deterministic KAg, there is a unique aggregated key per signing group, and the adversary wins with probability 1. □

Note that the impossibility result from above immediately rules out the strongest privacy notions for all existing multi-signatures that follow the classic (deterministic) definition from Sect. 2.1, which we have shown to be translatable into the MSvKA framework in Construction 1.

Our adversarial model, granting the adversary access to all secret keys, is stronger than the real-world scenario we have envisioned. Thus, one may question whether the impossibility result for deterministic schemes is a consequence of this (too) strong model, and they could actually satisfy a relaxed yet equally meaningful security notion. It is easy to see that this is not the case, as the attack solely uses knowledge of the public keys and the fact that apk is deterministically derived from them. Thus, even a significantly weaker model, where we don't give the adversary any secret keys or even oracle access to them, could still not be satisfied by any deterministic scheme.

Relations Among Games. We now show that FullPriv is strictly stronger than SetPriv, which in turn is strictly stronger than MemPriv. We omit the dedicated mentioning of the KPK model here, as our results also hold for the AbOPK model that we introduce later in this work. An overview of these results is available in Fig. 8.

Theorem 4 (FullPriv $\Rightarrow$ SetPriv). *For any* MSvKA *scheme it holds that* FullPriv *implies – and is strictly stronger than –* SetPriv.

We need to prove two statements here: the first is that every FullPriv-secure scheme is also SetPriv-secure; the second is that there are schemes that achieve the SetPriv notion, but not FullPriv. The full proof is given in the full paper [29].

The first is intuitively rather straightforward. If the aggregated key and signatures are fully indistinguishable from standard signatures and keys, then the aggregated values can not leak any information about the contained individual signers or group size. The proof is given in the full version of the paper [29] and is slightly more elaborate, as both games have different structures and challenges.

To show that there are schemes that achieve the SetPriv but not FullPriv, we start with a scheme Π that satisfies both and transform it into Π' that loses the FullPriv property but is still SetPriv secure. The idea is rather simple: Let Π' be exactly as Π, with the only difference that the apk' returned from Π'.KAg adds an extra bit, i.e., $apk' = apk\|1$. All algorithms of Π' that work with the aggregated key remove the last bit from apk' and then run identically as Π. This makes the aggregated public key clearly distinguishable from a standard one, so Π' loses the FullPriv property. As the extra bit is independent of the contained signers it does not give the adversary in the SetPriv game any advantage.

Theorem 5 (SetPriv $\Rightarrow$ MemPriv). *For any* MSvKA *scheme it holds that* SetPriv *implies – and is strictly stronger than –* MemPriv.

We again need to prove this in two steps. The first is proving that every SetPriv-secure scheme is also MemPriv-secure. This is straightforward, as both properties are expressed through the same security game, except that MemPriv makes an additional limitation on $\mathcal{A}$'s choice of challenge sets.

For the proof that MemPriv does not imply SetPriv, we must come up with a scheme that satisfies the former but not the latter. We start with a scheme Π that has both properties and change that into Π'. Π' behaves as Π, except that key aggregation now appends the set size to the aggregated key:

$$\Pi'.\mathsf{KAg}(PK) : (apk, \pi) \leftarrow \Pi.\mathsf{KAg}(PK); c := |PK| \; ; \; \textbf{return } (apk' := apk\|c, \pi)$$

The algorithms of Π' taking $apk' = apk\|c$ as input, remove the group size c again and invoke the algorithms of Π on apk. In the MemPriv game, both challenge sets S_0 and S_1 must have the same size, and thus this leaked group size does not give the adversary any advantage, i.e., Π' is still MemPriv-secure. In the SetPriv game, the adversary can now win trivially by submitting two challenge groups of different sizes, regardless of the security of Π. We give a full proof of this idea in the full version of the paper [29].

5   Our Multi-Signature Constructions

We now present our multi-signatures, which are the first schemes that achieve privacy in the KPK model. Our first scheme (randBLS-1) is a simple modification

Fig. 8. Relation between our definitions under different models. $A{\rightarrow}B$ means A implies B (any scheme has property A, also has property B). $A{\not\rightarrow}B$ means A does not imply B (there exists a scheme s.t. has property A, but not property B). Properties with green boxes are achievable by BLS-dMS and MuSig multi-signature schemes. (Color figure online)

of the BLS multi-signature from Boneh et al. [12] and satisfies the strongest privacy guarantee FullPriv-KPK. Regarding unforgeability, it only achieves MSvKA-UNF-1 security which is the same security level as the original scheme. Using our UNF-1 to UNF-3 transformation from Sect. 3, we turn this into a variant (randBLS-2) which has the strongest unforgeability – but for the price of losing the FullPriv property, as this now requires key-prefixing (which is not considered standard in BLS signatures). This randBLS-2 scheme still satisfies the SetPriv-KPK and MemPriv-KPK properties, which again improves the state of the art for MSvKA-UNF-3 secure scheme. In fact, our randBLS-2 scheme still provides aggregated signatures that are indistinguishable from standard BLS signatures *with* public-key prefixing. Thus, in applications where such prefixing is done already – such as in public ledgers – this construction blends in perfectly.

5.1   Our randBLS-1 Construction

Existing constructions cannot achieve any privacy property in the KPK setting, due to their deterministic key aggregation. Thus, the main task is to turn key aggregation into a probabilistic algorithm that allows the verifiability of a group only with the knowledge of a dedicated proof π. We achieve this by a simple twist in the BLS-based multi-signature scheme of Boneh et al. [12].

Our scheme has identical key generation and signature verification algorithms as the original BLS signature and BLS multi-signatures. The main difference is that we include a random r in the exponent hash $\mathsf{H}_1(pk, PK, r)$ that is used for key aggregation and signature combination. This random r is our proof π, and verifying an aggregated key is recomputing the product using the same ("random") hash. We further move the exponentiation with this hash from MulSign to Combine, which is due to our choice to only include π in Combine but not in MulSign (which was mainly for efficiency purposes and has no impact on the achievable unforgeability notion).

Construction 3 (randBLS-1). *Our first construction* randBLS-1 *uses a bilinear group generator* BGGen, *two hash functions* $\mathsf{H}_0 : \{0,1\}^* \to \mathbb{G}$ *and* $\mathsf{H}_1 : \{0,1\}^* \to \mathbb{Z}_p$ *and is defined as follows:*

$\mathsf{Pg}(1^\lambda)$: Return $(e, \mathbb{G}, \hat{\mathbb{G}}, g, \hat{g}, p) \leftarrow \mathsf{BGGen}(1^\lambda)$.
$\mathsf{Kg}(pp)$: Return $sk \leftarrow \mathbb{Z}_p^*$, $pk \leftarrow \hat{g}^{sk}$.

$\mathsf{KAg}(PK)$: $r \leftarrow \{0,1\}^\lambda$, $apk \leftarrow \prod_{pk_i \in PK} pk_i^{\mathsf{H}_1(pk_i, PK, r)}$. Return $(apk, \pi := r)$.

$\mathsf{VfKAg}(PK, apk, \pi)$: $apk' \leftarrow \prod_{pk_i \in PK} pk_i^{\mathsf{H}_1(pk_i, PK, \pi)}$. Return $apk = apk'$.

$\mathsf{MulSign}(sk_i, PK, apk, m)$: Return $s_i \leftarrow \mathsf{H}_0(m)^{sk_i}$.

$\mathsf{Combine}(PK, \pi, \{s_i\}_{pk_i \in PK})$: Return $\sigma \leftarrow \prod_{pk_i \in PK} s_i^{\mathsf{H}_1(pk_i, PK, \pi)}$.

$\mathsf{Vf}(apk, \sigma, m)$: Return $e(\sigma, \hat{g}) = e(\mathsf{H}_0(m), apk)$.

Unforgeability of randBLS-1. The unforgeability of BLS multi-signatures in the plain public-key model relies on the non-linear mapping in the key aggregation algorithm, and we must ensure that our randomization technique does not introduce a weakness. As the involved randomness in key aggregation is chosen by the adversary in our unforgeability games, he can try to perform attacks similar to rogue-key attacks to form an aggregated key which is independent of the challenge public key pk^*. This is not the case for our scheme, as we use the involved randomness as an additional input to the random oracle H_1. Even if the adversary chooses the randomness maliciously, he still cannot manipulate H_1's output to have a specific algebraic form to cancel pk^* out from the aggregated keys. Regarding the different unforgeability levels, MSvKA-UNF-1 is the best we can hope for, as MulSign is entirely independent of PK and apk.

Theorem 6 (Unforgeability of randBLS-1). *The* randBLS-1 *multi-signature scheme in Construction 3 is* MSvKA-UNF-1 *secure in the ROM for* q_{H_0} *and* q_{H_1} *oracle queries for random oracles* H_0 *and* H_1 *if the co-CDH assumption, Definition 1, holds and* $p > 8q_{\mathsf{H}_1}/\mu(\lambda)$.

Proof (Sketch). Our proof closely follows the unforgeability proof of deterministic BLS multi-signatures from [12]. We aim to build a co-CDH adversary using an efficient forger $\mathcal{A}$. Let us recap a proof strategy for original BLS signatures first [14]: Given a co-CDH problem instance $(A, B, \hat{B})$, the proof simulates an unforgeability game for $pk^* \leftarrow \hat{B}$. We set a $\mathsf{H}_0(m)$ query to $\mathsf{H}_0(m) \leftarrow A$, and hope to get a forgery σ for the message m. For a valid forgery, we have $e(A, pk^*) = e(\sigma, \hat{g})$, so σ is the solution for the given co-CDH instance.

The challenge in the multi-signature case is that the adversary does not output a forgery for pk^* directly, but an aggregated signature for some apk that contains pk^*. Thus, we need a way to get a valid signature for some $(pk^*)^c$ where c is a non-zero value (that will be known to the reduction). Our proof strategy is as follows: We first build an algorithm $\mathcal{B}$ which behaves as the co-CDH solver that uses the original BLS forger we explained above. This algorithm $\mathcal{B}$ only plays an intermediate role, and its task is to get an aggregated signature and key for some message in the simulated unforgeability game that embeds the co-CDH challenge. Our $\mathsf{VfKAg}()$ algorithm ensures that the set PK and the aggregated key apk that are chosen by the adversary satisfy that $pk^* \in PK$ and $apk = \prod_{pk_i \in PK} pk_i^{a_i}$ for $a_i = \mathsf{H}_1(pk_i, PK, \pi)$. We then use the Generalized Forking Lemma on the algorithm $\mathcal{B}$ to get two forgeries σ and σ' for aggregated keys apk and apk' such that $apk/apk' = (pk^*)^c$ for some non-zero c value. In particular, the forking lemma gives us two forgeries for the same set PK and the proof π. Further, all a_i values above are set to the same value except the $a_i = \mathsf{H}_1(pk_i, PK, \pi)$ for

$pk_i = pk^*$. For $pk_i = pk^*$, the random oracle is programmed to another value in the second forgery, so when we compute apk/apk' all values except pk^* cancel out. Finally, as we know that $e(A, apk) = e(\sigma, \hat{g})$ and $e(A, apk') = e(\sigma', \hat{g})$ holds, we also know that $e(A, apk/apk') = e(\sigma/\sigma', \hat{g})$, and thus the solution for the given co-CDH instance is $(\sigma/\sigma')^{1/c}$. The formal proof is in the full paper [29].

Privacy of randBLS-1. Our randBLS-1 construction achieves the strongest privacy notion FullPriv in the KPK model, i.e., produces indistinguishable aggregated keys and signatures from standard ones generated with BLSSign. This immediately implies that the notions of MemPriv and SetPriv are satisfied too.

Theorem 7 (Privacy of randBLS-1). *The* randBLS-1 *scheme in Construction 3 is* FullPriv-KPK *secure for* Sign = BLSSign *in ROM for* H_1 *as a random oracle.*

Proof (Sketch). In the FullPriv-KPK game, the adversary receives either an aggregated key and signatures (if $b = 0$) or a freshly sampled public key with the corresponding signatures (if $b = 1$) and must not be able to determine b. We prove this property through a series of games, where we end in a game where $\mathcal{A}$ always receives a freshly chosen (standard) key and signatures thereof.

First, we show that for an aggregated key apk^* in our scheme, we can generate a corresponding *aggregated secret key* $ask^* := \sum_{pk_i \in PK_{S^*}} sk_i \cdot H_1(pk_i, PK_{S^*}, \pi^*)$ that we can use to answer the signing queries using the plain BLS signing algorithm BLSSign$(ask^*, \cdot)$, instead of aggregating individual signatures. Subsequently, we show through several steps that this ask^* value is indistinguishable from a freshly sampled secret key. It is easy to see that ask^* (and apk^*) are uniformly random to a party who does not know the corresponding proof π^*, due to the random oracle involved in the computation. We then show that the proof π^* remains unknown to $\mathcal{A}$ even after outputting the challenge key and the corresponding signatures that implicitly contain π^*, which again stems from the random oracle property of H_1. In the final game, we replace (ask^*, apk^*) with a freshly sampled secret key, i.e., the game behaves identically for $b = 0$ and $b = 1$ and thus cannot reveal any information about the challenge bit b. The full proof is given in the full version of the paper [29].

5.2 Our randBLS-2 Construction

We now show how we can increase unforgeability to MSvKA-UNF-3, for the price of reducing privacy to SetPriv-KPK. This is done by simply applying the generic UNF-1 to UNF-3 transformation (from Construction 2) to randBLS-1. That is, the MulSign algorithm of our second scheme randBLS-2 now strictly binds each signature to the intended apk by including the key in the hash.

Construction 4 (randBLS-2). *The* randBLS-2 *is identical to* randBLS-1, *except for the following two algorithms:*

MulSign(sk_i, PK, apk, m): Return $s \leftarrow H_0(apk, m)^{sk_i}$
Vf(apk, σ, m): Return $e(\sigma, \hat{g}) = e(H_0(apk, m), apk)$.

Using Theorem 2, we conclude that the randBLS-2 scheme is MSvKA-UNF-3 secure if randBLS-1 is MSvKA-UNF-1 secure and key binding. The former was shown in Theorem 6, and thus what remains to be shown is that randBLS-1 is key binding, i.e., an adversary cannot come up with two sets $PK \neq PK'$ that map to the same aggregated key apk.

The simple proof of Theorem 8 is given in the full paper [29] and mainly relies on the fact that each aggregated key is sampled uniformly random by the random choice of r and H_1 being a random oracle, which ensures that collisions occur with negligible probability only. We can then conclude the Corollary 1.

Theorem 8. *The* randBLS-1 *scheme in Construction 3 is key-binding in the ROM for* H_1 *as a random oracle.*

Corollary 1 (Unforgeability of randBLS-2**).** *The* randBLS-2 *scheme in Construction 4 is* MSvKA-*UNF-3 secure in the ROM for* H_0 *and* H_1 *as random oracles if the co-CDH assumption holds and* $2^\lambda > 8q_H/\mu(\lambda)$ *for* q_H *oracle queries.*

As we now let Vf check the pairing for $H_0(apk, m)$ we can no longer achieve FullPriv for the *standard* BLSSign algorithm anymore (which uses $H_0(m)$). However, we still use the FullPriv game as a simple way to prove that the SetPriv-KPK is satisfied: we have shown in Theorem 4 that SetPriv is implied if a scheme satisfies FullPriv-KPK against *some* Sign algorithm. Thus, we simply prove FullPriv-KPK for the modified verification equation (but run for an individual signature, not an aggregated one) and then conclude SetPriv (which in turn implies MemPriv) from there. The proof of the Theorem 9 is the same as the proof of Theorem 7 except that we use a key-prefixed version of BLSSign instead of the standard one, and given in the full paper [29]. Using Theorem 4, we conclude the Corollary 2.

Theorem 9. *The* randBLS-2 *scheme in Construction 4 is* FullPriv-KPK *for the signing algorithm* $\mathsf{Sign}(sk, m) := H_0(\hat{g}^{sk}, m)^{sk}$ *in ROM for the random oracle* H_1.

Corollary 2 (Privacy of randBLS-2**).** *The* randBLS-2 *scheme in Construction 4 is* SetPriv-KPK *(and thus* MemPriv-KPK*) secure if* H_1 *is a random oracle.*

6   Weaker Privacy and Analysis of Existing Constructions

We have already shown that all existing multi-signature schemes cannot satisfy the privacy properties defined in Sect. 4, due to their deterministic key aggregation. As this is in contrast to what has been claimed, we investigate the weaker privacy guarantees that such deterministic systems can provide. We start by introducing our weaker "All-but-One-PK" (AbOPK) model that adapts the FullPriv, SetPriv and MemPriv definitions by restricting the adversary to knowing all individual public keys, except of one. We then analyze the most common BLS- and Schnorr-based multi-signatures and prove that they do achieve privacy in this weaker model. An overview of the security and privacy of the existing schemes and our new constructions is given in Fig. 9.

6.1   Privacy Model for Deterministic Schemes: AbOPK

As stated in Theorem 3, none of our privacy definitions is achievable when key aggregation is deterministic: the adversary can win each game trivially by comparing the aggregated key(s) he can compute for the challenge set(s) with the key he received from the challenger. To define the desirable privacy properties in such a deterministic environment, we need to capture and exclude the trivial yet inherent attacks imposed by this setting. This requires two changes:

- The adversary must not know all public keys anymore, i.e., at least one public key must remain secret.
- The adversary must not be able to receive aggregate keys or multi-signatures of the challenge group(s) outside the challenge oracle. This immediately rules out any unlinkability guarantees.

We realize both in our "All-but-One-PK" (AbOPK) model that we can apply to all three privacy games. In the AbOPK version of our games, the adversary will no longer receive all public keys, but all but one. Without loss of generality, we set pk_1 to be the unknown key. We also follow the modeling choice from Sect. 4 and generously give the adversary the secret key to every public key it is allowed to know. Thus, when generating all key pairs in our games, denoted as (SK, PK), the adversary now only gets $(SK \setminus \{sk_1\}, PK \setminus \{pk_1\})$. The AbOPK limitation has a strong impact on the overall privacy guarantees, as the adversary in all our games is now prevented from interacting with the holder of the "secret" public key at all.

Definition 8 (AbOPK Models). *A* MSvKA *scheme Π has the property* $\mathsf{X} \in \{\mathsf{SetPriv}, \mathsf{MemPriv}, \mathsf{FullPriv}\}$ *in the* AbOPK *model, if for all PPT adversaries $\mathcal{A}$ it holds that* $|\Pr[\mathsf{Exp}_{\Pi,\mathcal{A}}^{\mathsf{X-AbOPK}}(\lambda) = 1] - 1/2| \leq \mathsf{negl}(\lambda)$ *where* $\mathsf{Exp}_{\Pi,\mathcal{A}}^{\mathsf{X-AbOPK}}$ *is defined in Figs. 6 and 7.*

Impact of AbOPK. The most obvious change in our AbOPK model is that the adversary no longer receives all keys (SK, PK) in the second stage of our games, but only gets $(SK \setminus \{sk_1\}, PK \setminus \{pk_1\})$.

Another impact of our AbOPK models is that the challenge sets, that the adversary must output in all three games, become more restrictive. As the entire privacy now relies on the secrecy of pk_1, this public key must of course be part of the challenge sets – otherwise the adversary knows again all keys that will be aggregated into apk^*. This is modeled through additional abort conditions which check that 1 (as key index) is contained in all challenge sets. Putting both limitations – on the challenge sets and keys – together, this means that the adversary can never run any key aggregation or multi-signature algorithms for a *particular* challenge group (i.e., either S_0 and S_1 in the MemPriv, SetPriv games or S^* in the FullPriv game). Thus, also schemes that create aggregate keys and signatures that are linkable for each group PK can satisfy these weaker AbOPK privacy notions.

Obviously, the stronger KPK models are indeed strictly stronger than the weaker AbOPK ones. For completeness, we prove the relations in the full paper [29].

Scheme	Unforg.	FullPriv	SetPriv	MemPriv
BLS-dMS [12]	UNF-1	AbOPK	AbOPK	AbOPK
BLS-dMS + KeyPrefix (Cons. 2)	UNF-3	$-/(\text{AbOPK}^*)$	AbOPK	AbOPK
MuSig [31]	UNF-3	AbOPK*	AbOPK	AbOPK
Our Work (randBLS-1)	UNF-1	KPK	KPK	KPK
Our Work (randBLS-2)	UNF-3	$-/(\text{KPK}^*)$	KPK	KPK

Fig. 9. Comparison of existing and our new multi-signatures, regarding their unforgeability and privacy. *Note that there is a difference how "standard" the key-prefixing is that all UNF-3-secure schemes require. For Schnorr signatures, such prefixing, i.e., including the public key in the message hash, is often considered to be the standard – which is why MuSig achieves both UNF-3 and FullPriv security. For BLS signatures, key-prefixing is less standard, and thus all UNF-3 secure schemes that use such prefixing immediately lose the FullPriv privacy. If one considers including $(a)pk$ in the hash as standard for BLS too, then both UNF-3 secure BLS schemes also satisfy FullPriv.

6.2   Analysis of BLS and Schnorr Multi-Signatures

In this section, we summarize the analysis of the most common multi-signatures schemes, BLS-based by Boneh et al. [12] and Schnorr-based MuSig by Maxwell et al. [31]. We also note that our theorems and proofs can be easily adapted to other Schnorr multi-signatures with the same key aggregation technique (e.g., [25,33]).

We show that these schemes satisfy FullPriv-AbOPK privacy, i.e., produce multi-signatures and aggregate keys that are indistinguishable from individual ones (derived via SchnorrSign and BLSSign, respectively), if at least one public key remains unknown to the adversary. The formal theorems related to these properties and the proof of those theorems are in the full paper [29].

Originally, BLS-based multi-signature was proven to be MSdKA-UNF-1 secure and MuSig to be MSdKA-UNF-2 secure. Using our transformations from Sect. 3, we can conclude that the BLS-based scheme is MSvKA-UNF-1 secure and MuSig is MSvKA-UNF-3 secure. The difference in the unforgeability level originates from the fact, that Schnorr-schemes widely use the key-prefixed version, even in the stand-alone setting, and we followed that choice in our analysis. The BLS-based scheme needs to apply key-prefixing, which then allows us to prove UNF-3 security via our transformation in Theorem 2. This incurs a slight loss in privacy, as this scheme then only satisfies SetPriv-AbOPK.

7   Applications

We conclude by showing how our MSvKA schemes can be applied in the use case that was one of the main motivations of our work: public ledgers. Another application we envision is privacy-preserving authentication from hardware tokens, and refer to the full version of the paper [29] for a discussion of how this can be realized from our multi-signatures.

For the public ledger use case, we follow the simple example from the introduction. That is, we have three users – Alice, Bob, and Carol – each having their

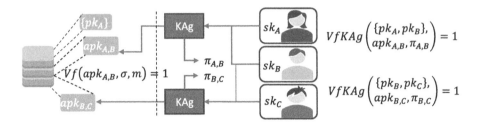

Fig. 10. Group signing using MSvKA in a public ledger.

own individual key pair, where one account is owned by Alice alone, the second by Alice and Bob, and the third by Bob and Carol. There are in fact different ways how our scheme could be used in this setting. The solution we sketch here is and is summarized in Fig. 10 is, to us, the most natural one.

Individual Setup. Every user generates their individual key pair, as $\mathsf{Kg}(pp) \to (sk_X, pk_X)$ for $X \in \{A, B, C\}$. We assume all public keys are publicly known to everyone, and the individual account by Alice is associated with pk_A.

Group Setup. When Alice wants to generate a joint account with Bob, either of them can trigger the key aggregation. Assuming this is done by Alice, she runs:

$$\mathsf{KAg}(PK_{A,B}) \to (apk_{A,B}, \pi_{A,B})$$

where $PK_{A,B} := \{pk_A, pk_B\}$. Alice locally stores the tuple $(Alice/Bob, apk_{A,B}, \pi_{A,B})$ and sends $(apk_{A,B}, \pi_{A,B})$ to Bob. Bob, upon receiving the tuple, now verifies that this aggregated public key is correctly formed by running:

$$\mathsf{VfKAg}(PK_{A,B}, apk_{A,B}, \pi_{A,B}) \to b$$

If $b = 1$, Bob stores $(Alice/Bob, apk_{A,B}, \pi_{A,B})$ and puts $apk_{A,B}$ on the ledger for the shared account.

For the shared account of Bob and Carol, the same procedure is used, and the resulting $apk_{B,C}$ gets associated with their account. At the end, Alice keeps $(Alice/Bob, apk_{A,B}, \pi_{A,B})$, Bob has $(Alice/Bob, apk_{A,B}, \pi_{A,B})$, $(Bob/Carol, apk_{B,C}, \pi_{B,C})$ and Carol stores $(Bob/Carol, apk_{B,C}, \pi_{B,C})$.

One could also assign one member of each group as the designated combiner, then only this party needs to keep the associated π. The values established for each group are not security-critical – their leakage have no impact on the guaranteed unforgeability, only on privacy. There is no privacy towards anyone knowing the proof π, so the value should be treated with some care but clearly does not have to be protected at the same level as the user's long-term secret key. What is important here is that each party stores the approved *apk* for each group, as this will be needed as trusted input for each signature contribution.

Group Signing. Whenever Alice and Bob want to make a transaction from their shared account protected with $apk_{A,B}$, both parties need to provide their signature contribution using their long-term key. Let us assume that Alice initiated the transaction. She computes her share as:

$$\mathsf{MulSign}(sk_A, PK_{A,B}, apk_{A,B}, m) \to s_A$$

Alice informs Bob about this request and sends him (s_A, m). If Bob agrees, he first computes his share and then combines both:

$$\mathsf{MulSign}(sk_B, PK_{A,B}, apk_{A,B}, m) \to s_B; \quad \mathsf{Combine}(PK_{A,B}, \pi_{A,B}, \{s_A, s_B\}) \to \sigma$$

Bob then sends (m, σ) to the ledger to release the transaction. Signatures for Bob/Carol are done analogously, and signatures for pk_A are just standard signatures.

Verification. Anyone on the ledger can verify the correctness of the transaction, e.g., for $apk_{A,B}$ by running $\mathsf{Vf}(apk_{A,B}, \sigma, m) \to b$. This verification does not require any individual keys or even knowledge of who the underlying signers are.

Privacy Guarantees. If a scheme with FullPriv privacy, such as randBLS-1 is used, then no one (except Alice and Bob) can even notice that $apk_{A,B}$ is an aggregated public key. If a scheme with Set/MemPriv privacy, such as randBLS-2 is used, then an outsider can see that this is an account controlled by multiple parties. However, the members of that group and the size of the group are still fully hidden. Our notion guarantees that privacy to anyone who is not part of the group, i.e., even a malicious Carol knowing all public keys and having a joint account with Bob cannot recognize that Bob also controls $apk_{A,B}$.

If key-prefixing in BLS is also done for standard signatures on the ledger, then aggregated keys and signatures from randBLS-2 are again fully indistinguishable from standard ones.

Unforgeability and Non-frameability Guarantees. For this application, our strongest notion UNF-3 is needed, which is satisfied only by randBLS-2. It ensures that all signature contributions are strictly bound to the context. That is, e.g., signature shares for $apk_{A,B}$ can neither be used for Alice's private account nor for the shared account Bob has with Carol.

Our schemes hide all information about their signers by default but also come with dedicated key verification. It is therefore important that this verification cannot be misused for framing attacks. Assume that Alice and Bob make a dubious transaction from their account $apk_{A,B}$, and later want to claim that this was actually done by Carol and Dave, e.g., by coming up with a proof π^* such that $\mathsf{VfKAg}(\{pk_C, pk_D\}, apk_{A,B}, \pi^*) = 1$. As non-frameability is guaranteed by all unforgeability notions, this is infeasible for every secure MSvKA scheme.

Acknowledgements. This research was partially funded by the HPI Research School on Data Science and Engineering. It was also supported by the German Federal Ministry of Education and Research (BMBF) through funding of the ATLAS project under reference number 16KISA037.

References

1. Bitcoin wiki. https://en.bitcoin.it/wiki/Multi-signature
2. Iohk musig2 implementation. https://github.com/input-output-hk/musig2
3. Ambrosin, M., Conti, M., Ibrahim, A., Neven, G., Sadeghi, A.R., Schunter, M.: SANA: secure and scalable aggregate network attestation. In: Proceedings of the 2016 ACM SIGSAC Conference on Computer and Communications Security (2016)
4. Backes, M., Hanzlik, L., Kluczniak, K., Scneider, J.: Signatures with Flexible Public Key: Introducing Equivalence Classes for Public Keys (2018), report Number: 191
5. Bagherzandi, A., Cheon, J.H., Jarecki, S.: Multisignatures secure under the discrete logarithm assumption and a generalized forking lemma. In: Proceedings of the 15th ACM conference on Computer and communications security - CCS '08, p. 449. Alexandria, Virginia, USA (2008)
6. Baird, L., et al.: Threshold signatures in the multiverse. In: 2023 IEEE Symposium on Security and Privacy (SP) (2023)
7. Baldimtsi, F., et al.: Subset-optimized BLS Multi-signature with Key Aggregation (2023). https://eprint.iacr.org/2023/498, report Number: 498
8. Bellare, M., Crites, E., Komlo, C., Maller, M., Tessaro, S., Zhu, C.: Better than advertised security for non-interactive threshold signatures. In: Advances in Cryptology – CRYPTO 2022 (2022)
9. Bellare, M., Dai, W.: Chain reductions for multi-signatures and the hbms scheme. In: Advances in Cryptology – ASIACRYPT 2021 (2021)
10. Bellare, M., Neven, G.: Multi-signatures in the plain public-key model and a general forking lemma. In: Proceedings of the 13th ACM Conference on Computer and Communications Security, CCS 2006 (2006)
11. Boldyreva, A.: Threshold signatures, multisignatures and blind signatures based on the gap-Diffie-Hellman-group signature scheme. In: Desmedt, Y.G. (ed.) PKC 2003. LNCS, vol. 2567, pp. 31–46. Springer, Heidelberg (2003). https://doi.org/10.1007/3-540-36288-6_3
12. Boneh, D., Drijvers, M., Neven, G.: Compact multi-signatures for smaller blockchains. In: Peyrin, T., Galbraith, S. (eds.) ASIACRYPT 2018. LNCS, vol. 11273, pp. 435–464. Springer, Cham (2018). https://doi.org/10.1007/978-3-030-03329-3_15
13. Boneh, D., Komlo, C.: Threshold signatures with private accountability. In: Advances in Cryptology – CRYPTO 2022 (2022). https://doi.org/10.1007/978-3-031-15985-5_19
14. Boneh, D., Lynn, B., Shacham, H.: Short signatures from the weil pairing. In: Advances in Cryptology - ASIACRYPT 2001 (2001)
15. Celi, S., Griffy, S., Hanzlik, L., Kempner, O.P., Slamanig, D.: SoK: Signatures With Randomizable Keys (2023), https://eprint.iacr.org/2023/1524, publication info: Preprint
16. Crites, E., Komlo, C., Maller, M.: How to Prove Schnorr Assuming Schnorr: Security of Multi- and Threshold Signatures (2021). https://eprint.iacr.org/2021/1375, report Number: 1375

17. Das, P., Faust, S., Loss, J.: A Formal Treatment of Deterministic Wallets. In: Proceedings of the 2019 ACM SIGSAC Conference on Computer and Communications Security, CCS 2019, pp. 651–668. Association for Computing Machinery, New York, November 2019. https://doi.org/10.1145/3319535.3354236, https://dl.acm.org/doi/10.1145/3319535.3354236
18. Das, S., Camacho, P., Xiang, Z., Nieto, J., Bunz, B., Ren, L.: Threshold Signatures from Inner Product Argument: Succinct, Weighted, and Multi-threshold (2023). https://eprint.iacr.org/2023/598, report Number: 598
19. Drijvers, M., Edalatnejad, K., Ford, B., Kiltz, E., Loss, J., Neven, G., Stepanovs, I.: On the Security of Two-Round Multi-Signatures. In: 2019 IEEE Symposium on Security and Privacy (SP) (2019)
20. Drijvers, M., Gorbunov, S., Neven, G., Wee, H.: Pixel: multi-signatures for consensus. In: Proceedings of the 29th USENIX Conference on Security Symposium (2020)
21. Eaton, E., Lepoint, T., Wood, C.A.: Security Analysis of Signature Schemes with Key Blinding (2023). https://eprint.iacr.org/2023/380, report Number: 380
22. Fleischhacker, N., Krupp, J., Malavolta, G., Schneider, J., Schröder, D., Simkin, M.: Efficient Unlinkable Sanitizable Signatures from Signatures with Re-Randomizable Keys (2015), report Number: 395
23. Garg, S., Jain, A., Mukherjee, P., Sinha, R., Wang, M., Zhang, Y.: hinTS: Threshold Signatures with Silent Setup (2023). https://eprint.iacr.org/2023/567, report Number: 567
24. Komlo, C., Goldberg, I.: FROST: flexible round-optimized schnorr threshold signatures. In: Selected Areas in Cryptography (2021)
25. Kılınç Alper, H., Burdges, J.: Two-round trip schnorr multi-signatures via delinearized witnesses. In: Malkin, T., Peikert, C. (eds.) CRYPTO 2021. LNCS, vol. 12825, pp. 157–188. Springer, Cham (2021). https://doi.org/10.1007/978-3-030-84242-0_7
26. Le, D.P., Yang, G., Ghorbani, A.: DDH-based Multisignatures with Public Key Aggregation (2019). https://eprint.iacr.org/2019/771, report Number: 771
27. Lee, K.: Decentralized Threshold Signatures for Blockchains with Non-Interactive and Transparent Setup (2023). https://eprint.iacr.org/2023/1206, report Number: 1206
28. Lee, K., Kim, H.: Two-round multi-signatures from okamoto signatures. Mathematics 11(14) (2023). https://doi.org/10.3390/math11143223
29. Lehmann, A., Özbay, C.: Multi-signatures for ad-hoc and privacy-preserving group signing. Cryptology ePrint Archive, Paper 2023/1884 (2023). https://eprint.iacr.org/2023/1884. https://eprint.iacr.org/2023/1884
30. Li, M., Zhang, M., Wang, Q., Ding, H., Meng, W., Zhu, L., Zhang, Z., Lin, X.: Decentralized Threshold Signatures with Dynamically Private Accountability, August 2023. http://arxiv.org/abs/2304.07937. arXiv:2304.07937 [cs]
31. Maxwell, G., Poelstra, A., Seurin, Y., Wuille, P.: Simple Schnorr multi-signatures with applications to Bitcoin. Des. Codes Crypt. 87(9), 2139–2164 (2019)
32. Micali, S., Ohta, K., Reyzin, L.: Accountable-subgroup multisignatures: extended abstract. In: Proceedings of the 8th ACM conference on Computer and Communications Security (2001)
33. Nick, J., Ruffing, T., Seurin, Y.: MuSig2: simple two-round schnorr multi-signatures. In: Malkin, T., Peikert, C. (eds.) CRYPTO 2021. LNCS, vol. 12825, pp. 189–221. Springer, Cham (2021). https://doi.org/10.1007/978-3-030-84242-0_8
34. Pan, J., Wagner, B.: Chopsticks: Fork-free two-round multi-signatures from non-interactive assumptions. In: Advances in Cryptology – EUROCRYPT 2023 (2023)

35. Pan, S., Chan, K.Y., Cui, H., Yuen, T.H.: Multi-signatures for ECDSA and its applications in blockchain. In: Information Security and Privacy (2022)
36. Ristenpart, T., Yilek, S.: The power of proofs-of-possession: securing multiparty signatures against rogue-key attacks. In: Naor, M. (ed.) EUROCRYPT 2007. LNCS, vol. 4515, pp. 228–245. Springer, Heidelberg (2007). https://doi.org/10.1007/978-3-540-72540-4_13
37. Syta, E., Tamas, I., Visher, D., Wolinsky, D.I., Jovanovic, P., Gasser, L., Gailly, N., Khoffi, I., Ford, B.: Keeping Authorities "Honest or Bust" with Decentralized Witness Cosigning, May 2016. arXiv:1503.08768 [cs]
38. Tessaro, S., Zhu, C.: Threshold and multi-signature schemes from linear hash functions. In: Advances in Cryptology – EUROCRYPT 2023 (2023), https://doi.org/10.1007/978-3-031-30589-4_22
39. Wuille, P., Nick, J., Towns, A.: Validation of taproot scripts. https://github.com/bitcoin/bips/blob/e918b50731397872ad2922a1b08a5a4cd1d6d546/bip-0342.mediawiki

ReSolveD: Shorter Signatures from Regular Syndrome Decoding and VOLE-in-the-Head

Hongrui Cui[1] , Hanlin Liu[2] , Di Yan[3] , Kang Yang[3]([✉]) , Yu Yu[1,2]([✉]) ,
and Kaiyi Zhang[1]

[1] Shanghai Jiao Tong University, Shanghai, China
{rickfreeman,kzoacn}@sjtu.edu.cn
[2] Shanghai Qi Zhi Institute, Shanghai, China
hans1024@sjtu.edu.cn, yuyu@yuyu.hk
[3] State Key Laboratory of Cryptology, Beijing, China
{yand,yangk}@sklc.org

Abstract. We present ReSolveD, a new candidate post-quantum signature scheme under the regular syndrome decoding (RSD) assumption for random linear codes, which is a well-established variant of the well-known syndrome decoding (SD) assumption. Our signature scheme is obtained by designing a new zero-knowledge proof for proving knowledge of a solution to the RSD problem in the recent VOLE-in-the-head framework using a sketching scheme to verify that a vector has weight exactly one. We achieve a signature size of 3.99 KB with a signing time of 27.3 ms and a verification time of 23.1 ms on a single core of a standard desktop for a 128-bit security level. Compared to the state-of-the-art code-based signature schemes, our signature scheme achieves 1.5×–2× improvement in terms of the common "signature size + public-key size" metric, while keeping the computational efficiency competitive.

1 Introduction

Zero-knowledge (ZK) proof is an important cryptographic tool that enables a prover to convince a verifier of the validity of a statement without revealing any further information. ZK proofs find a lot of applications in various contexts, e.g., secure multi-party computation (MPC), machine learning, and blockchain. Using the Fiat-Shamir heuristic [28], we can transform public-coin zero-knowledge proofs into signature schemes. In particular, this is the main approach to building code-based signature schemes. The recent call of NIST for standardizing post-quantum signatures expressed its primary interest in additional signature schemes that are not based on structured lattices [44], which promotes the research of non-lattice-based signature schemes, particularly code-based signatures.

The well-known syndrome decoding (SD) problem over a binary field $\mathbb{F}_2$ asks, given a matrix $\mathbf{H} \in \mathbb{F}_2^{(m-k) \times m}$ and a target vector $\boldsymbol{y} \in \mathbb{F}_2^{m-k}$, to recover a noise vector $\boldsymbol{e} \in \mathbb{F}_2^m$ such that $\mathbf{H} \cdot \boldsymbol{e} = \boldsymbol{y}$ for some sparse $\boldsymbol{e}$ of exact weight $w \ll m$.

Q. Tang and V. Teague (Eds.): PKC 2024, LNCS 14601, pp. 229–258, 2024.
https://doi.org/10.1007/978-3-031-57718-5_8

The worst-case SD problem in certain parameter regimes is known to be NP-hard [6,13], and its average-case analogue is one of the most promising assumptions for post-quantum cryptography. In the seminal work from three decades ago, Stern [51] introduced the first zero-knowledge proof to prove knowledge of a solution to the SD problem. However, the communication cost is significant due to the high soundness error, and thus the signature size would be very large (i.e. about 37 KB for 128-bit security), when being compiled using the Fiat-Shamir transform. Since then, a few prior works (e.g., [2,20,29,41,52]) optimized Stern's protocol, but the communication cost is still high. To avoid the issue of high soundness error, subsequent code-based signature schemes resort to different code-based problems, e.g., (a) LESS (and some subsequent improvements) [5,14,47] adopts the linear/permutation code equivalence problem, and (b) Durandal [3] depends on the rank SD problem over $\mathbb{F}_{2^m}$. Recently, based on the SD problem, the works [1,15,18,26,27,30,42] obtain significantly lower soundness errors by building zero-knowledge proofs based on the MPC-in-the-head paradigm [35], and achieve the best efficiency for now in terms of the common "signature size + public-key size" metric. We summarize the efficiency and assumptions of recent code-based signature schemes in Table 1. Among these schemes, Wave [22] is the only signature scheme that departs from the line that transforms zero-knowledge proofs with Fiat-Shamir. Instead, Wave adopts the hash-and-sign paradigm that depends on the existence of a code-based trapdoor permutation, which leads to a very large size of public keys. Wave achieves smaller signature sizes but relies on a non-standard code-based assumption. For the common "signature size + public-key size" metric, the Fiat-Shamir-based schemes still offer better performance.

In this work, we focus on designing a new code-based signature scheme under the regular syndrome decoding (RSD) assumption [4], a well-established variant of the well-known SD assumption. Specifically, RSD is the same as SD, except for requiring that the noise vector e is regular, i.e., $e \in \mathbb{F}_2^m$ is divided into w consecutive blocks of length m/w, where each block has exactly one noisy coordinate. Recent works [26,38] presented a reduction from SD to RSD, which builds confidence in the hardness of the RSD problem from a theoretic point of view. Furthermore, the hardness of the RSD problem was thoroughly analyzed by Carozza et al. [18], which gives us more confidence. As far as we know, the regular structure of noises does not lead to significantly better attacks when the code rate is kept large (and thus the recent algebraic attack [17] can be bypassed).

1.1   Our Contributions

In this paper, we put forward a new zero-knowledge (ZK) protocol on proving knowledge of a solution to the RSD problem over $\mathbb{F}_2$. By using the Fiat-Shamir transform, we compile the zero-knowledge protocol into a code-based signature scheme (called ReSolveD). Compared to the state-of-the-art code-based signature schemes, ReSolveD reduces the total size of the signature and public key by a factor of 1.5×–2×, while keeping the signing and verification performance competitive. In Table 1, we compare the efficiency of ReSolveD with the recent code-based signature schemes at the 128-bit security level. Note that LESS [47]

Table 1. Comparison of code-based signature schemes for 128-bit security level. Reported runtimes are extracted from original publications, using a 3.5 GHz Intel Xeon E3-1240 v5 for Wave [22], a 2.8 GHz Intel Core i5-7440HQ for Durandal [3], a 2.1 GHz Intel Core i7-12700 CPU for LESS [47], a 3.8 GHz Intel Core i7 supports AVX2 and AES instructions for [26,27], a 3.1 GHz Intel Core i9-9990K using AVX2 for [1], an Intel Xeon E-2378 with frequency fixed at 2.6 GHz for [42] and a conservative upper bound assuming a 3.8 GHz CPU for [18]. We benchmarked our ReSolveD-128 on a Ubuntu 20.04 LTS machine with AMD Ryzen 5 3600 CPU and 16 GB of RAM using AVX2.

Scheme	Sizes in KB			Runtimes in ms		Assumption
	$|\text{sig}|$	$|\text{pk}|$	$|\text{sig}| + |\text{pk}|$	t_{sign}	t_{verify}	
Wave [22]	1.59	3276.8	3278.39	300	–	large-weight SD over $\mathbb{F}_3$, $(U, U + V)$-codes indist.
Durandal-I [3]	4.06	15.25	19.31	4	5	Rank-SD over $\mathbb{F}_{2^m}$
Durandal-II [3]	5.02	18.61	23.63	5	6	Rank-SD over $\mathbb{F}_{2^m}$
LESS-FM-I [5]	15.2	9.77	24.97	–	–	Linear Code Equivalence
LESS-FM-II [5]	5.25	205.74	210.95	–	–	Perm. Code Equivalence
LESS-FM-III [5]	10.39	11.57	21.96	–	–	Perm. Code Equivalence
LESS-1b [47]	8.4	13.6	22	125.52	129.24	Linear Code Equivalence
LESS-1i [47]	5.8	40.8	46.6	121.10	125.43	Linear Code Equivalence
LESS-1s [47]	5.0	95.2	100.2	98.38	101.62	Linear Code Equivalence
CF-LESS-1($s = 2$) [21]	2.42	13.61	16.04	–	–	CF Code Equivalence
CF-LESS-1($s = 4$) [21]	1.80	40.81	42.61	–	–	CF Code Equivalence
GFS-256 [30]	23.98	0.11	24.09	–	–	SD over $\mathbb{F}_{256}$
GFS-1024 [30]	19.76	0.12	19.88	–	–	SD over $\mathbb{F}_{1024}$
FJR21-fast [27]	22.6	0.09	22.69	12.9	12.2	SD over $\mathbb{F}_2$
FJR21-short [27]	16.0	0.09	16.09	62.3	56.6	SD over $\mathbb{F}_2$
BGKM-Sig1 [15]	24.0	0.1	24.1	–	–	SD over $\mathbb{F}_2$
BGKM-Sig2 [15]	19.3	0.2	19.5	–	–	(QC)SD over $\mathbb{F}_2$
BGKM-Sig3 [15]	15.6	0.2	15.8	–	–	(QC)SD over $\mathbb{F}_2$
FJR22-Var1f [26]	15.6	0.09	15.69	–	–	SD over $\mathbb{F}_2$
FJR22-Var1s [26]	10.9	0.09	10.99	–	–	SD over $\mathbb{F}_2$
FJR22-Var2f [26]	17.0	0.09	17.09	13.4	12.7	SD over $\mathbb{F}_2$
FJR22-Var2s [26]	11.8	0.09	11.89	64.2	60.7	SD over $\mathbb{F}_2$
FJR22-Var3f [26]	11.5	0.14	11.64	6.4	5.9	SD over $\mathbb{F}_{256}$
FJR22-Var3s [26]	8.26	0.14	8.4	29.5	27.1	SD over $\mathbb{F}_{256}$
AGH$^+$-fast [1]	11.83	0.14	11.97	1.30	0.98	SD over $\mathbb{F}_{256}$
AGH$^+$-short [1]	8.28	0.14	8.42	2.87	2.59	SD over $\mathbb{F}_{256}$
AGH$^+$-shorter [1]	6.63	0.14	6.77	26.43	25.79	SD over $\mathbb{F}_{256}$
AGH$^+$-shortest [1]	5.56	0.14	5.7	320.66	312.67	SD over $\mathbb{F}_{256}$
MHJ$^+$-Vanilla-short [42]	8.27	0.14	8.6	4.5	4.17	SD over $\mathbb{F}_{256}$
MHJ$^+$-Vanilla-shorter [42]	6.6	0.14	6.94	45.06	42.02	SD over $\mathbb{F}_{256}$
MHJ$^+$-PoW-short [42]	7.78	0.14	8.11	4.34	4	SD over $\mathbb{F}_{256}$
MHJ$^+$-PoW-shorter [42]	6.06	0.14	6.34	42.55	39.75	SD over $\mathbb{F}_{256}$
CCJ-rsd-f [18]	12.52	0.09	12.61	2.8*	–	RSD over $\mathbb{F}_2$
CCJ-rsd-m1 [18]	9.69	0.09	9.78	17*	–	RSD over $\mathbb{F}_2$
CCJ-rsd-m2 [18]	9.13	0.09	9.22	31*	–	RSD over $\mathbb{F}_2$
CCJ-rsd-s [18]	8.55	0.09	8.64	65*	–	RSD over $\mathbb{F}_2$
ReSolveD-128-Var1	3.99	0.08	4.07	27.3	23.1	RSD over $\mathbb{F}_2$
ReSolveD-128-Var2	3.43	0.08	3.51	158.73	153.11	RSD over $\mathbb{F}_2$

and CF-LESS [21] lack of parameter sets for 128-bit security, instead we use their parameters for NIST category 1 security. While the work [1] describes three variants of their code-based signature scheme, Table 1 only shows the third one that has the best performance among the three. The shortest version of the signature scheme [1] has a signature size that is closest to the first variant of ReSolveD among prior code-based signature schemes, but the signing and verification timings are more than $10\times$ larger than our scheme. Notice that the shortest version of [1] also offers the smallest size in the "signature + public key" metric. Our second variant achieves $1.5\times$ improvement in terms of that metric with half of the running time. In Sect. 6.2, we also compare ReSolveD with other kinds of post-quantum signature schemes.

While most code-based signature schemes in the Fiat-Shamir line adopt the MPC-in-the-head framework to design ZK proofs, we construct a ZK proof on RSD problems in the VOLE-in-the-head framework [10]. In the VOLE-in-the-head framework, Baum et al. present a non-interactive version of the SoftSpokenOT technique [49] to generate information-theoretic message authentication codes (IT-MACs), and then transform a designated-verifier ZK proof based on IT-MACs (e.g., QuickSilver [56]) to a publicly-verifiable ZK proof. Our starting point is to prove knowledge of a solution to the RSD problem using a ZK proof based on IT-MACs, and then transform it to a public-coin ZK proof using the VOLE-in-the-head paradigm. Due to the additive homomorphism and unforgeability of IT-MACs, the equation $\mathbf{H} \cdot \boldsymbol{e} = \boldsymbol{y}$ is easy to prove. The key point is to prove that $\boldsymbol{e}$ is a regular noise with an exact Hamming weight t.

Notice that we can use the approaches implied in previous code-based signature schemes (e.g., [1,26]) to prove the validity of $\boldsymbol{e}$, but fail to obtain a code-based signature scheme with signature size shorter than the state-of-the-art schemes listed in Table 1. This requires us to exploit an approach that has better compatibility with VOLE-in-the-head. In particular, we refine the sketching technique [16], which is used in verifiable function secret sharing (FSS), to prove the constraint on noise $\boldsymbol{e}$. Additionally, we adopt the recent half-tree technique [32] to optimize the computation of GGM-based random vector commitments. See Sect. 1.2 for more details of our technique.

1.2   Technical Overview

We give a high-level overview of the technical route underlying the ReSolveD signature scheme, then we highlight the technical contributions, which include a novel method for validating the noise vector of an RSD problem and the half-tree optimization integrated into the VOLE-in-the-Head framework.

Code-Based Signatures from VOLE-in-the-Head. A canonical paradigm in code-based signatures is to first design a public-coin ZK proof for code-based problems and then apply the Fiat-Shamir transform to make it a signature scheme. While there are multiple choices in the design of ZK proofs, the recent VOLE-in-the-Head framework [10] provides a promising new direction. In particular, within this framework, we can generate IT-MAC relations in a public-coin fashion and then convert designated-verifier ZK (which relies on such relations) into publicly-verifiable ones. Given the rapid development of designated-verifier ZK [7,8,11, 23,24,53–56], this inspires us to design a designated-verifier ZK tailored to the RSD problem and convert it into a code-based signature scheme using VOLE-in-the-Head.

In more detail, the IT-MAC generation of VOLE-in-the-Head begins with the prover committing to a series of GGM trees. For each tree, the prover opens all but one leaf node to the verifier, which allows them to generate a small field VOLE correlation with the punctured index as the global key using the technique in SoftSpokenOT [49]. By applying de-randomization and consistency checking [37,45,46,49], the small field VOLE correlations can be aggregated so that the global key size is large enough to ensure the binding property of IT-MAC. Then the generated IT-MAC correlations are utilized by the subsequent designated-verifier ZK protocol.

One caveat of the above process is that to open the GGM-based vector commitment, the prover needs to know the punctured index, which is also the IT-MAC global key. Nevertheless, once the global key is known by the prover, the binding property fails to hold, and so does the soundness of the designated-verifier ZK upon which it relies. The crucial observation in [10,19] is that since the DVZK proof is public-coin, the vector commitment opening can be postponed until the proof has been completed. In this way, even if the prover learns the global key, it can no longer change the proof messages that have already been sent.

Checking the Noise Vector Using IT-MAC. We introduce the design of IT-MAC-based designated-verifier ZK for the RSD problem. Our starting point is the QuickSilver protocol [56] that provides an efficient method to verify the quadratic relations among multiple IT-MAC authenticated triples. We now explain how the validity check of the RSD noise vector can be streamlined into the verification of multiple quadratic relations, a task in which the QuickSilver protocol excels.

We assume without loss of generality that the public matrix $\mathbf{H}$ is in the systematic form, i.e., $\mathbf{H} = [\mathbf{I} \| \mathbf{H_B}]$ and that the witness is split accordingly as $e = [e_{\mathbf{A}} \| e_{\mathbf{B}}]$. Since IT-MACs are linearly homomorphic, the prover can commit to $e_{\mathbf{B}}$ and both parties check the Hamming weight constraint on the "virtual" witness $e = [y - \mathbf{H_B} \cdot e_{\mathbf{B}} \| e_{\mathbf{B}}]$ to implicitly check the linear constraint.

Instead of relying on polynomials [1,26] or share-conversions [18] to check the weight constraint, we prove the validity for each noise block by utilizing the sketching technique introduced by Boyle, Gilboa and Ishai [16]. More concretely, when proving the validity of the solution $e = [e_0 \| e_1 \| \dots \| e_{w-1}] \in \mathbb{F}_2^m$ to a RSD problem, we first define w matrices $L^i \in \mathbb{F}_{2^\lambda}^{4 \times m/w}$ each consisting of four rows for all $i \in [0, w)$ (i.e., the linear sketches). The first two rows are uniformly sampled and defined as $r_0^i, r_1^i \leftarrow \mathbb{F}_{2^\lambda}^{m/w}$. The third row is defined as the component-wise product of the first two rows, namely $r_0^i \circ r_1^i$. The last row is an all-1 vector. Then we can compute the sketch $[\![z^i]\!]$ by right-multiplying L^i with $[\![e_i]\!]$ where $[\![e_i]\!]$ is the noise block authenticated using IT-MAC [12,43].

$$\llbracket z^i \rrbracket = \begin{bmatrix} \llbracket z_0^i \rrbracket \\ \llbracket z_1^i \rrbracket \\ \llbracket z_2^i \rrbracket \\ \llbracket z_3^i \rrbracket \end{bmatrix} = \begin{bmatrix} (\boldsymbol{r}_0^i)^T \\ (\boldsymbol{r}_1^i)^T \\ (\boldsymbol{r}_0^i \circ \boldsymbol{r}_1^i)^T \\ 1 \dots 1 \end{bmatrix} \cdot \llbracket \boldsymbol{e}_i \rrbracket.$$

Finally, the verification procedure checks that the sketch $z^i = (z_0^i, z_1^i, z_2^i, z_3^i)$ satisfies the condition that $z_0^i \cdot z_1^i - z_2^i = 0$ and $z_3^i - 1 = 0$ for all $i \in [0, w)$. We view the above expression as a degree-2 polynomial in $r_0^i, r_1^i, \dots, r_{m/w}^i$ whose coefficients are determined by $\boldsymbol{e}_i$. Note that if $\boldsymbol{e}_i$ is not a unit vector, then the condition holds with probability less than $2/2^\lambda$ from Schwartz-Zippel Lemma [50,59].

Using the sketching technique, we can convert the validity check of each noise block into the verification of a simple multiplication relation. By running the QuickSilver protocol which shows a way to prove low-degree polynomials with very high efficiency, we can reduce all w linear checks to a single check by a random-linear combination. We note that due to the application of the sketching technique, our protocol still outperforms the polynomial-based protocols of [1,26] even if we replace the MPC-in-the-Head proof with VOLE-in-the-Head.

Half-Tree Optimization. We observe that a large portion of the computational overhead in the VOLE-in-the-Head framework originates from generating the vector commitments. By applying the half-tree technique [32] we can populate the GGM tree with half the number of calls to symmetric-key ciphers in the random permutation model [31]. In VOLE-in-the-Head, the number of GGM trees is linearly correlated with the communication overhead. Therefore, by optimizing the computational complexity in GGM tree generation, we can use fewer but deeper trees, opening more possibilities in the communication-computation trade-off.

1.3 Paper Organization

This paper is organized as follows: In Sect. 2 and Sect. 3, we introduce notations and definitions for necessary background knowledge on regular syndrome decoding problem, VOLE-in-the-Head paradigm and linear sketching technique. We present our more efficient zero-knowledge proof and signature scheme which yields shorter proof and signature size in Sect. 4 and Sect. 5 respectively. To conclude, we provide experimental evaluations of our construction and make comparisons with other state-of-the-art signature schemes in Sect. 6.

2 Preliminaries

2.1 Notation

We use λ to denote the computational security parameter. We use log to denote logarithms in base 2. We define $[a, b) = \{a, \dots, b-1\}$ and write $[a, b] = \{a, \dots, b\}$ and $[n] = [1, n]$. We write $x \leftarrow S$ to denote sampling x uniformly at random from a finite set S. We use $\{x_i\}_{i \in S}$ to denote the set that consists of all elements

Table 2. Symbols and their meanings in this paper.

Notation	Meaning
$a, [\![a]\!]$	A vector and its authentication
$a_i, a[i,j]$	The i-th coordinate and sub-vector with indices $[i,j]$ of a
$\mathbf{U}, \mathbf{U}[i], \mathbf{U}_j$	A matrix, its i-th row and its j-th column
$\mathbf{I}_k$	The $k \times k$ identity matrix
$\mathsf{M}[a], \mathsf{K}[a]$	IT-MAC tag and local key
m	Length of the noise vector in RSD
$m - k$	Length of the syndrome vector in RSD
w, d	Hamming weight of the noise vector in RSD
$\mathbb{F}_2, \mathbb{F}_{2^{\tau'}}, \mathbb{F}_{2^{\tau\tau'}}$	The base field in syndrome decoding and two extension fields
τ, τ'	Degrees of field extensions where $\tau' = O(\log(\lambda))$ and $\tau\tau' \geq \lambda$
$\mathrm{diag}(\mathbf{\Delta})$	The diagonal matrix with vector $\mathbf{\Delta}$ on its diagonal
$[a\|b], [\mathbf{A}\|\mathbf{B}]$	The concatenation of two vectors or two matrices
$[1\ldots 1]$	The all-one row vector
$a \circ b$	The component-wise multiplication between two vectors
$\mathrm{len}(a), \mathrm{wt}(a)$	The length and Hamming weight of a vector a

with indices in set S. When the context is clear, we abuse the notation and use $\{x_i\}$ to denote such a set.

We use bold lower-case letters like a for column vectors and bold uppercase letters like $\mathbf{A}$ for matrices. We let a_i denote the i-th component of a (with a_0 the first entry) and $a[i,j]$ denote the subvector of a with indices $[i,j]$. Let $\mathrm{len}(a)$ be the length of the vector a. Let $\mathrm{wt}(a)$ be the Hamming weight of the vector a and let $[a\|b]$, $[\mathbf{A}\|\mathbf{B}]$ denote the concatenation of two vectors and matrices, respectively. Let $\mathbf{I}_k$ denote the $k \times k$ identity matrix and $[1\ldots 1]$ denote the all-one row vector where the dimension is implicit in the context. Let $\mathrm{diag}(a)$ be the diagonal matrix with the vector a on its main diagonal. We use the notation $a \circ b$ to denote the component-wise multiplication between two vectors a and b.

We consider the regular syndrome decoding problem over $\mathbb{F}_2$ in this work. Let $\tau, \tau' \in \mathbb{N}$ and fix two monic irreducible polynomials $f_1(X), f_2(X)$ of degrees τ, τ' respectively. We define $\mathbb{F}_{2^{\tau'}} \cong \mathbb{F}_2[X]/f_2(X)$ and $\mathbb{F}_{2^{\tau\tau'}} \cong \mathbb{F}_{2^{\tau'}}[X]/f_1(X)$. Therefore, we can *pack* τ elements in $\mathbb{F}_{2^{\tau'}}$ or $\tau\tau'$ elements in $\mathbb{F}_2$ into one element in $\mathbb{F}_{2^\lambda}$. We also require $\tau\tau' \geq \lambda$. We list the symbols and their definitions of this paper in Table 2.

2.2   Hash Functions

In our protocol, we utilize universal hash functions and circular correlation robust hash functions. Following prior works [31], we define the security requirements in Definition 1 and Definition 2.

Definition 1. *A linear ϵ-almost universal family of hashes is a family of matrices $\mathcal{H} \subseteq \mathbb{F}_2^{r \times (n+h)}$ such that for any nonzero $v \in \mathbb{F}_2^{n+h}$, $\Pr_{\mathsf{H} \leftarrow \mathcal{H}}[\mathsf{H} \cdot v = 0] \leq \epsilon$. A matrix H is n-hiding if the distribution $\mathsf{H} \cdot v$ is independent of $v[0,n)$ for a uniformly random $v \leftarrow \mathbb{F}_2^{n+h}$. The hash family $\mathcal{H}$ is n-hiding if every hash function in this family is n-hiding.*

Definition 2. *Let* $\mathsf{H} : \{0,1\}^\lambda \to \{0,1\}^\lambda$ *be a function. For* $\Gamma \in \{0,1\}^\lambda$, *define* $\mathcal{O}_\Delta^{\mathsf{ccr}}(x,b) = \mathsf{H}(x \oplus \Gamma) \oplus b \cdot \Gamma$. *We don't allow the distinguisher to query the same* x *with both 0 and 1 to avoid the trivial attack. For a distinguisher* $\mathcal{D}$, *we define the following advantage*

$$\mathsf{Adv}_\mathsf{H}^{\mathsf{ccr}} := \left| \Pr_{\Gamma \leftarrow \{0,1\}^\lambda} [\mathcal{D}^{\mathcal{O}_\Delta^{\mathsf{ccr}}(\cdot)}(1^\lambda) = 1] - \Pr_{f \leftarrow \mathcal{F}_{\lambda+1,\lambda}} [\mathcal{D}^{f(\cdot)}(1^\lambda) = 1] \right|,$$

where $\mathcal{F}_{\lambda+1,\lambda}$ *denotes the set of all functions mapping* $(\lambda+1)$-*bit inputs to* λ-*bit outputs.* H *is* (t, q, ϵ)-*circular correlation robust if for all* $\mathcal{D}$ *running in time* t *and making at most* q *queries to the oracle we have* $\mathsf{Adv}_\mathsf{H}^{\mathsf{ccr}} \le \epsilon$.

2.3 Regular Syndrome Decoding

We recall the regular syndrome decoding problem (RSD) where the noise vector is the concatenation of several *unit vectors*. We inherit the notations from [26] (named *d*-split syndrome decoding in that paper).

Definition 3. *Let* m, k, w, d *be positive integers such that* $m > k$, $m > w$ *and* $d = w$. *The regular noise syndrome decoding problem with parameters* (m, k, w, d) *is the following problem: Let* $\mathbf{H}, \mathbf{e}$ *and* $\mathbf{y}$ *be such that:*

1. $\mathbf{H}$ *is uniformly sampled from* $\mathbb{F}_2^{(m-k) \times m}$,
2. $\mathbf{e}$ *is uniformly sampled from* $\{[\mathbf{e}_0 \| ... \| \mathbf{e}_{w-1}] : \forall i \in [0, w), \mathbf{e}_i \in \mathbb{F}_2^{\frac{m}{w}}, \|\mathbf{e}_i\|_0 = 1\}$,
3. $\mathbf{y}$ *is defined as* $\mathbf{y} := \mathbf{H} \cdot \mathbf{e}$. *From* $(\mathbf{H}, \mathbf{y})$, *find* $\mathbf{e}$.

Systematic Form of RSD. Following previous works [18,26] we assume without loss of generality that the matrix $\mathbf{H}$ is in the systematic form, i.e., $\mathbf{H} = [\mathbf{I}_{m-k} \| \mathbf{H_B}]$. Therefore, in the zero-knowledge protocol, the solution $\mathbf{e} = [\mathbf{e_A} \| \mathbf{e_B}]$ can be compressed into a smaller one $\mathbf{e_B}$ since the complete witness can be linearly expressed as $\mathbf{e} = [\mathbf{y} - \mathbf{H_B} \cdot \mathbf{e_B} \| \mathbf{e_B}]$.

The benefit of this optimization is two-fold. Firstly, by compressing the witness we can reduce the communication complexity of the ZK protocol, and therefore the signature size. Secondly, the linear expression implicitly enforces the constraint that $\mathbf{H} \cdot \mathbf{e} = \mathbf{y}$, and thus we only need to check the Hamming weight constraint on the "virtual" vector $\mathbf{e} = [\mathbf{y} - \mathbf{H_B} \cdot \mathbf{e_B} \| \mathbf{e_B}]$ in the ZK protocol.

The Hardness of RSD. A number of works studied the hardness of regular syndrome decoding under different parameter regimes [33,38]. In particular, some recent works utilize the regular noise structure into the state-of-the-art cryptanalysis algorithms of syndrome decoding [17,18,25]. To the best of our knowledge, the chosen parameters for our signature scheme lie in a region where the exact relationship between the hardness of RSD and SD remains unclear [25]. In Table 3, we choose parameters such that the RSD solution is unique $(\left(\frac{m}{w}\right)^w < 2^{m-k})$ while the same parameter would lead to multiple solutions if we drop the regularity constraint $(\binom{m}{w} > 2^{m-k})$. In this region, the regular structure of noises does not lead to significantly better attacks [17,18,25].

Functionality $\mathcal{F}_{\mathsf{DVZK}}$

This functionality runs with a prover $\mathcal{P}$ and a verifier $\mathcal{V}$, and operates as follows:

- Upon receiving $(\mathsf{dvzk}, sid, \ell, \{[\![x_i]\!], [\![y_i]\!], [\![z_i]\!]\}_{i \in [0,\ell)})$ from $\mathcal{P}$ and $\mathcal{V}$ if there exists some $i \in [0, \ell)$ such that one of $[\![x_i]\!], [\![y_i]\!], [\![z_i]\!]$ is not valid, output (sid, false) to $\mathcal{V}$ and abort.
- Check that $z_i = x_i \cdot y_i$ for all $i \in [0, \ell)$. If the check passes, then output (sid, true) to $\mathcal{V}$, else output (sid, false) to $\mathcal{V}$.

Fig. 1. Functionality for DVZK proofs of authenticated multiplication triples.

2.4 Information-Theoretic Message Authentication Codes

We use information-theoretic message authentication codes (IT-MACs) [12,43] over $\mathbb{F}_{2^\lambda}$. Specifically, let $\Delta \in \mathbb{F}_{2^\lambda}$ be a *global key*. We use $[\![x]\!] = (\mathsf{K}[x], \mathsf{M}[x], x)$ to denote that an element $x \in \mathbb{F}$ (where $\mathbb{F} \in \{\mathbb{F}_2, \mathbb{F}_{2^\lambda}\}$ known by one party can be authenticated by the other party who holds Δ and a *local key* $\mathsf{K}[x] \in \mathbb{F}_{2^\lambda}$, where a MAC tag $\mathsf{M}[x] = \mathsf{K}[x] + x \cdot \Delta$ is given to the party holding x. For a vector $\boldsymbol{x} \in \mathbb{F}_{2^\lambda}^\ell$, we denote by $[\![\boldsymbol{x}]\!] = ([\![x_0]\!], ..., [\![x_{\ell-1}]\!])$ a vector of authenticated values. For a constant value $c \in \mathbb{F}_{2^\lambda}$, it is easy to define $[\![c]\!] = (-c \cdot \Delta, 0, c)$. It is well known that IT-MACs are additively homomorphic. That is, given public coefficients $c_0, c_1, \ldots, c_\ell \in \mathbb{F}_{2^\lambda}$, two parties can *locally* compute $[\![y]\!] := \sum_{i=0}^{\ell-1} c_i \cdot [\![x_i]\!] + c_\ell$.

The IT-MAC authenticated value $[\![x]\!]$ can be opened by revealing x and $\mathsf{M}[x]$ and the validity can be enforced by checking that $\mathsf{M}[x] = \mathsf{K}[x] + x \cdot \Delta$. The security holds since opening $[\![x]\!]$ to any other value $(\mathsf{K}[x], \mathsf{M}[x'], x')$ is equivalent to guessing the global key since $\Delta = (\mathsf{M}[x] - \mathsf{M}[x']) \cdot (x - x')^{-1}$.

We can open multiple values $[\![x_0]\!], ..., [\![x_{\ell-1}]\!]$ in a batch by sending one MAC tag as follows. The sender first reveals $x'_0, ..., x'_{\ell-1}$, then using the additive homomorphism of IT-MAC, both parties can define $[\![y_i]\!] = [\![x_i]\!] - x'_i$ for $i \in [0, \ell)$. Now it suffices to check that $\forall i \in [0, \ell), y_i = 0$.

For task of checking multiple zero values $[\![y_0]\!], ..., [\![y_{\ell-1}]\!]$, we can save communication by opening a random linear combination $\chi_0 \cdot [\![y_0]\!] + ... + \chi_{\ell-1} \cdot [\![y_{\ell-1}]\!]$. In particular, the sender can only send $\sum_{i=0}^{\ell-1} \chi_i \cdot \mathsf{M}[y_i]$ since $\sum_{i=0}^{\ell-1} \chi_i \cdot y_i = 0$ for uniformly random $\chi_i \leftarrow \mathbb{F}_{2^\lambda}$.

2.5 Designated-Verifier Zero-Knowledge for Quadratic Relations

Based on IT-MACs, a family of streamable designated-verifier zero-knowledge (DVZK) proofs with fast prover time and a small memory footprint has been proposed [7,8,11,23,24,53–56]. While these DVZK proofs can prove arbitrary circuits, we only need them to prove a simple multiplication relation for our purpose. Specifically, given a set of authenticated triples $\{([\![x_i]\!], [\![y_i]\!], [\![z_i]\!])\}_{i \in [0,\ell)}$ over $\mathbb{F}_{2^\lambda}$, these DVZK protocols can enable a prover $\mathcal{P}$ to convince a verifier $\mathcal{V}$ that $z_i = x_i \cdot y_i$ for all $i \in [0, \ell)$. This is modeled by an ideal functionality shown in Fig. 1. In this functionality, an authenticated value $[\![x]\!]$ is input by two parties $\mathcal{P}$ and $\mathcal{V}$, meaning that $\mathcal{P}$ inputs (x, M) and $\mathcal{V}$ inputs (K, Δ). We say that $[\![x]\!]$ is valid, if $\mathsf{M} = \mathsf{K} + x \cdot \Delta$.

QuickSilver. We use the QuickSilver protocol [56] to instantiate $\mathcal{F}_{\mathsf{DVZK}}$. The benefit of using this protocol is two-fold. Firstly, the protocol is public-coin in the $\mathcal{F}_{\mathsf{sVOLE}}$-hybrid model, making it compatible with the VOLE-in-the-Head technique to be explained next. Secondly, the QuickSilver protocol excels at proving many quadratic relations as required in proving the Hamming weight constraint in the RSD problem, which only requires sending 2λ bits in total.

We briefly sketch how to prove multiple quadratic constraints in QuickSilver. Suppose the prover wants to prove $z_i = x_i \cdot y_i$ for $i \in [0, \ell)$, the verifier samples random challenges $\chi_0, ..., \chi_{\ell-1} \in \mathbb{F}$ and evaluates the following value using the IT-MAC relation $\mathsf{M}[x] = \mathsf{K}[x] + x \cdot \Delta$.

$$\sum_{i \in [0,\ell)} \chi_i \cdot (\mathsf{K}[x_i] \cdot \mathsf{K}[y_i] + \Delta \cdot \mathsf{K}[z_i]) = \sum_i \chi_i \cdot (x_i y_i - z_i) \cdot \Delta^2$$

$$+ \sum_i \chi_i \cdot (-x_i \mathsf{M}[y_i] - y_i \mathsf{M}[x_i] + \mathsf{M}[z_i]) \cdot \Delta + \sum_i \chi_i \cdot \mathsf{M}[x_i] \mathsf{M}[y_i].$$

If the quadratic relations hold then this value should be a linear function of Δ. To prove this, $\mathcal{P}$ simply sends the masked coefficients c_1, c_0 of that function to $\mathcal{V}$, who checks that $c_1 \cdot \Delta + c_0$ equals the masked left-hand side.

2.6   The Zero-Knowledge Functionality

We recall the definition of the ideal zero-knowledge functionality in Fig. 2. Looking ahead, we will construct a public-coin designated-verifier zero-knowledge protocol that realizes the functionality $\mathcal{F}_{\mathsf{RSD-ZK}}$ in the $\mathcal{F}_{\mathsf{sVOLE}}$-hybrid model, which can then be transformed into a publicly-verifiable zero-knowledge protocol using the techniques in [10].

Functionality $\mathcal{F}_{\mathsf{RSD-ZK}}$

Both parties $\mathcal{P}$ and $\mathcal{V}$ have access to the RSD instance $\boldsymbol{y} = \mathbf{H} \cdot \boldsymbol{e}$ for $\boldsymbol{y} \in \mathbb{F}_2^{m-k}$ and $\mathbf{H} \in \mathbb{F}_2^{(m-k) \times m}$. We assume the matrix $\mathbf{H} = [\mathbf{I}_{m-k} \| \mathbf{H_B}]$ is in the systematic form.

- **Input.** Upon receiving $(\mathtt{input}, \boldsymbol{e})$ from $\mathcal{P}$ and $(\mathtt{input})$ from $\mathcal{V}$, the functionality stores the input $\boldsymbol{e}$. Let $\boldsymbol{e} = [\boldsymbol{e}_0 \| ... \| \boldsymbol{e}_{w-1}]$, where $\mathsf{len}(\boldsymbol{e}_i) = m/w$ for $i \in [0, w)$.
- **Prove.** Upon receiving $(\mathtt{prove})$ from both parties, the functionality checks that $\boldsymbol{e}$ satisfies the following two constraints:
  - Linear Constraint: It holds that $\mathbf{H} \cdot \boldsymbol{e} = \boldsymbol{y}$.
  - Hamming Weight Constraint: It holds that $\mathsf{wt}(\boldsymbol{e}_i) = 1$ for $i \in [0, w)$.
  If both constraints are satisfied, the functionality sends true to $\mathcal{V}$. Otherwise, it sends false.

Fig. 2. The zero-knowledge functionality for regular syndrome decoding

3 VOLE-in-the-Head and Linear Sketching

In this section, we recapture the VOLE-in-the-head technique in [10] as well as the sketching technique of [16] that form the basis of our signature scheme in Sect. 5.

3.1 VOLE-in-the-Head

VOLE-in-the-Head is a technique proposed by Baum et al. [10] which allows transforming the public-coin designated-verifier zero-knowledge protocols in the VOLE-hybrid model into the publicly verifiable counterparts[1]. At the core of this technique is the observation that GGM-style vector commitment can realize an all-but-one random oblivious transfer functionality, which can then be transformed into a VOLE protocol using the technique in SoftSpokenOT [49]. One caveat is that to facilitate the simulation of OT from commitment, the verifier has to send its choice in the clear; Nevertheless, this suffices for a public-coin protocol since the verifier's action is merely sending public coins and the OT's output can be delayed to the very end of the protocol.

GGM-Style Vector Commitment. Given a n-level GGM tree, let r_j^i denotes the j-th node on the i-th level where $0 \leq i < n$ and $0 \leq j < 2^i$. It's well-known that if the root node is uniformly random and the tree is generated as $r_{2j}^{i+1} \| r_{2j+1}^{i+1} := \mathsf{PRG}(r_j^i)$ for some length-doubling PRG then the leaf nodes are pseudorandom. Moreover, for each leaf node, we can derive a random message and an authenticator. Then all messages can be committed by hashing the authenticators while all but one of them can be opened by presenting the sibling nodes on the punctured path and the authenticator of the punctured message. We model this vector commitment as an ideal functionality $\mathcal{F}_{\mathsf{VC}}$ in Fig. 3.

Functionality $\mathcal{F}_{\mathsf{VC}}$

Let $\tau' \in \mathbb{N}$, $\tau' \geq 1$ and $N = 2^{\tau'}$. The functionality is run between two parties $\mathcal{P}$ and $\mathcal{V}$ which are possibly corrupted by the adversary $\mathcal{A}$. We have the following commands.

- Upon receiving (commit) from $\mathcal{P}$ and $\mathcal{V}$, the functionality samples $m_i \leftarrow \{0,1\}^\lambda$ for $i \in [0, N)$. If $\mathcal{P}$ is corrupted then it receives $\{m_i\}_{i \in [0,N)}$ from the adversary and locally records the values. Then it sends (done) to both parties.
- Upon receiving (get, α) from $\mathcal{P}$ and $\mathcal{V}$, the functionality sends $\{m_i\}_{i \in [0,N), i \neq \alpha}$ to $\mathcal{V}$.

Fig. 3. The ideal vector commitment scheme supporting all-but-one opening.

---

[1] This technique somewhat resembles the classical MPC-in-the-head technique.

SoftSpokenOT. Let $\mathsf{PRG} : \mathbb{F}_2^\lambda \to \mathbb{F}_2^n$ be a pseudorandom generator. SoftSpo-kenOT [49] utilizes the fact that the all-but-one OT correlation is equivalent to the subfield VOLE correlation over the polynomial-sized extension field $\mathbb{F}_{2^{\tau'}}$. Let $\Delta \in \mathbb{F}_{2^{\tau'}}$ be the OT index. The key observation (which is implicit in the classical IKNP protocol) is that by defining $\boldsymbol{u}' := \sum_{i \in [0, 2^{\tau'})} \mathsf{PRG}(m_i)$, $\boldsymbol{v} := \sum_{i \in [0, 2^{\tau'})} i \cdot \mathsf{PRG}(m_i)$, and $\boldsymbol{w}' := \sum_{i \in [0, 2^\ell)} (i + \Delta) \cdot \mathsf{PRG}(m_i)$, the sender and receiver can locally compute the respective values and the transformation from OT to subfield VOLE can be done non-interactively. Notice that in the expression of $\boldsymbol{w}'$, the value $\mathsf{PRG}(m_\Delta)$ which is unknown to the receiver is multiplied by 0 and the receiver can efficiently compute $\boldsymbol{w}'$. Therefore, $\boldsymbol{w}' = \boldsymbol{v} + \boldsymbol{u}' \cdot \Delta$.

Since the field $\mathbb{F}_{2^{\tau'}}$ need to be enumerated, we require that $\tau' = O(\log \lambda)$ (i.e. small-field VOLE). Nevertheless, the VOLE global key needs to contain enough entropy to ensure soundness. Therefore, we need to repeat the base protocol $\lceil \frac{\lambda}{\tau'} \rceil$ times and apply a consistency checking protocol to ensure that the same vector $\boldsymbol{u}$ is used in all small-field VOLE instances (so that the global keys can be concatenated).

In particular, the sender and receiver would run the above small-field VOLE protocol for $\tau := \lceil \frac{\lambda}{\tau'} \rceil$ times, acquiring $[\![\boldsymbol{u}'_0]\!], ..., [\![\boldsymbol{u}'_{\tau-1}]\!]$, where $\boldsymbol{u}'_i \in \mathbb{F}_2^{n+h}$. Then by viewing each row of the concatenated matrix $\mathbf{U}' := [\boldsymbol{u}'_0 \| ... \| \boldsymbol{u}'_{\tau-1}]$ as a noisy codeword of the length-τ repetition code, as the sender sends the syndrome $\mathbf{C}$ of all the codewords to the receiver. Then the sender corrects the matrix $\mathbf{U}'$ into a structured matrix $\mathbf{U} := [1 ... 1] \cdot \boldsymbol{u}$ where each row is a repetition codeword while the receiver sets $\mathbf{W} = \mathbf{W}' + [0 \| \mathbf{C}] \cdot \mathrm{diag}(\boldsymbol{\Delta})$ where $\boldsymbol{\Delta}$ denotes the concatenation of all small-field VOLE global keys. Notice that with the matrix $\mathbf{U}$ being structured, we can transform each row of $\mathbf{W}, \mathbf{V}$ as well as $\boldsymbol{\Delta}$ as elements in the extension field $\mathbb{F}_{2^\lambda}$, which gives the IT-MAC format.

Finally, we need to check that $\mathbf{U}$ is indeed structured. We do this by sacrificing the last h rows of $\mathbf{U}$. In particular, the sender sends $\tilde{\boldsymbol{u}} = \mathsf{H}^{\mathsf{UHF}} \cdot \boldsymbol{u}$ and $\tilde{\mathbf{V}} = \mathsf{H}^{\mathsf{UHF}} \cdot \mathbf{V}$ for some linear universal hash function $\mathsf{H}^{\mathsf{UHF}} \in \mathbb{F}_2^{r \times (n+h)}$ while the receiver checks that $\tilde{\mathbf{V}} + \tilde{\boldsymbol{u}} \cdot [1 ... 1] \cdot \mathrm{diag}(\boldsymbol{\Delta}) = \mathsf{H}^{\mathsf{UHF}} \cdot \mathbf{W}$.

VOLE-in-the-Head. Now we can put together all the pieces and explain the technique in [10]. Recall that our goal is to transform a designated-verifier zero-knowledge protocol in the VOLE-hybrid model into a publicly verifiable one. We additionally require that the DVZK protocol be public-coin. The transformation proceeds as follows. We state the protocol in the interactive setting but the interaction can be removed using Fiat-Shamir [28].

1. The prover locally runs the SoftSpokenOT protocol, instantiating the all-but-one random OT with vector commitment. In particular, the prover generates the GGM trees and sends the commitments to the verifier. Then the prover simulates the SoftSpokenOT protocol, sending the correction syndrome and checking information to the verifier.
2. With the IT-MAC correlations from previous step, the parties simulate the zero-knowledge protocol using the previous subfield VOLE correlations.

3. When all interactions of the zero-knowledge protocol are completed, the verifier simply sends the VOLE global key Δ to the prover, who then replies with the corresponding vector de-commitment. The verifier then checks that

(a) the vector commitment openings are correct;
(b) the consistency checks inside SoftSpokenOT are correct;
(c) the zero-knowledge verification passes.

If all checks pass then the verifier accepts. Otherwise, it rejects the proof.

Intuitively, since the inner ZK protocol in the $\mathcal{F}_{\text{sVOLE}}$-hybrid model is public-coin, the parties can still simulate the protocol before sampling the global key Δ, and since the proof information is already sent in step 2, revealing the global key in step 3 does not grant the prover any advantage. In [10], this intuition is characterized by an ideal functionality $\mathcal{F}_{\text{sVOLE}}^{p,q,S_\Delta,\mathcal{C},\ell,\mathcal{L}}$ where the receiver's outputs are revealed after the prover commits to its inputs. In this work, we only consider a special case of it, namely we only consider using repetition code and fixing the set S_Δ to be the entire field $\mathbb{F}_{2^{\tau'}}$. We recall the functionality in Fig. 4.

Functionality $\mathcal{F}_{\text{sVOLE}}$

The functionality is parameterized by the base field $\mathbb{F}_2$ and its extension $\mathbb{F}_{2^{\tau'}}$. We also define an integer n as the number of random sVOLE correlations to produce and τ as the repetition parameter such that $\tau\tau' \geq \lambda$.
Upon receiving (init) from $\mathcal{P}$ and $\mathcal{V}$, the functionality does the following.

- Sample $\boldsymbol{u} \leftarrow \mathbb{F}_2^n$, $\mathbf{V} \leftarrow \mathbb{F}_{2^{\tau'}}^{n \times \tau}$ and $\boldsymbol{\Delta} \leftarrow \mathbb{F}_{2^{\tau'}}^\tau$. Let $\mathbf{W} = \mathbf{V} + \boldsymbol{u} \cdot [1 \ldots 1] \cdot \text{diag}(\boldsymbol{\Delta})$.
  - If $\mathcal{P}$ is corrupted, then receive $\boldsymbol{u}, \mathbf{V}$ from the adversary $\mathcal{A}$ and recompute $\mathbf{W}$.
  - If $\mathcal{V}$ is corrupted, then receive $\boldsymbol{\Delta}, \mathbf{W}$ from the adversary $\mathcal{A}$ and recompute $\mathbf{V} = \mathbf{W} - \boldsymbol{u} \cdot [1 \ldots 1] \cdot \text{diag}(\boldsymbol{\Delta})$.
- Send $(\boldsymbol{u}, \mathbf{V})$ to $\mathcal{P}$.
- If $\mathcal{P}$ is corrupted, then receive a leakage query L from $\mathcal{A}$.

Upon receiving (get) from $\mathcal{P}$ and $\mathcal{V}$, the functionality does the following.

- If $\boldsymbol{\Delta} \notin L$, then send (check-failed) to $\mathcal{V}$ and abort.
- Otherwise, send $(\boldsymbol{\Delta}, \mathbf{W})$ to $\mathcal{V}$.

Fig. 4. The subspace VOLE functionality.

3.2 The Linear Sketching Technique

To verify the Hamming weight constraint, we use the linear sketching technique of Boyle et al. [16]. For general field $\mathbb{F}$, given an IT-MAC authenticated vector $[\![\boldsymbol{u}]\!]$ where $\boldsymbol{u} \in \mathbb{F}^n$, we can easily check that $\|\boldsymbol{u}\|_0 = 1$. We first sample two public random vectors $\boldsymbol{r}_0, \boldsymbol{r}_1 \in \mathbb{F}^n$ and define z_0, z_1, z_2, z_3 as follows.

$$
\boldsymbol{z} = \begin{bmatrix} z_0 \\ z_1 \\ z_2 \\ z_3 \end{bmatrix} = \begin{bmatrix} \boldsymbol{r}_0^T \\ \boldsymbol{r}_1^T \\ (\boldsymbol{r}_0 \circ \boldsymbol{r}_1)^T \\ 1 \ldots 1 \end{bmatrix} \cdot \boldsymbol{u}.
$$

Here ∘ denotes the component-wise product between two vectors. Finally, we check that $z_0 \cdot z_1 = z_2$ and that $z_3 = 1$. The first check ensures that $\|\boldsymbol{u}\|_0 \leq 1$. Conditioned on passing the first check, the second check ensures that $\boldsymbol{u}$ is a unit vector. The second check is straightforward and we will elaborate on the intuition of the first check.

When viewing $(\boldsymbol{r}_0 \circ \boldsymbol{r}_1)^T \cdot \boldsymbol{u} - (\boldsymbol{r}_0^T \cdot \boldsymbol{u}) \cdot (\boldsymbol{r}_1^T \cdot \boldsymbol{u})$ as a multivariate polynomial over $\boldsymbol{r}_0, \boldsymbol{r}_1$, we have that if $\|\boldsymbol{u}\|_0 > 1$ then the polynomial is non-zero and has degree of two. Therefore, with the Schwartz-Zippel lemma [50,59], we can show that the equation $z_2 = z_0 \cdot z_1$ holds except with probability $\frac{2}{|\mathbb{F}|}$ over the choices of $r_0, ..., r_{n-1}$. Formally, we have the following lemma by Boyle et al. [16].

Lemma 1. *Let $\mathbb{F}$ be any finite field. Suppose $\boldsymbol{u} \in \mathbb{F}^n$ is not a unit vector then we have the probability*

$$\Pr[L \leftarrow \mathcal{L}(\mathbb{F}, n), \boldsymbol{z} = L \cdot \boldsymbol{u} : z_0 \cdot z_1 = z_2 \wedge z_3 = 1] \leq \frac{2}{|\mathbb{F}|},$$

where the distribution $\mathcal{L}(\mathbb{F}, n)$ is defined by sampling $\boldsymbol{r}_0, \boldsymbol{r}_1 \leftarrow \mathbb{F}^n$ and returning

$$L = \begin{bmatrix} \boldsymbol{r}_0^T \\ \boldsymbol{r}_1^T \\ (\boldsymbol{r}_0 \circ \boldsymbol{r}_1)^T \\ 1 \dots 1 \end{bmatrix}.$$

Notice that since IT-MAC is linear homomorphic, we can get the authentication of $\boldsymbol{z}$ by evaluating $[\![\boldsymbol{z}]\!] = L \cdot [\![\boldsymbol{u}]\!]$. Then, we can use the IT-MAC opening operation to check that $z_3 = 1$ and use QuickSilver to prove that $z_0 \cdot z_1 = z_2$.

In our protocol, we perform the checking on $\boldsymbol{u} \in \mathbb{F}_2$ over the extension field $\mathbb{F}_{2^\lambda}$ to get negligible soundness error. For RSD over larger fields, we can adapt the above method to prove that the non-zero element is equal to an arbitrary value in the field. Nevertheless, we focus on RSD over $\mathbb{F}_2$ in this work and using the above sketching technique is sufficient.

4 Designated-Verifier ZK from Linear Sketching

In this section, we present an efficient zero-knowledge proof for the RSD problem in the $\mathcal{F}_{\mathsf{sVOLE}}$-hybrid model and give a security proof for its soundness and zero-knowledge property.

4.1 Protocol Description

Since we may view the matrix $\mathbf{H}$ in its systematic form and therefore implicitly enforce the linear constraint, we can turn our focus to proving the Hamming weight constraint. Using the linear sketching technique [16] we can check that the segment of the witness vector has a Hamming weight of exactly 1 by verifying a quadratic relation and performing an IT-MAC opening. Using the QuickSilver protocol, we can prove all w quadratic relations corresponding to the entire

Protocol $\Pi_{\mathsf{RSD-DVZK}}$

Both parties $\mathcal{P}$ and $\mathcal{V}$ have access to the RSD instance $(\mathbf{H}, \boldsymbol{y})$ where $\mathbf{H} \in \mathbb{F}_2^{(m-k) \times m}$ and $\boldsymbol{y} = \mathbf{H} \cdot \boldsymbol{e}$. $\mathcal{P}$ has the witness $\boldsymbol{e} = [\boldsymbol{e}_0\|...\|\boldsymbol{e}_{w-1}]$ where $\|\boldsymbol{e}_i\|_0 = 1$ for $i \in [0, w)$. We assume the matrix $\mathbf{H} = [\mathbf{I}_{m-k}\|\mathbf{H_B}]$ is in the systematic form and the vector $\boldsymbol{e}$ is split into $\boldsymbol{e_A}$ and $\boldsymbol{e_B}$. We assume without loss of generality that $\tau\tau' = \lambda$.

Input: The prover commits to the witness as follows.

1. Both parties call $\mathcal{F}_{\mathsf{sVOLE}}$ on input (init) and $\mathcal{P}$ gets $\boldsymbol{u} \in \mathbb{F}_2^n$ and $\mathbf{V} \in \mathbb{F}_{2^{\tau'}}^{n \times \tau}$. Let $n = k + \lambda$. For $i \in [0, k)$ the prover defines $\mathbf{V}_i \hookrightarrow \mathsf{M}[u_i]$. The prover lifts the last λ coordinates of $\boldsymbol{u}$ into a mask $u^{\mathsf{QS}} \in \mathbb{F}_{2^\lambda}$ and we define its IT-MAC tag $\mathsf{M}[u^{\mathsf{QS}}]$ similarly by lifting the respective rows in $\mathbf{V}$. Finally, the prover sends $\boldsymbol{d} = \boldsymbol{e_B} - \boldsymbol{u}[0, k)$ to the verifier.

Prove: The parties check that the committed witness is valid as follows.

2. The verifier samples the sketch functions $L^{(i)}$ according to Lemma 1 for $i \in [0, w)$ and random challenges $\boldsymbol{\chi}^{\mathsf{QS}}, \boldsymbol{\chi}^{\mathsf{open}} \leftarrow \mathbb{F}_{2^\lambda}^w$ and sends them to the prover.
3. The prover defines $\mathsf{M}[\boldsymbol{e_B}]$ as the first k coordinates of $\mathsf{M}[\boldsymbol{u}]$ and reconstructs $\mathsf{M}[\boldsymbol{e}]$ using the linear relation $\boldsymbol{e} = [\boldsymbol{y} - \mathbf{H_B} \cdot \boldsymbol{e_B}\|\boldsymbol{e_B}]$. Let $\boldsymbol{e} = [\boldsymbol{e}_0\|...\|\boldsymbol{e}_{w-1}]$. Using the linear homomorphism of IT-MAC, we define the authentication of $\boldsymbol{z}^{(i)} = L^{(i)} \cdot \boldsymbol{e}_i$ for $i \in [0, w)$.

   Then the prover uses QuickSilver to prove that $z_0^{(i)} \cdot z_1^{(i)} = z_2^{(i)}$ for $i \in [0, w)$. In particular, it computes $m_0^{\mathsf{QS}} = \mathsf{M}[u^{\mathsf{QS}}] + \sum_{i \in [0, w)} \chi_i^{\mathsf{QS}} \cdot \mathsf{M}[z_0^{(i)}] \cdot \mathsf{M}[z_1^{(i)}]$ and $m_1^{\mathsf{QS}} = u^{\mathsf{QS}} + \sum_{i \in [0, w)} \chi_i^{\mathsf{QS}} \cdot (z_0^{(i)} \cdot \mathsf{M}[z_1^{(i)}] + z_1^{(i)} \cdot \mathsf{M}[z_0^{(i)}] + \mathsf{M}[z_2^{(i)}])$. The prover also defines $m_0^{\mathsf{open}} = \sum_{i \in [0, w)} \chi_i^{\mathsf{open}} \cdot \mathsf{M}[z_3^{(i)}]$. The prover sends $m_0^{\mathsf{QS}}, m_1^{\mathsf{QS}}, m_0^{\mathsf{open}}$ to the verifier.
4. Both parties call the functionality $\mathcal{F}_{\mathsf{sVOLE}}$ on input (get) and the verifier gets $\boldsymbol{\Delta} = (\Delta_0, ..., \Delta_{\tau-1}) \in \mathbb{F}_{2^{\tau'}}^\tau$ and $\mathbf{W} \in \mathbb{F}_{2^{\tau'}}^{n \times \tau}$. The verifier defines $\boldsymbol{\Delta} \hookrightarrow \Delta$ and $\mathbf{W}_i \hookrightarrow \mathsf{K}[u_i]$ for $i \in [0, k)$ as well as the IT-MAC local key $\mathsf{K}[u^{\mathsf{QS}}]$ using the last λ rows of $\mathbf{W}$. Then it defines $\mathsf{K}[\boldsymbol{e_B}] = \mathsf{K}[\boldsymbol{u}[0, k)] + \boldsymbol{d} \cdot \Delta$ and reconstructs $\mathsf{K}[\boldsymbol{e}]$ using the linear relation $\boldsymbol{e} = [\boldsymbol{y} - \mathbf{H_B} \cdot \boldsymbol{e_B}\|\boldsymbol{e_B}]$. It also defines the IT-MAC local keys of $\boldsymbol{z}^{(i)}$ for $i \in [0, w)$. The verifier accepts if the following relation holds and rejects otherwise.

$$m_0^{\mathsf{QS}} + m_1^{\mathsf{QS}} \cdot \Delta = \mathsf{K}[u^{\mathsf{QS}}] + \sum_{i \in [0, w)} \chi_i^{\mathsf{QS}} \cdot (\mathsf{K}[z_0^{(i)}] \cdot \mathsf{K}[z_1^{(i)}] + \Delta \cdot \mathsf{K}[z_2^{(i)}]) \text{ and}$$

$$m_0^{\mathsf{open}} + (\sum_{i \in [0, w)} \chi_i^{\mathsf{open}}) \cdot \Delta = \sum_{i \in [0, w)} \chi_i^{\mathsf{open}} \cdot \mathsf{K}[z_3^{(i)}] .$$

Fig. 5. The ZK protocol for syndrome decoding based on linear sketch in the $\mathcal{F}_{\mathsf{sVOLE}}$-hybrid model.

witness vector in a batch using a random linear combination, with essentially the same communication cost as proving one quadratic relation. The cost of w openings can also be reduced using another random linear combination. We describe the protocol in detail in Fig. 5 and prove its security in the next sub-section.

4.2 Security Proof

We prove that the protocol $\Pi_{\mathsf{RSD-DVZK}}$ is an honest verifier zero-knowledge protocol for regular syndrome decoding in the $\mathcal{F}_{\mathsf{sVOLE}}$-hybrid model in Theorem 1. Our proof is a straightforward extension of the proof in [10]. The only difference is that we use the linear sketch technique from [16] to check the validity of the witness vector.

Theorem 1. *The protocol $\Pi_{\mathsf{RSD-DVZK}}$ realizes the functionality $\mathcal{F}_{\mathsf{RSD-ZK}}$ in the $\mathcal{F}_{\mathsf{sVOLE}}$-hybrid model. The security holds against a malicious prover or a semi-honest verifier and the soundness error in the former case is bounded by $\frac{7}{2^\lambda}$.*

Proof. Correctness of the proof follows by definition. In the following, we construct simulators for the malicious prover and verifier cases to argue soundness and zero-knowledge properties respectively.

Malicious Prover. The simulator $\mathcal{S}_\mathcal{P}$ is constructed as follows.

1. $\mathcal{S}_\mathcal{P}$ simulates the (init) command of the functionality $\mathcal{F}_{\mathsf{sVOLE}}$ by receiving the $\boldsymbol{u}, \mathbf{V}$ values from $\mathcal{A}$. It also receives the difference vector $\boldsymbol{d}$ and recovers the witness $\boldsymbol{e_B} = \boldsymbol{d} + \boldsymbol{u}[0, k)$. Let $\boldsymbol{e} = [\boldsymbol{y} - \mathbf{H_B} \cdot \boldsymbol{e_B} \| \boldsymbol{e_B}]$. $\mathcal{S}_\mathcal{P}$ sends message (input, $\boldsymbol{e}$) to the functionality $\mathcal{F}_{\mathsf{RSD-ZK}}$.
2. $\mathcal{S}_\mathcal{P}$ samples the random challenges $L^{(i)}$ for $i \in [0, w)$ and $\chi^{\mathsf{QS}}, \chi^{\mathsf{open}} \leftarrow \mathbb{F}_{2^\lambda}^w$ and sends them to the adversary.
3. $\mathcal{S}_\mathcal{P}$ receives the QuickSilver proof messages $m_0^{\mathsf{QS}}, m_1^{\mathsf{QS}}, m_0^{\mathsf{open}}$ from the adversary.
4. $\mathcal{S}_\mathcal{P}$ simulates the (get) command of $\mathcal{F}_{\mathsf{sVOLE}}$ and the QuickSilver checking phase. In particular, $\mathcal{S}_\mathcal{P}$ sends $\perp$ to the ideal functionality in the following two cases.
   - Let $\boldsymbol{e} = [\boldsymbol{e_0} \| ... \| \boldsymbol{e_{w-1}}]$. There exists $i \in [0, w)$ s.t. $\|\boldsymbol{e_i}\|_0 \neq 1$ or $\|\boldsymbol{e_i}\|_0 = 1$ but the non-zero element is not 1.
   - Let $e_0^{\mathsf{QS}} = \mathsf{M}[u^{\mathsf{QS}}] + \sum_{i\in[0,w)} \chi_i^{\mathsf{QS}} \cdot \mathsf{M}[z_0^{(i)}] \cdot \mathsf{M}[z_1^{(i)}] - m_0^{\mathsf{QS}}$ and $e_1^{\mathsf{QS}} = u^{\mathsf{QS}} + \sum_{i\in[0,w)} \chi_i^{\mathsf{QS}} \cdot (z_0^{(i)} \cdot \mathsf{M}[z_1^{(i)}] + z_1^{(i)} \cdot \mathsf{M}[z_0^{(i)}] - \mathsf{M}[z_2^{(i)}]) - m_1^{\mathsf{QS}}$ be the errors in the QuickSilver messages while $e_0^{\mathsf{open}} = \sum_{i\in[0,w)} \chi_i^{\mathsf{open}} \cdot \mathsf{M}[z_3^{(i)}] - m_0^{\mathsf{open}}$ be the error in the opening message. We have $e_0^{\mathsf{QS}} \neq 0$ or $e_1^{\mathsf{QS}} \neq 0$ or $e_0^{\mathsf{open}} \neq 0$.

   Otherwise, $\mathcal{S}_\mathcal{P}$ sends continue to the ideal functionality.

Since the protocol is public-coin, the simulation of the verifier's messages is identically distributed with the interaction of the real verifier. Now we analyze the soundness error, which captures the difference between the abort probability of the real case and the ideal case. If the verifier in the real world rejects, then either the relation does not hold (i.e. the witness has too large or zero Hamming weight) or the QuickSilver messages are malformed. In both cases, the ideal verifier also rejects the proof.

Now we focus on the case where the real verifier accepts while the simulator rejects. If the extracted witness e does not satisfy the Hamming weight constraint, then by Lemma 1 we conclude that except with probability $\frac{2}{2^\lambda}$ there exists at least one index $i \in [0, w)$ such that the quadratic relation $z_0^{(i)} \cdot z_1^{(i)} = z_2^{(i)}$ and $z_3^{(i)} = 1$ does not hold. In this case, we can re-write the real verifier's first acceptance condition as follows.

$$m_0^{\mathsf{QS}} + m_1^{\mathsf{QS}} \cdot \Delta = \mathsf{K}[u^{\mathsf{QS}}] + \Big(\sum_{i \in [0,w)} \chi_i^{\mathsf{QS}} \cdot (z_0^i \cdot z_1^i - z_2^i) \Big) \cdot \Delta^2$$
$$+ \sum_{i \in [0,w)} \chi_i^{\mathsf{QS}} \cdot (z_0^i \cdot \mathsf{M}[z_1^i] + z_1^i \cdot \mathsf{M}[z_0^i] + \mathsf{M}[z_2^i]) \cdot \Delta$$
$$+ \sum_{i \in [0,w)} \chi_i^{\mathsf{QS}} \cdot \mathsf{M}[z_0^i] \cdot \mathsf{M}[z_1^i]$$

Since the χ^{QS} challenge is sampled uniformly at random and independent from other randomness, except with probability $\frac{1}{2^\lambda}$ the quadratic term of the above equation is non-zero. In this case, there exists at most two solutions to the equation. Since Δ is sampled uniformly at random and independent from other randomness, the equation holds with at most $\frac{2}{2^\lambda}$ probability.

Moreover, if $z_3^{(i)} \neq 1$ for some $i \in [0, w)$, since χ^{open} is uniformly random over $\mathbb{F}_{2^\lambda}^w$, the equality $\sum_{i \in [0,w)} \chi_i^{\mathsf{open}} \cdot z_3^{(i)} = \sum_{i \in [0,w)} \chi_i^{\mathsf{open}}$ holds except with $\frac{1}{2^\lambda}$ probability. Assuming the equality does not hold, the adversary can pass the check except it correctly guesses the Δ value, which happens except with $\frac{1}{2^\lambda}$ probability. Using the union bound, we conclude that the soundness error is upper bounded by $\frac{7}{2^\lambda}$.

Semi-Honest Verifier. The simulator $\mathcal{S}_\mathcal{V}$ is constructed as follows.

1. $\mathcal{S}_\mathcal{V}$ simulates the (init) command of the functionality $\mathcal{F}_{\mathsf{sVOLE}}$ and receives the messages Δ and $\mathbf{W}'$ from the adversary. Then it samples $d \leftarrow \mathbb{F}_2^k$ and sends it to the adversary.
2. $\mathcal{S}_\mathcal{V}$ receives the random challenges $L^{(i)}$ for $i \in [0, w)$ and $\chi^{\mathsf{QS}}, \chi^{\mathsf{open}} \in \mathbb{F}_{2^\lambda}^w$ from the adversary.
3. $\mathcal{S}_\mathcal{V}$ samples a random value $m_1^{\mathsf{QS}} \leftarrow \mathbb{F}_{2^\lambda}$ and computes $m_0^{\mathsf{QS}} = \mathsf{K}[u^{\mathsf{QS}}] + \sum_{i \in [0,w)} \chi_i^{\mathsf{QS}} \cdot (\mathsf{K}[z_0^{(i)}] \cdot \mathsf{K}[z_1^{(i)}] + \Delta \cdot \mathsf{K}[z_2^{(i)}]) - m_1^{\mathsf{QS}} \cdot \Delta$. It also prepares $m_0^{\mathsf{open}} = \sum_{i \in [0,w)} \chi_i^{\mathsf{open}} \cdot (\mathsf{K}[z_3^{(i)}] + \Delta)$. It sends $m_0^{\mathsf{QS}}, m_1^{\mathsf{QS}}, m_0^{\mathsf{open}}$ to the adversary.
4. $\mathcal{S}_\mathcal{V}$ simulates the (get) command of $\mathcal{F}_{\mathsf{sVOLE}}$ by sending $\Delta, \mathbf{W}'$ to the adversary.

Notice that we only argue for security against a semi-honest adversary. Due to the masking of $u[0, k)$, the message d is uniformly random in the view of the adversary. Also due to the masking of $u[k, k + \lambda)$, the message m_1^{QS} is also uniformly random. Moreover, the messages $m_0^{\mathsf{QS}}, m_0^{\mathsf{open}}$ can be deterministically evaluated using $\Delta, d, \{L^{(i)}\}, \chi^{\mathsf{QS}}, \chi^{\mathsf{open}}, \mathbf{W'}, m_1^{\mathsf{QS}}$. Therefore, we conclude that the adversary's view is identical between the simulated case and the real case.

5 ReSolveD: Shorter Signatures from RSD and VOLEitH

We apply the generic transformation in [10] to convert the public-coin protocol $\Pi_{\mathsf{RSD-DVZK}}$ in the $\mathcal{F}_{\mathsf{sVOLE}}$-hybrid model into a publicly-verifiable zero-knowledge proof $\Pi_{\mathsf{RSD-PVZK}}$. Then we apply the Fiat-Shamir transform and present ReSolveD, a post-quantum digital signature scheme from RSD and VOLE-in-the-Head. We present the signature scheme in Fig. 6.

- KeyGen()
  1. Samples a generator matrix in systematic form $\mathbf{H} = [\mathbf{I}\|\mathbf{H_B}] \in \mathbb{F}_2^{(m-k) \times m}$ as well as a regular noise $\boldsymbol{e} \in \mathbb{F}_2^m$.
  2. Output $\mathsf{pk} = (\mathbf{H}, \boldsymbol{y} = \mathbf{H} \cdot \boldsymbol{e})$, $\mathsf{sk} = (\mathsf{pk}, \boldsymbol{e})$.
- Sign(sk, m)
  1. The signer executes the prover's actions of $\Pi_{\mathsf{RSD-PVZK}}$. For all challenges $\mathsf{H}^{\mathsf{UHF}}, \chi^{\mathsf{QS}}, \chi^{\mathsf{open}}, \Delta$, the signer sends the protocol's transcript concatenated with the message m to the random oracle to get the respective challenges.
  2. Output signature σ as complete transcript of $\Pi_{\mathsf{RSD-PVZK}}$.
- Verify(pk, m, σ)
  1. The verifier executes the verifier's actions of $\Pi_{\mathsf{RSD-PVZK}}$. The verifier uses the prover's messages extracted from the signature σ while for the verifier's challenges, the verifier also hashes the partial transcript concatenated with the signed message m.
  2. The verifier accepts the signature if in the simulated execution of $\Pi_{\mathsf{RSD-PVZK}}$, the simualted verifier also accepts. It rejects if otherwise.

Fig. 6. The ReSolveD signature scheme. We assume that the unary form of the security parameter λ is the implicit input of all three algorithms.

5.1 Signature Description

We describe the protocol $\Pi_{\mathsf{RSD-PVZK}}$ in Fig. 8. We apply the half-tree optimization [32] when constructing the vector commitment scheme, which we recall in Fig. 7 and prove its security in Lemma 2. Notice that in this construction, we utilize the circular correlation robustness property which is usually instantiated in the ideal cipher model [31], of which we recall a simplified version in Definition 2.

Lemma 2. *Let G_1, G_2 be two random oracles and H be a (t, q, ϵ)-circular correlation robust hash function. Then the vector commitment scheme $\Pi_{\mathsf{VC-cGGM}}$ (Fig. 7) securely implements the vector commitment functionality $\mathcal{F}_{\mathsf{VC}}$ (Fig. 3).*

Protocol $\Pi_{\mathsf{VC-cGGM}}$

Let $G_1 : \{0,1\}^* \to \{0,1\}^{2\lambda}, G_2 : \{0,1\}^{\lambda} \to \{0,1\}^{\lambda} \times \{0,1\}^{2\lambda}$ be two random oracles and $\mathsf{H} : \{0,1\}^{\lambda} \times \{0,1\}^{\lambda} \to \{0,1\}^{\lambda}$ be a hash function. Let $\tau' \in \mathbb{N}$ be the tree depth and define $N = 2^{\tau'}$.

- For the **commit** command, $\mathcal{P}$ and $\mathcal{V}$ perform the following steps.
  1. $\mathcal{P}$ samples $\Gamma \leftarrow \mathbb{F}_2^{\lambda}$, $r_0^1 \leftarrow \mathbb{F}_2^{\lambda}$ and computes $r_1^1 = r_0^1 \oplus \Gamma$. It evaluates the full binary tree using the recursive relation $r_{2j}^{i+1} = \mathsf{H}(r_j^i)$, $r_{2j+1}^{i+1} = \mathsf{H}(r_j^i) \oplus r_j^i$ for $i \in [2, \tau)$, $j \in [0, 2^i)$ and computes $(m_i, \mathsf{com}_i) \leftarrow G_2(r_i^{\tau'})$ for $i \in [0, 2^{\tau'})$ and the sum of all even indexed nodes on each level $\{K_0^i\}_{i \in [1, \tau']} = \sum_{j \in [0, 2^{i-1})} r_{2j}^i$.
  2. $\mathcal{P}$ sends the commitment $\mathsf{com} := G_1(\mathsf{com}_0, ..., \mathsf{com}_{N-1})$ to $\mathcal{V}$ and locally stores the de-commitment information $\mathsf{decom} := (\Gamma, \{K_0^i\}_{i \in [1, \tau']})$ and the messages $\{m_i\}_{i \in [0, N)}$.
- For the (get, α) command, $\mathcal{P}$ and $\mathcal{V}$ perform the following steps.
  1. Let $\alpha_1, \alpha_2, ..., \alpha_{\tau'}$ be the binary decomposition of $\alpha \in [0, N)$, $\mathcal{P}$ sends the opening information $\mathsf{decom}_\alpha := (\{K_{\bar{\alpha}_i}^i := K_0^i \oplus \bar{\alpha}_i \cdot \Gamma\}_{i \in [1, \tau']}, \mathsf{com}_\alpha)$ to $\mathcal{V}$.
  2. Upon receiving the opening information, $\mathcal{V}$ defines $r_{\bar{\alpha}_1}^1 = K_{\bar{\alpha}_1}^1$ from decom_α. For $i \in [2, \tau']$, $j \in [0, 2^{i-1})$ and $j \neq \alpha_1 \| ... \| \alpha_{i-1}$, it evaluates $r_{2j}^i = \mathsf{H}(r_j^{i-1})$ and $r_{2j+1}^i = \mathsf{H}(r_j^{i-1}) \oplus r_j^{i-1}$ and defines $r_{\alpha_1 \| ... \| \alpha_{i-1} \| \bar{\alpha}_i}^i = K_{\bar{\alpha}_i}^i \oplus \sum_{j \in [2^{i-1}], j \neq \alpha_1 \| ... \| \alpha_{i-1}} r_{2j+\bar{\alpha}_i}^i$.
  3. For each leaf node $i \in [0, N) \setminus \alpha$, $\mathcal{V}$ derives $(m_i, \mathsf{com}_i) = G_2(r_i^{\tau'})$. $\mathcal{V}$ checks that $\mathsf{com} = G_1(\mathsf{com}_0, ..., \mathsf{com}_{N-1})$ using the com_α information in decom_α. If the equality does not hold then it outputs $\bot$. Otherwise, it outputs $\{m_i\}_{i \in [0, N), i \neq \alpha}$.

Fig. 7. The correlated GGM tree construction.

Proof. The protocol correctness follows by definition. Now we argue security against a malicious $\mathcal{P}$ and $\mathcal{V}$ respectively.

Malicious Prover. The simulator $\mathcal{S}_\mathcal{P}$ receives the commitment com from the adversary and then recovers the hashed values $\{\mathsf{com}_i\}_{i \in [0, N)}$ and $\{r_i^{\tau'}\}_{i \in [0, N)}$ from the random oracle queries and send $\{m_i\}_{i \in [0, N)}$ to $\mathcal{F}_{\mathsf{VC}}$ where $(m_i, \mathsf{com}_i) = G(r_i^{\tau'})$ for $i \in [0, N)$.

For the (get, α) command, $\mathcal{S}_\mathcal{P}$ receives the de-commitment information $\mathsf{decom}_\alpha = \{K_{\bar{\alpha}_i}^i\}_{i \in [1, \tau']}$ from the adversary and runs the checking procedures of the verifier. If the check fails then it sends $\bot$ to $\mathcal{F}_{\mathsf{VC}}$.

Unless there exists a collision in the random oracle queries, then the ideal execution successfully extracts the committed messages. The collision probability is upper bounded by $\frac{Q}{2^{\lambda}}$ where Q is the number of random oracle queries from by $\mathcal{A}$.

Malicious Verifier. The simulator $\mathcal{S}_\mathcal{V}$ samples $\mathsf{com} \leftarrow \{0,1\}^{\lambda}$ and sends it to $\mathcal{A}$ to simulate (commit). For the (get, α) command, the simulator samples $K_{\bar{\alpha}_i}^i \leftarrow$

$\{0,1\}^\lambda$ for $i \in [1, \tau']$, $com_\alpha \leftarrow \{0,1\}^\lambda$ and sends them to $\mathcal{A}$. Then it receives the $\{m_i\}_{i\in[0,N),i\neq\alpha}$ message from $\mathcal{F}_{VC}$ and programs the random oracle such that when evaluating the leaf nodes $r_i^{\tau'}$ for $i \in [0, N), i \neq \alpha$ the verification process would pass.

We argue indistinguishability via a hybrid argument.

- **Hybrid$_1$**. This is the real distribution of a malicious verifier.
- **Hybrid$_2$**. In this hybrid, we sample com_α uniformly at random and update $com = G_2(com_0, ..., com_{N-1})$ accordingly. Since G_2 is a random oracle, the only way that an adversary can distinguish between **Hybrid$_1$** and **Hybrid$_2$** is by querying the pre-image of com_α in **Hybrid$_1$**, which implies extracting Γ and contradicts the CCR security of H.
- **Hybrid$_3$**. In this hybrid, we sample $\{K_{\bar{\alpha}_i}^i\}_{i\in[1,\tau']}$ uniformly at random. We show in Lemma 3 that the adversary's advantage can be bounded by the CCR security of H.
- **Hybrid$_4$**. This is the ideal distribution, which is identical to **Hybrid$_3$**.

Lemma 3. *The advantage of distinguishing* **Hybrid$_2$** *and* **Hybrid$_3$** *in the proof of Lemma 2 can be bounded by the circular correlation robustness of the hash function* H.

Proof. We can sample the adversary's view using an oracle $\mathcal{O}(\cdot)$ such that the view corresponds to **Hybrid$_2$** (resp. **Hybrid$_3$**) if $\mathcal{O}$ is the real oracle $\mathcal{O}_\Gamma^{ccr}$ (resp. the ideal oracle f) as follows.

- For $i = 1$, we sample $K_{\bar{\alpha}_1}^1$ uniformly at random.
- For $i \in [2, \tau']$ we compute

$$K_{\bar{\alpha}_i}^i = \begin{cases} \mathcal{O}(\bigoplus_{j=1}^{i-1} K_{\bar{\alpha}_j}^j, 0) & \text{if } \bar{\alpha}_i = 0, \\ \mathcal{O}(\bigoplus_{j=1}^{i-1} K_{\bar{\alpha}_j}^j, 1) \oplus_{j=1}^{i-1} K_{\bar{\alpha}_j}^j & \text{if } \bar{\alpha}_i = 1. \end{cases}$$

- Sample com_α uniformly at random and compute $com = G_2(com_0, ..., com_{N-1})$.

Notice that if $\mathcal{O}$ is a random function then the output distribution is **Hybrid$_3$** whereas if $\mathcal{O} = \mathcal{O}_\Gamma^{ccr}(\cdot)$ then we have if $\bar{\alpha}_i = 0$ then

$$K_{\bar{\alpha}_i}^i = H(\bigoplus_{j=1}^{i-1} K_{\bar{\alpha}_j}^j)$$
$$= H(r_{\alpha_{i-1}\|...\|\alpha_1}^{i-1})$$

And if $\bar{\alpha}_i = 1$ then

$$K_{\bar{\alpha}_i}^i = H(\bigoplus_{j=1}^{i-1} K_{\bar{\alpha}_j}^j) \oplus \Delta \oplus \bigoplus_{j=1}^{i-1} K_{\bar{\alpha}_j}^j$$
$$= H(r_{\alpha_{i-1}\|...\|\alpha_1}^{i-1}) \oplus r_{\alpha_{i-1}\|...\|\alpha_1}^{i-1},$$

which is the same as in **Hybrid$_2$**.

Remark 1. We note that the construction of CCR hash functions in the random permutation model [31] requires a permutation on λ-bit strings. For some block ciphers (e.g. AES-128) the offered security level matches the block size and we can model the block cipher as a random permutation and apply the construction in [31]. Whereas other block ciphers with λ-bit security level do not provide a permutation on λ-bit strings (e.g. AES-192 and AES-256 has block size of 128 bits despite having higher security levels.) In this case, we use the standard GGM tree construction based on length-doubling PRG. We leave the efficient construction of CCR hash functions at the security level beyond 128 from standard symmetric primitives in the latter case (e.g. AES-192 and AES-256) as a future work.

5.2 Security Proof

We state the security of our protocol $\Pi_{\mathsf{RSD-PVZK}}$ under Fiat-Shamir transformation in Theorem 2. Since we prove the protocol $\Pi_{\mathsf{VC-cGGM}}$ securely realizes the vector commitment functionality $\mathcal{F}_{\mathsf{VC}}$ in Lemma 2, the security proof of the conversion from designated-verifier zero-knowledge (Fig. 5) to the non-interactive zero-knowledge is identical to the work of [10], we omit it in this paper.

Theorem 2. *Let* $\mathsf{PRG} : \{0,1\}^{\lambda} \to \mathbb{F}_2^n$ *be a pseudorandom generator, the zero-knowledge protocol* $\Pi_{\mathsf{RSD-PVZK}}$*, after Fiat-Shamir transformation, is a zero-knowledge non-interactive proof system in the random oracle model.*

5.3 Communication

We theoretically estimate the communication cost of $\Pi_{\mathsf{RSD-PVZK}}$. Firstly, during the inner protocol $\Pi_{\mathsf{RSD-DVZK}}$ the prover needs to send $\boldsymbol{d}$ and $m_0^{\mathsf{QS}}, m_1^{\mathsf{QS}}, m_0^{\mathsf{open}}$, which takes k elements in $\mathbb{F}_2$ and 3 elements in $\mathbb{F}_{2^\lambda}$ respectively.

Moreover, during the simulation of the $\mathcal{F}_{\mathsf{sVOLE}}$ setup, the prover needs to run τ instances of the vector commitment protocol $\Pi_{\mathsf{VC-cGGM}}$, each of which the communication cost is $(\tau' + 4) \cdot \lambda$ bits. Then, in SoftSpokenOT the prover needs to send the de-randomization matrix $\mathbf{C}$ as well as the checking information $\tilde{\boldsymbol{u}}, \tilde{\mathbf{V}}$, which takes $(\tau - 1) \cdot (k + \lambda + h)$ elements in $\mathbb{F}_2$, r elements in $\mathbb{F}_2$ and $r \cdot \tau$ elements in $\mathbb{F}_{2^{\tau'}}$ respectively.

Optimizations. We can use some existing techniques in the literature to optimize communication [9,18]. We list three main optimizations as follows.

- When running τ instances of $\Pi_{\mathsf{VC-cGGM}}$ the commitment message com can be combined by hashing all the leaf nodes across τ binary trees at once, saving $2\lambda \cdot (\tau - 1)$ bits of communication.
- Since in the RSD witness all elements in a block XOR to 1, the prover can commit to the first $\frac{m}{w} - 1$ coordinates of each block and linearly express the remaining element. Thus, we can reduce the witness length by a ratio of $\frac{w}{m}$.
- The values $\tilde{\mathbf{V}}, m_0^{\mathsf{QS}}, m_0^{\mathsf{open}}$ can be computed by the verifier and therefore to check for equality, it suffices for the prover to send a hash of those values.

Protocol $\Pi_{\mathsf{RSD-PVZK}}$

Both parties $\mathcal{P}$ and $\mathcal{V}$ have access to the RSD instance $(\mathbf{H}, \boldsymbol{y})$ where $\mathbf{H} \in \mathbb{F}_2^{(m-k) \times m}$ and $\boldsymbol{y} = \mathbf{H} \cdot \boldsymbol{e}$. The prover also knows the witness $\boldsymbol{e} = [\boldsymbol{e}_0\|...\|\boldsymbol{e}_{w-1}]$ where $\|\boldsymbol{e}_i\|_0 = 1$ for $i \in [0, w)$. We assume the matrix $\mathbf{H} = [\mathbf{I}_{m-k}\|\mathbf{H_B}]$ is in the systematic form and the vector $\boldsymbol{e}$ is split into $\boldsymbol{e_A}$ and $\boldsymbol{e_B}$. Let $n = k + \lambda$, $N = 2^{\tau'}$ and $\mathcal{H}^{\mathsf{UHF}} \subseteq \mathbb{F}_2^{r \times (n+h)}$ be a family of n-hiding, ϵ-universal hash function. Let $\mathsf{PRG} : \{0, 1\}^\lambda \to \mathbb{F}_2^{n+h}$ be a pseudorandom generator. We assume without loss of generality that $\tau\tau' = \lambda$.

1. $\mathcal{P}$ and $\mathcal{V}$ run τ instances of the vector commitment functionality $\mathcal{F}_{\mathsf{VC}}$ and send (commit) to them. Denote the messages as $\{k_j^i\}$ for $i \in [0, \tau)$, $j \in [0, N)$. The prover then defines $\mathbf{U}', \mathbf{V}$ for the index $i \in [0, \tau)$.

$$\mathbf{U}' = \left[\cdots \sum_j \mathsf{PRG}(k_j^i) \cdots \right], \quad \mathbf{V} = \left[\cdots \sum_j j \cdot \mathsf{PRG}(k_j^i) \cdots \right]$$

The prover also defines $\boldsymbol{u} = \mathbf{U}'[0]$ as the first column of $\mathbf{U}'$ and $\mathbf{C} := [\mathbf{U}'[1] \oplus \boldsymbol{u}\| \cdots \|\mathbf{U}'[\tau-1] \oplus \boldsymbol{u}] \in \mathbb{F}_2^{n \times (\tau-1)}$ where $\mathbf{U}'[i]$ denotes the i-th column of $\mathbf{U}'$. $\mathcal{P}$ sends $\mathbf{C}$ to $\mathcal{V}$.

2. $\mathcal{V}$ samples random challenge $\mathsf{H}^{\mathsf{UHF}} \leftarrow \mathcal{H}^{\mathsf{UHF}}$ and sends it to $\mathcal{P}$.

3. $\mathcal{P}$ defines the SoftSpokenOT check messages $\tilde{\boldsymbol{u}} = \mathsf{H}^{\mathsf{UHF}} \cdot \boldsymbol{u}$ and $\tilde{\mathbf{V}} = \mathsf{H}^{\mathsf{UHF}} \cdot \mathbf{V}$ and sends them to $\mathcal{V}$.

4. $\mathcal{P}$ and $\mathcal{V}$ run step 1–3 of $\Pi_{\mathsf{RSD-DVZK}}$ using the first n rows of $\boldsymbol{u}$ and $\mathbf{V}$.

5. $\mathcal{V}$ samples the random challenge $\boldsymbol{\Delta} = (\Delta_0, ..., \Delta_{\tau-1})$ and call (get, Δ_i) for $i \in [0, \tau)$. With the opened messages, it computes

$$\mathbf{W}' := \left[\sum_j (j + \Delta_0) \cdot \mathsf{PRG}(k_j^0) \cdots \sum_j (j + \Delta_{\tau-1}) \cdot \mathsf{PRG}(k_j^{\tau-1}) \right]$$

If the following two checks pass then $\mathcal{V}$ accepts the proof. Otherwise, $\mathcal{V}$ rejects.

– **SoftSpokenOT.** $\mathcal{V}$ checks that

$$\tilde{\mathbf{V}} + \tilde{\boldsymbol{u}} \cdot [1 ... 1] \cdot \mathsf{diag}(\boldsymbol{\Delta}) = \mathsf{H}^{\mathsf{UHF}} \cdot \left(\mathbf{W}' + [0\|\mathbf{C}] \cdot \mathsf{diag}(\boldsymbol{\Delta}) \right) .$$

– **QuickSilver.** The verifier runs the consistency check in step 4 of $\Pi_{\mathsf{RSD-DVZK}}$.

Fig. 8. The publicly verifiable zero-knowledge protocol for regular syndrome decoding.

Taking into account all the optimizations outlined above, we conclude the theoretical estimate of the communication of $\Pi_{\mathsf{RSD-PVZK}}$ as follows.

$$\mathsf{Comm} = \underbrace{\left((1 - \frac{w}{m})k + \lambda + h \right) \cdot (\tau - 1) + \underbrace{r}_{\tilde{u}} + \underbrace{(1 - \frac{w}{m})k}_{d}}_{\mathbf{C}}$$

$$+ \underbrace{\lambda}_{m_1^{\mathsf{QS}}} + \underbrace{((\tau' + 2) \cdot \tau + 2) \cdot \lambda}_{\text{VC Openings}} + \underbrace{2\lambda}_{\text{Equality Check}} \quad \text{bits.}$$

6   Performance Evaluation

In this section, we implement the ReSolveD signature scheme, which achieves highly competitive performance and a much smaller signature size when compared to other state-of-the-art code-based signature schemes. We first describe the parameters and implementation details of the scheme, then we report the evaluation results in terms of signature and key sizes as well as running time.

6.1   Parameters

We follow the approach from prior art [18] in the selection of parameters for the regular syndrome decoding instance. In particular, we select the minimal parameters that can offer the required bit security against state-of-the-art attacks that account for the regularity of the noise vector. Specifically, we estimate the complexity of the linearization attack, information syndrome decoding (ISD) attack and birthday paradox according to the formulas in [18] and take their minimal as the estimation of bit security. Using this estimation, we choose the smallest parameters that have complexity estimation of 2^{128}, 2^{143}, 2^{207} and 2^{272} according to the practice of previous works and the NIST's L1, L3 and L5 security levels.[2]

Table 3. The parameters for the ReSolveD signature scheme.

Parameter Set	m	k	w	τ	Estimated Bit Security
ReSolveD-128-Var1	1302	738	217	14	128.20
ReSolveD-128-Var2	1302	738	217	10	128.20
ReSolveD-L1	1470	834	245	11	143.20
ReSolveD-L3	2196	1248	366	17	207.48
ReSolveD-L5	2934	1668	489	22	272.29

Regarding the parameters of VOLE-in-the-Head, we follow the approach in the specification of FAEST [9]. In particular, with the security parameter λ and the repetition parameter τ, we compute $\tau_0' = \lceil \lambda/\tau \rceil$, $\tau_1' = \lfloor \lambda/\tau \rfloor$, and $\tau_0 = \lambda$ mod τ, $\tau_1 = \tau - \tau_0$. In this way, since $\tau_0\tau_0' + \tau_1\tau_1' = \lambda$, we can ensure that by sampling τ_0 instances of $\mathcal{F}_{VC}$ with depth τ_0' and τ_1 instances of $\mathcal{F}_{VC}$ with depth τ_1' we can get a global key with λ bits of entropy.

We select parameters such that our scheme demonstrates better performance in terms of the "signature size + public-key size" metric while still maintaining comparable running time compared to other NIST submissions. The parameters

---

[2] We select the parameters of ReSolveD-128 and ReSolveD-L{1,3,5} independently, because the former targets at signatures with 128-bit security while the latter targets other NIST submissions.

are shown in Table 3. We note that the parameter selection listed in Table 3 has considered recent attacks that exploit the regular noise structure [17,25].

We implement our signature scheme by adapting the implementation of FAEST[3].

We run the experiments on a Ubuntu 20.04 LTS machine with an AMD Ryzen 5 3600 CPU and 16 GB of RAM. For the time being, we only optimized the 128-bit version of ReSolveD with the AVX2 instruction set while we leave the respective optimization of ReSolveD-L1, ReSolveD-L3 and ReSolveD-L5 to a future work. The performance of ReSolveD under the first two sets of parameters with AVX2 optimization is reported in Table 1, while we compare the unoptimized version of ReSolveD under the other three sets of parameters with the reference implementation of other NIST submissions in the next subsection.

6.2 Comparison with Other Post-Quantum Signature Schemes

We give a detailed comparison between ReSolveD and NIST's new submissions SDitH [40] and FAEST [9] in Table 4. This is because SDitH shares a similarity in the underlying intractability assumption and FAEST utilizes the same VOLE-in-the-Head technique. In summary, ReSolveD and FAEST share almost the same

Table 4. Detailed comparison of ReSolveD compared to NIST's new submissions SDitH and FAEST with its EM variants for NIST security L1, L3 and L5.

Scheme	Sizes in Bytes				Runtimes in ms			Assumption
	$|\mathsf{sig}|$	$|\mathsf{sk}|$	$|\mathsf{pk}|$	$|\mathsf{sig}| + |\mathsf{pk}|$	t_{keygen}	t_{sign}	t_{verify}	
ReSolveD-L1	3916	32	96	4012	4.36	97.51	80.21	RSD over $\mathbb{F}_2$
ReSolveD-L3	8532	48	143	8675	9.97	257.37	226.71	RSD over $\mathbb{F}_2$
ReSolveD-L5	14944	64	191	15135	17.66	537.54	469.72	RSD over $\mathbb{F}_2$
FAEST-L1-S	5006	32	32	5038	0.19	129.14	124.89	AES
FAEST-L3-S	12744	56	64	12808	1.01	401.76	371.87	AES
FAEST-L5-S	22100	64	64	22164	1.47	624.62	586.12	AES
FAEST_EM-L1-S	4566	32	32	4598	0.18	112.06	108.85	EM-AES
FAEST_EM-L3-S	10824	48	48	10872	0.46	297.66	288.40	EM-AES
FAEST_EM-L5-S	20956	64	64	21020	1.41	540.35	540.04	EM-AES
SDitH-L1-gf256	8224	404	120	8344	6.08	33.23	28.62	SD over $\mathbb{F}_{256}$
SDitH-L1-gf251	8224	404	120	8344	4.41	14.76	12.32	SD over $\mathbb{F}_{251}$
SDitH-L3-gf256	19544	616	183	19727	7.31	113.98	98.82	SD over $\mathbb{F}_{256}$
SDitH-L3-gf251	19544	616	183	19727	5.30	34.46	28.32	SD over $\mathbb{F}_{251}$
SDitH-L5-gf256	33992	812	234	34226	10.59	209.67	186.77	SD over $\mathbb{F}_{256}$
SDitH-L5-gf251	33992	812	234	34226	8.74	59.33	54.85	SD over $\mathbb{F}_{251}$

---

[3] We adapted the reference implementation of FAEST at https://github.com/faest-sign/faest-ref. We also note that OpenSSL is required to facilitate fast evaluation.

Table 5. Comparison of signature sizes and runtimes at NIST L1 security for some standardized schemes and previous/new submissions from the NIST PQC standardization project. Numbers for Picnic are taken from [36] running on a 3.6 GHz Intel Xeon W-2133, others are taken from their technical report with a base clock frequency of up 2.6 GHz Intel Core i7-6600U CPU for Dilithium, a 2.3 GHz Intel Core i5-8259U for Falcon, a 3.1 GHz Intel Xeon E3-1220 CPU for SPHINCS$^+$ and a 3.6 GHz AMD Ryzen 5 3600 CPU for SPHNICS-α.

Scheme	Sizes in KB			Runtimes in ms		Assumption
	$|\text{sig}|$	$|\text{pk}|$	$|\text{sig}| + |\text{pk}|$	t_{sign}	t_{verify}	
Dilithium2 [39]	2.36	1.28	3.64	0.128	0.046	MLWE
Falcon-512 [48]	0.65	0.88	1.53	0.168	0.036	NTRU
SPHINCS$^+$-SHAKE-L1-F [34]	16.69	0.03	16.72	18.37	1.08	Hash
SPHINCS$^+$-SHAKE-L1-S [34]	7.67	0.03	7.70	355.64	0.38	Hash
SPHINCS$^+$-SHA2-L1-F [34]	16.69	0.03	16.72	10.86	0.69	Hash
SPHINCS$^+$-SHA2-L1-S [34]	7.67	0.03	7.70	207.98	0.28	Hash
SPHINCS-α-SHAKE-L1-F [58]	16.33	0.03	16.36	15.85	0.99	Hash
SPHINCS-α-SHAKE-L1-S [58]	6.72	0.03	6.75	316.60	1.36	Hash
SPHINCS-α-SHA2-L1-F [58]	16.33	0.03	16.36	7.40	0.56	Hash
SPHINCS-α-SHA2-L1-S [58]	6.72	0.03	6.75	149.18	0.75	Hash
Picnic1-L1-FS [57]	32.09	0.03	32.12	1.37	1.10	AES
Picnic2-L1-FS [57]	12.05	0.03	12.08	40.95	18.20	AES
Picnic3-L1 [57]	12.30	0.03	12.33	5.17	3.96	AES
Picnic3-L1-K12 [57]	12.30	0.03	12.33	3.98	2.87	AES
Picnic3-L1-64 [57]	11.14	0.03	11.17	23.25	17.21	AES
Picnic3-5-L1 [57]	13.38	0.03	13.41	5.59	4.63	AES
ReSolveD-L1	3.82	0.09	3.91	95.51	80.21	RSD

secret key size, but ReSolveD is smaller in signature size while faster in signing and verification time than the short version of FAEST and its EM variant, with only slightly larger public key size and slower key generation time in the same security level. The size of ReSolveD outperforms SDitH where the signature size (resp., secret key size) is more than 2× (resp., 12×) smaller than that in SDitH. However, the running time of our scheme is much slower.

We also compare our ReSolveD with post-quantum signature schemes to be standardized by NIST including Dilithium [39], Falcon [48] and SPHINCS$^+$ [34] and other previous/new submissions to NIST such as Picnic [57] and SPHINCS-α [58] in Table 5. Lattice-based signatures are currently the most efficient post-quantum signature schemes which achieve both smaller signature sizes and faster running times. However, these schemes are based on structured lattice problems such as Ring/Module-LWE and NTRU, on the contrary, our ReSolveD relies on no algebraic or geometric structures. Meanwhile, ReSolveD is competitive with Dilithium in the "signature size + public-key size" metric (with the former being 3.91 KB and the latter being 3.64 KB), although the runtimes of Dilithium significantly outperform us. Compared with the SPHINCS family and the Picnic family, our ReSolveD also achieves about $2\times$–$4\times$ smaller in sizes than SPHINCS$^+$ and SPHINCS-α, and is more than $3\times$ smaller than Picnic. Nevertheless, our ReSolveD is slower in terms of signing and verification. We plan to develop an optimized implementation of our scheme in the future work.

Acknowledgements. We thank anonymous reviewers for their helpful comments. Yu Yu is supported by the National Key Research and Development Program of China (Grant No. 2020YFA0309705), the National Natural Science Foundation of China (Grant Nos. 62125204 and 92270201), and the Major Program of Guangdong Basic and Applied Research (Grant No. 2019B030302008). Yu Yu also acknowledges the support from the XPLORER PRIZE. Kang Yang is supported by the National Natural Science Foundation of China (Grant Nos. 62102037 and 61932019).

References

1. Aguilar Melchor, C., Gama, N., Howe, J., Hülsing, A., Joseph, D., Yue, D.: The return of the SDitH. LNCS, vol. 14008, pp. 564–596. Springer, Heidelberg (2023). https://doi.org/10.1007/978-3-031-30589-4_20
2. Alaoui, S.M.E.Y., Cayrel, P., Bansarkhani, R.E., Hoffmann, G.: Code-based identification and signature schemes in software. In: Cuzzocrea, A., Kittl, C., Simos, D.E., Weippl, E.R., Xu, L. (eds.) Security Engineering and Intelligence Informatics - CD-ARES 2013 Workshops: MoCrySEn and SeCIHD, Regensburg, Germany, 2–6 September 2013, Proceedings. LNCS, vol. 8128, pp. 122–136. Springer, Heidelberg (2013). https://doi.org/10.1007/978-3-642-40588-4_9
3. Aragon, N., Blazy, O., Gaborit, P., Hauteville, A., Zémor, G.: Durandal: a rank metric based signature scheme. In: Ishai, Y., Rijmen, V. (eds.) EUROCRYPT 2019, Part III. LNCS, vol. 11478, pp. 728–758. Springer, Heidelberg (2019). https://doi.org/10.1007/978-3-030-17659-4_25
4. Augot, D., Finiasz, M., Sendrier, N.: A fast provably secure cryptographic hash function. Cryptology ePrint Archive, Report 2003/230 (2003). https://eprint.iacr.org/2003/230
5. Barenghi, A., Biasse, J.F., Persichetti, E., Santini, P.: LESS-FM: fine-tuning signatures from the code equivalence problem. In: Cheon, J.H., Tillich, J.P. (eds.) Post-Quantum Cryptography - 12th International Workshop, PQCrypto 2021. LNCS, vol. 12841, pp. 23–43. Springer, Heidelberg (2021). https://doi.org/10.1007/978-3-030-81293-5_2
6. Barg, S.: Some new NP-complete coding problems. Probl. Inf. Transm. **30**(3), 209–214 (1994)
7. Baum, C., Braun, L., Munch-Hansen, A., Razet, B., Scholl, P.: Appenzeller to Brie: efficient zero-knowledge proofs for mixed-mode arithmetic and Z2k. In: Vigna, G., Shi, E. (eds.) ACM CCS 2021, pp. 192–211. ACM Press, November 2021. https://doi.org/10.1145/3460120.3484812
8. Baum, C., Braun, L., Munch-Hansen, A., Scholl, P.: Moz$\mathbb{Z}_{2^k}$arella: efficient vector-OLE and zero-knowledge proofs over $\mathbb{Z}_{2^k}$. In: Dodis, Y., Shrimpton, T. (eds.) CRYPTO 2022, Part IV. LNCS, pp. 329–358. Springer, Heidelberg (2022). https://doi.org/10.1007/978-3-031-15985-5_12

9. Baum, C., et al.: FAEST: algorithm specifications. Technical report, National Institute of Standards and Technology (2023). https://faest.info/faest-spec-v1.1.pdf
10. Baum, C., et al.: Publicly verifiable zero-knowledge and post-quantum signatures from VOLE-in-the-Head. In: Handschuh, H., Lysyanskaya, A. (eds.) CRYPTO 2023, Part V. LNCS, vol. 14085, pp. 581–615. Springer, Heidelberg (2023). https://doi.org/10.1007/978-3-031-38554-4_19
11. Baum, C., Malozemoff, A.J., Rosen, M.B., Scholl, P.: Mac'n'Cheese: zero-knowledge proofs for boolean and arithmetic circuits with nested disjunctions. In: Malkin, T., Peikert, C. (eds.) CRYPTO 2021, Part IV. LNCS, vol. 12828, pp. 92–122. Springer, Heidelberg (2021). Virtual Event, https://doi.org/10.1007/978-3-030-84259-8_4
12. Bendlin, R., Damgård, I., Orlandi, C., Zakarias, S.: Semi-homomorphic encryption and multiparty computation. In: Paterson, K.G. (ed.) EUROCRYPT 2011. LNCS, vol. 6632, pp. 169–188. Springer, Heidelberg (2011). https://doi.org/10.1007/978-3-642-20465-4_11
13. Berlekamp, E.R., McEliece, R.J., van Tilborg, H.C.A.: On the inherent intractability of certain coding problems (Corresp.). IEEE Trans. Inf. Theory 24(3), 384–386 (1978). https://doi.org/10.1109/TIT.1978.1055873
14. Biasse, J.F., Micheli, G., Persichetti, E., Santini, P.: LESS is more: code-based signatures without syndromes. In: Nitaj, A., Youssef, A.M. (eds.) AFRICACRYPT 2020. LNCS, vol. 12174, pp. 45–65. Springer, Heidelberg (2020). https://doi.org/10.1007/978-3-030-51938-4_3
15. Bidoux, L., Gaborit, P., Kulkarni, M., Mateu, V.: Code-based signatures from new proofs of knowledge for the syndrome decoding problem. Des. Codes Cryptogr. 91(2), 497–544 (2023). https://doi.org/10.1007/s10623-022-01114-3
16. Boyle, E., Gilboa, N., Ishai, Y.: Function secret sharing: improvements and extensions. In: Weippl, E.R., Katzenbeisser, S., Kruegel, C., Myers, A.C., Halevi, S. (eds.) ACM CCS 2016, pp. 1292–1303. ACM Press, October 2016. https://doi.org/10.1145/2976749.2978429
17. Briaud, P., Øygarden, M.: A new algebraic approach to the regular syndrome decoding problem and implications for PCG constructions. In: Hazay, C., Stam, M. (eds.) Advances in Cryptology – EUROCRYPT 2023. LNCS, vol. 14008, pp. 391–422. Springer, Heidelberg (2023). https://doi.org/10.1007/978-3-031-30589-4_14
18. Carozza, E., Couteau, G., Joux, A.: Short signatures from regular syndrome decoding in the head. In: Hazay, C., Stam, M. (eds.) Advances in Cryptology – EUROCRYPT 2023. LNCS, vol. 14008, pp. 532–563. Springer, Heidelberg (2023). https://doi.org/10.1007/978-3-031-30589-4_19
19. Cascudo, I., Damgård, I., David, B., Döttling, N., Dowsley, R., Giacomelli, I.: Efficient UC commitment extension with homomorphism for free (and applications). In: Galbraith, S.D., Moriai, S. (eds.) ASIACRYPT 2019, Part II. LNCS, vol. 11922, pp. 606–635. Springer, Heidelberg (2019). https://doi.org/10.1007/978-3-030-34621-8_22
20. Cayrel, P., Véron, P., Alaoui, S.M.E.Y.: A zero-knowledge identification scheme based on the q-ary syndrome decoding problem. In: Biryukov, A., Gong, G., Stinson, D.R. (eds.) SAC 2010. LNCS, vol. 6544, pp. 171–186. Springer, Heidelberg (2010). https://doi.org/10.1007/978-3-642-19574-7_12
21. Chou, T., Persichetti, E., Santini, P.: On linear equivalence, canonical forms, and digital signatures. Cryptology ePrint Archive, Paper 2023/1533 (2023). https://eprint.iacr.org/2023/1533

22. Debris-Alazard, T., Sendrier, N., Tillich, J.P.: Wave: a new family of trapdoor one-way preimage sampleable functions based on codes. In: Galbraith, S.D., Moriai, S. (eds.) ASIACRYPT 2019, Part I. LNCS, vol. 11921, pp. 21–51. Springer, Heidelberg (2019). https://doi.org/10.1007/978-3-030-34578-5_2

23. Dittmer, S., Ishai, Y., Lu, S., Ostrovsky, R.: Improving line-point zero knowledge: two multiplications for the price of one, pp. 829–841. ACM Press (2022). https://doi.org/10.1145/3548606.3559385

24. Dittmer, S., Ishai, Y., Ostrovsky, R.: Line-point zero knowledge and its applications. In: 2nd Conference on Information-Theoretic Cryptography (2021)

25. Esser, A., Santini, P.: Not just regular decoding: asymptotics and improvements of regular syndrome decoding attacks. Cryptology ePrint Archive, Paper 2023/1568 (2023). https://eprint.iacr.org/2023/1568

26. Feneuil, T., Joux, A., Rivain, M.: Syndrome decoding in the head: shorter signatures from zero-knowledge proofs. In: CRYPTO 2022, Part II, pp. 541–572. LNCS, Springer, Heidelberg (2022). https://doi.org/10.1007/978-3-031-15979-4_19

27. Feneuil, T., Joux, A., Rivain, M.: Shared permutation for syndrome decoding: new zero-knowledge protocol and code-based signature. Des. Codes Cryptogr. **91**(2), 563–608 (2023). https://doi.org/10.1007/s10623-022-01116-1, First appeared online at https://eprint.iacr.org/2021/1576

28. Fiat, A., Shamir, A.: How to prove yourself: practical solutions to identification and signature problems. In: Odlyzko, A.M. (ed.) CRYPTO 1986. LNCS, vol. 263, pp. 186–194. Springer, Heidelberg (1987). https://doi.org/10.1007/3-540-47721-7_12

29. Gaborit, P., Girault, M.: Lightweight code-based identification and signature. In: IEEE International Symposium on Information Theory, ISIT 2007, Nice, France, 24–29 June 2007, pp. 191–195. IEEE (2007). https://doi.org/10.1109/ISIT.2007.4557225

30. Gueron, S., Persichetti, E., Santini, P.: Designing a practical code-based signature scheme from zero-knowledge proofs with trusted setup. Cryptography **6**(1), 5 (2022). https://doi.org/10.3390/cryptography6010005

31. Guo, C., Katz, J., Wang, X., Yu, Y.: Efficient and secure multiparty computation from fixed-key block ciphers. In: 2020 IEEE Symposium on Security and Privacy, pp. 825–841. IEEE Computer Society Press, May 2020. https://doi.org/10.1109/SP40000.2020.00016

32. Guo, X., et al.: Half-Tree: halving the cost of tree expansion in COT and DPF. In: Hazay, C., Stam, M. (eds.) EUROCRYPT 2023, Part I. LNCS, vol. 14004, pp. 330–362. Springer, Heidelberg (2023). https://doi.org/10.1007/978-3-031-30545-0_12

33. Hazay, C., Orsini, E., Scholl, P., Soria-Vazquez, E.: TinyKeys: a new approach to efficient multi-party computation. In: Shacham, H., Boldyreva, A. (eds.) CRYPTO 2018, Part III. LNCS, vol. 10993, pp. 3–33. Springer, Heidelberg (2018). https://doi.org/10.1007/978-3-319-96878-0_1

34. Hülsing, A., et al.: SPHINCS$^+$. Technical report, National Institute of Standards and Technology (2022). https://csrc.nist.gov/Projects/post-quantum-cryptography/selected-algorithms-2022

35. Ishai, Y., Kushilevitz, E., Ostrovsky, R., Sahai, A.: Zero-knowledge from secure multiparty computation. In: Johnson, D.S., Feige, U. (eds.) 39th ACM STOC, pp. 21–30. ACM Press, June 2007. https://doi.org/10.1145/1250790.1250794

36. Kales, D., Zaverucha, G.: Improving the performance of the Picnic signature scheme. IACR TCHES **2020**(4), 154–188 (2020). https://doi.org/10.13154/tches.v2020.i4.154-188, https://tches.iacr.org/index.php/TCHES/article/view/8680

37. Keller, M., Orsini, E., Scholl, P.: Actively secure OT extension with optimal overhead. In: Gennaro, R., Robshaw, M.J.B. (eds.) CRYPTO 2015, Part I. LNCS, vol. 9215, pp. 724–741. Springer, Heidelberg (2015). https://doi.org/10.1007/978-3-662-47989-6_35

38. Liu, H., Wang, X., Yang, K., Yu, Y.: The hardness of LPN over any integer ring and field for PCG applications. Cryptology ePrint Archive, Report 2022/712 (2022). https://eprint.iacr.org/2022/712

39. Lyubashevsky, V., et al.: CRYSTALS-DILITHIUM. Technical report, National Institute of Standards and Technology (2022). https://csrc.nist.gov/Projects/post-quantum-cryptography/selected-algorithms-2022

40. Melchor, C.A., et al.: The Syndrome Decoding in the Head (SD-in-the-Head) signature scheme. Technical report, National Institute of Standards and Technology (2023). https://csrc.nist.gov/csrc/media/Projects/pqc-dig-sig/documents/round-1/spec-files/SDitH-spec-web.pdf

41. Melchor, C.A., Gaborit, P., Schrek, J.: A new zero-knowledge code based identification scheme with reduced communication. In: 2011 IEEE Information Theory Workshop, ITW 2011, Paraty, Brazil, 16–20 October 2011, pp. 648–652. IEEE (2011). https://doi.org/10.1109/ITW.2011.6089577

42. Melchor, C.A., Hülsing, A., Joseph, D., Majenz, C., Ronen, E., Yue, D.: SDitH in the QROM. In: Guo, J., Steinfeld, R. (eds.) ASIACRYPT 2023, Part VII. LNCS, vol. 14444, pp. 317–350. Springer, Heidelberg (2023). https://doi.org/10.1007/978-981-99-8739-9_11

43. Nielsen, J.B., Nordholt, P.S., Orlandi, C., Burra, S.S.: A new approach to practical active-secure two-party computation. In: Safavi-Naini, R., Canetti, R. (eds.) CRYPTO 2012. LNCS, vol. 7417, pp. 681–700. Springer, Heidelberg (2012). https://doi.org/10.1007/978-3-642-32009-5_40

44. NIST: Call for additional digital signature schemes for the post-quantum cryptography standardization process (2022). https://csrc.nist.gov/csrc/media/Projects/pqc-dig-sig/documents/call-for-proposals-dig-sig-sept-2022.pdf

45. Orrù, M., Orsini, E., Scholl, P.: Actively secure 1-out-of-N OT extension with application to private set intersection. In: Handschuh, H. (ed.) CT-RSA 2017. LNCS, vol. 10159, pp. 381–396. Springer, Heidelberg (2017). https://doi.org/10.1007/978-3-319-52153-4_22

46. Patra, A., Sarkar, P., Suresh, A.: Fast actively secure OT extension for short secrets. In: NDSS 2017. The Internet Society, February/March 2017

47. Persichetti, E., Santini, P.: A new formulation of the linear equivalence problem and shorter less signatures. Cryptology ePrint Archive, Paper 2023/847 (2023). https://eprint.iacr.org/2023/847

48. Prest, T., et al.: FALCON. Technical report, National Institute of Standards and Technology (2022). https://csrc.nist.gov/Projects/post-quantum-cryptography/selected-algorithms-2022

49. Roy, L.: SoftSpokenOT: quieter OT extension from small-field silent VOLE in the minicrypt model. In: CRYPTO 2022, Part I. LNCS, vol. 13507, pp. 657–687. Springer, Heidelberg (2022). https://doi.org/10.1007/978-3-031-15802-5_23

50. Schwartz, J.T.: Fast probabilistic algorithms for verification of polynomial identities. J. ACM 27(4), 701–717 (1980). https://doi.org/10.1145/322217.322225

51. Stern, J.: A new identification scheme based on syndrome decoding. In: Stinson, D.R. (ed.) CRYPTO 1993. LNCS, vol. 773, pp. 13–21. Springer, Heidelberg (1994). https://doi.org/10.1007/3-540-48329-2_2

52. Véron, P.: Improved identification schemes based on error-correcting codes. Appl. Algebra Eng. Commun. Comput. **8**(1), 57–69 (1996). https://doi.org/10.1007/s002000050053
53. Weng, C., Yang, K., Katz, J., Wang, X.: Wolverine: fast, scalable, and communication-efficient zero-knowledge proofs for boolean and arithmetic circuits. In: 2021 IEEE Symposium on Security and Privacy, pp. 1074–1091. IEEE Computer Society Press, May 2021. https://doi.org/10.1109/SP40001.2021.00056
54. Weng, C., Yang, K., Xie, X., Katz, J., Wang, X.: Mystique: efficient conversions for zero-knowledge proofs with applications to machine learning. In: Bailey, M., Greenstadt, R. (eds.) USENIX Security 2021, pp. 501–518. USENIX Association, August 2021
55. Weng, C., Yang, K., Yang, Z., Xie, X., Wang, X.: AntMan: interactive zero-knowledge proofs with sublinear communication, pp. 2901–2914. ACM Press (2022). https://doi.org/10.1145/3548606.3560667
56. Yang, K., Sarkar, P., Weng, C., Wang, X.: QuickSilver: efficient and affordable zero-knowledge proofs for circuits and polynomials over any field. In: Vigna, G., Shi, E. (eds.) ACM CCS 2021, pp. 2986–3001. ACM Press, November 2021. https://doi.org/10.1145/3460120.3484556
57. Zaverucha, G., et al.: Picnic. Technical report, National Institute of Standards and Technology (2020). https://csrc.nist.gov/projects/post-quantum-cryptography/post-quantum-cryptography-standardization/round-3-submissions
58. Zhang, K., Cui, H., Yu, Y.: SPHINCS-alpha. Technical report, National Institute of Standards and Technology (2023). https://csrc.nist.gov/Projects/pqc-dig-sig/round-1-additional-signatures
59. Zippel, R.: Probabilistic algorithms for sparse polynomials. In: Ng, E.W. (ed.) Symbolic and Algebraic Computation, EUROSAM 1979, An International Symposium on Symbolic and Algebraic Computation, Marseille, France, June 1979, Proceedings. LNCS, vol. 72, pp. 216–226. Springer, Heidelberg (1979). https://doi.org/10.1007/3-540-09519-5_73

Probabilistic Hash-and-Sign with Retry in the Quantum Random Oracle Model

Haruhisa Kosuge[1](✉) and Keita Xagawa[2]📷

[1] Japan Ministry of Defense, Tokyo, Japan
`harucrypto@gmail.com`
[2] Technology Innovation Institute, Abu Dhabi, UAE
`keita.xagawa@tii.ae`

Abstract. A hash-and-sign signature based on a preimage-sampleable function (Gentry et al., STOC 2008) is secure in the quantum random oracle model if the preimage-sampleable function is collision-resistant (Boneh et al., ASIACRYPT 2011) or one-way (Zhandry, CRYPTO 2012). However, trapdoor functions in code-based and multivariate-quadratic-based signatures are not preimage-sampleable functions; for example, underlying trapdoor functions of the Courtois-Finiasz-Sendrier, Unbalanced Oil and Vinegar (UOV), and Hidden Field Equations (HFE) signatures are not surjections. Thus, such signature schemes adopt *probabilistic hash-and-sign with retry*. While Sakumoto et al. in PQCRYPTO 2011 showed the security of this paradigm in the classical random oracle model, their proof contains an error. Also, there is currently no known security proof for the probabilistic hash-and-sign with retry in the quantum random oracle model. We correct the proof in the random oracle model and give the first security proof in the quantum random oracle model for the probabilistic hash-and-sign with retry, assuming that the underlying trapdoor function is non-invertible, that is, it is hard to find a preimage of a given random value in the range. Our reduction from the non-invertibility assumption is tighter than the existing ones that apply only to signature schemes based on preimage-sampleable functions. We apply the security proof to code-based and multivariate-quadratic-based signatures. Additionally, we extend the proof into the multi-key setting and propose a generic method that provides security reduction without any security loss in the number of keys.

Keywords: Post-quantum cryptography · digital signature · hash-and-sign · quantum random oracle model · preimage sampleable function

1 Introduction

Hash-and-Sign Signature in the Random Oracle Model (ROM): A digital signature is an essential and versatile primitive since it supports non-repudiation and

The full version is available at https://eprint.iacr.org/2022/1359.
K. Xagawa–Part of the work done while at NTT Corporation.

Q. Tang and V. Teague (Eds.): PKC 2024, LNCS 14601, pp. 259–288, 2024.
https://doi.org/10.1007/978-3-031-57718-5_9

authentication; if a document is signed, the signer indeed signed it and cannot repudiate the signature. The standard security notion of the digital signature is existential unforgeability against chosen-message attack (EUF-CMA) [24]. Roughly speaking, a signature scheme is said to be EUF-CMA-secure if no efficient adversary can forge a signature even if the adversary can access a signing oracle, which captures non-repudiation and authentication. Hash-and-sign [4,5] is a widely adopted paradigm for constructing practical signatures, along with Fiat-Shamir [21], in the ROM [4]. This paper focuses on hash-and-sign.

A hash-and-sign signature scheme is realized by a hard-to-invert function $F \colon \mathcal{X} \to \mathcal{Y}$, its trapdoor $I \colon \mathcal{Y} \to \mathcal{X}$, and a hash function $H \colon \{0,1\}^* \to \mathcal{Y}$ modeled as a random oracle. To sign on a message m, a signer first computes $y = H(r, m)$, where r is a random string, computes $x = I(y)$, and outputs $\sigma = (r, x)$ as a signature. A verifier verifies the signature σ with the verification key F by checking if $H(r, m) = F(x)$ or not. We refer to this construction as *probabilistic hash-and-sign*; if r is an empty string, then *deterministic hash-and-sign*. The security properties of the trapdoor function are outlined as follows.

Non-invertibility (INV): It is hard to find a preimage of a challenge y that is uniformly chosen [27].

One-wayness (OW): It is hard to find a preimage of a challenge $y = F(x)$ for x chosen from some distribution on $\mathcal{X}$ [4].

Collision-resistance (CR): It is hard to find a collision pair of F.

A prime example is a deterministic hash-and-sign using a trapdoor permutation such as RSA, which is EUF-CMA-secure in the ROM, assuming the OW of the trapdoor permutation [4]. Gentry, Peikert, and Vaikuntanathan proposed deterministic/probabilistic hash-and-sign based on a preimage-sampleable function (PSF) [23], which is a trapdoor function with additional conditions, e.g., surjection. Gentry et al. showed a tight reduction from the CR assumption of PSF to the *strong* EUF-CMA (sEUF-CMA) security of the deterministic/probabilistic hash-and-sign, and they constructed a collision-resistant PSF from lattices. Unfortunately, it is hard to build PSFs in code-based and multivariate-quadratic-based (MQ-based) cryptography; for example, F is not a surjection. In this case, the trapdoor I fails to invert y whose preimage does not exist. For such trapdoor functions, we employ the probabilistic hash-and-sign *with retry*, where a signer takes randomness r until r allows inversion of $y = H(r, m)$. The Courtois-Finiasz-Sendrier (CFS) signature [13] in code-based cryptography and the Unbalanced Oil and Vinegar (UOV) [31] and Hidden Field Equations (HFE) signatures [39] in MQ-based cryptography use this paradigm. Sakumoto et al. [42] gave a security proof of the probabilistic hash-and-sign with retry in the ROM. However, their proof has a flaw in the simulation of the random oracle, which is pointed out by Chatterjee et al. [12].

Hash-and-Sign Signature in Quantum Random Oracle Model (QROM): Large-scale quantum computers will be able to break widely deployed public-key cryptography such as RSA and ECDSA because of Shor's algorithm [43]. Consequently, there has been a growing interest in post-quantum cryptography

Table 1. Summary of the security proofs for hash-and-sign in the QROM. DHaS, PHaS, and PHaSwR denote deterministic hash-and-sign, probabilistic hash-and-sign, and probabilistic hash-and-sign with retry. ϵ denotes the adversary's advantage in the game of the underlying assumption. q denotes the number of queries to the signing and random oracles.

Name	DHaS	PHaS	PHaSwR	Assumption	Security Bound
[9]	✓	✓	–	CR	$O(\epsilon_{cr})$
[47]	✓	✓	–	OW/INV	$O(q^2\sqrt{\epsilon_{ow/inv}})$
ext. of [45]	✓	✓	–	OW/INV	$O(q^4\epsilon_{ow/inv})$
[11]	–	✓	–	EUF-NMA	$O(\epsilon_{nma})$
Ours	-	✓	✓	INV	$O(q^2\epsilon_{inv})$

(PQC). Recently NIST selected PQC candidates of public-key encryption/key-encapsulation mechanism (KEM) and digital signature for standardization [38]. Furthermore, NIST initiated an additional call for PQC digital signatures [37]. In the context of PQC, it is essential for signature schemes to provide EUF-CMA security in the QROM [9] since it models real-world quantum adversaries having *offline* access to the hash function. Unfortunately, schemes that are secure in the ROM are not always secure in the QROM, as demonstrated by separation results, including a signature scheme, by Yamakawa and Zhandry [46].

Table 1 summarizes studies on the EUF-CMA security of hash-and-sign signatures in the QROM. Boneh et al. [9] showed a tight reduction from the CR assumption of PSF using the history-free reduction. Zhandry [47] gave a reduction from the OW/INV assumptions[1], using a technique called semi-constant distribution[2]. Unfortunately, the semi-constant distribution technique incurs a square-root loss in the success probability. Yamakawa and Zhandry [45] gave the lifting theorem that shows that any search-type game is hard in the QROM if the game is hard in the ROM. They used the lifting theorem to show that an EUF-NMA-secure signature in the ROM is EUF-NMA-secure in the QROM, where NMA stands for No-Message Attack. By extending the results of [45], we obtain a reduction from the OW/INV assumptions of PSF. Chailloux and Debris-Alazard [11] gave a security proof of the probabilistic hash-and-sign based on non-PSF trapdoor functions. Also, Grilo, Hövelmanns, Hülsing, and Majenz [25] gave a reduction from the EUF-RMA security of a signature scheme for fixed-length messages, where RMA stands for Random-Message Attack[3]. However, there is no known reduction to the EUF-RMA security of the underlying signature from the OW/INV assumptions of trapdoor functions.

---

[1] For PSF, tight reductions exist both from OW to INV and from INV to OW.

[2] Zhandry [47] proved the EUF-CMA security by assuming that the trapdoor permutation is one-way. The security proof applies to a case where the PSF is either one-way or non-invertible.

[3] A signer chooses r, computes $m' = H(r, m)$, and signs on m' by using a signing algorithm of the signature scheme for fixed-length messages, and outputs (r, σ).

Regarding the probabilistic hash-and-sign with retry, there is no valid proof even in the ROM. Naturally, there is no proof in the QROM, which has an impact on the security evaluation of code-based and MQ-based signatures. Our central question is:

Q1. Is there an EUF-CMA security proof for the probabilistic hash-and-sign with retry? How tight is the security proof?

Provable Security in Multi-key Setting: The EUF-CMA security is sometimes insufficient to ensure the security of the digital signature in the real world since exploiting one of many users may be sufficient for a real-world adversary to intrude into a system. We must consider the EUF-CMA security *in the multi-key setting*, the M-EUF-CMA security in short. The adversary, given multiple verification keys, tries to forge a valid signature for one of the verification keys. If the adversary can gain an advantage by targeting multiple keys (*multi-key attack*), the M-EUF-CMA security degrades with the number of keys (or users). NIST mentioned resistance to multi-key attacks as a "desirable property" in their call for proposals [36] of the PQC standardization project. We can ensure resistance against multi-key attacks if there is no security loss in the number of keys. Thus, our additional question is:

Q2. Is there an M-EUF-CMA security proof for hash-and-sign without any security loss in the number of keys?

The technique of including an entire verification key as part of the input for the hash function is known as *key prefixing*, which enables one to separate the domain of the hash function for each verification key. Schnorr signature adopts key prefixing to show a tight reduction in the multi-key setting [35]. Similarly, Duman et al. [19] proposed a technique called *prefix hashing* for the Fujisaki-Okamoto transform of KEM. Prefix hashing is a technique in which the hash function includes only a small unpredictable portion of a verification key, resulting in a smaller increase in execution time compared to the key prefixing.

1.1   Contributions

Security Proof of Probabilistic Hash-and-Sign with Retry in the QROM: We affirmatively answer Q1. We correct the existing proof of [42] in the ROM and establish a security proof in the QROM (*main theorem*) based on the corrected ROM proof. Additionally, the main theorem applies to the probabilistic hash-and-sign *without retry*. Furthermore, we show that a signature scheme is sEUF-CMA-secure if the underlying trapdoor function is an injection. Our reduction is tighter than the existing ones that apply to the probabilistic hash-and-sign without retry only [11,45,47]. Figure 1 shows a diagram of the reduction. The main theorem comprises two reductions; EUF-NMA $\Rightarrow$ EUF-CMA and INV $\Rightarrow$ EUF-NMA, where X $\Rightarrow$ Y inidicates a reduction from X to Y. The main theorem has a security bound $(2q_{\mathsf{qro}} + 1)^2 \epsilon_{\mathsf{inv}}$, where q_{qro} is a bound on the number of random oracle queries and ϵ_{inv} is an advantage of breaking the INV.

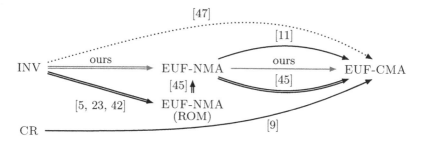

Fig. 1. A diagram illustrating reductions of hash-and-sign in the QROM. Red arrows represent our results, while solid, double, and dotted arrows represent tight reductions, reductions with linear or quadratic loss, and non-tight reductions. (Color figure online)

Proof Idea: We provide a technical overview of the main theorem. To prove EUF-NMA $\Rightarrow$ EUF-CMA, we assume that the following two values are statistically or computationally indistinguishable:

– x obtained after retrying y until y becomes invertible by the trapdoor I.
– x obtained by a simulator that does not use the trapdoor I.

The proof by Sakumoto et al. [42] simulates the signing oracle by programming H such that $H(r, m)$ outputs $F(x)$ for (r, x) chosen without using I. Since we do not assume that $F(x)$ is uniform, the output of H may become biased. Therefore, their proof is flawed, and the following two additional steps are required.

First, we *adaptively* reprogram the random function. Given a message m, the signing oracle repeatedly reprograms H such that $H(r, m) = y$ holds for randomly chosen $(r, y) \in \mathcal{R} \times \mathcal{Y}$, and this reprogramming continues until the trapdoor I can provide a preimage $x \in \mathcal{X}$ of y ($F(x) = y$). In the ROM, this reprogramming is feasible as long as r chosen in the signing oracle has not been queried in advance. In the QROM, we employ the tight adaptive reprogramming technique [25].

Next, we cancel the reprogramming during retries, specifically, reprogramming for (r, y) such that $I(y)$ fails to invert, to make the simulation feasible based on the aforementioned assumption. We utilize the fact that r is chosen independently of the queried m in the signing oracle, which allows us to choose r used for reprogramming during retries at the beginning of the game. We define a set of such prechosen r as $\mathcal{S}$. Then, we *puncture* H on $\mathcal{S}$ [1], that is, a modification of H such that the adversary cannot make a query for H on $\mathcal{S}$. In the ROM, this punctuation is feasible as long as the adversary does not make queries for H on $\mathcal{S}$. In the QROM, we utilize the semi-classical One-way to Hiding lemma [1]. As a result, we can cancel the reprogramming, as the adversary cannot distinguish whether H is reprogrammed during retries or not. After the cancelation, the EUF-NMA adversary can simulate the signing oracle.

Regarding INV $\Rightarrow$ EUF-NMA, the INV adversary gives his challenge y to the EUF-NMA adversary and outputs x^* that is included in the final output

(m^*, r^*, x^*) of the EUF-NMA adversary. In the ROM, the INV adversary randomly selects one query to H and returns his challenge y as in [42]. In the QROM, we use the measure-and-reprogram technique developed by Don et al. [17], incurring a security loss of $(2q_{\mathsf{qro}} + 1)^2$. As far as we know, this usage is new in the context of the probabilistic hash-and-sign.

Applications: Applying the main theorem, we enhance the EUF-CMA security of Wave [2] and give the first proof for the sEUF-CMA security of the modified CFS signature [14] as well as the EUF-CMA security of Rainbow [16], GeMSS [10], MAYO [6], QR-UOV [22], and PROV [20] in the QROM. To the best of our knowledge, the main theorem encompasses all existing hash-and-sign signatures such that reductions of INV $\Rightarrow$ (s)EUF-CMA are known in the ROM. NIST has recently announced additional candidates for post-quantum signatures. NIST has the intention of standardizing schemes that are not based on structured lattices [37]. The main theorem has wide application in code-based and MQ-based cryptography, promising candidates for this call. The additional candidates include Wave, MAYO, QR-UOV, and PROV. Notably, QR-UOV and PROV have utilized the main theorem in their specifications [20,22].

Security Proof in Multi-key Setting: We introduce a generic method for establishing a reduction from the property of trapdoor functions in the single-instance setting to the security of the hash-and-sign with prefix hashing in the multi-key setting. The core idea behind this generic method is to apply pairs of randomly generated transformations $\{L_j, R_j\}_j$ to a single verification key F'. Here, F' belongs to another trapdoor function, assumed to be non-invertible. This process effectively simulates multiple verification keys through $\{L_j \circ F' \circ R_j\}_j$. Assuming the indistinguishability between $\{L_j \circ F' \circ R_j\}_j$ and real verification keys $\{F_j\}_j$, we show a reduction of INV $\Rightarrow$ M-EUF-CMA with a security bound $(2q_{\mathsf{qro}} + 1)^2 \epsilon_{\mathsf{inv}}$ and a tight reduction of CR $\Rightarrow$ M-sEUF-CMA. Since there is no security loss in the number of keys, we can affirmatively answer Q2. Furthermore, we apply the generic method to some hash-and-sign signatures. In these applications, we introduce some computational problems that can computationally ensure the indistinguishability between $\{L_j \circ F \circ R_j\}_j$ and $\{F_j\}_j$. However, establishing the hardness of these computational problems remains an open problem as they have not been extensively studied.

Concurrent Work: Liu, Jiang, and Zhao [32] show the EUF-CMA security of the deterministic/probabilistic hash-and-sign based on trapdoor permutations in the QROM by using the measure-and-reprogram technique by Don et al. [17]. Their security bound is $(2(q_{\mathsf{qro}} + q_{\mathsf{sign}} + 1) + 1)^2 \epsilon_{\mathsf{inv}}$, where q_{sign} is a bound on the number of signing queries. They also give an analysis for (H)IBE in the QROM. Our work has two advantages over their work on hash-and-sign. First, our work has wider applications since it has generality in its application to probabilistic hash-and-sign with/without retry, in contrast to the restriction of [32] to the deterministic/probabilistic hash-and-sign[4] and allows the usage of non-PSF trapdoor functions, generalization of trapdoor permutations. Second, the main theorem has the bound $(2q_{\mathsf{qro}} + 1)^2 \epsilon_{\mathsf{inv}}$, which does not include q_{sign}.

Two papers [3,15] recently pointed out a subtle flaw in the security proofs of Fiat-Shamir with aborts [33] in the QROM [25,29]. The flaw stems from the bias introduced by the simulation with abort, which we treat in EUF-NMA $\Rightarrow$ EUF-CMA carefully. We note that the games in the corrected proof in [3] are defined in the same spirit as our proof of EUF-NMA $\Rightarrow$ EUF-CMA while the proof techniques and the details are different.

Organization: Section 2 gives notations, definitions, and so on. Section 3 reviews the existing security proofs in the (Q)ROM. Section 4 presents the main theorem and discusses applications. In Sect. 5, we describe the generic method applied in the multi-key setting.

2   Preliminaries

2.1   Notations and Terminology

For $n \in \mathbb{N}$, we let $[n] := \{1, \ldots, n\}$. We write any symbol for sets in calligraphic font. For a finite set $\mathcal{X}$, $|\mathcal{X}|$ is the cardinality of $\mathcal{X}$ and $\mathsf{U}(\mathcal{X})$ is the uniform distribution over $\mathcal{X}$. By $x \leftarrow_\$ \mathcal{X}$ and $x \leftarrow \mathcal{D}_\mathcal{X}$, we denote the sampling of an element from $\mathsf{U}(\mathcal{X})$ and $\mathcal{D}_\mathcal{X}$ (distribution on $\mathcal{X}$). We denote a set of functions having a domain $\mathcal{X}$ and a range $\mathcal{Y}$ by $\mathcal{Y}^\mathcal{X}$.

We write any symbol for functions in sans-serif font and adversaries in calligraphic font. Let F be a function, and $\mathcal{A}$ be an adversary. We denote by $y \leftarrow \mathsf{F}^\mathsf{H}(x)$ and $y \leftarrow \mathcal{A}^\mathsf{H}(x)$ (resp., $y \leftarrow \mathsf{F}^{|\mathsf{H}\rangle}(x)$ and $y \leftarrow \mathcal{A}^{|\mathsf{H}\rangle}(x)$) probabilistic computations of F and $\mathcal{A}$ on input x with a classical (resp., quantum) oracle access to a function H. If F and $\mathcal{A}$ are deterministic, we write $y := \mathsf{F}^\mathsf{H}(x)$ and $y := \mathcal{A}^\mathsf{H}(x)$. For a random function H, we denote by $\mathsf{H}^{x^* \mapsto y^*}$ a function such that $\mathsf{H}^{x^* \mapsto y^*}(x) = \mathsf{H}(x)$ for $x \neq x^*$ and $\mathsf{H}^{x^* \mapsto y^*}(x^*) = y^*$. The notation $\mathsf{G}^\mathcal{A} \Rightarrow y$ denotes an event in which a game G played by $\mathcal{A}$ returns y.

We denote 1 if the Boolean statement is true $\top$ and 0 if the statement is false $\bot$. A binary operation $a \overset{?}{=} b$ outputs $\top$ if $a = b$ and outputs $\bot$ otherwise.

2.2   Digital Signature and Trapdoor Function

Definition 1 (Digital Signature). *A digital signature scheme* Sig *consists of three algorithms:*

$\mathsf{Sig.KeyGen}(1^\lambda)$: *This algorithm takes the security parameter* 1^λ *as input and outputs a verification key* vk *and a signing key* sk.
$\mathsf{Sig.Sign}(sk, m)$: *This algorithm takes a signing key* sk *and a message* m *as input and outputs a signature* σ.

---

[4] Although the deterministic hash-and-sign is not in our scope, it can be transformed into the probabilistic one with a small tweak.

Game: EUF-CMA	Sign(m_i)	Game: EUF-NMA
1 $Q := \emptyset$	1 $\sigma_i \leftarrow$ Sig.Sign(sk, m_i)	1 $(vk, sk) \leftarrow$ Sig.KeyGen(1^λ)
2 $(vk, sk) \leftarrow$ Sig.KeyGen(1^λ)	2 $Q := Q \cup \{m_i\}$	2 $(m^*, \sigma^*) \leftarrow \mathcal{A}_{nma}(vk)$
3 $(m^*, \sigma^*) \leftarrow \mathcal{A}_{cma}^{Sign}(vk)$	3 return σ_i	3 return Sig.Verify(vk, m^*, σ^*)
4 if $m^* \in Q$ then		
5 return 0		
6 return Sig.Verify(vk, m^*, σ^*)		

Fig. 2. EUF-CMA and EUF-NMA games

Sig.Vrfy(vk, m, σ): *This algorithm takes a verification key vk, a message m, and a signature σ as input, and outputs $\top$ (acceptance) or $\bot$ (rejection).*

We say Sig *is correct if, for all* $(vk, sk) \leftarrow$ Sig.KeyGen(1^λ) *and for all* $m \in \mathcal{M}$, $\Pr[\text{Sig.Vrfy}(vk, m, \text{Sig.Sign}(sk, m)) = \bot]$ *is negligible.*

Definition 2 (Security of Signature). *Let* Sig *be a signature scheme. Using games given in Fig. 2, we define advantage functions of adversaries playing* EUF-CMA *(Existential UnForgeability against Chosen-Message Attack) and* EUF-NMA *(No-Message Attack) games against* Sig *as* $\text{Adv}_{Sig}^{EUF\text{-}CMA}(\mathcal{A}_{cma}) = \Pr\left[\text{EUF-CMA}^{\mathcal{A}_{cma}} \Rightarrow 1\right]$ *and* $\text{Adv}_{Sig}^{EUF\text{-}NMA}(\mathcal{A}_{nma}) = \Pr\left[\text{EUF-NMA}^{\mathcal{A}_{nma}} \Rightarrow 1\right]$, *respectively. Also, we define an advantage function for an* sEUF-CMA *(strong* EUF-CMA*) game as* $\text{Adv}_{Sig}^{sEUF\text{-}CMA}(\mathcal{A}_{cma}) = \Pr\left[\text{sEUF-CMA}^{\mathcal{A}_{cma}} \Rightarrow 1\right]$, *where the* sEUF-CMA *game is identical to the* EUF-CMA *game except that Line 4 of the game is changed as "if* $(m^*, \sigma^*) \in Q$ *then" and Line 2 of the signing oracle is changed as "$Q := Q \cup \{(m_i, \sigma_i)\}$". We say* Sig *is* EUF-CMA*-secure,* sEUF-CMA*-secure, or* EUF-NMA*-secure if its corresponding advantage is negligible for any efficient adversary in the security parameter.*

Definition 3 (Trapdoor Function). *A trapdoor function* T *consists of three algorithms:*

Gen(1^λ): *This algorithm takes the security parameter 1^λ as input and outputs a function* F *with a trapdoor* I *of* F.
F(x): *This algorithm takes $x \in \mathcal{X}$ and deterministically outputs* F(x) $\in \mathcal{Y}$.
I(y): *This algorithm takes $y \in \mathcal{Y}$ and outputs $x \in \mathcal{X}$, s.t.,* F(x)$=y$, *or outputs* $\bot$.

Definition 4 (Security of Trapdoor Function). *Let* T *be a trapdoor function. Using games given in Fig. 3, we define advantage functions of adversaries playing the* INV *(non-INVertibility)[5],* OW *(One-Wayness), and* CR *(Collision-Resistance) games against* T *as* $\text{Adv}_T^{INV}(\mathcal{B}_{inv}) = \Pr[\text{INV}^{\mathcal{B}_{inv}} \Rightarrow 1]$, $\text{Adv}_T^{OW}(\mathcal{B}_{ow}) = \Pr[\text{OW}^{\mathcal{B}_{ow}} \Rightarrow 1]$, *and* $\text{Adv}_T^{CR}(\mathcal{B}_{cr}) = \Pr[\text{CR}^{\mathcal{B}_{cr}} \Rightarrow 1]$, *respectively. We say* T *is non-invertible, one-way, or collision-resistant if its corresponding advantage is negligible in the security parameter for any efficient adversary.*

---

[5] In general, *non-invertibility* of trapdoor functions is called *one-wayness* [11,23,42]. We make a distinction between them depending on the way to choose challenges (INV follows [27] and OW follows [4]).

GAME: INV	GAME: OW	GAME: CR
1 $(\mathsf{F},\mathsf{I}) \leftarrow \mathsf{Gen}(1^\lambda)$	1 $(\mathsf{F},\mathsf{I}) \leftarrow \mathsf{Gen}(1^\lambda)$	1 $(\mathsf{F},\mathsf{I}) \leftarrow \mathsf{Gen}(1^\lambda)$
2 $y \leftarrow_\$ \mathcal{Y}$	2 $x \leftarrow \mathcal{D}_\mathcal{X}$	2 $(x_1^*, x_2^*) \leftarrow \mathcal{B}_{\mathsf{cr}}(\mathsf{F})$
3 $x^* \leftarrow \mathcal{B}_{\mathsf{inv}}(\mathsf{F}, y)$	3 $y := \mathsf{F}(x)$	3 $\mathbf{return}\ \mathsf{F}(x_1^*) \overset{?}{=} \mathsf{F}(x_2^*)$
4 $\mathbf{return}\ \mathsf{F}(x^*) \overset{?}{=} y$	4 $x^* \leftarrow \mathcal{B}_{\mathsf{ow}}(\mathsf{F}, y)$	
	5 $\mathbf{return}\ \mathsf{F}(x^*) \overset{?}{=} y$	

Fig. 3. INV (non-INVertibility), OW (One-Wayness), and CR (Collision-Resistance) games

GAME: PS_b	$\mathsf{Sample}_0()$	$\mathsf{Sample}_1()$
1 $(\mathsf{F},\mathsf{I}) \leftarrow \mathsf{Gen}(1^\lambda)$	1 $\mathbf{repeat}$	1 $x_i \leftarrow \mathsf{SampDom}(\mathsf{F})$
2 $b^* \leftarrow \mathcal{D}_{\mathsf{ps}}^{\mathsf{Sample}_b}(\mathsf{F})$	2 $\quad y_i \leftarrow_\$ \mathcal{Y}$	2 $\mathbf{return}\ x_i$
3 $\mathbf{return}\ b^*$	3 $\quad x_i \leftarrow \mathsf{I}(y_i)$	
	4 $\mathbf{until}\ x_i \neq \bot$	
	5 $\mathbf{return}\ x_i$	

Fig. 4. PS (Preimage Sampling) game

2.3 Preimage-Sampleable Function

In the ROM, hash-and-sign is EUF-CMA-secure when instantiated with a preimage-sampleable function (PSF) [23]. We first define its weakened version.

Definition 5 (Weak Preimage-Sampleable Function (WPSF)). *A WPSF* T *is a trapdoor function that is equipped with an additional function* $\mathsf{SampDom}(\mathsf{F})$, *which takes as input* $\mathsf{F} \in \mathcal{Y}^\mathcal{X}$ *and outputs some* $x \in \mathcal{X}$.

We then review PSF:

Definition 6 (Preimage-Sampleable Function (PSF) [23]). *A WPSF* T *is said to be a PSF if it satisfies three conditions for any* $(\mathsf{F},\mathsf{I}) \leftarrow \mathsf{Gen}(1^\lambda)$:

Condition 1: $\mathsf{F}(x)$ *is uniform over* $\mathcal{Y}$ *for* $x \leftarrow \mathsf{SampDom}(\mathsf{F})$.
Condition 2: $x \leftarrow \mathsf{I}(y)$ *follows a distribution of* $x \leftarrow \mathsf{SampDom}(\mathsf{F})$ *given* $\mathsf{F}(x) = y$.
Condition 3: $\mathsf{I}(y)$ *outputs* x *satisfying* $\mathsf{F}(x) = y$ *for any* $y \in \mathcal{Y}$.

If T *is collision-resistant PSF, it satisfies the above conditions plus the following:*

Condition 4: *For any* $y \in \mathcal{Y}$, *the conditional min-entropy of* $x \leftarrow \mathsf{SampDom}(\mathsf{F})$ *given* $\mathsf{F}(x) = y$ *is at least* $\omega(\log(\lambda))$.

In the proof of EUF-CMA security, a trapdoor function may not be a PSF, but it must be a WPSF that satisfies a relaxed version of **Condition 2** that ensures indistinguishability between $x \leftarrow \mathsf{SampDom}(\mathsf{F})$ and $x \leftarrow \mathsf{I}(y)$. To define this relaxed condition, we introduce a game shown in Fig. 4.

Definition 7 (Preimage Sampling (PS) Game). *Let* T *be a WPSF. Using a game defined in Fig. 4, we define an advantage function of an adversary playing the PS game against* T *as* $\mathsf{Adv}_\mathsf{T}^{\mathrm{PS}}(\mathcal{D}_{\mathsf{ps}}) = \left| \Pr\left[\mathsf{PS}_0^{\mathcal{D}_{\mathsf{ps}}} \Rightarrow 1\right] - \Pr\left[\mathsf{PS}_1^{\mathcal{D}_{\mathsf{ps}}} \Rightarrow 1\right] \right|$. *We say* T *is preimage-simulatable if its advantage is negligible for any efficient adversary.*

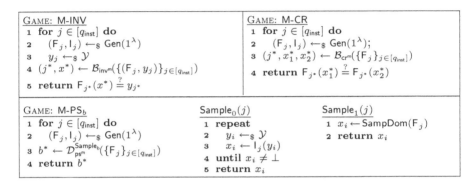

Fig. 5. M-EUF-CMA(Multi-key EUF-CMA) game

Fig. 6. M-INV, M-CR, and M-PS(Multi-instance INV, CR, and PS) games

2.4 Security Games in Multi-key/Multi-instance Settings

Definition 8 (Security of Signature in Multi-key Setting [30]). *Let* Sig *be a signature scheme. Using a game given in Fig. 5, we define advantage functions of adversaries playing the* M-EUF-CMA *and* M-sEUF-CMA *(Multi-key EUF-CMA/sEUF-CMA) games against* Sig *as* $\mathrm{Adv}_{\mathsf{Sig}}^{\mathrm{M\text{-}EUF\text{-}CMA}}(\mathcal{A}_{\mathsf{cma^m}}) = \Pr\left[\mathrm{M\text{-}EUF\text{-}CMA}^{\mathcal{A}_{\mathsf{cma^m}}} \Rightarrow 1\right]$ *and* $\mathrm{Adv}_{\mathsf{Sig}}^{\mathrm{M\text{-}sEUF\text{-}CMA}}(\mathcal{A}_{\mathsf{cma^m}}) = \Pr\left[\mathrm{M\text{-}sEUF\text{-}CMA}^{\mathcal{A}_{\mathsf{cma^m}}} \Rightarrow 1\right]$, *where the* M-sEUF-CMA *game is identical to the* M-EUF-CMA *game except that Line 5 of the game is changed as "if* $(j^*, m^*, \sigma^*) \in \mathcal{Q}$ *then" and Line 2 of the signing oracle is changed as "*$\mathcal{Q} := \mathcal{Q} \cup \{(j, m_i, \sigma_i)\}$*". We say* Sig *is* M-EUF-CMA-*secure or* M-sEUF-CMA-*secure if its corresponding advantage is negligible for any efficient adversary in the security parameter.*

Definition 9 (INV, CR, and PS in Multi-instance Setting). *Let* T *be a trapdoor function or WPSF. Using games given in Fig. 6, we define advantage functions of adversaries playing the* M-INV, M-CR, *and* M-PS *(Multi-instance non-invertibility, collision resistance, and preimage sampling) games against* T *as* $\mathrm{Adv}_{\mathsf{T}}^{\mathrm{M\text{-}INV}}(\mathcal{B}_{\mathsf{inv^m}}) = \Pr\left[\mathrm{M\text{-}INV}^{\mathcal{B}_{\mathsf{inv^m}}} \Rightarrow 1\right]$, $\mathrm{Adv}_{\mathsf{T}}^{\mathrm{M\text{-}CR}}(\mathcal{B}_{\mathsf{cr^m}}) = \Pr\left[\mathrm{M\text{-}CR}^{\mathcal{B}_{\mathsf{cr^m}}} \Rightarrow 1\right]$, *and* $\mathrm{Adv}_{\mathsf{T}}^{\mathrm{M\text{-}PS}}(\mathcal{D}_{\mathsf{ps^m}}) = \left|\Pr\left[\mathrm{M\text{-}PS}_0^{\mathcal{D}_{\mathsf{ps^m}}} \Rightarrow 1\right] - \Pr\left[\mathrm{M\text{-}PS}_1^{\mathcal{D}_{\mathsf{ps^m}}} \Rightarrow 1\right]\right|$, *respectively. We*

HaS[T, H].KeyGen(1^λ)	HaS[T, H].Sign(I, m)	HaS[T, H].Vrfy(F, m, (r, x))
1 (F, I) ← Gen(1^λ) 2 **return** (F, I)	1 **repeat** 2 $\quad r \leftarrow_\$ \mathcal{R}$ 3 $\quad x \leftarrow \mathsf{I}(\mathsf{H}(r, m))$ 4 **until** $x \neq \perp$ 5 **return** (r, x)	1 **return** $\mathsf{F}(x) \overset{?}{=} \mathsf{H}(r, m)$

Fig. 7. Algorithms of the probabilistic hash-and-sign with retry

say T *is multi-instance non-invertible, multi-instance collision-resistant, or multi-instance preimage-simulatable if its corresponding advantage is negligible in the security parameter for any efficient adversary.*

2.5 Hash-and-Sign Paradigm

Figure 7 shows algorithms of the probabilistic hash-and-sign with retry, and HaS[T, H] is a signature scheme using a trapdoor function T and a hash function H. If HaS[T, H].Sign outputs a signature without retry, HaS[T, H] instantiates the probabilistic hash-and-sign. If r is empty, HaS[T, H] instantiates the deterministic hash-and-sign.

2.6 Quantum Random Oracle Model (QROM)

In the ROM, a hash function H: $\mathcal{R} \times \mathcal{M} \rightarrow \mathcal{Y}$ is modeled as a random function H $\leftarrow_\$ \mathcal{Y}^{\mathcal{R} \times \mathcal{M}}$. The random function is under the control of the challenger, and the adversary makes queries to the random oracle (*random oracle queries*) to compute the hash values. In the ROM, the challenger can choose $y \leftarrow_\$ \mathcal{Y}$ and program H := $\mathsf{H}^{(r,m) \mapsto y}$ for queried (r, m) on-the-fly instead of choosing H $\leftarrow_\$ \mathcal{Y}^{\mathcal{R} \times \mathcal{M}}$ at the beginning (lazy sampling technique).

In the QROM, the adversary makes queries to H in a superposition of many different values, e.g., $\sum_{(r,m)} \alpha_{r,m} |r, m\rangle |y\rangle$. The challenger computes H and gives a superposition of the results to the adversary, $\sum_{(r,m)} \alpha_{r,m} |r, m\rangle |y \oplus \mathsf{H}(r, m)\rangle$. Due to the nature of superposition queries in the QROM, traditional proof techniques like lazy sampling used in the ROM cannot be directly applied in the QROM. However, some works enable one to adaptively reprogram H in the security game [17,25,28,44]. Among the works, we use the tight adaptive reprogramming technique [25] and the measure-and-reprogram technique [17]. Also, we use the semi-classical O2H technique [1].

2.7 Proof Techniques in QROM

We introduce three techniques employed in proving the main theorem.

Tight Adaptive Reprogramming Technique [25]: Figure 8 shows a game called AR (Adaptive Reprogramming) game, in which the adversary $\mathcal{D}_{\mathsf{ar}}$ attempts to distinguish H_0 (no reprogramming) from H_1 (reprogrammed by Repro). For i-th

$$
\begin{array}{ll}
\hline
\textsc{Game: } \mathrm{AR}_b & \mathsf{Repro}(m_i) \\
\hline
\text{1 } \mathsf{H}_0 \leftarrow_\$ \mathcal{Y}^{\mathcal{R} \times \mathcal{M}} & \text{1 } (r_i, y_i) \leftarrow_\$ \mathcal{R} \times \mathcal{Y} \\
\text{2 } \mathsf{H}_1 := \mathsf{H}_0 & \text{2 } \mathsf{H}_1 := \mathsf{H}_1^{(r_i, m_i) \mapsto y_i} \\
\text{3 } b^* \leftarrow \mathcal{D}_{\mathsf{ar}}^{|\mathsf{H}_b\rangle, \mathsf{Repro}}() & \text{3 } \mathbf{return } r_i \\
\text{4 } \mathbf{return } b^* & \\
\hline
\end{array}
$$

Fig. 8. AR (Adaptive Reprogramming) game

reprogramming query, the challenger reprograms H_1 for uniformly chosen (r_i, y_i), and gives r_i to $\mathcal{D}_{\mathsf{ar}}$. A distinguishing advantage of the AR game is defined by $\mathrm{Adv}_\mathsf{H}^{\mathrm{AR}}(\mathcal{D}_{\mathsf{ar}}) = \left| \Pr\left[\mathrm{AR}_0^{\mathcal{D}_{\mathsf{ar}}} \Rightarrow 1\right] - \Pr\left[\mathrm{AR}_1^{\mathcal{D}_{\mathsf{ar}}} \Rightarrow 1\right] \right|$.

Lemma 1 (Tight Adaptive Reprogramming Technique [25, Proposition 1]). *For any quantum AR adversary $\mathcal{D}_{\mathsf{ar}}$ issuing at most q_{rep} classical reprogramming queries and q_{qro} (quantum) random oracle queries to H_b, the distinguishing advantage of the AR game is bounded by*

$$
\mathrm{Adv}_\mathsf{H}^{\mathrm{AR}}(\mathcal{D}_{\mathsf{ar}}) \leq \frac{3}{2} q_{\mathsf{rep}} \sqrt{\frac{q_{\mathsf{qro}}}{|\mathcal{R}|}}.
$$

Measure-and-Reprogram Technique [17]: Let $\mathcal{A}$ be a quantum adversary playing a search-type game making q_{qro} quantum queries to $\mathsf{H} \leftarrow_\$ \mathcal{Y}^{\mathcal{R} \times \mathcal{M}}$. A two-stage algorithm S comprises S_1 and S_2, and it operates with black-box access to $\mathcal{A}$ as follows:

1. Choose $(i, b) \leftarrow_\$ ([q_{\mathsf{qro}}] \times \{0, 1\}) \cup \{(q_{\mathsf{qro}} + 1, 0)\}$.
2. Run $\mathcal{A}$ with H until i-th query.
3. Measure i-th query and output (r, m) as the output of S_1.
4. Given a random θ, reprogram $\mathsf{H}' = \mathsf{H}^{(r,m) \mapsto \theta}$.
5. If $i = q_{\mathsf{qro}} + 1$, then go to Step 8.
6. Answer i-th query with H (if $b = 0$) or H' (if $b = 1$).
7. Run $\mathcal{A}$ with H' until the end.
8. Output $\mathcal{A}$'s output z (possibly quantum) as the output of S_2.

Then, the following lemma holds for S and $\mathcal{A}$:

Lemma 2 (Measure-and-Reprogram Technique [17, Theorem 2]). *For any quantum adversary $\mathcal{A}$ issuing at most q_{qro} (quantum) random oracle queries to $\mathsf{H} \leftarrow_\$ \mathcal{Y}^{\mathcal{R} \times \mathcal{M}}$, there exists a two-stage algorithm S given uniformly chosen θ such that for any $(\hat{r}, \hat{m}) \in \mathcal{R} \times \mathcal{M}$ and any predicate V,*

$$
\Pr\left[(r, m) = (\hat{r}, \hat{m}) \wedge \mathsf{V}(r, m, \theta, z) : (r, m) \leftarrow \mathsf{S}_1^{\mathcal{A}}(), z \leftarrow \mathsf{S}_2^{\mathcal{A}}(\theta)\right]
$$
$$
\geq \frac{1}{(2q_{\mathsf{qro}} + 1)^2} \Pr\left[(r, m) = (\hat{r}, \hat{m}) \wedge \mathsf{V}(r, m, \mathsf{H}(r, m), z) : (r, m, z) \leftarrow \mathcal{A}^{|\mathsf{H}\rangle}()\right].
$$

Semi-classical O2H Technique [1]: We define *punctured oracle* following [7].

Definition 10 (Punctured Oracle [7, Definition 1]). *Let $\mathcal{S} \subset \mathcal{R} \times \mathcal{M}$ be a set. Let $f_{\mathcal{S}} \colon \mathcal{R} \times \mathcal{M} \to \{0,1\}$ be a predicate that returns 1 if and only if $(r,m) \in \mathcal{S}$. Punctured oracle $\mathsf{H}\backslash\mathcal{S}$ (H punctured by $\mathcal{S}$) of $\mathsf{H} \in \mathcal{Y}^{\mathcal{R} \times \mathcal{M}}$ runs as follows: on input (r,m), computes whether $(r,m) \in \mathcal{S}$ in an auxilliary qubit $|f_{\mathcal{S}}(r,m)\rangle$, measures $|f_{\mathcal{S}}(r,m)\rangle$, runs $\mathsf{H}(r,m)$, and returns the result. Let FIND be an event that any of measurements of $|f_{\mathcal{S}}(r,m)\rangle$ returns 1.*

The answer from the oracle $\mathsf{H}\backslash\mathcal{S}$ depends on the measurement results. Let us consider a query $\sum_{(r,m)} \alpha_{r,m}|r,m\rangle|y\rangle$. $\mathsf{H}\backslash\mathcal{S}$ computes $\sum_{(r,m)} \alpha_{r,m}|r,m\rangle|y\rangle|f_{\mathcal{S}}(r,m)\rangle$ and measures the third register. If the result is 0, then the query is transformed to $\sum_{(r,m)\notin\mathcal{S}} \alpha_{r,m}|r,m\rangle|y\rangle|0\rangle$ and $\mathsf{H}\backslash\mathcal{S}$ returns $\sum_{(r,m)\notin\mathcal{S}} \alpha_{r,m}|r,m\rangle|y \oplus \mathsf{H}(r,m)\rangle$ to the adversary. If the results is 1 (and thus, FIND $= \top$ holds), $\mathsf{H}\backslash\mathcal{S}$ returns $\sum_{(r,m)\in\mathcal{S}} \alpha_{r,m}|r,m\rangle|y \oplus \mathsf{H}(r,m)\rangle$ to the adversary. Thus, if FIND $= \bot$, then the adversary cannot obtain any information on $\mathsf{H}(r,m)$ for $(r,m) \in \mathcal{S}$. Hence, we have the following:

Lemma 3 (Indistinguishability of Punctured Oracles [1, Lemma 1]). *Let $\mathsf{H}_0, \mathsf{H}_1 \colon \mathcal{R} \times \mathcal{M} \to \mathcal{Y}$ and $\mathcal{S} \subset \mathcal{R} \times \mathcal{M}$, and z be a bitstring. ($\mathcal{S}$, H_0, H_1, and z are taken from arbitrary joint distribution satisfying $\mathsf{H}_0(r,m) = \mathsf{H}_1(r,m)$ for any $(r,m) \notin \mathcal{S}$.) For any quantum adversary $\mathcal{A}$ and any event E,*

$$\Pr\Big[E \wedge \mathrm{FIND} = \bot : b \leftarrow \mathcal{A}^{|\mathsf{H}_0\backslash\mathcal{S}\rangle}(z)\Big] = \Pr\Big[E \wedge \mathrm{FIND} = \bot : b \leftarrow \mathcal{A}^{|\mathsf{H}_1\backslash\mathcal{S}\rangle}(z)\Big].$$

The following lemma provides a bound on the advantage gap between the original game and a game with a punctured oracle by considering the probability of FIND $= \top$.

Lemma 4 (Semi-classical O2H Technique [1, Theorem 1]). *Let $\mathsf{H} \colon \mathcal{R} \times \mathcal{M} \to \mathcal{Y}$ and $\mathcal{S} \subset \mathcal{R} \times \mathcal{M}$, and z be a bitstring. ($\mathcal{S}$, H, and z are taken from arbitrary joint distribution.) For any quantum adversary $\mathcal{A}$ issuing at most q_{qro} (quantum) random oracle queries to H,*

$$\left| \Pr\Big[1 \leftarrow \mathcal{A}^{|\mathsf{H}\rangle}(z)\Big] - \Pr\Big[1 \leftarrow \mathcal{A}^{|\mathsf{H}\backslash\mathcal{S}\rangle}(z) \wedge \mathrm{FIND} = \bot\Big] \right|$$
$$\leq \sqrt{(q_{\mathsf{qro}} + 1)\Pr\Big[\mathrm{FIND} = \top : b \leftarrow \mathcal{A}^{|\mathsf{H}\backslash\mathcal{S}\rangle}(z)\Big]}.$$

Furthermore, the following provides a bound on $\Pr\big[\mathrm{FIND} = \top : b \leftarrow \mathcal{A}^{|\mathsf{H}\backslash\mathcal{S}\rangle}(z)\big]$.

Lemma 5 (Search in Semi-classical Oracle [1, Theorem 2 and Corollary 1]). *Let $\mathcal{A}$ be a quantum adversary issuing at most q_{qro} (quantum) random oracle queries to H. Let $\mathcal{B}^{|\mathsf{H}\rangle}(z)$ be an algorithm that runs as follows: Picks $i \leftarrow_\$ [q_{\mathsf{qro}}]$, runs $\mathcal{A}^{|\mathsf{H}\rangle}(z)$ until just before i-th query, measures a query input register in the computational basis, and outputs the measurement outcome as (r,m). Then,*

$$\Pr\Big[\mathrm{FIND} = \top : b \leftarrow \mathcal{A}^{|\mathsf{H}\backslash\mathcal{S}\rangle}(z)\Big] \leq 4q_{\mathsf{qro}} \Pr\Big[(r,m) \in \mathcal{S} : (r,m) \leftarrow \mathcal{B}^{|\mathsf{H}\rangle}(z)\Big].$$

In particular, if for each $(r, m) \in \mathcal{S}$, $\Pr[(r, m) \in \mathcal{S}] \leq \epsilon$ (conditioned on z, on other oracles $\mathcal{A}$ has access to, and on other outputs of H), then

$$\Pr\left[\mathrm{FIND} = \top : b \leftarrow \mathcal{A}^{|\mathsf{H}\backslash\mathcal{S}\rangle}(z)\right] \leq 4q_{\mathsf{qro}}\epsilon.$$

Table 2. Summary of the existing and our security proofs. In "Conditions of PSF", $\checkmark$ indicates this condition of PSF (see Definition 6) is necessary, and $\checkmark^1/\checkmark^2$ indicate that **Condition 2** is relaxed as "A bound δ on average of $\delta_{\mathsf{F,I}}$ is negligible" and "$\epsilon_{\mathsf{ps}} = \mathrm{Adv}_{\mathsf{T_{wpsf}}}^{\mathsf{PS}}(\mathcal{D}_{\mathsf{ps}})$ is negligible". In "Target scheme", d/p/pr stand for the deterministic hash-and-sign, probabilistic hash-and-sign, and probabilistic hash-and-sign with retry.

Security proof	Security Bound	Assumption	Conditions of PSF				Target scheme
			1	2	3	4	
[9]	$\frac{1}{1-2^{-\omega(\log(\lambda))}}\epsilon_{\mathsf{cr}}$	CR	$\checkmark$	$\checkmark$	$\checkmark$	$\checkmark$	d/p
[47]	$2\sqrt{\left(q_{\mathsf{sign}} + \frac{8}{3}(q_{\mathsf{sign}} + q_{\mathsf{qro}} + 1)^4\right)\epsilon_{\mathsf{ow/inv}}}$	OW/INV	$\checkmark$	$\checkmark$	$\checkmark$	$-$	d/p
ext. of [45]	$4q_{\mathsf{sign}}(q_{\mathsf{qro}} + 1)(2q_{\mathsf{qro}} + 1)^2\epsilon_{\mathsf{ow/inv}}$	OW/INV	$\checkmark$	$\checkmark$	$\checkmark$	$-$	d/p
[32]	$(2(q_{\mathsf{qro}} + q_{\mathsf{sign}} + 1) + 1)^2\epsilon_{\mathsf{ow/inv}}$	OW/INV	$\checkmark$	$\checkmark$	$\checkmark$	$-$	d/p
[11]	$\frac{1}{2}\left(\epsilon_{\mathsf{nma}} + \frac{8\pi}{\sqrt{3}}q_{\mathsf{qro}}^{\frac{3}{2}}\sqrt{\delta} + q_{\mathsf{sign}}\left(\delta + \frac{q_{\mathsf{sign}}}{|\mathcal{R}|}\right)\right)$	EUF-NMA	$-$	$\checkmark^1$	$\checkmark$	$-$	p
ours	$(2q_{\mathsf{qro}} + 1)^2\epsilon_{\mathsf{inv}} + \epsilon_{\mathsf{ps}} + \frac{3}{2}q_{\mathsf{sign}}'\sqrt{\frac{q_{\mathsf{sign}}' + q_{\mathsf{qro}} + 1}{|\mathcal{R}|}}$ $+ 2(q_{\mathsf{qro}} + 2)\sqrt{\frac{q_{\mathsf{sign}}' - q_{\mathsf{sign}}}{|\mathcal{R}|}}$	INV	$-$	$\checkmark^2$	$-$	$-$	p/pr
ours	$\epsilon_{\mathsf{nma}} + \epsilon_{\mathsf{ps}} + \frac{3}{2}q_{\mathsf{sign}}'\sqrt{\frac{q_{\mathsf{sign}}' + q_{\mathsf{qro}} + 1}{|\mathcal{R}|}}$ $+ 2(q_{\mathsf{qro}} + 2)\sqrt{\frac{q_{\mathsf{sign}}' - q_{\mathsf{sign}}}{|\mathcal{R}|}}$	EUF-NMA	$-$	$\checkmark^2$	$-$	$-$	p/pr
ours	$(2q_{\mathsf{qro}} + 1)^2\epsilon_{\mathsf{ow/inv}} + \frac{3}{2}q_{\mathsf{sign}}\sqrt{\frac{q_{\mathsf{sign}} + q_{\mathsf{qro}} + 1}{|\mathcal{R}|}}$	OW/INV	$\checkmark$	$\checkmark$	$\checkmark$	$-$	p

3   Existing Security Proofs

We review the existing security proofs, including our own, and summarize them in Table 2.

Security Proof in the ROM [5,23,42]: Let $\mathsf{T_{psf}}$ be a PSF. A reduction of INV $\Rightarrow$ EUF-CMA of $\mathsf{HaS}[\mathsf{T_{psf}}, \mathsf{H}]$ in the ROM is given by the lazy sampling and programming. The INV adversary $\mathcal{B}_{\mathsf{inv}}$, given a challenge (F, y), simulates the EUF-CMA game played by an adversary $\mathcal{A}_{\mathsf{cma}}$ as follows: For a random oracle query (r, m), $\mathcal{B}_{\mathsf{inv}}$ returns $\mathsf{F}(x)$ for $x \leftarrow \mathsf{SampDom}(\mathsf{F})$ and stores (r, m, x) in a database $\mathcal{D}$. If $(r, m, x) \in \mathcal{D}$ with some x, then $\mathcal{B}_{\mathsf{inv}}$ gives $\mathsf{F}(x)$ to $\mathcal{A}_{\mathsf{cma}}$. For a signing query m, $\mathcal{B}_{\mathsf{inv}}$ chooses (r, x) by $r \leftarrow_\$ \mathcal{R}$ and $x \leftarrow \mathsf{SampDom}(\mathsf{F})$. If $(r, m, *) \notin \mathcal{D}$, $\mathcal{B}_{\mathsf{inv}}$ returns (r, x) and stores (r, m, x) in $\mathcal{D}$; otherwise $\mathcal{B}_{\mathsf{inv}}$ returns stored (r, x). From **Condition 1** of PSF ($\mathsf{F}(x)$ is uniform), $\mathcal{B}_{\mathsf{inv}}$ can use $\mathsf{F}(x)$ as an output of the random function. Also from **Conditions 2** and **3**, $\mathcal{B}_{\mathsf{inv}}$ can simulate an honestly generated signature $x_i \leftarrow \mathsf{I}(\mathsf{H}(r_i, m_i))$ by $x_i \leftarrow \mathsf{SampDom}(\mathsf{F})$.

To win the INV game, $\mathcal{B}_{\text{inv}}$ gives his query y to $\mathcal{A}_{\text{cma}}$ in one of $(q_{\text{sign}} + q_{\text{ro}} + 1)$ queries to H. If $\mathcal{A}_{\text{cma}}$ outputs a valid signature (m^*, r^*, x^*) and $\mathsf{H}(r^*, m^*) = y$ holds, $\mathcal{B}_{\text{inv}}$ can win the INV game by outputting x^*. Since $\mathsf{H}(r^*, m^*) = y$ holds with $\frac{1}{q_{\text{sign}} + q_{\text{ro}} + 1}$, we have $\text{Adv}_{\mathsf{HaS}[\mathsf{T}_{\text{psf}}, \mathsf{H}]}^{\text{EUF-CMA}}(\mathcal{A}_{\text{cma}^c}) \leq (q_{\text{sign}} + q_{\text{ro}} + 1)\text{Adv}_{\mathsf{T}_{\text{psf}}}^{\text{INV}}(\mathcal{B}_{\text{inv}})$, where $\mathcal{A}_{\text{cma}^c}$ is an adversary who makes only classical queries[6].

Sakumoto et al. [42] extended the above proof to the probabilistic hash-and-sign with retry assuming non-PSF trapdoor functions. For a random oracle query (r, m), $\mathcal{B}_{\text{inv}}$ returns $y \leftarrow_\$ \mathcal{Y}$ and saves (r, m, y) in the database $\mathcal{D}'$. For a signing query m_i, $\mathcal{B}_{\text{inv}}$ takes $r_i \leftarrow_\$ \mathcal{R}$ and $x_i \leftarrow \mathsf{SampDom}(\mathsf{F})$. If $(r_i, *, *) \in \mathcal{D}'$, $\mathcal{B}_{\text{inv}}$ aborts the game; otherwise, $\mathcal{B}_{\text{inv}}$ stores $(r_i, m_i, \mathsf{F}(x_i))$ in $\mathcal{D}'$ and outputs (r_i, x_i). There is an issue in the programming $\mathsf{F}(x)$ instead of $y \leftarrow_\$ \mathcal{Y}$. Since we do not assume **Condition 1** of PSF, $\mathsf{F}(x)$ is not necessarily uniform. Therefore, the output of H becomes biased, and their security proof is flawed.

Security Proof by Semi-constant Distribution [47]: Zhandry showed the reduction from the OW assumption of trapdoor permutation in the QROM using a technique called *semi-constant distribution*, which leads to a reduction from the INV assumption of PSF. $\mathcal{B}_{\text{inv}}$ simulates the EUF-CMA game by generating signatures without the trapdoor as the above security proof in the ROM. Instead of adaptively programming H, $\mathcal{B}_{\text{inv}}$ replaces H as $\mathsf{H}' = \mathsf{F}(\mathsf{DetSampDom}(\mathsf{F}, \widetilde{\mathsf{H}}(r, m)))$, where $\mathsf{DetSampDom}$ is a deterministic function of $\mathsf{SampDom}$ and $\widetilde{\mathsf{H}} \leftarrow_\$ \mathcal{W}^{\mathcal{R} \times \mathcal{M}}$ is a random function to output randomness for $\mathsf{DetSampDom}$ [9]. From **Condition 1**, H' is indistinguishable from H.

The INV adversary $\mathcal{B}_{\text{inv}}$ programs H' that outputs y with probability ϵ (semi-constant distribution). In the signing oracle, if $\mathsf{H}'(r_i, m_i)$ outputs y, $\mathcal{B}_{\text{inv}}$ aborts this game. A bound on the statistical distance between the random function and the programmed one with the semi-constant distribution is $\frac{8}{3}(q_{\text{sign}} + q_{\text{qro}} + 1)^4 \epsilon^2$ [47, Corollary 4.3]. When $\mathcal{A}_{\text{cma}}$ wins the EUF-CMA game, $\mathcal{B}_{\text{inv}}$ can win the INV game with probability $(1 - \epsilon)^{q_{\text{sign}}} \epsilon \approx \epsilon - q_{\text{sign}} \epsilon^2$. Minimizing the bound $\frac{1}{\epsilon}\text{Adv}_{\mathsf{T}_{\text{psf}}}^{\text{INV}} + \left(q_{\text{sign}} + \frac{8}{3}(q_{\text{sign}} + q_{\text{qro}} + 1)^4\right)\epsilon$ gives [47, Theorem 5.3]

$$\text{Adv}_{\mathsf{HaS}[\mathsf{T}_{\text{psf}}, \mathsf{H}]}^{\text{EUF-CMA}}(\mathcal{A}_{\text{cma}}) \leq 2\sqrt{\left(q_{\text{sign}} + \frac{8}{3}(q_{\text{sign}} + q_{\text{qro}} + 1)^4\right)\text{Adv}_{\mathsf{T}_{\text{psf}}}^{\text{INV}}(\mathcal{B}_{\text{inv}})}.$$

Application of Lifting Theorem [45]: Yamakawa and Zhandry gave the lifting theorem for search-type games. As an application of the lifting theorem, they showed $\text{Adv}_{\mathsf{Sig}}^{\text{EUF-NMA}}(\mathcal{A}_{\text{nma}}) \leq (2q_{\text{qro}} + 1)^2 \text{Adv}_{\mathsf{Sig}}^{\text{EUF-NMA}}(\mathcal{A}_{\text{nma}^c})$, where $\mathcal{A}_{\text{nma}^c}$ is an EUF-NMA adversary making classical queries to H [45, Corollary 4.10]. For a hash-and-sign signature $\mathsf{HaS}[\mathsf{T}_{\text{psf}}, \mathsf{H}]$, they showed $\text{Adv}_{\mathsf{HaS}[\mathsf{T}_{\text{psf}}, \mathsf{H}]}^{\text{EUF-CMA}}(\mathcal{A}_{\text{cma}}) \leq 4q_{\text{sign}}\text{Adv}_{\mathsf{HaS}[\mathsf{T}_{\text{psf}}, \mathsf{H}]}^{\text{EUF-NMA}}(\mathcal{A}_{\text{nma}})$ [45, Theorem 4.11]. Extending the results of [45] using

---

[6] $\text{Adv}_{\mathsf{T}_{\text{psf}}}^{\text{INV}}(\mathcal{B}_{\text{inv}}) = \text{Adv}_{\mathsf{T}_{\text{psf}}}^{\text{OW}}(\mathcal{B}_{\text{ow}})$ holds ($\mathcal{D}_{\mathcal{X}}$ is defined as $\mathsf{SampDom}(\mathsf{F})$ in the OW game (see Fig. 3)) since the OW adversary can simulate the INV game by giving a uniform $y = \mathsf{F}(x)$ to the INV adversary, and vice versa.

the security proof in the ROM, we have a bound:

$$\mathrm{Adv}^{\text{EUF-CMA}}_{\text{HaS}[\mathsf{T}_{\text{psf}},\mathsf{H}]}(\mathcal{A}_{\text{cma}}) \leq 4q_{\text{sign}}(q_{\text{qro}}+1)(2q_{\text{qro}}+1)^2\mathrm{Adv}^{\text{INV}}_{\mathsf{T}_{\text{psf}}}(\mathcal{B}_{\text{inv}}).$$

Reduction from EUF-NMA *for WPSF* [11]: The security proofs mentioned above hold only if the underlying trapdoor function is PSF. To relax the conditions on trapdoor functions, Chailloux and Debris-Alazard gave EUF-NMA $\Rightarrow$ EUF-CMA for the probabilistic hash-and-sign[7]. The authors assumed a WPSF with **Condition 3** and a weaker version of **Condition 2**, that is, there is a bound δ on the average of statistical distance $\delta_{\mathsf{F},\mathsf{I}} = \Delta(\mathsf{SampDom}(\mathsf{F}),\mathsf{I}(\mathsf{U}(\mathcal{Y})))$ over all $(\mathsf{F},\mathsf{I}) \leftarrow \mathsf{Gen}(1^\lambda)$. Let T_{wpsf} be a WPSF. The EUF-NMA adversary $\mathcal{A}_{\text{nma}}$ replaces the random function H by H', which outputs $\mathsf{H}(r,m)$ with probability $\frac{1}{2}$ and $\mathsf{F}(\mathsf{DetSampDom}(\mathsf{F},w))$ with probability $\frac{1}{2}$. A bound on the advantage of distinguishing H from H' is $\frac{8\pi}{\sqrt{3}}q_{\text{qro}}^{3/2}\sqrt{\delta}$. The authors gave [11, Theorem 2]

$$\mathrm{Adv}^{\text{EUF-CMA}}_{\text{HaS}[\mathsf{T}_{\text{wpsf}},\mathsf{H}]}(\mathcal{A}_{\text{cma}}) \leq \frac{1}{2}\left(\mathrm{Adv}^{\text{EUF-NMA}}_{\text{HaS}[\mathsf{T}_{\text{wpsf}},\mathsf{H}]}(\mathcal{A}_{\text{nma}}) + \frac{8\pi}{\sqrt{3}}q_{\text{qro}}^{\frac{3}{2}}\sqrt{\delta} + q_{\text{sign}}\left(\delta + \frac{q_{\text{sign}}}{|\mathcal{R}|}\right)\right). \tag{1}$$

Reduction from Collision-Resistance [9]: Boneh et al. [9] gave a reduction from the CR of a PSF T_{psf} to the sEUF-CMA security of $\mathsf{HaS}[\mathsf{T}_{\text{psf}},\mathsf{H}]$. The CR adversary $\mathcal{B}_{\text{cr}}$ given F simulates the sEUF-CMA game for $\mathcal{A}_{\text{cma}}$. For a random function $\tilde{\mathsf{H}} \leftarrow_\$ \mathcal{W}^{\mathcal{R}\times\mathcal{M}}$, $\mathcal{B}_{\text{cr}}$ replaces H as $\mathsf{H}'(r,m) = \mathsf{F}(\mathsf{DetSampDom}(\mathsf{F},\tilde{\mathsf{H}}(r,m)))$, where H and H' are indistinguishable from **Condition 1**. Also, $\mathcal{B}_{\text{cr}}$ simulates the signing oracle using **Conditions 2** and **3**. If $\mathcal{A}_{\text{cma}}$ wins, then $\mathsf{F}(x^*) = \mathsf{H}'(r^*,m^*) = \mathsf{F}(x')$ holds for $x' = \mathsf{DetSampDom}(\mathsf{F},\tilde{\mathsf{H}}(r^*,m^*))$. When $x^* \neq x'$, $\mathcal{B}_{\text{cr}}$ can obtain a collision pair (x^*,x'). Since $x^* \neq x'$ holds with probability $1 - 2^{-\omega(\log(\lambda))}$ (see **Condition 4**),

$$\mathrm{Adv}^{\text{sEUF-CMA}}_{\text{HaS}[\mathsf{T}_{\text{psf}},\mathsf{H}]}(\mathcal{A}_{\text{cma}}) \leq \frac{1}{1-2^{-\omega(\log(\lambda))}}\mathrm{Adv}^{\text{CR}}_{\mathsf{T}_{\text{psf}}}(\mathcal{B}_{\text{cr}}). \tag{2}$$

Concurrent Work [32]: Liu, Jiang, and Zhao [32] showed OW $\Rightarrow$ EUF-CMA for the deterministic/probabilistic hash-and-sign based on trapdoor permutations in the QROM. Their reduction can be extended to INV $\Rightarrow$ EUF-CMA for the deterministic/probabilistic hash-and-sign based on PSFs. As in [9,12,47], the random function H is replaced as $\mathsf{H}' = \mathsf{F}(\mathsf{DetSampDom}(\mathsf{F},\tilde{\mathsf{H}}(m)))$ to answer the signing queries without using the trapdoor. From **Condition 1**, this modification does not incur any security loss. Then, their reduction uses the measure-and-reprogram technique [17, Theorem 2] (see Lemma 2 in Sect. 2.7) as in our security proof. Their reduction has a security bound that includes q_{sign} in the

---

[7] The authors of [11] defined a problem called *claw with random function problem*; however, its definition is identical to EUF-NMA game for hash-and-sign.

multiplicative loss:[8]

$$\mathrm{Adv}_{\mathsf{HaS}[\mathsf{T}_{\mathsf{psf}},\mathsf{H}]}^{\mathrm{EUF\text{-}CMA}}(\mathcal{A}_{\mathsf{cma}}) \leq (2(q_{\mathsf{qro}} + q_{\mathsf{sign}} + 1) + 1)^2 \mathrm{Adv}_{\mathsf{T}_{\mathsf{psf}}}^{\mathrm{INV}}(\mathcal{A}_{\mathsf{inv}}). \qquad (3)$$

4 New Security Proof

The main theorem is as follows:

Theorem 1 (INV $\Rightarrow$ EUF-CMA (Main Theorem)). *For any quantum EUF-CMA adversary $\mathcal{A}_{\mathsf{cma}}$ of $\mathsf{HaS}[\mathsf{T}_{\mathsf{wpsf}},\mathsf{H}]$ issuing at most q_{sign} classical queries to the signing oracle and q_{qro} (quantum) random oracle queries to $\mathsf{H} \leftarrow_{\$} \mathcal{Y}^{\mathcal{R} \times \mathcal{M}}$, there exist an INV adversary $\mathcal{B}_{\mathsf{inv}}$ of $\mathsf{T}_{\mathsf{wpsf}}$ and a PS adversary $\mathcal{D}_{\mathsf{ps}}$ of $\mathsf{T}_{\mathsf{wpsf}}$ issuing q_{sign} sampling queries such that*

$$\mathrm{Adv}_{\mathsf{HaS}[\mathsf{T}_{\mathsf{wpsf}},\mathsf{H}]}^{\mathrm{EUF\text{-}CMA}}(\mathcal{A}_{\mathsf{cma}}) \leq (2q_{\mathsf{qro}} + 1)^2 \mathrm{Adv}_{\mathsf{T}_{\mathsf{wpsf}}}^{\mathrm{INV}}(\mathcal{B}_{\mathsf{inv}}) + \mathrm{Adv}_{\mathsf{T}_{\mathsf{wpsf}}}^{\mathrm{PS}}(\mathcal{D}_{\mathsf{ps}})$$

$$+ \frac{3}{2}q'_{\mathsf{sign}}\sqrt{\frac{q'_{\mathsf{sign}} + q_{\mathsf{qro}} + 1}{|\mathcal{R}|}} + 2(q_{\mathsf{qro}} + 2)\sqrt{\frac{q'_{\mathsf{sign}} - q_{\mathsf{sign}}}{|\mathcal{R}|}}, \qquad (4)$$

where q'_{sign} is a bound on the total number of queries to H in all the signing queries, and the running times of $\mathcal{B}_{\mathsf{inv}}$ and $\mathcal{D}_{\mathsf{ps}}$ are about that of $\mathcal{A}_{\mathsf{cma}}$.

If $\mathcal{A}_{\mathsf{cma}}$ makes only classical random oracle queries q_{ro} times, then

$$\mathrm{Adv}_{\mathsf{HaS}[\mathsf{T}_{\mathsf{wpsf}},\mathsf{H}]}^{\mathrm{EUF\text{-}CMA}}(\mathcal{A}_{\mathsf{cma}}) \leq (q_{\mathsf{ro}} + 1)\mathrm{Adv}_{\mathsf{T}_{\mathsf{wpsf}}}^{\mathrm{INV}}(\mathcal{B}_{\mathsf{inv}}) + \mathrm{Adv}_{\mathsf{T}_{\mathsf{wpsf}}}^{\mathrm{PS}}(\mathcal{D}_{\mathsf{ps}})$$

$$+ q'_{\mathsf{sign}}\frac{q'_{\mathsf{sign}} + q_{\mathsf{ro}} + 1}{|\mathcal{R}|} + (q_{\mathsf{ro}} + 1)\frac{q'_{\mathsf{sign}} - q_{\mathsf{sign}}}{|\mathcal{R}|}.$$

Proof. In the beginning, we show that we can set q'_{sign} as $q'_{\mathsf{sign}} = \frac{c}{\rho}q_{\mathsf{sign}}$ for some constant $c > 1$, where $\rho = \Pr[x \neq \perp : y \leftarrow_{\$} \mathcal{Y}, x \leftarrow \mathsf{I}(y)]$. In q'_{sign} trials, at least q_{sign} signatures are generated if the number of successful trials (where $\mathsf{I}(\mathsf{H}(r,m))$ outputs a preimage) is q_{sign} or more. Let S be a random variable for the number of successful trials. $\mathbb{E}(S) = \rho q'_{\mathsf{sign}} = cq_{\mathsf{sign}}$ holds. From the Chernoff bound, we have $\Pr[S \leq (1 - \gamma)\mathbb{E}(S)] \leq e^{-\frac{1}{2}\gamma^2 \mathbb{E}(S)}$. Substituting $\gamma = \frac{\mathbb{E}(S) - q_{\mathsf{sign}} + 1}{\mathbb{E}(S)}$, the LHS becomes $\Pr[S \leq q_{\mathsf{sign}} - 1]$ that is a probability that we cannot generate q_{sign} signatures with q'_{sign} trials. Since we set $q'_{\mathsf{sign}} = \frac{c}{\rho}q_{\mathsf{sign}}$, the exponent of the RHS becomes $-\frac{((c-1)q_{\mathsf{sign}} + 1)^2}{2cq_{\mathsf{sign}}} \geq -\frac{c-1}{2c}q_{\mathsf{sign}}$ and the bound on $\Pr[S \leq q_{\mathsf{sign}} - 1]$ becomes negligible for $q_{\mathsf{sign}} = \omega(\log(\lambda))$.

In the upcoming proof, we will explain the proofs in parallel for both the ROM and QROM. For the figures, we will use notations assuming the QROM. EUF-NMA $\Rightarrow$ EUF-CMA: Figures 9 and 10 show the games and simulations described below. Without loss of generality, we assume that $\mathcal{A}_{\mathsf{cma}}$ makes a query (r^*, m^*) (the final ouput) to H. Then, the total number of queries to H is $q_{\mathsf{ro}} + 1$ (classical) or $q_{\mathsf{qro}} + 1$ (quantum).

---

[8] In the latest version of [32], a term q_{sign} has been removed from Eq. (3); however, we have identified a flaw in the proof (see the full version.).

GAME: G_0-G_1	$\text{Sign}^H(m_i)$ for G_0	$\text{Sign}^H(m_i)$ for G_1
1 $Q := \emptyset$	1 **repeat**	1 **repeat**
2 $H \leftarrow_\$ \mathcal{Y}^{\mathcal{R} \times \mathcal{M}}$	2 $r_i \leftarrow_\$ \mathcal{R}$	2 $r_i \leftarrow_\$ \mathcal{R}$
3 $(F, I) \leftarrow \text{Gen}(1^\lambda)$	3 $x_i \leftarrow I(H(r_i, m_i))$	3 $y_i \leftarrow_\$ \mathcal{Y}$
4 $(m^*, r^*, x^*) \leftarrow \mathcal{A}_{\text{cma}}^{\text{Sign}, |H\rangle}(F)$	4 **until** $x_i \neq \bot$	4 $x_i \leftarrow I(y_i)$
5 **if** $m^* \in Q$ **then**	5 $Q := Q \cup \{m_i\}$	5 $H := H^{(r_i, m_i) \mapsto y_i}$
6 **return** 0	6 **return** (r_i, x_i)	6 **until** $x_i \neq \bot$
		7 $Q := Q \cup \{m_i\}$
7 **return** $F(x^*) \stackrel{?}{=} H(r^*, m^*)$		8 **return** (r_i, x_i)

GAME: G_2	$\text{Sign}^H(m_i)$ for G_2
1 $Q := \emptyset$	1 **repeat**
2 $H \leftarrow_\$ \mathcal{Y}^{\mathcal{R} \times \mathcal{M}}$	2 $y_i \leftarrow_\$ \mathcal{Y}$
3 $ctr := 0$	3 $x_i \leftarrow I(y_i)$
4 $\mathcal{S} := \emptyset$	4 **if** $x_i = \bot$ **then**
5 **for** $j \in [q'_{\text{sign}} - q_{\text{sign}}]$ **do**	5 $ctr := ctr + 1$
6 $r \leftarrow_\$ \mathcal{R}$	6 $r_i := \mathcal{S}[ctr]$
7 $\mathcal{S} := \mathcal{S} \cup \{r\}$	7 **else**
8 $(F, I) \leftarrow \text{Gen}(1^\lambda)$	8 $r_i \leftarrow_\$ \mathcal{R}$
9 $(m^*, r^*, x^*) \leftarrow \mathcal{A}_{\text{cma}}^{\text{Sign}, |H\rangle}(F)$	9 $H := H^{(r_i, m_i) \mapsto y_i}$
10 **if** $m^* \in Q$ **then**	10 **until** $x_i \neq \bot$
11 **return** 0	11 $Q := Q \cup \{m_i\}$
	12 **return** (r_i, x_i)
12 **return** $F(x^*) \stackrel{?}{=} H(r^*, m^*)$	

GAME: G_3-G_5	$\text{Sign}^H(m_i)$ for G_3	$\text{Sign}^H(m_i)$ for G_4
1 $Q := \emptyset$	1 **repeat**	1 **repeat**
2 $H \leftarrow_\$ \mathcal{Y}^{\mathcal{R} \times \mathcal{M}}$	2 $y_i \leftarrow_\$ \mathcal{Y}$	2 $y_i \leftarrow_\$ \mathcal{Y}$
3 $\text{FIND} := \bot$	3 $x_i \leftarrow I(y_i)$	3 $x_i \leftarrow I(y_i)$
4 $ctr := 0$	4 **if** $x_i = \bot$ **then**	4 **until** $x_i \neq \bot$
5 $\mathcal{S} := \emptyset$	5 $ctr := ctr + 1$	5 $r_i \leftarrow_\$ \mathcal{R}$
6 **for** $j \in [q'_{\text{sign}} - q_{\text{sign}}]$ **do**	6 $r_i := \mathcal{S}[ctr]$	6 $H := H^{(r_i, m_i) \mapsto y_i}$
7 $r \leftarrow_\$ \mathcal{R}$	7 **else**	7 $Q := Q \cup \{m_i\}$
8 $\mathcal{S} := \mathcal{S} \cup \{r\}$	8 $r_i \leftarrow_\$ \mathcal{R}$	8 **return** (r_i, x_i)
9 $\mathcal{S}' := \{(r, m) : r \in \mathcal{S}, m \in \mathcal{M}\}$	9 $H := H^{(r_i, m_i) \mapsto y_i}$	
10 $(F, I) \leftarrow \text{Gen}(1^\lambda)$	10 **until** $x_i \neq \bot$	$\text{Sign}^H(m_i)$ for G_5
11 $(m^*, r^*, x^*) \leftarrow \mathcal{A}_{\text{cma}}^{\text{Sign}, |H \backslash \mathcal{S}'\rangle}(F)$	11 $Q := Q \cup \{m_i\}$	1 $x_i \leftarrow \text{SampDom}(F)$
12 **if** $m^* \in Q \vee \text{FIND} = \top$ **then**	12 **return** (r_i, x_i)	2 $r_i \leftarrow \mathcal{R}$
13 **return** 0		3 $H := H^{(r_i, m_i) \mapsto F(x_i)}$
		4 $Q := Q \cup \{m_i\}$
14 **return** $F(x^*) \stackrel{?}{=} H(r^*, m^*)$		5 **return** (r_i, x_i)

Fig. 9. Games for EUF-NMA $\Rightarrow$ EUF-CMA. The modifications from the previous game are highlighted in red text. (Color figure online)

GAME G_0 (EUF-CMA game): This is the original EUF-CMA game and $\Pr[G_0^{\mathcal{A}_{\text{cma}}} \Rightarrow 1] = \text{Adv}_{\text{HaS}[T_{\text{wpsf}}, H]}^{\text{EUF-CMA}}(\mathcal{A}_{\text{cma}})$ holds.

GAME G_1 (adaptive reprogramming of H): The signing oracle Sign^H uniformly chooses y_i and reprograms $H := H^{(r_i, m_i) \mapsto y_i}$ until $I(y_i)$ does not output $\bot$ (see Lines 3 to 5 in Sign^H for G_1). Considering the number of retries, H is reprogrammed for at most q'_{sign} times.

ROM: When the signing oracle has not chosen the same r_i in Line 2 of Sign^H more than twice, and the chosen r_i has not been queried to H in advance, there is no difference in the advantages between G_0 and G_1. There-

$\mathcal{D}_{\mathsf{ar}}^{\lvert H_b\rangle}()$ simulates G_0/G_1	$\mathsf{Sign}^{H_b,\mathsf{Repro}}(m_i)$
1 $\mathcal{Q} := \emptyset$	1 **repeat**
2 $(\mathsf{F},\mathsf{I}) \leftarrow \mathsf{Gen}(1^\lambda)$	2 $r_i \leftarrow \mathsf{Repro}(m_i)$
3 $(m^*,r^*,x^*) \leftarrow \mathcal{A}_{\mathsf{cma}}^{\mathsf{Sign},\lvert H_b\rangle}(\mathsf{F})$	3 $x_i \leftarrow \mathsf{I}(H_b(r_i,m_i))$
4 **if** $m^* \in \mathcal{Q}$ **then**	4 **until** $x_i \neq \perp$
5 **return** 0	5 $\mathcal{Q} := \mathcal{Q} \cup \{m_i\}$
	6 **return** (r_i,x_i)
6 **return** $\mathsf{F}(x^*) \stackrel{?}{=} H_b(r^*,m^*)$	

$\mathcal{D}_{\mathsf{ps}}^{\mathsf{Sample}_b}(\mathsf{F})$ simulates G_4/G_5	$\mathsf{Sign}^{H,\mathsf{Sample}_b}(m_i)$
1 $\mathcal{Q} := \emptyset$	1 $x_i \leftarrow \mathsf{Sample}_b()$
2 $H \leftarrow_\$ \mathcal{Y}^{\mathcal{R} \times \mathcal{M}}$	2 $r_i \leftarrow_\$ \mathcal{R}$
3 $\mathrm{FIND} := \perp$	3 $H := H^{(r_i,m_i) \mapsto \mathsf{F}(x_i)}$
4 $\mathcal{S} := \emptyset$	4 $\mathcal{Q} := \mathcal{Q} \cup \{m_i\}$
5 **for** $j \in [q'_{\mathsf{sign}} - q_{\mathsf{sign}}]$ **do**	5 **return** (r_i,x_i)
6 $r \leftarrow_\$ \mathcal{R}$	
7 $\mathcal{S} := \mathcal{S} \cup \{r\}$	
8 $\mathcal{S}' := \{(r,m) : r \in \mathcal{S}, m \in \mathcal{M}\}$	
9 $(m^*,r^*,x^*) \leftarrow \mathcal{A}_{\mathsf{cma}}^{\mathsf{Sign},\lvert H \setminus \mathcal{S}'\rangle}(\mathsf{F})$	
10 **if** $m^* \in \mathcal{Q} \vee \mathrm{FIND} = \top$ **then**	
11 **return** 0	
12 **return** $\mathsf{F}(x^*) \stackrel{?}{=} H(r^*,m^*)$	

$\mathcal{A}_{\mathsf{nma}}^{\lvert H\rangle}(\mathsf{F})$ simulates G_5	$\mathsf{Sign}^{H'}(m_i)$
1 $\mathcal{Q} := \emptyset$	1 $x_i \leftarrow \mathsf{SampDom}(\mathsf{F})$
2 $H' := H$	2 $r_i \leftarrow_\$ \mathcal{R}$
3 $\mathrm{FIND} := \perp$	3 $H' := H'^{(r_i,m_i) \mapsto \mathsf{F}(x_i)}$
4 $\mathcal{S} := \emptyset$	4 $\mathcal{Q} := \mathcal{Q} \cup \{m_i\}$
5 **for** $j \in [q'_{\mathsf{sign}} - q_{\mathsf{sign}}]$ **do**	5 **return** (r_i,x_i)
6 $r \leftarrow_\$ \mathcal{R}$	
7 $\mathcal{S} := \mathcal{S} \cup \{r\}$	
8 $\mathcal{S}' := \{(r,m) : r \in \mathcal{S}, m \in \mathcal{M}\}$	
9 $(m^*,r^*,x^*) \leftarrow \mathcal{A}_{\mathsf{cma}}^{\mathsf{Sign},\lvert H' \setminus \mathcal{S}'\rangle}(\mathsf{F})$	
10 **if** $m^* \in \mathcal{Q} \vee \mathrm{FIND} = \top$ **then**	
11 **return** 0	
12 **return** $\mathsf{F}(x^*) \stackrel{?}{=} H'(r^*,m^*)$	

Fig. 10. Simulations for EUF-NMA $\Rightarrow$ EUF-CMA

fore, $\left| \Pr\big[G_0^{\mathcal{A}_{\mathsf{cma}}} \Rightarrow 1\big] - \Pr\big[G_1^{\mathcal{A}_{\mathsf{cma}}} \Rightarrow 1\big] \right| \leq q'_{\mathsf{sign}} \frac{q'_{\mathsf{sign}}+q_{\mathsf{ro}}+1}{|\mathcal{R}|}$ holds.

QROM: The AR adversary $\mathcal{D}_{\mathsf{ar}}$ can simulate G_0/G_1 (the top row of Fig. 10). If $\mathcal{D}_{\mathsf{ar}}$ plays AR_0, $\mathcal{D}_{\mathsf{ar}}$ simulates G_0; otherwise it simulates G_1. From Lemma 1, we have $\left| \Pr\big[G_0^{\mathcal{A}_{\mathsf{cma}}} \Rightarrow 1\big] - \Pr\big[G_1^{\mathcal{A}_{\mathsf{cma}}} \Rightarrow 1\big] \right| \leq \mathrm{Adv}_H^{\mathrm{AR}}(\mathcal{D}_{\mathsf{ar}}) \leq \frac{3}{2}q'_{\mathsf{sign}}\sqrt{\frac{q'_{\mathsf{sign}}+q_{\mathsf{qro}}+1}{|\mathcal{R}|}}$.

GAME G_2 (pre-choosing r for unsuccessful trials): In the beginning, the challenger chooses $r \leftarrow_\$ \mathcal{R}$ for $q'_{\mathsf{sign}} - q_{\mathsf{sign}}$ times and keeps them in a sequence $\mathcal{S}$ (elements of $\mathcal{S}$ are ordered and may be duplicated.). In the signing oracle, $r_i = \mathcal{S}[ctr]$ is used for reprogramming if $\mathsf{I}(y_i)$ outputs $\perp$ for $y_i \leftarrow_\$ \mathcal{Y}$ (see Lines 6 and 9 of Sign^H for G_2), where $\mathcal{S}[j]$ is j-th element of $\mathcal{S}$ and ctr is a counter that increments just before using $\mathcal{S}[ctr]$.

ROM and QROM: In G_1, the challenger can choose r_i in the beginning since

r_i is chosen independently of m_i queried by $\mathcal{A}_{\text{cma}}$. Also, r_i is always uniformly chosen whatever $\mathsf{I}(y_i)$ outputs. Therefore, the challenger can use r_i chosen in the beginning only when $\mathsf{I}(y)$ outputs $\perp$. Hence, $\Pr\left[\mathsf{G}_1^{\mathcal{A}_{\text{cma}}} \Rightarrow 1\right] = \Pr\left[\mathsf{G}_2^{\mathcal{A}_{\text{cma}}} \Rightarrow 1\right]$ holds.

GAME G_3 (puncturing H): Let $\mathcal{S}' = \{(r,m) : r \in \mathcal{S}, m \in \mathcal{M}\}$ be a set induced by $\mathcal{S}$. Instead of H, $\mathcal{A}_{\text{cma}}$ makes queries to $\mathsf{H}\backslash\mathcal{S}'$ (H punctured by $\mathcal{S}'$). Also, G_3 outputs 0 if FIND $= \top$ (see the definitions of $\mathsf{H}\backslash\mathcal{S}'$ and FIND in Definition 10).

ROM: Since $\mathsf{H}\backslash\mathcal{S}'$ is purely classical, FIND becomes $\top$ with at most $(q_{\text{ro}}+1)\frac{q'_{\text{sign}} - q_{\text{sign}}}{|\mathcal{R}|}$; therefore, $\left|\Pr\left[\mathsf{G}_2^{\mathcal{A}_{\text{cma}}} \Rightarrow 1\right] - \Pr\left[\mathsf{G}_3^{\mathcal{A}_{\text{cma}}} \Rightarrow 1\right]\right| \le (q_{\text{ro}}+1)\frac{q'_{\text{sign}} - q_{\text{sign}}}{|\mathcal{R}|}$ holds.

QROM: We use Lemma 4 to bound $\left|\Pr\left[\mathsf{G}_2^{\mathcal{A}_{\text{cma}}} \Rightarrow 1\right] - \Pr\left[\mathsf{G}_3^{\mathcal{A}_{\text{cma}}} \Rightarrow 1\right]\right|$. Suppose that $\Pr\left[\mathsf{G}_2^{\mathcal{A}_{\text{cma}}} \Rightarrow 1\right] = \Pr\left[1 \leftarrow \mathcal{A}_{\text{cma}}^{\mathsf{Sign},|\mathsf{H}\rangle}(\mathsf{F})\right]$. Since G_3 uses $\mathsf{H}\backslash\mathcal{S}'$ and outputs 0 if FIND $= \top$, we have $\Pr\left[\mathsf{G}_3^{\mathcal{A}_{\text{cma}}} \Rightarrow 1\right] = \Pr\left[1 \leftarrow \mathcal{A}_{\text{cma}}^{\mathsf{Sign},|\mathsf{H}\backslash\mathcal{S}'\rangle}(\mathsf{F}) \wedge \text{FIND} = \perp\right]$ and $\Pr\left[\text{FIND} = \top : \mathsf{G}_3^{\mathcal{A}_{\text{cma}}} \Rightarrow b\right] = \Pr\left[\text{FIND} = \top : b \leftarrow \mathcal{A}_{\text{cma}}^{\mathsf{Sign},|\mathsf{H}\backslash\mathcal{S}'\rangle}(\mathsf{F})\right]$. Then,

$$\left|\Pr\left[\mathsf{G}_2^{\mathcal{A}_{\text{cma}}} \Rightarrow 1\right] - \Pr\left[\mathsf{G}_3^{\mathcal{A}_{\text{cma}}} \Rightarrow 1\right]\right| \le \sqrt{(q_{\text{qro}}+2)\Pr\left[\text{FIND} = \top : \mathsf{G}_3^{\mathcal{A}_{\text{cma}}} \Rightarrow b\right]}, \quad (5)$$

by Lemma 4. We will show a bound on Eq. (5) after defining G_4.

GAME G_4 (reprogramming only for successful trials): The signing oracle reprograms $\mathsf{H} := \mathsf{H}^{(r_i,m_i)\mapsto y_i}$ only for $r_i \leftarrow \mathcal{R}$, $y_i \leftarrow_\$ \mathcal{Y}$, and $x_i \leftarrow \mathsf{I}(y_i)$ satisfying $x_i \ne \perp$. Notice that $\mathcal{A}_{\text{cma}}$ makes queries to the punctured oracle $\mathsf{H}\backslash\mathcal{S}'$.

ROM: Since $\mathcal{A}_{\text{cma}}$ cannot distinguish whether H is reprogrammed for $(r,m) \in \mathcal{S}'$ if FIND $= \perp$, $\Pr\left[\mathsf{G}_3^{\mathcal{A}_{\text{cma}}} \Rightarrow 1\right] = \Pr\left[\mathsf{G}_4^{\mathcal{A}_{\text{cma}}} \Rightarrow 1\right]$ holds.

QROM: If the measurements of $|f_{\mathcal{S}'}(r,m)\rangle$ are 0 for all queries (FIND $= \perp$), then $\mathcal{A}_{\text{cma}}$'s queries never contain any $(r,m) \in \mathcal{S}'$ and $\mathcal{A}_{\text{cma}}$ cannot obtain $\mathsf{H}(r,m)$ for $(r,m) \in \mathcal{S}'$. Hence, if FIND $= \perp$, then $\mathcal{A}_{\text{cma}}$ cannot distinguish whether H is reprogrammed at $(r,m) \in \mathcal{S}'$ in G_3 or not in G_4 and we have

$$\Pr\left[\text{FIND} = \perp : \mathsf{G}_3^{\mathcal{A}_{\text{cma}}} \Rightarrow b\right] = \Pr\left[\text{FIND} = \perp : \mathsf{G}_4^{\mathcal{A}_{\text{cma}}} \Rightarrow b\right] \quad (6)$$

(as Lemma 3). Especially, if G_3 or G_4 outputs 1, then FIND should be $\perp$ (Line 12 of G_3-G_5). Thus, $\Pr\left[\mathsf{G}_3^{\mathcal{A}_{\text{cma}}} \Rightarrow 1\right] = \Pr\left[\mathsf{G}_4^{\mathcal{A}_{\text{cma}}} \Rightarrow 1\right]$ holds. Moreover, $\Pr\left[\text{FIND} = \top : \mathsf{G}_3^{\mathcal{A}_{\text{cma}}} \Rightarrow b\right] = \Pr\left[\text{FIND} = \top : \mathsf{G}_4^{\mathcal{A}_{\text{cma}}} \Rightarrow b\right]$ holds from Eq. (6).

Let G_4' be a game given in Fig. 11 (identical to G_4 except that $\mathcal{B}_{\text{cma}}$ outputs (r',m') and H is not punctured). Choosing $j \leftarrow_\$ [q_{\text{qro}}+1]$, $\mathcal{B}_{\text{cma}}$ runs $\mathcal{A}_{\text{cma}}$ playing G_4. Just before $\mathcal{A}_{\text{cma}}$ makes j-th query to H, $\mathcal{B}_{\text{cma}}$ measures a query input register of $\mathcal{A}_{\text{cma}}$ and outputs the measurement outcome as (r',m'). Since the oracles of G_4' reveal no information on $\mathcal{S}$, $\mathcal{B}_{\text{cma}}$ has no information on $\mathcal{S}$; therefore, $\Pr\left[\mathsf{G}_4'^{\mathcal{B}_{\text{cma}}} \Rightarrow 1\right] \le \Pr[r' \in \mathcal{S}] \le \frac{q'_{\text{sign}} - q_{\text{sign}}}{|\mathcal{R}|}$ holds. Hence, $\Pr\left[\text{FIND} = \top : \mathsf{G}_4^{\mathcal{A}_{\text{cma}}} \Rightarrow b\right] \le 4(q_{\text{qro}}+1)\frac{q'_{\text{sign}} - q_{\text{sign}}}{|\mathcal{R}|}$ holds from Lemma 5 and an upper bound on Eq. (5) is $2(q_{\text{qro}}+2)\sqrt{\frac{q'_{\text{sign}} - q_{\text{sign}}}{|\mathcal{R}|}}$.

GAME G_5 (simulating the signing oracle by SampDom): The signing oracle generates signatures by $r_i \leftarrow_\$ \mathcal{R}$ and $x_i \leftarrow$ SampDom(F).

ROM and QROM: The PS adversary $\mathcal{D}_{ps}$ can simulate G_4/G_5 as in the second row of Fig. 10. If $\mathcal{D}_{ps}$ plays PS_0, the procedures of the original and simulated G_4 are identical. If $\mathcal{D}_{ps}$ plays PS_1, he simulates G_5. Thus, we have $\left|\Pr[G_4^{\mathcal{A}_{cma}} \Rightarrow 1] - \Pr[G_5^{\mathcal{A}_{cma}} \Rightarrow 1]\right| \leq \mathrm{Adv}_{T_{wpsf}}^{PS}(\mathcal{D}_{ps})$.

GAME: G_4'	$\mathrm{Sign}^H(m_i)$ for G_4'
1 $\mathcal{Q} := \emptyset$	1 **repeat**
2 $H \leftarrow_\$ \mathcal{Y}^{\mathcal{R} \times \mathcal{M}}$	2 $y_i \leftarrow_\$ \mathcal{Y}$
3 $S := \emptyset$	3 $x_i \leftarrow I(y_i)$
4 **for** $j \in [q'_{sign}]$ **do**	4 **until** $x_i \neq \perp$
5 $r \leftarrow_\$ \mathcal{R}$	5 $r_i \leftarrow_\$ \mathcal{R}$
6 $S := S \cup \{r\}$	6 $H := H^{(r_i, m_i) \mapsto y_i}$
7 $S' = \{(r, m) : r \in S, m \in \mathcal{M}\}$	7 $\mathcal{Q} := \mathcal{Q} \cup \{m_i\}$
8 $(F, I) \leftarrow \mathrm{Gen}(1^\lambda)$	8 **return** (r_i, x_i)
9 $(r', m') \leftarrow \mathcal{B}_{cma}^{\mathrm{Sign}, |H\rangle}(F)$	
10 **return** $(r', m') \overset{?}{\in} S'$	

Fig. 11. A game G_4' used in the application of Lemma 5

We show that the EUF-NMA adversary $\mathcal{A}_{nma}$ can simulate G_5 as in the bottom row of Fig. 10. In the simulation, $\mathcal{A}_{cma}$ makes queries to $H' \backslash S'$, where H' outputs whatever H outputs except for $\{(r_i, m_i)\}_{i \in [q_{sign}]}$. Since $m^* \notin \mathcal{Q}$ holds if $\mathcal{A}_{cma}$ wins, $H'(r^*, m^*) = H(r^*, m^*)$ holds for (m^*, r^*, x^*) that $\mathcal{A}_{cma}$ returns. Therefore, $\mathcal{A}_{nma}$ wins his game if $\mathcal{A}_{cma}$ wins the EUF-CMA game. Hence, $\mathcal{A}_{nma}$ can perfectly simulate G_5 with the same number of queries and almost the same running time as $\mathcal{A}_{cma}$, and $\Pr[G_5^{\mathcal{A}_{cma}} \Rightarrow 1] \leq \mathrm{Adv}_{HaS[T_{wpsf}, H]}^{EUF-NMA}(\mathcal{A}_{nma})$ holds. We finally stress that the number of queries $\mathcal{A}_{nma}$ made to H is q_{qro} rather than $q_{qro} + q_{sign}$ since $\mathcal{A}_{nma}$ never queries to its random oracle in the simulation of the signature.

Summing up, we have

$$\mathrm{Adv}_{HaS[T_{wpsf}, H]}^{EUF-CMA}(\mathcal{A}_{cma}) \leq \mathrm{Adv}_{HaS[T_{wpsf}, H]}^{EUF-NMA}(\mathcal{A}_{nma}) + \mathrm{Adv}_{T_{wpsf}}^{PS}(\mathcal{D}_{ps})$$
$$+ \frac{3}{2} q'_{sign} \sqrt{\frac{q'_{sign} + q_{qro} + 1}{|\mathcal{R}|}} + 2(q_{qro} + 2) \sqrt{\frac{q'_{sign} - q_{sign}}{|\mathcal{R}|}}. \quad (7)$$

INV $\Rightarrow$ EUF-NMA: We use different techniques for the ROM and the QROM.

ROM: Given a challenge y, the INV adversary $\mathcal{B}_{inv}$ randomly picks one of queries to H and reprograms H and $H^{(r,m) \mapsto y}$. If $\mathcal{A}_{nma}$ wins his game with (m^*, r^*, x^*) and $H(r^*, m^*) = y$ holds, $\mathcal{B}_{inv}$ can win the INV game with x^*. Since $H(r^*, m^*) = y$ holds with probability $\frac{1}{q_{ro}+1}$, $\mathrm{Adv}_{HaS[T_{wpsf}, H]}^{EUF-NMA}(\mathcal{A}_{nma}) \leq (q_{ro} + 1)\mathrm{Adv}_{T_{wpsf}}^{INV}(\mathcal{B}_{inv})$.

QROM: We use Lemma 2. Let S be a two-stage algorithm that consists of S_1 and S_2 and runs $\mathcal{A}_{nma}$ in the EUF-NMA game as follows:

1. Choose $(i, b) \leftarrow_\$ ([q_{qro}] \times \{0, 1\}) \cup \{(q_{qro} + 1, 0)\}$.
2. Run $\mathcal{A}_{nma}$ with H until i-th query.
3. Measure i-th query and output (r, m) as the output of S_1.
4. Given a random θ, reprogram $H' = H^{(r,m) \mapsto \theta}$.
5. If $i = q_{qro} + 1$, then go to Step 8.
6. Answer i-th query with H (if $b = 0$) or H' (if $b = 1$).
7. Run $\mathcal{A}_{nma}$ with H' until the end.
8. Output $\mathcal{A}_{nma}$'s output (m^*, r^*, x^*) as the output of S_2.

The INV adversary $\mathcal{B}_{inv}$ runs S. Since y is uniform in the INV game, $\mathcal{B}_{inv}$ can set the input for S_2 as $\theta := y$. When the predicate is $F(x) \stackrel{?}{=} H(r, m)$, we have

$$\Pr\Big[(r, m) = (\hat{r}, \hat{m}) \wedge F(x) = y : (r, m) \leftarrow S_1^{\mathcal{A}_{nma}}(), (m, r, x) \leftarrow S_2^{\mathcal{A}_{nma}}(y)\Big]$$

$$\geq \frac{1}{(2q_{qro} + 1)^2} \Pr\Big[(r, m) = (\hat{r}, \hat{m}) \wedge F(x) = H(r, m) : (m, r, x) \leftarrow \mathcal{A}_{nma}^{|H\rangle}(F)\Big],$$

for any $(\hat{r}, \hat{m}) \in \mathcal{R} \times \mathcal{M}$ from Lemma 2. By summing over all $(\hat{r}, \hat{m}) \in \mathcal{R} \times \mathcal{M}$,

$$\Pr\Big[F(x) = y : (r, m) \leftarrow S_1^{\mathcal{A}_{nma}}(), (m, r, x) \leftarrow S_2^{\mathcal{A}_{nma}}(y)\Big]$$

$$\geq \frac{1}{(2q_{qro} + 1)^2} \Pr\Big[F(x) = H(r, m) : (m, r, x) \leftarrow \mathcal{A}_{nma}^{|H\rangle}(F)\Big]. \quad (8)$$

Notice that the probability in the RHS of Eq. (8) is the EUF-NMA advantage. Also, $\text{Adv}_{T_{wpsf}}^{INV}(\mathcal{B}_{inv}) \geq \Pr\Big[F(x) = y : (r, m) \leftarrow S_1^{\mathcal{A}_{nma}}(), (m, r, x) \leftarrow S_2^{\mathcal{A}_{nma}}(y)\Big]$ holds since $\mathcal{B}_{inv}$ runs S. Hence, we have

$$\text{Adv}_{HaS[T_{wpsf}, H]}^{EUF\text{-}NMA}(\mathcal{A}_{nma}) \leq (2q_{qro} + 1)^2 \text{Adv}_{T_{wpsf}}^{INV}(\mathcal{B}_{inv}). \quad (9)$$

From Eqs. (7) and (9), we have Eq. (4).   □

Theorem 1 has the following two advantages:

Advantage 1 (Wide applications): Our reduction gives security proofs for code-based and MQ-based hash-and-sign signatures. Relaxation of **Condition 2** is necessary for such applications. The existing security proofs replace the random function H with H' all at once, requiring statistical indistinguishability between H and H'. On the other hand, our proof adaptively reprograms H in each signing query. This approach enables us to provide the security proof under a weaker assumption compared to the one required by PSF, namely, a trapdoor function is WPSF and preimage-simulatable. When considering the PS advantage, the use of computational indistinguishability leads to further relaxation of requirements for the trapdoor function.

Advantage 2 (Tighter proof): Our reduction is tighter than the existing ones [45, 47]. While we cannot guarantee the optimality of our reduction, we can infer from several observations that a multiplicative loss of $(2q_{\mathsf{qro}} + 1)^2$ appears to be unavoidable in the generic (black-box) reduction. The reduction incurs a loss of the number of queries to H, even in the ROM (see Sect. 3). Second, the security loss of a generic reduction from ROM to QROM using the lifting theorem [45] is at least $(2q_{\mathsf{qro}} + 1)^2$. Third, in the Fiat-Shamir paradigm, a generic reduction from arbitrary ID schemes incurs the same security loss (see Remark 4).

We give some remarks on Theorem 1.

Remark 1. If $\mathsf{HaS}[\mathsf{T_{wpsf}}, \mathsf{H}]$ adopts the probabilistic hash-and-sign, then $q'_{\mathsf{sign}} = q_{\mathsf{sign}}$ holds and the last term of Eq. (4) becomes 0.

Remark 2. We have a tight reduction in EUF-NMA $\Rightarrow$ EUF-CMA with the security bound of Eq. (7). Comparing this bound with the one presented in [11] (refer to Eq. (1) in Sect. 3), we observe that our requirement for $\mathsf{T_{wpsf}}$ is weaker, and there are no square-root terms associated with **Condition 2**.

Remark 3. When the underlying trapdoor function is PSF (or trapdoor permutation), we have:

$$\mathrm{Adv}_{\mathsf{HaS}[\mathsf{T_{psf}}, \mathsf{H}]}^{\mathrm{EUF\text{-}CMA}}(\mathcal{A}_{\mathsf{cma}}) \leq (2q_{\mathsf{qro}} + 1)^2 \mathrm{Adv}_{\mathsf{T_{psf}}}^{\mathrm{INV}}(\mathcal{B}_{\mathsf{inv}}) + \frac{3}{2}q_{\mathsf{sign}}\sqrt{\frac{q_{\mathsf{sign}} + q_{\mathsf{qro}} + 1}{|\mathcal{R}|}}.$$

As $\mathsf{HaS}[\mathsf{T_{psf}}, \mathsf{H}].\mathsf{Sign}$ produces a signature without retry (**Condition 3**), $q'_{\mathsf{sign}} = q_{\mathsf{sign}}$ holds. In the PS game, the outputs of I and $\mathsf{SampDom}(\mathsf{F})$ are equivalent due to **Condition 2**, resulting in $\mathrm{Adv}_{\mathsf{T_{psf}}}^{\mathrm{PS}}(\mathcal{D}_{\mathsf{ps}}) = 0$. This bound is tighter than existing ones for $\mathsf{HaS}[\mathsf{T_{psf}}, \mathsf{H}]$ (see Table 2).

Remark 4. Grilo et al. showed a tight reduction of EUF-NMA $\Rightarrow$ EUF-CMA in the Fiat-Shamir paradigm, assuming that the underlying ID scheme is honest verifier zero-knowledge (HVZK) [25, Theorem 3]. Also, Don et al. gave a generic reduction in the Fiat-Shamir transform of arbitrary ID schemes with a security loss $(2q_{\mathsf{qro}} + 1)^2$ [18, Theorem 8]. The above reductions use the tight adaptive reprogramming technique and the measure-and-reprogram technique.

Remark 5. The Fiat-Shamir with aborts paradigm [33] shares a similar structure with the probabilistic hash-and-sign with retry. Concurrent works by Devevey et al. [15] and Barbosa et al. [3] demonstrate reductions of EUF-NMA $\Rightarrow$ EUF-CMA for the Fiat-Shamir with aborts. Devevey et al. rely on the strong HVZK assumption [15, Definition 6], which allows for statistical simulation of protocol outputs even in cases of failure. Their proof uses the tight adaptive reprogramming technique to alter the signing oracle such that the EUF-NMA adversary can simulate using the statistical HVZK. In contrast, Barbosa et al. assume a weaker assumption called *accepting* HVZK assumption, which assumes that protocol outputs can be statistically simulated if the protocol does not fail [3, Definition 1]. This assumption closely aligns with the idea that a WPSF is *statistically* preimage-simulatable (see Definition 7). Essentially, their approach aligns with ours, involving the adaptive reprogramming followed by canceling the reprogramming during retries.

4.1 Extension to SEUF-CMA Security

If F is injective, $\mathsf{HaS}[\mathsf{T_{wpsf}}, \mathsf{H}]$ is sEUF-CMA secure.

Corollary 1 (INV $\Rightarrow$ sEUF-CMA). *Suppose that* F *of* $\mathsf{T_{wpsf}}$ *is an injection. For any quantum* sEUF-CMA *adversary* $\mathcal{A}_{\mathsf{cma}}$ *of* $\mathsf{HaS}[\mathsf{T_{wpsf}}, \mathsf{H}]$ *issuing at most* q_{sign} *classical queries to the signing oracle and* q_{qro} *(quantum) random oracle queries to* $\mathsf{H} \leftarrow_\$ \mathcal{Y}^{\mathcal{R} \times \mathcal{M}}$, *there exist an* INV *adversary* $\mathcal{B}_{\mathsf{inv}}$ *of* $\mathsf{T_{wpsf}}$ *and a* PS *adversary* $\mathcal{D}_{\mathsf{ps}}$ *of* $\mathsf{T_{wpsf}}$ *issuing* q_{sign} *sampling queries such that*

$$\mathsf{Adv}_{\mathsf{HaS}[\mathsf{T_{wpsf}},\mathsf{H}]}^{\mathsf{sEUF\text{-}CMA}}(\mathcal{A}_{\mathsf{cma}}) \leq (2q_{\mathsf{qro}} + 1)^2 \mathsf{Adv}_{\mathsf{T_{wpsf}}}^{\mathsf{INV}}(\mathcal{B}_{\mathsf{inv}}) + \mathsf{Adv}_{\mathsf{T_{wpsf}}}^{\mathsf{PS}}(\mathcal{D}_{\mathsf{ps}})$$
$$+ \frac{3}{2}q'_{\mathsf{sign}}\sqrt{\frac{q'_{\mathsf{sign}} + q_{\mathsf{qro}} + 1}{|\mathcal{R}|}} + 2(q_{\mathsf{qro}} + 2)\sqrt{\frac{q'_{\mathsf{sign}} - q_{\mathsf{sign}}}{|\mathcal{R}|}}, \qquad (10)$$

where q'_{sign} *is a bound on the total number of queries to* H *in all the signing queries, and the running times of* $\mathcal{B}_{\mathsf{inv}}$ *and* $\mathcal{D}_{\mathsf{ps}}$ *are about that of* $\mathcal{A}_{\mathsf{cma}}$.

Proof. The sEUF-CMA game outputs 0 if $(m^*, r^*, x^*) \in \mathcal{Q}'$. Due to the injection of F, if $(m^*, r^*) = (m_i, r_i)$, it implies $x^* = x_i$. Therefore, we can rephrase the condition for outputting 0 as follows: the game outputs 0 if $(m^*, r^*) \in \mathcal{Q}'$, where $\mathcal{Q}' = \{(m_i, r_i)\}_{i \in [q_{\mathsf{sign}}]}$. With this reinterpretation, we demonstrate that the same bound as Eq. (7) holds for EUF-NMA $\Rightarrow$ sEUF-CMA.

In Corollary 1, we can use the same games as defined in Theorem 1, and the bound on $\left|\Pr[\mathsf{G}_0^{\mathcal{A}_{\mathsf{cma}}} \Rightarrow 1] - \Pr[\mathsf{G}_5^{\mathcal{A}_{\mathsf{cma}}} \Rightarrow 1]\right|$ remains unchanged. In the simulation of G_5 (see the bottom row of Fig. 10), $\mathcal{A}_{\mathsf{cma}}$ uses $\mathsf{H}' \backslash \mathcal{S}'$ reprogrammed on $\{(r_i, m_i)\}_{i \in [q_{\mathsf{sign}}]}$ instead of the original H. By $(m^*, r^*) \notin \mathcal{Q}'$, $\mathsf{H}'(r^*, m^*) = \mathsf{H}(r^*, m^*)$ holds and $\mathcal{A}_{\mathsf{nma}}$ can win his game if $\mathsf{F}(x^*) = \mathsf{H}'(r^*, m^*)$. Therefore, $\Pr[\mathsf{G}_5^{\mathcal{A}_{\mathsf{cma}}} \Rightarrow 1] \leq \mathsf{Adv}_{\mathsf{HaS}[\mathsf{T_{wpsf}},\mathsf{H}]}^{\mathsf{EUF\text{-}NMA}}(\mathcal{A}_{\mathsf{nma}})$ holds. Hence, Eq. (7) holds. $\square$

4.2 Applications of New Security Proof

By applying Theorem 1, we can establish security proofs for Wave [2], the original/modified UOV signatures [31,42], the modified HFE signature [42], and MAYO [6]. Additionally, by utilizing Corollary 1, we can provide a security proof for the modified CFS signature [14]. Essentially, it is sufficient to directly apply Theorem 1 or Corollary 1; however, we need to derive bounds on the PS advantage, denoted by ϵ_{ps}. We briefly explain ideas behind bounding ϵ_{ps} (see the complete proofs in the full paper.).

Modified CFS signature: An invertible subset of $\mathcal{Y}$, that is, $\mathcal{Y}' = \{y : \mathsf{I}(y) \neq \bot\}$, is a set of decodable syndromes of a Goppa code and the domain $\mathcal{X}$ of F is a set of corresponding errors. Given the relationship between $\mathcal{X}$ and $\mathcal{Y}'$, there exists a one-to-one correspondence between $x \in \mathcal{X}$ and $y \in \mathcal{Y}'$, and consequently, F is an injection (Corollary 1 is applied). Therefore, a preimage generated after retries is uniform over $\mathcal{X}$, and thus, $\mathsf{SampDom}(\mathsf{F})$, that is, $x \leftarrow_\$ \mathcal{X}$, can perfectly simulate the preimage. Hence, $\epsilon_{\mathsf{ps}} = 0$ holds.

Wave: Wave adopts the probabilistic hash-and-sign (Eq. (7) is applied.) and its trapdoor function is *average trapdoor PSF (ATPSF)* [11] that is a special case of WPSF satisfying:

1. There is a bound δ on the average of $\delta_{\mathsf{F},\mathsf{I}}$ over all $(\mathsf{F},\mathsf{I}) \leftarrow \mathsf{Gen}(1^\lambda)$, where $\delta_{\mathsf{F},\mathsf{I}} = \Delta(\mathsf{SampDom}(\mathsf{F}), \mathsf{I}(\mathsf{U}(\mathcal{Y})))$ is a statistical distance between $\mathsf{SampDom}(\mathsf{F})$ and $\mathsf{I}(y)$ for $y \leftarrow_\$ \mathcal{Y}$ (**relaxed Condition 2**).
2. $\mathsf{I}(y)$ outputs x satisfying $\mathsf{F}(x) = y$ for any $y \in \mathcal{Y}$ (**Condition 3**).

Applying the union bound over q_{sign} signing queries, we have $\epsilon_{\mathsf{ps}} \le q_{\mathsf{sign}}\delta$.

Original UOV signature: Since there is no known statistical bound on ϵ_{ps}, we must assume the computational hardness of the PS game.

Modified UOV/HFE signatures: Since a preimage generated after retries follows a uniform distribution as shown in [42], $x \leftarrow \mathsf{SampDom}(\mathsf{F})$, that is, $x \leftarrow_\$ \mathcal{X}$, can perfectly simulate the preimage; therefore, we have $\epsilon_{\mathsf{ps}} = 0$.

MAYO: MAYO adopts the probabilistic hash-and-sign (Eq. (7) is applied.) and its trapdoor I iteratively retries a part of x called *vinegar variables* until a specific condition is met. If I consistently outputs x without needing to retry the vinegar variables, then $\mathsf{SampDom}(\mathsf{F})$ $(x \leftarrow_\$ \mathcal{X})$ can perfectly simulate the preimage, and $\epsilon_{\mathsf{ps}} = 0$ holds. Let τ be a bound on the probability of I retrying the vinegar variables. MAYO's parameter sets ensure that $1 - q_{\mathsf{sign}}\tau > \frac{1}{2}$ holds, where the expected q_{sign} aligns with the security levels [6].

QR-UOV [22], PROV [20], and GeMSS [10] are provable secure since they follow the modified UOV/HFE signatures. If Rainbow [16] makes the same modification as the modified UOV signature, the scheme can be provably secure.

5 Security Proof of Hash-and-Sign with Prefix Hashing in Multi-key Setting

In prefix hashing, the hash function H includes a small unpredictable portion of the verification key. Let $\mathsf{H} \colon \mathcal{U} \times \mathcal{R} \times \mathcal{M} \to \mathcal{Y}$ be a hash function and $\mathsf{HaS^{ph}}[\mathsf{T}, \mathsf{H}, \mathsf{E}]$ be a signature scheme adopting the probabilistic hash-and-sign with retry and prefix hashing, where $\mathsf{E} \colon \mathcal{Y}^\mathcal{X} \to \mathcal{U}$ is a deterministic function to extract a small unpredictable part of F into a key ID $u \in \mathcal{U}$. We assume that $\mathsf{E}(\mathsf{F})$ is uniform over $\mathcal{U}$ for $(\mathsf{F},\mathsf{I}) \leftarrow \mathsf{Gen}(1^\lambda)$[9]. For a message m, $\mathsf{HaS^{ph}}[\mathsf{T}, \mathsf{H}, \mathsf{E}].\mathsf{Sign}$ repeats $r \leftarrow_\$ \mathcal{R}$ and $x \leftarrow \mathsf{I}(\mathsf{H}(\mathsf{E}(\mathsf{F}), r, m))$ until $x \neq \perp$ holds, and outputs (r, x). For a verification key F, a message m, and a signature (r, x), $\mathsf{HaS^{ph}}[\mathsf{T}, \mathsf{H}, \mathsf{E}].\mathsf{Vrfy}$ verifies by $\mathsf{F}(x) \overset{?}{=} \mathsf{H}(\mathsf{E}(\mathsf{F}), r, m)$.

We show that M-INV $\Rightarrow$ M-EUF-CMA and M-CR $\Rightarrow$ M-sEUF-CMA hold without any security loss in the number of keys q_{key} (see the full paper). We

---

[9] If unpredictable parts do not exist or are computationally expensive to include in H, a fixed nonce can be used instead (the nonce is put in the verification key).

note that there exist trivial reductions: $\mathrm{Adv}_{\mathsf{T}}^{\mathrm{M\text{-}INV}}(\mathcal{B}_{\mathsf{inv^m}}) \leq q_{\mathsf{key}}\mathrm{Adv}_{\mathsf{T}}^{\mathrm{INV}}(\mathcal{B}_{\mathsf{inv}})$ and $\mathrm{Adv}_{\mathsf{T}}^{\mathrm{M\text{-}CR}}(\mathcal{B}_{\mathsf{cr^m}}) \leq q_{\mathsf{key}}\mathrm{Adv}_{\mathsf{T}}^{\mathrm{CR}}(\mathcal{B}_{\mathsf{cr}})$. To address this issue, we propose a generic method to show reductions from INV or CR by assuming the hardness of the computational problem on keys' distributions.

GAME: ST_b	$\mathsf{NewKey}_0()$	$\mathsf{NewKey}_1()$
1 $(\mathsf{F}', \mathsf{I}') \leftarrow \mathsf{Gen}'(1^\lambda)$	1 $(\mathsf{F}_j, \mathsf{I}_j) \leftarrow \mathsf{Gen}(1^\lambda)$	1 $\mathsf{L}_j \leftarrow \mathcal{D}_\mathsf{L}$
2 $b^* \leftarrow \mathcal{D}_{\mathsf{st}}^{\mathsf{NewKey}_b}()$	2 return F_j	2 $\mathsf{R}_j \leftarrow \mathcal{D}_\mathsf{R}$
3 return b^*		3 $\mathsf{F}_j := \mathsf{L}_j \circ \mathsf{F}' \circ \mathsf{R}_j$
		4 return F_j

Fig. 12. ST(Sandwich Transformation) game

Let $\{\mathsf{F}_j\}_{j\in[q_{\mathsf{key}}]}$ be verification keys generated by Gen of a trapdoor function T. Given a verification key $\mathsf{F}': \mathcal{X}' \to \mathcal{Y}'$ generated by Gen' of another trapdoor function T', we simulate $\{\mathsf{F}_j\}_{j\in[q_{\mathsf{key}}]}$ by $\{\mathsf{L}_j \circ \mathsf{F}' \circ \mathsf{R}_j\}_{j\in[q_{\mathsf{key}}]}$, where $\mathsf{L}_j: \mathcal{Y}' \to \mathcal{Y}$ and $\mathsf{R}_j: \mathcal{X} \to \mathcal{X}'$. Let $\mathcal{D}_\mathsf{L}$ and $\mathcal{D}_\mathsf{R}$ be some distributions of L_j and R_j. We note that the domains and ranges of F' and F_j's may differ. We define a new game to give a bound on the distinguishing advantage of $\{\mathsf{F}_j\}_{j\in[q_{\mathsf{key}}]}$ and $\{\mathsf{L}_j \circ \mathsf{F}' \circ \mathsf{R}_j\}_{j\in[q_{\mathsf{key}}]}$.

Definition 11 (ST (Sandwich Transformation) Game). *Let* T *and* T' *be trapdoor functions. Using a game given in Fig. 12, we define an advantage function of an adversary* $\mathcal{D}_{\mathsf{st}}$ *playing the STgame against* T *and* T' *as* $\mathrm{Adv}_{\mathsf{T},\mathsf{T}'}^{\mathrm{ST}}(\mathcal{D}_{\mathsf{st}}) = \left|\Pr[\mathsf{ST}_0^{\mathcal{D}_{\mathsf{st}}} \Rightarrow 1] - \Pr[\mathsf{ST}_1^{\mathcal{D}_{\mathsf{st}}} \Rightarrow 1]\right|$.

We have the following reductions assuming some conditions on L_j and R_j (see the proofs in the full paper.).

Lemma 6 (INV + ST $\Rightarrow$ M-EUF-CMA). *Let* T' *be a trapdoor function with* $\mathsf{F}': \mathcal{X}' \to \mathcal{Y}$. *Suppose that* $\mathsf{L}_j: \mathcal{Y} \to \mathcal{Y}$ *and* $\mathsf{R}_j: \mathcal{X} \to \mathcal{X}'$ *are used to simulate* F_j *by* $\mathsf{L}_j \circ \mathsf{F}' \circ \mathsf{R}_j$ *in the STgame, where* L_j *is a bijection.*
For any quantum M-EUF-CMAadversary $\mathcal{A}_{\mathsf{cma^m}}$ *of* $\mathsf{HaS}^{\mathsf{ph}}[\mathsf{T}_{\mathsf{wpsf}}, \mathsf{H}, \mathsf{E}]$ *with* q_{key} *keys and issuing at most* q_{sign} *classical queries to the signing oracle and* q_{qro} *(quantum) random oracle queries to* $\mathsf{H} \leftarrow_\$ \mathcal{Y}^{\mathcal{U}\times\mathcal{R}\times\mathcal{M}}$, *there exist an INV adversary* $\mathcal{B}_{\mathsf{inv}}$ *of* T', *an M-PSadversary* $\mathcal{D}_{\mathsf{psm}}$ *of* $\mathsf{T}_{\mathsf{wpsf}}$ *with* q_{key} *instances and issuing* q_{sign} *sampling queries, and an STadversary* $\mathcal{D}_{\mathsf{st}}$ *of* $(\mathsf{T}_{\mathsf{wpsf}}, \mathsf{T}')$ *issuing* q_{key} *new key queries such that*

$$\mathrm{Adv}_{\mathsf{HaS}^{\mathsf{ph}}[\mathsf{T}_{\mathsf{wpsf}},\mathsf{H},\mathsf{E}]}^{\mathrm{M\text{-}EUF\text{-}CMA}}(\mathcal{A}_{\mathsf{cma^m}}) \leq (2q_{\mathsf{qro}}+1)^2\mathrm{Adv}_{\mathsf{T}'}^{\mathrm{INV}}(\mathcal{B}_{\mathsf{inv}}) + \mathrm{Adv}_{\mathsf{T}_{\mathsf{wpsf}}}^{\mathrm{M\text{-}PS}}(\mathcal{D}_{\mathsf{psm}})$$
$$+ \mathrm{Adv}_{\mathsf{T}_{\mathsf{wpsf}},\mathsf{T}'}^{\mathrm{ST}}(\mathcal{D}_{\mathsf{st}}) + \frac{3}{2}q'_{\mathsf{sign}}\sqrt{\frac{q'_{\mathsf{sign}}+q_{\mathsf{qro}}+1}{|\mathcal{R}|}}$$
$$+ 2(q_{\mathsf{qro}}+2)\sqrt{\frac{q'_{\mathsf{sign}}-q_{\mathsf{sign}}}{|\mathcal{R}|}} + \frac{q_{\mathsf{key}}^2}{|\mathcal{U}|}, \qquad (11)$$

where q'_{sign} *is a bound on the total number of queries to* H *in all the signing queries and the running times of* $\mathcal{B}_{\mathsf{inv}}$, $\mathcal{D}_{\mathsf{psm}}$, *and* $\mathcal{D}_{\mathsf{st}}$ *are about that of* $\mathcal{A}_{\mathsf{cma^m}}$.

Lemma 7 (CR + ST ⇒ M-sEUF-CMA). *Let* T' *be a trapdoor function with* $\mathsf{F}'\colon \mathcal{X}' \to \mathcal{Y}$. *Suppose that* $\mathsf{L}_j\colon \mathcal{Y}' \to \mathcal{Y}$ *and* $\mathsf{R}_j\colon \mathcal{X} \to \mathcal{X}'$ *are used to simulate* F_j *by* $\mathsf{L}_j \circ \mathsf{F}' \circ \mathsf{R}_j$ *in the* ST *game, where* L_j *and* R_j *are injections.*

For any quantum M-sEUF-CMA *adversary* $\mathcal{A}_{\mathsf{cma^m}}$ *of* $\mathsf{HaS^{ph}}[\mathsf{T}_{\mathsf{psf}},\mathsf{H},\mathsf{E}]$ *with* q_{key} *keys and issuing at most* q_{sign} *classical queries to the signing oracle and* q_{qro} *(quantum) random oracle queries to* $\mathsf{H} \leftarrow_{\$} \mathcal{Y}^{\mathcal{U} \times \mathcal{R} \times \mathcal{M}}$, *there exist a* CR *adversary* $\mathcal{B}_{\mathsf{cr}}$ *of* T' *and an* ST *adversary* $\mathcal{D}_{\mathsf{st}}$ *of* $(\mathsf{T}_{\mathsf{psf}},\mathsf{T}')$ *issuing* q_{key} *new key queries such that*

$$\mathsf{Adv}^{\mathrm{M\text{-}sEUF\text{-}CMA}}_{\mathsf{HaS^{ph}}[\mathsf{T}_{\mathsf{psf}},\mathsf{H},\mathsf{E}]}(\mathcal{A}_{\mathsf{cma^m}}) \leq \frac{1}{1-2^{-\omega(\log(\lambda))}}\left(\mathsf{Adv}^{\mathrm{CR}}_{\mathsf{T}'}(\mathcal{B}_{\mathsf{cr}})+\mathsf{Adv}^{\mathrm{ST}}_{\mathsf{T}_{\mathsf{psf}},\mathsf{T}'}(\mathcal{D}_{\mathsf{st}})\right) + \frac{q^2_{\mathsf{key}}}{|\mathcal{U}|},$$

where the running times of $\mathcal{B}_{\mathsf{cr}}$ *and* $\mathcal{D}_{\mathsf{st}}$ *are about that of* $\mathcal{A}_{\mathsf{cma^m}}$.

In the full paper, we apply the generic method to some frameworks of hash-and-sign signatures in lattice-based, code-based, and MQ-based cryptography. To bound the ST advantage, we introduce multi-instance variants of established computational problems in code-based and MQ-based cryptography, that is, permutation/linear equivalence [41] and morphism of polynomials [40].

Open Problems: There are two open problems for the generic method. First, the computational problems used for bounding the ST advantage have not been studied deeply; therefore, future studies are necessary to guarantee the hardness of the problems. Second, we currently fail to use the generic method to show the M-EUF-CMA security under *adaptive corruptions of signing keys*. Solving this issue is the second open problem.

References

1. Ambainis, A., Hamburg, M., Unruh, D.: Quantum security proofs using semi-classical oracles. In: Boldyreva and Micciancio [8], pp. 269–295. https://doi.org/10.1007/978-3-030-26951-7_10
2. Banegas, G., et al.: Wave. Technical report, National Institute of Standards and Technology (2023). https://wave-sign.org/wave_documentation.pdf
3. Barbosa, M., et al.: Fixing and mechanizing the security proof of fiat-shamir with aborts and dilithium. In: Handschuh and Lysyanskaya [26], pp. 358–389. https://doi.org/10.1007/978-3-031-38554-4_12
4. Bellare, M., Rogaway, P.: Random oracles are practical: a paradigm for designing efficient protocols. In: Denning, D.E., Pyle, R., Ganesan, R., Sandhu, R.S., Ashby, V. (eds.) ACM CCS 1993, pp. 62–73. ACM Press (1993). https://doi.org/10.1145/168588.168596
5. Bellare, M., Rogaway, P.: The exact security of digital signatures: how to sign with RSA and Rabin. In: Maurer [34], pp. 399–416. https://doi.org/10.1007/3-540-68339-9_34
6. Beullens, W., Campos, F., Celi, S., Hess, B., Kannwischer, M.: MAYO. Technical report, National Institute of Standards and Technology (2023). https://pqmayo.org/assets/specs/mayo.pdf

7. Bindel, N., Hamburg, M., Hövelmanns, K., Hülsing, A., Persichetti, E.: Tighter proofs of CCA security in the quantum random oracle model. In: Hofheinz, D., Rosen, A. (eds.) TCC 2019, Part II. LNCS, vol. 11892, pp. 61–90. Springer, Heidelberg (2019). https://doi.org/10.1007/978-3-030-36033-7_3
8. Boldyreva, A., Micciancio, D. (eds.): CRYPTO 2019, Part II. LNCS, vol. 11693. Springer, Heidelberg (2019)
9. Boneh, D., Dagdelen, Ö., Fischlin, M., Lehmann, A., Schaffner, C., Zhandry, M.: Random oracles in a quantum world. In: Lee, D.H., Wang, X. (eds.) ASIACRYPT 2011. LNCS, vol. 7073, pp. 41–69. Springer, Heidelberg (2011). https://doi.org/10.1007/978-3-642-25385-0_3
10. Casanova, A., Faugère, J.C., Macario-Rat, G., Patarin, J., Perret, L., Ryckeghem, J.: GeMSS. Technical report, National Institute of Standards and Technology (2020). https://csrc.nist.gov/projects/post-quantum-cryptography/post-quantum-cryptography-standardization/round-3-submissions
11. Chailloux, A., Debris-Alazard, T.: Tight and optimal reductions for signatures based on average trapdoor preimage sampleable functions and applications to code-based signatures. In: Kiayias, A., Kohlweiss, M., Wallden, P., Zikas, V. (eds.) PKC 2020, Part II. LNCS, vol. 12111, pp. 453–479. Springer, Heidelberg (2020). https://doi.org/10.1007/978-3-030-45388-6_16
12. Chatterjee, S., Das, M.P.L., Pandit, T.: Revisiting the security of salted UOV signature. In: Isobe, T., Sarkar, S. (eds.) Progress in Cryptology – INDOCRYPT 2022. LNCS, vol. 13774, pp. 697–719. Springer, Heidelberg (2022). https://doi.org/10.1007/978-3-031-22912-1_31
13. Courtois, N., Finiasz, M., Sendrier, N.: How to achieve a McEliece-based digital signature scheme. In: Boyd, C. (ed.) ASIACRYPT 2001. LNCS, vol. 2248, pp. 157–174. Springer, Heidelberg (2001). https://doi.org/10.1007/3-540-45682-1_10
14. Dallot, L.: Towards a concrete security proof of Courtois, Finiasz and Sendrier signature scheme. In: Lucks, S., Sadeghi, AR., Wolf, C. (eds.) WEWoRC 2007. LNCS, vol. 4945, pp. 65–77. Springer, Heidelberg (2007). https://doi.org/10.1007/978-3-540-88353-1_6
15. Devevey, J., Fallahpour, P., Passelègue, A., Stehlé, D.: A detailed analysis of fiat-shamir with aborts. In: Handschuh and Lysyanskaya [26], pp. 327–357. https://doi.org/10.1007/978-3-031-38554-4_11
16. Ding, J., et al.: Rainbow. Technical report, National Institute of Standards and Technology (2020). https://csrc.nist.gov/projects/post-quantum-cryptography/post-quantum-cryptography-standardization/round-3-submissions
17. Don, J., Fehr, S., Majenz, C.: The measure-and-reprogram technique 2.0: multi-round fiat-shamir and more. In: Micciancio, D., Ristenpart, T. (eds.) CRYPTO 2020, Part III. LNCS, vol. 12172, pp. 602–631. Springer, Heidelberg (2020). https://doi.org/10.1007/978-3-030-56877-1_21
18. Don, J., Fehr, S., Majenz, C., Schaffner, C.: Security of the Fiat-Shamir transformation in the quantum random-oracle model. In: Boldyreva and Micciancio [8], pp. 356–383. https://doi.org/10.1007/978-3-030-26951-7_13
19. Duman, J., Hövelmanns, K., Kiltz, E., Lyubashevsky, V., Seiler, G.: Faster lattice-based KEMs via a generic fujisaki-okamoto transform using prefix hashing. In: Vigna, G., Shi, E. (eds.) ACM CCS 2021, pp. 2722–2737. ACM Press (2021). https://doi.org/10.1145/3460120.3484819
20. Faugere, J.C., Fouque, P.A., Macario-Rat, G., Minaud, B., Patarin, J.: PROV. Technical report, National Institute of Standards and Technology (2023). https://csrc.nist.gov/csrc/media/Projects/pqc-dig-sig/documents/round-1/spec-files/prov-spec-web.pdf

21. Fiat, A., Shamir, A.: How to prove yourself: practical solutions to identification and signature problems. In: Odlyzko, A.M. (ed.) CRYPTO 1986. LNCS, vol. 263, pp. 186–194. Springer, Heidelberg (1987). https://doi.org/10.1007/3-540-47721-7_12

22. Furue, H., Ikematsu, Y., Hoshino, F., Kiyomura, Y., Saito, T., Takagi, T.: QR-UOV. Technical report, National Institute of Standards and Technology (2023). http://info.isl.ntt.co.jp/crypt/qruov/files/NISTPQC_QRUOV.pdf

23. Gentry, C., Peikert, C., Vaikuntanathan, V.: Trapdoors for hard lattices and new cryptographic constructions. In: Ladner, R.E., Dwork, C. (eds.) 40th ACM STOC, pp. 197–206. ACM Press (2008). https://doi.org/10.1145/1374376.1374407

24. Goldwasser, S., Micali, S., Rivest, R.L.: A digital signature scheme secure against adaptive chosen-message attacks. SIAM J. Comput. **17**(2), 281–308 (1988). https://doi.org/10.1137/0217017

25. Grilo, A.B., Hövelmanns, K., Hülsing, A., Majenz, C.: Tight adaptive reprogramming in the QROM. In: Tibouchi, M., Wang, H. (eds.) ASIACRYPT 2021, Part I. LNCS, vol. 13090, pp. 637–667. Springer, Heidelberg (2021). https://doi.org/10.1007/978-3-030-92062-3_22

26. Handschuh, H., Lysyanskaya, A. (eds.): CRYPTO 2023, Part V. LNCS, vol. 14085. Springer, Heidelberg (2023)

27. Hosoyamada, A., Yasuda, K.: Building quantum-one-way functions from block ciphers: Davies-Meyer and Merkle-Damgård constructions. In: Peyrin, T., Galbraith, S. (eds.) ASIACRYPT 2018, Part I. LNCS, vol. 11272, pp. 275–304. Springer, Heidelberg (2018). https://doi.org/10.1007/978-3-030-03326-2_10

28. Hülsing, A., Rijneveld, J., Song, F.: Mitigating multi-target attacks in hash-based signatures. In: Cheng, C.M., Chung, K.M., Persiano, G., Yang, B.Y. (eds.) PKC 2016, Part I. LNCS, vol. 9614, pp. 387–416. Springer, Heidelberg (2016). https://doi.org/10.1007/978-3-662-49384-7_15

29. Kiltz, E., Lyubashevsky, V., Schaffner, C.: A concrete treatment of Fiat-Shamir signatures in the quantum random-oracle model. In: Nielsen, J.B., Rijmen, V. (eds.) EUROCRYPT 2018, Part III. LNCS, vol. 10822, pp. 552–586. Springer, Heidelberg (2018). https://doi.org/10.1007/978-3-319-78372-7_18

30. Kiltz, E., Masny, D., Pan, J.: Optimal security proofs for signatures from identification schemes. In: Robshaw, M., Katz, J. (eds.) CRYPTO 2016, Part II. LNCS, vol. 9815, pp. 33–61. Springer, Heidelberg (2016). https://doi.org/10.1007/978-3-662-53008-5_2

31. Kipnis, A., Patarin, J., Goubin, L.: Unbalanced Oil and Vinegar signature schemes. In: Stern, J. (ed.) EUROCRYPT 1999. LNCS, vol. 1592, pp. 206–222. Springer, Heidelberg (1999). https://doi.org/10.1007/3-540-48910-X_15

32. Liu, Y., Jiang, H., Zhao, Y.: Tighter post-quantum proof for plain FDH, PFDH and GPV-IBE. Cryptology ePrint Archive, Report 2022/1441 (2022). https://eprint.iacr.org/2022/1441

33. Lyubashevsky, V.: Fiat-Shamir with aborts: applications to lattice and factoring-based signatures. In: Matsui, M. (ed.) ASIACRYPT 2009. LNCS, vol. 5912, pp. 598–616. Springer, Heidelberg (2009). https://doi.org/10.1007/978-3-642-10366-7_35

34. Maurer, U.M. (ed.): EUROCRYPT 1996. LNCS, vol. 1070. Springer, Heidelberg (1996)

35. Menezes, A., Smart, N.: Security of signature schemes in a multi-user setting. Des. Codes Cryptogr. **33**(3), 261–274 (2004). https://link.springer.com/article/10.1023/B:DESI.0000036250.18062.3f

36. NIST: Submission requirements and evaluation criteria for the post-quantum cryptography standardization process (2017). https://csrc.nist.gov/CSRC/media/Projects/Post-Quantum-Cryptography/documents/call-for-proposals-final-dec-2016.pdf
37. NIST: Call for additional digital signature schemes for the post-quantum cryptography standardization process (2022). https://csrc.nist.gov/csrc/media/Projects/pqc-dig-sig/documents/call-for-proposals-dig-sig-sept-2022.pdf
38. NIST: Status report on the third round of the NIST post-quantum cryptography standardization process (2022). https://csrc.nist.gov/publications/detail/nistir/8413/final
39. Patarin, J.: Hidden fields equations (HFE) and isomorphisms of polynomials (IP): two new families of asymmetric algorithms. In: Maurer [34], pp. 33–48. https://doi.org/10.1007/3-540-68339-9_4
40. Patarin, J., Goubin, L., Courtois, N.: Improved algorithms for isomorphisms of polynomials. In: Nyberg, K. (ed.) EUROCRYPT 1998. LNCS, vol. 1403, pp. 184–200. Springer, Heidelberg (1998). https://doi.org/10.1007/BFb0054126
41. Petrank, E., Roth, R.M.: Is code equivalence easy to decide? IEEE Trans. Inf. Theory **43**(5), 1602–1604 (1997). https://ieeexplore.ieee.org/document/623157
42. Sakumoto, K., Shirai, T., Hiwatari, H.: On provable security of UOV and HFE signature schemes against chosen-message attack. In: Yang, B.Y. (ed.) PQCrypto 2011, pp. 68–82. Springer, Heidelberg (2011). https://doi.org/10.1007/978-3-642-25405-5_5
43. Shor, P.W.: Algorithms for quantum computation: Discrete logarithms and factoring. In: 35th FOCS, pp. 124–134. IEEE Computer Society Press (1994). https://doi.org/10.1109/SFCS.1994.365700
44. Unruh, D.: Quantum position verification in the random oracle model. In: Garay, J.A., Gennaro, R. (eds.) CRYPTO 2014, Part II. LNCS, vol. 8617, pp. 1–18. Springer, Heidelberg (2014). https://doi.org/10.1007/978-3-662-44381-1_1
45. Yamakawa, T., Zhandry, M.: Classical vs quantum random oracles. In: Canteaut, A., Standaert, F.X. (eds.) EUROCRYPT 2021, Part II. LNCS, vol. 12697, pp. 568–597. Springer, Heidelberg (2021). https://doi.org/10.1007/978-3-030-77886-6_20
46. Yamakawa, T., Zhandry, M.: Verifiable quantum advantage without structure. In: 63rd FOCS, pp. 69–74. IEEE Computer Society Press (2022). https://doi.org/10.1109/FOCS54457.2022.00014
47. Zhandry, M.: Secure identity-based encryption in the quantum random oracle model. Cryptology ePrint Archive, Report 2012/076 (2012). https://eprint.iacr.org/2012/076

Formalizing Hash-then-Sign Signatures

Bertram Poettering[1] and Simon Rastikian[1,2]

[1] IBM Research Europe – Zurich, Rüschlikon, Switzerland
sra@zurich.ibm.com
[2] ETH Zurich, Zurich, Switzerland

Abstract. Many practical signature schemes follow the Hash-then-Sign (HtS) paradigm: Instead of signing messages directly, messages are first hashed and then their hash values are signed. Attractive properties of the HtS approach include that the core signing algorithm does not have to get involved with handling arbitrarily long message inputs, and that the tasks of hashing and signing can be performed by different entities. For instance, if a signing algorithm is implemented in a smartcard setting, then an HtS scheme can allow sending only the hash value to the smartcard, instead of the whole message.

While the HtS paradigm was introduced decades ago, most signature schemes leverage it, and many applications rely on it, security analyses for HtS signature schemes are typically conducted only holistically for the hash+sign hybrid. However, the corresponding security models (e.g., EUF-CMA) don't cover the fact that the separation of hashing and signing allows for more attacks than monolithic schemes. In particular, cases where an attacker can interact with a smartcard and request the creation of signatures on arbitrary hash values (for which it may or may not know the messages), remain unaddressed.

This work initiates a study of HtS signatures in the framework of provable security: After defining a precise syntax, we develop security notions that cover the artifacts of the separation of hashing and signing. We show that signature schemes exist that are weak in the HtS sense yet secure in the classic sense, demonstrating the relevance of our work. We then study the HtS security of a number of widely-standardized signature schemes, including of ECDSA. Finally, we propose a generic method for the secure separation of hashing and signing for signature schemes that use a Merkle–Damgård hash function.

Keywords: Digital Signature · Hash-then-Sign · Smartcard · Implementation

1 Introduction

HASH-THEN-SIGN SIGNATURES. Intuitively speaking, a signature scheme is of the hash-then-sign (**HtS**) type if the processes of signing a message and verifying a message-signature pair each consist of two strictly consecutive phases: For signing, first the (arbitrarily long) message is reduced with a hash function *hash* to a (constant-length) hash value, then a core signing routine *sgn* takes the hash

© International Association for Cryptologic Research 2024
Q. Tang and V. Teague (Eds.): PKC 2024, LNCS 14601, pp. 289–315, 2024.
https://doi.org/10.1007/978-3-031-57718-5_10

value and produces the signature. Similarly for verifying: First the message is reduced to its hash value, then a core verification routine *vfy* takes the hash value and the signature, and outputs a validity decision. In symbols: If (sk, vk) represents a signature key pair, a signature on message m is computed as per $\sigma \leftarrow sgn(sk, hash(m))$, and the validity of σ can be validated as per $0/1 \leftarrow vfy(vk, hash(m), \sigma)$.

PRACTICAL (NON-)EXAMPLES OF HTS SIGNATURES. Many signature schemes used in practice are of the HtS type. A classic example is the PKCS#1v1.5 [9] interpretation of Full-Domain-Hash RSA [1], where signatures under signing key (N, d) are generated as per $\sigma \leftarrow hash(m)^d$ (mod N, and for some hash function $hash: \{0,1\}^* \rightarrow \mathbb{Z}_N$). Another example is ECDSA [5], where a signature under signing key x consists of a solution (c, s) for the equation system $c = f(g^r) \wedge rs = cx + hash(m)$ (mod q, and for an ephemeral randomness r, a conversion function f, and a hash function $hash: \{0,1\}^* \rightarrow \mathbb{Z}_q$).

Practical signature schemes that are *not* HtS examples include all those derived via the Fiat–Shamir transform from a Sigma protocol, as the latter requires the combined hashing of message and zero-knowledge commitment. A concrete example for this are Schnorr signatures (e.g., ECSDSA [11] or EdDSA [8]), where the hash function is applied to the concatenation $R \parallel m$, where $R = g^r$ represents the commitment that is freshly created for each signing operation. Another signature scheme that is not of the HtS type is the original proposal of RSA-PSS [2], where, to achieve reduction tightness, a fresh randomizer is prepended to the message before it is hashed. (This is in contrast with the RSA-PSS variant standardized in PKCS#1v2.1 [7] which adds one more level of hashing.)

APPLICATIONS OF HTS SIGNATURES. The special structure of HtS signatures is attractive from the point of view of many applications, in particular if the separation of hashing and (the core of) signing/verifying naturally reflects different entities performing the two tasks. For instance, consider that the core routines of signature schemes are often non-trivial to implement, e.g., for requiring both big number arithmetic optimized in assembly (i.e., raw machine instructions) and effective protection against side-channel attacks, so that they are best implemented in specialized low-level system libraries. The messages to be signed or verified, however, may instead emerge in programs written in high-level language, for instance in Python or Java. As typical cryptographic hash functions like SHA256 are optimized for implementation in software, including in software written in high-level languages, it is often desirable to let the high-level components compute $h \leftarrow hash(m)$ on their messages m, and to let the low-level components finalize the operation by computing $\sigma \leftarrow sgn(sk, h)$ or $0/1 \leftarrow vfy(vk, h, \sigma)$. That is, the HtS property may remove the need for copying potentially very long messages from the high-level application to the low-level core; more generally, it allows for cleanly decoupling the different components of an implementation.

Another example where the hashing of the message and the execution of the signature core is performed by different entities is when the core routines are implemented in secure hardware. For concreteness, consider a smartcard (or a

Hardware Security Module (HSM), or a Trusted Platform Module (TPM)) that is connected to a host computer and tasked with both correctly implementing the core signing algorithm and physically protecting the signing key from read-out, while the host computer provides the messages that are to be signed. With a generic signature scheme, each signing operation would require the host computer to stream the full message into the smartcard, which is often prohibitively slow.[1] However, if an HtS scheme is used, the host computer could just locally derive $h \leftarrow hash(m)$ and ask the smartcard to complete the signature computation as per $\sigma \leftarrow sgn(sk, h)$. The PKCS#11 standard [12], which regulates smartcards and security tokens, defines an API for precisely this, for instance for RSA and DSA and ECDSA signatures.

1.1 Contributions

The above examples make evident that for certain applications it is desirable, if not technically mandatory, that an employed signature scheme is of the HtS type. However, as these applications merely try to exploit a *technical artifact* of some constructions, it is not given that this type of use is actually secure. Indeed, formal security arguments for signatures are typically only provided with respect to the standard EUF and SUF notions (existential/strong unforgeability), and these do not consider an internal separation of the signing process into a hashing phase and a core operation phase, executed by different entities. That is, generically speaking, the HtS use of a signature scheme that was not designed with the HtS setting in mind, and only was confirmed to provide protection with respect to the standard security notions, might not result in a secure system in practice.

This article initiates the formal study of HtS signatures. While, not surprisingly, our formalizations of syntax and semantics are fairly close to those of textbook signature schemes, our security definitions bring important new aspects to light that are not touched upon by the classic notions: As HtS signatures systematically distinguish between an entity that provides and hashes the message, and a second entity that implements the core signing routine, it is only meaningful to pay specific attention to cases where at least one of these entities does not always behave honestly. (For instance, malware on the host computer might try to interact with a connected smartcard in a malicious way.) Indeed, we are able to identify an HtS signature scheme that is provably secure in the standard EUF/SUF sense (i.e., assuming that *hash+sgn* are always executed together), but for which a single malicious interaction with the core signing routine is sufficient to fully compromise the keys. To formally cover this with a meaningful security model, our game-based definitions cleanly distinguish the different executing entities of HtS schemes by making the separation of hashing, signing, and verifying explicit. In our model, the insecure protocol suggested above is indeed identified as weak.

---

[1] Smartcard standard ISO 7816 defines that transferring a raw byte into the smartcard takes 372 clock cycles, and suggests a clock rate of (below) 5 MHz. Hence, streaming a 10 MB document into a smartcard takes at least 12.5 min.

After having developed a formal understanding of HtS signature schemes, we revisit a number of standardized DLP-based candidates (most prominently: ECDSA), and study how their direct HtS interpretations behave in our model.[2] We can, perhaps surprisingly, confirm their security in all cases; however, this requires fresh dedicated arguments.

We finally consider the general question of how to convert large classes of signature schemes to secure HtS instances without breaking compatibility, i.e., without requiring modifications of the regular signing and verification algorithms. As a result for the class of signature schemes that employ a Merkle–Damgård hash function (e.g., SHA1 or SHA2) to process the message, we can show that if one moves the final compression function invocation of the hash function from the *hash* to the *sgn* routine, unforgeability in the HtS sense can be proved generically, under the assumption that the compression function can be modeled as an ideal primitive (random oracle).

2 Preliminaries

2.1 Notation

We define security games using pseudo-code, in which we use the := operator to create notational aliases. Variables written with capital letters denote either sets or (associative) arrays, and the items stored in arrays are indexed via square bracket notation. We write A[·] to refer to *all* the elements of array A. We use symbol ⋄ as a special character that designates the empty element. If X and Y are two sets, we write $X \overset{\cup}{\leftarrow} Y$ shorthand for $X \leftarrow X \cup Y$.

Games terminate when executing a 'Stop with v' instruction with a Boolean value v. We compactly write 'Lose' for 'Stop with False', 'Win' for 'Stop with True', 'Promise C' for 'If $\neg C$: Win', 'Require C' for 'If $\neg C$: Lose', etc., where C is a Boolean condition. For a game G invoked with an adversary $\mathcal{A}$ we write $\Pr[G(\mathcal{A})]$ for the probability that the game terminates with True.

In games we write 'Share x' if value x shall be communicated to the adversary (i.e., become public information). One way to realize this is by initializing a log string L to the empty string when the game starts, to implement the 'Share' instruction by appending to the log string as per $L \leftarrow L \, \textrm{\tiny II} \, x$, and to let all oracles always return the current copy of L. Precise implementation details of the Share instruction don't really matter—as long as the contents of x are communicated to the adversary.

2.2 Signature Schemes

We recall the established notions of digital signature schemes. Our definitions of existential and strong unforgeability (EUF and SUF, respectively) are equivalent

---

[2] We refer to an HtS interpretation of a signature scheme as *direct* if the HtS hash function *hash* is identified with a standard hash function H used by the signature scheme, e.g., $H = \text{SHA256}$.

with the textbook notions, but, for alignment with the peculiarities of the generalized signature schemes that we study in the upcoming sections, our notation assumes an explicit verification oracle.

DSS. A *digital signature scheme* for a message space $\mathcal{M}$ consists of a signing key space $\mathcal{SK}$, a verification key space $\mathcal{VK}$, a signature space Σ, a key generation algorithm $gen \rightarrow \mathcal{SK} \times \mathcal{VK}$, a signing algorithm $\mathcal{SK} \times \mathcal{M} \rightarrow sgn \rightarrow \Sigma$, and a verification algorithm $\mathcal{VK} \times \mathcal{M} \times \Sigma \rightarrow vfy \rightarrow \{0,1\}$. Intuitively, for correctness we expect that for all $m \in \mathcal{M}$ after $(sk, vk) \leftarrow gen$ and $\sigma \leftarrow sgn(sk, m)$ and $v \leftarrow vfy(vk, m, \sigma)$ we have $v = 1$.

In the context of code-based specifications of verification algorithms, we may write 'Accept' for 'Return 1' and 'Reject' for 'Return 0'. (See Fig. 8 for an example.)

Definition 1 (Unforgeability). *Consider the* $\mathbf{UF}^e, \mathbf{UF}^s$ *games of Fig. 1. We define the unforgeability advantages of an adversary $\mathcal{A}$ as per* $\mathbf{Adv}^{uf\text{-}e}(\mathcal{A}) := \Pr[\mathbf{UF}^e(\mathcal{A})]$ *and* $\mathbf{Adv}^{uf\text{-}s}(\mathcal{A}) := \Pr[\mathbf{UF}^s(\mathcal{A})]$, *respectively. Intuitively, we say that a DSS is existentially (respectively, strongly) unforgeable if* $\mathbf{Adv}^{uf\text{-}e}(\mathcal{A})$ *(resp.,* $\mathbf{Adv}^{uf\text{-}s}(\mathcal{A})$*) is negligible for all realistic $\mathcal{A}$.*

INITIALIZATIONS: A, A˙, V, V˙ $\leftarrow \emptyset$

Game $\mathbf{UF}^{e,s}(\mathcal{A})$	**Oracle Sgn(m)**	**Oracle Vfy(m, σ)**
00 $sk, vk \leftarrow gen$	05 $\sigma \leftarrow sgn(sk, m)$	09 $v \leftarrow vfy(vk, m, \sigma)$
01 $\mathcal{A}(vk)$	06 Share σ	10 Share v
02^e Promise $V \subseteq A$	07 A $\overset{\cup}{\leftarrow} \{m\}$	11 If v: V $\overset{\cup}{\leftarrow} \{m\}$
03^s Promise $V\dot{} \subseteq A\dot{}$	08 A˙ $\overset{\cup}{\leftarrow} \{(m, \sigma)\}$	12 If v: V˙ $\overset{\cup}{\leftarrow} \{(m, \sigma)\}$
04 Lose		

Fig. 1. Games $\mathbf{UF}^e$ and $\mathbf{UF}^s$ for Definition 1: Line 02 is part of $\mathbf{UF}^e$ but not of $\mathbf{UF}^s$, while line 03 is part of $\mathbf{UF}^s$ but not of $\mathbf{UF}^e$. See Sect. 2.1 for the definitions of the instructions Promise, Lose, and Share. Set variable A records the authentic messages (i.e., those indeed considered by the signer) while set variable V records the verified messages (i.e., those accepted as valid by the verifier). The set variables A˙ and V˙ are similar, but they record message-signature pairs instead of messages. By line 02 the adversary wins the $\mathbf{UF}^e$ game if it concludes with $V \not\subseteq A$ (equivalently: $V \setminus A \neq \emptyset$), i.e., if there exists a verified message that is not authentic. The winning condition of the $\mathbf{UF}^s$ game is analogous.

3   Hash-then-Sign Signatures: HtS

We formalize HtS signatures by making the separation of hashing and signing explicit: We assume an explicit (possibly seeded) hash function *hash* that maps (hash seeds *hs* and) messages m to hash values hv, and we adapt the syntax of the *sgn* and *vfy* algorithms so that they operate on hash values hv instead of on messages m. We provide the syntax and security definitions of HtS schemes, specify how to recover a regular DSS scheme (in the sense of Sect. 2.2) from an HtS scheme, and, as a separation result, demonstrate that signature schemes can be secure in the DSS sense while being weak in the HtS sense.

HTS-DSS. A *hash-then-sign digital signature scheme* for a message space $\mathcal{M}$ consists of a signing key space $\mathcal{SK}$, a verification key space $\mathcal{VK}$, a signature space Σ, a hash seed space $\mathcal{HS}$, a hash value space $\mathcal{HV}$, a key generation algorithm $gen \to \mathcal{SK} \times \mathcal{VK} \times \mathcal{HS}$, a hash function $\mathcal{HS} \times \mathcal{M} \to hash \to \mathcal{HV}$, and algorithms $\mathcal{SK} \times \mathcal{HV} \to sgn \to \Sigma$ and $\mathcal{VK} \times \mathcal{HV} \times \Sigma \to vfy \to \{0,1\}$. By composing the latter components in the way specified in Fig. 2 we obtain the associated spaces $\mathcal{SK}' := \mathcal{SK} \times \mathcal{HS}$ and $\mathcal{VK}' := \mathcal{VK} \times \mathcal{HS}$, and the algorithms $gen' \to \mathcal{SK}' \times \mathcal{VK}'$ and $\mathcal{SK}' \times \mathcal{M} \to sgn' \to \Sigma$ and $\mathcal{VK}' \times \mathcal{M} \times \Sigma \to vfy' \to \{0,1\}$. For correctness we expect the same of an HtS-DSS as of a DSS, i.e., that for all $m \in \mathcal{M}$ after $(sk', vk') \leftarrow gen'$ and $\sigma \leftarrow sgn'(sk', m)$ and $v \leftarrow vfy'(vk', m, \sigma)$ we have $v = 1$.

Proc. gen'	**Proc.** $sgn'(sk', m)$	**Proc.** $vfy'(vk', m, \sigma)$
00 $sk, vk, hs \leftarrow gen$	04 $hv \leftarrow hash(hs, m)$	07 $hv \leftarrow hash(hs, m)$
01 $sk' := (sk, hs)$	05 $\sigma \leftarrow sgn(sk, hv)$	08 $v \leftarrow vfy(vk, hv, \sigma)$
02 $vk' := (vk, hs)$	06 **Return** σ	09 **Return** v
03 **Return** sk', vk'		

Fig. 2. Algorithms gen', sgn', vfy' associated with an HtS-DSS scheme $(gen, hash, sgn, vfy)$.

We provide a security definition for HtS-DSS in Definition 2. Recall that a main motivation of this work is to study how HtS-DSS behave if the message hashing on the signer side is not conducted in a trustworthy way. (For instance, if the signing algorithm is implemented on a smartcard and only message hashes are to be provided by the host PC, malware could impersonate the PC and ask the smartcard to sign maliciously chosen hash values.) Correspondingly, our adapted versions of the EUF/SUF games have a signing oracle Sgn that takes a hash value hv instead of a message m. The adversary is not restricted in how it chooses these values. In contrast, the verification oracle Vfy of our games continues to work with messages, and performs the hashing step itself. (As verifying is a public operation, there is no point in implementing it on a smartcard or on trusted hardware, as no secrets have to be protected.)

As the signing oracle doesn't see the messages behind the hash values hv provided by the adversary,[3] in our HtS games it is not meaningful to have a winning condition based on the authenticity of messages. (More technically speaking, the sets A and A' of Fig. 1 cannot be defined in the HtS setting.) We instead define unforgeability based on hash values: In correspondence with the variables A

---

[3] ... and, possibly, such messages don't even exist ....

and V of Fig. 1, in games $\mathbf{HUF}^e, \mathbf{HUF}^s$ of Fig. 3 we let game variables B and W record the authentic and verified hash values, respectively, with the augmentation to B˙ and W˙ to define strong unforgeability. The winning condition is now clear: The adversary is deemed successful if there exists a verified hash value that is not authentic.

Definition 2 (Unforgeability of HtS-DSS). *Consider the* $\mathbf{HUF}^e, \mathbf{HUF}^s$ *games of Fig. 3. We define the unforgeability advantages of an adversary $\mathcal{A}$ as per* $\mathbf{Adv}^{\text{huf-e}}(\mathcal{A}) := \Pr[\mathbf{HUF}^e(\mathcal{A})]$ *and* $\mathbf{Adv}^{\text{huf-s}}(\mathcal{A}) := \Pr[\mathbf{HUF}^s(\mathcal{A})]$, *respectively. Intuitively, we say that an HtS-DSS is existentially (respectively, strongly) unforgeable if* $\mathbf{Adv}^{\text{huf-e}}(\mathcal{A})$ *(resp.,* $\mathbf{Adv}^{\text{huf-s}}(\mathcal{A})$*) is negligible for all realistic $\mathcal{A}$.*

INITIALIZATIONS: $B, B˙, W, W˙ \leftarrow \emptyset$

Game $\mathbf{HUF}^{e,s}(\mathcal{A})$	Oracle Sgn(hv)	Oracle Vfy(m, σ)
00 $sk, vk, hs \leftarrow gen$	05 $\sigma \leftarrow sgn(sk, hv)$	09 $hv \leftarrow hash(hs, m)$
01 $\mathcal{A}(vk, hs)$	06 Share σ	10 $v \leftarrow vfy(vk, hv, \sigma)$
02^e Promise $W \subseteq B$	07 $B \overset{\cup}{\leftarrow} \{hv\}$	11 Share v
03^s Promise $W˙ \subseteq B˙$	08 $B˙ \overset{\cup}{\leftarrow} \{(hv, \sigma)\}$	12 If v: $W \overset{\cup}{\leftarrow} \{hv\}$
04 Lose		13 If v: $W˙ \overset{\cup}{\leftarrow} \{(hv, \sigma)\}$

Fig. 3. Games $\mathbf{HUF}^e$ and $\mathbf{HUF}^s$ for Definition 2: Line 02 is part of $\mathbf{HUF}^e$ but not of $\mathbf{HUF}^s$, while line 03 is part of $\mathbf{HUF}^s$ but not of $\mathbf{HUF}^e$. See Sect. 2.1 for the definitions of the instructions Promise, Lose, and Share. Set variable B records the authentic hash values (i.e., those indeed considered by the signer) while set variable W records the hash values of verified messages (i.e., those accepted as valid by the verifier). The set variables B˙ and W˙ are similar, but they record hash-value–signature pairs instead of just hash values. By line 02 the adversary wins the $\mathbf{HUF}^e$ game if it concludes with $W \nsubseteq B$ (equivalently: $W \setminus B \neq \emptyset$), i.e., if there exists a verified hash value that is not authentic. The winning condition of the $\mathbf{HUF}^s$ game is analogous.

3.1 DSS-UF Does Not Imply HtS-UF

Many common signature schemes have signing procedures that can be considered compositions of dedicated hashing and core signing steps, so that it might be tempting to consider them HtS instances. We demonstrate generically that even if such a scheme is provably unforgeable (as a DSS), then the same doesn't necessarily also hold for its HtS analogue.

Consider the DSS (gen^*, sgn^*, vfy^*) specified in Fig. 4 which is constructed from an underlying unforgeable DSS (gen, sgn, vfy) and a collision-resistant and one-way hash function H (think of SHA256 for concreteness). Note that, in this construction, keys are generated together with the hash value h_0 of a magic message m_0 that is drawn from a high entropy distribution (lines 01,02) and then disposed of. The signing algorithm sgn^* is such that if it is ever invoked on input a pre-image m of h_0, then the signing key is leaked by appending it to the signature (lines 08,09; note how lines 12,13 peel off such appended keys to ensure the scheme remains correct). Fortunately, as hash function H is assumed to be one-way, no adversary can find such a pre-image. As H is further assumed collision resistant, it is clear that the unforgeability of DSS (gen^*, sgn^*, vfy^*) can be reduced to that of DSS (gen, sgn, vfy).

Consider next the natural HtS-DSS interpretation of (gen^*, sgn^*, vfy^*) where $hash = H$ and the signing and verification algorithms are represented by the colored boxes in Fig. 4. Clearly, any adversary for the **HUF** games of Fig. 3 that invokes the Sgn oracle on input h_0 will learn sk and can forge signatures on arbitrary messages. That is, the scheme of Fig. 4 is not a secure HtS-DSS.

Proc. gen*	**Proc. sgn***(sk^*, m)	**Proc. vfy***(vk^*, m, σ)
00 $sk, vk \leftarrow gen$	06 $h \leftarrow H(m)$	11 $h \leftarrow H(m)$
01 $m_0 \leftarrow \$$	07 $\sigma \leftarrow sgn(sk, h)$	12 If $h = h_0$:
02 $h_0 \leftarrow H(m_0)$	08 If $h = h_0$:	13 $\sigma \parallel \_ \leftarrow \sigma$
03 $sk^* := (sk, h_0)$	09 $\sigma \leftarrow \sigma \parallel sk$	14 $v \leftarrow vfy(vk, h, \sigma)$
04 $vk^* := (vk, h_0)$	10 Return σ	15 Return v
05 Return sk^*, vk^*		

Fig. 4. Signature scheme that is secure in the DSS sense but not in the HtS sense. The colored boxes indicate the signing and verification algorithms of the HtS construction.

3.2 Practical Non-Examples of HtS-DSS

The separation example of Sect. 3.1 might seem far fetched. We note, however, that also widely deployed DSS like BLS and RSA-FDH (e.g., in the form of PKCS1v1.5), when naively implemented, are non-candidates for HtS-DSS despite their assumed unforgeability in the classic sense.[4]

Consider the BLS signature scheme [3], where key pairs have the form $(sk, vk) = (x, X)$ with $X = g^x$, and signatures are computed as per $\sigma \leftarrow H(m)^x$. Towards an HtS-DSS interpretation, let $hash = H$ and sgn be the algorithm that maps $hv \mapsto hv^x$. Specify a **HUF** adversary $\mathcal{A}$ that picks an arbitrary message m^*, computes the corresponding hash value $hv^* \leftarrow H(m^*)$, derives a masked hash value $hv \leftarrow hv^* g^r$ from it (for some blinding value r), queries hv to the signing oracle to receive $\sigma = hv^x = H(m^*)^x X^r$, and finally outputs m^* together with $\sigma^* = \sigma/X^r$ as a forgery candidate. It is easy to see that (1) the vfy algorithm will accept the forgery, (2) the **HUF** game, as $hv \neq hv^*$, will count the forgery as valid.

---

[4] For any DSS there might be multiple different interpretations as an HtS-DSS. The negative results presented here assume the most natural interpretation. For other interpretations it might be possible to establish positive results.

The attack on RSA-FDH [1] is very similar, but with a multiplicative masking using a factor of the form r^e which is removed from the signature by dividing by $r^{ed} = r$.

4   Case Study: DLP-Based Signature Schemes

We study several DSA-like signature schemes from the ISO 14888-3 standard [6] with respect to whether they can be operated securely in the HtS sense. (Many more schemes exist and deserve a similar analysis, but we leave this to future work.) Specifically, in this article, we investigate the Korean ECKCDSA, the American ECDSA, the Chinese SM2, and the Russian GOST. Possibly surprisingly, we conclude with positive results on all of them. While the four schemes are quite similar in nature, we note that their analyses are dedicated and lead to different bounds. For instance, our proof of ECKCDSA requires an additional mild assumption about the hash function whereas the proof of ECDSA requires modeling the "conversion function" as a composition of three different functions (like in [4]).

In the following sections, we let E be an elliptic curve over a finite field F and q be a prime that divides $\#E$. We also let $\mathcal{G}$ be a cyclic group of elliptic curve points of order q. We denote by G the generator of that group and 0 the identity element. We define in Definition 3 a security notion for hash functions that will be later used for proving the security of ECKCDSA and SM2.

Definition 3. *Let H be a hash function that maps its domain D to a range R. For any efficient adversary $\mathcal{A}$ we define the advantage of breaking random preimage resistance (**RPR**) of H as follows:*

$$\mathbf{Adv}^{\mathrm{rpr}}(\mathcal{A}) := \Pr\left[H(m) = hv \colon hv \xleftarrow{\$} R,\, m \leftarrow \mathcal{A}(hv),\, m \in D\right] \quad.$$

We argue that the above security definition is attainable by all the common hash functions used (SHA2, SHA3, SM3, GOST R 34.11-2012, ...). As a matter of fact, such security definition is extremely close to the one-wayness definition if we assume that the hash function is surjective.

4.1   ECKCDSA

The ECKCDSA (Elliptic Curve Korean Certificate-based Digital Signature Algorithm) is a Korean signature scheme standardized in [6] and analyzed in [10]. The key point in this scheme is that an xor operation is computed between the hash of the message and a function output that we denote f (check Fig. 5 line 07). We introduce the associated HtS scheme of ECKCDSA in Fig. 6 and prove in the random oracle model that if the DSS version of ECKCDSA is secure and the hash function used is random preimage resistant, then the HtS version of ECKCDSA is also secure.

Theorem 1. *Let $f\colon F \to \{0,1\}^{\lceil \log q \rceil}$ be modeled as a random oracle and H be a hash function mapping $H\colon \mathcal{G} \times \{0,1\}^* \to \{0,1\}^{\lceil \log q \rceil}$. For every adversary $\mathcal{A}$ playing the $\mathbf{HUF}^s$ (resp. $\mathbf{HUF}^e$) game instantiated with the HtS version of ECKCDSA defined over E (represented in Fig. 6), there exists an adversary $\mathcal{B}$ playing the $\mathbf{UF}^s$ (resp. $\mathbf{UF}^e$) game instantiated with the original ECKCDSA scheme defined over E (represented in Fig. 5) and an adversary $\mathcal{C}$ that attempts to break the random preimage resistance of H such that:*

$$\mathbf{Adv}^{\text{huf-s}}(\mathcal{A}) \leq \mathbf{Adv}^{\text{uf-s}}(\mathcal{B}) + Q\mathbf{Adv}^{\text{rpr}}(\mathcal{C}) + \frac{Q(4Q+1)}{q}$$

respectively

$$\mathbf{Adv}^{\text{huf-e}}(\mathcal{A}) \leq \mathbf{Adv}^{\text{uf-e}}(\mathcal{B}) + Q\mathbf{Adv}^{\text{rpr}}(\mathcal{C}) + \frac{Q(4Q+1)}{q}$$

where Q represents the number of queries the adversary poses to the available oracles.

Proc. gen	**Proc.** sgn(sk, m)	**Proc.** vfy(vk, m, σ)
00 $x \xleftarrow{\$} \mathbb{Z}_q^*$	04 $r \xleftarrow{\$} \mathbb{Z}_q^*$	12 If $s \notin \mathbb{Z}_q^*$: Reject
01 $X \leftarrow [x^{-1}]G$	05 $R \leftarrow [r]G$	13 $w \leftarrow c \oplus H(X \parallel m)$
02 $(sk, vk) := (x, X)$	06 $c \leftarrow f(R_x)$	14 $w \leftarrow \text{S2I}(w) \bmod q$
03 Return sk, vk	07 $w \leftarrow c \oplus H(X \parallel m)$	15 $R \leftarrow [s]X + [w]G$
	08 $w \leftarrow \text{S2I}(w) \bmod q$	16 $c' \leftarrow f(R_x)$
	09 $s \leftarrow x(r - w) \bmod q$	17 If $c \neq c'$: Reject
	10 $\sigma := (c, s)$	18 Accept
	11 Return σ	

Fig. 5. ECKCDSA scheme. We denote by S2I the mapping from string to integer. An interesting element in this DSA-like signature is the xor operation in lines 07 and 13.

Proof. We prove the statement for the strong unforgeability notion; The existential unforgeability can be proven analogously.

We present the reduction $\mathcal{B}$ in Fig. 7. First, when $\mathcal{A}$ calls the signing oracle, $\mathcal{B}$ simulates a signature (c, s), then keeps track of the pair (R_x, c) in line 24. Then, when $\mathcal{A}$ calls the random oracle on a value R_x, the reduction checks whether R_x was already stored. If so, then $\mathcal{B}$ outputs the corresponding simulated value c, otherwise, it calls the random oracle $\bar{f}$ from $\mathbf{UF}$. When $\mathcal{A}$ calls the verification oracle on (m, c, s), the reduction computes the value R. If the latter has not been stored previously, then $\mathcal{B}$ forwards the call to oracle Vf$\bar{y}$ from $\mathbf{UF}$ and updates its internal state in line 40, otherwise, $\mathcal{B}$ verifies the validity of this tuple. Now, if s is a fresh value, i.e. has not been previously simulated, then $\mathcal{B}$ calls the extractor (line 49) to extract the discrete logarithm (a.k.a. the secret

Proc. gen	**Proc.** sgn(sk, hv)	**Proc.** vfy(vk, hv, σ)
00 $x \xleftarrow{\$} \mathbb{Z}_q^*$	07 $r \xleftarrow{\$} \mathbb{Z}_q^*$	15 If $s \notin \mathbb{Z}_q^*$: Reject
01 $X \leftarrow [x^{-1}]G$	08 $R \leftarrow [r]G$	16 $w \leftarrow c \oplus hv$
02 $hs := X$	09 $c \leftarrow f(R_x)$	17 $w \leftarrow \text{S2I}(w) \mod q$
03 $(sk, vk) := (x, X)$	10 $w \leftarrow c \oplus hv$	18 $R \leftarrow [s]X + [w]G$
04 Return sk, vk, hs	11 $w \leftarrow \text{S2I}(w) \mod q$	19 $c' \leftarrow f(R_x)$
	12 $s \leftarrow x(r - w) \mod q$	20 If $c \neq c'$: Reject
Proc. hash(hs, m)	13 $\sigma := (c, s)$	21 Accept
05 $hv \leftarrow H(hs \mathbin{\|} m)$	14 Return σ	
06 Return hv		

Fig. 6. ECKCDSA in HtS syntax.

key) and forges a new signature. The forged signature is sent to Vfȳ along with the corresponding message.

Notice that the simulated value c is sampled uniformly at random mimicking the random oracle output $\bar{f}$. Similarly, a simulated s is picked independently and uniformly at random which makes it indistinguishable from an honestly generated $s' = x(r - w)$ where r and w are picked uniformly at random. This implies that, if no collisions occur between the simulated R_x and the ones input to the random oracle $\bar{f}$ (condition insured in line 22), then a simulated signature is indistinguishable from an honestly generated signature. The probability of line 22 aborting is upper-bounded by $\frac{2Q^2}{q}$ (The factor 2 is an artifact of the existence of $q/2$ different R_x values. In fact, for each query the adversary makes to the signing oracle, the probability that the simulated R_x was already in $\bar{\mathrm{F}}$ is upper-bounded by $Q/(q/2)$. Since the adversary can make Q oracle queries, we conclude the rough upper bound[5].) Similarly, line 23 aborts with probability upper-bounded by $\frac{2Q^2}{q}$; This line corresponds to the case where the two different simulated values lead to the same coordinate R_x.

It is clear that the output of the procedure f is indistinguishable from the output of a random oracle.

We now argue that the verification is computed properly. In fact, line 39 will allow $\mathcal{A}$ to win if the forgery is valid. In this case, since R_x has not been simulated in Sgn, then at least one element of the tuple (m, c, s) must be fresh which implies that the forgery itself is fresh. Lines 42 and 43,44 respectively reflect the cases where $\mathcal{A}$ presented an invalid forgery and a non-fresh forgery. Finally, if the forgery is fresh and valid but the computed value R_x is a previously simulated one, then it possible to extract the secret key in 49. This secret key can now be used to generate a valid signature (due to correctness of the scheme) that is forwarded to Vfȳ allowing $\mathcal{A}$ to win the game.

---

[5] It is possible to further refine the upper bound by counting the number of queries made to each of the different oracles, however this does not imply the absence of a quadratic term.

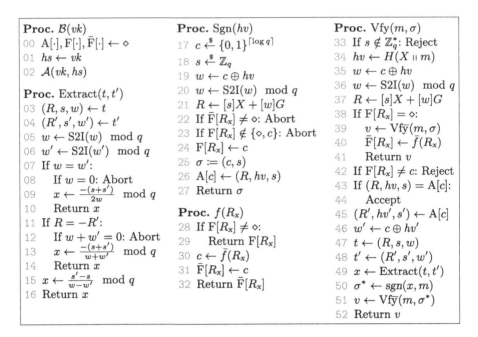

Proc. $\mathcal{B}(vk)$
00 $A[\cdot], F[\cdot], \bar{F}[\cdot] \leftarrow \diamond$
01 $hs \leftarrow vk$
02 $\mathcal{A}(vk, hs)$

Proc. Extract(t, t')
03 $(R, s, w) \leftarrow t$
04 $(R', s', w') \leftarrow t'$
05 $w \leftarrow \text{S2I}(w) \bmod q$
06 $w' \leftarrow \text{S2I}(w') \bmod q$
07 If $w = w'$:
08   If $w = 0$: Abort
09    $x \leftarrow \frac{-(s+s')}{2w} \bmod q$
10   Return x
11 If $R = -R'$:
12   If $w + w' = 0$: Abort
13    $x \leftarrow \frac{-(s+s')}{w+w'} \bmod q$
14   Return x
15 $x \leftarrow \frac{s'-s}{w-w'} \bmod q$
16 Return x

Proc. Sgn(hv)
17 $c \xleftarrow{\$} \{0,1\}^{\lceil \log q \rceil}$
18 $s \xleftarrow{\$} \mathbb{Z}_q$
19 $w \leftarrow c \oplus hv$
20 $w \leftarrow \text{S2I}(w) \bmod q$
21 $R \leftarrow [s]X + [w]G$
22 If $\bar{F}[R_x] \neq \diamond$: Abort
23 If $F[R_x] \notin \{\diamond, c\}$: Abort
24 $F[R_x] \leftarrow c$
25 $\sigma := (c, s)$
26 $A[c] \leftarrow (R, hv, s)$
27 Return σ

Proc. $f(R_x)$
28 If $F[R_x] \neq \diamond$:
29   Return $F[R_x]$
30 $c \leftarrow \bar{f}(R_x)$
31 $\bar{F}[R_x] \leftarrow c$
32 Return $\bar{F}[R_x]$

Proc. Vfy(m, σ)
33 If $s \notin \mathbb{Z}_q^*$: Reject
34 $hv \leftarrow H(X \parallel m)$
35 $w \leftarrow c \oplus hv$
36 $w \leftarrow \text{S2I}(w) \bmod q$
37 $R \leftarrow [s]X + [w]G$
38 If $F[R_x] = \diamond$:
39    $v \leftarrow \text{Vf}\bar{\text{y}}(m, \sigma)$
40    $\bar{F}[R_x] \leftarrow \bar{f}(R_x)$
41   Return v
42 If $F[R_x] \neq c$: Reject
43 If $(R, hv, s) = A[c]$:
44   Accept
45 $(R', hv', s') \leftarrow A[c]$
46 $w' \leftarrow c \oplus hv'$
47 $t \leftarrow (R, s, w)$
48 $t' \leftarrow (R', s', w')$
49 $x \leftarrow \text{Extract}(t, t')$
50 $\sigma^* \leftarrow \text{sgn}(x, m)$
51 $v \leftarrow \text{Vf}\bar{\text{y}}(m, \sigma^*)$
52 Return v

Fig. 7. ECKCDSA reduction from $\mathbf{HUF^s}$ to $\mathbf{UF^s}$. We superindex all the calls to the $\mathbf{UF^s}$ oracles by a bar (e.g. Vf$\bar{\text{y}}$ represents the call of the verification oracle in $\mathbf{UF^s}$). Line 08 aborts with negligible probability. If line 12 aborts, then it is possible to break $\mathbf{RPR}$ of H.

We now argue that the probability that Extract aborts during the Q queries is upper bounded by $\frac{Q}{q} + Q\mathbf{Adv}^{\text{rpr}}(\mathcal{C})$. As the matter of fact, on each call of Extract, the probability that line 08 aborts is the same as the probability of finding hv equals to a randomly generated c, i.e. $1/q$. Additionally, line 12 aborts only if the adversary manages to find a message m' that hashes to $hv' \leftarrow H(X \parallel m')$ where $hv' = c \oplus hv$ (here $c \oplus hv$ is known by the adversary but is uniformly random as c is picked uniformly at random). The probability of such event happening is upper bounded by the probability of breaking the $\mathbf{RPR}$ security notion of H, i.e., upper bounded by $\mathbf{Adv}^{\text{rpr}}(\mathcal{C})$. Notice that w can never be equals to w' in line 15 because in this case we know that $s \neq s'$, $r = r'$ and $c = c'$. The final equation can be thus concluded by combining all the previous bounds.

4.2   ECDSA

The ECDSA (Elliptic Curve Digital Signature Algorithm) is an American DSS also standardized in ISO 14888-3 [6]. We depict this scheme in Fig. 8: notice that part of the signature is computed using modular arithmetic of a field element mapped to an integer (check line 06 in Fig. 8). In order to prove the scheme secure, Fersch et al. [4] define this sequence of operations as a composition of three functions of which they model one as a bijective random oracle. In this work, we introduce an HtS variant of ECDSA in Fig. 9 and leverage on [4] to show that the unforgeability of DSS ECDSA reduces to the unforgeability of HtS ECDSA.

Theorem 2. *Let H be a hash function mapping $H \colon \{0,1\}^* \to \mathbb{Z}_q$. For every adversary $\mathcal{A}$ playing the $\mathbf{HUF}^e$ game instantiated with the HtS version of ECDSA defined over E (Fig. 9), there exists an adversary $\mathcal{B}$ playing the $\mathbf{UF}^e$ game instantiated with the original ECDSA scheme defined over E (Fig. 8) such that:*

$$\mathbf{Adv}^{\text{huf-e}}(\mathcal{A}) \le \mathbf{Adv}^{\text{uf-e}}(\mathcal{B}) + \frac{6Q^2}{q}$$

where Q is the number of queries $\mathcal{A}$ poses to the available oracles.

Proc. gen	Proc. sgn(sk, m)	Proc. vfy(vk, m, σ)
00 $x \xleftarrow{\$} \mathbb{Z}_q^*$	04 $r \xleftarrow{\$} \mathbb{Z}_q^*$	13 If $s = 0 \mod q$: Reject
01 $X \leftarrow [x]G$	05 $R \leftarrow [r]G$	14 If $c = 0 \mod q$: Reject
02 $(sk, vk) \coloneqq (x, X)$	06 $c \leftarrow \text{Fe2I}(R_x) \mod q$	15 $w \leftarrow H(m)$
03 Return sk, vk	07 If $c = 0$: goto line 04	16 $\alpha \leftarrow cs^{-1} \mod q$
	08 $w \leftarrow H(m)$	17 $\beta \leftarrow ws^{-1} \mod q$
	09 $s \leftarrow r^{-1}(cx + w) \mod q$	18 $R \leftarrow [\alpha]X + [\beta]G$
	10 If $s = 0$: goto line 04	19 $c' \leftarrow \text{Fe2I}(R_x) \mod q$
	11 $\sigma \coloneqq (c, s)$	20 If $c \ne c'$: Reject
	12 Return σ	21 Accept

Fig. 8. ECDSA scheme. We denote by Fe2I the mapping from field element to integer. This function is modeled as a bijective random oracle [4] in the proof.

Proc. gen	Proc. sgn(sk, hv)	Proc. vfy(vk, hv, σ)
00 $x \xleftarrow{\$} \mathbb{Z}_q^*$	07 $r \xleftarrow{\$} \mathbb{Z}_q^*$	16 If $s = 0 \mod q$: Reject
01 $X \leftarrow [x]G$	08 $R \leftarrow [r]G$	17 If $c = 0 \mod q$: Reject
02 $hs \coloneqq \varepsilon$	09 $c \leftarrow \text{Fe2I}(R_x) \mod q$	18 $w \leftarrow hv$
03 $(sk, vk) \coloneqq (x, X)$	10 If $c = 0$: goto line 07	19 $\alpha \leftarrow cs^{-1} \mod q$
04 Return sk, vk, hs	11 $w \leftarrow hv$	20 $\beta \leftarrow ws^{-1} \mod q$
	12 $s \leftarrow r^{-1}(cx + w) \mod q$	21 $R \leftarrow [\alpha]X + [\beta]G$
Proc. hash(hs, m)	13 If $s = 0$: goto line 07	22 $c' \leftarrow \text{Fe2I}(R_x) \mod q$
05 $hv \leftarrow H(m)$	14 $\sigma \coloneqq (c, s)$	23 If $c \ne c'$: Reject
06 Return hv	15 Return σ	24 Accept

Fig. 9. ECDSA in HtS syntax.

To prove such statement, we use the idea of Fersch, Kiltz and Poettering's work [4] that defines the conversion function in line 06 as a composition of three mappings $\psi \circ f \circ \phi$ from $\mathcal{G}$ to $\mathbb{Z}_q$. The first, ϕ, projects points in $\mathcal{G}$ to their x

component; The last, ψ, computes the modular arithmetic operation; The middle one, f, is a bijective function that disrupts the algebraic link between the domain and the range. The key point is to model f in the security proof by a bijective random oracle.

Proof. We give an overview of the proof, the detailed version can be found in Appendix A.1. The proof of such statement is similar to that of Theorem 1 of [4], except for the fact that collisions in H are not an issue here (e.g. in $\mathbf{HUF^e}$, $\mathcal{A}$ is rewarded when the presented hash value hv is fresh, not when the message m itself is fresh.) We illustrate the reduction in Fig. 10. In short, when $\mathcal{A}$ queries the signing oracle, the signature is simulated by the reduction and the simulated values are stored. When the adversary queries the bijective random oracle, the reduction outputs the simulated value if the input on which the random oracle has been queried is simulated, otherwise, the bijective random oracle (from game $\mathbf{HUF}$) is queried on the same input. The term $\frac{4Q^2}{q}$ is an artifact of lines 29, 30, and 31 which aim to prevent collisions between the bijective random oracle $\bar{f}$, $\bar{f}^{-1}$ and the simulated elements (R_x, hd). The verification is computed similarly to the previous proof: the adversary only wins if the input hv is fresh and the signature is valid. For this, oracle Vfy verifies locally the forgery if the hash value is not fresh (lines 50–56), otherwise it either directly calls Vfȳ on $\mathcal{A}$'s signature in line 61, or it is later called (line 71) after the secret key is extracted (line 69) then used to sign a message (line 70). The extractor here never aborts: for each of the three cases 07, 10 and 12, the denominator cannot be equals to zero. In fact, we know that $s, s' \in \mathbb{Z}_q^*$ and because of line 14 (Fig. 8) we have $c \neq 0$. Thus, for the first case, if $s = s'$ mod q then it is possible to deduce with basic linear algebra that $w = w'$ which contradicts line 50; the second case is settled straightforward; the third case is well defined because otherwise, if $s + s' = 0$ mod q where $s, s' \in \mathbb{Z}_q$ then we can deduce with simple linear algebra (setting $R = -R'$), that $w = w'$, which is contradicts line 09. With this we conclude our proof of Theorem 2.

4.3   SM2

The SM2 scheme is a Chinese DSS that is a variant of ECDSA (check Fig. 11). We modify SM2 in order to respect the HtS syntax in Fig. 12 and prove the security of this scheme. Our bounds comprises the probability of breaking $\mathbf{RPR}$ of the underlying hash function.

Theorem 3. *Let H be a hash function mapping $H\colon (\{0,1\}^* \times \mathcal{G}) \cup \{0,1\}^* \to \{0,1\}^{\lceil \log q \rceil}$. For every adversary $\mathcal{A}$ playing the $\mathbf{HUF^s}$ (resp. $\mathbf{HUF^e}$) instantiated with the HtS version SM2 defined over E (represented in Fig. 12), there exists an adversary $\mathcal{B}$ playing the $\mathbf{UF^s}$ (resp. $\mathbf{UF^e}$) instantiated with the original SM2 scheme defined over E (represented in Fig. 11) and $\mathcal{C}$ playing $\mathbf{RPR}$ game instantiated with H such that:*

$$\mathbf{Adv}^{\text{huf-s}}(\mathcal{A}) \leq \mathbf{Adv}^{\text{uf-s}}(\mathcal{B}) + Q\mathbf{Adv}^{\text{rpr}}(\mathcal{C}) + \frac{6Q^2}{q}$$

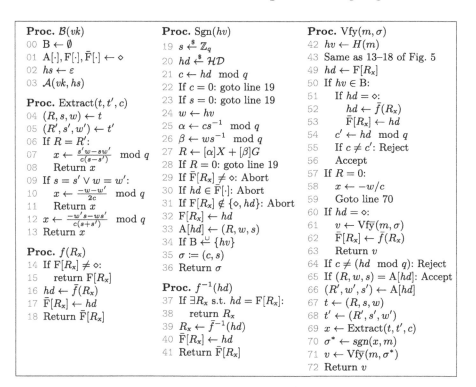

Proc. $\mathcal{B}(vk)$
00 $B \leftarrow \emptyset$
01 $A[\cdot], F[\cdot], \bar{F}[\cdot] \leftarrow \diamond$
02 $hs \leftarrow \varepsilon$
03 $\mathcal{A}(vk, hs)$

Proc. Extract(t, t', c)
04 $(R, s, w) \leftarrow t$
05 $(R', s', w') \leftarrow t'$
06 If $R = R'$:
07    $x \leftarrow \frac{s'w - sw'}{c(s - s')} \mod q$
08   Return x
09 If $s = s' \vee w = w'$:
10    $x \leftarrow \frac{-w - w'}{2c} \mod q$
11   Return x
12 $x \leftarrow \frac{-w's - ws'}{c(s + s')} \mod q$
13 Return x

Proc. $f(R_x)$
14 If $F[R_x] \neq \diamond$:
15   return $F[R_x]$
16 $hd \leftarrow \bar{f}(R_x)$
17 $\bar{F}[R_x] \leftarrow hd$
18 Return $\bar{F}[R_x]$

Proc. Sgn(hv)
19 $s \xleftarrow{\$} \mathbb{Z}_q$
20 $hd \xleftarrow{\$} \mathcal{HD}$
21 $c \leftarrow hd \mod q$
22 If $c = 0$: goto line 19
23 If $s = 0$: goto line 19
24 $w \leftarrow hv$
25 $\alpha \leftarrow cs^{-1} \mod q$
26 $\beta \leftarrow ws^{-1} \mod q$
27 $R \leftarrow [\alpha]X + [\beta]G$
28 If $R = 0$: goto line 19
29 If $\bar{F}[R_x] \neq \diamond$: Abort
30 If $hd \in \bar{F}[\cdot]$: Abort
31 If $F[R_x] \notin \{\diamond, hd\}$: Abort
32 $F[R_x] \leftarrow hd$
33 $A[hd] \leftarrow (R, w, s)$
34 If $B \xleftarrow{\cup} \{hv\}$
35 $\sigma := (c, s)$
36 Return σ

Proc. $f^{-1}(hd)$
37 If $\exists R_x$ s.t. $hd = F[R_x]$:
38   return R_x
39 $R_x \leftarrow \bar{f}^{-1}(hd)$
40 $\bar{F}[R_x] \leftarrow hd$
41 Return $\bar{F}[R_x]$

Proc. Vfy(m, σ)
42 $hv \leftarrow H(m)$
43 Same as 13–18 of Fig. 5
49 $hd \leftarrow F[R_x]$
50 If $hv \in B$:
51   If $hd = \diamond$:
52      $hd \leftarrow \bar{f}(R_x)$
53      $\bar{F}[R_x] \leftarrow hd$
54    $c' \leftarrow hd \mod q$
55   If $c \neq c'$: Reject
56   Accept
57 If $R = 0$:
58    $x \leftarrow -w/c$
59   Goto line 70
60 If $hd = \diamond$:
61    $v \leftarrow$ Vf$\bar{y}(m, \sigma)$
62    $\bar{F}[R_x] \leftarrow \bar{f}(R_x)$
63   Return v
64 If $c \neq (hd \mod q)$: Reject
65 If $(R, w, s) = A[hd]$: Accept
66 $(R', w', s') \leftarrow A[hd]$
67 $t \leftarrow (R, s, w)$
68 $t' \leftarrow (R', s', w')$
69 $x \leftarrow$ Extract(t, t', c)
70 $\sigma^* \leftarrow$ sgn(x, m)
71 $v \leftarrow$ Vf$\bar{y}(m, \sigma^*)$
72 Return v

Fig. 10. ECDSA reduction from **UF^e** to **HUF^e**. The conversion function is modeled as a composition of three functions. One of them, f is assumed to be a bijective random oracle. We superindex all the calls to the **UF^e** oracles by a bar. All the fractions in the extraction algorithm are well defined (check the proof for more details). We assume that the integers output by the bijective random oracle are picked from a set of integers $\mathcal{HD} := \mathbb{Z}_N$ where N is divisible by q. We call these integers 'handles' and denote them with hd.

respectively

$$\mathbf{Adv}^{\text{huf-e}}(\mathcal{A}) \leq \mathbf{Adv}^{\text{uf-e}}(\mathcal{B}) + Q\mathbf{Adv}^{\text{rpr}}(\mathcal{C}) + \frac{6Q^2}{q}$$

where Q is the number of queries $\mathcal{A}$ is allowed to make to the available oracles.

Proof. We give an overview of the proof here; the details can be found in Appendix A.2. The method for proving Theorem 3 is similar to that of ECDSA. We thus model the the conversion function in line 08 of Fig. 11 as a composition of three functions ϕ, f, ψ similarly to [4]. ϕ is a function mapping a group element to a field element by projecting the elliptic curve point to its first coordinate, f is a bijective random oracle that disrupts the algebraic links by mapping a field element to an integer, and ψ acts on integers and maps them to $\mathbb{Z}_q$ by computing the integer modulo q.

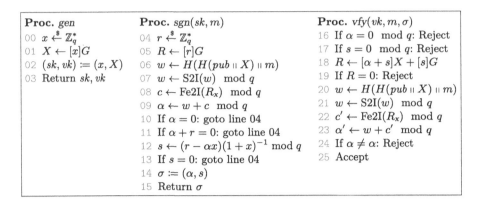

Proc. gen	**Proc.** sgn(sk, m)	**Proc.** vfy(vk, m, σ)
00 $x \xleftarrow{\$} \mathbb{Z}_q^*$	04 $r \xleftarrow{\$} \mathbb{Z}_q^*$	16 If $\alpha = 0 \mod q$: Reject
01 $X \leftarrow [x]G$	05 $R \leftarrow [r]G$	17 If $s = 0 \mod q$: Reject
02 $(sk, vk) := (x, X)$	06 $w \leftarrow H(H(pub \parallel X) \parallel m)$	18 $R \leftarrow [\alpha + s]X + [s]G$
03 Return sk, vk	07 $w \leftarrow \text{S2I}(w) \mod q$	19 If $R = 0$: Reject
	08 $c \leftarrow \text{Fe2I}(R_x) \mod q$	20 $w \leftarrow H(H(pub \parallel X) \parallel m)$
	09 $\alpha \leftarrow w + c \mod q$	21 $w \leftarrow \text{S2I}(w) \mod q$
	10 If $\alpha = 0$: goto line 04	22 $c' \leftarrow \text{Fe2I}(R_x) \mod q$
	11 If $\alpha + r = 0$: goto line 04	23 $\alpha' \leftarrow w + c' \mod q$
	12 $s \leftarrow (r - \alpha x)(1 + x)^{-1} \mod q$	24 If $\alpha \neq \alpha'$: Reject
	13 If $s = 0$: goto line 04	25 Accept
	14 $\sigma := (\alpha, s)$	
	15 Return σ	

Fig. 11. SM2 scheme (simplified). We denote by S2I the mapping from sting to integer and by Fe2I the mapping from field element to integer. The latter function is modeled as a bijective random oracle in the proof. In the specification, *pub* is a binary string made of the concatenation of some public data such as the bit-length of the signer's identifier, the verifier's identifier, the elliptic curve public parameters and the generator G.

We depict the adversary $\mathcal{B}$ in Fig. 13. $\mathcal{B}$ runs $\mathcal{A}$ and answers the signing queries by simulating in lines 13–22 properly. Right after the simulation, the reduction aborts on any possible collisions with the outputs of $\bar{f}, \bar{f}^{-1}$, then reprograms itself to answer the random oracle queries properly in lines 30 and 31. The verification oracle queries are answered with the same techniques as described in the section related to ECDSA, however of course, in a manner that is compatible with *vfy* function from Fig. 11.

We now focus on the extractor and argue why line 06 is well defined and why if line 10 aborts, then we can reduce the problem to breaking **RPR**.

First, the denominator on line 06 cannot be zero. In fact, we argue that when $r = r'$ (because $[r]G = R = R' = [r']G$), $w \neq w'$ which means that $s \neq s'$. Suppose that $w = w'$, then this implies that $\alpha' = w' + c = w + c = \alpha$. Combining this with the fact that $R = R'$ we thus have that $s = s'$. This case cannot happen generally after line 44 and particularly during the extraction process, as line 44 already eliminates the case where $(R', w', s') = (R, w, s) = A[hd]$. Next we notice that $[w + s + c]X + [s]G = R = R' = [w' + s' + c]X + [s']G$ which means that $[w - w' + s - s']X + [s - s']G = 0$. Thus if the denominator $w - w' + s - s'$ is actually equals to zero 0, then it must be that $s - s' = 0$ implying that $s = s'$. Because $R = R'$ the $s = s'$ implies that $w = w'$ which, again cannot be true as the same line 44 deals with such situation. This contradiction proves that when $R = R'$, $w - w' + s - s' \neq 0 \mod q$ in line 06.

As for the Abort line 10, we argue that this condition can only happen with probability $\mathbf{Adv}^{\text{rpr}}(\mathcal{C})$ for some adversary $\mathcal{C}$ and for each of the Q possible calls. In fact, we know that $[w + s + c]X + [s]G = R = -R' = [-w' - s' - c]X + [-s']G$ which leads to $[2c + w + w' + s + s']X + [s + s']G = 0$. If $2c + w + w' + s + s' = 0$ then it must be that $s + s' = 0 \mod q$. Replacing s by $(r - (w + c)x)(1 + x)^{-1}$ and s'

Proc. gen	Proc. sgn(sk, hv)	Proc. vfy(vk, hv, σ)
00 $x \xleftarrow{\$} \mathbb{Z}_q^*$	07 $r \xleftarrow{\$} \mathbb{Z}_q^*$	18 If $\alpha = 0 \mod q$: Reject
01 $X \leftarrow [x]G$	08 $R \leftarrow [r]G$	19 If $s = 0 \mod q$: Reject
02 $hs := pub \parallel X$	09 $w \leftarrow \text{S2I}(hv) \mod q$	20 $R \leftarrow [\alpha + s]X + [s]G$
03 $(sk, vk) := (x, X)$	10 $c \leftarrow \text{Fe2I}(R_x) \mod q$	21 If $R = 0$: Reject
04 Return sk, vk, hs	11 $\alpha \leftarrow w + c \mod q$	22 $w \leftarrow \text{S2I}(hv) \mod q$
	12 If $\alpha = 0$: goto line 07	23 $c' \leftarrow \text{Fe2I}(R_x) \mod q$
Proc. hash(hs, m)	13 If $\alpha + r = 0$: goto line 07	24 $\alpha' \leftarrow w + c' \mod q$
05 $hv \leftarrow H(H(hs) \parallel m)$	14 $s \leftarrow (r - \alpha x)(1 + x)^{-1} \mod q$	25 If $\alpha \neq \alpha'$: Reject
06 Return hv	15 If $s = 0$: goto line 07	26 Accept
	16 $\sigma := (\alpha, s)$	
	17 Return σ	

Fig. 12. SM2 in HtS syntax.

by $(-r - (w' + c)x)(1 + x)^{-1}$ we deduce that $w' = -(2c + w) \mod q$. Rewriting w' as $H(m^*)$ for some m^* and noticing that (all but one bit of) $-(2c+w) \mod q$ is uniformly random, then it is possible to reduce the problem of finding such m^* to breaking **RPR** of H for $\lceil \log q \rceil - 1$ bits.

4.4 GOST

GOST R 34.10-2012 is a Russian DSS standardized in ISO 14888-3 [6] under the acronym of ECRDSA. This scheme uses identical steps as ECDSA of Fig. 8 to compute part of the signature (denoted with c in Fig. 14). We present an HtS variant of GOST in Fig. 15 and employ a similar method as in the previous ECDSA analysis to show a reduction between **UF**^{e,s} instantiated with the DSS variant of GOST and **HUF**^{e,s} instantiated with the HtS variant of GOST.

Theorem 4. *Let H be a hash function mapping $H: \{0,1\}^* \to \mathbb{Z}_q$. For every adversary $\mathcal{A}$ playing the **HUF**^{s} (resp. **HUF**^{e}) instantiated with the HtS version of GOST defined over E (represented in Fig. 15), there exists an adversary $\mathcal{B}$ playing the **UF**^{s} (resp. **UF**^{e}) instantiated with the original GOST scheme defined over E (represented in Fig. 14) such that:*

$$\mathbf{Adv}^{\text{huf-s}}(\mathcal{A}) \leq \mathbf{Adv}^{\text{uf-s}}(\mathcal{B}) + \frac{6Q^2}{q}$$

respectively

$$\mathbf{Adv}^{\text{huf-e}}(\mathcal{A}) \leq \mathbf{Adv}^{\text{uf-e}}(\mathcal{B}) + \frac{6Q^2}{q}$$

where Q is the number of queries $\mathcal{A}$ is allowed to make to the available oracles.

Proof. We give an overview of the proof here; the details can be found in Appendix A.3. Our proof techniques are similar to that of SM2. Once again, we model the conversion function as a composition of three functions where the

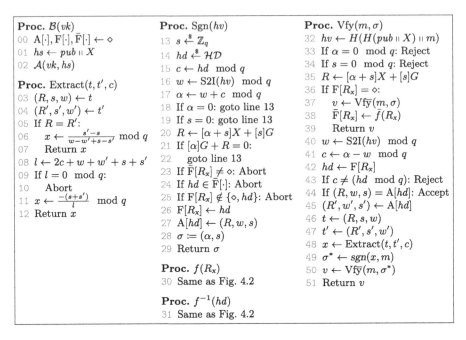

Proc. $\mathcal{B}(vk)$
00 $A[\cdot], F[\cdot], \bar{F}[\cdot] \leftarrow \diamond$
01 $hs \leftarrow pub \parallel X$
02 $\mathcal{A}(vk, hs)$

Proc. Extract(t, t', c)
03 $(R, s, w) \leftarrow t$
04 $(R', s', w') \leftarrow t'$
05 If $R = R'$:
06 $\quad x \leftarrow \frac{s'-s}{w-w'+s-s'} \bmod q$
07 $\quad$ Return x
08 $l \leftarrow 2c + w + w' + s + s'$
09 If $l = 0 \bmod q$:
10 $\quad$ Abort
11 $x \leftarrow \frac{-(s+s')}{l} \bmod q$
12 Return x

Proc. Sgn(hv)
13 $s \xleftarrow{\$} \mathbb{Z}_q$
14 $hd \xleftarrow{\$} \mathcal{HD}$
15 $c \leftarrow hd \bmod q$
16 $w \leftarrow$ S2I$(hv) \bmod q$
17 $\alpha \leftarrow w + c \bmod q$
18 If $\alpha = 0$: goto line 13
19 If $s = 0$: goto line 13
20 $R \leftarrow [\alpha + s]X + [s]G$
21 If $[\alpha]G + R = 0$:
22 $\quad$ goto line 13
23 If $\bar{F}[R_x] \neq \diamond$: Abort
24 If $hd \in \bar{F}[\cdot]$: Abort
25 If $F[R_x] \notin \{\diamond, hd\}$: Abort
26 $F[R_x] \leftarrow hd$
27 $A[hd] \leftarrow (R, w, s)$
28 $\sigma := (\alpha, s)$
29 Return σ

Proc. $f(R_x)$
30 Same as Fig. 4.2

Proc. $f^{-1}(hd)$
31 Same as Fig. 4.2

Proc. Vfy(m, σ)
32 $hv \leftarrow H(H(pub \parallel X) \parallel m)$
33 If $\alpha = 0 \bmod q$: Reject
34 If $s = 0 \bmod q$: Reject
35 $R \leftarrow [\alpha + s]X + [s]G$
36 If $F[R_x] = \diamond$:
37 $\quad v \leftarrow$ Vf$\bar{y}(m, \sigma)$
38 $\quad \bar{F}[R_x] \leftarrow \bar{f}(R_x)$
39 $\quad$ Return v
40 $w \leftarrow$ S2I$(hv) \bmod q$
41 $c \leftarrow \alpha - w \bmod q$
42 $hd \leftarrow F[R_x]$
43 If $c \neq (hd \bmod q)$: Reject
44 If $(R, w, s) = A[hd]$: Accept
45 $(R', w', s') \leftarrow A[hd]$
46 $t \leftarrow (R, s, w)$
47 $t' \leftarrow (R', s', w')$
48 $x \leftarrow$ Extract(t, t', c)
49 $\sigma^* \leftarrow$ sgn(x, m)
50 $v \leftarrow$ Vf$\bar{y}(m, \sigma^*)$
51 Return v

Fig. 13. SM2 reduction from $\mathbf{UF}^s$ to $\mathbf{HUF}^s$. The conversion function is modeled as a composition of three functions. One of them, f is assumed to be a bijective random oracle. We denote the range of f by $\mathcal{HD} := \mathbb{Z}_N$ and assume that N is divisible by q. We call the integers in $\mathcal{HD}$ 'handles' and denote them with hd. For simplicity, we superindex all the calls to the $\mathbf{UF}^s$ oracle by a bar (e.g. Vf$\bar{y}$ represents the call of the verification oracle in $\mathbf{UF}^s$). If the extraction algorithm aborts in line 10 then it is possible to define an adversary that breaks **RPR** of the hash function H.

middle one f is modeled as a bijective random oracle. As the previous proof, the signature process carefully simulates the pair (c, s) and aborts when a collision occurs with the random oracle output. In Fig. 16, the probability that any of the lines 18, 19 and 20 abort is upper-bounded by $3 \times \frac{2Q^2}{q}$. Next, during verification, the reduction isolates the cases where the delivered forgery is fresh and valid from all the other cases. In line 46 the extraction algorithm is called.

We argue that both lines 04 and 06 are well defined. For line 04, if $w = w'$ then it must be that $s = s'$. However this contradicts the fact that this case is already covered by line 42. As for line 06, if $w = -w'$ then still $s = s'$. This implies that $[sw^{-1}]G + [-cw^{-1}]X = R = -R' = -([-sw^{-1}]G + [cw^{-1}]X) = -R$ which means that $R = 0$ which contradicts the fact that this condition has already been checked by line 35. This concludes the proof of Theorem 4.

Proc. gen	Proc. sgn(sk, m)	Proc. vfy(vk, m, σ)
00 $x \xleftarrow{\$} \mathbb{Z}_q^*$	04 $r \xleftarrow{\$} \mathbb{Z}_q^*$	14 If $s = 0 \mod q$: Reject
01 $X \leftarrow [x]G$	05 $R \leftarrow [r]G$	15 If $c = 0 \mod q$: Reject
02 $(sk, vk) := (x, X)$	06 $w \leftarrow H(m)$	16 $w \leftarrow H(m)$
03 Return sk, vk	07 $c \leftarrow \text{Fe2I}(R_x) \mod q$	17 If $w = 0$: $w \leftarrow 1$
	08 If $c = 0$: goto line 04	18 $\alpha \leftarrow sw^{-1} \mod q$
	09 If $w = 0$: $w \leftarrow 1$	19 $\beta \leftarrow -cw^{-1} \mod q$
	10 $s \leftarrow (cx + rw) \mod q$	20 $R \leftarrow [\alpha]G + [\beta]X$
	11 If $s = 0$: goto line 04	21 If $R = 0$: Reject
	12 $\sigma := (c, s)$	22 $c' \leftarrow \text{Fe2I}(R_x) \mod q$
	13 Return σ	23 If $c \neq c'$: Reject
		24 Accept

Fig. 14. GOST scheme (simplified). We denote by Fe2I the mapping from field element to integer. This function is modeled as a bijective random oracle in the proof.

Proc. gen	Proc. sgn(sk, hv)	Proc. vfy(vk, hv, σ)
00 $x \xleftarrow{\$} \mathbb{Z}_q^*$	07 $r \xleftarrow{\$} \mathbb{Z}_q^*$	17 If $s = 0 \mod q$: Reject
01 $X \leftarrow [x]G$	08 $R \leftarrow [r]G$	18 If $c = 0 \mod q$: Reject
02 $hs := \varepsilon$	09 $w \leftarrow hv$	19 $w \leftarrow hv$
03 $(sk, vk) := (x, X)$	10 $c \leftarrow \text{Fe2I}(R_x) \mod q$	20 If $w = 0$: $w \leftarrow 1$
04 Return sk, vk, hs	11 If $c = 0$: goto line 07	21 $\alpha \leftarrow sw^{-1} \mod q$
	12 If $w = 0$: $w \leftarrow 1$	22 $\beta \leftarrow -cw^{-1} \mod q$
Proc. hash(hs, m)	13 $s \leftarrow (cx + rw) \mod q$	23 $R \leftarrow [\alpha]G + [\beta]X$
05 $hv \leftarrow H(m)$	14 If $s = 0$: goto line 07	24 If $R = 0$: Reject
06 Return hv	15 $\sigma := (c, s)$	25 $c' \leftarrow \text{Fe2I}(R_x) \mod q$
	16 Return σ	26 If $c \neq c'$: Reject
		27 Accept

Fig. 15. GOST in HtS syntax.

5   From MD-Based DSS to HtS-DSS

We introduce a generic conversion mechanism that allows any unforgeable signature scheme from Fig. 2 to be written in the HtS-DSS syntax while preserving unforgeability. This method can be utilized when the hash function is a Merkle–Damgård construction. The benefits of this conversion are threefold: (1) All DSS schemes from Fig. 2 where the underlying hash function is MD-based can benefit from it, including those schemes where the hash function is not originally outsourceable (check BLS, RSA-FDH and PKCS1v1.5 schemes in Sect. 3.2). (2) It requires no additional cryptographic primitives or hashing steps. (3) The signatures produced by the HtS-DSS signing algorithm are compatible with the original DSS verification algorithm.

In a nutshell, the conversion mechanism described in Fig. 17 strips off one compression function from the outsourced hash function and moves it into the signing algorithm. In particular, Fig. 17 bares in it two main steps.

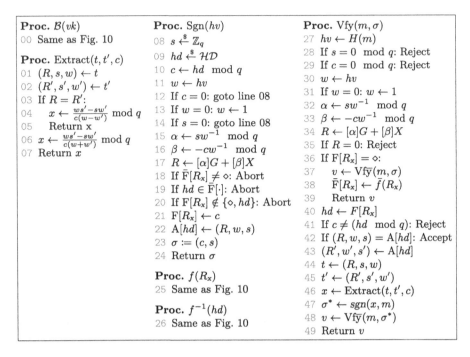

Proc. $\mathcal{B}(vk)$	**Proc.** Sgn(hv)	**Proc.** Vfy(m, σ)
00 Same as Fig. 10	08 $s \xleftarrow{\$} \mathbb{Z}_q$	27 $hv \leftarrow H(m)$
	09 $hd \xleftarrow{\$} \mathcal{HD}$	28 If $s = 0 \mod q$: Reject
Proc. Extract(t, t', c)	10 $c \leftarrow hd \mod q$	29 If $c = 0 \mod q$: Reject
01 $(R, s, w) \leftarrow t$	11 $w \leftarrow hv$	30 $w \leftarrow hv$
02 $(R', s', w') \leftarrow t'$	12 If $c = 0$: goto line 08	31 If $w = 0$: $w \leftarrow 1$
03 If $R = R'$:	13 If $w = 0$: $w \leftarrow 1$	32 $\alpha \leftarrow sw^{-1} \mod q$
04 $\quad x \leftarrow \frac{ws'-sw'}{c(w-w')} \mod q$	14 If $s = 0$: goto line 08	33 $\beta \leftarrow -cw^{-1} \mod q$
05 $\quad$ Return x	15 $\alpha \leftarrow sw^{-1} \mod q$	34 $R \leftarrow [\alpha]G + [\beta]X$
06 $x \leftarrow \frac{ws'-sw'}{c(w+w')} \mod q$	16 $\beta \leftarrow -cw^{-1} \mod q$	35 If $R = 0$: Reject
07 Return x	17 $R \leftarrow [\alpha]G + [\beta]X$	36 If $\mathrm{F}[R_x] = \diamond$:
	18 If $\bar{\mathrm{F}}[R_x] \neq \diamond$: Abort	37 $\quad v \leftarrow \overline{\mathrm{Vfy}}(m, \sigma)$
	19 If $hd \in \bar{\mathrm{F}}[\cdot]$: Abort	38 $\quad \bar{\mathrm{F}}[R_x] \leftarrow \bar{f}(R_x)$
	20 If $\mathrm{F}[R_x] \notin \{\diamond, hd\}$: Abort	39 $\quad$ Return v
	21 $\mathrm{F}[R_x] \leftarrow c$	40 $hd \leftarrow \mathrm{F}[R_x]$
	22 $\mathrm{A}[hd] \leftarrow (R, w, s)$	41 If $c \neq (hd \mod q)$: Reject
	23 $\sigma := (c, s)$	42 If $(R, w, s) = \mathrm{A}[hd]$: Accept
	24 Return σ	43 $(R', w', s') \leftarrow \mathrm{A}[hd]$
		44 $t \leftarrow (R, s, w)$
	Proc. $f(R_x)$	45 $t' \leftarrow (R', s', w')$
	25 Same as Fig. 10	46 $x \leftarrow$ Extract(t, t', c)
		47 $\sigma^* \leftarrow \mathrm{sgn}(x, m)$
	Proc. $f^{-1}(hd)$	48 $v \leftarrow \overline{\mathrm{Vfy}}(m, \sigma^*)$
	26 Same as Fig. 10	49 Return v

Fig. 16. GOST reduction from **UF**[s] to **HUF**[s]. The conversion function is modeled as a composition of three functions. One of them, f is assumed to be a bijective random oracle. We denote the range of f by $\mathcal{HD} := \mathbb{Z}_N$ and assume that N is divisible by q. We call the integers in $\mathcal{HD}$ 'handles' and denote them with hd. For simplicity, we superindex all the calls to the **UF**[s] oracles by a bar (e.g. $\overline{\mathrm{Vfy}}$ represents the call of the verification oracle in **UF**[s]). The extraction algorithm does not abort as all the fractions are well defined (check the proof for more details).

1. Pad the input message and split the padded message into a prefix m' and a suffix m^*. Then, perform a sequence of MD compression functions (denoted with h) with m' given as input.
2. Perform a single compression function over the chaining value and m^* then deliver the output value to the DSS signature algorithm.

Theorem 5 states that the mentioned conversion method preserves the security of the HtS-DSS scheme when the compression function is modeled as an ideal one.

We denote with CF the compression function and with *pad* the padding function. CF maps $\{0,1\}^c \times \{0,1\}^r$ to $\{0,1\}^r$ where c and r are positive integers, and *pad* maps bitstrings of arbitrary lengths to bitstrings of lengths multiples of c.

Theorem 5. *Let hash be a Merkle–Damgård (MD) construction that pads the input with pad then utilizes the underlying compression function* CF.

gen^*	$hash^*(hs, m)$	Proc. $sgn^*(sk, hv^*)$	Proc. $vfy^*(vk, hv^*, \sigma)$
00 $(sk, vk, hs) \leftarrow gen$	02 $m \leftarrow pad(m)$	07 $hv \leftarrow CF(cv^*, m^*)$	10 $hv \leftarrow CF(cv^*, m^*)$
01 Return sk, vk, hs	03 $m' \parallel m^* \leftarrow m$	08 $\sigma \leftarrow sgn(sk, hv)$	11 $v \leftarrow vfy(vk, hv, \sigma)$
	04 $cv^* \leftarrow h(hs, m')$	09 Return σ	12 Return v
	05 $hv^* := (cv^*, m^*)$		
	06 Return hv^*		

Fig. 17. (gen, sgn, vfy) are the "core" algorithms in Fig. 2. pad is an injective padding algorithm (used in real-world MD-based hash functions) and CF is the compression function. The sequence of compression functions calls that input the prefix m' are denoted by h. m^* is a bitstring of length equals the block size of the compression function. We assume here that $CF\colon \{0,1\}^c \times \{0,1\}^r \to \{0,1\}^r$ where c and r are positive integers, $\mathcal{HS} := \{0,1\}^c$, $\mathcal{HV} := \{0,1\}^r$ and $\mathcal{HV}^* := \{0,1\}^c \times \{0,1\}^r$.

Let (gen, sgn, vfy) be any DSS. Let S' be the DSS construction defined in Fig. 2 and $S^* := (gen^*, hash^*, sgn^*, vfy^*)$ be the HtS-DSS defined in Fig. 17.

Modeling CF as an ideal compression function, we have that, for every adversary $\mathcal{A}$ playing $\mathbf{HUF}^{e,s}$ instantiated with S^* there exists an adversary $\mathcal{B}$ playing $\mathbf{UF}^{e,s}$ instantiated with S' such that:

$$\mathbf{Adv}^{huf\text{-}e}(\mathcal{A}) \leq \mathbf{Adv}^{uf\text{-}e}(\mathcal{B}) + \frac{7Q^2}{2^c} + \frac{Q^2}{2^r - Q}$$

and

$$\mathbf{Adv}^{huf\text{-}s}(\mathcal{A}) \leq \mathbf{Adv}^{uf\text{-}s}(\mathcal{B}) + \frac{7Q^2}{2^c} + \frac{Q^2}{2^r - Q}$$

where Q is the total number of oracle queries $\mathcal{A}$ is allowed to make.

To prove the theorem, we build a reduction that keeps track of the 'history' of an input chaining value (the set of messages/chaining value pairs that led to this input chaining value). If the input chaining value is 'stray' (the reduction has never encountered the input chaining value before), then a message history is simulated and assigned to it. All output chaining values are computed using the external compression function oracle called on the message history (associated to the input chaining value) and the input message. This simulation algorithm is used to answer $\mathcal{A}$'s queries to both, the signing oracle and the compression function oracle. Of course, in the case of answering the queries to signing oracle, the reduction calls the external signing oracle on the simulated message history. The reduction can output coherent answers in both signing and compressing oracles. For the verification oracle, the external verification oracle is called on the given inputs.

Proof. We present the reduction in Fig. 18 of Appendix B. We exploit the specificity of S' (check Fig. 2) to prove Theorem 5. First, we argue why the procedure Sgn in Fig. 18 is indistinguishable from its corresponding oracle Sgn in Fig. 3. In fact, when $\overline{\text{Sgn}}$ is called in line 18 of Fig. 18, the oracle internally calls the MD construction (outputting a string picked uniformly at random) and signs the hash value using sgn. The outputs of sgn all share the same distributions when the inputs are uniformly random.

Similarly, we argue that if the reduction does not abort, then the output of $\overline{\text{CF}}$ is indistinguishable from the output of CF. In fact, in the latter, if the same elements are input twice, then the same value is output twice (line 21). Otherwise, the simulator Sim is called which in its turn calls $\bar{h}$ (line 29) that itself calls $\overline{\text{CF}}$ sequentially. The output from $\bar{h}$ is returned by CF which shows that CF is indistinguishable from $\overline{\text{CF}}$.

Left to show that if the reduction does not abort, then CF and Sgn are coherent in the sense of $\mathcal{A}$ cannot distinguish between the real world and the simulated world simply by alternating queries to the signing and compression function oracles. Before diving into the details of Sim notice that it is the same simulation algorithm that is called in lines 22 and 17. In line 25, the simulator uses Unroll to recover the full known history of the pair (cv^*, m^*); This is done by unwinding in lines 12–14. Notice that Unroll (proving by induction) never outputs cv such that $\text{PRE}[cv] = \Diamond$ because the base case leads to either the first line 11 aborting, or 12 is never executed meaning that $\text{PRE}[cv] \in \{\epsilon, \Diamond\}$. If the recovered chaining value is stray then line 27 is executed assigning a simulated message to this chaining value. Now, a sequence of compression functions is executed over the (potentially) simulated message along with the recovered message history (line 29). Of course the history table is updated in lines 31 and 08 (in other words, the random oracle is reprogrammed.) Because the history of a chain value cv^* is unique, and because the underlying compression functions are called to assign a new chaining value $\bar{cv}$ for a pair (cv^*, m^*), then it both Sgn and CF are consistent in their outputs.

We now calculate the probability of collisions occurring, i.e. the probability of $\mathcal{B}$ aborting. All the Abort statements can be found in the simulator Sim. Everytime Sim is called, PRE is updated at most 3 times in 07, 08 and 31. Observing that SimM picks a fresh, uniformly random string m', the probability of line 30 aborting can be upper-bounded by $\frac{3Q}{2^c}$ for each of the Q queries. Additionally, the only way of 11 aborting is that the adversary finds cv^* that is restricted ($\text{PRE}[cv^*] = \Diamond$). Finding such (secret) value is a pure luck matter since the restricted chaining values are output by $\overline{\text{CF}}$ and which the input is fresh and uniformly random. Thus the probability of 11 aborting is upper-bounded by $\frac{Q}{2^c}$ for each of the Q queries.

Finally, aborting in line 30 corresponds to one of the two cases: (1) either $\mathcal{A}$ manages to guess one of those secretly simulated m' from 04 (2) or it did not but line 29 output a value that collided with some previously generated chaining value (on different inputs). The probability of the first event happening can be upper-bounded by $\frac{Q}{2^r - Q}$ for each of the Q queries. The probability of the second event can be upper-bounded by $\frac{3Q}{2^c}$ for each of the Q queries Summing up the probabilities together, we conclude the proof of Theorem 5.

6 Conclusion

The common Hash-then-Sign (HtS) construction paradigm for signature schemes promotes hashing a message with a collision-resistant hash function before producing the signature from the hash with a signing core. However, the security of this approach is a priori unclear, in particular if the hashing is performed by a party that cannot be fully trusted. This work formalizes the syntax of HtS schemes and proposes corresponding security definitions. We analyze a selection of standardized DLP-based signature schemes (specifically ECKCDSA, ECDSA, SM2 and GOST) and are able to prove them secure according to our definitions. We further develop a technique that generically transforms Merkle–Damgård hashing based signature schemes into secure HtS instances.

A   Detailed Proofs

In this section, we provide detailed proofs for the three theorems Theorem 2, Theorem 3 and Theorem 4 in the strong unforgeability setting; the existential unforgeability can be proven analogously.

A.1   Detailed proof of ECDSA

We argue that the reduction $\mathcal{B}$ in Fig. 10 simulates properly an $\mathbf{HUF}^e$ interface. First, when $\mathcal{A}$ calls the signing oracle, $\mathcal{B}$ outputs a signature $\sigma := (c, s)$ where c and s are picked independently. s is picked uniformly at random from $\mathbb{Z}_q$ whereas c is computed the modular arithmetic of a uniformly random element from $\mathcal{HD}$. Since $\mathcal{HD} := \mathbb{Z}_N$ is assumed to have a size multiple of q, then c is a uniformly random element in $\mathbb{Z}_q$. In $\mathbf{HUF}^e$, Sgn returns a pair (c, s) where c is an output of a (bijective) random oracle evaluated on a freshly picked random input, and s is defined by $r^{-1}(xc + w) \mod q$ where r, x and c are independent and uniformly random and q is prime. The output of Sgn in $\mathcal{B}$ is indistinguishable from that of $\mathbf{HUF}^e$. Because, s, c and X are uniformly random, the simulated R value is also uniformly random (specifically its x coordinate R_x). This implies that when querying f^{-1}, the output is either the simulated R_x or the output of the random oracle $\bar{f}^{-1}$. In both cases, the simulation is indistinguishable from the output of $\bar{f}^{-1}$. In the case of f, the output is either the simulated uniformly random hd value or the output of the random oracle $\bar{f}$. Finally, we argue the output of the simulated verification oracle Vfy is indistinguishable from that of Vf$\bar{y}$. In fact, lines 13 and 14 (appearing in Fig. 8) return exactly the same Boolean constant as lines 16 and 17 of Fig. 9. Lines 50–56 simulate properly the case where the hash value is not fresh, thus $\mathcal{B}$ computes locally the verification of the forgery and returns the corresponding Boolean. Next, it is clear that line 63 returns a Boolean constant (computed in line 61) indistinguishable from the output of Vf$\bar{y}(m, \sigma)$. Line 64 of Fig. 10 computes the similar check (the only difference is the reprogramming of the random oracle f, f^{-1}) as line 23 of Fig. 9 and rejects. Line 65 of Fig. 10 accepts as $\mathcal{A}$ queried a non-fresh, authentic, pair (hv, σ). In fact, line 23 tests the authenticity of the queried c value, then because of line 65 we know that s and $w := hv$ is also authentic, thus the reduction $\mathcal{B}$ accepts as ECDSA is a correct scheme.

We now calculate the probability of having the reduction Abort. Line 29 prevents collisions between the simulated R_x and the ones queried to/generated by the random oracle in lines 16/39 from happening. Similarly, line 30 prevents collisions between the simulated hd and the ones queried to/generated by the random oracle in lines 39/16. Finally, line 31 aborts if a collision occurs between any of the simulated R_x in line 32. Each of these lines has a probability of aborting that is upper-bounded by $2Q^2/q$ where $\frac{q}{2}$ is the total number of different possible coordinates R_x.

Finally, we argue that Extract is well defined. In line 07 the denominator is not null as $c \neq 0$ (line 14 of Fig. 8). Additionally, if $s = s'$, $R = R'$ (line 06) and c is the same for both instances, then w must be equals to w': This case is handled in line 50 which contradicts running line 69. Since $c \neq 0$ then line 10 is also well defined. Since $R \neq R'$, and because c is the same for both (R, w, s) and (R', w', s'), then dealing away with collisions, we have $R_x = R'_x$ and $R = -R'$. This implies that, if $s + s' = 0 \mod q$ in line 12, then this implies that $w = w'$ which contradicts line 09. All of the lines 58,07, 10 and 12 allow the reduction to compute the secret key x in order to run this signing algorithm (line 70) generating a fresh forgery (m, σ^*). Line 71 always leads to a win. Bringing all the probabilities together, we conclude Theorem 2.

A.2   Detailed Proof of SM2

The procedure Sgn outputs $\sigma := (\alpha, s)$ where $\alpha = w + c \mod q$ and s are both uniformly random in $\mathbb{Z}_q^*$ (c is uniformly random because hd is uniformly random, the size of $\mathcal{HD} := \mathbb{Z}_N$ is a multiple of q and q is prime.) This output is indistinguishable from the output of the oracle $\overline{\mathrm{Sgn}}$ in which c is the random oracle output (thus α is independent uniformly random variable) and $s = (r - \alpha x)(1 + x)^{-1}$ of which r, x and α are independent uniformly random elements. Additionally, both f and f^{-1} are proper simulation of $\bar{f}$ and $\bar{f}^{-1}$ since in the case of f we have that c is chosen uniformly at random in line 15, and in the case of f^{-1}, the simulated R is computed according to line 20 of which both s and α are uniformly random elements. The verification procedure Vfy accepts if the provided tuple is authentic (line 44), rejects if the condition in line 43 is not met (reflects line 25 of Fig. 12), outputs the Boolean constant returned by the verification oracle $\overline{\mathrm{Vfy}}$ if the R_x is freshly (line 36). Finally, line 51 is never executed as the secret key x is extracted in line 48 and used to generate a fresh forged signature.

We argue that each of the following lines 23, 24 and 25 Aborts with a probability upper-bounded by $\frac{2Q^2}{q}$. In fact, line 23 tests the probability of collisions occurring between the simulated R_x and the ones that have previously been asked to the random oracle $\bar{f}$. Line 24 aborts when a collision between the simulated hd and the ones that have been previously asked to $\bar{f}^{-1}$ is detected. Line 25 aborts if two simulated R_x collide. Since, in total, there exists $\frac{q}{2}$ different R_x values, and since the adversary is allowed to make Q oracle queries, then we deduce the upper bound.

We now explain why, the only way for Extract to abort is in line 10. Firstly, the denominator in line 06 cannot be zero. In fact, we notice that $[w + s + c]X + [s]G = R = R' = [w' + s' + c]X + [s']G$ which means that $[w - w' + s - s']X + [s - s']G = 0$. Thus if the denominator $w - w' + s - s'$ is zero, then it must be that $s - s' = 0$ ($s = s'$). The conditions $r = r'$ and $s = s'$ imply that $\alpha = \alpha'$ and thus $w = w'$. This contradicts line 44 which occurs before extraction. We conclude that, when $R = R'$, $w - w' + s - s' \neq 0 \mod q$ in line 06.

We upper bound the probability that line 10 aborts. Starting from $R = -R'$ ($R_x = R'_x$ and $R \neq R'$) we have that $[w+s+c]X+[s]G = [-w'-s'-c]X+[-s']G$ which leads to $[2c + w + w' + s + s']X + [s + s']G = 0$. If $2c + w + w' + s + s' = 0 \mod q$ then $s+s' = 0 \mod q$ and $(r+r' - \alpha x - \alpha' x)(1+x)^{-1} = 0$ where $r = -r' \mod q$. This implies that $\alpha = -\alpha' \mod q$ or $w' = -(2c + w) \mod q$. Because $\lceil \log q \rceil - 1$ bits of $-(2c+w) \mod q$ are uniformly random (c is uniformly random and q is prime) then, the problem of finding such $w' := H(m')$ can be shifted to finding an m' that hashes to a random string of $\lceil \log q \rceil - 1$ bits (for each of the Q queries $\mathcal{A}$ can make). We conclude the term $\mathbf{Adv}^{\mathrm{rpr}}$ and thus Theorem 3.

A.3   Detailed Proof of GOST

In the reduction, the procedure Sgn outputs $\sigma := (c, s)$ where c and s are uniformly random from $\mathbb{Z}_q^*$ (c is a uniformly random element because hd is picked uniformly at random from $\mathcal{HD}$, the size of $\mathcal{HD} := \mathbb{Z}_N$ is a multiple of q and q is prime). This output is picked from the same distribution as that of $\overline{\mathrm{Sgn}}$ in which c is an output of a random oracle, and $s = (cx + rw)$ where both c and r are uniformly random elements. Both of the procedures f and f^{-1} output uniformly random elements if the inputs are fresh (f outputs either a uniformly random hd simulated in Sgn or calls $\bar{f}$. Same for f^{-1} which either outputs a uniformly random R_x simulated in Sgn or calls $\bar{f}^{-1}$). Finally, the Vfy procedure accepts if the input tuple is authentic (line 42) and rejects either if the computed R is zero (line 35 refers to line 21 of Fig. 14) or if the computed c is does not correspond to what has been simulated earlier (line 41 represents the condition in line 23 of Fig. 14). Finally, if the R_x coordinate of the computed R is fresh the $\overline{\mathrm{Vfy}}$ is called in line 37 and the output Boolean constant is returned. A (valid) forgery is delivered on line 48.

Line 18 aborts if a collision is detected between the simulated R_x and a previous value input to the random oracle. Line 19 aborts when a collision occurs between the simulated hd and a previous value input to the random oracle. Line 20 aborts if a collision occurs between all the simulated R_x values. Each of those lines abort with a probability that is upper-bounded by $2Q^2/q$ where $q/2$ is the number of different R_x values.

We now argue that the fractions in the extraction algorithm are always well defined. In line 04 we have that $c \neq 0 \mod q$ (line 29). Additionally, if $w = w'$ and because $r = r' \mod q$ ($R = R'$) then $s = s' \mod q$. However, having $(w, c, s) = (w', c, s')$ contradicts line 42.

In line 06, we also have that $c \neq 0 \mod q$ and that $r = -r' \mod q$. This implies that if $w = -w' \mod q$ then $s = cx + rw = cx + (-r')(-w') = cx + r'w' = s'$ which also contradicts line 42. With this, we conclude that Extract is indeed well defined. This algorithm extracts the secret key to be later used (in line 47) to forge a fresh valid signature and query the forgery to $\overline{\mathrm{Vfy}}$ which leads to winning the game.

Combining the advantages together, we conclude Theorem 4.

B   Reduction for Proving Theorem 5

We introduce in Fig. 18 the reduction we build from **UF** to **HUF** for Theorem 5.

INITIALIZATIONS: $M \leftarrow \emptyset$; $PRE[\cdot] \leftarrow \epsilon$

Proc. $\mathcal{B}(vk')$
00 $(vk, hs) \leftarrow vk'$
01 $PRE[hs] \leftarrow \diamond$
02 $\mathcal{A}(vk, hs)$
03 Abort

Proc. $SimM(cv)$
04 $m' \xleftarrow{\$} \{0,1\}^r \setminus M$
05 $cv' \leftarrow \overline{CF}(hs, m')$
06 Abort $PRE[cv'] \neq \epsilon$
07 $PRE[cv'] \leftarrow \Diamond$
08 $PRE[cv] \leftarrow (hs, m')$
09 $M \xleftarrow{\cup} \{m'\}$
10 Return m'

Proc. $Unroll(cv, m)$
11 Abort $PRE[cv] = \Diamond$
12 While $PRE[cv] \notin \{\epsilon, \diamond\}$:
13 $\quad (cv, m') \leftarrow PRE[cv]$
14 $\quad m \leftarrow m' \,\shortparallel\, m$
15 Return (cv, m)

Proc. $Sgn(hv^*)$
16 $(cv^*, m^*) \leftarrow hv^*$
17 $\_, \bar{m} \leftarrow Sim(cv^*, m^*)$
18 $\sigma \leftarrow \overline{Sgn}(\bar{m})$
19 Return σ

Proc. $CF(cv^*, m^*)$
20 If $\exists cv$ s.t. $PRE[cv] = (cv^*, m^*)$:
21 $\quad$ Return cv
22 $\bar{cv}, \_ \leftarrow Sim(cv^*, m^*)$
23 Return $\bar{cv}$

Proc. $Sim(cv^*, m^*)$
24 $m' \leftarrow \epsilon$
25 $(cv, m) \leftarrow Unroll(cv^*, m^*)$
26 If $PRE[cv] = \epsilon$:
27 $\quad m' \leftarrow SimM(cv)$
28 $\bar{m} \leftarrow m' \,\shortparallel\, m$
29 $\bar{cv} \leftarrow \bar{h}(hs, \bar{m})$
30 Abort $PRE[\bar{cv}] \notin \{\epsilon, (cv^*, m^*)\}$
31 $PRE[\bar{cv}] \leftarrow (cv^*, m^*)$
32 $M \xleftarrow{\cup} \{\bar{m}\}$
33 Return $\bar{cv}, \bar{m}$

Proc. $Vfy(m, \sigma)$
34 $v \leftarrow Vfy(m, \sigma)$
35 Return v

Fig. 18. SimM picks a fresh random message m' and associates the pair (hs, m') to the input chaining value cv by updating PRE (line 08); The output cv' of $\overline{CF}(hs, m')$ (line 05) is marked (line 07) to prevent any potential problems arising due to collisions. Unroll takes a chaining value cv as input and a message of length c bits. It traces back all of the previous message inputs that have been queried to the compression function or have been simulated. Both procedure Sgn and CF simulated in the same fashion (calling the simulator Sim in lines 17 and 22). Sgn then simply calls $\overline{Sgn}$ on the message output by the simulator (line 18) and returns the signature whereas CF returns the chaining value output by the simulator. The essence of the reduction is in the simulator Sim. The latter first unwinds the chaining value/message pair (line 25). If the unwound chaining value cv turns out to be 'stray' (meaning that $PRE[cv] = \epsilon$) then a pair (hs, m') is immediately assigned to it using SimM (line 27). Denoting with $\bar{h}$ the sequence of compression functions $\overline{CF}$ calls on its input, the simulator computes the final chaining value $\bar{cv}$ associated to the simulated messages $m' \,\shortparallel\, m$ and to hs (line 29). Sim aborts if a collision is detected (line 30). PRE is updated to keep coherence in the simulation and M is updated to prevent future collisions. We use two special symbols $\diamond$ and $\Diamond$ to detect collisions in arrays. These symbols shall be reserved as in $\mathcal{A}$ cannot query them. Notice that $\diamond$ symbol is used once and associated to hs. We assume that 2^r is bigger than Q, and thus the set $\{0,1\}^r \setminus M$ cannot be empty.

References

1. Bellare, M., Rogaway, P.: Random oracles are practical: a paradigm for designing efficient protocols. In: Denning, D.E., Pyle, R., Ganesan, R., Sandhu, R.S., Ashby, V. (eds.) ACM CCS 1993, pp. 62–73. ACM Press (1993). https://doi.org/10.1145/168588.168596
2. Bellare, M., Rogaway, P.: The exact security of digital signatures-how to sign with RSA and Rabin. In: Maurer, U. (ed.) EUROCRYPT 1996. LNCS, vol. 1070, pp. 399–416. Springer, Heidelberg (1996). https://doi.org/10.1007/3-540-68339-9_34
3. Boneh, D., Lynn, B., Shacham, H.: Short signatures from the Weil pairing. J. Cryptol. **17**(4), 297–319 (2004). https://doi.org/10.1007/s00145-004-0314-9
4. Fersch, M., Kiltz, E., Poettering, B.: On the provable security of (EC)DSA signatures. In: Weippl, E.R., Katzenbeisser, S., Kruegel, C., Myers, A.C., Halevi, S. (eds.) ACM CCS 2016, pp. 1651–1662. ACM Press (2016). https://doi.org/10.1145/2976749.2978413
5. FIPS 186-5: Digital Signature Standard (DSS). Federal Inf. Process. Stds. (NIST FIPS), National Institute of Standards and Technology, Gaithersburg, MD (2023). https://doi.org/10.6028/NIST.FIPS.186-5
6. ISO/IEC: IT security techniques - Digital signatures with appendix - Part 3: Discrete logarithm based mechanisms. ISO14888-3 (2018)
7. Jonsson, J., Kaliski, B.: Public-Key Cryptography Standards (PKCS) #1: RSA Cryptography Specifications Version 2.1. RFC 3447 (2003). https://doi.org/10.17487/RFC3447
8. Josefsson, S., Liusvaara, I.: Edwards-Curve Digital Signature Algorithm (EdDSA). RFC 8032 (2017). https://doi.org/10.17487/RFC8032
9. Kaliski, B.: PKCS #1: RSA Encryption Version 1.5. RFC 2313 (1998). https://doi.org/10.17487/RFC2313
10. Lim, C.H., Lee, P.J.: A study on the proposed korean digital signature algorithm. In: Ohta, K., Pei, D. (eds.) ASIACRYPT 1998. LNCS, vol. 1514, pp. 175–186. Springer, Heidelberg (2000). https://doi.org/10.1007/3-540-49649-1_15
11. TR-03111: Technical Guideline BSI TR-03111 v2.1: Elliptic Curve Cryptography. German Federal Office for Information Security (2018). https://www.bsi.bund.de/SharedDocs/Downloads/EN/BSI/Publications/TechGuidelines/TR03111/BSI-TR-03111_V-2-1_pdf.pdf?__blob=publicationFile&v=1
12. Zimman, C., Bong, D.: PKCS #11: Cryptographic Token Interface Current Mechanisms Specification Version 3.0 (2020). https://docs.oasis-open.org/pkcs11/pkcs11-curr/v3.0/pkcs11-curr-v3.0.html

Attacks

Breaking Parallel ROS: Implication for Isogeny and Lattice-Based Blind Signatures

Shuichi Katsumata[1] , Yi-Fu Lai[2(✉)] , and Michael Reichle[3]

[1] PQShield and AIST, Tokyo, Japan
shuichi.katsumata@pqshield.com
[2] Ruhr-Universität Bochum, Bochum, Germany
Yi-Fu.Lai@ruhr-uni-bochum.de
[3] ETH Zürich, Zürich, Switzerland
michael.reichle@inf.ethz.ch

Abstract. Many of the three-round blind signatures based on identification protocols are only proven to be ℓ-concurrently unforgeable for $\ell = \mathsf{polylog}(\lambda)$. It was only recently shown in a seminal work by Benhamouda et al. (EUROCRYPT'21) that this is not just a limitation of the proof technique. They proposed an elegant polynomial time attack against the ℓ-concurrently unforgeability of the classical blind Schnorr protocol for $\ell = \mathsf{poly}(\lambda)$. However, there are still many blind signatures following a similar recipe to blind Schnorr where the attack by Benhamouda et al. does not apply. This includes for instance the isogeny-based blind signature CSI-Otter by Katsumata et al. (CRYPTO'23), the lattice-based blind signatures Blaze+ by Alkeilani et al. (ACISP'20) and BlindOR by Alkeilani et al. (CANS'20).

In this work, we provide a simple and novel attack on blind signatures based on identification protocols performing *parallel repetition* to reduce the soundness error. Our attack translates to a polynomial time break for the ℓ-concurrent unforgeability of CSI-Otter, Blaze+, and BlindOR for $\ell = \mathsf{poly}(\lambda)$. More formally, we define an intermediate problem called Parallel Random inhomogeneities in an Overdetermined Solvable system of linear equations (pROS) problem and show that an attack against pROS implies an attack to the above blind signatures. One takeaway of our finding is that while parallel repetition allows to exponentially reduce the soundness error of an identification protocol, this has minimal effect on the resulting blind signature. Our attack is concretely very efficient and for instance breaks 4-concurrent unforgeability of CSI-Otter in time roughly 2^{34} hash computations.

1 Introduction

Blind signature is an interactive signing protocol between a signer and a user with an advanced privacy feature. Originally envisioned to be used for e-cash in the early 80's [12], we now have numerous applications in direct anonymous

© International Association for Cryptologic Research 2024
Q. Tang and V. Teague (Eds.): PKC 2024, LNCS 14601, pp. 319–351, 2024.
https://doi.org/10.1007/978-3-031-57718-5_11

attestation [10], privacy-preserving authentication tokens [22,32], cryptocurrencies and blockchains [11,14,34], to name a few.

Informally, *blindness* guarantees that a user with a message can obtain a signature from the signer, while the signer remains oblivious of the message it signed. Due to blindness, unforgeability can no longer be defined as in a standard signature; a challenger (playing the role of the signer) cannot decide if the forgery is on a message that it has not signed before. To this end, we define ℓ-*concurrent unforgeability* [1], guaranteeing that if a signer finished ℓ signing sessions, then no user can output $\ell + 1$ or more valid signatures. Importantly, we allow the user to *concurrently* open signing sessions. For instance, a malicious user may try to concurrently open ℓ signing sessions and mix them together to create $\ell + 1$ signatures.

3-Round Protocols. One of the popular approaches to construct blind signatures is to base on identification protocols. Starting with the blind Schnorr protocol based on the Schnorr identification protocol [13], this approach has been very successful, being instantiable from versatile assumptions including postquantum assumptions such as lattices and isogenies [3,5,6,20,21,25]. Compared to other approaches based on pairing specific techniques [2,9,27,28,30] and/or non-interactive zero-knowledge proofs [8,16,18,19,26], this approach is easier to generalize, leads to simpler constructions, and tends to be more efficient.

One peculiarity of many of the blind signatures based on this approach is that they were only proven to be ℓ-concurrent unforgeable for $\ell = \mathsf{polylog}(\lambda)$ with λ the security parameter. Interestingly, while the proof could not tolerate $\ell = \mathsf{poly}(\lambda)$, it was unclear whether this was an artifact of the proof technique or because there was a yet to be discovered attack. This issue was undesirable even from a practical point view as we did not know whether these blind signatures will remain secure when instantiated with concrete parameters, say what happens if the signer opened 128 concurrent sessions?

The ROS Attack. Schnorr [29] introduced the <u>R</u>andom inhomogeneities in an <u>O</u>verdetermined <u>S</u>olvable system of linear equations (ROS_ℓ) problem in dimension ℓ, and showed that a ROS_ℓ solver can be used to break the ℓ-concurrent unforgeability of the Schnorr signature. Wagner [33] soon after showed that the ROS_ℓ problem can be solved in subexponential time when ℓ grows asymptotically faster than $\mathsf{polylog}(\lambda)$. While this implies a subexponential timed attack on the ℓ-concurrent unforgeability of blind Schnorr for $\ell = \mathsf{poly}(\lambda)$, showing the (in)existence of a polynomial time attack remained elusive for nearly two decades.

It was only recently in a seminal work, Benhamouda et al. [7] proposed an elegant polynomial time attack against ROS_ℓ for $\ell = \mathsf{poly}(\lambda)$, finally *"partially"* closing the above issue: blind Schnorr is not ℓ-concurrent unforgeable for $\ell = \mathsf{poly}(\lambda)$. Their attack is very practical and for instance when $\ell = 128$, it only takes time roughly 2^{32} hash computations to break unforgeability.

---

[1] In the literature, this is typically coined as *one-more unforgeability*. We use our terminology throughout the introduction to be precise on the value of ℓ and concurrency.

Unaffected Schemes by the ROS Attack. The reason why we highlighted that the ROS attack by Benhamouda et al. is only a partial solution to the issue was because many of the post-quantum blind signatures [5,6,21,25] remain unaffected by the attack. For instance, the lattice-based blind signature by Hauck et al. [21] is related to a slightly generalized variant of the ROS problem for which the ROS attack by Benhamouda et al. does not seem to immediately apply.

The lattice-based blind signatures Blaze+, BlindOR [5,6] are even more different. The base identification protocol underlying these blind signatures has a small challenge set, and therefore, performs parallel repetition to reduce its soundness error. Due to this parallel repetition, the underlying problem is no longer the original ROS problem considered by Schnorr [29] and it is unclear whether the ROS attack of Benhamouda et al. applies. A related question is whether a blind Schnorr protocol constructed from a Schnorr identification protocol with parallel repetition can resurrect ℓ-concurrent unforgeability for $\ell = \mathsf{poly}(\lambda)$: while at the identification protocol layer, parallel repetition exponentially reduces the soundness error, how would this relate to ℓ-concurrent unforgeability?

Lastly, the recent isogeny-based blind signature CSI-Otter [25] also relies on a base identification protocol with parallel repetition. Adding to the complexity is that unlike lattices and classical groups that are modules, isogenies have a strictly weaker algebraic structure called group actions. As stated by Katsumata et al. [25], due to the lack of algebraic structures in isogenies, even defining an appropriate ROS problem underlying the security of CSI-Otter is non-trivial, and they left it as an open problem to examine the (in)security of their scheme for $\mathsf{poly}(\lambda)$ many concurrent sessions.

1.1   Contribution

In this work, we propose the *parallel* ROS ($\mathsf{pROS}_{\ell,\omega,\mathcal{C}}$) problem and show that it is solvable in polynomial time for appropriate parameters. As a consequence, we show that the lattice-based blind signatures Blaze+, BlindOR [5,6] and the isogeny-based blind signature CSI-Otter [25] are *not* ℓ-concurrently unforgeable when $\ell = \mathsf{poly}(\lambda)$. Our attack is very practical and for instance we can break the 4-concurrent unforgeability of CSI-Otter in time roughly 2^{34} hash computations.

In more detail, the $\mathsf{pROS}_{\ell,\omega,\mathcal{C}}$ problem captures the hardness of the ℓ-concurrent unforgeability of blind signatures based on an identification protocol with challenge space $\mathcal{C}$ performing ω parallel repetitions. For instance, when $\omega = 1$ and $\mathcal{C} = \mathbb{Z}_p$, the $\mathsf{pROS}_{\ell,\omega,\mathcal{C}}$ problem is identical to the standard ROS_ℓ problem, capturing the hardness of the ℓ-concurrent unforgeability of blind Schnorr. As another example, the $\mathsf{pROS}_{\ell,\omega,\mathcal{C}}$ problem underlying the hardness of the ℓ-unforgeability of CSI-Otter [25] is $\omega = \lambda$ and $\mathcal{C} = \{-1,1\}$. To be more precise, as discussed above, since isogenies are algebraically different from lattices and classical groups, we define two types of pROS problems over different mathematical structures capturing each cases: Group-$\mathsf{pROS}_{\ell,\omega,\mathcal{C}}$ for group actions (with a twist) and Ring-$\mathsf{pROS}_{\ell,\omega,\mathcal{C}}$ for modules.

Our main technical contribution is showing informally the following results:

- Group-pROS$_{\ell,\omega,\mathcal{C}}$ can be solved in time $\omega \cdot \text{poly}(|\mathcal{C}|)$ for any $\ell \geq \omega = \text{poly}(\lambda)$ and $\mathcal{C}$. When $|\mathcal{C}| = \text{poly}(\lambda)$, the attack runs in polynomial time.
- Ring-pROS$_{\ell,\omega,\mathcal{C}}$ can be solved in time $\omega \cdot \text{poly}(\log(|\mathcal{C}|))$ for any $\ell \geq \omega \cdot \log(|\mathcal{C}|) = \text{poly}(\lambda)$ and $\mathcal{C}$. Even if $|\mathcal{C}| = \exp(\lambda)$, the attack runs in polynomial time.

Importantly, parallel repetition only amplifies *linearly* the hardness of the ℓ-concurrent unforgeability. An immediate takeaway is that while parallel repetition allows to exponentially reduce the soundness error of an identification protocol, this has minimal effect on the resulting blind signature. Moreover, note that when $|\mathcal{C}| = \text{poly}(\lambda)$, our attack against Ring-pROS$_{\ell,\omega,\mathcal{C}}$ does not take advantage of the module structure as we can simply break Ring-pROS$_{\ell,\omega,\mathcal{C}}$ using the algorithm for breaking Group-pROS$_{\ell,\omega,\mathcal{C}}$. The technical overview of our attacks are provided in Sect. 3, where we further present a modified attack on Group-pROS$_{\ell,\omega,\mathcal{C}}$, leading to very practical attacks.

Using the above attack on the Group-pROS and Ring-pROS problems, we are able to break the ℓ-concurrent unforgeability for $\ell = \text{poly}(\lambda)$ of the following schemes:

- The isogeny-based blind signature CSI-Otter by [25]. (See Sect. 4.1.) Concretely, we can break 4-concurrent unforgeability in time roughly 2^{34} hash computations.
- Two lattice-based blind signatures Blaze+, BlindOR [5,6]. (See Sect. 4.2.) Concretely, we can break 4-concurrent unforgeability of both schemes in time roughly 2^{46} hash computations with a success probability of roughly 7.3%.
- Blind Schnorr with parallel repetition. (See Sect. 4.3.) For, e.g., 4 parallel repetitions, we can break 1024-concurrent unforgeability in time roughly 2^{11} hash computations.

We would like to emphasize that our attack does not contradict the security proof of ℓ-concurrent unforgeability for $\ell = \text{polylog}(\lambda)$ provided in previous works. Our asymptotic attack uses the fact that an adversary can initiate $\ell = \text{poly}(\lambda)$ concurrent sessions, a setting which previous works do not consider. Though, it is worth highlighting that our concrete attack indicates that in practice, ℓ can be quite small (i.e., $\ell = 4$ for CSI-Otter and $\ell \leq 16$ for Blaze+, BlindOR) to practically break the schemes.

Future Works. While our attack presents a concretely efficient break to the ℓ-concurrent unforgeability of the lattice-based blind signatures Blaze+, BlindOR [5,6] and the isogeny-based blind signature CSI-Otter [25], there may be ways to fix this using the techniques developed by Abe [1,24] or Tessaro and Zhu [31]. By tweaking the original blind Schnorr protocol in different ways, they are able to prove ℓ-concurrent unforgeability for $\ell = \text{poly}(\lambda)$ in either the generic group model or in the algebraic group model. Considering how simple and efficient Blaze+, BlindOR, and CSI-Otter are, it will be worthwhile to enhance their security with minimal modification while retaining efficiency.

We also leave analyzing the (in)security of the ℓ-concurrent unforgeability for $\ell = \text{poly}(\lambda)$ of the lattice-based blind signature by Hauck et al. [21] as an important open problem. Assuming the underlying polynomial ring R_q used in [21] splits into many fields, it almost seems that our pROS attack applies. However, due to lattice specific reasons, this attack does not seem to work.

This is because, unlike the use of decompositions and summations we will use in Sect. 4.2 against Blaze$^+$, there does not exist an efficient bijection between the original challenge space and the "parallelized" one due to the shortness requirement, leading to the inapplicability of our attack to [21]. As mentioned above, the ROS attack by Benhamouda et al. [7] does not immediately apply either.

2   Preliminary

Notation. We denote the set of natural numbers and integers by $\mathbb{N}$ and $\mathbb{Z}$, respectively. We define the ring of integers modulo N, i.e., $\mathbb{Z}_N$, with representatives in $[-q/2, q/2) \cap \mathbb{Z}$. For a positive integer k, we let $[k]$ denote the set $\{1, 2, ..., k\}$. For a distribution D, we write $x \leftarrow D$ to denote x is sampled according to D. For a finite set S, we denote $x \leftarrow S$ to sample x uniformly at random over S. We use $\odot$ to denote the component-wise multiplication of vectors in a multiplicative group $\mathcal{G}$. We sometimes use $\|$ to denote the concatenation of two strings. For an element g and vector $\mathbf{a} = (a_1, ..., a_n)$, we use $g^{\mathbf{a}}$ as a shorthand for $(g^{a_1}, ..., g^{a_n})$. Moreover, for any operation $*$ defined between two elements g and h and vectors $\mathbf{a} = (a_1, ..., a_n)$ and $\mathbf{b} = (b_1, ..., b_n)$, we use $g^{\mathbf{a}} * h^{\mathbf{b}}$ as a shorthand for $(g^{a_1} * h^{b_1}, ..., g^{a_n} * h^{b_1})$. We extend this notation to matrices naturally. For readability, we use the arrow notation (e.g. $\vec{d}$) or the bold lowercase letters (e.g. $\mathbf{e}$) to denote a vector. We use the bold uppercase letters (e.g. $\mathbf{A}$) to represent a matrix in the lattice context. For a matrix $\mathbf{A}$, we denote the i-th row of $\mathbf{A}$ to be $\mathbf{A}[i]$. Let $(\mathcal{G}, \cdot)$ be a group. Let $\mathbf{a} \in (\mathcal{G} \cup \{\bot\})^n$ and $\mathbf{b} \in \mathcal{G}^n$. We write $\|\mathbf{a}\|_\infty = 1$ if $\mathbf{a}$ has at most one non-bot entry α. Then, we define multiplication $\mathbf{a} \cdot \mathbf{b} := (\alpha \cdot b_k)_{k \in [n]}$. We extend this notation to matrices naturally.

2.1   Cyclic Effective Group Action Model

To describe the isogeny-based blind signature CSI-Otter [25], we adapt the cyclic effective group action model given in [17], which captures the essence of the isogeny group action used in the scheme.

Definition 2.1 (Cyclic Effective Group Action with Twists). *Let the group G act on the set $\mathcal{X}$ by $\diamond$. The tuple $(G, \mathcal{X}, \diamond, E_0)$ is said to be a cyclic effective group action with twists (CEGAwT) if*

1. *G is finite and cyclic of order N for some known $N \in \mathbb{N}$.*
2. *There exists a known generator $g \in G$ with known representation (i.e. $G = \langle g \rangle$).*
3. *There exist efficient algorithms for membership testing and to compute a unique representation for any element in $\mathcal{X}$.*
4. *The group action $(G, \mathcal{X}, \diamond)$ is regular.*

5. E_0 is a distinguished element in $\mathcal{X}$ with known representation.
6. There exists an algorithm such that for any element $a \in \mathbb{N}$ and $x \in \mathcal{X}$ the action $g^a \diamond x$ is efficiently computable.
7. There exists an efficient twisting algorithm on input $x' = h \diamond E_0$ computing $h^{-1} \diamond E_0$.

The isomorphism $G = \langle g \rangle \cong \mathbb{Z}_N$ gives a standard representation for G. This, in turn, naturally induces a CEGAwT $(\mathbb{Z}_N, \mathcal{X}, \star, E_0)$ where the action $m \star x := g^m \diamond x$. The structure of $\mathbb{Z}_N$ naturally gives efficient algorithms for membership testing, random sampling, and equality testing. Hence, on input $n \star E_0$, the twisting algorithm returns $-n \star E_0$.

Throughout this paper, we will use $(\mathbb{Z}_N, \mathcal{X}, \star, E_0)$ to represent a CEGAwT. For the sake of convenience, for any element $x' = h \star E_0 \in \mathcal{X}$, we will use the shorthand $x'^{-1} := h^{-1} \star E_0$. The notation is well-defined since for any $h_1 \star E_0 = h_2 \star E_0$, we have $h_1^{-1} \star E_0 = h_2^{-1} \star E_0$.

2.2 Lattices

We give a brief overview of the lattice foundations required to describe Blaze+ and BlindOR [4–6]. For readability, we simplify notation and focus on the essential parts that enable us to describe our attack. For a detailed overview, we refer to [4–6]. For any positive integer n, consider the polynomial ring $R_q = \mathbb{Z}_q[X]/(X^n + 1)$. Generally, we assume that n is a power of two. We consider the lattice R_q^m, where $m \in \mathbb{N}$.

Let $D_{\mathbb{Z}^n, \sigma, \mathbf{c}}$ be the discrete Gaussian distribution over $\mathbb{Z}^n$ with standard deviation $\sigma > 0$ and center $\mathbf{c}$. Throughout, we set $\chi = D_{\mathbb{Z}^n, \sigma, \mathbf{0}}$, for some implicit $\sigma > 0$, and $\chi_{\mathsf{rs}} = D_{\mathbb{Z}^n, s^*, \mathbf{0}}$, for some implicit $s^* > \sigma$. We denote by RejSamp an algorithm that carries out rejection sampling (with implicit parameters).

2.3 Blind Signature

Below, we recall the standard definition of (three-move) blind signatures.

Definition 2.2 (Blind Signature Scheme). *A* three-move *partially blind signature* BS = (BS.KGen, BS.S, BS.U, BS.Verify) *with an efficiently decidable public key space* $\mathcal{PK}$ *consists of the following PPT algorithms:*

BS.KGen(1^λ) $\to$ (pk, sk) : *On input the security parameter* 1^λ, *the key generation algorithm outputs a pair of public and secret keys* (pk, sk).
BS.S = (BS.S$_1$, BS.S$_2$) : *The interactive signer algorithm consists of two phases:*
    BS.S$_1$(sk) $\to$ (st$_\mathsf{S}$, $\rho_{\mathsf{S},1}$) : *On input a secret key* sk, *it outputs an internal signer state* st$_\mathsf{S}$ *and a first-sender message* $\rho_{\mathsf{S},1}$.[2]
    BS.S$_2$(st$_\mathsf{S}$, ρ_U) $\to$ $\rho_{\mathsf{S},2}$: *On input a signer state* st$_\mathsf{S}$ *and a user message* ρ_U, *it outputs a second-sender message* $\rho_{\mathsf{S},2}$.

---

[2] We assume without loss of generality that sk includes pk and st$_\mathsf{S}$ includes (pk, sk) and omit it when the context is clear. Below, we also assume that st$_\mathsf{U}$ includes M.

BS.U = (BS.U$_1$, BS.U$_2$) : *The interactive user algorithm consists of two phases:*
  BS.U$_1$(pk, M, $\rho_{S,1}$) $\to$ (st$_U$, ρ_U) : *On input a public key* pk $\in \mathcal{PK}$, *a message*
    M, *and a first-sender message* $\rho_{S,1}$, *it outputs an internal user state* st$_U$
    and a user message ρ_U.
  BS.U$_2$(st$_U$, $\rho_{S,2}$) $\to \sigma$: *On input a user state* st$_U$ *and a second-signer message*
    $\rho_{S,2}$, *it outputs a signature* σ.
BS.Verify(pk, M, σ) $\to$ 1 *or* 0 : *In input a public key* pk, *a message* M, *and a*
  signature σ, *the verification algorithm outputs* 1 *to indicate the signature is*
  valid, and 0 *otherwise.*

We define *correctness, blindness, and one-more unforgeability* of a blind signature scheme.

Perfect correctness ensures that when both the signer and the user adhere to the protocol specifications, the user's obtained signature will verify correctly. In the lattice-based setting (e.g. [5,6,21]), it is often acceptable to relax this requirement slightly, allowing for a scenario where the verification algorithm accepts with an overwhelming probability. Furthermore, it is acceptable that the signer aborts the protocol in advance.

The blindness property ensures that the signer cannot establish a link between the signing process and obtained signatures. This property preserves the privacy of the user's messages. As we are interested in forgery attacks, this notion is not important in our context and we omit details.

In this work, we focus on the one-more unforgeability (OMUF) notion of a blind signature. OMUF roughly ensures that at most one valid signature is generated after each full completion of a signing interaction. Formally, we have the following.

Definition 2.3 (One-More-Unforgeability). *We define ℓ-one-more unforgeability (ℓ-OMUF) for any $\ell \in \mathbb{N}$ of a three-move partially blind signature scheme* BS *via the following game between a challenger and an adversary $\mathcal{A}$:*

Setup. *The challenger samples* (pk, sk) $\leftarrow$ BS.KGen(1^λ) *and runs $\mathcal{A}$ on input*
  pk. *It further initializes* $\ell_{\mathsf{closed}} = 0$ *and* opened$_{\mathsf{sid}}$ = false *for all* sid $\in \mathbb{N}$.
Online Phase. *$\mathcal{A}$ is given access to oracles* S$_1$ *and* S$_2$, *which behave as follows.*
  Oracle S$_1$: *The oracle samples a fresh session identifier* sid. *It sets*
    opened$_{\mathsf{sid}}$ $\leftarrow$ true *and generates* (sts$_{S,sid}$, $\rho_{S,1}$) $\leftarrow$ BS.S$_1$(sk). *Then it*
    returns sid *and the first-sender message* $\rho_{S,1}$ *to $\mathcal{A}$.*
  Oracle S$_2$: *On input of a user message* ρ_U *and a session identifier* sid,
    if $\ell_{\mathsf{closed}} \geq \ell$ *or* opened$_{\mathsf{sid}}$ = false, *then it returns* $\perp$. *Otherwise, it*
    sets opened$_{\mathsf{sid}}$ = false. *It then computes the second-signer message*
    $\rho_{S,2} \leftarrow$ BS.S$_2$(sts$_{S,sid}$, ρ_U). *If* BS.S$_2$ *did not abort, then increments* ℓ_{closed}
    and returns $\rho_{S,2}$ *to $\mathcal{A}$. Else, returns* $\perp$.
Output Determination. *When $\mathcal{A}$ outputs distinct tuples* (M$_1$, σ_1), . . . ,
  (M$_k$, σ_k), *we say $\mathcal{A}$ wins if* $k \geq \ell_{\mathsf{closed}} + 1$ *and for all* $i \in [k]$,
  BS.Verify(pk, M$_i$, σ_i) = 1.

We say BS *is ℓ-one-more unforgeable (or ℓ-OMUF) if the advantage of $\mathcal{A}$ defined*
as Adv$_{\mathcal{A}}^{\mathsf{OMUF}}(\lambda)$:= Pr[$\mathcal{A}$ *wins*] *is negligible.*

2.4 ROS Problem

The ROS problem captures a concurrent and algebraic attack on one-more unforgeability of the classical Schnorr blind signature [29]. That is, if an adversary $\mathcal{A}$ can solve the $\mathsf{ROS}_{\ell,p}$ problem, then it can also break one-more unforgeability of the Schnorr blind signature. Here, the parameter p is the order of the underlying group and ℓ is the number of concurrent signing sessions. The problem is defined in Fig. 1. Later, we define natural extensions of ROS for parallel repetitions.

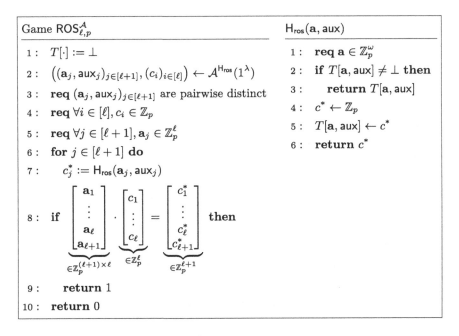

Fig. 1. Classical ROS problem over $\mathbb{Z}_p$. **req** returns 0 if the requirement does not hold.

3 Parallel ROS

We define two natural variants for the ROS problem for blind signatures based on parallel repetitions. The first variant Ring-pROS generalizes the standard ROS problem: the underlying algebraic structure is a ring $\mathcal{R}$ and we consider ω parallel repetitions. If we set $\mathcal{R} = \mathbb{Z}_p$ and $\omega = 1$, we obtain the classical ROS problem. The second variant Group-pROS is a harder variant of Ring-pROS: the underlying algebraic structure is a (multiplicative) group $\mathcal{G}$. Over groups, we have a single operation and thus, the adversary is much more restricted in its output (e.g., it cannot output arbitrary linear combinations).

Compared to ROS with a single repetition (i.e., $\omega = 1$), more parallel repetitions $\omega > 1$ require that we solve an overdetermined linear system with ω additional rows.

Perhaps surprisingly, we give two attacks on Ring-pROS and Group-pROS (with mild requirements). The first attack applies to both ROS variants and leverages that schemes with parallel repetitions often have a challenge space of polynomial size. The second attack generalizes the ROS attack from [7] and applies even for exponential challenge space. In Sect. 4, we apply our attacks to concrete schemes.

3.1 Definition of Parallel ROS

We define two problems Ring-pROS and Group-pROS.

For Rings Let $(\mathcal{R}, +, \cdot)$ be a ring.

Parallel ROS Problem for Rings. We define a ROS problem for rings with parallel repetitions. Let $\ell \in \mathbb{N}$ be the number of concurrent sessions and $\omega \in \mathbb{N}$ be the number of parallel repetitions. Let $\mathcal{R}_c \subseteq \mathcal{R}$ be the challenge space. For any adversary $\mathcal{A}$ with oracle access to $\mathsf{H}_{\mathsf{ros}}$, the problem $\mathsf{Ring\text{-}pROS}^{\mathcal{A}}_{\ell,\omega,\mathcal{R},\mathcal{R}_c}$ is defined in Fig. 2. We define the advantage of an adversary $\mathcal{A}$ against Ring-pROS as

$$\mathsf{Adv}^{\mathsf{Ring\text{-}pROS}}_{\mathcal{A},\ell,\omega,\mathcal{R},\mathcal{R}_c} := \Pr\left[b \leftarrow \mathsf{Ring\text{-}pROS}^{\mathcal{A}}_{\ell,\omega,\mathcal{R},\mathcal{R}_c}(\lambda) : b = 1 \right].$$

If the parameters are clear by context, we sometimes write Ring-pROS for short.

Remark 3.1. Note that for $\omega = 1, \mathcal{R} = \mathcal{R}_c = \mathbb{Z}_p$, this is the standard ROS problem (cf. Figure 1).

For Group Actions Let $(\mathcal{G}, \cdot)$ be a group.

Parallel ROS Problem for Group Actions. We define a ROS problem for groups with parallel repetitions. Let $\ell \in \mathbb{N}$ be the number of concurrent sessions and $\omega \in \mathbb{N}$ be the number of parallel repetitions. Let $\mathcal{G}_c \subseteq \mathcal{G}$ be the challenge space. For any adversary $\mathcal{A}$ with oracle access to $\mathsf{H}_{\mathsf{ros}}$, the problem $\mathsf{Group\text{-}pROS}^{\mathcal{A}}_{\ell,\omega,\mathcal{G},\mathcal{G}_c}$ is defined in Fig. 3. We define the advantage of an adversary $\mathcal{A}$ against Group-pROS as

$$\mathsf{Adv}^{\mathsf{Group\text{-}pROS}}_{\mathcal{A},\ell,\omega,\mathcal{G},\mathcal{G}_c} := \Pr\left[b \leftarrow \mathsf{Group\text{-}pROS}^{\mathcal{A}}_{\ell,\omega,\mathcal{G},\mathcal{G}_c}(\lambda) : b = 1 \right].$$

If the parameters are clear by context, we sometimes write Group-pROS for short.

3.2 Breaking Parallel ROS for Small Challenge Space

We provide an attack on Group-pROS with $\ell := \omega$ concurrent sessions if the challenge space is small, i.e., $|\mathcal{G}_c| = \mathsf{poly}(\lambda)$. Note that this also implies an attack on Ring-pROS (as the problem is more general) with the same parameters and complexity.

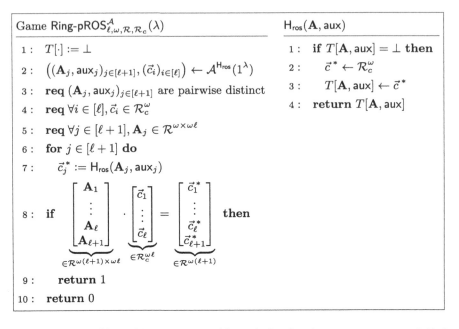

Fig. 2. Parallel ROS problem over ring $(\mathcal{R}, +, \cdot)$. In the above, **req** returns 0 if the requirement does not hold.

Overview. Our main observation is that since the challenge space is small, we can enforce specific values in a single coordinate of $\vec{c}_i^*$ by trying different auxiliary values. Roughly, we set up the first ℓ matrices $\mathbf{A}_j$ such that for each such matrix, we can find a trivial solution, i.e., the first $\omega\ell$ rows form an identity matrix (with $\perp$ symbols instead of zeros) and we pick the challenges as $\vec{c}_i = \vec{c}_i^*$. Next, we construct $\mathbf{A}_{\ell+1}$ with unit vectors as rows (with $\perp$ symbols instead of zeros) such that the ith row picks a single coordinate from the ith challenge vector $\vec{c}_i$. Then, we compute the challenge vector $\vec{c}_{\ell+1}^*$ and sample aux_i until each coordinate in $\vec{c}_{\ell+1}^*$ agrees with the picked coordinate in $\vec{c}_i$ for all $i \in [\omega]$. This constitutes a solution to the Group-pROS problem.

Finally, observe that we can replace all $\perp$ values with zeros to obtain a solution to the Ring-pROS problem.

The attack. First, for $i \in [\omega]$, we denote by $e_i^\perp := (\perp, \cdots, \perp, 1, \perp, \cdots \perp) \in (\mathcal{G} \cup \{\perp\})^k$ the vector of dimension $k \in \mathbb{N}$ with 1 at position i and all $\perp$ entries otherwise. Also, we write

$$\mathbf{I}_\omega^\perp := \begin{bmatrix} e_1^\perp \\ \vdots \\ e_\omega^\perp \end{bmatrix} \quad \text{and} \quad \mathbf{I}_{\omega\ell}^\perp := \begin{bmatrix} \mathbf{I}_\omega^\perp & \cdots & \perp \\ \vdots & \ddots & \vdots \\ \perp & \cdots & \mathbf{I}_\omega^\perp \end{bmatrix}$$

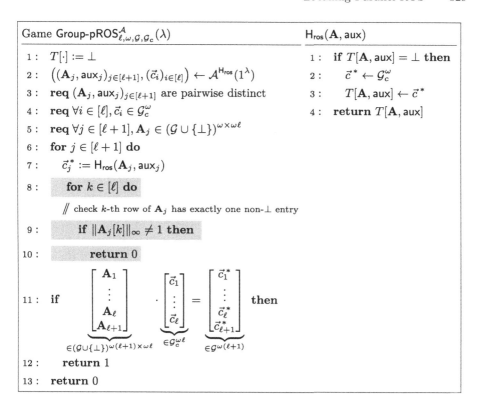

Fig. 3. Parallel ROS problem over a group $(\mathcal{G}, \cdot)$. In the above, **req** returns 0 if the requirement does not hold. The main difference between the parallel ROS problem over a ring $\mathcal{R}$ is highlighted. Recall we extend the operation $\cdot$ to vectors with the understanding that we ignore the $\perp \notin \mathcal{G}$ entries.

for identity matrices of dimension ω and $\omega\ell$, respectively, where zeros are replaced with $\perp$. Above, $e_i^{\perp}$ is of dimension ω. Next, set for $j \in [\ell]$ and $e_1^{\perp}$ of dimension ℓ

$$\mathbf{A}_j = \left[\perp \mid \cdots \mid \mathbf{I}_{\omega}^{\perp} \mid \cdots \mid \perp\right], \qquad \mathbf{A}_{\ell+1} = \begin{bmatrix} e_1^{\perp} & \cdots & \perp \\ \vdots & \ddots & \vdots \\ \perp & \cdots & e_1^{\perp} \end{bmatrix} \in (\mathcal{G} \cup \{\perp\})^{\omega \times \omega\ell}.$$

Note that in the definition of $\mathbf{A}_j$, the matrix $\mathbf{I}_{\omega}^{\perp}$ is placed at columns $(j-1)\omega + 1$ to $j\omega$. Set $\vec{c}_{\ell+1}^{\,*} = \mathsf{H}_{\mathsf{ros}}(\mathbf{A}_{\ell+1}, \mathsf{aux}_{\ell+1})$ for some arbitrary $\mathsf{aux}_{\ell+1}$. Then, for $i \in [\ell]$, sample aux_i until we have that $c_{i,1}^* = c_{\ell+1,i}^*$, where $\vec{c}_i^{\,*} = \mathsf{H}_{\mathsf{ros}}(\mathbf{A}_i, \mathsf{aux}_i)$. Since the size of $\mathcal{G}_c$ is polynomial, this sampling is efficient. Then, we have for $\vec{d} := ((\vec{c}_1^{\,*})^{\top}, \cdots, (\vec{c}_{\ell}^{\,*})^{\top})^{\top}$ that

$$
\mathbf{A}_{\ell+1} \cdot \vec{d} =
\begin{bmatrix}
e_1^{\perp} & \cdots & \perp \\
\vdots & \ddots & \vdots \\
\perp & \cdots & e_1^{\perp}
\end{bmatrix}
\cdot
\begin{bmatrix}
\vec{c}_1^{*} \\
\vdots \\
\vec{c}_{\ell}^{*}
\end{bmatrix}
=
\begin{bmatrix}
c_{1,1}^{*} \\
\vdots \\
c_{\ell,1}^{*}
\end{bmatrix}
= \vec{c}_{\ell+1}^{*}
\tag{1}
$$

Notably, the values $(\mathbf{A}_j, \mathsf{aux}_j)_{j \in [\ell+1]}$ and $(\vec{c}_i^{*})_{i \in [\ell]}$ form a valid Group-pROS solution since

$$
\begin{bmatrix}
\mathbf{A}_1 \\
\vdots \\
\mathbf{A}_{\ell} \\
\mathbf{A}_{\ell+1}
\end{bmatrix}
\cdot
\begin{bmatrix}
\vec{c}_1^{*} \\
\vdots \\
\vec{c}_{\ell}^{*}
\end{bmatrix}
=
\begin{bmatrix}
\mathbf{I}_{\omega\ell}^{\perp} \\
\mathbf{A}_{\ell+1}
\end{bmatrix}
\cdot \vec{d}
=
\begin{bmatrix}
\vec{d} \\
\mathbf{A}_{\ell+1} \cdot \vec{d}
\end{bmatrix}
\overset{(1)}{=}
\begin{bmatrix}
\vec{d} \\
\vec{c}_{\ell+1}^{*}
\end{bmatrix}
=
\begin{bmatrix}
\vec{c}_1^{*} \\
\vdots \\
\vec{c}_{\ell}^{*} \\
\vec{c}_{\ell+1}^{*}
\end{bmatrix}
$$

Complexity of the attack. Denote by $\xi = |\mathcal{G}_c|$ the size of the challenge space. For ω repetitions, the attack requires ω concurrent sessions. Also, for some fixed $\vec{c}_{\ell+1}^{*}$, the probability that $\vec{c}_{i,1}^{*} = \vec{c}_{\ell+1,i}^{*}$ is $1/\xi$, where $\vec{c}_i^{*}$ is sampled as in the attack. Since we require that this holds for all ω coordinates (i.e., for all $i \in [\omega]$), the attack requires $\mathcal{O}(\omega\xi)$ hash evaluations in expectation. Our attack has success probability 1.

In particular, the attack is PPT if $\omega = \mathsf{poly}(\lambda)$ and $\xi = \mathsf{poly}(\lambda)$. We refer to Sects. 4.1and 4.2 for an application of our attack on schemes from the literature.

Remark 3.2 (Guessing more coordinates at once). Our attack can be generalized in order to obtain a tradeoff between the number of required hash evaluations and the number of concurrent sessions. Let $N \in \mathbb{N}$. Recall that we sample $\vec{c}_i^{*}$ in such a way that $\vec{c}_{\ell+1,i}^{*} = \vec{c}_{i,1}^{*}$. We do this for all $i \in [\omega]$ in order to cover all coordinates of $\vec{c}_{\ell+1}^{*}$. The idea is to target N coordinates of $\vec{c}_{\ell+1}^{*}$ at the same time. That is, we sample auxiliary values until the first N coordinates in $\vec{c}_i^{*}$ agree with N coordinates in $\vec{c}_{\ell+1}^{*}$ until all coordinates of $\vec{c}_{\ell+1}^{*}$ are covered. The probability that N coordinates agree is $\frac{1}{\xi^N}$ and we require $\lceil \omega/N \rceil$ concurrent sessions to cover all coordinates of $\vec{c}_{\ell+1}^{*}$. The modifications are straightforward and we omit details. In total, we require only $\ell = \lceil \omega/N \rceil$ concurrent sessions and $\mathcal{O}(\ell \cdot \xi^N)$ hash evaluations. The success probability remains 1.

While the idea in Remark 3.2 is simple, it is powerful when applied to concrete schemes. For example, for $\omega = 128$ repetitions and challenge space $\{\pm 1\}$, set $N = 4$. Then, we require only $\ell = 4$ concurrent sessions for an attack that runs in 2^{34} time in expectation.

From the above discussions, we conclude the following statement.

Theorem 3.1. *Let $N \in \mathbb{N}$ and $\ell = \lceil \omega/N \rceil$. When $|\mathcal{G}_c| = \xi = \mathsf{poly}(\lambda)$ and $\omega = \mathsf{poly}(\lambda)$, there exists an PPT adversary against* Group-pROS, *parameterized by $(\ell, \omega, \mathcal{G}, \mathcal{G}_c)$, that makes $\mathcal{O}(\ell\xi^N)$ queries to the hash function in expectation, achieving an advantage of 1.*

3.3   Breaking Parallel ROS for Large Challenge Space

We provide an attack on Ring-pROS under the condition that non-zero challenge differences are invertible, i.e.,

$$(\mathcal{R}_c - \mathcal{R}_c) \setminus \{0\} \subseteq \mathcal{R}^\times. \tag{2}$$

Also, we assume that the size of the challenge space $|\mathcal{R}_c| = \Omega(2^\lambda)$ is exponential. In this case, the attack in Sect. 3.2 is infeasible[3]. Let $(B_\mu)_{\mu \in [\xi]}$ be a *binary generating set* for $\mathcal{R}$ of size ξ. That is, we assume that we can represent all elements $y \in \mathcal{R}$ as $y = \sum_{\mu \in [\xi]} B_\mu \cdot b_\mu$, where $b_\mu \in \{0, 1\}$. For example for $\mathcal{R} = \mathbb{Z}_p$, a good choice is $B_\mu = 2^{\mu-1}$ with $\xi = \lceil \log p \rceil$. We give an attack on the Ring-pROS problem with $\ell = \omega\xi$ concurrent sessions.

<u>Overview.</u> For a single parallel repetition (i.e., $\omega = 1$), the attack is identical to the ROS attack [7], albeit some minor changes and generalizations. If $\omega > 1$, we perform ω independent ROS attacks (using ξ concurrent sessions per attack) each targeting one coordinate of the target vector $\vec{c}_{\ell+1}^*$. We sketch the attack below.

First, we proceed as in Sect. 3.2. That is, we pick the first ℓ matrices $\mathbf{A}_i$ such that the first $\omega\ell$ rows form an identity matrix. Also, we pick the challenges as $\vec{c}_i = \vec{c}_i^*$. This yields ℓ trivial solutions for any choice of aux_i.

Then, we conceptually split the $\ell = \omega\xi$ concurrent sessions into ω many sets of ξ concurrent sessions. For each such set of ξ sessions, we choose two different auxiliary values aux_i^b per session which define two challenge vectors $\vec{c}_i^b$, for $b \in \{0, 1\}$. Then, we compute a linear polynomial f that allows us to express any element in $\mathcal{R}$, depending on the choice of the auxiliary values aux_i^b (within the current set of ξ sessions) using the binary generating set $(B_\mu)_{\mu \in [\xi]}$. This step also requires polynomial interpolation (which in turn requires Eq. 2).

We do this for all ω sets of ξ sessions and obtain ω polynomials $(f_\kappa)_{\kappa \in [\omega]}$. Using the fact that each polynomial is linear, we embed it in into the last matrix $\mathbf{A}_{\ell+1}$ such that each polynomial f_κ allows us to express one coordinate of the challenge vector $\vec{c}_{\ell+1}^*$ (via the binary choice of either aux_i^0 or aux_i^1 per session). After choosing the right aux_i^0 or aux_i^1 according to a binary decomposition with respect to $(B_\mu)_{\mu \in [\xi]}$, this yields a solution to the Ring-pROS problem.

<u>The attack.</u> First, we define ℓ matrices $\mathbf{A}_j$ such that we can find trivial solutions for ℓ concurrent sessions. That is, we define for $j \in [\ell]$ the matrix

$$\mathbf{A}_j = \begin{bmatrix} 0 \mid \cdots \mid \mathbf{I}_\omega \mid \cdots \mid 0 \end{bmatrix} \in \mathcal{R}^{\omega \times \omega\ell},$$

where the identity matrix $\mathbf{I}_\omega$ of dimension ω is placed at columns $(j-1)\omega+1$ to $j\omega$ and the remaining values are zeros. Set $\mathsf{aux}_j^0 \neq \mathsf{aux}_j^1$ arbitrarily, say $\mathsf{aux}_j^b := b$ for $b \in \{0, 1\}$, and define $\vec{c}_j^b = \mathsf{H}_{\mathsf{ros}}(\mathbf{A}_j, \mathsf{aux}_j^b)$. For some $\vec{b} \in \{0, 1\}^\ell$, let us denote by

$$\vec{d}_{\vec{b}} = ((\vec{c}_1^{b_1})^\top, \cdots, (\vec{c}_\ell^{b_\ell})^\top)^\top \tag{3}$$

---

[3] An exponential challenge space is not required for the attack but it simplifies the description (cf. Remark 3.3).

the vector in which we choose either $\vec{c}_j^{\,0}$ or $\vec{c}_j^{\,1}$ depending on b_j. Then, for any choice of $\mathbf{A}_{\ell+1}$ and $\vec{b}$, we have that

$$
\begin{bmatrix} \mathbf{A}_1 \\ \vdots \\ \mathbf{A}_\ell \\ \mathbf{A}_{\ell+1} \end{bmatrix} \cdot \begin{bmatrix} \vec{c}_1^{\,b_1} \\ \vdots \\ \vec{c}_\ell^{\,b_\ell} \end{bmatrix} = \begin{bmatrix} \mathbf{I}_{\omega\ell} \\ \mathbf{A}_{\ell+1} \end{bmatrix} \cdot \vec{d}_{\vec{b}} = \begin{bmatrix} \vec{d}_{\vec{b}} \\ \mathbf{A}_{\ell+1} \cdot \vec{d}_{\vec{b}} \end{bmatrix} = \begin{bmatrix} \vec{c}_1^{\,b_1} \\ \vdots \\ \vec{c}_\ell^{\,b_\ell} \\ \mathbf{A}_{\ell+1} \cdot \vec{d}_{\vec{b}} \end{bmatrix}.
$$

If we further have for some choice of $\vec{b}$ and $\mathsf{aux}_{\ell+1}$ that

$$
\mathbf{A}_{\ell+1} \cdot \vec{d}_{\vec{b}} = \vec{c}_{\ell+1}^{\,*} = \mathsf{H}_{\mathsf{ros}}(\mathbf{A}_{\ell+1}, \mathsf{aux}_{\ell+1}), \tag{4}
$$

then the values $(\mathbf{A}_j, \mathsf{aux}_j)_{j \in [\ell+1]}$ and $(\vec{c}_i)_{i \in [\ell]}$ form a valid Ring-pROS solution, where $\mathsf{aux}_i := \mathsf{aux}_i^{b_i}$ and $\vec{c}_i := \vec{c}_i^{\,b_i}$ for $i \in [\ell]$. Let $\mathsf{aux}_{\ell+1}$ be arbitrary. To conclude the attack, we define $\mathbf{A}_{\ell+1}$ and $\vec{b}$ such that Eq. 4 is satisfied.

Recall that $\ell = \omega\xi$. Let $\kappa \in [\omega]$. We construct some polynomial f_κ which depends on the challenges from the κth set of ξ concurrent sessions, i.e., the challenges $\{\vec{c}_{(\kappa-1)\xi+1}^{\,b}, \cdots, \vec{c}_{\kappa\xi}^{\,b} \mid b \in \{0,1\}\}$. For this, denote by $\vec{\gamma}_\kappa^{\,b} := \left(c_{(\kappa-1)\xi+1,1}^b, \cdots, c_{\kappa\xi,1}^b\right)^\top \in \mathcal{R}_c^\xi$ the vector which consists of the first coordinate of each such challenge for $b \in \{0,1\}$. Let $f_{\kappa,\mu} := \frac{X_\mu - \gamma_{\kappa,\mu}^0}{\gamma_{\kappa,\mu}^1 - \gamma_{\kappa,\mu}^0} \in \mathcal{R}[X_\mu]$ for $\mu \in [\xi]$. Note that here, we require that $\gamma_{\kappa,\mu}^1 - \gamma_{\kappa,\mu}^0 \in \mathcal{R}^\times$ which holds by assumption (cf. Equation 2), unless $\gamma_{\kappa,\mu}^1 = \gamma_{\kappa,\mu}^0$. The latter happens with negligible probability because we assume that the challenge space is exponential[4]. By construction, we have $f_{\kappa,\mu}(\gamma_{\kappa,\mu}^b) = b$. We now define the linear polynomial f_κ and parse its coefficients (without the constant term t_κ) in the vector $\vec{a}_\kappa$ as

$$
f_\kappa := \sum_{\mu \in [\xi]} B_\mu f_{\kappa,\mu} = t_\kappa + \sum_{\mu \in [\xi]} a_{\kappa,\mu} X_\mu \in \mathcal{R}[X_1, \ldots, X_\xi].
$$

Let $\vec{b}_\kappa \in \{0,1\}^\xi$ be arbitrary. (We choose concrete bit vectors later.) We denote by $\vec{\gamma}_{\vec{b}_\kappa} := \left(\gamma_{\kappa,1}^{b_{\kappa,1}}, \cdots, \gamma_{\kappa,\xi}^{b_{\kappa,\xi}}\right)$ the vector in which we choose either $\gamma_{\kappa,\mu}^0$ or $\gamma_{\kappa,\mu}^1$ dictated by $\vec{b}_\kappa$. Note that we have that

$$
\begin{aligned}
\left\langle \vec{a}_\kappa, \vec{\gamma}_{\vec{b}_\kappa} \right\rangle &= \sum_{\mu \in [\xi]} a_{\kappa,\mu} \cdot \gamma_{\kappa,\mu}^{b_{\kappa,\mu}} = f_\kappa\left(\gamma_{\kappa,1}^{b_{\kappa,1}}, \cdots, \gamma_{\kappa,\xi}^{b_{\kappa,\xi}}\right) - t_\kappa \\
&= \sum_{\mu \in [\xi]} B_\mu f_{\kappa,\mu}(\gamma_{\kappa,\mu}^{b_{\kappa,\mu}}) - t_\kappa = \sum_{\mu \in [\xi]} B_\mu b_{\kappa,\mu} - t_\kappa.
\end{aligned} \tag{5}
$$

---

[4] Concretely, we have $\gamma_{\kappa,\mu}^1 \neq \gamma_{\kappa,\mu}^0$ except with probability $1/|\mathcal{R}_c|$ since both values are distributed independently and uniformly at random in $\mathcal{R}_c$. Since we require this for all ℓ concurrent sessions, a union bound yields that we abort with probability at most $\ell/|\mathcal{R}_c|$. This probability is negligible for $\ell = \mathsf{poly}(\lambda)$ since we assume $|\mathcal{R}_c| = \Omega(2^\lambda)$. We refer to Remark 3.3 for a discussion on how to avoid aborts. For readability, we choose to abort here.

Denote $\vec{b} = (\vec{b}_1, \cdots, \vec{b}_\omega)^\top$. Next, we embed the coefficient vector $\vec{a}_\kappa$ in the κth row of $\mathbf{A}_{\ell+1}$ in such a way that it lines up with $\vec{\gamma}_{\vec{b}_\kappa}$ (filling the other coordinates with zeros appropriately), i.e., such that

$$\mathbf{A}_{\ell+1}[\kappa] \cdot \vec{d}_{\vec{b}} = \left\langle \vec{a}_\kappa, \vec{\gamma}_{\vec{b}_\kappa} \right\rangle, \tag{6}$$

where $\vec{d}_{\vec{b}}$ is defined as in Eq. (3). Recall that we choose the *first* coordinate of each challenge vector to define $\vec{\gamma}_{\vec{b}_\kappa}$, so we pad $\vec{a}_\kappa$ as follows. Let $\vec{a}^*_{\kappa,\mu} := (a_{\kappa,\mu}, 0, \cdots, 0) \in \mathcal{R}^\omega$ and $\vec{a}^*_\kappa := (\vec{a}^*_{\kappa,1}, \cdots, \vec{a}^*_{\kappa,\xi})^\top \in \mathcal{R}^{\omega\xi}$. Next, recall that each $\vec{\gamma}_{\vec{b}_\kappa}$ is constructed based on the challenges in the κth set of ξ concurrent sessions. Thus, to line up each coefficient, we set

$$\mathbf{A}_{\ell+1} := \begin{bmatrix} \vec{a}^*_1 & 0 & \cdots & & 0 \\ 0 & \vec{a}^*_2 & 0 & \cdots & 0 \\ \vdots & & \vdots & & \vdots \\ 0 & 0 & 0 & \cdots 0 & \vec{a}^*_\omega \end{bmatrix} \in \mathcal{R}^{\omega \times \omega\ell}.$$

With this choice of $\mathbf{A}_{\ell+1}$, Eq. (6) holds by construction.

We are now ready to choose $\vec{b}_\kappa$ concretely such that Eq. (4) holds. Set $\vec{c}^*_{\ell+1} = \mathsf{H}_{\mathsf{ros}}(\mathbf{A}_{\ell+1}, \mathsf{aux}_{\ell+1})$. For $\kappa \in [\omega]$, set $y_\kappa := c^*_{\ell+1,\kappa} + t_\kappa$ and decompose $y_\kappa = \sum_{\mu \in [\xi]} B_\mu b_{\kappa,\mu}$ in binary. Set $\vec{b}_\kappa := (b_{\kappa,1}, \cdots, b_{\kappa,\xi})$. By construction, we have for $\kappa \in [\omega]$ that

$$\mathbf{A}_{\ell+1}[\kappa] \cdot \vec{d}_{\vec{b}} \overset{(6)}{=} \left\langle \vec{a}_\kappa, \vec{\gamma}_{\vec{b}_\kappa} \right\rangle \overset{(5)}{=} \sum_{\mu \in [\xi]} B_\mu b_{\kappa,\mu} - t_\kappa = y_\kappa - t_\kappa = c^*_{\ell+1,\kappa}.$$

Since this holds for all $\kappa \in [\omega]$, Eq. (4) is satisfied and we found a solution to the Ring-pROS problem.

Complexity of the attack. The efficiency of the attack depends on the choice of the generating set. Given a binary generating set $(B_\mu)_{\mu \in [\xi]}$ of size ξ, the attack requires $\ell = \omega\xi$ concurrent sessions, where ω is the number of repetitions. Further, it requires $2\ell + 1$ hash evaluations, $\mathcal{O}(\ell)$ ring operations and ω decompositions of some ring element in the basis $(B_\mu)_{\mu \in [\xi]}$. The attack succeeds except with probability $\mathcal{O}(\frac{\ell}{2^\lambda}) = \mathsf{negl}(\lambda)$.

Remark 3.3 (No aborts). We present the attack with negligible abort probability for readability, but this is not inherent. It is possible to adapt the attack to always succeed. Observe that we abort only if there is a collision in the first coordinates $\gamma^0_{\kappa,\mu}$ and $\gamma^1_{\kappa,\mu}$ of $\vec{c}^0_i$ and $\vec{c}^1_i$, respectively, for appropriate $i \in [\ell]$. A simple fix is to resample the challenges in this case (by choosing different aux^b_i for $b \in \{0, 1\}$). A more direct approach is to instead setup the polynomials $f_{\kappa,\mu}$ using another coordinate of $\vec{c}^0_i$ and $\vec{c}^1_i$, where both challenge vectors have distinct values. Then, we have to change where to embed the coefficients in $\mathbf{A}_{\ell+1}$ but this is straightforward. In case both challenge vectors agree on all coordinates, we found a trivial collision (which yields a trivial solution).

We refer to Sect. 4.3 for an application of our attack with concrete parameters. The above considerations yield the following theorem.

Theorem 3.2. *Assume that* $(\mathcal{R}_c - \mathcal{R}_c) \setminus \{0\} \subseteq \mathcal{R}^{\times}$. *Let* $(B_\mu)_{\mu \in [\xi]}$ *be a binary generating set for* $\mathcal{R}$ *of size* ξ. *Assume that* $\omega = \mathsf{poly}(\lambda)$ *and* $\xi = \mathsf{poly}(\lambda)$. *Let* $\ell = \omega\xi$. *There exists an PPT adversary against* Ring-pROS, *parameterized by* $(\ell, \omega, \mathcal{R}, \mathcal{R}_c)$, *that makes at most* $2\ell + 1$ *queries to the hash function, achieving an advantage of* 1. *In total, the adversary performs* $\mathcal{O}(\ell)$ *ring operations and* ω *decompositions of some ring element with respect to* $(B_\mu)_{\mu \in [\xi]}$.

4 Implications of Attack

In this section, we apply our attacks on parallel ROS from Sect. 3 to several concrete blind signatures from the literature. In particular, we use the attack in Sect. 3.2 to provide efficient attacks on CSI-Otter [25], Blaze+ [4,5] and BlindOR [6]. Also, we give an attack on a conceptual variant of Schnorr with parallel repetitions to illustrate our attack in Sect. 3.3.

For each scheme, we first recall the (unblinded) interactive signing protocol. We remark that it suffices to present attacks on the unblinded version. Since an adversary against OMUF (i.e., a "malicious" user) does not care about blindness, which is a security notion for an "honest" user. Hence, an adversary can set the user's blinding randomnesses to be the identity elements so that the original CSI-Otter, Blaze, BlindOR trivially degenerate them to our unblinded variants we described. For instance, we can take $(\mathbf{d}, \mathbf{z}) = ((1, \cdots, 1), (0, \cdots, 0))$ in Fig. 2 of [25] and take $(\hat{e}, \hat{p}) = (1, \cdots, 1)$ in Fig. 5 of [5].

To improve readability, we only present the signer algorithms, key generation and verification, since these algorithms specify the OMUF game fully[5]. Then, we show that an adversary on Ring-pROS or Group-pROS (with appropriate parameters) allows to break OMUF of the scheme. Our attacks on Ring-pROS and Group-pROS from Sect. 3 yield concrete concurrent attacks on the scheme.

4.1 Isogeny-Based Blind Signature: CSI-Otter

Let $(\mathbb{Z}_N, \mathcal{X}, \star, E_0)$ be a CEGAwT and $\mathsf{H} : \{0,1\}^* \to \{-1,1\}^\omega$ be a collision-resistant hash function. We recall the interactive signing protocol, key generation and verification of CSI-Otter [25] in Fig. 4.

Our attack is summarized in the theorem below.

Theorem 4.1. *For any PPT adversary* $\mathcal{A}$ *on* Group-pROS$_{\ell, \omega, \{\pm 1\}, \{\pm 1\}}$, *there exists a PPT adversary* $\mathcal{B}$ *against* ℓ-OMUF *of* CSI-Otter *such that* $\mathsf{Adv}_{\mathcal{B}}^{\mathsf{OMUF}}(\lambda) = \mathsf{Adv}_{\mathcal{A}, \ell, \omega, \{\pm 1\}, \{\pm 1\}}^{\mathsf{Group\text{-}pROS}}(\lambda)$ *where* $\{\pm 1\}$ *forms a group with the multiplication.*

---

[5] In particular, we omit the user's algorithms which specify how a signature can be blinded. Since we provide attacks, these are not relevant in our context.

Signer($(X_0, X_1), (\delta, x_\delta)$)	User($(X_0, X_1), M$)
1: $\mathbf{y}_\delta \leftarrow \mathbb{Z}_N^\omega$	
2: $\mathbf{Y}_\delta \leftarrow \mathbf{y}_\delta \star E_0$	
3: $(\mathbf{c}_{1-\delta}, \mathbf{r}_{1-\delta}) \leftarrow \{-1, 1\}^\omega \times \mathbb{Z}_N^\omega$	
4: $\mathbf{Y}_{1-\delta} \leftarrow \mathbf{r}_{1-\delta} \star X_{1-\delta}^{\mathbf{c}_{1-\delta}}$	

$$(\mathbf{Y}_0, \mathbf{Y}_1) \xrightarrow{\hspace{3cm}}$$

	5: $\mathbf{c} = H(\mathbf{Y}_0, \mathbf{Y}_1, M)$

$$\xleftarrow{\hspace{1cm} \mathbf{c} \hspace{1cm}}$$

6: **req** $\vec{c} \in \{-1, 1\}^\omega$	
7: $\mathbf{c}_\delta = \mathbf{c} \odot \mathbf{c}_{1-\delta}$	
8: $\mathbf{r}_\delta = \mathbf{y}_\delta - a_\delta \cdot \mathbf{c}_\delta$	

$$\mathbf{r}_0, \mathbf{r}_1, \mathbf{c}_0, \mathbf{c}_1 \xrightarrow{\hspace{3cm}}$$

	9: $\sigma \leftarrow (\mathbf{c}_b, \mathbf{r}_b)_{b \in \{0,1\}}$

KeyGen(1^λ) :	Verify($(X_0, X_1), \sigma, M$) :
1: $\delta \leftarrow \{0, 1\}$	1: **parse** $\sigma = (\mathbf{c}_b, \mathbf{r}_b)_{b \in \{0,1\}}$
2: $(x_0, x_1) \leftarrow \mathbb{Z}_N^2$	2: $\mathbf{c}' \leftarrow H(\mathbf{r}_0 \star X_0^{\mathbf{c}_0}, \mathbf{r}_1 \star X_1^{\mathbf{c}_1}, M)$
3: $(X_0, X_1) \leftarrow (a_0 \star E_0, a_1 \star E_0)$	3: **req** $\mathbf{c}_0 \odot \mathbf{c}_1 = \mathbf{c}'$
4: **return** sk $= (\delta, x_\delta)$, pk $= (X_0, X_1)$	4: **return** 1

Fig. 4. The unblinded signing protocol, key generation and verification of CSI-Otter, where $H : \{0, 1\}^* \rightarrow \{\pm 1\}^\omega$ is a collision-resistant hash function. Here, $\odot$ denotes the entry-wise multiplication. In the signing protocol (resp. verification), **req** aborts (resp. returns 0) if the requirement does not hold. See Fig. 2 of [25] for the blinded version.

Proof. Let $\mathcal{A}$ be an adversary on Group-pROS$_{\ell, \omega, \{\pm 1\}, \{\pm 1\}}$ for some $\ell \in \mathbb{N}$. The adversary $\mathcal{B}$ against ℓ-OMUF of CSI-Otter with access to $\mathcal{A}$ proceeds as follows.

Adversary $\mathcal{B}$. First, $\mathcal{B}$ invokes the ℓ-OMUF experiment and obtains a public key (X_0, X_1). Also, $\mathcal{B}$ obtains access to the hash function H and the signing oracles S_1 and S_2. Next, $\mathcal{B}$ opens ℓ concurrent (signing) sessions via the S_1 oracle and obtains $(\mathbf{Y}_{i,0}, \mathbf{Y}_{i,1})$ from the ith session for each $i \in [\ell]$. Then, $\mathcal{B}$ sets up an empty table T and sets $\mathbf{Z}_b = (\mathbf{Y}_{1,b}^\top, \cdots, \mathbf{Y}_{\ell,b}^\top)^\top \in \mathbb{Z}_N^{\omega\ell}$ for $b \in \{0, 1\}$.

Let Q be the number of H_{ros} queries of $\mathcal{A}$ (including potential queries for verification of $\mathcal{A}$'s output). Assume without loss of generality that each H_{ros} query is distinct. Adversary $\mathcal{B}$ answers the ith query $(\mathbf{A}, \text{aux})$ as follows. If $\mathbf{A} \notin (\{\pm 1\} \cup \{\perp\})^{\omega \times \omega\ell}$ or $\|\mathbf{A}[k]\|_\infty \neq 1$ for some $k \in [\omega]$, returns $\vec{c}^* \leftarrow \{\pm 1\}^\omega$.

Otherwise, parses the kth row of $\mathbf{A}$ as $(\bot, \cdots, \alpha_k, \cdots, \bot) = \mathbf{A}[k]$, where $\alpha_k \in \{\pm 1\}$ is the non-$\bot$ entry in column ν_k. Computes

$$\mathbf{Y}_0^* = (\mathbf{Z}_{\nu_1}^{\alpha_1}, \cdots, \mathbf{Z}_{\nu_\omega}^{\alpha_\omega}) \quad \text{and} \quad \mathbf{Y}_1^* = (\mathbf{Z}_{\nu_1}, \cdots, \mathbf{Z}_{\nu_\omega}). \tag{7}$$

Note that $\mathbf{Y}_0^*, \mathbf{Y}_1^* \in \mathcal{X}^\omega$. Sets $\mathsf{M} = (\mathsf{aux}, i)$ and $\mathbf{c}^* = \mathsf{H}(\mathbf{Y}_0^*, \mathbf{Y}_1^*, \mathsf{M})$. Inserts $T[\mathbf{A}, \mathsf{aux}] = (\mathbf{Y}_0^*, \mathbf{Y}_1^*, \mathsf{M})$ into the table T and outputs $\mathbf{c}^*$. Note that by design, M is distinct for each distinct query.

After its query phase, $\mathcal{A}$ outputs $(\mathbf{A}_j, \mathsf{aux}_j)_{j \in [\ell+1]}$ and $(\mathbf{c}_i)_{i \in [\ell]}$. Adversary $\mathcal{B}$ checks if $\mathcal{A}$ succeeds; if not, outputs $\bot$ to the ℓ-OMUF game. Else, $\mathcal{B}$ closes the ith session with $\mathbf{c}_i \in \{\pm 1\}^\omega$ via the S_2 oracle and obtains $(\mathbf{r}_{i,0}, \mathbf{r}_{i,1}, \mathbf{c}_{i,0}, \mathbf{c}_{i,1})$ in response. Then, for $b \in \{0,1\}$, $\mathcal{B}$ sets $\mathbf{s}_b = (\mathbf{r}_{1,b}^\top, \cdots, \mathbf{r}_{\ell,b}^\top)$, $\mathbf{d}_b = (\mathbf{c}_{1,b}^\top, \cdots, \mathbf{c}_{\ell,b}^\top)^\top$. For each $j \in [\ell+1]$, parses $\mathbf{A}_j$ as above, i.e., for all rows $k \in [\omega]$, parses $(\bot, \cdots, \alpha_{j,k}, \cdots, \bot) = \mathbf{A}[k]$, where $\alpha_{j,k} \in \{\pm 1\}$ is the non-$\bot$ entry in column $\nu_{j,k}$. To generate the forgeries, for $b \in \{0,1\}$, sets

$$\mathbf{r}_{j,b}^* = (\alpha_{j,1}^{1-b} \cdot s_{b,\nu_{j,1}}, \cdots, \alpha_{j,\omega}^{1-b} \cdot s_{b,\nu_{j,\omega}}), \quad \mathbf{c}_{j,b}^* = (\alpha_{j,1}^{1-b} \cdot d_{b,\nu_{j,1}}, \cdots, \alpha_{j,\omega}^{1-b} \cdot d_{b,\nu_{j,\omega}}) \tag{8}$$

and parses $(\mathbf{Y}_{j,0}^*, \mathbf{Y}_{j,1}^*, \mathsf{M}_j) = T[\mathbf{A}_j, \mathsf{aux}_j]$. Finally, $\mathcal{B}$ sets $\sigma_j = (\mathbf{r}_{j,b}^*, \mathbf{c}_{j,b}^*)_{b \in \{0,1\}}$ and outputs the forgeries $(\sigma_j, \mathsf{M}_j)_{j \in [\ell+1]}$ to the ℓ-OMUF game.

Success probability. It is easy to see that $\mathcal{B}$ simulates H_{ros} perfectly. Thus, it suffices to show that the signatures $(\sigma_j, \mathsf{M}_j)_{j \in [\ell+1]}$ are valid if $\mathcal{A}$'s output forms a valid Group-pROS solution. In that case, we have that $(\mathbf{A}_j, \mathsf{aux}_j)_{j \in [\ell+1]}$ are pairwise distinct, $\mathbf{c}_i \in \{\pm 1\}^\omega$ and $\mathbf{A}_j \in (\{\pm 1\} \cup \{\bot\})^{\omega \times \omega \ell}$ with $\|\mathbf{A}_j[k]\|_\infty = 1$ for all $k \in [\omega]$. By construction, we know that $(\mathsf{M}_j)_{j \in [\ell+1]}$ are pairwise distinct. Further, we know that for $j \in [\ell+1]$ it holds that $\mathbf{A}_j \cdot \mathbf{d} = \mathsf{H}_{\text{ros}}(\mathbf{A}_j, \mathsf{aux}_j)$, where $\mathbf{d} = (\mathbf{c}_1^\top, \cdots, \mathbf{c}_\ell^\top)^\top$. With the above notation, this is equivalent to

$$(\alpha_{j,k} \cdot d_{\nu_{j,k}})_{k \in [\omega]} = \mathsf{H}(\mathbf{Y}_{j,0}^*, \mathbf{Y}_{j,1}^*, \mathsf{M}_j) := \mathbf{c}_j^* \tag{9}$$

by construction. For $i \in [\ell]$, we know that the signer's output satisfies $\mathbf{Y}_{i,0} = \mathbf{r}_{i,0} \star X_0^{\mathbf{c}_{i,0}}$, $\mathbf{Y}_{i,1} = \mathbf{r}_{i,1} \star X_1^{\mathbf{c}_{i,1}}$ and $\mathbf{c}_{i,0} \odot \mathbf{c}_{i,1} = \mathbf{c}_i$. With the above notation, this can be rewritten as

$$\mathbf{Z}_b = \mathbf{s}_b \star X_b^{\mathbf{d}_b} \quad \text{and} \quad \mathbf{d}_0 \odot \mathbf{d}_1 = \mathbf{d}. \tag{10}$$

We now show that $(\sigma_j, \mathsf{M}_j)_{j \in [\ell+1]}$ verify given the above. That is, $\mathbf{c}_{j,0}^* \odot \mathbf{c}_{j,1}^* = \mathbf{c}_j^*$ and that for $b \in \{0,1\}$, we have that $\mathbf{Y}_{j,b}^* = \mathbf{r}_{j,b}^* \star X_b^{\mathbf{c}_{j,b}^*}$. We verify that this holds for each coordinate. We have for $k \in [\omega]$ that

$$r_{j,b,k}^* \star X_b^{c_{j,b,k}^*} \stackrel{(8)}{=} (\alpha_{j,k}^{1-b} \cdot s_{b,\nu_{j,k}}) \star X_b^{\alpha_{j,k}^{1-b} \cdot d_{b,\nu_{j,k}}}$$
$$\stackrel{(10)}{=} Z_{b,\nu_{j,k}}^{\alpha_{j,k}^{1-b}}$$
$$\stackrel{(7)}{=} Y_{j,b,k}^*$$

and

$$c_{j,k}^* \overset{(9)}{=} \alpha_{j,k} \cdot d_{\nu_{j,k}} \overset{(10)}{=} \alpha_{j,k} \cdot d_{0,\nu_{j,k}} \cdot d_{1,\nu_{j,k}} \overset{(8)}{=} c_{j,0,k}^* \cdot c_{j,1,k}^*.$$

Thus, all signatures verify. $\qquad\qquad\qquad\qquad\qquad\qquad\qquad\qquad\qquad\qquad$ □

Remark 4.1. The above attack can be extended to encompass the general framework of CSI-Otter, wherein the groups $\mathcal{G}$ and $\mathcal{G}_c$, initially set as $\{\pm 1\}$, can be replaced by a cyclic group C_d of a higher order $d \in \mathbb{N}$. This substitution naturally corresponds the fact that the challenge space in CSI-Otter isomorphic to C_d as a group, where d corresponds to the d-th root of unity used within their generalized blind signature scheme.

Combining Theorem 4.1, Theorem 3.1, and the above remark, we obtain the following corollary.

Corollary 4.1. *Let $N \in \mathbb{N}$. Let the scheme CSI-Otter be parameterized by the challenge space $\{\pm 1\}$ with ω repetitions. Under this parameterization, there exists a PPT adversary against the ℓ-OMUF experiment of CSI-Otter for $\ell = \lceil \omega/N \rceil$ with expected $\mathcal{O}(\ell 2^N)$ queries to the hash function, achieving an advantage of 1. Furthermore, when ζ_d-CSI-Otter is parameterized by the challenge space $\langle \zeta_d \rangle$ of size d and ω repetitions, there exists a PPT adversary against the ℓ-OMUF experiment of ζ_d-CSI-Otter for $\ell = \lceil \omega/N \rceil$ with $\mathcal{O}(\ell d^N)$ queries to the hash functions, achieving an advantage of 1.*

Concretely, in CSI-Otter, ω is taken to be 128. With 128 concurrent sessions of CSI-Otter and expected 256 hash queries, we are able to break the 128-one-more unforgeability of it with an overwhelming probability. Also, with 4 concurrent sessions of CSI-Otter and expected 2^{34} hash queries, we are able to break 4-the one-more unforgeability of it with an overwhelming probability. In ζ_4-CSI-Otter, ω is taken to be 64. With 4 concurrent sessions of ζ_4-CSI-Otter, ω and expected 2^{34} hash queries, we are able to break the 4-one-more unforgeability of it with an overwhelming probability. Note that this does not contradict to the security proof of CSI-Otter where the reduction loss depends on the number of hash queries as given in [23].

4.2   Lattice-Based Blind Signatures: Blaze+ and BlindOR

In this subsection, we consider the lattice-based blind signatures Blaze+ [4,5] and BlindOR [6]. Let $R_q = \mathbb{Z}_q[X]/(X^n + 1)$, where $n \in \mathbb{N}$ is a power of two. We first define the two subsets of R_q

$$\mathbb{T} = \{(-1)^b \cdot X^k \mid b \in \{0,1\}, k \in [0, n-1]\},$$

$$\mathcal{C} = \{c \in R_q \mid c = \sum_{i \in [\omega]} \hat{c}_i \text{ for } \hat{c}_i \in \mathbb{T}\}.$$

The challenge space of BlindOR is $\mathbb{T}^\omega$. The challenge space of Blaze+ is $\mathcal{C}$, but during signing, this space is decomposed into $\mathbb{T}^\omega$. For this, we define the mapping $\mathsf{Decomp} : \mathcal{C} \to \mathbb{T}^\omega$. Given $c \in \mathcal{C}$, Decomp outputs $(\hat{c}_1, \cdots, \hat{c}_\omega)$ such that $c = \sum_{i \in [\omega]} \hat{c}_i$.

Further, let $B_{\mathsf{kg}} < B_{\mathsf{ver}}$ be two real numbers. The value B_{kg} is a norm bound for the vectors in the secret key and B_{ver} is a norm bound for the vectors in a signature. Also, we denote the abort probability of rejection sampling by δ_{rej}. We also denote by δ_{ver} the probability that a signature from an honest *unblinded* signing interaction (of Blaze+ or BlindOR) passes verification.

Blaze+ Here, we give a concrete attack on Blaze+. Let $\mathsf{H} : \{0,1\}^* \to \mathcal{C}$ be a collision-resistant hash function. Note that to generate the challenge c in Blaze+, the user evaluates the hash function $c \leftarrow \mathsf{H}(\mathsf{root}, \mathsf{M})$ on message M and a vector commitment root (i.e., a Merkle tree) to $w \in R_q$. Instead, we evaluate H on M and w to simplify presentation. The interactive signing protocol, key generation and verification is given in Fig. 5. We stress that this simplification is purely for readability, and an attack on the scheme in Fig. 5 immediately yields an attack on Blaze+ (by first committing to w in root).

Roughly, Blaze+ decomposes $c \in \mathcal{C}$ into ω monomials in $\mathbb{T}$ and runs ω parallel repetitions of a lattice-based identification protocol. For our attack, we observe that while the final signature in Blaze+ does not have explicit parallel repetitions, the signing protocol is parallelized. We can leverage this structure to attack the scheme. In particular, for $\ell \in \mathbb{N}$, we show that a successful adversary on $\mathsf{Group\text{-}pROS}_{\ell,\omega,\mathbb{T},\mathbb{T}}$ allows to break ℓ-OMUF with of Blaze+ with probability $\delta_{\mathsf{ver}}^\omega (1 - \delta_{\mathsf{rej}})^\omega$. Note that this is the probability that the signer does not abort in ℓ signing sessions and that all obtained signatures verify (i.e., all obtained signatures satisfy $\|(\mathbf{z}_{\delta,i}^\top, y_{\delta,i})_{i \in [\omega]}\| \leq B_{\mathsf{ver}}$). Then, we can apply the attack from Sect. 3.2 to obtain a concrete attack.

Theorem 4.2. *For any PPT adversary $\mathcal{A}$ on $\mathsf{Group\text{-}pROS}_{\ell,\omega,\mathbb{T},\mathbb{T}}$, there is an adversary $\mathcal{B}$ against ℓ-OMUF of Blaze+ such that $\mathsf{Adv}_{\mathcal{B}}^{\mathsf{OMUF}}(\lambda) = \delta_{\mathsf{ver}}^\ell (1 - \delta_{\mathsf{rej}})^\ell \cdot \mathsf{Adv}_{\mathcal{A},\ell,\omega,\mathbb{T},\mathbb{T}}^{\mathsf{Group\text{-}pROS}}(\lambda)$.*

Proof. Let $\mathcal{A}$ be an adversary on $\mathsf{Group\text{-}pROS}_{\ell,\omega,\mathbb{T},\mathbb{T}}$ for some $\ell \in \mathbb{N}$. We use $\mathcal{A}$ to construct an adversary $\mathcal{B}$ against ℓ-OMUF of Blaze+ as follows.

Adversary $\mathcal{B}$. Adversary $\mathcal{B}$ obtains a public key $(\mathbf{a}, t)$ and access to oracles H, S_1 and S_2. Then, $\mathcal{B}$ opens ℓ concurrent (signing) sessions via the S_1 oracle and obtains $(w_{i,k})_{k \in [\omega]}$ from the ith session. Next, $\mathcal{B}$ generates a table T initialized with $\perp$ entries. Sets $\mathbf{v} = (w_{1,1}, w_{1,2}, \cdots, w_{\ell,\omega}) \in R_q^{\omega\ell}$.

Let Q be the number of $\mathsf{H}_{\mathsf{ros}}$ queries of $\mathcal{A}$ (including potential queries for verification of $\mathcal{A}$'s output). Assume without loss of generality that each $\mathsf{H}_{\mathsf{ros}}$ query is distinct. For the ith such query $(\mathbf{A}, \mathsf{aux})$ to $\mathsf{H}_{\mathsf{ros}}$ of $\mathcal{A}$, adversary $\mathcal{B}$ proceeds as follows. If $\mathbf{A} \notin (\mathbb{T} \cup \{\perp\})^{\omega \times \omega\ell}$ or $\|\mathbf{A}[k]\|_\infty \neq 1$ for some $k \in [\omega]$, then returns $\vec{c}^* \leftarrow \mathbb{T}^\omega$. Else, sets $(w_1^*, \cdots, w_\omega^*)^\top = \mathbf{A} \cdot \mathbf{v}$ and $w^* \leftarrow \sum_{k \in [\omega]} w_k^*$. Also, sets $\mathsf{M} = (\mathsf{aux}, i)$ and $T[\mathbf{A}, \mathsf{aux}] = (w^*, \mathsf{M})$. Note that by construction, M is distinct for distinct queries. Sets $c^* = \mathsf{H}(w^*, \mathsf{M})$, decomposes $(\hat{c}_k)_{k \in [\omega]} = \mathsf{Decomp}(c^*)$ and outputs $\vec{c}^* = (\hat{c}_1, \cdots, \hat{c}_\omega)^\top$.

Signer$((\mathbf{a}, t), \mathbf{s})$	User$((\mathbf{a}, t), M)$

1 : **for** $i \in [\omega]$
2 : $(\mathbf{r}_i, e'_i) \leftarrow \chi_{rs}^m \times \chi_{rs}$
3 : $w_i = \mathbf{a}^\top \mathbf{r}_i + e'_i$

$$\xrightarrow{\quad (w_i)_{i \in [\omega]} \quad}$$

4 : $w \leftarrow \sum_{i \in [\omega]} w_i$
5 : $c \leftarrow \mathsf{H}(w, M)$
6 : $(\hat{c}_i)_{i \in [\omega]} \leftarrow \mathsf{Decomp}(c)$

$$\xleftarrow{\quad (\hat{c}_i)_{i \in [\omega]} \quad}$$

7 : **for** $i \in [\omega]$
8 :   **req** $\hat{c}_i \in \mathbb{T}$
9 : $\mathbf{z}_i \leftarrow \mathbf{s} \cdot \hat{c}_i + \mathbf{r}_i$
10 : $y_i \leftarrow e \cdot \hat{c}_i + e'_i$
11 : **req** $\mathsf{RejSamp}((\mathbf{z}_i, y_i)_{i \in [\omega]}) = 1$

$$\xrightarrow{\quad (\mathbf{z}_i, y_i)_{i \in [\omega]} \quad}$$

12 : $(\mathbf{z}, y) \leftarrow \left(\sum_{i \in [\omega]} \mathbf{z}_i, \sum_{i \in [\omega]} y_i \right)$
13 : $\sigma \leftarrow (\mathbf{z}, y, c)$

KeyGen(1^λ) :	Verify$((\mathbf{a}, t), \sigma, M)$:

1 : $\mathbf{a} \leftarrow R_q^m$ | 1 : **parse** $\sigma = (\mathbf{z}, y, c)$
2 : $(\mathbf{s}, e) \leftarrow \chi^m \times \chi$ | 2 : **req** $\|(\mathbf{z}^\top, y)\| \leq B_{ver}$
3 : **if** $(\|(\mathbf{s}^\top, e)\| > B_{kg})$ **then** | 3 : $w \leftarrow \mathbf{a}^\top \mathbf{z} + y - tc$
4 :   **goto** line 2 | 4 : **req** $c = \mathsf{H}(w, M)$
5 : $t \leftarrow \mathbf{a}^\top \mathbf{s} + e$ | 5 : **return** 1
6 : **return** $\mathsf{sk} = \mathbf{s}, \mathsf{pk} = (\mathbf{a}, t)$ |

Fig. 5. The unblinded signing protocol, key generation and verification Blaze+, where $\mathsf{H} : \{0,1\}^* \to \mathcal{C}$ is a collision-resistant hash function and $B_{kg}, B_{ver} \in R$ are fixed norm bounds. We also specify key generation and verification. In the signing protocol (resp. verification), **req** aborts (resp. returns 0) if the requirement does not hold. See Fig. 2 of [5] for the blinded version.

After $\mathcal{A}$'s query phase, it outputs $(\mathbf{A}_j, \mathsf{aux}_j)_{j \in [\ell+1]}$ and $(\vec{c}_i)_{i \in [\ell]}$. Adversary $\mathcal{B}$ checks if $\mathcal{A}$ is successful and outputs $\perp$ to the ℓ-OMUF game if not. If $\mathcal{A}$ was successful, then $\mathcal{B}$ parses $\vec{c}_i$ as $(\hat{c}_{i,k})_{k \in [\omega]} \in \mathbb{T}^\omega$. Then, $\mathcal{B}$ closes the ith

session with $(\hat{c}_{i,k})_{k\in[\omega]}$ via the S_2 oracle and obtains $(\mathbf{z}_{i,k}, y_{i,k})_{k\in[\omega]}$ if none of the sessions abort. For all $j \in [\ell + 1]$ and $k \in [\omega]$, parses the kth row of $\mathbf{A}_j$ as $(\bot, \cdots, \alpha_{j,k}, \cdots, \bot) = \mathbf{A}_j[k]$, where $\alpha_{j,k} \in \mathbb{T}$ is the non-$\bot$ entry at position $\nu_{j,k}$. Sets $\mu_{j,k} := (\nu'_{j,k}, \nu''_{j,k}) = (\lfloor \nu_{j,k}/\omega \rfloor, \nu_{j,k} \bmod \omega) \in [\ell] \times [\omega]$. We write $\mathbf{z}_{\mu_{j,k}} = \mathbf{z}_{\nu'_{j,k}, \nu''_{j,k}}$ for short, and extend this notation to $y_{\mu_{j,k}}, \hat{c}_{\mu_{j,k}}$ naturally. Using this notation, $\mathcal{B}$ constructs the values

$$\mathbf{z}_j^* = \sum_{k\in[\omega]} \alpha_{j,k} \cdot \mathbf{z}_{\mu_{j,k}} \quad \text{and} \quad y_j^* = \sum_{k\in[\omega]} \alpha_{j,k} \cdot y_{\mu_{j,k}}. \tag{11}$$

Also, $\mathcal{B}$ parses $(w_j^*, \mathsf{M}_j) \leftarrow T[\mathbf{A}_j, \mathsf{aux}_j]$. Note that by construction, we have that $w_j^* = \sum_{k\in[\omega]} \alpha_{j,k} \cdot w_{\mu_{j,k}}$. To generate the forgeries, $\mathcal{B}$ sets $c_j^* \leftarrow \mathsf{H}(w_j^*, \mathsf{M}_j)$ and $\sigma_j = (\mathbf{z}_j^*, y_j^*, \mathsf{M}_j)$. Finally, $\mathcal{B}$ outputs the forgeries $(\sigma_j, \mathsf{M}_j)_{j\in[\ell+1]}$ to the ℓ-OMUF game.

Success probability. Let us analyze the success probability. Recall that the random oracle H maps into $\mathcal{C}$, and for any $c \in \mathcal{C}$ we have that $\mathsf{Decomp}(c) \in \mathbb{T}^\omega$. Further, $\mathsf{Decomp}(c)$ is uniform over $\mathbb{T}^\omega$ for $c \leftarrow \mathcal{C}$ drawn at random. Thus, for each distinct $\mathsf{H}_{\mathsf{ros}}$ query, $\mathcal{B}$ outputs a random value in $\mathbb{T}^\omega$ as desired. Set $\mathbf{d} = (\vec{c}_1^\top, \cdots, \vec{c}_\ell^\top)^\top$. If $\mathcal{A}$ is successful, we have that $(\mathbf{A}_j, \mathsf{aux}_j)_{j\in[\ell+1]}$ are pairwise distinct, $(\hat{c}_{i,k})_{k\in[\omega]} = \vec{c}_i \in \mathbb{T}^\omega$ and $\mathbf{A}_j \in (\mathbb{T} \cup \{\bot\})^{\omega\times\omega\ell}$ with $\|\mathbf{A}_j[k]\|_\infty = 1$ for all $k \in [\omega]$. By construction, we know that $(\mathsf{M}_j)_{j\in[\ell+1]}$ are pairwise distinct.

Also, for all $j \in [\ell + 1]$ it holds that $\mathbf{A}_j \cdot \mathbf{d} = \mathsf{H}_{\mathsf{ros}}(\mathbf{A}_j, \mathsf{aux}_j)$. With the above notation, this is equivalent to $(\alpha_{j,k} \cdot \hat{c}_{\mu_{j,k}})_{k\in[\omega]} = \mathsf{H}_{\mathsf{ros}}(\mathbf{A}_j, \mathsf{aux}_j)$. Also, we have that $\mathsf{H}_{\mathsf{ros}}(\mathbf{A}_j, \mathsf{aux}_j) = \mathsf{Decomp}(\mathsf{H}(w_j^*, \mathsf{M}_j))$ by construction. Using both equalities and the definition of Decomp, we obtain for $j \in [\ell + 1]$ that

$$\mathsf{H}(w_j^*, \mathsf{M}_j) = \sum_{k\in[\omega]} \alpha_{j,k} \cdot \hat{c}_{\mu_{j,k}} \tag{12}$$

Also, if none of the ℓ signing sessions abort, we have that for all $(i, k) \in [\ell] \times [\omega]$ that

$$w_{i,k} = \mathbf{a}^\top \mathbf{z}_{i,k} + y_{i,k} - t \cdot \hat{c}_{i,k} \tag{13}$$

Combining the above observations, we obtain that $c_j^* = \mathsf{H}(w_j^*, \mathsf{M}_j)$ and

$$\begin{aligned}
w_j^* &= \sum_{k\in[\omega]} \alpha_{j,k} \cdot w_{\mu_{j,k}} \\
&\overset{(13)}{=} \sum_{k\in[\omega]} \alpha_{j,k}(\mathbf{a}^\top \mathbf{z}_{\mu_{j,k}} + y_{\mu_{j,k}} - t \cdot \hat{c}_{\mu_{j,k}}) \\
&= \mathbf{a}^\top \Big(\sum_{k\in[\omega]} \alpha_{j,k}\mathbf{z}_{\mu_{j,k}}\Big) + \Big(\sum_{k\in[\omega]} \alpha_{j,k}y_{\mu_{j,k}}\Big) - t \cdot \Big(\sum_{k\in[\omega]} a_{\mu_{j,k}}\hat{c}_{\mu_{j,k}}\Big) \\
&\overset{(11)}{=} \mathbf{a}^\top \mathbf{z}_j^* + y_j^* - t \cdot \Big(\sum_{k\in[\omega]} a_{\mu_{j,k}}\hat{c}_{\mu_{j,k}}\Big) \\
&\overset{(12)}{=} \mathbf{a}^\top \mathbf{z}_j^* + y_j^* - t \cdot \mathsf{H}(w_j^*, \mathsf{M}_j) \\
&= \mathbf{a}^\top \mathbf{z}_j^* + y_j^* - t \cdot c_j^*
\end{aligned}$$

Also, since δ_{rej} is the probability that a signing session aborts and since $\mathcal{B}$ opens ℓ sessions in total, we have that no session aborts with probability at least $(1 - \delta_{\text{rej}})^\ell$. It remains to show that $\|((\mathbf{z}_j^*)^\top, y_j^*)\| \leq B_{\text{ver}}$ with high probability. This follows as in the proof of correctness of Blaze+ [4, Theorem 1]. Roughly, observe that the multiplication with $\alpha_{j,k} \in \mathbb{T}$ does not increase the norm of $\mathbf{z}_{\mu_{j,k}}$ or $y_{\mu_{j,k}}$. Thus, the signatures output by $\mathcal{B}$ have the same norm distribution as honest (unblinded) signatures and consequently, the probability that all forgeries are valid is δ_{ver}^ℓ.

We can now combine Theorem 4.2 with our attack from Sect. 3.2 to break one-more unforgeability of Blaze+ in a concurrent setting.

Corollary 4.2. *Let $N \in \mathbb{N}$ and $\ell = \lceil \omega/N \rceil$. There is a PPT adversary on ℓ-OMUF of Blaze+ with success probability $\delta_{\text{ver}}^\ell (1 - \delta_{\text{rej}})^\ell$ with expected $\mathcal{O}(\ell(2n)^N)$ queries to the hash functions.*

Concretely, in the instantiation of Blaze+, we have $n = 1024$ and $\omega = 16$ for $\lambda = 128$. Also, the abort probability δ_{rej} for rejection sampling is at most $\delta_{\text{rej}} \leq 0.47$ in their instantiations, and the probability δ_{ver} that a honest signature verifies is at least $\delta_{\text{ver}} \geq 1 - 2^{-\lambda}$. By taking $N = 1$, with 16 concurrent sessions of Blaze+ and an expected number of 2^{15} hash queries, we obtain an attack on 16-one-more unforgeability of Blaze+ with the probability greater than $2.8 \cdot 10^{-5}$. For $N = 4$, with 4 concurrent sessions of Blaze+ and an expected number of 2^{46} hash queries, we are able to break the 4-one-more unforgeability of it with the probability at least 0.073.

Remark 4.2 (Variant with 4 rounds). Note that a 4-move version of Blaze+ is also presented in the appendix of [5]. Here, the user has the option to abort in case the blinding procedure fails. In the event of an abort, the user is required to provide a proof that no valid signature was obtained. Our attack works without change on this variant.

BlindOR Here, we give an efficient attack on BlindOR [6]. At a high-level, BlindOR runs two instances of Blaze$^+$ in parallel and combines them with the OR-proof technique (similar to CSI-Otter). That is, one instance is run as usual, whereas the other instance is simulated. Each instance uses one share $\mathbf{c}_0$ or $\mathbf{c}_1$ as challenge, where $\mathbf{c} = \mathbf{c}_0 \odot \mathbf{c}_1$ is output by a hash function. Further, BlindOR makes other design choices listed below.

Signer$((\mathbf{a}, t_0, t_1), (\delta, \mathbf{s}_\delta))$	**User$((\mathbf{a}, t_0, t_1), \mathsf{M})$**

1 :   **for** $i \in [\omega]$

2 : $(\mathbf{r}_{\delta,i}, e'_{\delta,i}) \leftarrow \chi^m_{\mathsf{rs}} \times \chi_{\mathsf{rs}}$

3 : $w_{\delta,i} \leftarrow \mathbf{a}^\top \mathbf{r}_{\delta,i} + e'_{\delta,i}$

4 : $\mathbf{c}_{1-\delta} \leftarrow \mathbb{T}^\omega$

5 : $(w_{1-\delta,i}, \mathbf{z}_{1-\delta,i}, y_{1-\delta,i})_{i \in [\omega]} \leftarrow \mathsf{Sim}(\mathbf{a}, t_{1-\delta}, \mathbf{c}_{1-\delta})$

$$\xrightarrow{\quad (w_{0,i}, w_{1,i})_{i \in [\omega]} \quad}$$

6 : $\mathbf{c} \leftarrow \mathsf{H}((w_{0,i}, w_{1,i})_{i \in [\omega]}, \mathsf{M})$

$$\xleftarrow{\quad \mathbf{c} \quad}$$

7 :   **req** $\mathbf{c} \in \mathbb{T}^\omega$

8 : $\mathbf{c}_\delta \leftarrow \mathbf{c} \odot \mathbf{c}_{1-\delta}$

9 :   **for** $i \in [\omega]$

10 : $\mathbf{z}_{\delta,i} \leftarrow \mathbf{s} \cdot c_{\delta,i} + \mathbf{r}_{\delta,i}$

11 : $y_{\delta,i} \leftarrow e \cdot c_{\delta,i} + e'_{\delta,i}$

12 :   **req** $\mathsf{RejSamp}((\mathbf{z}_i, y_i)_{i \in [\omega]})$

$$\xrightarrow{\quad (\mathbf{z}_{0,i}, y_{0,i}, \mathbf{z}_{1,i}, y_{1,i})_{i \in [\omega]}, \mathbf{c}_0, \mathbf{c}_1 \quad}$$

13 : $\sigma \leftarrow ((\mathbf{z}_{0,i}, y_{0,i}, \mathbf{z}_{1,i}, y_{1,i})_{i \in [\omega]}, \mathbf{c}_0, \mathbf{c}_1)$

Fig. 6. The unblinded signing protocol of BlindOR, where $\mathsf{H} : \{0,1\}^* \to \mathbb{T}^\omega$ is a collision-resistant hash function, $B_{\mathsf{ver}} \in R$ is some fixed norm bound, and $\odot$ is the entry-wise product. In the signing protocol, **req** aborts if the requirement does not hold. Key generation, verification and the simulator Sim are defined in Fig. 7. See Fig. 9 of [6] for the blinded version.

1. BlindOR uses challenges in $\mathbb{T}^\omega$ instead of $\mathcal{C}$ (as this allows to share the challenges multiplicatively over $\mathbb{T}$). On the other hand, Blaze$^+$ uses a single challenge $c \in \mathcal{C}$, but decomposes it into ω challenges in $\mathbb{T}$ during signing.
2. BlindOR performs η-many Blaze$^+$ protocols in parallel in S_1, but only a single protocol is completed in S_2. The completed protocol is the first for which rejection sampling succeeds (in random order).
3. Blaze$^+$ is described in the ring lattice setting, whereas BlindOR is described the module lattice setting.

For consistency, we present BlindOR in the ring setting (instead of in the module setting). We stress that this is purely to keep notation consistent and that it is straightforward to modify the attack to work in the module lattice setting. Also, since their instantiation uses $\eta = 1$, we omit the additional parallel executions

Verify$((\mathbf{a}, \mathbf{b}_0, \mathbf{b}_1), \sigma, \mathsf{M})$:	KeyGen(1^λ) :
1: **parse** $\sigma = ((\mathbf{z}_{0,i}, y_{0,i}, \mathbf{z}_{1,i}, y_{1,i})_{i \in [\omega]}, \mathbf{c}_0, \mathbf{c}_1)$	1: $\mathbf{a} \leftarrow R_q^m$
2: **for** $\delta \in \{0,1\}$	2: **for** $\delta \in \{0,1\}$
3: $\quad$ **req** $\|(\mathbf{z}_{\delta,i}^\top, y_{\delta,i})_{i\in[\omega]}\| \leq B_{\mathsf{ver}}$	3: $\quad (\mathbf{s}_\delta, e_\delta) \leftarrow \chi^m \times \chi$
4: $\quad$ **for** $i \in [\omega]$	4: $\quad$ **if** $(\|(\mathbf{s}_\delta^\top, e_\delta)\| > B_{\mathsf{kg}})$ **then**
5: $\quad\quad w_{\delta,i} \leftarrow \mathbf{a}^\top \mathbf{z}_{\delta,i} + y_{\delta,i} - t_\delta c_{\delta,i}$	5: $\quad\quad$ **goto** line 3
6: **req** $\mathbf{c}_0 \odot \mathbf{c}_1 = \mathsf{H}((w_{\delta,i}, w_{\delta,i})_{i\in[\omega]}, \mathsf{M})$	6: $\quad t_\delta \leftarrow \mathbf{a}^\top \mathbf{s}_\delta + e_\delta$
7: **return** 1	7: $\delta \leftarrow \{0,1\}$
	8: $\mathsf{sk} = (\delta, \mathbf{s}_\delta, e_\delta)$
Sim$(\mathbf{a}, t, \mathbf{c})$:	9: $\mathsf{pk} = (\mathbf{a}, t_0, t_1)$
	10: **return** sk, pk
1: **for** $i \in [\omega]$	
2: $\quad (\mathbf{z}_i, y_i) \leftarrow \chi_{\mathsf{rs}} \times \chi_{\mathsf{rs}}$	
3: $\quad w_i = \mathbf{a}^\top \mathbf{z}_i + y_i - t c_i$	
4: **return** $(w_i, \mathbf{z}_i, y_i)_{i\in[\omega]}$	

Fig. 7. The key generation and verification protocol for BlindOR, where $B_{\mathsf{kg}} \in R$ is some fixed norm bound, and $\odot$ is the entry-wise product. We also provide a description of the simulator Sim. In the verification, **req** returns 0 if the requirement does not hold. Note that instead of running the simulator again if it aborts as in [6], we define Sim such that it does not abort directly. The unblinded signing protocol is defined in Fig. 6.

in S_1 in our analysis. (We discuss in Remark 4.3 how to adapt the attack for $\eta > 1$.) Let $\mathsf{H} : \{0,1\}^* \to \mathbb{T}^\omega$ be a collision-resistant hash function. We describe the unblinded version of BlindOR in Figs. 6 and 7.

For our attack, we proceed as in our attack on Blaze+ (cf. Sect. 4.2) and handle the OR-proof as in our attack on CSI-Otter (cf. Sect. 4.1). We summarize our attack in the theorem below.

Theorem 4.3. *For any PPT adversary $\mathcal{A}$ on* Group-pROS$_{\ell,\omega,\mathbb{T},\mathbb{T}}$, *there is an adversary $\mathcal{B}$ against ℓ-OMUF of* BlindOR *such that* $\mathsf{Adv}_{\mathcal{B}}^{\mathsf{OMUF}}(\lambda) = \delta_{\mathsf{ver}}^{2\ell}(1 - \delta_{\mathsf{rej}})^\ell \cdot \mathsf{Adv}_{\mathcal{A},\ell,\omega,\mathbb{T},\mathbb{T}}^{\mathsf{Group\text{-}pROS}}(\lambda)$.

Proof. Let $\mathcal{A}$ be an adversary on Group-pROS$_{\ell,\omega,\mathbb{T},\mathbb{T}}$ for some $\ell \in \mathbb{N}$. We use $\mathcal{A}$ to construct an adversary $\mathcal{B}$ against ℓ-OMUF of BlindOR as follows.

Adversary $\mathcal{B}$. Adversary $\mathcal{B}$ obtains a public key $(\mathbf{a}, t_0, t_1)$ and access to oracles H, S_1 and S_2. Then, $\mathcal{B}$ opens ℓ concurrent (signing) sessions via the S_1 oracle and obtains $(w_{0,i,k}, w_{1,i,k})_{k\in[\omega]}$ from the ith session. Next, $\mathcal{B}$ generates a table T initialized with $\perp$ entries. Sets $\mathbf{v}_\delta = (w_{\delta,1,1}, w_{\delta,1,2}, \cdots, w_{\delta,\ell,\omega}) \in R_q^{\omega\ell}$ for $\delta \in \{0,1\}$.

Let Q be the number of $\mathsf{H}_{\mathsf{ros}}$ queries of $\mathcal{A}$ (including potential queries for verification of $\mathcal{A}$'s output). Assume without loss of generality that each $\mathsf{H}_{\mathsf{ros}}$ query is distinct. For the ith such query $(\mathbf{A}, \mathsf{aux})$ to $\mathsf{H_{ros}}$ of $\mathcal{A}$, adversary $\mathcal{B}$ proceeds as follows. If $\mathbf{A} \notin (\mathbb{T} \cup \{\bot\})^{\omega \times \omega\ell}$ or $\|\mathbf{A}[k]\|_\infty \neq 1$ for some $k \in [\omega]$, then returns $\mathbf{c}^* \leftarrow \mathbb{T}^\omega$. Else, parses the kth row of $\mathbf{A}$ as $(\bot, \cdots, \alpha_k, \cdots, \bot) = \mathbf{A}[k]$, where $\alpha_k \in \mathbb{T}$ is the non-$\bot$ entry in column ν_k. Sets $w^*_{0,k} = \alpha_k \mathbf{v}_{0,\nu_k}$ and $w^*_{1,k} = \mathbf{v}_{1,\nu_k}$ for $k \in [\omega]$. Note that $(w^*_{0,1}, \cdots, w^*_{0,\omega}) = \mathbf{A} \cdot \mathbf{v}_0$. Also, sets $\mathsf{M} = (\mathsf{aux}, i)$ and $T[\mathbf{A}, \mathsf{aux}] = ((w^*_{0,k}, w^*_{1,k})_{k \in [\omega]}, \mathsf{M})$. Note that by construction, M is distinct for distinct queries. Sets $\mathbf{c}^* = \mathsf{H}((w^*_{0,k}, w^*_{1,k})_{k \in [\omega]}, \mathsf{M})$ and outputs $\mathbf{c}^*$.

After $\mathcal{A}$'s query phase, it outputs $(\mathbf{A}_j, \mathsf{aux}_j)_{j \in [\ell+1]}$ and $(\mathbf{c}_i)_{i \in [\ell]}$. Adversary $\mathcal{B}$ checks if $\mathcal{A}$ is successful and outputs $\bot$ to the ℓ-OMUF game if not. If $\mathcal{A}$ was successful, $\mathcal{B}$ closes the ith session with $\mathbf{c}_i$ via the S_2 oracle and obtains $((\mathbf{z}_{i,0,k}, y_{i,0,k}, \mathbf{z}_{i,1,k}, y_{i,1,k})_{k \in [\omega]}, \mathbf{c}_{i,0}, \mathbf{c}_{i,1})$ if none of the sessions abort. For all $j \in [\ell+1]$ and $k \in [\omega]$, parses the kth row of $\mathbf{A}_j$ as above, i.e., $(\bot, \cdots, \alpha_{j,k}, \cdots, \bot) = \mathbf{A}_j[k]$, where $\alpha_{j,k} \in \mathbb{T}$ is the non-$\bot$ entry at position $\nu_{j,k}$. For $b \in \{0, 1\}$, sets $\mu_{j,b,k} := (\nu'_{j,k}, b, \nu''_{j,k}) = (\lfloor \nu_{j,k}/\omega \rfloor, b, \nu_{j,k} \bmod \omega) \in [\ell] \times \{0, 1\} \times [\omega]$. For values $\mathbf{x}$ indexed over $[\ell] \times \{0, 1\} \times [\omega]$, we write $\mathbf{x}_{\mu_{j,b,k}}$ short for $\mathbf{x}_{\nu'_{j,k}, b, \nu''_{j,k}}$. Using this notation, for $j \in [\ell+1]$ and $k \in [\omega]$, adversary $\mathcal{B}$ sets

$$
\begin{aligned}
\mathbf{z}^*_{j,0,k} &= \alpha_{j,k} \cdot \mathbf{z}_{\mu_{j,0,k}}, & y^*_{j,0,k} &= \alpha_{j,k} \cdot y_{\mu_{j,0,k}} & &\text{and} & \mathbf{c}^*_{j,0,k} &= \alpha_{j,k} \cdot \mathbf{c}_{\mu_{j,0,k}} \\
\mathbf{z}^*_{j,1,k} &= \mathbf{z}_{\mu_{j,0,k}}, & y^*_{j,1,k} &= y_{\mu_{j,1,k}} & & & \mathbf{c}^*_{j,1,k} &= \mathbf{c}_{\mu_{j,1,k}}
\end{aligned}
\tag{14}
$$

Sets $\mathbf{c}^*_{j,b} = (\mathbf{c}^*_{j,b,1}, \cdots, \mathbf{c}^*_{j,b,\omega})$. Also, $\mathcal{B}$ parses $((w^*_{j,0,k}, w^*_{j,1,k})_{k \in [\omega]}, \mathsf{M}_j) \leftarrow T[\mathbf{A}_j, \mathsf{aux}_j]$. Note that by construction, we have that

$$
w^*_{j,b,k} = \alpha^{1-b}_{j,k} \cdot w_{\mu_{j,b,k}}.
\tag{15}
$$

Finally, $\mathcal{B}$ sets $\sigma_j = ((\mathbf{z}^*_{j,0,k}, \mathbf{z}^*_{j,1,k}, y^*_{j,0,k}, y^*_{j,0,k})_{k \in [\omega]}, \mathbf{c}^*_{j,0}, \mathbf{c}^*_{j,1})$ and outputs the forgeries $(\sigma_j, \mathsf{M}_j)_{j \in [\ell+1]}$ to the ℓ-OMUF game.

Success probability. Let us analyze the success probability. It is easy to check that for each distinct $\mathsf{H_{ros}}$ query, $\mathcal{B}$ outputs a random value in $\mathbb{T}^\omega$ as desired. Set $\mathbf{d} = (\mathbf{c}_1^\top, \cdots, \mathbf{c}_\ell^\top)^\top$. If $\mathcal{A}$ is successful, we have that $(\mathbf{A}_j, \mathsf{aux}_j)_{j \in [\ell+1]}$ are pairwise distinct, $\mathbf{c}_i \in \mathbb{T}^\omega$ and $\mathbf{A}_j \in (\mathbb{T} \cup \{\bot\})^{\omega \times \omega\ell}$ with $\|\mathbf{A}_j[k]\|_\infty = 1$ for all $k \in [\omega]$. Also, we know that $(\mathsf{M}_j)_{j \in [\ell+1]}$ are pairwise distinct by construction. Further, for all $j \in [\ell+1]$ it holds that $\mathbf{A}_j \cdot \mathbf{d} = \mathsf{H_{ros}}(\mathbf{A}_j, \mathsf{aux}_j) := \mathbf{c}^*_j$. Using the above notation, this is equivalent to $\alpha_{j,k} \mathbf{d}_{\nu_{j,k}} = \mathbf{c}^*_{j,k}$ for all $k \in [\omega]$. By construction, we have that $\mathsf{H_{ros}}(\mathbf{A}_j, \mathsf{aux}_j) = \mathsf{H}((w^*_{j,0,k}, w^*_{j,1,k})_{k \in [\omega]}, \mathsf{M}_j)$. Using both equalities, we obtain for $j \in [\ell+1]$ that

$$
\mathsf{H}((w^*_{j,0,k}, w^*_{j,1,k})_{k \in [\omega]}, \mathsf{M}_j) = (\alpha_{j,k} \cdot \mathbf{d}_{\nu_{j,k}})_{k \in [\omega]}
\tag{16}
$$

Also, if none of the ℓ signing sessions abort, we have that for all $(i, b, k) \in [\ell] \times \{0, 1\} \times [\omega]$ that

$$
\begin{aligned}
w_{i,b,k} &= \mathbf{a}^\top \mathbf{z}_{i,b,k} + y_{i,b,k} - t_b \cdot \mathbf{c}_{i,b,k} \\
\mathbf{c}_i &= \mathbf{c}_{i,0} \odot \mathbf{c}_{i,1}
\end{aligned}
\tag{17}
$$

Combining the above observations, we obtain for all $j \in [\ell], b \in \{0,1\}, k \in [\omega]$ that

$$
\begin{aligned}
w_{j,b,k}^* &\overset{(15)}{=} \alpha_{j,k}^{1-b} \cdot w_{\mu_{j,b,k}} \overset{(17)}{=} \alpha_{j,k}^{1-b} (\mathbf{a}^\top \mathbf{z}_{\mu_{j,b,k}} + y_{\mu_{j,b,k}} - t_b \cdot \mathbf{c}_{\mu_{j,b,k}}) \\
&= \mathbf{a}^\top (\alpha_{j,k}^{1-b} \cdot \mathbf{z}_{\mu_{j,b,k}}) + (\alpha_{j,k}^{1-b} \cdot y_{\mu_{j,b,k}}) - t_b \cdot (\alpha_{j,k}^{1-b} \cdot \mathbf{c}_{\mu_{j,b,k}}) \\
&\overset{(14)}{=} \mathbf{a}^\top \mathbf{z}_{j,b,k}^* + y_{j,b,k}^* - t_b \cdot \mathbf{c}_{j,b,k}^*
\end{aligned}
$$

and

$$
\mathsf{H}((w_{j,0,k}^*, w_{j,1,k}^*)_{k \in [\omega]}, \mathsf{M}_j) \overset{(16)}{=} \alpha_{j,k} \cdot \mathbf{d}_{\nu_{j,k}} \overset{(17)}{=} \alpha_{j,k} \cdot \mathbf{c}_{\mu j,0,k} \cdot \mathbf{c}_{\mu j,1,k} \overset{(14)}{=} \mathbf{c}_{j,0,k}^* \cdot \mathbf{c}_{j,1,k}^*
$$

Also, since δ_{rej} is the probability that rejection sampling fails and since $\mathcal{B}$ opens ℓ sessions in total, we have that no session aborts with probability at least $(1 - \delta_{\mathsf{rej}})^\ell$. We can show that $\|((\mathbf{z}_{j,b,k}^*)^\top, y_{j,b,k}^*)\| \leq B_{\mathsf{ver}}$ as in the proof of Corollary 4.2 (i.e., our attack on Blaze$^+$). Since we obtain two Blaze$^+$ signatures per signature, the norm bound holds for all signatures with probability $\delta_{\mathsf{ver}}^{2\ell}$. $\quad\square$

Corollary 4.3. *Let $N \in \mathbb{N}$ and $\ell = \lceil \omega/N \rceil$. There exists a PPT adversary on ℓ-OMUF of $\mathsf{BlindOR}$ with success probability $\delta_{\mathsf{ver}}^{2\ell}(1 - \delta_{\mathsf{rej}})^\ell$ and with expected $\mathcal{O}(\ell(2n)^N)$ queries to the hash functions.*

For concrete numbers, we refer to the analysis of Blaze$^+$ (cf. Sect. 4.2)[6]. Note that the success probability is to be multiplied with $(1 - 2^\lambda)^\ell \approx 1$ due to the additional factor 2 in the exponent of δ_{ver}.

Remark 4.3. To reduce the abort probability δ_{rej} due to the signer's rejection sampling in S_2, $\mathsf{BlindOR}$ gives the option to initiate $\eta > 1$ signing sessions of S_1 concurrently, but only a single session is finished (if any). This session is the first session (chosen at random) where rejection sampling does not abort in S_2. Our attack can be adapted to this setting by guessing which session is finished. Then, we can proceed with our attack as before. The probability that we guess correctly in our attack is at least $(1/\eta)^\ell$.

4.3 Blind Signature Based on Parallel Schnorr

Let $(\mathbb{G}, +)$ be a group with prime order p. We use additive notation. Let $g \in \mathbb{G}$ be a generator. We define a natural variant of blind Schnorr with ω parallel repetitions. The interactive signing protocol, key generation and verification is

---

[6] Since BlindOR runs two Blaze$^+$ instances in parallel, the efficiency of the attack is identical for shared concrete parameters. Note that we presented our attack in the ring lattice setting, but as mentioned above, it is straightforward to adapt it to the module lattice setting of the BlindOR instantiation.

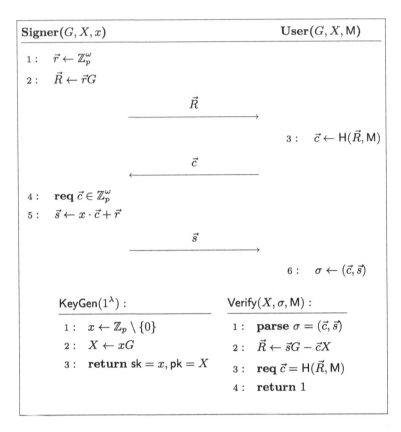

Fig. 8. An interactive signing protocol for Schnorr with ω parallel repetitions. We also specify key generation and verification. In the signing protocol (resp. verification), **req** aborts (resp. returns 0) if the requirement does not hold.

defined in Fig. 8. We also provide a full specification in Fig. 9 (without security proofs). We analyze it exclusively for illustrative purposes and note that the benefit compared to the original blind Schnorr is marginal.

Conceptually, the use of both parallel repetitions *and* exponential challenge space should make the scheme more secure. For example for the standard Schnorr Σ-protocol, the soundness error $\varepsilon := 1/p$ can be exponentially reduced with ω parallel repetitions to ε^ω [15]. Since blind Schnorr remains secure for $o(\log p)$-many concurrent sessions, perhaps its security can be amplified in a similar manner due to the exponential challenge space. We show that this intuition is wrong and there is an efficient attack on the scheme.

In more detail, we show that a successful adversary on $\mathsf{Ring}\text{-}\mathsf{pROS}_{\ell,\omega,\mathbb{Z}_p,\mathbb{Z}_p}$ allows to break the ℓ-OMUF of parallel blind Schnorr with ω repetitions. Then, we can apply the attack from Sect. 3.3 since $\mathbb{Z}_p$ is a field and binary decomposition is efficient over $\mathbb{Z}_p$.

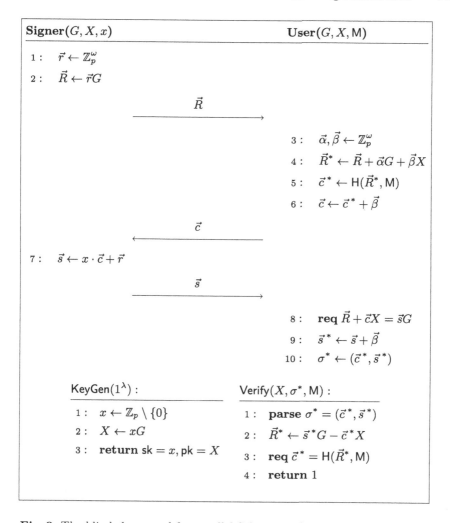

Fig. 9. The blinded protocol for parallel Schnorr with ω parallel repetitions.

Theorem 4.4. *For any PPT adversary* $\mathcal{A}$ *on* $\mathsf{Ring\text{-}pROS}_{\ell,\omega,\mathbb{Z}_p,\mathbb{Z}_p}$, *there is an adversary* $\mathcal{B}$ *against* ℓ-OMUF *of parallel blind Schnorr such that* $\mathsf{Adv}_{\mathcal{B}}^{\mathsf{OMUF}}(\lambda) =$ $\mathsf{Adv}_{\mathcal{A},\ell,\omega,\mathcal{R},\mathcal{R}_c}^{\mathsf{Ring\text{-}pROS}}(\lambda)$.

Proof. Let $\mathcal{A}$ be an adversary on $\mathsf{Ring\text{-}pROS}_{\ell,\omega,\mathbb{Z}_p,\mathbb{Z}_p}$ for some $\ell \in \mathbb{N}$. We construct an adversary $\mathcal{B}$ against ℓ-OMUF of parallel blind Schnorr with ω parallel repetitions using $\mathcal{A}$.

Adversary $\mathcal{B}$. Initially, $\mathcal{B}$ obtains a public key X and access to oracles H, S_1 and S_2. Then, $\mathcal{B}$ opens ℓ concurrent (signing) sessions via the S_1 oracle. It obtains $\vec{R}_i$ from the ith session. Then, $\mathcal{B}$ generates a table T initialized with $\perp$ entries. Sets $\vec{S} \leftarrow (\vec{R}_1^\top, \cdots, \vec{R}_\ell^\top)^\top \in \mathbb{G}^{\omega \cdot \ell}$.

Let Q be the number of H_{ros} queries of $\mathcal{A}$ (including potential queries for verification of $\mathcal{A}$'s output). Assume without loss of generality that each H_{ros} query is distinct. For the ith such query $(\mathbf{A}, \mathsf{aux})$ to H_{ros} of $\mathcal{A}$, adversary $\mathcal{B}$ proceeds as follows. If $\mathbf{A} \notin \mathbb{Z}_p^{\omega \times \omega \ell}$, then returns $\vec{c}^* \leftarrow \mathbb{Z}_p^\omega$. Otherwise, sets $\vec{R}^* \leftarrow \mathbf{A} \cdot \vec{S}$ and $\mathsf{M} = (\mathsf{aux}, i)$. Sets $T[\mathbf{A}, \mathsf{aux}] = (\vec{R}^*, \mathsf{M})$. Note that by construction, M is distinct for distinct queries. Outputs $\mathsf{H}(\vec{R}^*, \mathsf{M})$.

After $\mathcal{A}$'s query phase, it outputs $(\mathbf{A}_j, \mathsf{aux}_j)_{j \in [\ell+1]}$ and $(\vec{c}_i)_{i \in [\ell]}$. Adversary $\mathcal{B}$ checks if $\mathcal{A}$ is successful and outputs $\perp$ to the ℓ-OMUF game if not. Next, closes the ith session with $\vec{c}_i$ via the S_2 oracle and obtains $\vec{s}_i$. Sets $\vec{t} \leftarrow (\vec{s}_1^\top, \cdots, \vec{s}_\ell^\top)^\top$. Now, $\mathcal{B}$ parses $(\vec{R}_j^*, \mathsf{M}_j) \leftarrow T[\mathbf{A}_j, \mathsf{aux}_j]$. Sets $\vec{s}_j^* \leftarrow \mathbf{A}_j \cdot \vec{t}$, $\vec{c}_j^* \leftarrow \mathsf{H}(\vec{R}_j^*, \mathsf{M}_j)$, and $\sigma_j = (\vec{c}_j^*, \vec{s}_j^*)$. Finally, outputs the forgeries $(\sigma_j, \mathsf{M}_j)_{j \in [\ell+1]}$ to the ℓ-OMUF game.

Success probability. Let us analyze the success probability. Recall that the random oracle H maps into $\mathbb{Z}_p^\omega$. Thus, for each distinct H_{ros} query, $\mathcal{B}$ outputs a random value in $\mathbb{Z}_p^\omega$ as desired. Set $\vec{d} := (\vec{c}_1^\top, \cdots, \vec{c}_\ell^\top)^\top \in \mathbb{Z}_p^{\omega \ell}$. If $\mathcal{A}$ is successful, we have that $(\mathbf{A}_j, \mathsf{aux}_j)_{j \in [\ell+1]}$ are pairwise distinct, $\vec{c}_i \in \mathbb{Z}_p^\omega$ and $\mathbf{A}_j \in \mathbb{Z}_p^{\omega \times \omega \ell}$. Also, for all $j \in [\ell+1]$ it holds that $\mathbf{A}_j \cdot \vec{d} = \mathsf{H}_{ros}(\mathbf{A}_j, \mathsf{aux}_j)$. Thus, we know that $(\mathsf{M}_j)_{j \in [\ell+1]}$ are pairwise distinct by construction. Also, all forgeries are valid since $\vec{c}_j^* = \mathsf{H}(\vec{R}_j^*, \mathsf{M}_j)$ and

$$\begin{aligned}
\vec{R}_j^* &= \mathbf{A}_j \cdot \vec{S} = \mathbf{A}_j \cdot (\vec{R}_1^\top, \cdots, \vec{R}_\ell^\top)^\top \\
&= \mathbf{A}_j \cdot ((\vec{s}_1 G - \vec{c}_1 X)^\top, \cdots, (\vec{s}_\ell G - \vec{c}_\ell X)^\top)^\top \\
&= \mathbf{A}_j \cdot (\vec{t} G - \vec{d} X) \\
&= (\mathbf{A}_j \cdot \vec{t}) G - (\mathbf{A}_j \cdot \vec{d}) X \\
&= \vec{s}_j^* G - \mathsf{H}_{ros}(\mathbf{A}_j, \mathsf{aux}_j) X \\
&= \vec{s}_j^* G - \mathsf{H}(\vec{R}_j^*, \mathsf{M}_j) X \\
&= \vec{s}_j^* G - \vec{c}_j^* X.
\end{aligned}$$

$\square$

Set $B_\mu = 2^{\mu-1}$. If we combine Theorem 4.4 with Theorem 3.2 (i.e., the attack from Sect. 3.3 with binary generating set $(B_\mu)_{\mu \in [\lceil \log p \rceil]}$), we obtain an attack on parallel blind Schnorr. Since any value in $\mathbb{Z}_p$ can be decomposed in binary efficiently, the attack runs in $\mathcal{O}(\ell)$ for $\ell \geq \omega \lceil \log p \rceil$. Note that in practice, we often have $\lceil \log p \rceil = 256$ and the attack remains concretely efficient for a large number of parallel repetitions ω.

Corollary 4.4. *Let $n \in \mathbb{N}$ and $\ell \geq \omega \lceil \log p \rceil$. There exists an PPT adversary on ℓ-OMUF of parallel Schnorr with success probability 1 that runs in time $\mathcal{O}(\ell)$, counting hash queries, binary decompositions and operations in $\mathbb{Z}_p$ and $\mathbb{G}$.*

Acknowledgements. Shuichi Katsumata was supported by JST CREST Grant Number JPMJCR22M1, JST AIP Acceleration Research JPMJCR22U5, and JSPS KAKENHI Grant Number JP19H01109, Japan. Yi-Fu Lai was supported in part by the Ministry for Business, Innovation and Employment of New Zealand and was also supported by the European Union (ERC AdG REWORC - 101054911).

References

1. Abe, M.: A secure three-move blind signature scheme for polynomially many signatures. In: Pfitzmann, B. (ed.) EUROCRYPT 2001. LNCS, vol. 2045, pp. 136–151. Springer, Heidelberg (2001). https://doi.org/10.1007/3-540-44987-6_9
2. Abe, M., Groth, J., Haralambiev, K., Ohkubo, M.: Optimal structure-preserving signatures in asymmetric bilinear groups. In: Rogaway, P. (ed.) CRYPTO 2011. LNCS, vol. 6841, pp. 649–666. Springer, Heidelberg (2011). https://doi.org/10.1007/978-3-642-22792-9_37
3. Abe, M., Okamoto, T.: Provably secure partially blind signatures. In: Bellare, M. (ed.) CRYPTO 2000. LNCS, vol. 1880, pp. 271–286. Springer, Heidelberg (2000). https://doi.org/10.1007/3-540-44598-6_17
4. Alkeilani Alkadri, N., El Bansarkhani, R., Buchmann, J.: BLAZE: practical lattice-based blind signatures for privacy-preserving applications. In: Bonneau, J., Heninger, N. (eds.) FC 2020. LNCS, vol. 12059, pp. 484–502. Springer, Cham (2020). https://doi.org/10.1007/978-3-030-51280-4_26
5. Alkeilani Alkadri, N., El Bansarkhani, R., Buchmann, J.: On lattice-based interactive protocols: an approach with less or no aborts. In: Liu, J.K., Cui, H. (eds.) ACISP 2020. LNCS, vol. 12248, pp. 41–61. Springer, Cham (2020). https://doi.org/10.1007/978-3-030-55304-3_3
6. Alkeilani Alkadri, N., Harasser, P., Janson, C.: BlindOR: an efficient lattice-based blind signature scheme from OR-proofs. In: Conti, M., Stevens, M., Krenn, S. (eds.) CANS 2021. LNCS, vol. 13099, pp. 95–115. Springer, Cham (2021). https://doi.org/10.1007/978-3-030-92548-2_6
7. Benhamouda, F., Lepoint, T., Loss, J., Orrù, M., Raykova, M.: On the (in)security of ROS. In: Canteaut, A., Standaert, F.-X. (eds.) EUROCRYPT 2021. LNCS, vol. 12696, pp. 33–53. Springer, Cham (2021). https://doi.org/10.1007/978-3-030-77870-5_2
8. Beullens, W., Lyubashevsky, V., Nguyen, N.K., Seiler, G.: Lattice-based blind signatures: short, efficient, and round-optimal. Cryptology ePrint Archive, Paper 2023/077
9. Blazy, O., Fuchsbauer, G., Pointcheval, D., Vergnaud, D.: Short blind signatures. J. Comput. Secur. **21**(5), 627–661 (2013)
10. Brickell, E., Camenisch, J., Chen, L.: Direct anonymous attestation. In: ACM CCS 2004, pp. 132–145 (2004)
11. Buser, M., et al.: A survey on exotic signatures for post-quantum blockchain: Challenges & research directions. ACM Comput. Surv. **55**, 1–32 (2023)
12. Chaum, D.: Blind signatures for untraceable payments. In: Chaum, D., Rivest, R.L., Sherman, A.T. (eds.) Advances in Cryptology, pp. 199–203. Springer, Boston, MA (1983). https://doi.org/10.1007/978-1-4757-0602-4_18
13. Chaum, D., Pedersen, T.P.: Wallet databases with observers. In: Brickell, E.F. (ed.) CRYPTO 1992. LNCS, vol. 740, pp. 89–105. Springer, Heidelberg (1993). https://doi.org/10.1007/3-540-48071-4_7

14. Conti, M., Kumar, E.S., Lal, C., Ruj, S.: A survey on security and privacy issues of bitcoin. IEEE Commun. Surv. Tutorials **20**(4), 3416–3452 (2018)
15. Damgård, I.: On σ-protocols. Lecture Notes, University of Aarhus, Department for Computer Science, pp. 84 (2010)
16. R. del Pino and S. Katsumata. A new framework for more efficient round-optimal lattice-based (partially) blind signature via trapdoor sampling. In: Dodis, Y., Shrimpton, T. (eds.) CRYPTO 2022, Part II, pp. 306–336 (2022). https://doi.org/10.1007/978-3-031-15979-4_11
17. Duman, J., Hartmann, D., Kiltz, E., Kunzweiler, S., Lehmann, J., Riepel, D.: Generic models for group actions. Cryptology ePrint Archive, Report 2023/186
18. Fischlin, M.: Round-optimal composable blind signatures in the common reference string model. In: Dwork, C. (ed.) CRYPTO 2006. LNCS, vol. 4117, pp. 60–77. Springer, Heidelberg (2006). https://doi.org/10.1007/11818175_4
19. Fuchsbauer, G., Wolf, M.: (concurrently secure) blind schnorr from schnorr. IACR Cryptol. ePrint Arch., page 1676
20. Hauck, E., Kiltz, E., Loss, J.: A modular treatment of blind signatures from identification schemes. In: Ishai, Y., Rijmen, V. (eds.) EUROCRYPT 2019. LNCS, vol. 11478, pp. 345–375. Springer, Cham (2019). https://doi.org/10.1007/978-3-030-17659-4_12
21. Hauck, E., Kiltz, E., Loss, J., Nguyen, N.K.: Lattice-based blind signatures, revisited. In: Micciancio, D., Ristenpart, T. (eds.) CRYPTO 2020. LNCS, vol. 12171, pp. 500–529. Springer, Cham (2020). https://doi.org/10.1007/978-3-030-56880-1_18
22. Hendrickson, S., Iyengar, J., Pauly, T., Valdez, S., Wood, C.A.: Private access tokens. internet-draft draft-private-access-tokens-01
23. Kastner, J., Loss, J., Xu, J.: The Abe-Okamoto partially blind signature scheme revisited. In: Agrawal, S., Lin, D. (eds.) ASIACRYPT 2022, Part IV, vol. 13794, pp. 279–309. Springer, Cham (2022). https://doi.org/10.1007/978-3-031-22972-5_10
24. Kastner, J., Loss, J., Xu, J.: On pairing-free blind signature schemes in the algebraic group model. In: Hanaoka, G., Shikata, J., Watanabe, Y. (eds.) PKC 2022, Part II, vol. 13178, pp. 468–497. Springer, Cham (2022). https://doi.org/10.1007/978-3-030-97131-1_16
25. Katsumata, S., Lai, Y.F., LeGrow, J.T., Qin, L.: CSI-Otter: isogeny-based (partially) blind signatures from the class group action with a twist. In: Handschuh, H., Lysyanskaya, A. (eds.) Crypto, vol. 14083. Springer, Cham. https://doi.org/10.1007/978-3-031-38548-3_24
26. Katsumata, S., Reichle, M., Sakai, Y.: Practical round-optimal blind signatures in the ROM from standard assumptions. In: Guo, J., Steinfeld, R. (eds.) ASIACRYPT 2023. LNCS, vol. 14439, pp. 383–417. Springer, Singapore (2023)
27. Khalili, M., Slamanig, D., Dakhilalian, M.: Structure-preserving signatures on equivalence classes from standard assumptions. In: Galbraith, S.D., Moriai, S. (eds.) ASIACRYPT 2019. LNCS, vol. 11923, pp. 63–93. Springer, Cham (2019). https://doi.org/10.1007/978-3-030-34618-8_3
28. Meiklejohn, S., Shacham, H., Freeman, D.M.: Limitations on transformations from composite-order to prime-order groups: the case of round-optimal blind signatures. In: Abe, M. (ed.) ASIACRYPT 2010. LNCS, vol. 6477, pp. 519–538. Springer, Heidelberg (2010). https://doi.org/10.1007/978-3-642-17373-8_30
29. Schnorr, C.P.: Security of blind discrete log signatures against interactive attacks. In: Qing, S., Okamoto, T., Zhou, J. (eds.) ICICS 2001. LNCS, vol. 2229, pp. 1–12. Springer, Heidelberg (2001). https://doi.org/10.1007/3-540-45600-7_1

30. Seo, J.H., Cheon, J.H.: Beyond the limitation of prime-order bilinear groups, and round optimal blind signatures. In: Cramer, R. (ed.) TCC 2012. LNCS, vol. 7194, pp. 133–150. Springer, Heidelberg (2012). https://doi.org/10.1007/978-3-642-28914-9_8

31. Tessaro, S., Zhu, C.: Short pairing-free blind signatures with exponential security. In: Dunkelman, O., Dziembowski, S. (eds.) EUROCRYPT 2022, Part II, vol. 13276, pp. 782–811. Springer, Cham (2022).https://doi.org/10.1007/978-3-031-07085-3_27

32. VPN by Google one, explained. https://one.google.com/about/vpn/howitworks

33. Wagner, D.: A generalized birthday problem. In: Yung, M. (ed.) CRYPTO 2002. LNCS, vol. 2442, pp. 288–304. Springer, Heidelberg (2002). https://doi.org/10.1007/3-540-45708-9_19

34. Yi, X. and Lam, K.Y.: A new blind ECDSA scheme for bitcoin transaction anonymity. In: ASIACCS 19, pp. 613–620 (2019)

On the Possibility of a Backdoor
in the Micali-Schnorr Generator

Hannah Davis[1], Matthew D. Green[2], Nadia Heninger[3] ⓘ, Keegan Ryan[3] ⓘ,
and Adam Suhl[3]([✉])

[1] Seagate Technology, Scotts Valley, USA
hannah.e.davis@seagate.com
[2] Johns Hopkins University, Baltimore, USA
mgreen@cs.jhu.edu
[3] University of California, San Diego, La Jolla, USA
nadiah@cs.ucsd.edu, {kryan,asuhl}@ucsd.edu

Abstract. In this paper, we study both the implications and potential impact of backdoored parameters for two RSA-based pseudorandom number generators: the ISO-standardized Micali-Schnorr generator and a closely related design, the RSA PRG. We observe, contrary to common understanding, that the security of the Micali-Schnorr PRG is not tightly bound to the difficulty of inverting RSA. We show that the Micali-Schnorr construction remains secure even if one replaces RSA with a publicly evaluatable PRG, or a function modeled as an efficiently invertible random permutation. This implies that any cryptographic backdoor must somehow exploit the algebraic structure of RSA, rather than an attacker's ability to invert RSA or the presence of secret keys. We exhibit two such backdoors in related constructions: a family of exploitable parameters for the RSA PRG, and a second vulnerable construction for a finite-field variant of Micali-Schnorr. We also observe that the parameters allowed by the ISO standard are incompletely specified, and allow insecure choices of exponent. Several of our backdoor constructions make use of lattice techniques, in particular multivariate versions of Coppersmith's method for finding small solutions to polynomials modulo integers.

1 Introduction

In 2013, a collection of leaks due to Edward Snowden revealed the existence of a large-scale U.S. government effort called the SIGINT Enabling Project., intended to compromise the integrity of cryptographic systems. Equipped with a $200M annual budget, the project sought to "insert vulnerabilities into commercial encryption systems" and to "influence policies, standards and specification for commercial public key technologies" [3]. These leaks also revealed that the U.S. National Security Agency authored and maintained sole editorial control of the 2005 ISO 18031 standard on random bit generation [55], a standard that was largely incorporated into the U.S. ANSI X9.82 standard. A draft of the ANSI

ⓒ International Association for Cryptologic Research 2024
Q. Tang and V. Teague (Eds.): PKC 2024, LNCS 14601, pp. 352–386, 2024.
https://doi.org/10.1007/978-3-031-57718-5_12

standard in turn forms the basis for the U.S. National Institute for Standards and Technology's NIST Special Publication 800-90A, which defines requirements for random bit generation in government-approved cryptographic products.

Even before the Snowden leaks, the NIST/ANSI and ISO standards have drawn scrutiny for their inclusion of a number-theoretic PRG known as the Dual Elliptic Curve Deterministic Random Bit Generator (Dual EC DRBG), a construction that is exploitable by a party that generates the system public parameters and retains a secret trapdoor [62]. The Snowden leaks inspired renewed investigation of this standard and its deployment, revealing that Dual EC was more widely deployed than many academic researchers had realized. Moreover, later investigation revealed that TLS and IPsec implementations incorporating Dual EC [17,18] also made specific implementation decisions that rendered them practically exploitable by an adversary who possesses the Dual EC trapdoor.

Even if the standardized parameters were not *deliberately* backdoored, the mere possibility of such parameters poses a threat to users of a standardized PRG. In one noteworthy case, an undocumented implementation of Dual EC in Juniper NetScreen's firewalls appears to have been exploited in practice; in 2012 an outside group compromised the NetScreen codebase and replaced Juniper's Dual EC constants with parameters of their own devising [17]. These parameters were in place for over three years, presumably enabling the outside group to decrypt the communications of Juniper NetScreen customers, which at the time included the U.S. Federal Government. Demonstrating the existence, or ruling out the possibility, of methods to backdoor the parameter generation process is the only way to mitigate the risk of parameter substitution attacks which otherwise undermine the security of commercial encryption technology.

The MS DRBG Generator. While Dual EC is the only number-theoretic generator adopted as a NIST standard, the current draft of ISO 18031 (and early drafts of the ANSI X9.82 standard) also include a second public-key generator that has received surprisingly little successful analysis. Based on a design by Micali and Schnorr [50,51], the MS DRBG algorithm is a pseudorandom number generator whose security is purportedly related to the hardness of breaking RSA. In brief, the algorithm is instantiated using a state s_0 and an RSA public key (N, e), and at each stage the algorithm applies the RSA function to the state to obtain an integer $z_{i+1} = s_i^e \bmod N$. The most significant bits of z_{i+1} become the new state s_{i+1} for the next iteration of the algorithm, and the least significant bits of z_{i+1} are the output b_{i+1} of the pseudorandom number generator for that iteration.

While RSA (and Rabin)-based pseudorandom generators have been studied in the academic literature for many years [13,32,33,50,51,63], two aspects of the MS DRBG standard draw attention. First, in contrast with common practice for RSA-based generators, the generator outputs up to a $1 - 2/e$ fraction of the bits (or up to 864 bits for a 1024-bit modulus with a claimed 80-bit security level.)[1]

---

[1] Previous RSA-based generators (including some early drafts of MS DRBG) recommend outputting $\lg \lg N$ bits at each iteration (where lg denotes base-2 logarithm). MS DRBG's larger output is justified by a novel pseudorandomness assumption introduced by Micali and Schnorr [51].

More critically, the MS DRBG standard includes a design choice that is reminiscent of the Dual EC generator: namely, it incorporates a series of recommended public parameters that are intended to be used in production as the modulus N. As with Dual EC, the provenance of these moduli is not documented in the standard. However, correspondence from the ANSI standards process (revealed under the Freedom of Information Act [52]) supports the conclusion that both Dual EC and MS DRBG were authored by the National Security Agency, which also generated the parameters for both specifications. Unlike the Dual EC parameters (which could conceivably have been generated such that the generating party would not learn a trapdoor) according to the standard the MS DRBG moduli are the product of primes p, q chosen by the standard author. The NSA's knowledge of this secret factorization calls into question the security of the generator when used in a setting where the NSA is adverse to its user.

MS DRBG has not, to our knowledge, been used in any real-world systems. This is perhaps unsurprising; there is virtually no reason ever to use a number theoretic DRBG instead of one based on symmetric cryptography: symmetric DRBGs have much better performance and still derive their security from well-studied cryptographic assumptions. However, several surprisingly widespread implementations of Dual EC DRBG (e.g., Juniper's NetScreen implementation) were unknown to researchers and were only discovered by chance long after the deprecation of Dual EC. MS DRBG, though still in the ISO standard, has received far less attention than Dual EC from the research community. It is possible there were (or are) MS DRBG implementations used in production that have not received public scrutiny.

Given the known vulnerabilities in Dual EC DRBG and the (allegedly) identical provenance of MS DRBG, it is therefore reasonable to ask whether MS DRBG is vulnerable to an analogous attack. Concretely:

Does knowledge of the factors of (or malicious construction of) the recommended moduli imply a practical attack on the MS DRBG generator?

This question is surprisingly difficult to answer. While the literature is replete with studies of RSA-based generators, the majority of this work naturally assumes that the factorization of N is kept secret. In that setting, standard results on RSA hardcore bits can be used to argue the indistinguishability of generator output. Clearly such arguments no longer apply in settings where the factorization is *known* to the attacker. And yet in contrast to many other RSA-based constructions, knowledge of the factorization does not point to an obvious attack strategy against MS DRBG or similar RSA-based generators. Such gaps between "best reduction" and "best attack" are hardly unknown in the literature. We argue, however, that the history and provenance of the MS DRBG standard make it worthy of a closer look.

Our Results. We study both the implications and potential impact of backdoored parameters for the Micali-Schnorr generator and for the RSA PRG, a closely related design that was never standardized. To our knowledge, we are the first to identify vulnerabilities in these algorithms from this perspective in the literature.

First, we observe that the security of the Micali-Schnorr PRG is not tightly bound to the difficulty of inverting RSA. We show that the Micali-Schnorr construction remains secure even if one replaces RSA with a publicly evaluatable PRG or an ideal (and efficiently invertible) random permutation. While these results appear obvious in hindsight, they do not appear to have been articulated in the literature on RSA-based generators nor to have been known to the standards bodies. These observations imply that any cryptographic backdoor must somehow exploit the algebraic structure of RSA, rather than an attacker's ability to merely invert RSA or the presence of secret keys. We exhibit two such backdoors in related constructions: a family of exploitable parameters for the RSA PRG, and a second vulnerable construction for a finite-field variant of Micali-Schnorr. We also observe that the parameters allowed by the ISO standard are incompletely specified, and allow insecure choices of exponent. Several of our backdoor constructions make use of lattice techniques, in particular multivariate versions of Coppersmith's method for finding small solutions to polynomials modulo integers. We evaluate the impact of our attacks in the context of network protocols and find that the ISO weak exponent vulnerability would be exploitable in the context of IPsec.

Ultimately, although we were unsuccessful in fully solving the question we set out to answer, that of either finding an efficiently exploitable backdoor for the Micali-Schnorr generator or ruling out the possibility, we hope that this work will bring more attention to this unsolved problem and point the way to potentially fruitful cryptanalytic advances.

1.1 Technical Overview

Our goal in this work is to evaluate the hypothesis that the standardization of ISO/ANSI MS DRBG may represent an intentional attempt to subvert cryptographic systems. This possibility is intriguing for two different reasons: first, a better understanding would offer new historical context on the development of public-key standards and the intentions of nation-state cryptologic agencies. From a technical perspective, detailed investigation of this question might uncover the existence of heretofore non-public attacks on public-key cryptosystems. While factoring-based PRG constructions are some of the earliest work in this area, they appear to have received surprisingly little attention from a modern perspective, and this question shines new light on the tightness of the connection between the hardness assumptions and the security of the output.

Our approach is to assume the worst case: that the authors of the standard retained the factorization of each recommended modulus (or maliciously generated these moduli), and additionally possessed techniques that enabled them to practically exploit this knowledge. From this starting point we then attempt to "re-derive" the necessary techniques and to evaluate whether they can be used in practical settings. Our primary focus in this work is on techniques that enable state recovery given some quantity of generator output, since knowledge of the internal generator state would enable a passive attacker to obtain future generator output and possibly compromise the security of encryption protocols.

Indistinguishability, State Recovery and Backtracking Resistance. Like most standardized generators, MS DRBG uses an iterated construction. The generator is initially seeded with a state s_0 that is updated through application of a purported one-way function. The same function is also used to produce output bits. As with any PRG, knowledge of previous outputs must not provide an attacker with a meaningful advantage in predicting future output bits. This can only be achieved if all internal states remain secret until the generator is reseeded, since knowledge of any state permits the prediction of all future states and outputs. Both ISO and ANSI require an even stronger security property: the compromise of any intermediate state s_i must not enable prediction or distinguishing of generator outputs from *previous* cycles. We show that neither MS DRBG nor RSA PRG achieve this property when the factorization of N is known.

Eliminating the Obvious. A natural approach for a subversion attacker[2] to break these PRGs is to simply invert the RSA function to recover some internal generator state after observing generator output. However, in MS DRBG (as well as more traditional RSA and Rabin-based generators) this direct approach fails because the construction does not output all bits of RSA function output.

While the security assumptions that underlie the security proof for MS DRBG [51] are clearly false if the factorization of the modulus N is known, straightforward attempts to reverse the security reduction are also futile, for a similar reason. Micali and Schnorr's reduction relies on two elements: a novel indistinguishability assumption for partial RSA outputs (repeated herein as Assumption 1), which is combined with rejection sampling and the ACGS algorithm of Alexi, Chor, Goldreich, and Schnorr [5] (in Theorem 1) to reduce this to the hardness of the RSA problem. An adversary who can falsify Assumption 1 still does not obtain all bits of the ciphertext from the generator's output. Even when the attacker has access to an inversion oracle, both sides of the reduction are efficient to solve, so even reversing this portion of the reduction is unlikely to lead to a practical subversion attack. Moreover, the running time of this reduction algorithm for parameters of practical interest is much more expensive than simply brute forcing the unknown state would be, which makes Theorem 1 vacuous in the case of MS DRBG.[3]

Eliminating Black Box Attacks. Given the above, we turn our attention to whether being able to falsify Assumption 1 in a black box way suffices for a distinguishing attack on MS DRBG. Stated broadly, this assumption implies that for some length-expanding function $F : \{0,1\}^k \to \{0,1\}^n$ with $k \ll n$, the ensemble $\{b_1, b_2, \ldots, b_h\}$ is indistinguishable from random, when each $b_i \leftarrow F(s_{i-1}) \bmod 2^{n-k}$ and $s_i \leftarrow \lfloor F(s_{i-1})/2^{n-k} \rfloor$ (with s_0 a random k-bit string, and h an arbitrary number of outputs). It is relatively easy to argue this assumption holds when F is itself a PRG (or is modeled as a random function or permu-

---

[2] An attacker with backdoor information; see Sect. 5.1.
[3] Naturally ISO has specified parameters so that brute force and collision attacks against the state are infeasible.

tation on $\{0,1\}^n)$ as we prove in Sect. 4. We observe that the MS PRG construction instantiated with such a random permutation remains secure even when the inverse oracle is available to an adversary, or when the function contains no secrets or keys. Indeed, this construction is analogous to several common PRG constructions based on hash functions. The theorems we prove are straightforward, and their implications are obvious in retrospect, but they encode observations about the security of the MS DRBG construction that do not appear to have been formalized in the literature.

The main question then is whether such an assumption can hold when F is realized via the RSA function in the unusual setting where the factorization is known. These results suggest that any attacks on the MS or RSA PRGs must exploit *algebraic* properties of RSA and modular exponentiation, rather than being able to take advantage of factorization in a black-box way.

Algebraic Attacks. After eliminating the possibility of an "obvious" factoring-based backdoor, we give several candidate backdoor constructions and algorithmic weaknesses for RSA PRG and MS PRG that exploit algebraic properties of modular exponentiation. Most of our state recovery attacks make use of lattice-based techniques, in particular variants of multivariate Coppersmith's method. A straightforward application of Coppersmith-type methods to break MS and RSA PRG is ruled out by the ISO parameters; such attacks seem unlikely to allow recovery of a state larger than n/e bits for generic parameters (for RSA exponent e), while the ISO parameters set the state size at $2n/e$ bits.

We give backdoor constructions that introduce additional structure that results in feasible attacks that work beyond these known bounds. For RSA PRG, we show how to efficiently generate RSA moduli that embed cyclic and linear recurrence relations in the PRG output and how to hide these recurrences in the factorization of N; we also give an algorithm exploiting these recurrences for an efficient full state recovery attack from parameter ranges that were not known to be previously exploitable. Unfortunately, extending this idea to MS PRG does not seem to result in an efficiently exploitable backdoor without some further structure that allows us to simplify the exponentially many polynomial terms generated by the recurrence relations. We illustrate such an algebraic structure by showing that a variant of MS PRG defined over small-characteristic finite fields is trivially broken by using the linearity of the Frobenius endomorphism.

Finally, we show that the existence of RSA decryption exponents allows the efficient generation of apparently unnoticed weak exponent choices for MS PRG that are not ruled out by the parameters in the ISO standard. These weak exponents allow an efficient state recovery attack for the output lengths and state sizes in the ISO standard from a single PRG output block. We further observe that if this PRG were used to generate nonces and secret keys in the IPsec protocol (as Dual EC was in real-world implementations), this attack would allow an efficient state recovery attack from a single handshake nonce generated from raw PRG output.

358 H. Davis et al.

Future Directions. The problem of designing an efficient backdoor for the Micali-Schnorr scheme has floated around the cryptographic community as an open problem since at least 2013 [37], with little success.

In this work, we rule out some obvious-seeming approaches that are dead ends, and illuminate some potentially fruitful directions for future exploration. In the end, we leave the question of identifying or ruling out an efficiently exploitable general backdoor in the Micali Schnorr algorithm unsolved in this paper. Ultimately, a solution to this problem may involve new ideas in the cryptanalysis of RSA.

2   Background

The ISO, NIST, and ANSI standards refer to the (pseudo)random number generation algorithms they describe as *random bit generators* (RBGs) and to deterministic pseudorandom number generation algorithms as *deterministic random bit generators* (DRBGs).

ISO-18031 lists a number of (informal) security requirements for RBGs. We list the most relevant of these below, and mark the exact text from the standard in quotes. We have given names to these properties for future convenience.

Indistinguishability "Under reasonable assumptions, it shall not be feasible to distinguish the output of the RBG from true random bits that are uniformly distributed." Indistinguishability has been extensively studied in the academic literature [14,65].

State Compromise Resistance "The RBG shall not leak relevant secret information (e.g., internal state of a DRBG) through the output of the RBG." While indistinguishability is the main requirement for a PRG in the academic literature, the focus of many practical attacks is a full state compromise [17,18,20].

The following properties[4] are listed as optional requirements:

Backtracking Resistance "Given all accessible information about the RBG (comprising some subset of inputs, algorithms, and outputs), it shall be computationally infeasible (up to the specified security strength) to compute or predict any previous output bit."

Prediction Resistance "Given all accessible information about the RBG (comprising some subset of inputs, algorithms, and outputs), it shall be infeasible (up to the specified security strength) to compute or predict any future output bit at the time that [prediction resistance] was requested."

---

[4] The standard calls these properties "backward secrecy" and "forward secrecy", but in the opposite way from the academic literature; we rename these properties to avoid confusion.

We will use the term "PRG" to refer to the algorithms in this paper, and the term DRBG when we specifically reference the ISO standard. There have also been extensive academic efforts to formalize requirements for pseudorandom number generation under various attack models including recovery from state compromise [28].

2.1 The RSA PRG

The ISO standard introduces MS DRBG as a variant of the "so-called RSA generator", which iteratively applies RSA encryption to a starting seed to generate a sequence of states and outputs some least significant bits of each state as output. Micali and Schnorr [50] name this algorithm "the 'incestuous' generator".

We summarize this algorithm in Algorithm 1 below. Let N be an integer RSA modulus of length $\lg N = n$. Let k be the length of the PRG output on a single iteration, so we have $k < n$. The length of the state is $r = n$ bits. e will be a positive integer that is the RSA exponent; in order for (N, e) to be valid RSA parameters e should be relatively prime to $\varphi(N)$. (The choice $e = 2$ is the Rabin generator used in Blum-Blum-Shub [13].)

Algorithm 1: RSA PRG

Input : A number of iterations h
Output: hk pseudorandom bits
1 Sample initial state $s_0 \xleftarrow{\$} [1, N]$ using truly random coins.
2 **for** $i \leftarrow 1$ **to** h **do**
3 $\quad$ $s_i \leftarrow s_{i-1}^e \bmod N$
4 $\quad$ $b_i \leftarrow s_i \bmod 2^k$
5 **end**
6 Output the concatenation $b_1||b_2||\ldots||b_h$.

There is a simple formula for the ith state in terms of the initial state:

$$s_i \equiv s_0^{e^i} \bmod N$$

Output Length. There are several choices of output lengths discussed in the literature on this PRG.

- $k = \lg n$. Micali and Schnorr [51] show that the RSA PRG is secure for $k = \lg n$ bits of the RSA function, based on the Alexi-Chor-Goldreich-Schnorr theorem [5] that these bits are hardcore.
- $k = 1$. Fischlin and Schnorr [33] improve the running time of the ACGS reduction and use this running time to propose concrete parameters of $k = 1$ bit of output with a 1000-bit modulus N.
- $k = (1/2 - 1/e - \epsilon - o(1))n$. Steinfeld, Pieperzyk, and Wang [63] prove the security of outputting more bits under the hardness of improving on the Coppersmith bound for solving polynomials modulo RSA moduli [21].

2.2 The Micali-Schnorr PRG (MS PRG)

Like the RSA PRG, the Micali-Schnorr PRG iteratively applies the RSA function, but it separates the bits used to generate the next state from the bits that are output. It splits each RSA output into its most and least significant bits. The least significant bits become PRG output, while the most significant bits become the RSA input for the PRG's next iteration.

Let N be an integer RSA modulus of length $\lg N = n$. Let k be the length of the PRG output on a single iteration, so we have $k < n$. r will be the internal state length; for the Micali-Schnorr algorithm we have $r = n - k$. e will be a positive integer that is the RSA exponent; this is specified so that e is relatively prime to $\varphi(N)$.

Micali-Schnorr as Published in Their Papers. There are two published versions of the Micali-Schnorr paper. The first version, "Efficient, Perfect Random Number Generators," appeared in CRYPTO '88 [50]. The journal version of the paper, "Efficient, Perfect Polynomial Random Number Generators," was published in the Journal of Cryptology in 1991 [51].

The algorithm for the Micali-Schnorr PRG as published in the original paper takes as input a requested number of iterations h and outputs hk pseudorandom bits. Micali and Schnorr refer to this construction as the "sequential polynomial generator of the weaning type."

Algorithm 2: The Micali-Schnorr algorithm

    Input   : A number of iterations h
    Output: hk pseudorandom bits
1 Sample initial state $s_0 \xleftarrow{\$} [1, N2^{-k}]$ using truly random coins.
2 **for** $i \leftarrow 1$ **to** h **do**
3 | $z_i \leftarrow s_{i-1}^e \mod N$
4 | $b_i \leftarrow z_i \mod 2^k$
5 | **if** *version from [50]* **then**
6 | | $s_i \leftarrow \lfloor z_i 2^{-k} \rfloor + 1$;
7 | **else if** *ISO-18031 version* **then**
8 | | $s_i \leftarrow \lfloor z_i 2^{-k} \rfloor$;
9 **end**
10 Output $b_1 || b_2 || \ldots || b_h$.

Output Length. In the original paper, Micali and Schnorr discuss the following choices for k and n.

- $k = O(\lg n) = O(\lg \lg N)$ They list this as a suitable choice for the PRG. The algorithm in Micali and Schnorr's reduction runs in time polynomial in $2^k n e^{-1}$ so if the PRG is insecure for $k = O(\lg n)$ then this gives a polynomial time RSA decryption algorithm.

- $k = O(n^{1/3})$ They argue that this choice is suitable by comparing the resulting reduction time to the running time of the number field sieve for factoring, and note that if the algorithm is insecure for this parameter, it would beat the number field sieve.
- $k = n(1 - 1/e)$ is clearly insecure. For this choice, the security proof does not apply because $s_0^e < N$, so no mod operation occurs and "RSA" decryption is easy in this case.
- $k = n(1 - 2/e)$ is left as an open question, but Micali and Schnorr promote this choice as one that would produce an efficient generator if indeed it is secure. The security of this choice is based on the indistinguishability of RSA encryptions of short ($n - k$-bit) plaintexts from random integers modulo N. This is the value chosen by the ISO standard.

D.2 Default moduli for the MS_DRBG ( )

D.2.1 Introduction to MS_DRBG default moduli

Each modulus is of the form $n = pq$ with $p = 2p_1 + 1$, $q = 2q_1 + 1$, where p_1 and q_1 are $(\lg(n)/2 - 1)$-bit primes.

D.2.2 Default modulus n of size 1024 bits

The hexadecimal value of the modulus n is:

```
b66fbfda fbac2fd8 2eb13dc4 4fa170ff c9f7c7b5 1d55b214 4cc2257b 29df3f62
b421b158 0753f304 a671ff8b 55dd8abf b53d31ab a0ad742f 21857acf 814af3f1
e126d771 a61eca54 e62bfdb5 85c311b0 58e9cd3f aab758a5 e2896849 6ec1dd51
d0355aa1 55d4d912 6140dcfa b9b03f62 a5032d06 536d8574 0988f384 27f35885
```

D.2.3 Default modulus n of size 2048 bits

Fig. 1. A portion of ISO 18031 Appendix D.2 with the default 1024-bit modulus [43].

ISO/IEC 18031 Micali-Schnorr. The Micali-Schnorr algorithm was standardized in ISO/IEC 18031 as a deterministic random bit generator, named MS DRBG, alongside the Dual EC DRBG design. Dual EC was removed from ISO 18031 in a 2014 Technical Corrigendum.

The version of the Micali-Schnorr algorithm that appears in ISO/IEC 18031 [43] differs in one minor respect from the academic publication. Specifically, it alters line 6 so that $s_i \leftarrow \lfloor z_i 2^{-k} \rfloor$. (That is, it does not increment the result.) It isn't clear what effect, if any, this change has on the security of the scheme, and it is not documented in either publication. In personal communication, Micali told us he does not recall the reason for the original choice or the change.

Output Length. The ISO standard requires that the output length satisfies $8 \leq k \leq \min(n - 2\gamma, n(1 - 2/e))$, where γ is the target security level. The default k is the largest value this inequality allows, rounded down to a multiple of 8.

The introduction to MS DRBG (section C.4.3.1) applies very different output security bounds to RSA PRG than MS DRBG: it states that the $k = \lg \lg N$ least significant bits the RSA generator outputs "are (asymptotically in N) known to

be as secure as the RSA function f. The Micali-Schnorr generator MS_DRBG()
uses the same e and N to produce many more random bits per iteration, while
eliminating the reuse of bits as both output and seed" [43].

Modulus and Exponent Generation. The ISO standard states that implementations "shall" permit either an implementation-generated "private modulus" or
the use of one of the default moduli in the standard (see Fig. 1). The standard requires the length of the modulus to conform to the requested security
strength: a 1024-bit N for $\gamma = 80$; 2048 bits for $\gamma = 112$; 3072 for $\gamma = 128$; 7680
for $\gamma = 192$; and 15360 for $\gamma = 256$.

The ISO standard also specifies that custom RSA moduli should be generated
so that $p-1$, $p+1$, $q-1$, and $q+1$ have a prime factor of at least γ bits. It also
states that the default moduli have been generated so that $p = 2p_1+1, q = 2q_1+1$
for p_1, q_1 primes, and that $p+1$ and $q+1$ have "the required large prime factor".

It is also required that e be relatively prime to $(p-1)(q-1)$. While this is
necessary for these to be well-defined RSA parameters, the decryption exponent
$d = e^{-1} \bmod (p-1)(q-1)$ is never used in the normal course of random number
generation, so it is not clear why this requirement needs to be present.

The default moduli are stated to have "strong" primes as factors, which
"essentially guarantees" that $\varphi(N)$ will be relatively prime to odd e, but the
factorization of these default moduli is not given, so users are unable to verify
this for themselves when using the default moduli with user-generated e. If a
user-generated exponent is not supplied, the default $e = 3$ is used.

Backtracking and Prediction Resistance. The standard states: "[backtracking
resistance] is inherent in the algorithm, even if the internal state is compromised."
This is not true against an adversary who knows the factors of the modulus: if
the state and all but a few previous output bits are compromised, the adversary
can learn the remaining bits by decrypting the candidate z_i values and checking
whether the result is less than $N/2^k$. The standard ensures prediction resistance
by requiring the implementation to reseed every 50,000 outputs.

ANSI X9.82. The Dual EC and MS DRBG algorithms were the two number-
theoretic (public-key cryptographic) PRG designs promoted by the NSA for
inclusion in ANSI X9.82 [45]. A version of MS DRBG was present in early drafts
of the ANSI X9.82 specification from 2004 until it was removed in August 2005.

The text of the entire X9.82 DRBG specification is largely identical to the
standard ultimately published by ISO in 2005 [43]. A number of draft versions
of the X9.82 standard as well as internal discussions and documentation have
been made available as part of a FOIA request from NIST in 2014 and 2015 [52],
which provide interesting insights into the development of the standard. There
is evidence that this text was written by the US government [11].

There appear to have been differing views among committee members on the
number of bits that should be output from MS PRG. Early proposals suggested
outputting far fewer bits than the ISO version ultimately standardized. A set of

2004 slides from the NSA at a NIST workshop suggested outputting only the "hardcore" bits for each modulus size, which are provably as hard to predict as the entire state under the RSA assumption. For a 1024-bit RSA modulus the suggestion was 10 bits, and for 2048 and 3072-bit moduli the suggestion was 11 bits [45].

An undated (but apparently early) draft of X9.82 includes the comments "The MS generator allows a much larger percentage of N bits to be used on each iteration, and has an additional advantage that no output bits are used to propagate the sequence. (It does, however, rely on a stronger assumption for its security than the intractability of integer factorization.) As the X9.82 standard evolved, committee members argued for restricting the number of bits generated on each exponentiation to $O(\lg \lg N)$ *hard* bits, as is done in Blum-Blum-Shub. The result is that the efficiency argument for choosing MS over BBS doesn't apply. Nonetheless, a user does have more options in the choice of parameters" [2]. Later drafts of the text mention only the larger output lengths ultimately adopted by ISO.

The sole comments we have located that justify the decision to drop Micali-Schnorr from the standard come from a document titled "DRBG recommendations from the X9.82 Editing Group" which states "We recommend keeping DUAL_EC_DRBG. Despite the fact that it is much slower than the other DRBGs, it offers a third distinct technology that can serve as a hedge against breakthroughs in cryptanalysis of hashes and block ciphers. ... We suggest dropping HASH_DRBG and the MS_DRBG, as well as support for the other NIST curves in the DUAL_EC_DRBG" [1].

2.3   Related Work

Backdoored Random Number Generation. In addition to works cited in the introduction, a long line of literature considers the possibility of *algorithm substitution attacks* (previously referred to as "subversion" and "kleptographic") attacks [8,10,19,31,56,60,66,67]. To formalize this work into the setting of PRGs, Dodis et al. [27] give a formal treatment and prove that such schemes are equivalent to public-key encryption schemes with pseudorandom ciphertexts. Degabriele et al. [25] extend these results to consider backdoored PRNGs (which unlike PRGs may take additional inputs for prediction resistance).

Backdoored RSA Parameters. There is a surprisingly long line of work on generating "backdoored" RSA parameters [7,16,23,46,54,64,66–68]. These works focus on trapdoors that admit efficient factorization or recovery of private keys given only a public key (N, e). In contrast, our work begins from the assumption that the adversary possesses the factorization of N and addresses the problem of compromising an algorithm using this knowledge.

MS DRBG. Some previous works have considered MS DRBG. Fouque, Vergnaud, and Zapalowicz give a time/memory tradeoff for recovering the state faster than brute force [34], and Fouque and Zapalowicz study the statistical distance of short RSA [35]. In a 2013 blog post Matthew Green posed the problem of finding a practical attack against MS DRBG when the factors are known [37]. Antonio Sanso suggested in a 2017 blog post that Mersenne or other special-form primes might lead to a backdoor in Micali-Schnorr [61]. Lynn Engelberts extended Sanso's analysis of special form primes in a 2020 masters thesis. [30]

Security Proofs for Number-Theoretic PRGs. The limited applicability of asymptotic security proofs on concrete parameters for number-theoretic PRGs has been studied by Koblitz and Menezes [48].

3   Security Reductions for the MS and RSA PRGs

The security reduction that Micali and Schnorr give to their "sequential" construction has two steps. First, they define a security question, which they label **Q1**. We rephrase this as an assumption below:

Assumption 1 [51] **(Q1).** *The following distributions are polynomially indistinguishable (for public e and N)*

- $(N, s^e \bmod N)$ *for* $s \xleftarrow{\$} [1, N2^{-k}]$
- (N, r) *for* $r \xleftarrow{\$} [1, N]$.

The authors next provide a polynomial-time reduction that transforms a distinguisher algorithm for the Micali-Schnorr PRG into a distinguisher for Assumption 1. The proof uses a hybrid argument. It is this assumption that is used to justify the large output sizes used in the ISO version of MS PRG. The second half of the reduction completes the reduction to the hardness of RSA inversion, and gives a security reduction for both MS PRG and RSA PRG.

Theorem 1 [51]. *Let N be an RSA modulus. Every probabilistic algorithm that ϵ-rejects ciphertexts of random messages $s \xleftarrow{\$} [1, N2^{-k}]$ can be transformed into a probabilistic algorithm for decrypting arbitrary RSA ciphertexts; this algorithm terminates after at most $(2^k \epsilon^{-1} n)^{O(1)}$ steps.*

This reduction contains several steps that are fundamentally exponential time in k, the number of bits of output. In particular, the algorithm samples 2^k messages until it expects to find one with the required number of zeros. Thus, this reduction is only polynomial time for $\lg n$ bits of output. Fischlin and Schnorr [33] have improved the running time of the ACGS algorithm [5] used in the decryption step, but the reduction remains exponential in k.

In addition to being exponential time in the output length k, running the reduction will be more expensive than simply brute forcing the unknown bits of the plaintext when $k > n/2$, that is, when the output is larger than the state. In fact, the constants hidden in the $O(1)$ result in significantly worse parameters.

The exponential cost in the reduction in the proof of Theorem 1 appears to be the reason for only outputting $\lg n$ bits of output for the RSA PRG. It is interesting that the ISO standard accepts much more generous parameters for Micali-Schnorr output than for the RSA PRG without having attempted to find an analogously relaxed assumption that might permit more generous outputs as Steinfeld, Pieprzyk, and Wang [63] ultimately did.

Statistical Indistinguishability Results and Mod p Variants. Micali and Schnorr also consider a variant of their PRG defined modulo a prime p, and hypothesize that this variant is still secure despite the fact that their factoring-based assumptions no longer hold. The journal version of their paper [51] contains theorems proving the statistical randomness of the $(n/2 - k - (\lg n)^2)$ least significant bits of $s^e \bmod N$ for $s \xleftarrow{\$} [1, N^{2^{-k}}]$ when N is prime or an RSA modulus.

Fouque and Zapalowicz [35] give a more general version of this theorem for RSA moduli that applies to size bounds above $\sqrt{N}$ and prove that the $\lg N$ least significant bits of $s^e \bmod N$ for $s < M$ for a chosen bound $M < N$ are statistically indistinguishable from uniform. They apply their bounds to Micali-Schnorr and find that asymptotically, this bound dictates that the output is not statistically indistinguishable when more than $n/3$ bits are output.

These statistical indistinguishability results provide evidence that least significant bits of modular exponentiation (modulo primes or RSA moduli) are indistinguishable from uniform at much less aggressive parameters than ISO chose. However, such statistical indistinguishability results cannot apply when the output exceeds the length of the seed. Thus they do not rule out the possibility of attacks on the PRG with long or multiple outputs.

4 Ruling Out Black-Box Attacks

In this section, we will try to make more precise the intuition that the security of MS and RSA PRG is more closely related to the assumption of pseudorandomness of RSA ciphertexts than the hardness of inverting RSA. This offers a more formal explanation for why there does not appear to be a black-box way to use an RSA decryption oracle to break the security of MS PRG.

We begin by defining a generic Micali-Schnorr-type construction, which we call MS-f-PRG. In this variant the RSA operation is replaced by some function f. That is, Step 3 of Algorithm 2 in Sect. 2.2 becomes $z_i \leftarrow f(s_{i-1})$, for f that we will instantiate below.

4.1 Micali-Schnorr Is Secure with a PRG

The Micali-Schnorr construction is still secure when instantiated with a PRG.

Theorem 2. *If $f : [1, 2^{n-k}] \rightarrow [1, 2^n]$ is a secure pseudorandom generator, then the output of MS-f-PRG is pseudorandom.*

The proof is the same as the proof of Theorem 5.1 in [51], substituting the pseudorandomness of f for Assumption 1.

While this finding is not surprising, it illustrates that the security of MS-f-PRG need not depend on any secret information. This informs how a provably secure variant of MS PRG could be instantiated, but unfortunately it does not enable a proof for the variants with RSA modulus N or prime modulus p (as discussed in the original work of Micali and Schnorr [51]). In the context of an adversary who knows the factorization of N, $f(s) = s^e \bmod N$ with short seed $s < 2^{n-k}$ is distinguishable from random: simply decrypt $f(s)$ and check if the seed is short. This function is clearly not a PRG, and so we gain no information about the security of this construction. A similar argument applies in the prime modulus case $f(x) = x^e \bmod p$.

4.2 MS PRG Is Still Secure When Implemented with a Random Permutation

We next show that the Micali-Schnorr construction is secure when the one-way RSA function is replaced with a public (invertible) random permutation. While this analysis is clearly quite artificial, it offers a useful bound on the efficiency of *generic attacks* (i.e., attacks that do not exploit special properties of the RSA function) when the factorization of N is known.[5] This suggests that if it is indeed possible to backdoor the Micali-Schnorr construction, the backdoor must take advantage of some nontrivial algebraic property of RSA.

We begin by defining our variant of the MS PRG in which RSA encryption is replaced with a publicly accessible random permutation. Concretely, at line 3 of Algorithm 2 we replace the RSA evaluation $z_i \leftarrow s_{i-1}^e \bmod N$ with $z_i \leftarrow f(s_{i-1})$ where $f : [1, N-1] \to [1, N-1]$ is a publicly accessible random permutation. We give the attacker the ability to decrypt by making the inverse permutation f^{-1} publicly accessible. With this modification, we obtain the following theorem.

Theorem 3. *No adversary $\mathcal{A}$ that makes q total queries to black-box oracles for random permutations f and f^{-1} can distinguish the hk-bit output string of our modified variant of Algorithm 2 from a random hk-bit string with advantage greater than $\frac{(h+1)^2}{2N} + \frac{2hq}{N2^{-k}} + \frac{hq}{N} + \frac{2hq}{N-q} + \varepsilon$ (for some negligible ε).*

A proof of Theorem 3 can be found in the full version [24].

4.3 RSA-PRG as a Sponge

The iterative construction of RSA-PRG—apply a transformation to the state, then output a fraction of the bits—is widely used in symmetric cryptography and is known as the sponge construction. If we replace RSA encryption with a random function f in the RSA PRG construction, we can use theorems developed for cryptographic sponge constructions to obtain strong bounds on the security of the resulting construction. These theorems hold for functions that are fixed public and efficiently invertible permutations.

---

[5] More critically, this construction does not have any implications for the security of MS PRG instantiated with the RSA function, since RSA encryption quite clearly behaves differently than a random function.

Theorem 4. *Let f-PRG be the RSA PRG construction except replacing the $x \mapsto x^e \bmod N$ operation with a fixed, public, efficiently invertible random permutation $f : \mathbb{Z}_N \rightarrow \mathbb{Z}_N$. Then the output of f-PRG is indistinguishable from random to any adversary that runs in time polynomial in $\lg N - k$ and has black-box access to f and f^{-1}.*

Proof. f-PRG follows the sponge construction, with state size $\lg N$, rate k, and capacity $c = \lg N - k$. As Bertoni, Daemen, Peeters, and Van Assche show in Eq. 6 of [12], the Random Oracle ($\mathcal{RO}$) differentiating advantage against the sponge construction when used with a random permutation is upper bounded by $((1 - 2^{-k})m^2 + (1 + 2^{-k})m)2^{-(c+1)}$, where m is the number of calls to the underlying transformation.[6] The $\mathcal{RO}$-differentiation game models an adversary with query access to f and f^{-1}. Thus no $poly(\lg N - k)$-time adversary can distinguish f-PRG from a random oracle with more than negligible probability, even with query access to f and f^{-1}.

We remark that SHAKE-128 (from the SHA-3 standard [4]) is an XOF (and thus also a PRG) constructed as a sponge with state size 1600, outputting 5/6 of the state (1344 bits) per iteration, and the function f it uses to transform its state is a fixed, public, efficiently invertible permutation. This is a smaller state size than ISO MS DRBG uses ($\lg N = 3072$ for 128-bit security), and a larger fraction of bits that are output (5/6, compared to 1/3 for ISO using the default exponent $e = 3$).

5   Algebraic Attacks

Here we present several attacks against RSA PRG and variants of MS PRG. These results are not as compelling as the attack against Dual EC, but they illustrate different properties of the algebraic structure of RSA-based PRGs that may ultimately lead to either the development or ruling out of such a backdoor in the MS PRG.

5.1   Notions of Cryptographic Subversion

A growing body of work considers *algorithm substitution attacks* (ASAs) against cryptographic implementations. In this setting, a known cryptographic algorithm is replaced with a subverted algorithm designed by an attacker, who retains secret knowledge that allows for exploitation [8,10,19,31,56,60,66,67]. This effectively models our assumptions for a subversion attack on MS DRBG. We do not present formal definitions here, and refer the reader to e.g., [8,60] for details.

The MALICIOUS Framework. Peyrin and Wang [56] describe the MALICIOUS framework that includes several informal properties required by a subverted symmetric construction such as an RNG. Inspired by their definitions, we provide the following shorthand characterization for our asymmetric backdoor constructions.

---

[6] [12] requires $m \ll 2^c$, as is the case here.

Undiscoverability: An outside observer should be unable to find the hidden backdoor, even if the general form of the backdoor is known [56].

Practical Construction: The backdoor designer should be able to efficiently construct parameters that allow for backdoor exploitation.

Practical Exploitation: An attacker should be able to efficiently violate the security properties of the scheme if they know the secret information required to exploit the backdoor.

Plausible Deniability: To an external observer, the public parameters, keys, and structure of the cryptosystem should appear to be "properly" generated.

Relationship to Formal Definitions of ASAs. Bellare, Paterson and Rogaway formalized a framework for *algorithm substitution attacks* (ASAs) [8]. Informally, the framework captures the properties described above using two independent security games.[7] In the first game, a *detection adversary* ($\mathcal{D}$) represents the defender, and is used to define the undiscoverability of a cryptographic backdoor. In this framework, the detection adversary is asked to distinguish between the correct algorithm (e.g., an implementation of MS DRBG in which the modulus N is generated honestly at random and no secret factorization is retained) and a second *subverted* algorithm (such as the ISO standard with attacker-known or chosen factorization). The subverted algorithm passes this test if $\forall$ probabilistic polynomial time (PPT) algorithms $\mathcal{D}$, $\mathcal{D}$ distinguishes the input/output behavior of the subverted implementation from the correct implementation with at most negligible advantage.[8]

In the second game a *subversion adversary* ($\mathcal{S}$) is given access to secret knowledge about the subverted algorithm (for example, knowledge of the secret factorization of the modulus N.) The minimal criteria for a subversion attack is that there must exist some PPT $\mathcal{S}$ that distinguishes the input/output behavior of the subverted and non-subverted implementations with non-negligible advantage. If the non-subverted implementation is itself a secure PRG, then the ability to distinguish between subverted and unsubverted implementations naturally implies an attack that distinguishes the output of the subverted algorithm from random bits. In practice, subversion attackers may also be able to carry out more powerful attacks, such as state recovery and future output prediction.

5.2   Algorithmic Background: Multivariate Coppersmith's Method

Several of our attacks make use of the following version of multivariate Coppersmith's method. For a basic review of lattices and terminology, see [49].

---

[7] The "Practical Construction" requirement is captured formally by requiring that both honest and subverted algorithm have a polynomial-time *setup* algorithm that (in the subverted case) produces the subverted implementation and secret trapdoors.

[8] Subsequent definitions by Russell *et al.* extend this notion to one in which the detection adversary (in this work called an "online watchdog") is also allowed to observe interactions between the implementation and an attacker. We do not consider this scenario in our work, since we primarily focus on passive eavesdropping attacks.

Review of Coppersmith's Method. Coppersmith's method uses lattice reduction (typically LLL [49][9]) to find small solutions to polynomials modulo integers. For univariate polynomials, this method is fully rigorous, and has a clean bound: for a degree-d polynomial $f(x) \in \mathbb{Z}[x]$ and $N \in \mathbb{Z}$, all roots $r \in \mathbb{Z}$ satisfying $f(r) \equiv 0 \bmod N$ can be found for $|r| < N^{1/d}$ in polynomial time in d and $\lg N$ [21].

The multivariate generalization of this method that we need for our attacks does not have a clean theorem statement, and in fact a fully rigorous generalization cannot exist [22]. Nevertheless, a heuristic generalization of this method often works in practice ([47], see also [44]), and it is this heuristic version that we will use. We will derive the relevant bounds using ad hoc, problem-specific constructions.

The following lemma tells us the condition under which we expect to succeed.

Lemma 1. *Let $\{f_i(\boldsymbol{x})\}_{i=1}^{w}$ be integer polynomials in m variables $\boldsymbol{x} = (x_1, \ldots, x_m)$ and let $N \in \mathbb{Z}$. We wish to find one or more solutions $\boldsymbol{r} = (r_1, \ldots, r_m)$ simultaneously satisfying $\{f_i(\boldsymbol{r}) \equiv 0 \bmod N\}_{i=1}^{w}$.*

If we can find m auxiliary polynomials $Q_1, \ldots, Q_m$ such that

$$Q_j(r_1, \ldots, r_m) \equiv 0 \bmod N^t \qquad \text{and} \qquad |Q_j(r_1, \ldots, r_m)| < N^t$$

for some integer $t \geq 1$ then each Q_j satisfies $Q_j(r_1, \ldots, r_m) = 0$ over the integers. If in addition the Q_j are algebraically independent, then we can solve for a bounded number of possible solutions.

We sketch a general method to solve this problem in Algorithm 3 below. The details of Step 3 are application dependent; we elaborate on this in the full version [24].

The value t and choice of polynomial shifts $x_1^{a_1} \ldots x_m^{a_m}$ in Step 1 of Algorithm 3 are chosen as part of the optimization process. We will refer to t as the *multiplicity* of the roots. The lattice dimension is determined by the number of distinct monomials in the set of polynomials $\{g\}$ used to generate the lattice. In general, the dimension is exponential in the number of variables.

To apply Lemma 1 we bound $|g(\boldsymbol{r})| < |\sigma(g)|_1$, so we want to find m vectors in the lattice whose ℓ_1 norms are less than N^t. For a random lattice L, the successive minima $\lambda_i(L)$ often have close to the same length, and in practice LLL [49] typically finds vectors of length $1.02^{\dim L}(\det L)^{1/\dim L}$ or $1.02^{\dim L}\lambda$ [53].

These vectors are guaranteed to be linearly independent as coefficient vectors, but the corresponding polynomials are not guaranteed to be algebraically independent. Nevertheless, the polynomials found by this algorithm for random problem instances with optimal parameters are often algebraically independent.

We expect the algorithm to succeed when Condition 1 is satisfied.

---

[9] Given a lattice, the LLL algorithm computes in polynomial time a basis whose vectors satisfy heuristic and provable length bounds.

Algorithm 3: Multivariate Coppersmith Method (Sketch)

Input : $\{f_i(\boldsymbol{x})\}_{i=1}^{w} \in \mathbb{Z}[x_1,\ldots,x_m]^w, N \in \mathbb{Z}, \{R_j\}_{j=1}^{m}$
Output: $\{r_j\}_{j=1}^{m}$ satisfying $|r_j| < R_j$ and $f_i(\boldsymbol{r}) \equiv 0 \bmod N$
1 Generate a basis of auxiliary polynomials of the form

$$g_{a,b}(\boldsymbol{x}) = \left(\prod_j x_j^{a_j}\right)\left(\prod_i f_i^{b_i}\right) N^{t-\sum_i b_i}.$$

2 Map each polynomial to a scaled coefficient vector embedding:
$$\sigma : g(\boldsymbol{x}) = \sum_i g_i x_1^{c_{i,1}} x_2^{c_{i,2}} \ldots x_m^{c_{i,m}} \mapsto (g_1 R_1^{c_1,1} \ldots R_m^{c_1,m}, \ldots)$$
3 Construct a lattice basis B of coefficient vector embeddings $\sigma(g)$ for a carefully chosen subset of the gs generated in step 1.
4 LLL-reduce the lattice basis.
5 Construct a Gröbner basis of the polynomials $\sigma^{-1}(v)$ of all vectors v in the reduced basis whose ℓ_1 norms $|v|_1$ are shorter than N^t.
6 Enumerate the candidate solutions given by the Gröbner basis and verify whether each is a valid solution for the r_i.

Condition 1 (Heuristic Multivariate Coppersmith) *Algorithm 3 will heuristically find all suitable roots if the basis for lattice L constructed in Step 3 of Algorithm 3 satisfies*

$$1.02^{\dim L}(\det L)^{1/\dim L} < N^t.$$

Applying Coppersmith's Method to MS and RSA PRG. It is tempting to try to apply a multivariate Coppersmith approach directly to MS or RSA PRG to carry out a state recovery attack. In particular, such an attack involves finding a small solution of a degree-e polynomial modulo N, which is precisely the problem that Coppersmith-type methods solve.

In this section, we will sketch this attack and observe that it is ruled out by the parameter choices made by ISO for MS.

MS PRG. An attempted state recovery attack from two outputs would start from the polynomial relations between the unknown states s_i:

$$s_0^e - 2^k s_1 - b_1 \equiv 0 \bmod N$$
$$s_1^e - 2^k s_2 - b_2 \equiv 0 \bmod N$$

Let $|s_i| < R$. Construct the lattice basis

$$B = \begin{bmatrix} R^e & 0 & -2^k R & 0 & -b_1 \\ 0 & R^e & 0 & -2^k R & -b_2 \\ 0 & 0 & NR & 0 & 0 \\ 0 & 0 & 0 & NR & 0 \\ 0 & 0 & 0 & 0 & N \end{bmatrix}$$

We have $\det L(B) = R^{2e+2}N^3$ and $\dim L(B) = 5$. Omitting approximation factors in such small dimension, and setting $t = 1$, Condition 1 tells us we expect to succeed if

$$(\det L(B))^{1/\dim L(b)} = (R^{2e+2}N^3)^{1/5} < N$$

which applies when $R < N^{1/(e+1)}$. In other words, the bit length of the state size $r = n - k$ should satisfy $r < n/(e+1)$. Attempted improvements from higher degree polynomials and root multiplicities seem to give the same bound, even if more than two outputs are available.

This attack is ruled out by the choice of ISO parameters $r = 2n/e$. This makes sense because this attack does not even require the factorization of N.

RSA PRG. Steinfeld, Pieprzyk, and Wang [63] do a similar analysis of RSA PRG and obtain a heuristic bound of $r < n/(e+1)$ for the unknown portion of the state. Herrmann and May [39] improve this to n/e when the PRG outputs the most significant bits of the state.

Simpler attacks when $r < n/e$. A state size bound of $r < n/e$ is a degenerate case for both RSA and MS PRGs, since there is no modular reduction performed when computing $s_i^e \bmod N$. Fouque, Vergnaud, and Zapalowicz point out that one can recover the state via Hensel lifting [34].

5.3   Attacks on RSA PRG

In this section, we show how to construct backdoor parameters for the RSA PRG. The states (and thus the output) generated by the RSA PRG have an iterative structure that cycles modulo a divisor of $\varphi(\varphi(N))$. This means that an attacker who can control the generation of N and e can embed a chosen relationship among outputs that enables efficient distinguishing and state recovery attacks.

e has Short Period (eSP) attack mod $\varphi(\varphi(N))$ In our first backdoor construction, we show that it is possible to efficiently construct RSA parameters for which the output of RSA PRG produces extremely short cycles. This violates indistinguishability, but would be observable by any attacker. We then show that it is possible to somewhat obscure the most obvious cyclic behavior in the output, which leads to an efficiently generatable and exploitable backdoor. While this behavior alone doesn't lead to a fully undiscoverable backdoor, it provides intuition for a more sophisticated backdoor we construct later in the section.

Recall that the multiplicative order of an integer modulo N is a divisor of $\varphi(N)$. In the RSA-PRG generator with modulus N and exponent e, we have state s_i satisfying $s_i = s_0^{e^i} \bmod N$. Micali and Schnorr (as well as Blum, Blum, and Shub [13]) note that the period of the sequence of outputs generated by s_0 will thus be a divisor of $\varphi(\varphi(N))$ [51]. They say that "in general" the period "will be a large factor of $\varphi(\varphi(N))$ and will be much larger than $\sqrt{N}$ which is the average period of a random recursion in $\mathbb{Z}_N$. It is conceivable that the number $\varphi(\varphi(N))$ somewhat affects the output distribution of the generator and not only its period." They do not appear to have considered the possibility of malicious parameter generation.

In particular, the period can be made a *small* factor of $\varphi(\varphi(N))$. Suppose e generates a small subgroup of $\mathbb{Z}_{\varphi(N)}^*$. That is, suppose $e^j \equiv 1 \bmod \varphi(N)$ for some small j. Then $s_j = s_0^{e^j \bmod \varphi(N)} = s_0$, and PRG cycles with period j. A similar technique is possible when e shares a factor with $\varphi(N)$, we describe it in the full version [24]. One algorithm, given a specific e, to find primes p such that e has small order modulo $\varphi(p)$ is shown in Algorithm 4.

Algorithm 4: Constructing prime p s.t. e has small order mod $\varphi(p)$.

Input : An integer e
Output: A prime p such that e has small order modulo $\varphi(p)$.
1 Choose a cycle length ℓ.
2 Compute small prime factors p_i of $e^\ell - 1$ using the elliptic curve method or other factoring methods that are efficient for small factors.
3 Choose a subset of the p_i (and optionally also the composite cofactor) computed in the previous step, and check if $1 + \prod_i p_i$ is prime. (In order to generate odd primes, we will need one of the p_i to be 2.)

This algorithm is reasonably efficient in practice for parameters of interest. For example, for $e = 5$ and $\ell = 504$, it took 10 s on a laptop with a dual-core Intel i7-6500 CPU to find an 880-bit prime with these properties using Sage with ECM for factorization, aborting factorization when it started to get slow. We tried a few candidates for e and ℓ within this range. To generate a hard-to-factor modulus N, one could generate two primes using this algorithm.

Partially Hidden Cycling Behavior. Cycles in the output would be easy to notice for any user who generates enough outputs, so the previous construction would be easily discoverable. But if e generates cycles of length ℓ mod p, but not mod q, the outputs would not have as obvious cycling behavior to the end user. By choosing q such that $e^\ell \equiv c_q \bmod \varphi(q)$ for some c_q small enough that finding roots mod q of degree c_q polynomials is feasible, an adversary who knows the factorization and observes the sequence of outputs can efficiently recover the full state, as we will show in Theorem 5. Such a q can be generated similarly to Algorithm 4, but factoring $e^\ell - c_q$ instead of $e^\ell - 1$.

With such parameters, an attacker can recover the full state using only the first and $(\ell+1)$th PRG outputs, assuming each output has length $k \geq n/2$. (If RSA PRG parameters were set following the ISO parameters for MS DRBG, this will be the case for all $e \geq 5$.) The attack is given in Algorithm 5.

As a proof of concept, we generate (for public exponent $e = 5$) a 2048-bit backdoored $N = pq$ such that $5^{504} \equiv 1 \pmod{p-1}$ and $5^{504} \equiv 187 \pmod{q-1}$. We include it in the full version [24]. The state recovery attack (implemented in Sage) using this modulus took 31 s.

However, while practical to construct and practical to exploit, this "backdoor" is not undiscoverable (regardless of how q is generated) because a user could exploit the relationships modulo p to efficiently factor N as follows. They choose an initial state s_0, and compute the sequence of states $s_i = s_{i-1}^e \bmod N$. If they discover a state s_ℓ where $\gcd(s_\ell - s_0, N)$ is nontrivial, then they can use this to factor N. (Note that this algorithm is similar to the Pollard rho algorithm but with a different "pseudorandom" walk.)

Algorithm 5: eSP attack in the "partially hidden cycle" case.

---

1 Let b_1 and $b_{\ell+1}$ be two outputs. Without loss of generality assume $s_{\ell+1} \geq s_1$.
2 Observe that $b_{\ell+1} - b_1 \equiv (s_{\ell+1} - s_1) \bmod 2^k$. Observe further that
   $s_{\ell+1} - s_1 \equiv 0 \bmod p$, and $0 \leq (s_{\ell+1} - s_1)/p < q < 2^k$.
3 Let $m = (b_{\ell+1} - b_1)p^{-1} \bmod 2^k$, reduced such that $0 \leq m < 2^k$. Now
   $m = (s_{\ell+1} - s_1)/p$ as integers.
4 Solve the polynomial congruence $y^{c_q} - y - pm \equiv 0 \bmod q$. (Recall
   $c_q \equiv e^\ell \bmod \varphi(q)$.) (The degree c_q is small and q is prime, so this is feasible.)
5 One of the roots will be $s_1 \bmod q$, because mod q we have
   $s_1^{c_q} \equiv s_1^{e^\ell} \equiv s_{\ell+1} \equiv pm + s_1$.
6 For each root α, use CRT to recover $\tilde{s}_1 \in [0, 2^k q)$ such that $\tilde{s}_1 \equiv b_1 \pmod{2^k}$
   and $\tilde{s}_1 \equiv \alpha \pmod q$, and check whether $\tilde{s}_1$ would produce correct outputs b_i.
7 Since $s_1 < pq < 2^k q$, when $\alpha = s_1 \bmod q$, we will get $\tilde{s}_1 = s_1$ over the integers.

We summarize these results in the following informal theorem:

Theorem 5. *An attacker can efficiently generate RSA parameters $(N = pq, e)$ such that e has a chosen (small) order $\ell > \log_e \varphi(p)$ modulo $\varphi(p)$. This attacker can then carry out an efficient state recovery attack after observing at least $\ell + 1$ RSA PRG outputs of length $k \geq n/2$ bits generated using these parameters. This backdoor has efficient parameter generation and exploitation but is discoverable.*

These constructions can be extended in a straightforward manner in the case where N is a multi-prime or unbalanced RSA modulus.

While these ideas do not generate a fully satisfactory backdoor, they provide intuition for the construction in the next section, where we will replace the relationship $e^\ell \equiv 1 \bmod \varphi(N)$ (or $\bmod \varphi(p)$) with a more complex polynomial.

The SUS Backdoor for RSA-PRG. In order to conceal the discoverable cyclic behavior of the eSP backdoor, we augment this idea to generate moduli that embed a small, sparse polynomial relationship satisfied by the exponent e modulo $\varphi(N)$ or $\varphi(p)$. We will call this "Small Unknown Solution" or SUS.

Parameter Generation. Let $f(x) = \sum_{i \in S} c_i x^i$ be a sparse polynomial that will remain secret, where the c_i are all ± 1 and are roughly balanced. A correspondingly backdoored prime p will satisfy the relation $f(e) \equiv 0 \bmod p - 1$. This implies a relation between PRG states $\prod_{i \in S} s_i^{c_i} \equiv 1 \pmod p$, where $s_i = s_0^{e^i}$. To backdoor an RSA modulus N, we either ensure $f(e) \equiv 0 \bmod \varphi(N)$, or (like the "partially hidden cycle" eSP variant) $f(e) \equiv 0 \bmod \varphi(p)$ but not $\bmod \varphi(q)$.

Theorem 6. *SUS prime and RSA modulus generation is polynomial time in the length of the modulus.*

Proof. We apply Algorithm 4 except that we replace the desired relation $e^\ell - 1 \bmod p - 1$ with a sparse polynomial $f(e) = \sum_i c_i e^i$. To generate an RSA modulus, we can either generate two primes from different subsets of the factors in Step 3 (so that $f(e) \equiv 0 \bmod \varphi(N)$), or we can backdoor p and choose q normally (so that $f(e) \equiv 0 \bmod \varphi(p)$). The latter allows arbitrarily large N with fixed-size p, because the backdoor does not depend on the choice of q.

SUS State Recovery Attack. The state recovery algorithm uses multivariate Coppersmith. We write $s_0^{e^i} = s_i = b_i + 2^k r_i$, using the outputs b_i and unknown state MSBs r_i, with $0 \leq r_i < R = N/2^k$. For ease of exposition let us assume for now that $f(e) \equiv 0 \bmod \varphi(N)$; applying our backdoor polynomial f we obtain

$$\prod_{i \in S} \left(2^k r_i + b_i\right)^{c_i} \equiv 1 \bmod N$$

This is a low-degree multivariate polynomial modulo N whose roots are the unknown portions of each state. Recall all c_i are ± 1, with roughly balanced sets S^+ of positive c_i and S^- of negative c_i. This gives

$$\prod_{i \in S^+} (2^k r_i + b_i) - \prod_{i \in S^-} (2^k r_i + b_i) \equiv 0 \bmod N$$

Our polynomial degree is $\max(|S^+|, |S^-|)$, which is independent of e. We can then recover the r_i using multivariate Coppersmith.

If instead we had $f(e) \equiv 0 \bmod \varphi(p)$ but not mod $\varphi(q)$, we would instead recover the r_i mod p. But as long as $p > R$ this is the same as recovering r_i over the integers.

Example. Suppose $f(e) = e^{200} + e^{20} - e^{180} - e^0 \equiv 0 \pmod{\varphi(N)}$; we have $|S^+| = |S^-| = 2$. The Coppersmith polynomial in unknowns $r_{200}, r_{20}, r_{180}, r_0$ is

$$f(s) = (r_{200} + 2^{-k} b_{200})(r_{20} + 2^{-k} b_{20}) - (r_{180} + 2^{-k} b_{180})(r_0 + 2^{-k} b_0).$$

We apply Algorithm 3 with $t = 1$ and no extra shifts to generate a lattice with dim $L = 7$ and det $L = R^8 N^6$ (where R is our bound on the r_i). Applying Condition 1 (and omitting the approximation factor in dimension 7), we expect to succeed when $(R^8 N^6)^{1/7} < N$, or when $R < N^{1/8}$. Had we instead had $f(e) \equiv 0 \bmod \varphi(p)$, our success condition would instead be that $R < p^{1/8}$. In either case, this bound is independent of e.

As a demonstration, we generated a 1024-bit RSA modulus N satisfying $e^{200} - e^{180} + e^{20} - 1 \equiv 0 \bmod \varphi(N)$ for $e = 17$. We include it in the full version [24]. Parameter generation took 19 s using Sage on a single core of an Intel E5-2699 processor. Using these parameters with $k = 896$-bit outputs, our attack successfully recovered the state in 213 milliseconds from 200 PRG outputs. For these parameters, the fraction of bits output is below the $(1 - 1/e)$ fraction required by Herrmann and May [39]; that is, our attack requires less output to succeed than theirs. In fact, the fraction of bits output is smaller than $(1 - 2/e)$, the maximum fraction of output bits recommended in the ISO parameters for Micali-Schnorr — although when N is 1024 bits (at the 80-bit security level) the ISO standard recommends only 864 bit outputs, to ensure at least 160 bits remain unknown. In practice, however, LLL reduction of this Coppersmith lattice yields shorter vectors than predicted, and our attack empirically succeeds for these example parameters with ISO-sized $k = 864$ outputs, and even with outputs as small as $k = 856$ bits.

Using a higher multiplicity (and thus a larger-dimension lattice) allows the attack to succeed with even smaller outputs:

Theorem 7. *A SUS-backdoored modulus N of length n with backdoor polynomial f of degree ℓ and $|S|$ nonzero coefficients allows an efficient state recovery attack after observing ℓ outputs of length $k > n(1 - 1/c_S)$ for a constant c_S that depends only on $|S|$, and not on the exponent e.*

When f has $|S| = 2$ terms, $c_S = 2$, when f has $|S| = 4$ terms, $c_S < 6.55$, and when $|S| = 6$ terms, $c_S < 16.96$.

The attack requires only $|S|$ outputs within this range at specified positions.

Proof. The recovery algorithm works as follows. Let $f(x) = \sum_i c_i x^i$. Let $S^+ = \{i \mid c_i > 0\}$ and $S^- = \{i \mid c_i < 0\}$. Apply multivariate Coppersmith's method to solve for the unknown r_i in $\prod_{i \in S^+} (2^k r_i + b_i)^{c_i} - \prod_{i \in S^-} (2^k r_i + b_i)^{|c_i|} \equiv 0 \bmod p$.

For $|S| = 2$, we can construct a full-rank 3-dimensional lattice with multiplicity $t = 1$ to obtain the above bound. This case is degenerate: a polynomial with coefficients $+1, -1$ will generate output that cycles. We obtain the stated bound for $|S| = 4$ from a full-rank 1365-dimensional lattice with $t = 8$; for $|S| = 6$, a 1443-dimensional lattice with $t = 4$. For details see the full version [24].

We have chosen these values so that running LLL for these lattices is within feasible range today; one can get improved bounds for the c_S by choosing larger multiplicities and generating larger (but still polynomially sized) lattices.

Optimized lattice construction methods, like Herrmann and May's technique of unravelled linearization [39], seem to not apply here. We give more analysis in the full version [24].

Undiscoverability vs. Practical Exploitation. We hypothesize that SUS-backdoored parameters could be undiscoverable, if the sparse backdoor polynomial f is properly chosen. However, making the backdoor harder to discover seems to make it harder to exploit.

The backdoor polynomial f in the SUS attack is a sparse polynomial with the property that $f(e) \equiv 0 \bmod \varphi(N)$ or $\bmod \varphi(p)$. More terms in f make it harder to guess, but it also significantly increases the required fraction of output bits or the dimension of the lattice reduced using Coppersmith's method.

If f has too few terms, it becomes possible to guess f by brute force, and then verify a guess by checking (for some arbitrary a) whether $a^{f(e)} \equiv 1 \bmod N$ (if $f(e) = 0 \bmod \varphi(N)$) or if $\gcd(a^{f(e)} - 1, N)$ is nontrivial (if $f(e) = 0 \bmod \varphi(p)$).

As an example, suppose we want f to have eight nonzero terms. The multivariate polynomial to be solved using Coppersmith will have degree 4 ($|S^+| = |S^-| = 4$). If we assume the RSA PRG is reseeded every 50000 outputs (as the ISO standard recommends for MS DRBG), the degree of f must be less than 50000, since any outputs after the first 50000 will not be related. The size of the search space for f would be roughly $\binom{50000}{7} \approx 2^{97}$. (It is 7 and not 8 because $f(e) \equiv 0 \Rightarrow e^j f(e) \equiv 0$ implies the existence of a backdoor polynomial with degree exactly 49999).

A meet-in-the-middle attack does better than brute force. If $f(e) \equiv 0$ mod $\varphi(N)$, split $f = f_0 + f_1$ into the first 3 and last 4 unknown terms. Since $a^{f_0(e)+f_1(e)} \equiv 1$ mod N, precompute possible $a^{f_0(e)}$ terms and check for collisions with $a^{-f_1(e)}$. This takes $\binom{50000}{4} \approx 2^{58}$ time and $\binom{50000}{3} \approx 2^{44}$ space. A similar meet-in-the-middle is possible when the backdoor relation is mod $\varphi(p)$ but not mod $\varphi(N)$, using fast multipoint evaluation; see the full version [24] for details. We conjecture that no faster attack is possible; we leave this question open.

To illustrate the tradeoffs, in addition to the earlier example, we generated two backdoored parameter sets: one requires as high as the 3500th output, took 4 core-hours to exploit, and we conjecture is 2^{25}-undiscoverable; the other requires only as high as the 150th output, took 3 core-minutes to exploit, but is conjectured only 2^9-undiscoverable.[10] We give these (and other) parameters and discuss the tradeoffs further in the full version [24].

Both the construction and the discoverability analysis extend to unbalanced or multi-prime RSA. Exploitation of the backdoor is most efficient if the output is as large as possible, so the attacker would want to work modulo $\varphi(N)$ or modulo $\varphi(p)$ for a large prime factor p.

Extending this Idea to Micali-Schnorr. Our attempts to extend this idea from RSA PRG to Micali-Schnorr have encountered some barriers.

First, the output of MS PRG does not follow the clean iterative structure of the RSA PRG. For RSA PRG, we can write the ith block of output b_i as a value that is close to a power of the initial state $s_i \equiv s_{i-1}^e \equiv s_0^{(e^i)}$ mod N, or a single monomial like x^{e^i} in a polynomial equation. For MS PRG, writing the ith block of output in terms of the initial state by iteratively expanding the expression

$$s_i \equiv 2^{-k}(s_{i-1}^e - b_i) \text{ mod } N,$$

yields a polynomial with exponentially many terms involving previous outputs.

The minimum degree of our backdoor polynomial $\sum_{i \in S} \pm e^i \equiv 0$ mod $p - 1$ needs to be $\log_e \varphi(p)$ to embed information mod p, so our polynomial expression will have exponentially many terms in $\lg p$. Using larger coefficients in the polynomial to generate terms like ce^i increases the degree of the lattice polynomial.

Another way of viewing this obstacle is that the high-degree non-sparse relation between states is due to the simultaneous presence of addition, multiplication, and exponentiation modulo N (or p) in the state update function. If only exponentiation were involved, as is the case of RSA-PRG, we can simplify the expression as above. If only multiplication by a constant and addition were involved, all s_i are affine functions of s_0. When all three operations are involved, however, the resulting expression is a polynomial with exponentially many terms.

---

[10] Example code is available at https://github.com/ucsd-hacc/msdrbg_code.

One path forward would be to generate some algebraic structure that permits simplification or elimination of enough cross-terms that the polynomial no longer has exponentially many terms. (We give an example of such a structure in the next section.) Alternatively, we observe that these polynomials will have linear depth if evaluated as a circuit. Exploiting this idea would require new algorithmic ideas, since a lattice attack requires writing down the polynomial to be solved.

5.4   Attacks on MS PRG

Finite Field MS-PRG Is Insecure. In this section we define a variant of Micali-Schnorr over finite fields of small characteristic, and detail a straightforward state-recovery attack on this variant that involves no backdoors.

This attack does not imply anything about the existence of an attack (or a feasible backdoor) on standard MS DRBG, but it demonstrates that the pseudorandomness of modular exponentiation depends on the choice of field and illustrates algebraic structure that eliminates the exponential blow-up in terms that kept us from extending the ideas in the SUS backdoor to MS-PRG. This attack works for any choice of output length k, unlike the other attacks we detail.

Finite Field Micali-Schnorr. Our finite field variant of the Micali-Schnorr PRG is presented in Algorithm 6. Our eventual backdoor will rely on the characteristic of the field matching the exponent e, which we will take to be a small prime.

Let $\mathbb{F}_{e^n}$ be the finite field of size e^n. We can represent elements of $\mathbb{F}_{e^n}$ as polynomials in the quotient ring $\mathbb{F}_e[x]/N(x)$ (with N monic, irreducible, and $\deg(N) = n$) or as coefficient vectors in $(\mathbb{F}_e)^n$. Addition, multiplication, and exponentiation are defined in the standard ways.

Theorem 8 (Informal). *Finite-field Micali-Schnorr with state size n and output size k allows an efficient probabilistic state recovery attack when $\lceil (n-k)/k \rceil$ outputs are observed.*

Attacking FF-MS-PRG. Our attack relies on the linearity of the Frobenius endomorphism $x \mapsto x^e$ to limit the complexity introduced by exponentiation. This means the entire update step $s_i \leftarrow x^{-k}(s_{i-1}^e - b_i)$ is affine in terms of previous, and therefore also the initial, state. The bound $\deg(s_i) < n - k$ means several elements are 0 when interpreted as a coefficient vector, and this constraint allows the attacker to formulate a linear system of equations involving the known 0-elements of s_i, the unknown initial state s_0, and the known outputs b_i.

Algorithm 6: Finite-Field Micali-Schnorr

Input : Parameters $e \in \mathbb{Z}$, $N \in \mathbb{F}_e[x]$, a number of iterations h
Output: hk output values in $[0, e-1]$
1 Sample initial state $s_0 \in \mathbb{F}_e[x]/N$ of degree $< n - k$ using truly random coins.
2 **for** $i \leftarrow 1$ **to** h **do**
3 $\quad\big|\quad z_i \leftarrow s_{i-1}^e \bmod N(x)$
4 $\quad\big|\quad$ Write $z_i = x^k s_i + b_i$ for $\deg(s_i) < n - k$ and $\deg b_i < k$.
5 **end**
6 Output $b_1 || b_2 || \dots || b_h$.

The attacker observes output until this linear system is overdetermined, and then solves it. A solution giving s_0 is guaranteed to exist. Although the solution is not always unique, in practice this method appears to recover a solution close to the initial state after $\lceil (n-k)/k \rceil$ outputs.

This attack is efficient. With $n = 1024$ and $k = 341$, recovering the FF-MS-PRG state from 9 outputs took 7 min implemented in Sage; the unoptimized construction of the linear system was the bottleneck. Further details of this attack are included in the full version [24].

The Bad-e (Be) Attack. In this section, we describe choices for the exponent e that lead to efficient state-recovery attacks for the Micali-Schnorr generator. The particular choices of e we make are unusual, but allowed by the ISO standard, and are efficient to exploit with the output sizes recommended by ISO.

As observed in Sect. 5.2, a straightforward application of multivariate Coppersmith's method for a state recovery attack against MS PRG is ruled out by the parameters specified by ISO. We can circumvent these restrictions by choosing a large e such that $e^{-1} \bmod \varphi(N)$ is small.

Flexible Choice of e. ISO specifies that "The implementation should allow the application to request any *odd* integer e in the range $1 < e < 2^{\lg(N)-1} - 2 \cdot 2^{\lg N/2}$."

Our attack instantiates the public exponent e with a value other than the default exponent $e = 3$. Using larger e results in a larger output length k under the recommended parameters. Interestingly, while MS DRBG can be instantiated with almost any non-default e, there are more requirements on the public modulus : N may either be one of the default moduli or randomly generated.

Theorem 9 ($e = d^{-1}$ **for Small d Is Insecure**). *Instantiating Micali-Schnorr with RSA using exponent $e = d^{-1} \bmod \varphi(N)$ for d small allows an efficient state recovery attack from a single output when the state has length $r < n/(\binom{d}{2} + 1)$, in time polynomial in d and $\lg N$.*

Proof. One output b_1 yields a degree-d polynomial relating states s_0 and s_1.

$$s_0^e = (2^k s_1 + b_1) \bmod N$$
$$s_0 - (2^k s_1 + b_1)^d = 0 \bmod N$$

A straightforward application of multivariate Coppersmith results in a lattice of dimension $d + 2$ and determinant $R^{\binom{d}{2}+1}N^{d+1}$ for R the bound on the size of the state. Applying Condition 1 and omitting the approximation factor if we expect d to be a small constant, we expect to succeed when $r(\binom{d}{2} + 1) < n$.

We can verify that this attack is allowed by the ISO parameters. When e is large, which is what we expect for $d^{-1} \mod \varphi(N)$ for d small, the ISO parameters set $r = 2\gamma$ where γ is the security parameter. Thus we expect this attack to work when $\gamma(d^2 - d + 2) < n$. To be concrete, for the ISO security parameters (listed in Sect. 2), this inequality is satisfied for $d = 3$ for all parameter sizes, for $d = 5$ at $\gamma = 128$ and above, and $d = 7$ for $\gamma = 256$.

This exponent can be efficiently computed from knowledge of the factorization of N, and we expect it to be large since $\varphi(N) \mid de - 1$. This choice of e is arguably not a plausibly deniable "backdoor" since in practice e is almost always chosen to be small. In addition, it is efficiently discoverable for any small d via the Boneh and Durfee attack on small private RSA exponents [15]. However, in cryptographic protocols in which parameters are negotiated by machines making basic validity checks rather than actively looking for suspicious parameters, even such a discoverable backdoor could easily go undiscovered.

The attack can be generalized to $e = e_0 e_1^{-1}$ for small e_0, e_1, which enables efficient attacks on ISO security levels $\gamma = 112$ through 256, although the generalized attack is still detectable. We refer to the full version [24] for details.

6   Impact on Cryptographic Protocols

Deployed cryptographic systems typically use random numbers as input to a cryptographic protocol. The precise interaction between protocol, implementation and a subverted RNG impact the exploitability of a system. We now briefly consider how our attacks on MS and RSA PRG may affect common protocols.

Case Study: Using MS DRBG State Recovery to Subvert IPsec. IPsec [29] is an encryption protocol often used for VPNs. We focus on the key agreement protocol, typically IKE. During the period of standardization (approximately 2004–2007), the current version of the protocol was IKEv1 [38].

As noted in previous analyses [17,18,20] many IKE implementations use a single PRG to generate both unencrypted nonces, encryption padding and ephemeral secret keys for Diffie-Hellman key agreement. An attacker wishing to passively exploit the "Bad-e" state recovery attack in Sect. 5.4 would observe protocol handshakes, use the nonces to recover the state, and then iterate the state forward to recover the secret Diffie-Hellman exponent, recover the shared secret, and derive the symmetric session keys to decrypt the session data.

For the simplest attack described in Theorem 9, state recovery is feasible for all security parameters with exponent $e = 3^{-1} \mod \varphi(N)$ and requires observing at least $3n/4$ bits of output. For $n = 1024$ this is 96 bytes and for $n = 2048$ it is 192 bytes, both within the 256-byte upper limit on a variable-length nonce.

Extracting Generator Output from Public Nonces. The most likely source for public output is the random nonces in each key agreement: these range from 8–256 bytes in IKE. Thus in IKE a single nonce is conceptually sufficient to recover a single generator output block using a 1024-bit or 2048-bit modulus.

Extracting Generator Output from RSA Padding. Some configurations of the IKEv1 protocol employ RSA-PKCS#1v1.5 encryption to authenticate endpoints. In this configuration, one party encrypts a nonce to the other party's encryption key. Assuming an attacker can interact with the server once, it may therefore obtain raw PRG output in the padding of the RSA ciphertext.

With an RSA public key of length $\bar{n}$ bytes and a nonce of length m bytes, each ciphertext contains $\bar{n} - 3 - m$ bytes of *non-zero* RSA padding bytes, in addition to the m-byte nonce.[11] Assuming a 32-byte nonce, this provides 93 bytes of padding (or 125 bytes for padding and nonce combined) for a 1024-bit RSA encryption key and 221 bytes (or 253 bytes for both) for a 2048-bit encryption key. The 93-byte padding is less than the 96 output bytes required for a 1024-bit key, but the remaining bytes could be recovered via brute force.

Case Study: TLS. SSL/TLS [6,36] are the most common secure communications protocols used on the Internet. SSL and TLS each combine the use of long-term keys or secrets, as well as a key agreement protocol and symmetric encryption scheme for transmission of secure data into a single protocol. Common versions between 2004–2007 included SSL version 3 [36] and TLS 1.0–1.2 [6,26,57].

The random portion of an SSL/TLS nonce is 28 bytes long.[12] For SSL/TLS or IKE implementations with smaller nonces, an attacker would need to obtain several nonces over multiple key exchanges (≈ 4 at the 28 bytes length) in order to recover sufficient state to obtain one 108-byte MS DRBG output at the 1024-bit security level. Even this approach poses a challenge: for our basic attacks, the recovered output bytes must be *consecutive*. In a naive implementation of either protocol, the generation of nonces may be interspersed with other uses of the PRG: as a result, only fragments of each output block would be available. There are two potential engineering solutions that could mitigate this result:

1. During the standardization period, the NSA proposed and co-authored numerous IETF draft extensions to SSL/TLS [40–42,58,59] that cause servers and clients to output much longer nonces on request. At least one extension was ultimately deployed in the BSAFE commercial cryptography library [9]. The occasional use of such extensions by any client would provide eavesdroppers with an arbitrary amount of generator output that could be used to recover secret keys until the generator was reseeded.
2. Some commercial implementations of IKE *pre-generate* nonces in advance of a handshake, storing the results in a queue for later use [17]. Such implementations have been discovered in devices implementing the Dual EC DRBG

---

[11] The PKCS#1v1.5 standard requires that all padding bytes be non-zero, since the 0 byte is used as a delimiter. Recovering the raw byte stream would thus require some additional steps depending on how this string is generated.

[12] Each nonce is 28 bytes of random data concatenated with a 4-byte timestamp.

generator, a design choice that maximizes the practical impact of a subversion attack. A similar implementation decision could allow the exfiltration of multiple consecutive bytes of generator output over several handshakes.

There are also some algorithmic exploitation possibilities:

1. Multivariate Coppersmith methods can be used to solve for multiple nonconsecutive chunks of output; the exact bounds would depend on the details of the implementation.
2. Our SUS backdoor for RSA PRG exploits sequences of non-consecutive blocks of output, albeit selected to satisfy the linear backdoor recurrence embedded in the modulus. A more moderate improvement in the bounds might allow a recovery attack of this form.

7 Conclusion

In this paper, we studied the question of whether an adversary who controls the generation of the parameters used for the Micali-Schnorr PRG can break the security of the algorithm. To that end, we identified vulnerable parameters permitted by the ISO standard for Micali-Schnorr, and developed a novel backdoor algorithm for the closely-related RSA PRG that permits efficient state recovery attacks beyond previously known bounds. However, we encountered barriers in adapting our backdoor technique to MS PRG for realistic parameters, and thus the main question we set out to solve remains open.

A solution to this problem may involve the development of new ideas in the cryptanalysis of RSA. For example, the small characteristic finite field case has exploitable structure. Taking advantage of this structure leads to improvements in algorithms like the function field sieve for discrete logarithms over small-characteristic finite fields. An analogous improvement for the integers that allows simplifications of the recurrences might open doors (or be related to existing advances) in the study of factorization or RSA cryptanalysis algorithms.

Acknowledgments. We thank Emmanuel Thomé and Antonio Sanso as well as numerous attendees of CHES 2016 for enjoyable conversations about this problem. Bor de Kock contributed to an early version of this project. This work was supported by NSF under awards CNS-1653110, CNS-1801479, DMS-1913210, and CNS-2048563, and by DARPA under Contract No. HR001120C0084. Any opinions, findings and conclusions or recommendations expressed in this material are those of the authors and do not necessarily reflect the views of the United States Government or DARPA.

References

1. DRBG Recommmendations from the x9.82 Editing Group. https://github.com/matthewdgreen/nistfoia/blob/master/6.4.2014%20production/055%20-%20DRBG%20Recomm%20from%20X9.82%20Editing%20Group.pdf
2. DRBGs Based on Hard Problems. https://github.com/matthewdgreen/nistfoia/blob/master/6.4.2014%20production/039%20-%20DRBGs%20Based%20on%20Hard%20Problems.pdf
3. Excerpt from 2013 Intelligence Budget Request: SIGINT ENABLING. Media leak (2013). https://archive.nytimes.com/www.nytimes.com/interactive/2013/09/05/us/documents-reveal-nsa-campaign-against-encryption.html
4. SHA-3 Standard: permutation-based hash and extendable-output functions (2015-08-04 2015). https://doi.org/10.6028/NIST.FIPS.202
5. Alexi, W., Chor, B., Goldreich, O., Schnorr, C.P.: RSA/Rabin bits are $1/2 + 1/\text{poly}(\log N)$ secure. In: 25th FOCS, pp. 449–457. IEEE Computer Society Press (1984). https://doi.org/10.1109/SFCS.1984.715947
6. Allen, C., Dierks, T.: The TLS Protocol Version 1.0. RFC 2246 (1999). https://doi.org/10.17487/RFC2246, https://www.rfc-editor.org/info/rfc2246
7. Anderson, R.J.: Practical RSA Trapdoor. Electron. Lett. **29**, 995–995 (1993)
8. Bellare, M., Paterson, K.G., Rogaway, P.: Security of symmetric encryption against mass surveillance. In: Garay, J.A., Gennaro, R. (eds.) CRYPTO 2014. LNCS, vol. 8616, pp. 1–19. Springer, Heidelberg (2014). https://doi.org/10.1007/978-3-662-44371-2_1
9. Benjamin, D.: Additional TLS 1.3 Results from Chrome (December 2017). https://mailarchive.ietf.org/arch/msg/tls/i9blmvG2BEPf1s1OJkenHknRw9c/
10. Berndt, S., Liskiewicz, M.: Algorithm substitution attacks from a steganographic perspective. In: Thuraisingham, B.M., Evans, D., Malkin, T., Xu, D. (eds.) ACM CCS 2017, pp. 1649–1660. ACM Press (2017). https://doi.org/10.1145/3133956.3133981
11. Bernstein, D.J., Lange, T., Niederhagen, R.: Dual EC: A Standardized Back Door, pp. 256–281. Springer, Heidelberg (2016). https://doi.org/10.1007/978-3-662-49301-4_17
12. Bertoni, G., Daemen, J., Peeters, M., Van Assche, G.: On the indifferentiability of the sponge construction. In: Smart, N.P. (ed.) EUROCRYPT 2008. LNCS, vol. 4965, pp. 181–197. Springer, Heidelberg (2008). https://doi.org/10.1007/978-3-540-78967-3_11
13. Blum, L., Blum, M., Shub, M.: A simple unpredictable pseudo-random number generator. SIAM J. Comput. **15**(2), 364–383 (1986). https://doi.org/10.1137/0215025
14. Blum, M., Micali, S.: How to generate cryptographically strong sequences of pseudo random bits. In: 23rd FOCS, pp. 112–117. IEEE Computer Society Press (1982). https://doi.org/10.1109/SFCS.1982.72
15. Boneh, D., Durfee, G.: Cryptanalysis of RSA with private key d less than $N^{0.292}$. In: Stern, J. (ed.) EUROCRYPT 1999. LNCS, vol. 1592, pp. 1–11. Springer, Heidelberg (1999). https://doi.org/10.1007/3-540-48910-X_1
16. Cesati, M.: A new idea for RSA backdoors. arXiv preprint arXiv:2201.13153 (2022).
17. Checkoway, S., et al.: A systematic analysis of the juniper dual EC incident. In: Weippl, E.R., Katzenbeisser, S., Kruegel, C., Myers, A.C., Halevi, S. (eds.) ACM CCS 2016, pp. 468–479. ACM Press (2016). https://doi.org/10.1145/2976749.2978395

18. Checkoway, S., et al.: On the practical exploitability of dual EC in TLS implementations. In: Fu, K., Jung, J. (eds.) USENIX Security 2014, pp. 319–335. USENIX Association (2014)
19. Chow, S.S.M., Russell, A., Tang, Q., Yung, M., Zhao, Y., Zhou, H.S.: Let a non-barking watchdog bite: cliptographic signatures with an offline watchdog. In: Lin, D., Sako, K. (eds.) PKC 2019. LNCS, vol. 11442, pp. 221–251. Springer, Heidelberg (2019). https://doi.org/10.1007/978-3-030-17253-4_8
20. Cohney, S.N., Green, M.D., Heninger, N.: Practical state recovery attacks against legacy RNG implementations. In: Lie, D., Mannan, M., Backes, M., Wang, X. (eds.) ACM CCS 2018, pp. 265–280. ACM Press (2018). https://doi.org/10.1145/3243734.3243756
21. Coppersmith, D.: Small solutions to polynomial equations, and low exponent RSA vulnerabilities. J. Cryptol. **10**(4), 233–260 (1997). https://doi.org/10.1007/s001459900030
22. Coppersmith, D.: Finding small solutions to small degree polynomials. In: Silverman, J.H. (ed.) Cryptography and Lattices, pp. 20–31. Springer, Heidelberg (2001). https://doi.org/10.1007/3-540-44670-2_3
23. Crépeau, C., Slakmon, A.: Simple backdoors for RSA key generation. In: Joye, M. (ed.) CT-RSA 2003. LNCS, vol. 2612, pp. 403–416. Springer, Heidelberg (2003). https://doi.org/10.1007/3-540-36563-X_28
24. Davis, H., Green, M., Heninger, N., Ryan, K., Suhl, A.: On the possibility of a backdoor in the Micali-Schnorr generator. Cryptology ePrint Archive, Paper 2023/440 (2023). https://eprint.iacr.org/2023/440
25. Degabriele, J.P., Paterson, K.G., Schuldt, J.C.N., Woodage, J.: Backdoors in pseudorandom number generators: possibility and impossibility results. In: Robshaw, M., Katz, J. (eds.) CRYPTO 2016, LNCS, vol. 9814, pp. 403–432. Springer, Heidelberg (2016). https://doi.org/10.1007/978-3-662-53018-4_15
26. Dierks, T., Rescorla, E.: The Transport Layer Security (TLS) Protocol Version 1.1. RFC 4346 (2006). https://doi.org/10.17487/RFC4346
27. Dodis, Y., Ganesh, C., Golovnev, A., Juels, A., Ristenpart, T.: A formal treatment of backdoored pseudorandom generators. In: Oswald, E., Fischlin, M. (eds.) EUROCRYPT 2015. LNCS, vol. 9056, pp. 101–126. Springer, Heidelberg (2015). https://doi.org/10.1007/978-3-662-46800-5_5
28. Dodis, Y., Pointcheval, D., Ruhault, S., Vergnaud, D., Wichs, D.: Security analysis of pseudo-random number generators with input: /dev/random is not robust. In: Sadeghi, A.R., Gligor, V.D., Yung, M. (eds.) ACM CCS 2013, pp. 647–658. ACM Press (2013). https://doi.org/10.1145/2508859.2516653
29. Doraswamy, N., Glenn, K.R., Thayer, R.L.: IP Security Document Roadmap. RFC 2411 (1998). https://doi.org/10.17487/RFC2411, https://www.rfc-editor.org/info/rfc2411
30. Engelberts, L.: Analysis of the Micali-Schnorr PRNG with known factorisation of the modulus. Master's thesis, University of Oxford (2020)
31. Fischlin, M., Mazaheri, S.: Self-guarding cryptographic protocols against algorithm substitution attacks. In: Chong, S., Delaune, S. (eds.) CSF 2018 Computer Security Foundations Symposium, pp. 76–90. IEEE Computer Society Press (2018). https://doi.org/10.1109/CSF.2018.00013
32. Fischlin, R., Schnorr, C.P.: Stronger security proofs for RSA and Rabin bits. In: Fumy, W. (ed.) EUROCRYPT 1997. LNCS, vol. 1233, pp. 267–279. Springer, Heidelberg (1997). https://doi.org/10.1007/3-540-69053-0_19
33. Fischlin, R., Schnorr, C.P.: Stronger security proofs for RSA and Rabin bits. J. Cryptol. **13**(2), 221–244 (2000). https://doi.org/10.1007/s001459910008

34. Fouque, P.A., Vergnaud, D., Zapalowicz, J.C.: Time/memory/data tradeoffs for variants of the RSA problem. In: Du, D.Z., Zhang, G. (eds.) Computing and Combinatorics, pp. 651–662. Springer, Heidelberg (2013). https://doi.org/10.1007/978-3-642-38768-5_57

35. Fouque, P.A., Zapalowicz, J.C.: Statistical properties of short RSA distribution and their cryptographic applications. In: Cai, Z., Zelikovsky, A., Bourgeois, A. (eds.) Computing and Combinatorics, pp. 525–536. Springer, Cham (2014). https://doi.org/10.1007/978-3-319-08783-2_45

36. Freier, A.O., Karlton, P., Kocher, P.C.: The Secure Sockets Layer (SSL) Protocol Version 3.0. RFC 6101 (2011). https://doi.org/10.17487/RFC6101, https://www.rfc-editor.org/info/rfc6101

37. Green, M.: A few more notes on NSA random number generators (2013). https://web.archive.org/web/20230109062504/https://blog.cryptographyengineering.com/2013/12/28/a-few-more-notes-on-nsa-random-number/

38. Harkins, D., Carrel, D.: The Internet Key Exchange (IKE). IETF RFC 2409 (Proposed Standard) (1998)

39. Herrmann, M., May, A.: Attacking power generators using unravelled linearization: when do we output too much? In: Matsui, M. (ed.) ASIACRYPT 2009. LNCS, vol. 5912, pp. 487–504. Springer, Heidelberg (2009). https://doi.org/10.1007/978-3-642-10366-7_29

40. Hoffman, P.E.: Additional Random Extension to TLS. Internet-Draft draft-hoffman-tls-additional-random-ext-01, Internet Engineering Task Force (2010). Work in Progress. https://datatracker.ietf.org/doc/draft-hoffman-tls-additional-random-ext/01/

41. Hoffman, P.E.: Additional Master Secret Inputs for TLS. RFC 6358 (2012). https://doi.org/10.17487/RFC6358, https://www.rfc-editor.org/info/rfc6358

42. Hoffman, P.E., Solinas, J.: Additional PRF Inputs for TLS. Internet-Draft draft-solinas-tls-additional-prf-input-01, Internet Engineering Task Force (2009). Work in Progress. https://datatracker.ietf.org/doc/draft-solinas-tls-additional-prf-input/01/

43. International Organization for Standardization: ISO/IEC 18031:2011 Information Technology—Security Techniques—Random Bit Generation (2011). https://www.iso.org/standard/54945.html

44. Jochemsz, E., May, A.: A strategy for finding roots of multivariate polynomials with new applications in attacking RSA variants. In: Lai, X., Chen, K. (eds.) ASIACRYPT 2006. LNCS, vol. 4284, pp. 267–282. Springer, Heidelberg (2006). https://doi.org/10.1007/11935230_18

45. Johnson, D.B.: X9.82 part 3: number theoretic DRBGs. Presented at the NIST RNG Workshop (2004). https://csrc.nist.gov/CSRC/media/Events/Random-Number-Generation-Workshop-2004/documents/NumberTheoreticDRBG.pdf

46. Joye, M.: RSA moduli with a predetermined portion: Techniques and applications. In: Chen, L., Mu, Y., Susilo, W. (eds.) Information Security Practice and Experience, pp. 116–130. Springer, Heidelberg (2008). https://doi.org/10.1007/978-3-540-79104-1_9

47. Jutla, C.S.: On finding small solutions of modular multivariate polynomial equations. In: Nyberg, K. (ed.) EUROCRYPT 1998. LNCS, vol. 1403, pp. 158–170. Springer, Heidelberg (1998). https://doi.org/10.1007/BFb0054124

48. Koblitz, N., Menezes, A.: Another look at "provable security". II. (invited talk). In: Barua, R., Lange, T. (eds.) INDOCRYPT 2006. LNCS, vol. 4329, pp. 148–175. Springer, Heidelberg (2006). https://doi.org/10.1007/11941378_12

49. Lenstra, A.K., Lenstra, H.W., Jr., Lovász, L.: Factoring polynomials with rational coefficients. Math. Ann. **261**(4), 515–534 (1982)
50. Micali, S., Schnorr, C.P.: Efficient, perfect random number generators. In: Goldwasser, S. (ed.) CRYPTO 1988. LNCS, vol. 403, pp. 173–198. Springer, Heidelberg (1990). https://doi.org/10.1007/0-387-34799-2_14
51. Micali, S., Schnorr, C.P.: Efficient, perfect polynomial random number generators. J. Cryptol. **3**(3), 157–172 (1991). https://doi.org/10.1007/BF00196909
52. National Institute of Standards and Technology. Results of a recent FOIA for NIST documents related to the design of Dual EC DRBG (2015). https://github.com/matthewdgreen/nistfoia/
53. Nguyen, P.Q., Stehlé, D.: Lll on the average. In: Hess, F., Pauli, S., Pohst, M. (eds.) Algorithmic Number Theory, pp. 238–256. Springer, Heidelberg (2006). https://doi.org/10.1007/11792086_18
54. Patsakis, C.: Number theoretic SETUPs for RSA like factoring based algorithms. J. Inf. Hiding Multim. Signal Process. **3**(2), 191–204 (2012)
55. Perlroth, N., Larson, J., Shane, S.: N.S.A. able to foil basic safeguards of privacy on web. New York Times (2013). https://www.nytimes.com/2013/09/06/us/nsa-foils-much-internet-encryption.html
56. Peyrin, T., Wang, H.: The MALICIOUS framework: embedding backdoors into tweakable block ciphers. In: Micciancio, D., Ristenpart, T. (eds.) CRYPTO 2020. LNCS, vol. 12172, pp. 249–278. Springer, Heidelberg (2020). https://doi.org/10.1007/978-3-030-56877-1_9
57. Rescorla, E., Dierks, T.: The Transport Layer Security (TLS) Protocol Version 1.2. RFC 5246 (2008). https://doi.org/10.17487/RFC5246, https://www.rfc-editor.org/info/rfc5246
58. Rescorla, E., Salter, M.: Opaque PRF Inputs for TLS. Internet-Draft draft-rescorla-tls-opaque-prf-input-00, Internet Engineering Task Force (2006). Work in Progress. https://datatracker.ietf.org/doc/draft-rescorla-tls-opaque-prf-input/00/
59. Rescorla, E., Salter, M.: Extended Random Values for TLS. Internet-Draft draft-rescorla-tls-extended-random-02, Internet Engineering Task Force (2009). Work in Progress. https://datatracker.ietf.org/doc/draft-rescorla-tls-extended-random/02/
60. Russell, A., Tang, Q., Yung, M., Zhou, H.S.: Cliptography: clipping the power of kleptographic attacks. In: Cheon, J.H., Takagi, T. (eds.) ASIACRYPT 2016. LNCS, vol. 10032, pp. 34–64. Springer, Heidelberg (2016). https://doi.org/10.1007/978-3-662-53890-6_2
61. Sanso, A.: How to try to predict the output of Micali-Schnorr generator (MS-DRBG) knowing the factorization (2017). http://blog.intothesymmetry.com/2017/12/how-to-try-to-predict-output-of-micali.html
62. Shumow, D., Ferguson, N.: On the possibility of a back door in the NIST SP800-90 Dual Ec Prng. Presented at the Crypto 2007 rump session (2007). http://rump2007.cr.yp.to/15-shumow.pdf
63. Steinfeld, R., Pieprzyk, J., Wang, H.: On the provable security of an efficient RSA-based pseudorandom generator. In: Lai, X., Chen, K. (eds.) ASIACRYPT 2006. LNCS, vol. 4284, pp. 194–209. Springer, Heidelberg (2006). https://doi.org/10.1007/11935230_13
64. Wüller, S., Kühnel, M., Meyer, U.: Information hiding in the RSA modulus. In: Proceedings of the 4th ACM Workshop on Information Hiding and Multimedia Security, pp. 159–167 (2016)

65. Yao, A.C.C.: Theory and applications of trapdoor functions (extended abstract). In: 23rd FOCS, pp. 80–91. IEEE Computer Society Press (1982). https://doi.org/10.1109/SFCS.1982.45

66. Young, A., Yung, M.: The dark side of "black-box" cryptography, or: should we trust capstone? In: Koblitz, N. (ed.) CRYPTO 1996. LNCS, vol. 1109, pp. 89–103. Springer, Heidelberg (1996). https://doi.org/10.1007/3-540-68697-5_8

67. Young, A., Yung, M.: Kleptography: using cryptography against cryptography. In: Fumy, W. (ed.) EUROCRYPT 1997. LNCS, vol. 1233, pp. 62–74. Springer, Heidelberg (1997). https://doi.org/10.1007/3-540-69053-0_6

68. Young, A., Yung, M.: A space efficient backdoor in RSA and its applications. In: Preneel, B., Tavares, S. (eds.) SAC 2005. LNCS, vol. 3897, pp. 128–143. Springer, Heidelberg (2006). https://doi.org/10.1007/11693383_9

Cryptanalysis of the PEREGRINE Lattice-Based Signature Scheme

Xiuhan Lin[1], Moeto Suzuki[2], Shiduo Zhang[3], Thomas Espitau[4], Yang Yu[3,5,6,7](✉), Mehdi Tibouchi[2,8], and Masayuki Abe[2,8]

[1] School of Cyber Science and Technology, Shandong University, Qingdao, China
xhlin@mail.sdu.edu.cn
[2] Kyoto University, Kyoto, Japan
suzuki.moeto.56f@st.kyoto-u.ac.jp
[3] Institute for Advanced Study, Tsinghua University, Beijing, China
zsd19@mails.tsinghua.edu.cn, yu-yang@mail.tsinghua.edu.cn
[4] PQShield SAS, Paris, France
[5] BNRist, Tsinghua University, Beijing, China
[6] Zhongguancun Laboratory, Beijing, China
[7] National Financial Cryptography Research Center, Beijing, China
[8] NTT Social Informatics Laboratories, Tokyo, Japan
{mehdi.tibouchi,msyk.abe}@ntt.com

Abstract. The PEREGRINE signature scheme is one of the candidates in the ongoing Korean post-quantum cryptography competition. It is proposed as a high-speed variant of FALCON, which is a hash-and-sign signature scheme over NTRU lattices and one of the schemes selected by NIST for standardization. To this end, PEREGRINE replaces the lattice Gaussian sampler in the FALCON signing procedure with a new sampler based on the *centered binomial* distribution. While this modification offers significant advantages in terms of efficiency and implementation, it does not come with a provable guarantee that signatures do not leak information about the signing key. Unfortunately, lattice-based signature schemes in the hash-and-sign paradigm that lack such a guarantee (such as GGH, NTRUSign or DRS) have generally proved insecure.

In this paper, we show that PEREGRINE is no exception, by demonstrating a practical key recovery attack against it. We observe that the distribution of PEREGRINE signatures is a *hidden transformation* of some public distribution and still leaks information about the signing key. By adapting the parallelepiped-learning technique of Nguyen and Regev (Eurocrypt 2006), we show that the signing key can be recovered from a relatively small number of signatures. The learning technique alone yields an approximate version of the key, from which we can recover the exact key using a decoding technique due to Thomas Prest (PKC 2023).

For the reference implementation (resp. the official specification version) of PEREGRINE–512, we fully recover the secret key with good probability in a few hours given around 25,000 (resp. 11 million) signature samples.

© International Association for Cryptologic Research 2024
Q. Tang and V. Teague (Eds.): PKC 2024, LNCS 14601, pp. 387–412, 2024.
https://doi.org/10.1007/978-3-031-57718-5_13

Keywords: Cryptanalysis · Lattice-based signature · Statistical learning · NTRU

1 Introduction

As the potential advent of large-scale quantum computers puts all currently deployed public-key cryptography at risk, preparing the transition to post-quantum cryptography (PQC) is of great importance. To that end, NIST initiated its PQC standardization process in 2016, and announced in 2022 an initial batch of algorithms to be standardized by 2024, while other schemes remain under consideration for future standardization. Concurrently, other standardization bodies have launched their own processes and competitions for post-quantum cryptography, such as those in China[1], recently concluded, and the Republic of Korea[2], currently ongoing. In all these standardization efforts, constructions based on structured lattices have been of particular interest, as their good balance of performance and bandwidth requirements have made them some of the top contenders both for public-key encryption/KEMs and signatures.

Lattice-based signature candidates can be roughly divided into two families according to their design paradigm: they either rely on the Fiat–Shamir heuristic (often but not always paired with Lyubashevsky's aborting technique) or on the hash-and-sign framework based on lattice trapdoors. The two lattice-based signatures already selected for standardization in the NIST process, namely Dilithium [LDK+22] and Falcon [PFH+22], each represent one of those two paradigms: Dilithium is a Fiat–Shamir with aborts scheme, while Falcon is a hash-and-sign construction. They both have their pros and cons: Dilithium is a simpler design that is easier to implement securely, whereas Falcon tends to be faster and more compact at the cost of a much greater complexity of implementation and a somewhat reduced versatility in terms of parameter selection.

Hash-and-sign lattice-based signatures in general rely on the construction of a certain lattice with a "good" and a "bad" basis, that play the role of the secret signing key and the public verification key respectively. The good basis, also called the *trapdoor*, has relatively short and fairly orthogonal vectors, and as such can be used to approximate the closest vector problem to a good approximation factor. The bad basis on the other hand consists of much larger vectors, and is of little help in finding close vectors, even though it can still of course be used to check lattice membership. The signing procedure can then be described roughly as follows. The message to be signed is hashed to a random point in the ambient space of the lattice, and the signer uses the trapdoor to compute some lattice point close to that random point, and outputs it as the signature. The verification consists in checking that the signature is indeed a lattice point (which can be done with the "bad" public basis) and that it is sufficiently close to the hashed message.

---

[1] https://www.cacrnet.org.cn/site/content/854.html.
[2] https://kpqc.or.kr/.

That general framework is the one followed by the first proposed lattice-based signature schemes in the late 1990s, like GGH [GGH97] and NTRUSign [HHP+03]. Unfortunately, those early constructions turned out to be insecure: Nguyen and Regev [NR06] showed that each signature would leak some information about the secret trapdoor, and that a few tens of thousands of signatures could suffice to reconstruct the entire signing key. Several heuristic countermeasures against this kind of statistical attacks were subsequently proposed and promptly broken again, until Gentry, Peikert, and Vaikuntanathan [GPV08] finally presented a provably secure solution to that issue. The crux of what is now called the GPV framework is to randomize the signature generation in such a way that signatures follow a distribution *independent* of the trapdoor (usually a certain discrete Gaussian distribution supported on the lattice). This is the approach followed by most of the secure hash-and-sign lattice-based signatures proposed afterward, including Falcon. The reliance on Gaussian sampling, however, is also one of the source of Falcon's greater complexity compared to schemes like Dilithium.

Several variants of Falcon [EFG+22, KTW+22, ENS+23] have recently been proposed to mitigate its shortcomings with respect to implementation complexity while remaining firmly within the GPV framework and its provable security guarantees. Nevertheless, trying to do away with the GPV framework altogether and adopt more efficient countermeasures against statistical attacks may appear like a tempting choice. This idea is the basic design principle of the PEREGRINE signature scheme, one of the candidates in the ongoing first round of the Korean PQC competition. PEREGRINE avoids the Gaussian sampling in its signature generation procedure entirely. Instead, it uses Babai's round-off algorithm [Bab86] to first compute a vector $\mathbf{v}$ close to the hashed message and then adds a random noise $\mathbf{e} = \mathbf{Br}$ to get the signature $\mathbf{s} = \mathbf{v} + \mathbf{e}$ where $\mathbf{B}$ is the trapdoor and $\mathbf{r}$ is a random vector with coefficients following a *centered binomial* distribution. The addition of $\mathbf{e}$ is presented as an effective countermeasure against the Nguyen–Regev statistical attack [NR06] mentioned above. As noted in [SKLN22], the rationale underlying this choice is that the centered binomial distribution has "characteristics similar to a discrete Gaussian", although it does not offer a proof of security.

Hash-and-sign lattice signatures lacking such a proof, including the GGH and NTRUSign schemes already mentioned, as well as newer proposals like DRS [PSDS17], have generally been broken by statistical attacks [GS02, NR06, DN12, YD18]. Since PEREGRINE employs an additional countermeasure to specifically thwart this class of attacks, it is natural to analyze to what extent it succeeds in doing so.

Our Contributions. In this work, we show that, unfortunately, PEREGRINE is no exception and can indeed be defeated with a statistical learning attack similar to [NR06]. As experimental validation, we implement a practical key recovery attack that effectively recovers the PEREGRINE signing key from a few tens of thousands to a few million signature samples, depending on the precise variant under consideration.

As mentioned before, the PEREGRINE signature can be written as $\mathbf{s} = \mathbf{v} + \mathbf{Br}$ where $\mathbf{v}$ is in the parallelepiped spanned by the trapdoor $\mathbf{B}$, and $\mathbf{r}$ is drawn from a centered binomial distribution. The support of PEREGRINE signatures is now a set of *adjacent parallelepipeds* rather than a sole parallelepiped, and these adjacent parallelepipeds are labeled by $\mathbf{r}$. For random messages, the signatures are uniformly distributed in each parallelepiped and the probability of a random signature in a certain parallelepiped only depends on the label $\mathbf{r}$. We observe that the signature distribution can be obtained by applying the linear transformation of $\mathbf{B}$ on some *publicly known* distribution. We call this general problem the *hidden transformation* problem (HTP), and propose to revisit the classical parallelepiped-learning technique of [NR06] in that context.

We show that this attack applies to PEREGRINE, allowing to fully exploit the statistical leak on $\mathbf{B}$, and demonstrate that it leads to a practical key recovery. In particular, we notice that the reference implementation of PEREGRINE does not coincide with the algorithmic description in the official specification. Hence, we mount the attack on those two versions of PEREGRINE, and manage to break both of them. Our attack combines several techniques in the literature. We make use of the gradient descent algorithm in [TW20] as an improvement of the original method in [NR06]. We also employ a decoding technique inspired by Prest [Pre23] to recover the exact key from the approximation derived from statistical learning. Finally, we show that around 25,000 (resp. 11 million) signatures suffice to successfully recover the full key within a few hours with good probability for the reference implementation (resp. the official specification version) of PEREGRINE–512.

Roadmap. We start in Sect. 2 with the notations and background. Section 3 briefly describes the PEREGRINE signature scheme. In Sect. 4, we extend the parallelepiped-learning technique to "learning a hidden transformation". In Sect. 5, we analyze and carry out practical attacks against both the reference implementation and the official specification of PEREGRINE–512. Finally, we conclude in Sect. 6 and suggest some possible avenues for future work.

2   Preliminaries

2.1   Notation

We denote by $\mathrm{GL}_n(\mathbb{R})$ be the group of $n \times n$ invertible matrices with real coefficients and $\mathbb{S}^{n-1}$ be the unit sphere of $\mathbb{R}^n$.

We describe (column) vectors in bold lowercase and write b_i as the i-th coordinate of vector $\mathbf{b}$, i.e. $\mathbf{b} = (b_1, \ldots, b_n)$. Given $\mathbf{a} = (a_1, \ldots, a_n)$, $\mathbf{b} = (b_1, \ldots, b_n) \in \mathbb{R}^n$, the inner product is $\langle \mathbf{a}, \mathbf{b} \rangle = \sum_{i=1}^{n} a_i b_i$. For $\mathbf{a} \in \mathbb{R}^n$, the ℓ_2-norm is $\|\mathbf{a}\| = \sqrt{\langle \mathbf{a}, \mathbf{a} \rangle}$, the ℓ_1-norm is $\|\mathbf{a}\|_1 = \sum_i |a_i|$ and ℓ_∞-norm is $\|\mathbf{a}\|_\infty = \max_i |a_i|$. The operation $\lfloor x \rceil$ means rounding x to the closest integer and is naturally extended to the vector $\mathbf{x}$ by taking rounding coefficient-wisely. We describe matrices in bold uppercase and denote by $\mathbf{b}_i$ for the i-th column of matrix $\mathbf{B}$, i.e. $\mathbf{B} = (\mathbf{b}_1, \ldots, \mathbf{b}_n)$. We use $\mathbf{B}^t$ (resp. $\mathbf{B}^{-1}$) to denote the transpose (resp. inverse) of $\mathbf{B}$. Let $\mathbf{I}_n$ be $n \times n$ identity matrix. Given a differentiable function $f \colon \mathbb{R}^n \to \mathbb{R}$, the gradient of f at $\mathbf{w} \in \mathbb{R}^n$ is $\nabla f(\mathbf{w}) = (\frac{\partial f}{\partial x_1}(\mathbf{w}), \ldots, \frac{\partial f}{\partial x_n}(\mathbf{w}))$.

2.2   Lattices

A lattice $\mathcal{L}$ is a discrete subgroup of $\mathbb{R}^m$. It is the set of all integer combinations of linearly independent vectors $\mathbf{b}_1, \ldots, \mathbf{b}_n \in \mathbb{R}^m$, i.e. $\mathcal{L} = \{\sum_{i=1}^{n} x_i \mathbf{b}_i \mid x_i \in \mathbb{Z}\}$. The matrix $\mathbf{B} = (\mathbf{b}_1, \ldots, \mathbf{b}_n)$ is called the basis and n the rank of $\mathcal{L}$. When $n = m$, the lattice is said to be full-rank. We write $\mathcal{L}(\mathbf{B})$ to denote the lattice generated by a basis $\mathbf{B} \in \mathrm{GL}_n(\mathbb{R})$. Given $\mathbf{B} \in \mathrm{GL}_n(\mathbb{R})$, the parallelepiped spanned by $\mathbf{B}$ is $\mathcal{P}(\mathbf{B}) = \{\mathbf{xB} \mid \mathbf{x} \in [-\frac{1}{2}, \frac{1}{2})^n\}$. The parallelepiped $\mathcal{P}(\mathbf{B})$ is a fundamental region of the lattice $\mathcal{L}(\mathbf{B})$.

2.3   Statistics and Probability

For a distribution D, we write $y \leftarrow D$ when the random variable y is sampled from D. We also write $y \sim D$ a random variable y following the distribution D. Let $U(S)$ be the uniform distribution over the set S. Let $\#S$ be the number of elements in the set S. We denote by $\mathbb{E}[y]$ the expectation of the random variable y. A distribution D over $\mathbb{R}$ is called *centered* when $\mathbb{E}_{y \leftarrow D}[y] = 0$. For a distribution D over $\mathbb{R}^n$, we denote by $\mathbf{Cov}[D] = \mathbb{E}_{\mathbf{x} \leftarrow D}[\mathbf{xx}^t]$ its covariance matrix.

Given an even integer μ, the *centered binomial* distribution B_μ is defined over $[-\frac{\mu}{2}, \frac{\mu}{2}] \cap \mathbb{Z}$ by the probability density function $P[X = x] = \frac{\mu!}{(\frac{\mu}{2}+x)!(\frac{\mu}{2}-x)!} \cdot 2^{-\mu}$.

2.4   Cyclotomic Rings and NTRU

Let $\mathcal{R} = \mathbb{Z}[x]/(x^{n/2} + 1)$ with $n \geq 4$ a power of 2. Given $h \in \mathcal{R}$ and q a rational prime with h invertible modulo q, the lattice $\mathcal{L}_{NTRU} = \{(s_1, s_2) \in \mathcal{R}^2 \mid s_1 + s_2 h = 0 \bmod q\}$ is called an NTRU lattice. In a typical NTRU cryptosystem, the public key is $h = g/f \bmod q$ where (f, g) is a pair of short polynomials in $\mathcal{R}$ and used as the secret key. For short $(F, G) \in \mathcal{R}^2$ such that $fG - gF = q$,
$$\mathbf{B}_{f,g} = \begin{pmatrix} g & G \\ -f & -F \end{pmatrix} \in \mathcal{R}^{2 \times 2}$$
is an NTRU trapdoor basis of $\mathcal{L}_{NTRU}$.

3   The PEREGRINE Signature Scheme

Let us briefly describe the PEREGRINE signature scheme. We omit some details that are not necessary for understanding our work and refer to [SKLN22] for the complete description. PEREGRINE is specified by the parameters of Table 1.

As an NTRU-based hash-and-sign signature scheme, PEREGRINE uses an NTRU trapdoor basis $\mathbf{B}_{f,g}$ as the secret key and the public key is $h = g/f \bmod q$.

Table 1. Parameters of PEREGRINE.

Symbol	Description
$n/2$ (a power of two)	degree of the underlying ring $\mathcal{R} = \mathbb{Z}[x]/(x^{n/2} + 1)$
q	modulus
(μ_1, μ_2)	parameters of the binomial distributions in signing
$\lfloor \beta^2 \rfloor$	signature acceptance bound

Signing Procedure. The signing algorithm of PEREGRINE is described in Algorithm 1. It proceeds in two steps. The first step is in essence Babai's round-off algorithm [Bab86] outputting some integer vector (I_1, I_2) such that $\mathbf{B}_{f,g} \cdot \begin{pmatrix} I_1 \\ I_2 \end{pmatrix}$ is close to the hashed message $\begin{pmatrix} c \\ 0 \end{pmatrix}$. This is implemented with a so-called ModDown function, and the details are irrelevant to our attack. The second step, perhaps inspired by the Gaussian sampling techniques [GPV08, Pei10], is randomizing the close vector $\mathbf{B}_{f,g} \cdot \begin{pmatrix} I_1 \\ I_2 \end{pmatrix}$, which is attempted to defeat the parallelepiped-learning attack [NR06]. The randomization is performed by adding a binomial vector (J_1, J_2) to (I_1, I_2) without using Gaussian distribution.

Algorithm 1: Sign

Input: A message msg, an NTRU trapdoor $\mathbf{B}_{f,g}$.
Output: A signature (r, s_2).

1 $r \overset{\$}{\leftarrow} \{0,1\}^{320}$, $c \leftarrow H(msg\|r)$
2 $(I_1, I_2) \leftarrow \left(\left\lceil -\frac{cF}{q} \right\rceil, \left\lfloor \frac{cf}{q} \right\rfloor \right)$
3 **repeat**
4 $\quad (J_{1,0}, \ldots, J_{1,n/2-1}) \leftarrow B_{\mu_1}^{n/2}, (J_{2,0}, \ldots, J_{2,n/2-1}) \leftarrow B_{\mu_2}^{n/2}$
5 $\quad J_1 \leftarrow \sum_{i=0}^{n/2-1} J_{1,i} \cdot x^i$, $J_2 \leftarrow \sum_{i=0}^{n/2-1} J_{2,i} \cdot x^i$
6 $\quad \begin{pmatrix} s_1 \\ s_2 \end{pmatrix} \leftarrow \begin{pmatrix} c \\ 0 \end{pmatrix} - \mathbf{B}_{f,g} \cdot \begin{pmatrix} I_1 + J_1 \\ I_2 + J_2 \end{pmatrix}$
7 **until** $\|(s_1, s_2)\| \leq \lfloor \beta^2 \rfloor$
8 **return** (r, s_2)

Concrete Parameters. This work focuses on the parameter set of PEREGRINE–512 that was claimed to reach NIST security level I, in which $(n/2, q) = (512, 12289)$. We noted some discrepancies between the reference *implementation* and the official *specification*.

1. As per the specification, the key generation of PEREGRINE is almost the same with that of Falcon, except that the coefficients of (f, g) are drawn

from the binomial distribution B_{26}. The key generation should check if the Gram–Schmidt norms of $\mathbf{B}_{f,g}$ are bounded by $1.17\sqrt{q}$ to ensure the optimal trapdoor quality [DLP14]. However, this check is commented out in the reference implementation, which yields the risk of weak keys. We follow the key generation with such a check, while it would not affect our attack.

2. While the specification suggests $\mu_1 = \mu_2 = 26$, the reference implementation in effect works with $(\mu_1, \mu_2) = (6, 0)$. We mount the attack on both the reference implementation and the specification version. The reference implementation uses much smaller (μ_1, μ_2) narrowing the support of signatures, which greatly facilitates the attack in practice. However, larger binomial parameters in the specification still cannot be an effective countermeasure.

Signature Distribution. The signing procedure of PEREGRINE boils down to solving the approximate CVP in the NTRU lattice. The signature[3] (s_1, s_2) is the difference between the CVP solution to the target $(c, 0)$. It can be rewritten as

$$\begin{pmatrix} s_1 \\ s_2 \end{pmatrix} = \mathbf{B}_{f,g} \cdot \begin{pmatrix} R_1 - J_1 \\ R_2 - J_2 \end{pmatrix}$$

where $\begin{pmatrix} R_1 \\ R_2 \end{pmatrix} = \mathbf{B}_{f,g}^{-1} \cdot \begin{pmatrix} c \\ 0 \end{pmatrix} - \begin{pmatrix} I_1 \\ I_2 \end{pmatrix}$. It is known that (R_1, R_2) is uniformly distributed over $\left[-\frac{1}{2}, \frac{1}{2} \right)^n$ over the randomness of signed messages, then the distribution of (s_1, s_2) is a hidden linear transformation (i.e. $\mathbf{B}_{f,g}$) of a known distribution. As a consequence, the statistics of (s_1, s_2) would leak secret information, which opens up the avenue of cryptanalysis.

4   Learning a Hidden Transformation

As shown in Sect. 3, the distribution of PEREGRINE signatures is a hidden linear transformation of some known distribution. Learning the hidden transformation enables a key recovery attack against PEREGRINE.

In this section, we extend the Nguyen-Regev parallelepiped-learning attack [NR06] to more general *Hidden Transformation Problem* (HTP) defined as follows.

Definition 1 (HTP$_D$). *Let D be a public distribution over $\mathbb{R}^n$. Given a hidden matrix $\mathbf{B} = (\mathbf{b}_1, \dots, \mathbf{b}_n) \in GL_n(\mathbb{R})$ and a certain number of independent samples $\mathbf{y} = \mathbf{B}\mathbf{x}$ with $\mathbf{x} \leftarrow D$, find an approximation of $\pm\mathbf{b}_i$'s.*

4.1   The Algorithmic Framework

As our main use case is for D being the joint distribution of $(x_1, \dots, x_n)$ with x_i independently drawn from some centered distribution D_i, we choose to present our exploitation in this restricted setting for the sake of clarity. The adaptation to a general form of distribution is straightforward from there.

---

[3] The term s_1 can be recovered from the actual signature s_2 along with the NTRU public key and the hashed message.

4.1.1 Distribution Deformation

Let σ_i be the standard deviation of D_i and $D(\mathbf{B})$ denote the distribution of $\mathbf{y} = \mathbf{B}\mathbf{x}$ with $\mathbf{x} \leftarrow D$. We first describe the covariance of the transformed distribution $D(\mathbf{B})$.

Lemma 1. *Let* $\mathbf{B} \in \mathrm{GL}_n(\mathbb{R})$, *then* $\mathbf{Cov}[D(\mathbf{B})] = \mathbf{B}\boldsymbol{\Sigma}\mathbf{B}^t$ *where* $\boldsymbol{\Sigma} = \mathrm{diag}(\sigma_1^2, \ldots, \sigma_n^2)$.

Proof. For $\mathbf{y} \sim D(\mathbf{B})$, let $\mathbf{y} = \mathbf{B}\mathbf{x}$ where $\mathbf{x} \sim D$. Then we have

$$\mathbf{Cov}[D(\mathbf{B})] = \mathbb{E}[\mathbf{y}\mathbf{y}^t] = \mathbb{E}[\mathbf{B}\mathbf{x}\mathbf{x}^t\mathbf{B}^t] = \mathbf{B}\,\mathbb{E}[\mathbf{x}\mathbf{x}^t]\mathbf{B}^t.$$

Since D_i's are centered, then $\mathbb{E}[\mathbf{x}\mathbf{x}^t] = \boldsymbol{\Sigma}$ and the proof is completed.   □

The covariance leakage shown in Lemma 1 allows us to reduce the general hidden transformation problem to the case in which the covariance leakage is $\mathbf{I}_n$, by applying the exact matrix to de-bias the distribution.

Lemma 2. *Let* $\mathbf{B} \in \mathrm{GL}_n(\mathbb{R})$ *and* $\mathbf{K} = \mathbf{Cov}[D(\mathbf{B})]$. *Let* $\mathbf{P} \in \mathrm{GL}_n(\mathbb{R})$ *such that* $\mathbf{P}\mathbf{P}^t = \mathbf{K}^{-1}$. *Then the distribution of* $\mathbf{P}^t\mathbf{y}$ *with* $\mathbf{y} \sim D(\mathbf{B})$ *is* $D(\mathbf{C})$ *with* $\mathbf{C} = \mathbf{P}^t\mathbf{B}$ *such that* $\mathbf{Cov}[D(\mathbf{C})] = \mathbf{I}_n$. *In particular,* $\mathbf{C}$ *is orthogonal when* $\mathbf{Cov}[D] = \mathbf{I}_n$.

Proof. Lemma 1 shows that $\mathbf{K} = \mathbf{B}\boldsymbol{\Sigma}\mathbf{B}^t$ and then $\mathbf{K}^{-1} = \mathbf{B}^{-t}\boldsymbol{\Sigma}^{-1}\mathbf{B}^{-1}$. By definition, $\mathbf{y} \sim D(\mathbf{B})$ can be written into $\mathbf{y} = \mathbf{B}\mathbf{x}$ with $\mathbf{x} \sim D$. It follows that $\mathbf{P}^t\mathbf{y} = \mathbf{P}^t\mathbf{B}\mathbf{x}$ follows the distribution $D(\mathbf{C})$ with $\mathbf{C} = \mathbf{P}^t\mathbf{B}$. Moreover, $\mathbf{Cov}[D(\mathbf{C})] = \mathbf{C}\boldsymbol{\Sigma}\mathbf{C}^t = \mathbf{P}^t\mathbf{K}\mathbf{P} = \mathbf{I}_n$.   □

Lemma 2 translates directly into Algorithm 2, when we don't have access to the covariance of $D(\mathbf{B})$ itself, but we only have a family of samples of this distribution. Hence, we first approximate the covariance as precisely as possible, and then compute the square root as in Lemma 1 and apply the transformation to correct it. The estimation of the covariance is dependent of the prior we have on D. In the most general context, we rely on the computation of the *sample covariance matrix*[4]:

$$\mathbf{K} = \frac{1}{\#S - 1} \sum_{\mathbf{x} \in S} \mathbf{x}\mathbf{x}^t.$$

4.1.2 Mounting the Recovery

We next generalize the statistical analysis of the parallelepiped-learning attack [NR06] to the HTP_D setting. Algorithm 2 reduces the HTP instance regarding $(D, \mathbf{B})$ to the one regarding $(D, \mathbf{C})$ such that $\mathbf{Cov}[D(\mathbf{C})] = \mathbf{I}_n$. Let $\mathbf{D} = \mathrm{diag}(\sigma_1, \ldots, \sigma_n)$ and D' be the distribution of $\mathbf{D}^{-1}\mathbf{x}$ for $\mathbf{x} \sim D$, then $\mathbf{Cov}[D'] = \mathbf{I}_n$. Let $\mathbf{C}' = \mathbf{C}\mathbf{D}$, then $D(\mathbf{C}) = D'(\mathbf{C}')$ and $\mathbf{C}'$ is orthogonal. Hence, the rest of this section focuses on the HTP instance in which the hidden matrix $\mathbf{C}$ is orthogonal and the public distribution D satisfying $\mathbf{Cov}[D] = \mathbf{I}_n$.

---

[4] We recall that we supposed here that the distributions are centered. The term $\#S-1$ is the standard *Bessel correction* and is necessary to get an unbiased estimator.

Algorithm 2: Deform

Input: A distribution D and a set S of samples drawn from $D(\mathbf{B})$.
Output: A matrix $\mathbf{L}$ deforms samples from $D(\mathbf{B})$ into samples from a distribution close to $D(\mathbf{C})$ s.t. $\mathbf{C} = \mathbf{LB}$ and $\mathrm{Cov}[D(\mathbf{C})] = \mathbf{I}_n$.

1 Using the samples in S to compute an approximation $\mathbf{K}$ of $\mathrm{Cov}[D(\mathbf{B})]$
2 Compute $\mathbf{K}^{-1}$ and $\mathbf{P}$ such that $\mathbf{K}^{-1} = \mathbf{PP}^t$
3 **return** $\mathbf{L} = \mathbf{P}^t$

Let $\mathbf{m} = \sum_{i=1}^{n} z_i \mathbf{c}_i$ with $z_i \sim D_i$, then $\mathbf{m} \sim D(\mathbf{C})$. The fourth moment of $D(\mathbf{C})$ over $\mathbf{w} \in \mathbb{R}^n$ is defined as

$$M_{D(\mathbf{C}),4}(\mathbf{w}) = \mathbb{E}[\langle \mathbf{m}, \mathbf{w} \rangle^4].$$

Let $\alpha_i = \mathbb{E}[z_i^4]$. It holds that

$$M_{D(\mathbf{C}),4}(\mathbf{w}) = \mathbb{E}[\langle \mathbf{m}, \mathbf{w} \rangle^4] = \mathbb{E}\left[\left(\sum_{i=1}^{n} z_i \langle \mathbf{c}_i, \mathbf{w} \rangle \right)^4 \right]$$

$$= \sum_{i=1}^{n} \mathbb{E}[z_i^4] \langle \mathbf{c}_i, \mathbf{w} \rangle^4 + 3 \sum_{i \neq j} \langle \mathbf{c}_i, \mathbf{w} \rangle^2 \langle \mathbf{c}_j, \mathbf{w} \rangle^2$$

$$= 3\|\mathbf{w}\|^4 - \sum_{i=1}^{n} (3 - \alpha_i) \langle \mathbf{c}_i, \mathbf{w} \rangle^4.$$

Without loss of generality, we assume $\alpha_1 \leq \alpha_2 \leq \ldots \leq \alpha_n$. Lemma 3 shows the local minima of the fourth moment over all unit $\mathbf{w}$'s.

Lemma 3. *Suppose that $\alpha_i < 3$ for all $1 \leq i \leq n$, the local minimum of $M_{D(\mathbf{C}),4}(\mathbf{w})$ over all unit vectors $\mathbf{w}$ is obtained at $\pm\mathbf{c}_1, \ldots, \pm\mathbf{c}_n$. There are no other local minima.*

Proof. Since $\mathbf{C}$ is orthogonal, $M_{D(\mathbf{I}),4}(\mathbf{w}) = 3\|\mathbf{w}\|^4 - \sum_{i=1}^{n}(3 - \alpha_i)w_i^4$ has the same local extrema with $M_{D(\mathbf{C}),4}(\mathbf{w})$. Under the orthogonal transformation, the local extreme points of two functions are one-to-one.

Let $\beta_i = 3 - \alpha_i > 0$, then the minima of $M_{D(\mathbf{I}),4}(\mathbf{w})$ are the maxima of $f(\mathbf{w}) = \sum_{i=1}^{n} \beta_i w_i^4$ as $\|\mathbf{w}\| = 1$. It suffices to study the local maxima of $f(\mathbf{w})$. Using the method of Lagrange multipliers, we consider

$$F(\mathbf{w}) = \sum_{i=1}^{n} \beta_i w_i^4 - \lambda \left(\sum_{i=1}^{n} w_i^2 - 1 \right).$$

In order to meet $\nabla F = 0$, each w_i is either zero or $\pm\sqrt{\frac{\lambda}{2\beta_i}}$ and λ is determined by the number of non-zero w_i's. These points can be divided into two sets: the points in the first set are $\pm\mathbf{e}_i$'s where $\mathbf{e}_i$ is the i-th column of the identity matrix and the other set $\mathcal{I}$ contains the points with at least two non-zero coefficients.

We first prove that $\pm\mathbf{e}_i$ is a local maximum. Let $\mathbf{w} = (1 - \epsilon_i)\mathbf{e}_i + \sum_{j \neq i} \epsilon_j \mathbf{e}_j$ be some vector in $\mathcal{B} = \{\mathbf{w} : \|\mathbf{w} - \mathbf{e}_i\|^2 < \epsilon, \|\mathbf{w}\| = 1, \epsilon_i > 0\}$. Then

$$
\begin{aligned}
f(\mathbf{w}) &= \beta_i(1 - \epsilon_i)^4 + \sum_{j \neq i} \beta_j \epsilon_j^4 \\
&\leq \beta_i - \beta_i \epsilon_i + \max_{j \neq i} |\epsilon_j| \cdot \sum_{j \neq i} \beta_j \epsilon_j^2 \\
&\leq \beta_i - \beta_i \epsilon_i + \max_{j \neq i} |\epsilon_j| \cdot \beta_1 \left(1 - (1 - \epsilon_i)^2\right) \\
&\leq \beta_i - \beta_i \epsilon_i + \max_{j \neq i} |\epsilon_j| \cdot 2\beta_1 \epsilon_i \\
&\leq \beta_i + \left(\max_{j \neq i} |\epsilon_j| \cdot 2\beta_1 - \beta_i\right)\epsilon_i \\
&< \beta_i = f(\mathbf{e}_i).
\end{aligned}
$$

Above inequalities hold when $\epsilon < \min\{\frac{1}{4}, \frac{\beta_i}{2\beta_1}\}$, thus $\pm\mathbf{e}_i$ is indeed the local maximum of $f(\mathbf{w})$.

Then we prove that $\mathbf{w} = \sum_{i=1}^n \eta_i \mathbf{e}_i \in \mathcal{I}$ is not a local maximum. Let $\mathcal{K}_\mathbf{w} = \{\mathbf{e}_i : \langle \mathbf{w}, \mathbf{e}_i \rangle \neq 0\}$ and $k = \#\mathcal{K}_\mathbf{w}$. Let $\mathcal{S}$ be the subspace spanned by $\mathbf{e}_i \in \mathcal{K}_\mathbf{w}$ and $|_\mathcal{S}$ denote the directly dimensional reduction into $\mathcal{S}$. We next prove that $\mathbf{w}|_\mathcal{S}$ forms the local minima of $f|_\mathcal{S}$, which implies $\mathbf{w}$ is no longer the local maximum of f. The bordered Hessian matrix of Lagrange function $F|_\mathcal{S}$ on the point $\mathbf{w}|_\mathcal{S}$ has the form $\mathbf{H} = \begin{pmatrix} 0 & 2\mathbf{w}^t|_\mathcal{S} \\ 2\mathbf{w}|_\mathcal{S} & d\mathbf{I} \end{pmatrix} \in \mathbb{R}^{(k+1)\times(k+1)}$ and $d > 0$ is a constant related to η_i. Notice that $\det(\mathbf{H}) = \det(d\mathbf{I})\det(0 - \mathbf{w}^t|_\mathcal{S}(d\mathbf{I})^{-1}\mathbf{w}|_\mathcal{S}) = -d^{k-1} < 0$. Similarly, all leading principle minors of $\mathbf{H}$ have a negative determinant. The above negative leading principle minors show that the $\mathbf{w}|_\mathcal{S}$ form the local minima of $f|_\mathcal{S}$.

In conclusion, only $\pm\mathbf{e}_i$'s are the local maximum of $f(\mathbf{w})$. This also means the local minima of $M_{D(\mathbf{C}),4}$ are only located at $\pm\mathbf{c}_i$'s. $\square$

Now that we know that the secrets are exactly the local minima of the fourth moment, we can retrieve them by gradient descent. Note that we have an explicit expression of the gradient: for a unit vector $\mathbf{w}$, the gradient of $M_{D(\mathbf{C}),4}(\mathbf{w})$ is

$$
\nabla M_{D(\mathbf{C}),4}(\mathbf{w}) = 12\mathbf{w} - \sum_{i=1}^n (12 - 4\alpha_i)\langle \mathbf{c}_i, \mathbf{w}\rangle^3 \mathbf{c}_i.
$$

The descent is implemented as a geodesic flow, similarly to [TW20], which is significantly more efficient than the naive approach of [NR06]. Pseudocode is provided in Algorithm 3. We point out that the gradient is not known exactly so we need to approximate it using all the samples of S at each step, similarly to that the covariance of $D(\mathbf{B})$ is only known up to the best approximation allowed by S.

Algorithm 3: Descent

Input: A distribution D such that $\mathbf{Cov}[D] = \mathbf{I}_n$ and a set S of samples from $D(\mathbf{C})$ where $\mathbf{CC}^t = \mathbf{I}_n$.
Output: An approximation of one column of $\pm\mathbf{C}$.

1   Choose a random vector $\mathbf{w}$ uniformly over the unit sphere $\mathbb{S}^{n-1}$
2   Use the samples in S to compute (an approximation of) the gradient
     $\mathbf{g} = \nabla M_{D(\mathbf{C}),4}(\mathbf{w})$
3   $\mathbf{h} \leftarrow -\mathbf{g} + \langle \mathbf{g}, \mathbf{w} \rangle \mathbf{w}$
4   $\mathbf{h} \leftarrow \mathbf{h}/\|\mathbf{h}\|$
5   $\theta \leftarrow \theta_0$
6   **while** $\theta \geq \theta_{min}$ **do**
7       $\mathbf{w}_{new} \leftarrow \mathbf{w} \cdot \cos\theta + \mathbf{h} \cdot \sin\theta$
8       $\mathbf{w}_{new} \leftarrow \mathbf{w}_{new}/\|\mathbf{w}_{new}\|$
9   **if** $\left| M_{D(\mathbf{C}),4}(\mathbf{w}_{new}) - M_{D(\mathbf{C}),4}(\mathbf{w}) \right| < \frac{1}{2} \cdot \theta \cdot \langle \mathbf{h}, \mathbf{g} \rangle$ **then**
10   **goto** Step 14
11   **end if**
12       $\theta \leftarrow \nu \cdot \theta$
13 **end while**
14 $\mathbf{w} \leftarrow \mathbf{w}_{new}$
15 **if** $\theta < \theta_0$ **then**
16       $\theta_0 \leftarrow \theta/\nu$
17   **goto** Step 2
18 **end if**
19 **return** $\mathbf{w}$

To sum up, after putting everything together, the general hidden transformation problem can be solved by Algorithm 4.

4.2 The Case of PEREGRINE

While Sect. 4.1 depicts the generic algorithmic framework for learning the hidden transformation, we now discuss the concrete attack for PEREGRINE in more details.

Exploiting the Ring Structure. PEREGRINE is built over $\mathbb{Z}[x]/(x^{n/2}+1)$ and such a ring structure can be used to greatly improve practical attacks [DN12]:

– We can generate $\frac{n}{2}$ additional samples from one signature transcript using the ring automorphisms, i.e., by multiplying x^i. This makes the approximations more accurate for the same amount of traces collected, for instance for the empirical covariance estimation, we have:

$$\mathbf{K} = \frac{2}{n\#S - 2} \sum_{\mathbf{x} \in S} \sum_{i=0}^{n/2-1} \text{vec}(x^i \cdot \mathbf{x})\text{vec}(x^i \cdot \mathbf{x})^t$$

where vec denotes the vector representation of the polynomial.

Algorithm 4: Solver

Input: A distribution D and a set S of samples drawn from $D(\mathbf{B})$.
Output: An approximation of one column of $\pm\mathbf{B}$.

1 $\mathbf{L} \leftarrow \text{Deform}(D, S)$
2 $S' \leftarrow \{\mathbf{Ls} \mid \mathbf{s} \in S\}$
3 $\mathbf{D} \leftarrow \text{diag}(\sigma_1, \ldots, \sigma_n)$
4 Let D' be the distribution of $\mathbf{D}^{-1}\mathbf{x}$ for $\mathbf{x} \sim D$
5 $\mathbf{w} \leftarrow \text{Descent}(D', S')$
6 **return** $\sigma_i^{-1}\mathbf{L}^{-1}\mathbf{w}$ for i minimizing $\mathbb{E}_{z_i \leftarrow D'_i}[z_i^4]$

- All involved matrices (i.e. Σ, $\mathbf{B}$ and $\mathbf{K}$) are now 2-by-2 over $\mathcal{K}_{\mathbb{R}} = \mathbb{R}[x]/(x^{n/2} + 1)$, which allows to make the computation of the Gram root $\mathbf{P}$ much faster. In particular, our practical attacks leverage the Denman–Beavers iteration [DJ76], *at the ring level* to compute an approximate $\mathbf{P}$ over $\mathcal{K}_{\mathbb{R}}^{2 \times 2}$ in *quasi-linear time* instead of requiring full rounds of linear algebra (which would requires at least $O(n^\omega)$ time, with ω the exponent of matrix multiplication).

We now derive the formulas for the fourth moment and its gradient for both versions of PEREGRINE, namely the one appearing in the specification and the one in the implementation code.

General Computation. In the general setting considered at the start of this section, where D is the product of centered independent distributions D_i of standard deviations σ_i not necessarily equal to 1, the discussion of Sect. 4.1.2 shows that the fourth moment and its gradient have the following expressions:

$$M_{D(\mathbf{C}),4}(\mathbf{w}) = 3\|\mathbf{w}\|^4 - \sum_{i=1}^{n}(3 - \alpha_i)\langle \mathbf{c}_i, \mathbf{w}\rangle^4,$$

$$\nabla M_{D(\mathbf{C}),4}(\mathbf{w}) = 12\mathbf{w} - \sum_{i=1}^{n}(12 - 4\alpha_i)\langle \mathbf{c}_i, \mathbf{w}\rangle^3 \mathbf{c}_i.$$

where $\alpha_i = \mathbb{E}[z_i^4]$, for z_i distributed according to $\frac{1}{\sigma_i} \cdot D_i$. In particular, if we denote by $\mu_{4,i}$ the fourth moment of D_i, we have $\alpha_i = \mu_{4,i}/\sigma_i^4$.

For the distributions D_i of relevance to PEREGRINE, we can easily compute those values α_i using moment generating functions. In all cases, D_i is a convolution $D_i = U([-1/2, 1/2)) + B_\mu$ for some $\mu \geq 0$. Now the moment generating function of $U([-1/2, 1/2))$ is given by:

$$\text{MGF}_{U([-1/2,1/2))}(t) = \frac{e^{t/2} - e^{-t/2}}{t} = \frac{\sinh(t/2)}{t/2},$$

and that of B_μ for any even $\mu \geq 0$ is given by:

$$\text{MGF}_{B_\mu}(t) = \left(\frac{e^{t/2} + e^{-t/2}}{2}\right)^\mu = \cosh(t/2)^\mu.$$

As a result:

$$\text{MGF}_{D_i}(t) = \frac{\sinh(t/2) \cdot \cosh(t/2)^\mu}{t/2}$$

by multiplicativity in convolutions. On the other hand, by definition:

$$\text{MGF}_{D_i}(t) = 1 + \frac{\sigma_i^2}{2!} \cdot t^2 + \frac{\mu_{4,i}}{4!} \cdot t^4 + o(t^4).$$

Thus, it suffices to obtain a 4th order Taylor expansion of (4.2) to compute α_i.

Specification Version. According to the specification parameters,

$$D_i = U\big([-1/2, 1/2)\big) + B_\mu \quad \text{with} \quad \mu = 26$$

for all $1 \leq i \leq n$. Thus:

$$\text{MGF}_{D_i}(t) = \frac{\sinh(t/2) \cdot \cosh(t/2)^{26}}{t/2} = 1 + \frac{79}{24} \cdot t^2 + \frac{10141}{1920} \cdot t^4 + o(t^4).$$

As a result:

$$\alpha_i = \frac{4! \cdot 10141/1920}{(2! \cdot 79/24)^2} = \frac{91269}{31205}$$

for all $1 \leq i \leq n$. Hence, we obtain the corresponding fourth moment function as:

$$M_{D(\mathbf{C}),4}(\mathbf{w}) = 3\|\mathbf{w}\|^4 - \frac{2346}{31205} \sum_{i=1}^{n} \langle \mathbf{c}_i, \mathbf{w}\rangle^4$$

and its gradient as:

$$\nabla M_{D(\mathbf{C}),4}(\mathbf{w}) = 12\mathbf{w} - \frac{9384}{31205} \sum_{i=1}^{n} \langle \mathbf{c}_i, \mathbf{w}\rangle^3 \mathbf{c}_i.$$

Reference Implementation Version. The reference implementation uses more aggressive parameters: the binomial parameters $(\mu_1, \mu_2) = (6, 0)$. Hence,

$$D_i = \begin{cases} U\big([-1/2, 1/2)\big) + B_\mu & \text{with} \quad \mu = 6 \quad \text{for } 1 \leq i \leq n/2; \\ U\big([-1/2, 1/2)\big) & \text{for } n/2 + 1 \leq i \leq n. \end{cases}$$

For $1 \leq i \leq n/2$, we therefore get:

$$\text{MGF}_{D_i}(t) = \frac{\sinh(t/2) \cdot \cosh(t/2)^6}{t/2} = 1 + \frac{19}{24} \cdot t^2 + \frac{541}{1920} \cdot t^4 + o(t^4)$$

and hence:
$$\alpha_i = \frac{4! \cdot 541/1920}{(2! \cdot 19/24)^2} = \frac{4869}{1805}.$$

On the other hand, for $n/2 + 1 \leq i \leq n$, we simply have:

$$\mathrm{MGF}_{D_i}(t) = \frac{\sinh(t/2)}{t/2} = 1 + \frac{1}{24} \cdot t^2 + \frac{1}{1920} \cdot t^4 + o(t^4)$$

and hence:
$$\alpha_i = \frac{4!/1920}{(2!/24)^2} = \frac{9}{5}.$$

We therefore obtain the fourth moment function and its gradient for this version as:

$$M_{D(\mathbf{C}),4}(\mathbf{w}) = 3\|\mathbf{w}\|^4 - \frac{546}{1805} \sum_{i=1}^{n/2} \langle \mathbf{c}_i, \mathbf{w} \rangle^4 - \frac{6}{5} \sum_{i=n/2+1}^{n} \langle \mathbf{c}_i, \mathbf{w} \rangle^4,$$

$$\nabla M_{D(\mathbf{C}),4}(\mathbf{w}) = 12\mathbf{w} - \frac{2184}{1805} \sum_{i=1}^{n/2} \langle \mathbf{c}_i, \mathbf{w} \rangle^3 \mathbf{c}_i - \frac{24}{5} \sum_{i=n/2+1}^{n} \langle \mathbf{c}_i, \mathbf{w} \rangle^3 \mathbf{c}_i.$$

5   Practical Key Recovery Attack Against PEREGRINE

By combining the statistical learning in Sect. 4 and the trick of [Pre23], we propose a full key recovery attack against PEREGRINE–512. For both specification and reference implementation versions, our attack is able to fully recover the secret key of PEREGRINE in practice. In this section, we present the relevant implementation details and collect the experimental results of our attacks.

5.1   Gradient Descent

As discussed in the previous section, our attack uses gradient descent to find an approximation of secret vectors. The original gradient descent in [NR06] computes a step δ for the iteration where $\mathbf{w}_{new} = \mathbf{w} - \delta\mathbf{g}$ and $\mathbf{g}$ is the gradient $\nabla M_{D(\mathbf{C}),4}(\mathbf{w})$. This converges slowly and does not behave well in our case. To overcome this limitation, we instead implement the gradient descent following the one in [TW20], as described in Algorithm 3. This algorithm takes adaptive steps along geodesic paths on the unit sphere to search for a local minimum of $M_{D(\mathbf{C}),4}(\mathbf{w})$ restricted to the sphere, until $\|\mathbf{h}\|$ becomes sufficiently small. This improves the speed of convergence and proves quite effective in our setting. For simplicity's sake, our attack uses the same gradient descent parameters as in [TW20], namely $\theta_0 = 0.25$, $\theta_{min} = 0.005$ and $\nu = 0.8$.

5.2 Correcting Approximate Errors with Lattice Decoding

Once it converges, the gradient descent of Algorithm 4 outputs a vector which essentially follows a normal distribution centered at one of the basis vectors. Equivalently, it can be expressed as one of the basis vector plus some normal error vector, whose magnitude depends on the number of signatures in the attack. In order to recover the basis vector and actually break the scheme, a post-processing step is needed to correct the error.

The Nguyen–Regev Decoding Techniques. In their original attack against GGH and NTRUSign [NR06], Nguyen and Regev mentioned two possible approaches to carry out this post-processing. The first approach is simply to hope that the error becomes less than $1/2$ in infinity norm, so that the basis vector can be directly obtained by coefficient-wise rounding. This is simple but typically requires a relatively large number of signatures. The second approach is to use lattice reduction: the search for the target basis vector is viewed as a bounded distance decoding problem in the public lattice, which can be solved using standard techniques (Nguyen and Regev suggested applying Babai's nearest plane algorithm after reducing the public basis with BKZ; one could also reduce to unique SVP with Kannan's embedding technique and try to solve that unique SVP instance with BKZ).

The same two approaches can also be applied in our setting. However, due to the added noise in PEREGRINE, the magnitude of the error is substantially larger than in GGH and NTRUSign (especially in the "specification" version of PEREGRINE), and lattice dimensions are much larger than those considered in [NR06]. This tends to make lattice reduction-based decoding fairly impractical: the complexity of lattice reduction attacks, while it quickly falls below the claimed security level of the scheme itself, tends to remain too large to carry out the decoding in practice right up until the point where coefficient-wise rounding becomes feasible[5]. This leaves component-wise rounding, possibly complemented by "meet-in-the-middle" type combinatorial improvements, as the better suited approach in our case, and it requires lots of signatures to succeed.

Prest's Trick. Fortunately, since PEREGRINE is an NTRU-based scheme, one can do better than either of the Nguyen–Regev decoding techniques. As pointed out by Prest in [Pre23], it suffices to correctly recover *half* of the coefficients of a basis vector to break the scheme, since the remaining half can be deduced from the first using the NTRU equation (in much the same way as signature compression works in those schemes).

Formally, let $\mathbf{b} = (b^{(1)}, b^{(2)}) \in \mathcal{L}_{\mathrm{NTRU}}$ be the target vector to be recovered and $\mathbf{b}' = \big((b')^{(1)}, (b')^{(2)}\big)$ be the approximation output by Algorithm 4. Suppose that we know at least $n/2$ indices i such that the rounding $\lfloor b'_i \rceil$ matches the corresponding coefficient $\mathbf{b}_i$ of $\mathbf{b}$. This means that the difference $\mathbf{d} = \lfloor \mathbf{b}'_i \rceil - \mathbf{b} =$

---

[5] For the practical exploitation we propose, the required block size would be of the order of 200, which is intractable on a reasonable machine and orders of magnitude larger than the simple exploitation via linear algebra.

$(d^{(1)}, d^{(2)})$ has zeros in at least $n/2$ known positions. Now we have $b^{(1)} + b^{(2)} \cdot h = 0 \bmod q$ by definition of the NTRU lattice, and therefore:

$$\left\lfloor (b')^{(1)} \right\rceil + \left\lfloor (b')^{(2)} \right\rceil \cdot h = d^{(1)} + d^{(2)} \cdot h \bmod q.$$

This is an equation of polynomials of degree $n/2$, and we know the entire left-hand side; moreover, there are at most $n/2$ unknowns on the right-hand side. Therefore, we can solve the linear system for $\mathbf{d}$ (which is of course exactly revealed by its remainder modulo q since it is small) and hence recover $\mathbf{b}$ exactly.

In order to apply this idea, one then needs to determine a subset of at least $n/2$ coefficients of $\mathbf{b}'$ that are likely to be correctly rounded to the corresponding coefficient of $\mathbf{b}$. In [Pre23], Prest does so by selecting a certain threshold $\varepsilon \in (0, 1/2)$ and regarding a coefficient of $\mathbf{b}'$ as correctly rounded when its fractional part doesn't exceed ε.

We proceed in a slightly different way, which bypasses the need to select a threshold value, and which has some additional benefits discussed later in this section: our approach is simply to select the $n/2$ coefficients that have the highest probability of rounding correctly.

Rounding the Best Half of the Coefficients. As discussed earlier, by standard properties of the gradient descent, we can model the vector $\mathbf{b}'$ as a normal vector centered around $\mathbf{b}$. In particular, any fixed coefficient b' of $\mathbf{b}'$ follows a normal distribution $\mathcal{N}(b, \sigma^2)$ centered at the corresponding coefficient of $\mathbf{b}$, and of a certain variance σ^2 (not *a priori* the same for all coefficients).

Then, we claim that the probability of correct rounding (i.e., the probability that $\lfloor b' \rceil = b$) is a function of the fractional part $x = b' - \lfloor b' \rceil$ (which is a known value) and of σ (which we assume can be estimated in our setting). It can be expressed as follows.

Lemma 4. *Let $b' \sim \mathcal{N}(b, \sigma^2)$ for some unknown integer center b, and known standard deviation σ. Let $x = b' - \lfloor b' \rceil$. The probability that $\lfloor b' \rceil = b$ is given by:*

$$\psi_\sigma(x) = \frac{\rho_\sigma(x)}{\rho_\sigma(x + \mathbb{Z})}$$

where we let as usual $\rho_\sigma(t) = \exp\left(-t^2/(2\sigma^2)\right)$.

Proof. Let $e = b' - b \sim \mathcal{N}(0, \sigma^2)$. Then $e - x = \lfloor b' \rceil - b$ is an integer, and is zero exactly when $\lfloor b' \rceil = b$. Therefore, the probability $\psi_\sigma(x)$ of correct rounding is given by:

$$\psi_\sigma(x) = \Pr\left[e = x \middle| e \in x + \mathbb{Z}\right] = \frac{\rho_\sigma(x)}{\rho_\sigma(x + \mathbb{Z})}$$

since ρ_σ is up to a constant factor the probability density function of the normal distribution $\mathcal{N}(0, \sigma^2)$ of e. □

Now, let us first analyze our approach in a simple model where the distribution of the entire vector $\mathbf{b}'$ is a spherical Gaussian $\mathcal{N}(\mathbf{b}, \sigma^2 \cdot \mathbf{I}_n)$ of known standard deviation σ. In particular, the correct rounding probability p_i of the i-th coefficient is given by $\psi_\sigma(x_i)$ for all i, with $\mathbf{x} = (x_1, \ldots, x_n) = \mathbf{b}' - \lfloor \mathbf{b}' \rceil$. Furthermore, all the coefficients are independent; therefore, if we denote by:

$$0 \leq p_{(1)} \leq p_{(2)} \leq \cdots \leq p_{(n)} \leq 1$$

the probabilities p_i sorted in increasing order, the probability that the $n/2$ coefficients of $\mathbf{b}'$ with the highest probability of correct rounding are in fact correctly rounded is given by:

$$p_{\text{succ}} = \prod_{k=n/2+1}^{n} p_{(k)}.$$

In order to analyze our probability of success, we can estimate the expectation of $\log p_{\text{succ}}$ (which is somewhat better behaved than p_{succ} itself). To that end, we show that the sum of the top half (or any constant fraction) of the order statistics of n independent and identically distributed random variables has a relatively convenient expression as follows.

Lemma 5. *Let $X_1, \ldots, X_n$ be independent and identically distributed real-valued random variables with probability density function f_X and CDF F_X. Denote by $X_{(1)} \leq \cdots \leq X_{(n)}$ the corresponding values in non-decreasing order (the order statistics). Fix furthermore some constant $\alpha \in (0,1)$ and let:*

$$E_{n,\alpha} = \mathbb{E}\left[\sum_{k > \alpha n} X_{(k)} \right].$$

Then the following asymptotic equivalence holds:

$$E_{n,\alpha} \underset{n \to +\infty}{\sim} n \int_{F_X^{-1}(\alpha)}^{+\infty} x \cdot f_X(x)\, dx = n \int_{\alpha}^{1} F_X^{-1}(u)\, du.$$

Proof. The well-known expression of the probability density function of $X_{(k)}$ is given by (see e.g. [DN03, Eq. (2.1.6)]):

$$f_{(k)}(x) = \frac{n!}{(k-1)!(n-k)!} f_X(x) \cdot F_X(x)^{k-1} \left(1 - F_X(x)\right)^{n-k}.$$

Thus, we get:

$$E_{n,\alpha} = \int_{-\infty}^{+\infty} x \cdot \frac{f_X(x)}{F_X(x)} \sum_{k > \alpha n} k \binom{n}{k} F_X(x)^k \left(1 - F_X(x)\right)^{n-k}\, dx$$

$$= \int_{-\infty}^{+\infty} x \cdot f_X(x) \cdot n\varphi_{n,\alpha}\left(F_X(x)\right)\, dx$$

where we have let:

$$\varphi_{n,\alpha}(p) = \frac{1}{np} \sum_{k > \alpha n} k \binom{n}{k} p^k (1-p)^{n-k}.$$

In particular, $\varphi_{n,\alpha}(p) = \frac{1}{p}\mathbb{E}\left[\frac{1}{n}Z \mid \frac{1}{n}Z > \alpha\right]$ for $Z \sim \text{Binomial}(n,p)$. Now $\frac{1}{n}Z$ concentrates rapidly around p for large n. Therefore, $\frac{1}{n}Z > \alpha$ happens with probability very close to 1 if $p > \alpha$, and very close to 0 if $p < \alpha$. It easily follows that $\varphi_{n,\alpha}(p)$ converges pointwise to 0 for $p < \alpha$ and to $\frac{1}{p}\mathbb{E}\left[\frac{1}{n}Z\right] = p/p = 1$ for $p > \alpha$. A dominated convergence arguments then yields:

$$E_{n,\alpha} \sim n \int_{-\infty}^{+\infty} x \cdot f_X(x) \cdot [\![F_X(x) > \alpha]\!] \, dx = n \int_{F_X^{-1}(\alpha)}^{+\infty} x \cdot f_X(x) \, dx.$$

Making the change of variables $u = F_X(x)$, hence $x = F_X^{-1}(u)$, $du = f_X(x)\,dx$, we also obtain:

$$E_{n,\alpha} \sim n \int_\alpha^1 F_X^{-1}(u) \, du$$

as required.

Based on the above, we conclude that

$$\mathbb{E}\left[\log p_{\text{succ}}\right] = \mathbb{E}\left[\sum_{k > n/2} \log p_{(k)}\right] \underset{n \to +\infty}{\sim} n \int_{1/2}^1 F^{-1}(u)\,du$$

where F is the common CDF of the $\log p_i = \log \psi_\sigma(x_i)$. We can compute, for all $t \leq 0$:

$$F(t) = \Pr\left[\log \psi_\sigma(x_i) \leq t\right] = \Pr\left[\psi_\sigma(x_i) \leq e^t\right] = \Pr\left[|x_i| \geq \psi_\sigma^{-1}(e^t)\right]$$

since ψ_σ is decreasing on $[0, 1/2]$ and even (and $x_i \in [-1/2, 1/2)$). Now if we again let $e_i = b_i' - b_i \sim \mathcal{N}(0, \sigma^2)$, we have $x_i = e_i - \lfloor e_i \rceil$, so that:

$$F(t) = \Pr\left[|e_i - \lfloor e_i \rceil| \geq \psi_\sigma^{-1}(e^t)\right] = 1 - 2\Pr\left[0 \leq |e_i - \lfloor e_i \rceil| < \psi_\sigma^{-1}(e^t)\right]$$

$$= 1 - 2\Pr\left[e_i \in [0, \psi_\sigma^{-1}(e^t)) + \mathbb{Z}\right] = 1 - \sum_{k \in \mathbb{Z}} \text{erf}\left(\frac{\psi_\sigma^{-1}(e^t) + k}{\sigma\sqrt{2}}\right) - \text{erf}\left(\frac{k}{\sigma\sqrt{2}}\right).$$

This expression is somewhat cumbersome, but our attack approach is only workable when σ is small compared to 1, in which case all the terms in the sum over k are actually negligible except for $k = 0$. Therefore, for small σ, the following approximation holds:

$$F(t) \approx 1 - \text{erf}\left(\frac{\psi_\sigma^{-1}(e^t) + k}{\sigma\sqrt{2}}\right).$$

And as a result, by inverting this formula we similarly obtain:

$$F^{-1}(u) \approx \log \psi_\sigma\left(\sigma\sqrt{2} \cdot \text{erf}^{-1}(1-u)\right).$$

Finally, recall that:

$$\psi_\sigma(x) = \frac{\rho_\sigma(x)}{\rho_\sigma(x + \mathbb{Z})} = \frac{\exp\left(-\frac{x^2}{2\sigma^2}\right)}{\sum_{k \in \mathbb{Z}} \exp\left(-\frac{(x-k)^2}{2\sigma^2}\right)} = \frac{1}{\sum_{k \in \mathbb{Z}} \exp\left(\frac{2kx - k^2}{2\sigma^2}\right)}.$$

For σ small compared to 1, most of the terms in the sum in the denominator are negligibly small. Keeping only the terms $k \in \{-1, 0, 1\}$ provides a very close approximation in the range of interest. Hence:

$$\psi_\sigma(x) \approx \frac{1}{1 + \exp\left(\frac{2x-1}{2\sigma^2}\right) + \exp\left(\frac{-2x-1}{2\sigma^2}\right)} = \frac{1}{1 + 2\exp(-1/2\sigma^2)\cosh(x/\sigma^2)}.$$

Putting all together, we finally obtain the following approximation of $\mathbb{E}\left[\log p_{\mathrm{succ}}\right]$, valid for large n and σ small compared to 1:

$$\mathbb{E}\left[\log p_{\mathrm{succ}}\right] \approx -n \int_{1/2}^1 \log\left(1 + 2e^{-1/2\sigma^2}\cosh\left(\frac{\sqrt{2}}{\sigma}\mathrm{erf}^{-1}(1-u)\right)\right) du$$

(which can be simplified a bit further with the change of variables $u \mapsto 1 - u$). This expression is convenient for numerical computation, and lets us obtain the plot of $\exp\mathbb{E}\left[\log p_{\mathrm{succ}}\right]$ (which by Jensen's inequality is a lower bound of $\mathbb{E}\left[p_{\mathrm{succ}}\right]$) according to σ given in Fig. 1.

Modeling the Gaussian Error. As discussed above, a somewhat simple model of the error $\mathbf{e} = \mathbf{b}' - \mathbf{b}$ is that it is distributed as a spherical Gaussian vector $\mathcal{N}(0, \sigma^2 \cdot \mathbf{I}_n)$ of standard deviation σ depending on the number N of signatures used in the attack. As usual, we more precisely expect the standard deviation to decrease proportionally[6] to $\sqrt{N}$. In this model, we thus have $\sigma \approx C_\sigma/\sqrt{N}$ for some constant C_σ that can be derived experimentally by curve fitting.

We for example find that the size of the error in the attack against the specification version of PEREGRINE–512 is well-described by this model with $C_\sigma \approx 840$ (see Sect. 5.3 below). Plugging back the corresponding value of σ in our estimate of the probability of success p_{succ}, we obtain the graph in Fig. 2 of $\exp\left(\mathbb{E}\left[\log p_{\mathrm{succ}}\right]\right)$ as a function of N, which already captures the behavior of the attack fairly accurately as will be shown in Sect. 5.3.

However, it is not entirely accurate to model the error vector $\mathbf{e}$ as a spherical Gaussian. Indeed, the gradient descent is not directly carried out with respect to the original basis $\mathbf{B}$ of which $\mathbf{b}$ is a vector, but with respect to the deformed basis $\mathbf{LB}$. Therefore, a more accurate model describes the output $\mathbf{w}$ of the Descent algorithm as a spherical[7] Gaussian vector of covariance $(\sigma')^2 \cdot \mathbf{I}_n$, whereas the recovered vector $\mathbf{b}'$ output by Solver is given by an expression of the form $\mathbf{b}' = \mathbf{L}_0^{-1}\mathbf{w}$. As a result, the error $\mathbf{e} = \mathbf{b}' - \mathbf{b}$ is indeed Gaussian, but with a known

---

[6] In the Nguyen–Regev simple version of the gradient descent, the fact that the standard deviation is $\propto N^{-1/2+o(1)}$ is a consequence of the analysis of [NR06, Sec. 6]. The Tibouchi–Wallet gradient descent [TW20] is trickier to analyze, but expectedly follows the same asymptotic behavior in experiments.

[7] In fact, since the gradient descent is carried out on the unit sphere, it would be even more correct to model $\mathbf{w}$ as a Gaussian on the sphere, seen as a Riemannian manifold, so that the corresponding error is essentially a centered spherical Gaussian not in the whole space but on the tangent hyperplane. We ignore this further refinement in what follows.

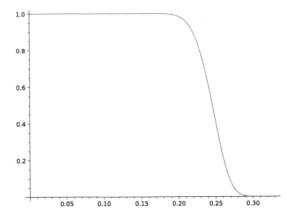

Fig. 1. Expected success probability (more precisely $\exp\left(\mathbb{E}\left[\log p_{\mathrm{succ}}\right]\right) \leq \mathbb{E}\left[p_{\mathrm{succ}}\right]$) of our decoding approach for $n = 1024$ (i.e., PEREGRINE–512), assuming a spherical Gaussian error of standard deviation σ.

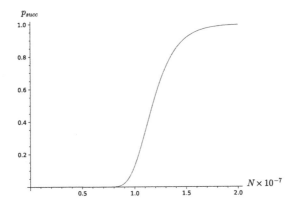

Fig. 2. Expected success probability (more precisely $\exp\left(\mathbb{E}\left[\log p_{\mathrm{succ}}\right]\right)$) of our decoding approach for the attack on the specification version of PEREGRINE–512, as a function of the number N of signatures.

covariance matrix $\boldsymbol{\Sigma} = (\sigma')^2 \cdot \mathbf{L}_0^{-1}(\mathbf{L}_0^{-1})^t$ which is no longer scalar in general. As before, σ' decreases like the square root of the number of signatures: we have another constant $C_{\sigma'}$, derived experimentally, such that $\sigma' \approx C_{\sigma'}/\sqrt{N}$.

In this more accurate model, each of the coefficients e_i of $\mathbf{e}$ remain normally distributed, but with potentially distinct[8] standard deviations σ_i. We therefore use those values σ_i to compute the probabilities of correct rounding $\psi_{\sigma_i}(x_i)$ of

---

[8] In fact, the symmetry provided by the ring structure ensures that there are at most two distinct values of the σ_i's, and those two values are moreover fairly close in the specification version of PEREGRINE. They are however markedly different in the reference implementation version, due to the two different binomial parameters involved.

Table 2. The number of the successful key recovery on the reference implementation for each instance and all 5 starting points.

$N \times 10^{-3}$	10	15	20	25	30	35	40	45	50
Instance 1	0	0	0	2	4	5	5	4	5
Instance 2	0	0	1	1	5	3	5	5	5
Instance 3	0	0	2	3	3	4	5	5	5
Instance 4	0	0	0	0	5	5	5	5	5
Instance 5	0	0	0	3	1	5	5	5	5
Instance 6	0	0	0	3	5	5	5	5	5
Instance 7	0	0	0	1	4	4	5	5	5
Instance 8	0	0	0	3	5	3	5	5	5
Instance 9	0	0	0	0	5	5	5	5	5
Instance 10	0	0	0	4	2	5	5	5	5

the various coefficients, and still keep the top half most likely to be correctly rounded when applying Prest's trick.

This provides a practical improvement in our experiments compared to the simpler model when all the σ_i's are assumed to be equal. This holds even though we still ignore the fact that the covariance Σ need not be diagonal, so that there the various coefficients may not be independent. It might be possible to improve the attack further by leveraging the entire covariance matrix Σ instead of only its diagonal coefficients, but we have not found a practical way to do so yet.

5.3 Experimental Results

We implemented the aforementioned key recovery attack against PEREGRINE. The statistical learning part is implemented in Rust using f64 precision, and some parallelization is used to compute the covariance, the fourth moment and the gradient descent. The decoding part is implemented in Python. The code of the attack can be found at https://github.com/lxhcrypto/Peregrine_attack.

We validated the attack on both the reference implementation and the specification version of PEREGRINE–512. We performed experiments over 10 instances and for each sample size N, we randomly chose 5 starting points in the gradient descent. For each instance and sample size, the attack is counted a success if it recovers the full secret key via decoding at least one approximation output by the statistical learning algorithm with some starting point.

Based on experimental measures and curve fitting in the original basis (resp. the deformed basis), we get the following estimates for the constants C_σ and $C_{\sigma'}$ describing the respective magnitude of the error vectors:

- $C_\sigma \approx 840$ and $C_{\sigma'} \approx 1.4$ for the specification version;
- $C_\sigma \approx 41$ and $C_{\sigma'} \approx 0.15$ for the reference implementation.

The curves are shown in Fig. 3.

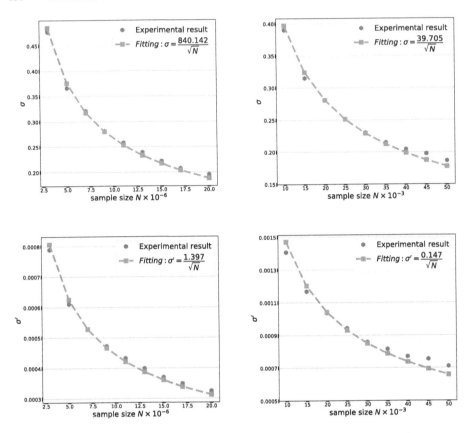

Fig. 3. Experimental measure of the constants C_σ (above) and $C_{\sigma'}$ (below) by curve fitting. The left-hand graphs are for the specification version and the right-hand ones for the reference implementation version. Experimental values measure over 10 PERE-GRINE–512 instances and for each sample size, we use 5 random starting points in the gradient descent.

Key Recovery Attack Against the Reference Implementation. The attack on the reference implementation is highly efficient. When $N \gtrsim 50{,}000$, one can get a good approximation $\mathbf{b}'$ such that $\|\lfloor \mathbf{b}' \rceil - \mathbf{b}\|_1 \le 7$ with a good probability, which allows to completely recover the key by a simple exhaustive search within half an hour. In order to further reduce the number of required signatures, one can employ the decoding technique in Table 2 and give a successful key recovery with 20,000 signatures on 2 out of 10 instances, and with 25,000 signatures on 8 out of 10 instances.

Key Recovery Attack Against the Specification. The attack on the specification version is more costly, as the specification uses larger binomial parameters. It now requires around 20 million signatures to succeed in key recovery by a simple exhaustive search within half an hour. By resorting to the decoding technique of

Table 3. The number of the successful key recovery on the specification version for each instance and all 5 starting points.

$N \times 10^{-6}$	3	5	7	9	11	13	15	17	20
Instance 1	0	0	0	0	3	5	5	5	5
Instance 2	0	0	0	0	0	4	3	5	5
Instance 3	0	0	0	0	0	5	5	5	5
Instance 4	0	0	0	0	0	2	4	5	5
Instance 5	0	0	0	0	3	3	3	5	5
Instance 6	0	0	0	0	1	5	5	5	5
Instance 7	0	0	0	0	4	3	5	5	5
Instance 8	0	0	0	0	2	3	2	5	5
Instance 9	0	0	0	0	0	5	5	5	5
Instance 10	0	0	0	0	3	3	5	5	5

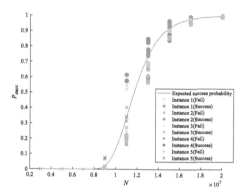

Fig. 4. Visualization of the "best half" decoding technique on the attack against the specification version of PEREGRINE–512.

Sect. 5.2, we achieve a successful attack with 11 million signatures on 6 out of 10 instances, as shown in Table 3. A visualization of the behavior of the decoding technique is provided in Fig. 4 (on the first 5 instances so as not to crowd the graph): each color represents a different instance, and each data point shows, for a particular run of the gradient descent, the predicted probability of success $p_{\text{succ}} = \prod_{k=n/2+1}^{n} \psi_{\sigma_i}(x_i)$ as well as the actual outcome (success or failure). As we can see, the results closely match the model depicted in Fig. 2.

6   Conclusion and Perspectives

We have shown that the PEREGRINE signature scheme is vulnerable to a practical statistical attack. More concretely, for the reference implementation (resp. the specification) of PEREGRINE–512, we completely recover the signing key within a few hours, provided that around 25,000 (resp. 11 million) signatures samples are available. The same attack is expected to break the PEREGRINE–1024 parameters as well.

The design weakness of PEREGRINE revealed by our attack does not seem easy to fix. For secure hash-and-sign lattice signatures, the signature distribution is supposed to be simulatable without knowing the signing key. Currently, there are two main approaches to do so: Gaussian sampling due to [GPV08] and rejection sampling due to [LW15]. Adapting PEREGRINE to either of those approaches would negate its claimed efficiency advantage over schemes like Falcon. At the same time, continuing to pursue a strategy of heuristic countermeasures without provable security guarantees appears increasingly hopeless.

This is especially the case as our attack can be further improved in various ways, which we leave as possible avenues for future work:

- in our experiments, we only carry out the attack on 5 random starting points per key instance. We could easily increase our success rate (and hence decrease the required number of signatures) by simply retrying with more random starting points, as already noted in [NR06];
- moreover, up to negacyclic rotation and sign flips, there are only two equivalence classes of basis vectors in the NTRU basis. As a result, given k starting points in our attack, we expect to collect around $k/2$ approximation of each of those two basis vectors. Averaging out or using majority vote is thus expected to reduce the standard deviation of the error by a factor $\sqrt{k/2}$, and hence significantly improve the success rate. We only had time to carry out partial experiments with that idea, but we could already confirm that it consistently recovers the key in the specification version of PEREGRINE–512 with 9 million signatures samples;
- similarly, even when applying the attack with a single starting point, we can use the methodology of Sect. 5.2 to estimate the expected number of incorrectly rounded coefficient among the "best half" (in the specification version of PEREGRINE–512, it is e.g. ≈ 3.8 for 9 million signatures and ≈ 7.1 for 8 million). Decoding those remaining errors using combinatorial techniques (ranging from a simple exhaustive search to basic meet-in-the-middle to advanced algorithms like those of May [May21] and Kirshanova–May [KM21]) should therefore let us reduce the required number of signatures for full recovery significantly;
- on the implementation side, the limiting factor in our experiments is the speed of gradient descent in our relatively basic CPU implementation. We expect that a GPU implementation would greatly increase performance. Also, tuning the parameters of the descent algorithm of [TW20], although time consuming, may provide significant speed-ups as well.

Acknowledgements. Xiuhan Lin, Shiduo Zhang and Yang Yu are supported by the National Key R&D Program of China (2023YFA1009500), the National Natural Science Foundation of China (62102216), the Mathematical Tianyuan Fund of the National Natural Science Foundation of China (12226006), the National Key R&D Program of China (2018YFA0704701,2022YFB2702804), the Major Program of Guangdong Basic and Applied Research (2019B030302008), Major Scientific and Technological Innovation Project of Shandong Province, China (2019JZZY010133), and Shandong Key Research and Development Program (2020ZLYS09).

References

[Bab86] Babai, L.: On Lovász' lattice reduction and the nearest lattice point problem. Combinatorica **6**, 1–13 (1986)

[DN03] David, H.A., Nagaraja, H.N.: Order Statistics, 3rd edn. Wiley, Hoboken (2003)

[DJ76] Denman, E.D., Beavers, A.N., Jr.: The matrix sign function and computations in systems. J. Appl. Math. Comput. **2**, 63–94 (1976)

[DLP14] Ducas, L., Lyubashevsky, V., Prest, T.: Efficient identity-based encryption over NTRU lattices. In: Sarkar, P., Iwata, T. (eds.) ASIACRYPT 2014. LNCS, vol. 8874, pp. 22–41. Springer, Heidelberg (2014). https://doi.org/10.1007/978-3-662-45608-8_2

[DN12] Ducas, L., Nguyen, P.Q.: Learning a zonotope and more: cryptanalysis of NTRUSign countermeasures. In: Wang, X., Sako, K. (eds.) ASIACRYPT 2012. LNCS; vol. 7658, pp. 433–450. Springer, Heidelberg (2012). https://doi.org/10.1007/978-3-642-34961-4_27

[EFG+22] Espitau, T., et al.: MITAKA: a simpler, parallelizable, maskable variant of FALCON. In: Dunkelman, O., Dziembowski, S. (eds.) EUROCRYPT 2022, vol. 13277, pp. 222–253. Springer, Heidelberg (2022). https://doi.org/10.1007/978-3-031-07082-2_9

[ENS+23] Espitau, T., Nguyen, T.T.Q., Sun, C., Tibouchi, M., Wallet, A.: Antrag: annular NTRU trapdoor generation. In: Guo, J., Steinfeld, R. (eds.) ASIACRYPT 2023 (2023). https://doi.org/10.1007/978-981-99-8739-9_1

[GPV08] Gentry, C., Peikert, C., Vaikuntanathan, V.: Trapdoors for hard lattices and new cryptographic constructions. In: Ladner, R.E., Dwork, C. (eds.) 40th ACM STOC, pp. 197–206. ACM Press (2008)

[GS02] Gentry, C., Szydlo, M.: Cryptanalysis of the revised NTRU signature scheme. In: Knudsen, L.R. (ed.) EUROCRYPT 2002. LNCS, vol. 2332, pp. 299–320. Springer, Heidelberg (2002). https://doi.org/10.1007/3-540-46035-7_20

[GGH97] Goldreich, O., Goldwasser, S., Halevi, S.: Public-key cryptosystems from lattice reduction problems. In: Kaliski, B.S. (ed.) CRYPTO 1997. LNCS, vol. 1294, pp. 112–131. Springer, Heidelberg (1997). https://doi.org/10.1007/BFb0052231

[HHP+03] Hoffstein, J., Howgrave-Graham, N., Pipher, J., Silverman, J.H., Whyte, W.: NTRUSIGN: digital signatures using the NTRU lattice. In: Joye, M. (ed.) CT-RSA 2003. LNCS, vol. 2612, pp. 122–140. Springer, Heidelberg (2003). https://doi.org/10.1007/3-540-36563-x_9

[KTW+22] Kim, K., et al.: SOLMAE: submission to the Korea post-quantum cryptography competition round 1. Technical report (2022). https://www.kpqc.or.kr/competition.html

[KM21] Kirshanova, E., May, A.: How to find ternary LWE keys using locality sensitive hashing. In: Paterson, M.B. (ed.) 18th IMA International Conference on Cryptography and Coding. LNCS, vol. 13129, pp. 247–264. Springer, Heidelberg (2021). https://doi.org/10.1007/978-3-030-92641-0_12

[LDK+22] Lyubashevsky, V., et al.: Crystals-Dilithium. Technical report, National Institute of Standards and Technology (2022). https://csrc.nist.gov/Projects/post-quantum-cryptography/selected-algorithms-2022

[LW15] Lyubashevsky, V., Wichs, D.: Simple lattice trapdoor sampling from a broad class of distributions. In: Katz, J. (ed.) PKC 2015. LNCS, vol. 9020, pp. 716–730. Springer, Heidelberg (2015). https://doi.org/10.1007/978-3-662-46447-2_32

[May21] May, A.: How to meet ternary LWE keys. In: Malkin, T., Peikert, C. (eds.) CRYPTO 2021. LNCS, vol. 12826, pp. 701–731. Springer, Cham (2021). https://doi.org/10.1007/978-3-030-84245-1_24

[NR06] Nguyen, P.Q., Regev, O.: Learning a parallelepiped: cryptanalysis of GGH and NTRU signatures. In: Vaudenay, S. (ed.) EUROCRYPT 2006. LNCS, vol. 4004, pp. 271–288. Springer, Heidelberg (2006). https://doi.org/10.1007/11761679_17

[Pei10] Peikert, C.: An efficient and parallel gaussian sampler for lattices. In: Rabin, T. (ed.) CRYPTO 2010. LNCS, vol. 6223, pp. 80–97. Springer, Heidelberg (2010). https://doi.org/10.1007/978-3-642-14623-7_5

[PSDS17] Plantard, Y., Sipasseuth, A., Dumondelle, C., Susilo, W.: DRS. Technical report, National Institute of Standards and Technology (2017). https://csrc.nist.gov/projects/post-quantum-cryptography/post-quantum-cryptography-standardization/round-1-submissions

[Pre23] Prest, T.: A key-recovery attack against mitaka in the t-probing model. In: Boldyreva, A., Kolesnikov, V. (eds.) PKC 2023. Part I, volume 13940 of LNCS, pp. 205–220. Springer, Heidelberg (2023). https://doi.org/10.1007/978-3-031-31368-4_8

[PFH+22] Prest, T., et al.: FALCON. Technical report, National Institute of Standards and Technology (2022). https://csrc.nist.gov/Projects/post-quantum-cryptography/selected-algorithms-2022

[SKLN22] Seo, E.Y., Kim, Y.S., Lee, J.W., No, J.S.: Peregrine: Submission to the Korea post-quantum cryptography competition round 1. Technical report (2022). https://www.kpqc.or.kr/competition.html

[TW20] Tibouchi, M., Wallet, A.: One bit is all it takes: a devastating timing attack on BLISS's non-constant time sign flips. J. Math. Cryptol. **15**(1), 131–142 (2020)

[YD18] Yang, Yu., Ducas, L.: Learning strikes again: the case of the DRS signature scheme. In: Peyrin, T., Galbraith, S. (eds.) ASIACRYPT 2018. Part II, volume 11273 of LNCS, pp. 525–543. Springer, Heidelberg (2018). https://doi.org/10.1007/s00145-020-09366-9

Improved Cryptanalysis of HFERP

Max Cartor[1], Ryann Cartor[2(✉)], Hiroki Furue[3], and Daniel Smith-Tone[1,4]

[1] University of Louisville, Louisville, KY, USA
maxwell.cartor@louisville.edu
[2] Clemson University, Clemson, SC, USA
rcartor@clemson.edu
[3] Department of Mathematical Informatics, The University of Tokyo, Tokyo, Japan
furue-hiroki261@g.ecc.u-tokyo.ac.jp
[4] National Institute of Standards and Technology, Gaithersburg, MD, USA
daniel.smith@nist.gov

Abstract. In this paper we introduce a new attack on the multivariate encryption scheme HFERP, a big field scheme including an extra variable set, additional equations of the UOV or Rainbow shape as well as additional random polynomials. Our attack brings several parameter sets well below their claimed security levels. The attack combines novel methods applicable to multivariate schemes with multiple equation types with insights from the Simple Attack that broke Rainbow in early 2022, though interestingly the technique is applied in an orthogonal way. In addition to this attack, we apply support minors techniques on a Min-Rank instance drawing coefficients from the big field, which was effective against other multivariate big field schemes. This work demonstrates that there exist previously unknown impacts of the above works well beyond the scope in which they were derived.

Keywords: Multivariate Cryptography · HFERP · Cryptanalysis · MinRank · Simple Attack

1 Introduction

With advancements towards widespread quantum computing, the need for accurate analysis of quantum-resistant cryptosystems is of high priority. Multivariate cryptography offers a possible path forward, providing an alternative to other post-quantum cryptosystems based on, for example, lattices or codes.

The characteristics of multivariate cryptosystems can be attractive, depending, of course, on the performance characteristics required for the application. Multivariate encryption schemes typically have quite fast encryption and relatively short ciphertexts in comparison to other post-quantum schemes. To date, this efficiency is more than counter-balanced by the extreme decryption times or

This work was partially supported by a grant from the Simons Foundation (712530, DCST).

Q. Tang and V. Teague (Eds.): PKC 2024, LNCS 14601, pp. 413–440, 2024.
https://doi.org/10.1007/978-3-031-57718-5_14

decryption failure issues, see [1,27], for example. Additionally, the multitude of attacks, even practical attacks [2,6,26,29], have brought their practicality into question.

The need for accurate cryptanalysis of multivariate cryptosystems is illustrated by the call from the National Institute of Standards and Technology (NIST) for a supplementary digital signature scheme standardization track as part of their ongoing post-quantum cryptography project. The aim of this call is to obtain secure signature schemes whose security does not rely on structured lattices, which makes multivariate signature schemes of particular interest. While the scheme we attack in this paper is an encryption scheme, history has shown that multivariate cryptanalysis in one arena can often be transferred to another; thus, we expect the analysis completed in this paper to have applications across multivariate cryptography.

HFERP, which was first proposed in 2018 [14], is a multivariate encryption scheme in the lineage of HFE. The basic construction is supported by a central map containing polynomials of HFE shape, see [21], Rainbow shape, [11], as well as random quadratic polynomials. The performance characteristics of HFERP are fairly typical for a multivariate encryption scheme; it has public key and secret key sizes of (93.6 KB, 31.7 KB) for 80-bit bit security and (552.3 KB, 226.0 KB) for 128-bit security, has fast encryption and quite slow decryption.

Several recent results inspire the need to reevaluate the cryptographic security of HFERP. The attack of [29] illustrates how the use of extra variables can be mostly ignored for MinRank style attacks. The improvement of [2] shows how the above attack can be performed with the support minors methodology of [3] even when coefficients are from an extension field. The attack of [6] demonstrates how different equation types can be exploited statistically to improve the power of an attack.

Some of the relevant pieces, however, from the above recent results do not naturally apply in the case of HFERP. For example, the attacks considered in [2,29] do not consider the effect of other equations that do not have a component of HFE shape. In the other direction, the attack of [6] relies on the specific structure of Rainbow, which is not a big field scheme.

1.1   Our Contribution

We introduce a new attack which considerably reduces the security levels of some parameters of HFERP. This attack is a MinRank attack boosted with the same kind of "Simple Attack" observation noted in [6]. While the attack of [6] slices the public key, viewed as a 3-tensor, in a nonstandard way (i.e., not along public equations), our attack utilizes the same statistical observation to improve the standard MinRank attack. Significantly, this attack is insensitive to the degree of the hidden HFE component; thus, for parameters where this attack is cheap, HFERP is reduced to a less efficient version of HFE.

In addition to the above attack, we also modify and apply the Big-Field Support Minors MinRank attack from [2] to HFERP. Support minors techniques have been shown effective against GeMSS and Rainbow in previous works, which have central maps polynomials of only single types. We show the far reaching potential of the support minors technique by applying it to the central map of HFERP, which has a central map containing polynomials of HFE, UOV, and random polynomials. This attack has complexity far below the claimed security levels.

The article is organized as follows. In Sect. 2, we introduce some historically relevant schemes. Next, in Sect. 3, we describe the updated multivariate cryptanalyst's toolkit, including all of the relevant attacks affecting the selection of parameters for HFERP. In the subsequent section, we apply the "Simple Attack" approach to HFERP and describe the algebraic methods of the cryptanalysis. We then compute updated complexities for MinRank cryptanalysis of HFERP in Sect. 6, verifying that the security provided by HFERP is significantly reduced by our methods. Finally, we conclude, reflecting on the recent changes in multivariate cryptanalysis and suggesting new directions to explore.

2   Schemes

2.1   C*

The C^* Cryptosystem was introduced by Matsumoto and Imai at Eurocrypt'88 ([18]) and was the first mainstream multivariate cryptosystem. The scheme hides the easily invertible central map $f : \mathbb{K} \to \mathbb{K}$, using linear maps $S, T : \mathbb{F}_q^n \to \mathbb{F}_q^n$ and a vector space isomorphism $\phi : \mathbb{F}_q^n \to \mathbb{K}$. The central map f is the $\mathbb{F}_q$-quadratic function $f(X) = X^{q^\theta + 1}$ where θ is a positive integer such that $gcd(1 + q^\theta, q^n - 1) = 1$. The public key $P : \mathbb{F}_q^n \to \mathbb{F}_q^n$ is computed as $P(x) = T \circ \phi^{-1} \circ f \circ \phi \circ S(x)$. C^* was broken in [20] by Patarin.

2.2   HFE and Variants

Hidden Field Equations. The HFE cryptosystem, introduced in [21], is a big field scheme which replaces the monomial map of C^* with a polynomial with degree bound D. We once again consider $\mathbb{F}_q, \mathbb{K}$, and ϕ as described in Sect. 2.1. Then for degree bound D we define the central map $f : \mathbb{K} \to \mathbb{K}$ as

$$f(X) = \sum_{\substack{i \leq j}}^{q^i + q^j < D} \alpha_{ij} X^{q^i + q^j} + \sum_{q^i < D} \beta_i X^{q^i} + \gamma.$$

Given invertible affine maps $S, T : \mathbb{F}_q^n \to \mathbb{F}_q^n$, the public key $P : \mathbb{F}_q^n \to \mathbb{F}_q^n$ is defined as

$$P(\mathbf{x}) = T \circ \phi^{-1} \circ f \circ \phi \circ S(\mathbf{x}),$$

and the private key is (S, f, T).

To encrypt a plaintext message $\mathbf{x} \in \mathbb{F}_q^n$, compute $P(\mathbf{x})$. To invert a ciphertext $\mathbf{y} \in \mathbb{F}_q^n$, compute $\mathbf{v} = T^{-1}(\mathbf{y})$ then solve $\phi(\mathbf{v}) = f(\mathbf{s})$ for $\mathbf{s} \in \mathbb{F}_{q^n}$ using the Berlekamp algorithm. The plaintext is then $\mathbf{x} = S^{-1}(\phi^{-1}(\mathbf{s}))$.

The degree bound of the central map is utilized to keep the use of Berlekamp's algorithm efficient during decryption. However, a small degree bound D has adverse effects on the security. HFE is weak against rank attacks due to the existence of a low rank linear combination of the public quadratic forms shown in [4].

HFEv⁻ After the break of HFE, HFEv⁻ was introduced in [23]. This scheme takes an HFE scheme and adds a vinegar and a minus modifier. The minus modifier removes a small number of equations from the public key and the vinegar modifier parameterizes the central map by adding supplementary variables called vinegar variables which occupy a small subspace of the input space.

The central map $f : \mathbb{F}_{q^n} \times \mathbb{F}_q^v \to \mathbb{F}_{q^n}$ is randomly generated of the form

$$f(X, x_1, ..., x_v) = \sum_{\substack{i,j \in \mathbb{N}}}^{q^i+q^j \leq D} \alpha_{ij} X^{q^i+q^j} + \sum_{\substack{i \in \mathbb{N}}}^{q^i \leq D} \beta_i(x_1, ..., x_v) X^{q^i} + \gamma(x_1, ..., x_v)$$

where $\alpha_{i,j} \in \mathbb{F}_{q^n}$, $\beta_i : \mathbb{F}_q^v \to \mathbb{F}_{q^n}$ are linear maps, and $\gamma : \mathbb{F}_q^v \to \mathbb{F}_{q^n}$ is a quadratic map in the vinegar variables $x_1, ..., x_v$. Two random affine maps $T : \mathbb{F}_q^n \to \mathbb{F}_q^{n-a}$ and $S : \mathbb{F}_q^{n+v} \to \mathbb{F}_q^{n+v}$ of maximal rank bookend the central map to hide the structure of f. This results in a private key of the three maps (T, f, S).

To generate the public key, we let ϕ be the vector space isomorphism previously defined. Next, let $\psi : \mathbb{F}_q^{n+v} \to \mathbb{F}_{q^n} \times \mathbb{F}_q^v$ be $\psi = \phi^{-1} \times id_v$ where id_v is the identity map over $\mathbb{F}_q^v$. Then, the composition function $\phi \circ \psi : \mathbb{F}_q^{n+v} \to \mathbb{F}_q^n$ is a quadratic multivariate function. The public key P is then defined as

$$P = T \circ \phi \circ f \circ \psi \circ S : \mathbb{F}_q^{n+v} \to \mathbb{F}_q^{n-q}.$$

2.3   Unbalanced Oil and Vinegar

The Oil and Vinegar signature scheme was introduced in [22] as another response to Patarin's break of C^*. The system uses two types of variables, oil variables and vinegar variables, over a finite field $\mathbb{F}_q$. Originally, the number of oil and vinegar variables were equal, but Kipnis and Shamir broke the balanced oil and vinegar scheme [17]. We now only consider the Unbalanced Oil and Vinegar scheme [16] where the number of vinegar variables is strictly greater than the number of oil variables.

Let $\mathbf{x} = (x_1, ..., x_v, x_{v+1}, ..., x_n) \in \mathbb{F}_q^n$. The variables $x_1, ..., x_v$ are the vinegar variables while $x_{v+1}, ..., x_n$ are the oil variables. The central map is defined as $F = (f_1, f_2, ..., f_{v+1})$ where each f is of the form

$$f_k(x) = \sum_{i=1}^{v}\sum_{j=1}^{v} \alpha_{ijk} x_i x_j + \sum_{i=1}^{v}\sum_{j=v+1}^{n} \beta_{ijk} x_i x_j + \sum_{i=1}^{n} \gamma_{ik} x_i + \delta_k.$$

Then, to create the public key equations P, we compose F with an invertible affine map $U : \mathbb{F}_q^n \to \mathbb{F}_q^n$ to get $P = F \circ U$.

The map F is a quadratic map, but it is linear in the oil variables, which is imperative to obtain a signature for a message $\mathbf{m}$. Inversion of the central map is completed by choosing random values from $\mathbb{F}_q$ for each of the vinegar variables then setting each equation equal to $\mathbf{m}$ and using Gaussian Elimination to solve for the remaining oil variables. If no solution is found, the process is repeated with choosing different values for the vinegar variables. The process is repeated until a solution for the set of oil variables is found. We then apply U^{-1} to find the final signature.

2.4 Rainbow

The Rainbow signature scheme introduced in [11] is constructed of L many UOV layers. Rainbow was the only multivariate signature scheme in the third round of the NIST standardization process, but has recently faced major attacks [5,6].

Each layer of UOV in the Rainbow signature scheme will have a different number of vinegar variables. Consider the sequence of integer values $0 < v_1 < v_2 < \ldots < v_L = n$ and a corresponding set of variables $V_1 = (x_1, \ldots, x_{v_1}), V_2 = (x_1, \ldots, x_{v_1}, \ldots, x_{v_2}), \ldots, V_L = (x_1, \ldots, x_{V_L})$ that contain the vinegar variables for the 1st, 2nd, ..., and Lth layers, respectively. Note, for each layer ℓ, the oil variables will contain $O_\ell = (x_{v_\ell+1}, \ldots, x_n)$. So, we have the relationships $V_1 \subset V_2 \subset \ldots \subset V_L$ and $O_L \subset O_{L-1} \subset \ldots \subset O_1$.

Each layer ℓ is composed of $n - v_\ell = o_\ell$ equations. The kth polynomial in the ℓth layer is of the form

$$f_k = \sum_{i=1}^{v_\ell} \sum_{j=1}^{v_\ell} \alpha_{ijk} x_i x_j + \sum_{i=1}^{v_\ell} \sum_{j=v_\ell+1}^{v_{\ell+1}} \beta_{ijk} x_i x_j + \sum_{i=1}^{n} \gamma_{i\ell} x_i + \delta_k,$$

where we normally consider $\delta_\ell = 0$. The public key is formed by composing the central map with two affine maps, U and T, to get $P = T \circ F \circ U$. In practice, we let $L = 2$. This means that $v_1 = v$, and $v_2 = n$. To speed up key generation, it is convention to use homogeneous polynomials f_i.

To invert the central map $F = (f_1, \ldots, f_n)$, we peel off the layers in the same fashion we invert the single layer UOV system. We choose values for the first layer vinegar variables $x_1, \ldots, x_{v_1}$ and substitute these values into the first layer maps $f_1, \ldots, f_{v_1}$. We then solve the resulting linear system in the first layer oil variables $x_{v_1+1}, \ldots, x_{v_2}$. We next substitute the values of these variables into the central maps $f_{v_1+1}, \ldots, f_n$.

2.5 HFERP

HFERP was introduced in [14] after SRP (introduced in [31]) was broken in [24]. The goal of SRP was to add an invertible system to UOV so that there is a way to uniquely solve for the vinegar variables instead of choosing random values. SRP used a square map, which left it susceptible to the MinRank attack. HFERP continues this goal by using an instance of HFE with a higher Q-rank (defined in Sect. 5) to protect against the attacks utilizing the low Q-rank of the Square map. HFERP utilizes a single layer of UOV with $v = d$ vinegar variables where d is the degree of the extension field used in the HFE scheme. HFERP also utilizes a plus modifier, adding p additional random equations to the central map to secure the system from rank attacks and to make decryption failures less likely.

Notation. We consider d to be the degree of the extension field in the HFE map, D the degree bound of the HFE central map, $\delta := \lceil \log_q(D) \rceil$, o is the number of oil variables in the UOV map, r a positive integer, and s is the number of added plus polynomials. For ease of notation, we will define $n := d+o$, $m := d+o+r+s$, and $t := m - d = o + r + s$. We will sometimes consider the linear maps T and U in their matrix representations, which we will denote as $\mathbf{T}$ and $\mathbf{U}$.

Key Generation and Encryption. To construct an HFERP system, choose a finite field $\mathbb{F}_q$ and a degree d extension $\mathbb{F}_{q^d}$ over $\mathbb{F}_q$. Let $\phi : \mathbb{F}_q^d \to \mathbb{F}_{q^d}$ be an $\mathbb{F}_q$-vector space isomorphism and o, r and s be non-negative integers.

The central map of HFERP is the concatenation of an HFE map, F_{HFE}, a single layer Rainbow map, $F_R = (f_1, ..., f_{o+r})$, and a plus modifier, F_p. These maps are defined as follows.

- $F_{HFE} : \mathbb{F}_q^n \to \mathbb{F}_q^d$ is the composition of

$$\mathbb{F}_q^n \xrightarrow{\pi_d} \mathbb{F}_q^d \xrightarrow{\phi} \mathbb{F}_{q^d} \xrightarrow{\mathcal{F}} \mathbb{F}_{q^d} \xrightarrow{\phi^{-1}} \mathbb{F}_q^d$$

  where $\mathcal{F}$ is the map in the extension field described in Sect. 2.2 and $\pi_d : \mathbb{F}_q^n \to \mathbb{F}_q^d$ is the projection onto the first d coordinates.
- The Rainbow component is an instance of UOV defined as

$$F_R = (f_1, ..., f_{o+r}) : \mathbb{F}_q^n \to \mathbb{F}_q^{o+r}.$$

  The variables $x_1, ..., x_d$ are the vinegar variables and remaining $x_{d+1}, ..., x_n$ are the oil variables. Each map f_i is defined as in Sect. 2.4.
- The plus modifier $F_p = (g_1, ..., g_s) : \mathbb{F}_q^n \to \mathbb{F}_q^s$ consists of s randomly generated quadratic polynomials.

To generate the public key, let $F = F_{HFE}||F_R||F_P$ (where $||$ denotes concatenation) and let $U : \mathbb{F}_q^n \to \mathbb{F}_q^n$ be an affine embedding of full rank and $T : \mathbb{F}_q^m \to \mathbb{F}_q^m$ be an affine isomorphism. Then, the public key is defined as $P = T \circ F \circ U : \mathbb{F}_q^n \to \mathbb{F}_q^m$.

Encryption Algorithm. Given a message $\mathbf{x} \in \mathbb{F}_q^n$, the ciphertext is computed as $P(\mathbf{x}) = \mathbf{y} \in \mathbb{F}_q^m$.

Decryption Algorithm. Given a ciphertext $\mathbf{y} = (y_1, ..., y_m) \in \mathbb{F}_q^m$, we start the decryption process by computing $\mathbf{y}' = (y_1', ..., y_m') = T^{-1}(\mathbf{y})$. The next step is to then compute $\mathbf{Y}' = \phi(y_1', ..., y_d') \in \mathbb{F}_{q^d}$. We then use the Berlekamp algorithm to compute the inverse of the HFE polynomials to recover $\mathbf{v} = (v_1, ..., v_d)$, which will be our vinegar variables. Once we have obtained the vinegar values $v_1, ..., v_d$, we then solve the system of $o + r$ linear equations in the $n - d = o$ variables $o_{d+1}, ..., o_n$ given by

$$g^{(k)}(v_1, ..., v_d, o_{d+1}, ..., o_n) = y_{d+k}',$$

for $k = 1, ..., o + r$. We denote the solution as $(v_{d+1}, ..., v_n)$. The final step is to compute the plaintext $\mathbf{x} \in \mathbb{F}_q^n$ by finding the preimage of $(v_1, ..., v_n)$ under the affine map U. Once a solution is found, check to see if it is consistent under the plus polynomials. If so, a valid decryption has been found. If not, repeat the process for a new solution $(v_1', ..., v_n')$ until we find a consistent solution.

3 Relevant Attacks

There is a standard suite of attacks commonly used in multivariate cryptography. In this section we provide a brief summary of relevant techniques.

3.1 Direct Attack

The most generic attack on a multivariate cryptosystem is the direct attack. In the context of encryption, the direct attack sets the public equations equal to a ciphertext value and attempts to solve the system algebraically. The complexity of the direct attack depends on a few factors.

First, by way of specializing some number of variables, one assumes that the ideal generated by these equations is zero-dimensional. In practice, if the field size is small, one should specialize more variables, attempting to solve the system by guessing some correct values of variables. This method is called the hybrid approach.

Second, the solving degree must be determined. This quantity is the degree at which the values of all monomials in the system of equations are determined uniquely. This phenomenon occurs when the number of linearly independent equations equals the number of monomials. The solving degree for a system of equations will be specific to each algorithm.

Finally, the complexity is dependent on the algorithm used to solve the system. If the system is relatively small (not cryptographic scale), then it is often beneficial to take advantage of the reduction to normal form occurring in the F4 algorithm [12]. For larger parameters, we expect it to be better to use the XL algorithm [9], not only for time complexity, but, perhaps more importantly, for memory complexity.

Given a system of m equations in n variables over $\mathbb{F}_q$, we may specialize k variables and in the case that $n < m$ we have the complexities of F4 and XL at solving degree d_s to be

$$\mathcal{O}\left(q^k \binom{n-k+d_s-1}{d_s}^\omega\right) \text{ and } \mathcal{O}\left(3q^k \binom{n-k+1}{2}\binom{n-k+d_s-1}{d_s}^2\right),$$

where ω is the linear algebra exponent.

3.2 MinRank Attacks

Many multivariate cryptosystems have been shown to be vulnerable against Min-Rank attacks. We can define the MinRank problem as follows:

Problem 1 (MinRank Problem) *Given matrices* $A_1, \ldots, A_K \in \mathbb{F}_q^{M \times N}$ *and* $R \in \mathbb{N}$, *decide if there exists a linear combination* $y_1, \ldots, y_K \in \mathbb{F}_q$ *(not all zero) such that*

$$rank\left(\sum_{i=1}^{K} y_i A_i\right) \leq R.$$

The goal of MinRank attacks is to try to find linear combinations of the public matrices that result in a matrix with low rank. This is an effective technique against schemes such as HFE as it allows an adversary to gain information about the low rank central maps. The MinRank attack was first introduced in [15], and other methods have since followed, including minors modeling and support minors modeling [3,13]. The complexity of MinRank attacks are tied to the complexity of polynomial solvers, such as the XL algorithm [10].

There are various methods to solve the MinRank problem. These methods vary from simply enumerating the space of linear combinations to constructing systems of equations with large sets of variables.

The simplest and most direct is simply exhaustive search. In this model one simply guesses linear combinations and computes the rank until a solution is found. The complexity of this version of MinRank is $q^K N^\omega$, where $2 \leq \omega \leq 3$ is the linear algebra exponent.

A simple general improvement to exhaustive search is called the combinatorial method, or sometimes linear algebra search. In this method, one guesses $\lceil \frac{K}{M} \rceil$ kernel vectors $\mathbf{v}_i$ and solves

$$\sum_{j=1}^{K} x_j \mathbf{A}_j \mathbf{v}_i = 0$$

linearly for $\mathbf{x}$. Simultaneously guessing two kernel vectors of a rank R matrix takes approximately $q^{\lceil \frac{K}{M} \rceil R}$ attempts on average. Thus, this technique has complexity

$$\mathcal{O}\left(q^{\lceil \frac{K}{M} \rceil R}\left(K^\omega + N^\omega\right)\right).$$

The support minors method of MinRank, see [3], is built from decomposition modeling. Given that the matrix $\mathbf{\Sigma} = \sum_{i=1}^{K} x_i \mathbf{A}_i$ has rank R, there exist matrices $\mathbf{S} \in \mathbb{F}_q^{M \times R}$ and $\mathbf{C} \in \mathbb{F}_q^{R \times N}$ such that $\mathbf{\Sigma} = \mathbf{SC}$. Specifically, the rowspace of $\mathbf{C}$ is the rowspace of $\mathbf{\Sigma}$, and so appending a row π of $\mathbf{\Sigma}$ to $\mathbf{C}$ results in an $(R+1) \times N$ matrix of rank R. The support minors modeling computes the maximal minors of such a matrix and solves the system for $\mathbf{x}$.

The complexity of solving the MinRank problem using Support Minors Modeling given K many matrices, M equations, N variables, and a target rank of R can be estimated as

$$\min_{M' \leq M} 3(K-1)(R+1) \binom{M'}{R}^2 \binom{K+b-2}{b}^2 \tag{1}$$

where b is the smallest integer such that

$$\binom{M'}{R}\binom{K+b-2}{b} - 1 \leq \sum_{i=1}^{b}(-1)^{i+1}\binom{M'}{R+1}\binom{N+i-1}{i}\binom{K+b-i}{b-i}. \tag{2}$$

As indicated in Equation (1) above, the number of columns used can be optimized to lower the complexity of the attack. One often finds that even a larger value of b along with a smaller M' may result in a more efficient attack.

Which MinRank technique is best in which parameter regime is a very interesting and subtle question. In general, smaller field sizes paired with either small target rank or a small search space offer more opportunities for the combinatorial search methods to be superior. If the field size is larger, or if the target rank is moderate; however, support minors are often more powerful.

The above techniques do not form a complete list of MinRank techniques. Other well-known techniques include minors modeling [4] and Kipnis-Shamir modeling [17]. Typically parameter sets for which these techniques can be effective are outperformed by support minors modeling.

3.3 Simple Attack

In 2022, the security of Rainbow took a major blow with the release of Beullens' simple attack from [6]. The Simple Attack is a differential attack, meaning it will make use of the discrete differential $DF(x,y) = F(x+y) - F(x) - F(y) + F(0)$. For our purposes in MPK cryptography, we have $P(0) = 0$ for a public key P. The simple attack utilizes a few key aspects to the Rainbow trapdoor function.

Recall from Sect. 2.4, an instance of Rainbow relies on q, the characteristic of the finite field, n, the number of variables, m, the number of public key equations, and o_2, which is the dimension of both the second layer oil subspace $O_2 \subset \mathbb{F}_q^n$ and the image of O_1 under the public key P. We will mirror the notation from [6] and set $P(O_1) = W \subset \mathbb{F}_q^m$ (Fig. 1).

From [6], it is known that for any $\mathbf{x} \in \mathbb{F}_q^n$ and any $\mathbf{o}_2 \in O_2$ that $DP(\mathbf{x}, \mathbf{o}_2) \in W$ and that $P(O_2) = \{0\}$. So, for a randomly chosen nonzero $\mathbf{x} \in \mathbb{F}_q^n$, construct the differential map

$$D_{\mathbf{x}} : \mathbb{F}_q^n \to \mathbb{F}_q^m : \mathbf{y} \mapsto DP(\mathbf{x}, \mathbf{y})$$

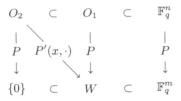

Fig. 1. Structure of nested subspaces.

where DP is defined as above. $D_\mathbf{x}$ is a linear map which sends O_2 to W. We know that $\dim(O_2) = o_2 = \dim(W)$, so the probability that D_x has a kernel vector in O_2 is the same probability that a random $o_2 \times o_2$ matrix over $\mathbb{F}_q$ is singular. This probability is known to be

$$1 - \prod_{i=0}^{o_2-1} (1 - q^{i-o_2}) \approx q^{-1}.$$

The goal in constructing this mapping is to find a nontrivial intersection between the kernel of the $D_\mathbf{x}$ map and the O_2 subspace. To search for the possible nontrivial intersection, the simple attack sets up the following system of equations:

$$\begin{cases} D_\mathbf{x}(\mathbf{o}) = 0 \\ P(\mathbf{o}) = 0. \end{cases} \tag{3}$$

The resulting system has m homogeneous linear equations and m homogenous quadratic equations in the n variables of $\mathbf{o}$. The simple attack then uses the m linear equations to eliminate m of the variables from the quadratic equations. This yields a system of m homogenous equations in only $n - m$ variables. Using Beullens' notation, let $\mathbf{B} \in \mathbb{F}_q^{n \times (n-m)}$ be a matrix whose columns form a basis for $\ker(D_\mathbf{x})$. Then the process reduces to finding a solution to $\mathbf{o} \in \mathbb{F}_q^{n-m}$ such that $P(\mathbf{Bo}) = 0$. If such a solution is found, then with high probability $\mathbf{o} \in O_2$. If no solution exists, randomly choose a new nonzero $\mathbf{x} \in \mathbb{F}_q^n$ and repeat the process. Once an O_2 vector is found, the second layer of Rainbow can be removed and the complexity is reduced to an instance of UOV with $m - o_2$ equations in $n - o_2$ variables.

3.4   Other Techniques

The work of Tao et al. in [29] presents a MinRank key recovery attack on HFEv$^-$ cryptosystem with complexity

$$\mathcal{O}\left(\binom{\hat{n} + \hat{d} + v + 1}{\hat{d} + 1}^\omega\right),$$

where $\hat{n}$ is the degree of the extension field, v is the number of vinegar variables, $\hat{d} = \lceil \log_q(D) \rceil$, D is the degree bound of the central HFE polynomial, and ω

is the linear algebra constant. This paper illustrates that the minus modifier does not increase the security of HFE type cryptosystems as the complexity is independent of a, the number of public equations deleted. The vinegar modifier only increases the complexity by a polynomial factor.

Given the public key $P = T \circ F \circ S$, the attack starts by recovering a map equivalent to the private map S by solving a MinRank problem over the base field with target rank d. Equivalent maps to the private T and F are then found by solving a system of linear and nonlinear equations. The work in [2] shows how to use Support Minors modeling for the problem, and results in a total break of GeMSS. The GeMSS cryptosystem can be thought of as a specific example of HFEv$^-$ and was a candidate in the NIST standardization process.

4   HFERP Simple Attack: Divide and Conquer

We introduce an attack that significantly diminishes the security levels of some HFERP parameter sets. This attack uses some similar tools as the Simple Attack against Rainbow, and is thus named accordingly. The goal of this attack is to find an HFE map hiding in a subspace of the public equations, which is defined based on the kernel of a linear combination of rectangular slices of the 3-tensor representation of the public key. Membership in the kernel provides linear relations that can be used to essentially remove variables from the MinRank modeling, making it much easier to solve a MinRank instance whose solution is an HFE polynomial. From there we are able to obtain maps equivalent to the secret maps U and T and then attack each section of the central map individually. We describe this attack on HFERP with only a single Rainbow layer (i.e., a UOV map), but the attack can easily be adjusted for more Rainbow layers.

Although this attack was inspired by the Simple Attack on Rainbow, there are some subtle differences in technique. In the basic Simple Attack against Rainbow, an adversary searches for an o_2 vector by finding a solution to the system of equations $\{D_{\mathbf{x}}(\mathbf{y}) = 0, P(\mathbf{y}) = 0\}$. Similarly, the combined attack of [6] on Rainbow, mostly relevant for the larger category III and V parameter sets, combines the kernel condition (the first equation above) with the rectangular MinRank attack. This technique essentially removes m of the n distinct $n \times m$ matrices of the rectangular MinRank attack, a significant improvement.

Our attack is similar, but has some notable differences. First, HFERP is an encryption scheme, and so must have at least as many equations as variables. Therefore, while we use a rectangular matrix similar to that used in the rainbow attack, it makes the most sense to consider kernel elements on the opposite side (corresponding to the output space as opposed to the input space of the HFERP public key). When the kernel of such a map intersects the subspace of HFE maps, the vectors contained in the intersection produce low rank linear combinations of the public maps.

The works of [2,29] are also related to this attack, as we are using MinRank techniques on the public matrices to find equivalent linear transformations as those used in the secret key. Although both of these attacks are exploiting the low rank properties of the HFE central map, our attack uses the MinRank techniques to strategically filter out the Rainbow and plus polynomials.

4.1   Finding y Vector

Let $\mathbf{P}_i$ be the matrix representation of the ith public polynomial p_i such that $\mathbf{x}\mathbf{P}_i\mathbf{x}^\top = p_i(\mathbf{x})$ for $\mathbf{x} \in \mathbb{F}_q^n$. Choose a random row vector $\mathbf{z} \in \mathbb{F}_q^n$ and compute the $m \times n$ matrix

$$
\mathbf{A}_z = \begin{bmatrix} \mathbf{z}\mathbf{P}_1 \\ \mathbf{z}\mathbf{P}_2 \\ \vdots \\ \mathbf{z}\mathbf{P}_m \end{bmatrix}.
$$

We hope to find a $\mathbf{z}$ such that the subspace of the rows of $\mathbf{A}_z$ with the structure of HFE has nontrivial left kernel. We let $\mathrm{Ker}_L(\mathbf{A}_z)$ denote the left kernel of $\mathbf{A}_z$. Recall that the set of HFE maps forms a dimension d subspace of the span of the $\mathbf{P}_i$ which has support on a d-dimensional subspace of $\mathbb{F}_q^n$. Thus for any $\mathbf{z}$, the map $\mathbf{A}_z$ restricted to the HFE subspace is a map from a d-dimensional space to a d-dimensional space. Under the heuristic assumption that this restricted map acts as a random $d \times d$ matrix the probability that the restricted map is singular is

$$
1 - \prod_{i=0}^{d-1}(1 - q^{i-d}),
$$

which for large q is approximately q^{-1}.

Our goal is to find a vector $\mathbf{y} \in \mathbb{F}_q^m$ such that

$$
\begin{cases} \mathbf{y} \in \mathrm{Ker}_L(\mathbf{A}_z) \\ \mathrm{Rank}\left(\displaystyle\sum_{i=1}^{m} y_i\mathbf{P_i}\right) \leq d. \end{cases} \tag{4}
$$

If the maps $\mathbf{P}_i$ were generic then the probability that even a single map in their span is of rank d would be very close to zero. We therefore work under the following heuristic assumption, well-supported by experimental data

Heuristic Assumption 1 *The only nonzero maps in the span of the $\mathbf{P}_i$ that have rank bounded by d are in the span of the maps $\mathbf{U}\mathbf{F}_i\mathbf{U}^\top$ for $i = 1, \ldots, d$, i.e. the HFE maps.*

Thus, we expect that any such solution $\mathbf{y}$ to (4) has the form

$$
\mathbf{y}\mathbf{T} = (\mathbf{a}\|\mathbf{0}) \implies \mathbf{y} = (\mathbf{a}\|\mathbf{0})\mathbf{T}^{-1}, \tag{5}
$$

where $\mathbf{a}$ is a length d vector and $\mathbf{0}$ is the length t zero vector. Note that for each public polynomial we have:

$$
p_i = \sum_{k=1}^{m} t_{ik}(f_k \circ U),
$$

where f_k represents the kth central map. The linear combination in question then becomes

$$\sum_{\ell=1}^{m} y_\ell \mathbf{P}_\ell = \sum_{\ell=1}^{m} y_\ell \left(\sum_{k=1}^{m} t_{\ell k} (\mathbf{UF}_k \mathbf{U}^\top) \right) = \sum_{k=1}^{m} \sum_{\ell=1}^{m} y_\ell t_{\ell k} (\mathbf{UF}_k \mathbf{U}^\top)$$

$$= \sum_{k=1}^{d} a_k \left(\mathbf{UF}_k \mathbf{U}^\top \right) + \sum_{k=d+1}^{m} 0 \left(\mathbf{UF}_k \mathbf{U}^\top \right).$$

This behavior is illustrated in Fig. 2.

To find such a vector y, we will compute a basis $\{\mathbf{v}_1, \ldots, \mathbf{v}_{r+s}\}$ for the left kernel of the $m \times n$ matrix $\mathbf{A}_z$. For each basis vector $\mathbf{v}_j$, we then compute the matrix

$$\mathbf{W}_j = \sum_{i=1}^{m} v_{ji} \mathbf{P}_i.$$

The vector $\mathbf{y}$ that we want is a linear combination of the basis vectors, so we can write $\mathbf{y} = \sum_{j=1}^{r+s} \lambda_j \mathbf{v}_j$. We can also write $\sum_{i=1}^{m} y_i \mathbf{P}_i$ as a linear combination of the $\mathbf{W}_j$ matrices as follows:

$$\sum_{i=1}^{m} y_i \mathbf{P}_i = \sum_{i=1}^{m} \left(\sum_{j=1}^{r+s} \lambda_j v_j \right)_i \mathbf{P}_i$$

$$= \sum_{i=1}^{m} \sum_{j=1}^{r+s} \lambda_j v_{ji} \mathbf{P}_i$$

$$= \sum_{j=1}^{r+s} \lambda_j \left(\sum_{i=1}^{m} v_{ji} \mathbf{P}_i \right)$$

$$= \sum_{j=1}^{r+s} \lambda_j \mathbf{W}_j.$$

We can then use MinRank on the $r + s$ many $\mathbf{W}_j \in \mathbb{F}_q^{n \times n}$ matrices with target rank d in order to find the weights λ_j that will give us the vector $\mathbf{y}$ we are interested in. When q is small, it appears the exhaustive search version of MinRank will be the most efficient way to find $\mathbf{y}$. For large q, Linear Algebra Search or Support Minors may be used to find $\mathbf{y}$.

4.2   Inverting U

We will use the obtained $\mathbf{y}$ to uncover the oil and vinegar subspaces of the UOV maps. We will denote the Oil and Vinegar subspaces in the public basis as O and V, respectively. Recall that $O, V \subset \mathbb{F}_q^n$, $O + V = \mathbb{F}_q^n$, $O \cap V = \{0\}$, $\dim(O) = o$, $\dim(V) = d$, and for any $x \in O$, $f_i(x) = 0$ for $1 \leq i \leq d + o + r$.

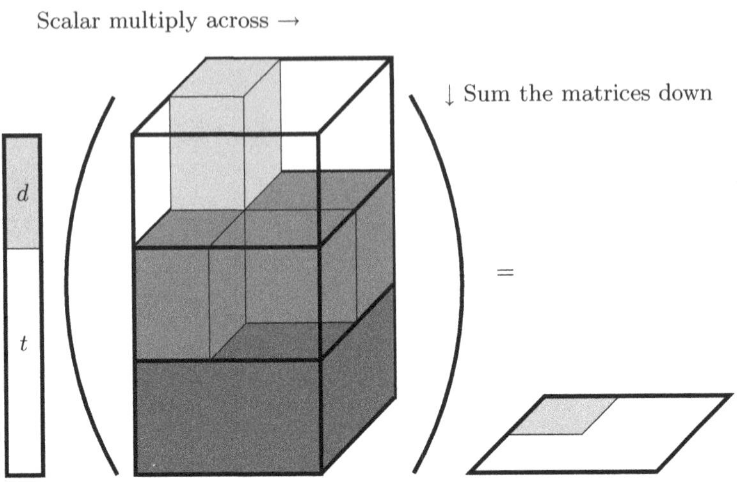

Scalar multiply across →

Fig. 2. We can consider the m many $n \times n$ matrix representations of each f_i as a 3 tensor where each $n \times n$ matrix F_i is stacked on top of F_{i+1}. We denote zero coordinates as white, and the gray areas represent nonzero coordinates. Let $\mathbf{y}$ be a vector that satisfies Eq. 5. The figure represents the linear combination $\sum_{i=1}^{m} (\mathbf{yT})_i \mathbf{F}_i$.

Once a $\mathbf{y} \in \mathbb{F}_q^m$ satisfying (4) is found, we then compute the $n \times n$ matrix

$$\mathbf{P_y} = \sum_{i=1}^{m} y_i \mathbf{P}_i.$$

We note a couple of things about $\mathbf{P_y}$. First, by Heuristic Assumption 1, we have that $\mathbf{P_y}$ is in the span of the HFE maps $\mathbf{UF}_i\mathbf{U}^\top$ for $i = 1, \ldots, d$. Second, since $\mathbf{y} \in \ker(\mathbf{A_z})$, we have that

$$0 = \sum_{i=1}^{m} y_i \mathbf{zP}_i = \mathbf{z} \sum_{i=1}^{m} y_i \mathbf{P}_i = \mathbf{zP_y};$$

therefore, $\mathbf{z} \in \ker(\mathbf{P_y})$. Thus, since we do not expect $\mathbf{z} \in O$, the rank of $\mathbf{P_y}$ is expected to be $d - 1$.

Note that O is a corank 1 subspace of $\ker(\mathbf{P_y})$. Therefore, restricting any HFE or oil-vinegar map to this subspace results in a map of rank at most 2, since all such maps are identically zero on the oil subspace O. (Prepending $\mathbf{z}$ to an ordered basis of O provides a projection onto $\ker(\mathbf{P_y})$ that sends any HFE or oil-vinegar quadratic form to an $(o+1) \times (o+1)$ symmetric matrix with nonzero entries in only the first row and column.) Thus we may recover multiple maps in the span of the HFE and oil-vinegar maps by solving easy instances of MinRank at rank 2.

Finding two such rank 2 maps $\mathbf{C}$ and $\mathbf{D}$ in the span of the public key restricted to $\ker(\mathbf{P_y})$ is sufficient to recover O. Since the kernels of all HFE and oil-vinegar maps are interlaced, the $(m - s)$-dimensional subspace of rank 2 restricted maps all have their kernels contained in O. Therefore, as long as $\ker(\mathbf{C}) \neq \ker(\mathbf{D})$, we have that $\mathrm{Span}(\ker(\mathbf{C}), \ker(\mathbf{D})) = O$.

Let $\{\beta_1, \ldots, \beta_o\}$ be a basis for the recovered oil subspace O and define $\mathbf{B_1}$ to be the $o \times n$ matrix whose jth row is β_j. Next, we complete the basis $\{\beta_1, \ldots, \beta_o\}$ with some arbitrary linearly independent set $\{\alpha_1, \ldots, \alpha_d\} \subset \mathbb{F}_q^n$. Let $\mathbf{B_2}$ be the $d \times n$ matrix whose jth row is α_j. We then vertically adjoin $\mathbf{B_2}$ and $\mathbf{B_1}$ to generate the $n \times n$ matrix

$$\widehat{\mathbf{B}} := \begin{bmatrix} \mathbf{B_2} \\ \mathbf{B_1} \end{bmatrix} = [\alpha_1^\top \cdots \alpha_d^\top \ \beta_1^\top \cdots \beta_o^\top]^\top .$$

Let $\mathbf{G}$ be in the span of the public quadratic forms and consider the matrix multiplication

$$\widehat{\mathbf{B}}\mathbf{G}\widehat{\mathbf{B}}^T = \begin{bmatrix} \alpha_1\mathbf{G}\alpha_1^\top & \cdots & \alpha_1\mathbf{G}\alpha_d^\top & \alpha_1\mathbf{G}\beta_1^\top & \cdots & \alpha_1\mathbf{G}\beta_o^\top \\ \vdots & \ddots & \vdots & \vdots & \ddots & \vdots \\ \alpha_d\mathbf{G}\alpha_1^\top & \cdots & \alpha_d\mathbf{G}\alpha_d^\top & \alpha_d\mathbf{G}\beta_1^\top & \cdots & \alpha_d\mathbf{G}\beta_o^\top \\ \beta_1\mathbf{G}\alpha_1^\top & \cdots & \beta_1\mathbf{G}\alpha_d^\top & \beta_1\mathbf{G}\beta_1^\top & \cdots & \beta_1\mathbf{G}\beta_o^\top \\ \vdots & \ddots & \vdots & \vdots & \ddots & \vdots \\ \beta_o\mathbf{G}\alpha_1^\top & \cdots & \beta_o\mathbf{G}\alpha_d^\top & \beta_o\mathbf{G}\beta_1^\top & \cdots & \beta_o\mathbf{G}\beta_o^\top \end{bmatrix} .$$

Consider the case in which $\mathbf{G}$ is in the span of $\mathbf{UF}_i\mathbf{U}$ for $i = 1, \ldots, d$, i.e. the HFE maps. Then the (i, j)th coordinate of $\widehat{\mathbf{B}}\mathbf{G}\widehat{\mathbf{B}}^T$ is of the form $\alpha_i\mathbf{G}\beta_{j-d}^\top$ when $i \leq d$ and $d < j \leq n$. Notice that because $\mathbf{G}$ is symmetric and each β_k is in O, and hence in the left kernel of $\mathbf{G}$, we have that

$$\mathbf{0}^\top = (\beta_k\mathbf{G})^\top = \mathbf{G}^\top\beta_k^\top = \mathbf{G}\beta_k^\top .$$

Thus, these coordinates are all zero. The (i, j)th coordinate of $\widehat{\mathbf{B}}\mathbf{G}\widehat{\mathbf{B}}^T$ is zero for $d < i \leq n, j \leq d$ by symmetry. Similarly, when $d < i, j \leq n$ the (i, j)th coordinate of $\widehat{\mathbf{B}}\mathbf{G}\widehat{\mathbf{B}}^T$ is zero for the same reason. Thus $\widehat{\mathbf{B}}\mathbf{G}\widehat{\mathbf{B}}^T$ may only be nonzero in its upper left $d \times d$ block, having the same structure as an HFE map.

Next, consider the case in which $\mathbf{G}$ is in the span of the $\mathbf{UF}_i\mathbf{U}$ for $i = d + 1, \ldots, d + o$, i.e. the oil-vinegar maps. In this case, the (i, j)th coordinate of $\widehat{\mathbf{B}}\mathbf{G}\widehat{\mathbf{B}}^T$ is $\beta_{i-d}\mathbf{G}\beta_{j-d}^\top$ when $d < i, j \leq n$. Since $\mathbf{G}$ is identically zero on O, we have that the coordinate is zero. Thus, $\mathbf{G}$ has a lower right $o \times o$ block of zeros, the same structure as an oil-vinegar map. We have thus verified the following proposition.

Proposition 1 *The oil subspace O is invariant under the map $U \circ \widehat{\mathbf{B}}$.*

4.3 Inverting T

Once we have obtained $\widehat{\mathbf{B}}$, we effectively have a way to circumnavigate the linear transformation on the input. Now, we wish to find a map T' that is equivalent to the linear transformation on the outputs.

Consider the structure of the public key.

$$P = T \circ \begin{bmatrix} F_{HFE} \\ F_{UOV} \\ F_{Plus} \end{bmatrix} \circ U$$

We may represent the function compositions as matrix multiplications in the following way:

$$\begin{bmatrix} p_1(\mathbf{x}) \\ \vdots \\ p_m(\mathbf{x}) \end{bmatrix} = \mathbf{T} \times \begin{bmatrix} \mathbf{x}\mathbf{U}\mathbf{F}_1\mathbf{U}^\top\mathbf{x}^\top \\ \vdots \\ \mathbf{x}\mathbf{U}\mathbf{F}_m\mathbf{U}^\top\mathbf{x}^\top \end{bmatrix}$$

$$\mathbf{P}_i = \sum_{k=1}^m t_{ik}\mathbf{U}\mathbf{F}_k\mathbf{U}^\top$$

$$\mathbf{P}_i = \mathbf{U}\left(\sum_{k=1}^m t_{ik}\mathbf{F}_k\right)\mathbf{U}^\top$$

For each public equation, we have the relationship that

$$\widehat{\mathbf{B}}\mathbf{P}_i\widehat{\mathbf{B}}^\top = \sum_{k=1}^m t_{ik}\left(\widehat{\mathbf{B}}\mathbf{U}\mathbf{F}_k\mathbf{U}^\top\widehat{\mathbf{B}}^\top\right) = \widehat{\mathbf{B}}\mathbf{U}\left(\sum_{k=1}^m t_{ik}\mathbf{F}_k\right)\mathbf{U}^\top\widehat{\mathbf{B}}^\top. \quad (6)$$

By construction, we know that $\mathbf{F}_k$ will have specific traits depending on k. These properties are listed in Table 1.

Table 1. The table summarizes notable properties of the symmetric matrices corresponding to the F_{HFE}, F_R, and F_P polynomials.

	$1 \leq k \leq d$	$d+1 \leq k \leq o+r$	$o+r+1 \leq k \leq m$
Structure of $\mathbf{F}_k$			
Rank($\mathbf{F}_k$) $\leq$	d	d	n
Guaranteed zeros	Rows $d \leq i \leq m$ Columns $d \leq j \leq m$	Lower right $o \times o$ submatrix	None

The next phase of the attack is to invert the output transformation T. We will denote $\widehat{\mathbf{P}}^{(i)} := \widehat{\mathbf{B}}\mathbf{P}_i\widehat{\mathbf{B}}^\top$ and for any matrix $\mathbf{M}$ we will let $\mathbf{M}_{[i:j]}$ denote the submatrix of $\mathbf{M}$ containing columns i through j. We consider that

$$\widehat{\mathbf{P}}^{(i)} = \sum_{k=1}^m t_{ik}\mathbf{F}_k.$$

Our goal now is to find $\mathbf{c} \in \mathbb{F}_q^m$ such that

$$\sum_{i=1}^{m} c_i \widehat{\mathbf{P}}_{[d+1:n]}^{(i)} = \mathbf{0}_{n \times o}. \qquad (7)$$

If such a $\mathbf{c}$ is found, we obtain

$$\sum_{i=1}^{m} c_i \widehat{\mathbf{P}}_{[d+1:n]}^{(i)} = \sum_{i=1}^{m} c_i \left(t_{i1} \mathbf{F}_{1,[d+1:n]} + \cdots + t_{im} \mathbf{F}_{m,[d+1:n]} \right)$$

$$= \sum_{i=1}^{m} c_i \left(t_{i1} \mathbf{F}_{d+1,[d+1:n]} + \cdots + t_{im} \mathbf{F}_{m,[d+1:n]} \right),$$

since $\mathbf{F}_{i,[d+1:n]} = \mathbf{0}_{n \times o}$. Thus we obtain a $\mathbf{c}$ that is in $\ker \left(\mathbf{T}_{[d+1:m]} \right)$. We can compute the left kernel of $\mathbf{T}_{[d+1:m]}$ by finding all solutions to Eq. 7. We will let $\{\tau_1, \ldots, \tau_d\} \subseteq \mathbb{F}_q^m$ be a basis for the left kernel of $\mathbf{T}_{[d+1:m]}$.

We will repeat the process described, but now we will consider the lower right $o \times o$ submatrix of each $\widehat{\mathbf{P}}$. Notice from Table 1 that these submatrices will be zero in $\mathbf{F}_k$ when $1 \le k \le d+o+r$. By finding all solutions to the linear combination of the public key equations that make the lower coordinates zero, we will find the left kernel of $\mathbf{T}_{[d+o+r+1:m]}$. Notice that $\{\tau_1, \ldots, \tau_d\} \subseteq \ker(\mathbf{T}_{[d+o+r+1:m]})$. We can append $o+r$ linearly independent kernel vectors to extend the set $\tau_1, \ldots, \tau_d$ to a basis of the entire space. We will denote this as $\{\tau_1, \ldots, \tau_d, \tau_{d+1}, \ldots, \tau_{d+o+r}\}$. We can take this set and extend it to a basis of $\mathbb{F}_q^m$. Let Γ be the basis matrix whose jth row is τ_j.

This basis acts on the public key equations in such a way that the first d equations of $\Gamma \circ P \circ \widehat{\mathbf{B}}$ will be HFE maps, the next $o+r$ maps will be rainbow maps, and the final s equations are plus polynomials. Let $\widehat{P}_i$ be the polynomial represented by $\widehat{\mathbf{B}}\mathbf{P}_i\widehat{\mathbf{B}}^\top$. Then,

$$\Gamma \circ \widehat{P} = \begin{bmatrix} \tau_1 \\ \vdots \\ \tau_{d+1} \\ \vdots \\ \tau_m \end{bmatrix} \begin{bmatrix} \widehat{P_1} \\ \vdots \\ \widehat{P_{d+1}} \\ \vdots \\ \widehat{P_m} \end{bmatrix} = \begin{bmatrix} \tau_1 \left(\mathbf{T}_{1,*}[f_1 \cdots f_m]^\top \right) \\ \vdots \\ \tau_{d+1} \left(\mathbf{T}_{d+1,*}[f_1 \cdots f_m]^\top \right) \\ \vdots \\ \tau_m \left(\mathbf{T}_{m,*}[f_1 \cdots f_m]^\top \right) \end{bmatrix}$$

$$= \begin{bmatrix} \sum_{i=1}^{d} \tilde{t}_{1,i} f_i \\ \vdots \\ \sum_{i=1}^{d+o+r} \tilde{t}_{d+1,i} f_i \\ \vdots \\ \sum_{i=1}^{m} \tilde{t}_{m,i} f_i \end{bmatrix} = \begin{bmatrix} \widetilde{F}_{HFE} \\ \widetilde{F}_R \\ \widetilde{F}_P \end{bmatrix}.$$

4.4   Divide and Conquer

At this point, we have equivalent keys for every part of the secret key. The security of HFERP is thus reduced to that of its HFE component effectively breaking the scheme. Once the HFE maps are recovered, a full message recovery or key recovery is then reduced to the task of breaking the embedded HFE instance. Having access to the oil and vinegar spaces, the remainder of inversion is just as in oil-vinegar.

5   HFERP Support Minors Direct Attack

The prior attack first separates the different layers of the HFERP central map, and can then break the isolated HFE scheme. Another technique would be to perform a big-field MinRank attack using Support Minors Modeling directly on the entire system, without first separating the layers. For many of the proposed parameter sets, this attack is more efficient than separating the scheme as in the Simple Attack. The complexity of this attack, however, depends on the degree bound of the HFE polynomial, δ, whereas the simple attack does not. This fact implies that the scheme is fully broken for all feasible parameter sets.

We will apply the techniques from [2] to implement an attack on the big-field HFE system within the HFERP scheme. The work of [2] describes a total break of the GeMSS cryptosystem using Support Minors Modeling. The big-field support minors technique helps deal with the fact that the MinRank system over the public keys will not have a unique solution, as the big-field structure will result in n solutions. This means we cannot directly apply an XL algorithm. The solution will be the $d-$dimensional kernel of the Macaulay matrix at the appropriate degree.

In MinRank attacks against big-field multivariate schemes, the min-Q-rank is commonly considered. Given a quadratic polynomial $f : \mathbb{F}_{q^d} \to \mathbb{F}_{q^d}$, we call the $d \times d$ matrix $\mathbf{F}$ the quadratic form of f when

$$f(X) = \left(X\ X^q\ \ldots\ X^{q^{d-1}} \right) \mathbf{F} \left(X\ X^q\ \ldots\ X^{q^{d-1}} \right)^{\top}.$$

We call the rank of the quadratic form the Q-rank of the polynomial. In the case of HFERP, the central map of the HFE polynomial will have a Q-rank of δ over the extension field $\mathbb{F}_{q^d}$. In this attack, we can directly apply the big-field MinRank attack with target rank δ to find an equivalent HFE central map.

Let $\hat{U} := U^{-1} \circ \pi_d^{-1} \circ \phi^{-1}$, where π_d^{-1} maps an element to a preimage under π_d. This can be represented as a matrix $\hat{U} \in \mathbb{F}_{q^d}^{d \times n}$. Denote $\delta := \lceil \log_q D \rceil$. Let $\mathbf{P}_1, \ldots, \mathbf{P}_m \in \mathbb{F}_q^{n \times n}$ denote the symmetric matrices associated with the public key and let $(\mathbf{e}_1, \ldots, \mathbf{e}_n)$ be the canonical basis for $\mathbb{F}_q^n$. For $1 \leq i \leq n$ we define the matrix $\mathbf{M}_i \in \mathbb{F}_q^{m \times n}$ by

$$\mathbf{M}_i := \begin{pmatrix} \mathbf{e}_i \mathbf{P}_1 \\ \vdots \\ \mathbf{e}_i \mathbf{P}_m \end{pmatrix}.$$

Consider the MinRank problem of finding a solution $\mathbf{v} \in \mathbb{F}_{q^d}^n$ such that

$$\text{rank}\left(\sum_{i=1}^{n} v_i \mathbf{M}_i\right) \leq \delta.$$

We see that for any row $\hat{u} = (u_1, \ldots, u_n)$ of $\widehat{\mathbf{U}}$, $\sum_{j=1}^{n} u_i \mathbf{M}_i$ is a solution to the MinRank problem (see Theorem 2 in [29] for details). We define

$$\mathbf{Z} := \sum_{i=1}^{n} u_i \mathbf{M}_i \in \mathbb{F}_q[\mathbf{u}]^{m \times n}. \tag{8}$$

We consider the Support Minors equations obtained by choosing $m' \in [2\delta + 1, m]$ columns in $\mathbf{Z}^\top$, with coefficients in $\mathbb{F}_q$ and solutions in $\mathbb{F}_{q^d}$. Moreover, we fix the variables in the support minors system $u_n = 1$ and $c_{\{1\ldots d\}} = 1$. This system has $n\binom{m'}{\delta+1}$ affine bilinear equations in $n\binom{m'}{\delta}$ monomials, of which $(n-1)\left(\binom{m'}{\delta} - 1\right)$ of them are bilinear monomials. We call this Modeling 1.

Using Assumption 1 from [2], when $m' \geq 2\delta + 1$, we can expect that the number of linearly independent equations in Modeling 1 is equal to $\mathcal{N}_1 := n\binom{m'}{\delta} - d$.

The attack continues in two steps. The first step is to form linear combinations between the equations from Modeling 1 to produce a system $\mathcal{L}$ of degree 1 polynomials. From Fact 3 in [2], we know that the number of linearly independent degree 1 polynomials, $\mathcal{N}_L$, that we can generate, is bounded below by $\binom{m'}{\delta} + n - d - 1$.

Once we have these linear polynomials, we can substitute variables in Modeling 1 to obtain what we call Modeling 2. Modeling 2 will consist of the quadratic system in $d_u = d - 1$ linear variables $u_1, \ldots, u_{d-1}$ obtained by plugging in the linear polynomials of $\mathcal{L}$ into the equations from Modeling 1. By Proposition 1 from [2], we find that the solving degree for a Gröbner basis algorithm on Modeling 2 will be 2.

We assume that $m' \geq 2\delta + 1$ and that the reduced row echelon form of the Macauley matrix of $\mathcal{L}$ is of the form

$$\mathcal{L} = \begin{pmatrix} I_{n_{C_T}} & * \\ 0 & \mathbf{K} \end{pmatrix} \in \mathbb{F}_q^{\mathcal{N}_L \times (n_{C_T} + n)},$$

where n_{C_T} is the number of minors variables and $\mathbf{K} \in \mathbb{F}_q^{(\mathcal{N}_L - n_{C_T}) \times n}$. The number of degree 2 affine equations which remain after the linear algebra step in Modeling 1 is equal to

$$\mathcal{N}_1 - \mathcal{N}_L = (n-1)\left(\binom{m'}{\delta} - 1\right).$$

We cannot construct more degree falls between the two sets, so the linear span of the equations contains an equation with leading monomial $u_i c_T$ for any T, $\#T = \delta$, $T \neq \{1 \ldots \delta\}$ and any $1 \leq i \leq n - 1$. Let

$$L^{(h)} := \begin{pmatrix} \mathbf{I}_{n_{C_T}} & \mathbf{0} & \mathbf{Y} \\ \mathbf{0} & \mathbf{I}_{n-d} & \mathbf{W} \end{pmatrix} \in \mathbb{F}_q^{\mathcal{N}_L \times (n_{C_T} + n - 1)}$$

where $\mathbf{Y} \in \mathbb{F}_q^{n_{C_T} \times d_u}$ and $\mathbf{W} \in \mathbb{F}_q^{n-d \times d_u}$. Let $\mathbf{c}$ denote the row vector whose components are the minor variables and $(u_1, \ldots, u_{n-1}) := (u_+, u_-)$ where u_+ is of length d_u (remaining linear variables) and u_- is of length $n - d_u$ (removed linear variables). Then there is a vector of constants $\alpha \in \mathbb{F}_q^{n_{C_T}}$ such that

$$\mathbf{c}^\top = -\mathbf{Y} u_+^\top - \alpha^\top.$$

Since $\mathbf{Y}$ is of full rank, the linear system can be inverted when $n_{C_T} \geq d_u$ and therefore all $\binom{d}{2}$ quadratic leading monomials can be found in the span of modeling 2.

To complete step 1, we can either use Strassen's Algorithm [28] or Wiedemann's Algorithm [30], which give the complexities listed below.

Using Strassen's Algorithm:

$$\mathcal{O}\left(\left(n\binom{2\delta+1}{\delta}\right)^\omega\right).$$

Using Wiedemann Algorthm:

$$\mathcal{O}\left(dn^3(\delta+1)\binom{2\delta+1}{\delta}^2\right)$$

The complexity of solving step 2 of the attack is

$$\mathcal{O}\left(\left(\binom{2\delta+1}{\delta}-1\right)(n-1)\binom{d+1}{2}^{\omega-1}\right).$$

Note that the complexity of solving the system is heavily dependent on the degree of the HFE polynomial.

6   Updated Complexities

6.1   Simple Attack: Divide and Conquer

Here we discuss the complexity of finding equivalent T, F, and U maps. The general outline of the complexity of the simple attack is

(comp. of finding $\mathbf{z}$) (comp. of finding $\mathbf{y}$) (comp. of solving syst of linear eq).

We estimate the probability of finding an appropriate $\mathbf{z}$ is q^{-1}, so we will expect to search for $\mathbf{y}$ about q times. The complexity of solving systems of linear equations and computing kernels is negligible. The most computationally expensive part of the attack is using MinRank techniques to find $\mathbf{y}$, which must be done for each guess $\mathbf{z}$.

Using the complexity estimate formulas for each type of MinRank attacks, we find that the optimal MinRank techniques for all parameters are combinatorial, in spite of the high target rank of the MinRank instances. Even more surprising is the fact that the best MinRank technique for attacking the parameter set targeting 80-bit of security is the exhaustive search method, which significantly outperforms the linear algebra search method. For parameters targeting 128-bit of security, the linear algebra search method performs the best. In particular, the linear algebra search MinRank technique breaks a parameter set targeting 128-bit security. These results are summarized in Table 2.

Table 2. Complexity of the Simple Attack on proposed parameters of HFERP, where $D = 3^7 + 1$ is the degree bound of the HFE central map polynomial. See Appendix B for notes on other parameters.

(q, d, o, r, s)	Claimed Sec	Simple Attack	MinRank Type
$(3, 42, 21, 15, 17)$	80 bit	$3 \cdot 3^{32} \cdot 63^{\omega} \approx 2^{69}$	Search
$(3, 63, 21, 11, 10)$	80 bit	$3 \cdot 3^{21} \cdot 84^{\omega} \approx 2^{52}$	Search
$(3, 60, o_i = 40, r_i = 23, 40)$	128 bit	$3 \cdot 3^{59} (86^{\omega} + 140^{\omega}) \approx 2^{115}$	Lin Alg

Naturally, if the security of HFERP is no more than the security of the embedded HFE instance, the construction is broken. Still, for a full key recovery it remains necessary to break the embedded HFE instance. The complexity of this last step is reported in Table 3.

Table 3. Complexity of the HFE attack step on proposed parameters of HFERP.

(q, d, o, r, s)	Degree Bound	Claimed Sec	HFE Step	MinRank Type
$(3, 42, 21, 15, 17)$	$D = 3^7 + 1$	80 bit	2^{55}	Support Minors
$(3, 63, 21, 11, 10)$	$D = 3^7 + 1$	80 bit	2^{57}	Support Minors
$(3, 60, o_i = 40, r_i = 23, 40)$	$D = 3^9 + 1$	128 bit	2^{65}	Support Minors

In addition, we performed some experiments of the attack on toy examples of the scheme. The experiments we performed using the MAGMA Computer Algebra System[1], see [7], on a 2.3 GHz Intel® Xeon® E5-2650 v3 processor with 10 cores. The results support our theoretical conclusions, up to the noise expected from a statistical attack. In particular, since the optimal MinRank method for these

---

[1] Any mention of commercial products does not indicate endorsement by NIST.

parameters is exhaustive search, the complexity increases by roughly a factor of q when $r + s$ is incremented, with any discrepancy from this quantity due to the number of vectors $\mathbf{z} \in \mathbb{F}_q^n$ required to successfully recover a map of HFE shape. The results of the experiments are reported in Table 4, and confirm the feasibility of this attack. This toy code can be found at [8].

Table 4. Experimental Results on the entire key recovery. Num. Iter. refers to the number of vectors $\mathbf{z} \in \mathbb{F}_q^n$ randomly chosen in the attack.

(q,d,o,r,s)	Num. Iter.	Time (ms)	(q,d,o,r,s)	Num. Iter.	Time (ms)
$(3,42,21,3,3)$	2	170	$(3,63,21,3,3)$	4	450
$(3,42,21,4,3)$	4	730	$(3,63,21,4,3)$	2	620
$(3,42,21,4,4)$	5	2590	$(3,63,21,4,4)$	3	2500
$(3,42,21,5,4)$	2	3150	$(3,63,21,5,4)$	3	7380
$(3,42,21,5,5)$	4	18870	$(3,63,21,5,5)$	5	36930
$(3,42,21,6,5)$	3	43150	$(3,63,21,6,5)$	3	67270
$(3,42,21,6,6)$	3	130470	$(3,63,21,6,6)$	5	339670

6.2 Big-Field Support Minors MinRank Attack

In Table 5 we summarize the complexity of the direct application of big-field support minors MinRank attack. We see that the scheme has dropped below NIST level 1 security levels for every proposed parameter set. See [8] for more details.

Table 5. Complexity of the Big-Field Support Minors attack on proposed parameters of HFERP. See Appendix B for notes on other parameters.

(q,d,o,r,s)	Degree Bound	Claimed Sec	Update Comp	Algth Type
$(3,42,21,15,17)$	$D = 3^7 + 1$	80 bit	2^{57}	Wiedemann
$(3,63,21,11,10)$	$D = 3^7 + 1$	80 bit	2^{59}	Strassen
$(3,85,o_i = 70, r_i = 89, 61)$	$D = 3^9 + 1$	128 bit	2^{63}	Strasssen
$(3,60,o_i = 40, r_i = 23, 40)$	$D = 3^9 + 1$	128 bit	2^{69}	Wiedemann

7 Conclusion

Accurate and systematic cryptanalysis of post-quantum cryptosystems is of utmost importance as we transition into a world in which post-quantum schemes are ubiquitous. This maxim is highlighted now that NIST has announced selections for post-quantum standards to diversify the types of hard problems that our public key infrastructure is based on and the work towards the post-quantum transition has already begun.

Recent work from [2,6,29] have had serious impacts on some of the oldest multivariate schemes in the literature, rightly causing concern for the viability of such schemes for widespread use. The field of multivariate cryptography once again finds itself in a situation in which there is rapid change, both in the development of new schemes and techniques for avoiding a collection of new attacks and in determining ways to extend these new attack ideas into new domains.

In this vein, we draw inspiration from the new "Simple Attack" of [6], extending the idea into the realm of big field schemes. Interestingly, this improvement to the MinRank attack, in the case of square $n \times n$ matrices, is a super-powered instance of the type of attack outlined in [19,25], but was not noticed in the context of HFERP before now. It is the significance of the "Simple Attack" on Rainbow that draws attention to these structures in private keys.

We find a completely new context for the application of the Simple Attack. Specifically, we find that the standard MinRank instance used in attacks used to set the parameters of HFERP is sufficiently empowered by the Simple Attack to significantly break most of the parameter sets. The divide and conquer technique may have further implications on other layered schemes.

Further, we extended the reach of the new support minors technique to a strong cryptanalysis of HFERP in a MinRank attack with coefficients coming from the big field. Although past results of [2,29] had only equations of the HFE type, HFERP has equations of multiple forms (namely HFE, UOV, and random polynomials). This attack is completely detrimental against all proposed parameters. This not only has implications against the HFERP scheme, but speaks to the far reaching power of the support minors technique.

A   Toy Example

We present in this appendix a toy example of the cryptanalysis of HFERP. First, we derive a public key. We choose the parameters $q = 31$, $d = 4$, degree bound $D = 2 * 31^3$ (so, in fact, the HFE map is generic quadratic) and $o = r = s = 2$. These parameters establish $n = 6$ and $m = 10$.

Public Key Generation

We select two random invertible transformations in $\mathrm{GL}_n(\mathbb{F}_q)$ and $\mathrm{GL}_m(\mathbb{F}_q)$:

$$U = \begin{bmatrix} 13 & 4 & 8 & 0 & 28 & 10 \\ 29 & 21 & 11 & 14 & 13 & 2 \\ 16 & 25 & 26 & 25 & 17 & 18 \\ 11 & 4 & 6 & 14 & 17 & 4 \\ 4 & 24 & 29 & 17 & 6 & 12 \\ 13 & 19 & 7 & 6 & 2 & 10 \end{bmatrix}$$

$$T = \begin{bmatrix} 7 & 16 & 11 & 8 & 30 & 17 & 27 & 13 & 28 & 25 \\ 18 & 18 & 7 & 4 & 1 & 10 & 26 & 23 & 17 & 11 \\ 22 & 9 & 29 & 7 & 11 & 14 & 6 & 7 & 19 & 4 \\ 0 & 21 & 16 & 13 & 14 & 13 & 3 & 2 & 25 & 3 \\ 24 & 28 & 2 & 21 & 26 & 22 & 20 & 15 & 1 & 2 \\ 7 & 3 & 30 & 25 & 9 & 18 & 7 & 13 & 26 & 5 \\ 14 & 25 & 1 & 4 & 1 & 14 & 26 & 15 & 15 & 24 \\ 21 & 7 & 10 & 17 & 11 & 26 & 18 & 20 & 1 & 10 \\ 16 & 10 & 24 & 14 & 30 & 0 & 0 & 0 & 11 & 3 \\ 5 & 23 & 18 & 18 & 15 & 18 & 15 & 13 & 6 & 14 \end{bmatrix}.$$

After selecting the central map $F = F_{HFE}\|F_R\|F_P$, we compose $P = T \circ F \circ U$ producing:

$$P_0 = \begin{bmatrix} 2 & 22 & 0 & 4 & 29 & 19 \\ 22 & 6 & 18 & 29 & 26 & 3 \\ 0 & 18 & 5 & 20 & 26 & 1 \\ 4 & 29 & 20 & 4 & 14 & 7 \\ 29 & 26 & 26 & 14 & 27 & 11 \\ 19 & 3 & 1 & 7 & 11 & 19 \end{bmatrix} \quad P_1 = \begin{bmatrix} 5 & 12 & 3 & 9 & 0 & 17 \\ 12 & 23 & 29 & 19 & 11 & 4 \\ 3 & 29 & 28 & 1 & 10 & 4 \\ 9 & 19 & 1 & 12 & 3 & 25 \\ 0 & 11 & 10 & 3 & 22 & 29 \\ 17 & 4 & 4 & 25 & 29 & 24 \end{bmatrix} \quad P_2 = \begin{bmatrix} 30 & 4 & 24 & 25 & 4 & 6 \\ 4 & 8 & 14 & 30 & 6 & 8 \\ 24 & 14 & 12 & 29 & 22 & 11 \\ 25 & 30 & 29 & 14 & 4 & 1 \\ 4 & 6 & 22 & 4 & 7 & 11 \\ 6 & 8 & 11 & 1 & 11 & 30 \end{bmatrix}$$

$$P_3 = \begin{bmatrix} 26 & 3 & 17 & 19 & 0 & 0 \\ 3 & 20 & 1 & 10 & 5 & 7 \\ 17 & 1 & 14 & 14 & 27 & 19 \\ 19 & 10 & 14 & 23 & 3 & 23 \\ 0 & 5 & 27 & 3 & 23 & 21 \\ 0 & 7 & 19 & 23 & 21 & 29 \end{bmatrix} \quad P_4 = \begin{bmatrix} 29 & 5 & 22 & 4 & 26 & 22 \\ 5 & 3 & 5 & 16 & 20 & 15 \\ 22 & 5 & 14 & 16 & 22 & 6 \\ 4 & 16 & 16 & 29 & 21 & 10 \\ 26 & 20 & 22 & 21 & 9 & 4 \\ 22 & 15 & 6 & 10 & 4 & 20 \end{bmatrix} \quad P_5 = \begin{bmatrix} 18 & 14 & 23 & 6 & 14 & 11 \\ 14 & 18 & 19 & 17 & 23 & 25 \\ 23 & 19 & 27 & 6 & 10 & 30 \\ 6 & 17 & 6 & 2 & 19 & 0 \\ 14 & 23 & 10 & 19 & 28 & 18 \\ 11 & 25 & 30 & 0 & 18 & 30 \end{bmatrix}$$

$$P_6 = \begin{bmatrix} 14 & 7 & 15 & 16 & 22 & 4 \\ 7 & 7 & 27 & 10 & 9 & 12 \\ 15 & 27 & 5 & 5 & 25 & 4 \\ 16 & 10 & 5 & 13 & 12 & 16 \\ 22 & 9 & 25 & 12 & 1 & 13 \\ 4 & 12 & 4 & 16 & 13 & 25 \end{bmatrix} \quad P_7 = \begin{bmatrix} 28 & 23 & 2 & 18 & 26 & 11 \\ 23 & 1 & 2 & 27 & 9 & 30 \\ 2 & 2 & 16 & 5 & 17 & 20 \\ 18 & 27 & 5 & 20 & 5 & 2 \\ 26 & 9 & 17 & 5 & 5 & 0 \\ 11 & 30 & 20 & 2 & 0 & 6 \end{bmatrix} \quad P_8 = \begin{bmatrix} 5 & 4 & 17 & 26 & 1 & 16 \\ 4 & 20 & 10 & 6 & 4 & 10 \\ 17 & 10 & 26 & 18 & 29 & 15 \\ 26 & 6 & 18 & 20 & 13 & 4 \\ 1 & 4 & 29 & 13 & 11 & 10 \\ 16 & 10 & 15 & 4 & 10 & 8 \end{bmatrix}$$

$$P_9 = \begin{bmatrix} 14 & 24 & 4 & 19 & 16 & 17 \\ 24 & 22 & 0 & 0 & 7 & 0 \\ 4 & 0 & 13 & 18 & 0 & 12 \\ 19 & 0 & 18 & 2 & 10 & 19 \\ 16 & 7 & 0 & 10 & 10 & 4 \\ 17 & 0 & 12 & 19 & 4 & 7 \end{bmatrix}.$$

Simple Attack

The first step of the attack is to randomly select a vector $\mathbf{z} \in \mathbb{F}_q^n$. For our example we select $\mathbf{z} = \begin{bmatrix} 27 & 20 & 11 & 2 & 8 & 12 \end{bmatrix}$ and compute $\mathbf{A_z}$ as in Sect. 4. We compute

$$\mathbf{K} = \ker(\mathbf{A_z}) = \begin{bmatrix} 30 & 0 & 0 & 0 & 2 & 18 & 1 & 7 & 24 & 3 \\ 0 & 30 & 0 & 0 & 25 & 2 & 4 & 10 & 25 & 15 \\ 0 & 0 & 30 & 0 & 23 & 30 & 20 & 29 & 30 & 29 \\ 0 & 0 & 0 & 30 & 2 & 7 & 3 & 21 & 18 & 13 \end{bmatrix}.$$

Now, there exists an element in the left kernel of $\mathbf{K}^\top$ that also produces a rank d linear combination of the public matrices. Creating the system of equations (4), we find a 1-dimensional solution space containing

$$\mathbf{y} = \begin{bmatrix} 23 & 2 & 0 & 30 & 30 & 23 & 3 & 26 & 5 & 7 \end{bmatrix}^\top.$$

Setting $\mathbf{P_y} = \sum_{i=0}^{m-1} y_i \mathbf{P}_i$, we obtain the rank d matrix in the span of the HFE polynomials. To recover a correct input basis, we compute the left kernel

$$\ker(\mathbf{P_y}) = \begin{bmatrix} 30 & 0 & 0 & 18 & 22 & 18 \\ 0 & 30 & 0 & 10 & 0 & 5 \\ 0 & 0 & 30 & 22 & 27 & 2 \end{bmatrix},$$

which reveals a projection onto an $o+1$ dimensional subspace containing the oil subspace. We solve two MinRank instances at rank 2, recover the oil space as the span of the left kernels. We extend this basis to cover all of $\mathbb{F}_q^n$ and obtain the full basis:

$$\mathbf{U}'^{-1} = \begin{bmatrix} 30 & 0 & 0 & 0 & 0 & 21 \\ 0 & 30 & 0 & 0 & 0 & 13 \\ 0 & 0 & 30 & 0 & 0 & 26 \\ 0 & 0 & 0 & 30 & 0 & 5 \\ 0 & 0 & 0 & 0 & 30 & 14 \\ 30 & 23 & 15 & 16 & 20 & 28 \end{bmatrix}.$$

Once an equivalent input basis is known, finding an output transformation that "unmixes" the key is easy. We merely find linear combinations of $\mathbf{U}'^{-1}\mathbf{P}_i\mathbf{U}'^{-\top}$ with HFE shape, find additional linear combinations orthogonal to the recovered HFE maps that have UOV shape and complete the basis. We recover

$$\mathbf{H}_0' = \begin{bmatrix} 0 & 10 & 20 & 8 & 0 & 0 \\ 10 & 20 & 16 & 20 & 0 & 0 \\ 20 & 16 & 8 & 0 & 0 & 0 \\ 8 & 20 & 0 & 8 & 0 & 0 \\ 0 & 0 & 0 & 0 & 6 & 27 \\ 0 & 0 & 0 & 0 & 27 & 9 \end{bmatrix} \quad \mathbf{H}_1' = \begin{bmatrix} 24 & 20 & 15 & 27 & 0 & 0 \\ 20 & 25 & 25 & 22 & 0 & 0 \\ 15 & 25 & 7 & 13 & 0 & 0 \\ 27 & 22 & 13 & 22 & 0 & 0 \\ 0 & 0 & 0 & 0 & 5 & 25 \\ 0 & 0 & 0 & 0 & 25 & 24 \end{bmatrix} \quad \mathbf{H}_2' = \begin{bmatrix} 0 & 8 & 21 & 6 & 18 & 15 \\ 8 & 13 & 6 & 7 & 13 & 28 \\ 21 & 6 & 5 & 27 & 10 & 4 \\ 6 & 7 & 27 & 1 & 12 & 26 \\ 18 & 13 & 10 & 12 & 28 & 16 \\ 15 & 28 & 4 & 26 & 16 & 10 \end{bmatrix}$$

$$\mathbf{H}_3' = \begin{bmatrix} 18 & 12 & 25 & 3 & 10 & 27 \\ 12 & 21 & 13 & 2 & 30 & 11 \\ 25 & 13 & 9 & 20 & 22 & 15 \\ 3 & 2 & 20 & 16 & 18 & 6 \\ 10 & 30 & 22 & 18 & 2 & 3 \\ 27 & 11 & 15 & 6 & 3 & 28 \end{bmatrix} \quad \mathbf{H}_4' = \begin{bmatrix} 28 & 27 & 12 & 10 & 12 & 28 \\ 27 & 30 & 30 & 24 & 20 & 1 \\ 12 & 30 & 3 & 6 & 27 & 21 \\ 10 & 24 & 6 & 29 & 20 & 12 \\ 12 & 20 & 27 & 20 & 0 & 0 \\ 28 & 1 & 21 & 12 & 0 & 0 \end{bmatrix} \quad \mathbf{H}_5' = \begin{bmatrix} 15 & 13 & 29 & 4 & 17 & 2 \\ 13 & 13 & 29 & 8 & 10 & 13 \\ 29 & 29 & 13 & 30 & 6 & 14 \\ 4 & 8 & 30 & 7 & 30 & 28 \\ 17 & 10 & 6 & 30 & 0 & 0 \\ 2 & 13 & 14 & 28 & 0 & 0 \end{bmatrix}$$

$$\mathbf{H}_6' = \begin{bmatrix} 27 & 1 & 29 & 5 & 20 & 20 \\ 1 & 24 & 27 & 17 & 14 & 10 \\ 29 & 27 & 24 & 17 & 4 & 27 \\ 5 & 17 & 17 & 2 & 10 & 24 \\ 20 & 14 & 4 & 10 & 0 & 0 \\ 20 & 10 & 27 & 24 & 0 & 0 \end{bmatrix} \quad \mathbf{H}_7' = \begin{bmatrix} 3 & 1 & 14 & 12 & 30 & 19 \\ 1 & 10 & 8 & 25 & 30 & 23 \\ 14 & 8 & 6 & 29 & 21 & 6 \\ 12 & 25 & 29 & 0 & 5 & 30 \\ 30 & 30 & 21 & 5 & 21 & 10 \\ 19 & 23 & 6 & 30 & 10 & 0 \end{bmatrix} \quad \mathbf{H}_8' = \begin{bmatrix} 15 & 20 & 22 & 13 & 17 & 8 \\ 20 & 21 & 27 & 26 & 26 & 19 \\ 22 & 27 & 7 & 7 & 20 & 23 \\ 13 & 26 & 7 & 8 & 2 & 3 \\ 17 & 26 & 20 & 2 & 17 & 17 \\ 8 & 19 & 23 & 3 & 17 & 29 \end{bmatrix}$$

$$\mathbf{H}_9' = \begin{bmatrix} 4 & 22 & 28 & 6 & 8 & 0 \\ 22 & 19 & 26 & 13 & 27 & 25 \\ 28 & 26 & 21 & 30 & 13 & 4 \\ 6 & 13 & 30 & 2 & 25 & 30 \\ 8 & 27 & 13 & 25 & 8 & 14 \\ 0 & 25 & 4 & 30 & 14 & 7 \end{bmatrix} \quad \text{and} \quad \mathbf{T}' = \begin{bmatrix} 15 & 11 & 4 & 20 & 17 & 28 & 0 & 5 & 11 & 1 \\ 16 & 8 & 10 & 18 & 16 & 3 & 4 & 17 & 11 & 4 \\ 15 & 1 & 28 & 13 & 29 & 27 & 28 & 3 & 2 & 25 \\ 3 & 5 & 22 & 15 & 22 & 16 & 25 & 14 & 25 & 6 \\ 28 & 8 & 27 & 23 & 12 & 8 & 27 & 0 & 7 & 19 \\ 16 & 8 & 22 & 4 & 6 & 9 & 27 & 13 & 18 & 14 \\ 16 & 9 & 26 & 27 & 25 & 19 & 17 & 3 & 19 & 4 \\ 16 & 11 & 24 & 25 & 18 & 23 & 27 & 23 & 25 & 1 \\ 7 & 28 & 30 & 25 & 0 & 18 & 14 & 4 & 14 & 27 \\ 20 & 7 & 20 & 0 & 25 & 6 & 11 & 0 & 27 & 22 \end{bmatrix}$$

One easily checks that $P = T' \circ F' \circ U'$, where U' and T' are the linear transformations defined by $\mathbf{U}'$ and $\mathbf{T}'$ and F' is the map defined coordinate-wise by the matrices $\mathbf{H}_i'$ above.

B   Note on Updated Complexities

It is worth noting that the parameters $q = 3$, $d = 85$ $o_i = 70$, $r_i = 89$, and $s = 61$ were proposed in [14] as having 128 bits of security against a direct attack. Upon closer evaluation, it appears a direct attack against these parameters would actually have bit complexity closer to 187. Using the divide and conquer approach (Simple Attack) against these parameters we have around 158 bits of security $(3 \cdot 3^{85} (239^\omega + 225^\omega) \approx 2^{158}$ using linear algebra search), which beats the best known direct attack. Furthermore, these parameters provide only 63 bits of security against the Big-Field Support Minors attack.

References

1. Apon, D., Moody, D., Perlner, R.A., Smith-Tone, D., Verbel, J.A.: Combinatorial rank attacks against the rectangular simple matrix encryption scheme. In: Ding, J., Tillich, J. (eds.) Post-Quantum Cryptography, PQCrypto 2020. LNCS, vol. 12100, pp. 307–322. Springer, Cham (2020). https://doi.org/10.1007/978-3-030-44223-1_17

2. Baena, J., Briaud, P., Cabarcas, D., Perlner, R.A., Smith-Tone, D., Verbel, J.A.: Improving support-minors rank attacks: applications to GeMSS and rainbow. In: Dodis, Y., Shrimpton, T. (eds.) Advances in Cryptology, CRYPTO 2022. LNCS, vol. 13509, pp. 376–405. Springer, Cham (2022). https://doi.org/10.1007/978-3-031-15982-4_13

3. Bardet, M., et al.: Improvements of algebraic attacks for solving the rank decoding and minrank problems. In: Moriai, S., Wang, H. (eds.) Advances in Cryptology, ASIACRYPT 2020. LNCS, vol. 12491, pp. 507–536. Springer, Cham (2020). https://doi.org/10.1007/978-3-030-64837-4_17

4. Bettale, L., Faugère, J., Perret, L.: Cryptanalysis of HFE, multi-HFE and variants for odd and even characteristic. Des. Codes Cryptogr. **69**(1), 1–52 (2013). https://doi.org/10.1007/s10623-012-9617-2

5. Beullens, W.: Improved cryptanalysis of UOV and rainbow. In: Canteaut, A., Standaert, F. (eds.) Advances in Cryptology, EUROCRYPT 2021. LNCS, vol. 12696, pp. 348–373. Springer, Cham (2021). https://doi.org/10.1007/978-3-030-77870-5_13

6. Beullens, W.: Breaking rainbow takes a weekend on a laptop. In: Dodis, Y., Shrimpton, T. (eds.) Advances in Cryptology, CRYPTO 2022. LNCS, vol. 13508, pp. 464–479. Springer, Cham (2022). https://doi.org/10.1007/978-3-031-15979-4_16

7. Bosma, W., Cannon, J., Playoust, C.: The magma algebra system I: the user language. J. Symb. Comput. **24**(3–4), 235–265 (1997). https://doi.org/10.1006/jsco.1996.0125

8. Cartor, M., Cartor, R., Furue, H., Smith-Tone, D.: Magma Code for Improved Cryptanalysis of HFERP (2024). https://github.com/maxcartor/HFERP-Cryptanalysis

9. Courtois, N.T., Klimov, A., Patarin, J., Shamir, A.: Efficient algorithms for solving overdefined systems of multivariate polynomial equations. In: Preneel, B. (ed.) Advances in Cryptology, EUROCRYPT 2000. LNCS, vol. 1807, pp. 392–407. Springer, Cham (2000). https://doi.org/10.1007/3-540-45539-6_27

10. Courtois, N.T., Klimov, A., Patarin, J., Shamir, A.: Efficient algorithms for solving overdefined systems of multivariate polynomial equations. In: Preneel, B. (ed.) Advances in Cryptology, EUROCRYPT 2000. LNCS, vol. 1807, pp. 392–407. Springer, Cham (2000). https://doi.org/10.1007/3-540-45539-6_27

11. Ding, J., Schmidt, D.: Rainbow, a new multivariable polynomial signature scheme. In: Ioannidis, J., Keromytis, A.D., Yung, M. (eds.) Applied Cryptography and Network Security, Third International Conference, ACNS 2005. LNCS, vol. 3531, pp. 164–175. Springer, Cham (2005). https://doi.org/10.1007/11496137_12

12. Faugere, J.C.: A new efficient algorithm for computing gröbner bases (f4). J. Pure Appl. Algebra **139**(1–3) 61–88 (1999)

13. Faugère, J., Levy-dit-Vehel, F., Perret, L.: Cryptanalysis of minrank. In: Wagner, D.A. (ed.) Advances in Cryptology, CRYPTO 2008. LNCS, vol. 5157, pp. 280–296. Springer, Cham (2008). https://doi.org/10.1007/978-3-540-85174-5_16

14. Ikematsu, Y., Perlner, R.A., Smith-Tone, D., Takagi, T., Vates, J.: HFERP - a new multivariate encryption scheme. In: Lange, T., Steinwandt, R. (eds.) Post-Quantum Cryptography. LNCS, vol. 10786, pp. 396–416. Springer, Cham (2018). https://doi.org/10.1007/978-3-319-79063-3_19

15. Kipnis, A., Shamir, A.: Cryptanalysis of the HFE public key cryptosystem by relinearization. Advances in Cryptology, CRYPTO 1999. LNCS, vol. 1666, pp. 19–30. Springer, Heidelberg (1999). https://doi.org/10.1007/3-540-48405-1_2

16. Kipnis, A., Patarin, J., Goubin, L.: Unbalanced oil and vinegar signature schemes. In: Stern, J. (ed.) Advances in Cryptology, EUROCRYPT 1999. LNCS, vol. 1592, pp. 206–222. Springer, Heidelberg (1999). https://doi.org/10.1007/3-540-48910-X_15

17. Kipnis, A., Shamir, A.: Cryptanalysis of the oil and vinegar signature scheme. In: Krawczyk, H. (ed.) Advances in Cryptology, CRYPTO 1998. LNCS, vol. 1462, pp. 257–266. Springer, Heidelberg (1998). https://doi.org/10.1007/BFb0055733

18. Matsumoto, T., Imai, H.: Public quadratic polynominal-tuples for efficient signature-verification and message-encryption. In: Günther, C.G. (ed.) Advances in Cryptology, EUROCRYPT 1988. LNCS, vol. 330, pp. 419–453. Springer, Heidelberg (1988). https://doi.org/10.1007/3-540-45961-8_39

19. Moody, D., Perlner, R.A., Smith-Tone, D.: An asymptotically optimal structural attack on the ABC multivariate encryption scheme. In: Mosca, M. (ed.) Post-quantum Cryptography, PQCrypto 2014. LNCS, vol. 8772, pp. 180–196. Springer, Cham (2014). https://doi.org/10.1007/978-3-319-11659-4_11

20. Patarin, J.: Cryptanalysis of the matsumoto and IMAI public key scheme of Eurocrypt 1988. In: Coppersmith, D. (ed.) Advances in Cryptology, CRYPTO 1995. LNCS, vol. 963, pp. 248–261. Springer, Heidelberg (1995). https://doi.org/10.1007/3-540-44750-4_20

21. Patarin, J.: Hidden fields equations (HFE) and isomorphisms of polynomials (IP): two new families of asymmetric algorithms. In: Maurer, U.M. (ed.) Advances in Cryptology, EUROCRYPT 1996. LNCS, vol. 1070, pp. 33–48. Springer, Heidelberg (1996). https://doi.org/10.1007/3-540-68339-9_4

22. Patarin, J.: The oil and vinegar signature scheme. Presented at the Dagstuhl Workshop on Cryptography (1997)

23. Patarin, J., Courtois, N.T., Goubin, L.: Quartz, 128-bit long digital signatures. In: Naccache, D. (ed.) Topics in Cryptology, CT-RSA 2001. LNCS, vol. 2020, pp. 282–297. Springer, Heidelberg (2001). https://doi.org/10.1007/3-540-45353-9_21

24. Perlner, R.A., Petzoldt, A., Smith-Tone, D.: Total break of the SRP encryption scheme. In: Adams, C., Camenisch, J. (eds.) Selected Areas in Cryptography, SAC 2017. LNCS, vol. 10719, pp. 355–373. Springer, Cham (2017). https://doi.org/10.1007/978-3-319-72565-9_18

25. Perlner, R.A., Smith-Tone, D.: A classification of differential invariants for multivariate post-quantum cryptosystems. In: Gaborit, P. (ed.) Post-quantum Cryptography, PQCrypto 2013. LNCS, vol. 7932, pp. 165–173. Springer, Heidelberg (2013). https://doi.org/10.1007/978-3-642-38616-9_11

26. Smith-Tone, D.: Practical cryptanalysis of k-ary c*. In: Ding, J., Tillich, J. (eds.) Post-Quantum Cryptography, PQCrypto 2020. LNCS, vol. 12100, pp. 360–380. Springer, Cham (2020). https://doi.org/10.1007/978-3-030-44223-1_20

27. Smith-Tone, D., Tone, C.: A multivariate cryptosystem inspired by random linear codes. Finite Fields Their Appl. **69**, 101778 (2021). https://doi.org/10.1016/j.ffa.2020.101778

28. Strassen, V.: Gaussian elimination is not optimal. Numerische Mathematik **13**, 354–356 (1969). http://eudml.org/doc/131927

29. Tao, C., Petzoldt, A., Ding, J.: Efficient key recovery for all HFE signature variants. In: Malkin, T., Peikert, C. (eds.) Advances in Cryptology, CRYPTO 2021. LNCS, vol. 12825, pp. 70–93. Springer, Cham (2021). https://doi.org/10.1007/978-3-030-84242-0_4

30. Wiedemann, D.H.: Solving sparse linear equations over finite fields. IEEE Trans. Inf. Theory **32**(1), 54–62 (1986). https://doi.org/10.1109/TIT.1986.1057137

31. Yasuda, T., Sakurai, K.: A multivariate encryption scheme with rainbow. In: Qing, S., Okamoto, E., Kim, K., Liu, D. (eds.) Information and Communications Security, ICICS 2015. LNCS, vol. 9543, pp. 236–251. Springer, Cham (2015). https://doi.org/10.1007/978-3-319-29814-6_19

Author Index

Printed in the United States
by Baker & Taylor Publisher Services